CHILD PSYCHOPATHOLOGY

CHILD PSYCHOPATHOLOGY

Edited by

Eric J. Mash
University of Calgary

and

Russell A. Barkley
University of Massachusetts Medical Center

Foreword by Alan E. Kazdin

THE GUILFORD PRESS
New York   London

© 1996 The Guilford Press
A Division of Guilford Publications, Inc.
72 Spring Street, New York, NY 10012

Printed in the United States of America

This book is printed on acid-free paper.

Last digit is print number: 9   8   7   6   5   4   3

Library of Congress Cataloging-in-Publication Data

Child psychopathology / edited by Eric J. Mash and Russell A. Barkley.
    p. cm.
  Includes bibliographical references and index.
  ISBN 1-57230-065-5
  1. Child psychopathology.   I. Mash, Eric J.   II. Barkley, Russell
A., 1949–   .
  [DNLM: 1. Mental Disorders—in infancy & childhood.   2. Child
Psychiatry.   WS 350 C5377 1996]
RJ499.C4863   1996
618.92'89—dc20
DNLM/DLC
for Library of Congress   96-4857
                                           CIP

The fool tells me his reasons,
the wise man persuades me with my own.

—ARISTOTLE

*In loving memory of a very wise man,
my dear friend, teacher, and confidant*

Gerald M. Phillips

—E.J.M.

Contributors

Anne Marie Albano, Ph.D., Center for Stress and Anxiety Disorders, The State University of New York at Albany; present address: Department of Psychology, University of Louisville, Kentucky

Carolyn A. Anderson, Ph.D., Stanford University Medical Center, Stanford, California

Joan Rosenbaum Asarnow, Ph.D., UCLA Neuropsychiatric Institute, University of California, Los Angeles

Robert F. Asarnow, Ph.D., UCLA Neuropsychiatric Institute, University of California, Los Angeles

Russell A. Barkley, Ph.D., Department of Psychiatry, University of Massachusetts Medical Center, Worcester

David H. Barlow, Ph.D., Center for Stress and Anxiety Disorders, The State University of New York at Albany

Diane Benoit, M.D., Department of Psychiatry, Hospital for Sick Children, University of Toronto, Ontario, Canada

Carolyn M. D. Black, M.S., Graduate School of Applied and Professional Psychology, Rutgers University, Busch Campus, Piscataway, New Jersey

Bruce F. Chorpita, A.B., Center for Stress and Anxiety Disorders, The State University of New York at Albany

Geraldine Dawson, Ph.D., Psychology Department, University of Washington, Seattle

David J. A. Dozois, M.Sc., Clinical Psychology Programme, University of Calgary, Alberta, Canada

Elisabeth M. Dykens, Ph.D., UCLA Neuropsychiatric Institute, University of California, Los Angeles

David W. Evans, Ph.D., Child Study Center, Yale University, New Haven, Connecticut

Kenneth E. Fletcher, Ph.D., Department of Psychiatry, University of Massachusetts Medical Center, Worcester

Constance Hammen, Ph.D., Department of Psychology, University of California, Los Angeles

Cynthia Harbeck-Weber, Ph.D., Children's Hospital, Columbus, Ohio

Karen Heffernan, M.S., Graduate School of Applied and Professional Psychology, Rutgers University, Busch Campus, Piscataway, New Jersey

Stephen P. Hinshaw, Ph.D., Department of Psychology, University of California, Berkeley

Robert M. Hodapp, Ph.D., Special Education, Graduate School of Education, University of California, Los Angeles

Robert A. King, M.D., Child Study Center, Yale University, New Haven, Connecticut

Laura Grofer Klinger, Ph.D., Psychology Department, University of Alabama, Tuscaloosa

James F. Leckman, M.D., Child Study Center, Yale University, New Haven, Connecticut

G. Reid Lyon, Ph.D., Human Learning and Behavior Branch, Center for Research for Mothers and Children, National Institute of Child Health and Human Development, National Institutes of Health, Bethesda, Maryland

Karlen Lyons-Ruth, Ph.D., Department of Psychiatry, Harvard Medical School, Cambridge, Massachusetts

Eric J. Mash, Ph.D., Department of Psychology, University of Calgary, Alberta, Canada

Lizette Peterson, Ph.D., Department of Psychology, University of Missouri—Columbia

Kenneth H. Rubin, Ph.D., Center for Children, Relationships, and Culture, University of Maryland, College Park

Karen D. Rudolph, Ph.D., Department of Psychology, University of California, Los Angeles

Shannon L. Stewart, Ph.D., Department of Psychology, University of Waterloo, Ontario, Canada

Christine Wekerle, Ph.D., Department of Psychology, The University of Western Ontario, London, Ontario, Canada

G. Terence Wilson, Ph.D., Graduate School of Applied and Professional Psychology, Rutgers University, Busch Campus, Piscataway, New Jersey

David A. Wolfe, Ph.D., Department of Psychology, The University of Western Ontario, London, Ontario, Canada

Charles H. Zeanah, Jr., M.D., Division of Infant, Child, and Adolescent Psychiatry, Louisiana State University School of Medicine, New Orleans

Foreword

Until quite recently, emotional behavioral, and learning problems of children and adolescents have been neglected in the mental health and related professions. In light of advances in the diagnosis, assessment, and treatment of adult psychopathology, this neglect was particularly conspicuous. It can be traced to a number of influences, both within the mental health profession and society at large. Among the constraints on the study of child psychopathology are the following: a conceptual view that emphasizes the limitations and deficits of children's psychology; assumptions, but also some evidence, that disturbed and disturbing behavior early in life is often transient; and the view that many childhood problems, such as fears and anxiety, language deficits, stuttering, and bedwetting, are "normal." Perhaps the most significant factor thwarting progress in this area is the simple fact that children have little or no direct social and political influence. This neglect of children and adolescents, the personal and social consequences of that neglect, and constructive suggestions for how to redress these issues have been outlined in many reports (e.g., Carnegie Council on Adolescent Development, 1995; Committee for the Study of Research on Child and Adolescent Mental Disorders, 1995; Hechinger, 1992; Institute of Medicine, 1989; U.S. Congress, 1986, 1991).

More recently, attention has been turned to these problems in children, which can be traced to a number of realizations on the part of the field. First, even if one were interested only in understanding adult psychopathology, there would still be an urgent need to mobilize research on children and adolescents—we now recognize many continuities of dysfunction over the lifespan, beyond the more extreme forms of dysfunction such as autism and severe mental retardation. Second, the scope of impairment among children and adolescents is great—debilitating emotional, behavioral, and developmental problems are evident among 15–20% of youth. Also, the criteria (cut-off scores) for delineating various diagnoses are difficult to justify. Individuals who fail to meet diagnostic criteria for various disorders still may show impairment in everyday functioning and remain at risk for untoward outcomes in adulthood. Consequently, there remains the haunting prospect that with some changes in definitions, the percentage of youth in need of care would increase. Third, contemporary society harbors a number of influences that have a significant impact on children's mental health–high rates of teen pregnancy and parenting; poverty and unemployment; breakdown and reconfiguration of the family; homelessness; exposure to family, neighborhood, and media violence; and the accessibility of illicit substances and weapons have heightened the awareness of the problems children face and the urgency of intervening. The enormous financial costs of services for children (e.g., in education, mental health, social services, and juvenile justice) have helped to mobilize concern and social and legislative attention. The enormous and often tragic personal costs to families have played a central role in generating attention, action, research, and social programs, for example, parent-initiated organizations designed to decrease substance use and abuse, crime, and driving while intoxicated.

In the past decade, particularly, there have been converging interests, efforts, and advances in the study of child development and clinical dysfunction and adaptation. The field of developmental psychopathology has emerged as the study of adjustment, maladjustment, and adaptation over the course of development, that is, the life span. This field accords major attention to children and adolescents but has potential implications for reconceptualizing adulthood as well. The study of psychopathology in childhood raises many challenges. The subject matter demands an interdisciplinary focus. Theory and research draw heavily on such diverse disciplines as epidemiology, genetics, neurology, pediatrics, psychiatry, psychology, and sociology, among others. In addition, as there are major differences between periods of development (e.g., infancy and adolescence), the study of development is highly specialized. Also, the range of influences that converge on the child during any particular developmental stage must be viewed in a broader context.

Child Psychopathology is a remarkable book in its presentation of this subject matter. The chapters address a broad range of disorders of childhood and adolescence, including emotional and behavioral problems, developmental and learning disorders, precursors of dysfunction that emerge in infancy and early childhood, and health-related disorders. Apart from the scope of coverage, the manner in which the topics are addressed is special. Several themes are woven into the chapters, including the importance of developmental processes, the interrelations of multiple levels of analyses, adaptive and maladaptive patterns and how they emerge developmentally, and current theories of etiology and their supportive research. Key topics such as risk and protective factors, vulnerability and resilience, underpinnings and substrates of dysfunction,

developmental paths and trajectories, and the onset and the long-term course of development are carefully documented within the chapters. Careful editorial guidance as this book was developed has achieved a discernible consistency in focus and organization among the chapters.

Clinical dysfunction and development are examined in context, that is, in a bio-psycho-social-environmental matrix. Recognition of multiple levels of influences and dynamic interchanges among them is the way to capture, to the extent possible, the developmental process. The different levels of analyses in relation to context, including family, culture, and ethnicity, convey the richness of the domains that the field must integrate. This book presents the challenges of and accomplishments in understanding the emergence of adaptive and maladaptive functioning.

The individual writings of Eric Mash and Russell Barkley over the years have had significant impact on the field. Their collaboration here has produced a unique book. We would expect that the editors would bring together an authoritative set of contributors whose chapters would present the latest advances in theory and research. High expectations for the chapters to follow will not be dashed. The latest findings, when as superbly organized as they are in this book, would be enough to warrant accolades. However, there is much more.

What is needed in the field is a conceptual vision that integrates and brings cohesion to the subject matter, and this book provides a novel statement of the field's goals and achievements and provides an overarching developmental-process view that permits the integration of the many topics, research methods, and foci of the field. This view emphasizes the interrelations of child, system, and contextual relations and variation in development as a function of such pervasive influences as age, sex, culture and ethnicity, and the socioeconomic status of the child and family. The book embraces the complexities of development, provides a model for its investigation, conveys exciting findings from studies that exemplify early returns from such research, and suggests exciting opportunities in the field as a whole, as well as within particular domains of interest. By showing how much can be accomplished when multiple disciplines converge and by raising many provocative questions about how and why particular paths emerged the book inspires reflection. After finishing it, I wished I was not already in the field of development and psychopathology, so that I could join it anew and devote time to the many research opportunities and needs the chapters present.

Alan E. Kazdin
Yale University

REFERENCES

Carnegie Council on Adolescent Development. (1995). *Great transitions: Preparing adolescents for a new century*. New York: Carnegie Corporation.

Hechinger, F.M. (1992). *Fateful choices: Healthy youth for the 21st century*. New York: Carnegie Corporation.

Committee for the Study of Research on Child and Adolescent Mental Disorders. (1995). *Report card on the National Plan for Research on Child and Adolescent Mental Disorders: The midway report*. Washington, DC: American Academy of Child and Adolescent Psychiatry.

Institute of Medicine. (1989). *Research on children and adolescents with mental, behavioral, and developmental disorders*. Washington, DC: National Academy Press.

United States Congress, Office of Technology Assessment. (1986). *Children's mental health: Problems and services—A background paper* (OTA-BP-H-33). Washington, DC: U.S. Government Printing Office.

United States Congress, Office of Technology Assessment. (1991). *Adolescent health* (OTA-H-468). Washington, DC: U.S. Government Printing Office.

Preface

Research in child and developmental psychopathology has flourished over the past two decades, with many previously known disorders being further delineated and new ones being discovered along the way. The exponential rate at which new findings are published each month in journals on this topic is nothing short of extraordinary. The scientific experts themselves are oft-heard to complain of how difficult it is becoming even to keep up with their relevant literatures. Woe to the clinical professionals dealing with these childhood disorders who fail to keep up with their journals for even a year or two—they may find, once they return to their unread stacks, that they are hopelessly behind in the advancements made in understanding these clinical conditions. Child psychopathology as an area of multidisciplinary study clearly epitomizes the dynamic, accumulative, and self-correcting nature of scientific knowledge. New findings expand upon and are assimilated with the established facts, often challenging older theoretical or conceptual models of the disorders, and at times even leading to mini-paradigm shifts in theoretical perspectives. Old questions find answers, yet in the pursuit of precise comprehension, in this case of childhood maladies, they inevitably raise ever-more questions along the way. The current level of excitement may vary across different areas of child psychopathology, yet within each it remains palpable and about each we can surely say that we know far more about this childhood disorder today than we did even as little as 6 years ago.

How to capture the current status of this rapidly evolving state of affairs? Identify those who have dedicated their professional careers to each disorder and let them tell us what they have learned. Our intention in creating this volume, therefore, was a quite simple one: Find the most knowledgeable professionals on a given disorder and give them free rein to provide as up-to-date and comprehensive a summary as possible of the nature of the disorder in which they have specialized. We asked only that they provide as current an overview as possible based on the research literature, and unfettered for the moment by clinical concerns such as the assessment and treatment of these disorders.

In essence, each author was challenged to answer the basic question, "What do we know about this disorder?," where "knowing" refers to scientifically acquired knowledge about the condition.

If sound theoretical or conceptual models of the disorder exist, then these are referenced in the reviews. In answering the basic question, our experts were asked to cover (1) the nature of the behaviors or symptoms that typify the disorder; (2) a brief historical perspective; (3) any criteria that exist to establish its presence (diagnosis) and the experts' candid assessment of these criteria; (4) epidemiological knowledge pertaining to the prevalence, gender distribution, and ethnic and cultural factors associated with the disorder; (5) the developmental courses and pathways known to be associated with each disorder; (6) the psychiatric, psychological, and social disorders or difficulties most likely to coexist with it (comorbidity); and (7) a survey of those things believed to give rise to the disorder (etiology). We believe that the authors chosen here, each an experienced, nationally recognized scientific expert on a specific disorder, have accomplished their charge admirably. We trust the reader will concur with our assessment.

We are indebted to the professionals who agreed to write for us on the respective disorders in which they specialize. We fully and genuinely appreciate the more-than-generous time commitment they gave to their chapters, stealing as it must have from their hectic scientific, academic, and clinical schedules. In the process of preparing this volume, others deserve our gratitude as well. At The Guilford Press, we are most appreciative of Anna Brackett for shepherding the book through the production process and to Marian Robinson and the rest of the marketing department for their talent in marketing this intellectual product. We also cannot help but renew our gratitude here to Seymour Weingarten, Editor-in-Chief, and Robert Matloff, President, not simply for their encouragement and acceptance of this volume, but for their more than 16 years of friendship and collaboration on this and other works as well. Lastly, we must thank our families, Heather Mash and Pat, Steve, and Ken Barkley, for their patience with the demands such a project makes on our time with them and for their encouragement and support of its accomplishment.

Eric J. Mash, Ph.D.
University of Calgary

Russell A. Barkley, Ph.D.
University of Massachusetts
Medical Center

Contents

I. INTRODUCTION

ONE Child Psychopathology: A Developmental-
Systems Perspective   3
Eric J. Mash and David J. A. Dozois

II. BEHAVIOR DISORDERS

TWO Attention-Deficit/Hyperactivity Disorder   63
Russell A. Barkley

THREE Conduct and Oppositional Defiant Disorders   113
Stephen P. Hinshaw and Carolyn A. Anderson

III. EMOTIONAL AND SOCIAL DISORDERS

FOUR Childhood Depression   153
Constance Hammen and Karen D. Rudolph

FIVE Childhood Anxiety Disorders   196
*Anne Marie Albano, Bruce F. Chorpita,
and David H. Barlow*

SIX Childhood Posttraumatic Stress Disorder   242
Kenneth E. Fletcher

SEVEN Social Withdrawal   277
Kenneth H. Rubin and Shannon L. Stewart

IV. DEVELOPMENTAL AND LEARNING DISORDERS

EIGHT Autistic Disorder 311
Laura Grofer Klinger and Geraldine Dawson

NINE Childhood-Onset Schizophrenia 340
Joan Rosenbaum Asarnow and Robert F. Asarnow

TEN Mental Retardation 362
Robert M. Hodapp and Elisabeth M. Dykens

ELEVEN Learning Disabilities 390
G. Reid Lyon

TWELVE Tic Disorders 436
David W. Evans, Robert A. King, and James F. Leckman

V. INFANTS AND CHILDREN AT RISK FOR DISORDER

THIRTEEN Disorder and Risk for Disorder during Infancy 457
and Toddlerhood
*Karlen Lyons-Ruth, Charles H. Zeanah,
and Diane Benoit*

FOURTEEN Child Maltreatment 492
Christine Wekerle and David A. Wolfe

VI. HEALTH DISORDERS

FIFTEEN Eating Disorders 541
*G. Terence Wilson, Karen Heffernan,
and Carolyn M. D. Black*

SIXTEEN Health-Related Disorders 572
Cynthia Harbeck-Weber and Lizette Peterson

Author Index 603

Subject Index 637

CHILD PSYCHOPATHOLOGY

I

INTRODUCTION

Child Psychopathology
A Developmental–
Systems Perspective

Eric J. Mash
David J. A. Dozois

This volume provides a comprehensive account of the characteristics, definitions, developmental course, correlates, causes, contexts, and outcomes of psychopathology in children.[1] Our knowledge base for child and developmental psychopathology has grown exponentially over the past decade (Cicchetti & Cohen, 1995; Hersen & Ammerman, 1995; Lewis & Miller, 1990; Ollendick & Hersen, 1989). However, this knowledge base is compromised by the atheoretical, unsystematic, and somewhat fragmented fashion in which research findings in child psychopathology have accrued and by the conceptual and research complexities inherent in the study of such a rapidly changing and socially embedded organism as the child. In this introductory chapter, we address several central themes and issues related to conceptualizing childhood dysfunction and its determinants. In doing so, we provide a developmental–systems framework for understanding child psychopathology that emphasizes the role of developmental processes, the importance of context, and the influence of multiple and interacting events and processes in shaping adaptive and maladaptive development.

Almost since the time that modern views of mental illness began to emerge in the late 18th and early 19th centuries, less attention has been given to the study of psychopathology in children than adults. Benjamin Rush, the first American psychiatrist, suggested that children were less likely to suffer from mental illness than adults because the immaturity of their developing brains would prevent them from retaining the mental events that caused insanity (Donohue, Hersen, & Ammerman, 1995). More recently, interest in the study of child psychopathology has increased dramatically. In part, this is due to a growing realization that: (1) many childhood problems have lifelong consequences for the child and for society; (2) most adult disorders are rooted in early childhood conditions and/or experiences; and (3) a better understanding of childhood disorders may provide the basis for designing more effective intervention and prevention programs.

Issues concerning how psychopathology in children should be conceptualized and defined continue to be vigorously debated, debates that are no doubt fueled by the relative absence of well-controlled research studies with children as compared with adults. Until recently, much of the field's accumulated knowledge about child psychopathology, its causes, and its outcomes was extrapolated from theory and research on adult disorders. For example, it has only been in the last 5 years that child-focused models and research into disorders such as childhood depression (Hammen & Rudolph, Chapter 4, this volume) and anxiety (Albano, Chorpita, & Barlow, Chapter 5, this volume; Bernstein & Borchardt, 1991; Ollendick, Mattis, & Neville, 1994) have begun to emerge.

Even in studies conducted with children, much of our knowledge is based on findings obtained at a single point in the child's development and in a single context. Although useful, such findings provide still photographs of moving targets and fail to capture the dynamic changes that characterize most forms of child psychopathology. In addition, prior studies have not given sufficient attention to the social and cultural milieu in which deviant child development occurs. Although longitudinal approaches (e.g., Robins, 1966) and contextual models (e.g., Bronfenbrenner, 1977) have been available in the field of child study for some time, it is only in the last decade that the research enterprise has begun to take seriously the study of developmental trajectories utilizing longitudinal methods and the need to construct developmentally sensitive and systems-oriented models to account for the emergence of psychopathology in children (Lyons-Ruth, 1995).

The study of child psychopathology is further complicated by the facts that childhood problems do not come in neat packages and that most forms of psychopathology in children are known to overlap and/or to coexist with other disorders. For example, there is much overlap among problems such as violence, emotional and behavioral disorders, child maltreatment, substance abuse, delinquency, and learning difficulties (e.g., Greenbaum, Prange, Friedman, & Silver, 1991) and also between childhood anxiety and depression (e.g., Brady & Kendall, 1992). Many behavioral and emotional disturbances in children are also associated with specific physical symptoms and/or medical conditions. For example, a significant relationship between atopic rhinitis (hay fever) and chronic overanxious disorder in boys has recently been reported (Hart, Lahey, Hynd, Loeber, & McBurnett, 1995). Such an association, if confirmed, may have value in helping to identify the neurophysiological mechanisms underlying anxiety disorders, for example, hypothesized dysregulation of adrenergic and cholinergic functioning (E. L. Hart et al., 1995).

It is also the case that distinct boundaries between many commonly occurring childhood difficulties (e.g., noncompliance, defiance) and those childhood problems that come to be labeled as "disorders" (e.g., oppositional defiant disorder)

are not easily drawn. Judgments of deviancy usually depend as much on the child's related characteristics (e.g., age, gender, intelligence), the situational appropriateness of the child's behavior, the social and cultural context in which judgments are made, and the characteristics of adults who make these judgments as they do on any specific behaviors displayed by the child (Mash & Terdal, 1988a).

It has become increasingly evident that most forms of child psychopathology cannot be attributed to a single unitary cause. Although some rare disorders such as phenylketonuria (PKU) or fragile X mental retardation may be caused by a single gene, current models in behavioral genetics (e.g., quantitative trait loci) recognize that more common and complex disorders are the result of the operation of multigene systems containing varying effect sizes (Plomin, 1995). Child and family disturbances are likely to result from multiple, frequently co-occurring, reciprocal, and interacting risk factors, causal events, and processes (e.g., Ge, Conger, Lorenz, Shanahan, & Elder, 1995). Contextual events exert considerable influence in producing child and adolescent disorders, an influence that is almost always equivalent to or greater than those factors usually thought of as residing "within" the child. Some of the determinants of child psychopathology that have been identified include: hypo- or hyperreactive early infant dispositions (e.g., Kagan, Resnick, & Snidman, 1988, 1990); insecure child–parent attachments (e.g., Bretherton, 1995); difficult child behavior (e.g., Emery, Binkoff, Houts, & Carr, 1983); social–cognitive deficits (e.g., Crick & Dodge, 1994); deficits in social learning (e.g., Patterson, 1982; Patterson, Reid, & Dishion, 1992), emotion regulation (Cicchetti, Ackerman, & Izard, 1995), and/or impulse control (Barkley, 1996); neuropsychological and/or neurobiological dysfunction (e.g., Barkley, Grodzinsky, & DuPaul, 1992); genetic influences (e.g., Plomin, 1995); maladaptive patterns of parenting (e.g., Dumas, LaFreniere, & Serketich, 1995; Shaw & Bell, 1993); maternal depressed mood (e.g., Downey & Coyne, 1990); marital discord (e.g., Davies & Cummings, 1994); limited family resources and other poverty-related life stressors (e.g., Felner et al., 1995); and a host of other potential factors. These factors cannot be understood in isolation, and, for most disorders, research does not support granting central etiological status to any *single* risk or causal factor (e.g., Seifer, Sameroff, Baldwin, & Baldwin, 1992).

Since the causes and outcomes of child psycho-pathology operate in dynamic and interactive ways over time, they are not easy to disentangle. The designation of a specific factor as a cause or an outcome of child psychopathology usually reflects the point in an ongoing developmental process that the child is observed and the perspective of the observer. For example, a language deficit may be viewed as a disorder in its own right (e.g., mixed receptive–expressive language disorder), the cause of other difficulties (e.g., impulsivity), or the out-come of some other condition or disorder (e.g., autistic disorder). In addition, biological and environmental determinants interact at all periods of development. Dawson, Hessl, and Frey (1994), for example, noted that the characteristic styles used by parents in responding to their infants' emotional expressions may influence the manner in which patterns of cortical mappings and connec-tions within the limbic system are established in the infant. Similarly, Hart, Gunnar, and Cic-chetti (1995) have reported that maltreated preschoolers showed reduced cortisol activity in response to stress relative to controls, a finding that suggests altered activity of the stress-regulating hypothalamic–pituitary–adrenocortical (HPA) sys-tem among children who have been maltreated. These and other findings suggest that early expe-riences may shape neural structure and function, which may then create dispositions that direct and shape the child's later experiences.

Recent conceptualizations have focused on the etiologies and outcomes of psychopathology in children with an enhanced sensitivity to develop-mental continuities and discontinuities, develop-mental pathways, coexisting conditions, and con-textual influences. These conceptualizations view both normal and deviant developmental pro-cesses as involving multidirectional, reciprocal, and dynamic interactions among genetic, neural, behavioral, and environmental influences over time (Cicchetti & Tucker, 1994). And, consistent with this view, recent work derives from theory and empirical research on genetic and neurobio-logical influences (e.g., Pennington & Ozonoff, 1991; Torgersen, 1993), cognitive processing (e.g., Crick & Dodge, 1994; Strassberg & Dodge, 1995), emotion regulation (Cicchetti et al., 1995), and psychosocial processes (Patterson, 1982).

As will be discussed throughout this volume, current models of child psychopathology also seek to incorporate neurobiological factors, early parent–child relationships, attachment processes, a long-term memory store that develops with age

and experience, micro- and macrosocial influ-ences, cultural factors, age and gender, and re-actions from the social environment as variables and processes that interact and transform one another over time. In short then, current ap-proaches view the roots of developmental and psychiatric disturbances in children as the result of complex interactions over the course of devel-opment between the biology of brain maturation and the multidimensional nature of experience (Cicchetti & Tucker, 1994).

The experience and the expression of psycho-pathology in children are known to have cogni-tive, affective, physiological, and behavioral com-ponents and, in light of this, many differing descriptions and definitions of dysfunctionality in children have been proposed. However, a com-mon theme in defining child psychopathology has been that of *adaptational failure* in one or more of these components or in the ways in which these components are integrated (Garber, 1984; Lease & Ollendick, 1993; Mash, 1989; Sroufe & Rutter, 1984). Adaptational failure may involve deviation from age-appropriate norms, exaggeration or di-minishment of normal developmental expres-sions, interference in normal developmental progress, failure to master age-salient develop-mental tasks, and/or failure to develop a specific function or regulatory mechanism (Edelbrock, 1984; Loeber, 1991). The intensity, frequency, duration, patterning, situational appropriateness, and quality of the child's cognitions, emotions, and/or behaviors also represent important param-eters for conceptualizing and assessing child de-viancy (Garber, 1984).

There are a multitude of etiological models and treatment approaches that have been proposed to explain and remediate psychopathology in chil-dren. Unfortunately, most of these have yet to be substantiated, or for that matter even tested (Kazdin, 1988a). These models and approaches have differed in their relative emphasis on cer-tain causal mechanisms and constructs, often using very different terminology and concepts to describe seemingly similar child characteristics and behaviors. Although useful, many of these earlier models are based on what seem to be faulty premises concerning singular pathways of causal influence that do not capture the complexi-ties of child psychopathology suggested by recent research findings (Kazdin & Kagan, 1994).

In this regard, biological paradigms have em-phasized genetic mutations, neuroanatomy, and neurobiological mechanisms as factors contributing to psychopathology; psychodynamic models have focused on intrapsychic mechanisms, conflicts, and defenses; attachment models have emphasized the importance of early relationships and the ways in which internal representations of these relationships provide the foundation for constructing working models of self, others, and relationships more generally; behavioral/reinforcement models have emphasized excessive, inadequate, or maladaptive reinforcement and/or learning histories; social learning models have emphasized the importance of observational learning, vicarious experience, and reciprocal social interactions; cognitive models generally focus on the child's distorted or deficient cognitive structures and processes; affective models have emphasized dysfunctional emotion regulatory mechanisms; and family systems models have conceptualized child psychopathology within a framework of intra- and intergenerational family systems and subsystems and have emphasized the structural and/or functional elements that surround family relational difficulties.

The distinctiveness of each of the aforementioned models is in the relative importance it attaches to certain events and processes. However, it should be stressed that despite these variations in the relative emphasis given to certain causes versus others, most models recognize the role of multiple interacting influences. For example, although they differ in their relative emphasis, social learning and affective models both place importance on the role of symbolic representational processes in explaining childhood dysfunction. There is a growing recognition of the need to integrate currently available models through intra- and interdisciplinary research efforts. Such integration generally requires looking beyond the emphasis of single-cause theories to see what can be learned from other approaches as well as a general openness to relating concepts and findings from diverse theories (cf. Arkowitz, 1992).

Interdisciplinary perspectives on child psychopathology mirror the considerable investment in children on the part of many different disciplines and professions. The study of the etiology and maintenance of psychopathology in children has been and continues to be the subject matter of psychology, education, psychiatry, social work, medicine, and numerous other disciplines. Clearly, there is no one discipline that has proprietary rights to the study of childhood disturbances. Each discipline has formulated child psychopathology in terms of its own unique perspective. Particularly relevant in the context of this

chapter, is that child psychopathology/normality in medicine and psychiatry has typically been conceptualized and defined categorically in terms of the presence or absence of a particular disorder or syndrome that is believed to exist "within in the child." In contrast, psychology has more often conceptualized psychopathology/normality as representing an extreme occurrence on a continuum or dimension of characteristic(s) and has also focused on the role of environmental influences that operate "outside the child." However, the boundaries between categories and dimensions, or between inner and outer conditions and causes, are arbitrarily drawn, and there is a need to find workable ways of integrating the two different world views of psychiatry/medicine and psychology (Richters & Cicchetti, 1993).

As the chapters in this volume attest to, research into child psychopathology is accelerating at a remarkable rate. This in turn has resulted in a rapidly expanding and changing knowledge base. Each of the chapters in this volume provides a comprehensive review of current research and theory for a specific form of child psychopathology and a discussion of new developments and directions related to this disorder. The purposes of this introductory chapter are to provide a selective overview and discussion of: historical developments in the study of child psychopathology; current approaches to the definition and classification of childhood disorders; common types of psychopathology in children; important philosophical and epistemological assumptions that have guided theory and research; predominant theories regarding etiology; and prevalent and recurrent conceptual and methodological issues that cut across the wide spectrum of disorders represented in this volume. Particular emphasis is given to concepts, methods, and strategies that capture the complexities, reciprocal influences, and divergent pathways that current models and research have identified as crucial for understanding child psychopathology.

HISTORICAL CONTEXT FOR CHILD PSYCHOPATHOLOGY

Brief Historical Overview

Historical developments surrounding the emergence of child psychopathology as a field of study have been documented in a number of excellent sources and are considered only briefly here (see Achenbach, 1982; Cicchetti, 1990; Donohue et al., 1995; Kanner, 1962; Rie, 1971; Rubinstein, 1948). In general, the emergence of concepts of child psychopathology was inextricably related to the broader philosophical and societal changes in the ways in which children have been viewed and treated by adults over the course of history (Aries, 1962; Borstelmann, 1983; French, 1977). In ancient Greek and Roman societies, child behavior disorders were believed to result from organic imbalances, and children with physical or mental handicaps, disabilities, or deformities were viewed as a source of economic burden and/or social embarrassment to be scorned, abandoned, or put to death (French, 1977). This mistreatment, by today's standards, was common throughout the middle ages (A.D. 500–1300). In Colonial America, as many as two-thirds of all children died prior to the age of 5 years, and those who survived continued to be subjected to harsh treatment by adults. For example, the Stubborn Child Act of 1654 permitted a parent to put "stubborn" children to death for noncompliance, and insane children were kept in cages and cellars into the mid-1800s (Donohue et al., 1995).

There appeared to be a complete absence of references to emotional disorders in children prior to the 18th century, and when references to disordered child behavior began to emerge at the end of that century, they were usually presented in terms of the problem child's behavior as inherently evil (Kanner, 1962). Bizarre behaviors in children were attributed to satanic possession and evil spirits during the Spanish Inquisition, and both Calvin and Luther viewed mentally retarded children as filled with Satan. And, as noted by Rie (1971), "No distinct concept of disordered behavior in children could emerge so long as possession by the devil excluded other notions of causality" (p. 8).

Although all varieties of aberrant behavior in children have existed for millennia, the formal study of such behavior is relatively recent. Following a comprehensive review of historical developments in child psychopathology, Rie (1971) concluded: "There is a consensus, then, about the absence of any substantial body of knowledge—prior to the twentieth century—concerning disordered behavior in childhood; about the inconsistencies and discontinuities of efforts on behalf of disturbed children; and about the relative absence of those professional specialities which now concern themselves with such problems" (p. 6).

Rubinstein (1948) noted that: (1) there was not a single article dealing with insanity in childhood in any of the first 45 volumes of the *Journal of Insanity*; (2) there was no discovery or theory of importance to child psychiatry in the American literature prior to 1900, and no research today stems from any of these writings; and (3) the only significant work with children prior to this century focused on the care, treatment, and training of "mental defectives."

Increased concern for the plight and welfare of children with mental and behavioral disturbances was the result of two important sources of influence. First, advances in general medicine, physiology, and neurology led to the reemergence of the organic disease model and a concomitant emphasis on more humane forms of treatment. Second, the growing influence of the philosophies of Locke, Pestalozzi, and Rousseau led to the view that children needed moral guidance and support. With these changing views came an increased concern for moral education, compulsory education, and improved health practices. These early influences also provided the foundation for evolving views of child psychopathology as dependent on both organic and environmental causes.

Masturbatory Insanity: An Example

Societal and clinical views regarding masturbation in children can be used to illustrate the ways in which conceptualizations of child psychopathology have changed over time as well as several general issues related to its definition, study, and treatment. In addition to the historical significance of masturbation as the first disorder described as unique to children and adolescents (Rie, 1971), early conceptualizations of masturbatory insanity illustrate a view of mental illness as residing within the child (Cattell, 1938; Rees, 1939; Rie, 1971; Szasz, 1970).

Society's objections to masturbation originated from Orthodox Jewish codes and from Judeo–Christian dogmata (Szasz, 1970). It was not until the 18th century, with a decline in the domination of religious thought, coupled with the augmented influence of science, that masturbation came to be viewed as particularly harmful (Rie, 1971; Szasz, 1970). An anonymous clergyman who later became a physician wrote a dissertation entitled *Onania, or the Heinous Sin of Self-Pollution* (circa 1710, cited in Szasz, 1970). It was this manuscript that initially transformed the moral convictions regarding the wrongfulness of masturbation into a physiological explanation with severe medical ramifications. Following this exposition, numerous books appeared claiming that masturbation was a predominant etiological cause of both physical disease and mental illness. Thus, the notion that sexual overindulgences were deleterious to one's health was accepted, "virtually unaltered, first by the Church and then by Medicine" (Szasz, 1970, p. 182). Although the medical view of masturbation first emphasized the adverse impact upon physical health, by the middle of the 19th century, the dominant thought shifted to a focus on the presumed negative effects on mental health and nervous system functioning. By the latter part of the 19th century, masturbation was the most frequently mentioned "cause" of psychopathology in children. In fact, Spitzka (1890; cited in Rie, 1971) attributed approximately 25% of all psychiatric cases to this etiological factor.

Views of masturbatory insanity emerged, and were maintained, in the absence of any thought to the contrary and without any consideration of the base rate of masturbation in the general population. Although interest in masturbatory insanity began to wane in the latter half of the 19th century, the argument endured, albeit in milder forms, during the early 20th century when psychoanalytic theory gained rapid acceptance. Freud suggested that masturbation was one of the precipitants of neurasthenia, hypochondriasis, and anxiety neurosis (Rees, 1939). Apart from his own theories regarding the pathogenesis of neuroses, however, Freud did not present any real evidence for this view (Szasz, 1970). Eventually, the notion of masturbatory insanity gave way to the concept of neurosis, but it was still not until much later in the 20th century that the misguided and illusory belief in a relationship between masturbation and mental illness was dispelled.

As conceptualizations of childhood psychopathology evolved, and several variants of psychotherapy and residential treatments were developed (see Grellong, 1987, and Roberts & Kurtz, 1987), the search for determinants of psychiatric disorders in children became increasingly more sophisticated, thorough, and systematic (Rie, 1971). With this increased refinement of theory and research, there remained only fragments of the etiological hypothesis of masturbation. For example, in some psychoanalytic circles, enuresis was thought to symbolize suppressed masturbation (Rees, 1939; Walker, Kenning, & Faust-Campanile, 1989). Eventually masturbation came to be viewed as entirely harmless (Szasz, 1970).

This brief historical review illustrates a number of points. First, it provides an example of how the political and social climates influence our definitions of child psychopathology. The impact of religious thought was clearly reflected in the transformation from the moral judgment against the sins of the flesh to the medical opinion that masturbation was harmful to one's physical health, to the psychiatric assertion that sexual overindulgence caused insanity.

Second, the review points out the need to be cognizant of the ways in which moral convictions, idiosyncratic definitions of normalcy or pathology, and personal expectations influence what one looks for and ultimately finds in the name of science. In the case of masturbation, misleading findings resulted because hypotheses were "tested" with a mentality of confirmation rather than falsification (see Maxwell & DeLaney, 1990). Szasz (1970), in writing about the powerful authority of America's historical psychiatric figures such as Benjamin Rush, noted that there is a tendency among scientists to "attend only to those of their observations that confirm the accepted theories of their age, and reject those that refute them" (p. 187).

Third, masturbatory insanity illustrates the potential dangers that ensue when treatment decisions are made on the basis of deficient theoretical exposition and in the absence of empirical data. For example, early treatments consisted of clitoridectomies for women and spiked-toothed rings placed on the penises of men (Szasz, 1970). Finally, the example of masturbatory insanity portrays the longstanding view of psychopathology as residing within the child and the essential neglect of the role of his or her surroundings, context, relationships, and the interactions among these variables. The focus of current theory, research, and practice reflects a shift toward acknowledging developmental factors and including the family, peer group, school, and other sources of influence in conceptualizing and understanding child psychopathology (Fauber & Long, 1991; Kazdin, 1993; Mash, 1989).

SIGNIFICANCE OF CHILD PSYCHOPATHOLOGY

There has been and continues to be a great deal of misinformation and folklore concerning disorders of childhood. Many unsubstantiated theories have existed in both the popular and scientific literatures. These have ranged from mid-19th century views that overstimulation in the schools causes insanity (Makari, 1993) to mid-20th century views that autism is caused by inadequate parenting (Bettelheim, 1967). In addition, many of the constructs used to describe the characteristics and conditions of psychopathology in children have been globally and/or poorly defined (e.g., adjustment problem, emotional disturbance). However, despite the limitations, uncertainties, and definitional ambiguities that exist in the field, it is also evident that psychopathology during childhood represents a frequently occurring and significant societal concern (Institute of Medicine, 1989). Support for the significance of the problem comes from several sources.

First, psychopathology in children is a relatively common occurrence. Overall estimates of developmental, emotional, and behavioral disorders in children have ranged from 14% to 22% of all children (Brandenburg, Friedman, & Silver, 1990) with more severe forms of diagnosable mental disturbances estimated to occur in approximately 8% to 10% of all children (Boyle et al., 1987; Costello, 1989; Offord et al., 1987; Rutter, 1989). Moreover, these estimates do not include a substantial number of children who manifest subclinical or undiagnosed disturbances that may place them at high risk for the later development of more severe clinical problems. For example, McDermott and Weiss (1995) reported that of the children in their national sample who were classified as adjusted, 34.4% were classified as being only "marginally" adjusted.

Second, there are continuities across ages for many forms of child psychopathology. A significant proportion of children do not grow out of their childhood difficulties, although the ways in which these difficulties are expressed are likely to change in both form and severity over time. Even when diagnosable psychopathology is not evident at later ages, the child's failure to adjust during earlier developmental periods may still have a lasting negative impact on later family, occupational, and social adjustment. And, some forms of child psychopathology, for example antisocial patterns of behavior in boys, are known to be highly predictive of a variety of negative psychosocial, educational, and health outcomes in adolescence and adulthood (Hinshaw & Anderson, Chapter 3, this volume).

Third, recent social changes and conditions may place children at increasingly greater risk for the development of disorders and also for the development of more severe problems at younger ages (Duncan, Brooks-Gunn, & Klebanov, 1994). These social changes and conditions include multigenerational adversity in inner cities,

chronic poverty in women and children, pressures of family break-up, single parenting, homelessness, problems of the rural poor, difficulties of North American Native American children, adjustment problems of children in immigrant families, and conditions associated with the impact of prematurity, HIV, cocaine, and alcohol on children's growth and development (National Commission on Children, 1991). In addition to sociocultural changes, medical advances associated with higher rates of fetal survival may also contribute to a greater number of children showing serious behavior problems and learning disorders at a younger age.

Fourth, a significant number of children in North America are being subjected to maltreatment, and chronic maltreatment and psychopathology in children are highly associated (Wekerle & Wolfe, Chapter 14, this volume). Although precise estimates of the rates of occurrence of maltreatment are difficult to obtain because of the covert nature of the problem and other sampling and reporting biases (Mash & Wolfe, 1991), the numbers appear to be large. There were between 2 and 3 million reports of physical child abuse in 1990 in the United States resulting in 1,200 fatalities and 160,000 serious physical injuries (U.S. General Accounting Office, 1992). It has been estimated that each year at least 2,000 infants and young children die from abuse or neglect at the hands of their parents or caregivers (U.S. Advisory Board on Child Abuse and Neglect, 1995). Moreover, many reports of "accidental" injuries in children may be the result of unreported mistreatment by parents or siblings (Peterson & Brown, 1994). It would appear, then, that the total number of children who are adversely affected by the psychological and physical impact of maltreatment in North American society is staggering.

Fifth, the lifelong consequences associated with child psychopathology are exceedingly costly in terms of their economic impact and toll on human suffering. The costs are enormous with respect to demands on community resources (e.g., health, education, mental health, and criminal justice systems), loss in productivity, the need for repeated and long-term interventions, and with respect to the human suffering of both the afflicted children and the family and community members with whom they come into contact.

Sixth, as many as 70% of children in need of special attention do not receive services, and empirically validated prevention and treatment programs for many childhood disorders are currently unavailable (Kazdin & Kagan, 1994; Mash, 1989). There is a pressing need for the development and evaluation of prevention and intervention programs that are grounded in theory and research on child development in general and developmental psychopathology in particular (Jensen et al., 1993; Hibbs, 1995).[2]

EPIDEMIOLOGICAL CONSIDERATIONS

Prevalence

Epidemiological studies seek to determine the prevalence and distribution of disorders and their correlates in particular populations of children who vary in age, sex, social class, race, ethnicity, or other characteristics (Costello, 1989). As noted earlier, the overall prevalence rates for childhood problems are estimated to be high and in the order of 14% to 22% of all children. Rutter, Tizard, and Whitmore (1970), in the classic Isle of Wight Study, found the overall rate of child psychiatric disorders to be 6% to 8% in 9- to 11-year-old children. Richman, Stevenson, and Graham (1975), in the London Epidemiological Study, found moderate to severe behavior problems for 7% of the population with an additional 15% of children having mild problems. Boyle et al. (1987) and Offord et al. (1987), in the Ontario Child Health Study, reported that 19% of boys and 17% of girls had one or more disorders. Other epidemiological studies by Costello and Angold (1993), Earls (1980), Lapouse and Monk (1958), MacFarlane, Allen, and Honzik (1954), Verhulst and Koot (1992), and Werner, Bierman, and French (1971) have reported similar overall rates of prevalence.

Perhaps the most consistent general conclusions to be drawn from these epidemiological studies are that prevalence rates for childhood problems are generally high but that rates are likely to vary with the nature of the disorder, the age, sex, social class, and ethnicity of the child, the criteria used to define the problem, the method used to gather information (e.g., interview, questionnaire), the source of information (e.g., child, parent, teacher, or professional), sampling considerations, and a host of other factors.

Age Differences

Bird, Gould, Yager, Staghezza, and Camino (1989) reported no significant age differences for children aged 4 to 16 years in the total number of DSM-III disorders diagnosed at each age. Some studies of nonclinical samples of children have found a general decline in overall problems with age (e.g., Achenbach & Edelbrock, 1981), whereas similar studies of clinical samples have found an opposite trend (e.g., Achenbach, Howell, Quay, and Conners, 1991). Some studies have reported interactions among number of problems, age, sex of child, problem type, clinical status, and source of information (e.g., Achenbach et al., 1991; Offord, Boyle, & Racine, 1989). For example, Achenbach et al. (1991) found that externalizing problems showed a decline with age relative to internalizing problems but only for those children who had been referred for treatment, and Offord et al. (1989) found complex interactions between age and sex of the child with the findings also depending on whether the informant was a child, parent, or teacher.

These and other findings raise numerous questions concerning age differences in children's problem behaviors. Answers to even a seemingly simple question such as "do problem behaviors decrease (or increase) with age?" are complicated by: (1) a lack of uniform measures of behavior that can be used across a wide range of ages; (2) qualitative changes in the expression of behavior with development; (3) the interactions between age and sex of the child; (4) the use of different sources of information; (5) the specific problem behavior(s) of interest; (6) the clinical status of the children being assessed; and (7) the use of different diagnostic criteria for children of different ages.

Notwithstanding the above, both longitudinal (MacFarlane et al., 1954) and cross-sectional (Achenbach & Edelbrock, 1981; Achenbach et al., 1991) general population surveys are informative in depicting changes in the proportions of specific parent-, teacher- or child-reported problem behaviors with age (e.g., hyperactivity, argues, is lonely) as well as the manner in which the age changes vary as a function of problem type, sex, and clinical status of the child. However, it should be emphasized that general age trends are based on group statistics that may obscure the nonlinear and nonnormative changes that can occur for individual children. Additionally, these general surveys do not provide information concerning the processes underlying age changes. Studies of change in individual children over time and of the context in which this change occurs are needed if such processes are to be understood (e.g., Francis, Fletcher, Stuebing, Davidson, & Thompson, 1991).

Socioeconomic Status

It is estimated that 20% or more of children in the United States are poor (U.S. Bureau of the Census, 1993) and that as many as 20% of children growing up in inner-city poverty are impaired to some degree in their social, behavioral, and academic functioning (Duncan et al., 1994; Institute of Medicine, 1989; Schteingart, Molnar, Klein, Lowe, & Hartmann, 1995). The impact of socioeconomic disadvantage on children derives from the fact that socioeconomic status (SES) is a composite variable that includes many potential sources of negative influence. In addition to low income, low SES is often accompanied by low maternal education, a low level of employment, single-parent status, limited resources, and negative life events (e.g., poor nutrition, exposure to violence). Since overall indices of SES may include one or more of these variables in any given study, the relationship that is reported between SES and child psychopathology may vary as a function of the particular index used.

Lower-SES children have been reported to display more psychopathology and other problems than upper-SES children (e.g., Hollingshead & Redlich, 1958). Achenbach et al. (1991), for example, found significantly higher scores for lower-SES children versus higher-SES children for almost all parent-reported problem behaviors and syndromes. However, it is critical to note that *none of the reported SES differences accounted for more than 1% of the variance.* So although the reported relationships between SES and child psychopathology are statistically significant, the effects are small and should be interpreted cautiously. More importantly these findings suggest that global estimates of SES often tell us little about the associated processes through which SES exerts its influence on the child. Knowledge of such processes is needed to inform our understanding of the disorder. To illustrate, in investigating the relationship between SES and aggression, Guerra, Tolan, Huesmann, Van Acker, and Eron (1995) found that the effects of SES were explained mostly by the effects of stressful life events and beliefs that were accepting of aggression.

Research findings related to child psychopathology are frequently confounded by a failure to control for SES. For example, although it has been found that physically abused children show higher levels of externalizing problems than nonabused children (Mash, Johnston, & Kovitz, 1983), it is unclear as to whether or not physical abuse and externalizing problems are associated when the effects of social class are controlled for (Cummings, Hennessy, Rabideau, & Cicchetti, 1994; Wolfe & Mosk, 1983). The relationships among SES, maltreatment, and behavior disorders are further complicated by other findings that the effects of physical abuse on internalizing disorders may be independent of social class, whereas the effects of abuse on externalizing disorders may be dependent on social-class-related conditions (Okun, Parker, & Levendosky, 1994).

Sex Differences

Although sex differences in the expression of psychopathology have been formally recognized since the time that Freud presented his views at the beginning of this century, until very recently psychopathology in girls has received far less research attention than psychopathology in boys (Eme, 1979). Many studies have either excluded girls from their samples entirely or have examined all children together without considering findings for girls separately. For example, there is a paucity of studies on disruptive behavior disorders in girls (Zoccolillo, 1993). This is related to the perception that these disorders are much more common in boys than in girls, sampling biases in which boys, who are more severely disruptive, are also more likely to be referred and studied, and to the use of inclusionary diagnostic criteria that were derived and validated largely from studies with boys (Spitzer, Davies, & Barkley, 1990).

Early research into sex differences focused mainly on descriptive comparisons of the frequencies of different problems for boys versus girls at different ages. For example, Weisz and Suwanlert (1989) studied children in the United States and Thailand and found that boys were rated higher than girls on every problem for which there was a significant sex difference, including total problems, undercontrolled problems, overcontrolled problems, and culture-specific problems. Across cultures, boys have been found to display more fighting, impulsivity, and other uncontrolled behaviors than girls (Olweus, 1979). Epidemiological findings suggest that externalizing problems are more prevalent in boys than in girls, whereas internalizing problems are more prevalent in girls than in boys (Achenbach et al., 1991; Anderson, Williams, McGee, & Silva, 1987; Bird et al., 1989; Offord et al., 1987; Verhulst, Akkerhuis, & Altaus, 1985).

It has been found that boys show greater difficulties than girls during early or middle childhood, particularly with respect to disruptive behavior disorders (MacFarlane et al., 1954). Girls' problems may increase during adolescence, with higher prevalence rates for depression and dysphoric mood from midadolescence through adulthood. For example, conduct disorders and hyperactivity have been found to be more frequent in 12- to 16-year-old boys than girls, whereas emotional problems have been found to be more frequent for girls than boys in this age group (Boyle et al., 1987; Offord et al., 1987). Additionally, early signs of aggression have been found to predict later antisocial behavior for boys but not for girls (Tremblay et al., 1992).

However, not all studies have reported significant sex differences in overall rates of problem behavior (e.g., Achenbach & Edelbrock, 1981; Velez, Johnson, & Cohen, 1989). And, as was the case for SES, even when significant overall sex differences have been found, they tend to be small and to account for only a small proportion of the variance. It has also been found that although there is a much larger predominance of externalizing problems in boys and of internalizing problems in adolescent girls in samples of children who are referred for treatment, sex differences in externalizing versus internalizing problems are minimal in nonreferred samples of children (Achenbach et al., 1991).

Comparisons of the behavioral and emotional problems in boys versus girls over time can provide useful information about sex-related characteristics. However, taken in isolation, such global comparisons do not address possible qualitative differences in: (1) how psychopathology is expressed in boys versus girls; (2) the processes underlying these expressions; (3) the long-term consequences of certain behaviors for boys versus girls; and/or (4) the impact of certain environmental events on boys versus girls (Zahn-Waxler, 1993). As noted by Hops (1995), it seems likely that "the pathways from childhood to adolescence and adult pathology are age and gender specific and that these differences may be the result of different social contexts that nurture the development of health or pathology for female and male individuals" (p. 428). In addition to differential socialization practices, there are likely to be differences in the expression and outcome of psychopathology in boys versus girls as a function of biologically based differences. For example, in a study of the psychophysiology of disruptive behavior in boys versus girls, Zahn-Waxler, Cole, Welsh, and Fox (1995) found that disruptive girls

showed high electrodermal responding relative to disruptive boys and were also highly activated by a sadness mood induction. These investigators suggest that girls' disruptive behavior may be more closely connected to experiences of anxiety than boys' disruptive behavior.

There may also be differences in the processes underlying the expression of psychopathology and distress in boys versus girls. For example, recent findings suggest that the emergent sexuality of adolescents may create special difficulties with the parent of the opposite sex and that distress in adolescent males may be particularly disruptive for mothers and daughters (Ge et al., 1995). Others studies have found that daughters of depressed mothers may be at greater risk for the development of internalizing disorders than sons (Gelfand & Teti, 1990) and that sons of fathers showing avoidant patterns of adjustment to marital distress may be particularly susceptible to internalizing disorders (Katz & Gottman, 1993).

It has also been found that the types of childrearing environments predicting resilience to adversity may differ for boys and girls. Resilience in boys is associated with households in which there is a male model (e.g., father, grandfather, older sibling), structure, rules, and some encouragement of emotional expressiveness. In contrast, resilient girls come from households that combine risk taking and independence with support from a female caregiver (e.g., mother, grandmother, older sister) (Werner, 1995).

Zahn-Waxler et al. (1995) refer to the "gender paradox of comorbidities," which is that although the prevalence of disruptive behavior is lower in female than in male individuals, the risk of comorbid conditions such as anxiety is higher in female samples. In explaining this paradox, Zahn-Waxler et al. (1995) suggest that girls' heightened level of interpersonal sensitivity, caring, and empathy may be a protective factor in insulating them from developing antisocial behavior. However, at the same time, girls' overreceptivity to the plight of others, and their reluctance to assert their own needs in situations involving conflict and distress, may elevate their risk for the development of internalizing problems.

Although findings relating to sex differences and child psychopathology are complex, inconsistent, and frequently difficult to interpret, the cumulative findings from recent studies strongly indicate that the effects of gender are critical to understanding the expression and course of most forms of childhood disorder (Kavanagh & Hops, 1994). It is particularly important to understand the processes and mechanisms underlying these gender effects, recognizing that biological differences and differential socialization practices are likely to interact in accounting for any differences between the sexes that are found.

Rural versus Urban Differences

Although there is a general belief that rates of child behavior disorder are higher in urban than in rural areas, research findings in support of this view are weak and/or inconsistent. Findings from the Isle of Wight, Inner London Borough, and Ontario Child Mental Health Studies reveal prevalence rates of problem behavior that were higher for urban than rural children (Offord et al., 1987; Rutter, 1981). On the other hand, in a cross-cultural investigation, Weisz and Suwanlert (1991) found few differences in parent or teacher ratings of child problems as a function of rural versus urban status in either of the cultures that were studied (United States and Thailand). In a detailed analysis that controlled for the effects of SES and ethnicity and also looked at gradations of urbanization, Achenbach et al. (1991) found few differences in children's behavior problems or competencies as a function of rural versus urban status, although there was a significant but very small effect indicating higher delinquency scores for children in urban environments. These investigators concluded that earlier findings of higher rates of problem behavior in urban than rural areas "may have reflected the tendency to combine areas of intermediate urbanization with large urban areas for comparison with rural areas as well as a possible lack of control for demographic differences" (p. 86).

Ethnicity and Culture

Ethnicity

Numerous terms have been used to describe ethnic influences. These include ethnicity, race, ethnic identity, ethnic orientation, acculturation, bicultural orientation, and culture. As pointed out by Foster and Martinez (1995), there is a need to recognize the diversity of terminology that has been used in describing ethnicity and the fact that these terms refer to related but different things. Despite the growing ethnic diversity of the North American population, ethnic representation in research studies and the study of ethnicity-related issues more generally have received relatively little attention in studies of child psychopathology. In lamenting this state of affairs, Foster and Martinez (1995) state: "The under-representation of children from diverse backgrounds is accompanied by a dearth of empirical literature on the origins, correlates, and treatment of child psychopathology in different ethnic groups within the United States. Instead, investigators have based theories of child behavior, both normal and deviant, on data drawn largely from European-American culture" (p. 214).

Research into child psychopathology has generally been insensitive to possible differences in prevalence, age of onset, developmental course, and risk factors related to ethnicity (Kazdin & Kagan, 1994). In addition, few studies have compared ethnic groups while controlling for other important variables such as SES, sex, age, and geographic region (Achenbach et al., 1991).

Some studies that have included a small number of African-American children in their samples have reported somewhat higher rates of externalizing problems for this group (Costello, 1989; Velez et al., 1989). However, other studies with much larger national samples that included non-Hispanic white, African-American, and Hispanic children have reported either no or very small differences related to race or ethnicity when SES, sex, age, and referral status were controlled for (Achenbach & Edelbrock, 1981; Achenbach et al., 1991; Lahey et al., 1995). So, although externalizing problems have been reported to be more common among African-American children, this finding is likely an artifact related to SES. Externalizing disorder is associated with both ethnicity and with SES, and, since there is an overrepresentation of minority status children in low SES groups in North America, caution must be exercised in interpreting the relationships among SES, ethnicity, and aggression (Guerra et al., 1995; Lahey et al., 1995).

In contrast to the mixed findings for conduct disorder, race has not been found to be strongly associated with risk for eating disorders (Leon, Fulkerson, Perry, & Early-Zald, 1995). However, Catalano et al. (1993) have reported different patterns of substance abuse related to ethnicity. More research is needed, but these and other findings suggest that the effects of ethnicity will likely vary with the problem under consideration.

As was the case for SES and gender, global comparisons of the prevalence of different types of problems for different ethnic groups are not likely to be very revealing. On the other hand, studies into the processes affecting the form, associated factors, and outcomes of different disorders for various ethnic groups hold promise for increasing our understanding of the relationship between ethnicity and child psychopathology.

Culture

Since the meaning of children's social behavior is influenced by cultural and societal values, it should not be surprising that the form of expression, frequency of occurrence, and predictive significance of various forms of child psychopathology may vary across cultures or that cultural attitudes may influence patterns of referral for treatment (Lambert & Weisz, 1992). For example, shyness and oversensitivity in children have been found to be associated with peer rejection and social maladjustment in Western cultures but with leadership, school competence, and academic achievement in Chinese children in Shanghai (Chen, Rubin, & Li, 1995). Similarly, Lambert and Weisz (1989) found that overcontrolled problems were reported significantly more often for Jamaican than American youngsters, a finding that is consistent with Afro-British Jamaican cultural attitudes and practices that discourage child aggression and other undercontrolled behavior and that foster inhibition and other overcontrolled behavior.

Weisz and Sigman (1993), using parent-reports of behavioral and emotional problems in 11- to 15-year-old children from Kenya, Thailand, and the United States, found that Kenyan children were rated particularly high on overcontrolled problems (e.g., fears, feelings of guilt, somatic concerns), due primarily to numerous reports of somatic problems. In this mixed-race sample, whites were rated particularly high on undercontrolled problems (e.g., arguing, disobedient at home, cruel to others). Weisz and Suwanlert (1987) compared 6- to 11-year-old children in the Buddhist-oriented, emotionally controlled culture of Thailand with American 6- to 11-year-olds. Parent reports revealed Thai–United States differences in 54 problem behaviors, most of which were modest in magnitude. Thai children were rated higher than American children on problems involving overcontrolled behaviors such as anxiety and depression, whereas American children were rated higher than Thai children on undercontrolled behaviors such as disobedience and fighting.

Weisz and Suwanlert (1991) compared ratings of behavior and emotional problems of 2- to 9-year-old children in Thailand and the United States. Parents and teachers in Thailand rated both overcontrolled problems and undercontrolled problems as less serious, less worrisome, less likely to reflect personality traits, and more likely to improve with time. These findings suggest that there may be cultural differences in the meanings ascribed to problem behaviors across cultures.

Findings from these studies suggest that the expression of, and tolerance for, many child behavioral and emotional disturbances are clearly related to social and cultural values. The processes that mediate this relationship are in need of further investigation. In this regard, it is important that research on child psychopathology not be generalized from one culture to another unless there is support for doing so. The rates of expression of some disorders, particularly those with a strong neurobiological basis (e.g., attention-deficit/hyperactivity disorder [ADHD], autistic disorder), may be less susceptible to cultural influences than others. However social and cultural beliefs and values are likely to influence the meaning given to these behaviors, the way in which they are responded to, their form of expression, and their outcomes.

An important distinction to be made with respect to cross-cultural comparisons is whether or not there are real differences in the rates of the disorder, or differences in the criteria used to make judgments about these problems. For example, Weisz and Suwanlert (1989) compared the teacher-reported behavioral/emotional problems of Thai and U.S. children (ages 6–11 years). It was found that Thai teachers were confronted with students who were more prone to behavioral and emotional problems at school than were teachers in the United States but that they applied different judgments to the behaviors they observed.

Cultural factors are known to influence not only informal labeling processes but formal diagnostic practices as well. For example, reported prevalence rates of ADHD in Britain are much lower than in the United States because of differences in the way in which diagnostic criteria for ADHD are applied in the two countries. Such differences in diagnostic practices may lead to spurious differences in reported prevalence rates for different forms of child psychopathology across cultures.

BASIC ISSUES IN CHILD PSYCHOPATHOLOGY

There are a number of recurrent and overlapping issues that have characterized the study of psychopathology in children (Rutter & Garmezy, 1983). This section briefly highlights a number of these including: (1) difficulties in conceptualizing psychopathology and normality in children; (2) the need to consider healthy child functioning and adjustment; (3) questions concerning developmental continuities/discontinuities; (4) the concept of developmental pathways; (5) risk and resilience; and (6) the role of contextual influences.

Psychopathology/Normality

Conceptualizing child psychopathology and attempting to establish boundaries between what constitutes abnormal versus normal functioning are arbitrary processes at best. Traditional approaches to mental disorders in children have emphasized concepts such as symptoms, diagnosis, illness, and treatment, and by doing so, they have strongly influenced the way we think about child psychopathology and related questions (Richters & Cicchetti, 1993). Childhood disorders have most commonly been conceptualized in terms of deviancies involving breakdowns in adaptive functioning, statistical deviation, unexpected distress or disability, and/or biological impairment.

Wakefield (1992) has proposed an overarching concept of mental disorder as "harmful dysfunction." This concept encompasses the child's physical and mental functioning and includes both value- and science-based criteria. In the context of child psychopathology, the child's condition is viewed as a disorder only if: (1) it causes harm or deprivation of benefit to the child, as judged by social norms; and (2) it results from the failure of some internal mechanism to perform its natural function (e.g., "an effect that is part of the evolutionary explanation of the existence and structure of the mechanism," p. 384). This view of mental disorder focuses attention on internally evolved mechanisms. Nevertheless, as pointed out by Richters and Cicchetti (1993), it only identifies

the decisions that need to be made in defining mental disorders but does not specify *how* such decisions are to be made. As is the case for most definitions of mental disorder that have been proposed, questions related to defining the boundaries between normal and abnormal, understanding the differences between normal variability and dysfunction, defining what constitutes "harmful conditions," linking dysfunctions causally with these conditions, and circumscribing the domain of "natural," or of other proposed mechanisms, are still matters of considerable controversy (Lilienfeld & Marino, 1995; Richters & Cicchetti, 1993). Categories of mental disorder stem from man-made linguistic distinctions and abstractions and boundaries between what constitutes normal and abnormal conditions, or different abnormal conditions, are not easily drawn. Although it may sometimes appear that efforts to categorize mental disorders are carving "nature at its joints," whether or not such "joints" actually exist is open to debate (e.g., Cantor, Smith, French, & Mezzich, 1980; Lilienfeld & Marino, 1995).

Healthy Functioning

The study of psychopathology in children requires concomitant attention to adaptive developmental processes for several reasons. First, judgments of deviancy require knowledge of normative developmental functioning, both with respect to the child's performance relative to same-age peers and with respect to the child's own baseline of development. Second, maladaptation and adaptation represent two sides of the same coin in that dysfunction in a particular domain of development (e.g., the occurrence of inappropriate behaviors) is usually accompanied by a failure to meet developmental tasks and expectations in the same domain (e.g., the nonoccurrence of appropriate behaviors). Third, in addition to the specific problems that lead to referral and diagnosis, disturbed children are also likely to show impairments in other areas of adaptive functioning. For example, in addition to their core symptoms of impulsivity and inattention, children with ADHD also show lower-than-average levels of functioning in their socialization, communication, and activities of daily living (e.g., Stein, Szumowski, Blondis, & Roizen, 1995). Fourth, most children with specific disorders are known to cope effectively in some areas of their lives. Understanding the child's strengths informs our knowledge of the disorder and provides a basis for the development of effective treatment strategies. Fifth, children move between pathological and nonpathological forms of functioning over the course of their development. Individual children may have their "ups and downs" in problem type and frequency over time (MacFarlane et al., 1954). Finally, many child behaviors that are not classifiable as deviant at a particular point in time may nevertheless represent less extreme expressions or compensations of an already-existing disorder or early expressions of a later progression to deviant extremes as development continues (Adelman, 1995). Therefore, understanding child psychopathology requires that we also attend to these less extreme forms of difficulty.

For these and other reasons to be discussed, the study of child psychopathology requires an understanding of both abnormal and healthy functioning. As noted by Cicchetti and Richters (1993), "it is only through the joint consideration of adaptive and maladaptive processes within the individual that it becomes possible to speak in meaningful terms about the existence, nature, and boundaries of the underlying psychopathology" (p. 335). To date, far greater attention has been devoted to the description and classification of psychopathology in children than to healthy child functioning, nonpathological psychosocial problems related to emotional upset, misbehavior, and learning, and factors that promote the successful resolution of developmental tasks (Adelman, 1995; Loeber, 1991). In light of this imbalance, there is currently a need for studies of normal developmental processes (Lewis, 1990; Sroufe & Rutter, 1984), investigations of normative and representative community samples of children (Kazdin, 1989; National Institute of Mental Health, 1990), and studies of "resilient" children who show normal development in the face of adversity (Rutter, 1987; Rutter & Rutter, 1993).

Developmental Continuities and Discontinuities

A central issue for theory and research in child psychopathology concerns the continuity of disorders identified from one time to another and the relationship between child and adult disorders (Garber, 1984; Kazdin & Johnson, 1994; Pennington & Ozonoff, 1991; Rutter & Rutter, 1993; Sroufe & Jacobvitz, 1989). Over the past decade, research into early attachment has stimulated general interest in the roles of relational processes and internalized representational systems as the bases for understanding continuities and discontinuities in psychopathology over time and across generations (Lyons-Ruth, 1995).

Some childhood disorders, such as mental retardation or autistic disorder, are chronic conditions that will persist throughout childhood and into adulthood. Other disorders, such as functional enuresis and encopresis, occur during childhood and only rarely manifest themselves in adults (Walker et al., 1989). And, other disorders (e.g., mood disorders, schizophrenia, generalized anxiety disorder) are expressed, albeit in modified forms, in both childhood and adulthood and exhibit varying degrees of continuity over time (American Psychiatric Association, 1994; Garber, 1984).

Evidence in support of the continuity between child and adult disorders is equivocal and depends on a number of methodological factors related to research design, assessment instruments, the nature of the study sample, and the type and severity of the disorder (Garber, 1984). In general, the literature suggests that child psychopathology is continuous with adult disorders for some but not all problems. As we discuss, there is evidence that appears to favor the stability of externalizing problems over internalizing problems. However, previous findings may reflect the severity and pervasiveness of the disorders assessed, referral biases, and the fact that longitudinal investigations of children with internalizing disorders are just beginning to emerge (Albano, Chorpita, & Barlow, Chapter 5, this volume; Ollendick & King, 1994; Rubin & Stewart, Chapter 7, this volume). One recent study of self-reported anxious symptoms in children in the first grade found that such symptoms were stable over a 4-month period and were predictive of poorer reading achievement over this time period (Ialongo, Edelsohn, Werthamer-Larsson, Crockett, & Kellam, 1994).

The possible mechanisms underlying the relationships between early maladaptation and later disordered behavior are numerous and can operate in both direct and indirect ways (Garber, 1984; Rutter, 1994a; Rutter & Rutter, 1993; Sroufe & Rutter, 1984). Some examples of direct relationships between early and later difficulties include: (1) the development of a disorder during infancy or childhood which then persists over time; (2) experiences that alter the infant's or child's physical status (e.g., neural plasticity), which in turn influence later functioning (Courchesne, Chisum, & Townsend, 1994); and (3) the acquisition of early patterns of responding (e.g., compulsive compliance) that may be adaptive in light of the child's current developmental level and circumstances, but may result in later psychopathology when circumstances change and new developmental challenges arise.

Some examples of indirect associations between child and adult psychopathology may involve: (1) early predispositions that eventually interact with environmental experiences (e.g., stressors), the combination of which leads to dysfunction. For example, Egeland and Heister (1995) found that the impact of daycare on disadvantaged high-risk children at 42 months of age was related to the child's attachment quality at 12 months of age, with securely attached children more likely to be negatively affected by early out-of-home care; (2) experiences that contribute to an altered sense of self-esteem (e.g., peer rejection), or that create a negative cognitive set, that then lead to later difficulties; and (3) experiences providing various opportunities or obstacles that then lead to the selection of particular environmental conditions and by doing so guide the child's course of development (Rutter, 1987; Sroufe & Rutter, 1984).

Recent longitudinal studies have documented impressive continuities for some behavioral problems, particularly conduct disorders in boys, whereas other behavioral difficulties appear to be more transient (Edelbrock, 1984). With respect to conduct disorders, official court records indicate that 50% to 70% of youths arrested for delinquent acts during childhood or adolescence are arrested in adulthood. Graham and Rutter (1973) found that 75% of children diagnosed with conduct disorder still evidenced this disorder at adolescence. Consistent with this finding, Offord et al. (1992) also found considerable stability of conduct disorder, with approximately 45% of the children with conduct disorder at ages 4 to 12 years still meeting criteria for this diagnosis at 4-year follow-up. Lahey et al. (1995) reported that about one-half of the youths in their sample who met criteria for conduct disorder at time one also met criteria at time two. These investigators also noted a high likelihood that the criteria for conduct disorder would be met at least one or more times over a 3-year interval. In other words, children who were diagnosed with conduct disorder were rarely symptom-free.

Research efforts have focused not only on the continuities and discontinuities in childhood disorders but also on the identification of factors that predict them. One factor that has been studied in the context of conduct disorder is age of onset, with early onset usually viewed as the occurrence of conduct-disorder symptoms prior to age 12 years (Loeber & Dishion, 1983; O'Donnell, Hawkins, & Abbott, 1995). It has been found that early onset of symptoms relates to higher rates and more serious antisocial acts over a longer period of time for both boys and girls. However, psychosocial variables that are present prior to and following onset may influence the seriousness and chronicity more than age of onset per se (Tolan & Thomas, 1995). An issue that needs to be addressed concerns whether or not early age of onset operates in a causal fashion for later problems, and if so, how?

Although research supports the notion of continuity of disorders, it does not support the continuity of identical symptoms over time (e.g., homotypic correspondence). Continuity over time for patterns of behavior rather than for specific symptoms is the norm. For example, although externalizing disorders in boys are stable over time, the ways in which these behavioral patterns are expressed are likely to change dramatically over the course of development (Olweus, 1979). Even with wide fluctuations in the expression of behavior over time, "children may show consistency in their general adaptive or maladaptive pattern of organizing their experiences and interacting with the environment" (Garber, 1984, p. 34). A number of research findings can be used to illustrate this notion of consistent "patterns of organization." For example, early behavioral inhibition may affect later adjustment by influencing the way in which the child adapts to new and unfamiliar situations and the ensuing person–environment interactions over time (Hirshfeld et al., 1992; Kagan, 1994a; Kagan, Resnick, Clark, Snidman, & Garcia-Coll, 1984; Kagan, Resnick, & Snidman, 1987; Kagan et al., 1988). Another example of a consistent pattern of organization is that of early attachment quality and the development of internal working models that children carry with them into their later relationships (Bowlby, 1988; Goldberg, 1991). Internal working models of self and relationships may remain relatively stable over time at the same time that the behavioral expressions of these internal models change with development. From a neuroscientific perspective, Pennington and Ozonoff (1991) argue that certain genes and neural systems also play a significant predisposing role in influencing the continuity of psychopathology, and that the "discontinuities at one level of analyses—that of observable behavior—may mask continuities at deeper levels of analysis; those concerned with the mechanisms underlying observable behavior" (p. 117).

Given that developmental continuity is reflected in general patterns of organization over time rather than in isolated behaviors or symptoms, the relationships between early adaptation and later psychopathology are not likely to be direct or uncomplicated (Sroufe & Rutter, 1984). The connections between child and adult psychopathology are marked by *both* continuities and discontinuities. The degree of continuity/discontinuity will vary as a function of changing environmental circumstances and transactions between the child and environment that affect the child's developmental trajectory.

Developmental Pathways

The concept of "developmental pathways" is crucial for understanding continuities and discontinuities in psychopathology. Such pathways are not directly observable but function as metaphors that are inferred from repeated assessments of individual children over time (Loeber, 1991). A pathway, according to Loeber (1991), "defines the sequence and timing of behavioral continuities and transformations and, ideally, summarizes the probabilistic relationships between successive behaviors" (p. 98). In attempting to identify developmental pathways as either "deviant" or "normal," it is important to recognize that: (1) different pathways may lead to similar expressions of psychopathology (i.e., equifinality); and (2) similar initial pathways may result in different forms of dysfunction (i.e., multifinality) depending on the organization of the larger system in which they occur (Lewis, 1990; Loeber, 1991; Sroufe & Jacobvitz, 1989).

Research findings related to child maltreatment provide an example of a possible developmental pathway. It has been found that physically abused children are more likely to develop insecure attachments, view interpersonal relationships as being coercive and threatening, become vigilant and selectively attend to hostile cues, instantly classify others as threatening or nonthreatening, and acquire aggressive behavioral strategies for solving interpersonal problems (Wekerle & Wolfe, Chapter 14, this volume). These children bring representational

models to peer relationships that are negative, conflictual, and unpredictable. They process social information in a biased and deviant manner, and develop problems with peer relationships that involve social withdrawal, unpopularity, and overt social rejection by peers (Dodge, Pettit, & Bates, 1994).

In another context, Lizardi et al. (1995) found that adult patients with early-onset dysthymia reported childhood experiences of greater physical and sexual abuse, poorer relationships with both their mothers and fathers, lower levels of maternal and paternal care, and greater maternal and paternal overprotection than normal controls. In contrast, patients with episodic major depression also reported greater childhood adversity, but they differed from normal controls only with respect to a history of sexual abuse, quality of relationship with father, and maternal overprotection. Although these findings are retrospective and need to be interpreted cautiously, they illustrate how different patterns of early relationships may be associated with different pathways to the development of different types of affective disorder at a later age.

The systematic delineation of developmental pathways offers several advantages for the study of the etiology and outcomes of childhood disorders and may also suggest strategies for intervention. Loeber (1991, p. 99) describes these advantages as "attempts to capture the changing manifestations and variable phenotype of a given disorder" over time. In this way, the study of developmental pathways includes etiological considerations, the assessment of comorbidities as they accrue over time, and a sensitivity to diverse outcomes.

Risk and Resilience

Most studies of child psychopathology have focused on elucidating the developmental pathways for deviancy and maladjustment to the relative exclusion of those for competency and adjustment (Loeber, 1991; but see Luthar, 1993; Rutter, 1985, 1987, 1994b; and Rutter & Rutter, 1993, for exceptions). However, a significant proportion of children who are at-risk do not develop later problems. There is a growing recognition of the need not only to examine risk factors but also those conditions that protect vulnerable children from dysfunction and lead to successful adaptations despite adversity (Cicchetti & Garmezy, 1993; Garmezy, 1985).

Although the term "resilience" has not been clearly operationalized, it is generally used to describe children who: (1) manage to avoid negative outcomes and/or to achieve positive outcomes despite being at significant risk for the development of psychopathology (Luthar, 1993; Rutter, 1987); (2) display sustained competence under stress; or (3) show recovery from trauma (Werner, 1995). Risk is usually defined in terms of child characteristics that are known to be associated with negative outcomes, for example, difficult temperament (Rende, 1993; Rothbart & Ahadi, 1994; Thomas, Chess, & Birch, 1968) or early conduct disorder, and/or in terms of a child's exposure to extreme or disadvantaged environmental conditions such as poverty or abuse. Individual children who are predisposed to develop psychopathology and who show a susceptibility to negative developmental outcomes under high-risk conditions are referred to as "vulnerable." Genetic make-up and temperament are two factors that are presumed to contribute to susceptibility for children who are exposed to high-risk environments (Rutter, 1985).

Zimmerman and Arunkumar (1994) have noted that research on resiliency has lacked a consistent vocabulary, conceptual framework, and methodological approach. It is particularly important to ensure that resilience not be defined as a universal, categorical, or fixed attribute of the child. Individual children may be resilient in relation to specific stressors but not resilient with respect to others, and resiliency may vary over time and across contexts. As noted by Zimmerman and Arunkumar (1994, p. 4), "research on resiliency can only identify those particular risk circumstances when environmental conditions, individual factors, and developmental tasks interact to help children and adolescents avoid negative consequences."

One problem in research on resilience has been an absence of agreed-upon criteria for defining positive developmental outcomes (see Kaufman, Cook, Arny, Jones, & Pittinsky, 1994 for a review of the ways in which positive outcomes in studies of resilience have been operationalized). Variations across studies in the source of information (e.g., parent or teacher), the type of assessment method (e.g., interview, questionnaire, observation), and the number and timing of assessments can easily influence the proportion of children who are designated as resilient or not in any particular investigation (Kaufman et al., 1994). And, there is also some confusion about and circularity in how the term resiliency has been used, in that it has been used to refer to both an outcome and to the cause of an outcome. Several different models of resiliency have also been proposed, the most common ones being a compensatory model, a challenge model (e.g., stress inoculation), and a protective factors model (Garmezy, Masten, & Tellegen, 1984).

Rather than a direct causal pathway leading to a particular outcome, resilience involves ongoing interactions between a series of protective and/or vulnerability factors within the child and his or her surroundings and particular risk factors. Protective or vulnerability factors need to be conceptualized as processes rather than as absolutes, since the same event or condition (e.g., early out-of-home placement) can operate as a protective or vulnerability factor as a function of the overall context in which it occurs (Rutter, 1987).

A variety of protective and vulnerability factors have been found to influence children's reactions to potential risk factors or stressors. These include factors within the child, the family, and the community (Werner & Smith, 1992). Common risk factors that have been found to adversely affect the child encompass both acute stressful situations and chronic adversity, and they include events such as chronic poverty, serious caregiving deficits, parental psychopathology, death of a parent, community disasters, homelessness, family breakup, and perinatal stress.

Protective factors within the child that have been identified include an easy temperament (e.g., a child who is energetic, affectionate, cuddly, good-natured, and/or easy to deal with) that makes the child engaging to other people, early coping strategies that combine autonomy with help-seeking when needed, high intelligence and scholastic competence, effective communication and problem-solving skills, positive self-esteem, and high self-efficacy (Werner, 1995). An example of a possible protective factor within the child is illustrated in a study by Katz and Gottman (1995), who found that high vagal tone, taken as an index of the child's ability to regulate emotion via self-soothing, focused attention, and organized and goal-directed behavior, can buffer children from the increases in externalizing behaviors that are often associated with exposure to marital hostility and discord.

At a family level, protective factors that have been identified include the opportunity to establish a close relationship with at least one person who is attuned to the child's needs, positive parenting, availability of resources (e.g., childcare), a talent or hobby that is valued by adults or peers, and family religious beliefs that provide stability and meaning during times of hardship or adversity (Werner & Smith, 1992). Protective factors in the community include extrafamilial relationships with caring neighbors, community elders, or peers, an effective school environment with teachers who serve as positive role models and sources of support, and opening of opportunities at major life transitions (e.g., adult education, voluntary military service, church or community participation, a supportive friend or marital partner).

Thus, early patterns of adaptation influence later adjustment in complex and reciprocal ways. Adverse conditions, early adaptational struggles, and failure to meet developmental tasks do not inevitably lead to a fixed and unmalleable dysfunctional path. Rather, many different factors, including chance events and encounters, can provide turning points whereby success in a particular developmental task (e.g., educational advances, peer relationships) alters a child's course onto a more adaptive trajectory (e.g., Rutter, 1987). Conversely, there are numerous events and circumstances that may deflect the child's developmental trajectory toward that of maladaptation (e.g., dysfunctional home environment, peer rejection, difficulties in school, parental psychopathology, intergenerational conflict).

The interrelated issues of developmental continuities/discontinuities and developmental pathways are far from being resolved or well understood. The multitude of interdependent and reciprocal influences, mechanisms, and processes involved in the etiology and course of child psychopathology clearly suggest a need for more complex theories (e.g., chaos theory) (Barton, 1994; Haynes & Blaine, 1995), research designs, and data-analytic strategies (Kazdin & Kagan, 1994).

Contextual Influences

Messick (1983) cogently argues that any consideration of psychopathology in childhood and adolescence must consider and account for three sets of contextual variables: (1) the child *as* context—the idea that there are unique child characteristics, predispositions, and traits that influence the course of development; (2) the child *of* context—the notion that the child comes from a background of interrelated family, peer, classroom,

teacher, school, community, and cultural influences; and (3) the child *in* context—the understanding that the child is a dynamic and rapidly changing entity and that descriptions taken at one point in time or in one situation may yield very different information than those taken at other times or in other contexts.

Research has increasingly come to recognize the reciprocal transactions between the developing child and the multiple social and environmental contexts in which development occurs. Understanding context requires a consideration of both proximal and distal events, events that impinge directly on the child in a particular situation at a particular point in time, extrasituational events that affect the child indirectly (e.g., a parent's work-related stress), and temporally remote events that continue to affect the child through their representation in the child's current cognitive/affective data base.

Defining context has been, and continues to be, a matter of some complexity (Mischel, 1968). The context of maltreatment provides an illustration of difficulties in definition. Maltreatment can be defined in terms of its type, frequency, severity, and chronicity in the family. Each of these parameters may contribute to child outcomes but in different ways. For example, Manly, Cicchetti, and Barnett (1994) studied different types of maltreatment and found that outcomes generally did not differ for children who were categorized as neglected versus abused. However, a regression analysis indicated that neglect accounted for more of the variance in child problems than other types of abuse. In this study, sexually abused children were also found to be more socially competent than children exposed to other forms of maltreatment. This may reflect a lack of chronicity associated with sexual abuse, or that problems related to sexual abuse may not reveal themselves until later periods in the child's development when issues concerning sexuality become more salient. Other studies have found that psychological maltreatment and emotional abuse account for most of the distortions in development and have the most negative consequences for the child (Crittenden, Claussen, & Sugarman, 1994).

The example of maltreatment illustrates how contexts for development encompass heterogeneous sets of circumstances and how child outcomes may vary as a function of the configuration of these circumstances over time, when and where outcomes are assessed, and the specific aspects of development that are affected. More precise definitions are needed if the impact of maltreatment, or for that matter any contextual event (i.e., parent disciplinary styles, family support, intellectual stimulation), is to be understood.

Even for those forms of child psychopathology for which there are strong neurobiological influences, the expression of the disorder is likely to interact with contextual demands. For example, Iaboni, Douglas, and Baker (1995) found that although the overall pattern of responding that characterized children with ADHD was indicative of a generalized inhibitory deficit, the self-regulatory problems of these children became more evident with continuing task demands for inhibition and/or deployment of effort.

Child psychopathology research has increasingly focused on the role of the family system, the complex relationships within families, and the reciprocal influences among various family subsystems. There is a need to consider the processes occurring within disturbed families and the common and unique ways in which these processes affect both individual family members and subsystems. Within the family, the role of the mother–child and marital subsystems have received the most research attention to date, with less attention given to the role of siblings (Hetherington, Reiss, & Plomin, 1994) or fathers (Phares & Compas, 1992). For the most part, research into family processes and child psychopathology has not kept pace with family theory and practice, and there is a need for the development of sophisticated methodologies and valid measures that will capture the complex relationships that have been hypothesized to be operative in disturbed and normal family systems (Bray, 1995; Bray, Maxwell, & Cole, 1995). This task is complicated by a lack of consensus concerning how dysfunctional or healthy family functioning should be defined or what specific family processes are important to assess (Bray, 1994; Mash & Johnston, 1995).

DEFINING CHILD PSYCHOPATHOLOGY

There has been, and continues to be, a lack of consensus concerning how psychopathology in children should be defined. Comparisons of findings across studies are extremely difficult to make because of the idiosyncratic ways in which samples of children have been constituted. For example, children described as "hyperactive" in different studies have varied widely with respect to their symptoms and conditions, problem severities, comorbidities, and levels of cognitive functioning (Barkley, Chapter 2, this volume).

More recently, researchers and clinicians have come to define psychopathology in children using standardized diagnostic systems such as DSM-IV (American Psychiatric Association, 1994) and ICD-10 (World Health Organization, 1992). The diagnostic criteria utilized in each of these systems are the ones most commonly used, and these are presented for the individual childhood disorders described in each of the chapters of this volume. However, the increased use and acceptance of these diagnostic systems should not be taken as an indication of widespread agreement regarding the fundamental nature of what constitutes psychopathology in children or the specific criteria that should be used in defining such psychopathology. In many ways, the increased use of these systems seems to reflect both some degree of resignation on the part of researchers and clinicians concerning the prospect of developing a better alternative approach and a growing consensus concerning the need to achieve some level of standardization, albeit an imperfect one, in defining childhood disorders.

There are several fundamental questions that have characterized most discussions concerning how child psychopathology should be defined. These include:

1. Should child psychopathology be viewed as a disorder that occurs within the individual child, as a relational disturbance, as a reaction to environmental circumstances, or as some combination of all of these?
2. Does child psychopathology constitute a qualitatively different condition than normality, an extreme point on a continuous trait or dimension, or some combination of the two?
3. Can homogeneous disorders be identified, or is child psychopathology best defined as a configuration of co-occurring disorders or as a profile of traits and characteristics?
4. Can child psychopathology be defined as a static entity at a particular point in time, or do the realities of development necessitate that it be defined as a dynamic and ongoing process that expresses itself in different ways over time and across contexts?
5. Is child psychopathology best defined in terms of its current expression, or do defi-

nitions also need to incorporate nonpathological conditions that may constitute risk factors for later problems?

There are currently no definitive answers to these questions. More often, the way in which they are answered is a reflection of theoretical or disciplinary preferences and specific purposes and goals (e.g., defining samples for research studies or determining program or insurance eligibility).

Psychopathology as Adaptational Difficulty

A common theme in defining child psychopathology has been that of adaptational difficulty or failure (Garber, 1984; Mash, 1989; Sroufe & Rutter, 1984). Sroufe and Rutter (1984) note that regardless of whether "particular patterns of early adaptation are to a greater or lesser extent influenced by inherent dispositions or by early experience, they are nonetheless patterns of adaptation" (p. 23). Developmental competence is reflected in the child's ability to use internal and external resources to achieve a successful adaptation (Waters & Sroufe, 1983), and problems occur when the child fails to adapt successfully. The term adaptational failure has been used in various ways to describe a child's deviation from age-appropriate norms, an exaggeration of normal developmental trends, an interference in normal developmental progress, or a failure to obtain a specific developmental function or mechanism (Edelbrock, 1984; Garber, 1984; Kazdin, 1988b; Mash, 1989). Even with wide variations in terminology and proposed explanatory mechanisms across theories, there is general agreement that maladaptation represents a pause, a regression, or a deviation in development (Garber, 1984; Simeonsson & Rosenthal, 1992). As noted nearly 50 years ago by Cattell (1938): "The forms which adjustment difficulties assume differ slightly under different cultural, economic, and religious conditions and in different periods of history; but most significantly they differ with age. Every age of man has its specific hurdles; and those who leap over one most easily may be least adapted to leap another of a different type" (p. 170).

In conceptualizing and defining psychopathology as adaptational difficulty, it also becomes essential to conceptualize and identify the specific developmental tasks that are important for children at various ages and periods of development and the many contextual variables that derive from and surround the child (Garber, 1984; Mash, 1989; Messick, 1983). In this regard, the study of psychopathology in children and the study of development and context are for all intents and purposes inseparable.

In determining whether a given behavior should be considered to be deviant in relation to stage-salient developmental issues, Garber (1984) stresses the need to understand four important parameters. The first, "intensity," refers to the magnitude of behavior as excessive or deficient. The second, "frequency," refers to the severity of the problem behavior, or how often it does or does not occur. Third, the "duration" of behavior must be considered. Some difficulties are transient and spontaneously remit whereas others persist over time. It is crucial that the intensity, frequency, and duration of the child's behavior be appraised with respect to what is considered normative for a given age. The final parameter of deviance concerns the "number of different symptoms" and their "configuration." Each of these parameters is central to research and theory and to one's specific definition of adaptational failure, regression, stagnation, or deviation.

Social Judgment

The diagnosis of psychopathology in children is almost always a reflection of both the characteristics and behavior of the child *and* of significant adults and professionals. Research findings utilizing behavior problem checklists and interviews indicate that there can be considerable disagreement across informants (e.g., parents, teachers, professionals) concerning problem behaviors in children (Achenbach, McConaughy, & Howell, 1987). Mothers typically report more problems than fathers (e.g., Achenbach et al., 1991), and across a range of domains, teachers identify more problems than other sources used to assess the same domain. For example, in a study with maltreated children, only 21% of children were classified as resilient by teachers, whereas 64% of children were so classified based on reports from other sources (Kaufman et al., 1994).

Issues regarding disagreement/agreement among informants are complicated by that fact that the amount of agreement will vary with the age and sex of the child (Offord et al., 1989), the nature of the problem being reported on (e.g., internalizing vs. externalizing), and the method used to gather information (e.g., interview versus questionnaire). For example, Tarullo, Richardson, Radke-Yarrow, and Martinez (1995) found that both mother–child and father–child agreement was higher for preadolescent than adolescent children. Disagreements among informants create methodological difficulties in interpreting epidemiological data when such data are obtained from different sources and also in how specific diagnoses are arrived at in research and practice.

Also of importance is how disagreements among informants are interpreted. For example, disagreements may be viewed as: (1) bias or error on the part of one of the informants; (2) evidence for the variability of children's behavior across the situations in which they are observed by others; (3) lack of access to certain types of behavior (i.e., private events) on the part of one informant; (4) denial of the problem; or (5) active distortion of information in the service of some other goal (i.e., defensive exclusion, treatment eligibility).

Parental psychopathology may "color" descriptions of child problems as may occur when abusive or depressed mothers provide negative or exaggerated descriptions of their children (Mash et al., 1983; Richters, 1992) or when dismissive/avoidant adult informants deny the presence of emotional problems at the same time that professionals observe a high level of symptoms (Dozier & Lee, 1995). These latter types of problems in reporting may be especially likely given the frequent lack of correspondence between the expression and the experience of distress for many child and adult disturbances. Hypothesized relationships between parental psychopathology and reports of exaggerated child symptoms have received mixed support. For example, recent work has failed to find evidence for distorted reports by depressed mothers (Tarullo et al., 1995).

TYPES OF CHILD PSYCHOPATHOLOGY

The types of problems for which children are referred for treatment are reflected in the different approaches that have been used to conceptualize and classify these problems. Among the more common of these approaches are:

1. General and specific behavior problem checklists that enumerate individual child symptoms, for example, the Child Behavior Checklist (Achenbach, 1991) and the Children's Depression Inventory (Kovacs & Beck, 1977).
2. Dimensional approaches that focus on symptom clusters or syndromes derived from behavior problem checklists, for example, the Child Behavior Checklist and Profile (Achenbach, 1993).
3. Categorical approaches that use predetermined diagnostic criteria to define the presence or absence of a particular disorder(s), for example, the DSM-IV (American Psychiatric Association, 1994) and ICD-10 (World Health Organization, 1992).

Issues related to the use of these different classification approaches are discussed in a later section of this chapter. What follows is a brief description of each of the aforementioned approaches that is intended to provide an overview of the types of problem behaviors, dimensions, and disorders that occur during childhood and that are the focus of the chapters of this volume.

Individual Symptoms

The individual behavioral and emotional problems (e.g., symptoms) that characterize most forms of child psychopathology have been found to occur in almost all children at one time or another during their development (e.g., Achenbach & Edelbrock, 1981; Achenbach et al., 1991; MacFarlane et al., 1954). When taken in isolation, specific symptoms have generally shown little correspondence to the child's overall current adjustment or to later outcomes. This is the case even for many symptoms previously hypothesized to be significant indicators of psychopathology in children, for example, thumbsucking after 4 years of age (Friman, Larzelere, & Finney, 1994). It is usually the age appropriateness, clustering, and patterning of symptoms that serve to define child psychopathology rather than the presence of individual symptoms.

Many of the individual behavior problems displayed by children who are referred for treatment are similar to those that occur in less extreme forms in the general population or in children of younger ages. For example, Achenbach et al. (1991) found that although referred children scored higher than nonreferred children on 209 of 216 parent-rated problems, only 9 of the 209 items showed effects related to clinical status that were considered to be large (accounting for more than 13.8% of the variance) according to criteria specified by Cohen (1988). To illustrate the kinds of individual symptoms that are more common in referred than nonreferred children, individual parent-reported symptoms that accounted for 10% or more of the variance in clinical status in the Achenbach et al. (1991) study are shown in Table 1.1. It can be seen that even problems that best discriminate between referred and non-referred children are relatively common behaviors that occur to some extent in all children—they are not particularly strange or unusual behaviors. In addition, most *individual* problem behaviors (approximately 90% of those on behavior problem checklists) do not, by themselves, discriminate between groups of clinic and non-clinic children. Nondiscriminating items include some problems for children in both groups that are relatively common (e.g., brags, screams) and others that occur less frequently (e.g., sets fires, bowel movements outside the toilet).

Dimensions of Child Psychopathology

A second approach to describing child psychopathology identifies symptom clusters or "syndromes" derived through the use of multivariate statistical procedures such as factor analysis or cluster analysis (e.g., Achenbach, 1993; McDermott, 1993; McDermott & Weiss, 1995). Research has identified two broad dimensions of child psychopathology, one reflecting externalizing or undercontrolled problems and the other reflecting internalizing or overcontrolled problems (Reynolds, 1992). The externalizing dimension encompasses behaviors often thought of as directed at others, whereas the internalizing dimension describes feelings or states that are commonly viewed as "inner directed."

Within the two broad dimensions of externalizing and internalizing disorders are specific subdimensions or syndromes. Some of the subdimensions of child psychopathology that have commonly been identified in research are presented in Table 1.2. They include: withdrawn, somatic complaints, anxious/depressed, social problems, thought problems, attention problems, delinquent behavior, and aggressive behavior (Achenbach, 1993). Examples of the specific problem behaviors that comprise each of these subdimensions are also included in Table 1.2. The particular subdimensions that are identified may vary from study to study as a function of the item pool from which they are derived, the age and sex of children in the sample, the methods of assessment, and the informants.

Recent taxometric efforts have also described groups of children in terms of consistently identified profiles of scores on the various syndromes (Achenbach, 1993). Such profiles have been reliably identified and appear to have promise in addressing problems related to comorbidity (see section on Comorbidity, below). At present, however, our nomenclature for describing these profiles is limited, and they have yet to be widely validated or used in clinical research and practice.

Categories of Child Psychopathology

The DSM-IV diagnostic system (American Psychiatric Association, 1994) provides comprehen-

TABLE 1.1. Individual Parent-Rated Problems Accounting for More than 10% of the Variance in Clinical Status of Children Aged 4–16

Poor school work (19%)[a]°
Can't concentrate, can't pay attention for long (18%)°
Lacks self-confidence (17%)°
Punishment doesn't change his/her behavior (17%)°
Disobedient at home (15%)°
Has trouble following directions (15%)°
Sad or depressed (15%)°
Uncooperative (14%)°
Nervous, high-strung, or tense (14%)°
Feels he/she can't succeed (13%)
Feels worthless or inferior (13%)
Disobedient at school (13%)
Easily distracted (13%)
Lies (13%)
Looks unhappy without good reason (13%)
Fails to finish things he/she starts (12%)
Defiant (12%)
Doesn't get along with other kids (12%)
Has a hard time making friends (12%)
Doesn't seem to feel guilty after misbehavior (12%)
Needs constant supervision (12%)
Sudden changes in mood or feelings (12%)
Angry moods (11%)
Impulsive or acts without thinking (11%)
Irritable (11%)
Temper tantrums or hot temper (10%)
Does things slowly and incorrectly (10%)
Loses train of thought (10%)
Loss of ability to have fun (10%)
Passive or lacks initiative (10%)

Note. From Achenbach et al. (1991, pp. 107–115). Copyright 1991 by the Society for Research in Child Development. Adapted by permission.
[a]Number in parentheses indicates the percentage of variance accounted for by this problem behavior.
°Items accounting for 14% or more of the variance are designated as having a large effect size according to criteria presented by Cohen (1988).

TABLE 1.2. Commonly Identified Dimensions of Child Psychopathology and Examples of Items That Reflect Each of the Dimensions[a]

Withdrawn

Would rather be alone
Refuses to talk
Secretive
Shy, timid
Stares blankly
Sulks
Underactive
Unhappy, sad, depressed
Withdrawn

Somatic complaints

Feels dizzy
Overtired
Aches, pains
Headaches
Nausea
Eye problems
Rashes, skin problems
Stomachaches
Vomiting

Anxious/depressed

Lonely
Cries a lot
Fears impulses
Needs to be perfect
Feels unloved
Feels persecuted
Feels worthless
Nervous, tense
Fearful, anxious
Feels too guilty
Self-conscious
Suspicious
Unhappy, sad, depressed
Worries
Harms self
Thinks about suicide
Overconforms
Hurt when criticized
Anxious to please
Afraid of mistakes

Social problems

Acts too young
Too dependent
Doesn't get along with peers
Gets teased
Not liked by peers
Clumsy
Prefers younger children
Overweight
Withdrawn
Lonely
Cries
Feels unloved
Feels persecuted
Feels worthless
Accident prone

Thought problems

Can't get mind off thoughts
Hears things
Repeats acts
Sees things
Strange behavior
Strange ideas
Stares blankly
Harms self
Fears
Stores up things

Attention problems

Acts too young
Can't concentrate
Can't sit still
Confused
Daydreams
Impulsive
Nervous, tense
Poor school work
Clumsy
Stares blankly
Twitches
Hums, odd noises
Fails to finish
Fidgets
Difficulty with directions
Difficulty learning
Apathetic
Messy work
Inattentive
Underachieving
Fails to carry out tasks

Delinquent behavior

Lacks guilt
Bad companions
Lies
Prefers older kids
Runs away from home
Sets fires
Steals at home
Swearing, obscenity
Truancy
Alcohol, drugs
Thinks about sex too much
Vandalism
Tardy

Aggressive behavior

Argues
Brags
Mean to others
Demands attention
Destroys own things
Destroys others' things
Disobedient at school
Jealous
Fights
Attacks people
Screams
Shows off
Stubborn, irritable
Sudden mood changes
Talks too much
Teases
Temper tantrums
Threatens
Loud
Disobedient at home
Defiant
Disturbs others
Talks out of turn
Disrupts class
Explosive
Easily frustrated

Note. From Achenbach (1993, pp. 41–43). Copyright 1993 by T. M. Achenbach. Adapted by permission.
[a]Dimensions are based on analyses across informants (e.g., parents, teachers, and children) and assessment methods (Child Behavior Checklist, Youth Self-Report Form, and Teacher Report Form).

sive coverage of the general types of symptom clusters displayed by children characterized as having mental disorders. To illustrate, DSM-IV categories that apply to children are listed in Tables 1.3 to 1.6. These tables are not intended to be exhaustive of all DSM-IV diagnoses that may apply to children. Rather, they are intended to provide an overview of the range and variety of disorders that typically occur during childhood. Specific DSM-IV disorders and their subtypes are discussed in detail in each of the individual chapters of this volume.

Table 1.3 lists DSM-IV developmental and learning disorders categories including mental retardation, pervasive developmental disorders such as autistic disorder, specific problems related to reading and mathematics, and communication difficulties. Many of these disorders constitute chronic conditions that often reflect deficits in capacity rather than performance difficulties per se.

Table 1.4 lists DSM-IV categories for disorders that are usually first diagnosed in infancy, childhood, or adolescence. These disorders have traditionally been thought of as first occurring in childhood, or as exclusive to childhood, and as requiring operational criteria different from those used to define disorders in adults.

Table 1.5 lists disorders that can be diagnosed in children (e.g., mood disorders, anxiety disorders) but that are not listed in DSM-IV as distinct disorders that first occur during childhood, or that require operational criteria that are different from those used for adults. In many ways the DSM-IV distinction between child and adult categories is an arbitrary one and more a reflection of our current lack of knowledge concerning the continuities between child and adult disorders than of the existence of qualitatively distinct conditions. Recent efforts to diagnose ADHD in adults illustrate this problem. Although the criteria for ADHD were derived from work with children and the disorder is included in the child section of DSM-IV, these criteria are being used to diagnose adults even though they do not fit the expression of the disorder in adults very well.

The more general issue here is whether there is a need for separate diagnostic criteria for children versus adults, or whether one can use the same criteria by adjusting them to take into account differences in developmental level. For instance, the childhood category of overanxious disorder in DSM-III-R (American Psychiatric Association, 1987) was subsumed under the cat-

TABLE 1.3. DSM-IV Categories for Developmental and Learning Disorders Usually First Diagnosed in Infancy, Childhood, or Adolescence

Mental Retardation
Mild, Moderate, Severe, Profound, Severity Unspecified

Learning Disorders
Reading Disorder
Mathematics Disorder
Disorder of Written Expression
Learning Disorder Not Otherwise Specified

Motor Skills Disorder
Developmental Coordination Disorder

Communication Disorders
Expressive Language Disorder
Mixed Receptive–Expressive
Language Disorder
Phonological Disorder
Stuttering
Communication Disorder Not Otherwise Specified

Pervasive Developmental Disorders
Autistic Disorder
Rett's Disorder
Childhood Disintegrative Disorder
Asperger's Disorder
Pervasive Developmental Disorder Not Otherwise Specified

egory generalized anxiety disorder in DSM-IV (American Psychiatric Association, 1994). With this change, the number of criteria required for children to meet this diagnosis was also altered.

Finally, Table 1.6 lists DSM-IV categories for other conditions that are not defined as mental disorders but that may be a focus of clinical attention during childhood. The categories that are included are the ones that seem especially relevant to children in that they emphasize relational problems, maltreatment, and academic and adjustment difficulties.

APPROACHES TO THE CLASSIFICATION AND DIAGNOSIS OF CHILD PSYCHOPATHOLOGY

The formal and informal classification systems that have been used by psychiatrists, psychologists, and educators to categorize the different forms of child psychopathology have played a central role in defining the field. For example, in referring to these systems, Adelman (1995) states: "They determine the ways individuals are de-

TABLE 1.4. DSM-IV Categories for Disorders Usually First Diagnosed in Infancy, Childhood, or Adolescence

Attention Deficit and Disruptive Behavior Disorders
Attention-Deficit/Hyperactivity Disorder
    Predominantly Inattentive Type
    Predominantly Hyperactive–Impulsive Type
    Combined Type
    Attention-Deficit/Hyperactivity Disorder
        Not Otherwise Specified
Disruptive Behavior Disorders
    Conduct Disorder
    Oppositional Defiant Disorder
    Disruptive Behavior Disorder Not Otherwise
        Specified

Feeding and Eating Disorders of Infancy or Early Childhood
Pica
Rumination Disorder
Feeding Disorder of Infancy or Early Childhood

Tic Disorders
Tourette's Disorder
Chronic Motor or Vocal Tic Disorder
Tic Disorder Not Otherwise Specified

Elimination Disorders
Encopresis
Enuresis

Other Disorders of Infancy, Childhood, or Adolescence
Separation Anxiety Disorder
Selective Mutism
Reactive Attachment Disorder of Infancy or Early
    Childhood
Stereotypic Movement Disorder
Disorder of Infancy, Childhood, or Adolescence Not
    Otherwise Specified

TABLE 1.5. Selected Categories for Disorders of Childhood or Adolescence That Are Not Listed Separately in DSM-IV as Those Usually First Diagnosed in Infancy, Childhood, or Adolescence

Mood Disorders
Depressive Disorders
    Major Depressive Disorder
    Dysthymic Disorder
Bipolar Disorders

Anxiety Disorders
Specific Phobia, Social Phobia, Obsessive–Compulsive
Disorder, Posttraumatic Stress Disorder,
Acute Stress Disorder, Generalized Anxiety
Disorder, Anxiety Disorder Due to . . .
(Specific Medical Condition)

Somatoform Disorders
Factitious Disorders
Dissociative Disorders
Sexual and Gender Identity Disorders
Eating Disorders
Sleep Disorders
Schizophrenia and Other Psychotic Disorders
Substance-Related Disorders
Impulse-Control Disorders Not Elsewhere Classified
Adjustment Disorders
Personality Disorders

been weak, nondiscriminating, or open to systematic bias. Similarly, comparisons between studies have often been vitiated because cases have been defined differently, because the settings have been noncomparable, or because the measures focused on different aspects of behavior" (p. 865).

TABLE 1.6. Selected DSM-IV Categories for Other Conditions That May Be a Focus of Clinical Attention during Childhood That Are Not Defined as Mental Disorders

Relational Problems
Relational Problem Related to a General Mental
    Disorder or General Medical Condition
Parent–Child Relational Problem
Partner Relational Problem
Sibling Relational Problem
Relational Problem Not Otherwise Specified

Problems Related to Abuse or Neglect
Physical Abuse of Child
Sexual Abuse of Child
Neglect of Child

Bereavement
Borderline Intellectual Functioning
Academic Problem
Child or Adolescent Antisocial Behavior
Identity Problem

scribed, studied, and served; they shape prevailing practices related to intervention, professional training, and certification; and they influence decisions about funding. It is not surprising, therefore, that debates about classification schemes, specific diagnostic procedures, and the very act of labeling are so heated" (p. 29).

Although early conceptualizations of psychopathology included underdeveloped and global descriptions of childhood disorders (e.g., adjustment problem), this state of affairs has been steadily improving. Nevertheless, problems and issues in describing and classifying childhood disorders continue to plague the field (e.g., Quay, Routh, & Shapiro, 1987). As noted by Rutter and Garmezy (1983): "All too frequently findings have been inconclusive because the measures employed have

There is general agreement in medicine and psychiatry regarding the need for a system of classification for childhood disorders. However, major areas of contention have arisen around such issues as which disorders should be included in the system, what the optimal strategies are for organizing and grouping disorders, and what specific criteria should be used to define a particular disorder (Achenbach, 1985; Achenbach & Edelbrock, 1989; Clementz & Iacono, 1993; Mash & Terdal, 1988a; Routh, 1990).

The two most common approaches to the diagnosis and classification of child psychopathology involve the use of: (1) "categorical" classification systems that are based primarily on informed clinical consensus, an approach that has and continues to dominate the field (American Psychiatric Association, 1994); and (2) empirically based "dimensional" classification schemes derived through the use of a variety of multivariate statistical techniques (Achenbach, 1993). In addition, alternative and/or derivative approaches to classification have been proposed to address perceived deficiencies associated with the use of categorical and dimensional approaches. These have included developmentally based approaches (Clementz & Iacono, 1993; Garber, 1984), the use of performance-based measures (Kazdin & Kagan, 1994), prototype classification (Cantor et al., 1980), and behavioral classification based on behavioral excesses, deficits, and faulty stimulus control (Adams, Doster, & Calhoun, 1977; Kanfer & Saslow, 1969; Mash & Hunsley, 1990). Although each of these alternative approaches has something to offer to the classification of childhood disorders, they are generally underdeveloped, unstandardized, and have not been widely accepted or used in either research or practice.

To date, there is no single classification scheme for childhood disorders that has established adequate reliability and validity (Garber, 1984; Mash & Terdal, 1988a). Concerns continue to be expressed by many researchers and clinicians that current diagnostic and classification systems: (1) underrepresent disorders of infancy and childhood; (2) are inadequate in representing the interrelationships and overlap that exists among many childhood disorders; and (3) are not sufficiently sensitive to the developmental, contextual, and relational parameters that are known to characterize most forms of psychopathology in children.

Categorical Approaches

Categorical approaches to the classification of childhood disorders have included systems developed by the Group for the Advancement of Psychiatry (1974), the World Health Organization (ICD-10; 1992), the American Psychiatric Association (DSM-IV; 1994), and the Zero to Three/National Center for Clinical Infant Programs (DC:0–3; 1994). Although a detailed review of all of these systems is beyond the scope of this chapter, a brief history of the development of the *Diagnostic and Statistical Manuals of Mental Disorders* (DSM) will be presented to illustrate issues associated with categorical approaches, the growing concern for more reliable classification schemes for childhood disorders, and the evolving conceptualizations of childhood disorders that have emerged over the past half century. Also, the recently developed *Diagnostic Classification of Mental Health and Developmental Disorders of Infancy and Early Childhood* (Diagnostic Classification: 0–3; Zero to Three/National Center for Clinical Infant Programs, 1994) will be presented to illustrate a categorical approach that attempts to integrate developmental and contextual information into the diagnosis of problems of infants and young children.

DSM-IV

One of the first efforts to collect data on mental illness was in the U.S. census of 1840, which recorded the frequency of a single category of "idiocy/insanity." Forty years later, seven categories of mental illness were identified: dementia, dipsomania, epilepsy, mania, melancholia, monomania, and paresis (American Psychiatric Association, 1994). Much later (in the 1940s), the World Health Organization (WHO) classification system emerged with the manuals of the *International Classification of Diseases* (ICD), whose 6th edition included, for the first time, a section for mental disorders (American Psychiatric Association, 1994; Clementz & Iacono, 1993).

In response to perceived inadequacies of the ICD system for classifying mental disorders, the American Psychiatric Association Committee on Nomenclature and Statistics developed its own *Diagnostic and Statistical Manual of Mental Disorders* (DSM-I) in 1952 (American Psychiatric Association, 1952). There were three major categories of dysfunction in the DSM-I: organic brain syndromes, functional disorder, and mental deficiency (Kessler, 1971). The term "reaction" was used throughout the text, which reflected Adolf Meyer's psychobiological view that mental illness involves reactions of the personality to psychological, social, and biological factors (American Psychiatric Association, 1987, 1994). Cass and Thomas (1979) noted that children were virtually neglected in the early versions of DSM with most childhood disorders relegated to the adult categories. In fact, DSM-I included only one child category of "adjustment reactions of childhood and of adolescence," which was included under the heading of "transient situational disorders."

As reflected in the use of the term "reaction," psychoanalytic theory had a substantial impact on the classification of both child and adult psychopathology (Clementz & Iacono, 1993). Although the term "reaction" was eliminated from DSM-II (American Psychiatric Association, 1968), a separate section was reserved for classifying neuroses, and diagnoses could be made based on an assessment of either the client's presenting symptomatology or inferences about his or her unconscious processes (Clementz & Iacono, 1993). Once again, apart from conditions subsumed under the adult categories, DSM-II gave little recognition to childhood difficulties save mental retardation and schizophrenia–childhood type (Cass & Thomas, 1979).

As a formal taxonomy, DSM-III (American Psychiatric Association, 1980) represented a significant advance over the earlier editions of the DSM. The first and second editions contained only narrative descriptions of symptoms, and clinicians had to draw on their own definitions for making a diagnosis (American Psychiatric Association, 1980). In DSM-III, these descriptions were replaced by explicit criteria, which, in turn, enhanced diagnostic reliability (Achenbach, 1985; American Psychiatric Association, 1980). Moreover, unsubstantiated inferences that were heavily embedded in psychoanalytic theory were dropped, more child categories were included, a multiaxial system was adopted, and a greater emphasis was placed on empirical data (Achenbach, 1985). These changes reflected the beginnings of a conceptual shift in both diagnostic systems and etiological models away from an isolated focus of psychopathology as existing within the child alone toward an increased emphasis on his or her surrounding context. DSM-III was revised in 1987 (DSM-III-R) to help clarify the numerous inconsistencies and ambiguities that were noted in its use. For example, empirical data at that time did not support the category of attention deficit disorder *without* hyperactivity as a unique symptom cluster (Routh, 1990), and this category was removed from DSM-III-R. DSM-III-R was also developed to be polythetic in that a child could be diagnosed with a certain subset of symptoms without having to meet all criteria. This was an important change, especially in light of the heterogeneity and rapidly changing nature of most childhood disorders (Mash & Terdal, 1988a). Relative to its predecessors, far greater emphasis was also placed on empirical findings in the development of the DSM-IV, particularly for the child categories (American Psychiatric Association, 1994).

DSM-IV is a multiaxial system that includes five different axes. Axis I is used to report *Clinical Disorders and Other Conditions That May Be a Focus of Clinical Attention*. The various Axis I diagnostic categories that apply to infants, children, and adolescents are listed in Tables 1.3 to 1.6 of this chapter. Axis II includes *Personality Disorders and Mental Retardation*. The remaining Axes pertain to *General Medical Conditions* (Axis III), *Psychosocial and Environmental Problems* (Axis IV) and *Global Assessment of Functioning* (Axis V).

Although DSM-III-R (American Psychiatric Association, 1987) and DSM-IV (American Psychiatric Association, 1994) include numerous improvements over the previous DSMs, with their greater emphasis on empirical research and more explicit diagnostic criteria sets and algorithms, there have also been criticisms raised with the DSM system. One major criticism is the static nature of DSM categories, especially when one considers the dynamic nature of development in children (Mash & Terdal, 1988a; Routh, 1990). Another source of dissatisfaction is that DSM-IV categorical scheme may contribute minimally to meeting children's needs. For example, it may be necessary for a child to meet specific diagnostic criteria for a learning disability in order to qualify for a special education class. However, if the child's problems are subclinical, or the child's problems relate to more than one DSM category, then he or she may be denied services (Achenbach, 1990). Another problem with DSM-IV relates to the wording and the lack of empirical adequacy for certain criterion sets. For example, the words "often" in ADHD and conduct disorder criteria or "persistent" and "recurrent" in separation anxiety disorder criteria are not clearly defined. This ambiguity poses a particular problem when one considers that the primary source of assessment information is often the child's parents, whose perception and understanding of these terms may be idiosyncratic or inaccurate (cf. Mash & Terdal, 1988a).

A further difficulty with DSM-IV diagnostic criteria is the lack of emphasis on the situational or contextual factors surrounding and contributing to various disorders. This is a reflection of the fact that DSM-IV continues to view mental disorder as individual psychopathology or risk for psychopathology rather than in terms of problems in psychosocial adjustment. The consideration in DSM-IV of factors such as culture, age, and gender associated with the expression of each disorder is laudable as is the increased recognition of the importance of family problems and extrafamilial relational difficulties.

The changes in the DSMs from 1952 to 1994 reflect increasing diagnostic accuracy and sophistication. The transition from "reactive" diagnoses (DSM-I) and the virtual neglect of childhood criteria (DSM-I, DSM-II), to an increased number of child categories, more explicit criteria, and multiaxial evaluation (DSM-III, DSM-III-R), to an even greater emphasis on empirical research to guide nomenclature as well as the increased awareness (and inclusion) of contextual and developmental considerations (DSM-IV) exemplify important shifts in how psychopathology in children has come to be conceptualized.

Diagnostic Classification: 0–3

In addition to the limitations noted above, DSM-IV does not provide in-depth coverage of the mental health and developmental problems of infants and young children for whom family relationships are especially salient. To address this perceived deficiency, the DC:0–3 was recently developed by the Diagnostic Classification Task Force of the Zero to Three/National Center for Clinical Infant Programs (Zero to Three/National Center for Clinical Infant Programs, 1994). DC:0–3 is intended to provide a comprehensive system for classifying problems during the first 3 to 4 years of life (Greenspan & Wieder, 1994). Unlike DSM-IV, DC:0–3 is based on the explicit premise that diagnosis must be guided by the principle that all infants and young children are active participants in relationships within the fam-

ily. Hence, a description of infant–caregiver interaction patterns and the links between these interaction patterns and adaptive and maladaptive patterns of infant and child development constitute an essential part of the diagnostic process.

In explicitly recognizing the significance of relational problems, DC:0–3 includes a relationship disorder classification as a separate axis (Axis II) in its multiaxial approach (Axis I, primary diagnosis; Axis III, medical and developmental disorders and conditions; Axis IV, psychosocial stressors; Axis V, functional emotional developmental level). The diagnosis of relationship disturbances or disorders is based on observations of parent–child interaction and the parent's verbal report regarding his or her subjective experience of the child. Relational difficulties are rated with respect to their intensity, frequency, and duration, and classified as a perturbation, a disturbance, or a disorder. In making the DC:0–3 Axis II relationship disorder diagnosis, three aspects of the relationship are considered: (1) behavioral quality of the interaction (e.g., sensitivity or insensitivity in responding to cues); (2) affective tone (e.g., anxious/tense, angry); and (3) psychological involvement (e.g., parents' perceptions of the child and what can be expected in a relationship).

Axis V of DC:0–3, functional emotional development level, includes the ways in which infants or young children organize their affective, interactive, and communicative experiences. Axis V assessment is based, in large part, on direct observations of parent–child interaction. The various levels include social processes such as mutual attention, mutual engagement or joint emotional involvement, reciprocal interaction, and affective/symbolic communication. Problems may reflect constrictions in range of affect within levels, or under stress, or failure to reach expected levels of emotional development.

DC:0–3 is laudable in recognizing: (1) the significance of early relational difficulties; (2) the need to integrate diagnostic and relational approaches in classifying child psychopathology (Lyons-Ruth, 1995); and (3) the need to apply both quantitative and qualitative criteria in describing relational problems. In addition, the dimensions and specific processes that are used for classification (e.g., negative affect, unresponsivity, uninvolvement, lack of mutual engagement, lack of reciprocity in interaction) include those that have been identified as important by recent developmental and clinical research studies on early relationships, and the system is decidedly more sensitive to developmental and contextual parameters than DSM-IV. However, although promising, DC:0–3 is new and untested, was generated on the basis of uncontrolled clinical observations, is of unknown reliability and validity, and suffers from many of the same criticisms that have been noted for DSM-IV. Nevertheless, the scheme provides a rich descriptive base for further exploration of the ways in which psychopathology is expressed during the first few years of life and calls attention to the need to examine potential continuities between such early problems and later individual and/or family disorders.

Dimensional Approaches

Dimensional approaches to classification assume that there are a number of independent dimensions or traits of behavior and that all children possess these to varying degrees. These traits or dimensions are typically derived through the use of multivariate statistical methods such as factor analysis or cluster analysis (Achenbach, 1993). Although empirically derived schemes are more objective and potentially more reliable than clinically derived classification systems, there are a number of problems associated with their use including the dependency of the derived dimensions on sampling, method, and informant characteristics, and on the age and sex of the child (Mash & Terdal, 1988a). As a result there can be difficulties in integrating information obtained from different methods, informants, over time, or across situations. Dimensional approaches have also shown a lack of sensitivity to contextual influences, although there have been some recent efforts to develop dimensional classification schemes based on item pools that include situational content (e.g., McDermott, 1993).

The recent growth in the use of multivariate classification approaches in child and family assessment has been fueled by the extensive work of Thomas Achenbach and his colleagues with the various parent, teacher, youth, observer, and interview versions of the Child Behavior Checklist and Profile (Achenbach, 1993). For a comprehensive discussion of this approach, and to the use of empirically derived classification schemes more generally, the reader is referred to Achenbach (1985, 1993) and Mash and Terdal (1988a).

It should also be noted that there has been a trend toward greater convergence of the categorical and dimensional approaches to classification. Many of the items that were retained in DSM-IV child categories were derived from findings from multivariate studies, and the process that led to the development of DSM-IV treated most childhood disorders as dimensions, albeit that the use of cutoff scores on item lists arbitrarily created categories out of these dimensions (Spitzer et al., 1990, p. 695).

Performance-Based Diagnostic Information

Performance-based information and/or observational measures provide additional sources of diagnostic information that may be sensitive to differences among children exhibiting similar self- or other-reported symptoms (Kazdin & Kagan, 1994). These measures assess children's performance on standardized tasks, usually ones that reflect basic biological, cognitive, affective, or social functioning. For example, tasks involving recall memory under stressful conditions, delayed response times to threatening stimuli, and the potentiation of the blink reflex following exposure to a threatening stimulus have all been suggested as potentially useful in diagnosing groups and/or subgroups of children with anxiety disorders (Kazdin & Kagan, 1994). Similarly, behavioral-inhibition tasks such as the stop-signal paradigm (Logan, 1994) and tasks involving sustained attention such as the continuous performance test (Verbaten & Overtoom, 1994) have been suggested as useful for understanding the difficulties of children with ADHD.

A study by Rubin, Coplan, Fox, and Calkins (1995) illustrates the utility of performance-based diagnostic information. These researchers differentiated groups of preschool children based on the two dimensions of emotionality (i.e., threshold and intensity of emotional response) and soothability (i.e., recovery from emotional reaction based on soothing by self and others), and on their amount of social interactions with peers. Children's dispositional characteristics and behavioral styles were used to predict outcomes. Asocial children with poor emotion regulation had more internalizing problems. In contrast, social children with poor emotion regulation were rated as having more externalizing difficulties. By incorporating behavioral and emotional dimensions into classification, it was possible to make finer predictions, for example, that only some types of asocial children (i.e., reticent children with poor emotion regulation) would display later problems.

The use of performance-based measures in diagnosis is predicated on the availability of reliable and valid performance indicators for groups of children with known characteristics. Although such data are available in varying amounts for a wide range of disorders, there is a need to validate such findings for the purposes of diagnosis and against other sources of information. It is also the case that performance criteria for these measures are based on information obtained from children who were themselves previously identified using other diagnostic procedures. This raises the question of nonindependence and representativeness of data sources. There is also little information available regarding the base rates of children in the general population who exhibit certain patterns of responding on these tasks.

ISSUES IN CLASSIFICATION

Categories, Dimensions, or Both?

Psychological studies of child psychopathology have tended to conceptualize behavior, affect, and cognition on quantitative/continuous dimensions, whereas child psychiatry has tended to conceptualize child psychopathology in categorical terms. Both approaches are relevant to classifying childhood disorders in that some disorders may be best conceptualized as qualitatively distinct conditions and others as extreme points on one or more continuous dimensions. Kazdin and Kagan (1994) argue for greater research attention to qualitatively distinct categories of disorder based on illustrative findings from studies suggesting that the emotional arousal generated by unfamiliarity, threat, and attack is not a continuous dimension, or that it is possible to identify different subgroups of aggressive children based on varying levels of adrenaline in their urine.

There is currently little agreement as to which childhood disorders are best conceptualized as categories and which as dimensions, except perhaps in the case of a few rare conditions such as autistic disorder. Moreover, since any classification scheme represents a construction rather than a reality, it seems unlikely that most disorders will fall neatly into one designation or the other (Lilienfeld & Marino, 1995). Whether or not particular conditions are construed as qualitatively distinct categories, or as continuous dimensions, or as both, will likely depend on the utility, validity, and predictive value of particular groupings and subgroupings for certain purposes related to understanding and remediating child psychopathology. Research into such subgroupings is just beginning to emerge.

Comorbidity

An issue that has important ramifications for theory and research in defining and classifying child psychopathology is that of comorbidity (Achenbach, 1995; Carey & DiLalla, 1994; Caron & Rutter, 1991). Comorbidity generally refers to the manifestation of two or more disorders whose co-occurrence is greater than what would be expected by chance alone. For example, although the base rates for ADHD and conduct disorder (CD) in the general population are less than 10% for each disorder, epidemiological studies have found that among children diagnosed with ADHD, approximately 50% are also diagnosed with CD (Kazdin & Johnson, 1994; Loeber & Keenan, 1994; Offord et al., 1992). Comorbidity has been reported to be as high as 50% in community samples and even higher in clinic samples (Anderson et al., 1987; Bird et al., 1988; Caron & Rutter, 1991). Some of the more commonly occurring child and adolescent disorders include CD and ADHD, autistic disorder and mental retardation, childhood depression and anxiety, and Tourette's syndrome and ADHD.

There is continuing debate regarding the definition and nature of comorbidity (Blashfield, McElroy, Pfohl, & Blum, 1994; Caron & Rutter, 1991; Lilienfeld, Waldman, & Israel, 1994; Robins, 1994; Rutter, 1994b; Spitzer, 1994; Widiger & Ford-Black, 1994). Some researchers, for example Lilienfeld et al. (1994), contend that the term is wholly inadequate because it does not distinguish accurately between manifest conditions seen in organic medicine (e.g., diseases) and latent conditions described in mental health (e.g., syndromes and disorders). Others argue that the dispute over whether one should use the term comorbidity, co-occurrence, or covariation is largely a semantic one (Rutter, 1994b; Spitzer, 1994; Widiger & Ford-Black, 1994).

Several reasons that comorbidity may be exaggerated or artificially produced have been identified in the literature (Caron & Rutter, 1991; Lilienfeld et al., 1994; Rutter, 1994b; Verhulst & van der Ende, 1993). There may be a sampling bias operating that occurs whenever there are fewer numbers of individuals who are referred to clinics than who exhibit a given disorder (Caron & Rutter, 1991; Verhulst & van der Ende, 1993). In such cases, the clinic samples will contain a disproportionately large number of subjects who display comorbid conditions. This phenomenon occurs because the probability of being referred to mental health services is higher for a child with a comorbid condition than for one with only one disorder. Related to this sampling bias are various other referral factors that may inflate the degree of co-occurring disorders among clinic samples. Clinics and clinicians who specialize in treating more complicated cases, for example, may be more likely to receive referrals in which comorbid conditions are present. In addition, children with internalizing difficulties such as depression are more likely to be referred by their parents or the school system if they also show externalizing symptoms, largely because externalizing problems are viewed as more disruptive by the referral source (Verhulst & van der Ende, 1993).

Comorbidity may also reflect various sources of nosological confusion arising from the manner in which different childhood disorders have been conceptualized and organized. For instance, Widiger and Ford-Black (1994) claim that excessive rates of co-occurrence seemed to appear concomitant with the changes that occurred in DSM-III (e.g., increased coverage, divisions of diagnostic categories, the provision of separate and multiple axes). Another example is that DSM-IV makes it possible to have multiple diagnoses in the absence of multiple syndromes (Robins, 1994). One source of confusion stems from the overlapping criterion sets within contemporary classification schemes. In DSM-IV, diagnoses are based on a set of polythetic criteria that includes specific symptom constellations. In many cases, the presence of concomitant symptoms of a different kind are ignored, resulting in an increased likelihood that the accompanying symptoms will be represented in a different diagnostic category (Caron & Rutter, 1991).

Apart from the various artifactual contributors to comorbidity, there are also indicators in support of "true" comorbidity (Rutter, 1994b). It is possible that general propensities toward and/or struggles with adaptation are at the core of every disorder, but how the phenotype is expressed is contingent upon a myriad of environmental conditions and person–environment interactions (Caron & Rutter, 1991). Consistent with this notion, Lilienfeld and his colleagues (1994) maintain that comorbidity in childhood disorders may be partly a function of developmental level—that is, of underlying processes that have not yet achieved full differentiation. Differing rates of comorbidity with age may also reflect the fact that the appearance of one disorder or problem may precede the appearance of the other, for example, as is the case for anxiety preceding depression (Brady & Kendall, 1992) or for impulsivity preceding attentional problems (Barkley, Chapter 2, this volume).

In summary, it would appear that some cases of comorbidity may be the result of ambiguity in the definition of dysfunctionality that is used or of artifactual/methodological issues. However, as noted by Kazdin and Kagan (1994), "the broader point is still relevant and not controverted with specific diagnostic conundrums—namely, multiple symptoms often go together in packages" (p. 40). This is not to suggest that all disorders cluster together into packages; but rather, the fact that many frequently do has important implications for how child psychopathology is conceptualized. The complexity of comorbidity behooves researchers to move beyond singular models and to examine multiple expressions, etiologies, and pathways of childhood dysfunction (Kazdin & Johnson, 1994).

THEORY AND CHILD PSYCHOPATHOLOGY

The Role of Theory in Child Psychopathology

Every step in the research process is influenced by the investigator's preconceptions and ideologies (Kuhn, 1962; Maxwell & Delaney, 1990). As the history of child psychopathology has shown, an overemphasis on a grand theory or explanatory model in the absence of data can perpetuate false ideas and seriously impede our understanding of childhood disorders. On the other hand, "data gathering in the absence of hypotheses can become an inconsequential exercise in gathering inconsequential facts" (Rutter & Garmezy, 1983, p. 870). The value of theory lies not just in providing answers but also in raising new questions, which arise not only in addressing new problems but also in looking at familiar problems in different ways. One cannot consider theory, research, and practice in childhood psychopathology without also having some understanding of the underlying philosophical and epistemological assumptions that have guided work in this area. In this context, Overton and Horowitz (1991) discuss four levels of science: (1) epistemology; (2) guidelines, rules, and definitions of scientific knowing; (3) metatheoretical principles; and (4) theory.

The first level, "epistemology," defined as a theory about the nature of knowledge itself, impacts upon the general rules of science, the metatheoretical assumptions about the nature of humankind, and the specific theoretical models and research designs that arise out of such assumptions. One epistemological stance (i.e., "realism") asserts that knowledge exists independently of one's own perceptual and cognitive processes (Maxwell & Delaney, 1990; Overton & Horowitz, 1991). "Logical positivism," a view that has guided most of our past and present research efforts in child psychopathology, reflects this stance. A second philosophical position is that of "rationalism." Rationalists contend that the knower of scientific knowledge actively constructs what is known (Maxwell & Delaney, 1990). Instead of there being a fixed and absolute knowledge base to unveil, rationalists assume that knowledge derives from the exercise of relating and interpreting observables to latent constructs (Overton & Horowitz, 1991). Within this metatheoretical position there lies a continuum between the belief, at one end, that our knowledge base will always be uncertain and the conviction, at the other end, that there must be some omniscient truth that lies beyond our interpretive schemes.

At the second level of scientific knowledge, that of guidelines, rules, and definitions, it becomes evident that epistemology exerts a strong influence. Logical positivism, for instance, distinguishes scientific knowledge from knowledge that accumulates from other modes of knowing by requiring that all theoretical constructs be reducible to stable, objective, and observable knowledge (Maxwell & Delaney, 1990; Overton & Horowitz, 1991). This view maintains that theoretical constructs are to be mathematically related (via correspondence rules) to directly observable behavior and events. Theory, under this argument, advances by means of the empirical method. A hypothesis is tested and, when enough hypotheses have been independently and empirically supported, generalizations can be made (via the inductive process) to form a theoretical model.

At the third level of scientific knowledge identified by Overton and Horowitz (1991), "metatheoretical principles" guide the development of more specific theories. Two metaphors have been dominant in guiding scientific metatheory: the "machine" and the "organic" metaphors (Overton & Horowitz, 1991; Simeonsson & Rosenthal, 1992). The machine metaphor adopts a metatheoretical principle that views the child as reactive and influences as linear. The organic metaphor, on the other hand, underlies theories that view the child as an active construer and contributor to his or her circumstances. These basic assumptions regarding human nature, in turn, guide the conceptualizations and research strategies of child psychopathology. One example of the way in which metatheory guides research may be highlighted from the mechanistic view. Mechanistic models attempt to resolve or eliminate apparent paradoxes within the data by controlling for superfluous variance (i.e., "error") through experimental (e.g., random selection and random assignment) or statistical means (e.g., analysis of covariance) or by transforming them into linear conjunctives or disjunctives (Kazdin & Kagan, 1994; Overton & Horowitz, 1991).

In a manner that parallels the mechanistic versus organismic distinction, theoretical models have also varied according to whether the role of the child and/or the environment is viewed as passive or active (Lewis, 1990; Sameroff, 1993). The passive child–passive environment view stems from the ideas of John Locke and David Hume. According to this view, the environment does not actively seek to influence the child's behavior, and the child passively receives information from his or her world. Such models currently receive little attention.

A second view emphasizes an active environment and the child as a passive recipient of external influences. Radical behaviorists would assert, for instance, that behavior is strictly a function of the contingencies of reinforcement (Lewis, 1990). The Watsonian belief that, given enough time, one could turn a child into anything (e.g., a thief or a doctor) is indicative of this position. A third view is of the child as active and the environment as passive. Constructivist theories, which regard the child's reality as socially and cognitively constructed, are representative of this view. A fourth and final view regards both the child and the environment as active contributors to adaptive and maladaptive behavior (Lewis, 1990). Examples of this approach include interactive and transactional models (Sameroff, 1993), the goodness-of-fit model (Lewis, 1990; Thomas & Chess, 1977), and models of risk and resilience (Rutter, 1985, 1987, 1994a, 1994b; Rutter & Rutter, 1993).

There is currently a shift in child psychopathology toward the integration of divergent metatheoretical foundations under the active child–active environment position. This trend is reflected in the emergence of integrative theoretical paradigms such as developmental psychopathology, the increased use of research designs incorporating a larger number of reciprocally related variables, and the emergence of statistical techniques that permit the analysis of such complex processes (e.g., structural equation modeling, latent growth-curve analyses).

Finally, the aforementioned levels of scientific knowledge (epistemology, scientific guidelines, and metatheory) contribute to the development of "theories," or the specific systems of explanatory concepts in child psychopathology. Some of these theories are highlighted in the section that follows. There is no single integrative theory that fully captures the diversity of perspectives and findings represented by current research in child psychopathology. Although the overarching theories (e.g., psychodynamic, cognitive–structural, behavioral) that have guided the study of child development and psychopathology during its formative stage have contributed to our knowledge base, at present these theories seem insufficient to account for the dynamic and interacting contextual, developmental, and system influences that have been identified as important in recent research. Many of the existing theories do not take into account the broader developmental, social, cognitive, affective, biological, family, community, and cultural contexts in which psychopathology develops.

As noted earlier, logical positivism dominated the scientific scene and concomitant scientific goals set out to simplify and isolate variables, provide operational definitions to test the reliability and validity of constructs, and experimentally or statistically control for unwanted variance (e.g., the theory of true and error score; Ghiselli, Campbell, & Zedeck, 1981; Kazdin & Kagan, 1994; Overton & Horowitz, 1991). This has perpetuated an oversimplified view of the etiology of child psychopathology in terms of singular pathways and outcomes. Beck's notion of a cognitive triad consisting of a negative view of oneself, the world, and the future as the causal source of major depression is one of many such examples (Beck, Rush, Shaw, & Emery, 1979). Rather than identifying and allowing for several possible pathways leading to depression (e.g., genetic factors, early loss, reinforcement history, peer relational difficulties), the cognitive model assumes that maladaptive thought processes are the principal antecedent factors of depression for virtually all individuals. It is becoming increasingly evident, however, that similar outcomes may be associated with heterogeneous influences and that similar risk factors may be related to disparate outcomes.

Related to the notion of singular causal pathways has been the emphasis in models of child psychopathology on main effects and linear relations. "Main effects and linear relations" models assume that the impact of a single variable will be the same across varying conditions (e.g., outcomes associated with marital discord will be the same for children of all ages and both sexes) and across a wide range of values (e.g., more severe stressors lead to poorer outcomes in a continuous and graded fashion), respectively. Although main effects and linear models may apply to some aspects of child psychopathology, when they become the primary focus of theory and research, amidst much evidence for interactive effects and nonlinearity, they may obscure important trends in the data, oversimplify or mask salient relations, and become detrimental to research progress (Kazdin & Kagan, 1994).

As noted by Rutter and Garmezy (1983), "the limitations inherent in the current data base render premature any effort to construct a global overarching theory of the psychopathology of development" (p. 870). Furthermore, any single overarching theory is unlikely to be appropriate to explain all forms of child psychopathology or to account for the full range of contributory child and family influences. Nevertheless, the developmental psychopathology perspective described below provides a useful working framework for conceptualizing and understanding child psychopathology. This perspective integrates and coordinates a wide range of theories (e.g., psychodynamic, behavioral, cognitive, biological, family systems, and sociological), each of which focuses on different sets of variables, methods, and explanations (Achenbach, 1990).

Developmental Psychopathology Perspective

A developmental psychopathology perspective provides a broad template and general principles for understanding the range of processes and mechanisms underlying how and why psychopathology in children emerges, how it changes over time, and how it is influenced by the child's developmental capacities and by the contexts in which development occurs (Cicchetti & Richters, 1993). Viewed as a macroparadigm that subsumes several theoretical approaches (Cicchetti, 1984; Cicchetti & Cohen, 1995; Lease & Ollendick, 1993; Lewis, 1990; Sroufe & Rutter, 1984), developmental psychopathology has been defined as *"the study of the origins and course of individual patterns of behavioral maladaptation,* whatever the age of onset, whatever the causes, whatever the transformations in behavioral manifestation, and however complex the course of the developmental pattern may be" (Sroufe & Rutter, 1984, p. 18; italics in original). Put simply, developmental psychopathology provides a general framework from which to understand both normal development and its maladaptive deviations. Its main focus is an elucidation of developmental processes and how they function through an examination of extremes in developmental outcome and of variations between normative outcomes and negative and positive extremes (Cicchetti & Richters, 1993). Developmental psychopathology does not focus exclusively on the study of childhood disorders but serves to inform the understanding and treatment of disorders through the study of a full range of developmental processes and outcomes.

A developmental psychopathology perspective is consistent with both transactional and ecological views and assumes that within ongoing change and transformation, there is coherence and predictability for adaptive and maladaptive development (Campbell, 1989). This perspective also emphasizes the importance of family, social, and cultural factors in predicting and understanding developmental changes (Achenbach, 1990; Campbell, 1989; Lewis, 1990). In this way, developmental psychopathology attempts to address the complex influences surrounding the development of the child across the lifespan. In attempting to do so, it draws on knowledge from multiple fields of inquiry including psychology, psychiatry, sociology, education, criminology, epidemiology, and neuroscience and attempts to integrate this knowledge within a developmental framework (Cicchetti & Richters, 1993).

The focus of developmental psychopathology is on normal developmental patterns, continuities and discontinuities in functioning, and transformational interactions over different developmental periods that produce adaptive or maladaptive outcomes (Lease & Ollendick, 1993). The processes underlying both healthy and pathological development are seen as stemming from idiosyncratic transactions between the child and his or her unique context (Achenbach, 1990; Lease & Ollendick, 1993; Sroufe & Rutter, 1984). Thus, a central tenet of this approach states that to understand maladaptive behavior adequately, one needs to view it in relation to what may be considered normative for a given period of development (Edelbrock, 1984). A significant challenge for research then is to differentiate those developmental deviations that are within normative ranges from those that are not and to ascertain which among the plethora of interacting variables account for developmental deviation.

A developmental psychopathology perspective is also guided by a number of the assumptions that characterize organizational theories of development more generally (Cicchetti & Tucker, 1994). These include the following:

1. The individual child plays an active role in his or her own developmental organization.
2. Self-regulation occurs at multiple levels, and the quality of integration within and among the child's biological, cognitive, emotional, and social systems needs to be considered (Cicchetti & Richters, 1993).
3. There is a dialectic between canalization of developmental process and ongoing changes through the life process.
4. Developmental outcomes are best predicted through consideration of prior experience and recent adaptations examined in concert.
5. Individual choice and self-organization play an important role in determining the course of development.
6. Transitional turning points or sensitive periods in development represent times when developmental processes are most susceptible to positive and/or negative self-organizational efforts (Cicchetti & Tucker, 1994).

The developmental psychopathology perspective is still in its own developmental infancy and until recently has been more of a conceptual enterprise than a well-validated approach (Lewis, 1990). However, in a very short period of time, it has proven to be an enormously useful framework for understanding and guiding research in child psychopathology and represents an important shift in thinking away from single causal hypotheses toward a view based on complex and multiple pathways of influence.

Disorder-Specific Models

In addition to a need for an integrative framework such as developmental psychopathology, there is a parallel need for more focused disorder- and problem-specific theories and hypotheses to account for the different forms of psychopathology in children, the different pathways through which similar forms of psychopathology emerge, and the reasons that seemingly similar developmental pathways may lead to different outcomes. Kazdin and Kagan (1994) rightfully argue that the best explanatory models are likely to be different depending on the specific disorder and/or differences related to gender, ethnicity, social class, and a host of other conditions. A key issue is to identify the range of conditions under which particular models are or are not applicable.

Several disorder- and problem-focused theories have recently been proposed. These models are empirically based and are sensitive to the specific characteristics and processes that research has identified as important for understanding a particular disorder or problem. A few examples of recent models include: Barkley's (1996) theory of "inhibitory dysfunction," which proposes that behavioral inhibition is the primary and central deficit underlying the attentional, cognitive, affective, and social difficulties that characterize children with ADHD; Cummings and Davies' (1995) and Davies and Cummings' (1994) "emotional security hypothesis," which proposes that emotional insecurity resulting from a number of sources (e.g., maternal depression, marital conflict) may lead to child difficulties in self-regulation, efforts to overregulate others, and maladaptive relational representations; Feldman and Downey's (1994) proposal that the impact of family violence on adult attachment behavior is mediated by an increased sensitivity to rejection, which is a motive to avoid rejection that is evidenced in social encoding biases, expectancies, values, and regulatory plans; Dodge's revised model of social information-processing deficits in

aggressive children, which views aggression as the outcome of the child's use of biased or distorted interpretational processes in social situations (Crick & Dodge, 1994); Bugental's (Bugental, 1993) model of abusive parent–child relationships, which focuses on "low personal control over failure," perceived power disadvantage, and a maladaptive defensive coping style to child behaviors that are perceived by the parent as potentially threatening; and, Mundy's (1995) proposed "social-approach disturbance" in children with autism, a disturbance which is hypothesized to be related to the compromised integrity of the neurological system that mediates social stimulus approach behaviors. This dysfunction is hypothesized to lead to an attenuation of the tendency to initiate affectively positive social behaviors, which in turn restricts the interactions that are needed to develop the social–cognitive capacities that regulate adaptive social interchange.

Other theories that have been proposed to account for these and other problems and disorders are presented in each of the chapters of this volume. The growth in the number of such theories reflects an increasing trend toward models that focus on the processes underlying specific forms of child psychopathology rather than on child psychopathology in general and a concomitant recognition of the importance of disorder-specific theories to guide research and practice. Recent research findings indicate that there are likely to be both common factors (e.g., insecure models of attachment) that apply across many different types of disorder, as well as specific factors that play a particularly crucial role in understanding individual disorders (e.g., impulsivity and ADHD). Identifying both common and specific factors and their relationship to one another is an important task for future research.

INFLUENCES ON CHILD PSYCHOPATHOLOGY

All forms of child psychopathology are influenced by the complex interactions among person variables (e.g., genetics) and the environmental context for development and behavior. Adelman and Taylor (1993, p. 64) have presented a useful conceptual framework that describes a representative range of factors that are related to emotional, behavioral, and learning problems in children. This framework is shown in Table 1.7. In elaborating on this framework, Adelman (1995) has described children's emotional, behavioral, and learning problems based on paradigmatic causes that include those that are primarily within the child, the environment, or in mismatches between the child and the environment. Many of the different theories of child psychopathology have differed in the emphasis given to the influences and interactions that are described in Table 1.7.

GENERAL THEORIES OF CHILD PSYCHOPATHOLOGY

Several major theories have been proposed to account for the emergence of psychopathology in children. These are listed in Table 1.8 and include: psychodynamic (Dare, 1985; Shapiro & Esman, 1992), attachment (Bowlby, 1973, 1988), behavioral/reinforcement (Bijou & Baer, 1961; Skinner, 1953), social learning (Bandura, 1977, 1986), cognitive (Beck et al., 1979), neurobiological/constitutional (e.g., Pennington & Ozonoff, 1991; Torgersen, 1993), affective (Cicchetti & Izard, 1995; Fox, 1994b), and family systems (Jacob, 1987) models. A detailed discussion of the basic tenets of each of these general theories is beyond the scope of this chapter. For comprehensive discussions of these theories, the reader is directed to original sources and to specific references cited throughout this volume. What follows is a discussion of several general points related to these theories.

Each general theoretical approach reflects a diversity of viewpoints. For example, psychodynamic theory encompasses traditional Freud-

TABLE 1.7. Factors Instigating Emotional, Behavioral, and Learning Problems

Environment (E)	Person (P)	Interactions and transactions between E and P[a]
1. Insufficient stimuli (e.g., prolonged periods in impoverished environments; deprivation of learning opportunities at home or school, such as lack of play and practice situations and poor instruction; inadequate diet) 2. Excessive stimuli (e.g., overly demanding home, school, or work experiences, such as overwhelming pressure to achieve and contradictory expectations; overcrowding) 3. Intrusive and hostile stimuli (e.g., medical practices, especially at birth, leading to physiological impairment; contaminated environments; conflict in home, school, workplace; faulty child-rearing practices, such as long-standing abuse and rejection; dysfunctional family; migratory family; language used is a second language; social prejudices related to race, sex, age, physical characteristics and behavior)	1. Physiological insult (e.g., cerebral trauma, such as accident or stroke, endocrine dysfunctions and chemical imbalances; illness affecting brain or sensory functioning) 2. Genetic anomaly (e.g., genes that limit, slow down, or lead to any atypical development) 3. Cognitive activity and affective states experienced by self as deviant (e.g., lack of knowledge or skills such as basic cognitive strategies; lack of ability to cope effectively with emotions, such as low self-esteem) 4. Physical characteristics shaping contact with environment and/or experienced by self as deviant (e.g., visual, auditory, or motoric deficits; excessive or reduced sensitivity to stimuli; easily fatigued; factors such as race, sex, age or unusual appearance that produce stereotypical responses) 5. Deviant actions of the individual (e.g., performance problems, such as excessive errors in performing; high or low levels of activity)	1. Severe to moderate personal vulnerabilities and environmental defects and differences (e.g., a person with extremely slow development in a highly demanding environment, all of which simultaneously and equally instigate the problem) 2. Minor personal vulnerabilities not accommodated by the situation (e.g., person with minimal CNS disorders resulting in auditory perceptual disability trying to do auditory-loaded tasks; very active person forced into situations at home, school, or work that do not tolerate this level of activity) 3. Minor environmental defects and differences not accommodated by the individual (e.g., person is in the minority racially or culturally and is not participating in many social activities because he or she thinks others may be unreceptive)

Note. From Adelman & Taylor (1993, p. 24). Copyright 1993 by Wadsworth, Inc. Reprinted by permission of Brooks/Cole Publishing Company.

[a]May involve only one P and one E variable or may involve multiple combinations.

TABLE 1.8. General Models Used to Conceptualize Child Psychopathology[a]

Psychodynamic Models
Inborn drives, intrapsychic mechanisms, conflicts, defenses, psychosexual stages, fixation and regression.

Attachment Models
Early attachment relationships, internal working models of self, others, and relationships in general.

Behavioral/Reinforcement Models
Excessive, inadequate, or maladaptive reinforcement and/or learning histories.

Social Learning Models
Vicarious and observational experience, reciprocal parent–child interactions.

Cognitive Models
Distorted or deficient cognitive structures and processes.

Constitutional/Neurobiological Models
Temperament, genetic mutations, neuroanatomy, neurobiological mechanisms.

Affective Models
Dysfunctional emotion regulatory mechanisms.

Family Systems Models
Intra- and intergenerational family systems, and the structural and/or functional elements within families.

[a]Models are highlighted in terms of their relative emphasis. Most models are overlapping and recognize the role of multiple influences as contributors to child psychopathology.

ian and Kleinian psychoanalytic constructs and their many derivatives as reflected in ego-analytic and object relations theory (Lesser, 1972). Behavioral/reinforcement perspectives include traditional operant/classical conditioning constructs, mediational models, and contemporary theories of learning (Klein & Mower, 1989; Krasner, 1991; Viken & McFall, 1994). Cognitive theories include cognitive-structural models, models of cognitive distortion, and models of faulty information processing (Kendall & Dobson, 1993). Family systems theories include systemic, structural, and social learning models (Jacob, 1987). Therefore, when discussing any theory, it is critical to distinguish among the different perspectives encompassed by the approach.

Many theories of child psychopathology are derivatives of earlier approaches. For example, psychodynamic theories dominated thinking about child psychopathology for the first half of this century. These theories contributed to our understanding of child psychopathology through their emphasis on the importance of relationships, early life experiences, mental mechanisms, and unconscious processes, and they spawned a number of other models, for example, attachment theory (Rutter, 1995). However, in referring to the relationship between psychoanalytic theory and attachment theory, Rutter (1995) states: "Although it is important not to throw out the baby with the bathwater, there is an awful lot of psychoanalytic water that needs to go down the plughole, and we also need to appreciate that psychoanalysis is only one of the parents of the baby and that the growing infant differs in very important ways from its progenitors" (p. 561).

The emergence of attachment theory reflected a shifting of attention from the more traditional psychoanalytic role of intrapersonal defenses to that of interpersonal relationships (Bretherton, 1995). Similarly, the emergence of social learning theory reflected a disenchantment with non-mediational models of learning and a growing interest in the role of symbolic processes.

A number of general points can be made regarding theories of child psychopathology:

1. Each theory offers an explanation regarding the etiology of child psychopathology. The strength of each theory rests on its specificity in predicting various forms of psychopathology and its degree of empirical support.

2. The varying degrees of support for each conceptualization suggest that no single model can fully explain the complexities involved in understanding child psychopathology. In light of this, increased understanding may accrue if greater integrative and collaborative efforts are undertaken.

3. Many explanations of childhood disorders implicitly or explicitly assume a simple association between a limited number of antecedents and a given disorder. However, as we have discussed, the concept of multiple pathways that lead to different outcomes depending on the circumstances represents a more viable framework in light of current research findings.

4. Although the testing of specific models is consistent with the spirit of parsimony, far greater attention needs to be given to the unique contexts and conditions under which a particular model does or does not apply.

5. Research on dysfunction frequently examines static conditions and influences such as the expression of a disorder at a given age or the influence of a specific stressor. However, evidence

indicates that the expression and etiology of psychopathology in children are continuously changing over time, and theories need to account for these types of changes (Garber, 1984; Kazdin & Kagan, 1994).

Current models are becoming increasingly sensitive to the many different components of childhood dysfunction. Indeed, constitutional, behavioral, cognitive, emotional, and social factors cross a number of theoretical domains as reflected in the emergence of hybrid models (e.g., cognitive-behavioral; social-information processing) as well as the inclusion of family and ecological constructs across many different theories. Behavioral models, which have frequently been characterized as having a narrow emphasis on conditioning principles, are also becoming increasingly sensitive to systems influences. For example, Viken and McFall (1994) state:

> Basic research increasingly is concerned with the kinds of complex, multidetermined behavioral systems that therapists face every day. Current topics include long-term effects of reinforcement procedures, constraints on the organization of behavior in time, enduring changes in free baselines, effects of free responding on responses to schedule constraints, new work on the distinction between intrinsic and extrinsic reinforcement, constraints involving more than two responses, resistance to schedule constraints, response substitution within functional classes of behaviors, the biological substrates regulating reinforcement processes, and the measurement of underlying equilibrium states when extended baselines are not available. Thus, contemporary reinforcement theory is relevant to a wide variety of basic research issues in cognitive science, neuroscience, and education." (p. 124)

Four theoretical approaches have received increased attention in current research on child psychopathology: (1) attachment theory; (2) cognitive theories; (3) affective models; and (4) constitutional/neurobiological models. Each of these approaches is highlighted in the sections that follow.

Attachment Theory

Bowlby's (1973, 1988) theory of attachment is based on both an ethological and a psychoanalytic perspective. Nevertheless, Bowlby rejected the psychoanalytic ideas that individuals passed through a series of stages where fixation at or regression to an earlier state could occur and that emotional bonds were derived from drives based on food or sex. Drawing on ethology and control theory, Freudian concepts of motivation based on psychic energy were replaced with cybernetically controlled motivational-behavioral systems organized as plan hierarchies (Bowlby, 1973; Bretherton, 1995). Within attachment theory, instinctive behaviors are not rigidly predetermined but rather become organized into flexible goal-oriented systems through learning and goal-corrected feedback. Behavioral/motivational systems (e.g., attachment, exploration) regulate time-limited consummatory behaviors and time-extended instinctive behaviors that maintain an organism in relation to its environment. Attachment belongs to a group of stress-reducing behavioral systems that operate in conjunction with physiological arousal-regulating systems. The child is motivated to maintain a balance between familiarity-preserving, stress-reducing behaviors, and exploratory and information-seeking behaviors. Self-reliance develops optimally when an attachment figure provides a secure base for exploration (Bretherton, 1995).

It is via the attachment relationship that the infant develops an "internal working model" of the self and others. Bowlby (1988) argued that the development of psychopathology is directly related to the inability of the caregiver to respond appropriately to the child's needs. This assertion is, however, a point of contention among researchers. Sroufe (1985), for example, has questioned the direct role of parental influence arguing that infant temperament, and the reciprocal interaction of a "difficult temperament" with parental response may better account for the variance in the attachment relationship and its ensuing insecure attachment difficulties. On the basis of a review of several studies that examined infant temperament and attachment, Sroufe (1985) suggests that although some studies have supported the notion that differences between secure and insecure attachments may be due to temperament, the bulk of evidence suggests that infants change their attachment patterns with different caregivers.

In postulating an association between early attachment and later psychopathology, one must exercise caution in that there does not appear to be one specific subtype of attachment that leads to one particular childhood disorder; rather, the trajectory for developmental pathways and manifestations of psychopathology emerge as the result of environmental experience, biological predispositions, and learning. When identifying possible developmental paths as factors related to subsequent psychopathology, the concept of the child's internal working model is useful, but it is important to bear in mind that the internal working model represents a set of active constructions that are subject to change and that the association with later psychopathology is probabilistic rather than absolute.

Rutter (1995) has highlighted a number of key issues surrounding current work on attachment including: (1) the need to identify mechanisms involved in proximity-seeking behavior; (2) broadening the basis for measuring attachment to include dimensions as well as categories; (3) studying relationship qualities that may not be captured by "insecurity"; (4) understanding the relationship between temperament and attachment; (5) dealing with how discrepant relationships are translated into individual characteristics; (6) operationalizing internal working models; (7) attachment quality across the lifespan and whether or not meanings are equivalent at different ages; (8) determining how one relationship affects others; and (9) identifying the boundaries of attachment vis-à-vis other aspects of relationships. Understanding the association between attachment and later functioning, parenting and attachment quality, the adaptive value of secure attachment (e.g., insecure attachment does not equal psychopathology), disorders of attachment associated with abuse and neglect, and the diffuse attachments associated with institutionalization are all issues in need of further investigation.

Bowlby's attachment theory has played an important role in focusing attention on the quality of parent–child relationships, the interaction between security in relationships and the growth of independence, the importance of placing emergent human relationships within a biological/evolutionary context (e.g., Kraemer, 1992), the concept of internal working models, and insecure early attachments as the basis for the development of psychopathology (Rutter, 1995).

Cognitive Theories

Considerable research has focused on the role of cognitions in both adult and child psychopathology (Kendall & Dobson, 1993). There are several theoretical perspectives that have been concerned with childhood cognitions. These have included cognitive-structural models (Selman, Beardslee, Schultz, Krupa, & Poderefsky, 1986), information-processing approaches (Crick & Dodge, 1994), and cognitive-behavioral approaches (Meichenbaum, 1977). Representative examples of the information-processing and cognitive-behavioral approaches are described below.

Information Processing

Faulty information processing has been implicated in a number of childhood disorders. For example, socially aggressive children have been found to display negative attributional biases (Dodge & Crick, 1990), and children with anxiety disorders show attentional biases to threatening stimuli (Vasey, Daleiden, Williams, & Brown, 1995). Research into faulty information processing and child psychopathology has emanated from two streams, one focusing on deficits in basic information processing related to attention, memory, and other cognitive functions (e.g., Carter & Swanson, 1995) and the other related to social information processing (Crick & Dodge, 1994).

Dodge's model as applied to socially aggressive boys illustrates the social information-processing approach (Dodge & Newman, 1981; Dodge & Somberg, 1987). In this model, a series of thought processes are postulated to occur during the course of appropriate social interactions and to be absent or distorted during inappropriate social interactions. The thinking of aggressive children in social situations is characterized by deficits in one or more of the following processes: (1) the way in which social cues are "encoded" (searching for and focusing one's attention on pertinent external stimuli); (2) the "interpretation" or derivation of meaning from cues that previously became the focus of one's initial attention; (3) "response search" or the generation of response alternatives; (4) "response decision"; and (5) the ability to "enact" the most appropriate response.

Recently, Dodge and his colleagues (Crick & Dodge, 1994; Dodge & Crick, 1990) have expanded their conceptual framework to reflect more accurately contemporary theoretical and empirical advances in the domains of developmental psychopathology, clinical psychology, and cognitive psychology. The reformulated model continues to posit the same basic information-processing steps but, at each stage, there is ongoing reciprocal interaction between the information-processing skills required during social transactions in context and the individual's "data base" (a collection of social schemas, memories, social knowledge, and cultural values or rules) (Crick & Dodge, 1994). Instead of a linear processing model, there is also the inclusion of cyclical feedback loops connecting all of the stages of processing. Increased recognition of the influence of peer appraisal and response, emotional processes, and the development and acquisition of cognitive skills as important contributors to social adjustment are meaningful additions to the reformulated model. In addition to the enhanced sensitivity to developmental trajectories, the reformulated model also emphasizes the role of early dispositions (e.g., temperament) and other factors (e.g., age, gender, social context) that serve to moderate the relationship between information processing and social adjustment. Specifically, the model asserts that parent–child interactions and the quality of early attachments may be important contributors to the ongoing formulation of the child's data base. Crick and Dodge's (1994) reformulated model is a good illustration of the current trend toward models of child psychopathology that attempt to integrate the structural aspects of cognition with ongoing cognitive processes, and with emotions, as they interact with one another across time and contexts.

Cognitive-Behavioral Theories

Cognitive-behavioral theories stem from a rational epistemological viewpoint: "a purposeful attempt to preserve the positive features of the behavioral approaches, while also working to incorporate into a model the cognitive activity and information-processing factors of the individual" (Kendall & MacDonald, 1993, p. 387; also see Kendall, Howard, & Epps, 1988). Importantly, cognitive-behavioral models also consider the role of affect and increasingly recognize the importance of contextual variables (e.g., family, peers) in both the etiology and maintenance of psychopathology (Kendall, 1991, 1993; Kendall & Dobson, 1993; Kendall & Morris, 1991).

Cognitive-behavioral theories assert that maladaptive cognitive processes predispose an individual to psychopathology and that it is these cognitive distortions that maintain the dysfunctional patterns and developmental anomalies (Beck,

1963, 1964; Beck et al., 1979). Cognitive models place a primary emphasis on the role of cognitive distortions, insufficient cognitive mediation, and/or attributional styles and expectations as important determinants in the development of behavioral and emotional maladies (Kendall et al., 1988). Four elements of cognition are distinguished for the purpose of understanding the pathogenesis of psychiatric disturbances: cognitive structures, cognitive content, cognitive operations, and cognitive products (Beck et al., 1979; Dobson & Kendall, 1993; Ingram & Kendall, 1986; Kendall, 1991, 1993; Kendall & Dobson, 1993). "Cognitive structures" represent the way in which information is organized and stored in memory and serve the function of filtering or screening ongoing experiences. "Cognitive content" (or propositions) refers to the information that is stored in memory (i.e., the substance of the cognitive structures). Together, cognitive structures and content make up what is termed "the schema." The schema stems from a child's processing of life experiences and acts as a guideline or core philosophy influencing expectations and filtering information in a fashion consistent with the child's core philosophy. As such, cognitive schemata have also been referred to as "filters" or "templates" (see Kendall & MacDonald, 1993). The schema is postulated to effect the relative observed consistency in the child's cognition, behavior, and affect (Stark, Rouse, & Livingston, 1991). According to Beck's model, maladaptive schemata develop in early childhood and remain dormant until some untoward event triggers the latent schemata, and the individual begins to encode, process, and interpret information in a schema-congruent way. Individuals with a depressive schema, for instance, process and interpret information about themselves, the world, and the future in a negatively biased fashion (the cognitive triad; Beck et al., 1979), whereas persons with an anxiety schema interpret environmental stimuli with a cognitive focus on future threat (Kendall et al., 1988).

Cognitive processes or operations pertain to the manner by which the cognitive system functions. Thus, cognitive processes, which are guided by the schema, suggest the mode by which an individual perceives and interprets both internal and external stimuli. Finally, cognitive products are the ensuing thoughts that stem from the simultaneous and reciprocal interactions between the various components of the cognitive system.

According to the cognitive model, each (or all) of these components may become dysfunctional and precipitate the expression of psychopathology (Beck, 1964; Beck et al., 1979; Kendall, 1991, 1993; Kendall et al., 1988; Stark et al., 1991). Within the adult literature, Beck and his colleagues (1979) have, for example, identified a number of cognitive distortions (by-products of the misperception of objective reality; cognitive content and processes) that tend to characterize the depressive process. Such faulty information-processing strategies include such systematic errors as dichotomous thinking, arbitrary inference, personalization, magnification and minimization, emotional reasoning, and overgeneralization (Beck et al., 1979).

Particularly important in the area of child psychopathology is the distinction between cognitive deficits versus cognitive distortions. Kendall (1993) argues that this distinction is useful in describing, classifying and understanding a variety of disorders of youth. "Deficits" refer to an absence of thinking where it would be beneficial. Aggressive youths, for example, frequently lack the ability to solve social problems adequately (Crick & Dodge, 1994; Lochman & Dodge, 1994), and impulsive children often fail to think before they respond (Moore & Hughes, 1988). Conversely, children who display cognitive "distortions" typically do not lack the ability to organize or process information; rather, their thinking is described as biased, dysfunctional, or misguided (Kendall, 1993; Kendall & MacDonald, 1993). The depressed individual's negative view of him- or herself, the world, and the future is an example of distorted thinking. Kendall (1985, 1993) notes that the distinction between deficient and distorted thinking is relevant to the distinction that has been made between externalizing and internalizing disorders (cf. Achenbach, 1990). Generally, internalizing disorders are related to distortions in thinking, whereas externalizing disorders are more commonly associated with cognitive deficits. Empirical evidence suggests that aggressive behaviors usually include both distortions and deficits (Lochman, White, & Wayland, 1991; comprehensive reviews of the empirical evidence in support of this distinction are found in Kendall, 1993, and Kendall & MacDonald, 1993).

A number of strengths and limitations of cognitive models may be delineated. A particularly important strength of cognitive-behavioral theory is that it examines the areas of cognition, affect, behavior, and social functioning as indicators of the etiology and maintenance of childhood disorders and possesses strong theory-to-assessment-to-treatment links (Kendall et al., 1988; Stark et al., 1991). Based on the theoretical model that a latent schema develops in childhood and remains dormant until an event triggers its structure, assessment functions to determine the severity and content of the maladaptive cognitive processes and products, and therapy serves to build new cognitive structures that serve as templates for coping (Beck et al., 1979; Kendall, 1993; Kendall & MacDonald, 1993; Stark et al., 1991).

One important limitation of cognitive-behavioral approaches pertains to tests of their etiological assumptions. There is an assumption that maladaptive thinking leads to (i.e., causes) maladaptive behavior. Although there is research support for faulty cognition as a concomitant of various adult (Dobson & Shaw, 1987; Lewinsohn, Steinmetz, Larson, & Franklin, 1981; Silverman, Silverman, & Eardley, 1984) and child disorders (Tems, Stuart, Skinner, Hughes, & Emslie, 1993), evidence for the causal hypothesis is presently mixed and equivocal. For example, Tems and her colleagues (1993) recently examined the cognitive patterns of depressed children and adolescents. Although depressed children displayed more cognitive distortion than controls, no significant differences between groups remained upon remission. This finding is neither unique to the childhood literature (for similar findings with adult depression see Lewinsohn et al., 1981; Dobson & Shaw, 1987; or Silverman et al., 1984) nor to internalizing disorders. Indeed, studies of the treatment of aggression have revealed, in some cases, that the alteration of cognitive processes does not necessarily lead to changes in behavior (Dodge, 1989).

Affective Models

Emotion and its regulatory functions are constructs that cross several conceptual models including psychodynamic theory with its concept of defense mechanisms, cognitive-behavioral theory, which stresses the role of thought patterns and behavior as determinants of emotion, attachment theory with its premise that an internal working model is formed on the basis of early relations and continues to regulate emotion in

subsequent relationships (Cassidy, 1994), and biological theories that emphasize the structural and neuropharmacological correlates of emotion regulation (Pennington & Ozonoff, 1991). Emotion and emotion regulation played a central role in the conceptual paradigms of early models of child psychopathology. For example, psychoanalytic theory emphasized the regulation of emotions through the use of defense mechanisms, with an absence of such regulation leading to anxiety and psychopathology (see Cole, Michel, & Teti, 1994). By affording the opportunity to avoid, minimize, or convert emotions, defense mechanisms were hypothesized to serve the function of regulating emotional experiences that are too difficult to deal with at the conscious level.

Although the advent and growth of cognitive and behavioral models shifted attention away from an interest in affective processes, the study of emotional processes in child psychopathology has recently experienced a resurgence of interest (Cicchetti & Izard, 1995; Fox, 1994b; Kagan, 1994b). In part, this renewed interest reflects the growing recognition that children's emotional experience, expression, and regulation are likely to affect the quality of their social interactions and relationships (e.g., Garber & Dodge, 1991). From a functionalist perspective, emotions are viewed as playing a causal role in organizing and directing the way in which children react to environmental events. This perspective is illustrated by findings showing that induced negative child emotions increase children's distress, negative expectations, and appraisals of adult conflict, whereas induced positive emotions have the opposite effect (Davies & Cummings, 1995). Several recent discussions have focused on the development of emotion regulation and its ability to influence both adaptive and maladaptive functioning (Cassidy, 1994; Cole et al., 1994; Kagan, 1994b; Mayer & Salovey, 1995; Thompson, 1994).

Emotion systems have as their primary functions the motivation/organization of behavior and communication with self and with others. Emotions represent patterns that include at least several of the following components: (1) activating neural, sensorimotor, cognitive, and/or affective stimulus event(s); (2) dedicated neural processes; (3) changes in physiological responses; (4) changes in motoric/expressive behavior; (5) related cognitive appraisals; and (6) concomitant alterations in subjective experiences or feeling states (Cicchetti et al., 1995; Izard, 1993; Kagan, 1994b).

Different theories have viewed child psychopathology as emanating from: (1) unrestrained emotions (i.e., emotions that are unconnected to cognitive or affective-cognitive control processes); (2) deficits or distortions in cognitions and behaviors that interfere with emotion modulation (i.e., emotions connected to cognitive processes and behavior that are situationally inappropriate); (3) emotional interference with planful cognitive processes (i.e., emotional flooding); (4) dysfunctional patterns of emotion processing and communication involving problems with recognition, interpretation, and expression; and (5) difficulties in coordinating emotional and cognitive processes in the regulation of emotion (Cicchetti et al., 1995).

Emotion dysfunction may emanate from several sources including variations in biological vulnerability and stress. In studying child psychopathology, it is important not to focus on negative emotions without also recognizing the beneficial and buffering effects of positive emotions, the adaptive value and facilitating effects of negative emotions of moderate or at times even extreme intensity, and the ongoing importance of emotion content and meaning for the child's behavior. Also, since negative emotions are neither topographically nor functionally unidimensional, it is important to identify the *discrete* emotions and emotional patterns underlying different forms of child psychopathology (Cicchetti et al., 1995). For example, the negative affect that is associated with depression may involve sadness, anger, or guilt in the same way that negative behaviors in depressed children may be both aggressive/confrontational and depressive/distressed (Hops, 1995).

It is useful to distinguish between the two dimensions of emotion reactivity versus emotion regulation. Reactivity refers to individual differences in the threshold and intensity of emotional experience, whereas regulation describes processes that operate to control or modulate reactivity (e.g., attention, inhibition, approach/avoidance, coping styles) (Rubin et al., 1995). According to Rubin et al. (1995), this distinction is important because it highlights the need to focus on the dynamic interaction between general temperament and specific regulatory mechanisms and, in turn, the need to recognize that emotional arousal (reactivity) can serve to inhibit,

facilitate, or disrupt behavior. The distinction can also be made between problems in regulation and problems in dysregulation, with regulation problems involving weak or absent control structures or structures overwhelmed by disabling input, and dysregulation involving existing control structures that operate in a maladaptive manner and direct emotion toward inappropriate goals (Cicchetti et al., 1995). Functions of emotion involve the emotion knowledge of self and others in identifying feelings and behavior, including monitoring of self and environment. Absent or weak monitoring may result in dissociated emotional and cognitive processes and emotional leakage, whereas excessive monitoring may lead to a narrow sampling of emotional signals and excessive use of specific emotions in communication (Cicchetti et al., 1995).

Of interest to the present chapter is the manner in which emotion regulation has been defined and conceptualized with respect to psychopathology. The processes of emotion regulation include the attenuation or deactivation of an ongoing emotion, amplification of an ongoing emotion, activation of a desired emotion, and the masking of emotional states (Cicchetti et al., 1995). Thompson (1994) defines emotion regulation as consisting of "the extrinsic and intrinsic processes responsible for monitoring, evaluating, and modifying emotional reactions, especially their intensive and temporal features, to accomplish one's goals" (p. 27). This definition, highlights several important characteristics of emotion regulation. First, emotion regulation involves enhancing, maintaining, or inhibiting emotional arousal for the purpose of meeting one's goals. Second, there are both internal and external factors that influence the development and use of emotion regulatory strategies. Finally, there is a temporal dimension: sometimes there are sudden and transitory changes in emotional arousal that must be dealt with (e.g., acute or state anxiety), whereas at other times there are longer-lasting ramifications of emotional arousal created by years of experience (e.g., chronic or trait anxiety; Kagan, 1994b; Terr, 1991).

The development of emotion regulation or dysregulation is thought to derive from both innate predispositions and from socialization. At the level of constitutional factors are various neural circuits and temperamental characteristics. For example, inhibited children appear to bring a high state of reactivity into their environment, particularly in novel or unfamiliar situations (Rubin & Stewart, Chapter 7, this volume). This biological propensity is thought to be the result of a number of neurological factors that include interrelating messages sent to and from neuroanatomical structures (vis-à-vis neuroelectricity and neuropharmacology) to the central and peripheral nervous system (Fox, 1994a; Kagan, 1994b).

Cognitive and language development also contribute to emotion regulation. Growth in cognitive development allows the child to increasingly differentiate and cope with a diverse set of emotion-arousing stimuli. The development of emotion language also affords an opportunity for the communication of emotion meaning to others and its management through self-regulatory mechanisms (Cole et al., 1994; Thompson, 1994).

Finally, emotion regulation is also embedded within the unique context of the child. Socialization influences within the family and culture are important in the development and expression of emotion and may support or hinder emotion regulation in a variety of ways. One important influence is the way in which parents respond to the child's initial expressions of emotion, and how emotions are communicated in the context of the ongoing interactions between parent and child (Cassidy, 1994). The development of emotion regulation may also come about through the modeling of appropriate or inappropriate emotional expression. Finally, the rules or boundaries of emotional expression, which are established by both the family and the community at large, also impact upon the development of emotion regulation (Cole et al., 1994).

Emotion dysregulation begins as contextually bound regulatory events that may then develop into more stable patterns of responding and thereby contribute to the development of psychopathology. The determination of emotion regulation as adaptive or maladaptive varies with the circumstances but generally involves the degree of flexibility of the response, the perceived conformity of the response to cultural and familial rules and boundaries, and the outcome of the response relative to the child's and parent's short- and long-term goals (Thompson, 1994).

Some forms of emotion dysregulation may be adaptive in one environment, or at one time, but maladaptive in other situations. For example, in discussing children who have been emotionally and sexually abused, Terr (1991) describes the

process of "numbing" (a symptom of a posttraumatic stress reaction) that serves to protect the child from overwhelming pain and trauma. However, when numbing becomes a characteristic way of coping with stressors later in life, it may interfere with adaptive functioning and with long-term goals. Another example stems from studies on attachment quality. In response to attachment figures who are rejecting or inconsistent, infants may develop an insecure/avoidant attachment in which emotional expression is minimized. The infant's reduced emotional expression, while serving the strategic function within the attachment relationship of minimizing loss by reducing investment in the relationship, may establish a pattern of emotional responding that is maladaptive for the development of subsequent relationships (Cassidy, 1994).

In summary, emotion theorists conceptualize the development of emotion regulation as involving a variety of increasingly complex developmental tasks. The degree of interference with these tasks depends on the fit between the child, her or his environment, and their interaction. Emotional dysregulation is believed to be the consequence of interference in the associated developmental processes. Dysregulation is associated with a wide range of emotions and, depending on the overall context, may or may not become a stylistic pattern, and may or may not lead to later psychopathology.

Constitutional/Neurobiological Models

In attempting to understand child psychopathology, constitutional/neurobiological models recognize both the physical make-up and tendencies of humans in general, as well as variations and individual differences in neurobiologically based characteristics and processes. These theories have emphasized genetic influences, constitutional factors, neuroanatomy, neuropharmacological mechanisms, and rates of maturation (e.g., onset of puberty). From a neurobiological perspective all mental disorders are believed to be represented in the brain as a biological entity. Somehow, an array of biochemicals and neurohormones interact to influence several brain regions, causing the individual to experience emotional and/or behavioral dysfunction (Kaplan & Sadock, 1991). The goals of research are to ascertain what specific genetic mutations are associated with structural and biochemical impairments and psychopathology.

In considering general human characteristics for behavior, emotion, and cognition, Richters and Cicchetti (1993) identify a number of important functions of the human nervous system that include the capacity for emotion recognition and expression, cooperation, formation of attachments, self-awareness, learning from experience, withholding or delaying a response, anticipating the future, recognizing and avoiding danger, generating strategies for action and choosing among them, and social communication. Since there are an unlimited number of ways to conceptualize the adaptive functions of the nervous system and its dysfunctions, it becomes necessary to circumscribe which of these and other functions of the nervous system are the most causally relevant to a particular childhood disorder (e.g., recognizing and avoiding danger in the case of anxiety disorders or delaying a response in the case of ADHD).

Genetic Influences

There has been some ambivalence regarding the significance of genetic influences in child psychopathology (Torgersen, 1993). Recent findings and technological advances in behavioral genetics have, to some extent, altered this view (e.g., Carey & DiLalla, 1994; Fox, 1994b; Lewis & Miller, 1990; Lombroso, Pauls, & Leckman, 1994; Plomin, 1995). Clearly, both constitutional and environmental factors contribute to children's behavioral/emotional disorders (Willis & Walker, 1989). As Torgersen (1993) states, "No behavior is independent of inborn endowments, and any behavior requires an environment in order to take place" (p. 42). Thus, asking whether a specific form of child psychopathology is due to genetics or environmental influences is both naive and futile. Rather, the more appropriate question is: to what extent are given behaviors due to variations in genetic endowment, variations within the environment, or the interaction between these two factors?

Over the past few decades, significant advances have been made in behavioral genetics with the identification of underlying genetic mechanisms involved in a plethora of medical illnesses and neurological disorders (e.g., Huntington's chorea, cystic fibrosis) (Lombroso et al., 1994; Willis & Walker, 1989). Genetic factors have been implicated in a number of childhood disorders (e.g., autistic disorder, ADHD, CD, Tourette's disorder, mood disorders, schizophrenia; see

Lombroso et al., 1994, and Torgersen, 1993, for reviews), and recent empirical evidence is accumulating in support of the role of genetic influences on temperament (e.g., behavioral inhibition; Kagan et al., 1988) and emotion regulation (Baum, Grunberg, & Singer, 1992; Fox, 1994a). Despite recent support and enthusiasm for the role of genetic influences in childhood dysfunction, however, no specific mutations have yet been isolated or identified in their pathogenesis (Lombroso et al., 1994).

Familial aggregation is frequently an initial step in understanding the function of genetic mechanisms. Once familial clustering is demonstrated, more in-depth and costly twin studies, adoption studies, segregation analyses, and linkage studies can be conducted (cf. Szatmari, Boyle, & Offord, 1993). Familial aggregation refers to the nonrandom clustering of disorders or characteristics within a given family relative to the random distribution of these disorders or characteristics in the general population (Szatmari et al., 1993). This paradigm rests on the premise that if there is a genetic component to a given disorder, the frequency of the phenotype (or manifest pathology) will be higher among biological relatives of the proband than the prevalence rates in the general population (Deutsch & Kinsbourne, 1990; Lombroso et al., 1994; Torgersen, 1993).

Several studies conducted by Cynthia Last and her associates (Last, Francis, Hersen, Kazdin, & Strauss, 1987; Last, Hersen, Kazdin, Francis, & Grubb, 1987; Last, Phillips, & Statfeld, 1987) have found that parents of children with overanxious disorder or separation anxiety disorder tend to have higher rates of anxiety in their own childhood histories relative to normative prevalence rates. In a community sample, Szatmari and colleagues (1993) also found evidence for familial aggregation of conduct problems and emotional difficulties. It is important to point out, however, that in these and similar studies, the researchers were unable to control for environmental variables that also contribute to an individual's pathology.

Twin studies are beneficial in helping to ascertain the contribution of genetic factors in the etiology of child psychopathology. The twin study approach emerged from the long-standing nature versus nurture or genetic versus environment debate (Lombroso et al., 1994). Although twin studies provide a powerful research strategy for examining the role of genetic influences in both psychiatric and nonpsychiatric disorders, there are numerous methodological issues which necessitate that caution be exercised in interpreting findings. For example, although Willerman (1973) found a concordance rate for hyperactivity of approximately 70%, this does not necessarily mean that 70% of the variance in hyperactivity is accounted for by genetic variation. Research suggests, for instance, that monozygotic (MZ) twins spend more time together, frequently engage in similar activities, and have many of the same friends in common (Torgersen, 1993). Thus, the common or shared environment presents a potential confound in any twin study, and, unless twins are reared apart, it becomes impossible to separate the effects of genetic and environmental influences (Deutsch & Kinsbourne, 1990). The representativeness and generalizability to the general population exemplify other problems with twin studies (Lombroso et al., 1994; Torgersen, 1993). Growing up with a sibling of an identical age, for example, introduces its own special challenges (e.g., competition between siblings, greater dependency on each other) that make the twin environment unique.

Adoption studies have been used to circumvent some of the problems with twin and familial aggregation studies. They explicitly attempt to control for environmental variation in the heritability equation. The assumption behind this strategy is that when a disorder has a genetic etiology, the frequency of its expression among biological relatives should be greater than the frequency of the disorder among adoptive relatives. Conversely, when environmental factors assume a larger role in the etiology of psychopathology, the frequency of the disorder would be expected to be greater among the parents of adoptive relatives than among biological parents (Lombroso et al., 1994; Torgersen, 1993). Lombroso and his collaborators reviewed the extant adoptive studies of childhood psychopathology and concluded that there was a paucity of research in this important area.

Several reasons may be advanced to account for the sparse number of investigations using the adoptive strategy. One obstacle has been the difficulty of attaining reliable information regarding the biological parents of adoptees. The timing of adoption placements also represents a potential confound. Since children are typically adopted at different ages, it is difficult to determine what environmental influences the biological parents may have had during the earliest years of life (Lombroso et al., 1994). Similarly, many children

are placed in residential settings prior to adoption; these conditions, which may affect the child's development, would be unaccounted for by an adoptive strategy. A confound analogous to the problem of timing is the high probability of being placed in an adoptive home that is similar to the home environment of the biological family. For instance, adoption agencies are quite strict in their criteria for adequate placements, and the adoptive home must, at minimum, meet current middle-class standards (Torgersen, 1993).

Many genetic research strategies are still in their technological infancy, and the goal of translating information from behavioral genetics to the implementation of treatment strategies (e.g., psychopharmacology) is far from being realized. Nevertheless, as discussed in the chapters of this volume, genetic factors have been implicated in a number of disorders including autism, personality disorders, substance abuse and dependency, anxiety disorders, mood disorders, schizophrenia, ADHD, and reading disorders (Lombroso et al., 1994; Pennington & Ozonoff, 1991; Torgersen, 1993). Genetic factors are increasingly implicated in a variety of psychiatric disturbances, and there is a broadened interest in including environmental considerations into genetic models (see Pennington & Ozonoff, 1991; Torgersen, 1993).

Behavioral Inhibition

Research on behavioral inhibition illustrates how constitutionally based traits represent predispositions or diatheses that may or may not contribute to later psychopathology. Evidence from various lines of research suggests that at least some behavioral traits, such as extreme shyness, are stable characteristics of a person's personality that stem from inborn predispositions to respond to environmental stimuli in certain ways (Aspendorpf, 1993; Rubin & Stewart, Chapter 7, this volume). In their studies of human infants, Kagan and his colleagues (Hirshfeld et al., 1992; Kagan et al., 1984, 1987, 1988; Rosenbaum et al., 1988) have found evidence for what is referred to as "behavioral inhibition to the unfamiliar." An interest in this area began several years ago when Kagan found that traits such as dependence, aggression, dominance, and competitiveness are transient and fluctuate over time from age 2 or 3 years to age 20 years. However, the trait of behavioral inhibition showed considerable stability across time. As adults, the inhibited children displayed elevated and unusually stable increases in their heart rates in response to mild stress.

Kagan and his colleagues (1984) followed the development of 43 extremely inhibited and uninhibited children by tracking their heart rates and behavioral responses in novel situations at 21 months and later at 4 years. By the age of 4 years, the 22 inhibited children had more stable heart rates, were more reluctant to perform various tasks, and were more passive than the 21 children who were uninhibited at 21 months of age. Kagan et al. (1984) suggested that this inhibition to the unfamiliar was moderately stable and may be the result of biological factors. Similar findings were obtained by Kagan et al. in their 1987 and 1988 studies. The behaviorally inhibited children's pupils were more dilated, and they had faster and more stable heart rates indicating that their sympathetic nervous system was chronically activated. These temperamental characteristics were so stable that Kagan and his colleagues could predict scores on several measures at 5 and 7 years on the basis on behavioral inhibition at 21 months (see Biederman et al., 1993, and Hirshfeld et al., 1992, for recent replications and extensions of these findings).

Kagan and his coworkers (1987) argued that the reactions that behaviorally inhibited children display center on a feedback loop connecting the hypothalamus with the pituitary and adrenal glands. A stressor triggers a series of chemical reactions. When the emotional centers in the brain (e.g., the limbic system) are activated, the neurotransmitters serotonin and norepinephrine are sent to the hypothalamus, which results in a secretion of corticotropin-releasing hormones. This release then causes the pituitary gland to circulate adrenocorticotropic hormone into the bloodstream, which, in turn, stimulates the adrenal glands to distribute cortisol (a hormone) to manage the stressor that is reflected in dilated pupils, increased heart rate, blood pressure, and muscle tone—the general fight or flight response (Kagan & Snidman, 1991; see also Asher, 1987; Baum et al., 1992).

Does behavioral inhibition embody a risk factor for later anxiety? Consistent with the description of the elevated autonomic nervous system arousal seen in behaviorally inhibited children, Klein and Gorman (1987) hypothesize that anxiety is due to an over-active adrenergic system in the central nervous system. Moreover, Thomas and Chess (1977) found that infants with withdrawal tendencies (e.g., behavioral inhibition)

were at risk for the development of overanxious or avoidant disorder in childhood. Recent longitudinal investigations conducted by Rubin and his associates have also demonstrated that social isolation and withdrawal are associated with internalizing (and, in some instances externalizing) problems in subsequent years (Hymel, Rubin, Rowden, & LeMare, 1990; Rubin, Chen, & Hymel, 1993; Rubin, Hymel, & Mills, 1989; Rubin & Mills, 1988, 1990, 1991).

Rosenbaum et al. (1988) investigated behavioral inhibition as a risk factor for later (i.e., adult) agoraphobia and panic disorder. Fifty-six children ages 2 to 7 years were matched for age, sex, ethnicity, and ordinal position. The rates of behavioral inhibition in children of adults with panic disorder and agoraphobia were significantly higher than the children of parents without these difficulties. Of course one cannot rule out the influence of the environment in this study, but there is additional evidence for the innate nature of behavioral inhibition.

Support for the biological nature of this disposition stems from some earlier studies using monkeys by Suomi and Harlow in the 1960s and 1970s (cited in Asher, 1987). These researchers found characteristics similar to Kagan's behaviorally inhibited subjects in depression-prone monkeys. These results suggest that extreme shyness may have a genetic component. Additional evidence for innate predispositions to anxiety also stems from genetic and familial studies. Torgersen (1983), for example, found that, for anxiety, there was a higher concordance for MZ twins than for dizygotic (DZ) twins. Moreover, several studies conducted by Cynthia Last and her colleagues point to the high overlap among childhood anxiety disorders as well as the familial concordance found in children of adults with anxiety disorders (e.g., Last, Phillips, & Statfeld, 1987). Research on the structural properties of the brain also enhances the idea of a biological predisposition. Recent anatomical research indicates that highly reactive individuals (e.g., inhibited children) are more likely to have right frontal lobe activation relative to controls. In contrast, uninhibited children tend to show more left side activation on the frontal pole (Fox, 1994a; Kagan, 1994b).

It would be naive to think of biology as the only etiological factor involved in anxious–withdrawn patterns of behavior. In contrast to the biological predisposition hypothesis, Messer and Biedel (1994) found, for example, that children with anxiety disorders tend to report that they come from families in which their autonomy is restricted. Biological support for behavioral inhibition does not mean that children with this tendency are destined to a life of anxiety or social withdrawal. Analogously, the absence of behavioral inhibition does not mean that a child will not later develop an anxiety disorder; rather, a particular outcome appears to be based on a series of reciprocal interactions between innate predispositions (debilitative or protective) and situational circumstances (i.e., a supportive or maladaptive environment). For instance, the probability that extreme shyness will continue in later years depends on how parents and other socializing agents respond to the child's inhibition (Fox, 1994a). If the child's caregivers accept his or her withdrawn behavior, then inhibition will be more likely to become entrenched than if caregivers foster approach behavior through gentle encouragement.

In sum, behavioral inhibition provides an example of a biological propensity that contributes to the likelihood of ensuing anxiety and states of elevated arousal. How this proclivity becomes effectual in leading to further anxiety and social withdrawal/isolation, however, is dependent on a myriad of additional situations that reside within the unique environmental context of the child and his or her interactions with it.

SUMMARY AND CONCLUSIONS

In this chapter we have described a developmental-systems framework for child psychopathology that emphasized three central themes: (1) the need to study child psychopathology in relation to ongoing normal and pathological developmental processes; (2) the importance of context in determining the expression and outcome of childhood disorders; and (3) the role of multiple and interacting events and processes in shaping both adaptive and maladaptive development. The research findings that are presented in each of the chapters of this volume illustrate the importance of these themes for understanding children and adolescents displaying a wide range of problems and/or conditions.

A developmental-systems framework (see also Mash, 1989; Mash & Terdal, 1988a) eschews simple linear models of causality and advocates for a greater emphasis on systemic and developmental factors and their interactions in understanding child psychopathology. Multiple etiologies and

their interplay represent the norm for most forms of child psychopathology. For example, in the study of conduct disorders, insecure attachment relationships, impulsivity, biased cognitive processing, parental rejection, a lack of parental supervision, interpersonal difficulties, reduced concentration of serotonin metabolite 5–HIAA in cerebrospinal fluid, a low baseline autonomic activity, and many other influences have been implicated. However, many of these influences have also been implicated in other disorders, and all children who experience them do not display conduct disorders. There is a need for research that will help to disentangle the role of these multiple sources of influence and their interactions in relation to different childhood disorders.

We have argued that all forms of child psychopathology are best conceptualized in terms of developmental trajectories, rather than as static entities, and that the expression and outcome for any problem will depend on the configuration and timing of a host of surrounding circumstances that include events both within and outside of the child. For any dynamically changing developmental trajectory there also exists some degree of continuity and stability of structure, process, and function across time. Understanding such continuity and stability in the context of change represents a challenge for future research and necessitates that psychopathology in children be studied over time, from a number of different vantage points, utilizing multiple methods, and drawing on knowledge from a variety of different disciplines.

Given the complexities associated with a developmental-systems framework for understanding child psychopathology, there is a clear need for theories to guide our research efforts. We have argued that a developmental psychopathology perspective provides a broad macroparadigm for conceptualizing and understanding childhood disorders in general and that complementary disorder- and problem-specific theories are also needed to account for the specific configuration(s) of variables that are commonly associated with particular disorders. Such problem-specific theories are presented in each of the chapters of this volume. The conceptualization of child psychopathology in terms of developmental trajectories, multiple influences, probabilistic relationships, and diverse outcomes suggests that there are likely to be some influences that are common to many different disorders and others that are specific to particular problems. Our theories need to account for both types of influence.

The problems of childhood are universal, and as a result there is much folklore and many unsubstantiated theories concerning both the causes of childhood difficulties and their remedies. Childhood disorders constitute a significant societal problem, and in the absence of an empirically grounded knowledge base, unsubstantiated theories have frequently been used as the basis for developing solutions to these problems. There is a pressing need for longitudinal research to inform our intervention and prevention efforts (Verhulst & Koot, 1991). Such research will likely require new ways of conceptualizing childhood disorders, far greater collaboration among disciplines than has previously been the case, and the use of more sophisticated design strategies and statistical tools that are sensitive to the multiple interacting influences and changes over time that we have outlined in this chapter (Mash & Krahn, 1995). This research agenda is reflected in the following statement from the *National Plan for Research on Child and Adolescent Mental Disorders* that was recently presented by the United States National Institute of Mental Health (NIMH):

> Clinical and basic research on child and adolescent disorders require the innovative application of existing statistical techniques from relevant disciplines, as well as the development of new techniques where appropriate. Areas in particular need of attention include the sequencing of risk factors, reducing long lists of measures, developing analytic methods for subsamples and single cases, developing taxonomic constructs from multisource data, extrapolating from studies in animal models to human subjects, and examining interactions between and among risk factors (rather than their simple linear effects). (Jensen et al., 1993, p. 560)

The chapters in this volume provide a state-of-the-art review and critique of current definitions, theories, and research for a wide range of childhood disorders. They also identify current needs and, consistent with the aforementioned statement from NIMH, forecast likely future directions for research into child psychopathology.

ACKNOWLEDGMENTS

During the preparation of this chapter, E. J. Mash was supported by a research grant from the Alberta Mental Health Research Fund and by a sabbatical fellowship from the University of Calgary. D. J. A. Dozois

was supported by an award from the Medical Research Council of Canada. This support is gratefully acknowledged.

NOTES

1. As a matter of convenience we use the terms "children" and "child" in this chapter and volume to refer to children of all ages from infancy through adolescence. The diversity within this wide age range will necessitate the use of more specific designations of age and developmental level as appropriate to the discussion. We have also opted to use the term "child psychopathology" rather than "developmental psychopathology." Either term would have been appropriate, since we view all disorders of childhood and adolescence as embedded in developmental processes and sequences. However, we use "child psychopathology" as the more general and theoretically neutral term to describe the full range of disorders that occur during childhood and adolescence. For the most part, the two terms are used interchangeably in this volume. Other terms that have been used to describe problems during childhood are "abnormal child psychology," "childhood disorders," "atypical child development," "childhood behavior disorders," and "exceptional child development." These differences in terminology reflect the many disciplines and theoretical perspectives that have been concerned with understanding and helping disturbed children.

2. We recognize that theory and research in child psychopathology need to be put to the test in the applied arena. However, we do not, in this volume, consider in any detail the range of assessment, treatment, or prevention strategies that are available for the problems under discussion. Our decision to not address assessment, treatment, and prevention in this volume was based on: (1) the perceived need for a substantive review of what we currently know about childhood disorders. Many current treatments for childhood disorders are untested (Kazdin, 1988a, 1993; Mash & Barkley, 1989), and it was felt that future efforts to test treatment approaches would benefit from a detailed discussion of our current knowledge base for child psychopathology; (2) a desire not to dilute the discussion of theory and research in child psychopathology by attempting to provide cursory coverage to assessment and intervention. Instead we refer the reader to companion volumes to this one that have as their primary focus either child assessment (Mash & Terdal, 1988b, in press) or child treatment (Mash & Barkley, 1989), respectively.

REFERENCES

Achenbach, T. M. (1982). *Developmental psychopathology* (2nd ed.). New York: Wiley.

Achenbach, T. M. (1985). *Assessment and taxonomy of child and adolescent psychopathology*. Beverly Hills, CA: Sage.

Achenbach, T. M. (1990). Conceptualization of developmental psychopathology. In M. Lewis & S. M. Miller (Eds.), *Handbook of developmental psychopathology* (pp. 3–14). New York: Plenum Press.

Achenbach, T. M. (1991). *Manual for the Child Behavior Checklist/4–18 and 1991 Profile*. Burlington, VT: University of Vermont Department of Psychiatry.

Achenbach, T. M. (1993). *Empirically based taxonomy: How to use syndromes and profile types derived from the CBCL/4–18, TRF, and YSR*. Burlington, VT: University of Vermont, Department of Psychiatry.

Achenbach, T. M. (1995). Diagnosis, assessment, and comorbidity in psychosocial treatment research. *Journal of Abnormal Psychology, 23*, 45–65.

Achenbach, T. M., & Edelbrock, C. (1981). Behavioral problems and competencies reported by parents of normal and disturbed children aged four through sixteen. *Monographs of the Society for Research in Child Development, 46* (1, Serial No. 188).

Achenbach, T. M., & Edelbrock, C. (1989). Diagnostic, taxonomic, and assessment issues. In T. H. Ollendick & M. Hersen (Eds.), *Handbook of child psychopathology* (2nd ed., pp. 53–73). New York: Plenum Press.

Achenbach, T. M., Howell, C. T., Quay, H. C., & Conners, C. K. (1991). National survey of problems and competencies among four- to sixteen-year-olds. *Monographs of the Society for Research in Child Development, 56* (3, Serial No. 225).

Achenbach, T. M., McConaughy, S. H., & Howell, C. T. (1987). Child/adolescent behavioral and emotional problems: Implications of cross-informant correlations for situational specificity. *Psychological Bulletin, 101*, 213–232.

Adams, H. E., Doster, J. A., & Calhoun, K. S. (1977). A psychologically-based system of response classification. In A. R. Ciminero, K. S. Calhoun, & H. E. Adams (Eds.), *Handbook of behavioral assessment* (pp. 47–78). New York: Wiley.

Adelman, H. S. (1995). Clinical psychology: Beyond psychopathology and clinical interventions. *Clinical Psychology: Science and Practice, 2*, 28–44.

Adelman, H. S., & Taylor, L. (1993). *Learning problems and learning disabilities: Moving forward*. Pacific Grove, CA: Brooks/Cole.

American Psychiatric Association. (1952). *Diagnostic and statistical manual of mental disorders*. Washington, DC: Author.

American Psychiatric Association. (1968). *Diagnostic and statistical manual of mental disorders* (2nd ed.). Washington, DC: Author.

American Psychiatric Association. (1980). *Diagnostic and statistical manual of mental disorders* (3rd ed.). Washington, DC: Author.

American Psychiatric Association. (1987). *Diagnostic and statistical manual of mental disorders* (3rd ed., rev.). Washington, DC: Author.

American Psychiatric Association. (1994). *Diagnostic and statistical manual of mental disorders* (4th ed.). Washington, DC: Author.

Anderson, J. C., Williams, S., McGee, R., & Silva, P. A. (1987). DSM III-disorders in preadolescent children: Prevalence in a large sample from the general population. *Archives of General Psychiatry, 44*, 69–76.

Aries, P. (1962). *Centuries of childhood*. New York: Vintage Books.

Arkowitz, H. (1992). Integrative theories of therapy. In D. K. Freedheim (Ed.), *History of psychotherapy: A cen-*

tury of change (pp. 261–303). Washington, DC: American Psychological Association.

Asher, J. (1987). Born to be shy? *Psychology Today, 21,* 56–64.

Aspendorpf, J. B. (1993). Abnormal shyness in children. *Journal of Child Psychology and Psychiatry, 34,* 1069–182.

Bandura, A. (1977). *Social learning theory.* Englewood Cliffs, NJ: Prentice Hall.

Bandura, A. (1986). *Social foundations of thought and action: A social cognitive theory.* Englewood Cliffs, NJ: Prentice-Hall.

Barkley, R. A. (1996). *Behavioral inhibition and executive functions: Constructing a unifying theory of ADHD.* Manuscript submitted for publication.

Barkley, R. A., Grodzinsky, G., & DuPaul, G. (1992). Frontal lobe functions in attention deficit disorder with and without hyperactivity: A review and research report. *Journal of Abnormal Child Psychology, 20,* 163–188.

Barton, S. (1994). Chaos, self-organization, and psychology. *American Psychologist, 49,* 5–14.

Baum, A., Grunberg, N. E., & Singer, J. E. (1992). Biochemical measurements in the study of emotion. *Psychological Science, 3,* 56–59.

Beck, A. T. (1963). Thinking and depression: Idiosyncratic content and cognitive distortions. *Archives of General Psychiatry, 9,* 324–333.

Beck, A. T. (1964). Thinking and depression: Theory and therapy. *Archives of General Psychiatry, 10,* 561–571.

Beck, A. T., Rush, A. J., Shaw, B. F., & Emery, G. (1979). *Cognitive therapy of depression.* New York: Guilford Press.

Bernstein, G. A., & Borchardt, C. M. (1991). Anxiety disorders of childhood and adolescence: A critical review. *Journal of the American Academy of Child and Adolescent Psychiatry, 30,* 519–532.

Bettelheim, B. (1967). *The empty fortress.* New York: The Free Press.

Biederman, J., Rosenbaum, J. F., Bolduc-Murphy, E. A., Faraone, S. V., Chaloff, J., Hirshfeld, D. R., & Kagan, J. (1993). A 3-year follow-up of children with and without behavioral inhibition. *Journal of the American Academy of Child and Adolescent Psychiatry, 32,* 814–821.

Bijou, S. W., & Baer, D. M. (1961). *Child development: Systematic and empirical theory.* New York: Appleton-Century-Crofts.

Bird, H. R., Canino, G., Rubio-Stipec, M., Gould, M. S., Ribera, J., Sesman, M., Woodbury, M., Huertas-Goldman, S., Pagan, A., Sanchez-Lacay, A., & Moscoso, M. (1988). Estimates of the prevalence of childhood maladjustment in a community survey of Puerto Rico: The use of combined measures. *Archives of General Psychiatry, 45,* 1120–1126.

Bird, H. R., Gould, M. S., Yager, T., Staghezza, B., & Camino, G. (1989). Risk factors for maladjustment in Puerto Rican children. *Journal of the American Academy of Child and Adolescent Psychiatry, 28,* 847–850.

Blashfield, R. K., McElroy, R. A., Jr., Pfohl, B., & Blum, N. (1994). Comorbidity and the prototype model. *Clinical Psychology: Science and Practice, 1,* 96–99.

Borstelmann, L. J. (1983). Children before psychology: Ideas about children from antiquity to the late 1800s. In P. H. Mussen (Series Ed.) & W. Kessen (Vol. Ed.), *Handbook of child psychology: Vol. 1. History, theory, and methods* (4th ed., pp. 1–40). New York: Wiley.

Bowlby, J. (1973). *Attachment and loss: Vol. 2. Separation: Anxiety and anger.* New York: Basic Books.

Bowlby, J. (1988). *A secure base: Parent–child attachment and healthy human development.* New York: Basic Books.

Boyle, M. H., Offord, D. R., Hoffman, H. G., Catlin, G. P., Byles, J. A., Cadman, D. T., Crawford, J. W., Links, P. S., Rae-Grant, N. I., & Szatmari, P. (1987). Ontario Child Health Study: I. Methodology. *Archives of General Psychiatry, 44,* 826–831.

Brady, E. U., & Kendall, P. C. (1992). Comorbidity of anxiety and depression in children and adolescents. *Psychological Bulletin, 111,* 244–255.

Brandenburg, N. A., Friedman, R. M., & Silver, S. E. (1990). The epidemiology of childhood psychiatric disorders: Prevalence findings from recent studies. *Journal of the American Academy of Child and Adolescent Psychiatry, 29,* 76–83.

Bray, J. H. (1994). *Family assessment: Current issues in evaluating families.* Unpublished manuscript, Department of Family Medicine, Baylor College of Medicine, Houston, TX.

Bray, J. H. (1995). Methodological advances in family psychology research: Introduction to the special section. *Journal of Family Psychology, 9,* 107–109.

Bray, J. H., Maxwell, S. E., & Cole, D. (1995). Multivariate statistics for family psychology research. *Journal of Family Psychology, 9,* 144–160.

Bretherton, I. (1995). Attachment theory and developmental psychopathology. In D. Cicchetti & S. L. Toth (Eds.), *Emotion, cognition, and representation* (Rochester Symposium on Developmental Psychopathology). Rochester, NY: University of Rochester Press.

Bronfenbrenner, U. (1977). Toward an experimental ecology of human development. *American Psychologist, 32,* 513–531.

Bugental, D. B. (1993). Communication in abusive relationships: Cognitive constructions of interpersonal power. *American Behavioral Scientist, 36,* 288–308.

Campbell, S. B. (1989). Developmental perspectives. In T. H. Ollendick & M. Hersen (Eds.), *Handbook of child psychopathology* (2nd ed., pp. 5–28). New York: Plenum Press.

Cantor, N., Smith, E. E., French, R. deS., & Mezzich, J. (1980). Psychiatric diagnosis as prototype categorization. *Journal of Abnormal Psychology, 89,* 181–193.

Carey, G., & DiLalla, D. L. (1994). Personality and psychopathology: Genetic perspectives. *Journal of Abnormal Psychology, 103,* 32–43.

Caron, C., & Rutter, M. (1991). Comorbidity in child psychopathology: Concepts, issues, and research strategies. *Journal of Child Psychology and Psychiatry, 32,* 1063–1080.

Carter, J. D., & Swanson, H. L. (1995). The relationship between intelligence and vigilance in children at risk. *Journal of Abnormal Child Psychology, 23,* 201–220.

Cass, L. K., & Thomas, C. B. (1979). *Childhood pathology and later adjustment.* New York: Wiley.

Cassidy, J. (1994). Emotion regulation: Influences of attachment relationships. In N. A. Fox (Ed.), *Monographs of the society for research in child development, 59* (2–3, Serial No. 240), 228–249.

Catalano, R. F., Hawkins, J. D., Krenz, C., Gilmore, M., Morrison, D., Wells, E., & Abbott, R. (1993). Using research to guide culturally appropriate drug abuse prevention. *Journal of Consulting and Clinical Psychology, 61,* 804–811.

Cattell, R. B. (1938). *Crooked personalities in childhood and after.* New York: Appleton-Century.

Chen, X., Rubin, K. H., & Li, Z. Y. (1995). Social functioning and adjustment in Chinese children: A longitudinal study. *Developmental Psychology, 31,* 531–539.

Cicchetti, D. (1984). The emergence of developmental psychopathology. *Child Development, 55,* 1–7.

Cicchetti, D. (1990). An historical perspective on the discipline of developmental psychopathology. In J. Rolf, A. Masten, D. Cicchetti, K. Nuechterlein, & S. Weintraub (Eds.), *Risk and protective factors in the development of psychopathology* (pp. 2–28). New York: Cambridge University Press.

Cicchetti, D., Ackerman, B. P., & Izard, C. E. (1995). Emotions and emotion regulation in developmental psychopathology. *Development and Psychopathology, 7,* 1–10.

Cicchetti, D., & Cohen, D. J. (1995). *Developmental psychopathology* (Vols. 1 and 2). New York: Wiley.

Cicchetti, D., & Garmezy, N. (1993). Prospects and promises in the study of resilience. *Development and Psychopathology, 4,* 497–502.

Cicchetti, D., & Izard, C. E. (Eds.). (1995). Special issue: Emotions in developmental psychopathology. *Developmental Psychopathology, 7* (whole No. 1).

Cicchetti, D., & Richters, J. E. (1993). Developmental considerations in the investigation of conduct disorder. *Development and Psychopathology, 5,* 331–344.

Cicchetti, D., & Tucker, D. (1994). Development and self-regulatory structures of the mind. *Development and Psychopathology, 6,* 533–549.

Clementz, B. A., & Iacono, W. G. (1993). Nosology and diagnosis. In A. S. Bellack & M. Hersen (Eds.), *Psychopathology in adulthood* (pp. 3–20). Boston: Allyn & Bacon.

Cohen, J. (1988). *Statistical power analysis for the behavioral sciences* (2nd ed.). New York: Academic Press.

Cole, P. M., Michel, M. K., & Teti, L. O. (1994). The development of emotion regulation and dysregulation: A clinical perspective. *Monographs of the Society for Research in Child Development, 59,* 53–72.

Costello, E. J. (1989). Developments in child psychiatric epidemiology. *Journal of the American Academy of Child and Adolescent Psychiatry, 28* 836–841.

Costello, E. J., & Angold, A. (1993). Toward a developmental epidemiology of the disruptive behavior disorders. *Development and Psychopathology, 5,* 91–101.

Courchesne, E., Chisum, H., & Townsend, J. (1994). Neural-activity dependent brain changes in development: Implications for psychopathology. *Development and Psychopathology, 6,* 697–722.

Crick, N. R., & Dodge, K. A. (1994). A review and reformulation of social information-processing mechanisms in children's social adjustment. *Psychological Bulletin, 115,* 73–101.

Crittenden, P. M., Claussen, A. H., & Sugarman, D. B. (1994). Physical and psychological maltreatment in middle childhood and adolescence. *Development and Psychopathology, 6,* 145–164.

Cummings, E. M., & Davies, P. T. (1995). The impact of parents on their children: An emotional security perspective. *Annals of Child Development, 10,* 167–208.

Cummings, E. M., Hennessy, K. D., Rabideau, G. J., & Cicchetti, D. (1994). Responses of physically abused boys to interadult anger involving their mothers. *Development and Psychopathology, 6,* 31–41.

Dare, C. (1985). Psychoanalytic theories of development. In M. Rutter & L. Hersov (Eds.), *Child and adolescent psychiatry: Modern approaches* (2nd ed., pp. 205–215). Oxford, UK: Blackwell Scientific Publications.

Davies, P. T., & Cummings, E. M. (1994). Marital conflict and child adjustment: An emotional security hypothesis. *Psychological Bulletin, 116,* 387–411.

Davies, P. T., & Cummings, E. M. (1995). Children's emotions as organizers of their reactions to interadult anger: A functionalist perspective. *Developmental Psychology, 31,* 677–684.

Dawson, G., Hessl, D., & Frey, K. (1994). Social influences on early developing biological and behavioral systems related to risk for affective disorder. *Development and Psychopathology, 6,* 759–779.

Deutsch, C. K., & Kinsbourne, M. (1990). Genetics and biochemistry in attention deficit disorder. In M. Lewis & S. M. Miller (Eds.), *Handbook of developmental psychopathology* (pp. 93–107). New York: Plenum Press.

Dobson, K. S., & Kendall, P. C. (1993). Future trends for research and theory in cognition and psychopathology. In K. S. Dobson & P. C. Kendall (Eds.), *Psychopathology and cognition* (pp. 475–486). San Diego: Academic Press.

Dobson, K. S., & Shaw, B. F. (1987). Specificity and stability of self-referent encoding in clinical depression. *Journal of Abnormal Psychology, 96,* 34–40.

Dodge, K. A. (1989). Problems in social relationships. In E. J. Mash & R. A. Barkley (Eds.), *Treatment of childhood disorders* (pp. 222–244). New York: Guilford Press.

Dodge, K. A., & Crick, N. R. (1990). Social information-processing bases of aggressive behavior in children. *Personality and Social Psychology Bulletin, 16,* 8–22.

Dodge, K. A., & Newman, J. P. (1981) Biased decision-making processes in aggressive boys. *Journal of Abnormal Psychology, 90,* 375–379.

Dodge, K. A., Pettit, G. S., & Bates, J. E. (1994). Effects of physical maltreatment on the development of peer relations. *Development and Psychopathology, 6,* 43–55.

Dodge, K. A., & Somberg, D. R. (1987). Hostile attributional biases among aggressive boys are exacerbated under conditions of threats to the self. *Child Development, 58,* 213–224.

Donohue, B., Hersen, M., & Ammerman, R. T. (1995). Historical overview. In M. Hersen & R. T. Ammerman (Eds.), *Advanced abnormal child psychology* (pp. 3–19). Hillsdale, NJ: Erlbaum.

Downey, G., & Coyne, J. C. (1990). Children of depressed parents: An integrative review. *Psychological Bulletin, 116,* 29–45.

Dozier, M., & Lee, S. (1995). Discrepancies between self- and other-report of psychiatric symptomatology: Effects of dismissing attachment strategies. *Development and Psychopathology, 7,* 217–226.

Dumas, J. E., LaFreniere, P. J., & Serketich, W. J. (1995). "Balance of power": A transactional analysis of control in mother–child dyads involving socially competent, aggressive, and anxious children. *Journal of Abnormal Psychology, 104,* 104–113.

Duncan, G. J., Brooks-Gunn, J., & Klebanov, P. K. (1994). Economic deprivation and early-childhood development. *Child Development, 65,* 296–318.

Earls, F. J. (1980). Prevalence of behavior problems in 3-year-old children. *Archives of General Psychiatry, 37,* 1153–1157.

Edelbrock, C. (1984). Developmental considerations. In T. H. Ollendick & M. Hersen (Eds.), *Child behavioral as-*

sessment: Principles and procedures (pp. 20–37). New York: Pergamon Press.

Egeland, B., & Heister, M. (1995). The long-term consequences of infant day-care and mother-infant attachment. Child Development, 66, 474–485.

Eme, R. F. (1979). Sex differences in childhood psychopathology: A review. Psychological Bulletin, 86, 574–595.

Emery, R. E., Binkoff, J. A., Houts, A. C., & Carr, E. G. (1983). Children as independent variables: Some clinical implications of child effects. Behavior Therapy, 14, 398–412.

Fauber, R. L., & Long, N. (1991). Children in context: The role of the family on child psychotherapy. Journal of Consulting and Clinical Psychology, 59, 813–820.

Feldman, S., & Downey, G. (1994). Rejection sensitivity as a mediator of the impact of childhood exposure to family violence on adult attachment behavior. Development and Psychopathology, 6, 231–247.

Felner, R. D., Brand, S., DuBois, D. L., Adan, A. M., Mulhall, P. F., & Evans, E. G. (1995). Socioeconomic disadvantage, proximal environmental experiences, and socioemotional and academic adjustment in early adolescence: Investigation of a mediated effects model. Child Development, 66, 774–792.

Foster, S. L., & Martinez, C. R., Jr. (1995). Ethnicity: Conceptual and methodological issues in child clinical research. Journal of Clinical Child Psychology, 24, 214–226.

Fox, N. A. (1994a). Dynamic cerebral processes underlying emotion regulation. Monographs of the Society for Research in Child Development, 59 (2–3, Serial No. 240), 152–166.

Fox, N. A. (Ed.). (1994b). The development of emotion regulation: Biological and behavioral considerations. Monographs of the Society for Research in Child Development, 59 (2–3, Serial No. 240).

Francis, D. J., Fletcher, J. M., Stuebing, K. K., Davidson, K. C., & Thompson, N. M. (1991). Analysis of change: Modeling individual growth. Journal of Consulting and Clinical Psychology, 59, 27–37.

French, V. (1977). History of the child's influence: Ancient Mediterranean civilizations. In R. Q. Bell & L. V. Harper (Eds.), Child effects on adults (pp. 3–29). Hillsdale, NJ: Erlbaum.

Friman, P. C., Larzelere, R., & Finney, J. W. (1994). Exploring the relationship between thumbsucking and psychopathology. Journal of Pediatric Psychology, 19, 431–441.

Garber, J. (1984). Classification of childhood psychopathology: A developmental perspective. Child Development, 55, 30–48.

Garber, J., & Dodge, K. A. (Eds.). (1991). The development of emotion regulation and dysregulation. New York: Cambridge University Press.

Garmezy, N. (1985). Stress-resistant children: The search for protective factors. In J. E. Stevenson (Ed.), Recent research in developmental psychology. Journal of Child Psychology and Psychiatry Book Supplement, 4, 213–233.

Garmezy, N., Masten, N. S., & Tellegen, A. (1984). The study of stress and competence in children: A building block of developmental psychopathology. Child Development, 55, 97–111.

Ge, X., Conger, R. D., Lorenz, F. O., Shanahan, M., & Elder, G. H., Jr. (1995). Mutual influences in parent and adolescent distress. Developmental Psychology, 31, 406–419.

Gelfand, D. M., & Teti, D. M. (1990). The effects of maternal depression on children. Clinical Psychology Review, 10, 329–353.

Ghiselli, E. E., Campbell, J. P., & Zedeck, S. (1981). Measurement theory for the behavioral sciences. New York: W. H. Freeman.

Goldberg, S. (1991). Recent developments in attachment theory and research. Canadian Journal of Psychiatry, 36, 393–400.

Graham, P. J., & Rutter, M. (1973). Psychiatric disorder in the young adolescent: A follow-up study. Proceedings of the Royal Society of Medicine, 66, 1226–1229.

Greenbaum, P. E., Prange, M. E., Friedman, R. M., & Silver, S. E. (1991). Substance abuse prevalence and comorbidity with other psychiatric disorders among adolescents with severe emotional disturbances. Journal of the American Academy of Child and Adolescent Psychiatry, 30, 575–583.

Greenspan, S. I., & Wieder, S. (1994). Diagnostic classification of mental health and developmental disorders of infancy and early childhood. Zero to Three, 14(6), 34–41.

Grellong, B. A. (1987). Residential care in context: Evolution of a treatment process in response to social change. Residential Treatment for Children and Youth, 4, 59–70.

Group for the Advancement of Psychiatry. (1974). Psychopathological disorders in childhood: Theoretical considerations and a proposed classification. New York: Jason Aronson.

Guerra, N. G., Tolan, P. H., Huesmann, L. R., Van Acker, R., & Eron, L. D. (1995). Stressful events and individual beliefs as correlates of economic disadvantage and aggression among urban children. Journal of Consulting and Clinical Psychology, 63, 518–528.

Hart, E. L., Lahey, B. B., Hynd, G. W., Loeber, R., & McBurnett, K. (1995). Association of chronic overanxious disorder with atopic rhinitis in boys: A four-year longitudinal study. Journal of Clinical Child Psychology, 24, 332–337.

Hart, J., Gunnar, M., & Cicchetti, D. (1995). Salivary cortisol in maltreated children: Evidence of relations between neuroendocrine activity and social competence. Development and Psychopathology, 7, 11–26.

Haynes, S. N., & Blaine, D. (1995). Dynamical models for psychological assessment: Phase space functions. Special section: Chaos theory and psychological assessment. Psychological Assessment, 7, 17–24.

Hersen, M., & Ammerman, R. T. (Eds.). (1995). Advanced abnormal child psychology. Hillsdale, NJ: Erlbaum.

Hetherington, E. M., Reiss, D., & Plomin, R. (Eds.). (1994). Separate social worlds of siblings: The impact of nonshared environment on development. Hillsdale, NJ: Erlbaum.

Hibbs, E. D. (Ed.). (1995). Special Issue: Psychosocial treatment research. Journal of Abnormal Psychology, 23, 1–156.

Hirshfeld, D. R., Rosenbaum, J. F., Biederman, J., Bolduc, E. A., Faraone, S. V., Snidman, N., Reznick, J. S., & Kagan, J. (1992). Stable behavioral inhibition and its association with anxiety disorder. Journal of the American Academy of Child and Adolescent Psychiatry, 31, 103–111.

Hollingshead, A. B., & Redlich, F. C. (1958). Social class and mental illness. New York: Wiley.

Hops, H. (1995). Age- and gender-specific effects of parental depression: A commentary. Developmental Psychology, 31, 428–431.

Hymel, S., Rubin, K. H., Rowden, L., & LeMare, L. (1990). Children's peer relationships: Longitudinal prediction of internalizing and externalizing problems from middle to late childhood. *Child Development, 61,* 2004–2021.

Iaboni, F., Douglas, V. I., & Baker, A. G. (1995). Effects of reward and response costs on inhibition in ADHD children. *Journal of Abnormal Psychology, 104,* 232–240.

Ialongo, N., Edelsohn, G., Werthamer-Larsson, L., Crockett, L., & Kellam, S. (1994). The significance of self-reported anxious symptoms in the first grade. *Journal of Abnormal Child Psychology, 22,* 441–455.

Ingram, R. E., & Kendall, P. C. (1986). Cognitive clinical psychology: Implications of an information processing perspective. In R. E. Ingram (Ed.), *Information processing approaches to clinical psychology* (pp. 3–21). New York: Academic Press.

Institute of Medicine. (1989). *Research on children and adolescents with mental, behavioral and developmental disorders.* Washington, DC: National Academy Press.

Izard, C. E. (1993). Four systems for emotion activation: Cognitive and noncognitive processes. *Psychological Review, 100,* 68–90.

Jacob, T. (Ed.). (1987). *Family interaction and psychopathology: Theories, methods, and findings.* New York: Plenum Press.

Jensen, P. S., Koretz, D., Locke, B. Z., Schneider, S., Radke-Yarrow, M., Richters, J. E., & Rumsey, J. M. (1993). Child and adolescent psychopathology research: Problems and prospects for the 1990s. *Journal of Abnormal Child Psychology, 21,* 551–580.

Kagan, J. (1994a). *Galen's prophecy: Temperament in human nature.* New York: Basic Books.

Kagan, J. (1994b). On the nature of emotion. In N. A. Fox (Ed.), *Monographs of the society for research in child development, 59* (2–3, Serial No. 240), 7–24.

Kagan, J., Resnick, J. S., Clark, C., Snidman, N., & Garcia-Coll, C. (1984). Behavioral inhibition to the unfamiliar. *Child Development, 55,* 2212–2225.

Kagan, J., Resnick, J. S., & Snidman, N. (1987). The physiology and psychology of behavioral inhibition in children. *Child Development, 58,* 1459–1473.

Kagan, J., Resnick, J. S., & Snidman, N. (1988). Biological bases of childhood shyness. *Science, 240,* 167–171.

Kagan, J., Resnick, J. S., & Snidman, N. (1990). The temperamental qualities of inhibition and lack of inhibition. In M. Lewis & S. M. Miller (Eds.), *Handbook of developmental psychopathology* (pp. 219–226). New York: Plenum.

Kagan, J., & Snidman, N. (1991). Temperamental factors in human development. *American Psychologist, 46,* 856–862.

Kanfer, F. H., & Saslow, G. (1969). Behavioral diagnosis. In C. M. Franks (Ed.), *Behavior therapy: Appraisal and status* (pp. 417–444). New York: McGraw-Hill.

Kanner, L. (1962). Emotionally disturbed children: A historical review. *Child Development, 33,* 97–102.

Kaplan, H. I., & Sadock, B. J. (1991). *Synopsis of psychiatry* (6th ed.). Baltimore: Williams & Wilkins.

Katz, L. F., & Gottman, J. M. (1993). Patterns of marital conflict predict children's internalizing and externalizing behaviors. *Developmental Psychology, 29,* 940–950.

Katz, L. F., & Gottman, J. M. (1995). Vagal tone protects children from marital conflict. *Development and Psychopathology, 7,* 83–92.

Kaufman, J., Cook, A., Arny, L., Jones, B., & Pittinsky, T. (1994). Problems defining resiliency: Illustrations from the study of maltreated children. *Development and Psychopathology, 6,* 215–229.

Kavanagh, K., & Hops, H. (1994). Good girls? Bad boys?: Gender and development as contexts for diagnosis and treatment. In T. H. Ollendick & R. J. Prinz (Eds.), *Advances in clinical child psychology* (Vol. 16, pp. 45–79). New York: Plenum Press.

Kazdin, A. E. (1988a). *Child psychotherapy: Developing and identifying effective treatments.* New York: Pergamon Press.

Kazdin, A. E. (1988b). The diagnosis of childhood disorders: Assessment issues and strategies. *Behavioral Assessment, 10,* 67–94.

Kazdin, A. E. (1989). Developmental psychopathology: Current research, issues and directions. *American Psychologist, 44,* 180–187.

Kazdin, A. E. (1993). Psychotherapy for children and adolescents: Current progress and future. *American Psychologist, 48,* 644–657.

Kazdin, A. E., & Johnson, B. (1994). Advances in psychotherapy for children and adolescents: Interrelations of adjustment, development, and intervention. *Journal of School Psychology, 32,* 217–246.

Kazdin, A. E., & Kagan, J. (1994). Models of dysfunction in developmental psychopathology. *Clinical Psychology: Science and Practice, 1,* 35–52.

Kendall, P. C. (1985). Toward a cognitive-behavioral model of child psychopathology and a critique of related interventions. *Journal of Abnormal Child Psychology, 13,* 357–372.

Kendall, P. C. (1991). Guiding theory for therapy with children and adolescents. In P. C. Kendall (Ed.), *Child and adolescent therapy: Cognitive-behavioral procedures* (pp. 3–22). New York: Guilford Press.

Kendall, P. C. (1993). Cognitive-behavioral therapies with youth: Guiding theory, current status, and emerging developments. *Journal of Consulting and Clinical Psychology, 61,* 235–247.

Kendall, P. C., & Dobson, K. S. (1993). On the nature of cognition and its role in psychopathology. In K. S. Dobson & P. C. Kendall (Eds.), *Psychopathology and cognition* (pp. 3–17). San Diego: Academic Press.

Kendall, P. C., Howard, B. L., & Epps, J. (1988). The anxious child: Cognitive-behavioral treatment strategies. *Behavior Modification, 12,* 281–310.

Kendall, P. C., & MacDonald, J. P. (1993). Cognition in the psychopathology of youth and implications for treatment. In K. S. Dobson & P. C. Kendall (Eds.), *Psychopathology and cognition* (pp. 387–427). San Diego: Academic Press.

Kendall, P. C., & Morris, R. J. (1991). Child therapy: Issues and recommendations. *Journal of Consulting and Clinical Psychology, 59,* 777–784.

Kessler, J. W. (1971). Nosology in child psychopathology. In H. E. Rie (Ed.), *Perspectives in child psychopathology* (pp. 85–129). Chicago: Aldine-Atherton.

Klein, D. F., & Gorman, J. M. (1987). A model of panic and agoraphobia development. *Acta Psychiatrica Scandinavica, 76* (Suppl. 335), 87–95.

Klein, S. B., & Mower, R. R. (Eds.). (1989). *Contemporary learning theories: Instrumental conditioning theory and the impact of biological constraints on learning.* Hillsdale, NJ: Erlbaum.

Kovacs, M., & Beck, A. T. (1977). An empirical clinical approach towards a definition of childhood depression. In J. G. Schulterbrandt & A. Raskin (Eds.), *Depression in*

children: Diagnosis, treatment, and conceptual models (pp. 1–25). New York: Raven Press.

Kraemer, G. W. (1992). A psychobiological theory of attachment. *Behavioral and Brain Sciences, 15,* 493–541.

Krasner, L. (1991). History of behavior modification. In A. S. Bellack & M. Hersen (Eds.), *International handbook of behavior modification and therapy* (2nd ed., pp. 3–25). New York: Plenum Press.

Kuhn, T. S. (1962). *The structure of scientific revolutions.* Chicago: University of Chicago Press.

Lahey, B. B., Loeber, R., Hart, E. L., Frick, P. J., Applegate, B., Zhang, Q., Green, S. M., & Russo, M. F. (1995). Four-year longitudinal study of conduct disorder in boys: Patterns and predictors of persistence. *Journal of Abnormal Psychology, 104,* 83–93.

Lambert, M. C., & Weisz, J. R. (1989). Over- and under-controlled clinic referral problems in Jamaican clinic-referred children: Teacher reports for ages 6–17. *Journal of Abnormal Child Psychology, 17,* 553–562.

Lambert, M. C., & Weisz, J. R. (1992). Jamaican and American adult perspectives on child psychopathology: Further exploration of the threshold model. *Journal of Consulting and Clinical Psychology, 60,* 146–149

Lapouse, R., & Monk, M. A. (1958). An epidemiologic study of behavior characteristics in children. *American Journal of Public Health, 48,* 1134–1144.

Last, C. G., Francis, G., Hersen, M., Kazdin, A. E., & Strauss, C. C. (1987). Separation anxiety and school phobia: A comparison using DSM-III criteria. *American Journal of Psychiatry, 144,* 653–657.

Last, C. G., Hersen, M., Kazdin, A. E., Francis, G., & Grubb, H. J. (1987). Psychiatric illness in the mothers of anxious children. *American Journal of Psychiatry, 144,* 1580–1583.

Last, C. G., Phillips, J. E., & Statfeld, A. (1987). Childhood anxiety disorders in mothers and their children. *Child Psychiatry and Human Development 18,* 103–109.

Lease, C. A., & Ollendick, T. H. (1993). Development and psychopathology. In A. S. Bellack & M. Hersen (Eds.), *Psychopathology in adulthood* (pp. 89–103). New York: Allyn and Bacon.

Leon, G. R., Fulkerson, J. A., Perry, C. L., & Early-Zald, M. B. (1995). Prospective analysis of personality and behavioral vulnerabilities and gender influences in later development of disordered eating. *Journal of Abnormal Psychology, 104,* 140–149.

Lesser, S. T. (1972). Psychoanalysis of children. In B. B. Wolman (Ed.), *Manual of child psychopathology* (pp. 847–864). New York: McGraw-Hill.

Lewinsohn, P. M., Steinmetz, J. L., Larson, D. W., & Franklin, J. (1981). Depression-related cognitions: Antecedent or consequence? *Journal of Abnormal Psychology, 90,* 213–219.

Lewis, M. (1990). Models of developmental psychopathology. In M. Lewis & S. M. Miller (Eds.), *Handbook of developmental psychopathology* (pp. 15–27). New York: Plenum Press.

Lewis, M., & Miller, S. M. (Eds.). (1990). *Handbook of developmental psychopathology.* New York: Plenum Press.

Lilienfeld, S. O., & Marino, L. (1995). Mental disorder as a Roschian concept: A critique of Wakefield's "harmful dysfunction" analysis. *Journal of Abnormal Psychology, 104,* 411–420.

Lilienfeld, S. O., Waldman, I. D., & Israel, A. C. (1994). A critical examination of the use of the term and concept

of comorbidity in psychopathology research. *Clinical Psychology: Science and Practice, 1,* 71–83.

Lizardi, H., Klein, D., Ouimette, P. C., Riso, L. P., Anderson, R. L., & Donaldson, S. K. (1995). Reports of childhood home environment in early-onset dysthymia and episodic major depression. *Journal of Abnormal Psychology, 104,* 132–139.

Lochman, J. E., & Dodge, K. A. (1994). Social-cognitive processes of severely violent, moderately aggressive, and nonaggressive boys. *Journal of Consulting and Clinical Psychology, 62,* 366–374.

Lochman, J. E., White, K. J., & Wayland, K. K. (1991). Cognitive-behavioral assessment with aggressive children. In P. C. Kendall (Ed.), *Child and adolescent therapy: Cognitive-behavioral procedures* (pp. 25–65). New York: Guilford Press.

Loeber, R. (1991). Questions and advances in the study of developmental pathways. In D. Cicchetti & S. L. Toth (Eds.), *Rochester symposium on developmental psychopathology: Vol. 3. Models and integrations* (pp. 97–116). New York: University of Rochester Press.

Loeber, R., & Dishion, T. (1983). Early predictors of male delinquency: A review. *Psychological Bulletin, 93,* 68–99.

Loeber, R., & Keenan, K. (1994). Interaction between conduct disorder and its comorbid conditions: Effects of age and gender. *Clinical Psychology Review, 14,* 497–523.

Logan, G. D. (1994). On the ability to inhibit thought and action: A users' guide to the stop signal paradigm. In T. H. Carr & D. Dagenbach (Eds.), *Inhibitory processes in attention, memory, and language* (pp. 189–239). San Diego: Academic Press.

Lombroso, P. J., Pauls, D. L., & Leckman, J. F. (1994). Genetic mechanisms in childhood psychiatric disorders. *Journal of the American Academy of Child and Adolescent Psychiatry, 33,* 921–938.

Luthar, S. S. (1993). Annotation: Methodological and conceptual issues in research on childhood resilience. *Journal of Child Psychology and Psychiatry, 34,* 441–453.

Lyons-Ruth, K. (1995). Broadening our conceptual frameworks: Can we reintroduce relational strategies and implicit representational systems to the study of psychopathology? *Developmental Psychology, 31,* 432–436.

MacFarlane, J. W., Allen, L., & Honzik, M. P. (1954). *A developmental study of the behavior problems of normal children between twenty-one months and fourteen years.* Berkeley: University of California Press.

Makari, G. J. (1993). Educated insane: A nineteenth-century psychiatric paradigm. *Journal of the History of the Behavioral Sciences, 29,* 8–21.

Manly, J. T., Cicchetti, D., & Barnett, D. (1994). The impact of subtype, frequency, chronicity, and severity of child maltreatment on social competence and behavior problems. *Development and Psychopathology, 6,* 121–143.

Mash, E. J. (1989). Treatment of child and family disturbance: A behavioral-systems perspective. In E. J. Mash & R. A. Barkley (Eds.), *Treatment of childhood disorders* (pp. 3–38). New York: Guilford Press.

Mash, E. J., & Barkley, R. A. (Eds.). (1989). *Treatment of childhood disorders.* New York: Guilford Press.

Mash, E. J., & Hunsley, J. (1990). Behavioral assessment: A contemporary approach. In A. S. Bellack & M. Hersen (Eds.), *International handbook of behavior modification and behavior therapy* (2nd ed., pp. 87–106). New York: Plenum Press.

Mash, E. J., & Johnston, C. (1995). Family relational problems. In V. E. Caballo, G. Buela-Casal, & J. A. Carrobles (Eds.), *Handbook of psychopathology and psychiatric disorders* (Vol. 2). Madrid: Siglo XXI.

Mash, E. J., Johnston, C., & Kovitz, K. (1983). A comparison of the mother-child interactions of physically abused and non-abused children during play and task situations. *Journal of Clinical Child Psychology, 12,* 337–346.

Mash, E. J., & Krahn, G. L. (1995). Research strategies in child psychopathology. In M. Hersen & R. T. Ammerman (Eds.), *Advanced abnormal child psychology* (pp. 105–133). Hillsdale, NJ: Erlbaum.

Mash, E. J., & Terdal, L. G. (1988a). Behavioral assessment of child and family disturbance. In E. J. Mash & L. G. Terdal (Eds.), *Behavioral assessment of childhood disorders* (2nd ed., pp. 3–65). New York: Guilford Press.

Mash, E. J., & Terdal, L. G. (Eds.). (1988b). *Behavioral assessment of childhood disorders* (2nd ed.). New York: Guilford Press.

Mash, E. J., & Terdal, L. G. (Eds.). (in press). *Behavioral assessment of childhood disorders* (3rd ed.). New York: Guilford Press.

Mash, E. J., & Wolfe, D. A. (1991). Methodological issues in research on physical child abuse. *Criminal Justice and Behavior, 18,* 8–30.

Maxwell, S. E., & Delaney, H. D. (1990). *Designing experiments and analyzing data: A model comparison perspective.* Belmont: Wadsworth.

Mayer, J. D., & Salovey, P. (1995). Emotional intelligence and the construction and regulation of feelings. *Applied and Preventive Psychology, 4,* 197–208.

McDermott, P. A. (1993). National standardization of uniform multisituational measures of child and adolescent behavior pathology. *Psychological Assessment, 5,* 413–424.

McDermott, P. A., & Weiss, R. V. (1995). A normative typology of healthy, subclinical, and clinical behavior styles among American children and adolescents. *Psychological Assessment, 7,* 162–170.

Meichenbaum, D. (1977). *Cognitive-behavior modification: An integrative approach.* New York: Plenum Press.

Messer, S. C., & Beidel, D. C. (1994). Psychosocial correlates of childhood anxiety disorders. *Journal of the American Academy of Child and Adolescent Psychiatry, 33,* 975–983.

Messick, S. (1983). Assessment of children. In P. H. Mussen (Series Ed.) & W. Kessen (Vol. Ed.), *Handbook of child psychology: Vol. 1. History, theory, and methods* (4th ed., pp. 477–526). New York: Wiley.

Mischel, W. (1968). *Personality and assessment.* New York: Wiley.

Moore, L. A., & Hughes, J. N. (1988). Impulsive and hyperactive children. In J. N. Hughes (Ed.), *Cognitive behavior therapy with children in schools* (pp. 127–159). Toronto: Pergamon Press.

Mundy, P. (1995). Joint attention and social-emotional approach behavior in children with autism. *Development and Psychopathology, 7,* 137–162.

National Commission on Children. (1991). *Beyond rhetoric: A new American agenda for children and families: The final report of the National Commission on Children.* Washington, DC: U.S. Government Printing Office.

National Institute of Mental Health. (1990). *National plan for research on child and adolescent mental disorders: A report requested by the U.S. Congress* (DHHS Publication No. ADM 90–1683). Washington, DC: U.S. Government Printing Office.

O'Donnell, J., Hawkins, J. D., & Abbott, R. D. (1995). Predicting serious delinquency and substance abuse among aggressive boys. *Journal of Consulting and Clinical Psychology, 63,* 529–537.

Offord, D. R., Boyle, M. H., & Racine, Y. A. (1989). Ontario Child Health Study: Correlates of disorder. *Journal of the American Academy of Child and Adolescent Psychiatry, 28,* 856–860.

Offord, D. R., Boyle, M. H., Racine, Y. A., Fleming, J. E., Cadman, D. T., Blum, H. M., Byrne, C., Links, P. S., Lipman, E. L., MacMillan, H. L., Grant, N. I. R., Sanford, M. N., Szatmari, P., Thomas, H., & Woodward, C. A. (1992). Outcome, prognosis, and risk in a longitudinal follow-up study. *Journal of the American Academy of Child and Adolescent Psychiatry, 31,* 916–923.

Offord, D. R., Boyle, M. H., Szatmari, P., Rae-Grant, N. I., Links, P. S., Cadman, D. T., Byles, J. A., Crawford, J. W., Blum, H. M., Byrne, C., Thomas, H., & Woodward, C. A. (1987). Ontario Child Health Study: II. Six-month prevalence of disorder and rates of service utilization. *Archives of General Psychiatry, 44,* 832–836.

Okun, A., Parker, J. G., & Levendosky, A. A. (1994). Distinct and interactive contributions of physical abuse, socioeconomic disadvantage, and negative life events to children's social, cognitive, and affective adjustment. *Development and Psychopathology, 6,* 77–98.

Ollendick, T. H., & Hersen, M. (Eds.). (1989). *Handbook of child psychopathology* (2nd ed.). New York: Plenum Press.

Ollendick, T. H., & King, N. J. (1994). Diagnosis, assessment, and treatment of internalizing problems in children: The role of longitudinal data. *Journal of Consulting and Clinical Psychology, 62,* 918–927.

Ollendick, T. H., Mattis, S. G., & Neville, J. K. (1994). Panic in children and adolescents: A review. *Journal of Child Psychology and Psychiatry, 35,* 113–134.

Olweus, D. (1979). Stability of aggressive reaction patterns in males: A review. *Psychological Bulletin, 86,* 852–875.

Overton, W. F., & Horowitz, H. A. (1991). Developmental psychopathology: Integrations and differentiations. In D. Cicchetti & S. L. Toth (Eds.), *Rochester symposium on developmental psychopathology: Vol. 3. Models and integrations* (pp. 1–42). New York: University of Rochester Press.

Patterson, G. R. (1982). *Coercive family process.* Eugene, OR: Castalia.

Patterson, G. R., Reid, J. B., & Dishion, T. J. (1992). *Antisocial boys.* Eugene, OR: Castalia.

Pennington, B. F., & Ozonoff, S. (1991). A neuroscientific perspective on continuity and discontinuity in developmental psychopathology. In D. Cicchetti & S. L. Toth (Eds.), *Rochester symposium on developmental psychopathology: Vol. 3. Models and integrations* (pp. 117–159). New York: University of Rochester Press.

Peterson, L., & Brown, D. (1994). Integrating child injury and abuse-neglect research: Common histories, etiologies, and solutions. *Psychological Bulletin, 116,* 293–315.

Phares, V., & Compas, B. (1992). The role of fathers in child and adolescent psychopathology: Make room for daddy. *Psychological Bulletin, 111,* 387–412.

Plomin, R. (1995). Molecular genetics and psychology. *Current Directions in Psychological Science, 4,* 114–117.

Quay, H. C., Routh, D. K., & Shapiro, S. K. (1987). Psychopathology of childhood: From description to validation. *Annual Review of Psychology, 38,* 491–532.

Rees, J. R. (1939). Sexual difficulties in childhood. In R. G. Gordon (Ed.), *A survey of child psychiatry* (pp. 246–256). Oxford, UK: Oxford University Press.

Rende, R. D. (1993). Longitudinal relations between temperament traits and behavior syndromes in middle childhood. *Journal of the American Academy of Child and Adolescent Psychiatry, 32,* 287–290.

Reynolds, W. M. (Ed.). (1992). *Internalizing disorders in children and adolescents.* New York: Wiley.

Richman, N., Stevenson, J. E., & Graham, P. J. (1975). Prevalence of behaviour problems in 3-year-old children: An epidemiological study in a London borough. *Journal of Child Psychology and Psychiatry, 16,* 277–287.

Richters, J. E. (1992). Depressed mothers as informants about their children: A critical review of the evidence for distortion. *Psychological Bulletin,112,* 485–499.

Richters, J. E., & Cicchetti, D. (1993). Mark Twain meets DSM-III-R: Conduct disorder, development, and the concept of harmful dysfunction. *Development and Psychopathology, 5,* 5–29.

Rie, H. E. (1971). Historical perspective of concepts of child psychopathology. In H. E. Rie (Ed.), *Perspectives in child psychopathology* (pp. 3–50). Chicago: Aldine-Atherton.

Roberts, A. R., & Kurtz, L. F. (1987). Historical perspectives on the care and treatment of the mentally ill. *Journal of Sociology and Social Welfare, 14,* 75–94.

Robins, L. N. (1966). *Deviant children grown up.* Baltimore: Williams & Wilkins.

Robins, L. N. (1994). How recognizing "comorbidities" in psychopathology may lead to an improved research nosology. *Clinical Psychology: Science and Practice, 1,* 93–95.

Rosenbaum, J. F., Biederman, J., Gersten, M., Hirshfeld, D., Meminger, S., Herman, J. B., Kagan, J., Resnick, S., & Snidman, N. (1988). Behavioral inhibition in children of parents with panic disorder and agoraphobia. *Archives of General Psychiatry, 45,* 463–470.

Rothbart, M. K., & Ahadi, S. A. (1994). Temperament and the development of personality. *Journal of Abnormal Psychology, 103,* 55–66.

Routh, D. K. (1990). Taxonomy in developmental psychopathology: Consider the source. In M. Lewis & S. M. Miller (Eds.), *Handbook of developmental psychopathology* (pp. 53–62). New York: Plenum Press.

Rubin, K. H., Chen, X., & Hymel, S. (1993). Socioemotional characteristics of withdrawn and aggressive children. *Merrill-Palmer Quarterly, 39,* 518–534.

Rubin, K. H., Coplan, R. J., Fox, N. A., & Calkins, S. D. (1995). Emotionality, emotion regulation, and preschoolers' social adaptation. *Development and Psychopathology, 7,* 49–62.

Rubin, K. H., Hymel, S., & Mills, R. S. L. (1989). Sociability and social withdrawal in childhood: Stability and outcomes. *Journal of Personality, 57,* 237–255.

Rubin, K. H., & Mills, R. S. L. (1988). The many faces of social isolation in childhood. *Journal of Consulting and Clinical Psychology, 56,* 916–924.

Rubin, K. H., & Mills, R. S. L. (1990). Maternal beliefs about adaptive and maladaptive social behaviors in normal, aggressive, and withdrawn preschoolers. *Journal of Abnormal Child Psychology, 18,* 419–435.

Rubin, K. H., & Mills, R. S. L. (1991). Conceptualizing developmental pathways to internalizing disorders in childhood. *Canadian Journal of Behavioral Science, 23,* 300–317.

Rubinstein, E. (1948). Childhood mental disease in America: A review of the literature before 1900. *American Journal of Orthopsychiatry, 18,* 314–321.

Rutter, M. (1981). The city and the child. *American Journal of Orthopsychiatry, 51,* 610–625.

Rutter, M. (1985). Resilience in the face of adversity: Protective factors and resistance to psychiatric disorder. *British Journal of Psychiatry, 147,* 598–611.

Rutter, M. (1987). Psychosocial resilience and protective mechanisms. *American Journal of Orthopsychiatry, 57,* 316–331.

Rutter, M. (1989). Isle of Wight revisited: Twenty-five years of child psychiatric epidemiology. *Journal of the American Academy of Child and Adolescent Psychiatry, 28,* 633.

Rutter, M. (1994a). Beyond longitudinal data: Causes, consequences, and continuity. *Journal of Consulting and Clinical Psychology, 62,* 928–940.

Rutter, M. (1994b). Comorbidity: Meanings and mechanisms. *Clinical Psychology: Science and Practice, 1,* 100–103.

Rutter, M. (1995). Clinical implications of attachment concepts: Retrospect and prospect. *Journal of Child Psychology and Psychiatry, 36,* 549–571.

Rutter, M., & Garmezy, N. (1983). Developmental psychopathology. In P. H. Mussen (Series Ed.) & E. M. Hetherington (Vol. Ed.), *Handbook of child psychology: Vol. 4. Socialization, personality, and social development* (4th ed., pp. 775–911). New York: Wiley.

Rutter, M., & Rutter, M. (1993). *Developing minds: Challenge and continuity across the life span.* New York: Basic Books.

Rutter, M., Tizard, J., & Whitmore, K. (Eds.). (1970). *Education, health, and behaviour.* London: Longman.

Sameroff, A. J. (1993). Models of development and developmental risk. In C. H. Zeanah, Jr. (Ed.), *Handbook of infant mental health* (pp. 3–13). New York: Guilford Press.

Schteingart, J. S., Molnar, J., Klein, T. P., Lowe, C. B., & Hartmann, A. H. (1995). Homelessness and child functioning in the context of risk and protective factors moderating child outcomes. *Journal of Clinical Child Psychology, 24,* 320–331.

Seifer, R., Sameroff, A. J., Baldwin, C. P., & Baldwin, A. (1992). Child and family factors that ameliorate risk between 4 and 13 years of age. *Journal of the American Academy of Child and Adolescent Psychiatry, 31,* 893–903.

Selman, R. L., Beardslee, W., Schultz, L. H., Krupa, M., & Poderefsky, D. (1986). Assessing adolescent interpersonal negotiation strategies: Toward the integration of structural and functional models. *Developmental Psychology, 22,* 450–459.

Shapiro, T., & Esman, A. (1992). Psychoanalysis and child and adolescent psychiatry. *Journal of the American Academy of Child and Adolescent Psychiatry, 31,* 6–13.

Shaw, D. S., & Bell, R. Q. (1993). Developmental theories of parental contributors to antisocial behavior. *Journal of Abnormal Child Psychology, 21,* 493–518.

Silverman, J. S., Silverman, J. A., & Eardley, D. A. (1984). Do maladaptive attitudes cause depression? *Archives of General Psychiatry, 41,* 28–30.

Simeonsson, R. J., & Rosenthal, S. L. (1992). Developmental models and clinical practice. In C. E. Walker & M. C. Roberts (Eds.), *Handbook of clinical child psychology* (2nd ed., pp. 19–31). New York: Wiley.

Skinner, B. F. (1953). *Science and human behavior.* New York: Macmillan.

Spitzer, R. L. (1994). Psychiatric "co-occurrence"? I'll stick with "comorbidity." *Clinical Psychology: Science and Practice, 1,* 88–92.

Spitzer, R. L., Davies, M., & Barkley, R. A. (1990). The DSM-III-R field trial of disruptive behavior disorders. *Journal of the American Academy of Child and Adolescent Psychiatry, 29,* 690–697.

Sroufe, L. A. (1985). Attachment classification from the perspective of infant–caregiver relationships and infant temperament. *Child Development, 56,* 1–14.

Sroufe, L. A., & Jacobvitz, D. (1989). Diverging pathways, developmental transformations, multiple etiologies and the problem of continuity in development. *Human Development, 32,* 196–203.

Sroufe, L. A., & Rutter, M. (1984). The domain of developmental psychopathology. *Child Development, 55,* 17–29.

Stark, K. D., Rouse, L. W., & Livingston, R. (1991). Treatment of depression during childhood and adolescence: Cognitive-behavioral procedures for the individual and family. In P. C. Kendall (Ed.), *Child and adolescent therapy: Cognitive-behavioral procedures* (pp. 165–206). New York: Guilford Press.

Stein, M. A., Szumowski, E., Blondis, T. A., & Roizen, N. J. (1995). Adaptive skills dysfunction in ADD and ADHD children. *Journal of Child Psychology and Psychiatry, 36,* 663–670.

Strassberg, Z., & Dodge, K. (1995). *Maternal physical abuse of the child: A social information processing perspective.* Manuscript submitted for publication.

Szasz, T. S. (1970). *The manufacture of madness.* New York: Dell.

Szatmari, P., Boyle, M. H., & Offord, D. R. (1993). Familial aggregation of emotional and behavioral problems of childhood in the general population. *American Journal of Psychiatry, 150,* 1398–1403.

Tarullo, L. B., Richardson, D. T., Radke-Yarrow, M., & Martinez, P. E. (1995). Multiple sources in child diagnosis: Parent–child concordance in affectively ill and well families. *Journal of Clinical Child Psychology, 24,* 173–183.

Tems, C. L., Stewart, S. M., Skinner, J. R., Hughes, C. W., & Emslie, G. (1993). Cognitive distortions in depressed children and adolescents: Are they state dependent or traitlike? *Journal of Clinical Child Psychology, 22,* 316–326.

Terr, L. C. (1991). Childhood traumas: An outline and overview. *American Journal of Psychiatry, 148,* 10–20.

Thomas, A., & Chess, S. (1977). *Temperament and development.* New York: Brunner/Mazel.

Thomas, A., Chess, S., & Birch, H. (1968). *Temperament and behavior disorders in children.* New York: New York University Press.

Thompson, R. A. (1994). Emotion regulation: A theme in search of definition. *Monographs of the Society for Research in Child Development, 59,* 25–52.

Tolan, P., & Thomas, P. (1995). The implications of age of onset for delinquency risk II: Longitudinal data. *Journal of Abnormal Child Psychology, 23,* 157–181.

Torgersen, S. (1983). Genetic factors in anxiety disorders. *Archive of General Psychiatry, 140,* 1085–1089.

Torgersen, S. (1993). Genetics. In A. S. Bellack & M. Hersen (Eds.), *Psychopathology in adulthood* (pp. 41–56). New York: Allyn and Bacon.

Tremblay, R. E., Masse, B., Perron, D., LeBlanc, M.,

Schwartzman, A., & Ledingham, J. E. (1992). Early disruptive behavior, poor school achievement, delinquent behavior, and delinquent personality: Longitudinal analyses. *Journal of Consulting and Clinical Psychology, 60,* 64–72.

U.S. Advisory Board on Child Abuse and Neglect. (1995). *A nation's shame: Fatal child abuse and neglect in the United States.* Washington, DC: National Clearinghouse on Child Abuse and Neglect.

U.S. Bureau of the Census. (1993). *Poverty in the United States: 1992* (Current Population Reports, Series P-60, No. 185). Washington, DC: U.S. Government Printing Office.

U.S. General Accounting Office. (1992). *Child abuse: Prevention programs need greater emphasis.* Washington, DC: Author.

Vasey, M. W., Daleiden, E. L., Williams, L. L., & Brown, L. M. (1995). Biased attention in childhood anxiety disorders: A preliminary study. *Journal of Abnormal Child Psychology, 23,* 267–279.

Velez, C. N., Johnson, J., & Cohen, P. (1989). A longitudinal analysis of selected risk factors for childhood psychopathology. *Journal of the American Academy of Child and Adolescent Psychiatry, 28,* 861–864.

Verbaten, M. N., & Overtoom, C. C. E. (1994). Methylphenidate influences on both early and late ERP waves of ADHD children in a Continuous Performance Test. *Journal of Abnormal Child Psychology, 22,* 561–578.

Verhulst, F. C., Akkerhuis, G. W., & Altaus, M. (1985). Mental health in Dutch children: 1. A cross-cultural comparison. *Acta Psychiatrica Scandinavica, 72* (Suppl. 323).

Verhulst, F. C., & Koot, H. M. (1991). Longitudinal research in child and adolescent psychiatry. *Journal of the American Academy of Child and Adolescent Psychiatry, 30,* 361–368.

Verhulst, F. C., & Koot, H. M. (1992). *Child psychiatric epidemiology: Concepts, methods, and findings.* Newbury Park, CA: Sage.

Verhulst, F. C., & van der Ende, J. (1993). "Comorbidity" in an epidemiological sample: A longitudinal perspective. *Journal of Child Psychology and Psychiatry, 34,* 767–783.

Viken, R. J., & McFall, R. M. (1994). Paradox lost: Contemporary reinforcement theory for behavior therapy. *Current Directions in Psychological Science, 3,* 123–125.

Wakefield, J. C. (1992). The concept of mental disorder: On the boundary between biological facts and social values. *American Psychologist, 47,* 373–388.

Walker, C. E., Kenning, M., & Faust-Campanile, J. (1989). Enuresis and encopresis. In E. J. Mash & R. A. Barkley (Eds.), *Treatment of childhood disorders* (pp. 423–448). New York: Guilford Press.

Waters, E., & Sroufe, L. A. (1983). Social competence as a developmental construct. *Developmental Review, 3,* 79–97.

Weisz, J. R., & Sigman, M. (1993). Parent reports of behavioral and emotional problems among children in Kenya, Thailand, and the United States. *Child Development, 64,* 98–109.

Weisz, J. R., & Suwanlert, S. (1987). Epidemiology of behavioral and emotional problems among Thai and American children: Parent reports for ages 6 to 11. *Journal of the American Academy of Child and Adolescent Psychiatry, 26,* 890–897.

Weisz, J. R., & Suwanlert, S. (1989). Over- and under-controlled referral problems among children and adolescents from Thailand and the United States: The wat and wai of cultural differences. *Journal of Consulting and Clinical Psychology, 55,* 719–726.

Weisz, J. R., & Suwanlert, S. (1991). Adult attitudes toward over- and undercontrolled child problems: Urban and rural parents and teachers from Thailand and the United States. *Journal of Child Psychology and Psychiatry and Allied Disciplines, 32,* 645–654.

Werner, E. E. (1995). Resilience in development. *Current Directions in Psychological Science, 4,* 81–85.

Werner, E. E., Bierman, J. M., & French, F. E. (1971). *The children of Kauai: A longitudinal study from the prenatal period to age ten.* Honolulu: University of Hawaii Press.

Werner, E. E., & Smith, R. S. (1992). *Overcoming the odds: High risk children from birth to adulthood.* Ithaca, NY: Cornell University Press.

Widiger, T. A., & Ford-Black, M. M. (1994). Diagnoses and disorders. *Clinical Psychology: Science and Practice, 1,* 84–87.

Willerman, L. (1973). Activity level and hyperactivity in twins. *Child Development, 44,* 1411–1415.

Willis, D. J., & Walker, C. E. (1989). Etiology. In T. H. Ollendick & M. Hersen (Eds.), *Handbook of child psychopathology* (2nd ed., pp. 29–51). New York: Plenum Press.

Wolfe, D. A., & Mosk, M. D. (1983). Behavioral comparisons of children from abusive and distressed families.

Journal of Consulting and Clinical Psychology, 51, 702–708.

World Health Organization. (1992). *The ICD-10 classification of mental and behavioural disorders: Clinical descriptions and diagnostic guidelines.* Geneva, Switzerland: Author.

Zahn-Waxler, C. (1993). Warriors and worriers: Gender and psychopathology. *Development and Psychopathology, 5,* 79–89.

Zahn-Waxler, C., Cole, C. M., Welsh, J. D., & Fox, N. A. (1995). Psychophysiological correlates of empathy and prosocial behaviors in preschool children with behavior problems. *Development and Psychopathology, 7,* 27–48.

Zero to Three/National Center for Clinical Infant Programs. (1994). *Diagnostic classification of mental health and developmental disorders of infancy and early childhood (Diagnostic Classification: 0–3).* Washington, DC: Author.

Zimmerman, M. A., & Arunkumar, R. (1994). Resiliency research: Implications for schools and policy. *Social Policy Report, 8*(4), 1–17.

Zoccolillo, M. (1993). Gender and the development of conduct disorder. *Development and Psychopathology, 5,* 65–78.

II

BEHAVIOR
DISORDERS

Attention-Deficit/ Hyperactivity Disorder

Russell A. Barkley

It is commonplace for children, especially young preschool children, to be active, energetic, and exuberant and to flit from one activity to another as they explore their environment and its novelties. They are also notorious for getting bored easily with tasks that lack intrinsic appeal for them and for acting without much forethought, responding on impulse to events that occur around them, often with their emotional reactions to these events being readily apparent. And if opportunities arise that offer the promise of immediate reward or gratification to them, then their indulgence in them is to be expected without much regard for the restraint or self-control that would be demanded of someone older. But when children persistently display levels of activity that are far in excess of their age group, when they are unable to sustain their attention, interest, or persistence as well as their peers to their activities, longer-term goals, or the tasks assigned to them by others, or when their impulse control and self-regulation lag far behind expectations for their developmental level, they are no longer simply expressing the *joie de vivre* that characterizes childhood. They are, instead, highly likely to experience a number of problems in their social, cognitive, academic, familial, and emotional domains of development and adjustment. And they are at great risk for falling substantially behind other children in their ability to meet the demands increasingly placed upon them for daily adaptive functioning.

Such demands will include the need to become more personally organized and self-sufficient, more reflective, objective, and measured in their consideration of events and their choice of actions, and more responsible and self-caring. They also will need to become more planful and concerned about the future, more independent from but thoughtful of others, and better able to adhere to progressively more numerous and complex social rules. They will be expected increasingly to turn away from the pleasures and seductions of the moment, and even engage in self-deprivation, so as to concentrate their attention on maximizing future gains, incrementally more distant in time, through various acts of deferred gratification. And the social pressure to organize their own behavior ever more toward time and the future, and ever less to the immediate context, will prove unrelenting.

Highly active, inattentive, and impulsive youngsters will find themselves far less able than their peers to cope successfully with these developmental progressions toward self-regulation, time, and the future. And they will often experience the harsh judgments, punishments, moral denigration, and social rejection and ostracism reserved for those society views as lazy, unmotivated, selfish, thoughtless, immature, and willfully irresponsible. Such children may both fascinate and repel us, giving us at once concern as to why they cannot seem to control their own behavior, follow through on what they are told to

do, and pay attention to getting ready for the future, while simultaneously shocking our sensibilities with their often heedless risk-taking, disregard for others, devil-may-care attitudes, and hell-bent, seemingly self-destructive ways. As a result, they have captured public interest and commentary for at least 130 years, and scientific interest for nearly 100 of these. And while the diagnostic labels for disorders of inattention and impulsiveness have changed numerous times over this century, their actual nature has changed little, if at all, from descriptions at the turn of the century (Still, 1902). This constellation of behavior problems may constitute one of the most well-studied childhood disorders of our time. Yet these children remain an enigma to Western societies who are now struggling to accept the notion that the disorder may be a developmental disability when nothing apparently seems physically or outwardly to be wrong with them.

Children who are excessively active, are unable to sustain their attention, and are deficient in their impulse control to a degree that is deviant for their developmental level, are now given the clinical diagnosis of attention-deficit/hyperactivity disorder (ADHD; American Psychiatric Association, 1994). Their problematic behavioral characteristics are thought to arise early, often before age 7 years, and to be persistent over development in most cases. The purpose of the present chapter is to provide an overview of the nature of this disorder, briefly consider its history, and describe its diagnostic criteria, developmental courses and outcomes, and its causes. Some of the critical issues related to these matters will be raised along the way. Given the thousands of scientific papers on this topic, however, an overview of these various subjects is all that space here can afford. But in this overview, a new theoretical model of ADHD will be presented that should provide a more parsimonious accounting of the many features of the disorder while it points to numerous promising directions for future research. The end result should be a deeper appreciation in the reader for the developmental significance of this problem and the seriousness with which it should be taken. Perhaps then it will become clearer why continuing to refer to this disorder as simply an attention deficit may be a gross understatement of what has become increasingly evident in contemporary research: ADHD is most likely a developmental disorder of behavioral inhibition that interferes with self-regulation and the cross-temporal organization of behavior.

HISTORICAL CONTEXT

Literary references to individuals having serious problems with inattention, hyperactivity, and poor impulse control have been with us for some time. Shakespeare made reference to a malady of attention in one of his characters in *King Henry VIII*. A later description specifically of a hyperactive child can be found in the middle of the 1800s, when the poem "Fidgety Phil" was penned by the German physician, Heinrich Hoffman (see Stewart, 1970). William James (1890), in his *Principles of Psychology*, described a normal variant of character which he called the "explosive will" that resembles the difficulties experienced by those who today are called ADHD: "There is a normal type of character, for example, in which impulses seem to discharge so promptly into movements that inhibitions get no time to arise. These are the 'dare-devil' and 'mercurial' temperaments, overflowing with animation, and fizzling with talk . . ." (p. 800).

Yet serious clinical interest in children with this constellation of symptoms seems to have first occurred in three subsequently published lectures of the English physician George Still (1902) before the Royal Academy of Physicians. Still reported on a group of 20 children in his clinical practice whom he defined as having a deficit in "volitional inhibition" (p. 1008) or a "defect in moral control" (p. 1009) over their own behavior. Aggressive, passionate, lawless, inattentive, impulsive, and overactive were descriptions he applied to these children, many of whom today would be diagnosed not only as ADHD but also as having oppositional defiant disorder (ODD) (see Chapter 3, Hinshaw & Anderson, this volume). Still's observations were quite astute, describing many of the associated features of ADHD that would come to be corroborated in research more than 50 to 90 years later: (1) an overrepresentation of male subjects (ratio of 3:1 in Still's sample); (2) an aggregation of alcoholism, criminal conduct, and depression among the biological relatives; (3) a familial predisposition to the disorder, likely hereditary; (4) yet with the possibility of the disorder also arising from acquired injury to the nervous system.

Initial interest in children with similar characteristics seems to have arisen in North America around the time of the great encephalitis epidemics of 1917–1918. Children surviving these brain infections were noted to have many behavioral problems similar to those comprising contempo-

rary ADHD (Ebaugh, 1923; Hohman, 1922; Stryker, 1925). These cases and others known to have arisen from birth trauma, head injury, toxin exposure, and infections (see Barkley, 1990) gave rise to the concept of a brain-injured child syndrome (Strauss & Lehtinen, 1947), often associated with mental retardation, that would eventually become applied to children manifesting these same behavior features but without evidence of brain damage or retardation (Dolphin & Cruickshank, 1951; Strauss & Kephardt, 1955). This concept would later evolve into that of minimal brain damage, and eventually minimal brain dysfunction (MBD), as challenges were raised to the label in view of the dearth of evidence of brain injury in many of these cases (see Kessler, 1980, for a more detailed history of MBD).

At this same time (the 1950s), others became interested in the more specific behaviors of hyperactivity and poor impulse control, labeling the condition as "hyperkinetic impulse disorder" and attributing it to cortical overstimulation due to poor thalamic filtering of stimuli entering the brain (Knobel, Wolman, & Mason, 1959; Laufer, Denhoff, & Solomons, 1957). These and other papers at the time gave rise to the notion of the "hyperactive child syndrome" (Burks, 1960; Chess, 1960) typified by daily motor movement that was far in excess of that seen in normal children of the same age. Despite a continuing belief among clinicians and researchers of this era that the condition had some sort of neurological origin, the larger influence of psychoanalytic thought held sway. And so, when the second edition of *Diagnostic and Statistical Manual of Mental Disorders* (DSM-II) appeared, all childhood disorders were described as "reactions," and the hyperactive child syndrome became "hyperkinetic reaction of childhood" (American Psychiatric Association, 1968). It was defined simply (and completely) as follows: "This disorder is characterized by overactivity, restlessness, distractibility, and short attention span, especially in young children; the behavior usually diminishes in adolescence. If this behavior is caused by organic brain damage, it should be diagnosed under the appropriate non-psychotic organic brain syndrome" (p. 50).

Important in this definition was the inclusion of problems with attention and distractibility along with those of hyperactivity/restlessness already being emphasized in the existing research literature of the time. Another important distinction was the assertion that the condition seemed developmentally benign, diminishing as it did at adolescence. Also, the recognition that the disorder was *not* caused by brain damage seemed to follow a similar argument made somewhat earlier by the prominent child psychiatrist Stella Chess (1960) and created the beginnings of the major departure between professionals in North America and those in Europe that continues, to some extent, to the present. Europe continued to view hyperkinesis as a relatively rare condition of extreme overactivity often associated with mental retardation or evidence of organic brain damage. This discrepancy in perspectives in conceptualizations seems to be closing recently, at least between scientists on both continents (compare, for instance, Barkley, 1990, with Taylor, 1986) and, more recently, in diagnostic criteria (see DSM-IV and ICD-10 criteria below). Nevertheless, the manner in which clinicians and educators on both continents view the disorder remains quite disparate; in North America such children are labeled as having ADHD, a developmental disorder, whereas in Europe they are viewed as having conduct problem or disorder, a behavioral disturbance arising out of family dysfunction and social disadvantage.

By the 1970s, research was appearing that emphasized the importance of problems with sustained attention and impulse control in addition to hyperactivity in understanding the nature of the disorder (Douglas, 1972). Douglas (1980, 1983) would eventually come to theorize that the disorder was comprised of four major deficits, these being in (1) the investment, organization, and maintenance of attention and effort; (2) the ability to inhibit impulsive behavior; (3) the ability to modulate arousal levels to meet situational demands; and (4) an unusually strong inclination to seek immediate reinforcement. Significant, in retrospect, but apparently unnoticed at the time was the observation by Douglas, akin to that of Still some 70 years earlier, that the disorder was associated with significant problems in moral development. The repeated noticing of this association, as will be shown later, is not merely coincidental. Douglas's seminal paper along with the numerous studies of attention, impulsiveness, and other cognitive sequelae of this disorder that followed (see Douglas, 1983; and Douglas & Peters, 1978, for reviews) eventually led to retitling the disorder as attention deficit disorder (ADD) in 1980 when the third revision of DSM appeared (DSM-III; American Psychiatric Association, 1980). No longer was the disorder viewed

as simply a behavioral reaction of childhood in keeping with a psychoanalytic perspective. Instead, the cognitive and developmental nature of the disorder was emphasized, and more explicit criteria for defining and diagnosing the condition were now provided. Specifically, symptom lists and cutoff scores were recommended for each of the three major symptoms to assist with identification of the condition.

Equally as significant, historically, as the renaming of the condition was the distinction in DSM-III between two types of ADD: those with hyperactivity and those without it. Little research existed at the time on the latter subtype that would have supported such a distinction being made in an official and increasingly prestigious diagnostic taxonomy. Yet, in hindsight, this bald assertion led to further valuable research on the differences between these two forms of ADD that otherwise would never have taken place. That research may have been fortuitous, as will be discussed below. It may be leading to the conclusion that ADD without hyperactivity is actually a separate, distinct, and newly recognized disorder of attention rather than being a related subtype of a single disorder with a shared, common impairment in attention (Barkley, DuPaul, & McMurray, 1990; Carlson, 1986; Goodyear & Hynd, 1992).

Nevertheless, within a few years of the creation of the label ADD, concern arose that problems with hyperactivity and impulse control were features critically important to differentiating the disorder from other conditions and to predicting later developmental risks (Barkley, 1990; Weiss & Hechtman, 1993). And so these symptoms seemed to warrant a return to top billing in the name for the condition. In 1987, the disorder was renamed as attention-deficit hyperactivity disorder in DSM-III-R (American Psychiatric Association, 1987), and a single list of items incorporating all three symptoms with a single threshold for diagnosis was specified. Also important here was the placement of the condition of ADD without hyperactivity, later named undifferentiated attention-deficit disorder, in a separate section of the manual from ADHD with the specification that insufficient research existed to guide in the construction of diagnostic criteria for it at that time.

During the 1980s, reports began to appear that challenged the notion that ADHD was primarily a disturbance in attention and focused instead on problems with motivation generally, and an insensitivity to response consequences specifically (Barkley, 1989a; Glow & Glow, 1979; Haenlein & Caul, 1987). Research was demonstrating that children with ADHD did not respond the same to alterations in contingencies of reinforcement or punishment than did normal children—under conditions of continuous reward, their performances were often indistinguishable from normal children on various lab tasks but when reinforcement patterns shifted to partial reward or to extinction (no reward) conditions, children with ADHD showed significant declines in their performance (Douglas & Parry, 1983, 1994; Parry & Douglas, 1983). It was also becoming evident to me that deficits in the manner in which rules and instructions governed behavior characterized these children (Barkley, 1981, 1989a, 1990). When rules specifying behavior were given that competed with the prevailing immediate consequences in the setting for other forms of action, the rules did not control behavior as well as in normal children. Thus, I hypothesized that the class of human behavior initiated and sustained by rules (and language), called "rule governed" behavior by behaviorists (Hayes, 1989; Skinner, 1953) may be impaired in those with ADHD.

Over the past decade, researchers employing information-processing paradigms to study ADHD were having a difficult time demonstrating that the problems these children had with attending to tasks were actually attentional in nature. Problems in response inhibition and motor-system control were more reliably demonstrated instead (Barkley, Grodzinsky, & DuPaul, 1992; Schachar & Logan, 1990; Sergeant, 1988; Sergeant & Scholten, 1985a, 1985b). Researchers, moreover, were finding that the problems with hyperactivity and impulsivity were not separate symptoms but formed a single dimension of behavior (Achenbach & Edelbrock, 1983; Goyette, Conners, & Ulrich, 1978; Lahey et al., 1988), which I previously described as "disinhibition" (Barkley, 1990). The symptoms of hyperactivity and impulsivity seemed to be both a single and signal problem for the disorder. All of this led to the creation of two separate lists of items and thresholds for ADHD when DSM-IV was published (American Psychiatric Association, 1994); one for inattention and another for hyperactive–impulsive behavior. Unlike its predecessor, DSM-III-R, the establishment of the inattention list once again permitted the diagnosis of a subtype of ADHD that consisted principally of problems with attention (ADHD predominantly inattentive type). It also permitted, for the first time,

the distinction of a subtype of ADHD that consisted chiefly of hyperactive–impulsive behavior without significant inattention (ADHD, predominantly hyperactive–impulsive type). Children having significant problems from both item lists were titled ADHD, combined type. The specific criteria from DSM-IV are set forth and discussed in more detail below (see "Diagnostic Criteria and Related Issues").

In conclusion, as of this writing, debate continues over the core deficit(s) in ADHD with increasing weight being given to the central problem of behavioral inhibition. The nature of the problems with sustaining attention demonstrated by these children remains controversial but apparently must be explained by deficiencies within the anterior motor control systems of the brain rather than in the more posterior sensory or information-processing systems themselves. Likewise, controversy continues to swirl around the place of a subtype composed primarily of inattention within the larger condition of ADHD, with many viewing it as having distinctive features more akin to other internalizing rather than externalizing disorders (Barkley, 1990; Barkley, Grodzinsky, & DuPaul, 1992; Lahey & Carlson, 1992; Goodyear & Hynd, 1992; Hinshaw, 1994).

DESCRIPTION AND DIAGNOSIS

The Core Symptoms

As discussed above, ADHD is generally viewed at this time as comprising two major symptoms: (1) inattention, and (2) hyperactive–impulsive behavior (disinhibition) (American Psychiatric Association, 1994).

Inattention

The problem with attention is witnessed in the child's inability to sustain attention or respond to tasks or play activities as long as others of the same age and to follow through on rules and instructions as well as others. It is also seen in the child being more disorganized, distracted, and forgetful than others of the same age. Parents and teachers frequently complain that these children do not seem to listen as well as they should for their age, cannot concentrate, are easily distracted, fail to finish assignments, daydream, and change activities more often than others (Barkley, DuPaul, & McMurray, 1990). Research employ-

ing objective measures of these attributes corroborates their presence in ADHD in that such children, when compared to normal children, are often recorded as being more "off-task," less likely to complete as much work as others, looking away more from the activities they are requested to do (including television), persisting less in correctly performing boring activities, such as in continuous performance tasks, and being slower and less likely to return to an activity once interrupted (Barkley & Ullman, 1975; Corkum & Siegel, 1993; Luk, 1985; Milich & Lorch, 1994; Schachar, Tannock, & Logan, 1993). These behaviors have also been noted to distinguish them from children with learning disabilities (Barkley, DuPaul, & McMurray, 1990) or other psychiatric disorders (Werry, Elkind, & Reeves, 1987). Yet, objective research does not find children with ADHD to be generally more distracted by extraneous events occurring during their task performance, although they may be so distracted if the irrelevant stimuli are embedded within the task itself (Campbell, Douglas, & Morgenstern, 1971; Cohen, Weiss, & Minde, 1972; Rosenthal & Allen, 1980; Steinkamp, 1980).

Hyperactive–Impulsive Behavior (Disinhibition)

The problems with disinhibition noted in children with ADHD are manifest in difficulties with fidgetiness, staying seated when required, moving about, running, and climbing more than other children, playing noisily, talking excessively, interrupting others' activities, and being less able than others to wait in line or take turns in games (American Psychiatric Association, 1994). Parents and teachers describe them as acting as if driven by a motor, incessantly in motion, always on the go, and unable to wait for events to occur. Research objectively documents them to be more active than other children (Barkley & Ullman, 1975; Barkley & Cunningham, 1979a; Luk, 1985; Porrino et al., 1983; Zentall, 1985), to be less mature in controlling motor overflow movements (Denckla & Rudel, 1978), to have considerable difficulties with stopping an ongoing behavior (Schachar et al., 1993; Milich, Hartung, & Haigler, 1994), to talk more than others (Barkley, Cunningham, & Karlsson, 1983), to interrupt others' conversations (Malone & Swanson, 1993), to be less able to resist immediate temptations and delay gratification (Anderson, Hinshaw, & Simmel, 1994; Campbell, Szumowski, Ewing, Gluck, &

Breaux, 1982; Rapport, Tucker, DuPaul, Merlo, & Stoner, 1986), and to respond too quickly and too often when they are required to wait and watch for events to happen, as is often seen in impulsive errors on continuous performance tests (Corkum & Siegel, 1993). Although less frequently examined, differences in activity and impulsiveness have been found between children with ADHD and those with learning disabilities (Barkley, DuPaul, & McMurray, 1990) and other psychiatric disorders (Halperin, Matier, Bedi, Sharpin, & Newcorn, 1992; Roberts, 1990; Werry et al., 1987).

Interestingly, recent research shows that the problems with disinhibition arise first (at age 3–4 years) with those related to inattention emerging in the developmental course of ADHD (at age 5–7 years), or by entry into formal schooling, or, even later by the early to middle elementary school grades if only the problems with attention are the principle difficulties (Hart et al., in press; Loeber, Green, Lahey, Christ, & Frick, 1992). And, whereas the symptoms of disinhibition in the DSM item lists seem to decline with age, those of inattention remain relatively stable during the elementary grades (Hart et al., in press). Yet even they decline by adolescence (Fischer, Barkley, Fletcher, & Smallish, 1993a). Why the inattention arises later than the disinhibitory symptoms and does not decline when the latter do over development remains an enigma. One explanation of this will be presented below in discussion of a theoretical model of ADHD, which I have recently advanced (Barkley, 1994, 1997).

Situational and Contextual Factors

The symptoms comprising ADHD are greatly affected in their level of severity by a variety of situational and contextual factors; an observation that is true for most forms of childhood psychopathology. Douglas (1972) commented on the greater variability of task performances made by ADHD compared to control children. Many others since then have found that when the ADHD child must perform multiple trials within a task assessing attention and impulse control, the range of scores around that child's own mean performance is frequently greater than in normal children (see Douglas, 1983). The finding is sufficiently common in measures of reaction time (Chee, Logan, Schachar, Lindsay, & Wachsmuth, 1989; Zahn, Krusei, & Rapoport, 1991) to have led to several developers of continuous perfor-

mance tests marketed for commercial use in diagnosing ADHD to recommend that the variability in this measure serve as an indicator for the disorder (Conners, 1995; Greenberg & Waldman, 1992).

A number of other factors have been noted to influence the ability of children with ADHD to sustain their attention to task performance, control their impulses to act, regulate their activity level, and to produce work consistently. These include: (1) time of day or fatigue (Porrino et al., 1983; Zagar & Bowers, 1983); (2) increasing task complexity such that organizational strategies are required (Douglas, 1983); (3) extent of restraint demanded for the context (Barkley & Ullman, 1975; Luk, 1985); (4) level of stimulation within the setting (Zentall, 1985); (5) the schedule of immediate consequences associated with the task (Barkley, Copeland, & Sivage, 1980; Douglas & Parry, 1983, 1994); and (6) the absence of adult supervision during task performance (Draeger, Prior, & Sanson, 1986; Gomez & Sanson, 1994).

Besides the aforementioned factors, which chiefly apply to task performance, variability has also been documented across more macroscopic settings. For instance, using a rating scale of 16 different contexts within the home (the Home Situations Questionnaire), it has been shown that children with ADHD are most problematic in their behavior when persistence in work-related tasks is required (i.e., chores, homework, etc.) or where behavioral restraint is necessary, especially in settings involving public scrutiny (i.e., in church, in restaurants, when a parent is on the phone, etc.) (Altepeter & Breen, 1992; Barkley & Edelbrock, 1987; DuPaul & Barkley, 1992). Such children are least likely to pose behavioral management problems during free play, when little self-control is required. Although they will be more disruptive when their fathers are at home than during free play, children with ADHD are still rated as much less problematic when the father is at home than in most other contexts. Fluctuations in the severity of ADHD symptoms have also been documented across a variety of school contexts (Barkley & Edelbrock, 1987; DuPaul & Barkley, 1992). In this case, contexts involving task-directed persistence are the most problematic, with significantly fewer degrees of problems posed by contexts involving an absence of supervision (i.e., at lunch, in hallways, at recess, etc.), and even fewer problems being posed during special events (i.e., field trips, assemblies, etc.) (Altepeter & Breen, 1992).

Associated Cognitive Impairments

Although ADHD is defined by the presence of the two major symptom dimensions noted above (inattention, disinhibition), research finds that such children often demonstrate deficiencies in many other abilities. Among these, the most reliably demonstrated are difficulties with: (1) *motor coordination and sequencing* (Barkley, 1997; Barkley, DuPaul, & McMurray, 1990; Breen, 1989; Denckla & Rudel, 1978; Mariani & Barkley, 1995); (2) *working memory and mental computation* (Barkley, 1997; Mariani & Barkley, 1995; Zentall & Smith, 1993); (3) *planning and anticipation* (Barkley, Grodzinsky, & DuPaul, 1992; Douglas, 1983; Grodzinsky & Diamond, 1992); (4) *verbal fluency and confrontational communication* (Grodzinsky & Diamond, 1992; Zentall, 1988); (5) *effort allocation* (Douglas, 1983; Sergeant & van der Meere, 1994; Voelker, Carter, Sprague, Gdowski, & Lachar, 1989); (6) *applying organizational strategies* (Hamlett, Pellegrini, & Connors, 1987; Voelker et al., 1989; Zentall, 1988); (7) *the internalization of self-directed speech* (Berk & Potts, 1991; Copeland, 1979); (8) *adhering to restrictive instructions* (Barkley, 1985; Danforth, Barkley, & Stokes, 1991; Roberts, 1990; Routh & Schroeder, 1976); and (9) *self-regulation of emotional arousal* (Barkley, 1997; Cole, Zahn-Waxler, & Smith, 1994; Douglas, 1983; Hinshaw, Buhrmeister, & Heller, 1989). Several studies have also demonstrated what both Still (1902) and Douglas (1972) noted anecdotally years ago—ADHD may be associated with less mature or diminished moral reasoning (Hinshaw, Herbsman, Melnick, Nigg, & Simmel, 1993; Nucci & Herman, 1982; Simmel & Hinshaw, 1993).

The commonality among most or all of these seemingly disparate abilities is that all have been considered to fall within the domain of "executive functions" in the field of neuropsychology (Denckla, 1994; Torgesen, 1994) or "metacognition" in developmental psychology (Flavell, 1970; Torgesen, 1994; Welsh & Pennington, 1988), or to be affected by these functions. And all have been considered to be mediated by the frontal cortex, and particularly the prefrontal lobes (Fuster, 1989; Stuss & Benson, 1986). Executive functions have been defined as those neuropsychological processes that permit or assist with human self-regulation (Barkley, 1997), which itself has been defined as any behavior by a person that modifies the probability of a sub-

sequent behavior by that person so as to alter the probability of a later consequence (Kanfer & Karoly, 1972; Skinner, 1953). By classifying cognitive actions or thinking as private behavior, one can understand how these private self-directed, cognitive (executive) actions fall within the definition of human self-regulation—they are private behaviors (cognitive acts) that modify other behaviors so as to alter the likelihood of later consequences for the individual. And, by appreciating the role of the frontal lobes generally, and the prefrontal cortex particularly, in these executive abilities, it is easy to see why researchers have repeatedly speculated that ADHD probably arises out of some disturbance or dysfunction of this brain region (Benton, 1991; Heilman, Voeller, & Nadeau, 1991; Levin, 1938; Mattes, 1980).

THEORETICAL FRAMEWORK

Many different theories of ADHD have been proposed over the past century to account for the diversity of findings so evident in this disorder. Some of these were discussed above (see "Historical Context"), such as Still's (1902) notion of defective volitional inhibition and moral regulation of behavior, Douglas's (1972, 1983) theory of deficient attention, inhibition, arousal, and preference for immediate reward, and the attempts to view ADHD as a deficit in sensitivity to reinforcement (Haenlein & Caul, 1987) or rule-governed behavior (Barkley, 1981, 1989a). More recently, Quay (1989), relying on Gray's neuropsychological model of anxiety (Gray, 1982), proposed that ADHD represented a deficit in the brain's behavioral inhibition system (BIS). However, as Quay rightly noted (1990), such an extrapolation would imply that those with ADHD should demonstrate little if any difficulties with anxiety disorder (as this is due to an overaroused BIS in Gray's model) and this is not the case. Anxiety disorders occur in as many as 15% to 40% of children with ADHD (Russo & Biedel, 1994; Tannock, in press) (see "Comorbid Conditions" below). Nevertheless, Quay's hypothesis has resulted in increased research on inhibitory and activation (reinforcement) processes in both ADHD (Milich et al., 1994) and conduct disorder (see Chapter 3, Hinshaw & Anderson, this volume). Relying on Logan's "race" model of inhibition, Schachar and Logan (1990) have also argued for a central defi-

cit in inhibitory processes in those with ADHD. In this model, an event or stimulus is hypothesized to trigger both an activating or primary response and an inhibitory response creating a competition or race between the two as to which will be executed first. Disinhibited individuals, such as those with ADHD, are viewed as having slower initiation of inhibitory processes relative to normal children (Schachar, Tannock, & Logan, 1993).

There is little doubt that poor behavioral inhibition plays a central role in ADHD (see Barkley, 1990, 1994, 1997; Barkley, Grodzinsky, & DuPaul, 1992, for reviews). Although important in the progress of our understanding about ADHD, this conclusion still leaves at least two important questions on the nature of ADHD unresolved: (1) How does this account for the numerous other associated symptoms found in ADHD (described above) and apparently subsumed under the concept of executive functions? (2) How does this account for the involvement of the separate problem with inattention (poor sustained attention) in the disorder? A recently proposed theoretical model of ADHD not only encompasses many of these earlier explanations but may hold the answers to these questions as well as some unexpected directions that future research on ADHD might wish to pursue (Barkley, 1994, 1997).

Inhibition, Executive Functions, and Time

The model of ADHD set forth below and in Figure 2.1 places behavioral inhibition at a central point in its relation to four other executive functions dependent upon it for their own effective execution. These four executive functions, as suggested above, permit and subserve human self-regulation, bringing behavior progressively more under the control of time and the influence of future over immediate consequences. The end result is a greater capacity for predicting and controlling one's environment (and one's own behavior within it) so as to maximize future consequences to the individual. More generally, the interaction of these executive functions permits far more effective adaptive functioning.

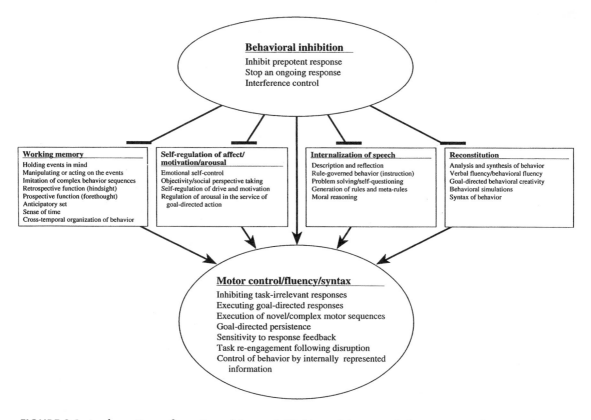

FIGURE 2.1. A schematic configuration of the model linking inhibition with four executive functions that then influence motor control. From Barkley (1997). Copyright 1997 by the American Psychological Association. Reprinted by permission.

Several assumptions are important in understanding the model as it is applied to ADHD: (1) The capacity for behavioral inhibition begins to emerge first in development, ahead of these four executive functions. (2) These executive functions emerge at different times in development, may have different developmental trajectories, and are interactive. (3) The impairment that ADHD creates in these executive functions is *secondary* to the primary deficit it creates in behavioral inhibition (improve the inhibition and these executive functions should likewise improve). (4) The deficit in behavioral inhibition arises principally from genetic and neurodevelopmental origins, rather than purely social ones, although its expression is certainly influenced by social factors over development. (5) The secondary deficits in self-regulation created by the primary deficiency in inhibition feed back to contribute further to poor behavioral inhibition given that self-regulation contributes to the enhancement of self-restraint (inhibition). Finally, (6) the model does not apply to those having ADD without hyperactivity or what is now called ADHD, predominantly inattentive type. The model has been derived from earlier theories on the evolution of human language (Bronowski, 1977) and the functions of the prefrontal cortex (Fuster, 1989). The evidence for the model as applied to ADHD and for the above assertions is reviewed elsewhere (Barkley, 1994, 1997).

"Behavioral inhibition" is viewed as being comprised of two related processes: (1) the capacity to inhibit prepotent responses, either prior to or once initiated, creating a delay in the response to an event (response inhibition); and (2) the protection of this delay, the self-directed actions occurring within it, and the goal-directed behaviors they create from interference by competing events and their prepotent responses (interference control). "Prepotent responses" are defined as those for which immediate reinforcement is available for their performance or for which there is a strong history of reinforcement in this context. Through the postponement of the prepotent response and the creation of this protected period of delay, the occasion is set for four other executive functions to act effectively in modifying the individual's eventual response(s) to the event. This is done to achieve a net maximization of both temporally distant and immediate consequences rather than immediate consequences alone for the individual. The chain of goal-directed, future-oriented behaviors set in motion by these acts of self-regulation is then also pro-

tected from interference during its performance by this same process of inhibition (interference control). And even if disrupted, the individual retains the capacity or intention (via working memory) to return to the goal-directed actions until the outcome is successfully achieved or judged to be no longer necessary.

Prolongation/Working Memory

The capacity to inhibit an initial prepotent response to an event creates a delay in responding. Humans have evolved the capability during this delay to retain a mental representation of the event in mind (Bronowski, 1977). The capacity for "prolongation" of mental representations of events is dependent upon inhibition and allows even infants to successfully perform delayed response tasks to a limited degree (Diamond, 1990; Diamond, Cruttenden, & Niederman, 1994; Goldman-Rakic, 1987). As this capacity increases developmentally, it forms the basis for "working memory," which has been defined as the ability to maintain mental information on-line while acting upon it. The information so retained pertains to action and has been called "provisional memory" (Fuster, 1989) to distinguish it from the stage of brief retention of information known as "short-term memory." It is provisional in that once the information has served to prepare and execute a response, it is removed from working memory. These prolonged mental representations of events can also be stored in long-term memory for later retrieval back into working memory as their information may be pertinent to considering a response to a current event. This recall of past events for the sake of preparing a current response is known as "hindsight" or the "retrospective function" of working memory (Bronowski, 1977; Fuster, 1989). To carry out such a process, events must be tagged in some way concerning their sequence or temporal order. And this retention of events in a temporal sequence has been shown to contribute to the "subjective estimation of time" (Michon, 1985). Analysis of temporal sequences of events for recurring patterns can then be used to conjecture hypothetical future events—the individual's best guess as to what may happen next or later in time based on the detection of recurring patterns in past event sequences. This permits the individual to create a preparation to act, sometimes called an "anticipatory set" or intention to act (Fuster, 1989). This extension of hindsight forward into time also creates "forethought" or the "prospec-

tive function" of working memory, forming a temporally symmetrical counterpart to the retrospective function of hindsight (Bronowski, 1977; Fuster, 1989). And from this sense of future likely emerges the progressively greater valuation of future consequences over immediate ones that takes place throughout not only child development but adult life as well (Green, Fry, & Meyerson, 1994).

Important in this model for understanding the linkage of inattention to disinhibition in ADHD is the critical role played by working memory in maintaining on-line ones' intentions to act ("plans") so as to guide the construction and execution of complex chains of goal-directed actions over time (Fuster, 1989). Such sustained chains of goal-directed actions create persistence of responding, as William James (1890) recognized nearly a century ago, giving rise to the capacity of humans to sustain attention (responding) for dramatically long periods of time in pursuit of future goals. And so, as James so eloquently described, the capacity for prolongation of mental events underlies human will, volition, or self-discipline: *"The essential achievement of the will, in short, when it is most 'voluntary,' is to ATTEND to a difficult object and hold it fast before the mind"* (p. 815); and, "Everywhere then the function of the effort [voluntary or free will] is the same: to keep affirming and adopting a thought which, if left to itself, would slip away" (p. 818).

The human capacity to prolong mental representations of events permits a number of important and related mental functions to occur, including working memory, hindsight, forethought, sense of time, and anticipatory set. In so doing, individuals are now capable of the cross-temporal organization of behavior; that is, the linking of events, responses, and their eventual consequences via their representation in working memory despite what may be considerable gaps among them in real time. Thus, self-regulation relative to time arises as a consequence of prolongation and working memory providing a human ability of substantial cultural, and possibly evolutionary, importance. And since language is used, in part, to express cognitive content, references to time, sense of past, and sense of future in verbal interactions with others should become increasingly frequent in the developmental course of children as this sense of time develops.

As extrapolated to those with ADHD, the model predicts that deficits in behavioral inhibition lead to deficiencies in prolongation and

working memory thus giving rise to particular forms of forgetfulness in those with the disorder (forgetting to act at certain critical points in time). But the effect of the disinhibition on working memory will also be to diminish the individual's subjective sense of time and his or her reliance on both hindsight and forethought in governing his or her behavior. This will lead to a reduction in the creation of anticipatory sets or preparations for action toward future predictable events in those with ADHD. Consequently, the capacity for the cross-temporal organization of behavior in those with ADHD is diminished, disrupting the ability to string together complex chains of actions directed, over time, to a future goal. The greater the degree to which time separates the components of the behavioral contingency (event, response, consequence), the more difficult the task will prove for those with ADHD. Research is beginning to demonstrate some of these deficits in those with ADHD, although others remain unstudied (Barkley, 1997). Also unstudied is the prediction that references to time, past, and future in verbal interactions with others will be diminished in those with ADHD relative to peers of the same developmental level. Yet, clinical descriptions of those with ADHD abound with references to deficits in forgetfulness (to act), organization, preparedness, meeting deadlines, and planning (Barkley, 1990; Ingersoll, 1988; Hallowell & Ratey, 1994).

Self-Regulation of Affect

The model in Figure 2.1 states that behavioral inhibition sets the occasion for the development of self-regulation of affect in children. The inhibition of the initial prepotent response includes the inhibition of the initial emotional valence that it may have elicited. It is not that the child does not experience emotion but that the behavioral reaction to or expression of that emotion is delayed along with any motor behavior associated with it. The delay in responding to this emotion allows the child time to engage in self-directed behaviors that will modify both the eventual response to the event as well as the emotional reaction that may accompany it. This has been called "separation of affect" (Bronowski, 1977) and is believed to permit greater objectivity on the part of the child in determining an eventual response to an event. But it is not just affect that is being managed by the development of self-regulation but drive and motivation as well (Fuster, 1989). This permits the child

to actually learn to induce drive or motivational states that may be required for the initiation and maintenance of goal directed behavior.

Extending this model to ADHD leads to the following predictions. Those with ADHD should display: (1) greater emotional expression in their reactions to events; (2) less objectivity in the selection of a response to an event; (3) diminished social perspective taking as the child does not delay his or her initial emotional reaction long enough to take the view of others and their own needs into account; and (4) diminished ability to induce drive and motivational states in themselves in the service of goal-directed behavior. It is also conceivable that social perspicacity would be affected by the impairment in working memory noted above given its critical role in holding several events in mind to evaluate their relations. Those with ADHD remain less mature in the self-regulation of emotion because of their deficiencies in behavioral inhibition. They may remain more dependent upon the environmental contingencies within a situation or task to determine their motivational or drive states than do others (Barkley, 1997).

Internalization of Speech

One of the more fascinating developmental processes witnessed in children is the progressive internalization or privatization of speech. During the early preschool years, speech, once developed, is initially employed for communication with others. As behavioral inhibition progresses, the delays in responding it permits allows language to be turned on the self. Language is now not just a means of influencing the behavior of others but provides a means of reflection (self-directed description) as well as a means for controlling one's own behavior (Berk & Potts, 1991; Bronowski, 1977; Vygotsky, 1978, 1987). Self-directed speech progresses from being public, to being subvocal, to finally being private, all over the course of perhaps 6 to 10 years (Berk & Potts, 1991). With this progressive privatization of speech, comes an increasing control it permits over one's own behavior (Berk & Potts, 1991; Kopp, 1982). Language in general, and rules (behavior-specifying stimuli) in particular, gain an increasing degree of stimulus control over motor behavior, providing a tremendously increased capacity for self-control, planfulness, and goal-directed behavior. It has even been conjectured (Barkley, 1997) that this internalization of speech

represents a larger process that may encompass the internalization of action or responding. Thus, not only speech becomes private, creating the means for verbal thought (Berk & Potts, 1991; Vygotsky, 1987), but other forms of self-directed behavior become private, permitting other modes of thinking as well. I have even gone so far as to speculate that this process of internalization of behavior may be related in some as yet unknown way to the same mechanism by which working memory arises, given that working memory seems to be self-directed private behavior. And so this component of the model may not be separate from that of prolongation/working memory discussed above.

For those with ADHD, the model stipulates that the privatization of speech should be less mature or advanced as it is in others of the same age, resulting in greater public speech (excessive talking), less reflection before acting, less organized and rule-oriented self-speech, and a diminished influence of self-directed speech in controlling one's own behavior. The self-control and rule-governed behavior permitted by the internalization of speech should, therefore, be diminished in those with ADHD as well (Barkley, 1997).

Reconstitution

It has been argued (Bronowski, 1977) that the use of language to represent objects, actions, and their properties provides a means by which the world, through internalized speech, can be taken apart and recombined just as is done with the parts of speech that represent that world. The delay in responding that behavioral inhibition permits allows time for events to be mentally prolonged and then disassembled so as to extract more information about the event before preparing a response to it. Internal speech permits *analysis* and out of this process comes its complement—*synthesis*. Just as the parts of speech can be recombined to form new sentences, the parts of the world represented in speech are, likewise, recombined to create entirely new ideas about the world (Bronowski, 1977) and entirely new responses to that world. The world is seen as having parts rather than inviolate wholes—parts capable of multiple and novel recombinations. As Bronowski (1977) has stated, this permits humans a far greater capacity for creativity and problem solving than is evident in our closest relatives, the primates. The process of reconstitution, he asserts, is evident in everyday speech in its flu-

ency. It becomes even more obvious when speech is task- or goal-directed as one can now witness the rapid, efficient, and often novel combination of the parts of speech into entire messages that represent the ideas of the individual.

As applied to ADHD, such a model predicts that those with ADHD will demonstrate a diminished use of analysis and synthesis in the formation of responses to events. The capacity to generate multiple plans of action (options) in the service of goal-directed behavior should, therefore, be diminished in those with ADHD as should goal-directed creativity more generally. And this impairment in reconstitution will be most evident in everyday verbal fluency when the person with ADHD is required by a task or situation to assemble rapidly, accurately, and efficiently the parts of speech into messages (sentences) so as to accomplish the goal or requirements of the task. The amount of evidence for a deficiency in verbal fluency in children with ADHD is limited, but what exists is highly consistent with this prediction (Barkley, 1997).

Motor Control/Fluency

If the deficit in behavioral inhibition proposed in the current model is housed within the brain's motor or output system, then its effects should also be evident in the planning and execution of motor actions. Complex fine and gross motor actions require inhibition to preclude the initiation of movements located in neural zones adjacent to those being activated. Inhibition provides an increasing "functional pruning" of the motor system such that only those actions required to accomplish the task are initiated by the individual. Although this pruning action is believed to be distinct from actual synaptic pruning that may occur in neural development, the two processes may not be entirely unrelated. Over development, such powers of inhibition also permit the construction and execution of lengthy, complex, and novel chains of goal-directed behavior, protecting them from disruption by interference until they have been completed. Both novelty and complexity are important in understanding the role of the prefrontal cortex in these aspects of motor planning and execution (Fuster, 1989). As applied to ADHD, the model stipulates that those with the disorder should display greater difficulties with the development of motor coordination and especially in the planning and execution of com-

plex, lengthy, and novel chains of goal-directed responses. There is substantial evidence already available for problems in motor development and motor execution in those with ADHD (see Barkley, 1997). It remains to be determined whether those with ADHD have more difficulties in producing, executing, and sustaining lengthy and complex chains of novel responses toward goals. Yet this is precisely what one could infer from the poor sustained attention so often attributed to and observed in those with ADHD.

Summary

The model portrayed in Figure 2.1 represents behavioral inhibition as a central and fundamental component in a theory of executive functions, generally, and ADHD, more specifically. In this model, behavioral inhibition sets the occasion for the efficient execution of four executive functions or self-directed actions that permit self-regulation, these being: (1) prolongation/working memory; (2) self-regulation of affect (drive and motivation); (3) the internalization of speech (and, perhaps behavior more generally); and (4) reconstitution (analysis/synthesis). These functions permit motor control/fluency and the cross-temporal organization of behavior (Fuster, 1989), allowing greater prediction and control of the individual over his or her environment and his or her own behavior within it (Bronowski, 1977) in the service of maximizing net long-term consequences for the individual (Barkley, 1997). The impairment in behavioral inhibition occurring in ADHD is hypothesized to disrupt the efficient execution of these four executive functions thereby delimiting the capacity of these individuals for self-regulation. The result is an impairment in the cross-temporal organization of behavior, in the prediction and control of one's own behavior and environment, and inevitably in the maximization of long-term consequences for the individual. That adaptive functioning would be impaired by ADHD, then, should go without saying.

The present model of ADHD shows how the findings noted above under "Associated Cognitive Impairments" can now be integrated into a single unifying theory of the disorder. Undoubtedly, this theory requires a great deal of research to clarify the nature of each component in the model, to evaluate the strength of the relationship of each component to behavioral inhibition and to the other components, to elucidate the developmental progression of each component

and their ordering, and to critically test some of the previously unexpected predictions of the model as applied to ADHD (i.e., diminished sense of time, reduced references to time in verbal interactions, the impact of ADHD on analysis/synthesis and creativity, etc.). Greater care in operationally specifying some of these executive functions or constructs is also required so as to make them more susceptible to measurement and tests of falsification. Certainly the complexity of the model is potentially problematic in that even when such efforts succeed at falsifying the model, it may prove tempting to explain their results by reference to the other intervening constructs in the model. What research is available, however, seems supportive of the model, and at least one critical test, that of impaired sense of time, has been borne out (Barkley, Koplowitz, Anderson, & McMurray, 1996; Cappella, Gentile, & Juliano, 1977; Koplowitz & Barkley, 1996).

To return to the second question raised earlier then, how is the problem with inattention and, more specifically, poor sustained attention, accounted for in this model? It is critical, first, to distinguish between two forms of sustained attention that are traditionally confused in the research literature on ADHD. The first I have called "contingency-shaped attention" (Barkley, 1997) and refers to continued responding in a situation or to a task as a function of the motivational or reinforcement properties of that context and specifically the contingencies of reinforcement provided by the task or activity. Responding that is maintained under these conditions is directly dependent on the immediate environmental contingencies and so is described as contingency-shaped attention or responding. And so it is not surprising that many factors can be found to affect this form of sustained attention or responding: (1) the novelty of the task, (2) the intrinsic interest the activity may hold for the individual, (3) the immediate reinforcement contingencies it provides for responding in the task, (4) the state of fatigue of the individual, and (5) the presence or absence of an adult supervisor (or other stimuli that signal other consequences for performance that are outside the task itself), among other factors. All are important to determining the extent to which the individual, or any animal, will sustain its responding within that context. This type of sustained attention is not affected by ADHD, according to this model (Barkley, 1997).

But as children mature, a second form of sustained attention emerges that is better termed "goal-directed persistence." It arises as a direct consequence of the development of self-regulation. This form of persistence derives from the development of a progressively greater capacity by the child to hold events, goals, and plans in mind (working memory), to adhere to rules governing behavior and to formulate and follow such rules as need be, and to self-induce motivational or drive states supportive of the plans and goals formulated by the individual so as to maintain goal-directed behavior. In short, the interaction of the components of the model in the performance of self-regulation permits substantially longer, complex, and even novel chains of behavior to be constructed and sustained, despite interruptions, until the goal is attained. Persistence of effort (Douglas, 1983), volition (Still, 1902), or will (James, 1890) may be other terms used to describe this capacity to initiate and sustain chains of goal-directed behavior in spite of the absence of immediate environmental contingencies for their performance. Such behavior is clearly less dependent on the current context and its immediate contingencies for its performance. And, more telling is that it may often be associated with a state of self-imposed deprivation from reinforcement or, less often, even infliction of immediate aversive or punitive states if, in so doing, later consequences are maximized over immediate ones. These acts of self-deprivation are often called deferred gratification, self-discipline, willpower, or resistance to temptation and result directly from acts of self-regulation. And it is this type of goal-directed persistence arising out of self-regulation that is so tragically disrupted by ADHD. This may help to account for why tasks assessing such resistance to temptation have often been successful in distinguishing children with ADHD from normal children (Barkley, 1996; Campbell et al., 1982; Hinshaw, Heller, & McHale, 1992).

This appreciation of the linkage among the executive functions in the model, the self-regulation they permit, and the goal-directed persistence that derives from self-control explains several important findings about the link between disinhibition (hyperactive–impulsive behavior) and inattention. It is possible to see, now, why the problems with hyperactive–impulsive behavior arise first in the development of ADHD to be followed within a few years by the problems with inattention. It is only when these executive functions and the rudimentary self-regulation they permit in early childhood have had adequate

opportunity to develop in normal children that those with ADHD will now be found wanting in this ability to engage in goal-directed persistence.

And it is also possible to understand why studies show that behavior ratings of inattention do not form a separate factor from those of hyperactive–impulsive behavior in preschool children until they reach early school age (Achenbach & Edelbrock, 1983, 1987). Furthermore, this makes it possible to understand why inattention even comes to form a separate, semi-independent factor from hyperactive–impulsive behavior by school age. It is because the inattention (goal-directed persistence) is one step removed from the problems with disinhibition via the toll the latter takes on working memory and the other components of the model and, hence, on self-regulation more generally. If this is so, it should be found that measures traditionally interpreted as assessing sustained attention in ADHD children should correlate significantly with measures of working memory, and they seem to do so forming a single dimension in early school-age children (Mariani & Barkley, 1995). Persistence requires working memory, among other components of the model, and working memory needs behavioral inhibition and the interference control it permits. The inattention so problematic in ADHD is but the third step in the developmental sequence from behavioral inhibition to self-regulation to persistence. Inhibition is the first.

DIAGNOSTIC CRITERIA AND RELATED ISSUES

DSM-IV Criteria

The most recent diagnostic criteria for ADHD as defined in DSM-IV (American Psychiatric Association, 1994) are set forth in Table 2.1. They stipulate that individuals have had their symptoms of ADHD for at least 6 months, that these symptoms be to a degree that is developmentally deviant, and that they have developed by 7 years of age. From the inattention item list, six of nine items must be endorsed as developmentally inappropriate. From the hyperactive–impulsive item lists, six of nine items, total, must be endorsed as deviant. Depending on whether criteria are met for either or both symptom lists will determine the type of ADHD that is to be diagnosed: predominantly inattentive, predominantly hyperactive–impulsive, and combined type.

These diagnostic criteria are some of the most rigorous and most empirically derived criteria ever available in the history of clinical diagnosis for this disorder. They were derived from a committee of some of the leading experts in the field, a literature review of ADHD, an informal survey of rating scales assessing the behavioral dimensions related to ADHD by the committee, and from statistical analyses of the results of a field trial of the items using 380 children from 10 different sites in North America (Lahey et al., in press).

Despite being an improvement over prior sets of DSM diagnostic criteria, some problems and critical issues still remain. For one thing, as alluded to above, *it is not clear that the predominantly inattentive type of ADHD (ADHD-PI) is actually a subtype of ADHD,* sharing a common attention deficit with the other types. This will be discussed further below. For another, it is also unclear whether the predominantly hyperactive–impulsive type (ADHD-PHI) is really a separate type from the combined type (ADHD-C) or simply an earlier developmental stage of it. The field trial found that ADHD-PHI was primarily comprised of preschool aged children, whereas ADHD-C was primarily school-aged children. As noted above, this is what one would expect to find given that research has previously found that the hyperactive–impulsive symptoms appear first, followed within a few years by those of inattention. If one is going to require that inattention symptoms be part of the diagnostic criteria, then the age of onset for such symptoms will necessitate that ADHD-C have a later age of onset than ADHD-PHI. Thus, it seems that these two types may actually be developmental stages of the same type of ADHD.

By permitting younger children to receive the diagnosis by meeting only the criteria for ADHD-PHI, however, the DSM-IV now may be capturing more of the preschool children referred to clinics with this behavior pattern who are impaired. Previously, under DSM-III-R, they might have gone undiagnosed for want of sufficient inattention to be eligible for diagnosis. This may be a good thing. Yet this also raises *the issue of whether or not the requirement for significant inattention to diagnose ADHD is even necessary* given that ADHD-PHI children are likely to eventually move into ADHD-C over time. Does the added requirement of significant inattention for the hyperactive–impulsive group add any greater power in predicting additional impairments not already achieved by the hyperactive–

TABLE 2.1. DSM-IV Criteria for ADHD

A. Either (1) or (2):

(1) six (or more) of the following symptoms of **inattention** have persisted for at least 6 months to a degree that is maladaptive and inconsistent with developmental level:

Inattention

(a) often fails to give close attention to details or makes careless mistakes in schoolwork, work, or other activities

(b) often has difficulty sustaining attention in tasks or play activities

(c) often does not seem to listen when spoken to directly

(d) often does not follow through on instructions and fails to finish schoolwork, chores, or duties in the workplace (not due to oppositional behavior or failure to understand instructions)

(e) often has difficulty organizing tasks and activities

(f) often avoids, dislikes, or is reluctant to engage in tasks that require sustained mental effort such as schoolwork or homework)

(g) often loses things necessary for tasks or activities (e.g., toys, school assignments, pencils, books, or tools)

(h) is often easily distracted by extraneous stimuli

(i) is often forgetful in daily activities

(2) six (or more) of the following symptoms of **hyperactivity–impulsivity** have persisted for at least 6 months to a degree that is maladaptive and inconsistent with developmental level:

Hyperactivity

(a) often fidgets with hands or feet or squirms in seat

(b) often leaves seat in classroom or in other situations in which remaining seated is expected

(c) often runs about or climbs excessively in situations in which it is inappropriate (in adolescents or adults, may be limited to subjective feelings of restlessness)

(d) often has difficulty playing or engaging in leisure activities quietly

(e) is often "on the go" or often acts as if "driven by a motor"

(f) often talks excessively

Impulsivity

(g) often blurts out answers before the questions have been completed

(h) often has difficulty awaiting turn

(i) often interrupts or intrudes on others (e.g., butts into conversations or games)

B. Some hyperactive–impulsive or inattentive symptoms that caused impairment were present before age 7 years.

C. Some impairment from the symptoms is present in two or more settings (e.g., at school [or work] and at home).

D. There must be clear evidence of clinically significant impairment in social, academic, or occupational functioning.

E. The symptoms do not occur exclusively during the course of a Pervasive Developmental Disorder, Schizophrenia, or other Psychotic Disorder and are not better accounted for by another mental disorder (e.g., Mood Disorder, Anxiety Disorder, Dissociative Disorder, or a Personality Disorder).

Code based on type:

314.01 Attention-Deficit/Hyperactivity Disorder, Combined Type: if both Criteria A1 and A2 are met for the past 6 months.

314.00 Attention-Deficit/Hyperactivity Disorder, Predominantly Inattentive Type: if Criterion A1 is met but Criterion A2 is not met for the past 6 months.

314.01 Attention-Deficit/Hyperactivity Disorder, PredominantlyHyperactive-Impulsive Type: if Criterion A2 is met but Criterion A1 is not met for the past 6 months.

Coding note: For individuals (especially adolescents and adults) who currently have symptoms that no longer meet full criteria, "In Partial Remission" should be specified).

Note. From American Psychiatric Association (1994, pp. 83–85). Copyright 1994 by the American Psychiatric Association. Reprinted by permission.

impulsive symptoms? Apparently not much, according to the results of the field trial (Lahey et al., in press). Significant levels of inattention mainly predicted additional problems with completing homework that were not as well predicted by the hyperactive–impulsive behavior. Otherwise, the latter predicted most of the other areas of impairment studied in this field trial. This is consistent with follow-up studies that have found that childhood symptoms of hyperactivity are related to adolescent negative outcomes whereas those of inattention are much less so, if at all (Fischer, Barkley, Fletcher, & Smallish, 1993b; Weiss & Hechtman, 1993).

Another critical issue deserving consideration is *how well the diagnostic thresholds set for the two symptom lists apply to age groups outside of those used in the field trial* (ages 4–16 years, chiefly). This concern arises out of the well-known findings that the behavioral items comprising these lists decline significantly with age. Applying the same threshold across such a declining developmental slope could produce a situation where a larger percentage of young preschool aged-children (ages 2–3 years) would be inappropriately diagnosed as ADHD (false positives), whereas a smaller than expected percentage of adults would meet the criteria (false negatives). Support of just such a problem with using these criteria for adults was found in a recent study (Murphy & Barkley, 1995) collecting norms for DSM-IV item lists on a large sample of adults ages 17 to 84 years. The threshold needed to place an individual at the 93rd percentile for that person's age group declined to four of nine inattention items and five of nine hyperactive–impulsive items for ages 17 to 29 years, then to four of nine on each list for the 30- to 49-year age group, then to three of nine on each list for those 50 years and older. Studies of the applicability of the diagnostic thresholds to preschool children remain to be done. Until then, it seems prudent to utilize the recommended symptom list thresholds only for children ages 4 to 16 years.

These developmental changes in symptom thresholds raise another critical issue for developing diagnostic criteria for ADHD, and this is *the appropriateness of the item set for different developmental periods.* Inspection of the item lists suggests that the items for inattention may have a wider developmental applicability across school-age ranges of childhood and even into adolescence and young adulthood. Those for hyperactivity, in contrast, seem much more applicable to young children and less appropriate or not at all to older teens and adults. The items for impulsivity are few and may or may not be as applicable to teens and adults as much as to children. Yet, as discussed in the theoretical model above, disinhibition may be the central feature of the disorder. Recall from above the observations found in recent research (Hart et al., in press) that the symptoms of inattention remain stable across middle childhood into early adolescence, whereas those for hyperactive–impulsive behavior decline significantly over this same course. Although this may represent a true developmental decline in the severity of the latter symptoms, and possibly in the severity and prevalence of ADHD itself,

with maturation, it could also represent an illusory developmental trend. That is, it might be an artifact of the developmental restrictedness of some items (hyperactivity) more than others (inattention) and the minimal sampling of impulsive behavior appropriate for the various developmental periods.

An analogy using mental retardation may be instructive. Consider the following items that might be chosen to assess developmental level in preschool-aged children: being toilet-trained, recognizing colors, counting to 10, repeating 5 digits, buttoning snaps on clothing, recognizing simple geometric shapes, and using a vocabulary repertoire of at least 50 words. Evaluating whether or not a child is able to do these things may prove to be very useful in distinguishing mentally retarded from nonretarded preschoolers. However, if one continued to use this same item set to assess retarded children as they grew older, one would find a decline in the severity of the retardation in such children as progressively more items were achieved with age. One would also find that the prevalence of retardation would decline with age as many formerly retarded children "outgrew" these problems. But we know this would be illusory because mental retardation represents a *developmentally relative deficit* in the achievement of these and other mental and adaptive milestones.

Returning to the diagnosis of ADHD, if the same developmentally restricted item sets are applied throughout development with no attempt to adjust either the thresholds or, more importantly, the types of items developmentally appropriate for different periods, we might see the same results as with the analogy to mental retardation shown here. The fact that similar results to this analogy do occur with ADHD should give one pause before one interprets the observed decline in symptom severity (and even the observed decline in apparent prevalence!) as being accurate. If the theoretical model developed above is at all accurate, then developmentally sensitive sets of items for disinhibition need to be created and tested for use in this disorder to more accurately capture its nature and the fact that it, like mental retardation, probably represents a developmentally relative deficit. As it now stands, ADHD is being defined mainly by one of its earliest developmental manifestations (hyperactivity) and one of its later (school-age) yet secondary sequelae (goal-directed persistence) and only minimally by its central feature (impulsivity).

The issue is not just speculative. My colleagues and I involved in follow-up research with ADHD children into their adulthood have been impressed at the chronicity of impairments created by the disorder despite an *apparent* decline in the percentage of cases continuing to meet diagnostic criteria and an *apparent* decline in the severity of the symptoms used in these criteria (Barkley, Fischer, Edelbrock, & Smallish, 1991; Fischer et al., 1993a). Making developmentally referenced adjustments to the diagnostic thresholds at their adolescent follow-up resulted in a larger number continuing to meet criteria for the disorder (from 71% to 84%). Such adjustments, however, did not correct for the potentially increasing inappropriateness of the item sets for this aging sample, and so it is difficult to say how many of those not meeting these adjusted criteria may still have had the disorder. More importantly, we have found few differences in our measures of impairment between those no longer meeting diagnostic criteria for ADHD and those still doing so (Fischer, Barkley, Edelbrock, & Smallish, 1990).

A somewhat different critical issue concerning the diagnostic criteria for ADHD in Table 2.1 pertains to *whether or not the criteria should be adjusted for the gender of the children being diagnosed.* Research evaluating these and similar item sets demonstrates that male youngsters display more of these items and to a more severe degree than do female youngsters in the general population of children (Achenbach & Edelbrock, 1983; DuPaul, 1991; Goyette et al., 1978). If so, then should the same threshold for diagnosis be applied to both genders? Doing so would seem to result in girls having to meet a higher threshold relative to other girls to be diagnosed as ADHD than do boys relative to other boys. The problem is further accentuated by the fact that the majority of individuals in the DSM field trial were boys. Not doing so, and adjusting the cutoff scores for each gender separately, might well result in nullifying the finding that ADHD is more common in male than female individuals by a ratio of roughly 3:1 (see below). A conference held at the National Institute of Mental Health in November of 1994 to discuss gender differences in ADHD did not recommend that this be done as yet. But a consensus emerged that sufficient evidence existed warranting further study to determine if girls with ADHD not meeting current diagnostic thresholds were actually impaired. If so, then gender-based thresholds for diagnosis would be necessary.

The requirement of an age of onset for ADHD symptoms (7 years) in the diagnostic criteria has also come under recent challenge from its own field trial (Applegate et al., 1995) as well as other longitudinal studies (McGee, Williams, & Feehan, 1992). Such a criterion for age of onset suggests that there may be qualitative differences between those who meet the criterion (early onset) and those who do not (late onset). Some results do suggest that those with an onset before age 6 years may have more severe and persistent conditions and more problems with reading and school performance more generally (McGee et al., 1992). But these were matters of degree and not kind in this study. The DSM-IV field trial also was not able to show any clear discontinuities in degree of ADHD or in the types of impairments it examined between those meeting and those not meeting the 7-year age of onset. It remains unclear at this time as to just how specific an age of onset may need to be for distinguishing ADHD from other disorders.

A related potential problem for these criteria occurs in their failure to stipulate a lower bound age group for giving the diagnosis below which no diagnosis should be made. This is important because research on preschool children has shown that a separate dimension of hyperactive–impulsive behavior from aggression or defiant behavior does not seem to emerge until about 3 years of age (Achenbach & Edelbrock, 1987; Campbell, 1990). Below this age, these behaviors cluster together to form what has been called behavioral immaturity or an undercontrolled pattern of conduct. All of this implies that the symptoms of ADHD may be difficult to distinguish from other early behavioral disorders until at least 3 years of age, and so this age might serve as a lower bound for diagnostic applications. Similarly, research discussed below ("ICD-10 Criteria") implies that a lower bound of IQ might also be important below which the nature of ADHD may be quite different.

Another issue pertinent to the above is the problem of the duration requirement being set at 6 months. This has been chosen mainly out of tradition with earlier DSMs with little or no research support for selecting this particular length of time for symptom presence. It is undoubtedly important that the symptoms be relatively persistent if we are to view this disorder as within the individual rather than arising purely from context or out of a transient, normal developmental stage. Yet specifying a precise duration is difficult in

the absence of much research to guide the issue. Research on preschool-aged children might prove helpful here, however. Such research has shown that many children aged 3 years (or younger) may have parents or preschool teachers who report concerns about the activity level or attention of the children, yet these concerns have a high likelihood of remission within 12 months (Beitchman, Wekerle, & Hood, 1987; Campbell, 1990; Lerner, Inui, Trupin, & Douglas, 1985; Palfrey, Levine, Walker, & Sullivan, 1985). It would seem for preschoolers, then, that the 6–month duration specified in the DSM-IV may be too brief, resulting in overidentification of ADHD children at this age (false positives). However, this same body of research found that for those children whose problems lasted at least 12 months or beyond age 4 years, a persistent pattern of this behavior was established that was highly predictive of its continuance into the school-age range. This suggests that a duration of symptoms of at least 12 months might prove more rigorous.

One debate in the scientific literature occurring over the last decade was whether or not ADHD represented a category or a dimension of behavior. The notion of applying categories for psychopathologies of children seems to derive from the medical model where such categories constitute disease states (Edelbrock & Costello, 1988). From this perspective, an individual either has the disorder or not. DSM, in one sense, uses this categorical approach (all or none) by requiring that certain thresholds be met to be placed within the category of ADHD. The view of psychopathologies in children as representing dimensions of behavior, or even typologies (profiles) of these dimensions, arises from the perspective of developmental psychopathology (Achenbach & Edelbrock, 1984). In this view, ADHD constitutes the extreme end of a dimension, or dimensions, of behavior that falls along a continuum with normal children. The dimensional view (more or less) does not necessarily see ADHD as a disease entity but as a matter of degree in what is otherwise a characteristic of normal children.

The debate as it pertains to ADHD seems to have lessened recently for several reasons, some of which relate to the construction of DSM-III-R and now DSM-IV. First, and not widely known, is the fact that the DSM-III-R committee relied on several of the most commonly used behavior rating scales (Conners scales, Child Behavior Checklist [CBC], Behavior Problem Checklist) as one source in selecting items to be included in the symptom list(s) and to be tested out in the field trials (Spitzer, Davies, & Barkley, 1990). Second, the casting of these symptoms into lists along which a threshold of severity is placed for granting a diagnosis tacitly represents the disorder as a dimension. Third, the ICD-10 criteria (see below) for this disorder formally recommend the use of standardized dimensional measures to assess the degree of deviancy of the individual in determining the presence of the disorder, a further acknowledgment of the dimensional nature of the disorder. Texts on the clinical diagnosis of ADHD in North America (Barkley, 1990; Goldstein & Goldstein, 1990; Hinshaw, 1994), likewise, recommend the addition of child behavior rating scales to the clinical assessment procedures for ADHD children lending further endorsement to the dimensional view of ADHD. A fourth line of evidence supporting the dimensional view has come from demonstrations that the majority of subjects placing at extreme ends of dimensions of behavior related to ADHD on rating scales will receive the diagnosis when structured interviews using the diagnostic criteria are given (Chen, Faraone, Biederman, & Tsuang, 1994; Edelbrock & Costello, 1988). This, of course, is not surprising given the previous three points bearing on this issue. The debate must ultimately be settled on whether or not qualitative differences exist between individuals who achieve the diagnostic threshold versus those who are subthreshold. Until such discontinuities are demonstrated, the categorical approach to ADHD remains one of convenience, parsimony, and tradition (Hinshaw, 1994) rather than one with empirical validation.

The DSM requirement that the symptoms be demonstrated in at least two of three environments so as to establish pervasiveness of symptoms is new to this edition and problematic. By stipulating that two of three sources of information (parent, teacher, employer) must agree on the presence of the symptoms, the criteria now confound settings with sources of information. Research shows that the degree of agreement between parents and teacher, for instance, is modest, often ranging between .30 and .50 depending on the behavioral dimension being rated (Achenbach, McConaughy, & Howell, 1987).

This sets an upper limit on the extent to which parents and teachers are going to agree on the severity of ADHD symptoms and, thus, on whether or not the child has the disorder in that setting. While such disagreements among sources certainly reflect differences in the child's behavior as a function of true differential demands of these settings, they also reflect differences in the attitudes and judgments between different people.

Insisting on such agreement on diagnostic criteria may reduce the application of the diagnosis to some children unfairly simply as a result of such well-established differences between parents' and teachers' opinions. It may also create a confounding of the disorder with issues of comorbidity with oppositional defiant disorder (ODD) (Costello, Loeber, & Stouthamer-Loeber, 1991). Parent-only identified ADHD children may have predominantly ODD with relatively milder ADHD, whereas teacher-only identified ADHD children may have chiefly ADHD and minimal or no ODD symptoms. Children identified by both parents and teachers as ADHD may, therefore, carry a higher likelihood of ODD. They may also simply reflect a more severe condition of ADHD than do the home- or school-only cases, being different in degree rather than in kind. Research is clearly conflicting on the matter (Cohen & Minde, 1983; Rapoport, Donelly, Zametkin, & Carrougher, 1986; Schachar, Rutter, & Smith, 1981; Taylor, Sandberg, Thorley, & Giles, 1991). Considering that teacher information on children is not always obtainable or convenient to obtain and that diagnosis based on parents' reports will lead to a diagnosis based on teacher reports 90% of the time (Biederman, Keenan, & Faraone, 1990), parent reports may suffice for diagnostic purposes for now. Until more research is done to address this issue, the requirement of pervasiveness should probably go unheeded.

Despite these numerous problematic issues for the DSM approach to diagnosis, the criteria are actually some of the best ever advanced for the disorder and represent a vast improvement over the state of affairs that existed prior to 1980. The various editions of DSM also have spawned a large amount of research into ADHD, its symptoms, subtypes, criteria, and even etiologies that likely would not have occurred had such criteria not been set forth for professional consumption and criticism. The most recent criteria provide clinicians with a set of guidelines more specific, reliable, empirically based or justifiable, and closer to the scientific literature on ADHD than earlier editions.

ICD-10 Criteria

The criteria for hyperkinetic disorders from the *International Classification of Diseases* (ICD-10) are shown in Table 2.2 (World Health Organization, 1990). They resemble DSM-IV in stressing lists of symptoms related to inattention, overactivity, and impulsivity, and in requiring that pervasiveness across settings be demonstrated. The specific item contents, manner of presenting these symptom lists and allowance for office observation of the symptoms clearly differs from DSM-IV. Despite these differences, ICD criteria suffer from all of the same problematic issues raised above for DSM. Indeed, the specification that symptoms be present in two of three settings is likely to have the effect of reducing the prevalence rate to below 1% of the population (Lambert, Sandoval, & Sassone, 1978; Szatmari, Offord, & Boyle, 1989), well below the 3% to 5% often cited for ADHD (see "Prevalence" below). In addition, the requirement that the child not meet criteria for depression or anxiety disorders is also troubling. Evidence indicates that these disorders may overlap with ADHD (see "Comorbid Conditions" below) but that most ADHD children do not experience these disorders, nor do most children with these disorders have ADHD. Anxiety disorders, at least, appear to be transmitted independently of ADHD in families (Biederman, Faraone, Keenan, & Tsuang, 1991). Where they seem to overlap, it may result from both disorders being present in the family background of such children. This may not be so for depression where evidence suggests that the risk for depression increases the familial risk for ADHD and vice versa (Biederman, Faraone, & Lapey, 1992).

Like the DSM-IV, the ICD-10 sets no lower limit of IQ for the diagnosis of ADHD. Minimal research seems to exist that speaks to the issue of a discontinuity or qualitative shift in the nature of ADHD in individuals below IQs of 50. Some indirect evidence implies that this may occur, however. Rutter and colleagues (Rutter, Bolton, et al., 1990; Rutter, Macdonald, et al., 1990) have concluded that children who fall below this level of IQ may have a qualitatively different form of mental retardation. This is inferred from findings

TABLE 2.2. ICD-10 Criteria for Hyperkinetic Disorder

Note: The research diagnosis of hyperkinetic disorder requires the definite presence of abnormal levels of inattention, hyperactivity, and restlessness that are pervasive across situations and persistent over time and that are not caused by other disorders such as autism or affective disorders.

G1. *Inattention.* At least six of the following symptoms of inattention have persisted for at least 6 months, to a degree that is maladaptive and inconsistent with the developmental level of the child:

   (1) often fails to give close attention to details, or makes careless errors in schoolwork, work, or other activities;

   (2) often fails to sustain attention in tasks or play activities;

   (3) often appears not to listen to what is being said to him or her;

   (4) often fails to follow through on instructions or to finish schoolwork, chores, or duties in the workplace (not because of oppositional behaviour or failure to understand instructions);

   (5) is often impaired in organizing tasks and activities;

   (6) often avoids or strongly dislikes tasks, such as homework, that require sustained mental effort;

   (7) often loses things necessary for certain tasks or activities, such as school assignments, pencils, books, toys, or tools;

   (8) is often easily distracted by external stimuli;

   (9) is often forgetful in the course of daily activities.

G2. *Hyperactivity.* At least three of the following symptoms of hyperactivity have persisted for at least 6 months, to a degree that is maladaptive and inconsistent with the developmental level of the child:

   (1) often fidgets with hands or feet or squirms on seat;

   (2) leaves seat in classroom or in other situations in which remaining seated is expected;

   (3) often runs about or climbs excessively in situtions in which it is inappropriate (in adolescents or adults, only feelings of restlessness may be present);

   (4) is often unduly noisy in playing or has difficulty in engaging quietly in leisure activities;

   (5) exhibits a persistent pattern of excessive motor activity that is not substantially modified by social context or demands.

G3. *Impulsivity.* At least one of the following symptoms of impulsivity has persisted for at least 6 months, to a degree that is maladaptive and inconsistent with the developmental level of the child:

   (1) often blurts out answers before questions have been completed;

   (2) often fails to wait in lines or await turns in games or group situations;

   (3) often interrupts or intrudes on others (e.g. butts into others' conversations or games);

   (4) often talks excessively without appropriate response to social constraints.

G4. Onset of the disorder is no later than the age of 7 years.

G5. *Pervasiveness.* The criteria should be met for more than a single situation, e.g. the combination of inattention and hyperactivity should be present both at home and at school, or at both school and another setting where children are observed, such as a clinic. (Evidence for cross-situationality will ordinarily require information from more than one source; parental reports about classroom behaviour, for instance, are unlikely to be sufficient.)

G6. The symptoms in G1–G3 cause clinically significant distress or impairment in social, academic, or occupational functioning.

G7. The disorder does not meet the criteria for pervasive developmental disorders (F84.–), manic episode (F30.–), depressive episode (F32.–), or anxiety disorders (F41.–).

Note. From World Health Organization (1993, pp. 155–156). Copyright 1993 by the World Health Organization. Reprinted by permission.

that this group is overrepresented for its position along a normal distribution and from findings that genetic defects contribute more heavily to this subgroup. Given this shift in the prevalence and causes of mental retardation below this level of IQ, a similar state of affairs might exist for the form of ADHD associated with it necessitating its distinction from the type of ADHD that occurs in individuals above this IQ level. Consistent with such a view have been findings that the percent- age of positive responders to stimulant medica- tion in those with ADHD falls off sharply below this threshold of IQ (Demb, 1991).

Is ADHD a Mental Disorder?

Social critics (Kohn, 1989; Schrag & Divoky, 1975) have charged that professionals have been too quick to label energetic and exuberant chil- dren as having a mental disorder and that educa-

tors also may be using these labels as an excuse for simply poor educational environments. In other words, children who are hyperactive or ADHD are actually normal but are being labeled as mentally disordered because of parent and teacher intolerance (Kohn, 1989). If this were actually true, then we should find no differences of any cognitive, behavioral, or social significance between children so labeled and normal children. We should also find that being labeled as ADHD is not associated with any significant later risks in development for maladjustment within any domains of adaptive functioning, social, or school performance. Furthermore, research on potential etiologies for the disorder should, likewise, come up empty-handed. This is hardly the case. Differences between ADHD and normal children are numerous, as noted above. And, as will be shown later, numerous developmental risks await the child meeting clinical diagnostic criteria for the disorder, and certain potential etiological factors are becoming consistently noted in the research literature.

Conceding all of this, however, does not automatically entitle ADHD to be placed within the realm of mental disorders. Wakefield (1992) has argued that mental disorders must meet several criteria to be viewed as such: (1) engender substantial harm to the individual or those around him or her and (2) incur dysfunction of natural mental mechanisms that have been selected in an evolutionary sense (have survival value). It should become clear from the totality of information on ADHD presented here and elsewhere (Barkley, 1990; Hinshaw, 1994) that the disorder handily meets both criteria. Those with ADHD, as described in the theory above, have significant deficits in behavioral inhibition and the executive functions dependent upon it that are critical for effective self-regulation. And, those with ADHD experience significant and numerous risks for harm to themselves over development.

EPIDEMIOLOGY OF ADHD

Prevalence

Szatmari (1992) has recently reviewed the findings of six large epidemiological studies that identified cases of ADHD within these samples. The prevalences found in these studies ranged from a low of 2% to a high of 6.3% with most falling within the range of 4.2% to 6.3%. Other studies not reviewed by Szatmari have also found simi-

lar prevalence rates in elementary school-aged children ([5–6%] DuPaul, 1991; [3.3–6.4%] Lambert et al., 1978; [2.5–4%] Pelham, Gnagy, Greenslade, & Milich, 1992) or even higher ones ([14.3%] Trites, Dugas, Lynch, & Ferguson, 1979). The differences in prevalence rates are, at least in part, due to different methods of selecting these populations, to the nature of the populations themselves (nationality or ethnicity, urban vs. rural, etc.), to the criteria used to define a case of ADHD within them, and certainly to the age range of the samples. For instance, prevalence rates may be 2% to 3% in girls but 6% to 9% in boys during the 6- to 12-year-old age period (Szatmari et al., 1989) but fall to 1% to 2% in girls and 3% to 4.5% in boys by adolescence (Lewinsohn, Hops, Roberts, Seeley, & Andrews, 1993; McGee et al., 1990; Szatmari et al., 1989).

The use of significantly elevated cutoff scores on parent or teacher rating scales, alone, tends to result in higher prevalence estimates (as in the Trites et al., 1979, study) than when high scores on both are required or when clinical diagnostic criteria, such as those from DSM, are employed (as in the studies reviewed by Szatmari, 1992). For instance, Lambert et al. (1978) found that prevalence estimates declined from 3.3% to 6.4% to 1% or less when agreement on the presence of hyperactivity was required among parents, teachers, and physicians. In contrast, when only the endorsement of the presence of the behavior of hyperactivity (not the clinical disorder) is required from either parent or teacher rating scales, prevalence rates can run as high as 22% to 57% (Lapouse & Monk, 1958; McArdle, O'Brien, & Kolvin, 1995; Werry & Quay, 1971). This underscores the point made earlier that being described as inattentive or overactive by a parent or teacher does not in and of itself constitute a disorder in a child. Thus, it is easy to see that some of the earliest estimates of prevalence rates given for ADHD as being 20% or more were clearly based on very generous criteria defining a case. Additional criteria establishing severity, pervasiveness, and impairment as well as ruling out other conditions need to be applied, as in DSM or ICD criteria, before the presence of a true disorder can be established. When this is done, prevalence rates fall to the 3% to 6% level as described in DSM.

Szatmari et al. (1989) found that the prevalence of ADHD in a large sample of children from Ontario, Canada also varied as a function of young age, male gender, chronic health problems, family dysfunction, low socioeconomic status, pres-

ence of a developmental impairment, and urban living. Others have found similar conditions associated with the risk for ADHD (Velez, Johnson, & Cohen, 1989). Important, however, was the additional finding in the Szatmari et al. (1989) study that when comorbidity with other disorders was statistically controlled in the analyses, gender, family dysfunction, and low socioeconomic status were no longer significantly associated with occurrence of the disorder. Health problems, developmental impairment, young age, and urban living remained significantly associated with the occurrence of the disorder.

As noted above in discussing DSM criteria, it may be that the declining prevalence of ADHD with age is partly or wholly artifactual. This could possibly result from the use of items in the diagnostic symptom lists that are chiefly applicable to young children. These items may reflect the underlying construct(s) of ADHD very well at younger ages but may be increasingly less applicable to ever-older age groups. This could create a situation where individuals remain impaired in the construct(s) comprising ADHD as they mature while outgrowing the symptom list for the disorder, resulting in an illusory decline in prevalence as was noted in the example above using mental retardation. Until more age-appropriate symptoms are studied for adolescent and adult populations, this issue remains unresolved.

Gender Differences

As noted above, gender appears to play a significant role in determining prevalence of ADHD within a population. On average, male children are between 2.5 and 5.6 times more likely than female children to be defined or diagnosed as having ADHD within epidemiological samples of children, with the average being roughly 3:1 (Lewinsohn et al., 1993; McGee et al., 1990; Szatmari, 1992). Within clinic-referred samples, the sex ratio can rise to 6:1 to 9:1 (Ross & Ross, 1982), suggesting that boys with ADHD are far more likely to be referred to clinics than girls, especially if they have a comorbid oppositional or conduct disorder. It is unclear at this time why boys should be more likely to have ADHD than girls. This could be an artifact of the common finding that male individuals are more aggressive and oppositional, and, because such behavior is often associated with ADHD, male individuals are also found to be more likely to have ADHD as well. The finding of Szatmari (1992) that gen-

der was no longer associated with the occurrence of ADHD once other comorbid conditions were controlled for in their statistical analyses implies that this may be the case. It could also be an artifact of applying a set of diagnostic criteria developed primarily on male subjects to female subjects. Male subjects may demonstrate more of the behaviors typical of ADHD than female. Using a predominantly male distribution to set diagnostic criteria could create a higher threshold for diagnosis for female subjects relative to other female populations than for male subjects relative to other male populations, as noted earlier in discussing DSM.

Socioeconomic Differences

Few studies have examined the relationship of ADHD to social class, and those that have are not especially consistent. Lambert et al. (1978) found only slight differences in the prevalence of hyperactivity across social class when parent, teacher, and physician all agreed on the diagnosis. However, social class differences in prevalence did arise when only two of these three sources had to agree, with there generally being more ADHD children in lower than higher social classes. For instance, when parent and teacher agreement (but not physician) was required, 18% of those identified as hyperactive were in the high social class, 36% in the middle, and 45% in the low social class. Where only the teacher's opinion was used, the percentages were 17%, 41%, and 41%, respectively. Likewise, Trites (1979) also found the prevalence of hyperactivity, as defined by a threshold on a teacher rating scale, to vary as a function of neighborhood and social class. As noted earlier, Szatmari (1992) found in his review that rates of ADHD tended to increase with lower socioeconomic status. However, in his own study (Szatmari et al., 1989), it was found that psychosocial variables, such as low socioeconomic status, were no longer associated with rates of ADHD when other comorbid conditions, such as conduct disorder, were controlled. For now, it is clear that ADHD occurs across all socioeconomic levels. Where differences in prevalence rates are found across levels of social class, they may be artifacts of the source used to define the disorder or of the comorbidity of ADHD with other disorders known to be related to social class, such as aggression and conduct disorder. Certainly, no one has made the argument that the nature or qualitative aspects of ADHD differ across social classes.

Ethnic/Cultural/National Issues

Early studies of the prevalence of hyperactivity, relying principally on teacher ratings, found significant disparities across four countries (United States, Germany, Canada, and New Zealand), ranging from 2% in girls and 9% in boys in the United States to 9% in girls and 22% in boys in New Zealand (Trites et al., 1979). Similarly, O'Leary, Vivian, and Nisi (1985) found rates of hyperactivity to be 3% in girls and 20% in boys in Italy using this same teacher rating scale and cutoff score. However, this may have resulted from the use of a threshold established on norms collected in the United States across these other countries, where the distributions were quite different from those found in the United States.

Among a Japanese sample (Kanbayashi, Nakata, Fujii, Kita, & Wada, 1994) using parent ratings of items from DSM-III-R, a prevalence rate of 7.7% of the sample was found, with rates falling from approximately 13% in boys in the age range of 4 to 9 years to 5.5% in the 10- to 12-year age group. For girls, rates were 7.9% for the 4- to 6-year-old group declining to 2.5% and 2.3% in the 7- to 9-year and 10- to 12-year-old age groups, respectively. Baumgartel (1994) used teacher ratings of DSM-III, DSM-III-R, and DSM-IV symptom lists in a large sample of German elementary school children and found rates of 4.8% for ADHD-C, 3.9% for ADHD-PHI, and 9% for ADHD-PI subtypes based on DSM-IV. Of those meeting criteria for ADHD on the earlier DSM item lists, 95% met criteria for the disorder using the more recent DSM-IV list. The remaining 5% who did not were mainly the ADHD-PI subtype for whom the earlier DSM provided little guidance for diagnosis. In India, among over 1,000 children screened at a pediatric clinic, 5.2% of children ages 3 to 4 years were found to have ADHD by DSM-III-R criteria, whereas the rate rose to over 29% for ages 11 to 12 years (Bhatia, Nigam, Bohra, & Malik, 1991). The male:female ratio was 4:1 within this sample. Problematic in this study, however, is the fact that it is not a true epidemiological sample. Differences in prevalence across ages could simply reflect cohort effects—children are referred to this clinic for different reasons at different ages.

An issue that must be kept in mind in such cross-cultural studies is that cultural differences in the interpretations given by teachers or parents for the same items may exist. People of different cultures interpret these items differently and may have different expectations for child behavior than in other cultures or countries. Also, most of these studies used teacher or parent ratings rather than clinical diagnostic criteria. As already noted above, prevalence rates of hyperactivity or ADHD are typically higher when simply a threshold on a rating scale is the only criteria for establishing a case of the disorder. Where clinical criteria are employed, rates are more conservative. Differences in prevalence across countries may also simply be an artifact of the different diagnostic practices employed within each (Pendergrast et al., 1988). Nevertheless, these studies show that hyperactivity or ADHD is present in all countries studied so far. Although it may not receive the same diagnostic label in each country, the behavior pattern comprising the disorder appears to be present internationally.

Differences among ethnic groups in rates of hyperactivity within the United States have been reported. Langsdorf, Anderson, Walchter, Madrigal, and Juarez (1979) reported that almost 25% of African-American children and 8% of Latino-Americans met a cutoff score on a teacher rating scale commonly used to define hyperactivity, whereas Ullmann (cited in O'Leary et al., 1985) reported rates of 24% for African-American children and 16% of white Americans on a teacher rating scale. Lambert et al. (1978) found higher rates of hyperactivity among African-American than white American children only when the teachers were the only ones reporting the diagnosis; Latino-American children were not found to differ from white American children in this respect. Such differences, however, may arise in part because of socioeconomic factors that are differentially associated with these ethnic groups in the United States. Such psychosocial factors are strongly correlated with aggression and conduct problems. And, as noted above, such psychosocial factors no longer make a significant contribution to the prevalence of ADHD when comorbidity for other disorders is controlled (Szatmari, 1992). Doing the same within studies of ethnic differences might well reduce or eliminate these differences in prevalence among them. Thus, it would seem that ADHD arises in all ethnic groups studied so far. Whether the differences in prevalence among these ethnic groups are real or are a function of the source of information about the symptoms of ADHD and, possibly, socioeconomic factors remains to be determined.

DEVELOPMENTAL COURSE AND ADULT OUTCOMES

Major follow-up studies of clinically referred hyperactive children have been ongoing during the last 25 years at five sites: (1) Montreal (Weiss & Hechtman, 1993), (2) New York City (Gittelman, Mannuzza, Shenker, & Bonagura, 1985; Mannuzza, Gittelman-Klein, Bessler, Malloy, & Lapadulo, 1993), (3) Iowa City (Loney, Kramer, & Milich, 1981), (4) Los Angeles (Satterfield, Hoppe, & Schell, 1982), and (5) Milwaukee (Barkley, Fischer, et al., 1990). Follow-up studies of children identified as hyperactive during epidemiological screenings of general populations have also been conducted in the United States (Lambert, 1988), New Zealand (McGee, Williams, & Silva, 1984; Moffitt, 1990), and England (Taylor et al., 1991), among others.

But before embarking on a summary of their results and inferring from these the developmental course likely to occur in children with ADHD, some cautionary notes are in order. First, the limited number of follow-up studies in existence do not permit a great deal of certainty to be placed in the specificity of the types and degrees of outcomes likely to be effected by ADHD. Even so, more can likely be said about the outcomes of ADHD children than about most other childhood mental disorders. Second, the discontinuities of measurement that exist in these follow-up studies between their different points of assessments of their subjects make straightforward conclusions about developmental course difficult. Third, the differing sources of subjects greatly affect the outcomes to be found, with subjects drawn from clinic-referred populations having two to three times the occurrence of some negative outcomes and more diverse negative outcomes than those drawn from population screens (i.e., Barkley, Fischer, et al., 1990, vs. Lambert, 1988). Fourth, the entry/diagnostic criteria used in each of the major follow-up studies must be kept in mind in interpreting their outcomes and cross-referencing them with those from other sites using very different criteria. Most studies selected for children known at the time as "hyperactive." Such children are most likely representative of the course of the ADHD-PHI or ADHD-C Types from the current DSM taxonomy. Even then, the degree of deviance of the samples on parent and teacher ratings of these symptoms was not established at the entry point in a few of these studies. These studies also cannot be viewed as representing the ADHD-PI subtype, for which no follow-up information is currently available. And fifth, the screening out of subjects with certain comorbid conditions at entry in some studies can substantially affect the findings at the outcome points among the different follow-up projects. The descriptions of clinic-referred ADHD children who are of similar age groups to those in the follow-up studies but who are not followed over time may help understand the risks associated with different points in development. However, these may also be contaminated by cohort effects at the time of referral and so can only be viewed as suggestive. Research by my colleagues and me with ADHD adolescents implies that such cohort effects may be minor; that is, adolescents with ADHD referred to clinics seem to have similar types and degrees of impairment as ADHD children followed up to adolescence (Barkley, Anastopoulos, Guevremont, & Fletcher, 1991; Barkley, Fischer, et al., 1990). In painting the picture of the developmental outcome of ADHD, then, broad strokes are permissible but the finer details await more and better-refined studies. I concentrate here on the course of the disorder itself, returning to the comorbid disorders and associated conditions likely to arise in the course of ADHD in a later section of this chapter ("Comorbid Psychiatric Disorders").

The onset of ADHD symptoms, as noted earlier, is often in the preschool years, typically at ages 3 to 4 years (Barkley, DuPaul, & McMurray, 1990; Loeber et al., 1992; Taylor et al., 1991) and, more generally, by entry into formal schooling. First to arise, also noted earlier, is the pattern of hyperactive–impulsive behavior and, in some cases, oppositional and aggressive conduct. Preschool-aged children with significant degrees of inattentive and hyperactive behavior who are difficult to manage for their parents or teachers and whose pattern of such behavior is persistent for at least a year or more are highly likely to have ADHD and to remain so into elementary school years (Beitchman et al., 1987; Campbell, 1990; Palfrey et al., 1985). This is especially likely to occur where difficulties characterized by conflict, greater maternal directiveness and negativity, and greater child defiant behavior exist in the parent–child interactions of such children (Campbell, March, Pierce, & Ewing, 1991; Richman, Stevenson, & Graham, 1982). More negative temperament and greater emotional reactivity to events are also more common in preschool ADHD children (Barkley, DuPaul, & McMurray, 1990; Campbell, 1990). It is little wonder that greater parenting stress is associated with preschool

ADHD children and seems to be at its highest relative to later age groups (Mash & Johnston, 1983a, 1983b). Within the preschool setting, ADHD children will be found to be more often out of their seats, wandering the classroom, being excessively talkative and vocally noisy, and disruptive of other children's activities (Campbell, Schleifer, & Weiss, 1978; Schleifer et al., 1975).

By the time ADHD children move into the elementary-age range of 6 to 12 years, the problems with hyperactive–impulsive behavior are likely to continue and to be joined now by difficulties with goal-directed persistence (sustained attention). As discussed earlier, the symptoms of inattention appear to arise by 5 to 7 years of age (Loeber et al., 1992; Hart et al., in press) and, in my opinion, emerge out of the increasing difficulties ADHD children are having with self-regulation and especially such self-regulation relative to time. Difficulties with work completion and productivity, distraction, forgetfulness related to doing, lack of planfulness, poor organization of work activities, trouble meeting deadlines associated with home chores, school assignments, and social promises or commitments to peers are now combined with the impulsive, heedless, and disinhibited behavior typifying these children since preschool age. Thus, it is highly likely that the preschool children with the ADHD-PHI subtype will move into the combined type as the problems with sustained attention/persistence come to the fore. Some research suggests that the level of hyperactive–impulsive behavior will decline across these school years, whereas that for inattention remains stable (Hart et al., in press). As suggested earlier, though, this may be an artifact of the items used to assess such behavior across this age range, whereas the larger class of developmentally relevant inhibitory and self-regulatory behaviors remain relatively undiminished.

It also seems to be during these early school-age years that problems with oppositional and socially aggressive behavior may develop in at least 40% to 70% of ADHD children (Barkley, 1990; Loeber et al., 1992; Taylor et al., 1991). By ages 8 to 12 years, these early forms of defiant and hostile behavior may evolve further into symptoms of conduct disorder in up to half of all children with ADHD (Barkley, Fischer, et al., 1990; Loeber et al., 1992; Taylor et al., 1991).

Certainly by now (ages 6 to 12 years) all of the deficits in the executive functions related to inhibition in the model presented earlier are likely to be arising and interfering with adequate self-regulation for age (Barkley, 1997). Not surprisingly, the overall adaptive functioning of ADHD children (Stein, Szumowski, Blondis, & Roizen, 1995) and adolescents (M. A. Stein, personal communication, February 1995) is falling significantly below their intellectual ability as the disorder takes its toll on self-care, personal responsibility, chore performance, trustworthiness, independence, appropriate social skills, and timeliness, specifically, and moral conduct generally (Koplowitz & Barkley, 1996; Pelham & Bender, 1982; Hinshaw et al., 1993).

If ADHD is present in clinic-referred children, the likelihood is that 50% to 80% will continue to have their disorder into adolescence (Barkley, Fischer, et al., 1990; Mannuzza & Klein, 1992). Using the same parent rating scales at both the childhood and adolescent evaluation points, Fischer et al. (1993a) were able to show that both hyperactive and control children demonstrated significant declines by adolescence on the Attention Problems scale of the CBC, the hyperactivity–impulsivity factor of the Conners Parent Rating Scale, and the number of problem settings and mean severity scores from the Home Situations Questionnaire, a measure of the pervasiveness of behavior problems at home. Moreover, the hyperactive group showed a far more marked decline than the control group on each of these scales, mainly because the former were so far from the mean of the normative group to begin with in childhood. Nevertheless, even at adolescence, the groups were still significantly different on these scales with the mean for the hyperactives remaining two standard deviations or more above the mean for the controls. This emphasizes the point made earlier that simply because severity levels of symptoms are declining over development does not mean hyperactive children are necessarily outgrowing their disorder relative to normal children; like mental retardation, the disorder of ADHD is defined by a developmentally relative deficiency, rather than an absolute one, that persists in most children over time.

The persistence of ADHD symptoms across childhood as well as into early adolescence appears, again, to be associated with initial degree of hyperactive–impulsive behavior in childhood, the coexistence of conduct problems or oppositional hostile behavior, poor family relations and specifically conflict in parent–child interactions, as well as maternal depression, and duration of mental health interventions (Fischer et al., 1993b; Taylor et al., 1991). These predictors have also been associated with the development and persistence of oppositional and conduct disorder into

this age range (12–17 years; Fischer et al., 1993b; Loeber, 1990; Mannuzza & Klein, 1992; Taylor et al., 1991).

Four of the sites in North America following clinic-referred children have been able to conduct evaluations of their subjects at adult outcome, but only two have reported their findings as yet (Montreal and New York City). The Milwaukee study by my colleagues and me will be completed within the year, and, hopefully, the Iowa City study will report its outcomes soon as well. Unfortunately, the Montreal study did not use any instruments evaluating DSM criteria at their adult follow-up, and so a direct estimate of the percentage continuing to be ADHD is not available from this study. The investigators of that study estimated, however, that at least half of their subjects were still impaired by some symptoms of their disorder in adulthood.

The New York City studies have used DSM-based criteria at their outcome points; but even here, it is difficult to determine precisely what percentage of children with ADHD continue to display the disorder into adulthood. This results, in part, from the fact that the criteria for diagnosing ADHD used now were not available at the time these subjects entered their respective studies, and so the percentage having the disorder at study entry cannot be directly determined. Accepting, for the moment that most children entering the study for hyperactivity would have been classified as ADHD at that time, then the New York City study suggests that 11% of hyperactive children continue to have ADHD into adulthood (Mannuzza & Klein, 1992).

Before rushing to proclaim that nearly 90% of clinic-referred hyperactive children will outgrow their disorder (ADHD), however, we must be cautious for several reasons: (1) This is a single study that deserves replication in the other ongoing follow-up studies to determine the generality of its findings. (2) The degree of deviance of the subjects at study entry using rating scales for the first cohort had to be determined by the subjective judgement of one of the investigators as norms for the rating scales were not yet available. (3) The investigators switched from using parent reports to determine presence of disorder in adolescence to using self-reports of symptoms in adulthood; a switch that may potentially underestimate the adult prevalence. (4) Children with conduct disorders were excluded from the study at entry, which can effectively eliminate up to half of all potentially eligible hyperactive children; these may represent the

more severe degrees of the disorder, and they likely represent the most persistent form, as noted above. (5) The application of DSM thresholds for diagnosis of adults is not appropriate as it sets too high a threshold for most adults to meet given that it was based on children (see discussion of DSM criteria above). (6) The content of most of the DSM items is probably not optimal for capturing the nature of ADHD (disinhibition and poor self-regulation) as it affects adult behavior. Thus, the results of the New York City study probably represent the best outcomes for hyperactive children one can expect and probably are underestimates of the real persistence of the disorder into adulthood.

This can be seen in comparing the adolescent outcomes for this study to our own Milwaukee study. The New York study found less than 50% of their subjects met criteria currently for ADHD in adolescence, whereas over 71% did so in the Milwaukee study (Barkley, Fischer, et al., 1990). More telling, however, was the fact that over 83% of the hyperactive subjects were still two standard deviations or more above the mean in the number of ADHD symptoms they currently displayed and thus still had the disorder—a finding supporting the point made earlier that applying childhood-based DSM criteria to adolescents and adults may be overly restrictive and lead to underestimates of the prevalence of the disorder at these ages. Furthermore, although not yet completed, the findings to date from the Milwaukee adult outcome evaluation indicate that the percentage remaining ADHD in adulthood in this sample will far exceed the prevalence found in the New York study. This probably results from the Milwaukee study using research diagnostic criteria (including the 98th percentile on parent rating scales) for defining subjects as hyperactive and not excluding children with conduct disorders at study entry. In conclusion, until more studies report adult outcomes for ADHD children using clinical diagnostic criteria appropriate for adults, the true persistence of the disorder into adulthood cannot be determined. At the very least, current research suggests it may be 30% to 50%, and likely higher among clinic-referred children followed to adulthood.

ASSOCIATED CONDITIONS

Individuals diagnosed with ADHD are often found to have a number of other conditions and impairments associated with the disorder. These are briefly described below.

Comorbid Psychiatric Disorders

Between 35% and 60% of clinic-referred children with ADHD will meet criteria for a diagnosis of ODD by 7 years of age or later and 30% to 50% will eventually meet criteria for CD (Barkley, 1990; Biederman et al., 1992). Perhaps 15% to 25% of clinic-referred children with ADHD will later qualify for a diagnosis of antisocial personality disorder (ASP) in adulthood (Biederman et al., 1992; Mannuzza & Klein, 1992; Weiss & Hechtman, 1993). Similar or only slightly lower degrees of overlap are noted in studies using epidemiologically identified samples rather than those referred to clinics. ADHD, therefore, has a strong association with antisocial disorders, such as ODD, CD, and ASP and has been found to be one of the most reliable early predictors of these disorders (Fischer et al., 1993b; Loeber, 1990; Mannuzza & Klein, 1992; Taylor et al., 1991). Familial associations among the disorders have also been found suggesting some common causal relationship among them (Biederman et al., 1992).

The overlap of anxiety disorders with ADHD has been found to be 25% to 40% in clinic-referred children (Biederman et al., 1992; Russo & Biedel, 1994; Tannock, in press). In longitudinal studies, however, the overlap of ADHD with anxiety disorders is reduced or nonexistent in adolescence (Russo & Biedel, 1994). This suggests that the two disorders may not be associated in any causal way. The association of anxiety disorders with ADHD has been shown to reduce the degree of impulsiveness relative to those ADHD children without anxiety disorders (Pliszka, 1992). Some research suggests that the disorders are transmitted independently in families and so are not linked to each other in any specific way (Biederman et al., 1991; Last, Hersen, Kazdin, Orvaschel, & Perrin, 1991). This may not be the case for the inattentive type of ADHD, where higher rates of anxiety disorders have been noted in these children (Russo & Biedel, 1994), though not always (Barkley, DuPaul, & McMurray, 1990), and in their first- and second-degree relatives (Barkley, DuPaul, & McMurray, 1990; Biederman et al., 1992) again, although not always (Lahey & Carlson, 1992). Regrettably, research on the overlap of anxiety disorders with ADHD has generally chosen to collapse across the types of anxiety disorders in evaluating this issue. Greater clarity and clinical utility from these findings might occur if the types of anxiety disorders present were to be examined separately.

The situation for ADHD and comorbid mood disorders is less clear. Studies exist that find no association, whereas other studies find as many as 75% of those with ADHD have a mood disorder (Biederman et al., 1992). Overall, the evidence suggests that there is some overlap, with perhaps as much as 40% to 50% of those with ADHD eventually developing a mood disorder of some form. Some evidence also suggests that these disorders may be related to each other in that familial risk for one increases the risk for the other (Biederman et al., 1991, 1992).

This does not seem to be the case for the comorbidity of bipolar (manic-depressive) disorder with ADHD (Carlson, 1990). Follow-up studies have not documented any significant increase in risk of bipolar disorder in children with ADHD followed into adulthood (Gittelman et al., 1985; Weiss & Hechtman, 1993), nor has an increased prevalence of bipolar disorder been noted among their biological relatives (Biederman et al., 1992; Lahey et al., 1988; Morrison & Stewart, 1973). In contrast, children and adolescents diagnosed as bipolar often have a significantly higher lifetime prevalence of ADHD, particularly in their earlier childhood years (Carlson, 1990; Strober et al., 1988). Recently, Biederman et al. (1995) found that nearly 60% of children diagnosed with prepubertal mania have abnormal scores (greater than two standard deviations above the mean) on the attention problems scale of the CBC. It is not clear if ADHD is actually present in such cases of bipolar disorder or if the high overlap with ADHD is partly or wholly an artifact of similar symptoms comprising the symptom lists used for both diagnoses (i.e., hyperactivity, distractibility, poor judgment, etc.). In any case, the overlap of ADHD with bipolar disorder appears to be unidirectional—a diagnosis of ADHD seems *not* to increase the risk for bipolar disorder, whereas a diagnosis of bipolar seems to elevate the risk of a prior or concurrent diagnosis of ADHD.

A similar state of affairs seems to exist for the comorbidity of tic disorders and Tourette syndrome (TS) with ADHD (see Evans et al., Chapter 12, this volume). That is, a diagnosis of ADHD does not appear to elevate the risk for a diagnosis of TS. However, among individuals with TS, an average of 48% may qualify for a diagnosis of ADHD (range 35–71%; Comings & Comings, 1988). Complicating matters is the fact that the onset of ADHD often seems to precede that of TS in cases of comorbidity (Comings & Comings, 1988). Yet Pauls et al. (1986) have shown that TS

and ADHD occur independently among relatives of each disorder, suggesting that a Berkson's bias (comorbidity with ADHD leads to clinic referral) may be operating in clinical referrals for TS.

Associated Problems with Academic Functioning

The vast majority of clinic-referred children with ADHD have difficulties with school performance, most often underproductivity of their work. ADHD children are often found to score below normal or control groups of children on standardized achievement tests (Barkley, DuPaul, & McMurray, 1990; Cantwell & Satterfield, 1978; Fischer et al., 1990). Surprisingly, however, these differences are likely to be found even in preschool-age children with ADHD (Mariani & Barkley, 1995), suggesting that the disorder may take a toll on the acquisition of academic skills and knowledge even before entry into first grade. This makes sense given that some of the executive functions believed to be disrupted by ADHD in the model presented earlier are also likely to be involved in some forms of academic achievement (i.e., working memory and mental arithmetic or spelling; internalized speech and reading comprehension; verbal fluency and oral narratives and written reports, etc.).

Between 19% and 26% of children with ADHD are likely to have at least one type of learning disability, conservatively defined as a significant delay in reading, arithmetic, or spelling relative to intelligence and achievement in one of these three areas at or below the 7th percentile (Barkley, 1990). If defined as simply a significant discrepancy between intelligence and achievement, then up to 53% of hyperactive children could be said to have a learning disability (Lambert & Sandoval, 1980). Or, if the criterion of simply two grades below grade level is used, then as many as 80% of ADHD children in late childhood (age 11 years) may have learning disorders (Cantwell & Baker, 1992). The finding that children with ADHD are more likely to have learning disabilities (Gross-Tsur, Shalev, & Amir, 1991) implies a possible genetic link between the two disorders. However, more recent research (Faraone et al., 1993; Gilger, Pennington, & DeFries, 1992) shows that the two disorders are transmitted independently in families, although some subtypes of reading disorders associated with ADHD may share a common genetic etiology (Gilger et al., 1992). This is consistent with research suggesting that early ADHD may predispose children toward certain types of reading problems, whereas early reading problems do not generally give rise to later symptoms of ADHD (Wood & Felton, 1994). The picture is less clear for spelling disorders, where a common or shared genetic etiology to both ADHD and spelling disorder has been shown in a joint analysis of twin samples from London and Colorado (Stevenson, Pennington, Gilger, DeFries, & Gillis, 1993). This may result from the fact that early spelling ability seems to be linked to the integrity of working memory (Mariani & Barkley, 1995; Levy & Hobbes, 1989) which has been demonstrated to be dependent on intact inhibitory processes (see theoretical model above).

A higher prevalence of speech and language disorders has also been documented in many studies of ADHD children typically ranging from 30% to 64% of the samples (Gross-Tsur et al., 1991; Hartsough & Lambert, 1985; Humphries, Koltun, Malone, & Roberts, 1994; Szatmari et al., 1989; Taylor et al., 1991). The converse is also true; children with speech and language disorders have a higher than expected prevalence of ADHD (approximately 30–58%), among other psychiatric disorders (Baker, Cantwell, & Mattison, 1980; Beitchman, Nair, Clegg, Ferguson, & Patel, 1986; Beitchman, Hood, Rochon, & Peterson, 1989; Beitchman, Hood, & Inglis, 1990). The link between ADHD and language disorders is not unexpected given the theoretical model presented earlier that hypothesizes a link between inhibitory problems in ADHD and the internalization of language as well as with motor control/fluency. And, although not well-documented, many clinical anecdotes have noted an association between ADHD and poor handwriting, consistent with the previously noted risk for motor coordination/fluency problems in children with ADHD. It is not surprising, then, that as many as 40% of children with ADHD have received some form of special educational assistance by adolescence, with 25% to 35% or more having been retained in grade at least once, 10% to 25% having been expelled, and between 10% and 35% never completing high school (Fischer et al., 1990; Weiss & Hechtman, 1993).

ADHD and Intelligence

As noted earlier, the inhibitory processes and the executive functions linked to them in the model

presented above could be expected to result in a small but significant relationship between ADHD and intelligence quotient (IQ), particularly verbal IQ. This is because the latter is likely to be related to working memory, internalized speech, and the eventual development of verbal thought. Studies using both normal samples (Hinshaw, Morrison, Carte, & Cornsweet, 1987; McGee, Williams, & Silva, 1984) and behavior-problem samples (Sonuga-Barke, Lamparelli, Stevenson, Thompson, & Henry, 1994) have found significant negative associations between degree of rated hyperactive–impulsive behavior and measures of intelligence. In contrast, associations between ratings of conduct problems and intelligence in children are often much smaller or even nonsignificant, particularly when hyperactive–impulsive behavior is partialed out of the relationship (Hinshaw et al., 1987; Lynam, Moffitt, & Stouthamer-Loeber, 1993; Sonuga-Barke et al., 1994). This implies that the relationship between IQ and disruptive behavior in children is relatively specific to the hyperactive–impulsive element of the disruptive behavior disorders (see Hinshaw, 1992, for a review).

When samples of hyperactive or ADHD children are selected for study without specifically equating groups for IQ, such studies often find these children to differ significantly from control groups in their intelligence, particularly verbal intelligence (Barkley, Karlsson, & Pollard, 1985; Mariani & Barkley, 1995; McGee et al., 1992; Moffitt, 1990; Stewart, Pitts, Craig, & Dieruf, 1966; Werry et al., 1987). Given that several of the subtests from intelligence tests, such as on the Wechsler Intelligence Scale for Children-III (WISC-III), are partly assessing working memory (mental arithmetic, digit span, etc.), it should not be surprising in view of the above theoretical model that ADHD is associated with decreased performance on these particular subtests (Anastopoulos, Spisto, & Maher, 1994; Lufi, Cohen, & Parrish-Plass, 1990). Differences in IQ have also been found between hyperactive boys and their normal siblings (Halperin & Gittelman, 1982; Tarver-Behring, Barkley, & Karlsson, 1985; Welner, Welner, Stewart, Palkes, & Wish, 1977). All of this suggests that impulsive–hyperactive behavior generally, and ADHD specifically, has an inherent association with diminished IQ, particularly verbal IQ (Halperin & Gittelman, 1982; Hinshaw, 1992; McGee et al., 1992; Sonuga-Barke et al., 1994; Werry et al., 1987). This small but significant relationship implies

that between 3% and 10% of the variance in IQ may be a function of symptoms of ADHD (hyperactive–impulsive behavior). As noted earlier, however, the far greater impact of ADHD seems to be on the children's application of their intelligence in day-to-day adaptive functioning (Stein et al., 1995).

Coexisting Social Problems

ADHD is classified in DSM-IV as a disruptive behavior disorder because of the significant difficulties it creates for children in disrupting their social conduct and general social adjustment. The interpersonal behaviors of those with ADHD, as noted earlier, are often characterized as more impulsive, intrusive, excessive, disorganized, engaging, aggressive, intense, and emotional. And so they are "disruptive" of the smoothness of the ongoing stream of social interactions, reciprocity, and cooperation that may constitute the children's daily life with others (Whalen & Henker, 1992). This makes sense given the theoretical model presented above; ADHD is associated with an impairment in self-regulation, and this impairment must radiate into the social ecology of these children, affecting others and the manner in which they may reciprocate.

Research finds that ADHD affects the interactions of children with their parents and, hence, the manner in which parents may respond to these children. Those with ADHD are more talkative, negative and defiant, less compliant and cooperative, more demanding of assistance from others, and less able to play and work independently of their mothers (Barkley, 1985; Danforth et al., 1991; Gomez & Sanson, 1994; Mash & Johnston, 1982). Their mothers are less responsive to the questions of their children, more negative and directive, and less rewarding of their children's behavior (Danforth et al., 1991). Mothers of ADHD children have been shown to give both more commands as well as more rewards to their ADHD sons than daughters (Barkley, 1989b; Befera & Barkley, 1984) but also to be more emotional and acrimonious in their interactions with their sons (Buhrmester, Camparo, Christensen, Gonzalez, & Hinshaw, 1992; Taylor et al., 1991). ADHD children seem to be somewhat less problematic for their fathers than their mothers (Buhrmester et al., 1992; Tallmadge & Barkley, 1983), but even the latter interactions are different from those of normal father–child dyads. Research has shown that

these mother–child conflicts may result in increased father–child conflict when mothers and fathers interact jointly (triadically) with their hyperactive children, especially in hyperactive boys (Buhrmester et al., 1992). Such increased maternal negativity and acrimony toward sons in these interactions has been shown to predict greater noncompliance in classroom and play settings and greater covert stealing away from home, even when the level of the child's own negativity and parental psychopathology are statistically controlled in the analyses (Anderson et al., 1994). These negative parent–child interaction patterns occur in the preschool age group (Cohen, Sullivan, Minde, Novak, & Keens, 1983) and may be at their most negative and stressful (to the parent) in this age range (Mash & Johnston, 1982, 1990). With increasing age, the degree of conflict in these interactions lessens but remains deviant from normal into later childhood (Barkley, Karlsson, & Pollard, 1985; Mash & Johnston, 1982) and adolescence (Barkley, Anastopoulos, Guevremont, & Fletcher, 1992; Barkley, Fischer, et al., 1991). Negative parent–child interactions in childhood have been observed to be significantly predictive of continuing parent–child conflicts 8 to 10 years later in adolescence in families with ADHD children (Barkley, Fischer, et al., 1991). Few differences are noted between the interactions of mothers of ADHD children with those children as compared to their interactions with the siblings of the ADHD children (Tarver-Behring et al., 1985).

Important in this line of family research has been the discovery that *it is the presence of comorbid ODD that is associated with most of the interaction conflicts* noted in the mother–child interactions of ADHD children and adolescents (Barkley, Anastopoulos, et al., 1992; Barkley, Fischer, et al., 1992). In a sequential analysis of these parent–teen interaction sequences, investigators have noted that it is the immediate or first lag in the sequence that is most important in determining the behavior of the other member of the dyad (Fletcher, Fischer, Barkley, & Smallish, in press). That is, the behavior of each member is determined mainly by the immediately preceding behavior of the other member and not by earlier behaviors of either member in the chain of interactions. The interactions of the comorbid ADHD/ODD group reflected a strategy best characterized as "tit for tat" in that the type of behavior (positive, neutral, or negative) of each member was most influenced by the same type

of behavior emitted immediately preceding it. Mothers of ADHD only and normal teens were more likely to utilize positive and neutral behaviors regardless of the immediately preceding behavior of their teens, characterized as a "be nice and forgive" strategy that is thought to be more mature and more socially successful for both parties in the long run (Fletcher et al., in press). Even so, those with ADHD alone are still found to be deviant from normal in these interaction patterns even though less so than the comorbid ADHD/ODD group. The presence of comorbid ODD has also been shown to be associated with greater maternal stress and psychopathology as well as marital difficulties (Barkley, Anastopoulos, et al., 1992; Barkley, Fischer, et al., 1992).

These interaction conflicts in families with ADHD children are not limited to just parent–child interactions. Increased conflicts have been observed between ADHD children and their siblings relative to normal child–sibling dyads (Mash & Johnston, 1983a; Taylor et al., 1991). Research on the larger domain of family functioning has shown that families of ADHD children experience more parenting stress and decreased sense of parenting competence (Fischer, 1990; Mash & Johnston, 1990), increased alcohol consumption in parents (Cunningham, Benness, & Siegel, 1988; Pelham & Lang, 1993), decreased extended family contacts (Cunningham et al., 1988), and increased marital conflict, separations, and divorce as well as maternal depression in parents of ADHD children (Befera & Barkley, 1984; Cunningham et al., 1988; Barkley, Fischer, et al., 1990; Lahey et al., 1988; Taylor et al., 1991). Again, it is the comorbid association of ADHD with ODD, or its later stage of conduct disorder, that is linked to even greater degrees of parental psychopathology, marital discord, and divorce than in ADHD only children (Barkley, Fischer, et al., 1990, 1991; Lahey et al., 1988; Taylor et al., 1991). Interestingly, Pelham and Lang (1993) have shown that the increased alcohol consumption in these parents is, in part, directly a function of the stressful interactions they have with their ADHD children.

Research has demonstrated that the primary direction of effects within these interactions is from child to parent (Fischer, 1990; Mash & Johnston, 1990) rather than the reverse. That is, much of the disturbance in the interaction seems to stem from the effects of the child's excessive, impulsive, unruly, noncompliant, and emotional behavior on the parent rather than from the

effects of the parent's behavior on the child. This was documented primarily through studies that evaluated the effects of stimulant medication on the behavior of the children and their interaction patterns with their mothers. Such research found that medication improves the compliance of those with ADHD and reduces their negative, talkative, and generally excessive behavior such that their parents reduce their levels of directive and negative behavior as well (Barkley & Cunningham, 1979b; Barkley et al., 1983; Danforth et al., 1991; Humphries, Kinsbourne, & Swanson, 1978). These effects of medication are noted even in the preschool-aged group of children with ADHD (Barkley, 1988) as well as in those in late childhood (Barkley, Karlsson, Pollard, & Murphy, 1985), and in both sexes of ADHD children (Barkley, 1989b). Besides a general reduction in the negative, disruptive, and conflictual interaction patterns of these children with parents resulting from stimulant medication, general family functioning also seems to improve when ADHD children are treated with stimulant medication (Schachar, Taylor, Weiselberg, Thorley, & Rutter, 1987).

These patterns of disruptive, intrusive, excessive, negative, and emotional social interactions of ADHD children have been found to occur in their interactions with teachers (Whalen, Henker, & Dotemoto, 1980) and peers (Clark, Cheyne, Cunningham, & Siegel, 1988; Cunningham & Siegel, 1987; Whalen, Henker, Collins, McAuliffe, & Vaux, 1979). It should come as no surprise, then, that those with ADHD are less liked by other children and have fewer friends as a consequence (Pelham & Bender, 1982). Once more, stimulant medication has been observed to decrease these negative and disruptive behaviors toward teachers (Whalen et al., 1980) and peers (Cunningham, Siegel, & Offord, 1985; Wallander, Schroeder, Michelli, & Gualtieri, 1987; Whalen et al., 1987) but may not result in any increase in more prosocial or positive initiatives toward peers (Wallander et al., 1987).

Medical Risks

What little research exists on the subject suggests that children with ADHD may be more prone to difficulties with their health, difficulties that may even begin prenatally. Mothers of hyperactive children reported a greater incidence of their own health and pre- and perinatal problems during their pregnancies with these children than did mothers of nonhyperactive children (Hartsough & Lambert, 1985). But others (Barkley, DuPaul, & McMurray, 1990; Gross-Tsur et al., 1991; Taylor et al., 1991) have not replicated such findings. The study by Gross-Tsur et al. (1991) did, however, find a significant association between intrauterine growth retardation and ADHD. One explanation for these inconsistencies across studies may rest in the results of a recent study showing that perinatal complications were significantly elevated only among the subgroup of ADHD children whose disorder appears to be nonfamilial or nongenetic, whereas cases of familial ADHD show no significant elevations in number of complications (Sprick-Buckminster, Biederman, Milberger, Faraone, & Lehman, 1993).

The postnatal course of those with hyperactivity has been shown to be subject to more stress and complications in several studies (Hartsough & Lambert, 1985; Stewart et al., 1966; Taylor et al., 1991). *Chronic health problems,* such as recurring upper respiratory infections, asthma, and allergies, have also been documented in the later preschool and childhood years of hyperactive children (Hartsough & Lambert, 1985; Mitchell, Aman, Turbott, & Manku, 1987; Szatmari et al., 1989). And, children with atopic (allergic) disorders have been shown to have more symptoms of ADHD (Roth, Beyreiss, Schlenzka, & Beyer, 1991). Yet, more careful research using better control groups, longitudinal samples, or analysis of the familial aggregation of disorders has not shown a specific association of these disorders with hyperactivity (Biederman, Milberger, Faraone, Guite, & Warburton, 1994; McGee, Stanton, & Sears, 1993; Mitchell et al., 1987; Taylor et al., 1991).

Accident proneness has also been documented in several studies of ADHD children with up to 46% being so described and 15% having had at least four or more serious injuries from these accidents (Hartsough & Lambert, 1985; Mitchell et al., 1987; Taylor et al., 1991). For instance, Stewart, Thach, and Freidin (1970) found that nearly 21% of hyperactive children had experienced at least one accidental poisoning versus only 8% of control children. Furthermore, research on children experiencing accidents suggests they are more likely to be overactive, impulsive, and defiant (Cataldo et al., 1992; Rosen & Peterson, 1990; Stewart et al., 1970). Pless, Taylor, and Arsenault (1995) found that children injured as pedestrians or bike riders in traffic accidents performed more poorly on tests of vigi-

lance and impulse control and received higher parent and teacher ratings of hyperactive/aggressive behavior. Other research, however, suggests that the association between accidents and hyperactivity may be more a function of the degree of aggression and conduct problems and not of overactivity or inattention (Davidson, Hughes, & O'Connor, 1988; Davidson, Taylor, Sandberg, & Thorley, 1992). Yet, a large population study of 10,394 British children found that *both* overactivity and aggression contributed independently to the prediction of accidents (Bijur, Golding, Haslum, & Kurzon, 1988). Thus, it may be that both ADHD and aggression are linked to accident proneness.

In the Canadian follow-up research of hyperactive children into adulthood, evidence emerged suggesting that such children, as young adults, may have *a higher risk for traffic accidents* (Weiss & Hechtman, 1993). The Milwaukee follow-up study, similarly, suggested that adolescents with ADHD were more likely to drive illegally before obtaining a permit. Group differences in auto accident rates were not significant, most likely because fewer than 20% had drivers' licenses at this follow-up point. A subsequent 3- to 5-year follow-up study of adolescents with ADHD into their early driving years was able to document an increased risk for traffic accidents and speeding tickets than in a control group followed contemporaneously (Barkley, Guevremont, Anastopoulos, DuPaul, & Shelton, 1993).

A few studies have suggested an association between hyperactivity and *sleep disturbances* (Kaplan, McNichol, Conte, & Moghadam, 1987; Stewart et al., 1966; Trommer, Hoeppner, Rosenberg, Armstrong, & Rothstein, 1988). Yet the studies are somewhat contradictory in the type of sleep problems associated with ADHD. One (Trommer et al., 1988) suggested that the problems are mainly longer time to fall asleep (56%), tired at awakening (55%), and frequent night wakings (32%), whereas another found only the latter problem to be significantly more frequent (38%) (Kaplan et al., 1987).

The relationships discussed above between ADHD and increased (1) accident proneness in childhood, (2) speeding and auto accidents in adolescence and young adulthood, (3) conduct problems, (4) crime, (5) substance use and abuse (alcohol and tobacco primarily) in adolescence and adulthood, and (6) a general pattern of risk-taking behavior all intimate that ADHD might be expected to be associated with a *reduced life ex-*

pectancy. The diminished regard for the future consequences of one's behavior, as discussed in the theoretical model, would also predict a reduced concern for health-conscious behavior, such as exercise, proper diet, and moderation in using legal substances (caffeine, tobacco, and alcohol) throughout life. No follow-up studies of hyperactive or ADHD children have lasted long enough to document such a reduction in life expectancy; the oldest subjects now appear to be entering their 40s (Weiss & Hechtman, 1993). Yet concern over life expectancy in ADHD is not unfounded given the recent findings from the follow-up study of Terman's original sample of highly intelligent children, most of whom are now in their 70s or older and half of whom are deceased (Friedman et al., 1995). That study indicated that the most significant childhood personality characteristic predictive of reduced life expectancy by all causes was related to impulsive, undercontrolled personality characteristics. Individuals classified as having this set of characteristics lived an average of 8 years less than those who did not (73 vs. 81 years). It will be critical for the next generation of child psychopathologists to carry on the ongoing follow-up studies of hyperactive/ADHD children discussed above into their later years of life to evaluate fully this apparent risk.

POTENTIAL ETIOLOGIES

At the outset, it must be stated that the precise causes of ADHD are unknown at the present time, if by cause one means the direct, immediate, necessary, and sufficient events that lead to this behavior pattern in children. But although such primary modes of causation in ADHD remain to be established, a number of factors have been shown to be associated with a significantly increased risk for ADHD children. It is among these more indirect forms of causation, which are implicated in their guilt by association, that one must be content to look for now. Numerous causes of ADHD have been proposed, but evidence for many has been weak or lacking entirely. For that reason, attention will not be given to most of these here, and the reader is directed to other reviews for a discussion of them (Barkley, 1990; Ingersoll & Goldstein, 1993; Ross & Ross, 1982). Not surprisingly, the vast majority of the potentially causative factors associated with ADHD that have received much research sup-

port are biological in nature; that is, they are known to be related to or have a direct effect on brain development and/or functioning. But the precise causal pathways by which these factors lead to ADHD are simply not known at this time. Even so, far less evidence is available to support any purely psychosocial etiology of ADHD. In the vast majority of cases where such psychosocial risks have been significantly associated with ADHD/hyperactivity—as in child-management methods used by parents, parenting stress, marital conflict, or parental psychopathology—more careful analysis of subgroups or later research has shown these to be either the result of ADHD in the child (i.e., child's effects on parents), or, far more often, are related to aggression, ODD, or CD rather than to ADHD. Furthermore, genetic studies discussed below have shown that environmental factors, such as parental child-rearing as well as all nongenetic sources of neurological impairment, combined account for less than 10% to 15% of the variance in ADHD symptoms (Goodman & Stevenson, 1989). The strong hereditary influence in ADHD may also contribute to an apparent link between poor child management by a parent and ADHD—a link that may be attributable to the parent's own ADHD (Frick & Jackson, 1993). As Plomin (1995) has noted, even aspects of the home environment once thought to be nongenetic may have genetic contributions to them. For this reason, the few assertions made that hyperactivity or ADHD may arise purely from poor child-rearing practices by parents (Silverman & Ragusa, 1992; Willis & Lovaas, 1977) must be viewed with much skepticism until these studies control for the potential presence of ADHD in the parent and its association with that parent's child-management ability. Therefore, purely psychosocial factors as causes of ADHD will not receive further attention here.

However, this should not be construed as meaning only that "biology is destiny." Environmental factors may well shape and mold the nature and severity of an initial biologically created vulnerability toward poor inhibition such that it rises to the level of clinical ADHD. And certainly the risk for certain comorbid disorders, such as ODD and CD, are largely related to family environmental factors as noted above. Given that such comorbid conditions have proven to be the most consistent predictors of later developmental risks and negative outcomes (Fischer, Barkley, Edelbrock, & Smallish, 1993; Weiss & Hechtman, 1993), the environment in which the child is raised and schooled may well play a large role in determining the outcomes of children with the disorder even if it plays much less a role in primary causation.

Neurological Factors

In Still's (1902) first description of ADHD children, he conjectured that the disorder most likely arose out of impairments within the brain and hereditary factors. These two sets of factors remain the potential causes for which the greatest evidence is available in research on ADHD. Throughout the century, investigators have repeatedly noted the similarities between symptoms of ADHD and those produced by lesions or injuries to the frontal lobes more generally and the prefrontal cortex specifically (Mattes, 1980; Benton, 1991; Heilman et al., 1991). Both children and adults suffering injuries to the prefrontal region demonstrate deficits in sustained attention, inhibition, regulation of emotion and motivation, and the capacity to organize behavior across time (Fuster, 1989; Grattan & Eslinger, 1991; Stuss & Benson, 1986).

Numerous other lines of evidence have been suggestive of a neurological origin to the disorder. The early onset of the symptoms in ADHD and their relatively persistent nature over time, their association with other developmental disorders believed to be associated with neurological development or impairment (i.e., learning disabilities, language disorders, motor abnormalities, and IQ), their significant relationship to peri- and postnatal adversities, and their relatively dramatic improvement by stimulant medication have conspired repeatedly to focus attention by researchers on neurodevelopmental factors as likely to be causal of the disorder. The repeated findings of deficient performances on some neuropsychological tests known to be associated with prefrontal lobe functions, such as inhibition, persistence, planning, working memory, motor control and fluency, and verbal fluency, as reviewed above, have further supported the view of a neuropsychological origin to ADHD (Barkley, 1990; Barkley, Grodzinsky, & DuPaul, 1992; Goodyear & Hynd, 1992). The significantly greater risk for the disorder in other family members (see "Genetic Factors" below) and the increased risk for these symptoms in children known to have been exposed to toxins (pre- or postnatally) have likewise fueled scientific speculation that biologi-

cal factors must be involved in this disorder. But is there more direct proof of this connection to brain function and morphology?

It has only been within the past 10 to 15 years that more direct research findings pertaining to neurological integrity in ADHD have increasingly supported the view of a neurodevelopmental origin to the disorder. Even here, however, far more research is needed before we can be as sanguine about the biological nature of ADHD as we might like to be. Studies using "psychophysiological measures" of nervous system (central and autonomic) electrical activity, variously measured (electroencephalograms, galvanic skin responses, heart-rate deceleration, etc.), have been inconsistent in demonstrating group differences between ADHD and control children. But where differences from normal are found, they are consistently in the direction of "diminished arousal or arousability" in those with ADHD (see Hastings & Barkley, 1978; Rosenthal & Allen, 1978; Ross & Ross, 1982, for reviews). Far more consistent have been the results of evoked response measures taken in conjunction with performance of vigilance tests (Frank, Lazar, & Seiden, 1992; Klorman, Salzman, & Borgstedt, 1988). ADHD children have been found to have smaller amplitudes in the late positive components of their responses. These late components are believed to be a function of the prefrontal regions of the brain, are related to poorer performances on vigilance tests, and are corrected by stimulant medication (Klorman et al., 1988). Thus, although the evidence is far from conclusive, evoked response patterns related to sustained attention and inhibition have been suggestive of an underresponsiveness of ADHD children to stimulation that is corrected by stimulant medication.

Several studies have also examined "cerebral blood flow" in ADHD and normal children. They have consistently shown decreased blood flow to the prefrontal regions and pathways connecting these regions to the limbic system via the caudate and specifically its anterior region known as the striatum (Lou, Henriksen, & Bruhn, 1984; Lou, Henriksen, Bruhn, Borney, & Nielsen, 1989). More recently, studies using "positron emission tomography" (PET) to assess cerebral glucose metabolism have found diminished metabolism in adults (Zametkin et al., 1990) and female adolescents with ADHD (Ernst et al., 1994) but have proven negative in male adolescents with ADHD (Zametkin et al., 1993). However, significant cor-

relations have been noted between diminished metabolic activity in the left anterior frontal region and severity of ADHD symptoms in adolescents with ADHD (Zametkin et al., 1993). This demonstration of an association between the metabolic activity of certain brain regions and symptoms of ADHD is critical in proving a connection between the findings pertaining to brain activation and the behavior comprising ADHD.

The gross structure of the brain as portrayed by "coaxial tomographic scan" (CT) has not shown differences between ADHD and normal children (Shaywitz, Shaywitz, Byrne, Cohen, & Rothman, 1983), but greater brain atrophy was found in adults with ADHD who had a history of substance abuse (Nasrallah et al., 1986). The latter, however, seems more likely to account for these results than the ADHD. More fine-grained analysis of brain structures using the higher resolution "magnetic resonance imaging" (MRI) devices has begun to suggest differences in some brain regions in those with ADHD relative to control groups. Much of this work has been done by Hynd and his colleagues. Initial studies from this group examined the region of the left and right temporal lobes associated with auditory detection and analysis (planum temporale) in ADHD, LD (reading), and normal children. For some time, researchers studying reading disorders have focused on these brain regions given their connection to the analysis of speech sounds. Both the ADHD and LD children were found to have smaller right hemisphere plana temporale than the control group, whereas only the LD subjects had a smaller left plana temporale (Hynd, Semrud-Clikeman, Lorys, Novey, & Eliopulos, 1990). In the next study, the corpus callosum was examined in those with ADHD. This structure assists with the interhemispheric transfer of information. Those with ADHD were found to have a smaller callosum, particularly in the area of the genu and splenium and that region just anterior to the splenium (Hynd, Semrud-Clikeman, et al., 1991). An attempt to replicate this finding, however, failed to show any differences between ADHD and control children in the size or shape of the entire corpus callosum with the exception of the region of the splenium (posterior portion), which again was significantly smaller in subjects with ADHD (Semrud-Clikeman et al., 1994). Because of the earlier research by Lou et al. (1984) demonstrating decreased blood flow in the caudate–striatal regions of the frontal region, a subsequent study concen-

2. Attention-Deficit/Hyperactivity Disorder | 97

trated on the morphology of this region in children with ADHD. Lesions of this region have been associated with symptoms very similar to ADHD. Results of this study indicated that children with ADHD had a significantly smaller left caudate nucleus creating a reversal of the normal pattern of left > right asymmetry of the caudate (Hynd et al., 1993). This finding is consistent with the earlier blood-flow studies of decreased activity in this brain region.

Important to understand here is the very small sample size employed in many of these studies. Such small samples typically fall well below levels needed for adequate statistical power and thus may obscure minor differences in brain structure/function that would be significant with larger samples. These small samples also tend to contribute to a high probability of failures by others, using similarly small samples, to replicate the original findings. The variability across studies using small samples has the potential to be quite large. Greater sample sizes are to be strongly encouraged in future research in this area. Also important is the fact that none of these studies found evidence of brain damage in any of these structures in those with ADHD. This is consistent with past reviews of the literature suggesting that brain damage was likely related to less than 5% of those with hyperactivity (Rutter, 1977, 1983). Where differences in brain structures are found, they are likely the result of abnormalities in brain development within these particular regions, the causes of which are unknown.

Genetic Factors

No evidence exists to show that ADHD is the result of abnormal chromosomal structures, as in Down syndrome, their fragility (as in fragile X) or transmutations, or of extra chromosomal material, as in XXY syndrome. Children with such chromosomal abnormalities may show greater problems with attention, but such abnormalities are very uncommon in children with ADHD. By far, the greatest research evidence suggests that ADHD is a trait that is highly hereditary in nature, making heredity one of the most well-substantiated etiologies for ADHD.

Multiple lines of research support such a conclusion. For years, researchers have noted the higher prevalence of psychopathology in the parents and other relatives of children with ADHD. In particular, higher rates of ADHD, conduct problems, substance abuse, and depression have

been repeatedly observed in these studies (Barkley, DuPaul, & McMurray, 1990; Biederman et al., 1992; Pauls, 1991). By separating the group of ADHD children into those with and without CD, it has been shown that the conduct problems, substance abuse, and depression in the parents are related more to the presence of CD than to ADHD (August & Stewart, 1983; Barkley, Fischer, et al., 1991; Lahey et al., 1988). Yet rates of hyperactivity or ADHD remain high even in relatives of the group of ADHD children without CD. Research shows that between 10% to 35% of the immediate family members of children with ADHD are also likely to have the disorder with the risk to siblings of the ADHD children being approximately 32% (Biederman et al., 1992; Biederman et al., 1991; Pauls, 1991; Welner et al., 1977).

Another line of evidence for genetic involvement in ADHD has emerged from studies of adopted children. Cantwell (1975) and Morrison and Stewart (1973) both reported higher rates of hyperactivity in the biological parents of hyperactive children than in adoptive parents having such children. Both studies suggest that hyperactive children are more likely to resemble their biological parents than their adoptive parents in their levels of hyperactivity. Yet, both studies were retrospective and both failed to study the biological parents of the adopted hyperactive children as a comparison group (Pauls, 1991). Cadoret and Stewart (1991) studied 283 male adoptees and found that if one of the biological parents had been judged delinquent or to have an adult criminal conviction, the adopted away sons had a higher likelihood of having ADHD. A later study (van den Oord, Boomsma, & Verhulst, 1994) using biologically related and unrelated pairs of international adoptees identified a strong genetic component (47% of the variance) for the attention problems dimension of the CBC, a rating scale commonly used in research in child psychopathology. This particular scale has a strong association with a diagnosis of ADHD (Biederman et al., 1994) and is often used in research in selecting subjects with the disorder. Thus, much as the family association studies discussed earlier, results of adoption studies point to a significant hereditary contribution to hyperactivity.

Studies of twins provide a third avenue of evidence for a genetic contribution to ADHD. Early studies demonstrated a greater agreement (concordance) for symptoms of hyperactivity and in-

attention between monozygotic (MZ) compared to dizogotic twins (DZ) (O'Connor, Foch, Sherry, & Plomin, 1980; Willerman, 1973). Studies of very small samples of twins (Heffron, Martin, & Welsh, 1984; Lopez, 1965) found complete (100%) concordance for MZ twins for hyperactivity and far less agreement for DZ twins. A later study (Stevenson, 1992) of a much larger sample of twins (570) found that approximately 50% of the variance in hyperactivity and inattention in this sample was due to heredity, whereas 0% to 30% may have been environmental. Examining only those twins with clinically significant degrees of ADHD within this sample revealed a heritability of 64% for hyperactivity and inattention. This implies that the more deviant or clinically serious the degree of symptoms of ADHD, the more genetic factors may be contributing to it. Other large-scale twin studies are also quite consistent with these findings (Edelbrock, Rende, Plomin, & Thompson, 1995; Levy & Hay, 1992). For instance, Gilger et al. (1992) found that if one twin was diagnosed as ADHD, the concordance for the disorder was 81% in MZ twins and 29% in DZ twins. Stevenson (1994) recently summarized the status of twin studies on symptoms of ADHD by stating that the average heritability is .80 for symptoms of this disorder (range .50–.90). Thus, twin studies add substantially more evidence to that already found in family and adoption studies supporting a genetic basis to ADHD and its behavioral symptoms.

Quantitative genetic analyses of the large sample of families studied in Boston by Biederman and his colleagues suggest that a single gene may account for the expression of the disorder (Faraone et al., 1992). The focus of research recently has been on the dopamine type 2 gene given findings of its increased association with alcoholism, Tourette syndrome, and ADHD (Comings et al., 1991), but others have failed to replicate this finding (Gelernter et al., 1991; Kelsoe et al., 1989). However, a more recent study has implicated the dopamine transporter gene in ADHD (Cook et al., 1995). Clearly research into the genetic mechanisms involved in the transmission of ADHD across generations will prove an exciting and fruitful area of research endeavor over the next decade as the human genome is mapped and better understood.

Environmental Toxins

As the twin and quantitative genetic studies have suggested, environmental causes of ADHD may exist, but this does not mean just those within the realm of psychosocial or family influences. Variance in the expression of ADHD that may result from environmental sources means all nongenetic sources more generally, and these include pre-, peri-, and postnatal complications, and malnutrition, diseases, trauma, and other neurologically compromising events that may occur during the development of the nervous system before and after birth. Among these various biologically compromising events, several have been repeatedly linked to risks for inattention and hyperactive behavior.

One such event is exposure to environmental toxins and specifically lead. *Elevated body lead* burden has been shown to have a small but consistent and statistically significant relationship to the symptoms comprising ADHD (Baloh, Sturm, Green, & Gleser, 1975; David, 1974; de la Burde & Choate, 1972, 1974; Needleman et al., 1979). However, even at relatively high levels of lead, less than 38% of children are rated as having the behavior of hyperactivity on a teacher rating scale (Needleman et al., 1979) implying that most lead-poisoned children do not develop symptoms of ADHD. And most ADHD children, likewise, do not have significantly elevated lead burdens, although their lead levels may be higher than in control subjects (Gittelman & Eskinazi, 1983). Studies that have controlled for the presence of potentially confounding factors in this relationship have found the association between body lead (in blood or dentition) and symptoms of ADHD to be .10–.19 with the more factors controlled, the more likely the relationship falls below .10 (Ferguson, Ferguson, Horwood, & Kinzett, 1988; Silva, Hughes, Williams, & Faed, 1988; Thompson et al., 1989). This suggests that no more than 4% (at best) of the variance in the expression of these symptoms in children with elevated lead is explained by their lead levels. Moreover, two serious methodological issues plague even the better-conducted studies in this area: (1) None of the studies has used clinical criteria for a diagnosis of ADHD to determine precisely what percentage of lead-burdened children actually have the disorder—all have simply used behavior ratings comprising only a small number of items of inattention or hyperactivity. (2) None of the studies assessed for the presence of ADHD in the parents and controlled its contribution to the relationship. Given the high heritability of ADHD, this factor alone could attenuate the already small correlation between lead and symptoms of ADHD by as much as a third to a half its present levels.

Other types of environmental toxins found to have some relationship to inattention and hyperactivity are prenatal exposure to alcohol and tobacco smoke (Bennett, Wolin, & Reiss, 1988; Denson, Nanson, & McWatters, 1975; Nichols & Chen, 1981; Shaywitz, Cohen, & Shaywitz, 1980; Streissguth et al., 1984). It has also been shown that parents of children with ADHD do consume more alcohol and smoke more tobacco than control groups even when not pregnant (Cunningham et al., 1988; Denson et al., 1975). Thus, it is reasonable for research to continue to pursue the possibility that these environmental toxins may be causally related to ADHD. However, as in the lead studies discussed above, research in this area suffers from the same two serious methodological limitations—the failure to utilize clinical diagnostic criteria to determine rates of ADHD in exposed children and to evaluate and control for the presence of ADHD in the parents. Until these steps are taken in future research, the relationships demonstrated so far between these toxins and ADHD must be viewed with some caution.

ADHD—PREDOMINANTLY INATTENTIVE TYPE

In 1980, the publication of DSM-III not only changed the name for the disorder from hyperkinetic reaction of childhood to attention deficit disorder, it now included a bifurcation of the disorder into two subtypes. One contained the symptoms of inattention, hyperactivity, and impulsivity and was termed attention deficit disorder with hyperactivity (ADD+H), whereas the other was thought to be comprised of just inattention and impulsivity, and was labeled as ADD without hyperactivity (ADD−H). This second subtype was quite unexpected given that there existed almost no research on such a subtype or its characteristics at that time. Its creation, however, resulted in a number of studies being conducted to investigate its nature and associated features. The result of nearly 15 years of investigation into this subtype seems to suggest the following: (1) The ADD−H subtype actually represents a disorder for which children are referred to clinics for evaluation and treatment. (2) The symptom of impulsiveness is associated with hyperactivity and not inattention as was originally set forth in DSM-III. (3) A separate dimension of inattention exists apart from that of hyperactivity–impulsivity such that a separate group of children having predominantly inattentive symptoms can be identified. (4) The ADD−H subtype is not associated with the other disruptive behavior disorders (ODD, CD) anywhere near as much as is ADD+H. (5) Children with ADD−H have distinctly different social problems with peers than do those with ADD+H (Barkley, 1990; Carlson, 1986; Lahey & Carlson, 1992).

Despite its appearance in DSM-III, the relatively small amount of research on the disorder that existed when DSM-III-R was being prepared resulted in its being relegated to an ill-defined category, known as undifferentiated ADD. This was done with the proviso that more research was needed before its rightful place within DSM generally, and the disruptive behavior disorders specifically, could be better specified. By the time DSM-IV was written, much more research was available to support the existence of such a disorder. Efforts also were made within the DSM-IV field trial to determine its most appropriate symptom list. The result was the creation of ADHD, predominantly inattentive type (ADHD-PI) within DSM-IV.

Controversy continues over whether this represents a true subtype of ADHD, sharing a common attentional disturbance with the combined type while being distinguished from it simply by the relative absence of significant hyperactivity–impulsivity. Several recent reviews of this literature have suggested that it is not a true subtype but actually a separate, distinct disorder having a different attentional disturbance than the one present in ADHD, combined type (Barkley, 1990; Barkley, Grodzinsky, & DuPaul, 1992; Goodyear & Hynd, 1992). Another review concluded that evidence for this subtype's existence was at least strong enough to place it within the DSM (under ADHD), to provide a better definition of it than in DSM-III-R, and to await more research on its course and treatment responsiveness to help clarify its status within this taxonomy of psychopathology (Lahey & Carlson, 1992).

There is no question that statistical (factor) analyses of teacher ratings of these symptoms typically produce a two-factor solution like that created in DSM-IV (inattention, hyperactivity–impulsivity) as these reviews have noted. These two dimensions often emerge in parent ratings of these symptoms as well, but not always and particularly not when preschool samples of children are studied separately (Achenbach & Edelbrock, 1987). In that age group, a single dimension exists similar to the older DSM-III-R structure for ADHD and is often associated with aggressive/oppositional behavior as well. Moreover, some

factor analyses of teacher ratings using a somewhat different set of inattention items revealed two dimensions of inattention (disorganized–distractible and sluggish–drowsy) hinting that the cognitive styles of the ADD–H and ADD+H subtypes, in fact, could be different. Factor analyses of direct observations of children's inattentive behavior collected in classrooms, likewise, indicated that the inattention dimension may actually be comprised of two types of inattention, one corresponding to an inattentive–passive form and the other to a problem with persistence (Achenbach, 1986).

The latter findings are important if only in reminding us that teacher and parent ratings consist of opinions about a child's behavior representing relatively crude judgments that may overlook or obscure important distinctions about behavior. This is well-demonstrated in the fact that neuropsychological research using laboratory measures often identifies at least four distinct components of attention (Barkley, 1994) and at least two of impulsivity (Milich & Kramer, 1984; Olson, 1989; Gerbing, Ahadi, & Patton, 1987). And research using clinician ratings has identified a third dimension of behavior labeled as sluggish tempo (Lahey et al., 1988). Thus, we should not be too complacent about the results of factor analyses of parent–teacher ratings of children's behavior as accurately reflecting the exact nature of these behavior problems or the clinical disorders comprised of them. The items in such rating scales, and indeed in DSM-IV, are relatively global in nature (i.e., difficulty finishing tasks, needs supervision, etc.) and could result from very different disturbances in attention in different children.

This may help to explain why initial research on ADHD-PI (or ADD–H) is suggestive of a different attentional disturbance in this group than that found in the combined type (ADHD-C or ADD+H). The very limited research available to date intimates that ADHD-PI children have more problems in the focused or selective component of attention, appear sluggish in their speed of information processing, and may have memory retrieval problems, whereas those with ADHD-C have more problems with persistence and, relatedly, working memory as well as inhibition (Barkley, DuPaul, & McMurray, 1990; Barkley, Grodzinsky, & DuPaul, 1992; Goodyear & Hynd, 1992; Lahey & Carlson, 1992). The results of such laboratory studies are not sufficiently consistent across studies, however, to conclude

unequivocally that these two subtypes have a different attentional disturbance.

Part of the problem with many of the studies, and especially those finding few if any differences in these subtypes, is that most of the measures selected are drawn from the research literature on ADD+H. If uncritically accepted, such research might show that any differences between the two subtypes are merely matters of degree. Yet it is important in research on this issue to choose attentional tasks that represent its distinct components so as to test for double-dissociation—one subtype may have problems in one component (inhibition and persistence) but not others, whereas the other subtype may show problems in a different component (being focused and selective) but not in that of the first subtype. Certainly, the theoretical model of ADHD developed above applies only to the ADD+H (ADHD-C and ADHD-PHI) subtype because of its emphasis on disinhibition as the central feature of the model. The components of the model, however, provide guidelines as to what other cognitive/motor domains may be useful in selecting measures that would distinguish these subtypes.

Psychophysiological studies, such as the program of research by Klorman and colleagues (Klorman, 1992; Klorman et al., 1988) on evoked responses in ADD+H, could be very fruitful in helping to distinguish the nature of these subtle distinctions in attention between these subtypes. A pilot study in my own lab with Ronald Cohen has revealed that early components of the evoked response may be disturbed in those with ADD–H, consistent with a problem in the initial processing of sensory information, whereas those with ADD+H show a diminished late component of the response at P300, identical to that found repeatedly by Klorman and colleagues, and suggestive of a problem with resource allocation (motor effort). More research of this type may be needed to sort out the differences in attentional disturbances in these two groups rather than to rely simply on global symptom ratings by adults to settle the debate.

Two other areas of functioning that appear to distinguish these two subtypes of ADHD are peer relations and the types of emotional disturbances and psychiatric disorders found to be comorbid with them. Research suggests that those with ADHD-PI (ADD–H) may be more anxious, are more likely to have anxiety disorders and perhaps other mood disorders, and are often rated as socially withdrawn, shy, reticent, or apprehensive

than those with ADHD-C (ADD+H). The latter group, in contrast, are more aggressive, defiant, and oppositional, are more likely to have oppositional or conduct disorder, and are more often rejected by their peers than those with ADHD-PI (Lahey & Carlson, 1992). The studies of comorbidity and family aggregation of psychiatric disorders by Biederman and colleagues (Biederman et al., 1992) suggest that those with ADHD-PI have far fewer comorbid psychiatric conditions and impairments than those with ADHD-C. Although more research on these distinctions is needed given the very limited number of studies examining them, what little evidence exists intimates at important differences between these subtypes. If replicated in later research, such distinctions would predict very different adolescent outcomes for these subtypes. Findings from follow-up studies (see "Developmental Course and Adult Outcomes," above) have shown that early hyperactive–impulsive behavior is associated with a greater risk for adolescent delinquency, early substance use and abuse, and school suspensions and expulsions, particularly when this is combined with early aggressive or defiant behavior. This implies that the ADHD-C (ADD+H) subtype is far more prone to these outcomes than is the ADHD-PI subtype (ADD–H).

Studies of the prevalence of these two subtypes of ADHD are few in number but suggest several important differences between them (Szatmari, 1992). ADHD-C (ADD+H) is far more common than is ADHD-PI (ADD–H) with approximately 85% or more of those having ADD falling into the "+H" subtype in childhood. In adolescence, however, the ADD–H subtype was more common but still less prevalent than the "+H" subtype. It remains unclear as to whether differences exist in the sex ratios of these two subtypes, though male subjects still seem to predominate in both subtypes relative to female subjects (Szatmari, 1992).

FUTURE DIRECTIONS

A number of issues have been raised throughout this chapter that point the way to potentially fruitful research. The theoretical model discussed above, alone, suggests numerous possibilities for studying working memory, time and its influence over behavior, the internalization of language, creativity and fluency, the self-regulation of affect and motivation, and motor fluency in those with ADHD. Such research will not only be theory-driven but should have the laudable outcome of linking studies of a child psychopathological condition with the larger literatures of developmental psychology, developmental neuropsychology, information processing, and behavior analysis—linkages already being examined in a general way for commonalities among their paradigms and findings (Lyon, 1995).

Certainly, the diagnostic criteria developed to date, even though the most rigorous and empirical ever provided, may still suffer from problems. The fact that such criteria are not theory-driven and developmentally referenced despite being empirically derived risks creating several difficulties for understanding the disorder and clinically applying these criteria, among these being: (1) apparent developmental declines in the disorder and its symptoms may be more illusion than fact; (2) subtypes of a disorder are created that may simply be developmental stages of the same disorder (ADHD-PHI and ADHD-C) or are different disorders entirely (ADHD-PI); (3) female subjects may be underidentified when criteria are developed predominantly from male populations; and (4) a criterion for pervasiveness that confounds the source of information with its setting may be resulting in overly restrictive criteria. These are just a few of the difficulties.

Important in future research will be efforts to understand the nature of the attentional problems in ADHD given that extant research seriously questions whether these problems are actually within the realm of attention at all. Most studies point to impairment within the motor, output, or motivational systems of the brain rather than the sensory processing systems where attention has been traditionally thought to reside. And the theoretical model presented here hypothesizes that even this supposed problem with sustained attention represents a deficiency in a more complex, developmentally later form of goal-directed persistence. It arises out of poor self-regulation rather than representing a disturbance in the more basic and traditional form of sustained responding that is contingency-shaped and maintained. Our understanding of the very nature of the disorder of ADHD is at stake in how research comes to resolve these issues.

That the field of behavioral genetics offers exciting prospects for future research on ADHD goes without saying given the evidence available to date for a strong hereditary influence in the behavior patterns comprising ADHD as well as the clinical disorder itself. As of this writing, the race

seems to be on to identify the mechanisms by which this trait(s) is transmitted within families and the location and nature of the very gene(s) that give rise to it. Such exciting prospects also exist within the domain of neurobiological and neuroimaging studies in view of present, albeit limited, evidence that diminished metabolic activity and even minute structural differences in brain morphology within highly specific regions of the prefrontal and limbic systems may be associated with this disorder. The increasing availability, economy, safety, and sensitivity of modern neuroimaging devices should result in a plethora of new studies on ADHD given the promising starts to date.

Key to understanding ADHD may be the notion that it is actually a disorder of performance and not of skill; of how one's intelligence is applied in everyday effective adaptive functioning and not in knowledge itself; of doing what you know rather than knowing what to do; and of *when* and not *how* in the performance of behavior generally. The concept of time, how it is sensed, and how it is used in self-regulation may come to be a critical element in our understanding of ADHD as it is coming to be in our understanding of the unique role of the prefrontal cortex more generally (Fuster, 1989). Likewise, the recent return to developing theories of mind, how events are mentally represented and prolonged in working memory, and how private thought arises out of initially public behavior through the developmental process of internalization hold important pieces of information for the understanding of ADHD itself.

ACKNOWLEDGMENTS

During the preparation of this chapter the author was supported, in part, by grants from the National Institute of Mental Health (Nos. MH45714, MH42181, MH41583) and the National Institute for Child Health and Human Development (No. HD28171).

REFERENCES

Achenbach, T. M. (1986). *Child Behavior Checklist: Direct observation form.* Burlington, VT: Author.

Achenbach, T. M., & Edelbrock, C. S. (1983). *Manual for the Child Behavior Profile and Child Behavior Checklist.* Burlington, VT: Author.

Achenbach, T. M., & Edelbrock, C. S. (1984). Psychopathology of childhood. *Annual Review of Psychology, 35,* 227–256.

Achenbach, T. M., & Edelbrock, C. S. (1987). Empirically based assessment of the behavioral/emotional problems of 2– and 3–year-old children. *Journal of Abnormal Child Psychology, 15,* 629–650.

Achenbach, T. M., McConaughy, S. H., & Howell, C. T. (1987). Child/adolescent behavioral and emotional problems: Implications of cross-informant correlations for situational specificity. *Psychological Bulletin, 101,* 213–232.

Altepeter, T. S., & Breen, M. J. (1992). Situational variation in problem behavior at home and school in attention deficit disorder with hyperactivity: A factor analytic study. *Journal of Child Psychology and Psychiatry, 33,* 741–748.

American Psychiatric Association. (1968). *Diagnostic and statistical manual of mental disorders* (2nd ed.). Washington, DC: Author.

American Psychiatric Association. (1980). *Diagnostic and statistical manual of mental disorders* (3rd ed.). Washington, DC: Author.

American Psychiatric Association. (1987). *Diagnostic and statistical manual of mental disorders* (3rd ed., rev.). Washington, DC: Author.

American Psychiatric Association. (1994). *Diagnostic and statistical manual of mental disorders* (4th ed.). Washington, DC: Author.

Anastopoulos, A. D., Spisto, M. A., & Maher, M. C. (1994). The WISC-III Freedom from Distractibility factor: Its utility in identifying children with attention deficit hyperactivity disorder. *Psychological Assessment, 6,* 368–371.

Anderson, C. A., Hinshaw, S. P., & Simmel, C. (1994). Mother–child interactions in ADHD and comparison boys: Relationships with overt and covert externalizing behavior. *Journal of Abnormal Child Psychology, 22,* 247–265.

Applegate, B., Lahey, B. B., Hart, E. L., Waldman, I., Biederman, J., Hynd, G. W., Barkley, R. A., Ollendick, T., Frick, P. J., Greenhill, L., McBurnett, K., Newcorn, J., Kerdyk, L., Garfinkel, B., & Shaffer, D. (1995). *The age of onset for DSM-IV attention-deficit hyperactivity disorder: A report of the DSM-IV field trials.* Manuscript submitted for publication.

August, G. J., & Stewart, M. A. (1983). Family subtypes of childhood hyperactivity. *Journal of Nervous and Mental Disease, 171,* 362–368.

Baker, L., Cantwell, D. P., & Mattison, R. E. (1980). Behavior problems in children with pure speech disorders and in children with combined speech and language disorders. *Journal of Abnormal Child Psychology, 8,* 245–256.

Baloh, R., Sturm, R., Green, B., & Gleser, G. (1975). Neuropsychological effects of chronic asymptomatic increased lead absorption. *Archives of Neurology, 32,* 326–330.

Barkley, R. A. (1981). *Hyperactive children: A handbook for diagnosis and treatment.* New York: Guilford Press.

Barkley, R. A. (1985). The social interactions of hyperactive children: Developmental changes, drug effects, and situational variation. In R. McMahon & R. Peters (Eds.), *Childhood disorders: Behavioral–developmental approaches* (pp. 218–243). New York: Brunner/Mazel.

Barkley, R. A. (1988). The effects of methylphenidate on the interactions of preschool ADHD children with their mothers. *Journal of the American Academy of Child and Adolescent Psychiatry, 27,* 336–341.

Barkley, R. A. (1989a). The problem of stimulus control and rule-governed behavior in children with attention deficit disorder with hyperactivity. In J. Swanson & L. Bloomingdale (Eds.), *Attention deficit disorders* (pp. 203–234). New York: Pergamon.

Barkley, R. A. (1989b). Hyperactive girls and boys: Stimulant drug effects on mother–child interactions. *Journal of Child Psychology and Psychiatry, 30,* 379–390.

Barkley, R. A. (1990). *Attention-deficit hyperactivity disorder: A handbook for diagnosis and treatment.* New York: Guilford Press.

Barkley, R. A. (1994). Impaired delayed responding: A unified theory of attention deficit hyperactivity disorder. In D. K. Routh (Ed.), *Disruptive behavior disorders: Essays in honor of Herbert Quay* (pp. 11–57). New York: Plenum Press.

Barkley, R. A. (1997). Behavioral inhibition sustained, attention, and executive functions: Constructing a unifying theory of ADHD. *Psychological Bulletin, 121,* 65–94.

Barkley, R. A., Anastopoulos, A. D., Guevremont, D. G., & Fletcher, K. F. (1991). Adolescents with attention deficit hyperactivity disorder: Patterns of behavioral adjustment, academic functioning, and treatment utilization. *Journal of the American Academy of Child and Adolescent Psychiatry, 30,* 752–761.

Barkley, R. A., Anastopoulos, A. D., Guevremont, D. G., & Fletcher, K. F. (1992). Adolescents with attention deficit hyperactivity disorder: Mother–adolescent interactions, family beliefs and conflicts, and maternal psychopathology. *Journal of Abnormal Child Psychology, 20,* 263–288.

Barkley, R., Copeland, A., & Sivage, C. (1980). A self-control classroom for hyperactive children. *Journal of Autism and Developmental Disorders, 10,* 75–89.

Barkley, R. A., & Cunningham, C. E. (1979a). Stimulant drugs and activity level in hyperactive children. *American Journal of Orthopsychiatry, 49,* 491–499.

Barkley, R. A., & Cunningham, C. E. (1979b). The effects of methylphenidate on the mother–child interactions of hyperactive children. *Archives of General Psychiatry, 36,* 201–208.

Barkley, R., Cunningham, C., & Karlsson, J. (1983). The speech of hyperactive children and their mothers: Comparisons with normal children and stimulant drug effects. *Journal of Learning Disabilities, 16,* 105–110.

Barkley, R. A., DuPaul, G. J., & McMurray, M.B. (1990). A comprehensive evaluation of attention deficit disorder with and without hyperactivity. *Journal of Consulting and Clinical Psychology, 58,* 775–789.

Barkley, R. A., & Edelbrock, C. S. (1987). Assessing situational variation in children's behavior problems: The Home and School Situations Questionnaires. In R. Prinz (Ed.), *Advances in behavioral assessment of children and families* (Vol. 3, pp. 157–176). Greenwich, CT: JAI Press.

Barkley, R. A., Fischer, M., Edelbrock, C. S., & Smallish, L. (1990). The adolescent outcome of hyperactive children diagnosed by research criteria: I. An 8 year prospective follow-up study. *Journal of the American Academy of Child and Adolescent Psychiatry, 29,* 546–557.

Barkley, R. A., Fischer, M., Edelbrock, C. S., & Smallish, L. (1991). The adolescent outcome of hyperactive children diagnosed by research criteria: III. Mother–child interactions, family conflicts, and maternal psychopathology. *Journal of Child Psychology and Psychiatry, 32,* 233–256.

Barkley, R. A., Grodzinsky, G., & DuPaul, G. (1992). Frontal lobe functions in attention deficit disorder with and without hyperactivity: A review and research report. *Journal of Abnormal Child Psychology, 20,* 163–188.

Barkley, R. A., Guevremont, D. G., Anastopoulos, A. D., DuPaul, G. J., & Shelton, T. L. (1993). Driving-related risks and outcomes of attention deficit hyperactivity disorder in adolescents and young adults: A 3–5 year follow-up survey. *Pediatrics, 92,* 212–218.

Barkley, R. A., Karlsson, J., & Pollard, S. (1985). Effects of age on the mother–child interactions of hyperactive children. *Journal of Abnormal Child Psychology, 13,* 631–638.

Barkley, R. A., Karlsson, J., Pollard, S., & Murphy, J. V. (1985). Developmental changes in the mother–child interactions of hyperactive boys: Effects of two dose levels of Ritalin. *Journal of Child Psychology and Psychiatry and Allied Disciplines, 26,* 705–715.

Barkley, R. A., Koplowitz, S., Anderson, T., & McMurray, M. (1996). *Sense of time in ADHD children: II. Duration, distraction, and medication effects.* Manuscript submitted for publication.

Barkley, R. A., & Ullman, D. G. (1975). A comparison of objective measures of activity level and distractibility in hyperactive and nonhyperactive children. *Journal of Abnormal Child Psychology, 3,* 213–244.

Baumgaertel, A. (1994, June). *Assessment of German school children using DSM criteria based on teacher report.* Paper presented at the Society for Research in Child and Adolescent Psychopathology, London, England.

Befera, M., & Barkley, R. A. (1984). Hyperactive and normal girls and boys: Mother–child interactions, parent psychiatric status, and child psychopathology. *Journal of Child Psychology and Psychiatry, 26,* 439–452.

Beitchman, J. H., Hood, J., & Inglis, A. (1990). Psychiatric risk in children with speech and language disorders. *Journal of Abnormal Child Psychology, 18,* 283–296.

Beitchman, J. H., Hood, J., Rochon, J., & Peterson, M. (1989). Empirical classification of speech/language impairment in children: II. Behavioral characteristics. *Journal of the American Academy of Child and Adolescent Psychiatry, 28,* 118–123.

Beitchman, J. H., Nair, R., Clegg, M., Ferguson, B., & Patel, P. G. (1986). Prevalence of psychiatric disorders in children with speech and language disorders. *Journal of the American Academy of Child and Adolescent Psychiatry, 25,* 528–535.

Beitchman, J. H., Wekerle, C., & Hood, J. (1987). Diagnostic continuity from preschool to middle childhood. *Journal of the American Academy of Child and Adolescent Psychiatry, 26,* 694–699.

Bennett, L. A., Wolin, S. J., & Reiss, D. (1988). Cognitive, behavioral, and emotional problems among school-age children of alcoholic parents. *American Journal of Psychiatry, 145,* 185–190.

Benton, A. (1991). Prefrontal injury and behavior in children. *Developmental Neuropsychology, 7,* 275–282.

Berk, L. E., & Potts, M. K. (1991). Development and functional significance of private speech among attention-deficit hyperactivity disorder and normal boys. *Journal of Abnormal Child Psychology, 19,* 357–377.

Bhatia, M. S., Nigam, V. R., Bohra, N., & Malik, S. C. (1991). Attention deficit disorder with hyperactivity among paediatric outpatients. *Journal of Child Psychology and Psychiatry, 32,* 297–306.

Biederman, J., Faraone, S. V., Keenan, K., & Tsuang, M. T. (1991). Evidence of a familial association between attention deficit disorder and major affective disorders. *Archives of General Psychiatry, 48,* 633–642.

Biederman, J., Faraone, S. V., & Lapey, K. (1992). Comorbidity of diagnosis in attention-deficit hyperactivity disorder. In G. Weiss (Ed.), *Child and adolescent psychiatric clinics of North America: Attention-deficit hyperactivity disorder* (pp. 335–360). Philadelphia: Saunders.

Biederman, J., Keenan, K., & Faraone, S. V. (1990). Parent-based diagnosis of attention deficit disorder predicts a diagnosis based on teacher report. *American Journal of Child and Adolescent Psychiatry, 29,* 698–701.

Biederman, J., Milberger, S., Faraone, S. V., Guite, J., & Warburton, R. (1994). Associations between childhood asthma and ADHD: Issues of psychiatric comorbidity and familiality. *Journal of the American Academy of Child and Adolescent Psychiatry, 33,* 842–848.

Biederman, J., Wozniak, J., Kiely, K., Ablon, S., Faraone, S., Mick, E., Mundy, E., & Kraus, I. (1995). CBCL clinical scales discriminate prepubertal children with structured-interview-derived diagnosis of mania from those with ADHD. *Journal of the American Academy of Child and Adolescent Psychiatry, 34,* 464–471.

Bijur, P., Golding, J., Haslum, M., & Kurzon, M. (1988). Behavioral predictors of injury in school-age children. *American Journal of Diseases of Children, 142,* 1307–1312.

Breen, M. J. (1989). Cognitive and behavioral differences in ADHD boys and girls. *Journal of Child Psychology and Psychiatry, 30,* 711–716.

Bronowski, J. (1977). Human and animal languages. In *A sense of the future* (pp. 104–131). Cambridge, MA: MIT Press.

Buhrmester, D., Camparo, L., Christensen, A., Gonzalez, L. S., & Hinshaw, S. P. (1992). Mothers and fathers interacting in dyads and triads with normal and hyperactive sons. *Developmental Psychology, 28,* 500–509.

Burks, H. (1960). The hyperkinetic child. *Exceptional Children, 27,* 18.

Cadoret, R. J., & Stewart, M. A. (1991). An adoption study of attention deficit/hyperactivity/aggression and their relationship to adult antisocial personality. *Comprehensive Psychiatry, 32,* 73–82.

Campbell, S. B. (1990). *Behavior problems in preschool children.* New York: Guilford Press.

Campbell, S. B., Douglas, V. I., & Morganstern, G. (1971). Cognitive styles in hyperactive children and the effect of methylphenidate. *Journal of Child Psychology and Psychiatry, 12,* 55–67.

Campbell, S. B., March, C. L., Pierce, E. W., Ewing, L. J., & Szumowski, E. K. (1991). Hard-to-manage preschool boys: Family context and the stability of externalizing behavior. *Journal of Abnormal Child Psychology, 19,* 301–318.

Campbell, S. B., Schleifer, M., & Weiss, G. (1978). Continuities in maternal reports and child behaviors over time in hyperactive and comparison groups. *Journal of Abnormal Child Psychology, 6,* 33–45.

Campbell, S. B., Szumowski, E. K., Ewing, L. J., Gluck, D. S., & Breaux, A. M. (1982). A multidimensional assessment of parent-identified behavior problem toddlers. *Journal of Abnormal Child Psychology, 10,* 569–592.

Cantwell, D. (1975). *The hyperactive child.* New York: Spectrum.

Cantwell, D. P., & Baker, L. (1992). Association between attention deficit-hyperactivity disorder and learning disorders. In S. E. Shaywitz & B. A. Shaywitz (Eds.), *Attention deficit disorder comes of age: Toward the twenty-first century* (pp. 145–164). Austin, TX: Pro-ed.

Cantwell, D. P., & Satterfield, J. H. (1978). The prevalence of academic underachievement in hyperactive children. *Journal of Pediatric Psychology, 3,* 168–171.

Cappella, B., Gentile, J. R., & Juliano, D. B. (1977). Time estimation by hyperactive and normal children. *Perceptual and Motor Skills, 44,* 787–790.

Carlson, C. (1986). Attention Deficit Disorder Without Hyperactivity: A review of preliminary experimental evidence. In B. Lahey & A. Kazdin (Eds.), *Advances in clinical child psychology* (Vol. 9, pp. 153–176). New York: Plenum Press.

Carlson, G. A. (1990). Child and adolescent mania—diagnostic considerations. *Journal of Child Psychology and Psychiatry, 31,* 331–342.

Cataldo, M. F., Finney, J. W., Richman, G. S., Riley, A. W., Hook, R. J., Brophy, C. J., & Nau, P. A. (1992). Behavior of injured and uninjured children and their parents in a simulated hazardous setting. *Journal of Pediatric Psychology, 17,* 73–80.

Chee, P., Logan, G., Schachar, R., Lindsay, P., & Wachsmuth, R. (1989). Effects of event rate and display time on sustained attention in hyperactive, normal, and control children. *Journal of Abnormal Child Psychology, 17,* 371–391.

Chen, W. J., Faraone, S. V., Biederman, J., & Tsuang, M. T. (1994). Diagnostic accuracy of the Child Behavior Checklist scales for attention-deficit hyperactivity disorder: A receiver-operating characteristic analysis. *Journal of Consulting and Clinical Psychology, 62,* 1017–1025.

Chess, S. (1960). Diagnosis and treatment of the hyperactive child. *New York State Journal of Medicine, 60,* 2379–2385.

Clark, M. L., Cheyne, J. A., Cunningham, C. E., & Siegel, L. S. (1988). Dyadic peer interaction and task orientation in attention-deficit-disordered children. *Journal of Abnormal Child Psychology, 16,* 1–15.

Cohen, N. J., & Minde, K. (1983). The "hyperactive syndrome" in kindergarten children: Comparison of children with pervasive and situational symptoms. *Journal of Child Psychology and Psychiatry, 24,* 443–455.

Cohen, N. J., Sullivan, J., Minde, K., Novak, C., & Keens, S. (1983). Mother-child interaction in hyperactive and normal kindergarten-aged children and the effect of treatment. *Child Psychiatry and Human Development, 13,* 213–224.

Cohen, N. J., Weiss, G., & Minde, K. (1972). Cognitive styles in adolescents previously diagnosed as hyperactive. *Journal of Child Psychology and Psychiatry, 13,* 203–209.

Cole, P. M., Zahn-Waxler, C., & Smith, D. (1994). Expressive control during a disappointment: Variations related to preschoolers behavior problems. *Developmental Psychology, 30,* 835–846.

Comings, D. E., & Comings, B. G. (1988). Tourette's syndrome and attention deficit disorder. In D. J. Cohen, R. D. Bruun, & J. F. Leckman (Eds.), *Tourette's syndrome and tic disorders: Clinical understanding and treatment* (pp. 119–136). New York: Wiley.

Comings, D. E., Comings, B. G., Muhleman, D., Dietz, G., Shahbahrami, B., Tast, D., Knell, E., Kocsis, P., Baumgarten, R., Kovacs, B. W., Levy, D. L., Smith, M., Borison, R. L., Evans, D. D., Klein, D. N., MacMurray, J., Tosk, J. M., Sverd, J., Gysin, R., & Flanagan, S. D. (1991). The dopamine D_2 receptor locus as a modifying gene in neuropsychiatric disorders. *Journal of the American Medical Association, 266,* 1793–1800.

Connors, C. K. (1995). *The Connors Continuous Performance Test.* North Tonawanda, NY: MultiHealth Systems.

Cook, E. H., Stein, M. A., Krasowski, M. D., Cox, N. J., Olkon, D. M., Kieffer, J. E., & Leventhal, B. L. (1995). Association of attention deficit disorder and the dopamine transporter gene. *American Journal of Human Genetics, 56,* 993–998.

Copeland, A. P. (1979). Types of private speech produced by hyperactive and nonhyperactive boys. *Journal of Abnormal Child Psychology, 7,* 169–177.

Corkum, P. V., & Siegel, L. S. (1993). Is the continuous performance task a valuable research tool for use with children with attention-deficit-hyperactivity disorder? *Journal of Child Psychology and Psychiatry, 34*, 1217–1239.

Costello, E. J., Loeber, R., & Stouthamer-Loeber, M. (1991). Pervasive and situational hyperactivity—Confounding effect of informant: A research note. *Journal of Child Psychology and Psychiatry, 32*, 367–376.

Cunningham, C. E., Benness, B. B., & Siegel, L. S. (1988). Family functioning, time allocation, and parental depression in the families of normal and ADDH children. *Journal of Clinical Child Psychology, 17*, 169–177.

Cunningham, C. E., & Siegel, L. S. (1987). Peer interactions of normal and attention-deficit disordered boys during free-play, cooperative task, and simulated classroom situations. *Journal of Abnormal Child Psychology, 15*, 247–268.

Cunningham, C. E., Siegel, L. S., & Offord, D. R. (1985). A developmental dose response analysis of the effects of methylphenidate on the peer interactions of attention deficit disordered boys. *Journal of Child Psychology and Psychiatry, 26*, 955–971.

Danforth, J. S., Barkley, R. A., & Stokes, T. F. (1991). Observations of parent–child interactions with hyperactive children: Research and clinical implications. *Clinical Psychology Review, 11*, 703–727.

David, O. J. (1974). Association between lower level lead concentrations and hyperactivity. *Environmental Health Perspective, 7*, 17–25.

Davidson, L. L., Hughes, S. J., & O'Connor, P. A. (1988). Preschool behavior problems and subsequent risk of injury. *Pediatrics, 82*, 644–651.

Davidson, L. L., Taylor, E. A., Sandberg, S. T., & Thorley, G. (1992). Hyperactivity in school-age boys and subsequent risk of injury. *Pediatrics, 90*, 697–702.

de la Burde, B., & Choate, M. (1972). Does asymptomatic lead exposure in children have latent sequelae? *Journal of Pediatrics, 81*, 1088–1091.

de la Burde, B., & Choate, M. (1974). Early asymptomatic lead exposure and development at school age. *Journal of Pediatrics, 87*, 638–642.

Demb, H. B. (1991). Use of Ritalin in the treatment of children with mental retardation. In L. L. Greenhill & B. B. Osmon (Eds.), *Ritalin: Theory and patient management* (pp. 155–170). New York: Mary Ann Liebert.

Denckla, M. B. (1994). Measurement of executive function. In G. R. Lyon (Ed.), *Frames of reference for the assessment of learning disabilities: New views on measurement issues* (pp. 117–142). Baltimore: Brookes.

Denckla, M. B., & Rudel, R. G. (1978). Anomalies of motor development in hyperactive boys. *Annals of Neurology, 3*, 231–233.

Denson, R., Nanson, J. L., & McWatters, M. A. (1975). Hyperkinesis and maternal smoking. *Canadian Psychiatric Association Journal, 20*, 183–187.

Diamond, A. (1990). The development and neural bases of memory functions as indexed by the AB and delayed response task in human infants and infant monkeys. In A. Diamond (Ed.), *The development and neuronal bases of higher cognitive functions. Annals of the New York Academy of Science, 608*, 276–317.

Diamond, A., Cruttenden, L., & Neiderman, D. (1994). AB with multiple wells: 1. Why are multiple wells sometimes easier than two wells? 2. Memory or memory + inhibition? *Developmental Psychology, 30*, 192–205.

Dolphin, J. E., & Cruickshank, W. M. (1951). Pathology of concept formation in children with cerebral palsy. *American Journal of Mental Deficiency, 56*, 386–392.

Douglas, V. I. (1972). Stop, look, and listen: The problem of sustained attention and impulse control in hyperactive and normal children. *Canadian Journal of Behavioural Science, 4*, 259–282.

Douglas, V. I. (1980). Higher mental processes in hyperactive children: Implications for training. In R. Knights & D. Bakker (Eds.), *Treatment of hyperactive and learning disordered children* (pp. 65–92). Baltimore: University Park Press.

Douglas, V. I. (1983). Attention and cognitive problems. In M. Rutter (Ed.), *Developmental neuropsychiatry* (pp. 280–329). New York: Guilford Press.

Douglas, V. I., & Parry, P. A. (1983). Effects of reward on delayed reaction time task performance of hyperactive children. *Journal of Abnormal Child Psychology, 11*, 313–326.

Douglas, V. I., & Parry, P. A. (1994). Effects of reward and non-reward on attention and frustration in attention deficit disorder. *Journal of Abnormal Child Psychology, 22*, 281–302.

Douglas, V. I., & Peters, K. G. (1978). Toward a clearer definition of the attentional deficit of hyperactive children. In G. A. Hale & M. Lewis (Eds.), *Attention and the development of cognitive skills* (pp. 173–248). New York: Plenum Press.

Draeger, S., Prior, M., & Sanson, A. (1986). Visual and auditory attention performance in hyperactive children: Competence or compliance. *Journal of Abnormal Child Psychology, 14*, 411–424.

DuPaul, G. J. (1991). Parent and teacher ratings of ADHD symptoms: Psychometric properties in a community-based sample. *Journal of Clinical Child Psychology, 20*, 245–253.

DuPaul, G. J., & Barkley, R. A. (1992). Situational variability of attention problems: Psychometric properties of the Revised Home and School Situations Questionnaires. *Journal of Clinical Child Psychology, 21*, 178–188.

Ebaugh, F. G. (1923). Neuropsychiatric sequelae of acute epidemic encephalitis in children. *American Journal of Diseases of Children, 25*, 89–97.

Edelbrock, C. S., & Costello, A. (1988). Convergence between statistically derived behavior problem syndromes and child psychiatric diagnoses. *Journal of Abnormal Child Psychology, 16*, 219–231.

Edelbrock, C. S., Rende, R., Plomin, R., & Thompson, L. (1995). A twin study of competence and problem behavior in childhood and early adolescence. *Journal of Child Psychology and Psychiatry, 36*, 775–786.

Ernst, M., Liebenauer, L. L., King, A. C., Fitzgerald, G. A., Cohen, R. M., & Zametkin, A. J. (1994). Reduced brain metabolism in hyperactive girls. *Journal of the American Academy of Child and Adolescent Psychiatry, 33*, 858–868.

Faraone, S. V., Biederman, J., Chen, W. J., Krifcher, B., Keenan, K., Moore, C., Sprich, S., & Tsuang, M. T. (1992). Segregation analysis of attention deficit hyperactivity disorder. *Psychiatric Genetics, 2*, 257–275.

Faraone, S. V., Biederman, J., Lehman, B., Keenan, K., Norman, D., Seidman, L. J., Kolodny, R., Kraus, I., Perrin, J., & Chen, W. (1993). Evidence for the independent familial transmission of attention deficit hyperactivity disorder and learning disabilities: Results from a family genetic study. *American Journal of Psychiatry, 150*, 891–895.

Fergusson, D. M., Fergusson, I. E., Horwood, L. J., & Kin-

zett, N. G. (1988). A longitudinal study of dentine lead levels, intelligence, school performance, and behaviour. *Journal of Child Psychology and Psychiatry, 29,* 811–824.

Fischer, M. (1990). Parenting stress and the child with attention deficit hyperactivity disorder. *Journal of Clinical Child Psychology, 19,* 337–346.

Fischer, M., Barkley, R. A., Edelbrock, C. S., & Smallish, L. (1990). The adolescent outcome of hyperactive children diagnosed by research criteria, II: Academic, attentional, and neuropsychological status. *Journal of Consulting and Clinical Psychology, 58,* 580–588.

Fischer, M., Barkley, R. A., Edelbrock, C. S., & Smallish, L. (1993). The stability of dimensions of behavior in ADHD and normal children over an 8–year follow-up. *Journal of Abnormal Child Psychology, 21,* 315–337.

Fischer, M., Barkley, R. A., Fletcher, K. & Smallish, L. (1993a). The stability of dimensions of behavior in ADHD and normal children over an 8 year period. *Journal of Abnormal Child Psychology, 21,* 315–337.

Fischer, M., Barkley, R. A., Fletcher, K., & Smallish, L. (1993b). The adolescent outcome of hyperactive children diagnosed by research criteria, V: Predictors of outcome. *Journal of the American Academy of Child and Adolescent Psychiatry, 32,* 324–332.

Flavell, J. H. (1970). Developmental studies of mediated memory. In H. W. Reese & L. P. Lipsett (Eds.), *Advances in child development and behavior* (pp. 181–211). New York: Academic Press.

Fletcher, K., Fischer, M., Barkley, R. A., & Smallish, L. (in press). A sequential analysis of the mother–adolescent interactions of ADHD, ADHD/ODD, and normal teenagers during neutral and conflict discussions. *Journal of Abnormal Child Psychology.*

Frank, Y., Lazar, J. W., & Seiden, J. A. (1992). Cognitive event-related potentials in learning-disabled children with or without attention-deficit hyperactivity disorder. *Annals of Neurology, 32,* 478 (abstract).

Frick, P. J., & Jackson, Y. K. (1993). Family functioning and childhood antisocial behavior: Yet another reinterpretation. *Journal of Clinical Child Psychology, 22,* 410–419.

Friedman, H. S., Tucker, J. S., Schwartz, J. E., Tomlinson-Keasey, C., Martin, L. R., Wingard, D. L., & Criqui, M. H. (1995). Psychosocial and behavioral predictors of longevity: The aging and death of the "Termites." *American Psychologist, 50,* 69–78.

Fuster, J. M. (1989). *The prefrontal cortex.* New York: Raven Press.

Garber, J., & Dodge, K. A. (Eds.). (1991). *The development of emotional regulation and dysregulation.* Cambridge, UK: Cambridge University Press.

Gelernter, J. O., O'Malley, S., Risch, N., Kranzler, H. R., Krystal, J., Merikangas, K., Kennedy, J. L., et al. (1991). No association between an allele at the D₂ dopamine receptor gene (DRD_2) and alcoholism. *Journal of the American Medical Association, 266,* 1801–1807.

Gerbing, D. W., Ahadi, S. A., & Patton, J. H. (1987). Toward a conceptualization of impulsivity: Components across the behavioral and self-report domains. *Multivariate Behavioral Research, 22,* 357–379.

Gilger, J. W., Pennington, B. F., & DeFries, J. C. (1992). A twin study of the etiology of comorbidity: Attention-deficit hyperactivity disorder and dyslexia. *Journal of the American Academy of Child and Adolescent Psychiatry, 31,* 343–348.

Gillis, J. J., Gilger, J. W., Pennington, B. F., & Defries, J. C. (1992). Attention deficit disorder in reading-disabled twins: Evidence for a genetic etiology. *Journal of Abnormal Child Psychology, 20,* 303–315.

Gittelman, R., & Eskinazi, B. (1983). Lead and hyperactivity revisited. *Archives of General Psychiatry, 40,* 827–833.

Gittelman, R., Mannuzza, S., Shenker, R., & Bonagura, N. (1985). Hyperactive boys almost grown up: I. Psychiatric status. *Archives of General Psychiatry, 42,* 937–947.

Glow, P. H., & Glow, R. A. (1979). Hyperkinetic impulse disorder: A developmental defect of motivation. *Genetic Psychological Monographs, 100,* 159–231.

Goldman-Rakic, P. S. (1987). Development of cortical circuitry and cognitive function. *Child Development, 58,* 601–622.

Goldstein, S., & Goldstein, M. (1990). *Managing attention disorders in children.* New York: Wiley.

Gomez, R., & Sanson, A. V. (1994). Mother–child interactions and noncompliance in hyperactive boys with and without conduct problems. *Journal of Child Psychology and Psychiatry, 35,* 477–490.

Goodman, J. R., & Stevenson, J. (1989). A twin study of hyperactivity: II. The aetiological role of genes, family relationships, and perinatal adversity. *Journal of Child Psychology and Psychiatry, 30,* 691–709.

Goodyear, P., & Hynd, G. (1992). Attention deficit disorder with (ADD/H) and without (ADD/WO) hyperactivity: Behavioral and neuropsychological differentiation. *Journal of Clinical Child Psychology, 21,* 273–304.

Goyette, C. H., Conners, C. K., & Ulrich, R. F. (1978). Normative data on revised Conners Parent and Teacher Rating Scales. *Journal of Abnormal Child Psychology, 6,* 221–236.

Grattan, L. M., & Eslinger, P. J. (1991). Frontal lobe damage in children and adults: A comparative review. *Developmental Neuropsychology, 7,* 283–326.

Gray, J. A. (1982). *The neuropsychology of anxiety.* New York: Oxford University Press.

Green, L., Fry, A. F., & Meyerson, J. (1994). Discounting of delayed rewards: A life-span comparison. *Psychological Science, 5,* 33–36.

Greenberg, L. M., & Waldman, I. D. (1992). *Developmental normative data on the Test of Variables of Attention (T.O.V.A.).* Minneapolis Department of Psychiatry, University of Minnesota Medical School.

Grodzinsky, G. M., & Diamond, R. (1992). Frontal lobe functioning in boys with attention-deficit hyperactivity disorder. *Developmental Neuropsychology, 8,* 427–445.

Gross-Tsur, V., Shalev, R. S., & Amir, N. (1991). Attention deficit disorder: Association with familial-genetic factors. *Pediatric Neurology, 7,* 258–261.

Haenlein, M., & Caul, W. F. (1987). Attention deficit disorder with hyperactivity: A specific hypothesis of reward dysfunction. *Journal of the American Academy of Child and Adolescent Psychiatry, 26,* 356–362.

Hallowell, E. M., & Ratey, J. J. (1994). *Driven to distraction.* New York: Pantheon.

Halperin, J. M., & Gittelman, R. (1982). Do hyperactive children and their siblings differ in IQ and academic achievement? *Psychiatry Research, 6,* 253–258.

Halperin, J. M., Matier, K., Bedi, G., Sharma, V., & Newcorn, J. H. (1992). Specificity of inattention, impulsivity, and hyperactivity to the diagnosis of attention-deficit hyperactivity disorder. *Journal of the American Academy of Child and Adolescent Psychiatry, 31,* 190–196.

Hamlett, K. W., Pellegrini, D. S., & Conners, C. K. (1987).

An investigation of executive processes in the problem-solving of attention deficit disorder-hyperactive children. *Journal of Pediatric Psychology, 12,* 227–240.

Hart, E. L., Lahey, B. B., Loeber, R., Applegate, B., Green, S., & Frick, P. J. (in press). *Developmental change in attention-deficit hyperactivity disorder in boys: A four-year longitudinal study.* New Haven, CT: Yale Child Study Center.

Hartsough, C. S., & Lambert, N. M. (1985). Medical factors in hyperactive and normal children: Prenatal, developmental, and health history findings. *American Journal of Orthopsychiatry, 55,* 190–210.

Hastings, J., & Barkley, R. A. (1978). A review of psychophysiological research with hyperactive children. *Journal of Abnormal Child Psychology, 7,* 413–337.

Hayes, S. (1989). *Rule–governed behavior.* New York: Plenum Press.

Heffron, W. A., Martin, C. A., & Welsh, R. J. (1984). Attention deficit disorder in three pairs of monozygotic twins: A case report. *Journal of the American Academy of Child Psychiatry, 23,* 299–301.

Heilman, K. M., Voeller, K. K. S., & Nadeau, S. E. (1991). A possible pathophysiological substrate of attention deficit hyperactivity disorder. *Journal of Child Neurology, 6,* 74–79.

Hinshaw, S. P. (1992). Externalizing behavior problems and academic underachievement in childhood and adolescence: Causal relationships and underlying mechanisms. *Psychological Bulletin, 111,* 127–155.

Hinshaw, S. P. (1994). *Attention deficits and hyperactivity in children.* Thousand Oaks, CA: Sage.

Hinshaw, S. P., Buhrmeister, D., & Heller, T. (1989). Anger control in response to verbal provocation: Effects of stimulant medication for boys with ADHD. *Journal of Abnormal Child Psychology, 17,* 393–408.

Hinshaw, S. P., Heller, T., & McHale, J. P. (1992). Covert antisocial behavior in boys with attention-deficit hyperactivity disorder: External validation and effects of methylphenidate. *Journal of Consulting and Clinical Psychology, 60,* 274–281.

Hinshaw, S. P., Herbsman, C., Melnick, S., Nigg, J., & Simmel, C. (1993, February). *Psychological and familial processes in ADHD: Continuous or discontinuous with those in normal comparison children?.* Paper presented at the Society for Research in Child and Adolescent Psychopathology, Santa Fe, NM.

Hinshaw, S. P., Morrison, D. C., Carte, E. T., & Cornsweet, C. (1987). Factorial dimensions of the Revised Behavior Problem Checklist: Replication and validation within a kindergarten sample. *Journal of Abnormal Child Psychology, 15,* 309–327.

Hohman, L. B. (1922). Post-encephalitic behavior disorders in children. *Johns Hopkins Hospital Bulletin, 33,* 372–375.

Humphries, T., Kinsbourne, M., & Swanson, J. (1978). Stimulant effects on cooperation and social interaction between hyperactive children and their mothers. *Journal of Child Psychology and Psychiatry, 19,* 13–22.

Humphries, T., Koltun, H., Malone, M., & Roberts, W. (1994). Teacher-identified oral language difficulties among boys with attention problems. *Developmental and Behavioral Pediatrics, 15,* 92–98.

Hynd, G. W., Hern, K. L., Novey, E. S., Eliopulos, D., Marshall, R., Gonzalez, J. J., & Voeller, K. K. (1993). Attention-deficit hyperactivity disorder and asymmetry of the caudate nucleus. *Journal of Child Neurology, 8,* 339– 347.

Hynd, G. W., Semrud-Clikeman, M., Lorys, A. R., Novey, E. S., & Eliopulos, D. (1990). Brain morphology in developmental dyslexia and attention deficit disorder/hyperactivity. *Archives of Neurology, 47,* 919–926.

Hynd, G. W., Semrud-Clikeman, M., Lorys, A. R., Novey, E. S., Eliopulos, D., & Lyytinen, H. (1991). Corpus callosum morphology in attention deficit-hyperactivity disorder: Morphometric analysis of MRI. *Journal of Learning Disabilities, 24,* 141–146.

Ingersoll, B. D. (1988). *Your hyperactive child.* New York: Doubleday.

Ingersoll, B. D., & Goldstein, S. (1993). *Attention deficit disorder and learning disabilities: Realities, myths, and controversial treatments.* New York: Doubleday.

James, W. (1890). *The principles of psychology.* London: Dover.

Kanbayashi, Y., Nakata, Y., Fujii, K., Kita, M., & Wada, K. (1994). ADHD-related behavior among non-referred children: Parents' ratings of DSM-III-R symptoms. *Child Psychiatry and Human Development, 25,* 13–29.

Kanfer, F. H., & Karoly, P. (1972). Self-control: A behavioristic excursion into the lion's den. *Behavior Therapy, 3,* 398–416.

Kaplan, B. J., McNichol, J., Conte, R. A., & Moghadam, H. K. (1987). Sleep disturbance in preschool-aged hyperactive and nonhyperactive children. *Pediatrics, 80,* 839–844.

Kelsoe, J. R., Ginns, E. I., Egeland, J. A., Gerhard, D. S., Goldstein, A. M., Bale, S. J., Pauls, D. L., et al. (1989). Re-evaluation of the linkage relationship between chromosome 11p loci and the gene for bipolar affective disorder in the Old Order Amish. *Nature, 342,* 238–243.

Kessler, J. W. (1980). History of minimal brain dysfunction. In H. Rie & E. Rie (Eds.), *Handbook of minimal brain dysfunctions: A critical view* (pp. 18–52). New York: Wiley.

Klorman, R. (1992). Cognitive event-related potentials in attention deficit disorder. In S. E. Shaywitz & B. A. Shaywitz (Eds.), *Attention deficit disorder comes of age: Toward the twenty-first century* (pp. 221–244). Austin, TX: Pro-ed.

Klorman, R., Salzman, L. F., & Borgstedt, A. D. (1988). Brain event-related potentials in evaluation of cognitive deficits in attention deficit disorder and outcome of stimulant therapy. In L. Bloomingdale (Ed.), *Attention deficit disorder* (Vol. 3, pp. 49–80). New York: Pergamon.

Knobel, M., Wolman, M. B., & Mason, E. (1959). Hyperkinesis and organicity in children. *Archives of General Psychiatry, 1,* 310–321.

Kohn, A. (1989, November). Suffer the restless children. *The Atlantic Monthly,* pp. 90–100.

Koplowitz, S., & Barkley, R. A. (1996). *Sense of time in ADHD children: I. Survey results and objective testing.* Unpublished manuscript, University of Massachusetts Medical Center, Worcester, MA.

Kopp, C. B. (1982). Antecedents of self-regulation: A developmental perspective. *Developmental Psychology, 18,* 199–214.

Lahey, B. B., Applegate, B., McBurnett, K., Biederman, J., Greenhill, L., et al. (in press). DSM-IV field trials for attention deficit/hyperactivity disorder in children and adolescents. *American Journal of Psychiatry.*

Lahey, B. B., & Carlson, C. L. (1992). Validity of the diagnostic category of attention deficit disorder without hyperactivity: A review of the literature. In S. E. Shaywitz

& B. A. Shaywitz (Eds.), *Attention deficit disorder comes of age: Toward the twenty-first century* (pp. 119–144). Austin, TX: Pro-ed.

Lahey, B. B., Pelham, W. E., Schaughency, E. A., Atkins, M. S., Murphy, H. A., Hynd, G. W., Russo, M., Hartdagen, S., & Lorys-Vernon, A. (1988). Dimensions and types of attention deficit disorder with hyperactivity in children: A factor and cluster-analytic approach. *Journal of the American Academy of Child and Adolescent Psychiatry, 27,* 330–335.

Lambert, N. M. (1988). Adolescent outcomes for hyperactive children. *American Psychologist, 43,* 786–799.

Lambert, N. M. & Sandoval, J. (1980). The prevalence of learning disabilities in a sample of children considered hyperactive. *Journal of Abnormal Child Psychology, 8,* 33–50.

Lambert, N. M., Sandoval, J., & Sassone, D. (1978). Prevalence of hyperactivity in elementary school children as a function of social system definers. *American Journal of Orthopsychiatry, 48,* 446–463.

Langsdorf, R., Anderson, R. F., Walchter, D., Madrigal, J. F., & Juarez, L. J. (1979). Ethnicity, social class, and perception of hyperactivity. *Psychology in the Schools, 16,* 293–298.

Lapouse, R., & Monk, M. (1958). An epidemiological study of behavior characteristics in children. *American Journal of Public Health, 48,* 1134–1144.

Last, C. G., Hersen, M., Kazdin, A., Orvaschel, H., & Perrin, S. (1991). Anxiety disorders in children and their families. *Archives of General Psychiatry, 48,* 928–934.

Laufer, M., Denhoff, E., & Solomons, G. (1957). Hyperkinetic impulse disorder in children's behavior problems. *Psychosomatic Medicine, 19,* 38–49.

Lerner, J. A., Inui, T. S., Trupin, E. W., & Douglas, E. (1985). Preschool behavior can predict future psychiatric disorders. *Journal of the American Academy of Child Psychiatry, 24,* 42–48.

Levin, P. M. (1938). Restlessness in children. *Archives of Neurology and Psychiatry, 39,* 764–770.

Levy, F., & Hay, D. (1992, February). *ADHD in twins and their siblings.* Paper presented at the Society for Research in Child and Adolescent Psychopathology, Sarasota, FL.

Levy, F., & Hobbes, G. (1989). Reading, spelling, and vigilance in attention deficit and conduct disorder. *Journal of Abnormal Child Psychology, 17,* 291–298.

Lewinsohn, P. M., Hops, H., Roberts, R. E., Seeley, J. R., & Andrews, J. A. (1993). Adolescent psychopathology: I. Prevalence and incidence of depression and other DSM-III-R disorders in high school students. *Journal of Abnormal Psychology, 102,* 133–144.

Loeber, R. (1990). Development and risk factors of juvenile antisocial behavior and delinquency. *Clinical Psychology Review, 10,* 1–42.

Loeber, R., Green, S. M., Lahey, B. B., Christ, M. A. G., & Frick, P. J. (1992). Developmental sequences in the age of onset of disruptive child behaviors. *Journal of Child and Family Studies, 1,* 21–41.

Loney, J., Kramer, J., & Milich, R. (1981). The hyperkinetic child grows up: Predictors of symptoms, delinquency, and achievement at follow-up. In K. Gadow & J. Loney (Eds.), *Psychosocial aspects of drug treatment for hyperactivity.* Boulder, CO: Westview Press.

Lopez, R. (1965). Hyperactivity in twins. *Canadian Psychiatric Association Journal, 10,* 421.

Lou, H. C., Henriksen, L., & Bruhn, P. (1984). Focal cerebral hypoperfusion in children with dysphasia and/or at-

tention deficit disorder. *Archives of Neurology, 41,* 825–829.

Lou, H. C., Henriksen, L., Bruhn, P., Borner, H., & Nielsen, J. B. (1989). Striatal dysfunction in attention deficit and hyperkinetic disorder. *Archives of Neurology, 46,* 48–52.

Lufi, D., Cohen, A., & Parish-Plass, J. (1990). Identifying ADHD with the WISC-R and the Stroop Color and Word Test. *Psychology in the Schools, 27,* 28–34.

Luk, S. (1985). Direct observations studies of hyperactive behaviors. *Journal of the American Academy of Child and Adolescent Psychiatry, 24,* 338–344.

Lynam, D., Moffitt, T., & Stouthamer-Loeber, M. (1993). Explaining the relation between IQ and delinquency: Class, race, test motivation, school failure, or self-control? *Journal of Abnormal Psychology, 102,* 187–196.

Lyon, G. R. (1995). *Attention, memory, and executive functions.* Baltimore: Brookes.

Malone, M. A., & Swanson, J. M. (1993). Effects of methylphenidate on impulsive responding in children with attention deficit hyperactivity disorder. *Journal of Child Neurology, 8,* 157–163.

Mannuzza, S., Gittelman-Klein, R., Bessler, A., Malloy, P., & LaPadula, M. (1993). Adult outcome of hyperactive boys: Educational achievement, occupational rank, and psychiatric status. *Archives of General Psychiatry, 50,* 565–576.

Mannuzza, S., & Klein, R. (1992). Predictors of outcome of children with attention-deficit hyperactivity disorder. In G. Weiss (Ed.), *Child and adolescent psychiatric clinics of North America: Attention-deficit hyperactivity disorder* (pp. 567–578). Philadelphia: Saunders.

Mariani, M., & Barkley, R. A. (1995). *Neuropsychological and academic functioning in preschool children with attention deficit hyperactivity disorder.* Manuscript submitted for publication.

Mash, E. J., & Johnston, C. (1982). A comparison of mother–child interactions of younger and older hyperactive and normal children. *Child Development, 53,* 1371–1381.

Mash, E. J., & Johnston, C. (1983a). Sibling interactions of hyperactive and normal children and their relationship to reports of maternal stress and self-esteem. *Journal of Clinical Child Psychology, 12,* 91–99.

Mash, E. J., & Johnston, C. (1983b). The prediction of mothers' behavior with their hyperactive children during play and task situations. *Child and Family Behavior Therapy, 5,* 1–14.

Mash, E. J., & Johnston, C. (1990). Determinants of parenting stress: Illustrations from families of hyperactive children and families of physically abused children. *Journal of Clinical Child Psychology, 19,* 313–328.

Mattes, J. A. (1980). The role of frontal lobe dysfunction in childhood hyperkinesis. *Comprehensive Psychiatry, 21,* 358–369.

McArdle, P., O'Brien, G., & Kolvin, I. (1995). Hyperactivity: Prevalence and relationship with conduct disorder. *Journal of Child Psychology and Psychiatry, 36,* 279–303.

McGee, R., Feehan, M., Williams, S., Partridge, F., Silva, P. A., & Kelly, J. (1990). DSM-III disorders in a large sample of adolescents. *Journal of the American Academy of Child and Adolescent Psychiatry, 29,* 611–619.

McGee, R., Stanton, W. R., & Sears, M. R. (1993). Allergic disorders and attention deficit disorder in children. *Journal of Abnormal Child Psychology, 21,* 79–88.

McGee, R., Williams, S., & Feehan, M. (1992). Attention deficit disorder and age of onset of problem behaviors. *Journal of Abnormal Child Psychology, 20,* 487–502.

McGee, R., Williams, S., & Silva, P. A. (1984). Behavioral and developmental characteristics of aggressive, hyperactive, and aggressive–hyperactive boys. *Journal of the American Academy of Child Psychiatry, 23,* 270–279.

Michon, J. (1985). Introduction. In J. Michon & T. Jackson (Eds.), *Time, mind, and behavior.* Berlin: Springer-Verlag.

Milich, R., Hartung, C. M., Matrin, C. A., & Haigler, E. D. (1994). Behavioral disinhibition and underlying processes in adolescents with disruptive behavior disorders. In D. K. Routh (Ed.), *Disruptive behavior disorders in childhood* (pp. 109–138). New York: Plenum Press.

Milich, R., & Kramer, J. (1984). Reflections on impulsivity: An empirical investigation of impulsivity as a construct. In K. Gadow & I. Bialer (Eds.), *Advances in learning and behavioral disabilities* (Vol. 3, pp. 57–94). Greenwich, CT: JAI Press.

Milich, R., & Lorch, E. P. (1994). Television viewing methodology to understand cognitive processing of ADHD children. In T. H. Ollendick & R. J. Prinz (Eds.), *Advances in Clinical Child Psychology* (Vol. 16, pp. 177–202). New York: Plenum Press.

Mitchell, E. A., Aman, M. G., Turbott, S. H., & Manku, M. (1987). Clinical characteristics and serum essential fatty acid levels in hyperactive children. *Clinical Pediatrics, 26,* 406–411.

Moffitt, T. E. (1990). Juvenile delinquency and attention deficit disorder: Boys' developmental trajectories from age 3 to 15. *Child Development, 61,* 893–910.

Morrison, J., & Stewart, M. (1973). The psychiatric status of the legal families of adopted hyperactive children. *Archives of General Psychiatry, 28,* 888–891.

Murphy, K., & Barkley, R. A. (1995). *The prevalence of DSM-IV symptoms of ADHD in a community sample of adults.* Manuscript submitted for publication.

Nasrallah, H. A., Loney, J., Olson, S. C., McCalley-Whitters, M., Kramer, J., & Jacoby, C. G. (1986). Cortical atrophy in young adults with a history of hyperactivity in childhood. *Psychiatry Research, 17,* 241–246.

Needleman, H. L., Gunnoe, C., Leviton, A., Reed, R., Peresie, H., Maher, C., & Barrett, P. (1979). Deficits in psychologic and classroom performance of children with elevated dentine lead levels. *New England Journal of Medicine, 300,* 689–695.

Nichols, P. L., & Chen, T. C. (1981). *Minimal brain dysfunction: A prospective study.* Hillsdale, NJ: Erlbaum.

Nucci, L. P., & Herman, S. (1982). Behavioral disordered children's conceptions of moral, conventional, and personal issues. *Journal of Abnormal Child Psychology, 10,* 411–426.

O'Connor, M., Foch, T., Sherry, T., & Plomin, R. (1980). A twin study of specific behavioral problems of socialization as viewed by parents. *Journal of Abnormal Child Psychology, 8,* 189–199.

O'Leary, K. D., Vivian, D., & Nisi, A. (1985). Hyperactivity in Italy. *Journal of Abnormal Child Psychology, 13,* 485–500.

Olson, S. L. (1989). Assessment of impulsivity in preschoolers: Cross-measure convergences, longitudinal stability, and relevance to social competence. *Journal of Clinical Child Psychology, 18,* 176–183.

Palfrey, J. S., Levine, M. D., Walker, D. K., & Sullivan, M. (1985). The emergence of attention deficits in early childhood: A prospective study. *Developmental and Behavioral Pediatrics, 6,* 339–348.

Parry, P. A., & Douglas, V. I. (1983). Effects of reinforcement on concept identification in hyperactive children. *Journal of Abnormal Child Psychology, 11,* 327–340.

Pauls, D. L. (1991). Genetic factors in the expression of attention-deficit hyperactivity disorder. *Journal of Child and Adolescent Psychopharmacology, 1,* 353–360.

Pauls, D. L., Hurst, C. R., Kidd, K. K., Kruger, S. D., Leckman, J. F., & Cohen, D. J. (1986). Tourette Syndrome and attention deficit disorder: Evidence against a genetic relationship. *Archives of General Psychiatry, 43,* 1177–1179.

Pelham, W. E., & Bender, M. E. (1982). Peer relationships in hyperactive children: Description and treatment. In K. D. Gadow & I. Bialer (Eds.), *Advances in learning and behavioral disabilities* (Vol. 1, pp. 365–436). Greenwich, CT: JAI Press.

Pelham, W. E., Gnagy, E. M., Greenslade, K. E., & Milich, R. (1992). Teacher ratings of DSM-III-R symptoms for the disruptive behavior disorders. *Journal of the American Academy of Child and Adolescent Psychiatry, 31,* 210–218.

Pelham, W. E., & Lang, A. R. (1993). Parental alcohol consumption and deviant child behavior: Laboratory studies of reciprocal effects. *Clinical Psychology Review, 13,* 763–784.

Pendergrast, M., Taylor, E., Rapoport, J. L., Bartko, J., Donnelly, M., Zametkin, A., Ahearn, M. B., Dunn, G., & Wieselberg, H. M. (1988). The diagnosis of childhood hyperactivity A U.S.–U.K. cross-national study of DSM-III and ICD-9. *Journal of Child Psychology and Psychiatry, 29,* 289–300.

Pless, I. B., Taylor, H. G., & Arsenault, L. (1995). The relationship between vigilance deficits and traffic injuries involving children. *Pediatrics, 95,* 219–224.

Pliszka, S. R. (1992). Comorbidity of attention-deficit hyperactivity disorder and overanxious disorder. *Journal of the American Academy of Child and Adolescent Psychiatry, 31,* 197–203.

Plomin, R. (1995). Genetics and children's experiences in the family. *Journal of Child Psychology and Psychiatry, 36,* 33–68.

Porrino, L. J., Rapoport, J. L., Behar, D., Sceery, W., Ismond, D. R., & Bunney, W. E., Jr. (1983). A naturalistic assessment of the motor activity of hyperactive boys. *Archives of General Psychiatry, 40,* 681–687.

Quay, H. C. (1989). The behavioral reward and inhibition systems in childhood behavior disorder. In L. M. Bloomingdale (Ed.), *Attention deficit disorder III: New research in treatment, psychopharmacology, and attention* (pp. 176–186). New York: Pergamon.

Quay, H. C. (1990, February). Presidential address to the Society for Research in Child and Adolescent Psychopathology, Irvine, CA.

Rapoport, J. L., Donnelly, M., Zametkin, A., & Carrougher, J. (1986). "Situational hyperactivity" in a U.S. clinical setting. *Journal of Child Psychology and Psychiatry, 27,* 639–646.

Rapport, M. D., Tucker, S. B., DuPaul, G. J., Merlo, M., & Stoner, G. (1986). Hyperactivity and frustration: The influence of control over and size of rewards in delaying gratification. *Journal of Abnormal Child Psychology, 14,* 181–204.

Richman, N., Stevenson, J., & Graham, P. (1982). *Preschool to school: A behavioural study.* New York: Academic Press.

Roberts, M. A. (1990). A behavioral observation method for differentiating hyperactive and aggressive boys. *Journal of Abnormal Child Psychology, 18,* 131–142.

Rosen, B. N., & Peterson, L. (1990). Gender differences in children's outdoor play injuries: A review and an integration. *Clinical Psychology Review, 10,* 187–205.

Rosenthal, R. H., & Allen, T. W. (1978). An examination of attention, arousal, and learning dysfunctions of hyperkinetic children. *Psychological Bulletin, 85,* 689–715.

Rosenthal, R. H., & Allen, T. W. (1980). Intratask distractibility in hyperkinetic and nonhyperkinetic children. *Journal of Abnormal Child Psychology, 8,* 175–187.

Ross, D. M., & Ross, S. A. (1982). *Hyperactivity: Research, theory and action.* New York: Wiley.

Roth, N., Beyreiss, J., Schlenzka, K., & Beyer, H. (1991). Coincidence of attention deficit disorder and atopic disorders in children: Empirical findings and hypothetical background. *Journal of Abnormal Child Psychology, 19,* 1–13.

Routh, D. K., & Schroeder, C. S. (1976). Standardized playroom measures as indices of hyperactivity. *Journal of Abnormal Child Psychology, 4,* 199–207.

Russo, M. F., & Beidel, D. C. (1994). Comorbidity of childhood anxiety and externalizing disorders: Prevalence, associated characteristics, and validation issues. *Clinical Psychology Review, 14,* 199–221.

Rutter, M. (1977). Brain damage syndromes in childhood: Concepts and findings. *Journal of Child Psychology and Psychiatry, 18,* 1–21.

Rutter, M. (1983). Introduction: Concepts of brain dysfunction syndromes. In M. Rutter (Ed.), *Developmental neuropsychiatry* (pp. 1–14). New York: Guilford Press.

Rutter, M., Bolten, P., Harrington, R., LeCouteur, A., Macdonald, H., & Simonoff, E. (1990). Genetic factors in child psychiatric disorders—I. A review of research strategies. *Journal of Child Psychology and Psychiatry, 31,* 3–37.

Rutter, M., Macdonald, H., LeCouteur, A., Harrington, R., Bolton, P., & Bailey, P. (1990). Genetic factors in child psychiatric disorders—II. Empirical findings. *Journal of Child Psychology and Psychiatry, 31,* 39–83.

Satterfield, J. H., Hoppe, C. M., & Schell, A. M. (1982). A prospective study of delinquency in 110 adolescent boys with attention deficit disorder and 88 normal adolescent boys. *American Journal of Psychiatry, 139,* 795–798.

Schachar, R. J., & Logan, G. D. (1990). Impulsivity and inhibitory control in normal development and childhood psychopathology. *Developmental Psychology, 26,* 710–720.

Schachar, R., Rutter, M., & Smith, A. (1981). The characteristics of situationally and pervasively hyperactive children: Implications for syndrome definition. *Journal of Child Psychology and Psychiatry, 22,* 375–392.

Schachar, R. J., Tannock, R., & Logan, G. (1993). Inhibitory control, impulsiveness, and attention deficit hyperactivity disorder. *Clinical Psychology Review, 13,* 721–740.

Schachar, R., Taylor, E., Weiselberg, M., Thorley, G., & Rutter, M. (1987). Changes in family function and relationships in children who respond to methylphenidate. *Journal of the American Academy of Child and Adolescent Psychiatry, 26,* 728–732.

Schleifer, M., Weiss, G., Cohen, N. J., Elman, M., Cvejic, H., & Kruger, E. (1975). Hyperactivity in preschoolers and the effect of methylphenidate. *American Journal of Orthopsychiatry, 45,* 38–50.

Schrag, P., & Divoky, D. (1975). *The myth of the hyperactive child.* New York: Pantheon.

Semrud-Clikeman, M., Filipek, P. A., Biederman, J., Steingard, R., Kennedy, D., Renshaw, P., & Bekken, K. (1994). Attention-deficit hyperactivity disorder: Magnetic resonance imaging morphometric analysis of the corpus callosum. *Journal of the American Academy of Child and Adolescent Psychiatry, 33,* 875–881.

Sergeant, J. (1988). From DSM-III attentional deficit disorder to functional defects. In L. Bloomingdale & J. Sergeant (Eds.), *Attention deficit disorder: Criteria, cognition, and intervention* (pp. 183–198). New York: Pergamon.

Sergeant, J., & Scholten, C. A. (1985a). On data limitations in hyperactivity. *Journal of Child Psychology and Psychiatry, 26,* 111–124.

Sergeant, J., & Scholten, C. A. (1985b). On resource strategy limitations in hyperactivity: Cognitive impulsivity reconsidered. *Journal of Child Psychology and Psychiatry, 26,* 97–109.

Sergeant, J., & van der Meere, J. P. (1994). Toward an empirical child psychopathology. In D. K. Routh (Ed.), *Disruptive behavior disorders in children* (pp. 59–86). New York: Plenum Press.

Shaywitz, B. A., Shaywitz, S. E., Byrne, T., Cohen, D. J., & Rothman, S. (1983). Attention deficit disorder: Quantitative analysis of CT. *Neurology, 33,* 1500–1503.

Shaywitz, S. E., Cohen, D. J., & Shaywitz, B. E. (1980). Behavior and learning difficulties in children of normal intelligence born to alcoholic mothers. *Journal of Pediatrics, 96,* 978–982.

Silva, P. A., Hughes, P., Williams, S., & Faed, J. M. (1988). Blood lead, intelligence, reading attainment, and behaviour in eleven year old children in Dunedin, New Zealand. *Journal of Child Psychology and Psychiatry, 29,* 43–52.

Silverman, I. W., & Ragusa, D. M. (1992). Child and maternal correlates of impulse control in 24-month old children. *Genetic, Social, and General Psychology Monographs, 116,* 435–473.

Simmell, C., & Hinshaw, S. P. (1993, March). *Moral reasoning and antisocial behavior in boys with ADHD.* Poster presented at the biennial meeting of the Society for Research in Child Development, New Orleans.

Skinner, B. F. (1953). *Science and human behavior.* New York: Macmillan.

Sonuga-Barke, E. J., Lamparelli, M., Stevenson, J., Thompson, M., & Henry, A. (1994). Behaviour problems and pre-school intellectual attainment: The associations of hyperactivity and conduct problems. *Journal of Child Psychology and Psychiatry, 35,* 949–960.

Spitzer, R. L., Davies, M., & Barkley, R. A. (1990). The DSM-III-R field trial for the disruptive behavior disorders. *Journal of the American Academy of Child and Adolescent Psychiatry, 29,* 690–697.

Sprick-Buckminster, S., Biederman, J., Milberger, S., Faraone, S. V., & Lehman, B. (1993). Are perinatal complications relevant to the manifestation of ADD? Issues of comorbidity and familiality. *Journal of the American Academy of Child and Adolescent Psychiatry, 32,* 1032–1037.

Stein, M. A., Szumowski, E., Blondis, T. A., & Roizen, N. J. (1995). Adaptive skills dysfunction in ADD and ADHD children. *Journal of Child Psychology and Psychiatry, 36,* 663–670.

Steinkamp, M. W. (1980). Relationships between environmental distractions and task performance of hyperactive and normal children. *Journal of Learning Disabilities, 13,* 40–45.

Stevenson, J. (1992). Evidence for a genetic etiology in hyperactivity in children. *Behavior Genetics, 22,* 337–343.

Stevenson, J. (1994, June). *Genetics of ADHD.* Paper presented at the Professional Group for ADD and Related Disorders, London.

Stevenson, J., Pennington, B. F., Gilger, J. W., DeFries, J. C., & Gilies, J. J. (1993). Hyperactivity and spelling disability: Testing for shared genetic aetiology. *Journal of Child Psychology and Psychiatry, 34,* 1137–1152.

Stewart, M. A. (1970). Hyperactive children. *Scientific American, 222,* 94–98.

Stewart, M. A., Pitts, F. N., Craig, A. G., & Dieruf, W. (1966). The hyperactive child syndrome. *American Journal of Orthopsychiatry, 36,* 861–867.

Stewart, M. A., Thach, B. T., & Friedin, M. R. (1970). Accidental poisoning and the hyperactive child syndrome. *Disease of the Nervous System, 31,* 403–407.

Still, G. F. (1902). Some abnormal psychical conditions in children. *Lancet, 1,* 1008–1012, 1077–1082, 1163–1168.

Strauss, A. A., & Kephardt, N. C. (1955). *Psychopathology and education of the brain-injured child: Vol. 2. Progress in theory and clinic.* New York: Grune & Stratton.

Strauss, A. A., & Lehtinen, L. E. (1947). *Psychopathology and education of the brain-injured child.* New York: Grune & Stratton.

Streissguth, A. P., Martin, D. C., Barr, H. M., Sandman, B. M., Kirchner, G. L., & Darby, B. L. (1984). Intrauterine alcohol and nicotine exposure: Attention and reaction time in 4–year-old children. *Developmental Psychology, 20,* 533–541.

Stryker, S. (1925). Encephalitis lethargica—The behavior residuals. *Training School Bulletin, 22,* 152–157.

Stuss, D. T., & Benson, D. F. (1986). *The frontal lobes.* New York: Raven Press.

Szatmari, P. (1992). The epidemiology of attention-deficit hyperactivity disorders. In G. Weiss (Ed.), *Child and adolescent psychiatric clinics of North America: Attention-deficit hyperactivity disorder* (pp. 361–372). Philadelphia: Saunders.

Szatmari, P., Offord, D. R., & Boyle, M. H. (1989). Correlates, associated impairments, and patterns of service utilization of children with attention deficit disorders: Findings from the Ontario Child Health Study. *Journal of Child Psychology and Psychiatry, 30,* 205–217.

Tallmadge, J., & Barkley, R. A. (1983). The interactions of hyperactive and normal boys with their mothers and fathers. *Journal of Abnormal Child Psychology, 11,* 565–579.

Tannock, R. (in press). Attention deficit disorders with anxiety disorders. In T. E. Brown (Ed.), *Subtypes of attention deficit disorders in children, adolescents, and adults.* Washington, DC: American Psychiatric Press.

Tarver-Behring, S., Barkley, R. A., & Karlsson, J. (1985). The mother–child interactions of hyperactive boys and their normal siblings. *American Journal of Orthopsychiatry, 55,* 202–209.

Taylor, E. (1986). *The overactive child.* Philadelphia: Lippincott.

Taylor, E., Sandberg, S., Thorley, G., & Giles, S. (1991). *The epidemiology of childhood hyperactivity.* Oxford, UK: Oxford University Press.

Thomson, G. O. B., Raab, G. M., Hepburn, W. S., Hunter, R., Fulton, M., & Laxen, D. P. H., (1989). Blood-lead levels and children's behaviour—Results from the Edinburgh lead study. *Journal of Child Psychology and Psychiatry, 30,* 515–528.

Torgesen, J. K. (1994). Issues in the assessment of of executive function: An information-processing perspective. In G. R. Lyon (Ed.), *Frames of reference for the assessment of learning disabilities: New views on measurement issues* (pp. 143–162). Baltimore: Brookes.

Trites, R. L. (1979). *Hyperactivity in children: Etiology, measurement, and treatment implications.* Baltimore: University Park Press.

Trites, R. L., Dugas, F., Lynch, G., & Ferguson, B. (1979). Incidence of hyperactivity. *Journal of Pediatric Psychology, 4,* 179–188.

Trommer, B. L., Hoeppner, J. B., Rosenberg, R. S., Armstrong, K. J., & Rothstein, J. A. (1988). Sleep disturbances in children with attention deficit disorder. *Annals of Neurology, 24,* 325.

van den Oord, E. J. C. G., Boomsma, D. I., & Verhulst, F. C. (1994). A study of problem behaviors in 10- to 15-year-old biologically related and unrelated international adoptees. *Behavior Genetics, 24,* 193–205.

Velez, C. N., Johnson, J., & Cohen, P. (1989). A longitudinal analysis of selected risk factors for childhood psychopathology. *Journal of the American Academy of Child and Adolescent Psychiatry, 28,* 861–864.

Voelker, S. L., Carter, R. A., Sprague, D. J., Gdowski, C. L., & Lachar, D. (1989). Developmental trends in memory and metamemory in children with attention deficit disorder. *Journal of Pediatric Psychology, 14,* 75–88.

Vygotsky, L. S. (1978). *Mind in society.* Cambridge, MA: Harvard University Press.

Vygotsky, L. S. (1987). Thinking and speech. In *The collected works of L. S. Vygotsky: Vol. 1. Problems in general psychology* (N. Minick, Trans.). New York: Plenum Press.

Wakefield, J. C. (1992). The concept of mental disorder: On the boundary between biological facts and social values. *American Psychologist, 47,* 373–388.

Wallander, J. L., Schroeder, S. R., Michelli, J. A., & Gualtieri, C. T. (1987). Classroom social interactions of attention deficit disorder with hyperactivity children as a function of stimulant medication. *Journal of Pediatric Psychology, 12,* 61–76.

Weiss, G., & Hechtman, L. (1993). *Hyperactive children grown up.* New York: Guilford Press.

Welner, Z., Welner, A., Stewart, M., Palkes, H., & Wish, E. (1977). A controlled study of siblings of hyperactive children. *Journal of Nervous and Mental Disease, 165,* 110–117.

Welsh, M. C., & Pennington, B. F. (1988). Assessing frontal lobe functioning in children: Views from developmental psychology. *Developmental Neuropsychology, 4,* 199– 230.

Werry, J. S., Elkind, G. S., & Reeves, J. S. (1987). Attention deficit, conduct, oppositional, and anxiety disorders in children: III. Laboratory differences. *Journal of Abnormal Child Psychology, 15,* 409–428.

Werry, J. S., & Quay, H. C. (1971). The prevalence of behavior symptoms in younger elementary school children. *American Journal of Orthopsychiatry, 41,* 136–143.

Whalen, C. K., & Henker, B. (1992). The social profile of attention-deficit hyperactivity disorder: Five fundamental facets. In G. Weiss (Ed.), *Child and adolescent psychiatric clinics of North America: Attention-deficit hyperactivity disorder* (pp. 395–410). Philadelphia: Saunders.

Whalen, C. K., Henker, B., Collins, B. E., McAuliffe, S., & Vaux, A. (1979). Peer interaction in structured communication task: Comparisons of normal and hyperactive boys and of methylphenidate (Ritalin) and placebo effects. *Child Development, 50,* 388–401.

Whalen, C. K., Henker, B., & Dotemoto, S. (1980). Methylphenidate and hyperactivity: Effects on teacher behaviors. *Science, 208,* 1280–1282.

Whalen, C. K., Henker, B., Swanson, J. M., Granger, D., Kliewer, W., & Spencer, J. (1987). Natural social behaviors in hyperactive children: Dose effects of methylphenidate. *Journal of Consulting and Clinical Psychology, 55,* 187–193.

Willerman, L. (1973). Activity level and hyperactivity in twins. *Child Development, 44,* 288–293.

Willis, T. J., & Lovaas, I. (1977). A behavioral approach to treating hyperactive children: The parent's role. In J. B. Millichap (Ed.), *Learning disabilities and related disorders* (pp. 119–140). Chicago: Yearbook Medical Publications.

Wood, F. B., & Felton, R. H. (1994). Separate linguistic and attentional factors in the development of reading. *Topics in language disorders, 14,* 52–57.

World Health Organization. (1993). *The ICD-10 classification of mental and behavioral disorders: Diagnostic criteria for research.* Geneva, Switzerland: Author.

Zagar, R., & Bowers, N. D. (1983). The effect of time of day on problem-solving and classroom behavior. *Psychology in the Schools, 20,* 337–345.

Zahn, T. P., Krusei, M. J. P., & Rapoport, J. L. (1991). Reaction time indices of attention deficits in boys with disruptive behavior disorders. *Journal of Abnormal Child Psychology, 19,* 233–252.

Zametkin, A. J., Liebenauer, L. L., Fitzgerald, G. A., King, A. C., Minkunas, D. V., Herscovitch, P., Yamada, E. M., & Cohen, R. M. (1993). Brain metabolism in teenagers with attention-deficit hyperactivity disorder. *Archives of General Psychiatry, 50,* 333–340.

Zametkin, A. J., Nordahl, T. E., Gross, M., King, A. C., Semple, W. E., Rumsey, J., Hamburger, S., & Cohen, R. M. (1990). Cerebral glucose metabolism in adults with hyperactivity of childhood onset. *New England Journal of Medicine, 323,* 1361–1366.

Zentall, S. S. (1985). A context for hyperactivity. In K. Gadow & I. Bialer (Eds.), *Advances in learning and behavioral disabilities* (Vol. 4, pp. 273–343). Greenwich, CT: JAI Press.

Zentall, S. S. (1988). Production deficiencies in elicited language but not in the spontaneous verbalizations of hyperactive children. *Journal of Abnormal Child Psychology, 16,* 657–673.

Zentall, S. S., & Smith, Y. S. (1993). Mathematical performance and behavior of children with hyperactivity with and without coexisting aggression. *Behavior Research and Therapy, 31,* 701–710.

Conduct and Oppositional Defiant Disorders

Stephen P. Hinshaw
Carolyn A. Anderson

The United States is currently witnessing an unprecedented surge in rates of violent crime among youth (Fingerhut & Kleinman, 1990), with ever-increasing numbers of children and adolescents serving as perpetrators of aggression, assault, and murder (Richters, 1993). Indeed, newspaper headlines that include graphic depictions of violence among children and adolescents are commonplace in the 1990s. Among youth, the highest rates of referral for mental health services involve aggressive, acting-out, and disruptive behavior patterns, tendencies that have shown a detectable increase over the past 20 years (Achenbach & Howell, 1993). The threat—or reality—of violence has created climates of fear, intimidation, and deprivation in many communities (Richters & Martinez, 1993). Furthermore, incarceration rates in the United States are at all-time highs (*The New York Times*, September 13, 1994). Thus, for reasons of social salience, increasing prevalence, and potential for psychological and physical harm to individuals and communities, the need for sound scientific efforts directed toward understanding the roots, classification, underlying mechanisms, and treatment of antisocial behavior has never been greater.

Considerable controversy exists, however, in the field. For one thing, there is dispute regarding the proper disciplines that should investigate antisocial activity and the optimal perspectives from which to view such behavior patterns. Because of the differing definitions of normative behavior across cultures, perhaps anthropological or sociological perspectives on antisocial functioning should receive primacy (e.g., Hirschi, 1969). Although our focus herein is directed more toward individual, familial, and social contextual influences than toward the role of culture per se, the ascription of antisocial behavior exclusively to intraindividual causes is a danger that we take pains to avoid. A pertinent question, in fact, is whether antisocial behavior patterns comprise psychological or psychiatric impairment ("mental disorders" in the terminology of the fourth edition of the *Diagnostic and Statistical Manual of Mental Disorders* (DSM-IV; American Psychiatric Association, 1994) as opposed to adaptive responses to aggression-provoking or criminogenic environments. The viability and validity of considering antisocial behavior patterns as psychopathological are foci herein, as is the need for subtyping both antisocial behavior and the individuals who commit such acts. We contend, in fact, that only a subset of individuals displaying antisocial behavior patterns should properly fall under the umbrella of mental disorder or impairment (see Richters & Cicchetti, 1993).

Overall, a salient theme throughout the chapter is that antisocial patterns, whether considered as dimensions of behavior or as distinct categorical entities, are heterogeneous with respect to constituent behaviors, causation, developmental mechanisms, and long-term course. Phrased alternatively, antisocial actions that appear similar at a given point in time may betray fundamentally disparate subtypes when viewed longitudinally (see especially Moffitt, 1993). Global, unidimensional theories of antisocial actions must give way to consideration of divergent underlying patterns and differing developmental trajectories for distinct subgroups of youngsters.

Our overarching goals for this chapter are to present current perspectives on the voluminous literature surrounding aggressive, antisocial, and psychopathic behavior patterns in childhood and adolescence and to illuminate current thinking with respect to definitions, conceptualization, prevalence, comorbidity, and etiology. We emphasize throughout that antisocial behavior develops in relation to multiple influences, including psychobiological variables, parent–child interactions, familial traits, school settings, social service agencies, cultural messages, and societal norms. Given the centrality of the domains in which antisocial youth display impairment—in particular, peer relationships, academic achievement, and family functioning—our hope is that the reader will leave these pages with an appreciation of the complexity of the issues surrounding this salient and troublesome type of behavioral disturbance.

The variegated nature of the subject matter—and the lack of consensus regarding underlying frameworks—necessitates our beginning by defining several key terms and by discussing a number of core conceptual issues regarding aggression and antisocial behavior. Following such coverage, we provide a brief historical account of conceptions of antisocial behavior and cover current diagnostic criteria and related issues. After discussion of prevalence and of developmental progressions—a key focus of the chapter—we highlight issues of gender, comorbidity, underlying mechanisms, and etiology, with strong consideration given to integrated, transactional causal models of the development of antisocial behavior. We conclude with discussion of key issues for the field. Note that page limitations necessitate our deemphasizing the important topics of assessment and intervention; for recent perspectives, see Hinshaw and Zupan (in press), Kazdin (1987), and Kolko (1994).

TERMINOLOGY AND CONCEPTS

Terms in Use to Define the Domain

Investigators, clinicians, and commentators have utilized a host of terms to describe *antisocial behavior* in children, adolescents, and adults, with resultant imprecision and confusion. To clarify the ensuing discussion, we briefly discuss several of the most widely used exemplars of such terminology. First, from a legal perspective, child and adolescent manifestations of antisocial behavior are termed "delinquent" and adult manifestations, "criminal." Indeed, with rates of imprisonment at an all-time high in the United States, legal definitions of antisocial activity are increasingly salient. Yet these terms have limitations for psychological analysis, including (1) the usual necessity of official apprehension in allowing their usage, (2) their neglect of the antisocial activities of young children, and (3) the ever-changing nature of the bounds of illicit behavior defined by legal standards.[1] Although the focus of the chapter is on chronic patterns of aggressive and antisocial behavior that transcend delinquency or criminal behavior per se, much of the current literature in the field focuses on delinquency. Clarification of sample definitions is essential in reading the literature on this topic.

Second, empirical psychological investigations often distinguish so-called externalizing behavior patterns—those marked by impulsive, overactive, aggressive, and antisocial actions—from internalizing (anxious, dysphoric, withdrawn, thought-disordered, somaticizing) features (Achenbach, 1991). Indeed, a long tradition of research posits fundamental distinctions between these two domains with respect to underlying behavioral components, etiological factors, and long-term course (e.g., Quay, 1986). Whereas the differentiation does appear valid, we highlight at the outset that, in the realm of severe psychopathology, overlap between these two areas is quite likely. Indeed, the association between antisocial behavior and internalizing syndromes of anxiety and depression receives subsequent commentary in our discussion of comorbidity.

Within the externalizing domain—also known as "acting-out," "disruptive," or "undercontrolled"[2] —a fundamental distinction exists between aggressive and antisocial behavior, on the one hand, and the spectrum of inattentive–impulsive–overactive symptoms on the other (Fergusson, Horwood, & Lloyd, 1991; Loney,

1987). Whereas these types of behavior frequently co-occur, as witnessed by their loading together on a higher-order externalizing dimension (Quay, 1986) and by the diagnostic overlap of categories reflecting oppositional or aggressive actions with attention-deficit disorders (see Biederman, Newcorn, & Sprich, 1991), the distinction has been validated in many investigations (for a review, see Hinshaw, 1987).[3] Because the overlap or comorbidity between aggressive/antisocial actions and inattentive–impulsive–overactive patterns is quite important for the development of long-term antisocial patterns (e.g., Moffitt, 1990), we expressly consider this association in the section on comorbidity.

Third, in the psychiatric tradition of forming diagnostic categories, the labels "conduct disorder" (CD) and, more recently, "oppositional defiant disorder" (ODD) are the two mainstays of the "disruptive behavior disorders" (American Psychiatric Association, 1994). ODD is denoted by the age-inappropriate and persistent display of angry, defiant, irritable, and oppositional behaviors; CD includes a far more severe list of aggressive and antisocial behaviors that involve the infliction of pain or the denial of the rights of others (e.g., initiating fights, breaking into others' homes, firesetting) (American Psychiatric Association, 1994). The intention behind these diagnostic categories is to include youngsters whose defiant or antisocial behavior patterns are persistent and clearly impairing. Thus, whereas many (if not most) youngsters diagnosed with CD will be apprehended as delinquent, only a minority of delinquent adolescents would qualify for a diagnosis of CD, given the transitory nature of much delinquency (Hinshaw, Lahey, & Hart, 1993; Moffitt, 1993). Elaboration of the diagnostic criteria for ODD and CD—and appraisal of their validity as categories—are central topics of this chapter.

Fourth, the term for adults with the persistent display of antisocial behavior patterns is "antisocial personality disorder," found on Axis II of the DSM-IV nosology (American Psychiatric Association, 1994). As we highlight subsequently, conceptions of antisocial personality disorder in recent decades have emphasized the repetitive display of multiple illegal behaviors, with the necessity of a history of conduct-disordered behavior before adulthood. This behaviorally based definition can be differentiated from the alternative conception of "psychopathy," which emphasizes a callous, manipulative, impulsive,

and remorseless psychological and interpersonal profile (Cleckley, 1976; Hare, Hart, & Harpur, 1991; Sutker, 1994). It is noteworthy that current research supports the viability of psychopathy per se as a separable taxon, whereas repetitive criminality is best conceived as dimensional in nature (Harris, Rice, & Quinsey, 1994). Although some rapprochement between definitions of antisocial personality disorder and psychopathy has emerged in recent years (American Psychiatric Association, 1994), the field is grappling with the differing underlying models of these conceptions (Hinshaw, 1994; Sutker, 1994).

In sum, the various terms in use for depicting the domain under consideration often hamper clear communication in the field. Although our primary focus herein is on the diagnostic categories of ODD and CD in childhood and adolescence, the heated debate in the field as to the utility of such categorical conceptions, the considerable research on dimensional approaches to aggression and antisocial behavior, and the voluminous literature on delinquency all necessitate our explicitly considering alternate frameworks in the sections that follow. Indeed, differences in conceptual focus and in sampling across investigations comprise a central problem for the field. In keeping with the present emphasis on the diversity of antisocial activity, we next consider the multiple types of activities that are subsumed by measured dimensions of aggressive and antisocial behaviors.

Subtypes of Aggression and Antisocial Behavior

Despite the cross-sectional and longitudinal coherence of severe antisocial behavior (e.g., Farrington, 1992), the constituent behavior patterns subsumed under aggressive and antisocial activities are quite variegated. Major reviews of the development of aggression (Feschbach, 1970; Parke & Slaby, 1983) emphasize the importance of subdividing the domain into theoretically and empirically distinguishable subcategories. Brief descriptions of several dichotomized distinctions may help to convey the diversity of the domain.

First, interpersonal aggression may be verbal (taunting, threatening, name calling, swearing) versus physical (bullying, fighting, assaulting). This distinction is evidenced not only descriptively but developmentally: Physical aggression emerges rather early in development, with peak levels during the preschool years, whereas ver-

bal aggression shows a later onset (Parke & Slaby, 1983). Thus, the persistence of high levels of physical aggression into middle childhood may signal the need for clinical attention, as might the early onset of noteworthy verbal aggression during the preschool years.

Next, aggression can be categorized as instrumental (goal directed) versus hostile (Feschbach, 1970); for the latter type, the infliction of pain is characterized as the intent of the behavior. Some levels of instrumental aggression are clearly normative for toddlers, whose cries of "mine" as they grab toys may signal a consolidating sense of self. On the other hand, hostile aggression (at extreme levels) demands further assessment at any age.

An understudied distinction pertains to aggression that is direct (cf. the verbal and physical manifestations noted above) versus indirect ("getting even" by having a third party retaliate, spreading rumors). Indirect aggression may pertain to girls more than to boys (Bjorkqvist, Osterman, & Kaukiainen, 1992); its consideration may illuminate (and mitigate) the oft-cited gender differences in rates of aggression and antisocial behavior (Goodman & Kohlsdorf, 1994; see also Crick & Grotpeter, 1995, for discussion of relational aggression, which may also predominate in girls).

Fourth, aggressive behavior may be proactive (bullying, threatening) versus reactive (retaliatory). In a systematic program of research, Dodge and colleagues (see Dodge, 1991; Dodge & Coie, 1987) have shown that reactive (but not proactive) aggression is marked by several sociocognitive information-processing deficits and distortions, including the underutilization of cues in reaching interpersonal decisions and a propensity to attribute hostile intent to others in ambiguous interpersonal situations, and by exposure to abusive environments. Thus, this distinction appears to have important theoretical and empirical underpinnings.

At a broader level, antisocial behavior can be classified as "overt"—exemplified by most of the types of aggressive actions noted in the preceding paragraphs—versus "covert" or nonaggressive. The latter category is characterized by such clandestine actions as lying, stealing, destroying property, abusing substances, being truant, and firesetting. On the widely used and well-validated Child Behavior Checklist (CBCL; Achenbach, 1991), the overt/covert distinction is evidenced by separate narrow-band scales of Aggressive and Delinquent. Although many severely antisocial youth display both types of anti-social activity, the overt/covert distinction is empirically robust (Loeber & Schmaling, 1985) with growing evidence for divergent external correlates and causal factors. For instance, the Aggression scale of the CBCL displays substantial heritability, but the Delinquent scale, covering covert behaviors, does not (Edelbrock, Rende, Plomin, & Thompson, 1995). These two domains are also marked by somewhat different familial child-rearing styles (Patterson & Stouthamer-Loeber, 1984) and disparate developmental trajectories (Loeber, 1990; Loeber, Wung, et al., 1993). Because the DSM-IV diagnosis of CD (as have all recent DSM editions) includes an admixture of overt and covert behavioral criteria—for example, assault and forced sexual activity as well as lying, shoplifting, and truancy—the CD diagnosis may confound disparate subtypes of antisocial youth (Achenbach, 1993). We return to this point in our subsequent discussion of diagnostic criteria.

Overall, even at the level of description of the constituent actions, the realm of aggression/antisocial behavior is complex and variegated. Much of the literature on aggression, antisocial activity, and delinquency confounds multiple subcategories of this domain, leading to difficulty in comparing investigations from different laboratories or from different time periods. Because precision in terminology is of paramount importance for the field, we argue throughout for careful attention to the definitions of antisocial behavior and to the subtypes of antisocial youth in various investigations.

Dimensions or Categories?

A key issue for the field of psychopathology pertains to the conception of deviance as dimensional or continuous, on the one hand, versus discrete or categorical on the other (see Eysenck, 1986, for pertinent discussion). For the domain under consideration, the question may be posed as follows: Is antisocial behavior in children and adolescents best conceived as a continuum, with quantitative (but not qualitative) differences between youngsters with respect to their constituent behaviors? Or do actual categories, diagnostic entities, or taxa (e.g., ODD or CD) exist? In other words, are there cutoff points for the underlying behavioral features (or for correlates of the symptom patterns) that reflect true discontinuities in the population? This deceptively simple dichotomy between dimensional and categorical perspectives is quite pertinent to any discussion of aggressive and antisocial behavior.

In the first place, our nosologies (e.g., DSM-IV) are presented largely in a Kraepelinian framework, in which distinct disorders—defined by inclusionary and exclusionary criteria—are held to be "present" versus "absent" and to be distinct from other diagnoses (see Achenbach, 1993). As argued by Hinshaw, Lahey, and Hart (1993), however, categorical approaches must reflect actual discontinuities in the underlying distributions of the constituent behavior patterns if they are to be viable. If such discontinuities are not found, the only advantages of categorical approaches would be convenience and the maintenance of tradition. Although few data address this issue regarding antisocial behavior, the empirical report of Robins and McEvoy (1990) is heuristic.

In this investigation, the question was whether the overt and covert symptoms of CD in childhood, assessed retrospectively by American adults who participated in the landmark Epidemiologic Catchment Area (ECA) study of the prevalence of mental disorders (Robins & Regier, 1991), could predict adolescent and adult patterns of substance abuse. Specifically, would the prediction be linear, with each successive number of aggressive/antisocial symptoms incrementing the predictive power in stepwise fashion, or would it increase precipitously when a certain diagnostic threshold was reached? The prediction function was, in fact, entirely linear: Each successively higher number of childhood CD symptoms incremented the prediction to later substance abuse, with no evidence for a "jump" in predictive power above any given cutoff. Overall, for this example, a conception of CD as continuous or dimensional appeared optimal.

With other types of mental and cognitive disorder, however—for example, severe forms of mental retardation—discontinuities with respect to causation and impairment appear when appropriate cutoffs are invoked for clearly dimensional measures (in this case, measured intelligence; see Rutter, Bolton, et al., 1990). In this case, thresholds regarding IQ and adaptive behavior do yield a viable category. It is also possible that, for antisocial behavior, criteria other than overt and covert behaviors themselves may be utilized to define distinct categories. In fact, Moffitt (1993) has summarized disparate evidence and concluded that (1) age of onset and (2) overlap with attention deficits, neuropsychological dysfunction, and family discord are joint markers of fundamentally divergent taxa, with an early-onset type manifesting clear psychopathology but adolescent-onset youngsters appearing within the normal range of developmental tendencies.

Dimensional and categorical approaches to psychopathology need not be mutually exclusive (Achenbach, 1993). For instance, groups of individuals with discrete psychopathology may emerge when cluster analytic approaches are applied to dimensional measures of behavioral disturbance; in other words, empirically derived typologies may emerge from quantitative, dimensional data, with the potential for validation of the resultant categories on the basis of external criterion measures. Indeed, renewed interest in underlying classes or taxa characterizes current conceptualization in developmental psychopathology (Kazdin & Kagan, 1994). In sum, dimensional and categorical approaches can provide complementary information regarding psychopathology. Initial quantitative measurement on continuous scales can be supplemented with additional developmental or diagnostic information and with appropriate statistical analyses to yield the possibility of categorical taxa. Before discrete categories are posited and reified, however, the field must establish clear evidence for their validity.

A related point bears mention. Particularly within the realm of antisocial behavior, for which multiple socioeconomic, familial, and societal influences are salient, it may be that classification into discrete categories—especially those with a psychiatric, intraindividual orientation—may blind the field to the very real social influences on these troublesome behavior patterns. Indeed, because treatment decisions are quite likely to follow from conceptions as to the locus of the problem, classification of the child as psychopathological may steer toward individual rather than systemic prevention or treatment strategies. Despite the scientific and practical benefits that may accrue to accurate classification, real dangers exist when labeling unjustly ascribes the underlying problem to psychopathology or to a mental disorder (Richters & Cicchetti, 1993). On the other hand, if viable categories are found to exist—and if some youngsters with antisocial behavior patterns evidence clear psychopathology—the resultant precision could aid in the mounting of therapeutic efforts (Harris et al., 1994; Moffitt, 1993). In the next section, we elaborate on the current diagnostic criteria for CD and ODD and pause to address the standards that should be invoked to decide if aberrant be-

havior patterns comprise mental disorders/psychopathology as opposed to social deviance or developmental variations.

DEFINITIONAL CRITERIA

Brief Historical Overview

Children and Adolescents

Some of the earliest applications of multivariate statistical analysis to child psychopathology helped to establish the psychometric viability of aggressive and antisocial behavior patterns in children and adolescents (e.g., Hewitt & Jenkins, 1946). This work also began the tradition of subtyping this domain. In brief, youngsters' social bonds and types of antisocial activities formed the basis of two discrete dimensions: (1) "undersocialized," marked by assaultive, aggressive behaviors committed alone, versus (2) "socialized" or group-delinquent, characterized by the presence of social connections and by covert as well as overt antisocial activity. This empirical distinction has continued to receive internal and external validation. Indeed, so-called socialized delinquency—which may be evidenced by gang membership—is typically marked by fewer indicators of psychopathological functioning and a better long-term course than the undersocialized variant (Quay, 1987). Accordingly, much of the psychological and psychiatric literature on aggression in childhood and adolescence has focused on youngsters who display an undersocialized pattern of antisocial behavior. Indeed, as we present later in the chapter, key psychobiological features and the presence of multiple familial risk factors are salient for the undersocialized group (who tend to display early onset and significant aggression) but not the socialized subcategory.

In the landmark 1980 publication of the third edition of the *Diagnostic and Statistical Manual of Mental Disorders* (DSM-III; American Psychiatric Association, 1980), which revolutionized psychiatric nosology in the United States, CD received "operational" criteria for the first time; these included a number of severe overt and covert manifestations of antisocial behavior. Only one constituent action, displayed over long time periods, was necessary for a diagnosis; overly inflated prevalence rates were a potential problem. DSM-III also listed four subcategories of CD, corresponding to the cells of a 2×2 matrix of (1) socialized versus undersocialized and (2) aggres-

sive versus nonaggressive dimensions. The reliability of classification into these subtypes was poor, however, largely because of the confounding of the two components (e.g., few undersocialized, nonaggressive youngsters were found).

In DSM-III-R (American Psychiatric Association, 1987), the number of conduct-disordered behaviors required for diagnosis was increased to three (from a list of 13), with each needing to be displayed for at least 6 months. This raising of the threshold reflected the established finding that the diversity (rather than any particular form) of antisocial activity—committed at early ages—best predicts chronic antisocial functioning and recidivism in adolescence and adulthood (see, e.g., Robins, 1966; Stattin & Magnusson, 1989). Furthermore, the subtyping scheme was simplified to the following: (1) a group (or socialized) type; (2) a solitary, aggressive subcategory; and (3) an undifferentiated type with mixed features.

DSM-III also included, for the first time, a milder variant of CD termed oppositional disorder. The intention behind this category was to capture early manifestations of aggressive, antisocial behavior that are exhibited in early to middle childhood. The constituent symptoms comprised irritable, stubborn, and defiant behavioral features, displayed at rates considered deviant developmentally. Because of the ubiquity of such behavioral features in young children, however, along with marginal reliabilities in empirical investigations, considerable doubt was raised as to the viability of this category (see Rey et al., 1988). The revision in DSM-III-R—with the name changed to oppositional defiant disorder, or ODD—included nine behavioral symptoms, five of which were necessary for diagnosis. Whether this definition captures a true developmental precursor to later CD (Loeber, Lahey, & Thomas, 1991) or fails to deserve the status of a bona fide disorder (Achenbach, 1993) has been the subject of continuing debate. We return to this controversy in our consideration of developmental factors and trajectories related to antisocial behavior patterns.

Adults

Regarding adult manifestations of chronic antisocial behavior, a sizable literature has appeared over the years with respect to so-called psychopathy or sociopathy, signified by a manipulative, exploitive, predatory lifestyle (see Cleckley, 1976). Psychopathy has been the subject of considerable research regarding its psychodynamic,

familial, and psychobiological underpinnings: Early socialization practices as well as the potential for impaired avoidance conditioning and diminished response to punishment have been implicated as key mechanisms for this disorder (see review of Sutker, 1994).

In DSM-III (American Psychiatric Association, 1980), Axis II personality disorders were presented for the first time, with the goal of operationalizing chronic, maladaptive traits that yield substantial impairment. Reflecting the DSM's adherence to nonetiologically oriented operational criteria, the new category of antisocial personality disorder (APD) borrowed heavily from the formulations of Robins (1966, 1978), who eschewed inferences of internal psychological processes and instead advocated a set of behavioral indicators of chronic antisocial functioning in adulthood. Many of the psychological and interpersonal hallmarks of psychopathy per se (e.g., callousness, manipulativeness, deceitfulness) were ignored in favor of multiple indicators of a persistent antisocial lifestyle (e.g., inconsistent work behavior, lack of monogamous relationships, aggression, multiple offenses). (For a review of assessment issues pertinent to psychopathy, see Lilienfeld, 1993.) In addition—and crucially for the subject matter of the present chapter—the diagnosis of APD mandated the presence of CD in childhood or adolescence. Thus, by definition in both DSM-III and DSM-III-R, antisocial behavior patterns beginning in youth were considered a necessary precondition for APD. This requirement has continued in DSM-IV, as we discuss below.

The exclusively behavioral focus of the APD criteria has been criticized by Hare et al. (1991), who contend that psychopathy comprises key psychological and interpersonal features (e.g., callousness and manipulation as well as shallow, nonempathic affect). Indeed, they contend that APD definitions run the risk of labeling repetitive criminality as a form of personality disorder, with pertinent psychological and interpersonal features ignored in the diagnostic criteria. As noted earlier, and in partial defense of their position, psychopathy per se has recently been found to behave as a discrete taxon, whereas repetitive criminality in adulthood appears to fit a dimensional characterization (Harris et al., 1994). Yet importantly, the optimal indicator of the category of psychopathy appears to be the development of persistent aggression and antisocial behavior patterns in childhood (Harris et al., 1994; Hinshaw, 1994). Investigation of the developmental roots of adult antisocial functioning, however characterized, is therefore crucial.

Current Definitions of ODD and CD

The DSM-IV definitional criteria for ODD are presented in Table 3.1, and the criteria for CD are listed in Table 3.2. As can be seen, ODD requires four of eight indicators of hostile, defiant, negativistic, and irritable behaviors for a duration of at least 6 months—present at levels considered developmentally extreme—whereas CD mandates three of 15 examples of more serious overt and covert antisocial behaviors. Several themes and issues regarding the definitions of these taxa bear extended discussion.

Viability of the Categories

A key means of appraising the validity of categories of antisocial behavior is to appraise their separability from other behavioral syndromes.

TABLE 3.1. DSM-IV Diagnostic Criteria for Oppositional Defiant Disorder

A. A pattern of negativistic, hostile, and defiant behavior lasting at least 6 months, during which four (or more) of the following are present:

    (1) often loses temper
    (2) often argues with adults
    (3) often actively defies or refuses to comply with adults' requests or rules
    (4) often deliberately annoys people
    (5) often blames others for his or her mistakes or misbehavior
    (6) is often touchy or easily annoyed by others
    (7) is often angry or resentful
    (8) is often spiteful or vindictive

    Note: Consider a criterion met only if the behavior occurs more frequently than is typically observed in individuals of comparable age and developmental level.

B. The disturbance in behavior causes significant impairment in social, academic, or occupational functioning.

C. The behaviors do not occur exclusively during the course of a Psychotic or Mood Disorder.

D. Criteria are not met for Conduct Disorder and, if the individual is age 18 years or older, criteria are not met for Antisocial Personality Disorder.

Note. From American Psychiatric Association (1994, pp. 93–94). Copyright 1994 by the American Psychiatric Association. Reprinted by permission.

TABLE 3.2. DSM-IV Criteria for Conduct Disorder

A. A repetitive and persistent pattern of behavior in which the basic rights of others or major age-appropriate societal norms or rules are violated, as manifested by the presence of three (or more) of the following criteria in the past 12 months, with at least one criterion present in the past 6 months:

Aggression to people and animals
(1) often bullies, threatens, or intimidates others
(2) often initiates physical fights
(3) has used a weapon that can cause serious physical harm to others (e.g., a bat, brick, broken bottle, knife, gun)
(4) has been physically cruel to people
(5) has been physically cruel to animals
(6) has stolen while confronting a victim (e.g., mugging, purse snatching, extortion, armed robbery)
(7) has forced someone into sexual activity

Destruction of property
(8) has deliberately engaged in fire setting with the intention of causing serious damage
(9) has deliberately destroyed others' property (other than by fire setting)

Deceitfulness or theft
(10) has broken into someone else's house, building, or car
(11) often lies to obtain goods or favors or to avoid obligations (i.e., "cons" others)
(12) has stolen items of nontrivial value without confronting a victim (e.g., shoplifting, but without breaking and entering; forgery)

Serious violations of rules
(13) often stays out at night despite parental prohibitions, beginning before age 13 years
(14) has run away from home overnight at least twice while living in parental or parental surrogate home (or once without returning for a lengthy period)
(15) often truant from school, beginning before age 13 years

B. The disturbance in behavior causes clinically significant impairment in social, academic, or occupational functioning.

C. If the individual is age 18 years or older, criteria are not met for Antisocial Personality Disorder.

Specify type based on age of onset:
   Childhood-Onset Type: onset of at least one criterion characteristic of Conduct Disorder prior to age 10 years
   Adolescent-Onset Type: absence of any criteria characteristic of Conduct Disorder prior to age 10 years

Specify severity:
   Mild: few if any conduct problems in excess of those required to make the diagnosis **and** conduct problems cause only minor harm to others
   Moderate: number of conduct problems and effect on others intermediate between "mild" and "severe"
   Severe: many conduct problems in excess of those required to make the diagnosis **or** conduct problems cause considerable harm to others

Note. From American Psychiatric Association (1994, pp. 90–91). Copyright 1994 by the American Psychiatric Association. Reprinted by permission.

As discussed earlier, ODD and CD display such distinctiveness from attention-deficit/hyperactivity disorder (ADHD), whether the domains are considered dimensionally or categorically (e.g., Fergusson et al., 1991; Hinshaw, 1987). Indeed, evidence for distinct etiological mechanisms is beginning to emerge (Biederman, Munir, & Knee, 1987). Yet the theoretical and empirical importance of the frequent overlap of these conditions bears further examination in the subsequent section on comorbidity.

With respect to predictive validity, it is clear that diverse aggressive and antisocial activities with an early onset strongly predict persistent antisociability as well as myriad adjustment difficulties (e.g., Robins, 1966; Stattin & Magnusson, 1989; Zoccolillo, Pickles, Quinton, & Rutter, 1992). More precise data regarding the predictive viability of current conceptions of ODD and

CD are the focus of the subsequent section on developmental progressions.

Another means of validation is to examine whether clear impairment accrues to the behavioral symptomatology. That is, we may ask the following questions:

1. Do the constituent behavioral features yield clear evidence of dysfunction in school, at home, and in interpersonal relationships?
2. Is there evidence for discontinuous levels of such impairment above the diagnostic thresholds?

As for the first question, the disruption, pain, and even tragedy related to conduct-disordered behavior patterns are clear; violence and property destruction take a considerable toll on individuals, families, and communities at large, and nonaggres-

sive aspects of CD can yield considerable harm to the self and to others as well. Indeed, youth with CD are at substantial risk for peer rejection, academic failure, and a persistent course, attesting to the virulence of the syndrome (Loeber, 1991). Yet, whereas the field trials for DSM-IV confirmed that three or more constituent symptoms are associated with marked impairment, it is not clear that a true discontinuity with respect to external criteria exists at or above any given threshold of the defining behaviors (e.g., Robins & McEvoy, 1990). In short, the viability of categorical notions of CD is an issue demanding continued investigation.

To an even greater extent, the validity of ODD as a diagnostic entity is an unresolved issue. Unlike most of the actions subsumed under the CD criteria—which involve severe manifestations of overt and covert behaviors—the constituent symptoms of ODD are clearly in the realm of normal developmental actions. Furthermore, the majority of youngsters reliably diagnosed with ODD in childhood will *not* progress to the more serious manifestations of CD (see subsequent discussion of developmental progressions). On the other hand, if the initial diagnosis must await the severe list of CD symptoms, intervention efforts may be overly delayed (Loeber et al., 1991). As a result, debate continues regarding the appropriateness of this category in formal nosologies (Achenbach, 1993; Loeber, Keenan, Lahey, Green, & Thomas, 1993). Indeed, recent critiques of the DSM-IV in the media have ridiculed the notion of ODD as a mental disorder (e.g., Kirk & Hutchins, 1994).

In sum, the coherence and distinctiveness of antisocial behavior patterns have been recognized for decades in the field of child psychopathology. Divergent validity from attention-disordered syndromes has been established (Hinshaw, 1987; Loney, 1987), and diverse antisocial behaviors emerging early in development are highly predictive of a persistent course. It is still unclear, however, whether current symptom cutoff scores yield truly discontinuous taxa; in particular, the viability of ODD is hotly debated. We turn now to additional issues raised by the categories of ODD and CD.

Admixture of Overt and Covert Symptomatology

Examination of Table 3.2 reveals clearly that a combination of overt and covert features is included in the diagnostic criteria for CD. Indeed, the subheadings for the criterion list highlight the disparate symptomatology among the 15 behavioral indicators. As noted by Achenbach (1993), as well as other investigators, this diverse listing—combined with the requirement of three symptoms for diagnosis—means that some youngsters with CD will have exclusively covert problems, some others will show only overt aggression, and still others will have mixed symptomatology. This state of affairs guarantees the heterogeneity of the diagnosis; indeed, most samples of youngsters diagnosed with CD are likely to contain fundamentally disparate subgroups. Because of the separability of overt and covert dimensions, the field would be well-served by investigations that identify the explicit types of behavioral symptoms that characterize CD samples.

Social/Environmental Context

In psychiatric nosologies the locus of deviant behavior is, by definition, intraindividual. As a result, the clear roles of poverty, traumatic stress, and violent communities in fostering antisocial behavior may be greatly underappreciated. To counter the overascription of all aggressive/antisocial activity to individual psychopathology, DSM-IV has incorporated the following wording regarding the diagnosis of CD (American Psychiatric Association, 1994, p. 88):

> Concerns have been raised that the Conduct Disorder diagnosis may at times be misapplied to individuals in settings where patterns of undesirable behavior are sometimes viewed as protective (e.g., threatening, impoverished, high-crime) . . . the Conduct Disorder diagnosis should be applied only when the behavior in question is symptomatic of an underlying dysfunction within the individual and not simply a reaction to the immediate social context. Moreover, immigrant youth from war-ravaged countries who have a history of aggressive behaviors that may have been necessary for their survival in that context would not necessarily warrant a diagnosis of Conduct Disorder. It may be helpful for the clinician to consider the social and economic context in which the undesirable behaviors have occurred.

We hasten to point out that the clinical realities of severe antisocial behavior are complex, without clear demarcations of contextual versus intraindividual "location" of the behavior patterns. An excellent example of this ambiguity is the provocative portrayal of mob boss John Gotti by Richters and Cicchetti (1993). Although Gotti developed and acted in a subculture that clearly

sanctioned extremes of aggression and violence, he appeared to display severe psychopathy as well, with a long history of brutality that transcended even his chosen environment. It must always be kept in mind that deviant behavior is multidetermined, with no clear separation of cultural, environmental, or intraindividual causal factors.

Mental Dysfunction or Disorder?

Indeed, what criteria should be invoked to decide that a certain individual suffers from psychopathology or a mental disorder? This issue has received close scrutiny by nosologists and critics alike. The perspective of Wakefield (1992) has been heuristic for the field. Not satisfied with the oft-utilized criteria for defining mental disorder of social deviance, personal distress, psychological handicap, and the like—standards that are too prone to cultural variation and that may not reflect actual psychopathology—Wakefield (1992) has invoked the dual criterion set of "harmful dysfunction" to characterize mental disorder per se. First, the deviant behavioral or emotional pattern must yield actual harm, in the form of meaningful suffering or impairment. This criterion is admittedly context dependent. Second, the pattern must be dysfunctional, in the sense of exemplifying aberrations in the abilities of mental mechanisms to perform natural functions, with the latter defined as having been selected by evolution for the good of the species. Through this latter criterion, Wakefield (1992) is attempting to transcend arbitrary, cultural definitions of deviance and posit underlying dysfunction in evolutionary terminology.

Few would doubt the clear harm yielded by conduct-disordered behavior patterns—and, to some extent, oppositional–defiant patterns—at least as defined by most cultures. Physical and sexual assault, property destruction, firesetting, and stealing are behaviors that understandably impart fear. Yet can it be asserted that the behavioral profile of CD reveals dysfunctional mental mechanisms? Indeed, not only is a fairly strong degree of antisocial behavior statistically normative for adolescents in Western societies, but most behavior patterns severe enough to yield a diagnosis of CD in adolescence are not linked with other manifestations of psychopathology. That is, there appears to be no cognitive disturbance, noteworthy family dysfunction, or history of associated attentional deficits for adolescent-onset

youth diagnosed with nonaggressive forms of CD (see Moffitt, 1993). Only a relatively rare type of antisocial youngster—marked by early developmental equivalents of overt and covert activities—may be considered to display putative dysfunctions of mental mechanisms that would yield evidence for mental disorder.[4] Because of the importance of considering the distinctions among antisocial youth based on age of onset, we now turn to such subtyping, the only officially recognized subcategorization of CD in DSM-IV.

Subtypes of CD Defined by Age of Onset

The DSM-IV criteria include childhood-onset versus adolescent-onset subtypes of youth with CD, with the difference relating to the presence of at least one constituent symptom prior to the age of 10 years. Although evidence for disparate types of antisocial youngsters based on age of onset has accumulated for years, Moffitt's (1993) recent synthesis has made a compelling case for a bifurcated developmental taxonomy.

Briefly, Moffitt (1993) describes the puzzling nature of the literature on antisocial behavior and delinquency, pointing to the troubling inconsistency in findings related to causal factors, correlates, underlying mechanisms, and response to intervention. She contends that such confusion stems largely from the confounding in most cross-sectional investigations of (1) a relatively small subgroup of youngsters (predominantly boys) with onset in childhood, who display a persistent course of antisocial activity that unfolds with development, with (2) a far larger category of adolescent-onset youth for whom forays into antisocial activity are time-limited. Importantly, the former group is characterized by several features that suggest chronic psychopathology: They tend to display neuropsychological deficits, comorbid attentional deficits and impulsivity, academic underachievement, violent assault and aggression, and family members within the antisocial spectrum. This early-onset group accounts for a disproportionate percentage of illegal antisocial acts; such youth are quite likely to persist with antisocial behavior across the lifespan (Moffitt, 1993).

Adolescent-onset youngsters, on the other hand, are as likely to be girls as boys and do not evidence the signs of psychopathology characteristic of their early-onset peers. Although they may display significant rates of antisocial activity dur-

ing adolescence, the behavioral profile is not nearly so likely to include violent offending. Furthermore, measures of neuropsychological abnormality and indices of family dysfunction are relatively absent in this group. Moffitt (1993) invokes the concept of social mimicry to explain the onset of antisocial behavior in such otherwise "normal" youth: Because of the ever-increasing gap between biological maturity and the opportunity for full psychological and educational independence in modern society, many adolescents mimic the antisocial actions of early-onset youngsters in an attempt to gain prestige and desired commodities (e.g., sexual partners, money, status).

The overriding message is that unless investigators and policy makers differentiate these disparate subgroups, little progress will accrue to efforts to understand, predict, and treat antisocial behavior in youth. The further contention is that only early-onset/persistent youngsters fall in the domain of psychopathology per se. Our sub-

sequent discussion of developmental progressions will return to the issue of the accuracy of prediction to adolescent and adult outcomes for early-onset CD youth.

Relation to ICD-10

The authors of both the DSM-IV (American Psychiatric Association, 1994) and the most recent edition of the *International Classification of Diseases* (ICD-10; World Health Organization, 1992) have been emphasizing greater convergence between the two nosologies. Table 3.3 lists the required symptom list for conduct disorders in the ICD-10. Following this list, the ICD-10 specifies several exclusionary criteria (which include dissocial personality disorder, schizophrenia, manic episode, depressive episode, pervasive developmental disorders, and hyperkinetic disorder), and a child- versus adolescent-onset subcategorization (similar to that of DSM-IV) is noted. Several subtypes are then listed: conduct

---

TABLE 3.3. ICD-10 Diagnostic Criteria for Conduct Disorders

There is a repetitive and persistent pattern of behaviour, in which either the basic rights of others or major age-appropriate societal norms or rules are violated, lasting at least 6 months, during which some of the following symptoms are present (see individual subcategories for rules or numbers of symptoms).

Note: The symptoms in 11, 13, 15, 16, 20, 21, and 23 need only have occurred once for the criterion to be fulfilled.

The individual:
 (1) has unusually frequent or severe temper tantrums for his or her developmental level;
 (2) often argues with adults;
 (3) often actively refuses adults' requests or defies rules;
 (4) often, apparently deliberately, does things that annoy other people;
 (5) often blames others for his or her own mistakes or misbehaviour;
 (6) is often "touchy" or easily annoyed by others;
 (7) is often angry or resentful;
 (8) is often spiteful or vindictive;
 (9) often lies or breaks promises to obtain goods or favours or to avoid obligations;
(10) frequently initiates physical fights (this does not include fights with siblings);
(11) has used a weapon that can cause serious physical harm to others (e.g., bat, brick, broken bottle, knife, gun);

(12) often stays out after dark despite parental prohibition (beginning before 13 years of age);
(13) exhibits physical cruelty to other people (e.g., ties up, cuts, or burns a victim);
(14) exhibits physical cruelty to animals;
(15) deliberately destroys the property of others (other than by firesetting);
(16) deliberately sets fires with a risk or intention of causing serious damage;
(17) steals objects of non-trivial value without confronting the victim, either within the home or outside (e.g., shoplifting, burglary, forgery);
(18) is frequently truant from school, beginning before 13 years of age;
(19) has run away from parental or parental surrogate home at least twice or has run away once for more than a single night (this does not include leaving to avoid physical or sexual abuse);
(20) commits a crime involving confrontation with the victim (including purse-snatching, extortion, mugging);
(21) forces another person into sexual activity;
(22) frequently bullies others (e.g., deliberate infliction of pain or hurt, including persistent humiliation, tormenting, or molestation);
(23) breaks into someone else's house, building, or car.

[See text for information about individual subcategories.]

Note. From World Health Organization (1993, pp. 157–159). Copyright 1993 by the World Health Organization. Reprinted by permission.

disorder confined to the family context, unsocialized conduct disorder, socialized conduct disorder, and oppositional defiant disorder. For the first three of these, at least three of the component symptoms from (9) to (23) are mandatory; for the oppositional defiant disorder subtype, four or more of the symptoms from (1) to (8) are required, but no more than two from (9) to (23). In general, there is extremely close correspondence between the symptom lists and operational criteria for ODD and CD in the DSM-IV and the ICD-10, as a comparison of Tables 3.1 and 3.2 with Table 3.3 indicates.

Current Definition of Antisocial Personality Disorder

Although the focus of this chapter is on child and adolescent antisocial behavior patterns, we mention briefly the DSM-IV (American Psychiatric Association, 1994) definition of APD. In contrast to the recent editions of the American nosology (DSM-III and DSM-III-R; American Psychiatric Association, 1980, 1987) that have defined APD almost exclusively in terms of antisocial behavior patterns (see earlier discussion), the DSM-IV definition has begun to integrate conceptions of psychopathy (Cleckley, 1976; Sutker, 1994) and psychopathic personality disorder (see Hare et al., 1991) with the behavioral indicators of antisocial activity (see Table 3.4). As can be seen, several psychological and interpersonal features are now displayed in the symptom list—e.g., deceitfulness, lack of remorse, impulsivity—supplementing the patterns of antisocial behavior, nonconformity, and aggression that have predominated in recent conceptions of APD. The field is still in flux as to the optimal definition of adult APD and psychopathy; DSM-IV appears to mark a step toward integration of the personological/interpersonal and the more behavioral definitions that have competed in recent decades. The viability and validity of this amalgamation of symptom patterns in the DSM-IV definition await empirical scrutiny.

PREVALENCE

Consideration of prevalence estimates for ODD and CD must immediately be qualified by several important considerations. First, definitions of these disorders have changed at a fast rate in recent years. Indeed, as discussed earlier, oppositional disorder was first introduced as a diagnostic category in 1980 (DSM-III), with ODD added in 1987 (DSM-III-R) and modified in 1994 (DSM-IV); the definition of CD was made significantly more stringent in DSM-III-R, with additional modifications in DSM-IV. Not only are epidemiological data with respect to the current definitional criteria lacking, but estimates of prevalence in recent years are highly dependent on the particular definitional criteria that are utilized.

Second, as we highlight in the subsequent section on developmental progressions, there are severe limitations to the viability of any cross-sectional definitions of oppositional–defiant or conduct-disordered behavior patterns. Indeed, only

---

TABLE 3.4. DSM-IV Diagnostic Criteria for Antisocial Personality Disorder

A. There is a pervasive pattern of disregard for and violation of the rights of others occurring since age 15 years, as indicated by three (or more) of the following:

  (1) failure to conform to social norms with respect to lawful behaviors as indicated by repeatedly performing acts that are grounds for arrest

  (2) deceitfulness, as indicated by repeated lying, use of aliases, or conning others for personal profit or pleasure

  (3) impulsivity or failure to plan ahead

  (4) irritability and aggressiveness, as indicated by repeated physical fights and assaults

  (5) reckless disregard for safety of self or others

  (6) consistent irresponsibility, as indicated by repeated failure to sustain consistent work behavior or honor financial obligations

  (7) lack of remorse, as indicated by being indifferent to or rationalizing having hurt, mistreated, or stolen from another

B. The individual is at least age 18 years.

C. There is evidence of Conduct Disorder [see Table 3.2] with onset before age 15 years.

D. The occurrence of antisocial behavior is not exclusively during the course of Schizophrenia or a Manic Episode.

Note. From American Psychiatric Association (1994, pp. 649–650). Copyright 1994 by the American Psychiatric Association. Reprinted by permission.

a minority of youngsters with diagnosed ODD will progress to CD, and only a minority of youth with CD will develop subsequent antisocial personality disorder as adults (see next section). Furthermore, the rates of overall conduct disorder that are yielded in adolescence may be over-inflated unless childhood-onset versus adolescent-onset subtypes are taken into account (Moffitt, 1993). Thus, it is crucial to specify the ages of onset in samples or populations of aggressive or conduct-disordered youth.

Third, the United States still lacks a thorough, national-scale, epidemiological data base with respect to psychopathology in childhood and adolescence. Thus, most estimates come from restricted geographic areas or from other nations. Fourth, as highlighted in our earlier discussion, categorical definitions of aggressive and antisocial behavior patterns may reflect rather arbitrary numbers of constituent symptoms. Thus, unless considerable efforts are made to index impairment that accrues to the disruptive behavior patterns, prevalence estimates may be misguided.

Overall, estimates of the prevalence of CD among children and adolescents range widely, from less than 1% to nearly 10% (see, e.g., Zoccolillo, 1993). Indeed, varying definitional criteria and sampling methods heavily influence results. The well-executed investigation of Offord and colleagues in Canada uncovered an overall rate among children and adolescents aged 4 to 16 years of 5.5% (8.1% for boys and 2.8% for girls), with DSM-III criteria defined by CBCL items serving as the operationalization of CD (Offord, Alder, & Boyle, 1986). Importantly, a clear majority of the youth diagnosed with CD had at least one additional psychiatric diagnosis as well, highlighting the widespread nature and the importance of co-morbidity for this disorder. Substantial impairment characterizes most youngsters meeting criteria for CD, in peer-related, academic, family, and personal/psychological domains. In addition, the behaviors subsumed under the CD diagnosis have been shown to be among the most "referable" for clinical services in all of child psychopathology (Weisz & Weiss, 1991).

Key intraindividual and systemic factors appear to influence prevalence of CD. For instance, most reports find substantially lower rates in girls than in boys, particularly for children; yet by adolescence, the gender disparity abates markedly (Zoccolillo, 1993). We pursue gender issues related to antisocial behavior subsequently. Furthermore, inner-city life and its attendant insults to the family and child (e.g., impoverishment) clearly increase the risk for CD (e.g., Rutter et al., 1974). In all, epidemiologists would do well to heed the advice of Costello and Angold (1993) regarding the importance of developmental perspectives on the epidemiology of disruptive behavior disorders. Clearly, ODD and CD are not static clinical entities, as the next section details; the field must begin to incorporate notions of flux and of developmental pathways into future nosological efforts.

DEVELOPMENTAL PROGRESSIONS

Heterotypic Continuity

Students of the development of aggression and antisocial behavior must come to terms with two competing facts: (1) measures of these behaviors show considerable stability across the lifespan, with correlations across lengthy intervals approaching those for IQ (e.g., Olweus, 1979; Loeber, 1982; Farrington, 1992); but (2) the form and composition of antisocial activity change markedly over the years (see, for example, Cairns, Cairns, Neckerman, Ferguson, & Gariepy, 1989). How can these seemingly disparate findings be rectified?

Increasingly, developmental psychopathologists recognize that predictability and congruence across development are not necessarily synonymous with simple consistency or similarity. That is, developmental precursors may relate in systematic and meaningful ways with subsequent outcomes even though the topographic patterns of behavior shift markedly with development. For instance, consistent security of attachment in infancy predicts social competence and resiliency in early and middle childhood (e.g., Erickson, Sroufe, & Egeland, 1985), although the means of expression of the latter constructs in a 7-year-old are quite different from the infant's use of the caretaker as a secure base for exploration of the environment. Analogously, antisocial traits may show moderate to strong stability over the course of development, yet the surface manifestations of the underlying propensity will shift with growth (see Patterson, 1993, who uses the term "chimera" to describe this phenomenon in relation to antisocial behavior). In other words, the constituent behavior patterns change with development. Such so-called "heterotypic continuity" is an important background concept for the topic at hand.

More specifically, in certain individuals the argumentative and defiant behaviors of preschool and early childhood predate the physical aggression and stealing in middle and late childhood and the sexual assault, substance abuse, and/or concentrated property destruction in adolescence. Extending the developmental span, infant and toddler behavioral patterns of irritability, overactivity, and fussiness may be part of the same continuum, as might the chronic criminality and interpersonal callousness of the psychopathic adult. At a basic level, the field can explore predictability: With what magnitude do such relationships hold? We address this question in the next section. The more theoretical issue relates to the mechanisms underlying such relationships: How and why could such predictability exist? Our subsequent discussion of biological, cultural, familial, and peer-related etiological influences is pertinent to uncovering the processes underlying developmental continuities. Indeed, it is clear that, as the age spectrum expands, prediction of antisocial functioning from one developmental stage to the next necessitates consideration of complex, transactional pathways involving the interplay of intraindividual, environmental, and cultural/social systemic factors (Moffitt, 1990; Hinshaw, 1994).

In our discussion of developmental progressions, we first discuss the linkage between ODD in early to middle childhood and CD in late childhood and early adolescence. Evidence regarding such predictability is crucial for validating both the diagnostic category of ODD and the concept of a childhood-onset variant of CD. Second, departing from formal nosological categorizations, we discuss alternative means of charting developmental progressions through childhood and adolescence, focusing on the work of Loeber and colleagues. Third, we note briefly extant evidence for linkages between syndromes of antisocial behavior in childhood/adolescence and adult antisocial personality dysfunction. We highlight, in passing, evidence for the predictability of antisocial behavior patterns from extremely early precursors in infancy or toddlerhood. Recognizing the rather descriptive focus of this discussion, we highlight that the subsequent material on (1) comorbidity with other childhood emotional and behavioral disturbance and (2) etiological factors is necessary for a full understanding of developmental processes (see Hinshaw, 1994, for elaboration of the comments below).

Developmental Trajectories: Progression from ODD to CD

We noted earlier the ongoing debate regarding the viability of ODD as a diagnostic category. Recent meta-analytic findings provide some corroboration of the ODD symptom complex (Frick et al., 1993; see also Loeber et al., 1991). As shown in Figure 3.1, the above-noted overt–covert continuum is supplemented in these analyses by an orthogonal destructive–nondestructive dimension. When these two dimensions of antisocial behavior are crossed, four quadrants of constituent behaviors emerge; the region defined by overt, nondestructive behaviors corresponds quite closely to the ODD symptom pattern in DSM-IV (e.g., argumentative, stubborn, defiant, angry). At least from a cross-situational perspective, the ODD behavioral complex has coherence.

Is there additional, more explicitly developmental evidence, supporting the viability of ODD? For one thing, behaviors characteristic of ODD emerge 2 to 3 years earlier than do CD symptoms (Loeber, Green, Lahey, Christ, & Frick, 1992): The average age of onset for the former is approximately 6 years, compared to 9 years for CD behaviors. Thus, it may be the case that the ODD pattern serves as a developmental precursor to CD (Loeber et al., 1991). Second, key risk factors—for example, impoverishment, family discord, family history of antisocial activity—appear salient for the development of both ODD and CD, but the magnitude of association between such factors and these behavioral repertoires is stronger for CD than for ODD (Lahey, Loeber, Quay, Frick, & Grimm, 1992). The suggestion, once again, is that ODD serves as a milder (and presumably earlier) variant of CD.

Such evidence, however, does not pertain directly to the predictive relationship between early ODD and subsequent CD. The Developmental Trends Study of Loeber, Lahey and colleagues provides an important data base regarding this issue (for a pertinent publication, see Loeber, Keenan, et al., 1993). In this investigation, a two-site sample of approximately 175 clinic-referred boys initially aged 7 to 12 years—recruited to reflect large proportions of disruptive and attention-deficit disorders at intake—has been followed prospectively, with a nearly universal retention rate of the sample across the longitudinal span of the study.

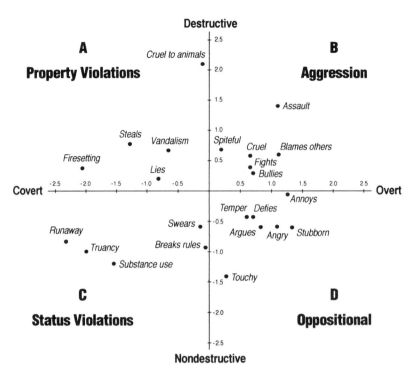

FIGURE 3.1. Results of meta-analysis of factor analyses of disruptive child behavior (see Frick et al., 1993). Copyright 1993 by Elsevier Science, Inc. Reprinted by permission.

First, newly developing cases of CD over the initial 3-year longitudinal interval were almost always preceded by ODD patterns earlier in development (Lahey et al., 1992). In addition, children with the severe behavioral profile comprising CD typically "retained" many of the features of ODD that had emerged earlier in development.[5] In conjunction with the evidence from the immediately preceding paragraph, it therefore appears that a developmental sequence exists linking ODD in middle childhood with CD in late childhood or early adolescence.

Yet despite the sensitivity of the prediction of CD from ODD—over 90% of youth with CD have previously met (and still retain) ODD criteria—the majority of youngsters with ODD do not appear to progress to the more severe constellation of antisocial behaviors characterizing CD. In the Developmental Trends Study, for example, only about a quarter of the boys with ODD had developed CD by the initial 3-year follow-up interval (see review in Hinshaw et al., 1993). Thus, the positive predictive power (PPP)

of the association was far lower than the sensitivity.[6] Approximately one-half of the ODD-diagnosed youth maintained this diagnosis over the 3-year period but without progression to CD, and a final quarter desisted from diagnostic criteria for ODD. In short, whereas a clear developmental progression appears to exist from ODD to CD, it does so for only a minority of children with the former diagnosis. (We note, in passing, that an underexplored issue is whether other diagnoses or impairments accrue to those youngsters with early ODD who do not progress to CD.)

Different scientists have formed divergent conclusions regarding such findings. Loeber et al. (1991) contend that such predictive validity signifies the importance of the ODD taxon; without this category, they contend, early manifestations of later CD would be missed, depriving the child, family, and community of important early-intervention strategies. Waiting for a child to display the severe symptom constellation characterizing CD may well overlook, in early childhood, the oppositional–defiant patterns that serve as a

sensitive predictor. Yet, with a PPP of only one-fourth—or possibly somewhat higher over longer time intervals—it is apparent that most youngsters with ODD will not develop CD, meaning that early identification and/or treatment may be misguided. Indeed, Achenbach (1993) views the evidence as supporting the contention that ODD does *not* merit separate demarcation as a category of psychopathology, given its similar pattern of risk factors and the likelihood that, for selected cases, the constituent symptoms simply reflect earlier developmental manifestations of an unfolding antisocial pattern rather than a separate category per se.

In all, whereas CD is nearly universally preceded by ODD, in only a minority of cases does the latter symptom pattern predict the former. For a subgroup of youngsters, then, ODD appears to have heterotypic continuity with subsequent antisocial activity—signifying clear harm and possible dysfunction, in terms of the criterion set of Wakefield (1992)—but in most instances ODD may signify an extreme of normal developmental variation, linked with important triggering factors (e.g., family discord, extremes of temperament) but likely to be transitory in nature. Highly needed is precise specification of (1) the behavioral and familial markers of predisposition to ODD patterns in infancy or early childhood; (2) those risk factors that propel certain cases of ODD toward a continuing antisocial trajectory[7]; and (3) the protective factors that aid in desistence. We note in passing that nearly all of the evidence cited in this section has pertained to male subjects. For female subjects, different predictive relationships appear to hold across development (see subsequent section on gender).

Progression to Adult Antisocial Personality Disorder

A parallel set of findings to those presented immediately above for ODD–CD relationships appears to hold regarding the linkage between CD in childhood or adolescence and APD in adulthood. That is, (1) adults with APD have nearly universally met criteria for CD earlier in their development, signifying the extremely high sensitivity of the CD–APD link; but (2) only a minority of youth with CD go on to develop the chronic antisocial behavior patterns characteristic of APD, highlighting the rather low PPP of the predictive relationship (see reviews of Hinshaw, 1994; Robins, 1978). The PPP appears to range from approximately one-quarter to 40% (Robins, 1966; Zoccolillo et al., 1992). It is noteworthy also that if the adult outcome is broadened to include exclusive substance use, the predictive power increases significantly (Robins, 1991).

Several additional findings supplement these descriptive, predictive statistics. First, several replicated variables increment the predictability of adult antisocial personality from childhood manifestations, including early onset of diverse aggressive and antisocial behaviors and persistence of symptomatology in childhood (Robins, 1978, 1991). A host of additional factors (academic underachievement, family variables, impoverishment) will receive additional attention subsequently. Second, the predictive relationship toward adult disorder appears to differ in female subjects as opposed to male subjects; as we discuss in the subsequent section on gender, CD in girls is a strong predictor of later *internalizing* disorders and features as well as antisocial tendencies (Robins, 1986). Third, despite the rather low PPP statistics for predicting APD from CD, the clear majority of youth displaying CD will show substantial social and personal impairment in adulthood, even if full diagnostic criteria for APD are not met (Zoccolillo et al., 1992). In other words, the lack of perfect prediction to adult APD should not lead to the conclusion that CD has a benign outcome in most cases. Fourth, the predictive relationships to adult antisocial personality dysfunction have been obtained almost exclusively with respect to the more behavioral conceptions of APD rather than to the psychological/interpersonal features of psychopathy; far less is known about the developmental roots of psychopathy per se.

In sum, virtually all individuals meeting criteria for adult APD will have begun their antisocial activity earlier in development; indeed, a requirement for the DSM-IV APD diagnosis is categorization as CD before the age of 15. Yet the predictive validity—like that for ODD–CD links—is far lower, on the order of one-third. Spanning across early childhood to adulthood, then, only 10% or so of youngsters (multiplying the approximate rate of the ODD–CD linkage by the CD–APD progression rate) with ODD will progress to persistent adult manifestations of APD; those who do will inevitably have displayed the symptomatology of CD "en route." Also, only a handful of investigations have prospectively linked CD in childhood or adolescence with APD or psychopathy in adulthood; prospective data are

critically needed to help elucidate mechanisms underlying developmental links.

Alternative Perspectives on Progressions in Childhood and Adolescence

Loeber (1988) has provided evidence regarding developmental pathways leading to delinquency or persistent antisocial behavior that transcend DSM-style nosological conceptions. One such trajectory is an "exclusive substance use" path, which involves progression from more accessible to "harder" substances but does not include aggression or covert activities other than drug use. The onset of substance use for youth following this trajectory is typically rather late. Another path is a "nonaggressive" (or covert) trajectory, and a third is a pernicious "aggressive/versatile" pathway, with the latter involving early onset and linkages with ADHD as well as escalation into increasing violence (Loeber, 1990; see subsequent section on comorbidity). It is noteworthy that all three paths contribute to adolescent substance abuse, exemplifying equifinality—the presence of similar outcomes from disparate paths (Cicchetti & Richters, 1993).

More recently, Loeber, Wung, et al. (1993) have proposed expanded versions of such pathways, with origins earlier in development. Their evidence for these trajectories is based on prospective data from high-risk youth. The "authority conflict" trajectory typically pertains to defiant, oppositional patterns that progress to more serious conflict with adults; the "overt" path progresses from early fighting and overt aggression to assault; and the "covert" pathway focuses on links between shoplifting and property defacement and more serious property crime later in development. Most pertinent to the ongoing discussion is that most antisocial youngsters do not stay in any one path but tend to "expand" into multiple trajectories over time. The identification and validation of separate paths point to the importance of subdividing the domain of antisocial behavior; the tendency of youth to cross over into several paths highlights the clinically significant pattern of diversification among seriously at-risk youngsters.

Before leaving the topic of developmental progressions, it is important to ask whether antisocial tendencies can be predicted with any confidence from extremely early behavioral manifestations or risk tendencies. Although indices of difficult temperament in infancy appear to be only weakly correlated with later behavioral manifestations, Campbell and Ewing (1990) and White, Moffitt, Earls, Robins, and Silva (1990) have shown that extremes of early childhood problems can predict later hyperactive and antisocial tendencies at rates far above chance levels. As we highlight in the upcoming section on etiological factors, such developmental pathways typically involve multiple risk factors, including socioeconomic disadvantage, family adversity, victimization by abuse, achievement problems, neuropsychological deficits, and—later in development—a peer network that supports antisocial activity. Thus, pathways to extremes of antisocial behavior are quite likely to include a multiplicity of interacting and transacting variables (Capaldi & Patterson, 1994; Moffitt, 1993).

Conclusions

Antisocial behavior patterns in adulthood appear de novo in only extremely rare cases, signalling the sensitivity of early manifestations of overt and covert activities in childhood in presaging such activity. Yet only a minority of oppositional, defiant, and aggressive youth progress to diagnosable CD in adolescence, and despite the continuing interpersonal, academic, and personal adjustment problems of a majority of adolescents with CD, only a minority of youth with this disorder develop the adult manifestations of APD. Such information highlights once again the importance of identifying an early-onset subgroup of youngsters with early manifestations of antisocial behavior. Current perspectives point to the interaction of multiple risk factors in predicting extremes of antisocial activity later in life. Finally, as noted earlier, nearly all of the information presented in this section regarding developmental trajectories is available for male samples only; of crucial importance is examination of female samples with extremes of aggression and antisocial behavior.

ISSUES RELATED TO GENDER

Rates of Aggression, Antisocial Behavior, and CD

Gender differences in the quantity and quality of aggression and antisocial behavior are well documented and often cited; they pertain to investigations using either categorical or dimensional defi-

nitions of disruptive behavior. Indeed, investigations utilizing continuous measures of aggression consistently demonstrate elevated rates in boys as compared to girls (see review by Parke & Slaby, 1983). Such differences pertain to verbal as well as physical aggression; they are supported by evidence from cross-cultural studies (Parke & Slaby, 1983). If rates of violent crime are considered in adolescence and adulthood, gender disparities are marked (Chesney-Lind & Shelden, 1992).

As discussed in the section on definitions of aggressive activity, however, some investigators have contended that qualitatively different forms of antisocial behavior—in particular, aggression that is indirect, involving tattling, "getting even," or having a third person retaliate—are typically overlooked. Because these types of behavior appear at higher rates in female individuals than in male individuals (Bjorkqvist et al., 1992), the often-cited male predominance in aggressive activity may be overstated. Indeed, as we discuss below, nonaggressive or covert forms of antisocial behavior are of crucial importance for discussions of the development of antisocial activity in females.

With respect to categorical definitions, gender has been identified as the most consistently documented risk factor for CD (Robins, 1991). Through childhood, boys greatly outnumber girls with respect to diagnosed CD, with ratios of 4:1 commonly reported (e.g., American Psychiatric Association, 1987). ODD is also believed to be more common in boys than girls (American Psychiatric Association, 1987), at least through preadolescence. Yet, as we highlight next, developmental factors are quite salient in the accurate portrayal of gender-related rates of antisocial behavior (see Goodman & Kohlsdorf, 1994, and Chesney-Lind & Shelden, 1992, for additional findings and synthesis).

Developmental Trajectories and Gender

Whereas boys clearly display greater rates of conduct problems than girls in preadolescence (Anderson, Williams, McGee, & Silva, 1987; Rutter, Tizard, & Whitmore, 1970), more controversy exists with regard to the picture during adolescence. Indeed, in a seminal review, Zoccolillo (1993) has contended that, by adolescent years, the male predominance in rates of CD is no longer statistically significant. Is it, in fact, the case that girls "catch up" to boys with respect to antisocial behavior during the teenage years? If so, what mechanisms account for this fact?

Responses to these questions require acknowledgment of our often-voiced need for subcategorizing (1) the constituent behaviors comprising the CD diagnosis and (2) the types of youngsters who develop antisocial behavior patterns. First, it does appear that CD typically has a later onset in girls than in boys. Epidemiological data from New Zealand (see Anderson et al., 1987; McGee, Feehan, Williams, & Anderson, 1992) illustrate such a developmental shift, whereby the male predominance regarding ODD and CD in preadolescence is replaced by similar prevalence rates by age 15 years. The increase in rates of female conduct problems in adolescence is accounted for primarily by a rise in nonaggressive or covert antisocial activity; overt aggression and violent offending remain far lower in girls than in boys throughout the lifespan (McGee et al., 1992; Moffitt, 1993; Robins, 1991). As a result, criteria emphasizing overt aggression lead to higher rates of diagnosed CD in male subjects as opposed to female subjects, whereas nonaggressive forms of CD appear to display a nearly equal prevalence during the teenage years (Zoccolillo, 1993). The admixture of overt and covert symptomatology in the official diagnostic criteria for CD (see earlier discussion) tends to cloud the nature of this gender-related developmental shift in conduct problems.

Such results are also consistent with the theoretical and empirical formulations that posit two discrete taxa comprising CD-related behaviors (Moffitt, 1993). Boys appear to predominate among "aggressive/versatile" youth (Loeber, 1990), who are characterized by mixed aggressive–covert symptom pictures, onset in early to middle childhood, and a persistent course; a far higher proportion of girls characterizes the "nonaggressive" path, marked by a relative absence of violence, adolescent onset, and substantial rates of recovery.

Although CD typically appears to begin later in girls than in boys, an alternate explanation is that early signs of conduct problems are more effectively detected in male subjects (Zoccolillo, 1993), presumably because of the more overtly aggressive form of the syndrome in boys. Indeed, Zoccolillo (1993) contends that preliminary symptoms of CD may be qualitatively different in female subjects, requiring different diagnostic criteria for the two genders and mandating lower thresholds of traditional CD symptoms for girls. Candidates for such differential sympto-

matology in girls could be extensive rule violations or medically unexplained somatic complaints, the latter related to higher rates of conversion disorder in adult female biological relatives of individuals with APD. Zoccolillo's (1993) controversial proposal, then, is both to reduce the quantity and intensity of the criterion number of CD symptoms for girls and to reconstruct diagnostic criterion lists regarding distinct gender-related forms of an underlying "antisocial" trait.

In response to this idea—and sparking a lively interchange—Zahn-Waxler (1993) rejects the idea of the field's promoting decreases in symptom thresholds for a CD diagnosis in girls. Such alterations could be seen as stigmatizing for female individuals, according to Zahn-Waxler (1993), by indicating that relatively low levels of aggression or conduct problems in girls would receive diagnostic labeling. Overemphasis on nonaggressive symptomatology for female subjects could also lead to an overlooking of the serious problems of interpersonal aggression and violence in our society. Instead, Zahn-Waxler (1993) argues strongly for intensified investigations of the biological, familial, and social systemic influences that lead to a greater likelihood of display of aggression in boys and male adolescents.

Indeed, as just one example, provocative evidence suggests differential risk and protective factors across the genders. Caspi, Lynam, Moffitt, and Silva (1993) noted that early onset of menarche in females predicted increased delinquency, with the effects largely restricted to females who attended mixed-gender schools. Presumably, the modeling of antisocial behavior by boys—as well as the increased pressure for early sexual relations—interacted with physical maturation to promote antisocial behavior in girls. We focus more specifically on etiological factors in subsequent sections.

Differential Long-Term Outcomes of CD for Male and Female Subjects

Although prospective data are quite sparse, it appears that the long-range course of CD diverges between the genders. We discussed earlier the extremely high sensitivity and the moderate PPP of the predictive relationship between CD in adolescence and APD in adulthood for male subjects. For female subjects, the data of Robins (1986) paint a different picture. Utilizing retrospective accounts of childhood CD symptoms from adults in the ECA investigations, Robins (1986) found, first, that girls appear to display the same developmental progressions in antisocial symptomatology through childhood as do boys—for example, school discipline problems and underachievement predate fighting and stealing, which precede arrest and school expulsion. For girls, however, these progressions emerge later in childhood, as discussed in the section above; the onset of CD does appear to be delayed.

Second, and crucially, although such early conduct problems for girls do predict, at above-chance levels, later APD and substance use disorder, the base rates of these latter disorders are far higher for boys, as are the predictive risks from early to later forms of antisociability. It is not the case, however, that child/adolescent CD is an insensitive predictor for girls; rather, this symptom complex is a better predictor of internalizing syndromes such as anxiety, mood, and somatization disorders in females (Robins, 1986). Thus, constellations of childhood antisocial behavior in girls presage a far wider symptom spectrum in adulthood than they do in boys; investigators and clinicians must be aware of the diversity of negative sequelae—including poor parenting skills in adulthood—for girls who display conduct-disordered behavior patterns (see Lewis et al., 1991). A key task for developmental psychopathologists will be to ascertain the mechanisms that link externalizing, antisocial activity in girls and female adolescents during early development with depression and somatic symptomatology later in life. Indeed, echoing the comments of Zoccolillo (1993), Robins (1991), and Zahn-Waxler (1993), we emphasize that intensified investigation of antisocial behavior patterns in girls and women should greatly enhance the field's power to test important etiological hypotheses and uncover pertinent developmental mechanisms.

COMORBIDITY

Comorbidity signifies a greater-than-chance association between two or more independent disorders. Such overlap between conditions is receiving increased attention, in part because of evidence for widespread comorbidity across multiple childhood behavioral/emotional disorders and in part because of the theoretical importance of such cross-domain linkages (Caron &

Rutter, 1991; Hinshaw et al., 1993). Whereas a great deal of so-called comorbidity in child psychopathology may relate to poor or ambiguous definitions of mental disorders[8] or to conflation of developmental progressions as the overlap of two independent conditions (Caron & Rutter, 1991), true comorbidity challenges univariate conceptions of the genesis of disorders; investigation of such comorbidity may help to uncover relevant developmental mechanisms of psychopathology. In the case of ODD and CD, there is substantial evidence for comorbidity with several important child disorders, and such syndromal overlap is quite crucial for understanding developmental trajectories. In the interest of space, we restrict our discussion of comorbidity to the following domains: attentional deficits/hyperactivity, underachievement, and key internalizing disorders.

ADHD

When considered dimensionally, scales of attentional deficits or impulsivity/hyperactivity correlate significantly with counterpart dimensions of overt and covert antisocial actions (Hinshaw, 1987; Quay, 1986); when viewed categorically, substantial overlap between ADHD and either ODD or CD is apparent (Biederman et al., 1991; Offord et al., 1986). Although the two broad domains—attention deficits/hyperactivity and conduct problems—as well as the major subdomains within each (attentional problems vs. hyperactivity/impulsivity and overt vs. covert antisocial behavior) show partial independence, the frequent overlap between the areas is of clinical and theoretical importance.

Indeed, given current evidence, it is impossible to assert that the domain of conduct problems/aggression yields a completely separable syndrome from attention deficits/hyperactivity. For one thing, despite diverging family histories, truly independent etiologies have not been discovered, and there is no conclusive evidence for differential treatment response (Hinshaw, 1987). In addition, with the effects of measurement error removed, the association between the two domains is quite strong (Fergusson et al., 1991). Given the severity of their symptomatology and impairment and the likelihood of their early onset, the group of youngsters with comorbid ADHD and ODD or CD merits further discussion.

First, the overlapping subgroup with conduct problems and attention deficits/impulsivity displays a far more pernicious form of psychopathology than does either single-diagnosis category: Such youngsters display more physical aggression, a greater range and greater persistence of antisocial activity, more severe academic underachievement, and higher rates of peer rejection (see review by Hinshaw et al., 1993). All of these factors have been shown to be strong predictors of negative outcomes in later life (e.g., Parker & Asher, 1987). As demonstrated by Walker, Lahey, Hynd, and Frame (1987), such greater impairment accrues specifically to the comorbidity of CD with ADHD and not to the overlap of CD with other symptom patterns.

Second, the conjoint presence of ADHD serves to propel an earlier onset of CD symptomatology (Hinshaw et al., 1993). Such early onset of antisocial behavior continues to be the strongest predictor of the subsequent development of antisocial patterns in adolescence and adulthood. Indeed, Robins (1991) has shown that the age of onset of CD symptomatology remains an independent predictor of APD in adulthood even when the number and diversity of CD symptoms in childhood is controlled statistically.

Given the predictability of later antisocial behavior patterns from early indices of aggression and extreme oppositionality (see prior section), the question remains as to whether ADHD symptomatology—either alone or when linked with CD—is an independent predictor of subsequent antisocial behavior. Evidence here is controversial. Earlier investigations (see, for example, Satterfield, Hoppe, & Schell, 1982) contended that ADHD syndromes were strong predictors of adolescent delinquency. A key critique of such reports, however, has been that the assessment tools utilized were not able to differentiate clearly between attentional and conduct-disordered behavior problems in childhood (see Hinshaw, 1987). Thus, it may have been the case that the "ADHD" samples under investigation were highly contaminated with comorbid antisocial conditions. Utilizing evaluation instruments that can separate the two domains, more recent work has concluded that childhood aggression and antisocial behavior are stronger predictors of later antisocial tendencies than are attention problems per se (e.g., Barkley, Fischer, Edelbrock, & Smallish, 1990; see review of Lilienfeld & Waldman, 1990).

Two key European investigations, however (see Farrington, Loeber, & Van Kammen, 1990; Magnusson, 1987) have demonstrated that dimensions of hyperactivity, impulsivity, and inattentiveness

(HIA) in childhood independently predict antisocial outcomes in adulthood. Indeed, Farrington et al. (1990) showed that HIA indices, measured in middle childhood, predicted age-25 chronic offending as well as did childhood aggression, with no interaction between the two dimensions found. Furthermore, the prospective American investigation of Mannuzza et al. (1991) concluded that ADHD youngsters without childhood CD still showed a strong risk for substance abuse and antisocial disorders in young adulthood. It is conceivable, however, that such ADHD samples could have displayed ODD (or other forerunners of CD) in childhood and that the oppositional behavior pattern, rather than the attention deficits, presaged the later antisociability; without assessment of antisocial behavior patterns that is sensitive to developmental stages, predictive relationships could well remain ambiguous.[9]

Perhaps the safest conclusion from this controversial area is that ADHD clearly increases the risk for early onset of ODD and CD; its ability to predict later antisocial patterns over and above such facilitation of early aggressive behavior is questionable. There is no doubt, however, that the comorbid presence of ADHD and ODD/CD in childhood signals a persistent, early-developing, treatment-refractory subcategory of youngsters who are deserving of research and clinical attention (see Loeber, 1990). Indeed, in Moffitt's (1993) exposition on early-onset/life-course-persistent antisocial youth, the presence of ADHD syndromes in early childhood is a key aspect of the symptom picture. Indeed, the behavioral impulsivity that is a central facet of the psychopathology of ADHD appears to be a significant predictor of antisocial behavior (White et al., 1994; see also Barkley, 1994). Furthermore, Moffitt's (1990) investigation points to the complexity of developmental trajectories for the subgroup of aggressive–hyperactive children: Early attention problems display statistical interactions with (1) family adversity and (2) low verbal IQ in predicting adolescent antisocial patterns, signifying that cognitive functioning and psychosocial variables propel the risk for poor outcome among comorbid youth. We provide extended coverage of such interacting causal factors in subsequent sections.

Academic Underachievement/ Learning Disabilities

Another important comorbid condition or associated dimension pertains to the domain of academic failure. For years, linkages between aggressive/delinquent behavior patterns and underachievement have been noted, but only recently have several key developmental manifestations of this important comorbidity been clarified. At the outset, we note that the field recognizes many forms and definitions of academic underachievement; because such variables as grade retention, placement in special education, and suspension or expulsion are known to relate rather directly to acting-out behavior patterns, we focus our attention on academic underachievement per se.[10]

Hinshaw (1992) recently presented an integrated account of the association between antisocial behavior and academic underachievement; in the interests of space, we highlight key conclusions herein. First, developmental shifts in this relationship are salient. Despite many assertions to the contrary, the specific association in early to middle childhood is between ADHD—and not ODD or CD—and underachievement. The apparent link between the aggressive disorders and learning failure before adolescence relates to the overlap of antisocial-spectrum disorders and ADHD (Frick et al., 1991). By the teenage years, delinquency and antisocial behavior patterns are clearly associated with underachievement, but not in all cases. The data of Moffitt (1990) are again instructive here: For child-onset antisocial youth, early development is marked by several interacting risk factors, including behavior patterns in the ADHD spectrum, family discord, neuropsychological deficits, and underachievement.

Second, unilateral, "main effect" models that aspire to account for the relationship between externalizing behavior problems and underachievement are typically overstated. That is, whereas in some individuals early underachievement may predict later antisocial behavior (via demoralization, frustration, and the like), and whereas in others early aggression and defiance may precipitate learning failure (via poor classroom behavior, oppositional attitudes, etc.), the association between inattentive and aggressive behavior patterns and risk for school failure often appears quite early in development, before the start of formal schooling. This state of affairs strongly suggests that underlying "third variables"—for example, language deficits, socioeconomic disadvantage, neurodevelopmental delay—require further exploration as mechanisms underlying the subsequent comorbidity (see Hinshaw, 1992, for elaboration). In other

words, the association between academic failure and antisocial behavior, which specifically appears in the adolescent years, is marked by a complex, developmental trajectory in most instances, with intraindividual and familial variables predating the formal comorbidity.

Third, and related to the point just made, the effects of underachievement and antisocial behavior are likely to be reciprocally deterministic, "snowballing" across development. The child with subtle language deficits may have difficulty with the phonological processes necessary for mastery of reading; he or she may also have developed contentious relationships with parents and peers, setting the stage for oppositional/defiant behavior patterns. In addition, evidence exists that early school failure exacerbates preexisting acting-out tendencies (McGee et al., 1986); as stated above, a combination of attention deficits with low achievement and neuropsychological impairment is a hallmark of children who develop into chronically antisocial individuals (Moffitt, 1993). Over time, the early adolescent with poor academic preparation is increasingly likely to lose motivation for schooling and to associate with deviant, antisocial peers, intensifying his or her own aggression and antisocial behavior patterns. It must be noted, however, that differential trajectories appear for different subgroups; for some underachieving children, antisocial behavior may follow from learning failure without childhood signs of aggression (Maughan, Gray, & Rutter, 1985), whereas in most youth the comorbid pattern is evident early in development. In all, the relationship between underachievement and school failure, on the one hand, and antisocial behavior, on the other, is complex and laden with developmental significance; understanding this comorbidity is necessary for a full understanding of the unfolding of conduct problems.

Internalizing Disorders

Although internalizing conditions such as anxiety disorders and depression may appear, at first glance, to be diametric opposites of such prototypically externalizing difficulties as aggression and antisocial behavior, dimensional and categorical investigations reveal substantially above-chance rates of overlap for these two domains (e.g., Offord et al., 1986; see review in Zoccolillo, 1992). Such comorbidity presents challenges to simplistic, univariate views of causation; additional study of diagnostic overlap will be essential for elucidating etiology. In this still-underexplored area, we highlight two issues: the comorbidity of aggression/antisocial behavior with anxiety disorders, and the overlap with depression. Space limitations necessitate only a brief summary of pertinent findings; for a comprehensive review, see Zoccolillo (1992).

Recent work suggests strongly that preadolescent boys with comorbid CD and anxiety disorders are a less aggressive and assaultive subgroup than their CD peers without anxiety conditions. Covert symptomatology, on the other hand, does not appear to differentiate the subgroups (Walker et al., 1991). Yet prospective data reveal a more complex relationship over time. Specifically, in the aforementioned Developmental Trends Study, whereas physical aggression and anxiety symptomatology were inversely related during the initial years of the assessment procedures, serious aggression began to increase in the CD-anxiety-disordered group until it outstripped that of the solely CD boys (see discussion in Hinshaw et al., 1993). Clearly, additional prospective data will be necessary to untangle the complex relationships that develop over time.

CD and depressive syndromes also display comorbidity at significant levels (see Kovacs, Paulauskas, Gatsonis, & Richards, 1988; Puig-Antich, 1982). At present, it is indeterminate whether (1) major depression precipitates acting-out behavior, (2) CD and its associated impairment lead to demoralization and dysphoria, or (3) uniform underlying causal factors—psychological, familial, or psychobiological—trigger the joint display of such symptomatology (for empirical data related to this issue, see Patterson, Reid, & Dishion, 1992). It is likely to be the case that each of these causal scenarios applies to certain subgroups. The comorbidity between these domains is important theoretically, from both psychodynamic and biological perspectives. Dynamically, depression is believed to emanate from loss events, with aggressive impulses introjected and displayed against the self. Thus, the dynamic boundary between self-directed and other-directed aggression may be a narrow one. This relationship is also demonstrated by the increased likelihood of suicidal behavior among youth with both conduct-disordered and depressive features (e.g., Shaffi, Carrigan, Whittinghill, & Derrick, 1985). Psychobiologically, in fact, decreased serotonergic activity is associated with dimensions of impulsivity and aggression and with suicidal behavior (Brown & Van Praag, 1991; see review in Lahey, Hart, Pliszka, Applegate, & McBurnett, 1993). In all, research strategies that focus on CD,

depressed, and comorbid subgroups will be necessary to uncover important relationships between these domains (for exemplary research, see Capaldi, 1991).

Summary

The field of developmental psychopathology is increasingly recognizing that it is an exception for child disorders to occur in isolation; indeed, comorbidity is the typical state of affairs for clinical samples (Biederman et al., 1991; Caron & Rutter, 1991). For youth with ODD or CD, overlap with ADHD is commonplace, and such comorbidity is clearly associated with an early onset of aggression and with substantial impairment in personal, interpersonal, and family domains. In particular, the impulse control problems pertinent to youngsters with joint attention deficits and aggression appear to propel a negative course. Next, academic underachievement often appears in youngsters with early-onset conduct problems and in delinquent adolescents; in childhood, such learning failure is linked specifically with ADHD, but over time, antisocial behavior and underachievement appear reciprocally deterministic. Understanding the unfolding interplay between cognitive, academic, and behavioral factors in aggression and conduct disorder can help to elucidate important clinical and theoretical issues. Finally, internalizing disorders (anxiety disorders, depression) also appear alongside aggression and antisocial behavior at above-chance rates; enhanced understanding of such comorbidity may also help to uncover causal pathways to suicidality and to adult manifestations of depression and antisocial personality disorder. In sum, it is nearly a necessity for future research efforts regarding aggression and antisocial behavior patterns in children and adolescents to include information on association or comorbidity with other dimensions or disorders; without such information, mistaken attributions related to the etiology and underlying mechanisms of aggression and conduct problems are likely to be the rule.

ETIOLOGICAL HYPOTHESES AND THEORETICAL FRAMEWORKS

In presenting information regarding causal factors, we first point out that the act of subdividing this section—into segments on biological, familial, sociocognitive/peer-related, and wider contextual influences—belies the actual state of affairs with regard to etiology, namely, that causal mechanisms are multifaceted and transactional. Indeed, important work in the field regarding biological and familial mechanisms points strongly to gene–environment correlations as crucial for the development of persistent antisocial behavior patterns (Caspi & Moffitt, 1995). Overall, models integrating psychobiological, personological, familial, neighborhood, and socio-economic causal factors are gaining ascendancy in the field, transcending univariate, main-effect perspectives (e.g., Capaldi & Patterson, 1994; Frick & Jackson, 1993; Lahey et al., 1993; Moffitt, 1990). Although we have chosen to subdivide this etiological section for organizational reasons, we fully recognize the futility of attempting to make overly rigid demarcations among causal influences.

Psychobiological Factors

Although psychobiological research on child psychopathology has lagged behind similar work on adult disorders, a number of recent investigations have focused on psychophysiological and neurophysiological aspects of conduct-disordered behavior, with most reports featuring physical aggression as the salient feature of antisocial behavior under investigation (Quay, 1988). Whereas few findings have received cross-validation—related, in part, to imprecise sampling and unreliable measurement of key constructs—progress in the field is accumulating.

At the outset of their excellent review of work in this area, Lahey et al. (1993) state clearly that investigation of biological variables—for example, neurotransmitter systems, skin conductance, event-related potentials, or hormonal influences—does not rule out important roles for psychosocial factors in the genesis or maintenance of antisocial behavior. It is conceivable, in fact, "that a socioenvironmental event (e.g., abnormal infant experience) could be one of the *causes* of aggression, but that the effect of this experience on aggression is *mediated* by alterations in neurotransmitter activity" (Lahey et al., 1993, p. 142). Furthermore, as pointed out by Richters and Cicchetti (1993), it is plausible that the autonomic underreactivity characteristic of extreme antisocial behavior and psychopathy could, in part, emanate from a chronically violent lifestyle (see also Susman, 1993). Given the practical and theoretical importance of elucidating causal mechanisms for antisocial disorders, the

field can no longer afford the "either–or," biological versus environmental rancor that has plagued debate for many years (see Dodge, 1990).

The plethora of neurotransmitters, neuropsychological measures, neuroanatomical regions, brain imaging techniques, hormonal pathways, and peripheral psychophysiological variables can lend a somewhat chaotic feel to research in this area. Providing an important theoretical orientation to biologically oriented research, McBurnett and Lahey (1994) discuss both traditional and updated theories related to the key constructs of arousal and reactivity, which have been heuristic for investigations of adult psychopathy and APD. Importantly, Quay (1988, 1993) has integrated the complex neurobiological and neuroanatomical theorizing of Jeffrey Gray with current research, focusing on a behavioral activation (or reward) system, a behavioral inhibition system, and a generalized arousal (fight/flight) system, with each comprising distinct neuroanatomical regions and neurotransmitter pathways (see McBurnett, 1992, and Quay, 1993, for explication). Such theoretical integration provides a framework for interpreting diverse findings as well as a foundation for subsequent research. The complexity of findings and measures from this emerging field permits only summary discussion of key directions.

Youngsters diagnosed with CD who display (1) early onset, (2) aggressive features, and (3) "undersocialized" symptom patterns appear to differ from normal and clinical comparison samples in two important ways. First, they demonstrate low psychophysiological or cortical arousal; and second, they display low autonomic reactivity on a variety of relevant indices. Such findings are strongly reminiscent of findings with adult samples composed of psychopathic individuals (see Fowles & Missel, 1994, for a review). Importantly, this pattern is almost completely reversed in youth with nonaggressive, socialized, and/or late onset CD; these latter subgroups often display arousal and reactivity responses that are elevated above those of not only the aforementioned CD subgroups but of normal comparison samples as well (see McBurnett & Lahey, 1994, for details). The assumption is that the low arousal and low reactivity associated with the early-onset group diminish avoidance conditioning to socialization stimuli, fueling poor response to punishment and, eventually, a career marked by undersocialization and psychopathic functioning. Related findings with neurotransmitter

metabolites (see, for example, Rogeness, Javors, Maas, & Macedo, 1990) and experimental tasks designed to elicit reward dominance (e.g., Daugherty & Quay, 1991) have been interpreted in terms of an imbalance favoring the behavioral activation/reward system over the behavioral inhibition system in youth with undersocialized, aggressive conduct disorder (Quay, 1993; see also Kruesi et al., 1990).

Research on hormonal influences is less conclusive, with inconsistent findings pertinent to cortisol levels. Cortisol secretion may, however, be related to comorbid anxiety disorders in CD samples (McBurnett & Lahey, 1994), necessitating the consideration of such comorbidity to clarify hormonal effects. Testosterone influences have received incomplete support regarding their relationship to some indices of aggression (McBurnett & Lahey, 1994). We reiterate that many potentially important psychobiological investigations have suffered from small and/or incompletely specified samples; many intriguing patterns of findings in the field mandate replication and cross-validation (e.g., Kruesi et al., 1992).

With regard to neuropsychological variables, Moffitt and Lynam (1994) have provided an important synthesis. Their initial contention is that the oft-cited IQ deficit (approaching half a standard deviation) in antisocial and delinquent samples is actually far greater (over a full standard deviation) in early-onset youth with CD and is not explicable on the basis of such factors as official detection of delinquency, motivation, racial or socioeconomic status, or school failure (Lynam, Moffitt, & Stouthamer-Loeber, 1993; Moffitt & Silva, 1988). This IQ deficit is, in their view, an indicator of broad-based neuropsychological dysfunction. Such a perspective has been criticized, however, by those who contend that IQ scores should not be automatically conflated with neuropsychological performance (Block, 1995).

Moving to more specific types of neuropsychological dysfunction, Moffitt and Lynam (1994) contend that deficits in (1) verbal reasoning and (2) "executive" functioning characterize the profiles of early-onset, aggressive antisocial youngsters who are comorbid for ADHD. Such deficits, which appear at quite early ages, yield cumulative effects on antisocial behavior over the course of development, by promoting impulsive responding, facilitating disruption of early caretaker–child relationships, precipitating harsh or inconsistent parenting, and presaging academic underachievement. This framework thus holds

that even subtle neuropsychological deficits will interact with a host of other variables—including parental socialization influences—to produce indirect and distal effects on the development and intensification of antisocial behavior. Indeed, one contention is that neuropsychological difficulties may increase vulnerability to pathological environmental circumstances (Moffitt & Lynam, 1994).

Overall, the range of potential psychobiological influences on antisocial behavior is wide, and replication of predictive findings is crucial. Research on female samples is urgently needed in the field. Interactions of neurophysiological and neuropsychological risk with pathogenic environmental circumstances are strongly implicated in the genesis and maintenance of antisocial behavior patterns; given their long-established role in promoting antisociability, we turn next to the wide range of familial influences on aggression and antisocial behavior.

Familial Influences

Parent Psychopathology and Possible Genetic Contribution

At the outset, we alert the reader to the obvious but overlooked fact that, in biological families, familial influences on child development may be psychological in nature, may be genetically mediated, or may result from correlated (or interacting) joint influences of genes and environment. Indeed, for decades investigators have sought to ascertain whether antisocial behavior patterns are heritable. Much early research in the field of behavior genetics had implicit (if not explicit) eugenic underpinnings; and psychobiological research today is still embedded in sociopolitical contexts (Lahey et al., 1993). Whether research in this area can enhance policy and intervention that are empowering rather than discriminatory is still an open question. Finally, as will become apparent, promising leads regarding genetic influences are likely to be confirmed only if investigators pay careful attention to subtypes and subdivisions within the domain of antisocial behavior.

In the first place, intergenerational linkages with respect to criminal behavior have been demonstrated for some time (see review in Frick & Jackson, 1993), and evidence is mounting that certain types of parental psychopathology are associated with child aggression and antisocial behavior. Parental antisocial personality is strongly and specifically related to child CD

(Faraone, Biederman, Keenan, & Tsuang, 1991; Lahey, Piacentini, et al., 1988). This association is particularly clear for fathers (Frick et al., 1992), as is a link between (1) paternal substance abuse disorders and (2) maternal histrionic personality configurations and child antisocial behavior patterns (Lahey, Piacentini, et al., 1988). Intriguingly, children's aggression is also associated with their parents' childhood aggression at the same age (Huesmann, Eron, Lefkowitz, & Walder, 1984). Maternal depression has also been implicated in linkages to child aggression, with an association found in some investigations but not in others. One explanation for such inconsistency is that maternal depression is a nonspecific risk factor for child maladjustment, predicting a wide range of psychopathology (Downey & Coyne, 1990).[11]

Are such associations genetically mediated? Until recently, despite evidence for heritable components to adult antisocial behavior (diLalla & Gottesman, 1991), hereditary influences on child and adolescent aggression and antisocial behavior had been supported only weakly (see Rutter, Macdonald, et al., 1990). It is conceivable, however, that subtyping and subcategorizing may lead to different conclusions for restricted domains of antisocial behavior. Indeed, as highlighted at the outset of the chapter, Edelbrock et al. (1995) have found rather strong heritabilities for the Aggression (overt antisocial behavior) scale of the CBCL but lower figures for the Delinquency (covert antisocial behavior) scale. Furthermore, whereas adolescent-onset, nonpersistent antisocial patterns appear to yield little heritability, the more aggressive and persistent child-onset variant may reflect some degree of genetic contribution (Frick & Jackson, 1993).[12] Given the potential for genetic transmission of severely antisocial behavior patterns, other family socialization influences that are allegedly psychosocial in nature must be scrutinized; the field requires more complex models incorporating heritable *and* psychosocial components that examine the "double risk" of genetic predisposition in combination with chaotic and stressful upbringing in predicting antisocial behavior patterns (Frick & Jackson, 1993).

Family Functioning and Parent–Child Interaction

Several variables indicating dysfunctional familial functioning—including marital conflict, di-

vorce, and child abuse—have been implicated in the onset and maintenance of antisocial behavior in youth (e.g., Emery, 1982; Dodge, Bates, & Pettit, 1990). These variables appear to relate in complex ways to such behavior patterns, however, bespeaking the need to consider mediating and moderating variables. For example, effects of marital conflict and hostility on aggressive behavior patterns appear to be mediated by parental lack of availability to and negativity with the child (Olweus, 1979). Also, the effects of parental anger and discord on young children's aggressive and angry behavior are mediated by a host of developmental and contextual factors (see the programatic work of Cummings and colleagues; e.g., Cummings, Simpson, & Wilson, 1993). Also, whereas divorce has been implicated in the onset of conduct problems in boys, increasing evidence points to preexisting and ongoing marital conflict in the parents and preexisting behavior patterns of the child as the stronger causal influences (Amato & Keith, 1991). Furthermore, Lahey, Hartdagen, et al. (1988) discovered that the effects of divorce on boys' conduct problems were almost entirely related to diagnoses of antisocial personality disorders in the parents. We must highlight that, in this brief discussion, variables such as marital conflict or discord are far from unidimensional; greater specificity in linking discrete conflictual processes in marriage with diverse child outcomes is emerging (Fincham & Osborne, 1993; Katz & Gottman, 1993).

With respect to effects of abuse and family violence, Dodge, Bates, et al. (1990) discovered that early physical abuse was a clear risk factor for later aggressive behavior reported in school settings, even with statistical control of family ecological variables and child temperament. Indeed, intergenerational effects of abuse are empirically validated (Widom, 1989), strongly supporting the need for prevention and early intervention efforts in this area. Intriguingly, the effects of familial abuse on children's antisocial tendencies appear to be mediated, in part, by a pattern of sociocognitive information-processing variables that emanate from the abuse experience and that appear related to reactive, retaliatory aggression (Dodge, 1991; Dodge, Bates, et al., 1990; see subsequent section). Furthermore, for girls, sexual abuse may be a salient risk factor (Chesney-Lind & Shelden, 1992), albeit one that has diffuse and nonspecific effects on a host of behavioral and psychological facets of later functioning.

Several indices of parent–child interaction display moderate to strong relationships with children's aggressive and antisocial behavior (see Loeber & Stouthamer-Loeber, 1986): (1) low levels of parental involvement in their children's activities, (2) poor supervision of offspring, and (3) harsh and inconsistent discipline practices. The most comprehensive model in the field is the coercion theory of Patterson (1982; Patterson et al., 1992), which is supported by microanalyses of in-home observations of family interaction.[13] What emerges is a pattern of harsh, ultimately unsuccessful interchanges between parent and child, leading to the development and intensification of antisocial behavior. In brief, by backing down from requests and adhering to the child's escalating demands, parents negatively reinforce the child's increasingly defiant and aggressive behavior patterns; similarly, harsh and abusive discipline practices, displayed when the child escalates to severe misbehavior, are rewarded by the child's temporary capitulation (see Patterson, 1982). Such mutual training in aversive responding fuels both aggressive child behavior and greater levels of harsh, nonresponsive parenting. (Note that, in Wahler's alternative formulation, the child's misbehavior serves to reduce the uncertainty associated with inconsistent parental responses.) Aversive interchanges serve to intensify aggressive behavior outside the home and to precipitate a widening array of negative consequences for the child and family, including risk for academic underachievement and peer rejection by the child, depressed mood in family members, and a strong likelihood of persisting antisocial behavior (Patterson et al., 1992).

Research on family socialization related to aggression increasingly recognizes bidirectional influences in which child behavior influences parent behavior as well as the converse (Lytton, 1990). It is conceivable, in fact, that negative parenting is largely a reaction to the difficult, oppositional, and aggressive behaviors displayed by the child with developing conduct disorder. K. Anderson, Lytton, and Romney (1986) performed an intriguing experimental study in which mothers of CD and comparison boys interacted with (1) their own son, (2) another boy with a diagnosis of CD, and (3) another comparison boy. Mothers in both groups displayed more negativity and made more requests with conduct-disordered youngsters, strongly supporting child-to-parent effects in eliciting coercive interchange. Importantly, however, mothers of the CD young-

sters responded with the most negativity to their own boys, suggesting that a history of negative interactions plays an important role. Indeed, recent research with clinical samples demonstrates that maternal coercion during parent–child interactions predicts ADHD children's independently observed overt and covert antisocial behaviors over and above the effects of the child's negativity during the interaction and maternal indices of psychopathology (C. Anderson, Hinshaw, & Simmel, 1994). Understanding the "ultimate" cause (parent- vs. child-related) of the escalating behavior patterns is probably futile; reciprocal determinism is likely to paint the most accurate picture (Dodge, 1990; Wahler, 1990).

The most conclusive evidence for the causal role of parenting practices in promoting antisocial behavior would emanate from experimental investigations with interventions designed to reduce coercive interchange. In fact, Dishion, Patterson, and Kavanagh (1992) demonstrated that in families randomly assigned to receive intensive behavioral intervention, the risk for child antisocial behavior was markedly reduced, with indices of parenting skill following treatment serving as predictors of teacher-reported antisocial behavior patterns. Thus, despite the potential for genetic mediation or for bidirectional effects, ineffective parenting practices play a causal role in the genesis of antisocial behavior. Yet it is also clear that coercive family interchange is embedded in a rich array of wider contextual variables (Capaldi & Patterson, 1994; Wahler & Dumas, 1989); discussion of these appears in a subsequent section.

Attachment and Multiple Family Risk Factors

A different approach to the development of conduct problems has been taken by theorists and investigators within the attachment tradition, with primary focus to date on the development of problem behavior early in life. Attachment theory focuses on the quality of parent–child relationships (not only in infancy but across the lifespan) to explain the development of psychopathology; behavior problems in children are often seen as strategies for receiving attention or gaining proximity to caregivers who may not respond to other approach signals (e.g., Greenberg & Speltz, 1988).

Empirical studies of attachment security have found that some of the behaviors differentiating securely attached from insecurely attached chil-

dren are identical to symptoms of early disruptive behavior disorders (Greenberg, Speltz, & deKlyen, 1993). Furthermore, investigations linking infant attachment status with behavior problems in the preschool years have yielded provocative (but inconsistent) findings. The anxious–avoidant attachment pattern is prospectively linked to oppositional–defiant problems in the preschool years (Erickson et al., 1985); and the newer disorganized/disoriented classification, at 18 months, predicts subsequent behavior problems of a hostile nature (Lyons-Ruth, Alpern, & Repacholi, 1993). Negative findings have also been reported, however (e.g., Fagot & Kavanagh, 1990), in samples that are not defined as high risk and/or do not include the disorganized/disoriented category.

Across longer time intervals, insecure attachment has been linked with aggression in elementary school boys (Renken, Egeland, Marvinney, Mangelsdorf, & Sroufe, 1989) but not in girls (see review in Greenberg et al., 1993). Again, predictions are strongly enhanced in the presence of additional environmental or familial risk factors. In a recent study, Easterbrooks, Davidson, and Chazan (1993) found that attachment status assessed during a reunion paradigm at age 7 years concurrently predicted multiple behavior problems on the teacher report form of the CBCL over and above the effects of other risk factors and verbal IQ. Insecure attachment was also found to be pervasive within clinical samples of preschool-aged boys (but not girls) with ODD (Greenberg, Speltz, deKlyen, & Endriga, 1991; Speltz, Greenberg, & deKlyen, 1990).

In all, Greenberg et al. (1993) summarize extant results by concluding that main effects from insecure attachment to child antisocial behavior have not been found. Instead, attachment relationships interact statistically with gender, biological/temperamental aspects of the child, family ecological variables, and parent management practices to precipitate antisocial behavior (note the positive results in high-risk samples, which by definition include additional risk factors). Thus, as noted at the outset of the section on etiology, multivariate, transactional causal pathways are gaining ascendancy in the field.

Sociocognitive Variables

One mechanism by which both psychobiological and familial factors may exert effects on antisocial behavior patterns is through the child's means

of perceiving, construing, and evaluating the social world. In this section—necessarily brief because of space limitations—we focus on the seminal work of Dodge and colleagues, who have provided a multistage social information-processing model designed to enhance understanding of both normal and atypical peer relationships and social adjustment. Spanning developmental, cognitive, and clinical child psychology, this work has proven heuristic for aggressive behavior.

In the most recent formulation of this model (Crick & Dodge, 1994), a dynamic, transactional network of cognitive processes is held to mediate children's interpersonal responses and ultimate social adjustment. These processes include, at early stages of information processing, the encoding and interpretation of social cues and the clarification of social goals; at intermediate stages, response access/construction and response decision; and finally, behavioral enactment, with consequent peer evaluation and response. Interrelationships among these stages are believed to be fluid and nonlinear, with continual interplay among biological predispositions, environmental cues, information-processing variables per se, and feedback from the interpersonal behavior and peer response (Crick & Dodge, 1994).

A programmatic series of investigations has revealed that aggressive youngsters display deficits and distortions at various levels of this information-processing model. At an overview level, such children and adolescents (in comparison with nonaggressive youth) underutilize pertinent social cues, misattribute hostile intent to ambiguous peer provocations, generate fewer assertive solutions to social problems, and expect that aggressive responses will lead to reward (e.g., Dodge & Frame, 1982; Dodge, Price, Bachorowski, & Newman, 1990; see review in Crick & Dodge, 1994). Importantly, such effects are found in both community and clinical samples of aggressive youth, including severely violent offenders (Lochman & Dodge, 1994). More specific examination of subgroups, however, reveals that such "early stage" deficits as cue underutilization and attributional distortions pertain specifically to the subgroup of aggressive youngsters with comorbid ADHD (Milich & Dodge, 1984) or to the earlier-noted "reactive–aggressive" subtype (see Dodge, 1991). Presumably, the impulsive cognitive style displayed by these children limits a full scanning of pertinent social cues before behavioral decisions are made, and ambiguous interpersonal situations are (mis)-construed as threats to the self. In contrast, proactively aggressive children, whose aggression subserves instrumental goals, may show their primary information-processing differences at later stages of the model that incorporate the expectation of positive outcomes from aggressive acts (Dodge, 1991). In short, the model has allowed for specificity with respect to subcategories of aggressive youth.

As highlighted throughout the chapter, interplay among causal factors and underlying mechanisms is increasingly recognized as critical for accurate formulation of aggressive behavior patterns. It is certainly conceivable, for example, that certain temperamental styles in children may relate to impulsive cognitive processing. Furthermore, as discussed earlier regarding familial influences, punitive and abusive parenting practices appear to influence aggressive behavior through their instigation of early-stage information processing deficits and distortions (Dodge et al., 1990). In other words, a child exposed to a harsh, abusive upbringing may begin to attribute malevolent intent to others, fueling negative and aggressive interchanges that reinforce the biased attribution. In passing, we must point out that despite the elegance of the sociocognitive information-processing model, large-effect sizes are the exception rather than the rule (Crick & Dodge, 1994); sociocognitive factors are not sufficient in providing explanation of persistent antisocial behavior. A key goal for the field will be to construct and test multivariate models that can predict and explain, with greater precision, the complex interrelationships among causal and risk factors.

Wider Contextual Factors

For many years investigators have noted a clear link between measures of psychosocial adversity—including impoverishment, high rates of crime in the neighborhood, family crowding, parental psychopathology, deviant peer groups, and related factors—and children's risk for antisocial behavior. Indeed, the risk for antisocial activity is far higher in crowded, poverty-stricken, inner-city areas than in rural settings (Rutter et al., 1974). Whereas a thorough review of the long history of research regarding social/cultural influences on antisocial behavior and delinquency is beyond the scope of this chapter, a key issue is whether such socioeconomic, familial, neighborhood, and peer-related factors directly contribute to antisocial behavior patterns or whether

their effects are mediated by more specific variables, such as parent–child interactions or sociocognitive processes.

We first consider briefly the long-held contention that deviant peer groups are a primary influence on antisocial behavior. Debate is strong about this issue. Block, Block, and Keyes (1988) have challenged the traditional notion that peers are the primary influence on such variables as substance abuse by demonstrating that early family socialization practices exert causal influence. For late-onset antisocial youngsters, however, exposure to deviant peers was recently found to have a direct influence on delinquency (Capaldi & Patterson, 1994). From a microanalytic perspective, Coie and Lenox (1994) provide important detail regarding the processes by which aggressive children who are also rejected by their peers display a qualitatively distinct pattern of peer interactions that promotes further escalation of aggressive behavior. In brief, rejected/aggressive children fail to heed social disapprobation for hostile activities, stigmatizing themselves and fueling social isolation. Overall, whereas peer rejection and antisocial behavior are not inevitably linked (French, 1988), aggressive and antisocial children with peer rejection (who are quite likely to be those youngsters with comorbid ADHD; Milich & Landau, 1988) are at particularly strong risk for persistent antisocial activity (Coie & Lenox, 1994).

Moving to a broader perspective, in a masterful synthesis, Capaldi and Patterson (1994) have examined a wide array of contextual factors for their predictive relationships to antisocial behavior patterns for male youth, testing for direct versus indirect effects of such factors (see also Wahler & Hann, 1987). The research program is provocative in that Patterson and colleagues are conceptualizing a far broader network for the development of aggressive and conduct-disordered behavior than microsocial parent–child interactions per se. First, high levels of family adversity and several related contextual factors (multiple family transitions, unemployment, and low socioeconomic status [SES]) were shown to relate specifically to early-onset (but not adolescent-onset) conduct disorders. This list of factors adds to those proposed by Moffitt (1993) for the child-onset group, which included neuropsychological dysfunction and attention deficits as well as discordant family interchange. Early-onset, persistent antisocial behavior patterns are clearly overdetermined.

Second, as indicated above, evidence supported the direct (as opposed to mediated) effects on antisocial behavior of the contextual factor of exposure to a deviant peer group, particularly for boys without a childhood onset of antisocial behavior. High rates of such association strongly influence delinquency (Sampson & Groves, 1989). This finding once again underscores the importance of subtyping aggression and antisocial behavior; direct effects of deviant peer groups pertain chiefly to adolescent-onset youngsters (see Moffitt, 1993). Third, the effects of several important contextual factors on antisocial behavior were reduced or rendered nonsignificant when parenting variables were added to the predictive equations of Capaldi and Patterson (1994). The direct effects of low SES, in particular, were erased when parent management variables were included (see also Dodge, Pettit, & Bates, 1994); the roles of family transitions, stress, and unemployment also appeared to be indirect. Fourth, community and other contextual variables related to antisocial outcomes in a "chain reaction" fashion (Capaldi & Patterson, 1994), whereby unemployment (for example) predicted greater levels of stress and greater numbers of family transitions, which in turn reduced family involvement and monitoring and predicted higher levels of coercive parenting.

In a research paradigm with a nonclinical sample, Richters and Martinez (1993) examined the role of children's exposure to community violence in predicting maladjustment. Whereas such exposure predicted youths' self-reported symptomatology, the effects were mitigated when indices of family stability were controlled statistically. In this instance, family-level variables served as a protective factor against the risk incurred by high-frequency encounter of significant violence in the neighborhood and community.

Finally, we note that the lack of direct effects for many wider contextual variables does not reduce their importance in explaining antisocial behavior. Indeed, researchers and policy makers must be aware of the economic and community-level factors that predispose certain families to provide markedly poor socialization for their offspring. Antisocial behavior patterns are not only intergenerational but are intertwined with important economic, community, and family ecological factors.

Summary of Causal Influences

Table 3.5 presents, in summary form, the causal variables that we have discussed in this chapter, indicating those with evidence for direct influences

on clinical-level aggression and antisocial behavior and those with evidence for indirect effects. We caution immediately against any inference of linear relationships from the table; indeed, the two-dimensional nature of the printed page fails utterly to account for (1) the strong likelihood of transactional, reciprocal relationships among these variables and (2) the constant interplay of "cause" and "effect" in the genesis and maintenance of antisocial behavior patterns. Indeed, as discussed earlier, such putative predisposing variables as psychophysiological arousal or conditionability may be consequences rather than precursors of an antisocial lifestyle (Richters & Cicchetti, 1993). Furthermore, the field is moving headlong toward models of psychopathology that transcend the types of linear, variable-centered effects that have pervaded the field for decades (e.g., Magnusson & Bergman, 1990). We present this table as a summary heuristic to aid the reader in deciphering the complex information we have presented herein.

TABLE 3.5. Summary of Causal Influences on and Sequelae of Clinical-Level Aggression and Antisocial Behavior

---

<u>Early onset</u>

Precursors
Male gender (D)
Genetic risk (D?)
Neuropsychological deficits/lowered verbal IQ (D, I)
Altered psychophysiological parameters—arousal, reactivity (D? I?)
Attention deficits/hyperactivity (D, I)
Marital discord (I)
Discordant parent–child interactions/abuse history (D)
Attachment disruption (I)
Early-stage sociocognitive deficits and distortions (cue underutilization, hostile attribution bias)—reactive subtype only (D)
Later-stage sociocognitive patterns (expectation in value of aggressive behavior)—proactive subtype only (D?)
Lowered socioeconomic status and other neighborhood influences (I)

Sequelae
Academic underachievement
Peer rejection
Neuropsychological deficits secondary to violence/head injury
Altered psychophysiological parameters—arousal, reactivity—secondary to violent lifestyle

<u>Adolescent onset</u>

Precursors
Association with deviant peer network (D)

Note. Regarding precursors, "D" indicates evidence for direct causal link; "I" indicates evidence for indirect or mediated causal link; "?" indicates doubt about viability or strength of relationship because of insufficient data. It must be remembered that, in actuality, many of the factors indicated are linked in transactional fashion with aggression and antisocial behavior; separation into causes and effects may be misleading.

CONCLUDING COMMENTS

We reiterate several key themes regarding the development of severe aggression and antisocial behavior that have been the focus of our chapter. First, important subtypes and subcategories of this domain exist, and their recognition is essential for progress in the field. Second, these behavior patterns are multidetermined and multigenerational; breaking cycles of aggression that are mediated by abuse, poverty, despair, and cultural acceptance of violence is a daunting goal. Third, causal pathways are complex and transactional: The interplay of psychobiological, psychological, familial, sociocognitive, socioeconomic, and sociocultural factors in shaping different types of antisocial behaviors and antisocial individuals is intriguing and challenging. Fourth, enhanced understanding of underlying mechanisms and of effective preventive intervention strategies is essential for individual and societal well-being.

Regarding research strategies and priorities, we make several predictions for the next decade. (1) Investigations across multiple areas of interest will derive increasing benefit from important work on subtyping. As we have repeatedly asserted, the assumption of homogeneity across individuals with antisocial behavior is doomed to theoretical and clinical failure. (2) Prospective studies of antisocial behavior from extremely early development (e.g., infancy) will come of age. Given the relative intractability of early-onset antisocial behavior patterns in childhood—much less adolescence—and given the theoretical richness of the domains of temperament and attachment, high-risk investigations from early ages are clearly needed. (3) Designs explicitly incorporating integration of biological, psychosocial, and wider systems contexts will become de rigeur. The field must recognize the multivariate nature of the phenomenon, mandating large-scale investigations. (4) Intervention trials will be recognized not only for their clinical importance but also for their ability to yield causal inferences about underlying psychopathological mechanisms. As

shown by Dishion et al. (1992), controlled treatment studies can yield crucial data about the causal role of parenting practices; other mechanisms can be tested rigorously as well. In all, the field is maturing at a rapid pace, but in light of the havoc wreaked by persistent antisocial behavior patterns, progress is achingly slow. There can be cause for optimism only if ideological rancor gives way to concentrated scientific efforts aimed at understanding and reducing aggression and antisocial activity.

Transcending methodological and scientific trends per se, what does the future hold with regard to the prevalence and expression of aggressive and antisocial behavior patterns? Many historic issues pertinent to psychopathology tend to be cyclic in nature; for example, patterns of use and abuse of different substances have ebbed and flowed in recent years, as a function of availability, cost, shifting legal strictures, and the like. It is therefore conceivable that rates of violence and antisocial activity, which have precipitously increased in recent years, will taper off with a renewal of economic prosperity or as other secular trends unfold. On the other hand, the ever-growing portrayal of violence in public media, the increasing rates of blended families, and easy access to dangerous weapons in our society may portend a continuing escalation of aggressive behavior patterns. Furthermore, following Moffitt's (1993) analysis, the disparity between biological and psychosocial maturity in our culture is likely to widen rather than narrow in future years, as a function of earlier physical maturity in an increasingly technological age. Such trends presage continuing escalations in adolescent-onset antisocial activity. It is conceivable, as well, that the constellation of teratogenic and perinatal factors, disrupted attachments, and poor educational preparation that accrue to ever-escalating numbers of stressed, impoverished families will also propel an increase in multiproblem, early-onset, life-course-persistent antisocial youth. Overall, it is not the time to rest on the laurels of the field's quite real scientific gains of recent decades but rather to redouble scientific and policy-related efforts.

ACKNOWLEDGMENTS

Work on this chapter was supported by National Institute of Mental Health Grant Nos. R01 MH45064 and U01 MH50461.

NOTES

1. We should note that because key differences pertain to those youth who become officially apprehended versus those with similar behavior patterns who escape detection, "self-reported" delinquency is typically distinguished from "official" delinquency.

2. The term "undercontrolled" may be a misnomer in the view of Block and Gjerde (1986), who contend that a disruptive, aggressive behavioral style may be associated with either an undercontrolled (impulsive) or an overcontrolled (planful, psychopathic) cognitive structure.

3. In addition, regarding the realm of attention deficit/hyperactivity, research has converged on the finding of a fundamental distinction between (a) inattentive–disorganized versus (b) impulsive–hyperactive behaviors (see also Barkley, Chapter 2, this volume).

4. We hasten to add that some might dispute whether even these criteria signify true dysfunction in Wakefield's sense. In other words, can the field assert unequivocally that such disturbances reflect mental mechanisms selected by evolutionary processes? The probable lack of consensus regarding such criteria casts doubt on the universality of Wakefield's "dysfunction" criterion.

5. In fact, the criteria in the DSM specify that a diagnosis of CD supersedes a diagnosis of ODD.

6. Sensitivity refers to the proportion of "cases" who display the early risk factor or precursor diagnosis, whereas PPP signifies the proportion of those with the risk factor/early diagnosis who go on to become cases.

7. It is known, for example, that the emergence of fighting and stealing in early to middle childhood appears to be a key link for youngsters progressing from ODD to CD (Hinshaw et al., 1993). For extended theoretical treatment of the complex factors that "conspire" to propel certain individuals to a persistent antisocial course, see Caspi and Moffitt (1995).

8. In adult psychopathology, for example, the ambiguously defined nature of Axis II personality disorders leads to extremely high rates of "comorbidity," signified by the ascription of multiple personality disorders to the same individual. Such overlap of disorders may, in part, be an artifact of a lack of coherence of the definitional criteria.

9. Along this line, Satterfield, Swanson, Schell, and Lee (1994) reanalyzed the data from Satterfield et al. (1982), accounting for attention-disordered subgroups in childhood with and without accompanying aggressive/defiant symptomatology. Whereas the risk for adolescent antisocial behavior was markedly elevated in the comorbid subgroup, antisocial behavior in later life was also found at above-base-rate levels in the exclusively attention-disordered youngsters. The suggestion from this report is that whereas "pure" hyperactivity

in childhood still incurs risk for antisocial outcomes, this risk is exacerbated significantly when ADHD is comorbid with oppositionality and defiance.

10. A contentious debate in the field pertains to the importance of "specific learning problems," signified by academic achievement significantly below that predicted by both age or grade and intellectual potential, versus general learning difficulties, which may well be accompanied by subaverage IQ. Although our discussion focuses on specific learning disabilities, the achievement problems of youth without IQ-discrepant learning handicaps are also of theoretical and clinical importance. Indeed, a consistently found correlate of antisocial and delinquent behavior patterns is lowered verbal intelligence. Lynam et al. (1993) contend that this IQ–delinquency linkage is of moderate magnitude, is not explainable by other constructs (e.g., low motivation, socioeconomic status, racial background) or by official versus self-reported delinquent status, and is revealing of an important neuropsychological substrate to delinquent/antisocial behavior patterns. Whereas the nature of the IQ–antisocial behavior linkage is controversial (Block, 1995), its presence is well established, mandating careful theoretical attention in causal accounts of persistent antisociability.

11. Richters (1992) provides thoughtful commentary on the nature of the association between mothers' depression and their often-noted tendency to rate their own children at high levels on scales measuring externalizing tendencies. Whereas definitive results await better-designed investigations, it appears that, rather than reflecting distorted or biased ratings, the linkage may well reflect accurate detection by mothers of independently corroborated acting-out behavior.

12. If validated, genetic mechanisms contributing to antisocial behavior may be found to operate through those biological mechanisms discussed in the previous section: (a) neurotransmitter abnormalities, possibly at receptor sites; (b) alterations in autonomic reactivity; or (c) deficits in arousal (see Frick & Jackson, 1993).

13. Space permits only brief mention of another seminal set of works regarding parent socialization and child aggression, namely, those by Wahler and colleagues. Over many years Wahler has emphasized the roles of maternal coercion and maternal attention/neglect in shaping aggressive behavior (e.g., Wahler & Dumas, 1987), with important consideration of such social-ecological variables as maternal isolation/insularity and family stress (e.g., Wahler & Dumas, 1989; Wahler & Hann, 1987). Wahler's work provides an important counterpoint to the seminal model of Patterson.

REFERENCES

Achenbach, T. M. (1991). *Manual for the Child Behavior Checklist/4–18 and 1991 profile.* Burlington, VT: University of Vermont, Department of Psychiatry.

Achenbach, T. M. (1993). Taxonomy and comorbidity of conduct problems: Evidence from empirically based approaches. *Development and Psychopathology, 5,* 51–64.

Achenbach, T. M., & Howell, C. T. (1993). Are American children's problems getting worse? A 13-year comparison. *Journal of the American Academy of Child and Adolescent Psychiatry, 32,* 1145–1154.

Amato, P. R., & Keith, B. (1991). Parental divorce and the well-being of children: A meta-analysis. *Psychological Bulletin, 110,* 26–46.

American Psychiatric Association. (1980). *Diagnostic and statistical manual of mental disorders* (3rd ed.). Washington, DC: Author.

American Psychiatric Association. (1987). *Diagnostic and statistical manual of mental disorders* (3rd ed., rev.). Washington, DC: Author.

American Psychiatric Association. (1994). *Diagnostic and statistical manual of mental disorders* (4th ed.). Washington, DC: Author.

Anderson, C. A., Hinshaw, S. P., & Simmel, C. (1994). Mother–child interactions in ADHD and comparison boys: Relationships to overt and covert externalizing behavior. *Journal of Abnormal Child Psychology, 22,* 247–265.

Anderson, J. C., Williams, S., McGee, R., & Silva, P. (1987). DSM-III disorders in preadolescent children. *Archives of General Psychiatry, 44,* 69–76.

Anderson, K. E., Lytton, H., & Romney, D. M. (1986). Mothers' interactions with normal and conduct-disordered boys: Who affects whom? *Developmental Psychology, 22,* 604–609.

Barkley, R. A. (1994). Impaired delayed responding: A unified theory of attention-deficit hyperactivity disorder. In D. K. Routh (Ed.), *Disruptive behavior disorders in childhood: Essays in honor of Herbert C. Quay* (pp. 11–57). New York: Plenum Press.

Barkley, R. A., Fischer, M., Edelbrock, C. S., & Smallish, L. (1990). The adolescent outcome of hyperactive children diagnosed by research criteria: I. An 8-year prospective follow-up study. *Journal of the American Academy of Child and Adolescent Psychiatry, 29,* 546–557.

Biederman, J., Munir, K., & Knee, D. (1987). Conduct and oppositional disorder in clinically referred children with attention deficit disorder: A controlled family study. *Journal of the American Academy of Child and Adolescent Psychiatry, 26,* 724–727.

Biederman, J., Newcorn, J., & Sprich, S. E. (1991). Comorbidity of attention deficit hyperactivity disorder with conduct, depressive, anxiety, and other disorders. *American Journal of Psychiatry, 148,* 564–577.

Bjorkqvist, K., Osterman, K., & Kaukiainen, A. (1992). The development of direct and indirect aggressive strategies in males and females. In K. Bjorkqvist & P. Niemala (Eds.), *Of mice and women: Aspects of female aggression* (pp. 51–64). New York: Academic Press.

Block, J. (1995). On the relation between IQ, impulsivity, and delinquency: Remarks on the Lynam, Moffitt, and Stouthamer-Loeber (1993) interpretation. *Journal of Abnormal Psychology, 104,* 395–398.

Block, J., Block, J. H., & Keyes, S. (1988). Longitudinally foretelling drug usage in adolescence: Early childhood peer and environmental precursors. *Child Development, 59,* 336–355.

Block, J., & Gjerde, P. (1986). Distinguishing between antisocial behavior and undercontrol. In D. Olweus, J. Block, & M. Radke-Yarrow (Eds.), *Development of anti-*

social and prosocial behavior: Research, theories, and issues (pp. 177–206). Orlando, FL: Academic Press.

Brown, S., & van Praag, H. M. (Eds.). (1991). *The role of serotonin in psychiatric disorders.* New York: Brunner/Mazel.

Cairns, R. B., Cairns, B. D., Neckerman, H. J., Ferguson, L. L., & Gariepy, J. (1989). Growth and aggression: I. Childhood to early adolescence. *Developmental Psychology, 25,* 320–330.

Campbell, S. B., & Ewing, L. J. (1990). Follow-up of hard-to-manage preschoolers: Adjustment at age 9 and predictors of continuing symptoms. *Journal of Child Psychology and Psychiatry, 31,* 871–889.

Capaldi, D. M. (1991). Co-occurrence of conduct problems and depressive symptoms in early adolescent boys: I. Familial factors and general adjustment in Grade 6. *Development and Psychopathology, 3,* 277–300.

Capaldi, D. M., & Patterson, G. R. (1994). Interrelated influences of contextual factors on antisocial behavior in childhood and adolescence for males. In D. C. Fowles, P. Sutker, & S. H. Goodman (Eds.), *Progress in experimental personality and psychopathology research* (pp. 165–198). New York: Springer.

Caron, C., & Rutter, M. (1991). Comorbidity in child psychopathology: Concepts, issues, and research strategies. *Journal of Child Psychology and Psychiatry, 32,* 1063–1080.

Caspi, A., & Moffitt, T. E. (1995). The continuity of maladaptive behavior: From description to understanding in the study of antisocial behavior. In D. Cicchetti & D. J. Cohen (Eds.), *Developmental psychopathology* (Vol. 2, pp. 472–511). New York: Wiley.

Caspi, A., Lynam, D., Moffitt, T. E., & Silva, P. A. (1993). Unraveling girls' delinquency: Biological, dispositional, and contextual contributions to adolescent misbehavior. *Developmental Psychology, 29,* 19–30.

Chesney-Lind, M., & Shelden, R. G. (Eds.). (1992). *Girls: Delinquency and juvenile justice.* Pacific Grove, CA: Brooks/Cole.

Cicchetti, D., & Richters, J. (1993). Developmental considerations in the investigation of conduct disorder. *Development and Psychopathology, 5,* 331–344.

Cleckley, H. (1976). *The mask of sanity* (5th ed.). St. Louis: Mosby.

Coie, J. D., & Lenox, K. F. (1994). The development of antisocial individuals. In D. C. Fowles, P. Sutker, & S. H. Goodman (Eds.), *Progress in experimental personality and psychopathology research* (pp. 45–72). New York: Springer.

Costello, E. J., & Angold, A. (1993). Toward a developmental epidemiology of the disruptive behavior disorders. *Development and Psychopathology, 5,* 91–101.

Crick, N. R., & Dodge, K. A. (1994). A review and reformulation of social information processing mechanisms in children's social adjustment. *Psychological Bulletin, 115,* 74–101.

Crick, N. R., & Grotpeter, J. K. (1993). Relational aggression, gender, and social-psychological adjustment. *Child Development, 66,* 710–722.

Cummings, E. M., Simpson, K. S., & Wilson, A. (1993). Children's responses to interadult anger as a function of information about resolution. *Developmental Psychology, 29,* 978–985.

Daugherty, T. K., & Quay, H. C. (1991). Response perseveration and delayed responding in childhood behavior disorders. *Journal of Child Psychology and Psychiatry, 32,* 453–461.

DiLalla, L. F., & Gottesman, I. I. (1991). Biological and genetic contributors to violence: Widom's untold tale. *Psychological Bulletin, 109,* 125–129.

Dishion, T. J., Patterson, G. R., & Kavanagh, K. A. (1992). An experimental test of the coercion model: Linking theory, measurement, and intervention. In J. McCord & R. E. Tremblay (Eds.), *Preventing antisocial behavior: Interventions from birth through adolescence* (pp. 253–282). New York: Guilford Press.

Dodge, K. A. (1990). Nature versus nurture in child conduct disorder: It is time to ask a different question. *Developmental Psychology, 26,* 698–701.

Dodge, K. A. (1991). The structure and function of reactive and proactive aggression. In D. J. Pepler & K. H. Rubin (Eds.), *The development and treatment of childhood aggression* (pp. 201–218). Hillsdale, NJ: Erlbaum.

Dodge, K. A., Bates, J., & Pettit, G. S. (1990). Mechanisms in the cycle of violence. *Science, 250,* 1678–1683.

Dodge, K. A., & Coie, J. D. (1987). Social-information-processing factors in reactive and proactive aggression in children's peer groups. *Journal of Personality and Social Psychology, 53,* 1146–1158.

Dodge, K. A., & Frame, C. L. (1982). Social cognitive biases and deficits in aggressive boys. *Child Development, 53,* 629–635.

Dodge, K. A., Pettit, G. S., & Bates, J. E. (1994). Socialization mediators of the relation between socioeconomic status and child conduct problems. *Child Development, 65,* 649–665.

Dodge, K. A., Price, J. M., Bachorowski, J., & Newman, J. M. (1990). Hostile attributional biases in severely aggressive adolescents. *Journal of Abnormal Psychology, 99,* 385–392.

Downey, G., & Coyne, J. C. (1990). Children of depressed parents: An integrative review. *Psychological Bulletin, 108,* 50–76.

Easterbrooks, M. A., Davidson, C. E., & Chazan, R. (1993). Psychosocial risk, attachment, and behavior problems among school-aged children. *Development and Psychopathology, 5,* 389–402.

Edelbrock, C., Rende, R., Plomin, R., & Thompson, L. A. (1995). A twin study of competence and problem behavior in childhood and early adolescence. *Journal of Child Psychology and Psychiatry, 36,* 775–785.

Emery, R. E. (1982). Interparental conflict and the children of discord and divorce. *Psychological Bulletin, 92,* 310–330.

Erickson, M. F., Sroufe, L. A., & Egeland, B. (1985). The relationship between quality of attachment and behavior problems in preschool in a high-risk sample. In I. Bretherton & E. Waters (Eds.), *Growing points of attachment theory and research. Monographs of the Society for Research in Child Development, 50* (1–2, Serial No. 209), 147–166.

Eysenck, H. J. (1986). A critique of classification and diagnosis. In T. Millon & G. L. Klerman (Eds.), *Contemporary directions in psychopathology* (pp. 73–98). New York: Guilford Press.

Fagot, B. I., & Kavanagh, K. (1990). The prediction of antisocial behavior from avoidant attachment classifications. *Child Development, 61,* 864–873.

Faraone, S. V., Biederman, J., Keenan, K., & Tsuang, M. T. (1991). Separation of DSM-III attention deficit disorder and conduct disorder: Evidence from a family genetic study of American child psychiatry patients. *Psychological Medicine, 21,* 109–121.

Farrington, D. P. (1992). Explaining the beginning, progress, and ending of antisocial behavior from birth to adulthood. In J. McCord (Ed.), *Advances in criminological theory* (pp. 253–286). New Brunswick, NJ: Transaction Publishers.

Farrington, D. P., Loeber, R., & Van Kammen, W. B. (1990). Long-term criminal outcomes of hyperactivity-impulsivity-attention deficit and conduct problems in childhood. In L. N. Robins & M. Rutter (Eds.), *Straight and devious pathways from childhood to adulthood* (pp. 62–81). Cambridge, UK: Cambridge University Press.

Fergusson, D. M., Horwood, L. J., & Lloyd, M. (1991). Confirmatory factor analysis of attention deficit and conduct disorder. *Journal of Child Psychology and Psychiatry, 32,* 257–274.

Feshbach, S. (1970). Aggression. In P. H. Mussen (Ed.), *Carmichael's manual of child psychology* (pp. 159–259). New York: Wiley.

Fincham, F. D., & Osborne, L. N. (1993). Marital conflict and children: Retrospect and prospect. *Clinical Psychology Review, 13,* 75–88.

Fingerhut, L. A., & Kleinman, J. C. (1990). International and interstate comparisons of homicide among young males. *Journal of the American Medical Association, 263,* 3292–3295.

Fowles, D. C., & Missel, K. A. (1994). Electrodermal hyporeactivity, motivation, and psychopathy: Theoretical issues. In D. C. Fowles, P. Sutker, & S. H. Goodman (Eds.), *Progress in experimental personality and psychopathology research* (pp. 263–283). New York: Springer.

French, D. C. (1988). Heterogeneity of peer-rejected boys: Aggressive and nonaggressive subtypes. *Child Development, 59,* 976–985.

Frick, P. J., & Jackson, Y. K. (1993). Family functioning and childhood antisocial behavior: Yet another reinterpretation. *Journal of Clinical Child Psychology, 22,* 410–419.

Frick, P. J., Kamphaus, R. W., Lahey, B. B., Christ, M. A. G., Hart, E. L., & Tannenbaum, T. E. (1991). Academic underachievement and the disruptive behavior disorders. *Journal of Consulting and Clinical Psychology, 59,* 289–294.

Frick, P. J., Lahey, B. B., Loeber, R., Stouthamer-Loeber, M., Christ, M. A. G., & Hanson, K. (1992). Familial risk factors to oppositional defiant disorder and conduct disorder: Parental psychopathology and maternal parenting. *Journal of Consulting and Clinical Psychology, 60,* 49–55.

Frick, P. J., Lahey, B. B., Loeber, R., Tannenbaum, L., Van Horn, Y., Christ, M. A. G., Hart, E. L., & Hanson, K. (1993). Oppositional defiant disorder and conduct disorder: A meta-analytic review of factor analyses and cross-validation in a clinic sample. *Clinical Psychology Review, 13,* 319–340.

Goodman, S. H., & Kohlsdorf, B. (1994). The developmental psychopathology of conduct problems: Gender issues. In D. C. Fowles, P. Sutker, & S. H. Goodman (Eds.), *Progress in experimental personality and psychopathology research* (pp. 121–161). New York: Springer.

Greenberg, M. T., & Speltz, M. L. (1988). Attachment and the ontogeny of conduct problems. In J. Belsky & T. Nezworski (Eds.), *Clinical implications of attachment* (pp. 177–218). Hillsdale, NJ: Erlbaum.

Greenberg, M. T., Speltz, M. L., & DeKlyen, M. (1993). The role of attachment in the early development of disruptive behavior problems. *Development and Psychopathology, 5,* 191–213.

Greenberg, M. T., Speltz, M. L., DeKlyen, M., & Endriga, M. C. (1991). Attachment security in preschoolers with and without externalizing behavior problems: A replication. *Development and Psychopathology, 3,* 413–430.

Hare, R. D., Hart, S. D., & Harpur, T. J. (1991). Psychopathy and the *DSM-IV* criteria for antisocial personality disorder. *Journal of Abnormal Psychology, 100,* 391–398.

Harris, G. T., Rice, M. E., & Quinsey, V. L. (1994). Psychopathy as a taxon: Evidence that psychopaths are a discrete class. *Journal of Consulting and Clinical Psychology, 62,* 387–397.

Hewitt, L. E., & Jenkins, R. L. (1946). *Fundamental patterns of maladjustment: The dynamics of their origin.* Springfield, IL: State of Illinois.

Hinshaw, S. P. (1987). On the distinction between attentional deficits/hyperactivity and conduct problems/aggression in child psychopathology. *Psychological Bulletin, 101,* 443–463.

Hinshaw, S. P. (1992). Externalizing behavior problems and academic underachievement in childhood and adolescence: Causal relationships and underlying mechanisms. *Psychological Bulletin, 111,* 127–155.

Hinshaw, S. P. (1994). Conduct disorder in childhood: Conceptualization, diagnosis, comorbidity, and risk status for antisocial functioning in adulthood. In D. C. Fowles, P. Sutker, & S. H. Goodman (Eds.), *Progress in experimental personality and psychopathology research* (pp. 3–44). New York: Springer.

Hinshaw, S. P., Lahey, B. B., & Hart, E. L. (1993). Issues of taxonomy and comorbidity in the development of conduct disorder. *Development and Psychopathology, 5,* 31–49.

Hinshaw, S. P., & Zupan, B. A. (in press). Assessment of antisocial behavior and conduct disorder in children. In D. M. Stoff, J. Breiling, & J. D. Maser (Eds.), *Handbook of antisocial behavior.* New York: Wiley.

Hirschi, T. (1969). *Causes of delinquency.* Berkeley: University of California Press.

Huesmann, L. R., Eron, L. D., Lefkowitz, M. M., & Walder, L. O. (1984). Stability of aggression over time and generations. *Developmental Psychology, 20,* 1120–1134.

Katz, L. F., & Gottman, J. M. (1993). Patterns of marital conflict predict children's internalizing and externalizing behaviors. *Developmental Psychology, 29,* 940–950.

Kazdin, A. E. (1987). Treatment of antisocial behavior in children: Current status and future directions. *Psychological Bulletin, 102,* 187–203.

Kazdin, A. E., & Kagan, J. (1994). Models of dysfunction in developmental psychopathology. *Clinical Psychology: Science and Practice, 1,* 35–52.

Kirk, S. A., & Hutchins, H. (1994, June 20). Is bad writing a mental disorder? *New York Times,* pp. A11, A17.

Kolko, D. J. (1994). Conduct disorder. In M. Hersen, R. T. Ammerman, & L. A. Sisson (Eds.), *Handbook of aggressive and destructive behavior in psychiatric patients* (pp. 363–394). New York: Plenum Press.

Kovacs, M., Paulauskas, S., Gatsonis, C., & Richards, C. (1988). Depressive disorders in childhood: A longitudinal study of comorbidity with and risk for conduct disorders. *Journal of Affective Disorders, 15,* 205–217.

Kruesi, M. J. P., Hibbs, E. D., Zahn, T. P., Keysor, C. S., Hamburger, S. D., Bartko, J. J., & Rapoport, J. L. (1992). A 2-year prospective follow-up study of children and adolescents with disruptive behavior disorders. *Archives of General Psychiatry, 49,* 429–435.

Kruesi, M. J. P., Rapoport, J. L., Hamburger, S., Hibbs, E., Potter, W. Z., Lenane, M., & Brown, G. L. (1990). Cerebrospinal fluid monoamine metabolites, aggression, and impulsivity in disruptive behavior disorders of children and adolescents. *Archives of General Psychiatry, 47,* 419–426.

Lahey, B. B., Hart, E. L., Pliszka, S., Applegate, B., & McBurnett, K. (1993). Neurophysiological correlates of conduct disorder: A rationale and review of current research. *Journal of Clinical Child Psychology, 22,* 141–153.

Lahey, B. B., Hartdagen, S. E., Frick, P. J., McBurnett, K., Connor, R., & Hynd, G. W. (1988). Conduct disorder: Parsing the confounded relationship between parental divorce and antisocial personality. *Journal of Abnormal Psychology, 97,* 334–337.

Lahey, B. B., Loeber, R., Quay, H. C., Frick, P. J., & Grimm, S. (1992). Oppositional defiant and conduct disorders: Issues to be resolved for DSM-IV. *Journal of the American Academy of Child and Adolescent Psychiatry, 31,* 539–546.

Lahey, B. B., Piacentini, J. C., McBurnett, K., Stone, P., Hartdagen, S., & Hynd, G. (1988). Psychopathology and antisocial behavior in the parents of children with conduct disorder and hyperactivity. *Journal of the American Academy of Child and Adolescent Psychiatry, 27,* 163–170.

Lewis, D. O., Yeager, C. A., Cobham-Portorreal, C. S., Klein, N., Showalter, B. A., & Anthony, A. (1991). A follow-up of female delinquents: Maternal contributions to the perpetuation of deviance. *Journal of the American Academy of Child and Adolescent Psychiatry, 30,* 197–201.

Lilienfeld, S. O. (1993). Conceptual problems in the assessment of psychopathy. *Clinical Psychology Review, 14,* 17–38.

Lilienfeld, S. O., & Waldman, I. D. (1990). The relation between childhood attention-deficit hyperactivity disorder and adult antisocial behavior reexamined: The problem of heterogeneity. *Clinical Psychology Review, 10,* 699–725.

Lochman, J. E., & Dodge, K. A. (1994). Social-cognitive processes of severely violent, moderately aggressive, and nonaggressive boys. *Journal of Consulting and Clinical Psychology, 62,* 366–374.

Loeber, R. (1982). The stability of antisocial and delinquent child behavior: A review. *Child Development, 53,* 1431–1446.

Loeber, R. (1988). Natural histories of conduct problems, delinquency, and associated substance use: Evidence for developmental progressions. In B. B. Lahey & A. E. Kazdin (Eds.), *Advances in clinical child psychology* (pp. 73–124). New York: Plenum Press.

Loeber, R. (1990). Development and risk factors of juvenile antisocial behavior and delinquency. *Clinical Psychology Review, 10,* 1–41.

Loeber, R. (1991). Antisocial behavior: More enduring than changeable? *Journal of the American Academy of Child and Adolescent Psychiatry, 30,* 393–397.

Loeber, R., Green, S. M., Lahey, B. B., Christ, M. A. G., & Frick, P. J. (1992). Developmental sequences in the age of onset of disruptive child behaviors. *Journal of Child and Family Studies, 1,* 21–41.

Loeber, R., Keenan, K., Lahey, B. B., Green, S. M., & Thomas, C. (1993). Evidence for developmentally based diagnoses of oppositional defiant disorder and conduct disorder. *Journal of Abnormal Child Psychology, 21,* 377–410.

Loeber, R., Lahey, B. B., & Thomas, C. (1991). Diagnostic conundrum of oppositional defiant disorder and conduct disorder. *Journal of Abnormal Psychology, 100,* 379–390.

Loeber, R., & Schmaling, K. B. (1985). Empirical evidence for overt and covert patterns of antisocial conduct problems: A meta-analysis. *Journal of Abnormal Child Psychology, 13,* 337–352.

Loeber, R., & Stouthamer-Loeber, M. (1986). Family factors as correlates and predictors of juvenile conduct problems and delinquency. In M. Tonry & N. Morris (Eds.), *Crime and justice* (Vol. 17, pp. 29–149). Chicago: University of Chicago Press.

Loeber, R., Wung, P., Keenan, K., Giroux, B., Stouthamer-Loeber, M., Van Kammen, W. B., & Maughan, B. (1993). Developmental pathways in disruptive child behavior. *Development and Psychopathology, 5,* 103–133.

Loney, J. (1987). Hyperactivity and aggression in the diagnosis of attention deficit disorder. In B. B. Lahey & A. E. Kazdin (Eds.), *Advances in clinical child psychology* (Vol. 10, pp. 99–135). New York: Plenum Press.

Lynam, D., Moffitt, T. E., & Stouthamer-Loeber, M. (1993). Explaining the relation between IQ and delinquency: Race, class, test motivation, school failure, or self-control. *Journal of Abnormal Psychology, 102,* 187–196.

Lyons-Ruth, K., Alpern, L., & Repacholi, B. (1993). Disorganized infant attachment classification and maternal psychosocial problems as predictors of hostile–aggressive behavior in the preschool classroom. *Child Development, 64,* 572–585.

Lytton, H. (1990). Child and parent effects in boys' conduct disorder: A reinterpretation. *Developmental Psychology, 26,* 683–697.

Magnusson, D. (1987). Adult delinquency in the light of conduct and physiology at an early age: A longitudinal study. In D. Magnusson & A. Ohman (Eds.), *Psychopathology: An interactional perspective* (pp. 221–234). Orlando, FL: Academic Press.

Magnusson, D., & Bergman, L. R. (1990). A pattern approach to the study of pathways from childhood to adulthood. In L. N. Robins & M. Rutter (Eds.), *Straight and devious pathways from childhood to adulthood* (pp. 101–115). Cambridge, UK: Cambridge University Press.

Mannuzza, S., Klein, R. G., Bonagura, N., Malloy, P., Giampino, T. L., & Addalli, K. A. (1991). Hyperactive boys almost grown up: V. Replication of psychiatric status. *Archives of General Psychiatry, 48,* 77–83.

Maughan, B., Gray, G., & Rutter, M. (1985). Reading retardation and antisocial behavior: A follow-up into employment. *Journal of Child Psychology and Psychiatry, 26,* 741–758.

McBurnett, K. (1992). Psychobiological approaches to personality and their application to child psychopathology. In B. B. Lahey & A. E. Kazdin (Eds.), *Advances in clinical child psychology* (Vol. 14, pp. 107–164). New York: Plenum Press.

McBurnett, K., & Lahey, B. B. (1994). Neuropsychological and neuroendocrine correlates of conduct disorder and antisocial behavior in children and adolescents. In D. C. Fowles, P. Sutker, & S. H. Goodman (Eds.), *Progress in experimental personality and psychopathology research* (pp. 199–231). New York: Springer.

McGee, R., Feehan, M., Williams, S., & Anderson, J. (1992). DSM-III disorders from age 11 to age 15 years. *Journal of the American Academy of Child and Adolescent Psychiatry, 31,* 50–59.

McGee, R., Williams, S., Bradshaw, J., Chapel, J. L., Rubins, A., & Silva, P. A. (1986). The relationship between specific reading retardation, general reading backwardness, and behavioral problems in a large sample of Dunedin boys: A longitudinal study from five to eleven years. *Journal of Child Psychology and Psychiatry, 27,* 597–610.

Milich, R., & Dodge, K. A. (1984). Social information processing deficits in child psychiatry populations. *Journal of Abnormal Child Psychology, 12,* 471–489.

Milich, R., & Landau, S. (1988). The role of social status variables in differentiating subgroups of hyperactive children. In L. M. Bloomingdale & J. M. Swanson (Eds.), *Attention deficit disorder* (Vol. 4, pp. 1–16). Oxford, UK: Pergamon.

Moffitt, T. E. (1990). Juvenile delinquency and attention deficit disorder: Boys' developmental trajectories from age 3 to age 15. *Child Development, 61,* 893–910.

Moffitt, T. E. (1993). Life-course persistent and adolescence-limited antisocial behavior: A developmental taxonomy. *Psychological Review, 100,* 674–701.

Moffitt, T. E., & Lynam, D. (1994). The neuropsychology of conduct disorder and delinquency: Implications for understanding antisocial behavior. In D. C. Fowles, P. Sutker, & S. H. Goodman (Eds.), *Progress in experimental personality and psychopathology research* (pp. 233–262). New York: Springer.

Moffitt, T. E., & Silva, P. A. (1988). IQ and delinquency: A direct test of the differential detection hypothesis. *Journal of Abnormal Psychology, 97,* 330–333.

New York Times. (1994, September 13). More inmates in the U.S. than ever before. p. A8.

Offord, D. R., Alder, R. J., & Boyle, M. H. (1986). Prevalence and sociodemographic correlates of conduct disorder. *American Journal of Social Psychiatry, 4,* 272–278.

Olweus, D. (1979). Stability of aggressive reaction patterns in males: A review. *Psychological Bulletin, 86,* 852–875.

Parke, R. D., & Slaby, R. G. (1983). The development of aggression. In P. H. Mussen (Series Ed.) & E. M. Hetherington (Vol. Ed.), *Handbook of child psychology: Vol. 4. Socialization, personality, and social development* (pp. 547–641). New York: Wiley.

Parker, J. G., & Asher, S. R. (1987). Peer relations and later personal adjustment: Are low accepted children at risk? *Psychological Bulletin, 102,* 357–389.

Patterson, G. R. (1982). *Coercive family process.* Eugene, OR: Castalia.

Patterson, G. R. (1993). Orderly change in a stable world: The antisocial trait as a chimera. *Journal of Consulting and Clinical Psychology, 61,* 911–919.

Patterson, G. R., Reid, J. B., & Dishion, T. J. (1992). *Antisocial boys.* Eugene, OR: Castalia.

Patterson, G. R., & Stouthamer-Loeber, M. (1984). The correlation of family management practices and delinquency. *Child Development, 55,* 1299–1307.

Puig-Antich, J. (1982). Major depression and conduct disorder in prepuberty. *Journal of the American Academy of Child Psychiatry, 21,* 118–128.

Quay, H. C. (1986). Conduct disorders. In H. C. Quay & J. S. Werry (Eds.), *Psychopathological disorders of childhood* (3rd ed., pp. 35–72). New York: Wiley.

Quay, H. C. (1987). Patterns of delinquent behavior. In H. C. Quay (Ed.), *Handbook of juvenile delinquency* (pp. 118–138). New York: Wiley.

Quay, H. C. (1988). The behavioral reward and inhibition systems in childhood behavior disorders. In L. M. Bloomingdale (Ed.), *Attention deficit disorder* (Vol. 3, pp. 176–186). Oxford, UK: Pergamon.

Quay, H. C. (1993). The psychobiology of undersocialized aggressive conduct disorder: A theoretical perspective. *Development and Psychopathology, 5,* 165–180.

Renken, B., Egeland, B., Marvinney, D., Mangelsdorf, S., & Sroufe, L. A. (1989). Early childhood antecedents of aggression and passive-withdrawal in early elementary school. *Journal of Personality, 57,* 257–281.

Rey, J. M., Bashir, M. R., Schwarz, M., Richards, I. N., Plapp, J. M., & Stewart, G. W. (1988). Oppositional disorder: Fact or fiction? *Journal of the American Academy of Child and Adolescent Psychiatry, 27,* 157–162.

Richters, J. E. (1992). Depressed mothers as informants about their children: A critical review of the evidence for distortion. *Psychological Bulletin, 112,* 485–499.

Richters, J. E. (1993). Community violence and children's development: Toward a research agenda for the 1990's. *Psychiatry, 56,* 3–6.

Richters, J. E., & Cicchetti, D. (1993). Mark Twain meets DSM-III-R: Conduct disorder, development, and the concept of harmful dysfunction. *Development and Psychopathology, 5,* 5–29.

Richters, J. E., & Martinez, P. E. (1993). Violent communities, family choices, and children's chances: An algorithm for improving the odds. *Development and Psychopathology, 5,* 609–627.

Robins, L. N. (1966). *Deviant children grown up: A sociological and psychiatric study sociopathic personality.* Baltimore: Williams & Wilkins.

Robins, L. N. (1978). Aetiological implications in studies of childhood histories relating to antisocial personality. In R. D. Hare & D. Schalling (Eds.), *Psychopathic behaviour: Approaches to research* (pp. 255–271). Chichester, UK: Wiley.

Robins, L. N. (1986). The consequences of conduct disorder in girls. In D. Olweus, J. Block, & M. Radke-Yarrow (Eds.), *The development of antisocial and prosocial behavior: Research, theories, and issues* (pp. 385–414). Orlando, FL: Academic Press.

Robins, L. N. (1991). Conduct disorder. *Journal of Child Psychology and Psychiatry, 32,* 193–212.

Robins, L. N., & McEvoy, L. (1990). Conduct problems as predictors of substance abuse. In L. N. Robins & M. Rutter (Eds.), *Straight and devious pathways from childhood to adulthood* (pp. 182–204). Cambridge, UK: Cambridge University Press.

Robins, L. N., & Regier, D. A. (1991). *Psychiatric disorders in America: The Epidemiologic Catchment Area Study.* New York: Free Press.

Rogeness, G. A., Javors, M. A., Maas, J. W., & Macedo, C. A. (1990). Catecholamines and diagnoses in children. *Journal of the American Academy of Child and Adolescent Psychiatry, 29,* 234–241.

Rutter, M., Bolton, P., Harrington, R., Le Couteur, A., Macdonald, H., & Simonoff, E. (1990). Genetic factors in child psychiatric disorders—I. A review of research strategies. *Journal of Child Psychology and Psychiatry, 31,* 3–37.

Rutter, M., Macdonald, H., Le Couteur, A., Harrington, R., Bolton, P., & Bailey, A. (1990). Genetic factors in child psychiatric disorders—II. Empirical findings. *Journal of Child Psychology and Psychiatry, 31,* 39–83.

Rutter, M., Tizard, J., & Whitmore, K. (Eds.). (1970). *Education, health, and behaviour.* London: Longmans.

Rutter, M., Yule, B., Quinton, D., Rowlands, O., Yule, W., & Berger, M. (1974). Attainment and adjustment in two geographical areas: III—Some factors accounting for area differences. *British Journal of Psychiatry, 125,* 520–533.

Sampson, R. J., & Groves, W. B. (1989). Community structure and crime: Testing social-disorganization theory. *American Journal of Sociology, 94,* 774–802.

Satterfield, J. H., Hoppe, C. M., & Schell, A. M. (1982). A prospective study of delinquency in 110 adolescent boys with attention deficit disorder and 88 normal adolescent boys. *American Journal of Psychiatry, 139,* 795–798.

Satterfield, J., Swanson, J., Schell, A., & Lee, F. (1994). Prediction of antisocial behavior in attention-deficit hyperactivity disorder boys from aggression/defiance scores. *Journal of the American Academy of Child and Adolescent Psychiatry, 33,* 185–190.

Shaffi, N., Carrigan, S., Whittinghill, J. R., & Derrick, A. (1985). Psychological autopsy of completed suicide of children and adolescents. *American Journal of Psychiatry, 142,* 1061–1064.

Speltz, M. L., Greenberg, M. T., & deKlyen, M. (1990). Attachment in preschoolers with disruptive behavior: A comparison of clinic-referred and nonproblem children. *Development and Psychopathology, 2,* 31–46.

Stattin, H., & Magnusson, D. (1989). The role of early aggressive behavior in the frequency, seriousness, and types of later crime. *Journal of Consulting and Clinical Psychology, 57,* 710–718.

Susman, E. L. (1993). Psychological, contextual, and psychobiological interactions: A developmental perspective on conduct disorder. *Development and Psychopathology, 5,* 181–189.

Sutker, P. B. (1994). Psychopathy: Traditional and clinical antisocial concepts. In D. C. Fowles, P. Sutker, & S: H. Goodman (Eds.), *Progress in experimental personality and psychopathology research* (pp. 73–120). New York: Springer.

Wahler, R. G. (1990). Who is driving the interactions? A commentary on "Child and parent effects in boys' conduct disorder." *Developmental Psychology, 26,* 702–704.

Wahler, R. G., & Dumas, J. E. (1987). Family factors in childhood psychopathology: Toward a coercion–neglect model. In T. Jacob (Ed.), *Family interaction and psychopathology: Theories, methods, and findings* (pp. 581–627). New York: Plenum Press.

Wahler, R. G., & Dumas, J. E. (1989). Attentional problems in dysfunctional mother–child interactions: An interbehavioral model. *Psychological Bulletin, 105,* 116–130.

Wahler, R. G., & Hann, D. M. (1987). An interbehavioral approach to clinical child psychology: Toward an understanding of troubled families. In D. H. Ruben & D. J. Delprato (Eds.), *New ideas in therapy: Introduction to an interdisciplinary approach* (pp. 53–78). New York: Greenwood Press.

Wakefield, J. C. (1992). The concept of mental disorder: On the boundary between biological facts and social values. *American Psychologist, 47,* 373–388.

Walker, J. L., Lahey, B. B., Hynd, G. W., & Frame, C. L. (1987). Comparison of specific patterns of antisocial behavior in children with conduct disorder with or without coexisting hyperactivity. *Journal of Consulting and Clinical Psychology, 55,* 910–913.

Walker, J. L., Lahey, B. B., Russo, M. F., Christ, M. A. G., McBurnett, K., Loeber, R., Stouthamer-Loeber, M., & Green, S. M. (1991). Anxiety, inhibition, and conduct disorder in children: I. Relation to social impairment. *Journal of the American Academy of Child and Adolescent Psychiatry, 30,* 187–191.

Weisz, J. R., & Weiss, B. (1991). Studying the "referability" of child clinical problems. *Journal of Consulting and Clinical Psychology, 59,* 266–273.

White, J. L., Moffitt, T. E., Caspi, A., Bartusen, D., Needles, D., & Stouthamer-Loeber, M. (1994). Measuring impulsivity and examining its relation to delinquency. *Journal of Abnormal Psychology, 103,* 192–205.

White, J., Moffitt, T. E., Earls, F., Robins, L., & Silva, P. (1990). How early can we tell? Predictors of childhood conduct disorder and adolescent delinquency. *Criminology, 28,* 507–528.

Widom, K. S. (1989). Intergenerational transmission of child abuse. *Science, 244,* 160–166.

World Health Organization. (1992). *International statistical classification of diseases and related health problems* (10th ed.). Geneva, Switzerland: Author.

World Health Organization. (1993). *The ICD-10 classification of mental and behavioural disorders: Diagnostic criteria for research.* Geneva, Switzerland: Author.

Zahn-Waxler, C. (1993). Warriors and worriers: Gender and psychopathology. *Development and Psychopathology, 5,* 79–89.

Zoccolillo, M. (1992). Co-occurrence of conduct disorder and its adult outcomes with depressive and anxiety disorders: A review. *Journal of the American Academy of Child and Adolescent Psychiatry, 31,* 547–556.

Zoccolillo, M. (1993). Gender and the development of conduct disorder. *Development and Psychopathology, 5,* 65–78.

Zoccolillo, M., Pickles, A., Quinton, D., & Rutter, M. (1992). The outcome of conduct disorder: Implications for defining adult personality disorder and conduct disorder. *Psychological Medicine, 22,* 971–986.

EMOTIONAL AND SOCIAL DISORDERS

Childhood Depression

Constance Hammen
Karen D. Rudolph

Within a period of less than 20 years, several prevailing myths about depressive disorders in children and adolescents have been exposed and refuted, while an explosion of interest in the topic has led to a proliferation of theoretical and empirical developments. The myths included the idea that depression in children didn't exist at all; or that it was merely a transitory or developmentally normal state; or that it was most typically expressed indirectly, masked by "depression equivalents" such as somatic complaints, behavioral disruptions, or school difficulties.

It is well-known that psychoanalytic theories viewed depression in children as an impossibility because of lack of sufficiently developed superego with which to direct aggression inward against the self (Rochlin, 1959). Later, Lefkowitz and Burton (1978) concluded that evidence of early depression was "insufficient and insubstantial." Eventually, however, researchers began to demonstrate that children of all ages may show features of the syndrome of depression (reviewed in Cantwell & Carlson, 1983), that it may be extremely impairing, and that if we examine for it in children who may have been referred for treatment of disruptive behavior problems, it is not masked and may simply have been overlooked (e.g., Carlson & Cantwell, 1980).

Thus, from its origins as a problem that did not exist—or did not matter—childhood depression has emerged as an issue at the forefront of developmental psychopathology. It is a problem that stimulates enormous interest in issues of assessment and classification, in etiology and course, and in treatment. The publication in 1983 of *Affective Disorders in Childhood and Adolescence,* edited by Cantwell and Carlson, and in 1986 of *Depression in Young People,* edited by Rutter, Izard, and Read, indicated that some of the key figures in childhood psychopathology had turned their focus on childhood depression. Subsequent years have found a huge growth in the research literature on the topic as both its practical and theoretical importance have become apparent.

The goal of this chapter is to review the state of knowledge in several areas: characterization of childhood and adolescent depression, discussion of its course and epidemiology, and consideration of models of etiology and supporting evidence. As we shall see, diagnostic methods and etiological models originally imported from the adult depression field have provided starting points, but they are not wholly sufficient to capture important elements of childhood depression.

DEFINING CHILDHOOD DEPRESSION

Joey is a 10-year-old boy whose mother and teacher have shared their concerns about his irritability and temper tantrums displayed both at home and at school. With little provocation, he bursts into tears and yells and throws objects. In class he seems to have difficulty concentrating and seems easily distracted. Increasingly shunned

by his peers, he plays by himself at recess—and at home, spends most of his time in his room watching TV. His mother notes that he has been sleeping poorly and has gained 10 pounds over the past couple of months from constant snacking. A consultation with the school psychologist has ruled out learning disabilities or attention-deficit disorder; instead, she says, he is a deeply unhappy child who expresses feelings of worthlessness and hopelessness—and even a wish that he would die. These experiences probably began about 6 months ago when his father—divorced from the mother for several years—remarried and moved to another town where he spends far less time with Joey.

Diagnostic Criteria

The case of Joey is intended to illustrate three keys issues about the diagnosis of depression in youngsters. One is that the same criteria used for adults can be applied and that the essential features of the depression syndrome are as recognizable in children as in adults (Carlson & Cantwell, 1980; Mitchell, McCauley, Burke, & Moss, 1988). Second, because children's externalizing or disruptive behaviors attract more attention or are more readily expressed, compared to internal, subjective suffering, depression is sometimes overlooked. It may not be recognized, or it might not be assessed. As we note in a later section, "Definitional and Diagnostic Issues," the high level of comorbidity in childhood depression—especially that involving conduct and other disruptive behaviors—gave rise to the erroneous belief that depression is "masked." Third, there are a few features of the syndrome of depression, such as irritable mood, that are more likely to be typical of children than of adults, leading to age-specific modifications of the diagnostic criteria. Additionally, as we discuss below, certain features of depression are more typical at different ages.

Depressive disorders in children and adolescents are diagnosed with the same criteria as adults. Thus, for example, the fourth edition of *Diagnostic and Statistical Manual of Mental Disorders* (DSM IV; American Psychiatric Association, 1994) and the 10th edition of the *International Classification of Diseases* (ICD-10; World Health Organization, 1993) give criteria for major depressive episode and dysthymia that are to be used for both adults and children. As shown in Table 4.1, the two diagnostic systems use similar criteria for major depression (e.g., either depressed mood or equivalent or loss of interest or pleasure plus additional specific symptoms), with a duration of at least 2 weeks. Dysthymic disorder is a diagnosis of persistent, chronic depressive symptoms, with a duration of at least 1 year (in adults, duration is at least 2 years). According to a recent study of dysthymic disorder in children, it differs from major depression primarily in the emphasis on gloomy thoughts and other negative affect, with fewer symptoms such as anhedonia, social withdrawal, fatigue, and reduced sleep and poor appetite (Kovacs, Akiskal, Gatsonis, & Parrone, 1994).

TABLE 4.1. Diagnostic Criteria for Depressive Disorders

ICD-10	DSM IV
Note: General diagnostic criteria and clinical features are specified, but the following are the more precisely defined diagnostic criteria for research (for depressive episode and dysthymia).	Major Depressive Episode
	A. Five (or more) of the following symptoms during the same 2-week period; at least one of the symptoms is depressed mood or loss of interest or pleasure.
Depressive episode	
A. Symptoms must be present for at least 2 weeks; the person did not meet criteria for mania or hypomania at any time.	(1) depressed mood most of the day, nearly every day as indicated by subjective report or observation by others. Note: In children and adolescents, can be irritable mood.
B. (1) Depressed mood most of the day and almost every day, uninfluenced by circumstances;	(2) markedly diminished interest or pleasure in all or almost all activities most of the day, nearly every day (as indicated by subjective account or observation by others).
(2) loss of interest or pleasure in activities that are normally pleasurable;	
(3) increased fatiguability or decreased energy.	(3) significant weight loss when not dieting or weight gain (e.g., a change of more than 5% body weight in a month), or decrease or
C. (1) Loss of confidence or self-esteem;	

TABLE 4.1. (continued)

ICD-10	DSM IV
(2) unreasonable feelings of self-reproach or excessive and inappropriate guilt; (3) recurrent thoughts of death or suicide, or any suicidal behaviour; (4) complaints or evidence of diminished ability to think or concentrate, such as indecisiveness or vacillation; (5) change in psychomotor activity, with agitation or retardation (either subjective or objective); (6) sleep disturbance of any type; (7) change in appetite (decrease or increase) with corresponding weight change.	increase in appetite nearly every day. Note: In children consider failure to make expected weight gains. (4) insomnia or hypersomnia nearly every day. (5) psychomotor agitation or retardation nearly every day (observable by others). (6) fatigue or loss of energy nearly every day. (7) feelings of worthlessness or excessive or inappropriate guilt nearly every day. (8) diminished ability to think or concentrate, or indecisiveness, nearly every day (either subjective or observed by others). (9) recurrent thoughts of death (not just fear of dying), recurrent suicidal ideation without a specific plan, or a suicide attempt or a specific plan for committing suicide.

Note: Depressive episodes may be diagnosed as mild (at least two from B plus at least two from C for a total of at least four), moderate (at least two from B plus three or four from C for a total of at least six), severe without psychotic features (all three from B plus at least five from C for a total of at least eight; no hallucinations, delusions, or depressive stupor), or severe with psychotic features (all three from B plus at least five from C for a total of at least eight; presence of stupor, hallucinations, or delusions).

Depressive episodes may also be rated for the presence or absence of a "somatic syndrome" consisting of at least four of eight "melancholic" symptoms. If there has been at least one previous episode of depression, the diagnosis is recurrent depressive disorder (mild, moderate, or severe type).

Major Depressive Episode (unipolar) can be further specified as mild, moderate, severe (based on functional impairment and severity of symptoms), with or without psychotic features, with or without melancholic features, whether or not recurrent, or chronic.

Dysthymia

A. There must be a period of at least 2 years of constant or constantly recurring depressed mood. Intervening periods of normal mood rarely last for longer than a few weeks, and there are no episodes of hypomania.

B. None, or very few, individual episodes within the 2-year period are sufficiently severe or long-lasting to meet criteria for recurrent mild depressive disorder.

C. During at least some of the periods of depression at least three of the following should be present:

(1) reduced energy or activity;
(2) insomnia;
(3) loss of self-confidence or feelings of inadequacy;
(4) difficulty in concentrating;
(5) frequent tearfulness;
(6) loss of interest in or enjoyment of sex and other pleasurable activities;
(7) feeling of hopelessness or despair;
(8) a perceived inability to cope with the routine responsibilities of everyday life;
(9) pessimism about the future or brooding over the past;
(10) social withdrawal;
(11) reduced talkativeness.

Dysthymic Disorder

A. Depressed mood for most of the day, for more days than not, as indicated either by subjective account or observation by others, for at least 2 years. Note: In children and adolescents, mood can be irritable and duration must be at least 1 year.

B. Presence, while depressed, of two or more of the following:

(1) poor appetite or overeating
(2) insomnia or hypersomnia
(3) low energy or fatigue
(4) low self-esteem
(5) poor concentration or difficulty making decisions
(6) feelings of hopelessness

C. During the period of depression, the person has never been without symptoms in A or B for more than 2 months at a time. Also, the disturbance must not be better accounted for by chronic Major Depressive Disorder (or Major Depressive Disorder in partial remission)—i.e., no Major Depressive Disorder in the first 2 years of the disturbance (1 year for children and adolescents).

Note. ICD-10 criteria adapted from World Health Organization (1993, pp. 81–85, 88–89). Copyright 1993 by the World Health Organization. Adapted by permission. DSM-IV criteria adapted from American Psychiatric Association (1994, pp. 327, 349). Copyright 1994 by the American Psychiatric Association. Adapted by permission.

Age-Specific Diagnostic Criteria and Developmental Features

The only formal modification of adult criteria involves recognition by DSM-IV that irritability may be a significant feature of child and adolescent depression, and irritable mood may be substituted for depressed mood. This adjustment to the diagnostic criteria recognizes both that irritability is a common expression of distress in depressed youngsters—as shown in the case of Joey—and that young depressed children may not express subjective negative affect, as discussed further below. As an example of the frequency of irritability as a symptom of the syndrome of depression in youngsters, Goodyer and Cooper (1993) found that 80% of their sample of 11– to 16–year-old girls with major depressive episode reported irritability, and Ryan et al. (1987) observed irritability or anger in 83% of a child and adolescent clinic sample.

Table 4.2 presents frequency of Research Diagnostic Criteria symptoms seen in clinic-referred child and adolescent samples diagnosed with major depressive episode, based on data collected by Mitchell et al. (1988). These rates of specific diagnostic symptoms are quite similar to those reported by Ryan et al. (1987) in their prepubertal and pubertal samples of youngsters with major depressive episode. Table 4.2 shows that, in general, rates of symptoms for the two age groups are relatively similar. Mitchell et al. (1988) report that depressed adolescents have a significantly higher rate of hypersomnia than depressed children do but no other significant differences. Ryan et al. (1987) found similar effects with hypersomnia; they also observed significantly more weight loss in adolescents than children and more psychomotor agitation in children than adolescents.

There may be other developmental differences in the kinds of symptoms most likely to be present in the depression syndrome. Young depressed children, especially preschoolers and preadolescents, are unlikely to report subjective dysphoria and hopelessness (e.g., Ryan et al., 1987) but, instead, show depressed appearance (e.g., Carlson & Kashani, 1988). In adolescence, by contrast, depressed mood is commonly reported by more than 90% of those with major depression (e.g., Mitchell et al., 1988; Ryan et al., 1987). Also, younger depressed children are more likely to have physically unjustified or exaggerated somatic complaints (Kashani & Carlson, 1987; Ryan et al., 1987). In a community sample, depression symptoms were more associated with physical complaints among 12-year-olds than they were for 17-year-olds (Kashani, Rosenberg, & Reid, 1989). Younger children, as noted above, also show more irritability, uncooperativeness, apathy, and disinterest (Kashani, Holcomb, & Orvaschel, 1986).

In addition to the comparisons of depressed children and adolescents by Ryan et al. (1987) and Mitchell et al. (1988), two studies compared the symptoms of depressed youngsters and adults. Overall, several symptoms increase with age: anhedonia, psychomotor retardation, and diurnal variation; whereas several decrease with

TABLE 4.2. Percentages of Depressed Subjects Endorsing K-SADS Symptoms

Symptoms	Children ($n = 45$) (%)	Adolescents ($n = 50$) (%)
RDC		
Depressed mood	95	92
Guilt	44	56
Anhedonia	89	92
Fatigue	62	92
Concentration problems	80	82
Agitation	51	70
Retardation	56	48
Insomnia	82	64
Hypersomnia	24	60
Anorexia	56	48
Weight loss	18	32
Increased appetite	22	34
Weight gain	9	14
Suicidal ideation	67	68
Suicide attempts	39	39
Endogenous		
Quality of mood	53	56
Morning depression	15	20
Unrelated to events	68	59
Lack of reactivity of depression	98	91
Related		
Excessive worrying	76	86
Hopelessness	60	68
Hypochondriasis	16	24
Somatic complaints	77	78
Social withdrawal	78	73
Low self-esteem	93	94
Psychotic		
Manic symptoms	11	3
Hallucinations	31	22
Delusions	13	6

Note. All differences statistically insignificant except hypersomnia ($p < .05$ for hypersomnia). From Mitchell, McCauley, Burke, & Moss (1988, p. 14). Copyright 1988 by Williams & Wilkins. Reprinted by permission.

age: depressed appearance, somatic complaints, and poor self-esteem (Carlson & Kashani, 1988). Comparing combined child–adolescent groups with a sample of adults, Mitchell et al. (1988) found similar differences for self-esteem, somatic complaints, and diurnal variation and also found that adult depressed patients report less guilt and more early morning awakening and weight loss than do depressed youngsters.

The increased presence of vegetative, melancholic symptoms in adults could be due to more severe depression in the comparison adult (inpatient) sample compared to the child samples that were a mixture of inpatients and outpatients. Analyses of self-reported depressive symptoms (e.g., measured on the Children's Depression Inventory [CDI]; Kovacs, 1980) similarly suggest developmental differences. For example, Weiss et al. (1991a, 1991b) found vegetative symptoms loaded with negative affect in factor analyses in adolescence but not in childhood. Overall, despite these few age-related differences, most investigators have concluded that the adult criteria for depression may validly be applied to youngsters.

In addition to presentation of depressive symptoms, patterns of comorbid disorders are also likely to be somewhat different at different ages. For instance, depressed children (and young adolescents) are more likely than depressed older adolescents to display separation anxiety disorders, whereas adolescents report more eating disorders and substance use disorders (e.g., Fleming & Offord, 1990). Other kinds of anxiety disorders and disruptive behavioral disorders appear to coexist with depression for both children and adolescents. We explore the issue of comorbidity more fully in later sections.

Additional Diagnostic Features

Like adult depression, childhood depression sometimes includes psychotic symptoms and endogenous (melancholic) features. Hallucinations—especially auditory—were observed in 48% of a depressed sample of preadolescent patients (Chambers, Puig-Antich, Tabrizi, & Davies, 1982) and among 31% of the Mitchell et al. (1988) sample. Also, 31% of the Strober, Lampert, Schmidt, and Morrell (1993) sample of adolescent depressed inpatients were diagnosed as psychotic. These rates are higher than those typically reported for adult depressed patients (e.g., 9% in Mitchell et al., 1988). Delusions among depressed children and adolescents are less common (e.g., 7% in Chambers et al., 1982), although investigators note the difficulty in obtaining accurate information from children.

With respect to endogenous symptomatology, Ryan et al. (1987) reported that 48% of their prepubertal sample and 51% of the adolescent sample had symptoms such as lack of reactivity, distinct quality of mood, diurnal variation, and the like. Presence of the endogenous type of depression may predict a worse course with shorter time to relapse (McCauley et al., 1993). In addition, a certain number of depressed youngsters display—or are seen to experience during follow-up—manic or hypomanic symptoms suggestive of bipolar disorder. For instance, Strober et al. (1993) observed that 28% of the psychotic, depressed adolescent inpatients "switched" to bipolar disorder during a 2-year follow-up. Ryan et al. (1987) found that 4% of each of their prepubertal and pubertal depressed samples met criteria for mania or hypomania, and the figure was 8% in the Mitchell et al. (1988) study. According to longitudinal data collected over a period of up to 12 years, 13% of early-onset dysthymic children and 15% of those with initial major depressive episode developed bipolar disorder (Kovacs et al., 1994).

In addition to the specific diagnostic criteria for depressive disorders, there are several other symptoms frequently seen in children and adolescents. Social withdrawal, for example, is common—reported as a correlate of depressive symptoms in a community sample (Kashani et al., 1989), occurring in 93% to 100% of groups of depressed girls ranging between 11 and 16 years (Goodyer & Cooper, 1993), and in 76% of the Mitchell et al. (1988) sample. We discuss social functioning further in a later section, "Behavioral/Interpersonal Theories." Excessive worrying and other anxiety symptoms (e.g., Goodyer & Cooper, 1993; Mitchell et al., 1988) are common, as are oppositional and conduct problems. Indeed, the likelihood of comorbid anxiety and disruptive behavior disorder diagnoses is very high (e.g., 60–70%), and we discuss the matter of comorbidity in greater detail below. Somatic symptoms and bodily complaints are also frequently associated with depression, as noted above, and problems with self-esteem—and in adolescent girls, distress over negative body image—are also common associated symptoms of depression (e.g., Allgood-Merten, Lewinsohn, & Hops, 1990; Petersen, Sarigiani, & Kennedy, 1991).

Suicidal thoughts and attempts are among the diagnostic criteria for major depression. Suicidal ideation is quite common in depressed youngsters: in 67% of a small sample of preschoolers (Kashani & Carlson, 1987), 60% to 67% in prepubertal depressed children, and 61% to 68% in adolescents (Mitchell et al., 1988; Ryan et al., 1987). Actual suicidal attempts occurred in 39% of the preadolescent and adolescent samples of Mitchell et al. (1988), with 6% to 12% of the Ryan et al. (1987) child and adolescent samples making moderate or severe attempts. These rates appear to be higher among depressed youngsters than among depressed adults (e.g., Mitchell et al., 1988). Suicidality is not restricted to depressed youth, however, often occurring among those with substance use disorders and impulsive behavior disorders, and may be greatly affected by social environmental factors (such as a friend's or publicized suicide) as well as by depression as such (e.g., Lewinsohn, Rohde, & Seeley, 1994). Indeed, the correlates and predictors of childhood, or especially adolescent suicidality, represent an extensive body of work beyond the scope of this chapter, but see Berman and Jobes (1991) for further discussion.

DEFINITIONAL AND DIAGNOSTIC ISSUES

Confusion sometimes arises in the childhood depression field, as it does with adult depression, because of different usages of the term "depression" and associated differences in methods of assessment. For example, in studies of childhood and adolescent depression, the term is variously used to identify those with depressed mood, those with a constellation of mood and other symptoms forming a syndrome, or those with a set of symptoms meeting official diagnostic criteria for a depressive disorder. This distinction among mood, syndrome, and disorder has been discussed extensively elsewhere (e.g., Compas, Ey, & Grant, 1993). Each view of depression represents somewhat different assumptions and assessment procedures. For instance, mood measures refer to depression as a symptom indicating the presence of sad mood or unhappiness and are typically rated by self-report on scales. Depression as a syndrome (or more accurately, an anxious/depressed syndrome) has emerged from the multivariate statistical methods of assessing childhood emotional and behavioral problems (e.g.,

Achenbach, 1991). Each constellation of symptoms occurs together as a recognizable and statistically coherent pattern, and the anxious/depressed cluster identified in recent years may be rated by the child or adolescent, parents, and teachers on the Child Behavior Checklist, Youth Self-Report, or Teacher Report Form (Achenbach & Edelbrock, 1978; Achenbach, 1991). The items that clustered together, named as the anxious/depressed syndrome, include the following: lonely, cries a lot, fears impulses, perfectionism, feels unloved, feels persecuted, feels worthless, nervous, fearful, guilty, self-conscious, suspicious, unhappy, and worries. This definition of depression is an empirical one, and it makes no assumptions about a particular model of cause or status.

Depression as defined by the third approach, diagnosis of a disorder, refers to the presence of a set of currently agreed-upon indicators of a disease embodied in a categorical diagnostic system such as DSM-IV (American Psychiatric Association, 1994) or ICD-10 (World Health Organization, 1992). This model assumes that there are specific disorders with relatively distinct boundaries.

One of the implications of the different uses of the term depression (and the associated assessment methods) is whether depression is best construed as a dimension or a category. To some extent, as we note later, the finding of high levels of comorbidity of childhood depression is an artifact of a categorical method of defining disorders (e.g., present or absent, this one or that one). If depression is viewed as a dimension, then individuals differ mainly by degree regardless of whether or not they might also have other symptoms. Thus, occurrence of depressive symptoms along with other disorders would not be unexpected in a dimensional perspective.

Sources of Information in Defining Depression

An issue that arises above and beyond the question of the different meanings of the term depression is the matter of informants for depression. It is well known that, in general, subjects themselves, parents, peers, and teachers may give discrepant reports of symptomatology (Achenbach, McConaughy, & Howell, 1987). This complication arises in child and adolescent depression (e.g., Costello et al., 1988) and gives rise to two important issues. One is how to obtain the most valid picture of the existence of depression, and

the other is the question of whether mothers who are themselves depressed give negatively biased reports of their children's symptomatology.

The first question of valid diagnosis is typically resolved by using multiple informants and methods (e.g., Puig-Antich, Chambers, & Tabrizi, 1983; Rutter, 1986). Most diagnostic methods of assessing depression, such as the Schedule for Affective Disorders and Schizophrenia for School-Aged Children (K-SADS: Chambers et al., 1985) or Diagnostic Interview Schedule for Children (DISC: Costello, Edelbrock, Dulcan, Kalas, & Klaric, 1984; revised DISC: Shaffer, Fisher, Piacentini, Schwab-Stone, & Wicks, 1989), prescribe separate interviews for the child and a parent. The manner of combining the information may differ from method to method or project to project. The DISC, for example, is a highly structured interview administered by trained lay persons rather than clinicians, and it frequently uses a computer-based scoring algorithm for combining information about diagnostic criteria. The K-SADS, administered by clinicians, commonly uses a "best clinical guess" method, combining information from the child and the parent but weighted by the type of information given, according to clinicians' judgment. Internal symptoms such as depressed feelings and negative thoughts, for example, cannot readily be detected by parents, and therefore the child's report might be given greater weight in a diagnosis of depression. Certain kinds of conduct might also be hidden from parents (e.g., substance abuse), resulting in greater weight given to the youth's report. Other kinds of conduct problems such as lying, having problems sustaining attention, and the like might be more readily reported by parents than children.

The other issue concerning informants is the question of whether there might be systematic biases in the reports of certain informants. Specifically, some research has suggested that relatively depressed women might actually distort or exaggerate reports of their children's behavior as more negative than it actually is. However, a review of 22 studies by Richters (1992) found that such claims were based largely on inadequate designs, including simple associations between mothers' and children's symptoms that could actually be accurate given the common finding of disorders in offspring of depressed women. Only a small number of studies were located that were appropriate to test the question by including objective measures of children's behaviors

from comparable perspectives and comparing depressed and nondepressed women. Of those studies, none supported the idea that depressed women perceive more problem behaviors than actually exist—and two of the studies found that depressed women were actually more accurate in detecting true disorders in their children than were nondepressed women (Conrad & Hammen, 1989; Weissman et al., 1987).

Continuity of Self-Reported and Diagnosable Depression

Another key issue that emerges in childhood depression research using the various definitions and indicators of depression is whether they are measuring the same thing but at different levels of severity and specificity. Thus, when we present studies based on self-reports on questionnaires such as the Children's Depression Inventory (Kovacs, 1980) or Center for Epidemiological Studies-Depression (CES-D: Radloff, 1977) scores, are those results applicable to the phenomena of depression that are studied in a clinically diagnosed community or treatment sample?

One approach to this issue has been detailed by Compas et al. (1993) with respect to adolescent depressive phenomena. They review studies of the correspondence among measures of symptom, syndrome, and disorder and develop a sequential and hierarchical model of the interrelationships among them. They argue that the symptom of depressed mood is the broadest and most nonspecific indicator (with a point prevalence of 15–40% in adolescents); most such youngsters do not display a depressive syndrome, but a subset (approximately 5–6% of the total population) are classified as high scorers on the anxious/depressed syndrome of the Achenbach taxonomic approach. A further subset of these individuals (maybe 1–3% of the total population) meet diagnostic criteria for a depressive disorder. The three conditions share negative affectivity but differ in their symptom constellations, with the anxious/depressed syndrome including anxiety symptoms that are not part of a purely depressed mood, whereas depressive disorders include somatic and vegetative symptoms that are not included in the mood or syndrome definitions of depression (Compas et al., 1993). The authors further argue that the transition from depressed mood to a depressive syndrome is mediated by dysregulation of biological, stress, and/or coping processes. In short, these authors emphasize both

continuity and discontinuity in the different experiences of depression and urge further research that includes all three levels of assessment, longitudinal analysis of the unfolding of the hypothesized sequence, and analyses of the implications of different levels of symptom expression.

A somewhat different approach to the continuity issue is to compare the characteristics of those who score high on symptoms by self-report but who do not meet diagnostic criteria (false positives) with those who score high and who meet diagnostic criteria (true positives). Gotlib, Lewinsohn, and Seeley (1995) compared such groups of adolescents in the Oregon community study. They found that although the false-positive group did not attain diagnostic status, they were similar to the true-positive group on most measures of cognitive and psychosocial dysfunction, and they were significantly more impaired than nondepressed subjects (true negatives). Moreover, the nondiagnosed high-scorers were significantly more likely than true negatives to receive a psychiatric diagnosis in the subsequent 12-month period—especially major depressive episode and substance abuse. Subsequent diagnosable psychopathology occurred among the false-positive adolescents even after controlling for past history of depression. These findings—and others indicating impairment of functioning in groups identified only by high levels of depression scores on self-report measures—certainly suggest that elevated symptom levels are on the same scale as diagnosed depression but less severe.

As we have argued elsewhere with respect to the continuity issue in adult depression (Gotlib & Hammen, 1992), elevated scores alone do not necessarily provide comparability to diagnosed cases of depression. It is likely that duration and impairment of functioning are the variables that account for continuity between elevated scorers and clinically diagnosed cases. This may be even more the case in childhood and early adolescent depression, where even moderate symptoms may disrupt normal developmental processes contributing to impairment of functioning, and where syndromes are less distinct and boundaries less clear. Thus, even somewhat elevated scores for children—if they indicate protracted distress and are accompanied by impaired functioning—may be on the same continuum as clinical cases.

Comorbidity

The co-occurrence of multiple disorders is so common in youngsters as to challenge the conventional assumption of discrete conditions. Nowhere is comorbidity or covariation of symptoms more obvious and challenging than in childhood depression (Hammen & Compas, 1994). Although one might expect to find greater comorbidity in clinic-referred samples if the presence of multiple problems increases the likelihood of treatment-seeking, even community samples show rates of comorbid conditions that significantly exceed rates that would be expected if separate disorders occurred together by chance alone (Caron & Rutter, 1991).

How significant is the issue of comorbidity? Angold and Costello (1993) recently reviewed six community studies and found that the presence of depression in children and adolescents increased the probability of finding another disorder by at least 20 times. For example, Rohde, Lewinsohn, and Seeley (1991) reported a 42% comorbidity rate among adolescents diagnosed with depression in their large community study, and studies of clinical samples of depressed children and youth have found even higher rates (e.g., Kovacs, Feinberg, Crouse-Novak, Paulauskas, & Finkelstein, 1984; Mitchell et al., 1988).

The most common comorbid conditions are anxiety disorders and disruptive behavior disorders. For instance, Kovacs (1990) reviewed studies of depressed youngsters and concluded that 30% to 75% had diagnosable anxiety disorders. Brady and Kendall (1992) found up to 62% comorbidity of depression and anxiety disorders in their review. Kovacs, Paulauskas, Gatsonis, and Richards (1988) found that anxiety disorders develop most commonly before major depression. Comorbid anxiety disorders appear to include the full array: separation anxiety, overanxious (generalized anxiety) disorder, severe phobias, or obsessive–compulsive disorder. Kovacs (1990) speculated that sometimes anxiety and depression are actually a single disorder—although in other cases they are distinct but mark a particularly pernicious course and prognosis. In terms of depression measured as a constellation of symptoms rather than a diagnostic disorder, Achenbach (1991) failed to find a "pure" depression syndrome emerging from principal-components analyses of reports by youth, parents, and teachers. Instead, depression symptoms loaded on a factor that also included anxiety symptoms, leading to an anxious/depressed core syndrome in the current version of Achenbach's taxonomic procedures (see also Compas et al., 1993).

Depression also coexists commonly with conduct/behavioral disorders, including antisocial, oppositional, attention-deficit, and substance use disorders. The frequency of such combinations initially created the confusion of "masked" depression. Fleming and Offord (1990) offered the following summary of comorbid conditions in their review of community studies of depression: 17–79% comorbid with conduct disorder, 0–50% with oppositional defiant disorder, 0–57% with attention-deficit disorder, and 23–25% with alcohol or drug use disorder. Among specific studies, for example, Rohde et al. (1991) reported a lifetime comorbidity rate of 12.1% for conduct disorder in the depressed group (compared with just 6% in nondepressed subjects).

Clinical samples of depressed youngsters are highly likely to include coexisting conduct disorder (e.g., 33% reported by Puig-Antich, 1982; also Ryan et al., 1987), 36% lifetime conduct disorder reported by Kovacs et al. (1988), and concurrent rates of 16% in children and 14% in adolescents reported by Mitchell et al. (1988). Both community and treatment-referred sample studies also report elevations in rates of comorbid substance use disorders and attention-deficit/hyperactivity disorder (e.g., Kashani et al., 1987; Keller et al., 1988; review by Angold & Costello, 1993).

Studies of nondiagnosed depressions using self- and other-reported symptom scales similarly show covariation of depression and behavior-disorder symptoms. For instance, Cole and Carpentieri (1990) found a correlation of .73 between conduct-disorder symptoms and depression, after controlling for sources of shared method variance in reports by children, parents, and peers. Similarly, Quiggle, Garber, Panak, and Dodge (1992) also found high correlations between depression and aggression from various informants after controlling for method variance. Studies based on Achenbach's measures of core symptom clusters have also found that the anxious/depressed syndrome correlates highly with both internalizing clusters and externalizing (aggressive, attention problems) clusters (e.g., Achenbach, 1991).

What are the implications of such high levels of comorbidity of depression with other problems in children and adolescents? One is that our current definitions and measures of childhood depression may not be entirely appropriate. To some extent the comorbidity may be an artifact of a categorical diagnostic system with overly narrow boundaries on the one hand but overlapping symptoms on the other (e.g., negative mood and outlook, poor appetite and sleep patterns, restlessness and poor concentration may all occur in several different disorders). Perhaps the boundaries that have been drawn for adults do not apply to the actual phenomenology of depression in children; thus, the coexistence of depression and anxiety, and depression and anger in youngsters may reflect the true nature of how depression is experienced and expressed in youth (e.g., Achenbach, 1991; Renouf & Harter, 1990; see Hammen & Compas, 1994, for a more extended discussion). Early depression in children may simply be less differentiated than it is in adults, owing to different developmental experiences. For instance, neurological immaturity may prevent the manifestation of symptoms specific to particular disorders, such as pessimism or internalized negative self-referent thought, whereas maturity and learning experiences shape self-regulatory processes. The developmental aspects of the manifestations of distress and disorder are important not only for defining depression in youngsters, but also from a theoretical point of view concerning the interplay of affect expression, regulation, and coping.

Another implication of comorbidity is that its universality in depression suggests that we may not have fully explored the correlates and consequences specifically due to depressive conditions compared with those due to another condition. If most depressed children actually have mixed disorders, then much of the literature based on "depressed" children may actually reflect diverse disorders. This raises the need for longitudinal analysis of the course of "pure" versus mixed depression–internalizing or mixed depression–externalizing disorders. How do they differ, and what are the temporal patterns and trajectories of different combinations of disorders?

Finally, another implication of comorbidity is the challenge it presents for understanding etiological and risk mechanisms of depression. On the one hand, extensive comorbidity challenges the way we think about etiology, since coexistence of various symptoms suggests a dynamic interplay between the child's expressions and experiences and the environment. Thus, for example, we might question whether conduct disorder induces depression because of its disruptive effect on peer relationships and school success or whether depression induces (in some) conduct disorder as an expression of frustration, and anger toward the self and others? Similar examples arise in considering the co-occurrence of depression with anxiety disorders, eating disorders, and substance abuse. Clearly, the dynamic interplay be-

tween children's symptoms needs to be explored; we cannot simply conclude the presence of two or more disorders. The point is that the fact of comorbidity is one of several characteristics of depression in children that calls for a move away from static, intraindividual models of etiology toward more contextual and transactional models to help capture the processes of symptom development and expression over time.

On the other hand, comorbidity also creates a need to study the content of risk and causal factors in a different way than we study "pure" depression. Risk factors for different disorders might themselves occur together (e.g., parental depression associated with marital disruption). A single risk factor might be responsible for nonspecific outcomes (e.g., child maltreatment might increase risk for various symptoms). A risk factor might induce one condition that in turn leads to another condition (constitutional emotional reactivity and inhibition might lead to anxiety disorders that eventually cause depression). Certainly there are many possible complexities in studying etiological mechanisms and many candidates for risk factors that may have somewhat nonspecific consequences. The complexity of these matters is quite challenging and ultimately creates a need for sophisticated research designs and methods. It is entirely possible that the explanations for childhood-onset depression are somewhat different from those of adult-onset depression.

In summary, the issues of defining depression, measuring it, and exploring its developmental pathways present unique challenges that would seem to call for more than merely downward extensions of how we measure and define adult depression. The fact that we can employ adult criteria has ushered in an era of greater study of this important topic, but at the same time, it may have misled us into believing that the phenomena are the same and have similar consequences as adult depression.

EPIDEMIOLOGY OF CHILDHOOD DEPRESSION

Prevalence/Incidence

Only in recent years have investigators mounted methodologically sound epidemiological surveys of childhood disorders. Despite the advantage of large and reasonably representative samples, the studies have tended to use somewhat different methods of assessment and case identification processes (such issues and other methodological shortcomings are discussed in Fleming & Offord, 1990; see also Angold & Costello, 1993, for method differences).

Table 4.3 lists several of the largest and most comparable studies, and their reported rates of major depressive episode and dysthymic disorder. The rates reported may be further qualified by age, gender, and other sociodemographic factors as discussed later. Most of the studies report 6-month or 1-year prevalence. Collapsed across child and adolescent samples, the most frequent rates are in the 6% to 8% range for major depressive episode (the most striking exception is the Costello et al., 1988, report of 0.4% MDE for 7- to 11-year-olds). Even when diagnostic criteria are not met, subsyndromal depressive symptoms may also indicate high levels of distress. For instance, Cooper and Goodyer (1993) reported that 20.7% of their all-female sample of 11- to 16-year-olds had significant symptoms but fell short of diagnostic criteria.

Table 4.3 obscures important age-related effects: Children ages 6 to 11 have much lower rates of diagnoses of major depression (2–3%) than do adolescents (6–8%) (e.g., Angold & Rutter, 1992; Cohen et al., 1993); age differences as a function of gender are discussed further below. Rates of dysthymic disorder are variable but generally low. Depression in preschool children is apparently rare, occurring in less than 1% (Kashani & Carlson, 1987), but data in this age group are sparse, and children younger than about 7 years are typically not included in large-scale community surveys.

It should be noted that the rates of depressive disorders must be further qualified by the source of the diagnostic information. As noted earlier, children and adolescents report symptoms much more frequently than do their parents or teachers. The rates in Table 4.3 generally include information obtained from the child, but different studies used different methods of combining symptom data. Moreover, when self-report symptom scores, rather than diagnoses, are used to indicate depressive experiences, approximately 10% to 30% of adolescents exceed cutoffs for high levels (e.g., Albert & Beck, 1975; Garrison, Jackson, Marsteller, McKeown, & Addy, 1990; Reinherz et al., 1989; Roberts, Lewinsohn, & Seeley, 1991). Other cutoffs yield even higher levels of depressive symptoms. For example, Roberts, Andrews, Lewinsohn, and Hops (1990) in the Oregon sample reported that 46% of boys and 59% of girls scored 16 or

TABLE 4.3. Epidemiological Studies of Child and Adolescent Depression

Study	Sample	Method	6- or 12-month prevalence of depression
Ontario Child Health Study (Offord et al., 1987)	Ages 4–16 (n = 3,294)	Child, parent, teacher questionnaires (CBCL, YSR) adminsistered by interviewers	5.5% DSM-III-R major depression and dysthymia (see Angold & Costello, 1993)
Puerto Rico Child Epidemiologic Study (Bird et al., 1988)	Ages 4–16 (n = 386[a])	Child and parent interviewed by psychiatrist (DISC)	5.9% DSM-III major depression or dysthymia with CGAS impairment of functioning
Dunedin, New Zealand (Anderson et al., 1987; McGee et al., 1990)	Age 11 (n = 925); age 15 follow-up (n = 976)	Child interviewed by psychiatrist (DISC); parents, teachers completed questionnaires	0.5% DSM-III major depression; 0.4% dysthymia at age 11 (current); 2.5% DSM-III major depression; 1.5% dysthymia at age 15 (current)
Pittsburgh HMO Study (Costello et al., 1988)	Ages 7–11 (n = 300[a])	Child and parent interviewed (DISC)	0.4% DSM-III major depression; 1.3% dysthymia
New York Child Longitudinal Study (Cohen et al., 1989)	Ages 9–18 (n = 776)	Child and parent interviewed (DISC)	3.4% DSM-III-R major depression and dysthymia (see Angold & Costello, 1993)
New Jersey Study (Whitaker et al., 1990)	Ages 13–18 (n = 356[a])	Child interviewed by clinicians (based on DSM-III criteria)	4.0% DSM-III major depression; 4.9% dysthymia (lifetime)
Northeastern U.S. Longitudinal Study (Reinherz, Giaconia, Pakiz, et al., 1993)	Age 18 follow-up (n = 386)	Child interviewed by clinicians (DISC)	6.0% DSM-III-R major depression (9.4% lifetime)
Oregon Adolescent Depression Project (Lewinsohn, Hops, et al., 1993)	Ages 14–18 (n = 1,508)	Child interviewed by clinicians (K-SADS)	7.8% DSM-III-R major depression; 0.07% dysthymia

[a]Screened for further assessment from larger population.

higher on the CES-D, a cutoff that typically identifies 16% to 20% of the adult population. Rather than mere "adolescent turmoil," elevated self-report scores indicate impaired functioning (e.g., Lewinsohn, Hops, Roberts, Seeley, & Andrews, 1993) as well as diagnosis (Roberts et al., 1991) and later treatment seeking or hospitalization (e.g., Kandel & Davies, 1986). Taken together, both diagnoses and self-reported depressive symptoms indicate high rates of significant emotional distress in children and adolescents.

There is some evidence to suggest that the prevalence of depression in youngsters is increasing. Earlier reports of birth-cohort effects showing increased rates of major depression in those born more recently (e.g., Gershon, Hamovit, Guroff, & Nurnberger, 1987; Klerman et al., 1985) have been replicated by the Cross-National Collaborative Group (1992), indicating growing rates of childhood or adolescent onset of depression among those born in more recent decades. In a birth-cohort study specifically focused on chil-

dren, Ryan and his colleagues (1992) evaluated siblings of preadolescent depressed and normal children and concluded that rates of depression are higher in siblings born more recently for both the depressed and nonpsychiatric groups. Given the relatively restricted range of ages of the siblings, this finding provokes concern that the increases in depression rates in children may have accelerated in only the past few years. Also, Lewinsohn, Rohde, Seeley, and Fischer (1993) reported an age-cohort effect for their adolescent sample (at least for young women) indicating increases in depression rates among those born more recently. Various analyses of the sources of such increased rates have generally ruled out methodological artifacts, suggesting that at least some of the cause may be due to social changes that increase vulnerability to depression. Among such changes are family disruption and exposure to greater stressors along with reduced access to resources and supports.

Gender Differences

The only two controversies on this topic are *when* sex differences emerge, and *why*. The basic finding of higher rates of depression diagnoses and symptoms in girls in adolescence is well established (e.g., Lewinsohn, Hops, et al., 1993; McGee, Feehan, Williams, & Anderson, 1992; Petersen et al., 1991; Reinherz, Giaconia, Lefkowitz, Pakiz, & Frost, 1993; Whitaker et al., 1990; see also reviews by Fleming & Offord, 1990; Nolen-Hoeksema & Girgus, 1994). Studies of preadolescent children vary in their reports of whether boys' and girls' rates are equal (e.g., Angold & Rutter, 1992; Fleming, Offord, & Boyle, 1989) or boys' exceed girls' rates of depression (e.g., Costello et al., 1988) prior to adolescence. There are also divergent findings about the age at which adolescent girls' rates increase and differences appear, but most studies concur that it is in early to middle adolescence (e.g., Angold & Rutter, 1992; Cohen et al., 1993; Cooper & Goodyer, 1993; Petersen et al., 1991). Cohen et al. (1993), for example, reported a prevalence of 7.6% in 14- to 16-year-old girls compared with 1.6% for boys of the same ages, with a peak in the age differences at 14 years.

The issue of why sex differences emerge in adolescence has been explored from numerous perspectives, including hormonal and stress-coping perspectives, changing roles, and other psychosocial explanations and interactions among these variables. A complete discussion is beyond the scope of this chapter. Hormonal (pubertal) status as such does not appear to coincide precisely with depression level; using multiple definitions of depression in more than 3,500 clinical cases, Angold and Rutter (1992) determined that pubertal status did not affect depression when age was controlled. A link between self-esteem, body image, and depression has been reported by several investigators (e.g., Allgood-Merten et al., 1990; Reinherz et al. 1989), suggesting a vulnerability to depression due to attaching self-worth to perceived value to others (see also Brooks-Gunn, 1988).

Nolen-Hoeksema and Girgus (1994) reviewed the evidence for several explanations: (1) boys and girls have the same causal factors, but such factors become more prevalent for girls in adolescence; (2) factors leading to depression are different for boys and girls, and girls' factors become prevalent in adolescence; (3) gender differences in personality styles that are diatheses for depression are present before adolescence and interact with adolescent challenges that may be greater for girls, to cause greater depression in young women. Nolen-Hoeksema and Girgus (1994) conclude that the latter hypothesis is best supported; that girls' greater orientation toward sociality and cooperation, plus their more ruminative coping styles, put them at greater disadvantage in adolescence when they face somewhat greater biological and stressful role-related challenges than boys do. Other interpretations may be possible, but the most important point is that the phenomena of sex differences are a challenge to researchers. In view of the clear excess of female depression in adults (2 or 3:1), models of the origins and recurrence of depression must account for such gender differences and how they apparently arise in adolescence (e.g., Gotlib & Hammen, 1992).

Social Class Effects

Social class effects on depressive symptoms have been well documented in adult depressive symptoms and diagnoses. The results with children and adolescents are more mixed. Community studies based on diagnoses by Costello et al. (1988) with preadolescents and by Whitaker et al. (1990) with adolescents failed to find significant differences in depression rates associated with socioeconomic status, although Bird et al. (1988) did find differences for combined age groups, and Reinherz,

Giaconia, Pakiz, et al. (1993) found greater major depressive disorder rates in adolescents associated with lower SES. Studies of symptom levels rather than diagnoses have shown depression linked to lower SES (e.g., Gore, Aseltine, & Colton, 1993; Offord et al., 1992, using a broad category of "emotional disorder"; see also Fleming & Offord, 1990, for a review).

Socioeconomic status is measured in various ways and is probably not a very useful variable in understanding mechanisms of depression. Social disadvantage conferred by low socioeconomic status may consist of not only low income and restricted parental education but also chronic stress, family disruption, racial discrimination, blocked access to opportunities, and greater exposure to environmental adversities. As we explore later in greater detail, there is fairly consistent evidence of links between childhood depression and various indicators of adversity (see also Costello et al., 1988; Garrison et al., 1990; Kandel & Davies, 1986; McGee et al., 1992; Reinherz et al., 1989).

Ethnic and Cultural Differences

Few studies have included sufficient ethnically diverse samples to test the question of differences in depression rates. Costello et al. (1988) in their HMO sample did not find differences in depression rates comparing African-American and white youngsters, nor did Kandel and Davies (1982) find differences in symptom levels. Garrison et al. (1990) did find that blacks had higher CES-D scores than did whites in the initial wave (seventh grade), and by the third wave (in ninth grade), scores of black males had declined to the same levels as white males, whereas black females continued to score higher than white females. Further studies are needed to explore race effects, and to separate out effects that might be caused by different cultural expressions of depressive symptoms and adverse conditions associated with ethnic status.

DEVELOPMENTAL COURSE AND PROGNOSIS

Impairment of Functioning

Not surprisingly, diagnoses of depression or significant symptoms are associated with functional impairment. For instance, Whitaker et al. (1990) reported that the Global Adjustment Scale (based on rating procedures from the DSM-III) ratings reflected significant impairment defined by a particular cutoff score in a substantial proportion of youth with major depression (85%) and dysthymic disorder (87%)—more than any other diagnosis. Similarly, Lewinsohn, Hops, et al. (1993) found that the Global Assessment of Functioning scores of community adolescents who met criteria for major depressive episode were significantly lower than those of nondiagnosed youth.

School and academic disruption are a frequent, although not invariable, concomitant of depression. Puig-Antich et al. (1985a) reported significant school achievement and school behavior problems in their treated sample of children. Studies of children and adolescents scoring high on depressive symptoms have also found academic impairments (Cole, 1990; Forehand, Brody, Long, & Fauber, 1988; Nolen-Hoeksema, Girgus, & Seligman, 1986). Adolescents with higher depression scores were less likely to graduate from high school in the Kandel and Davies (1986) study. Children of depressed women—many of whom were depressed themselves—demonstrated significantly worse academic adjustment over time than did children of nonpsychiatric women (Anderson & Hammen, 1993). On the other hand, several studies have found no associations between depression and school performance (see Reinherz, Giaconia, Pakiz, et al., 1993, comparing depressed youngsters with those with no diagnosis; Costello et al., 1988, and McCauley et al., 1993, comparing depressed children with those having other psychiatric diagnoses).

Cognitive, family, and interpersonal impairments are also commonly observed in depressed youngsters. Cognitive difficulties include poor self-esteem and dysfunctional attitudes and beliefs. Family impairments may reflect observed or reported poor relationships between child and parents, and interpersonal difficulties reflect peer rejection, social withdrawal, low competence on measures of interpersonal problem solving or social perceptions. All of these areas of functioning are explored in greater depth later in the chapter.

In all these areas—school, interpersonal, and cognitive—the question arises whether these difficulties are concomitants, causes, or consequences of depressive symptoms (or even of comorbid conditions). Research has not fully clarified these issues in longitudinal studies, but later sections explore in greater detail the potential role such difficulties play as risk factors for

depression. Needless to say, whether or not they may be the original causes of children's depression, interpersonal and academic disruptions present significant developmental challenges that portend poor prognosis for adjustment. Youngsters who are unable to master necessary skills because of their depressive symptoms, for example, soon find themselves deprived of sources of reinforcement and self-esteem that support emotional adjustment and protect against maladaptive reactions to adversity. As we explore later on, a dynamic, transactional model of depression vulnerability may be needed to account for the sequence of experiences accompanying depression over time and development.

Age of Onset

Retrospective assessment among community adults typically indicates that mid to late adolescence is the most common age of onset of first major depression or significant symptoms. Lewinsohn, Hoberman, and Rosenbaum (1988) found that Oregon residents with histories of depression reported a mean age of onset of 14.3 years for major depressive disorder and 11.3 years for dysthymic disorder. The Epidemiological Catchment Area study of U.S. adults found that the highest rates for onset of major depressive disorder occurred between the ages of 15 and 19 years for both men and women (Burke, Burke, Regier, & Rae, 1990).

Among treated samples of depressed children, the longitudinal studies of Kovacs and colleagues (Kovacs, Feinberg, Crouse-Novak, Paulauskas, & Finkelstein, 1984) found onset of both major depression and dysthymic disorder at around age 11 years. Similarly, depressed children of depressed parents also have early onsets (average age 12–13) compared to onsets in youngsters of nonpsychiatric patients (around age 16–17) (Weissman et al., 1987; see also Hammen, Burge, Burney, & Adrian, 1990). Keller et al. (1988) report a mean age of major depression onset of 14 years in a mixed sample of offspring of depressed parents and community residents; Lewinsohn, Hops, et al. (1993) also report mean onset for major depression at around age 14 years for both boys and girls and about age 11 years for dysthymic disorder.

Age-of-onset information not only suggests that depression is commonly a disorder of relatively young onset, but it also has implications for prognosis. Earlier onset of depression, as with most disorders, appears to predict a more pro-tracted or more severe course of disorder in both children (e.g., Kovacs, Feinberg, Crouse-Novak, Paulauskas, & Finkelstein, 1984; although see McCauley et al., 1993) and adults (e.g., Bland, Newman, & Orn, 1986; Hammen, Davila, Brown, Gitlin, & Ellicott, 1992).

Duration of Major Depressive Episodes

Keller et al. (1988) reported a median length of episode of 16 weeks in their mixed sample of community adolescents and offspring of depressed parents—a result very similar to the inpatient sample of Strober et al. (1993). In an adolescent community sample, however, Lewinsohn, Hops, et al. (1993) reported a mean duration of 24 weeks, similar to the mean of 21 weeks in the Strober sample. McCauley et al. (1993) reported a mean of 36 weeks in their combined inpatient and outpatient sample (similar to that observed by Kovacs, Feinberg, Crouse-Novak, Paulauskas, & Finkelstein, 1984).

Course and Recurrence

Related to mean duration is the question of recovery. The great majority of child and adolescent depressives recover within a year, but a sizable minority remain depressed—21% in the Keller study (10% still depressed after 2 years), 19% in the Strober study (also 10% after 2 years), and 20% still depressed in the McCauley study (but less than 5% after 2 years). Kovacs, Feinberg, Crouse-Novak, Paulauskas, Pollack, and Finkelstein (1984) reported that 41% of their outpatient sample was still depressed after 1 year, and 8% after 2 years. Interestingly, McCauley et al. (1993) found that girls were significantly more likely than boys to have long episodes of depression, but the other studies either did not find, or did not examine, sex differences.

Recurrence of episodes is common among youth with major depression. Kovacs, Feinberg, Crouse-Novak, Paulauskas, Pollock, and Finkelstein (1984) reported that 26% had a new episode within 1 year of recovery, 40% within 2 years, and 72% within 5 years. Asarnow et al. (1988) found that 45% of their hospitalized sample were rehospitalized within 2 years. Lewinsohn, Hops, et al. (1993) found that 18% of their largely untreated community sample had a recurrence of major depression within 1 year, whereas McCauley et al. (1993) reported 25% relapse within 1 year (and 54% within 3 years).

The issue of chronicity of depressive symptoms has been addressed less often than episodic course. Keller et al. (1988), for instance, found that 24% of the youngsters with major depression also suffered from dysthymic disorder—in effect, double depression, with the dysthymia preceding the major depressive episodes. Kovacs, Feinberg, Crouse-Novak, Paulauskas, Pollack et al. (1984) also reported finding double depression, and such youngsters had a greater likelihood of relapse. Indeed, early onset dysthymia is strongly predictive of further affective disorder, with 81% of dysthymic children estimated to develop major depressive disorder (Kovacs et al., 1994); Kovacs and her colleagues argue that early onset dysthymia is a risk factor for recurrent mood disorder. Ryan et al. (1987) followed a sample of child and adolescent depressed patients and reported that nearly half of the sample had chronic major depression or fluctuating major depression with dysthymia over a 2-year course.

Studies of youth scoring high on self-report measures over repeated assessments suggest considerable stability of depressive symptoms (although of course, periodic rather than chronic elevations cannot be ruled out). Garrison and her colleagues (1990) found that the prior year's CES-D scores accounted for 12% to 20% of the variance in subsequent CES-D scores over three testings (seventh to ninth grades). Verhulst and van der Ende (1992) found that elevations of the anxious/depressed syndrome of the Child Behavior Checklist (CBCL) were fairly stable over four testings in 6 years; the odds ratio was 10:1 for having a high score at the final testing given a high score at the initial testing. Overall, 16% of the youngsters were high on all four testings (only 11% of those who were high at the first testing were below the 50th percentile at the final testing).

Continuity over Time

The growing body of longitudinal data on clinical course certainly suggests that children who are diagnosed with depression are likely to experience recurrences within a few years. Less information is available, however, on the continuity between child/adolescent depression and adult depression. Indirect evidence of continuity comes from the community study of adult depressives by Lewinsohn et al. (1988) who found that more cases of major depression occurred in young women and were actually recurrences presumably of adolescent-onset depressions. Similarly,

Burke et al. (1990) identified 1,000 cases of unipolar depression in the Epidemiological Catchment Area sites and asked such individuals when they had first became depressed. Both men and women reported a large peak onset in the age range of 15 to 19 years.

More direct evidence of continuity comes from longitudinal or follow-up studies. Kandel and Davies (1986) found that dysphoric feelings reported by adolescents predicted similar depressed feelings 9 years later in adulthood; women who reported such experiences in their teenage years were significantly more likely to be treated by mental health professionals. To date the longest and largest follow-up study of clinically depressed youngsters has been reported by Harrington, Fudge, Rutter, Pickles, and Hill (1990). The investigators recontacted former depressed patients who had been treated for depression an average of 18 years earlier. Sixty percent had experienced at least one recurrence of major depression during adulthood (and had elevated rates of other psychiatric disorders as well). Garber, Kriss, Koch, and Lindholm (1988) also reported on a follow-up of a small group of child patients and found that the majority had experienced recurrence of major depression in the 8-year period since discharge.

Overall, these few studies of continuity indicate that occurrence of depression in childhood or adolescence portends future depression—in keeping with the maxim in adult depression that the best predictor of future depression is past depression. Also, the relatively few longitudinal studies of the course of depression in young samples also indicate a pernicious course. The issue is why young depressives have recurrent episodes and a possibly dire course of disorder, and whether their disorders differ from those of people with adult onsets. It is easy to speculate about the developmental disruptions that might give rise to a self-perpetuating course of disorder, but longitudinal studies that adequately study such processes are sorely needed.

THEORETICAL MODELS OF CHILD DEPRESSION

Theoretical conceptualizations of the etiology, concomitants, and consequences of childhood depression largely have originated as extrapolations or adaptations of adult models. More recently, child psychopathologists have under-

scored the potential problems of uniformly applying adult models to children. This concern has provided an impetus for the introduction of developmentally sensitive models that account for the complex ontogenic processes involved in the evolution and persistence of vulnerability. We first present the major theoretical approaches, highlighting developmental issues that arise when these models are applied to the child depression literature and summarizing relevant empirical findings. Then we discuss how isolated theories have been integrated into multidimensional developmental models.

Genetic Models

The predominance of evidence concerning genetic influences on depression is based on studies of adult probands. These studies show clear evidence that depression runs in families (Hammen, 1991a), but few establish genetic rather than psychosocial transmission or clarify what it is that may be transmitted. Moreover, research on adult depression is hampered by the problem of heterogeneity of depression—an issue that certainly remains unresolved for children as well.

Genetic Studies: Child Probands

Despite the potential advantages of sampling families through child probands (see Todd, Neuman, Geller, Fox, & Hickok, 1993), few researchers have examined the family pedigrees of depressed youngsters. Puig-Antich et al. (1989) and Todd et al. (1993) reported a higher incidence of affective disorder in the first- and second-degree adult relatives and first cousins of clinically depressed children in comparison to normal controls. Significantly higher rates of affective disorder also have been found in the first-degree relatives of depressed adolescents compared to the relatives of adolescents with equally severe nondepressive diagnoses (Garber et al., 1988).

Unfortunately, few researchers have used designs that allow for the segregation of genetic and environmental determinants. In one small sample twin study, Wierzbicki (1987) reported a heritability of 35% for subclinical depressive symptoms. Rende, Plomin, Reiss, and Hetherington (1993) compared genetic and nongenetic influences on depressive symptomatology in adolescent siblings of different genetic relatedness in both nondivorced families (monozygotic twins, dizygotic

twins, full siblings) and stepfamilies (full siblings, half siblings, biologically unrelated siblings). Analyses revealed a significant genetic influence (individual heritability = 34%) and minimal environmental influence on individual differences in symptoms. However, an examination of extreme cases (CDI scores > 13) was suggestive of substantial shared environmental influence and a nonsignificant genetic influence (group heritability = 23%). Finally, Kendler (1990) used an algebraic model to derive an index of predicted risk for depression in close relatives due to shared nongenetic family risk factors. Comparisons of predicted and observed relative risk suggested that family environment (e.g., early parental loss and aversive childrearing style) may account for a significant proportion of the familial aggregation of depression.

Commentary

Overall, genetic studies consistently indicate familial aggregation of affective disorders, but these findings are compatible with both genetic and nongenetic transmission of disorder. The likelihood of high levels of disruption and stress in families with depressed members is significant (see below). Thus, children may inherit environmental risk factors in addition to a genetic liability. Additionally, genetic studies are limited by failure to include sufficient samples of groups with other, nondepressed, disorders to address the issue of specificity of genetic transmission for depression. Moreover, genetic effects are moderate at best and need to be more fully integrated with models of nongenetic effects—as well as applied more specifically to issues of onset, severity, and long-term course of depression.

Biological Models

The search for a biological marker of child depression has generally focused on circadian rhythm abnormalities. Two hypotheses have been proposed to describe the nature of possible disturbances: (1) the phase-advance hypothesis, in which the internal pacemaker that modulates rapid eye movement (REM) sleep propensity, plasma cortisol secretion, and body temperature is advanced relative to the pacemaker that modulates slow-wave sleep propensity and plasma growth hormone; and (2) the circadian dysregulation or attenuation hypothesis, in which circadian rhythms are marked by a loss of power or

stability (see Naylor et al., 1993; Teicher et al., 1993).

Neuroendocrine Regulation

Two approaches have been used to assess abnormalities of hypothalamic–pituitary–adrenal (HPA) axis functioning in child depression: assessment of baseline cortisol levels and evaluation of cortisol secretion in response to the dexamethasone suppression test (DST). Studies of prepubertal children (Puig-Antich et al., 1989) and adolescents (Dahl et al., 1989; Kutcher et al., 1991) have failed to find differences among depressed children, nondepressed psychiatric controls, and normal controls on multiple parameters of cortisol secretion. Overall, hypersecretion of cortisol was rare in both age groups. Dahl et al. (1991) found similar secretion patterns in depressed and nondepressed adolescents, but one significant difference did emerge: depressed adolescents demonstrated significantly elevated cortisol levels around the time of sleep onset, mainly accounted for by a subset of inpatient/suicidal depressed youngsters.

Some support for a link between cortisol dysregulation and depression in youngsters comes from several studies that have demonstrated an atypical DST response (nonsuppression of cortisol). Positive results have been reported more consistently in inpatient and/or suicidal samples; a meta-analysis of five studies revealed that 81.7% of inpatient depressed children and only 31.6% of outpatient depressed children were nonsuppressors (reviewed in Birmaher et al., 1992; see also Pfeffer, Stokes, & Shindledecker, 1991, who found significant associations between pre- but not post-DST cortisol levels and severity of suicidal behavior regardless of diagnosis, and Weller, Weller, Fristad, & Bowes, 1990, who found DST responses associated with suicidal ideation and behavior). In general, most findings suggest questionable specificity of abnormal DST responses to major depression in children (see Dahl et al., 1989; Puig-Antich et al., 1989).

Findings as to other neuroendocrine abnormalities in depressed youngsters are mixed. Studies of growth hormone (GH) response to pharmacological stimulation reveal decreased secretion in depressed prepubertal children and adolescents as compared to nondepressed psychiatric controls and normals (Dahl et al., 1992). Prepubertal depressed children also have been found to demonstrate increased sleep-stimulated GH secretion, whereas suicidal (but not nonsuicidal) depressed adolescents have been found to demonstrate blunted sleep-stimulated GH secretion (see Dahl et al., 1992). However, another study revealed nocturnal *hypersecretion* of GH in depressed adolescents, in addition to some elevation in thyroid-stimulating hormone secretion (Kutcher et al., 1991).

Sleep–Wake Cycle

Studies of sleep architecture in depressed youngsters have yielded significant variability. Dahl et al. (1989) and Puig-Antich et al. (1989) found no differences between depressed and nondepressed youngsters on several sleep parameters, including REM latency, delta sleep, total sleep time, and sleep efficiency. Two studies revealed increased sleep latency and reduced REM latency in depressed adolescents (Kutcher, Williamson, Marton, & Szalai, 1992) and in an inpatient/suicidal subgroup of depressed adolescents (Dahl et al., 1991). Other investigators have identified disturbances in sleep continuity, REM density, sleep efficiency, and frequency of awakenings in depressed youngsters, but nonsignificant findings also have been reported (see Kutcher et al., 1992, for a review).

Locomotor Activity

Teicher et al. (1993) examined circadian rhythms in depressed children and adolescents by monitoring locomotor activity for a 72-hour period. Strong support was gained for a circadian-dysregulation/attenuation hypothesis rather than a phase-advance hypothesis. The depressed group displayed a significant reduction in circadian amplitude, an enhancement in noncircadian oscillations, and a loss of circadian power/fit. Loss of fit was caused by an interaction of circadian and hemicircadian rhythms, which led to a blunting of the normal circadian peak and a shift in the apex of activity to later in the day. No evidence was found for a weakening in circadian entrainment (as would be reflected in a deviation from the optimal 24-hour circadian period). The authors note that this profile is consistent with biological rhythm abnormalities in adults and with clinical observations of diurnal variation (e.g., improved mood and energy later in the day), suggesting continuity in the chronobiological roots of adult and child depression.

Commentary

In general, evidence for reliable biological markers of childhood-onset depression is clearly more modest than in the adult literature. However, some relatively consistent trends suggest that depression may be linked more strongly to HPA axis dysfunction and sleep disturbance in adolescents than in preadolescents, which may reflect either maturational changes in CNS regulation of the neuroendocrine system or developmental shifts in the regulation of sleep itself (e.g., Dahl et al., 1991; Puig-Antich et al., 1989). Additionally, several studies have revealed a specific association between biological disturbance and suicidal behavior or inpatient status, which may indicate that particular subgroups of depressed youngsters evidence biological vulnerability. Also, biological dysfunction in depressed youngsters may be tied specifically to dysregulation of the sleep-onset mechanism (Dahl et al., 1991). Despite recognition of the impact of stress on neuroendocrine arousal (e.g., Birmaher et al., 1992; Dahl et al., 1989; Gold, Goodwin, & Chrousos, 1988), existing studies of HPA axis function in depressed children primarily have measured basal hormone levels or response to pharmacological challenge. One explanation for the modest findings to date may be that an underlying biochemical vulnerability assumes the form of oversensitivity to stress, rather than chronic hyperarousal. Granger, Weisz, and Kauneckis (1994) tested this hypothesis in an outpatient sample of children: HPA reactivity was ascertained by examining intraindividual changes between basal salivary cortisol level and cortisol level following exposure to a psychosocial challenge. Results indicated that neuroendocrine activation in response to the task (but not pretask cortisol level) was associated with anxiety and social inhibition, but was not associated with depression or with externalizing behavior. However, follow-up analyses revealed that hyperreactivity at the initial session predicted anxiety and depression 6 months later (Granger, Weisz, McCracken, Ikeda, & Douglas, 1995). These findings suggest that biochemical differences in depressed children *may* involve increased sensitivity to stress, rather than chronic dysregulation. Replication of these results in other samples and elucidation of reactivity profiles specific to depression are necessary.

Recent psychobiological theories of adult depression have implicated neurophysiological and biochemical abnormalities as both contributors to depression and possible consequences of alterations in brain structure and function resulting from prolonged (possibly childhood) exposure to stressful conditions associated with depression (e.g., Gold et al., 1988). Research into the biological substrates of child depression requires further study with longitudinal designs. For instance, Granger et al. (1995) suggested a possible developmental sequence in which repeated neuroendocrine activation increases children's susceptibility to internalizing problems. In turn, recurrent or chronic symptomatology may lead to exaggerated biological reactivity to psychosocial stress (see also Kagan, Reznick, & Gibbons, 1989).

Cognitive Theories

Cognitive theories emphasize the role played by negative or maladaptive belief systems in the onset and course of disorder. Below we survey traditional cognitive approaches, which primarily concentrate on cognitions about the self; later sections will include a discussion of children's interpersonal cognitions. Cognitive theories also have been expanded to encompass interactions between cognitions and stress; these diathesis–stress models will be introduced in our section on environmental theories.

Information-Processing/Cognitive Schemata

Cognitive theories were pioneered by Beck (e.g., Beck, Rush, Shaw, & Emery, 1979). Beck's information-processing model implicates three aspects of cognitive functioning in depression. First, depressed individuals are believed to engage in systematic biases or errors in thinking, which lead to idiosyncratic interpretations of situations and events—that is, negative "automatic thoughts." Second, depressed individuals are believed to exhibit negative cognitive schemata, which are viewed as stable internal structures in memory that guide information processing and stimulate the self-critical beliefs and attitudes characteristic of depression. Finally, depression is associated with the "negative cognitive triad," or a tendency to possess negative perceptions of the self, world, and future, as reflected in views of the self as worthless or inadequate, the world as mean or unfair, and the future as hopeless. The theory maintains that these cognitive styles heighten one's susceptibility to depression, especially when activated by external stressors. Moreover, because the rigid nature of cognitive schemata renders them highly

resistant to change even in the face of contradictory feedback, depressed individuals may be vulnerable to persistent difficulties.

Relatively sparse data are available regarding information-processing patterns in depressed children. Children with elevated levels of self-reported depressive symptoms have been found to make significantly more cognitive errors—overgeneralization, catastrophization, selective abstraction, and personalization—than do their nondepressed counterparts (Leitenberg, Yost, & Carroll-Wilson, 1986), although these errors may be restricted to certain domains such as the social arena (e.g., Robins & Hinkley, 1989). Symptoms also have been linked to maladaptive or distorted patterns of stimulus appraisal and idiosyncratic processing of positive and negative self-referent adjectives in normal school children (Hammen & Zupan, 1984; Moyal, 1977) and in clinically depressed youngsters (Haley, Fine, Marriage, Moretti, & Freeman, 1985).

Indirect support for the operation of depressogenic schemata also can be gleaned from examining the presumed end products of impaired information processing—that is, self-critical beliefs. Studies of general population samples have linked depression to diminished global self-esteem/self-worth, irrational beliefs, dysfunctional attitudes, negative automatic thoughts, and pessimism in children (e.g., Kaslow, Rehm, & Siegel, 1984; McGee, Anderson, Williams, & Silva, 1986; Robins & Hinkley, 1989) and adolescents (e.g., Garber, Weiss, & Shanley, 1993; Hops, Lewinsohn, Andrews, & Roberts, 1990; Lewinsohn, Roberts et al., 1994; Renouf & Harter, 1990). Studies of clinical depression also have confirmed the presence of negative cognitions about the self, the world, and the future, diminished self-perceptions of competence, negative automatic thoughts, and low self-concept/self-esteem (e.g., Asarnow, Carlson, & Guthrie, 1987; Gotlib, Lewinsohn, Seeley, Rohde, & Redner, 1993; King, Naylor, Segal, Evans, & Shain, 1993; Koenig, 1988; Laurent & Stark, 1993; Marton, Connolly, Kutcher, & Korenblum, 1993; McCauley, Mitchell, Burke, & Moss, 1988).

Attributional Style/Control-Related Beliefs

A second set of cognitive theories involves reformulations and extensions of Seligman's (1975) learned helplessness model. The original version posited that depression stems from the experience of uncontrollable, noncontingent events. A revision of this model (Abraham, Seligman, & Teasdale, 1978) relies more heavily on cognitions by introducing the notion of a "depressive attributional style," or a predisposition to attribute negative outcomes to internal, global, and stable factors, and to attribute positive outcomes to external, specific, and unstable factors. This conceptualization led to a distinction between "personal helplessness," which would result from beliefs that desired outcomes are not contingent on one's own responses and "universal helplessness," which would result from beliefs that desired outcomes are not contingent on one's own or relevant others' responses. In the most recent extension of this model, Abramson, Metalsky, and Alloy (1989) have described a subtype of "hopelessness" depression, which would evolve from the interaction between exposure to negative events and a depressogenic attributional style that encompasses pessimistic expectations about future outcomes. Relatedly, locus-of-control theory has implicated perceptions of control as precursors to depression. Expanding on this theory, Weisz and colleagues (e.g., Weisz, 1986; Weisz & Stipek, 1982) have articulated a two-dimensional model that represents control-related beliefs as the joint function of judgments about outcome contingency and personal competence.

Cross-sectional and longitudinal studies have linked depression in community and psychiatric samples of children and adolescents with negative attributional style and hopelessness about the future (e.g., Asarnow et al., 1987; Gotlib et al., 1993; Hops et al., 1990; Nolen-Hoeksema et al., 1986; Nolen-Hoeksema, Girgus, & Seligman, 1992; Quiggle et al., 1992; Seligman et al., 1984). Yet some authors have noted contradictory or only partial evidence for this connection (Hammen, Adrian, & Hiroto, 1988; Robins & Hinkley, 1989). In a study of *situation-specific* attributions, rather than habitual explanatory style, depressive symptoms were found to be unrelated to causal attributions following experimental manipulation of success or failure (Ward, Friedlander, & Silverman, 1987).

Both confirmatory (Moyal, 1977) and disconfirmatory (McCauley et al., 1988) data exist as to a depressive tendency toward an external locus of control. Early studies of perceived control by Weisz and colleagues supported the predicted link between depression and low perceived competence and control, but not noncontingency, in outpatient (Weisz, Weiss, Wasser-

man, & Rintoul, 1987) and inpatient (Weisz et al., 1989) samples of children and adolescents. These results led the authors to hypothesize that child depression may be more closely tied to "personal helplessness" than to "universal helplessness." However, a more recent study of normal school children, which included psychometrically stronger measures, revealed positive associations between depressive symptoms and competence and contingency beliefs (Weisz, Sweeney, Proffitt, & Carr, 1994).

Self-Control Cognitions

Rehm's (1977) self-control theory of depression presupposes that depression vulnerability derives from impairment in various stages of the self-regulatory process—that is, self-monitoring, self-evaluation, and self-reinforcement. For example, depressed individuals may selectively attend to negative aspects of their behavior, may engage in unrealistic and perfectionistic standard-setting, and may fail to provide themselves with sufficient rewards for success.

Relatively consistent support has been found for dysfunctional self-regulatory styles in depressed children. Assessing children's cognitions prior and subsequent to performance on a range of laboratory tasks, investigators have documented that mildly and clinically depressed groups manifest increased negative self-evaluation, more stringent criteria for failure, higher standard setting, lower pre- and posttask expectations for performance, and greater likelihood of recommending self-punishment rather than reward (Cole & Rehm, 1986; Kaslow et al., 1984; Kendall, Stark, & Adam, 1990; Meyer, Dyck, & Petrinack, 1989). However, nonsignificant findings have been reported for differences in self-reward (Cole & Rehm, 1986), performance expectations and self-evaluations (Perkins, Meyers, & Cohen, 1988), and extreme standard setting (Kendall et al., 1990).

Commentary

Ample evidence links child depression to dysfunctional patterns of attitudes about the self, styles of cognitive appraisal, and interpretation of personally relevant events and outcomes. Existing studies therefore justify cognitive approaches as a promising avenue for expansion, yet several issues await further clarification.

One critical task for child depression researchers will be to determine whether negative cognitive schemata and faulty information processing are unique to depression or whether they are indices of general psychopathology. Evidence is mixed on this question, with some studies pointing to syndrome-specific cognitions and others suggesting generalization to other internalizing and externalizing problems. Specific links have been found between depression and dysfunctional self-control cognitions (Kaslow et al., 1984), poor self-concept (Koenig, 1988), decreased self-worth (Marton et al., 1993), cognitive bias (Haley et al., 1985), and negative attributional style (Asarnow & Bates, 1988; McCauley et al., 1988). Other studies have revealed specificity only on certain measures or have failed to find any sign of specificity (Asarnow et al., 1987; Garber et al., 1993; Gotlib et al., 1993; Leitenberg et al., 1986; Quiggle et al., 1992).

More direct tests of content specificity have also yielded contradictory results. Laurent and Stark (1993) reported that endorsement of depressive and anxious cognitions on the Cognitions Checklist (CCL) failed to discriminate depressed from anxious children. Interestingly, less positive (but not more negative) views of the self, world, and future *specifically* characterized the depressed group. Garber et al. (1993) reported content specificity of depressive but not anxious cognitions in a sample of adolescents. Finally, Rudolph, Hammen, and Burge (1995) identified symptom-specific content in children's representations of self within the context of peer relationships: Anxiety contributed to low perceived self-competence, whereas depression contributed to low perceived self-worth. These findings provide some leads for future research on specificity, which may lead to more refined and developmentally sensitive cognitive models.

Relatedly, the comorbidity issue challenges researchers to determine the extent to which cognitive factors discriminate between subgroups of depressed children. Investigators rarely have compared depressive cognitions in groups of children with depression only versus those with additional diagnoses. Researchers have begun to note within-group differences in the expression of negative cognitions (e.g., Asarnow & Bates, 1988), although to date, diagnostic subgroup studies have yielded somewhat inconsistent results on cognitive measures (Gotlib et al., 1993; Laurent & Stark, 1993; Sanders, Dadds, Johnston, & Cash, 1992).

Several controversies are about the nature of depressive cognitions. Although the traditional approach of cognitive models is to view the negative belief systems of depressed youngsters as cognitive error reflecting biased interpretations, other investigators have proposed that negative cognitions might actually represent accurate appraisals of personal deficits and environmental realities. Weisz, Rudolph, Granger, and Sweeney (1992) reviewed relevant studies and generally concluded that findings support the actual deficit rather than cognitive distortion models; in a later section, "Interpersonal Relationships," we review evidence of interpersonal difficulties, for example. However, only a few investigators (e.g., Kendall et al., 1990; Meyer et al., 1989; Proffitt & Weisz, 1992) have provided both objective and subjective assessments that allowed for direct comparisons. Future endeavors to clarify this complex issue would carry significant ramifications for cognitive models of child depression.

Another unresolved controversy involves the generalization of negative cognitions. Initial research maintained a more simplistic focus on global cognitive constructs, such as self-esteem or self-worth, or examined cognitive differences averaged across numerous adjustment domains (e.g., academic, social, behavioral). However, research (King, Naylor, et al., 1993; Marton et al., 1993; Robins & Hinkley, 1989) indicating the occurrence of domain-specific negative cognitions—that is, self-criticism or tendencies to make cognitive errors only in certain competence realms—necessitates the formulation of more differentiated models accounting for *which* subgroups of depressed children will exhibit *which* types of maladaptive cognitions in *which* domains.

A final conceptual shortcoming of cognitive models is their frequently ahistorical outlook. Typically, minimal attention has been devoted to understanding the antecedents of cognitive vulnerability or the mechanisms underlying risk. Child depression researchers are therefore calling for theoretical models and empirical research designed to account for the emergence of negative cognitions and the interplay between negative cognitions and depression over time (Gotlib & Hammen, 1992; Hammen, 1990; Weisz et al., 1992).

A handful of studies provide an initial look at possible processes. Consistent with a social learning model, some researchers have discovered an association between maternal cognitions (e.g., attributional style, standard setting) or behavior (e.g., criticism of the child) and child cognitions (e.g., attributional style, standard setting, self-concept, self-schema) or behavior (e.g., self-criticism) (Cole & Rehm, 1986; Jaenicke et al., 1987; Seligman et al., 1984). These studies suggest that children not only may learn to imitate overt maternal behavior through observation, but they also may internalize aversive interactions in the form of self-blaming cognitive styles and negative beliefs about their own self-worth and adequacy. Regardless of the process believed to drive the formation of depressive cognitions, we will need to integrate data from clinical samples with the extensive knowledge base on normal cognitive development to obtain a complete picture (see Weisz et al., 1992).

Finally, in terms of etiological significance of dysfunctional cognitions, cognitive theories of depression historically have been presented as vulnerability models. However, relatively few studies have included prospective designs suitable for testing causal mechanisms. In support of causal claims, depressive attributional style, pessimism, and poor self-concept (Hammen, 1988; Lewinsohn, Roberts, et al., 1994; Nolen-Hoeksema et al., 1986, 1992; Seligman et al., 1984) have been found to predict subsequent depressive symptoms and diagnoses. Hops et al. (1990) presented data illustrating that low levels of negative attributional style may act as a protective factor against the *persistence* of symptoms. In contrast, others have demonstrated instability of negative cognitions during symptom remission, or failure of cognitions to predict future depression (e.g., Asarnow & Bates, 1988; Gotlib et al., 1993; Hammen et al., 1988; King, Naylor, et al., 1993; McCauley et al., 1988). One study noted *deterioration* in attributional style following depression onset and *stability* of pessimistic attributions even after a significant decline in symptoms (Nolen-Hoeksema et al., 1992). The authors interpreted these results as evidence that depression may leave a cognitive "scar," by leading the child to develop a negative explanatory style. Clearly, investigators need to be more active in pursuing alternative interpretations: whether depressive cognitions are mood dependent and simply more accessible during depression, whether they remain stable but latent in the absence of triggers, or whether they provide changing levels of risk or protective capabilities over time.

Behavioral/Interpersonal Theories

Lewinsohn (1974) has conceptualized depression as a reaction to low rates of response-contingent positive reinforcement, which may represent a final common pathway of various processes. First, competence deficits may interfere with the achievement of success or the formation of satisfactory interpersonal relationships, thereby creating an obstacle to positive environmental feedback. Alternatively, depression may result from the unavailability of reinforcers in the environment or from a decreased ability to appreciate positive experiences. Any one of these sources of reduced reinforcement then may lead to withdrawal, further functional impairment, and intensified feelings of depression.

Whereas traditional behavioral models primarily view depression as a *consequence* of skill deficits and an ensuing inability to elicit positive feedback, recent models have highlighted the transactional nature of social experience. In this vein, researchers (e.g., Barnett & Gotlib, 1988; Coyne, 1976; Gotlib & Hammen, 1992; Hammen, 1991b, 1992a) have argued that depressive symptoms and qualities of depression-prone individuals may foster problematic relationships. These interpersonal perspectives regard the link between depression and social impairment as a bidirectional partnership, in that depressed individuals both *react* and *contribute* to interpersonal difficulties. Thus, depressive behaviors may provoke aversive interpersonal encounters and rejection, which maintain or heighten depressed affect.

A growing data base confirms the presence of social impairment and competence deficits in depressed youngsters, including difficulties in interpersonal relationships, problem solving, coping, and academic functioning.

Interpersonal Relationships

A strong association has been observed between depression and children's perceptions of their social competence. Kennedy, Spence, and Hensley (1989) found that children who scored high on the CDI reported being less socially skilled and described themselves as less assertive and more submissive in comparison to nondepressed children. Depressive symptoms also have been linked to self-reported inappropriate assertiveness and impulsiveness (Helsel & Matson, 1984; Wierzbicki & McCabe, 1988) and to poor social self-concept (e.g., Altmann & Gotlib, 1988) in school-age children. In adolescents, one study (Buhrmester, 1990) revealed significant associations between depression/anxiety and lower levels of self- and peer-rated social competence, whereas another study (Forehand et al., 1988) yielded nonsignificant findings for teacher-rated social competence. Depressed adolescents also report greater interpersonal dependency, as reflected in their lack of social self-confidence, than do their nondepressed age mates (Marton et al., 1993).

In terms of self-perceived quality of peer relationships, depression in normal and psychiatric samples has been linked to less secure peer attachment—that is, low trust, poor communication, and alienation (Armsden & Greenberg, 1987; Armsden, McCauley, Greenberg, Burke, & Mitchell, 1990) and to reports of decreased social support from friends (Lewinsohn, Roberts, et al., 1994), although Barrera and Garrison-Jones (1992) found the opposite association. Using a behavioral approach to studying social isolation, Larson, Raffaelli, Richards, Ham, and Jewell (1990) found that depression was not associated with a greater amount of overall time spent alone, but depressed youth did spend less time in public places (vs. their bedrooms), and depressed boys spent less time with their friends.

Minimal data exist on observed peer interactions of depressed youngsters. In one inpatient sample, depressed children were found to engage in less social activity and to exhibit less affect-related expression than did nondepressed psychiatric controls (Kazdin, Esveldt-Dawson, Sherick, & Colbus, 1985). Altmann and Gotlib (1988) discovered that depressed mood in school children was associated with a greater amount of time spent alone on the playground and with more aversive and aggressive behavior. School children with relatively elevated CDI scores also have been found to evidence more difficulty in negotiating peer conflict and less adaptive affect regulation during stressful peer encounters, but they did not demonstrate decreased engagement (Rudolph, Hammen, & Burge, 1994).

With regard to sociometric status, depressed inpatient youngsters have been described by parents as less able to engage in positive peer relationships or to maintain special friendships than a "neurotic" control group (Puig-Antich et al., 1985a) and a normal comparison group (Puig-Antich et al., 1993). Self-, teacher, and peer reports of depressed mood have been found to be related to teacher and peer ratings of unpopularity and rejection in school children (Jacobsen,

Lahey, & Strauss, 1983; Kennedy et al., 1989; Proffitt & Weisz, 1992; Rudolph et al., 1994). Kennedy et al. (1989) also found that depressed children had an increased probability of both peer isolation and rejection.

Social Problem Solving

Some studies have revealed a positive correlation between depressed mood and deficits in the ability to generate effective alternative solutions to hypothetical problems (Kaslow et al. 1983; Sacco & Graves, 1984), yet others have failed to uphold these results (Doerfler, Mullins, Griffin, Siegel, & Richards, 1984; Mullins, Siegel, & Hodges, 1985). Social problem solving and interpersonal negotiation ability also failed to discriminate between depressed and nondepressed adolescents (Marton et al., 1993). Examining the *quality* of interpersonal problem-solving strategies, Rudolph et al. (1994) discovered that dysphoric children selected significantly fewer sociable/assertive and more hostile problem-solving strategies on a questionnaire measure than did nondepressed children, but groups did not differ in their endorsement of passive strategies. Likewise, Quiggle et al. (1992) found decreased endorsement of assertive questionnaire responses in depressed children.

Coping

Researchers have found a concurrent association between depressive symptoms and less effective coping styles (e.g., Hops et al., 1990; Lewinsohn, Roberts, et al., 1994). The coping profiles of dysphoric and depressed children are marked by lower levels of active, problem-solving, or problem-focused coping and elevated levels of passive, avoidant, ruminative, or emotion-focused coping (Compas & Grant, 1993; Ebata & Moos, 1991; Glyshaw, Cohen, & Towbes, 1989), although this pattern may be gender specific, as adolescent girls have been found to engage in more ruminative coping than do boys (Compas, Malcarne, & Fondacaro, 1988). Studying a closely related construct—affect regulation—Garber, Braafladt, and Zeman (1991) found that depressed children were more likely to recommend using active-avoidant strategies, passive-avoidant strategies, or negative behavior to manage their affect, whereas nondepressed youngsters were more likely to suggest problem-focused and active-distraction strategies. Finally, Nolen-Hoeksema et al. (1992) found that depressed children showed declines in their mastery orientation, as reflected by higher teacher ratings of helpless coping responses to interpersonal and academic challenges. Such patterns are similar to those observed in depressed young adults, who display a passive-ruminative response style, which entails excessive attention to depressive symptoms and their potential causes and consequences and which interferes with active and effective problem solving (e.g., Nolen-Hoeksema, 1991; Nolen-Hoeksema, Morrow, & Fredrickson, 1993).

Academic/Cognitive Competence

Contradictory evidence exists as to the relationship between depression and cognitive competence. With regard to self-reported ability, studies have linked depression to lower perceived cognitive competence and negative academic self-concept in normal and inpatient samples (e.g., Asarnow et al., 1987; McGee et al., 1986). Some investigators have found an association between depressive symptoms and impaired cognitive performance on laboratory tasks (Ward et al., 1987), whereas others have reported no differences between depressed and nondepressed children in actual performance, despite discrepancies in self-evaluation (Kendall et al., 1990; Meyer et al., 1989). Studies using academic grades as the criterion have generally revealed significant negative associations between CDI scores and grades (e.g., Forehand et al., 1988; Proffitt & Weisz, 1992). Finally, interviews with depressed adolescents and their mothers reveal an increased incidence of behavior problems at school, less positive relationships with teachers, and lower academic achievement ratings in comparison to nonpsychiatric controls (Puig-Antich et al., 1993).

These findings were confirmed in three studies evaluating dual- or multi-competence models (e.g., social, academic, behavioral). Deficits in each competence domain exerted additive effects on depressive symptoms. Overall, however, social rejection appeared to be a somewhat stronger predictor than did academic difficulties (Blechman, McEnroe, Carella, & Audette, 1986; Cole, 1991; Patterson & Stoolmiller, 1991). In general, scholastic achievement and academic performance seem to be more affected than actual intellectual potential, suggesting that symptoms (e.g., poor concentration, motivational deficits) may interfere with youngsters' application of their abilities (Kovacs & Goldston, 1991).

Commentary

Much of the work on children's behavioral and social competence is based on self-report, which may be open to distortion and lacks confirmation by additional informants or direct observation. Also, more research is needed on clinical samples.

Studies of interpersonal/behavioral competence have commonly disregarded questions of specificity. In fact, few researchers have demonstrated a unique link between particular social styles and depression, and indeed, analogous difficulties have sometimes been reported for anxious children (e.g., Strauss, Frame, & Forehand, 1987) and those with aggressive behavior patterns (e.g., Pelham & Bender, 1982). The few empirical tests of specificity have yielded inconsistent results. Goodyer, Wright, and Altham (1990) found that the experience of poor quality friendships was comparable in depressed and anxious youngsters, and Armsden et al. (1990) found that insecure peer attachment failed to discriminate depressed adolescents from psychiatric controls. Puig-Antich et al. (1985a) reported that decreased academic achievement was common to depressed and psychiatric control groups. However, Marton et al. (1993) found that decreased social self-confidence characterized a group of depressed outpatients, but not a nondepressed outpatient control group. Kennedy et al. (1989) discovered that self- and peer ratings depicted depressed school children as less socially competent and less accepted by their peers than a nondepressed, fearful group. Rudolph et al. (1994) found that decreased sociability, increased hostility, and peer rejection were specifically associated with depression, whereas decreased hostility was specifically associated with anxiety.

Obviously, specificity questions are complicated by the further matter of comorbidity. Although previous studies paint a consistent picture of general social disturbance in depressed children, closer scrutiny reveals quite heterogeneous interpersonal profiles, ranging from passivity, withdrawal, and peer isolation, to aggressiveness, impulsivity, and peer rejection. These conflicting findings may reflect the existence of subtypes of depressed children with distinct social problems. Some preliminary evidence suggests that diagnostic comorbidity may contribute to intragroup differences. Rudolph et al. (1994) compared low-symptom, pure-internalizing (depressed/anxious), pure-externalizing, and mixed-symptom groups. They reported an overall pattern of findings suggesting that pure internalizers may demonstrate a level of social dysfunction that lies somewhere between low- and mixed-symptom children. Additionally, the comorbid group appeared to account for the increased levels of peer rejection in depressed children, although the pure-internalizing group was still less popular than asymptomatic children. Other studies of nonreferred and inpatient children have led to similar conclusions that the *combination* of depressive and externalizing disorders, but not depression alone, may result in problematic social status (Asarnow, 1988; Cole & Carpentieri, 1990) or maladaptive coping styles (Asarnow et al., 1987).

As outlined above, behavioral/interpersonal models of depression differ in their predictions about the direction of influence between depression and sociobehavioral impairment. The nature of this link remains elusive, and support has been found for both models—interpersonal problems and skill deficits leading to depression versus depression leading to incompetence and troublesome relationships. The predominantly cross-sectional nature of the pertinent research precludes conclusions as to etiological relations. However, a few prospective studies may shed light on this issue. In support of Lewinsohn's (1974) model, Wierzbicki and McCabe (1988) demonstrated that child and parent evaluations of social skills added significantly to current depression in the prediction of later depressive symptoms. Goodyer et al. (1990) found that the quality of 7- to 16-year-old children's friendships predicted the onset of depressive disorders within a 12-month period. Finally, depressed children have been found to rate less enjoyment of lists of pleasant and ambiguous daily activities than do normal and psychiatric control groups (Shelton & Garber, 1987). Other longitudinal studies suggest that the interpersonal difficulties depressed children display may be enduring characteristics that remain even when symptoms have remitted (Lewinsohn, Roberts, et al., 1994; Nolen-Hoeksema et al., 1992; Puig-Antich et al., 1985b).

Together these findings suggest that impaired social functioning and low rates of environmental reinforcement may constitute a risk factor for depression onset or relapse. Nevertheless, the opposite may also be true: Depressive symptoms impair social functioning (e.g., Adrian & Hammen, 1993; Kazdin, Esveldt-Dawson, & Matson, 1982). Parallel to research with depressed adults (e.g., Coyne, 1976; Gurtman, 1986), depressive behaviors in children may un-

dermine the quality of dyadic peer transactions, induce negative affect, and elicit aversive responses from peers (Rudolph et al., 1994). Thus, further longitudinal research is needed to clarify the causal directions and mechanisms of the link between depression and social/behavioral difficulties. The final answer most likely will involve a cyclical process, proceeding from reduced competence to depressed affect to even more dysfunctional behavior, which then evokes negative consequences that perpetuate or exacerbate symptoms.

Family Theories

Literature on normal development emphasizes the contribution of the family to children's socioemotional adjustment. In turn, developmental psychopathologists have begun to implicate family factors in the origin of depression.

Psychodynamic Theories

Disruptions of caregiving relationships figure prominently in early etiological formulations of depression. Psychoanalytic and object relations theories both propose the experience of loss as a primary vulnerability factor for depression— either actual physical loss through death or separation or symbolic loss through emotional deprivation, rejection, or inadequate parenting (e.g., Fairbairn, 1952; Freud, 1917/1957). These theories hold in common the notion that depression arises from anger or hostility that initially is felt toward the lost object but then is directed inward in the form of self-criticism. Because children historically were believed to lack introjective abilities, early theories failed to recognize the occurrence of childhood depression. Rather, their emphasis lay in explaining how problematic childhood relationships may contribute to risk for depression in adults.

Attachment Theory

Contemporary conceptualizations expand on these approaches to account for early onset of depression. Most notably, attachment theory focuses on the adverse impact of dysfunctional parent–child relationships on children's subsequent functioning (Bowlby, 1969, 1980). Bowlby contended that establishment of a secure attachment relationship is dependent upon the ability of the caregiver to impart a sense of security and

trust to the infant and to comfort the infant when distressed. In the absence of conditions that would cultivate a healthy bond (e.g., accessibility, contingent responsivity, emotional supportiveness), the infant presumably becomes vulnerable to later adjustment problems. Based on Bowlby's original work that hypothesized depressive (and other psychopathological) reactions to disruptions in the attachment bond, theorists have implicated insecure attachment and ensuing "internal working models" of relationships (Bowlby, 1969, 1980; Main, Kaplan, & Cassidy, 1985) as specific risk factors for depression (e.g., Blatt & Homann, 1992; Cummings & Cicchetti, 1990; Hammen, 1992a).

Complementing these conceptual advances, researchers have begun to accumulate evidence for an association between early family experiences and childhood depression. Two separate bodies of literature have yielded important information about family functioning: studies of depressed parents and their offspring (high-risk studies) and studies of the families of depressed youngsters (reviewed in Kaslow, Deering, & Racusin, 1994; McCauley & Myers, 1992).

Parent–Child Relationships: Offspring/High-Risk Studies

As discussed above, the observed aggregation of depression in families in part may be due to genetic factors, but evidence indicates the additional influence of psychosocial factors in maintaining this generational cycle (Hammen, 1991a). Specifically, a burgeoning body of research attests to ongoing and pervasive patterns of dysfunctional interactions in families with affectively disordered parents (reviewed by Gelfand & Teti, 1990; Goodman, 1992; Hammen, 1991a). Because of the high risk for depression in offspring, these studies may advance our understanding of family processes relevant to child depression.

Early investigations based on self-reports of parenting indicated that clinically depressed mothers experienced decreased involvement, impaired communication, increased friction, lack of affection, and resentment of their children (e.g., Weissman, Paykel, & Klerman, 1972). Direct observations have suggested that symptomatic mothers demonstrate flat affect, provide less kinesthetic stimulation, and display less contingent responsivity and positive affection during interactions with their infants than do nondepressed mothers (e.g., Field, Healy, Goldstein, &

Guthertz, 1990; Fleming, Ruble, Flett, & Shaul, 1988). In contrast to this pattern of withdrawal and disengagement, maternal depression also has been associated with increased hostility, anger, and intrusiveness during mother–infant interactions (e.g., Cohn, Matias, Tronick, Connell, & Lyons-Ruth, 1986).

Similar disturbances emerge during the toddler and preschool years. Compared to nondepressed women, depressed mothers engage in less frequent verbalization, show less responsiveness to their children's speech (Breznitz & Sherman, 1987), and exhibit greater difficulty in the successful assertion of control and achievement of compromise with their children (Kochanska, Kuczynski, Radke-Yarrow, & Welsh, 1987). Other investigators have linked maternal depression to lower levels of reciprocity (Mills, Puckering, Pound, & Cox, 1985) and to decreased involvement and structure (Goodman & Brumley, 1990) during mother–preschooler transactions. Lovejoy (1991) found increased negativity but not decreased positivity or contingent responding in depressed mother–child dyads.

Troublesome interactions have also been noted between depressed mothers and their school-aged children and adolescents. During a conflict discussion task with their 8- to 16-year-old offspring, clinically depressed mothers demonstrated increased criticism, negativity, and off-task verbalizations in comparison to control groups of medically ill and normal mothers (Gordon et al., 1989). Studying natural interactions in the home, Hops and colleagues (Hops et al., 1987) observed that depressed mothers emitted higher rates of dysphoric affect and lower rates of happy affect than did normal mothers. An interesting interactive sequence also emerged in depressed families, in which maternal dysphoric affect and family aggressive affect formed a reciprocally suppressing cycle. However, two studies (Inoff-Germain, Nottelmann, & Radke-Yarrow, 1992; Tarullo, DeMulder, Martinez, & Radke-Yarrow, 1994) did not reveal increased negativity, critical/irritable behavior, or disengagement in unipolar depressed mothers interacting with their preadolescent and adolescent offspring.

The link between parent characteristics and child symptomatology is further illustrated by the behavior and general psychosocial adjustment of offspring. During interactions with depressed mothers, infants manifest less frequent positive and more frequent negative facial expression, fewer verbalizations, decreased activity level and playfulness, and greater reciprocity of the negative affective states of their mothers (e.g., Field et al., 1990). Infants and toddlers of depressed mothers have been found to exhibit emotional delays, disturbances in affect regulation, separation difficulties, and insecure attachment (Beardslee, Bemporad, Keller, & Klerman, 1983; Blatt & Homann, 1992; Radke-Yarrow, Cummings, Kuczynski, & Chapman, 1985; Teti, Gelfand, Messinger, & Isabella, 1991), although findings on attachment have been variable (DeMulder & Radke-Yarrow, 1991; Lyons-Ruth, Zoll, Connell, & Grunebaum, 1986). Toddlers and preschoolers of depressed women have been observed to demonstrate decreased verbalization with their mothers (Breznitz & Sherman, 1987), increased inhibition in unfamiliar situations (Kochanska, 1991), and socially inhibited/anxious behavior with peers (Rubin, Both, Zahn-Waxler, Cummings, & Wilkinson, 1991). School-age offspring show negativity and off-task behavior during mother–child interactions (Hammen, 1991a) and are less comfortable interacting with their mothers (Tarullo et al., 1994). More generally, they exhibit less initiative and more withdrawal, social isolation, inattentiveness, and impatience than do the children of normal parents. Disturbance during adolescence is reflected in excessive defiance, conflict, and withdrawal (reviewed by Beardslee et al., 1983; Orvaschel, Weissman, & Kidd, 1980). These behavioral profiles resemble those of depressed youngsters and provide clues as to the potential impact of parent psychopathology and negative parent–child relations on children's functioning. Establishing a more direct link, Burge and Hammen (1991) found that two dimensions of maternal behavior—negative affective quality and low task involvement—specifically predicted subsequent child affective diagnoses.

Parent–Child Relationships: Patient Samples

Additional information about family relationships comes from studies of children in treatment for depression. Clinical descriptions of the families of depressed children depict parents as more negative, critical, detached, punitive, angry, belittling, and psychologically abusive (Burbach & Borduin, 1986; Poznanski, Krahenbuhl, & Zrull, 1976). An observational task observed by Cole and Rehm (1986) revealed that the mothers of depressed children set higher standards for their children's success compared to mothers of

nondepressed patient children, and they provided fewer rewards during a challenging game than did mothers of a nonclinic group.

Based on parent interviews, Puig-Antich and colleagues (1985a) found that mother–child relationships of clinically depressed 6- to 12- year-olds were marked by poorer communication, decreased warmth, and increased hostility than were those of nondepressed emotionally disordered and normal control groups. Examination of family variables subsequent to the child's recovery revealed only partial improvement (Puig-Antich et al., 1985b). Similar differences have emerged between reports of mother–adolescent relationships in depressed and normal control groups (Puig-Antich et al., 1993). Significantly worse father–child, spousal, and sibling relationships were also evident in the depressed group.

Based on structured interviews, Amanat and Butler (1984) compared interactional patterns in families of 7- to 14-year-old depressed and overanxious children and characterized the family environments of depressed children as rigid power hierarchies in which parents occupied dominant and controlling positions, resulting in the suppression of self-expression and autonomy in their children. Finally, studies assessing *perceptions* of family interactions have revealed reports of insecure parental attachment in depressed inpatient adolescents (Armsden et al., 1990) and memories of increased parental rejection and deprivation during childhood in depressed outpatient adults (e.g., Lamont, Fischoff, & Gottlieb, 1976).

Parent–Child Relationships: Community Samples

Support for a connection between depression and family dysfunction in community samples comes largely from self-reports of family functioning. Kaslow et al. (1984) found that school-age children with higher levels of depressive symptoms report decreased parental psychological availability and less positive family relationships. Larson and colleagues (Larson et al., 1990) discovered that depressed youth preferred to be alone rather than with their families and were somewhat more likely to experience their families as less friendly than were nondepressed controls. Symptoms in adolescents have been associated with more negative attitudes toward parents, perceptions of decreased family support (Hops et al., 1990), and perceptions of less secure parent–child attach-

ment (Pappini, Roggman, & Anderson, 1991). Studies of young adults confirm a link between depression and recall of early parent–child relationships characterized by low maternal care, nurturance, and affection, and high punitiveness and overprotection (Blatt, Wein, Chevron, & Quinlan, 1979; Parker, 1981; see Blatt & Homann, 1992, for review).

Several studies have revealed that the families of depressed children are marked by increased family, marital, and sibling discord (reviewed by Kaslow et al., 1994; see Cole & McPherson, 1993; Kashani, Burbach, & Rosenberg, 1988). Two observational studies yielded comparable results. Forehand et al. (1988) found that CDI scores were negatively correlated with adolescents' problem-solving ability and positive communication during a conflict discussion task with their mothers. Kobak, Sudler, and Gamble (1991) observed mother–teen dyads during a problem-solving task and found that depressive symptoms were associated with elevated levels of dyadic dysfunctional anger and maternal dominance.

Contextual Family Variables

In addition to specific qualities of parent–child interaction, other negative family circumstances have been linked to depression. Substantial data indicate differences in the family atmosphere and home environment of depressed youngsters and offspring of depressed parents. Families with depressed members are perceived as less cohesive and adaptable, less open to emotional expressiveness, less democratic, more hostile and rejecting, more conflictual and disorganized, and less likely to engage in pleasant activities (Barrera & Garrison-Jones, 1992; Billings & Moos, 1985; Garrison et al., 1990; Hops et al., 1990; Lefkowitz & Tesiny, 1984; Oliver, Handal, Finn, & Herdy, 1987; Orvaschel et al., 1980). Controlling for statistical confounds in past studies, Cole and McPherson (1993) found that cohesion (particularly father–adolescent cohesion) but not expressiveness was associated with adolescent depressive symptoms. Research in the area of expressed emotion (EE) has revealed higher levels of criticism and emotional overinvolvement in the descriptions made by parents about their depressed children than about normal children (Asarnow, Tompson, Hamilton, Goldstein, & Guthrie, 1994).

Parental and child depression also occur in the context of increased family stressors, including negative life events and chronic strain—for ex-

ample, marital discord, maternal adversity, decreased family support, abuse/neglect (Billings & Moos, 1985; Goodyer, Wright, & Altham, 1988; Hammen et al., 1987; Kashani & Carlson, 1987). Despite early claims that death of a parent in childhood increases risk for depression, a review of the relevant research (based mainly on adults) indicates an indirect effect of parental death that is mediated by subsequent inadequate parenting or other associated risk factors (Marton & Maharaj, 1993).

Yet some data suggest that adverse family circumstances may be a nonspecific experience of psychiatrically disturbed youngsters. Kovacs and colleagues (Kovacs, Feinberg, Crouse-Novak, Paulauskas, & Finkelstein, 1984) observed no significant differences between depressed and nondepressed outpatient psychiatric groups on a number of variables reflecting a history of family disruption or interpersonal trauma (e.g., parental death, divorce/separation, or absence). Goodyer et al. (1988) found that maternal adversity and family life events were equally predictive of depressive and anxiety disorders. Burt, Cohen, and Bjorck (1988) reported comparable correlations between an aversive family climate and symptoms of depression and anxiety. Finally, Asarnow et al. (1987) found that perceived home environment did not discriminate between 8- to 13-year-old depressed and nondepressed inpatients (but did distinguish suicidal from nonsuicidal groups).

Commentary

Many gaps remain to be filled in the conceptual and empirical associations between family conditions and child and adolescent depression. Much of the suggestive evidence has come from offspring studies, and less from studies of depressed children—two groups that might have different causal mechanisms. Also, since much of the research has employed self-report data open to the effects of negative mood on reporting, additional observational studies are needed.

The familiar topics of specificity and comorbidity must also be raised. Researchers only recently have begun to examine the extent to which family models are unique to depression. Available data thus far are inconsistent, with studies alternately indicating little (e.g., Burbach, Kashani, & Rosenberg, 1989; Goodyer et al., 1988), partial (e.g., Cole & Rehm, 1986; Puig-Antich et al. 1985a), or complete (e.g., Armsden et al., 1990; Barrera & Garrison-Jones, 1992; Lamont et al., 1976) specificity. These discrepancies are not surprising in light of differences in samples, diagnostic comparison groups, family measures, and other important variables. Yet researchers will now need to move beyond hypotheses about general associations to the delineation of more specific models of risk that connect particular dimensions or constellations of family characteristics to particular disorders.

Information about family relationships in pure depressed versus comorbid groups is minimal. One study of EE suggested that the presence of comorbid disruptive behavior disorder was associated with higher levels of parental criticism in comparison to depression alone (Asarnow et al., 1994). Only one group, to our knowledge, has provided comparisons of observed family functioning associated with pure depression versus comorbid depression and externalizing disorder (Dadds, Sanders, Morrison, & Rebgetz, 1992; Sanders et al., 1992); results were complex and varied by group.

These initial findings highlight the importance of taking into account comorbid disorders when developing and testing family models of depression. To begin, the presence of unidentified comorbid subgroups may account for contradictory findings across studies. Furthermore, conceptual models will need to move to a higher level of complexity to explain the phenomenon of comorbidity. As discussed earlier, this complexity may involve the consideration of various explanations for co-occurring disorders, including shared family risk factors, nonspecific outcomes of particular family influences, or reciprocal effects of different symptom patterns.

Because much of the current evidence on family adjustment, particularly in studies of depressed youngsters, is correlational in nature, questions remain concerning the direction of influence between family dysfunction and child depression. Although one feasible hypothesis would assign problematic parent–child relationships and stressful family environments an etiological role in the onset and/or maintenance of depression, other processes must be considered. First, the observed associations may reflect the operation of a third variable, such as a common genetic vulnerability, that underlies parental psychopathology and parenting difficulties and at the same time increases children's susceptibility to depression.

Second, we must consider an alternate pathway whereby children's symptoms or dysfunctional

behavior evoke negative responses from their parents and impede adaptive family functioning. Hammen and colleagues tested a bidirectional model and found that depressed mothers and their offspring did indeed exert mutual (negative) influences on each other (Hammen, Burge, & Stansbury, 1990). Others also have found important interactions between mother and child impairment in determining the quality of behavioral transactions (e.g., Tarullo et al., 1994). Thus, impaired maternal behavior may result partly from the unrewarding nature of interactions with a depressed or maladjusted child. Future researchers therefore may do well to include a stronger emphasis on the reciprocal nature of parent–child relationships, the behavior of depressed children during family interactions, and the more global impact of child depression on the family.

A third explanation for family-depression linkages may be that maladaptive family patterns represent state-dependent concomitants of the acute episode of illness. On balance, however, relevant research tends to find that family interaction problems are relatively stable even when symptoms remit (e.g., Billings & Moos, 1985; Puig-Antich et al., 1985b). Other analyses of temporal relationships also have yielded preliminary support for causal hypotheses by showing that quality of interactions predicts subsequent course of children's depression (Asarnow, Goldstein, Tompson, & Guthrie, 1993; Hops et al., 1990—although see negative findings by Burt et al., 1988; Garrison et al., 1990).

Finally, considerably more research is needed to specify mechanisms by which family disturbances contribute to depression in youngsters. The development of more sophisticated models of family influence will require a richer understanding of the mechanisms by which impairment may render children vulnerable to depression. Understanding these processes no doubt will require adopting a developmental perspective.

To begin, it may be useful to consider how family relationships may affect patterns of growth at each stage of development and how disruption in these relationships may sacrifice children's adaptation. Based on the above research, deviant parent–child interactions associated with depression interfere with the mastery of different developmental tasks throughout childhood, from the formation of healthy attachment relationships and effective emotion-regulation abilities in infants and toddlers to the acquisition of skills necessary for self-regulation, autonomy, verbal

problem solving, and conflict resolution during childhood and adolescence (e.g., Burge & Hammen, 1991; Kochanska et al., 1987; Radke-Yarrow et al., 1985). Thus, ineffective parenting may influence children's risk for depression through different channels across development. An important goal for researchers will be to delineate the specific mode of transmission. This process most likely will include not only genetic risk factors and deficits in children's behavioral competencies, but also increases in exposure to stress in the family context, decreases in family support, and changes in the ways in which children view themselves and the world (cf. Blatt & Homann, 1992; Goodman, 1992; Hammen, 1991a).

Environmental Models

In line with current research efforts in children, our discussion of environmental theories of depression will focus primarily on the life-stress literature. Life-stress theories of adult depression have progressed in complexity in the past two decades. This evolution has been described in depth elsewhere (e.g., Gotlib & Hammen, 1992; Hammen, 1992b), and several variants of the life-stress approach and are summarized briefly below.

Stress-Reaction Models

Original life-stress theories viewed depression as a response to the experience of negative life events (e.g., Brown & Harris, 1978; Paykel, 1979). From this perspective, stress is viewed as a precursor and contributor to depression onset, persistence, or recurrence. To avoid the confounds associated with symptom-related stress, researchers initially concentrated on "fateful" life events, or events whose occurrence is independent of the individual. Furthermore, to avoid the confounds associated with idiosyncratic *perceptions* of events, researchers frequently used the "contextual threat" method (Brown & Harris, 1978) to determine the *objective* impact of stress independent of individuals' subjective reactions.

Life-stress research in children is still relatively sparse, but a few studies have linked stress with concurrent depression (Kashani et al., 1986, with preschoolers; Mullins et al., 1985, with school-aged children; Goodyer et al., 1990, with depressed children and adolescents; Burt et al., 1988; Garrison et al., 1990; Hops et al., 1990; Siegel & Brown, 1988, with adolescents). Good-

yer and Altham (1991a) gathered data from parents about lifetime "exit events," or the permanent removal of a significant other from the child's life. Results suggested that exposure to multiple (two or more) exit events was associated with increased risk for the development of a depressive disorder—although apparently not having a negative effect because of subsequent family adversity.

Going beyond correlational studies, some initial longitudinal data support a stress-reaction model. For example, Garrison et al. (1990) and Siegel and Brown (1988) found a prospective association between negative events and later depression. Hops et al. (1990) reported that microstressors, but not macrostressors, predicted increases in dysphoria over a follow-up period. Finally, Hammen and colleagues (Hammen, 1988; Hammen et al., 1988) found that the occurrence of stressful events predicted subsequent depression in the children of depressed mothers.

Diathesis–Stress Models

Proponents of diathesis–stress models argue that the impact of stress may be moderated by individual risk factors. Depression is therefore regarded as a function of the interaction between personal vulnerability and external stress. Most notably, vulnerability has been construed as a stable cognitive propensity toward depression-inducing interpretations or appraisals of events. Exposure to events is presumed to serve as a trigger that activates this underlying cognitive predisposition (cf. cognitive theories of Beck, Seligman, and others). Even more specifically, several theorists have speculated that the key determinant of depression onset and/or severity may be the *match* between an individual's particular cognitive vulnerability and the nature of the stressful event. In this respect, psychodynamic, cognitive, and life-stress models converge in the notion that individual vulnerability may be understood in terms of a tendency to base one's self-worth either on success in interpersonal relationships (called "dependency" or "sociotropy") or on individual achievement/mastery (called "autonomy") (e.g., Beck, 1983; Blatt & Homann, 1992; see Gotlib & Hammen, 1992, for review). Negative events would therefore induce depression to the extent that they precipitate a depletion or loss of self-worth in an individual's specific area of vulnerability.

Empirical findings concerning cognition–life event interactions to predict future depression are mixed. With respect to attributional style, Dixon and Ahrens (1992) found a significant interaction, Hammen et al. (1988) did not, and Nolen-Hoeksema et al. (1992) found an interaction in the prediction of depressive symptoms in older, but not younger, children. Defining stress as an increase in peer rejection, Panak and Garber (1992) demonstrated that attributional style moderated the impact of stress on depressive symptoms 1 year later.

Only a few studies have tested the cognitive–stress "match" model in depressed children. Turner and Cole (1994) found that cognitions—attributional style and cognitive errors—about the social and academic domains, but not the athletic domain, moderated the effects of negative daily events/activities in the same domain, but not in alternate domains (although support was obtained only in older children). Hammen and Goodman-Brown (1990) assessed the relative value placed by each *individual* child on particular competence domains (interpersonal vs. achievement). As predicted, the authors found an increased risk for the development of depression only in those children who experienced a preponderance of negative life events congruent with their specific vulnerabilities, particularly for the interpersonal schema types.

Mediation Models

Questioning the applicability of cognitive moderation models to young children, Cole and Turner (1993) proposed a related cognitive *mediation* model. These authors noted probable developmental differences in the interplay between cognitions and stress due to the absence of stable cognitive styles in early childhood. Instead, they suggested that adverse environmental events or other forms of pathogenic feedback may be internalized in the form of negative cognitions, which then predispose the child to depression. In this case, depressogenic cognitions would *arise from* rather than *interact with* life stress. Harter, Marold, and Whitesell (1992) have developed a mediation model that invokes similar constructs. Lack of social support from family and peers (which may be regarded as a type of stress) is believed to mediate the impact of negative self-concept on depressive symptoms. As in diathesis–stress "match" models, Harter emphasizes the importance of assessing domain-specific cognitions and appraising the value placed on particular competence domains. Distinct from modera-

tor models, low perceived (and actual) competence is believed to *contribute* to decreased support (increased stress).

Cole and Turner (1993) tested two cognitive mediation models that operationalized stress in terms of competence and life events. Findings confirmed that attributional style and cognitive errors completely mediated the relationship between competence and depression, and partially mediated the relationship between events and depression. Minimal support was obtained for a cognitive moderation model. As noted by the authors, the cross-sectional nature of the study precludes causal conclusions, but results are suggestive of a process in which aversive environmental feedback promotes a negative cognitive style, which then leads to depression. Harter et al. (1992) also gained support for their mediation model, but self-cognitions were found to exert both direct and indirect effects on depression.

Stress-Generation Models

Most recently, an alternative and complementary life-stress model has been introduced. Noting the impact of depression on people's lives, Hammen (1991b, 1992b) has proposed a stress-generation model of depression. Whereas traditional life-stress research focused on "fateful" life events, Hammen has emphasized that depression, associated impairment, and preexisting characteristics may act to promote dysfunction, such that depressed individuals actually *generate* stressful circumstances, which in turn trigger depressive reactions (especially in vulnerable domains). The effects are likely to be most apparent in interpersonal relationships. Applying this model to children, early onset of depression may interrupt normal development, creating maladaptive skills, leading to stress and risk for future maladjustment.

In support of a stress-generation model in children, Adrian and Hammen (1993) found that the offspring of depressed mothers displayed significantly higher rates of life events that they had at least partially caused, such as peer conflict events. These results are compatible with the hypothesis that life stress may not only be a *cause* of subsequent symptoms, but may also be a *consequence* of related impairment, yet they leave open the question of whether depression precedes event occurrence. In one study that examined stress generation more directly, Cohen, Burt, and Bjorck (1987) found that depressive symptoms in adolescents predicted the occurrence of sub-

sequent controllable negative events, whereas controllable stress failed to predict subsequent symptoms. Another study revealed that clinic-referred children in general experienced higher levels of events that were "confounded with their own maladjustment" (Jensen, Richters, Ussery, Bloedau, & Davis, 1991, p. 305).

Miscellaneous Environmental Influences

Investigators also have assessed the impact of other environmental/demographic risk factors and adverse conditions. For example, depression in youngsters has been linked to social/environmental disadvantage, parental unemployment, remarriage of a parent, living in a single-parent household, and coming from a larger family (e.g., King, Segal, Naylor, & Evans, 1993; Kovacs, Feinberg, Crouse-Novak, Paulauskas, & Finkelstein, 1984; Reinherz, Giaconia, Pakiz, et al., 1993; reviewed by Kaslow et al., 1994). Gore, Aseltine, and Colton (1992) hypothesized that stress (i.e., undesirable life events, chronic interpersonal strains) and poor quality social support may act as proximal risk factors that mediate the impact of background variables (i.e., family structure, gender, socioeconomic status, parent health) on depression. Findings confirmed that depression was directly associated with being a girl, living in a family with a lower standard of living and a lower level of parent education (in girls only), and having parents with higher levels of physical and mental illness. Depression was unrelated to family structure (i.e., single- or step-parent household) when economic conditions were controlled. Finally, results indicated that stress and social support accounted for the effects on depression of some background variables (i.e., parental mental illness and standard of living), but not others (i.e., gender, parent education).

Commentary

Although life-stress conceptualizations of depression have advanced in sophistication in the adult field in recent years, empirical research with children has lagged significantly behind. For one thing, child research has been based largely on self-report life event checklists, which provide little information about the context, impact, or meaning of an event—and which fail to distinguish between fateful and dependent, or controllable, events. Also, assessment methods have variously included episodic events, chronic adver-

sities, and minor hassles. Each of these types of stress may constitute an important source of vulnerability, and future investigators will need to assess their relative contribution to depression.

Few researchers have assessed the specificity of depressive reactions to stressors. Of the existing evidence, most points to a lack of specificity in the depression–stress relationship (e.g., Burt et al., 1988; Goodyer & Altham, 1991a, 1991b). Compas, Howell, Phares, Williams, and Giunta (1989) linked life events and daily hassles with internalizing *and* externalizing symptomatology in adolescents. These authors also found that both types of behavior problems predicted subsequent daily stress (but not major life events). The role of stress generation is unclear because of a lack of information about chronology. Examining a diathesis–stress model, Hammen (1988) found that the interaction of attributional style and negative events was predictive of nondepressive but not depressive symptoms. Finally, Kovacs, Feinberg, Crouse-Novak, Paulauskas, and Finkelstein (1984) reported that stressful family background variables were equally common in depressed and nondepressed referred children. In the only study supporting specificity, Shelton and Garber (1987) found that children with depressive disorders experienced significantly more unpleasant events than did a nondepressed psychiatric comparison group. To our knowledge, none has compared stress exposure in groups of depressed children with and without comorbid diagnoses.

Once again, our theoretical models must be expanded to incorporate hypotheses as to the mechanisms underlying diagnostic comorbidity (e.g, similar life experiences leading to nonspecific outcomes, co-occurring stressors resulting in multiple types of dysfunction, or perhaps, the interaction of stressors with other vulnerability factors producing comorbid symptomatology). Additionally, the role of comorbid disorder in the *generation* of stressors should be examined.

Despite widespread acknowledgment of the importance of diathesis–stress models of depression, life-stress researchers have considered a relatively restricted domain of individual vulnerabilities—cognitive or otherwise—as potential moderators or mediators of stress in children. Several likely candidates should be on the agenda for future research. For instance, other potential internal resources or risk factors may include genetic/biological influences, coping repertoires and problem-solving skills, beliefs about control

and self-efficacy, cognitive schemata, and sociodemographic variables. External resources may also intervene in the stress–depression link. For example, many depression researchers have pointed out the potential buffering effects of social support, which may protect children from the adverse consequences of stress (e.g., Hammen, Burge, & Adrian, 1991; Harter et al., 1992), but minimal empirical research examines this prediction in depressed children. Conversely, increased parental strain or psychopathology may exacerbate children's sensitivity to life stress (e.g., Compas et al., 1989; Hammen et al., 1987) or may even account for the increased exposure of clinic-referred children to stressful events (Adrian & Hammen, 1993; Jensen et al., 1991). The determinants of children's vulnerability and resilience to depression in the face of stress deserve further exploration as we are still far from tapping the many possibilities offered by this line of research.

CONCLUSIONS: THE NEED FOR INTEGRATIVE, DEVELOPMENTAL THEORIES

Throughout the chapter, we have identified methodological and empirical gaps in the study of child and adolescent depression. In addition, conceptual issues remain that highlight the differences between the child and adult depression fields. The abundance of well-validated theories of adult depression represents both an asset and a liability for child depression researchers. On the one hand, adult models have been indispensable as guides to research in youngsters. Yet as a consequence, the child depression literature has suffered from a relative dearth of developmentally grounded theories. Thus, existing models often neglect to take into account two critical and distinct components of child depression: the impact of development on depression and the impact of depression on development.

Several child psychopathologists have begun to articulate more cohesive developmental models of depression that advocate the adoption of multidimensional, transactional perspectives and that reflect a gradual convergence of cognitive, interpersonal, family, and life-stress approaches (e.g., Blatt & Homann, 1992; Cicchetti & Schneider-Rosen, 1986; Cummings & Cicchetti, 1990; Gotlib & Hammen, 1992; Hammen, 1992a). These models share many common features: the contribution of early family socialization to subsequent function-

ing, the emergence of internal representations or working models of relationships, the interplay between individual vulnerabilities and external experience, and the role of depression as both a consequence of prior psychosocial disturbance and as a risk factor for future difficulties.

Figure 4.1 depicts one possible multidimensional developmental model of depression. The model is intended to highlight the complex and reciprocal interplay among individual child characteristics, interpersonal experiences, and depressive symptomatology as described below. However, there are clearly many other variables and pathways that may be involved in shaping children's adjustment over time, and this model should be regarded as a starting point.

In brief, contemporary developmental psychopathology theories are based on the premise that experiences within the family are encoded in memory as a set of beliefs about the self and others and expectations about future interpersonal encounters. Children who are exposed to caregiving styles characterized by insensitivity or rejection would presumably develop generalized internal representations of the self as incompetent or unworthy, others as hostile or unresponsive, and interpersonal relationships as aversive or unpredictable. Dysfunctional relationships and negative cognitive styles in turn are believed to interfere with the maturation of emotion and behavior-regulation skills. This backdrop of cognitive, affective, and social impairment may directly precipitate depressive reactions or may drive maladaptive interpersonal behavior that is

met with conflict, rejection, or isolation, leading to depression. Alternatively, negative cognitive representations and poor social relationships may augment children's vulnerability to depression when they are faced with high levels of stress. Depression then may compromise future development by disrupting important social bonds, undermining existing competencies, inducing stress, and reaffirming children's negative views of themselves and the world.

To be sure, children's genetic or biological characteristics may enter into the cycle at any point. For instance, individual differences in temperament are likely to shape the nature of parent–child relationships and children's experiences in other interpersonal contexts. Biological vulnerability, such as a tendency toward neuroendocrine hyperarousal, inevitably will interact with psychosocial resources in determining children's ability to cope with external stress and their ensuing sensitivity to depression.

Depression onset early in childhood may be particularly deleterious. First, impairment during critical periods may redirect typical developmental trajectories, such that children are unable to compensate for skills that they have failed to learn. Second, early formation of negative and inflexible cognitive schemata may reduce the likelihood that children will attend to or incorporate future disconfirmatory feedback. Third, the connections among cognitive appraisal mechanisms, affective tendencies, behavioral patterns, and external stress may strengthen over time, resulting in a decreased threshold for activation of these

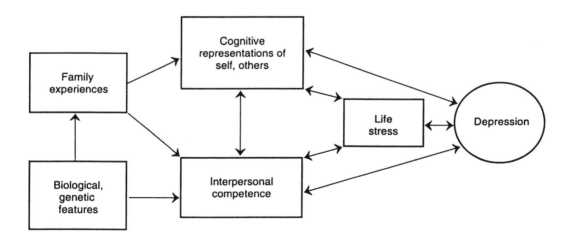

FIGURE 4.1. Multifactorial, transactional model of child and adolescent depression.

networks as children enter adolescence and adulthood (cf. Bower, 1981; Teasdale, 1983). Finally, the accumulated impact of chronic psychological and social stress over time may alter biological processes presumed to underlie depression vulnerability, particularly in young children whose systems are not fully matured (Gold et al., 1988; Granger, Weisz, & Kauneckis, 1994).

Integrative conceptual models of child depression are still relatively novel, and developmental psychopathologists have only begun to bring these ideas into the empirical domain. However, preliminary data on certain elements of these models suggest that they hold some promise. For example, some studies have revealed a relationship between maternal depression and insecure child attachment (e.g., Lyons-Ruth et al., 1986; Radke-Yarrow et al., 1985; Teti et al., 1991). Moreover, findings summarized above regarding the prevalence of negative perceptions of family and peers in depressed children and young adults (e.g., Armsden & Greenberg, 1987; Armsden et al., 1990; Blatt et al., 1979; Kaslow et al., 1984; Pappini et al., 1991; Parker, 1981) are consistent with predictions that depression may be associated with the formation of internalized representations of others as unresponsive, hostile, rejecting, and untrustworthy. Pursuing the conceptual model even further, Kobak et al. (1991) found that depressive symptoms were significantly associated with insecure and preoccupied attachment strategies in adolescents, while the occurrence of negative life events in the preceding year and poor quality of current mother–adolescent interactions added to the prediction of symptoms.

Recent studies examining interpersonal/attachment cognitions have also yielded some promising results. Hammen and colleagues (1995) tested a diathesis–stress model of depression in adolescents. Findings suggested that the interaction of insecure attachment cognitions and negative life events predicted depression onset or exacerbation 1 year later, but this link was nonspecific to depression. Testing a cognitive-interpersonal formulation in school-aged children, Rudolph et al. (1994b) found that elevations in depressive symptoms were associated with negative cognitive representations about self and others, negative expectations about social transactions, and biases in the processing of interpersonal information. Results also upheld an integrated model that established links among family representations, peer representations, interpersonal functioning, and depression.

Other investigators have tested more general multidimensional models to explore the relative contributions of cognitive, behavioral, and family variables to the prediction of depression. Stark, Humphrey, Laurent, Livingston, and Christopher (1993) found that pure depressed, pure anxious, and mixed depressed/anxious children were best discriminated by a combination of negative cognitions, aversive family conditions, and maladaptive social styles. Using a multifactor model to predict depression and aggression in high-risk children, Downey and Walker (1992) also confirmed the importance of considering both family-level influences and child-level influences in determining psychopathology.

These studies represent exciting starting points for future research on childhood depression. The next generation of theories clearly will need to involve comprehensive and developmental models that incorporate multiple domains of functioning and account for the reciprocal interplay among these domains across development. These conceptual gains also will need to be mirrored by empirical studies designed to address systematically the many important issues that have arisen from the past two decades of research.

REFERENCES

Abramson, L. Y., Metalsky, G. I., & Alloy, L. B. (1989). Hopelessness depression: A theory-based subtype of depression. *Psychological Review, 96,* 358–372.

Abramson, L. Y., Seligman, M. E., & Teasdale, J. D. (1978). Learned helplessness in humans: Critique and reformulation. *Journal of Abnormal Psychology, 37,* 49–74.

Achenbach, T. M. (1991). The derivation of taxonomic constructs: A necessary stage in the development of developmental psychopathology. In D. Cicchetti & S. Toth (Eds.), *Rochester Symposium on Developmental Psychopathology: Models and integrations* (Vol 3, pp. 43–74). Hillsdale, NJ: Erlbaum.

Achenbach, T. M., & Edelbrock, C. (1978). The classification of child psychopathology: A review and analysis of empirical efforts. *Psychological Bulletin, 85,* 1275–1301.

Achenbach, T. M., McConaughy, S. H., & Howell, C. T. (1987). Child/adolescent behavioral and emotional problems: Implications of cross-informant for situational stability. *Psychological Bulletin, 101,* 213–232.

Adrian, C., & Hammen, C. (1993). Stress exposure and stress generation in children of depressed mothers. *Journal of Consulting and Clinical Psychology, 61,* 354–359.

Albert, N., & Beck, A. (1975). Incidence of depression in early adolescence: A preliminary study. *Journal of Youth and Adolescence, 4,* 301–307.

Allgood-Merten, B., Lewinsohn, P., & Hops, H. (1990). Sex differences and adolescent depression. *Journal of Abnormal Psychology, 99,* 55–63.

Altmann, E. O., & Gotlib, I. H. (1988). The social behavior of depressed children: An observational study. *Journal of Abnormal Child Psychology, 16,* 29–44.

Amanat, E., & Butler, C. (1984). Oppressive behaviors in the families of depressed children. *Family Therapy, 11,* 65–76.

American Psychiatric Association. (1994). *Diagnostic and statistical manual of mental disorders* (4th ed.). Washington, DC: Author.

Anderson, C. A., & Hammen, C. L. (1993). Psychosocial outcomes of children of unipolar depressed, bipolar, medically ill, and normal women: A longitudinal study. *Journal of Consulting and Clinical Psychology, 61,* 448–454.

Anderson, J., Williams, S., McGee, R., Silva, P. (1987). DSM-III disorders in preadolescent children: Prevalence in a large sample from the general population. *Archives of General Psychiatry, 44,* 69–76.

Angold, A., & Costello, E. (1993). Depressive comorbidity in children and adolescents: Empirical, theoretical, and methodological issues. *American Journal of Psychiatry, 150,* 1779–1791.

Angold, A., & Rutter, M. (1992). Effects of age and pubertal status on depression in a large clinical sample. *Development and Psychopathology, 4,* 5–28.

Armsden, G. C., & Greenberg, M. T. (1987). The Inventory of Parent and Peer Attachment: Individual differences and their relationship to psychological wellbeing in adolescence. *Journal of Youth and Adolescence, 16,* 427–454.

Armsden, G. C., McCauley, E., Greenberg, M. T., Burke, P. M., & Mitchell, J. R. (1990). Parent and peer attachment in early adolescent depression. *Journal of Abnormal Child Psychology, 18,* 683–697.

Asarnow, J. R. (1988). Peer status and social competence in child psychiatric inpatients: A comparison of children with depressive, externalizing, and concurrent depressive and externalizing disorders. *Journal of Abnormal Child Psychology, 16,* 151–162.

Asarnow, J. R., & Bates, S. (1988). Depression in child psychiatric inpatients: Cognitive and attributional patterns. *Journal of Abnormal Child Psychology, 16,* 601–615.

Asarnow, J. R., Carlson, G. A., & Guthrie, D. (1987). Coping strategies, self-perceptions, hopelessness, and perceived family environments in depressed and suicidal children. *Journal of Consulting and Clinical Psychology, 55,* 361–366.

Asarnow, J., Goldstein, M., Carlson, G., Perdue, S., Bates, S., & Keller, J. (1988). Childhood-onset depressive disorders: A follow-up study of rates of rehospitalization and out-of-home placement among child psychiatric inpatients. *Journal of Affective Disorders, 15,* 245–253.

Asarnow, J. R., Goldstein, M. J., Tompson, M., & Guthrie, D. (1993). One-year outcomes of depressive disorders in child psychiatric inpatients: Evaluation of the prognostic power of a brief measure of expressed emotion. *Journal of Child Psychology and Psychiatry, 34,* 129–137.

Asarnow, J. R., Tompson, M., Hamilton, E. B., Goldstein, M. J., & Guthrie, D. (1994). Family-expressed emotion, childhood-onset depression, and childhood-onset schizophrenia spectrum disorders: Is expressed emotion a nonspecific correlate of child psychopathology or a specific risk factor for depression? *Journal of Abnormal Child Psychology, 22,* 129–146.

Barnett, P. A., & Gotlib, I. H. (1988). Psychosocial functioning and depression: Distinguishing among antecedents, concomitants, and consequences. *Psychological Bulletin, 104,* 97–126.

Barrera, M., & Garrison-Jones, C. (1992). Family and peer support as specific correlates of adolescent depressive symptoms. *Journal of Abnormal Child Psychology, 20,* 1–16.

Beardslee, W. R., Bemporad, J., Keller, M. B., & Klerman, G. L. (1983). Children of parents with major affective disorder: A review. *American Journal of Psychiatry, 140,* 825–832.

Beck, A. T. (1983). Cognitive therapy of depression: New perspectives. In P. J. Clayton & J. E. Barrett (Eds.), *Treatment of depression: Old controversies and new approaches* (pp. 265–290). New York: Raven Press.

Beck, A. T., Rush, A. J., Shaw, B. F., & Emery, G. (1979). *Cognitive therapy of depression.* New York: Guilford Press.

Berman, A., & Jobes, D. (1991). *Adolescent suicide: Assessment and intervention.* Washington, DC: American Psychological Association.

Billings, A. G., & Moos, R. H. (1985). Children of parents with unipolar depression: A controlled 1-year follow-up. *Journal of Abnormal Child Psychology, 14,* 149–166.

Bird, H. R., Canino, G., Rubio-Stipec, M., Gould, M. S., Ribera, J., Sesman, M., Woodbury, M., Huertas-Goldman, S., Pagan, A., Sanchez-Lacay, A., & Moscoso, M. (1988). Estimates of the prevalence of childhood maladjustment in a community survey in Puerto Rico. *Archives of General Psychiatry, 45,* 1120–1126.

Birmaher, B., Ryan, N. D., Dahl, R., Rabinovich, H., Ambrosini, P., Williamson, D. E., Novacenko, H., Nelson, B., Lo, E. E. S., & Puig-Antich, J. (1992). Dexamethasone suppression test in children with major depressive disorder. *Journal of the American Academy of Child and Adolescent Psychiatry, 31,* 291–297.

Bland, R. C., Newman, S. C., & Orn, H. (1986). Recurrent and nonrecurrent depression: A family study. *Archives of General Psychiatry, 43*(11), 1085–1089.

Blatt, S. J., & Homann, E. (1992). Parent–child interaction in the etiology of dependent and self-critical depression. *Clinical Psychology Review, 12,* 47–91.

Blatt, S. J., Wein, S. J., Chevron, E. S., & Quinlan, D. M. (1979). Parental representations and depression in normal young adults. *Journal of Abnormal Psychology, 88,* 388–397.

Blechman, E. A., McEnroe, M. J., Carella, E. T., & Audette, D. P. (1986). Childhood competence and depression. *Journal of Abnormal Psychology, 95,* 223–227.

Bower, G. (1981). Mood and memory. *American Psychologist, 36,* 129–148.

Bowlby, J. (1969). *Attachment and loss: Vol. I. Attachment.* New York: Basic Books.

Bowlby, J. (1980). *Loss: Sadness and depression.* New York: Basic Books.

Brady, E. U., & Kendall, P. C. (1992). Comorbidity of anxiety and depression in children and adolescents. *Psychological Bulletin, 111,* 244–255.

Breznitz, Z., & Sherman, T. (1987). Speech patterning of natural discourse of well and depressed mothers and their young children. *Child Development, 58,* 395–400.

Brooks-Gunn, J. (1988). Antecedents and consequences of variations in girls' maturational timing. *Journal of Adolescent Health Care, 9,* 365–373.

Brown, G. W., & Harris, T. (1978). *Social origins of depression: A study of psychiatric disorders in women.* New York: Free Press.

Buhrmester, D. (1990). Intimacy of friendship, interpersonal competence, and adjustment during preadolescence and adolescence. *Child Development, 61,* 1101–1111.

Burbach, D. J., & Borduin, C. M. (1986). Parent-child relations and the etiology of depression: A review of methods and findings. *Clinical Psychology Review, 6,* 133–153.

Burbach, D. J., Kashani, J. H., & Rosenberg, T. K. (1989). Parental bonding and depressive disorders in adolescents. *Journal of Child Psychology and Psychiatry, 30,* 417–429.

Burge, D., & Hammen, C. (1991). Maternal communication: Predictors of outcome at follow-up in a sample of children at high and low risk for depression. *Journal of Abnormal Psychology, 100,* 174–180.

Burke, K. C., Burke, J. D., Regier, D. A., & Rae, D. S. (1990). Age at onset of selected mental disorders in five community populations. *Archives of General Psychiatry, 47,* 511–518.

Burt, C. E., Cohen, L. H., & Bjorck, J. P. (1988). Perceived family environment as a moderator of young adolescents' life stress adjustment. *American Journal of Community Psychology, 16,* 101–122.

Cantwell, D. P., & Carlson, G. A. (Eds.). (1983). *Affective disorders in childhood and adolescence.* New York: Spectrum.

Carlson, G., & Cantwell, D. (1980). Unmasking masked depression in children and adolescents. *American Journal of Psychiatry, 137,* 445–449.

Carlson, G., & Kashani, J. (1988). Phenomenology of major depression from childhood through adulthood: Analysis of three studies. *American Journal of Psychiatry, 145,* 1222–1225.

Caron, C., & Rutter, M. (1991). Comorbidity in child psychopathology: Concepts, issues and research strategies. *Journal of Child Psychology and Psychiatry, 32,* 1063–1080.

Chambers, W., Puig-Antich, J., Hirsch, M., Paez, P., Ambrosini, P., Tabrizi, M., & Davies, M. (1985). The assessment of affective disorders in children and adolescents by semistructured interview: Test-retest reliability. *Archives of General Psychiatry, 42,* 696–702.

Chambers, W., Puig-Antich, J., Tabrizi, M., & Davies, M. (1982). Psychotic symptoms in prepubertal major depressive disorder. *Archives of General Psychiatry, 39,* 921–927.

Cicchetti, D., & Schneider-Rosen, K. (1986). An organizational approach to childhood depression. In M. Rutter, C. Izard, & P. Read (Eds.), *Depression in young people: Clinical and developmental perspectives* (pp. 71–134). New York: Guilford Press.

Cohen, L. H., Burt, C. E., & Bjorck, J. P. (1987). Life stress and adjustment: Effects of life events experienced by young adolescents and their parents. *Developmental Psychology, 23,* 583–592.

Cohen, P., Cohen, J., Kasen, S., Velez, C. N., Hartmark, C., Johnson, J., Rojas, M., Brook, J., & Streuning, E. L. (1993). An epidemiological study of disorders in late childhood and adolescence: I. Age and gender-specific prevalence. *Journal of Child Psychology and Psychiatry, 34,* 851–867.

Cohn, J. F., Matias, R., Tronick, E., Connell, D., & Lyons-Ruth, K. (1986). Face-to-face interactions of depressed mothers and their infants. In E. Tronick & T. Field (Eds.), *Maternal depression and infant disturbance* (New Directions for Child Development, No. 34, pp. 31–46). San Francisco: Jossey-Bass.

Cole, D. A. (1990). The relation of social and academic competence to depressive symptoms in childhood. *Journal of Abnormal Psychology, 99,* 422–429.

Cole, D. A. (1991). Preliminary support for a competency-based model of depression in children. *Journal of Abnormal Psychology, 100,* 181–190.

Cole, D. A., & Carpentieri, S. (1990). Social status and the comorbidity of child depression and conduct disorder. *Journal of Consulting and Clinical Psychology, 58,* 748–757.

Cole, D. A., & McPherson, A. E. (1993). Relation of family subsystems to adolescent depression: Implementing a new family assessment strategy. *Journal of Family Psychology, 7,* 119–133.

Cole, D. A., & Rehm, L. P. (1986). Family interaction patterns and childhood depression. *Journal of Abnormal Child Psychology, 14,* 297–314.

Cole, D. A., & Turner, J. E. (1993). Models of cognitive mediation and moderation in child depression. *Journal of Abnormal Psychology, 102,* 271–281.

Compas, B. E., Ey, S., & Grant, K. E. (1993). Taxonomy, assessment, and diagnosis of depression during adolescence. *Psychological Bulletin, 114,* 323–344.

Compas, B. E., & Grant, K. (1993, March). *Stress and adolescent depressive symptoms: Underlying mechanisms and processes.* Paper presented at the biennial meeting of the Society for Research in Child Development, New Orleans, Louisiana.

Compas, B. E., Howell, D. C., Phares, V., Williams, R. A., & Giunta, C. T. (1989). Risk factors for emotional/behavioral problems in young adolescents: A prospective analysis of adolescent and parental stress and symptoms. *Journal of Consulting and Clinical Psychology, 57,* 732–740.

Compas, B. E., Malcarne, V. L., & Fondacaro, K. M. (1988). Coping with stressful events in older and younger adolescents. *Journal of Consulting and Clinical Psychology, 56,* 405–411.

Conrad, M., & Hammen, C. (1989). Role of maternal depression in perceptions of child maladjustment. *Journal of Consulting and Clinical Psychology, 57,* 663–667.

Cooper, P. J., & Goodyer, I. (1993). A community study of depression in adolescent girls I: Estimates of symptom and syndrome prevalence. *British Journal of Psychiatry, 163,* 369–374.

Costello, A. J., Edelbrock, C., Dulcan, M. K., Kalas, R., & Klaric, S. H. (1984). *Development and testing of the NIMH Diagnostic Interview Schedule for Children in a clinic population* (Contract No. RFP-DB-81-0027). Rockville, MD: Center for Epidemiologic Studies, National Institute of Mental Health.

Costello, E. J., Costello, A. J., Edelbrock, C., Burns, B. J., Dulcan, M. K., Brent, D., & Janiszewski, S. (1988). Psychiatric disorders in pediatric primary care. *Archives of General Psychiatry, 45,* 1107–1116.

Coyne, J. C. (1976). Depression and the response of others. *Journal of Abnormal Psychology, 85,* 186–193.

Cross-National Collaborative Group. (1992). The changing rate of major depression: Cross-national comparisons. *Journal of the American Medical Association, 268,* 3098–3105.

Cummings, E. M., & Cicchetti, D. (1990). Toward a transactional model of relations between attachment and depression. In M. Greenberg, D. Cicchetti, & E. M. Cummings (Eds.), *Attachment in the preschool years: Theory, research, and intervention* (pp. 339–372). Chicago: University of Chicago Press.

Dadds, M. R., Sanders, M. R., Morrison, M., & Rebgetz, M. (1992). Childhood depression and conduct disorder: II. An analysis of family interaction patterns in the home. *Journal of Abnormal Psychology, 101,* 505–513.

Dahl, R., Puig-Antich, J., Ryan, N., Nelson, B., Novacenko, H., Twomey, J., Williamson, D., Goetz, R., & Ambrosini, P. J. (1989). Cortisol secretion in adolescents with major depressive disorder. *Acta Psychiatrica Scandanavia, 80,* 18–26.

Dahl, R. E., Ryan, N. D., Puig-Antich, J., Nguyen, N. A., Al-Shabbout, M., Meyer, V. A., & Perel, J. (1991). 24-Hour cortisol measures in adolescents with major depression: A controlled study. *Biological Psychiatry, 30,* 25–36.

Dahl, R. E., Ryan, N. D., Williamson, D. E., Ambrosini, P. J., Rabinovich, H., Novacenko, H., Nelson, B., & Puig-Antich, J. (1992). Regulation of sleep and growth hormone in adolescent depression. *Journal of the American Academy of Child and Adolescent Psychiatry, 31,* 615–621.

DeMulder, E. K., & Radke-Yarrow, M. (1991). Attachment with affectively ill and well mothers: Concurrent behavioral correlates. *Development and Psychopathology, 3,* 227–242.

Dixon, J. F., & Ahrens, A. H. (1992). Stress and attributional style as predictors of self-reported depression in children. *Cognitive Therapy and Research, 16,* 623–634.

Doerfler, L. A., Mullins, L. L., Griffin, N. J., Siegel, L. J., & Richards, C. S. (1984). Problem-solving deficits in depressed children, adolescents, and adults. *Cognitive Therapy and Research, 8,* 489–500.

Downey, G., & Walker, E. (1992). Distinguishing family-level and child-level influences on the development of depression and aggression in children at risk. *Development and Psychopathology, 4,* 81–95.

Ebata, A. T., & Moos, R. H. (1991). Coping and adjustment in distressed and healthy adolescents. *Journal of Applied Developmental Psychology, 12,* 33–54.

Fairbairn, W. (1952). An object relations theory of the personality. New York: Basic Books.

Field, T., Healy, B., Goldstein, S., & Guthertz, M. (1990). Behavior-state matching and synchrony in mother-infant interactions of nondepressed versus depressed dyads. *Developmental Psychology, 26,* 7–14.

Fleming, A., Ruble, D., Flett, G., & Shaul, D. (1988). Postpartum adjustment in first-time mothers: Relations between mood, maternal attitudes, and mother-infant interactions. *Developmental Psychology, 24,* 71–81.

Fleming, J. E., & Offord, D. R. (1990). Epidemiology of childhood depressive disorders: A critical review. *Journal of the American Academy of Child and Adolescent Psychiatry, 29,* 571–580.

Fleming, J. E., Offord, D. R., & Boyle, M. H. (1989). Prevalence of childhood and adolescent depression in the community. *British Journal of Psychiatry, 155,* 647–654.

Forehand, R., Brody, G. H., Long, N., & Fauber, R. (1988). The interactive influence of adolescent and maternal depression on adolescent social and cognitive functioning. *Cognitive Therapy and Research, 12,* 341–350.

Freud, S. (1917). Mourning and melancholia. *Standard Edition, 14.* London: Hogarth Press, 1957.

Garber, J., Braafladt, N., & Zeman, J. (1991). The regulation of sad affect: An information-processing perspective. In J. Garber & K. Dodge (Eds.), *The development of emotion regulation and dysregulation* (pp. 208–240). New York: Cambridge University Press.

Garber, J., Kriss, M. R., Koch, M., & Lindholm, L. (1988). Recurrent depression in adolescents: A follow-up study. *Journal of the American Academy of Child and Adolescent Psychiatry, 27,* 49–54.

Garber, J., Weiss, B., & Shanley, N. (1993). Cognitions, depressive symptoms, and development in adolescents. *Journal of Abnormal Psychology, 102,* 47–57.

Garrison, C. Z., Jackson, K. L., Marsteller, F., McKeown, R., & Addy, C. (1990). A longitudinal study of depressive symptomatology in young adolescents. *Journal of the American Academy of Child and Adolescent Psychiatry, 29,* 581–585.

Gelfand, D. M., & Teti, D. M. (1990). The effects of maternal depression on children. *Clinical Psychology Review, 10,* 320–354.

Gershon, E., Hamovit, J., Guroff, J., & Nurnberger, J. (1987). Birth-cohort changes in manic and depressive disorders in relatives of bipolar and schizoaffective patients. *Archives of General Psychiatry, 44,* 314–319.

Glyshaw, K., Cohen, L. H., & Towbes, L. C. (1989). Coping strategies and psychological distress: Prospective analyses of early and middle adolescents. *American Journal of Community Psychology, 17,* 607–623.

Gold, P. W., Goodwin, F. K., & Chrousos, G. P. (1988). Clinical and biochemical manifestations of depression: Relation to the neurobiology of stress. *New England Journal of Medicine, 319,* 348–353.

Goodman, S. H. (1992). Understanding the effects of depressed mothers on their children. In E. F. Walker, B. A. Cornblatt, & R. H. Dworkin (Eds.), *Progress in experimental personality and psychopathology research* (Vol. 15, pp. 47–109). New York: Springer.

Goodman, S. H., & Brumley, H. E. (1990). Schizophrenic and depressed mothers: Relational deficits in parenting. *Developmental Psychology, 26,* 31–39.

Goodyer, I. M., & Altham, P. M. E. (1991a). Lifetime exit events and recent social and family adversities in anxious and depressed school-age children and adolescents—I. *Journal of Affective Disorders, 21,* 219–228.

Goodyer, I. M., & Altham, P. M. E. (1991b). Lifetime exit events and recent social and family adversities in anxious and depressed school-age children and adolescents—II. *Journal of Affective Disorders, 21,* 229–238.

Goodyer, I., & Cooper, P. (1993). A community study of depression in adolescent girls II: The clinical features of identified disorder. *British Journal of Psychiatry, 163,* 374–380.

Goodyer, I., Wright, C., & Altham, P. M. E. (1988). Maternal adversity and recent life events in anxious and depressed school-age children. *Journal of Child Psychology and Psychiatry, 29,* 651–667.

Goodyer, I., Wright, C., & Altham, P. (1990). The friendships and recent life events of anxious and depressed school-age children. *British Journal of Psychiatry, 156,* 689–698.

Gordon, D., Burge, D., Hammen, C., Adrian, C., Jaenicke, C., & Hiroto, D. (1989). Observations of interactions of depressed women with their children. *American Journal of Psychiatry, 146,* 50–55.

Gore, S., Aseltine, R. H., & Colton, M. E. (1992). Social structure, life stress, and depressive symptoms in a high school-aged population. *Journal of Health and Social Behavior, 33,* 97–113.

Gore, S., Aseltine, R. H., & Colton, M. E. (1993). Gender, social-relational involvement, and depression. *Journal of Research on Adolescence, 3,* 101–125.

Gotlib, I. H., & Hammen, C. L. (1992). *Psychological aspects of depression: Toward a cognitive-interpersonal integration.* London: Wiley.

Gotlib, I. H., Lewinsohn, P. M., & Seeley, J. R. (1995). Symptoms versus a diagnosis of depression: Differences in psychosocial functioning. *Journal of Consulting and Clinical Psychology, 63,* 90–100.

Gotlib, I. H., Lewinsohn, P. M., Seeley, J. R., Rohde, P., & Redner, J. E. (1993). Negative cognitions and attributional style in depressed adolescents: An examination of stability and specificity. *Journal of Abnormal Psychology, 102,* 607–615.

Granger, D. A., Weisz, J. R., & Kauneckis, D. (1994). Neuroendocrine reactivity, internalizing behavior problems, and control-related cognitions in clinic-referred children and adolescents. *Journal of Abnormal Psychology, 103,* 267–276.

Granger, D. A., Weisz, J. R., McCracken, J. T., Ikeda, S., & Douglas, P. (1995). *Reciprocal influences among adrenocortical activation, psychosocial processes, and clinic-referred children's behavioral adjustment.* Manuscript submitted for publication.

Gurtman, M. B. (1986). Depression and the response of others: Reevaluating the reevaluation. *Journal of Abnormal Psychology, 95,* 99–101.

Haley, G. M., Fine, S., Marriage, K., Moretti, M. M., & Freeman, R. J. (1985). Cognitive bias and depression in psychiatrically disturbed children and adolescents. *Journal of Consulting and Clinical Psychology, 53,* 535–537.

Hammen, C. (1988). Self-cognitions, stressful events, and the prediction of depression in children of depressed mothers. *Journal of Abnormal Child Psychology, 16,* 347–360.

Hammen, C. (1990). Cognitive approaches to depression in children: Current findings and new directions. In B. Lahey & A. E. Kazdin (Eds.), *Advances in clinical child psychology* (Vol. 13, pp. 139–173). New York: Plenum Press.

Hammen, C. (1991a). Depression runs in families: The social context of risk and resilience in children of depressed mothers. New York: Springer-Verlag.

Hammen, C. (1991b). The generation of stress in the course of unipolar depression. *Journal of Abnormal Psychology, 100,* 555–561.

Hammen, C. (1992a). Cognitive, life stress, and interpersonal approaches to a developmental psychopathology model of depression. *Development and Psychopathology, 4,* 191–208.

Hammen, C. (1992b). Life events and depression: The plot thickens. *American Journal of Community Psychology, 20,* 179–193.

Hammen, C., Adrian, C., Gordon, D., Burge, D., Jaenicke, C., & Hiroto, D. (1987). Children of depressed mothers: Maternal strain and symptom predictors of dysfunction. *Journal of Abnormal Psychology, 96,* 190–198.

Hammen, C., Adrian, C., & Hiroto, D. (1988). A longitudinal test of the attributional vulnerability model in children at risk for depression. *British Journal of Clinical Psychology, 27,* 37–46.

Hammen, C., Burge, D., & Adrian, C. (1991). Timing of mother and child depression in a longitudinal study of children at risk. *Journal of Consulting and Clinical Psychology, 59,* 341–345.

Hammen, C., Burge, D., Burney, E., & Adrian, C. (1990). Longitudinal study of diagnoses in children of women with unipolar and bipolar affective disorder. *Archives of General Psychiatry, 47,* 1112–1117.

Hammen, C., Burge, D., Daley, S. E., Davila, J., Paley, B., & Rudolph, K. D. (1995). Interpersonal attachment cognitions and prediction of symptomatic responses to interpersonal stress. *Journal of Abnormal Psychology, 104,* 436–443.

Hammen, C., Burge, D., & Stansbury, K. (1990). Relationship of mother and child variables to child outcomes in a high risk sample: A causal modeling analysis. *Developmental Psychology, 26,* 24–30.

Hammen, C., & Compas, B. (1994). Unmasking unmasked depression: The problem of comorbidity in child and adolescent depression. *Clinical Psychology Review, 14,* 585–603.

Hammen, C., Davila, J., Brown, G., Gitlin, M., & Ellicott, A. (1992). Stress as a mediator of the effects of psychiatric history on severity of unipolar depression. *Journal of Abnormal Psychology, 101,* 45–52.

Hammen, C., & Goodman-Brown, T. (1990). Self-schemas and vulnerability to specific life stress in children at risk for depression. *Cognitive Therapy and Research, 14,* 215–227.

Hammen, C., & Zupan, B. A. (1984). Self-schemas, depression, and the processing of personal information in children. *Journal of Experimental Child Psychology, 37,* 598–608.

Harrington, R., Fudge, H., Rutter, M., Pickles, A., & Hill, J. (1990). Adult outcomes of childhood and adolescent depression: Psychiatric status. *Archives of General Psychiatry, 47,* 465–473.

Harter, S., Marold, D. B., & Whitesell, N. R. (1992). Model of psychosocial risk factors leading to suicidal ideation in young adolescents. *Development and Psychopathology, 4,* 167–188.

Helsel, W., & Matson, J. L. (1984). The assessment of depression in children: The internal structure of the Children's Depression Inventory. *Behaviour Research and Therapy, 22,* 289–298.

Hops, H., Biglan, A., Sherman, L., Arthur, J., Friedman, L., & Osteen, V. (1987). Home observations of family interactions of depressed women. *Journal of Consulting and Clinical Psychology, 55,* 341–346.

Hops, H., Lewinsohn, P. M., Andrews, J. A., & Roberts, R. E. (1990). Psychosocial correlates of depressive symptomatology among high school students. *Journal of Clinical Child Psychology, 3,* 211–220.

Inoff-Germain, G., Nottelmann, E. D., & Radke-Yarrow, M. (1992). Evaluative communications between affectively ill and well mothers and their children. *Journal of Abnormal Child Psychology, 20,* 189–212.

Jacobsen, R. H., Lahey, B. B., & Strauss, C. C. (1983). Correlates of depressed mood in normal children. *Journal of Abnormal Child Psychology, 11,* 29–40.

Jaenicke, C., Hammen, C., Zupan, B., Hiroto, D., Gordon, D., Adrian, C., & Burge, D. (1987). Cognitive vulnerability in children at risk for depression. *Journal of Abnormal Child Psychology, 15,* 559–572.

Jensen, P. S., Richters, J., Ussery, T., Bloedau, L., & Davis, H. (1991). Child psychopathology and environmental influences: Discrete life events versus ongoing adversity. *Journal of the American Academy of Child and Adolescent Psychiatry, 30,* 303–309.

Kagan, J., Reznick, J., & Gibbons, J. (1989). Inhibited and uninhibited types of children. *Child Development, 60,* 838–845.

Kandel, D. B., & Davies, M. (1982). Epidemiology of depressive mood in adolescents. *Archives of General Psychiatry, 39,* 1205–1212.

Kandel, D. B., & Davies, M. (1986). Adult sequelae of adolescent depressive symptoms. *Archives of General Psychiatry, 43,* 255–262.

Kashani, J. H., Burbach, D. J., & Rosenberg, T. K. (1988). Perception of family conflict resolution and depressive symptomatology in adolescents. *Journal of the American Academy of Child and Adolescent Psychiatry, 27,* 42–48.

Kashani, J. H., & Carlson, G. A. (1987). Seriously depressed preschoolers. *American Journal of Psychiatry, 144,* 348–350.

Kashani, J. H., Carlson, G. A., Beck, N. C., Hoeper, E. W., Corcoran, C. M., McAllister, J. A., Fallahi, C., Rosenberg, T. K., & Reid, J. C. (1987). Depression, depressive symptoms, and depressed mood among a community sample of adolescents. *American Journal of Psychiatry, 144,* 931–934.

Kashani, J. H., Holcomb, W. R., & Orvaschel, H. (1986). Depression and depressive symptoms in preschool children from the general population. *American Journal of Psychiatry, 143,* 1138–1143.

Kashani, J., Rosenberg, T., & Reid, J. (1989). Developmental perspectives in child and adolescent depressive symptoms in a community sample. *American Journal of Psychiatry, 146,* 871–875.

Kaslow, N. J., Deering, C. G., & Racusin, G. R. (1994). Depressed children and their families. *Clinical Psychology Review, 14,* 39–59.

Kaslow, N. J., Rehm, L. P., & Siegel, A. W. (1984). Social-cognitive and cognitive correlates of depression in children. *Journal of Abnormal Child Psychology, 12,* 605–620.

Kaslow, N. J., Tanenbaum, R. L., Abramson, L. Y., Peterson, C., & Seligman, M. E. P. (1983). Problem-solving deficits and depressive symptoms among children. *Journal of Abnormal Child Psychology, 11,* 497–502.

Kazdin, A. E., Esveldt-Dawson, K., & Matson, J. L. (1982). Changes in children's social skills performance as a function of preassessment experiences. *Journal of Clinical Child Psychology, 11,* 243–248.

Kazdin, A. E., Esveldt-Dawson, K., Sherick, R. B., & Colbus, D. (1985). Assessment of overt behavior and childhood depression among psychiatrically disturbed children. *Journal of Consulting and Clinical Psychology, 53,* 201–210.

Keller, M. B., Beardslee, W., Lavori, P. W., Wunder, J., Dorer, D. L., & Samuelson, H. (1988). Course of major depression in non-referred adolescents: A retrospective study. *Journal of Affective Disorders, 15,* 235–243.

Kendall, P. C., Stark, K. D., & Adam, T. (1990). Cognitive deficit or cognitive distortion in childhood depression. *Journal of Abnormal Child Psychology, 18,* 255–270.

Kendler, K. S. (1990). Familial risk factors and the familial aggregation of psychiatric disorders. *Psychological Medicine, 20,* 311–319.

Kennedy, E., Spence, S. H., & Hensley, R. (1989). An examination of the relationship between childhood depression and social competence amongst primary school children. *Journal of Child Psychology and Psychiatry, 30,* 561–573.

King, C. A., Naylor, M. W., Segal, H. G., Evans, T., & Shain, B. N. (1993). Global self-worth, specific self-perceptions of competence, and depression in adolescents. *Journal of the American Academy of Child and Adolescent Psychiatry, 32,* 745–752.

King, C. A., Segal, H. G., Naylor, M. W., & Evans, T. (1993). Family functioning and suicidal behavior in adolescent inpatients with mood disorders. *Journal of the American Academy of Child and Adolescent Psychiatry, 32,* 1198–1206.

Klerman, G. L., Lavori, P. W., Rice, J., Reich, T., Endicott, J., Andreasen, N. C., Keller, M. B., & Hirschfeld, R. M. A. (1985). Birth cohort trends in rates of major depressive disorder among relatives of patients with affective disorder. *Archives of General Psychiatry, 42,* 689–693.

Kobak, R. R., Sudler, N., & Gamble, W. (1991). Attachment and depressive symptoms during adolescence: A developmental pathways analysis. *Development and Psychopathology, 3,* 461–474.

Kochanska, G. (1991). Patterns of inhibition to the unfamiliar in children of well and affectively ill mothers. *Child Development, 62,* 250–263.

Kochanska, G., Kuczynski, L., Radke-Yarrow, M., & Welsh, J. D. (1987). Resolutions of control episodes between well and affectively ill mothers and their young children. *Journal of Abnormal Child Psychology, 15,* 441–456.

Koenig, L. J. (1988). Self-image of emotionally disturbed adolescents. *Journal of Abnormal Child Psychology, 16,* 111–126.

Kovacs, M. (1980). Rating scales to assess depression in school-aged children. *Acta Paedopsychiatry, 46,* 305–315.

Kovacs, M. (1990). Comorbid anxiety disorders in childhood-onset depressions. In J. D. Maser & C. R. Cloninger (Eds.), *Comorbidity of mood and anxiety disorders* (pp. 272–281). Washington, DC: American Psychiatric Press.

Kovacs, M., Akiskal, H. S., Gatsonis, C., & Parrone, P. L. (1994). Childhood-onset dysthymic disorder: Clinical features and prospective naturalistic outcome. *Archives of General Psychiatry, 51,* 365–374.

Kovacs, M., Feinberg, T. L., Crouse-Novak, M. A., Paulauskas, S. L., & Finkelstein, R. (1984). Depressive disorders in childhood: I. A longitudinal prospective study of characteristics and recovery. *Archives of General Psychiatry, 41,* 229–237.

Kovacs, M., Feinberg, T. L., Crouse-Novak, M., Paulauskas, S. L., Pollock, M., & Finkelstein, R. (1984). Depressive disorders in childhood: II. A longitudinal study of the risk for a subsequent major depression. *Archives of General Psychiatry, 41,* 643–649.

Kovacs, M., & Goldston, D. (1991). Cognitive and social cognitive development of depressed children and adolescents. *Journal of the American Academy of Child and Adolescent Psychiatry, 30,* 388–392.

Kovacs, M., Paulauskas, S., Gatsonis, C., & Richards, C. (1988). Depressive disorders in childhood: III. Longitudinal study of comorbidity with and risk for conduct disorders. *Journal of Affective Disorders, 15,* 205–217.

Kutcher, S., Malkin, D., Silverberg, J., Marton, P., Williamson, P., Malkin, A., Szalai, J., & Katic, M. (1991). Nocturnal cortisol, thyroid stimulating hormone, and growth hormone secretory profiles in depressed adolescents. *Journal of the American Academy of Child and Adolescent Psychiatry, 30,* 407–414.

Kutcher, S., Williamson, P., Marton, P., & Szalai, J. (1992). REM latency in endogenously depressed adolescents. *British Journal of Psychiatry, 161,* 399–402.

Lamont, J., Fischoff, S., & Gottlieb, H. (1976). Recall of parental behaviors in female neurotic depressives. *Journal of Clinical Psychology, 32,* 762–765.

Larson, R. W., Raffaelli, M., Richards, M. H., Ham, M., & Jewell, L. (1990). Ecology of depression in late childhood and early adolescence: A profile of daily states and activities. *Journal of Abnormal Psychology, 99,* 92–102.

Laurent, J., & Stark, K. D. (1993). Testing the cognitive content-specificity hypothesis with anxious and depressed youngsters. *Journal of Abnormal Psychology, 102,* 226–237.

Lefkowitz, M., & Burton, N. (1978). Childhood depression: A critique of the concept. *Psychological Bulletin, 85,* 716–726.

Lefkowitz, M. M., & Tesiny, E. P. (1984). Rejection and depression: Prospective and contemporaneous analyses. *Developmental Psychology, 20,* 776–785.

Leitenberg, H., Yost, L. W., & Carroll-Wilson, M. (1986). Negative cognitive errors in children: Questionnaire development, normative data, and comparisons between children with and without self-reported symptoms of depression, low self-esteem, and evaluation anxiety. *Journal of Consulting and Clinical Psychology, 54,* 528–536.

Lewinsohn, P. M. (1974). A behavioral approach to depression. In R. Friedman & M. Katz (Eds.), *The psychology of depression: Contemporary theory and research* (pp. 157–185). Washington, DC: Winston-Wiley.

Lewinsohn, P. M., Hoberman, H. M., & Rosenbaum, M. (1988). A prospective study of risk factors for unipolar depression. *Journal of Abnormal Psychology, 97,* 251–264.

Lewinsohn, P. M., Hops, H., Roberts, R. E., Seeley, J. R., & Andrews, J. A. (1993). Adolescent psychopathology: I. Prevalence and incidence of depression and other DSM-III-R disorders in high school students. *Journal of Abnormal Psychology, 102,* 133–144.

Lewinsohn, P. M., Roberts, R. E., Seeley, J. R., Rohde, P., Gotlib, I. H., & Hops, H. (1994). Adolescent psychopathology: II. Psychosocial risk factors for depression. *Journal of Abnormal Psychology, 103,* 302–315.

Lewinsohn, P., Rohde, P., & Seeley, J. (1994). Psychosocial risk factors for future adolescent suicide attempts. *Journal of Consulting and Clinical Psychology, 62,* 297–305.

Lewinsohn, P., Rohde, P., Seeley, J., & Fischer, S. (1993). Age-cohort changes in the lifetime occurrence of depression and other mental disorders. *Journal of Abnormal Psychology, 102,* 110–120.

Lovejoy, M. C. (1991). Maternal depression: Effects on social cognition and behavior in parent–child interactions. *Journal of Abnormal Child Psychology, 19,* 693–706.

Lyons-Ruth, K., Zoll, D., Connell, D., & Grunebaum, H. U. (1986). The depressed mother and her one-year-old infant: Environment, interaction, attachment, and infant development. In E. Tronick & T. Field (Eds.), *Maternal depression and infant disturbance* (New Directions for Child Development, No. 34, pp. 31–46). San Francisco: Jossey-Bass.

Main, M., Kaplan, N., & Cassidy, J. (1985). Security in infancy, childhood, and adulthood: A move to the level of representation. In I. Bretherton & E. Waters (Eds.), *Growing points in attachment theory and research. Monographs of the Society for Research in Child Development, 50,* 66–104.

Marton, P., Connolly, J., Kutcher, S., & Korenblum, M. (1993). Cognitive social skills and social self-appraisal in depressed adolescents. *Journal of the American Academy of Child and Adolescent Psychiatry, 32,* 739–744.

Marton, P., & Maharaj, S. (1993). Family factors in adolescent unipolar depression. *Canadian Journal of Psychiatry, 38,* 373–382.

McCauley, E., Mitchell, J. R., Burke, P., & Moss, S. (1988). Cognitive attributes of depression in children and adolescents. *Journal of Consulting and Clinical Psychology, 56,* 903–908.

McCauley, E., & Myers, K. (1992). Family interactions in mood-disordered youth. *Child and Adolescent Psychiatric Clinics of North America, 1,* 111–127.

McCauley, E., Myers, K., Mitchell, J., Calderon, R., Schloredt, K., & Treder, R. (1993). Depression young people: Initial presentation and clinical course. *Journal*

of the American Academy of Child and Adolescent Psychiatry, 32, 714–722.

McGee, R., Anderson, J., Williams, S., & Silva, P. A. (1986). Cognitive correlates of depressive symptoms in 11-year-old children. *Journal of Abnormal Child Psychology, 14,* 517–524.

McGee, R., Feehan, M., Williams, S., Partridge, F., Silva, P., & Kelly, J. (1990). DSM-III disorders in a large sample of adolescents. *Journal of the American Academy of Child and Adolescent Psychiatry, 29,* 611–619.

McGee, R., Feehan, M., Williams, S., & Anderson, J. (1992). DSM-III disorders from age 11 to age 15 years. *Journal of the American Academy of Child and Adolescent Psychiatry, 31,* 50–59.

Meyer, N. E., Dyck, D. G., & Petrinack, R. J. (1989). Cognitive appraisal and attributional correlates of depressive symptoms in children. *Journal of Abnormal Child Psychology, 17,* 325–336.

Mills, M., Puckering, C., Pound, A., & Cox, A. (1985). What is it about depressed mothers that influences their children's functioning? In J. E. Stevenson (Ed.), *Recent research in developmental psychopathology* (pp. 11–17). Oxford, UK: Pergamon Press.

Mitchell, J., McCauley, E., Burke, P. M., & Moss, S. J. (1988). Phenomenology of depression in children and adolescents. *Journal of the American Academy of Child and Adolescent Psychiatry, 27,* 12–20.

Moyal, B. R. (1977). Locus of control, self-esteem, stimulus appraisal, and depressive symptoms in children. *Journal of Consulting and Clinical Psychology, 45,* 951–952.

Mullins, L. L., Siegel, L. J., & Hodges, K. (1985). Cognitive problem-solving and life event correlates of depressive symptoms in children. *Journal of Abnormal Child Psychology, 13,* 305–314.

Naylor, M. W., King, C. A., Lindsay, K. A., Evans, T., Armelagos, J., Shain, B. N., & Greden, J. F. (1993). Sleep deprivation in depressed adolescents and psychiatric controls. *Journal of the American Academy of Child and Adolescent Psychiatry, 32,* 753–759.

Nolen-Hoeksema, S. (1991). Responses to depression and their effects on the duration of depressive episodes. *Journal of Abnormal Psychology, 100,* 569–582.

Nolen-Hoeksema, S., & Girgus, J. S. (1994). The emergence of gender differences in depression during adolescence. *Psychological Bulletin, 115,* 424–443.

Nolen-Hoeksema, S., Girgus, J. S., & Seligman, M. E. P. (1986). Learned helplessness in children: A longitudinal study of depression, achievement, and explanatory style. *Journal of Personality and Social Psychology, 51,* 435–442.

Nolen-Hoeksema, S., Girgus, J. S., & Seligman, M. E. P. (1992). Predictors and consequences of childhood depressive symptoms: A 5-year longitudinal study. *Journal of Abnormal Psychology, 101,* 405–422.

Nolen-Hoeksema, S., Morrow, J., & Fredrickson, B. L. (1993). Response styles and the duration of episodes of depressed mood. *Journal of Abnormal Psychology, 102,* 20–28.

Offord, D. R., Boyle, M. H., Szatmari, P., Rae-Grant, N., Links, P. S., Cadman, D. T., Byles, J., Crawford, J., Blum, H., Byrne, C., Thomas, H., & Woodward, C. (1987). Ontario Child Health Study: II. Six-month prevalence of disorder and rates of service utilization. *Archives of General Psychiatry, 44,* 832–836.

Offord, D. R., Boyle, M. H., Racine, Y. A., Fleming, J. E., Cadman, D. T., Blum, H, M., Byrne, C., Links, P. S.,

Lipman, E. L., MacMillan, H. L., Grant, N. I. R., Sanford, M. N., Szatmari, P., Thomas, H., & Woodward, C. A. (1992). Outcome, prognosis, and risk in a longitudinal follow-up study. *Journal of the American Academy of Child and Adolescent Psychiatry, 31,* 916–923.

Oliver, J. M., Handal, P. J., Finn, T., & Herdy, S. (1987). Depressed and nondepressed students and their siblings in frequent contact with their families. *Cognitive Therapy and Research, 11,* 501–515.

Orvaschel, H., Weissman, M. M., & Kidd, K. K. (1980). Children and depression: The children of depressed parents; the childhood of depressed patients; depression in children. *Journal of Affective Disorders, 2,* 1–16.

Panak, W. F., & Garber, J. (1992). Role of aggression, rejection, and attributions in the prediction of depression in children. *Development and Psychopathology, 4,* 145–165.

Pappini, D., Roggman, L., & Anderson, J. (1991). Early-adolescent perceptions of attachment to mother and father: A test of the emotional-distancing and buffering hypothesis. *Journal of Early Adolescence, 11,* 258–275.

Parker, G. (1981). Parental reports of depressives: An investigation of several explanations. *Journal of Affective Disorders, 3,* 131–140.

Patterson, G. R., & Stoolmiller, M. (1991). Replications of a dual failure model for boys' depressed mood. *Journal of Consulting and Clinical Psychology, 59,* 491–498.

Paykel, E. S. (1979). Recent life events in the development of the depressive disorders: Implications for the effects of stress. In R. A. Depue (Ed.), *The psychobiology of the depressive disorders* (pp. 245–262). New York: Academic Press.

Pelham, W. E., & Bender, M. E. (1982). Peer relationships in hyperactive children: Description and treatment. In K. D. Gadow & I. Bialer (Eds.), *Advances in learning and behavioral disabilities* (Vol. 1, pp. 365–436). Greenwich, CT: JAI Press.

Perkins, S. C., Meyers, A. W., & Cohen, R. (1988). Problem-solving ability and response to feedback in peer-nominated mildly depressed children. *Cognitive Therapy and Research, 12,* 89–102.

Petersen, A. C., Sarigiani, P. A., & Kennedy, R. E. (1991). Adolescent depression: Why more girls? *Journal of Youth and Adolescence, 20,* 247–271.

Pfeffer, C. R., Stokes, P., & Shindledecker, R. (1991). Suicidal behavior and hypothalamic–pituitary–adrenocortical axis indices in child psychiatric inpatients. *Biological Psychiatry, 29,* 909–917.

Poznanski, E. O., Krahenbuhl, V., & Zrull, J. P. (1976). Childhood depression: A longitudinal perspective. *Journal of the American Academy of Child Psychiatry, 15,* 491–501.

Proffitt, V. D., & Weisz, J. R. (1992). *Perceived incompetence and depression in childhood: Cognitive distortion or accurate appraisal.* Unpublished manuscript.

Puig-Antich, J. (1982). Major depression and conduct disorder in prepuberty. *Journal of the American Academy of Child and Adolescent Psychiatry, 21,* 118–128.

Puig-Antich, J., Chambers, W. J., & Tabrizi, M. A. (1983). The clinical assessment of current depressive episodes in children and adolescents: Interviews with parents and children. In D. P. Cantwell & G. A. Carlson (Eds.), *Affective disorders in childhood and adolescence* (pp.157–179). New York: Spectrum.

Puig-Antich, J., Dahl, R., Ryan, N., Novacenko, H., Goetz, D., Goetz, R., Twomey, J., & Klepper, T. (1989). Cortisol secretion in prepubertal children with major depressive disorder. *Archives of General Psychiatry, 46,* 801–809.

Puig-Antich, J., Kaufman, J., Ryan, N. D., Williamson, D. E., Dahl, R. E., Lukens, E., Todak, G., Ambrosini, P., Rabinovich, H., & Nelson, B. (1993). The psychosocial functioning and family environment of depressed adolescents. *Journal of the American Academy of Child and Adolescent Psychiatry, 32,* 244–253.

Puig-Antich, J., Lukens, E., Davies, M., Goetz, D., Brennan-Quattrock, J., & Todak, G. (1985a). Psychosocial functioning in prepubertal major depressive disorders: I. Interpersonal relationships during the depressive episode. *Archives of General Psychiatry, 42,* 500–507.

Puig-Antich, J., Lukens, E., Davies, M., Goetz, D., Brennan-Quattrock, J., & Todak, G. (1985b). Psychosocial functioning in prepubertal major depressive disorders: II. Interpersonal relationships after sustained recovery from affective episode. *Archives of General Psychiatry, 42,* 511–517.

Quiggle, N. L., Garber, J., Panak, W. F., & Dodge, K. A. (1992). Social information processing in aggressive and depressed children. *Child Development, 63,* 1305–1320.

Radke-Yarrow, M., Cummings, E. M., Kuczynski, L., & Chapman, M. (1985). Patterns of attachment in two-and-three-year olds in normal families and families with parental depression. *Child Development, 56,* 884–893.

Radloff, L. (1977). The CES-D Scale: A new self-report depression scale for research in the general population. *Applied Psychological Measurement, 1,* 385–401.

Rehm, L. P. (1977). A self-control model of depression. *Behavior Therapy, 8,* 787–804.

Reinherz, H. Z., Giaconia, R. M., Lefkowitz, E. S., Pakiz, B., & Frost, A. K. (1993). Prevalence of psychiatric disorders in a community population of older adolescents. *Journal of the American Academy of Child and Adolescent Psychiatry, 32,* 369–377.

Reinherz, H. Z., Giaconia, R. M., Pakiz, B., Silverman, A. B., Frost, A. K., & Lefkowitz, E. S. (1993). Psychosocial risks for major depression in late adolescence: A longitudinal community study. *Journal of the American Academy of Child and Adolescent Psychiatry, 32,* 1155–1163.

Reinherz, H. Z., Stewart-Berghauer, G., Pakiz, B., Frost, A. K., Moeykens, B. A., & Holmes, W. M. (1989). The relationship of early risk and current mediators to depressive symptomatology in adolescence. *Journal of the American Academy of Child and Adolescent Psychiatry, 28,* 942–947.

Rende, R. D., Plomin, R., Reiss, D., & Hetherington, E. M. (1993). Genetic and environmental influences on depressive symptomatology in adolescence: Individual differences and extreme scores. *Journal of Child Psychology and Psychiatry, 8,* 1387–1398.

Renouf, A. G., & Harter, S. (1990). Low self-worth and anger as components of the depressive experience in young adolescents. *Development and Psychopathology, 2,* 293–310.

Richters, J. E. (1992). Depressed mothers as informants about their children: A critical review of the evidence for distortion. *Psychological Bulletin, 112,* 485–499.

Roberts, R., Andrews, J., Lewinsohn, P., & Hops, H. (1990). Assessment of depression in adolescents using the Center for Epidemiologic Studies Depression Scale. *Psychological Assessment: A Journal of Consulting and Clinical Psychology, 2,* 122–128.

Roberts, R. E., Lewinsohn, P. M., & Seeley, J. R. (1991). Screening for adolescent depression: A comparison of

depression scales. *Journal of the American Academy of Child and Adolescent Psychiatry, 30,* 58–66.

Robins, C. J., & Hinkley, K. (1989). Social-cognitive processing and depressive symptoms in children: A comparison of measures. *Journal of Abnormal Child Psychology, 17,* 29–36.

Rochlin, G. (1959). The loss complex. *Journal of the American Psychoanalytic Association, 7,* 299–316.

Rohde, P., Lewinsohn, P., & Seeley, J. (1991). Comorbidity of unipolar depression: II. Comorbidity with other mental disorders in adolescents and adults. *Journal of Abnormal Psychology, 100,* 214–222.

Rubin, K. H., Both, L., Zahn-Waxler, C., Cummings, E. M., & Wilkinson, M. (1991). Dyadic play behaviors of children of well and depressed mothers. *Development and Psychopathology, 3,* 243–251.

Rudolph, K. D., Hammen, C., & Burge, D. (1994). Interpersonal functioning and depressive symptoms in childhood: Addressing the issues of specificity and comorbidity. *Journal of Abnormal Child Psychology, 22,* 355–371.

Rudolph, K. D., Hammen, C., & Burge, D. (1995). *A cognitive-interpersonal approach to depressive symptoms in childhood.* Manuscript submitted for publication.

Rutter, M. (1986). The developmental psychopathology of depression: Issues and perspectives. In M. Rutter, C. E. Izard, & P. B. Read (Eds.), *Depression in young people: Clinical and developmental perspectives* (pp. 3–30). New York: Guilford Press.

Rutter, M., Izard, C. E., & Read, P. B. (Eds.). (1986). *Depression in young people: Clinical and developmental perspectives.* New York: Guilford Press.

Ryan, N. D., Puig-Antich, J., Ambrosini, P., Rabinovich, H., Robinson, D., Nelson, B., Iyengar, S., & Twomey, J. (1987). The clinical picture of major depression in children and adolescents. *Archives of General Psychiatry, 44,* 854–861.

Ryan, N. D., Williamson, D. E., Iyengar, S., Orvaschel, H., Reich, T., Dahl, R. E., & Puig-Antich, J. (1992). A secular increase in child and adolescent onset affective disorder. *Journal of the American Academy of Child and Adolescent Psychiatry, 31,* 600–605.

Sacco, W. P., & Graves, D. J. (1984). Childhood depression, interpersonal problem solving and self-ratings of performance. *Journal of Clinical Child Psychology, 13,* 10–15.

Sanders, M. R., Dadds, M. R., Johnston, B. M., & Cash, R. (1992). Childhood depression and conduct disorder: I. Behavioral, affective, and cognitive aspects of family problem-solving interactions. *Journal of Abnormal Psychology, 101,* 495–504.

Seligman, M. E. P. (1975). *Helplessness: On depression, development, and death.* San Francisco: W. H. Freeman.

Seligman, M. E. P., Peterson, C., Kaslow, N. J., Tanenbaum, R. L., Alloy, L. B., & Abramson, L. Y. (1984). Attributional style and depressive symptoms among children. *Journal of Abnormal Psychology, 93,* 235–238.

Shaffer, D., Fisher, P., Piacentini, J., Schwab-Stone, M., & Wicks, J. (1989). *Diagnostic Interview Schedule for Children (DISC 2.1).* Rockville, MD: National Institute of Mental Health.

Shelton, M. R., & Garber, J. (1987). *The Children's Activity Inventory.* Unpublished manuscript, Vanderbilt University.

Siegel, J. M., & Brown, J. D. (1988). A prospective study of stressful circumstances, illness symptoms, and depressed mood among adolescents. *Developmental Psychology, 24,* 715–721.

Stark, K. D., Humphrey, L. L., Laurent, J., Livingston, R., & Christopher, J. (1993). Cognitive, behavioral, and family factors in the differentiation of depressive and anxiety disorders during childhood. *Journal of Consulting and Clinical Psychology, 5,* 878–886.

Strauss, C. C., Frame, C. L., & Forehand, R. (1987). Psychosocial impairment associated with anxiety in children. *Journal of Clinical Child Psychology, 16,* 235–239.

Strober, M., Lampert, C., Schmidt, S., & Morrell, W. (1993). The course of major depressive disorder in adolescents: Recovery and risk of manic switching in a 24-month prospective, naturalistic follow-up of psychotic and nonpsychotic subtypes. *Journal of the American Academy of Child and Adolescent Psychiatry, 32,* 34–42.

Tarullo, L. B., DeMulder, E. K., Martinez, P. E., & Radke-Yarrow, M. (1994). Dialogues with preadolescents and adolescents: Mother–child interaction patterns in affectively ill and well dyads. *Journal of Abnormal Child Psychology, 22,* 33–51.

Teasdale, J. D. (1983). Negative thinking in depression: Cause, effect, or reciprocal relationship? *Advances in Behaviour Research and Therapy, 5,* 3–25.

Teicher, M. H., Glod, C. A., Harper, D., Magnus, E., Brasher, C., Wren, F., & Pahlavan, K. (1993). Locomotor activity in depressed children and adolescents: I. Circadian dysregulation. *Journal of the American Academy of Child and Adolescent Psychiatry, 32,* 760–769.

Teti, D. M., Gelfand, D. M., Messinger, D., & Isabella, R. (1991, April). *Security of infant attachment and maternal functioning among depressed and nondepressed mothers and infants.* Paper presented at the biennial meeting of the Society for Research in Child Development, Seattle, WA.

Todd, R. D., Neuman, R., Geller, B., Fox, L. W., & Hickok, J. (1993). Genetic studies of affective disorders: Should we be starting with childhood onset probands? *Journal of the American Academy of Child and Adolescent Psychiatry, 32,* 1164–1171.

Turner, J. E., & Cole, D. A. (1994). Developmental differences in cognitive diatheses for child depression. *Journal of Abnormal Child Psychology, 22,* 15–32.

Verhulst, F. C., & van der Ende, J. (1992). Six-year developmental course of internalizing and externalizing problem behaviors. *Journal of the American Academy of Child and Adolescent Psychiatry, 31,* 924–931.

Ward, L. G., Friedlander, M. L., & Silverman, W. K. (1987). Children's depressive symptoms, negative self-statements, and causal attributions for success and failure. *Cognitive Therapy and Research, 11,* 215–227.

Weiss, B., Weisz, J. R., Politano, M., Carey, M., Nelson, W. M., & Finch, A. J. (1991a). Developmental differences in the factor structure of the Children's Depression Inventory. *Psychological Assessment: A Journal of Consulting and Clinical Psychology, 3,* 38–45.

Weiss, B., Weisz, J. R., Politano, M., Carey, M., Nelson, W. M., & Finch, A. J. (1991b). Relations among self-reported depressive symptoms in clinic-referred children versus adolescents. *Journal of Abnormal Psychology, 101,* 391–397.

Weissman, M. M., Paykel, E. S., & Klerman, G. L. (1972). The depressed woman as a mother. *Social Psychiatry, 7,* 98–108.

Weissman, M., Wickramarante, P., Warner, V., John, K., Prusoff, B. A., Merikangas, K. R., & Gammon, D. (1987). Assessing psychiatric disorders in children: Discrepancies between mothers' and children's reports. *Archives of General Psychiatry, 44,* 747–753.

Weisz, J. R. (1986). Understanding the developing under-standing of control. In M. Perlmutter (Ed.), *Social cognition: Minnesota symposia on child psychology* (Vol. 18, pp. 219–278). Hillsdale, NJ: Erlbaum.

Weisz, J. R., Rudolph, K. D., Granger, D. A., & Sweeney, L. (1992). Cognition, competence, and coping in child and adolescent depression: Research findings, developmental concerns, therapeutic implications. *Development and Psychopathology, 4,* 627–653.

Weisz, J. R., Stevens, J. S., Curry, J. F., Cohen, R., Craighead, W. E., Burlingame, W. V., Smith, A., Weiss, B., & Parmelee, D. X. (1989). Control-related cognitions and depression among inpatient children and adolescents. *Journal of the American Academy of Child and Adolescent Psychiatry, 28,* 358–363.

Weisz, J. R., & Stipek, D. J. (1982). Competence, contingency, and the development of perceived control. *Human Development, 25,* 250–281.

Weisz, J. R., Sweeney, L., Proffitt, V., & Carr, T. (1994). Control-related beliefs and self-reported depressive symptoms in late childhood. *Journal of Abnormal Psychology, 102,* 411–418.

Weisz, J. R., Weiss, B., Wasserman, A. A., & Rintoul, B. (1987). Control-related beliefs and depression among clinic-referred children and adolescents. *Journal of Abnormal Psychology, 96,* 149–158.

Weller, E. B., Weller, R. A., Fristad, M. A., & Bowes, J. M. (1990). Dexamethasone suppression test and depressive symptoms in bereaved children: A preliminary report. *Journal of Neuropsychiatry and Clinical Neurosciences, 2,* 418–421.

Wierzbicki, M. (1987). Similarity of monozygotic and dizygotic child twins in level and lability of subclinically depressed mood. *American Journal of Orthopsychiatry, 57,* 33–40.

Wierzbicki, M., & McCabe, M. (1988). Social skills and subsequent depressive symptomatology in children. *Journal of Clinical Child Psychology, 17,* 203–208.

Whitaker, A., Johnson, J., Shaffer, D., Rapoport, J. L., Kalikow, K., Walsh, B. T., Davies, M., Braiman, S., & Dolinsky, A. (1990). Uncommon troubles in young people: Prevalence estimates of selected psychiatric disorders in a nonreferred adolescent population. *Archives of General Psychiatry, 47,* 487–496.

World Health Organization. (1992). *International statistical classification of diseases and related health problems* (10th ed.). Geneva, Switzerland: Author.

World Health Organization. (1993). *The ICD-10 classification of mental and behavioural disorders: Diagnostic criteria for research.* Geneva, Switzerland: Author.

Childhood
Anxiety Disorders

Anne Marie Albano
Bruce F. Chorpita
David H. Barlow

Anxiety disorders are widely recognized as the most common class of psychiatric disorders affecting children and adolescents (Anderson, Williams, McGee, & Silva, 1987; Bell-Dolan & Brazeal, 1993; Kashani & Orvaschel, 1988; Orvaschel & Weissman, 1986). Although transient fears and anxieties are considered part of normal development, for a significant proportion of children, the anxiety experience becomes a stable negative force in their lives. Anxiety is associated with severe impairment in functioning, expressed in its most disabling form through a child's avoidance of activities such as school, peer involvement, and autonomous activities (Bell-Dolan & Brazeal, 1993; Kendall et al., 1992). Since the publication of the third edition of the *Diagnostic and Statistical Manual of Mental Disorders* (DSM-III; American Psychiatric Association, 1980), a multitude of studies have documented the incidence and prevalence of anxiety disorders in children and adolescents. Advances in child psychopathology research focused on these anxiety disorders have resulted in the recent nosological changes evident in DSM's fourth edition (DSM-IV; American Psychiatric Association, 1994). Although separation anxiety disorder (SAD) is the only remaining childhood anxiety disorder per se, the criteria of the "adult" anxiety disorders have been modified to include devel-

opmentally appropriate descriptors for accurate diagnosis in children. The present chapter examines the prevalence, expression, and developmental patterns of specific anxiety disorders in children and adolescents. Attention is directed toward clinical variables (e.g., age at onset, severity, comorbidity) and sociodemographic variables (e.g., gender, race, socioeconomic status) relative to each disorder. Clinical impairment in functioning is specified within a developmental context. These issues are discussed in terms of the course of childhood anxiety disorders. The chapter concludes with a review of current issues in the study of childhood anxiety and future directions.

BRIEF HISTORICAL CONTEXT

The study of children's anxieties and fears has been described in the literature for decades (see Barrios & O'Dell, 1989, for a review). Case studies of childhood fears formed the foundation for the development of both psychoanalytic and behavioral theory. In the classic case study of "Little Hans," Freud (1909/1955) defined and described several key unconscious processes operating in the development of phobia, such as the ego defense mechanisms of repression and displacement. Further, this case provided Freud with rich

clinical data for the explication of the "oedipal stage," perhaps the most controversial and critical stage of psychosexual development. Although the study of Little Hans has since been reformulated beyond Freud's initial conceptualization (e.g., A. Freud, 1965), its value and place in psychoanalytic theory remain firmly ingrained. Similarly, the conditioned fear of a white laboratory rat in young Albert provided early support for the classical conditioning of anxiety and behavioral theory (Harris, 1979; Watson & Rayner, 1920). Repeated pairings of a neutral stimulus (rat) and an aversive stimulus (loud noise), and the subsequent reaction of fear of the rat in 1-year-old Albert, provided Watson and Rayner with empirical support for behavioral theory. Additional support for the theory was soon to follow in yet another case study of a child, as Jones (1924a, 1924b) validated the behavioral tenet that all behavior is learned and hence can also be unlearned. Utilizing techniques incorporating modeling and desensitization, Jones described the treatment of 3-year-old Peter's fear of rabbits, which was successfully resolved.

Although these and similar case studies of children served to further the interest and support for specific theoretical models and related therapeutic interventions, the study of pathological anxiety conditions in children was (until relatively recently) essentially ignored. There exists a wealth of information and research spanning several decades on the developmental progression of children's fears and phobias, and several comprehensive reviews outline the historical progression of this research (Barrios & Hartmann, 1988; Barrios & O'Dell, 1989; King, Hamilton, & Ollendick, 1988; Ollendick & King, 1991). To summarize, prior to the publication of DSM-III (American Psychiatric Association, 1980), fears and anxiety reactions in children were classified according to etiology (Hebb, 1946) or empirically based factor groupings (Scherer & Nakamura, 1968; Miller, Barrett, Hampe, & Noble, 1972; Ollendick, 1983a). Such research has demonstrated that subclinical fears are common in children (e.g., Miller, 1983; Ollendick, 1983a), the number of fears reported by children declines with age (MacFarlane, Allen, & Honzik, 1954), and the focus of the fear changes over time (e.g., Bauer, 1976). In addition, across studies, girls consistently endorse a greater number of fears than boys (Abe & Masui, 1981; Lapouse & Monk, 1958, 1959).

In contrast to the wealth of studies examining subclinical fears in children, formal psychiatric classification systems have acknowledged the presence of pathological phobic reactions for only the past four decades. The publication of DSM's first edition (American Psychiatric Association, 1952) first identified phobias as psychoneurotic reactions, and subsequently in DSM-II (American Psychiatric Association, 1968), the diagnostic category changed to phobic neuroses. DSM-II introduced overanxious reaction as a distinct diagnostic category for children and adolescents. These early DSM systems were heavily tied to psychoanalytic theory, purporting an unconscious process or conflict as the etiological mechanism for the phobic or overanxious reaction (Barlow, 1988). The inclusion of overanxious reaction in the psychiatric nomenclature marked the beginning, albeit meager, of attention to anxious children and adolescents.

Over the past two decades, clinically significant phobias and anxiety conditions in childhood have begun to receive serious attention by clinicians and researchers alike. The failure to attend to childhood anxiety conditions may be due, in part, to long-standing disagreements within the field as to what constituted a clinical anxiety state from transient developmental fears and anxieties (Barrios & Hartmann, 1988; Strauss & Last, 1993). DSM-III (American Psychiatric Association, 1980) and DSM-III-R (American Psychiatric Association, 1987) represent the first attempts in the history of modern classification systems of psychopathology to delineate developmentally appropriate diagnostic criteria for anxiety and phobic disorders in children and adolescents. Separation anxiety disorder, avoidant disorder of childhood and adolescence, and overanxious disorder earned notoriety as the three distinct anxiety disorders of childhood. In total, children could be diagnosed with these three anxiety disorders in addition to adult anxiety disorders such as phobic disorder, obsessive–compulsive disorder, and posttraumatic stress disorder. Thus the DSM-III and subsequent DSM-III-R sparked a legion of studies examining the epidemiology and clinical characteristics of anxiety disorders in childhood (e.g., Flament et al., 1988; Francis, Last, & Strauss, 1987; Last, Francis, Hersen, Kazdin, & Strauss, 1987; Last, Hersen, Kazdin, Finkelstein, & Strauss, 1987; Last & Strauss, 1989a). Consequently, such studies have culminated in the recent changes and revisions in criteria for diagnosing anxiety disorders evidenced in DSM-IV (American Psychiatric Association, 1994) and the tenth edition of the *International Classification of Diseases* (World Health

Organization, 1992). These changes are discussed throughout this chapter.

Researchers over the past 20 years have witnessed a plethora of studies in the broad area of anxiety disorders, attending to both children and adults. The systematic examination of anxiety disorders in children continues to lag far behind adult psychopathology research, and several pressing issues underscore the crucial necessity for ongoing study in this area.

First, anxiety disorders are the most common *and most prevalent* category of psychiatric disorders in youth (Bernstein & Borchardt, 1991) and the primary reason for the referral of children and adolescents for mental health services (Beidel, 1991). Yet, fewer than 20% of all children requiring mental health services actually receive the necessary intervention (Kendall, 1994; Tuma, 1989). This underutilization of mental health services may partially result from a failure to identify adequately psychiatric disorders in children, particularly internalizing disorders such as anxiety. Children presenting with externalizing conditions such as conduct disorder (CD) and attention-deficit/hyperactivity disorder (ADHD) are more easily recognized by adult caretakers, particularly when the symptoms of these disorders begin to interfere with daily functioning and cause disruption in school and familial activities. Children with internalizing disorders, however, suffer for the most part in silence and are not easily identified as problematic. The limited utilization of mental health services in response to anxiety disorders in children and adolescents may well reflect the limited knowledge of what constitutes this type of mental health problem in children. Consequently, the result is a failure to recognize and intervene early in the development of these disorders.

Contributing to the problem of identifying pathological anxiety conditions in children is our inadequate understanding of what constitutes normal, developmentally appropriate anxiety reactions. Because all children are expected to display separation anxiety or specific fears at various times in their young lives, the intensity and duration of these developmentally appropriate episodes have not been adequately studied in comparison to pathological anxiety states. Early studies on the prevalence of fears, worries, and anxieties in children and adolescents reported estimates ranging from 3% to 18% (e.g., Abe & Masui, 1981; Orvaschel & Weissman, 1986; Werry & Quay, 1971). More recently, Bell-Dolan, Last, and Strauss (1990) examined the prevalence of anxiety symptoms in a sample on 62 never psychiatrically ill children and adolescents. A variety of anxiety symptoms, particularly fears of heights, public speaking, and somatic complaints were endorsed by approximately 20% of the subjects. These findings were higher than previous estimates reported in the literature, suggesting that anxiety symptoms at subclinical or clinical levels may occur with greater frequency in youth than previously expected. Overall, the authors called for a greater attention toward examining the patterns of expression of anxiety symptoms in children and for investigations into developmental and situational factors impacting upon these symptoms.

Second, research has demonstrated the negative impact of childhood anxiety on a broad range of psychosocial factors including academic performance (e.g., Dweck & Wortman, 1982) and social functioning (e.g., Strauss, Frame, & Forehand, 1987; Turner, Beidel, & Costello, 1987). Impairment in functioning may be adversely affected by the consistent finding of high comorbidity among the anxiety disorders and of anxiety with disorders such as depression and attention-deficit disorder (Keller et al., 1992). In such cases where anxiety is comorbid with an externalizing disorder or depression of sufficient intensity, it is likely that the latter disorder will become the focus of treatment and overshadow the anxiety disorder. Given that the impairment experienced by anxious children and adolescents cuts across a wide range of activities and situations, and that the diagnostic picture may be complicated by anxiety comorbidity, ongoing studies are sorely needed to evaluate fully the impact and course of these disorders on youth.

Finally, empirical data consistently support the findings that anxiety disorders have an early onset in childhood and adolescence and run a chronic course well into adulthood (cf. Barlow, 1988). Thus, the impairment associated with anxiety in youth hold long-term implications for adult functioning (Kendall, 1992), with research suggesting that anxiety symptoms may actually worsen over time (cf. Kendall, 1994) and possibly lead to depression (e.g., Alloy, Kelly, Mineka, & Clements, 1990). Attention to basic psychopathology research serves to advance our understanding of the nature and course of such disorders, but more importantly, it holds implications for the development of empirically based and efficacious prescriptive treatment protocols for the range of anxiety disorders in youth.

DESCRIPTION OF THE DISORDERS

In DSM-IV (American Psychiatric Association, 1994), children can be diagnosed with any of nine anxiety disorders: separation anxiety disorder, panic disorder, agoraphobia, generalized anxiety disorder (overanxious disorder), social phobia, specific (simple) phobia, obsessive–compulsive disorder, posttraumatic stress disorder, and acute stress disorder. These disorders share anxiety as the predominant feature, expressed through specific and discrete cognitive, physiological, and behavioral reactions. What distinguishes one anxiety disorder from the next is the focus of the child's anxiety. In this section we define the core and related symptoms of specific anxiety disorders affecting children and adolescents. A comparison of DSM-IV and ICD-10 criteria are provided in tabular form for each disorder. The reader interested in posttraumatic stress disorder and related reactions is referred to Fletcher (Chapter 6, this volume) for a comprehensive review.

Separation Anxiety Disorder

Core Symptoms

Separation anxiety disorder (SAD) is the only childhood anxiety disorder surviving the latest revision of American psychiatric nomenclature. First described in DSM-III, SAD was retained in the childhood disorders section of DSM-IV (American Psychiatric Association, 1994). The essential feature of SAD is excessive anxiety and fear concerning separation from home or from those to whom the child is attached. Such anxiety must be inappropriate given the child's age and expected developmental level, given that separation anxiety is a normal developmental phenomenon from approximately age 7 months to 6 years (Bernstein & Borchardt, 1991). The core fear of this disorder is evidenced through recurrent distress when separation is anticipated or occurs, avoidance of separation situations, and impairment in important areas of functioning. The primary cognitive distortion displayed by separation-anxious children is an overwhelming fear of losing or becoming separated from major attachment figures through catastrophic means. For example, children with SAD often fear that harm may befall a parent through accident, assault, or other catastrophe, or, that they themselves may become lost or get kidnapped and thus never see their parents again. It is common for

younger children with SAD to report recurrent nightmares characterized by separation themes (Bell-Dolan & Brazeal, 1993).

Separation-anxious children display a wide range of concomitant avoidance behaviors. Avoidance behaviors can be described along a continuum of severity, although no formal classification of SAD-related avoidance exists. Mild avoidance behavior may be characterized by the child wanting the parents to be available by phone during school hours or to be easily accessible when he or she is attending parties or other outings. Parents may notice the child's hesitation to leave home, procrastination during the morning routine, and incessant questioning about schedules. Moderate degrees of avoidance are often characterized by refusal to attend sleepovers or outings requiring separation of several hours from the parents. Younger children become very "clingy" with parents, often following their parents from room to room, whereas older children become reluctant to leave home or engage in peer activities in the absence of their parents (Bell-Dolan & Brazeal, 1993). Children who evidence severe avoidance behavior may refuse to attend school or to sleep in their own rooms and tend to shadow or cling to the parent(s) at all times. These children can become desperate in their attempts to contact parents, feigning illness and concocting fantastic excuses in their effort to escape or avoid the separation situation. It is not uncommon for separation-anxious children to leave schools or camps and attempt to reach home by walking or running away despite the structure and supervision of responsible adults.

The progression from mild to severe avoidance occurs through an insidious process beginning with deceivingly innocuous requests or complaints on the part of the child. For example, complaints of nightmares may first allow the child intermittent access to sleeping with the parents. Within a relatively short period of time, the child will be sleeping with one or both parents on a consistent basis. We have observed this pattern in children up to 13 years of age. Similarly, morning routines become disrupted by somatic complaints, resulting in delaying attendance or sporadic absence from school. This pattern of avoidance reaches its peak when the child clings and cries in anticipation of a separation situation and refuses to attend required activities such as school or to allow the parents to leave for work. The desperation of one child was evidenced in her repeated stories of having communicable ill-

nesses and multiple deaths in her family as reasons for having to leave school early each day. Likewise, physical symptoms progress from nonspecific complaints of stomachaches or headaches (Livingston, Taylor, & Crawford, 1988) to more serious concerns evidenced by children who vomit and experience panic attacks at separation. Observation of children with SAD invariably reveals a pattern to these complaints, as the symptoms occur on a fairly regular basis on weekdays but not on weekends or school holidays. In DSM-IV, children must evidence at least three of eight symptoms for at least 4 weeks to qualify for a diagnosis of SAD. Moreover, the disturbance must be accompanied by clinically significant distress or impairment in social, academic, or other important areas of functioning. Table 5.1 presents DSM-IV and ICD-10 criteria for SAD.

SAD is most often diagnosed in prepubertal children (Bowen, Offord, & Boyle, 1990; Kashani & Orvaschel, 1988), although it can occur at any age (Bell-Dolan & Brazeal, 1993). In one study examining the developmental differences in the expression of separation anxiety symptoms, Francis et al. (1987) found age differences but not gender differences with regard to which DSM-III criteria were most frequently endorsed. Young prepubertal children (ages 5–8) were most likely to report fears of harm befalling attachment figures, nightmares, or school refusal; children ages 9 to 12 endorsed excessive distress at the time of separation; and adolescents (ages 13–16) most often endorsed somatic complaints and school refusal. Moreover, younger children endorsed a greater number of symptoms relative to the adolescents.

Related Symptoms

Children diagnosed with SAD are more likely to report somatic complaints than children diagnosed with phobic disorders (Last, 1991). Children with SAD may also drop out of activities such as clubs or sports if their parents are not actively involved, but not for lack of interest in the activity. Friendships may wane due to the child's repeated refusal to attend activities away from home, although children with SAD in general are socially skilled and well liked by peers (Last, 1989). Academic performance can be compromised by repeated requests to leave class and the child's distress and preoccupation with separation concerns. In extreme form, children with SAD who refuse to attend school miss important social and academic experiences available only in the school setting. At times, efforts are made to provide these children with tutoring and assignments to complete at home, however repeated absences place a child at risk for failure to meet the standards for attendance set forth in state regulations. Consequently, some children are then required to repeat the academic year and, in extreme cases, are remanded to the legal system for compliance with school attendance.

Children who present with SAD often report a variety of specific fears in addition to their separation anxiety such as fears of monsters, animals, insects, and the dark (Last, 1989; Ollendick & Huntzinger, 1990), and such fears may or may not be of phobic proportion (Last, 1989). The most common fear expressed by children with SAD is of getting lost (Last, Francis, & Strauss, 1989). This fear differentiated children with SAD from children diagnosed with overanxious disorder and those with a "phobia of school" (Last et al., 1989). Moreover, the fears endorsed by children with SAD were different from those reported by children in the general population (cf. Last et al., 1989; Ollendick, Matson, & Helsel, 1985). Approximately one-third of children with SAD present with a concurrent overanxious disorder that is usually secondary to the separation anxiety; and one-third of children with SAD present with a comorbid depressive disorder that develops several months following the onset of SAD (Last, Strauss, & Francis, 1987). Separation-anxious children may threaten to harm themselves in attempts to escape or avoid separations; however serious suicidal symptomatology is rarely associated with SAD (Last, 1989). Given the recent nosological changes in the DSM-IV, it will be of interest to see whether children with SAD will meet criteria for generalized anxiety disorder, which has subsumed the former overanxious disorder of childhood.

Social Phobia

Core Symptoms

In DSM-IV, the essential feature of social phobia is a marked and persistent fear of one or more social or performance situations in which the person fears that embarrassment may occur. Upon exposure to the social or performance situation, the person almost invariably experiences an immediate anxiety response that may take the form of a panic attack. Individuals with social phobia may either avoid these situations or endure them with extreme distress. Due to

TABLE 5.1. Diagnostic Criteria for Separation Anxiety Disorder of Childhood

DSM-IV	ICD-10
A. Developmentally inappropriate and excessive anxiety concerning separation from home of from those to whom the individual is attached, as evidenced by three (or more) of the following:	A. At least three of the following must be present:
(1) recurrent excessive distress when separation from home or major attachment figures occurs or is anticipated	(1) unrealistic and persistent worry about possible harm befalling major attachment figures or about the loss of such figures (e.g., fear that they will leave and not return or that the child will not see them again), or persistent concerns about the death of attachment figures
(2) persistent and excessive worry about losing, or about possible harm befalling, major attachment figures	(2) unrealistic and persistent worry that some untoward event will separate the child from a major attachment figure (e.g., the child getting lost, being kidnapped, admitted to hospital, or killed)
(3) persistent and excessive worry that an untoward event will lead to separation from a major attachment figure (e.g., getting lost or being kidnapped)	(3) persistent reluctance or refusal to go to school because of fear over separation from a major attachment figure or in order to stay at home (rather than for other reasons such as fear over events at school)
(4) persistent reluctance or refusal to go to school or elsewhere because of fear of separation	(4) difficulty in separating at night, as manifested by any of the following:
(5) persistently and excessively fearful or reluctant to be alone or without major attachment figures at home or without significant adults in other settings	(a) persistent reluctance or refusal to go to sleep without being near an attachment figure
(6) persistent reluctance or refusal to go to sleep without being near a major attachment figure or to sleep away from home	(b) getting up frequently during the night to check on, or to sleep near, an attachment figure
(7) repeated nightmares involving the theme of separation	(c) persistent reluctance or refusal to sleep away from home
(8) repeated complaints of physical symptoms (such as headaches, stomach aches, nausea, or vomiting) when separation from major attachment figure occurs or is anticipated.	(5) persistent inappropriate fear of being alone, or otherwise without the major attachment figure, at home during the day
	(6) repeated nightmares involving themes of separation
B. The duration of the disturbance is at least 4 weeks.	(7) repeated occurrence of physical symptoms (such as nausea, stomach ache, headache, or vomiting) on occasions that involve separation from a major attachment figure, such as leaving home to go to school or on other occasions involving separation (holidays, camps, etc.)
C. The onset is before age 18 years.	(8) excessive, recurrent distress in anticipation of, during, or immediately following separation from a major attachment figure (as shown by: anxiety, crying, tantrums; persistent reluctance to go away from home; excessive need to talk with parents or desire to return home; misery, apathy, or social withdrawal)
D. The disturbance causes clinically significant distress or impairment in social, academic (occupational), or other important areas of functioning.	
E. The disturbance does not occur exclusively during the course of a Pervasive Developmental Disorder, Schizophrenia, or other Psychotic Disorder and, in adolescents and adults, is not better accounted for by Panic Disorder With Agoraphobia.	B. The criteria for generalized anxiety disorder of childhood (F93.80) are not met.
Specify if: **Early Onset**: if onset occurs before age 6 years	C. Onset is before the age of 6 years.
	D. The disorder does not occur as part of a broader disturbance of emotions, conduct, or personality, or of a pervasive developmental disorder, psychotic disorder, or psychoactive substance use disorder.
	E. Duration of the disorder is at least 4 weeks.

Note. DSM-IV criteria from American Psychiatric Association (1994, p. 113). Copyright 1994 by the American Psychiatric Association. Reprinted by permission. ICD-10 criteria from World Health Organization (1993, pp. 162–163). Copyright 1993 by the World Health Organization. Reprinted by permission.

cognitive–developmental limitations, children and adolescents may fail to recognize that this fear is unreasonable and excessive, although such insight is required to make the diagnosis in adults. In children and adolescents, the symptoms must be present for a minimum of 6 months and cause significant interference in functioning or marked distress in order to warrant the diagnosis. The DSM-III-R diagnosis avoidant disorder of childhood or adolescence has been deleted and subsumed within social phobia in DSM-IV. The essential feature of avoidant disorder was defined as an excessive shrinking from contact with unfamiliar people, for a minimum of 6 months and of sufficient intensity to interfere with the child's ability to foster and perform in peer relationships. Although social phobia and avoidant disorder shared many characteristics in DSM-III-R, the latter did not require that the fear focus on social evaluation but solely on contact with unfamiliar people (Vasey, 1995). In addition to developmental-specific changes in criteria, social phobia in DSM-IV has been expanded to include a fear of situations where the person is exposed to unfamiliar people. DSM-IV requires the qualifier "generalized" subtype if the fear includes most social situations, however, subtype distinctions have not been systematically examined in children and adolescents. Preliminary data suggest that the generalized subtype is the most common form of social phobia in children and adolescents (Albano, DiBartolo, Heimberg, & Barlow, 1995; Beidel & Morris, 1993). DSM-IV diagnostic criteria for social phobia and ICD-10 criteria for social anxiety disorder in children are found in Table 5.2.

Children and adolescents with social phobia often have few friends, are reluctant to join in group activities, and are considered shy and quiet by their parents and peers. In school situations, social-phobic children are extremely fearful of a wide range of situations including reading aloud or speaking in class, asking the teacher for help, unstructured peer encounters, gym activities, working on group projects, taking tests, and eating in the cafeteria. Social-phobic children may be described by teachers as "loners." During unstructured class time, these children are typically off by themselves or in the company of one specific friend. Social-phobic children and adolescents are reluctant to attend extracurricular events such as club meetings or school dances. These children need much encouragement to attend parties or similar social activities. Similar avoidance behavior may be observed in family

situations. Social-phobic children will shrink away from extended family gatherings, avoid answering the telephone or doorbell, and are reticent when meeting friends of family members. Older children may refuse to order for themselves in restaurants. The social-phobic adolescent lags behind peers in meeting age-specific developmental challenges such as dating and seeking employment. It is not uncommon for the parents of these adolescents to lament over not having to deal with typical teenage behavior, such as tying up the telephone lines or always being on the go.

In feared situations, the social-phobic child will experience excessive concerns about embarrassment, negative evaluation, and rejection. Observations and responses of social phobic children reveal their thoughts to be characterized by negative self-focus and self-deprecation and accompanied by a range of autonomic symptoms and sensations (Albano, DiBartolo, et al., 1995; Albano, Marten, Holt, Heimberg, & Barlow, 1995). Complaints of stomachaches and illness are common, especially among younger children. Older children and adolescents become overly concerned with the physical manifestations of anxiety, much like adult social phobics. Fears of blushing or shaking during an oral report, unsteady voice while speaking to peers, or sweating that others may notice serve to magnify the child's social phobia. Research has demonstrated that the aforementioned physical responses of social-phobic children are consistent with those of social-phobic adults (see Beidel & Morris, 1993, 1995). Behaviorally, younger children may manifest excessive clinging and crying, while the older child is likely to shrink from social contact and avoid being the focus of attention.

Social phobia is most often diagnosed in adolescents and rarely diagnosed in children younger than age 10 years (Vasey, 1995). Strauss and Last (1993) examined the sociodemographic differences between simple- ($n = 38$) and social- ($n = 29$) phobic children ages 4 through 17 years. Results indicated that both social- and simple-phobic children were referred for treatment approximately 3 years following the onset of their phobias and that equal proportions of male and female children were referred for both types of disorders (Strauss & Last, 1993). Simple-phobic children were found to be younger and to have an earlier age at onset. Consistent with this pattern, a significantly higher proportion of social-phobic children were found to be postpubertal. These results corroborate retrospective reports of adult social-phobic patients who placed the age

TABLE 5.2. Diagnostic Criteria for Social Phobia

DSM-IV	ICD-10
A. A marked and persistent fear of one or more social or performance situations in which the person is exposed to unfamiliar people or to possible scrutiny by others. The individual fears that he or she will act in a way (or show anxiety symptoms) that will be humiliating or embarrassing. **Note:** In children, there must be evidence of the capacity for age-appropriate social relationships with familiar people and the anxiety must occur in peer settings, not just in interactions with adults.	A. Persistent anxiety in social situations in which the child is exposed to unfamiliar people, including peers, is manifested by socially avoidant behavior.
B. Exposure to the feared social situation almost invariably provokes anxiety, which may take the form of a situationally bound or situationally predisposed Panic Attack. **Note:** In children, the anxiety may be expressed by crying, tantrums, freezing, or shrinking from social situations with unfamiliar people.	B. The child exhibits self-consciousness, embarrassment or overconcern about the appropriateness of his or her behavior when interacting with unfamiliar figures.
C. The person recognizes that the fear is excessive or unreasonable. **Note:** In children, this feature may be absent.	C. There is significant interference with social (including peer) relationships, which are consequently restricted: when new or forced social situations are experienced, they cause marked distress and discomfort as manifested by crying, lack of spontaneous speech, or withdrawal from the social situation.
D. The feared social or performance situations are avoided or else are endured with intense anxiety or distress.	D. The child has satisfying social relationships with familiar figures (family members or peers that he or she knows well).
E. The avoidance, anxious anticipation, or distress in the feared social or performance situation(s) interferes significantly with the person's normal routine, occupational (academic) functioning, or social activities or relationships, or there is marked distress about having the phobia.	E. Onset of the disorder generally coincides with a developmental phase where these anxiety reactions are considered appropriate. The abnormal degree, persistence over time, and associated impairment must be manifest before the age of 6 years.
F. In individuals under age 18 years, the duration is at least 6 months.	F. The criteria for generalized anxiety disorder of childhood (F93.80) are not met.
G. The fear or avoidance is not due to the direct physiological effects of a substance (e.g., a drug of abuse, a medication) or a general medical condition and is not better accounted for by another mental disorder (e.g., Panic Disorder With or Without Agoraphobia, Separation Anxiety Disorder, Body Dysmorphic Disorder, a Pervasive Developmental Disorder, or Schizoid Personality Disorder).	G. The disorder does not occur as part of broader disturbances of emotions, conduct, or personality, or of a pervasive developmental disorder, psychotic disorder, or psychoactive substance use disorder.
H. If a general medical condition or another mental disorder is present, the fear in Criterion A is unrelated to it, e.g., the fear is not of Stuttering, trembling in Parkinson's disease, or exhibiting abnormal eating behavior in Anorexia Nervosa or Bulimia Nervosa.	H. Duration of the disorder is at least 4 weeks.
Specify if: **Generalized:** if the fears include most social situations (also consider the additional diagnosis of Avoidant Personality Disorder)	

Note. DSM-IV criteria from American Psychiatric Association (1994, pp. 416–417). Copyright 1994 by the American Psychiatric Association. Reprinted by permission. ICD-10 criteria from World Health Organization (1993, pp. 163–164). Copyright 1993 by the World Health Organization. Reprinted by permission.

of onset of the disorder in adolescence (Thyer, Parrish, Curtis, Nessa, & Cameron, 1985).

Related Symptoms

Social phobia has recently been identified as the most common anxiety disorder affecting adults (Kessler et al., 1994), yet there is little information in the literature regarding this anxiety disorder in children and adolescents. In all likelihood, social phobia in children and adolescents is underreported and undertreated because these children are not readily recognized as clinically impaired (Albano, DiBartolo, et al., 1995). Because of the nature of the disorder, socially anxious children are more likely to endure anxiety-provoking social situations with distress than to call attention to themselves. Consequently, these children appear to be functioning adequately and, at most, may be considered quiet or shy. In our clinical experience, these children are brought to treatment when the disorder is of sufficient intensity to have interfered with academic progress (such as repeated absences from school) or because the parents report frequent somatic complaints (headaches, stomachaches) or avoidance behaviors that interfere with family and daily activities. Social-phobic children present with significantly higher levels of depressed mood than normal children (Francis, Last, & Strauss, 1992). Moreover, similar to social-phobic adults, these children endorse significantly lower perceptions of cognitive competence and higher trait anxiety (Beidel, 1991). Research has demonstrated that social-phobic children evidence higher state anxiety during an evaluative task than overanxious and normal control children (Beidel, 1991).

Children and adolescents who fear being the focus of attention during meals may refuse to eat during school hours. These children may spend their lunch time in study hall or the library, avoiding the social activity of the school cafeteria. One teenage girl seen at our clinic spent every lunch period during her freshman year of high school sitting in a bathroom stall. Ironically, the attention that these children attempt to avoid often comes back on them in the form of "growling" stomachs caused by hunger. Children and adolescents with social phobia may avoid school for a variety of reasons. Younger children may refuse to attend school because of fears of being teased or rejected by peers or fears of being called on by the teacher to read before the class. School refusal in the adolescent may be prompted by concerns about appearance, especially if the adolescent is required to change clothes in a locker room for gym class. Social-phobic youth go to great lengths to appear calm before their peers and to avoid any sort of attention at all costs. Therefore, children entering the middle school years who are sensitive to negative evaluation may be particularly vulnerable to social phobia. Changing classes, using lockers, larger classrooms, and working in groups will increase the number and types of social-evaluative situations to which a child may be exposed. Hence, middle school children who are school refusing constitute a significant proportion of the children referred to our anxiety clinic with social phobia. For children with significant school refusal behavior, the complications of nonattendance described for children with SAD will also apply.

Obsessive–Compulsive Disorder

Core Symptoms

The essential features of obsessive–compulsive disorder (OCD) are recurrent and intrusive obsessions and compulsions that are time consuming (greater than 1 hour per day) and cause either marked distress for the child or significant impairment in functioning (American Psychiatric Association, 1994). The symptoms of OCD in children and adolescents (Table 5.3) are consistent with those found in adults. Children will report obsessions involving contamination fears, sexual themes, religiosity, or aggressive/violent images. Some children complain of an inability to stop "hearing" intrusive and recurrent songs or rhymes. Fears of catching a life-threatening illness such as cancer or AIDS and excessive concern with morality and religion have also been reported. Compulsions involving repetition, washing, checking, ordering, and arranging are also common in child cases (Flament et al., 1988; Last & Strauss, 1989b; Riddle et al., 1990). Washing rituals have been identified as the most common symptom of OCD, affecting more than 85% of children in the National Institute of Mental Health (NIMH) cohort (Swedo, Rapoport, Leonard, Lenane, & Cheslow, 1989). Excessive washing may be expressed in repeated handwashing and elaborate bathing or shower rituals. Children with OCD often report that a specific washing and grooming pattern must be followed daily, and, if interrupted, then it must be repeated until "perfect."

TABLE 5.3. Diagnostic Criteria for Obsessive-Compulsive Disorder

DSM-IV	ICD-10

A. Either obsessions or compulsions:

Obsessions as defined by (1), (2), (3), and (4):
(1) recurrent and persistent thoughts, impulses, or images that are experienced, at some time during the disturbance, as intrusive and inappropriate and that cause marked anxiety or distress
(2) the thoughts, impulses, or images are not simply excessive worries about real-life problems
(3) the person attempts to ignore or suppress such thoughts, impulses, or images, or to neutralize them with some other thought or action
(4) the person recognizes that the obsessional thoughts, impulses, or images are a product of his or her own mind (not imposed from without as in thought insertion)

Compulsions as defined by (1) and (2):
(1) repetitive behaviors (e.g., hand washing, ordering, checking) or mental acts (e.g., praying, counting, repeating words silently) that the person feels driven to perform in response to an obsession, or according to rules that must be applied rigidly
(2) the behaviors or mental acts are aimed at preventing or reducing distress or preventing some dreaded event or situation; however, these behaviors or mental acts either are not connected in a realistic way with what they are designed to neutralize or prevent or are clearly excessive

B. The obsessions or compulsions cause marked distress, are time consuming (take more than 1 hour a day), or significantly interfere with the person's normal routine, occupational (or academic) functioning, or usual social activities or relationships.

C. If another Axis I disorder is present, the content of the obsessions or compulsions is not restricted to it (e.g., preoccupation with food in the presence of an Eating Disorder; hair pulling in the presence of Trichotillomania; concern with appearance in the presence in the presence of Body Dysmorphic Disorder; preoccupation with drugs in the presence of a Substance Use Disorder; preoccupation with having a serious illness in the presence of Hypochondriasis; preoccupation with sexual urges or fantasies in the presence of a Paraphilia; or guilty ruminations in the presence of Major Depressive Disorder).

D. The disturbance is not due to the direct physiological effects of a substance (e.g., a drug of abuse, a medication) or a general medical condition.

Specify if:
With Poor Insight: if, for most of the time during the current episode, the person does not recognize that the obsessions and compulsions are excessive or unreasonable

---

A. Either obsessions or compulsions (or both) are present on most days for a period of at least 2 weeks.

B. Obsessions (thoughts, ideas, or images) and compulsions (acts) share the following features, all of which must be present:
(1) They are acknowledged as originating in the mind of the patient, and are not imposed by outside persons or influences.
(2) They are repetitive and unpleasant, and at least one obsession or compulsion that is acknowledged as excessive or unreasonable must be present.
(3) The patient tries to resist them (but resistance to very long-standing obsessions or compulsions may be minimal). At least one obsession or compulsion that is unsuccessfully resisted must be present.
(4) Experiencing the obsessive thought or carrying out the compulsive act is not in itself pleasurable. (This should be distinguished from the temporary relief of tension or anxiety.)

C. The obsessions or compulsions cause distress or interfere with the patient's social or individual functioning, usually by wasting time.

D. *Most commonly used exclusion clause.* The obsessions or compulsions are not the result of other mental disorders, such as schizophrenia and related disorders (F20–F29) or mood [affective] disorders (F30–F39).

Note. DSM-IV criteria from American Psychiatric Association (1994, pp. 422–423). Copyright 1994 by the American Psychiatric Association. Reprinted by permission. ICD-10 criteria from World Health Organization (1993, pp. 97–98). Copyright 1993 by the World Health Organization. Reprinted by permission.

Compulsions associated with OCD must be distinguished from normal developmental rituals found in childhood. Nonanxious children will at times display preferences or ritual-like behaviors that are relatively innocuous. For example, arranging dolls or toys in a specified order and nighttime rituals with parents and siblings (e.g., "Goodnight John-Boy," "Goodnight Marybeth") are common in children. What distinguishes OCD from transient rituals or behavioral preferences is the child's distress if the ritual is prevented or the sequence interrupted. Normal developmental rituals are not excessive, differ in content from typical OCD rituals (e.g., washing), and typically dissipate by age 9 years (Leonard, Goldberger, Rapoport, Cheslow, & Swedo, 1990; Leonard et al., 1993). DSM-IV does not require children to recognize the excessive and unreasonable nature of OCD symptoms. Parents may become alert to OCD when the disorder begins to interfere with the child's or the family's functioning. For example, excessive slowness in grooming, touching, and arranging all personal belongings and repeated checking of locks will intrude upon family plans and could interfere with school attendance. Parents may observe their child repeating nonsensical behavioral patterns, such as tapping and touching food before eating or going back and forth through doorways for a certain number of times. One 12-year-old boy at our clinic had to repeat a series of dance-like footsteps prior to entering any room. This behavior caused him considerable embarrassment in peer situations, especially in middle school when he was required to change classes. In children, obsessions without compulsions are relatively rare, as is also true for adults. Conversely, in very young children (ages 6 to 8), rituals typically occur without cognitive obsessions (Swedo et al., 1989). These children may describe an irresistible urge or ritual without an identifiable cognitive precipitant. Interestingly, the literature reveals that in 90% of children with OCD the symptom patterns change over time (Swedo et al., 1989). For example, parents will report early symptoms involving checking locks and cupboards with such behaviors later being replaced by counting or arranging rituals.

Investigators have noted that as many as 50% to 60% of children diagnosed with OCD experience severe impairment in global functioning (Berg et al., 1989; Last & Strauss, 1989b; Whitaker et al., 1990). Such impairment reflects the interference of the disorder in the child's personal, social, and academic life. Children and adolescents with elaborate nighttime rituals are unable to invite friends to sleepovers and, likewise, must refuse to accept similar invitations. With increasing complexity, ordering and arranging rituals become difficult to hide from schoolmates. These rituals become more elaborate and time consuming as they evolve topographically, reflecting ever-increasing anxiety in the child. Homework may become an overwhelming struggle, as a child may spend hours with repeated checking and erasing. A straightforward multiple-choice test can trigger continuous checking rituals due to obsessional doubting, with the child failing to complete the test within the allotted time. Adolescents are particularly challenged by OCD. Instead of gaining independence from the family and testing skills in autonomous activities, adolescents with OCD will find their increased independence extremely anxiety provoking and difficult to master. Rituals may keep the adolescent from engaging in usual teenage activities, such as dating, working, or driving. Moreover, leaving home for college can be particularly challenging due to the impact of leaving a family system that has evolved around the OCD. The potential for being "discovered" by college peers may increase the adolescent's anxiety, and reinforce feelings of uncontrollability and helplessness.

Studies of OCD in children and adolescents place the mean age of onset around 10 years (see Albano, Knox, & Barlow, 1995; Leonard & Rapoport, 1991), although onset has been reported in cases younger than 7 years (Swedo et al., 1989). Onset appears earlier in male than female children, resulting in a predominance of boys in younger samples. However, gender differences disappear by middle childhood, with equal male-to-female ratios reported in older samples of children with OCD (see Albano, Knox, & Barlow, 1995). Interestingly, one study found female adolescents reporting more symptoms of compulsions and male adolescents reporting more obsessions (Valleni-Basile et al., 1994). The early onset of this disorder has also been confirmed by retrospective reports of adults with OCD (Lo, 1967).

Related Symptoms

Results of the extensive NIMH study of childhood OCD found depression to be the most common associated feature of this disorder (Swedo et al., 1989). Higher severity of depressive symp-

toms has been associated with an earlier onset of OCD (Rapoport et al., 1981). Other anxiety disorders, including specific phobia, overanxious disorder, and separation anxiety are often associated with OCD, as well (Last & Strauss, 1989b; March, Leonard, & Swedo, 1995). Although obsessions may involve seemingly bizarre content, thought disorder is not usually an associated feature of OCD (Wolff, 1989). There is a high incidence of OCD in children and adults with Tourette's disorder (35% to 50%); the incidence of Tourette's disorder in children and adults with OCD is lower, with estimates ranging between 5% and 7% (American Psychiatric Association, 1994).

Specific Phobias

Core Symptoms

Specific phobia (formerly "simple" phobia) refers to a marked and persistent fear of circumscribed objects or situations that are unrelated to fears of embarrassment in public or performance situations (social phobia) or fears of having a panic attack (panic disorder). Exposure to the phobic stimulus almost immediately provokes an anxiety response that may take the form of a panic attack. The phobic stimulus is avoided or may be endured with distress. Children may not recognize that the fear is excessive or unreasonable. Moreover, for children and adolescents, the fear must have persisted for 6 months and cause marked interference in functioning or distress to warrant the diagnosis (Table 5.4). Silverman and Rabian (1993) differentiate specific phobias from normal developmental fears in that the phobic reaction is excessive and out of proportion to the demands of the situation, occurs without volition, leads to avoidance, persists over time, and is maladaptive. Moreover, the convictions associated with a phobic reaction persist despite disconfirmatory evidence or attempts to reason with the child or adolescent. Table 5.5 lists the DSM-IV subtypes that have been delineated to indicate the focus of the fear or avoidance in specific phobia.

Common phobias of childhood include heights, darkness, loud noises including thunder, injections, insects, dogs, and other small animals (King, 1993; Silverman & Rabian, 1993; Strauss & Last, 1993). School phobia is also common in children, but the principal motivating condition for the school refusal behavior must be delineated for accurate differential diagnosis and prescrip-

tive treatment planning (Kearney, 1995). A child would be diagnosed with a specific phobia of school if the fear were circumscribed to a particular school-related situation (e.g., fire drills) as opposed to embarrassment or humiliation, in which case social phobia would be the appropriate diagnosis.

Responses of phobic children are manifested across the three components of anxiety (cognitive, behavioral, and physiological). Cognitions of phobic children are characterized by catastrophic predictions of some dreadful event occurring upon exposure to the feared stimulus. Most common are fears of threats to personal safety, such as fearing being bitten by a dog, struck by lightning, or stung by an insect. Phobic children also report anticipatory anxiety in the form of "What if" statements (Silverman & Rabian, 1993). For example, a child who is phobic of thunderstorms may lament "What if it storms on my way to school, and I get struck by lightning?" These catastrophic and worrisome thoughts preoccupy the child and result in extreme distress and interference in functioning. Behaviorally, avoidance is the predominant response of phobic children. Avoidance may take the form of screaming, crying, tantruming, or hiding in anticipation of confronting the feared stimulus. When contact with the phobic stimulus is unavoidable, clinging and begging the parents for help to escape the confrontation is not uncommon. Moreover, phobic children are apprehensive and appear constantly "on the look out" for the feared stimulus. For example, children fearful of thunderstorms may scan the weather channels and watch the sky prior to leaving home. Dog-phobic children may go to great lengths to avoid walking down a street where a dog may be penned behind a fence. Significant avoidance behavior is associated with the intensity of the fear and degree of interference in functioning (Silverman & Rabian, 1993). Simple-phobic children report physiological symptoms consistent with panic sensations, including rapid heart rate, sweating, hyperventilation, shakiness, and stomach upset.

Phobias of animals, darkness, insects, blood, and injury usually begin before age 7 years and are not typically linked to any traumatic event at onset (Marks & Gelder, 1966). These phobias parallel the onset of normal subclinical fears in children, although the phobic diagnosis suggests stability of the fear over time. Our understanding of the patterns of onset for childhood phobias is largely based on the retrospective report of

TABLE 5.4. Diagnostic Criteria for Specific Phobia

DSM-IV	ICD-10
A. Marked and persistent fear that is excessive or unreasonable, cued by the presence or anticipation of a specific object or situation (e.g., flying, heights, animals, receiving and injection, seeing blood).	A. The individual manifests a persistent or recurrent fear (phobia) that is developmentally phase-appropriate (or was so at the time of onset) but that is abnormal in degree and is associated with significant social impairment
B. Exposure to the phobic stimulus almost invariably provokes an immediate anxiety response, which may take the form of a situationally bound or situationally predisposed Panic Attack. **Note:** In children, the anxiety may be expressed by crying, tantrums, freezing, or clinging.	B. The criteria for generalized anxiety disorder of childhood (F93.80) are not met.
C. the person recognizes that the fear is excessive or unreasonable. **Note:** In children, this feature may be absent.	C. The disorder does not occur as part of a broader disturbance of emotions, conduct, or personality, or of a pervasive developmental disorder, psychotic disorder or psychoactive substance use disorder.
D. The phobic situations(s) is avoided or else is endured with intense anxiety or distress.	D. Duration of the disorder is at least 4 weeks.
E. The avoidance, anxious anticipation, or distress in the feared situation(s) interferes significantly with the person's normal routine, occupational (or academic) functioning, or social activities or relationships, or there is marked distress about having the phobia.	
F. In individuals under age 18 years, the duration is at least 6 months.	
G. The anxiety, Panic Attacks, or phobic avoidance associated with the specific object or situation are not better accounted for by another mental disorder, such as Obsessive–Compulsive Disorder (e.g., fear of dirt in someone with an obsession about contamination), Posttraumatic Stress Disorder (avoidance of stimuli associated with a severe stressor), Separation Anxiety Disorder (e.g., avoidance of school), Social Phobia (e.g., avoidance of social situations because of fear of embarrassment), panic Disorder With Agoraphobia, or Agoraphobia Without History of Panic Disorder.	

Specify type:
  Animal Type
  Natural Environment Type (e.g., heights, storms, water)
  Blood–Injection–Injury Type
  Situational Type (e.g., airplanes, elevators, enclosed places)
  Other Type (e.g., phobic avoidance of situations that may lead to choking, vomiting, or contracting an illness; in children, avoidance of loud sounds or costumed characters)

Note. DSM-IV criteria from American Psychiatric Association (1994, pp. 410–411). Copyright 1994 by the American Psychiatric Association. Reprinted by permission. ICD-10 criteria from World Health Organization (1993, p. 163). Copyright 1993 by the World Health Organization. Reprinted by permission.

TABLE 5.5. Specific Phobia Subtypes

Subtype	Description
Animal	Fear cued by animals or insects.
Natural	Fear cued by objects in the natural environment, such as storms, heights, darkness, or water.
Blood–injection–injury	Fear cued by seeing blood or an injury, or receiving an injection or other invasive medical procedure.
Situational	Fear cued by a specific situation such as public transportation, tunnels, bridges, elevators, flying, driving, or enclosed places.
Other	Fear cued by stimuli such as loud noise, costumed characters; fear and avoidance of such situations as vomiting, choking, or contracting an illness.

adult phobic patients. For example, adult phobic patients place the onset of animal phobia at 7 years, blood phobia at 9 years, and dental phobia at 12 years (Öst, 1987). Similarly, Liddell and Lyons (1978) reported the age of onset for blood phobia to be 8.8 years, dental phobia, 10.8 years, and thunderstorm phobia, 11.9 years. Evidence suggests that specific phobias occur across the lifespan, with elevations between the ages of 10 and 13 years (Strauss & Last, 1993).

Related Symptoms

Typically, the phobic child is brought to treatment when the intensity of the phobia causes significant interference with normal routine and functioning within the family. Some specific phobia stimuli can be avoided with little disruption in routine. For example, small animals can be kept out of sight of a phobic child visiting a relative's home. However, when a particular situation cannot be altered or avoided, the phobic child can become oppositional and aggressive in his or her struggle for escape. It is not uncommon for several adults to hold down a raging needle-phobic child for required injections. Children attempting to avoid specific situations may hide from parents, shout in rage, and attempt to punch or kick to avoid the stimulus. The intensity of such behavior represents the degree of distress experienced by the child and serves to reinforce frustration and helplessness on the part of the parents.

A vasovagal fainting response occurs in approximately 70% to 75% of blood-injection-injury type specific phobias (American Psychiatric Association, 1994; Antony, 1994). Estimates specific to children and adolescents are lacking at present. This physiological response is characterized by an initial brief acceleration of heart rate, followed by an immediate deceleration of heart rate and drop in blood pressure. This deceleration is unique to this subtype of specific phobia and is in contrast to the usual sustained acceleration of heart rate found in other specific phobia subtypes. In severe cases, children and adolescents who display this response may faint on exposure to stimuli that evoke images of blood or injury. Reading about bloody scenes in stories, viewing blood or injuries on television, or hearing about accidents and trauma in news reports may all evoke this fainting response. In a severe case of a 16-year-old girl, fainting occurred on average of four to eight times per week (Albano, Mitchell, Zarate, & Barlow, 1992). Even common everyday sayings, such as "Cut it out!" would evoke a sufficiently strong visual image of blood resulting in the fainting response for this particular adolescent. In this case, in addition to the potential detrimental effects of avoiding medical and dental care, this child was exposed to excessive teasing and ridicule from peers.

Generalized Anxiety Disorder (Overanxious Disorder)

Core Symptoms

The essential feature of generalized anxiety disorder (GAD) is excessive and uncontrollable anxiety and worry about a number of events and activities, occurring more days than not, for at least 6 months. In addition, diagnosis of GAD in children requires the presence of at least one accompanying physiological symptom. Table 5.6 outlines the diagnostic criteria for GAD.

Whether children and adolescents will "fit" with the new GAD criteria remains to be evaluated. In DSM-IV, the former overanxious disorder of childhood and adolescence (OAD) was subsumed under the revised GAD criteria. Nevertheless, our understanding of the symptoms and clinical presentation of GAD in youth is based largely on studies of children with OAD. The essential feature of OAD involved worry about a number of general life concerns, including the future, past behavior, and competence in

TABLE 5.6. Diagnostic Criteria for Generalized Anxiety Disorder

DSM-IV	ICD-10
A. Excessive anxiety and worry (apprehensive expectation), occurring more days than not for at least 6 months, about a number of events or activities (such as work or school performance).	*Note:* In children and adolescents the range of complaints by which the general anxiety is manifest is often more limited than in adults (see F41.1), and the specific symptoms of autonomic arousal are often less prominent. For these individuals, the following alternative set of criteria can be used if preferred:
B. The person finds it difficult to control the worry.	
C. The anxiety and worry are associated with three (or more) of the following six symptoms (with at least some symptoms present for more days than not for the past 6 months). **Note:** Only one item is required in children. (1) restlessness or feeling keyed up or on edge (2) being easily fatigued (3) difficulty concentrating or mind going blank (4) irritability (5) muscle tension (6) sleep disturbance (difficulty falling or staying asleep, or restless unsatisfying sleep)	A. Extensive anxiety and worry (apprehensive expectation) occur on at least half of the total number of days over a period of at least 6 months, the anxiety and worry referring to at least several events or activities (such as work or school performance). B. The individual finds it difficult to control the worry. C. The anxiety and worry are associated with at least three of the following symptoms (with at least two symptoms present on at least half of the total number of days): (1) restlessness, feeling "keyed up" or "on edge" (as shown for example, by feelings of mental tension combined with an inability to relax); (2) feeling tired, "worn out", or easily fatigued because of worry or anxiety; (3) difficulty in concentrating, or mind "going blank"; (4) irritability; (5) muscle tension; (6) sleep disturbance (difficulty in falling or staying asleep, or restless, unsatisfying sleep) because of worry or anxiety.
D. The focus of the anxiety and worry is not confined to features of an Axis I disorder, e.g., the anxiety or worry is not about having a Panic Attack (as in Panic Disorder), being embarrassed in public (as in Social Phobia), being contaminated (as in Obsessive–Compulsive Disorder), being away from home or close relatives (as in Separation Anxiety Disorder), gaining weight (as in Anorexia Nervosa), having multiple physical complaints (as in Somatization Disorder), or having a serious illness (as in Hypochondriasis), and the anxiety and worry do not occur exclusively during Posttraumatic Stress Disorder.	D. The multiple anxieties and worries occur across at least two situations, activities, contexts, or circumstances. Generalized anxiety does not present as discrete paraxysmal episodes (as in panic disorder), nor are the main worries confined to a single, major theme (as in separation anxiety disorder or phobic disorder of childhood). (When more focused anxiety is identified in the broader context of a generalized anxiety, generalized anxiety disorder takes precedence over other anxiety disorders.)
E. The anxiety, worry, or physical symptoms cause clinically significant distress or impairment in social, occupational, or other important areas of functioning.	E. Onset occurs in childhood or adolescence (before the age of 18 years).
F. The disturbance is not due to the direct physiological effects of a substance (e.g., a drug of abuse, a medication) or a general medical condition (e.g., hyperthyroidism) and does not occur exclusively during a Mood Disorder, a Psychotic Disorder, or a Pervasive Developmental Disorder.	F. The anxiety, worry, or physical symptoms cause clinically significant distress or impairment in social, occupational, or other important areas of functioning. G. The disorder is not due to the direct effects of a substance (e.g., psychoactive substances, medication) or a general medical condition (e.g., hyperthyroidism) and does not occur exclusively during a mood disorder, psychotic disorder, or pervasive developmental disorder.

Note. DSM-IV criteria from American Psychiatric Association (1994, pp. 435–436). Copyright 1994 by the American Psychiatric Association. Reprinted by permission. ICD-10 criteria from World Health Organization (1993, pp. 164–166). Copyright 1993 by the World Health Organization. Reprinted by permission.

areas such as sports, academics, and peer relationships. Children with OAD are typically described as "little worriers" by adult caretakers.

Unrealistic and excessive worrying about future events was present in over 95% of a clinic sample of children with OAD (Strauss, Lease, Last, & Francis, 1988). Future-oriented worries focus on a variety of situations and issues including the start of school, changes in family routine such as an upcoming vacation, social events and activities, and family members' health. It is not uncommon for these children to worry about a number of adult concerns as well, such as the family finances (Bell-Dolan & Brazeal, 1993). Children with OAD report worrying about being good at school, athletics, social relationships, and so on, to the point of being perfectionistic (Bell-Dolan & Brazeal, 1993; Strauss, 1990). Consequently, children with OAD place exceedingly high standards for achievement on themselves and are brutal in their self-reproach if they fail to meet these standards. In fact, worry associated with OAD persists in the absence of objective cause for concern. For example, children and adolescents with OAD who receive As on homework and tests will continue to worry about failure or falling below some self-generated standard.

Children with OAD are described as markedly self-conscious and require frequent reassurance from others (Eisen & Kearney, 1995; Silverman & Ginsburg, 1995; Strauss, 1990). Similar to children with specific phobia, "What if" statements also pervade these children's thinking. Unlike specific phobics however, cognitive distortions of OAD children are fairly continuous and not circumscribed to a particular stimulus or situation. Children with OAD overestimate the likelihood of negative consequences, exaggerate the predicted outcome to a catastrophic degree, and underestimate their ability to cope with less than ideal circumstances. Research has demonstrated that although nonreferred children also worry about low-frequency events (Silverman, LaGreca, & Wasserstein, 1995), children with OAD may not recognize that such events have a low probability of occurrence. The degree of worry evidenced by children with OAD ranges from several times per week to almost constant ruminations.

Studies examining DSM-III and DSM-III-R diagnoses suggested that OAD can begin at any age in childhood, with one study reporting OAD present as early as age 4 years (Beitchman, Wekerle, & Hood, 1987). The reported mean age of onset of OAD ranges from 10.8 years (Last, Strauss, & Francis, 1987) to 13.4 years (Last, Hersen, et al., 1987). OAD occurs in approximately 3% of children, whereas estimates in adolescents range from 6% to 7% (see Bell-Dolan & Brazeal, 1993). In clinic-referred samples, children with OAD are older than children with SAD or specific phobia (e.g., Albano, Chorpita, DiBartolo, & Barlow, 1995). Strauss, Lease, et al. (1988) examined the developmental characteristics of children with OAD and found that older children present with a higher total number of overanxious symptoms and self-report significantly higher levels of anxiety and depression than younger children.

Related Symptoms

In a study examining the developmental characteristics of OAD, Strauss, Lease, et al. (1988) found a sample of 55 overanxious children to present with a high rate of concurrent anxiety and affective disorders. Younger children (ages 5–11) tended to present with comorbid separation-anxiety concerns and attention-deficit disorder, whereas major depression and simple (specific) phobia were more common to the older children with OAD (ages 12–19; Strauss, Lease, et al., 1988). Somatic complaints are also found in children and adolescents diagnosed with OAD (Last, 1991). Headaches, stomachaches, muscle tension, sweating, and trembling are among the most commonly reported physical complaints of these children (Eisen & Engler, 1995). Accordingly, many children with OAD are referred for treatment by their pediatricians or by gastrointestinal specialists (Bell-Dolan & Brazeal, 1993). The criteria for OAD in DSM-III-R were rather vague with regard to somatic complaints. A child could endorse some physical complaint for which no physical basis could be established (e.g., headaches or stomachaches), or endorse marked feelings of tension or inability to relax. However, the child could meet full criteria for OAD in the absence of any somatic symptom, because DSM-III-R required four of seven symptoms for diagnosis (only two were somatic in nature). DSM-IV outlines six specific somatic symptoms of which one is required to make the diagnosis in children and adolescents. Headaches and stomachaches are conspicuously missing from this list. One avenue of investigation for psychopathology research is to examine whether the somatic symptom criteria will pose

problems in assigning the new GAD diagnosis to children.

Panic Disorder

Core Symptoms

Until recently, panic disorder had been considered an anxiety disorder of adulthood that did not occur in children and only rarely occurred in adolescents (see Kearney & Silverman, 1992; Moreau & Weissman, 1992; Nelles & Barlow, 1988). Because of the cognitive nature of this disorder, children were thought to be incapable of forming catastrophic misinterpretations of bodily sensations. However, literature is accumulating supporting the existence of panic attacks and panic disorder in youth (e.g., Griegel, Albano, & Barlow, 1991; Moreau & Follett, 1993; Ollendick, 1995; Ollendick, Mattis, & King, 1994; Vitiello, Behar, Wolfson, & Delaney, 1987; Vitiello, Behar, Wolfson, & McLeer, 1990).

Panic disorder is defined by the occurrence of at least one unexpected panic attack followed by a minimum of 1 month of any one (or more) of the following: persistent fear of experiencing future attacks, worry about the implications of the attack or its consequences, or a significant change in behavior related to the attacks (American Psychiatric Association, 1994). In addition, the panic attacks cannot result from the direct physiological effects of a substance, such as medications or caffeine, or a general medical condition (e.g., hyperthyroidism). Table 5.7 outlines the diagnostic criteria for panic disorder.

The diagnosis of panic disorder in children may be difficult to establish because of the cognitive-developmental limitations of the child. Young children report a fear of becoming sick, without specific reference to autonomic symptoms and misinterpretation of such symptoms. In our clinical practice, prepubescent children almost never verbalize specific fears of dying, going crazy, or losing control because of the presence of physiological symptoms. More often these children report nonspecific anxiety about suddenly becoming ill or express a fear of vomiting that the children find difficult to predict or control. In early adolescence, fears of specific autonomic symptoms begin to occur, including fears of breathlessness, tachycardia, depersonalization, and dizziness. According to Moreau and Follett (1993), the most commonly reported symptoms of panic in children and adolescents include trembling and shaking, palpitations, dizziness/faintness, dyspnea, sweating, and (in older children) fears of dying or losing control. Young children typically describe their emotional states in terms of physical illness. Thus, because of the cognitive nature of depersonalization (feeling out of one's body), this symptom is rarely reported by prepubescent children (Moreau & Follett, 1993). In addition, several investigators have noted the co-occurrence of panic attacks and refusal to eat due to fear of vomiting in children and adolescents (Ballenger, Carek, Steele, & Cornish-McTighe, 1989; Bradley & Hood, 1993; Manassis & Kalman, 1990).

There is a serious paucity of literature examining age and gender patterns in panic disorder relative to children. The extant literature is comprised largely of case reports and uncontrolled studies (e.g., Alessi & Magen, 1988; Alessi, Robbins, & Dilsaver, 1987; Ballenger et al., 1989; Hayward et al., 1992; Moreau, Weissman, & Warner, 1989; Vitiello et al., 1990). In a recent review of this literature, Ollendick and colleagues (1994) suggested that panic *attacks* are common among adolescents, with 40% to 60% of adolescents surveyed reporting having experienced a panic attack. Panic attacks and panic disorder occur in children but with less frequency than in adolescents (Ollendick et al., 1994). Results of an investigation of panic attacks in younger children revealed an interesting developmental trend (Hayward et al., 1992). Of 754 children aged 10.3 to 15.6 years, the increased occurrence of panic attacks was associated with pubertal progression as assessed through the Tanner self-staging method. Overall, panic attacks were more commonly reported by female subjects evidencing advanced pubertal development, regardless of age (Hayward et al., 1992). This apparent association of pubertal development and panic attacks warrants further study. Consistent with the gender pattern for adults with the disorder, panic disorder appears to be more common among female than male adolescents (Kearney & Allan, 1995; Ollendick et al., 1994).

Related Symptoms

In addition to panic symptoms, children and adolescents with panic disorder may display concomitant agoraphobia, defined as the fear of being in situations from which escape may be difficult or embarrassing, or in which help is not readily available in the event of a panic attack (American Psychiatric Association, 1994). Consequently,

these children and adolescents may attempt to avoid situations such as movie theaters, malls, playgrounds, or being home alone. The child's avoidance may also generalize to school situations such as riding the bus, gym class, or an outright refusal to attend school. Typically a parent or close friend becomes the child's "safety person," whereby activities are endured in the presence of this person. To ensure attendance, a parent may attempt to accompany the child during the school day. Although this behavior resembles separation anxiety disorder, the differential diagnosis must be made according to the focus of the child's fear. In panic disorder, the fear is of the physical sensations accompanying the panic attack or having the attack itself and not triggered by the fear of becoming lost or separated from a parent or loved one.

DEFINITIONAL AND DIAGNOSTIC ISSUES

When one is evaluating a child or adolescent patient with anxiety, care must be rendered in differentiating normal from pathological anxiety conditions. Anxiety is a basic human emotion, characterized by a diffuse, uncomfortable sense of apprehension, and often accompanied by autonomic symptoms (Barlow, 1988). At its basic level, anxiety serves an adaptive function to alert an individual to novel or threatening situations and, thus, to allow the person to confront or flee such situations. Thus, anxiety is also an integral part of the normal developmental progression from dependency to autonomy. Through repeated exposure to new and untried situations, individuals become "experienced" in the cycle of anxious arousal and the resultant habituation and abatement of sensations. For example, anxiety is considered normal for young children who confront situations such as the dark, separation from caretakers, or the first day of school. Similarly, adolescents will experience anxiety when learning to drive, or on their first date or job interview. Pathological anxiety, however, may be distinguished from normal, expected levels of anxiety on the basis of the intractability of the anxiety, the pervasiveness of the fear and avoidance, and the degree of interference in the child's daily functioning (Albano, DiBartolo, et al., 1995; Barrios & Hartmann, 1988). Our current diagnostic classification system attempts to account for each of these variables in the criteria for the individual anxiety disorders. Specific time intervals for the presence of significant symptomatology are specified within each diagnostic category. In addition, evidence of distress and significant interference in the child's normal routines (academic, social, occupational) are also required. These criteria alert the clinician to examine the presenting complaint in terms of normal, transient anxiety and fear experiences that are an expected and necessary part of development.

Early DSM systems represented the categorical classification approach, attempting to separate disorders into clinically derived and mutually exclusive diagnostic classes. The DSM system has been widely used by clinicians and researchers, fostering efficient means of communication among health care professionals. There exists considerable debate as to the usefulness of categorical systems such as DSM, largely due to the dissatisfaction with the categorical approach to psychopathology in general (e.g., Achenbach, 1980, 1988; Rutter & Tuma, 1988). Although a thorough review of the criticisms of the categorical approach is beyond the scope of this chapter, two problems in particular bear specifically on the diagnosis of children and adolescents. First, throughout early DSM versions, there existed a substantial amount of symptom overlap and heterogeneity among disorders. Such overlap raised questions regarding the discriminative validity and, ultimately, the clinical utility of a particular disorder. Perrin and Last (1995) reviewed the extant literature on the diagnostic comorbidity among DSM childhood anxiety disorders, concluding that the high degree of comorbidity reflected an "artificial" classification system and one only "loosely based on empirical research" (p. 431). Second, earlier DSM editions and similar categorical systems relied on the dichotomous nature of diagnosis. Categorical systems are explicit in that a certain number of symptoms must be present to assign a diagnosis. If symptoms of several different diagnoses are present in a child, but the child does not display the minimum number of required symptoms for any one diagnosis, then no diagnosis is assigned. Consequently, the child fails to meet the "threshold" (Frances, Widiger, & Fyer, 1990) for a disorder. Among the problems with this threshold approach is that appropriate treatment planning can be seriously compromised (Eisen & Kearney, 1995) because of the failure to identify subclinical and prodromal syndromes.

One alternative to categorical classification is an empirically derived dimensional system of classifi-

TABLE 5.7. Diagnostic Criteria for Panic Disorder

DSM-IV	ICD-10

DSM-IV

Panic Attack

Note: A Panic Attack is not a codable disorder. Code the specific diagnosis in which the Panic Attack occurs (e.g., Panic Disorder with Agoraphobia)

A discrete period of intense fear or discomfort, in which four (or more) of the following symptoms developed abruptly and reached a peak within 10 minutes:

(1) palpitations, pounding heart, or accelerated heart rate
(2) sweating
(3) trembling or shaking
(4) sensations of shortness of breath or smothering
(5) feeling of choking
(6) chest pain or discomfort
(7) nausea or abdominal distress
(8) feeling dizzy, unsteady, lightheaded, or faint
(9) derealization (feelings of unreality) or depersonalization (being detached from oneself)
(10) fear of losing control or going crazy
(11) fear of dying
(12) chills or hot flushes

Panic Disorder without Agoraphobia

A. Both (1) and (2):

(1) recurrent unexpected Panic Attacks
(2) at least one of the attacks has been followed by 1 month (or more) of one (or more) of the following:

(a) persistent concern about having additional attacks
(b) worry about the implications of the attack or its consequences (e.g., losing control, having a heart attack, "going crazy")
(c) a significant change in behavior related to the attacks

B. Absence of Agoraphobia.

C. The Panic Attacks are not due to the direct physiological effects of a substance (e.g., a drug of abuse, a medication) or a general medical condition (e.g., hyperthyroidism).

D. The Panic Attacks are not better accounted for by another mental disorder, such as Social Phobia (e.g., occurring on exposure to feared social situations), Specific Phobia (e.g., on exposure to a specific phobic situation), Obsessive–Compulsive Disorder (e.g., on exposure to dirt in someone with an obsession about contamination), Posttraumatic Stress Disorder (e.g., in response to stimuli associated with a severe stressor), or Separation Anxiety Disorder (e.g., in response to being away from home or close relatives).

ICD-10

A. The individual experiences recurrent panic attacks that are not consistently associated with a specific situation or object and that often occur spontaneously (i.e. the episodes are unpredictable). The panic attacks are not associated with marked exertion or with exposure to dangerous or life-threatening situations.

B. A panic attack is characterized by all of the following:

(1) it is a discrete episode of intense fear or discomfort;
(2) it starts abruptly;
(3) it reaches a maximum within a few minutes and lasts at least some minutes;
(4) at least four of the symptoms listed below must be present, one of which must be from items (a) to (d):

Autonomic arousal symptoms

(a) palpitations or pounding heart, or accelerated heart rate;
(b) sweating;
(c) trembling or shaking;
(d) dry mouth (not due to medication or dehydration);

Symptoms involving chest and abdomen

(e) difficulty in breathing;
(f) feeling of choking;
(g) chest pain or discomfort;
(h) nausea or abdominal distress (e.g. churning in stomach);

Symptoms involving mental state

(i) feeling dizzy, unsteady, faint, or light-headed;
(j) feelings that objects are unreal (derealization), or that the self is distant or "not really here" (depersonalization);
(k) fear of losing control, "going crazy," or passing out;
(l) fear of dying;

General symptoms

(m) hot flushes or cold chills;
(n) numbness or tingling sensations.

The range of individual variation in both content and severity is so great that two grades, moderate and severe, may be specified, if desired, with a fifth character:

F41.00 Panic disorder, moderate
At least four panic attacks in a 4-week period.

F41.01 Panic disorder, severe
At least four panic attacks per week over a 4-week period.

TABLE 5.7 (continued)

DSM-IV	ICD-10

<u>Panic Disorder with Agoraphobia</u>

A. Both (1) and (2):

   (1) recurrent unexpected Panic Attacks

   (2) at least one of the attacks has been followed by 1 month (or more) of one (or more) of the following:

     (a) persistent concern about having additional attacks

     (b) worry about the implications of the attack or its consequences (e.g., losing control, having a heart attack, "going crazy")

     (c) a significant change in behavior related to the attacks

B. The presence of Agoraphobia.

C. The Panic Attacks are not due to the direct physiological effects of a substance (e.g., a drug of abuse, a medication) or a general medical condition (e.g., hyperthyroidism).

D. The Panic Attacks are not better accounted for by another mental disorder, such as Social Phobia (e.g., occurring on exposure to feared social situations), Specific Phobia (e.g., on exposure to a specific phobic situation), Obsessive–Compulsive Disorder (e.g., on exposure to dirt in someone with an obsession about contamination), Posttraumatic Stress Disorder (e.g., in response to stimuli associated with a severe stressor), or Separation Anxiety Disorder (e.g., in response to being away from home or close relatives).

<u>Agoraphobia without History of Panic Disorder</u>

A. The presence of Agoraphobia related to fear of developing panic-like symptoms (e.g., dizziness or diarrhea).

B. Criteria have never been met for Panic Disorder.

C. The disturbance is not due to the direct physiological effects of a substance (e.g., a drug of abuse, a medication) or a general medical condition.

D. If an associated general medical condition is present, the fear described in Criterion A is clearly in excess of that usually associated with the condition.

Note. DSM-IV criteria from American Psychiatric Association (1994, pp. 395, 402, 404–405). Copyright 1994 by the American Psychiatric Association. Reprinted by permission. ICD-10 criteria from World Health Organization (1993, pp. 94–95). Copyright 1993 by the World Health Organization. Reprinted by permission.

cation. Dimensional systems are based on a quantitative analysis of those behaviors or symptoms that are correlated and cluster together most often (Eisen & Kearney, 1995). The best-known dimensional approach is Achenbach's internalizing–externalizing system (Achenbach, 1991, 1993; Achenbach & Edelbrock, 1983). Based on extensive empirical studies using the Child Behavior Checklist (CBCL; Achenbach, 1993), two broadband factors, "internalizing/overcontrolled" and "externalizing/undercontrolled" have been delineated. An anxious child may score highest on the "anxious/depressed" and "somatic complaints" narrow-band factors, with lesser loadings on conceptually unrelated factors such as delinquent and aggressive behavior. Developmental variables are accounted for in this system, which also provides clinical profiles for specific populations of children and adolescents. Although this system is grounded in empirical research, it has the disadvantage of not being widely adopted by clinicians and researchers. An additional disadvantage of the system is the high correlation between the two broadband factors when psychopathology is extensive (Hinshaw, 1992).

Clinical researchers are moving toward a combined approach to understanding psychopathology. For example, the current approach toward defining school refusal behavior represents a combination of an empirically derived categorical and dimensional system (Kearney & Silverman, 1993). Briefly, school refusal behavior is hypothesized to occur along four functional dimensions: (1) avoidance of negative affectivity (e.g., anxiety and depression), (2) escape from aversive social and/or evaluative situations (e.g., peer interactions, tests), (3) attention seeking (e.g., disruptive behavior), and (4) positive tangible reinforcement (e.g., watching television and sleeping late rather than attending class). Conditions 1 and 2 describe children who refuse school for negative reinforcement, whereas conditions 3 and 4 describe children who refuse school for positive reinforcement (Kearney, 1995). This functional approach toward defining school refusal behavior (Kearney & Silverman, 1996) is grounded in sound psychometric properties and allows for individual and developmental differences. Moreover, the system bridges the gap between assessment and treatment planning. The development of treatment goals and focus of treatment interventions can be derived from knowledge about the function of the school refusal behavior. Specifically, treatment success is enhanced by adapting specific therapeutic procedures and foci to specific functional components of the child's problem (e.g., Kearney & Silverman, 1990).

Research on the classification of psychological disorders has contributed to the delineations represented in the fourth revision of DSM. DSM-IV is based on the prototypical approach to classification (Barlow, 1992). Similar to the functional model of school refusal behavior, the prototypical approach also combines some features of both the categorical and dimensional approach. Briefly, this approach identifies essential symptoms of a disorder and concurrently allows for nonessential variations of symptoms to occur. Although an improvement over the previous DSM system, problems continue to accompany diagnosis with DSM-IV. First, the problem of diagnostic comorbidity as described above continues to blur diagnostic decisions (Barlow & Durand, 1995). Second, DSM-IV fails to provide operational definitions for the individual diagnostic criteria. For example, the term "persistent" is used throughout the criteria for separation anxiety disorder (see Table 5.1). As noted by Kearney, Eisen, and Schaefer (1995), specific guidelines for defining the term "persistent" are not provided in DSM, leaving the criteria open to interpretation and variability across clinicians. Third, DSM also fails to consider the variability of each diagnostic category across different developmental periods. With the exception of DSM disorders of childhood or adolescence, diagnostic criteria are based on the clinical presentation of each disorder in adults. DSM systems have repeatedly been criticized as being highly "adultomorphistic" (e.g., Phillips, Draguns, & Bartlett, 1975), where adult parameters of a disorder are automatically applied to children and adolescents. Thus, the reliability and validity of diagnoses as applied to children become questionable, especially when developmental fluctuations are left up to individual clinician judgment.

Clearly, the classification of psychopathology in children and adolescents remains controversial and represents a fast growing and exciting field (Kearney, Eisen, & Schaefer, 1995). The process of refining the aforementioned systems of classification will continue as our science advances. Of critical importance for improving the reliability and validity of diagnosis in children will be greater attention toward the explication of developmental factors and variations in symptoms, along with studies focused on the expres-

sion of such symptoms in nonreferred children. The internalizing/externalizing system and the functional approach toward school refusal behavior were developed in response to the dissatisfaction with and inadequacy of categorical approaches to defining psychopathology in youth. Nevertheless, the DSM system continues to be the most widely utilized classification approach to psychopathology. Hopefully, DSM-IV prototypical approach will stimulate progress toward refining and understanding fully the nature and presentation of these disorders in children.

DEVELOPMENTAL COURSE AND PROGNOSIS

Although anxiety symptoms are common in children and adolescents, information on the natural history of anxiety disorders in children and adolescents is sparse (Moreau & Follett, 1993). The extant literature is limited by a variety of methodological constraints, including small sample size, failure to conduct blind diagnostic assessments, lack of adequate follow-up assessments, and absence of appropriate psychiatric and nonreferred control groups. Nevertheless, evidence is accumulating to suggest that certain anxiety disorders in childhood begin relatively early and, if left untreated, may span a chronic course into adulthood.

Separation anxiety disorder has an acute and early onset (Last, Hersen, et al., 1987). Onset most often occurs following a major stressor, such as the start of school, death of a parent, or move to a new school or neighborhood (Last, 1989). The onset of SAD has been tied to developmental transition periods, such as entering kindergarten or making the change from elementary school to junior high school. Prolonged physical illness, causing the child to be housebound and away from school or peer activities, may also precipitate the disorder. In such cases, the child may continue to complain of physical symptoms despite resolution of the illness. Few studies have tracked the long-term course of SAD in children (Cantwell & Baker, 1989; Keller et al., 1992), however clinical experience suggests a variable course. Recurrence is typically tied to school holidays, prolonged illness, or a change in residence and/or school. Complete remission of all signs and symptoms may extend for years, with a relapse seeming to occur from "out of the blue" (see Black, 1995). However, clinical observation suggests that relapse occurs during times of signif-

icant developmental changes and demands or periods of increased stress. It has been suggested that children who do not recover completely from SAD may be at greater risk for developing anxiety or depressive disorders during adulthood (Black, 1995). Several studies suggest that children with SAD are at increased risk of developing depression and social phobia and that girls with SAD are especially at risk for panic disorder and agoraphobia (Beiderman et al., 1993b; Black & Robbins, 1990; Gittleman & Klein, 1985; Moreau & Follett, 1993).

In contrast to the wealth of literature documenting the natural course of fears in children, very little empirical research has been conducted on the course of phobic disorders in childhood. In a classic and widely cited study, Agras, Chapin, and Oliveau (1972) followed a community sample of phobic individuals comprised of 10 children under the age of 20 years, and 20 adults. Subjects were followed over a 5-year period during which none received treatment for his or her phobia. Results suggested that many phobic conditions resolve without active intervention and that children improve more rapidly than adults. Ollendick (1979) subsequently criticized the Agras et al. (1972) data, noting that the children were not completely asymptomatic over the course of the follow-up assessment. Similarly, in a study of 62 children (ages 6 to 15 years) treated for phobias, Hampe, Noble, Miller, and Barrett (1973) found 7% of the sample to exhibit phobias at 2-year follow-up. Overall, these studies suggest that symptoms of phobias persist over time for a proportion of children and adolescents and are consistent with the retrospective reports of adults with phobias (e.g., Öst, 1987; Thyer, Parrish, et al., 1985). These data must be interpreted with caution, however. At the time of these investigations, children were not assessed using DSM criteria, and each investigation was limited by methodological constraints. Moreover, because social phobia was not examined in these early studies, the natural course of this disorder in children has yet to be systematically investigated.

The literature on the course of childhood OCD is perhaps most unsettling, given the consistent finding supporting the chronicity and intractability of this anxiety disorder in youth. As in adults, OCD appears to follow a chronic but fluctuating course (Swedo et al., 1989). In a 2-year epidemiological follow-up study of adolescents, 31% of those who had received an initial current or lifetime diagnosis of OCD received a current diag-

nosis at follow-up, and an additional 25% received a residual diagnosis of subclinical OCD symptoms. Of those who had received an initial current or lifetime subclinical OCD diagnosis, 10% received a current diagnosis of OCD, and an additional 40% received a residual diagnosis of subclinical OCD symptoms (Berg et al., 1989). Recently, Leonard et al. (1993) reported the results of a prospective 2-to 7-year follow-up study of 54 pediatric OCD patients. Subjects in this study participated in controlled pharmacological treatment followed by a variety of uncontrolled treatments including behavior therapy. At follow-up, 43% of the subjects continued to meet diagnostic criteria for OCD, and only 11% were considered totally asymptomatic. Seventy percent of subjects were still taking psychoactive medication at follow-up. Overall, the authors considered the group improved from baseline despite continued OCD symptomatology and reported only 10 subjects (19%) as unchanged or worse. This study well illustrates the chronicity of OCD. Recently, leading investigators summarized the literature on childhood OCD (March et al., 1995), concluding that the majority of pediatric OCD patients, with a combination of pharmacological and cognitive-behavioral therapy, "can expect substantial improvement but not complete remission of symptoms over time" (p. 257).

With regard to the more traditional adult disorders, generalized anxiety disorder (GAD) and panic disorder with or without agoraphobia (PDA), information concerning the history and course of these disorders in youth is practically nonexistent. The limited data on GAD, interpreted from studies of overanxious children, suggest that the disorder is unstable over time (e.g., Cantwell & Baker, 1989; Last, Hersen, et al., 1987; Last, Perrin, Hersen, & Kazdin, 1992). For example, in a 5-year follow-up study of eight children diagnosed with OAD, Cantwell and Baker (1989) found an equal percentage of children either maintained or did not meet the diagnosis (25% each). However, the majority of the sample (50%) received an alternative diagnosis at follow-up. This finding may be suggestive of OAD being a prodromal form of other disorders. The natural course of panic disorder in children and adolescents has not been studied. Investigations with adult patients suggest that panic disorder tends to be a chronic and recurrent illness (see Barlow, 1988; Breier, Charney, & Heninger, 1986; Keller & Baker, 1992). History of childhood anxiety disorders (in addition to comorbid depression and personality disorder) has been associated with the chronicity and stability of

panic disorder in adults (Pollack, Otto, Rosenbaum, & Sachs, 1992).

EPIDEMIOLOGY

Population Studies

The incidence and course of anxiety disorders in children and adolescents have been explored in a number of studies using community and clinical samples. In two cross-sectional epidemiological studies (Kashani, Orvaschel, Rosenberg, & Reid, 1989; Kashani & Orvaschel, 1988), 21% of children sampled (ages 8, 12, or 17 years) reported symptoms consistent with the diagnosis of an anxiety disorder. Prevalence rates reported for these samples were 12.9% and 12.4% for SAD and OAD, respectively, 3.3% for simple phobia, and 1.1% for social phobia. Similar findings were obtained in a longitudinal study conducted in New Zealand (Anderson et al., 1987; McGee et al., 1990). In a sample of 792 children evaluated at age 11 years, the prevalence rates were 3.5% for SAD, 2.9% for OAD, 2.4% for simple phobia, and 1.0% for social phobia. When the children were reassessed at age 15 years (McGee et al., 1990), the overall prevalence rates were 5.9% for OAD, 2.0% for SAD, 3.6% for simple phobia, and 1.1% for social phobia. The rates reported for simple and social phobia are misleading, however, because the most common simple fear was the fear of public speaking. According to the criteria and descriptions outlined in DSM-III-R (American Psychiatric Association, 1987), phobia of public speaking should be considered a social phobia.

The first epidemiological study of OCD in children was conducted on the Isle of Wight (Rutter, Tizard, & Whitmore, 1970). Of the 2,199 children studied (ages 10 and 11), 0.3% were identified as "mixed obsessional/anxiety disorders." Results of the NIMH adolescent OCD study revealed a weighted point prevalence rate of 0.8% and a lifetime prevalence of 1.9% for the general adolescent population (Flament et al., 1988). These findings are more consistent with the estimated 2% prevalence in the general adult population (Karno, Golding, Sorenson, & Burnam, 1988). However, Valleni-Basile et al. (1994) reported a 3% prevalence rate for clinical OCD and 19% for subclinical OCD in their community sample of adolescents. A prevalence of 4% was found in one study of older Israeli adolescents (Zohar et al., 1992). Overall, these studies suggest that OCD is a relatively common disorder in adolescents.

Controversy regarding the occurrence of panic disorder in youth has most likely contributed to the paucity of studies investigating the epidemiology of this disorder in children and adolescents. Panic disorder is not mentioned in the most widely cited epidemiological studies of anxiety disorders in youth (e.g., Anderson et al., 1987; Kashani & Orvaschel, 1988; Rutter et al., 1970). However, several investigators have reported on the prevalence of this disorder in children and adolescents. In a sample of 388 adolescents ages 12 to 19 years, Warren and Zgourides (1988) reported 4.7% of the sample met DSM-III diagnostic criteria for panic disorder. Additionally, 60% of the sample reported having experienced at least one panic attack, and 31.9% reported having at least one attack meeting DSM-III criteria. Macaulay and Kleinknecht (1989) assessed 660 adolescents (ages 13–18) with a battery of panic-related questionnaires. For the sample, the authors found 35.7% reported no panic attacks, 47.5% reported mild panic, 10.4% moderate panic, and 5.4% reported severe panic. The frequency of panic reported by the severe subgroup averaged slightly less than DSM-III-R criteria (3.8 attacks as opposed to 4 attacks in 4 weeks). Moreover, 73.3% of the severe group were female adolescents. More recent epidemiological data suggest a lifetime prevalence for panic disorder of about 1% for adolescents (Lewinsohn, Hops, Roberts, Seeley, & Andrews, 1993; Whitaker et al., 1990). These data are fairly consistent with the adult lifetime prevalence rates estimated to be around 1.5% (see Ollendick et al., 1994).

Clinical Samples

Among clinic-referred samples of anxious children, Last, Francis, et al. (1987) reported 33% of their sample received a primary diagnosis of SAD, 15% had primary school phobia (described as social in origin), 15% had OAD, and 15% presented with a major affective disorder. High comorbidity rates were evidenced among childhood anxiety disorders, with one or more concurrent anxiety disorder diagnosed in 41% of the children with primary SAD, 63% of the school (social) phobia sample, and 56% of the children with primary OAD (Last, Hersen, et al., 1987).

In a recent study of 227 consecutive referrals to an outpatient child anxiety disorders clinic, 212 children (ages 7–17) received principal DSM-III-R diagnoses of an anxiety disorder (Albano, Chorpita, et al., 1995). Diagnoses were based on the Anxiety Disorders Interview Schedule, Child and Parent Versions (Silverman, 1991) and reflected the composite diagnosis based on the combined child and parent report. For the sample, 25.3% were social phobia, 17.5% OAD, 13.3% OCD, 11.4% SAD, 9.6% simple phobia, and 6.0% panic disorder or panic disorder with agoraphobia. Interestingly, 16.9% of the sample received coprincipal diagnoses, of which at least one was an additional anxiety disorder. In addition, the rate for OCD as a principal diagnosis was higher than previous reports of clinic samples (cf. Last & Strauss, 1989b). Prior research has consistently reported a higher prevalence of OCD in community as compared to clinic samples (see March et al., 1995). It has been suggested that a bias toward considering OCD as rare may have led clinicians to consider alternative diagnoses such as schizophrenia (Valleni-Basile et al., 1994).

Last, Perrin, Hersen, and Kazdin (1995) examined prospectively the course and outcome of DSM-III-R anxiety disorders in a clinical sample of 84 children over a 3- to 4-year period. The authors found that 82% of children were recovered from their initial anxiety disorders at the end of the follow-up period and that 68% of these children had recovered during the first year. Only 8% of children evidenced a relapse of anxiety disorders after a period of remission. SAD had the highest rate of recovery (96%) and specific phobia the poorest (69%). The majority of children with OAD recovered during follow-up (80%); however this disorder showed the slowest time to recovery and the highest rate of new disorders during follow-up (35%).

The systematic study of community and clinical samples of anxious youth provides invaluable information concerning the incidence and prevalence of these disorders, patterns of comorbidity, demographic factors, and examination of factors related to course and clinical outcome. Overall, studies such as Last et al. (1995) offer encouraging results and suggest that clinically referred children with anxiety disorders can expect a favorable recovery. Advances in the treatments of these disorders should further enhance prognosis.

Sociodemographic Variables

Racial and Social Class Factors

Lower socioeconomic status and lower parental education level have been associated with a greater prevalence and risk of SAD (Bird, Gould, Yager, Staghezza, & Canino, 1989; Last, Hersen, et al., 1987; Valez, Johnson, & Cohen, 1989).

In addition, reported samples of children with SAD were predominantly Caucasian. Samples of children with phobic disorders (simple and social combined) are predominantly Caucasian and middle to low-middle socioeconomic status (Strauss & Last, 1993). No information is available on the demographic composition of GAD in children and adolescents, however children with OAD are predominantly from middle- to upper-income families in clinical samples (e.g., Last, Hersen, et al., 1987; Last et al., 1992) and predominantly Caucasian (e.g., Last, Hersen, et al., 1987). No particular pattern has emerged for socioeconomic or racial data in children and adolescents with OCD (e.g., Last & Strauss, 1989b; Valleni-Basile et al., 1994).

In a study designed to evaluate racial similarities and differences in anxiety-disordered youth, Last and Perrin (1993) compared a clinical sample of African-American children ($n = 30$) to Caucasian children ($n = 139$) on sociodemographic variables, clinical characteristics, and lifetime rates of DSM-III-R anxiety disorders. Results suggest that African-American children and Caucasian children seeking treatment for anxiety disorders are more similar than different, as no significant differences were found with regard to age, sex, duration of disorder, or lifetime history of an affective disorder. There was a trend toward significance with Caucasian children being more likely to present with school refusal and higher diagnostic severity ratings, and African-American children being more likely to have a history of posttraumatic stress disorder. Moreover, African-American children tended to score higher on the Revised Fear Survey Schedule for Children (Ollendick, 1983b; cf. Neal, Lilly, & Zakis, 1993).

Sex Differences

Several studies have reported a greater prevalence of SAD in female as compared to male children (Anderson et al., 1987; Costello, 1989; Last, Hersen, et al., 1987), although others have reported no differences (Last et al., 1992; Bird et al., 1989). Last et al. (1992) reported that 44.3% of their social-phobic sample were female children, however Beidel and Turner (as cited in Beidel & Morris, 1995) reported 70% of their sample were female children. In a community study examining the relative prevalence of DSM-III phobic disorders, Anderson et al. (1987) found a male-to-female ratio of 6:1 for phobic disorder

in children and adolescents (excluding social phobia). Strauss and Last (1993) report equal male-to-female ratios for their clinic-referred sample of children with simple phobias. This apparent discrepancy between these studies may reflect methodological differences or the possibility that male and female children are referred for treatment of these disorders at a similar rate (Strauss & Last, 1993). A clear and stable gender difference for the blood phobia subtype has emerged, with the majority of cases being female ones (Marks, 1988).

Male cases predominate in samples of children with OCD (Swedo et al., 1989; Last & Strauss, 1989b), however this finding may be a function of age (see "Obsessive–Compulsive Disorder," above). The male-to-female ratio for OCD in adolescents is equivalent (Flament et al., 1988; Valleni-Basile et al., 1994). Several studies examining gender differences in OAD have suggested a preponderance of male cases (Cantwell & Baker, 1989; Verhulst, Akkerhuis, & Althaus, 1985; Verhulst & Akkerhuis, 1988), however referral biases may have contributed to these results. The gender ratio generally reported in both community and clinical samples is nearly equivalent, although it has been suggested that the disorder may be more common in females (Eisen & Kearney, 1995). GAD has been diagnosed more frequently in female adolescents than in males (Bowen et al., 1990; McGee et al., 1990).

In summary, little research has focused directly on the demographic composition of anxiety disorders in children and adolescents; consequently, the available data are limited by referral and methodological constraints. It is extremely difficult to draw any firm conclusions regarding racial, socioeconomic, or gender patterns of anxious youth. Studies vary on selection and recruitment procedures, geographical boundaries, incentives for participation, and opportunities for treatment. Cultural or racial biases may influence whether or not children from specific minority groups are referred for treatment of internalizing disorders such as anxiety. Moreover, of clinic-referred samples, the majority of studies in the literature stem from specialty clinics for anxiety disorders in youth. Thus, within clinic-referred samples, there is the potential for ascertainment bias in the patient population. Families who seek mental health services may have been in a better position to be referred or afford such services. The literature is best interpreted with these caveats in mind.

Cultural Variations

Investigations of the cultural aspects of childhood anxiety play an important role in determining which patterns of behavior are universal and which might be specific to particular groups or settings. By highlighting determinants of anxiety not accounted for by existing biological and psychosocial theory, cross-cultural perspectives help to clarify the underlying validity of our present conceptualization of childhood anxiety. Although cultural influences have received some attention in the adult anxiety literature (e.g., Barlow, 1988; Brown, Eaton, & Sussman, 1990; Friedman & Paradis, 1991; Neal & Turner, 1991), very few studies exist using child populations. The majority of the research has involved cross-cultural assessment using self-report measures developed in the United States. Only a few studies have examined differences in diagnostic patterns across cultural groups (Neal & Turner, 1991).

The Fear Survey Schedule for Children–Revised (FSSC-R; Ollendick, 1983b), an 80-item inventory of different fear stimuli and situations, has been used to assess differences in patterns of childhood fears across numerous cultural groups. The FSSC-R has been translated into a variety of languages and administered to children and adolescents in the United States, Portugal, Italy, Turkey, Australia, the Netherlands, Northern Ireland, China, and the United Kingdom (see Fonesca, Yule, & Erol, 1994, for a review). Examination of the main differences across groups is limited to those groups that have received the same 80-item adaptation, that is, Australia, the United States, the United Kingdom, Portugal, China, and the Netherlands. Results showed relatively similar scores for most of these countries; however, the Dutch sample scored lower, and the Portuguese sample scored higher than the other countries on total fear scores (Fonesca et al., 1994). One possible explanation for this difference is that the tendency for Latin cultures is to express fears more spontaneously, whereas Nordic cultures tend to control or conceal emotions (Fonesca et al., 1994). Across all groups, girls were found to score higher than boys. This does not necessarily imply a universal, "culture-free" gender pattern for fears however, because the role of women in these cultures is fairly homogeneous and may involve a higher risk for the development of anxiety (cf. Nolen-Hoeksema, 1987).

Examination of the most common fears across cultures shows striking commonalities. Children in the United Kingdom, the United States, Turkey, Portugal, and Australia all share the fear of being hit by a car as the most frequently endorsed childhood fear. Fears of not being able to breathe, a bomb attack or war, fire, a burglar, falling from a height, and death ranked in the top 10 fears of at least four of these countries. In addition, items appended to the original 80-item measure revealed that fear of a parent's death was considerable in all countries tested (United Kingdom, Turkey, Portugal), with endorsement ranging from 73% to 84% (Fonesca et al., 1994).

In a manner similar to the work of Ollendick and colleagues, Spielberger and colleagues (Spielberger & Diaz-Guerrero, 1986; Spielberger, Diaz-Guerrero, & Strelau, 1990) have fostered research examining self-reported trait anxiety across different cultures. The State–Trait Anxiety Inventory for Children (STAIC; Spielberger, 1973) is a measure of general anxiety or negative affect in school-aged children. At present, the majority of the cross-cultural research with the STAIC has involved validation of the instrument in a variety of countries. Currently, adaptations have been developed for Polish, Hungarian, Russian, Jordanian, Lebanese, and Bengali populations, most of which were comprised of students in middle to late adolescence. In one comparative study, Ahlawat (1986) found similar factor structures between the Arabic STAIC and the American version. In addition, sex differences were similar to those found in the United States, with girls scoring higher in trait anxiety than boys. In general, support for the use of the STAIC across different cultures is growing. These developments are particularly noteworthy given that not all attempts to validate self-report measures of childhood anxiety across cultures have been successful (e.g., Wilson, Chibaiwa, Majoni, Masakume, & Nkoma, 1990).

Guida and Ludlow (1989) examined the phenomenon of test anxiety in children from different cultural groups and evaluated the effects of socioeconomic status (SES), subject sex, and cultural background on self-reported test anxiety. Using the Test Anxiety Scale for Children (TASC; Sarason, Davidson, Lightfall, Waite, & Ruebush, 1960), the investigators compared samples of urban, African-American children, middle-class American children, upper-class American children, and a large sample of Chilean students. In the comparative analyses, the Chilean students scored higher on test anxiety than the American samples. Across groups, children with high SES

scored lower on the TASC than children with low SES. Within low-SES subjects, there was also a tendency for girls to score higher than boys on the test anxiety measure.

In an investigation of cultural influences on general child pathology, Weisz et al. (1987) used parent self-report measures to compare American children with children living in Thailand. The general pattern suggested that Thai children manifest more internalizing behavior (e.g., being withdrawn, anxious, or depressed) than do American children. The authors interpreted these findings as consistent with their hypothesis that the more emotionally controlled Thai culture would contribute to higher internalizing behavior in Thai children. Such findings are particularly interesting in light of the extant findings concerning the influence of a controlled environment on the development of anxiety and negative affect (e.g., Parker, 1983; Mineka, 1985).

In the literature examining cultural issues in childhood anxiety, diagnostic studies are certainly the fewest in number (see Neal & Turner, 1991). In one study using DSM-III nosology, Anderson and colleagues (1987) found separation anxiety disorder to be the most frequent childhood anxiety diagnosis in a New Zealand population. In another investigation, Orvaschel (1988) found a significantly lower prevalence of anxiety disorders among a Caucasian American sample when compared to a non-Caucasian sample. However, the number of non-Caucasians ($n = 8$) was too small to be representative of the population in general. In an examination of depression, anxiety, and substance abuse among Native American Alaskan adolescents, Dinges and Duong-Tran (1993) found that in adolescents diagnosed with depression (using the DISC), stressful life events had a significant relationship to comorbidity in both groups.

In general, the diversity of findings obscures any unified theory of cultural influence at present. There is undoubtedly a need for more comparative cultural studies using diagnostic criteria and for lines of research to continue to follow up the investigations of existing assessment studies. Cultural differences in the expression and conceptualization of anxiety disorders in adults have been well documented (see Barlow, 1988). Of interest to the cross-cultural study of children with anxiety disorders is the examination of cultural differences in the interpretation of the course of these disorders, symptom presentation, and intervention approaches. Culture-specific symptoms

and syndromes of anxiety have not been explored in children. For example, isolated sleep paralysis has been found to be more prevalent in African-Americans than in Caucasians and is conceptualized as a form of nocturnal panic (Barlow & Durand, 1995). Whether this phenomenon occurs in African-American children has yet to be evaluated. The efforts to understand the role of culture in childhood anxiety are only in their earliest stages.

ETIOLOGICAL MODELS OF ANXIETY DISORDERS IN CHILDREN

Biological Factors

In recent years attention has turned toward the examination of behavioral inhibition as a temperamental marker for the development of anxiety disorders (Biederman et al., 1993a, 1993b; Biederman et al., 1990; Hirshfeld et al., 1992; Rosenbaum et al., 1992; Rosenbaum, Biederman, Hirshfeld, Bolduc, & Chaloff, 1991; Rosenbaum et al., 1988; Rubin & Stewart, Chapter 7, this volume). Rosenbaum, Biederman, Hirshfeld, Bolduc, Faraone, et al. (1991) define temperament as a response disposition emerging early in life, enduring over time, and having an impact on later personality. The term behavioral inhibition (Kagan, 1982, 1989) refers to a particular temperamental style, evidenced by a child's degree of sociability as displayed by observable behaviors manifested along the approach–withdrawal dimension. As a result of years of longitudinal research, Kagan and colleagues (Kagan, Reznick, & Snidman, 1988) have reported on the distinction and course of inhibited and uninhibited children. According to their findings, some 10% to 15% of Caucasian American children are born predisposed to be irritable as infants. These children then become shy and fearful as toddlers, and quiet, cautious, and introverted by the start of their primary school years. In standardized behavioral test situations, inhibited children consistently refrain from spontaneous vocalizations when in the presence of a stranger and cry and cling to their mothers rather than explore play settings and approach other children. In contrast, 25% to 30% of the children studied demonstrated an opposing temperament of being sociable, bold, and gregarious. Moreover, as opposed to the inhibited cohort, these children were unperturbed by novel stimuli. Kagan et al. have followed

two independent cohorts of children over an extended (7-year) period. Children were originally identified as inhibited or uninhibited at either 21 or 31 months of age during standardized behavioral tests when exposed to unfamiliar settings, people, and objects. These differences in behavior were largely maintained through repeated assessments at 4, 5, and 7 years of age, suggesting that such differences represent an enduring temperamental trait (see Kagan, Reznick, & Gibbons, 1989; Kagan, Reznick, & Snidman, 1987; Kagan et al., 1988).

Kagan's original work on behavioral inhibition was designed to examine temperamental styles of infants, and as such no specific hypotheses regarding psychopathology were postulated. However, as attention turned toward the serious study of childhood anxiety disorders, the similarities between inhibited and anxious children became more apparent. For example, Gersten (1986) described the behavioral reactions of inhibited children on their first days of school as largely avoidant and consistent with symptoms of separation anxiety. The behaviors of Kagan's inhibited children were judged to be consistent with descriptions of children of agoraphobics who manifested anxiety symptoms (Berg, 1976) and to retrospective reports of agoraphobic adults about their own childhoods as well (Berg, Marks, McGuire, & Lipsedge, 1974; Deltito, Perugi, Maremmani, Mignani, & Cassano, 1986). The association between behavioral inhibition and childhood anxiety disorders was found in psychophysiological indices, as well. Kagan et al. (1987) demonstrated that as compared to uninhibited children, inhibited children show increased sympathetic activation on exposure to novel stimuli. Such activation is inferred from high heart rate, low heart rate variability, and acceleration of heart rate in response to mild stress. These findings suggested increased sympathetic tone in inhibited children and led Kagan et al. (1987) to postulate that inhibited children had a low arousal threshold in the amygdala and hypothalamus, especially when confronted with unfamiliar events. These physiological events, coupled with the behavioral responses of escape, avoidance, and passivity are consistent with current neurophysiological theories of the etiology of anxiety disorders, and they suggest that behavioral inhibition in early childhood may be a marker of anxiety proneness.

Further evidence for the association between behavioral inhibition and anxiety stems from investigations with primates (Suomi, 1984, 1986).

Suomi observed a subsample of young rhesus monkeys to display "anxiety-like" behaviors more easily than other monkeys in response to repeated forced separation. These monkeys tended to react to novel stimuli with retreat, diminished exploration, and increased physiological arousal. Suomi identified these monkeys as "high reactive," and postulated that the factors most predictive of developing this anxiety-like state were under genetic control. Further, Suomi estimated that 15% of his monkeys are born with the high-reactive predisposition. Although high reactivity appears to represent a form of anxiety proneness, much like behavioral inhibition in children, the development of anxiety symptoms would still be dependent on environmental factors such as separation. Reactions consistent with behavioral inhibition have also been observed in other species such as cats and dogs (see Reznick, 1989).

Expanding upon the work of Kagan and colleagues, investigators at the Harvard Medical School postulated that a diathesis of anxiety proneness, expressed as behavioral inhibition in infancy, represented an inherited physiological predisposition to the development of pathological anxiety (see Biederman et al., 1993b, and Rosenbaum, Biederman, Hirshfeld, Bolduc, & Chaloff, 1991). In a series of studies, the Harvard group assessed behavioral inhibition in high-risk children of parents with panic disorder with agoraphobia (PDAG). These children were compared with children of parents with other psychiatric diagnoses, including major depression (MDD), and with the inhibited and uninhibited children in Kagan's original longitudinal study of behavioral inhibition. For these studies, all assessments of behavioral inhibition were performed in Kagan's laboratory by staff who were blind to parental diagnoses. Psychopathology in the children and parents was assessed through structured diagnostic interviews. In addition, children attending a pediatric medicine outpatient clinic who had no history of anxiety or depression served as a normal comparison group for these studies.

Several provocative results have emerged from these investigations. First, parental PDAG, either alone or with comorbid major depressive disorder, is associated with behavioral inhibition in 85% and 70% of the children, respectively. However, major depression by itself and psychiatric disorder without MDD or PDAG do not predict such an association. Rates of behavioral inhibition were 50% and 15.4%, respectively. Second, evaluation of the children revealed a greater

prevalence of anxiety disorders in the inhibited children as compared to the not-inhibited and pediatric controls. These results were taken as evidence that behavioral inhibition is an expression of familial vulnerability to anxiety disorders (Biederman, Rosenbaum, Bolduc, Faraone, & Hirshfeld, 1991; Biederman et al., 1993a). Next, assessments were conducted on the parents and siblings of the children from the Kagan et al. (1988) longitudinal cohort and compared to evaluations of first-degree relatives of normal control children (Rosenbaum, Biederman, Hirshfeld, Bolduc, Faraone, et al., 1991). Results were consistent with the hypothesis that behavioral inhibition in children predicts increased rates of anxiety disorders in biological relatives. Specifically, as compared to normal controls, parents of inhibited children had higher rates of social phobia, history of childhood anxiety disorder, history of avoidant and overanxious disorders, and continuity of anxiety from childhood through adulthood. Moreover, siblings of inhibited children had higher rates of phobias than siblings of control children.

Although the evidence for a familial predisposition to anxiety disorders was supported by these series of studies, the data did not identify specific factors that would determine which inhibited children were at greater risk for developing a childhood anxiety disorder. In the study by Rosenbaum et al. (1992), parents of children with behavioral inhibition and multiple anxiety disorders had higher rates of multiple anxiety disorders themselves, as compared with parents of inhibited children without anxiety disorders and uninhibited, normal controls. Unfortunately, these data did not permit explication of the relative importance of parental psychopathology as a genetic or environmental risk factor for children with behavioral inhibition (Biederman et al., 1993b). Rather, the presence of parental anxiety disorders may help to identify the inhibited subgroup of children at risk for developing childhood anxiety disorders. In a 3-year follow-up study, children in the at-risk sample and the Kagan longitudinal cohort were reevaluated for presence of psychiatric disorders (Biederman, Rosenbaum et al., 1993a). Results indicated significant differences between all inhibited and all noninhibited children in the rates of multiple psychiatric and anxiety disorder diagnoses. Seventy-five percent of those who had SAD at baseline were found to have agoraphobia at follow-up. Moreover, inhibited children who were asymptomatic at baseline evidenced a greater probability of developing an anxiety disorder at follow-up as compared to noninhibited children.

Although the results of the Harvard studies are provocative and undoubtedly will provoke serious study, no firm conclusions can be drawn regarding a biological mechanism for the heritability of anxiety disorders. Upwards of 70% of the inhibited children in the Harvard sample were free of any anxiety disorder (Biederman et al., 1990). In addition, in the absence of parental disorders, behavioral inhibition is not predictive of later psychopathology (Biederman et al., 1993a). Behavioral inhibition itself is more prevalent than are anxiety disorders in the general population of children, suggesting that inhibition may be just one of several factors required for the development of pathological anxiety conditions (Biederman et al., 1993b). Moreover, two distinct phenotypes of behavioral inhibition have been identified in the Kagan et al. and Harvard cohorts (Kagan et al., 1989; Hirshfeld et al., 1992). Some inhibited children evidence a stable pattern of inhibition through age 7 years, display a high and stable heart rate during test situations in early childhood, tend to develop an anxiety disorder, and are positive for parental anxiety disorders. Children with unstable behavioral inhibition present with a variable pattern of behavioral and physiological responding. Childhood anxiety disorders and parental pathology are less strongly associated in this subgroup.

Psychosocial Factors

Recent psychosocial conceptualizations of childhood anxiety have now acknowledged the existence of the broader emotional construct of negative affect (Brady & Kendall, 1992; King, Ollendick, & Gullone, 1991; Watson & Clark, 1984). Thus, understanding the process of anxiety in children requires an examination of depression as well. Consistent with this notion, a number of diagnostic studies have cited findings of high comorbidity between anxiety and depressive disorders as support for a unitary construct (Strauss, Last, Hersen, & Kazdin, 1988; Strauss, Lease, et al., 1988). These findings have suggested not only conceptual overlap between the two disorders, but they also support the possibility of a developmental progression along a cognitive dimension hypothesized to distinguish between the two disorders (Barlow, 1991).

Interestingly, clinical theories of adult anxiety and depression offer a conceptualization of these

disorders quite consistent with emerging findings in the studies of children, making the connection between these two areas more salient. In recent adult theories, notions of the dimensional elements of disturbance, the relationship of normal to abnormal processes, the multiplicity of psychosocial and biological influences, and the continuity of anxious and depressive features have received increased emphasis (cf. Alloy et al., 1990; Barlow, 1988, 1991; Moras & Barlow, 1992). Although the expression of anxiety disorders is known to be topographically unique across developmental levels, the underlying constituents to the process of anxiety may be quite similar.

Benefiting from a focus on dimensional core elements, Barlow (1991) articulated such a model of emotional disorders, integrating the theoretical understanding of both anxiety and depression. Drawing from biological, cognitive, and emotion theory, the model offers a conceptualization of anxiety as a complex "blending" of cognitive and affective elements. Barlow (1991) further specifies these elements principally as high negative affect, a sense of uncontrollability, and attentional self-focus. This model is presented in Figure 5.1. The construct of anxiety, therefore, is uniquely characterized by its "state of 'helplessness' because of perceived inability to predict, control, or obtain desired results in certain upcoming situations or contexts" (Barlow, 1991, p. 60). Furthermore, the phenomenon of depression is postulated as being closely related to anxiety, sharing the same affective properties but involving a greater measure of uncontrollability on the cognitive dimension. Thus, the distinction between anxiety and depression is marked by the shift from a sense of limited control, eliciting autonomic arousal and the associated apprehensive action tendencies, to a sense of no control, characterized by anhedonia, disengagement, and inactivity. Other theorists have similarly concluded that anxiety and depression may represent a common core nosological construct, differing principally on a cognitive dimension (e.g., Alloy et al., 1990).

Etiologically, the process of anxiety is represented in Figure 5.2. This model posits an interaction of biological vulnerability (cf. temperament) and stressful life events influencing a diffuse stress response that involves a number of neurological subsystems, most notably hypothalamic–adrenocortical activation (e.g., Gray, 1982). Such activation may engender a psychological vulnerability characterized by a sense of low control over one's fear responses or stressful stimuli. This vulnerability is then attenuated or amplified by a number of secondary factors such as support networks, coping skills, or other resources.

As it applies to children, this model has strong implications for the role of early environment (Barlow, Chorpita, & Turovsky, in press; Chorpita & Barlow, 1995). Perception of control (or lack of control) has been suggested as the core feature of anxiety (Barlow, 1988; Barlow et al., in press). Early experience with uncontrollability is therefore seen as contributory to the development of childhood anxiety, and possibly later, depression. This notion highlights the consistency with other areas of research, such as conditioning studies (e.g., Mineka, Gunnar, & Champoux, 1986; see Mineka & Zinbarg, in press). For example, Mineka et al. (1986) reared two experimental groups of rhesus monkeys differing only in their response-contingent control over access to food, water, and other treats from 2 to 6 months of life. The yoked control group, which received the same amount of these reinforcers noncontingently, showed increased acquisition of fear and reduced exploratory behavior in a novel environment (cf. insecure attachment; Bowlby, 1969). These results are particularly noteworthy as an analogue for human anxiety. Further, the generality of the effects parallels long-standing observations of continuity in human infant behavior (e.g., Kagan et al., 1987).

These patterns related to controllability have been noted by prominent developmental researchers (e.g., Sroufe, 1990). Sroufe (1990) described the early process of negotiation between mother and infant as one in which effective communication plays an important role in regulating affect and arousal. As infants begin to become overaroused from social stimulation with the mother, they provide subtle clues to the mother (e.g., head turning). Mothers who successfully respond and deescalate the interaction prevent disorganized or fretful affect in the infant. Ultimately, in normal development, this regulation of affect and arousal is thought to become internalized. Similar to findings of Mineka et al. (1986), the early experience with relevant outcomes being contingent on one's behavior is related to positive long-term functioning.

A substantial body of literature has documented the relationship between stress and subsequent maladjustment in children (Garmezy, 1986; Garmezy & Rutter, 1985). Although definitional problems relevant to measurement of stressors have complicated and flawed some

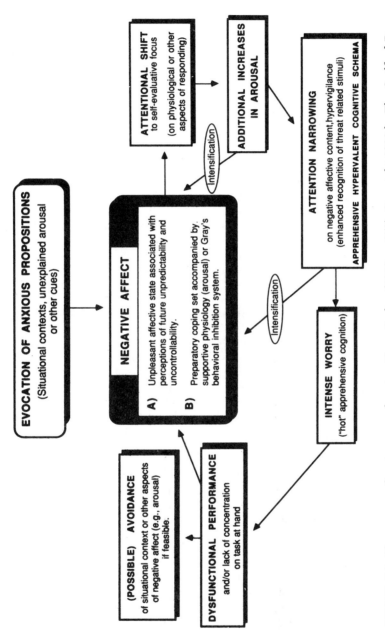

FIGURE 5.1. The process of anxious apprehension. From Barlow (1988, p. 250). Copyright 1988 by The Guilford Press. Reprinted by permission.

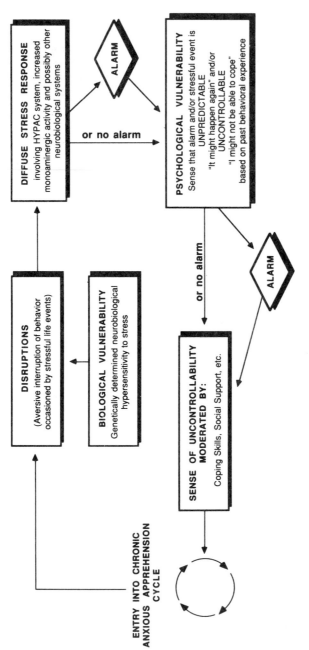

FIGURE 5.2. The origins of anxious apprehension. From Barlow (1988, p. 275). Copyright 1988 by The Guilford Press. Reprinted by permission.

of the research, a clear pattern exists suggesting that early experience with stress can have damaging effects in a child's development, at least under certain conditions. However, it appears that stressful events alone are not always sufficient to result in dysfunction and that conditions related to prediction and control may again be of considerable importance. Nonetheless, environmental stress has been associated with the onset and occurrence of anxiety symptoms in children (Kashani et al., 1990) and adolescents (Bernstein, Garfinkel, & Hoberman, 1989). As measured by the Life Events Checklist (Johnson & McCutcheon, 1980), children and adolescents with high levels of anxiety reported a significantly higher number of environmental stressors as compared to youngsters having low levels of anxiety (cf. Bernstein & Borchardt, 1991). Several investigators have suggested that environmental stress is a significant conditioning factor responsible for the development of phobias (Öst, 1987; Sheehan, Sheehan, & Minichiello, 1981; Thyer, Neese, Cameron, & Curtis, 1985) and most clearly present in the development of posttraumatic stress disorder (Barlow, 1988).

Although the relationship between stress and anxiety has been demonstrated, the mechanism of action maintaining or promoting a continued state of anxiety after the stressor has passed has not been fully explored. Garmezy (1986) identifies one of the possible explanations for the deleterious effects of stress on developing children. Citing Hebb's (1955) inverted U-shaped function relating arousal to performance, Garmezy (1986) argues that stress, leading to overarousal, may interfere with optimal communication, performance, and responsivity. Other formulations have been offered, however, that argue against this "arousal model." For example, Izard (e.g., Izard & Beuchler, 1979) described these states of arousal as emergence of basic human emotions. These emotional states are felt to emerge at the time when they are most necessary or adaptive. Thus, states of distress, anger, or fear in a young child may not necessarily represent compromised performance but, rather, may contribute to the difficult process of negotiation and coping in which an infant or young child must engage. Izard's formulation suggests that it may not be the topography of the individual's reaction to stress that is of concern. Rather, the degree to which the "basic emotion" is effective, or more precisely, operational, influences the subsequent development of the child.

Consistent with this theme of the importance of mastery, Masten, Best, and Garmezy (1991) reviewed conditions found to serve as protective factors in child development. For example, Bandura's (1986) conception of self-efficacy (cf. mastery and control) has been found to be related to positive development. "Resilient children may enter into a situation more prepared for effective action by virtue of their self-confidence; subsequently, successful mastery of a difficult situation would be expected to increase self-efficacy and reinforce efforts to take action" (Masten et al., 1991, p. 431). Intellectual skill and social–cognitive ability are also predictive of healthy development. These factors may share the same mechanism, namely increasing the degree of mastery and control one has over the environment.

The importance of caretakers in the development of this active approach to coping is well-documented. Previous reviews have described the importance of the attachment relationship in the development of autonomy and decreased inhibition (Sroufe, 1979). Crockenberg (1981) demonstrated the importance of even the very earliest experiences (i.e., before attachment relationships are conventionally assessed). Results of a longitudinal study indicated that maternal unresponsiveness to the infant at 3 months was associated with anxious attachment at 1 year in 10 of 11 children.

The conceptualization of the process of anxiety as involving a diminished sense of mastery and control is consistent with other lines of literature as well (see Chorpita & Barlow, 1995, for a review), for example, cognitive theories (Abramson, Seligman, & Teasdale, 1978; Alloy et al., 1990), sex differences in coping styles (Nolen-Hoeksema, 1987), neurophysiological models (e.g., Dienstbier, 1989; Gray, 1982), attachment theory (e.g., Bowlby, 1969), and clinical studies of the early development of negative affect (e.g., Parker, 1983). The evidence that early uncontrollable experience for children predisposes a cognitive "template" for helplessness is compelling. Not surprisingly, these ideas are reflected in the core elements of contemporary treatment strategies, which emphasize the importance of personal mastery (cf. "coping," Kendall, Kane, Howard, & Siqueland, 1990) and the critical role of parents in inhibiting or fostering a sense of control (e.g., Dadds, Heard, & Rappee, 1992).

Familial and Genetic Factors

The role of the family in the etiology of anxiety disorders is broadly recognized (e.g., Crowe, Noyes, Pauls, & Slymen, 1983; Goodyer, 1990;

Harris, Noyes, Crowe, & Chaudhry, 1983; Noyes et al., 1986). Because familial effects describe influences from both heritability and environmental variables, however, research on family factors related to anxiety has been diverse in goals and methods. The familial literature related to childhood anxiety involves several major lines of research, including twin methodology, study of offspring of anxiety disorder parents, patterns of family prevalence, and psychosocial analyses (e.g., examinations of parenting style).

Many of the twin studies on anxiety disorders were conducted prior to the acceptance of DSM-III or DSM-III-R terminology (see Silverman, Cerny, & Nelles, 1986, for a review). In the first large-scale twin study using DSM criteria, Torgersen (1983) studied a sample of 85 same-sex twin pairs (ages 18–66) to investigate the possibility of genetic transmission of anxiety disorders. Results demonstrated considerably high monozygotic concordance for the anxiety disorders other than GAD. Concordance rates were highest among panic disorder and panic disorder with agoraphobia. Torgersen interpreted these data to suggest that there is high heritability for most of the anxiety disorders, but not for GAD. The interpretation of these findings has subsequently been questioned, however (e.g., Turner et al., 1987). This confusion is due in part to Torgersen's (1983) hypotheses about heritability for specific disorders. Others have argued that genes play their greatest role in contributing to a general risk factor and are not disorder-specific (e.g., Kendler, Neale, Kessler, Heath, & Eaves, 1992; Turner et al., 1987). Viewed in this manner, nonspecific anxiety disorder concordance rate becomes the more critical variable, and Torgersen's data do support the notion of hereditary transmission of a broad predisposition or vulnerability for anxiety disorders in general.

In a more recent study of anxiety concordance in twins, Andrews, Stewart, Allen, and Henderson (1990) assessed a sample of 446 pairs of adult twins using a structured clinical interview. The purpose of the interview was to identify participants who met diagnostic criteria for an anxiety disorder as well as to assess for lifetime history of anxiety symptoms. Consistent with the revised interpretation of Torgersen's (1983) study, the results did not support the possibility of inheritance of specific disorders and seemed to suggest a genetic contribution to general symptomatology. Along similar lines, Kendler et al. (1992) have examined genetic contribution to nonspecific vulnerabilities for anxiety and depression using bivariate twin analysis. In a population of 1,033 female, same-sex twin pairs, additive genetic variance was found to represent a common influence on the presence of GAD and MDD. These findings are some of the most compelling support for the notion of a general risk factor for anxiety, or more broadly, disorders of negative affect. In addition, the models tested were able to demonstrate that much of the specific etiological influence stems from unshared environmental variance. That is, familial environment played no significant role in the etiology of either MDD or GAD. The implication, then, is that a shared genetic risk factor may be responsible for a basic vulnerability for the disorder, whose specific expression is modified by unique experience.

Other studies of familial influences have involved examination of patterns of pathology in offspring of clinically anxious parents. Turner et al. (1987), for example, evaluated the hypothesis of a general predisposition for anxiety disorders that has since received much support from twin methodology. Adults were classified using a structured diagnostic interview (ADIS; DiNardo, O'Brien, Barlow, Waddell, & Blanchard, 1983) into anxiety disorders, dysthymia, and normal control groups. Fifty-nine children of clinically anxious adults were found to have more worries, more somatic complaints, more intense fears, and were more withdrawn than controls, when assessed using the FSSC-R (Ollendick, 1983b), the STAIC (Spielberger, 1973), and a semistructured interview schedule, the Child Assessment Schedule (CAS; Hodges, McKnew, Cytryn, Stern, & Kline, 1982). In addition, information from the CAS suggested that the children studied were seven times as likely to meet criteria for an anxiety disorder compared to offspring of the normal controls and two times as likely when compared to offspring of the dysthymic controls. These findings were consistent with the idea of a general familial risk factor for anxiety disorders, with the child self-report data suggesting that symptomatology in these children may be best understood as dimensional (i.e., degree of symptomatology vs. disorder presence or absence).

In a similar investigation, Last, Hersen, Kazdin, Orvaschel, and Perrin (1991) assessed pathology in the first- and second-degree relatives of children with anxiety disorders. Results indicated that relatives of clinically anxious children showed a higher prevalence of anxiety over normal controls, as well as controls with attention-deficit/hyperactivity disorder. Consistent with previous familial studies, there were no significant findings

to indicate that specific anxiety diagnoses in children also exist in their relatives. The pattern once again suggested a family influence for general anxiety proneness.

Using a more dimensional approach similar to Turner and colleagues (1987), Silverman, Cerny, Nelles, and Burke (1988) examined the frequency of behavior problems in children of clinically anxious adults using the CBCL (Achenbach & Edelbrock, 1983). Adults diagnosed with an anxiety disorder were grouped diagnostically and ranked according to the amount of demonstrated avoidance behavior. The agoraphobic group was most severe, followed by a mixed phobic group, and then a panic disorder without agoraphobia group. Children of parents in each of these three groups demonstrated frequencies of problem behaviors as measured by the CBCL in the same rank order as their parents' avoidance. The authors concluded that avoidance behavior in parents was a critical variable in the expression of anxious behavior problems in their offspring. Consistent with other research, these findings reflect a general vulnerability influencing anxious behavior in children. However, it is premature to speculate whether the associated mechanisms of transmission are causally related to heritability or to parent behavior. Indeed, the majority of familial studies have failed to address directly issues of causality, with the exception of the twin methodology. Thus, while genetic mechanisms have received definitive support (e.g., Kendler et al., 1992), the psychosocial transmission of anxiety remains less well elaborated. Contemporary theoretical accounts of causal mechanisms have suggested that some children may imitate fears and anxieties of their parents and that parents of some anxious children may reward and negatively reinforce anxious and avoidant behavior (e.g., King et al., 1988).

Recent empirical research along these lines has involved a microsocial analysis of family behavior to identify relevant modeling or conditioning processes in family interactions (Barrett, Rapee, & Dadds, 1993; Dadds et al., 1992). In a group of studies, children were asked to complete an information-processing questionnaire similar to the ambiguous situations task outlined by Butler and Mathews (1983). The questionnaire required subjects to choose an interpretation and a plan of action in response to an ambiguous description of a hypothetical scene. The parents completed the same questionnaire, after which the family discussed their answers together to arrive at a mutual solution. The degree to which parents modeled, prompted, and rewarded anxiety in their children was assessed during the discussion. Results indicated that children with anxiety disorders not only perceived more threat than nonclinic controls, but they were also more sensitive to adopting a more anxious interpretation following the discussion with their parents (Barrett et al., 1993). Lending even greater support to the idea that parental behavior may influence the expression of anxiety phenomena, subsequent findings demonstrated that children and their parents who received a family intervention targeting these same communication variables responded better to treatment than those children who received traditional cognitive behavioral treatment alone (Barrett, Dadds, Rapee, & Ryan, 1994).

Other lines of research examining psychosocial mechanisms of transmission have suggested that broader dimensions of parenting style such as control and warmth are related to anxiety in offspring (e.g., Parker, 1983; Solyom, Silberfeld, & Solyom, 1976). Gerlsma, Emmelkamp, and Arrindell (1990) have summarized the extensive literature on the effects of parenting rearing style (PRS) on depression and anxiety. Much of the work in this area stems from attachment theory (Bowlby, 1973), which posits the relevance of unsuitable or disrupted parenting style as a determinant of anxiety. Research progressing along several different lines has demonstrated the importance of inadequate affection and excessive parental control as part of the early experiences of adults with anxiety disorders (e.g., Ehiobuche, 1988; Parker, 1981). Most findings implicate "affectionless control" (Parker, 1983) as a key variable in predicting general predisposition to anxiety or phobias (Gerlsma et al., 1990), with effect sizes generally larger for maternal PRS. Alnæs and Torgersen (1990), however, have emphasized that lack of paternal care may play an important role as well, particularly in the discrimination of anxiety and depression.

Attempting to identify how parental rearing style might discriminate among different anxiety disorders, Silove, Parker, Hadzi-Pavlovic, Manicavasagar, and Blaszczynski (1991) investigated PRS in patients with DSM-III-R diagnoses of panic disorder and generalized anxiety disorder. Results tentatively suggest that insufficient affection played a role for both disorders, however, control or overprotection seemed to be the more important variable associated with panic disorder. In general, the findings in the area of PRS are

limited by the fact that most PRS assessment has been conducted retrospectively, requiring individuals with anxiety to describe their perceptions of early parenting experiences. Although some evidence exists that these retrospective accounts may not be state dependent or otherwise biased (e.g., Parker, 1979), there is clearly a need to validate this line of work with an emphasis on cross-sectional or prospective designs (cf. Messer & Beidel, 1994).

COMMON COMORBIDITIES

The issue of comorbidity in the childhood anxiety disorders plays a critical role in the understanding of childhood anxiety more generally (e.g., Caron & Rutter, 1991). Certainly, the study of comorbid anxiety syndromes is essential to understanding the underlying risk factors, the relationships among anxiety symptoms, the developmental continuities and discontinuities, and the validity of the major anxiety syndromes themselves. Comorbid disorders in childhood tend to occur more often than "pure" diagnostic profiles (e.g., Anderson et al., 1987). As such, it is difficult to draw meaningful conclusions about the characteristics of any particular childhood anxiety syndrome without consideration of the comorbid disorders, their potential influences, and their underlying latent constructs (cf. Lillienfeld, Waldman, & Israel, 1994).

At present, disagreements exist about how comorbidity itself should best be defined. For example, the categorical nosology of the DSM classification system for anxiety disorders allows examination of comorbidity at the syndrome level only; meanwhile, others have argued that symptom comorbidity, or covariability within dimensional classification systems (cf. Achenbach & Edelbrock, 1983), might have greater utility (e.g., Brown & Barlow, 1992; Frances et al., 1990). In addition, Caron and Rutter (1991) proposed that syndromal comorbidity might arise for numerous reasons, many of which can be artifactual. These reasons include referral effects (e.g., Berkson, 1946), symptom criterion overlap, artificial dichotomizing of dimensional syndromes, and developmental progression (e.g., overanxious disorder as an early manifestation of generalized anxiety disorder). Such conceptual disagreements about comorbidity more generally may in part be responsible for the relative lack of research examining comorbidity among childhood anxiety disorders.

Some of the only research attention given to the comorbidity of childhood anxiety disorders involved an investigation by Last, Strauss, et al. (1987). Using DSM-III diagnostic criteria, the investigators examined the co-occurrence of diagnoses in an outpatient population of 73 children. The results demonstrated that OAD children demonstrated the highest rate of comorbidity, with 9% having three or more additional clinical diagnoses. In addition, children assigned principal diagnoses of OAD most frequently received social phobia or avoidant disorder as additional diagnoses. Overall, the patterns demonstrated high diagnostic comorbidity for all of the anxiety disorders studied, with additional diagnoses assigned to as many as 80% of cases for selected anxiety diagnoses (SAD, OAD, school phobia), and with additional anxiety diagnoses assigned to 100% of the children with a principal diagnosis of major depression.

Existing studies on OCD have found many disorders to be comorbid with this diagnosis. For example, the NIMH study of 70 children and adolescents found 26% of the sample presented with only OCD (Swedo et al., 1989). For this sample, the most common comorbid disorders were tic disorders (30%, excluding Tourette's disorder), major depression (26%), specific developmental disorder (24%), specific phobia (17%), overanxious disorder (16%), adjustment disorder with depressed mood (13%), oppositional disorder (11%), and attention-deficit disorder (10%). Similar rates of comorbidity have been reported in both community and clinical samples (e.g., Albano, Chorpita, et al., 1995; Flament et al., 1988; Last & Strauss, 1989b; Riddle et al., 1990; Valleni-Basile et al., 1994). It has been suggested that high rates of comorbidity among OCD and other anxiety and mood disorders are reflective of these disorders being associated features of OCD and/or that OCD symptoms are features of other disorders (Valleni-Basile et al., 1994). Further research is necessary to explore fully the hypothesis that anxiety and depression exist on a continuum representing the same underlying construct.

Often the study of comorbidity involves attempts to clarify difficult diagnostic boundary issues. Because closely related diagnostic categories that often co-occur may actually represent one underlying syndrome, it is important to examine the validity of such disorders. For example, children diagnosed with DSM-III-R avoidant disorder of childhood and adolescence were

found to be indistinguishable from children with DSM-III-R social phobia on measures of fear and depression, socioeconomic status, and gender and ethnicity ratios (Francis et al., 1992). In fact, these two disorders appeared to be best differentiated by age at intake, suggesting that avoidant disorder may be a temporal precursor to social phobia (i.e., developmental progression; cf. Caron & Rutter, 1991). Consistent with these findings, avoidant disorder of childhood and adolescence was not included in DSM-IV nosology, however the social phobia criteria were modified to account for developmental variation (see "Description of the Disorders," above).

The issue of whether high comorbidity indicates invalid division of latent constructs becomes more complex when one considers the more heterogeneous and yet common syndromes of childhood, such as school refusal or test anxiety. Indeed, because these syndromes are unique to childhood, their nosology has received relatively less empirical attention than the disorders common to both children and adults. Consequently, their relationship to DSM diagnostic nosology has been the subject of debate (e.g., Beidel & Turner, 1988; Kearney & Silverman, 1996). In a study of test anxiety, for example, Beidel and Turner found comorbidity of the test-anxious syndrome with DSM-III diagnoses of social phobia (24%), simple phobia (4%), separation anxiety (4%), and overanxious disorder (24%). Although it might be argued that test anxiety is perhaps best conceptualized along the dimension of DSM nosology, it is interesting to note that 40% of the test-anxious sample did not meet criteria for any DSM-III diagnosis.

Similar quandaries have arisen in the area of school refusal (Kearney & Silverman, 1996). Several attempts have been made to understand school refusal as a symptom of anxiety or affective disorders (Bernstein & Garfinkel, 1986; Last & Francis, 1988; Last, Francis, et al., 1987; Last & Strauss, 1990; Ollendick & Mayer, 1984), and there has been considerable debate as to how the phenomenon is principally related to the most frequent comorbid diagnostic categories, simple phobia and separation anxiety disorder (Last & Strauss, 1990). Complicating the issue still further, many researchers continue to use the terms "school phobia" and "school refusal" interchangeably, considering the school refusal syndrome to be more or less conceptually equivalent to simple phobia of school (Burke & Silverman, 1987). Recent evidence does not support this conten-

tion, however (Kearney & Silverman, 1996). In fact, the comorbidity of school refusal and DSM anxiety disorders suggests no clear overlap at all (e.g., Kearney, Eisen, & Silverman, 1995; Last & Francis, 1988; Last & Strauss, 1990). Rather, it appears that the school refusal syndrome may best be conceptualized along dimensions other than those included in DSM nosology (e.g., function of symptomatic behaviors; see Kearney & Silverman, 1996, for a full discussion).

Perhaps among the least understood syndromes of childhood anxiety are the diagnoses related to generalized anxiety. In DSM-III-R, GAD and OAD share overlapping features and represent conceptually similar syndromes thought to differ due to developmental presentation. However, the data on the comorbidity of these two syndromes are equivocal, mainly as the result of the absence of data on GAD in children. For example, Last et al. (1992) found no cases of GAD in a sample of 188 children and adolescents, yet 25 of these subjects were assigned principal diagnoses of OAD. Other studies have presented similar findings (e.g., Last, Strauss, et al., 1987). Emerging findings suggest that despite the similarity of GAD and OAD symptomatology, the disorders are not likely to be comorbid when assessed cross-sectionally. For example, in a sample of 174 children and adolescents, Albano, Chorpita, et al. (1995) found that of 29 children with a principal diagnosis of OAD, none were assigned a secondary diagnosis of GAD. Interestingly, GAD was found to be a secondary diagnosis and comorbid with social phobia in this sample. These apparently paradoxical findings can be better understood when one considers the notion that OAD and GAD might demonstrate high comorbidity longitudinally, that is, a child may have a history of OAD preceding the onset of GAD, but not cross-sectionally. The idea that OAD and GAD would not often be diagnosed concurrently is further supported by theoretical developments suggesting that generalized anxiety may be topographically distinct in children from that in adolescents or adults (see Vasey, 1993).

A similar debate continues concerning the comorbidity of SAD and PDA. Although these disorders can share features of restricted range of activity, necessity of a "safe" person, and the experience of fear without an external stressor, the data supporting their relationship are indeterminate (Ollendick et al., 1994). Data from the retrospective studies attempting to assess longitudinal comorbidity suggest that the link between SAD and PDA is not a strong one (Thyer, Neese,

et al., 1985; Thyer, Neese, Curtis, & Cameron, 1986; van der Molen, van der Hout, van Dieren, & Greiz, 1989), however, contrary evidence has also been noted (e.g., Allessi & Magen, 1988). Evaluating children for lifetime history of anxiety disorders, Last et al. (1992) found no significant relationship between SAD and the subsequent diagnosis of PD. In fact, their data supported the notion that OAD may be the most frequent diagnosis to precede PD, having emerged prior to PD in 90% of their subjects. Although not consistent with existing speculation about the relationship of panic and SAD, such findings compare favorably with existing theories about the relationship of chronic arousal and panic attacks (Barlow, 1988).

Research on comorbidity of the anxiety disorders has often extended into the realm of depressive disorders as well, notably, major depression and dysthymia. For example, Strauss, Last, et al. (1988) examined anxiety and depression in 106 outpatient children and adolescents using DSM-III criteria. For children diagnosed with an anxiety disorder, comorbidity with depression was extensive (28%), and those children with comorbid anxiety and depression showed more severe anxiety symptomatology than those children with anxiety disorders alone. In a similar manner, Strauss, Lease, et al. (1988), examined a broad age range of 55 children and adolescents diagnosed with DSM-III overanxious disorder. In a median split analysis of the sample, comorbid depression was found in 50% of the older children (ages 12–19 years) and in 20% of the younger children (ages 5–11 years). This suggests not only the overlap between the latent constructs of anxiety and depression, but it also supports the possibility of a developmental progression, whereby anxiety precedes depression. Similar evidence has been found in adult populations (cf. Barlow et al., in press).

CURRENT ISSUES AND FUTURE DIRECTIONS

The inclusion of the childhood anxiety disorders section within the publication of DSM-III sparked a legion of studies on the classification and diagnosis of these disorders in youth. Clearly, the increased attention to understanding the phenomenology and classification of these disorders has illuminated the high prevalence of these conditions in the general child and adolescent popu-

lation. Although the changes evident in the DSM-IV criteria remain to be evaluated, considerable debate regarding the occurrence of specific symptoms and disorders in youth exists. The presence of panic disorder in children remains controversial, and evidence for the disorder in adolescents has only recently emerged. Investigators are now turning toward explicating those cognitive-developmental variations in the expression of panic disorder in youth (see Ollendick et al., 1994). Similarly, Vasey, Crnic, and Carter (1994) are examining social–cognitive factors within a developmental context to understand worry in children. Investigators must approach the study of these conditions from a developmental perspective and avoid the tendency to apply adult symptom criteria to youth. Moreover, the structure and process of classification in children and adolescents remain areas of considerable study and debate. The utility of the categorical, dimensional, and integrated systems of classification must be explored further.

Studies of clinic-referred samples have furthered our understanding of the devastating impact of anxiety disorders on all areas of the child's functioning. Although the existing literature is growing, many questions remain regarding the expression, diagnosis, and treatment of these disorders in youth. Specifically, longitudinal studies are needed to explore fully the natural history of these disorders and the patterns of symptom expression in normal, nonreferred youth. Only with the systematic study of normal children will investigators begin to appreciate and understand those factors involved in the etiology and maintenance of these disorders. Moreover, studies of clinical samples must be directed toward examining prognostic factors, especially in children who have or have not received treatment. It is only relatively recently that studies examining the efficacy of prescriptive psychosocial treatment protocols have begun to appear in the literature (e.g., Albano, Marten, et al., 1995; Kearney & Silverman, 1990; Kendall, 1994; March, Mulle, & Herbel, 1994; Ollendick, 1995). With the exception of Kendall's (1994) clinical outcome study with overanxious youth, controlled investigations are lacking. Although several investigations are under way (see Hibbs & Jensen, in press), the long-term effectiveness of psychosocial treatments for anxiety disorders in youth remains largely unexplored. Similarly, research regarding the long-term effectiveness of pharmacological agents and their combination with

psychosocial treatments is sorely lacking (see March, 1995). Overall, questions regarding the prognosis for children with these disorders remain unanswered.

The continual study of developmental variations and influences will remain central to our further understanding of the nature of these disorders in youth. Elucidating the nature and mechanisms underlying certain vulnerability pathways such as inhibited temperament, environmental, and familial factors will no doubt occupy the attention of researchers well into the next century. Several compelling etiological models were reviewed in this chapter. Contemporary theorists point toward an integrated model, encompassing biological vulnerabilities, psychological constructs, as well as conditioning and environmental factors (see Barlow, 1988; Barlow et al., in press; and Hope, in press). The continued study of the interaction between biological and psychological factors in children and adolescents should continue to provide insights into the nature and correlates of these disorders. Again, longitudinal studies are needed to explicate the interaction of factors within these etiological models. Moreover, studies are needed to examine the long-term implications of enduring and fixed factors such as family environment or developmental disability on course and prognosis.

ACKNOWLEDGMENTS

The writing of this chapter was supported in part by National Institute of Mental Health (NIMH) Grant No. MH49691.

REFERENCES

Abe, K., & Masui, T. (1981). Age-sex trends of phobic and anxiety symptoms in adolescents. *British Journal of Psychiatry, 138,* 297–302.

Abramson, L. Y., Seligman, M. E. P., & Teasdale, J. (1978). Learned helplessness in humans: Critique and reformulation. *Journal of Abnormal Psychology, 87,* 49–74.

Achenbach, T. M. (1980). DSM-III in light of empirical research on the classification of child psychopathology. *Journal of the American Academy of Child and Adolescent Psychiatry, 19,* 395–412.

Achenbach, T. M. (1988). Integrating assessment and taxonomy. In M. Rutter, A. H. Tuma, & I. S. Lann (Eds.), *Assessment and diagnosis in child psychopathology.* New York: Guilford Press.

Achenbach, T. M. (1991). *Manual for the Child Behavior Checklist/4–18 and 1991 profile.* Burlington, VT: University of Vermont Department of Psychiatry.

Achenbach, T. M. (1993). Implications of multiaxial empirically based assessment for behavior therapy with children. *Behavior Therapy, 24,* 91–116.

Achenbach, T. M., & Edelbrock, C. (1983). *Manual for the Child Behavior Checklist and Revised Child Behavior Profile.* Burlington, VT: University of Vermont Department of Psychiatry.

Agras, W. S., Chapin, H. N., & Oliveau, D. C. (1972). The natural history of phobias: Course and prognosis. *Archives of General Psychiatry, 26,* 315–317.

Ahlawat, K. S. (1986). Cross-cultural comparison of anxiety for Jordanian and U.S. high school students. In C. D. Speilberger & R. Diaz-Guerrero (Eds.), *Cross cultural anxiety* (Vol. 3, pp. 93–112). Washington, DC: Hemisphere/Harper & Row.

Albano, A. M., Chorpita, B. F., DiBartolo, P. M., & Barlow, D. H. (1995). *Comorbidity of DSM-III-R anxiety disorders in children and adolescents.* Unpublished manuscript, State University of New York at Albany.

Albano, A. M., Knox, L. S., & Barlow, D. H. (1995). Obsessive–compulsive disorder. In A. R. Eisen, C. A. Kearney, & C. A. Schaefer (Eds.), *Clinical handbook of anxiety disorders in children and adolescents* (pp. 282–316). Northvale, NJ: Jason Aronson.

Albano, A. M., DiBartolo, P. M., Heimberg, R. G., & Barlow, D. H. (1995). Children and adolescents: Assessment and treatment. In R. G. Heimberg, M. R. Liebowitz, D. A. Hope, & F. R. Schneier (Eds.), *Social phobia: Diagnosis, assessment, and treatment* (pp. 387–425). New York: Guilford Press.

Albano, A. M., Marten, P. A., Holt, C. S., Heimberg, R. G., & Barlow, D. H. (1995). Cognitive-behavioral group treatment for adolescent social phobia: A preliminary study. *Journal of Nervous and Mental Disease, 183,* 685–692.

Albano, A. M., Mitchell, W. B., Zarate, R., & Barlow, D. H. (1992, July). *Applied tension and positive mood induction in the treatment of specific phobia of blood.* Paper presented at the Fourth World Congress of Behavior Therapy, Queensland, Australia.

Alessi, N. E., & Magen, J. (1988). Panic disorder in psychiatrically hospitalized children. *American Journal of Psychiatry, 145,* 1450–1452.

Alessi, N. E., Robbins, D. R., & Dilsaver, S. C. (1987). Panic and depressive disorders among psychiatrically hospitalized adolescents. *Psychiatry Research, 20,* 275–283.

Alloy, L. B., Kelly, K. A., Mineka, S., & Clements, C. M. (1990). Comorbidity of anxiety and depressive disorders: A helplessness–hopelessness perspective. In J. D. Maser & C. R. Cloninger (Eds.), *Comorbidity of mood and anxiety disorders* (pp. 499–543). Washington, DC: American Psychiatric Press.

Alnæs, R., & Torgersen, S. (1990). Parental representation in patients with major depression, anxiety disorder and mixed conditions. *Acta Psychiatrica Scandinavica, 80,* 518–522.

American Psychiatric Association. (1952). *Diagnostic and statistical manual of mental disorders.* Washington, DC: Author.

American Psychiatric Association. (1968). *Diagnostic and statistical manual of mental disorders* (2nd ed.). Washington, DC: Author.

American Psychiatric Association. (1980). *Diagnostic and statistical manual of mental disorders* (3rd ed.). Washington, DC: Author.

American Psychiatric Association. (1987). *Diagnostic and statistical manual of mental disorders* (3rd ed., rev.). Washington, DC: Author.

American Psychiatric Association. (1994). *Diagnostic and statistical manual of mental disorders* (4th ed.). Washington, DC: Author.

Anderson, D. J., Williams, S., McGee, R., & Silva, P. A. (1987). DSM-III disorders in preadolescent children: Prevalence in a large sample from the general population. *Archives of General Psychiatry, 44,* 69–76.

Andrews, G., Stewart, G., Allen, R., & Henderson, A. S. (1990). The genetics of six neurotic disorders: A twin study. *Journal of Affective Disorders, 19,* 23–29.

Antony, M. (1994). *Heterogeneity among specific phobia subtypes in DSM-IV.* Unpublished doctoral dissertation, Albany, State University of New York.

Ballenger, J. C., Carek, D. J., Steele, J. J., & Cornish-McTighe, D. (1989). Three cases of panic disorder with agoraphobia in children. *American Journal of Psychiatry, 146,* 922–924.

Bandura, A. (1986). *Social foundations of thought and action.* Englewood Cliffs, NJ: Prentice-Hall.

Barlow, D. H. (1988). *Anxiety and its disorders: The nature and treatment of anxiety and panic.* New York: Guilford Press.

Barlow, D. H. (1991). Disorders of emotion. *Psychological Inquiry, 2,* 58–71.

Barlow, D. H. (1992). Diagnosis, DSM-IV, and dimensional approaches. In A. Ehlers, W. Fiegenbaum, I. Florin, & J. Margraf (Eds.), *Perspectives and promises of clinical psychology* (pp. 13–21). New York: Plenum Press.

Barlow, D. H., Chorpita, B. F., & Turovsky, J. (in press). Fear, panic, anxiety, and the disorders of emotion. In D. A. Hope (Ed.), *Nebraska Symposium on Motivation: Integrated views of motivation and emotion* (Vol. 43). Lincoln: University of Nebraska Press.

Barlow, D. H., & Durand, V. M. (1995). *Abnormal psychology: An integrative approach.* Pacific Grove, CA: Brooks/Cole.

Barrett, P. M., Dadds, M. R., Rapee, R. M., & Ryan, S. (1994, November). *Effectiveness of group treatment for anxious children and their parents.* Paper presented at the 28th annual convention of the Association for Advancement of Behavior Therapy, San Diego, CA.

Barrett, P. M., Rapee, R. M., & Dadds, M. R. (1993, November). *Cognitive and family processes in childhood anxiety.* Paper presented at the 27th annual convention of the Association for Advancement of Behavior Therapy, Atlanta, GA.

Barrios, B. A., & Hartmann, D. P. (1988). Fears and anxieties. In E. J. Mash & L. G. Terdal (Eds.), *Behavioral assessment of childhood disorders* (2nd ed., pp. 196–262). New York: Guilford Press.

Barrios, B. A., & O'Dell, S. L. (1989). Fears and anxieties. In E. J. Mash & R. A. Barkley (Eds.), *Treatment of childhood disorders* (pp. 167–221). New York: Guilford Press.

Bauer, D. H. (1976). An exploratory study of developmental changes in children's fears. *Journal of Child Psychology and Psychiatry, 17,* 69–74.

Beidel, D. C. (1991). Social phobia and overanxious disorder in school-age children. *Journal of the American Academy of Child and Adolescent Psychiatry, 30,* 545–552.

Beidel, D. C., & Morris, T. L. (1993). Avoidant disorder of childhood and social phobia. *Child and Adolescent Psychiatric Clinics of North America, 2,* 623–638.

Beidel, D. C., & Morris, T. L. (1995). Social phobia. In J. S. March (Ed.), *Anxiety disorders in children and adolescents* (pp. 181–211). New York: Guilford Press.

Beidel, D. C., & Turner, S. M. (1988). Comorbidity of test anxiety and other anxiety disorders in children. *Journal of Abnormal Child Psychology, 16,* 275–287.

Beitchman, J. H., Wekerle, C., & Hood, J. (1987). Diagnostic continuity from preschool to middle childhood. *Journal of the American Academy of Child and Adolescent Psychiatry, 26,* 694–699.

Bell-Dolan, D., & Brazeal, T. J. (1993). Separation anxiety disorder, overanxious disorder, and school refusal. *Child and Adolescent Psychiatric Clinics of North America, 2,* 563–580.

Bell-Dolan, D., Last, C. G., & Strauss, C. C. (1990). Symptoms of anxiety disorders in normal children. *Journal of the American Academy of Child and Adolescent Psychiatry, 29,* 759–765.

Berg, C., Rapoport, J. L., Whitaker, A., Davies, M., Leonard, H., Swedo, S., Braiman, S., & Lenane, M. (1989). Childhood obsessive compulsive disorder: A two-year prospective follow-up of a community sample. *Journal of the American Academy of Child and Adolescent Psychiatry, 28,* 528–533.

Berg, I. (1976). School phobia in the children of agoraphobic women. *British Journal of Psychiatry, 128,* 86–89.

Berg, I., Marks, I., Maguire, R., & Lipsedge, M. (1974). School phobia and agoraphobia. *Psychological Medicine, 4,* 428–434.

Berkson, J. (1946). Limitations of the application of fourfold table analysis to hospital data. *Biometrics, 2,* 47–53.

Bernstein, G. A., & Borchardt, C. M. (1991). Anxiety disorders of childhood and adolescence: A critical review. *Journal of the American Academy of Child and Adolescent Psychiatry, 30,* 519–532.

Bernstein, G. A., & Garfinkel, B. D. (1986). School phobia: The overlap of affective and anxiety disorders. *Journal of the American Academy of Child and Adolescent Psychiatry, 145,* 70–74.

Bernstein, G. A., Garfinkel, B. D., & Hoberman, H. M. (1989). Self-reported anxiety in adolescents. *American Journal of Psychiatry, 146,* 384–386.

Biederman, J., Rosenbaum, J. F., Bolduc, E. A., Faraone, S. V., & Hirshfeld, D. R. (1991). A high risk study of young children of parents with panic disorder and agoraphobia with and without comorbid major depression. *Psychiatry Research, 37,* 333–348.

Biederman, J., Rosenbaum, J. F., Bolduc-Murphy, E. A., Faraone, S. V., Chaloff, J., Hirshfeld, D. R., & Kagan, J. (1993a). A three year follow-up of children with and without behavioral inhibition. *Journal of the American Academy of Child and Adolescent Psychiatry, 32,* 814–821.

Biederman, J., Rosenbaum, J. F., Bolduc-Murphy, E. A., Faraone, S. V., Chaloff, J., Hirshfeld, D. R., & Kagan, J. (1993b). Behavioral inhibition as a temperamental risk factor for anxiety disorders. *Child and Adolescent Psychiatric Clinics of North America, 2,* 667–684.

Biederman, J., Rosenbaum, J. F., Hirshfeld, D. R., Faraone, S. V., Bolduc, E. A., Gersten, M., Meminger, S. R., Kagan, J., Snidman, N., & Reznick, J. S. (1990). Psychiatric correlates of behavioral inhibition in young children of parents with and without psychiatric disorders. *Archives of General Psychiatry, 47,* 21–26.

Bird, H. R., Gould, M. S., Yager, T., Staghezza, B., & Canino, G. (1989). Risk factors for maladjustment in Puerto Rican children. *Journal of the American Academy of Child and Adolescent Psychiatry, 28,* 847–850.

Black, B. (1995). Separation anxiety disorder and panic disorder. In J. S. March (Ed.), *Anxiety disorders in children and adolescents* (pp. 212–234). New York: Guilford Press.

Black, B., & Robbins, D. R. (1990). Panic disorder in children and adolescents. *Journal of the American Academy of Child and Adolescent Psychiatry, 29*, 36–44.

Bowen, R. C., Offord, D. R., & Boyle, M. H. (1990). The prevalence of overanxious disorder and separation anxiety disorder: Results from the Ontario child health study. *Journal of the American Academy of Child and Adolescent Psychiatry, 29*, 753–758.

Bowlby, J. (1969). *Attachment and loss: Vol. 1. Attachment.* New York: Basic Books.

Bowlby, J. (1973). *Attachment and loss: Vol. 2. Separation.* New York: Basic Books.

Bradley, S. J., & Hood, J. (1993). Psychiatrically referred adolescents with panic attacks: Presenting symptoms, stressors, and comorbidity. *Journal of the American Academy of Child and Adolescent Psychiatry, 32*, 826–829.

Brady, E. U., & Kendall, P. C. (1992). Comorbidity of anxiety and depression in children and adolescents. *Psychological Bulletin, 111*, 244–255.

Breier, A., Charney, D. S., & Heninger, G. R. (1986). Agoraphobia and panic attacks: Development, diagnostic stability, and course of illness. *Archives of General Psychiatry, 43*, 1029–1036.

Brown, D. R., Eaton, W. W., & Sussman, L. (1990). Racial differences in prevalence of phobic disorders. *Journal of Nervous and Mental Disease, 178*, 434–441.

Brown, T. A., & Barlow, D. H. (1992). Comorbidity among anxiety disorders: Implications for treatment and DSM-IV. *Journal of Consulting and Clinical Psychology, 60*, 835–844.

Burke, A. E., & Silverman, W. K. (1987). The prescriptive treatment of school refusal. *Clinical Psychology Review, 7*, 353–362.

Butler, G., & Mathews, A. (1983). Cognitive processes in anxiety. *Advances in Behavior Research and Therapy, 5*, 51–62.

Cantwell, D. P., & Baker, L. (1989). Stability and natural history of DSM-III childhood diagnoses. *Journal of the American Academy of Child and Adolescent Psychiatry, 29*, 691–700.

Caron, C., & Rutter, M. (1991). Comorbidity in child psychopathology: Concepts, issues and research strategies. *Journal of Child Psychology and Psychiatry, 32*, 1063–1080.

Chorpita, B. F., & Barlow, D. H. (1995). *Control in the early environment: Implications for psychosocial models of childhood anxiety.* Unpublished manuscript, Albany, State University of New York.

Costello, E. J. (1989). Child psychiatric disorders and their correlates: A primary care pediatric sample. *Journal of the American Academy of Child and Adolescent Psychiatry, 28*, 851–855.

Crockenberg, S. (1981). Infant irritability, mother responsiveness, and social support influences on the security of infant–mother attachment. *Child Development, 52*, 857–865.

Crowe, R. R., Noyes, R., Pauls, D. L., & Slymen, D. (1983). A family study of panic disorder. *Archives of General Psychiatry, 40*, 1065–1069.

Dadds, M. R., Heard, P. M., & Rapee, R. M. (1992). The role of family intervention in the treatment of child anxiety disorders: Some preliminary findings. *Behavior Change, 9*, 171–177.

Deltito, J. A., Perugi, G., Maremmani, I., Mignani, V., & Cassano, G. B. (1986). The importance of separation anxiety in the differentiation of panic disorder from agoraphobia. *Psychiatric Development, 4*, 227–236.

Dienstbier, R. A. (1989). Arousal and physiological toughness: Implications for mental and physical health. *Psychological Review, 96*, 84–100.

DiNardo, P. A., O'Brien, G. T., Barlow, D. H., Waddell, M. T., & Blanchard, E. B. (1983). Reliability of DSM-III anxiety disorders using a new structured interview. *Archives of General Psychiatry, 22*, 1070–1078.

Dinges, N. G., & Duong-Tran, Q. (1993). Stressful life events and co-occurring depression, substance abuse, and suicidality among American Indian and Alaskan Native adolescents. *Culture, Medicine, and Psychiatry, 16*, 487–502.

Dweck, C., & Wortman, C. (1982). Learned helplessness, anxiety, and achievement. In H. Krone & L. Laux (Eds.), *Achievement, stress and anxiety* (pp. 93–125). New York: Hemisphere.

Ehiobuche, I. (1988). Obsessive–compulsive neurosis in relation to parental child rearing patterns amongst Greek, Italian, and Anglo-Australian subjects. *Acta Psychiatrica Scandinavica, 78*, 115–120.

Eisen, A. R., & Engler, L. B. (1995). Chronic anxiety. In A. R. Eisen, C. A. Kearney, & C. A. Schaefer (Eds.), *Clinical handbook of anxiety disorders in children and adolescents.* Northvale, NJ: Jason Aronson.

Eisen, A. R., & Kearney, C. A. (1995). *Practitioner's guide to treating fear and anxiety in children and adolescents: A cognitive-behavioral approach.* Northvale, NJ: Jason Aronson.

Flament, M. F., Whitaker, A., Rapoport, J. L., Davies, M., Zeremba-Berg, C., Kalikow, K. S., Sceery, W., & Shaffer, D. (1988). Obsessive compulsive disorder in adolescence: An epidemiological study. *Journal of the American Academy of Child and Adolescent Psychiatry, 27*, 764–771.

Fonesca, A. C., Yule, W., & Erol, N. (1994). Cross-cultural issues. In T. H. Ollendick, N. J. King, & W. Yule (Eds.), *International handbook of phobic and anxiety disorders in children and adolescents* (pp. 67–84). New York: Plenum Press.

Frances, A., Widiger, T., & Fyer, M. R. (1990). The influence of classification methods on comorbidity. In D. Maser & C. D. Cloninger (Eds.), *Comorbidity of anxiety and mood disorders.* Washington, DC: American Psychiatric Association Press.

Francis, G., Last, C. G., & Strauss, C. C. (1987). Expression of separation anxiety disorder: The roles of age and gender. *Child Psychiatry and Human Development, 18*, 82–89.

Francis, G., Last, C. G., & Strauss, C. C. (1992). Avoidant disorder and social phobia in children and adolescents. *Journal of the American Academy of Child and Adolescent Psychiatry, 31*, 1086–1089.

Freud, A. (1965). *Normality and pathology in childhood: Assessment of development.* New York: International Universities Press.

Freud, S. (1909). Analysis of a phobia in a five-year-old boy. *Standard Edition, 10*, 3–149. London: Hogarth Press, 1955.

Friedman, S., & Paradis, C. M. (1991). African-American patients with panic disorder and agoraphobia. *Journal of Anxiety Disorders, 5*, 35–41.

Garmezy, N. (1986). Developmental aspects of children's responses to the stress of separation and loss. In M. Rutter, C. E. Izard, & P. B. Read (Eds.), *Depression in young people: Developmental and clinical perspectives* (pp. 297–323). New York: Guilford Press.

Garmezy, N. & Rutter, M. (1985). *Stress, coping, and development in children.* New York: McGraw-Hill.

Gerlsma, C., Emmelkamp, P. M. G., & Arrindell, W. A. (1990). Anxiety, depression, and perception of early parenting: A meta-analysis. *Clinical Psychology Review, 10,* 251–277.

Gersten, M. (1986). *The contribution of temperament to behavior in natural contexts.* Unpublished doctoral dissertation, Harvard Graduate School of Education, Cambridge, MA.

Gittelman, R., & Klein, D. F. (1985). Childhood separation anxiety and adult agoraphobia. In A. H. Tuma & J. Maser (Eds.), *Anxiety and the anxiety disorders* (pp. 389–402). Hillsdale, NJ: Erlbaum.

Goodyer, I. N. (1990). Family relationships, life events, and child psychopathology. *Journal of Child Psychology and Psychiatry, 31,* 161–192.

Gray, J. A. (1982). *The neuropsychology of anxiety.* New York: Oxford University Press.

Griegel, L. E., Albano, A. M., & Barlow, D. H. (1991, November). *"Do children panic?" revisited: Yes they do!* Paper presented at the meeting of the Association for Advancement of Behavior Therapy, New York.

Guida, F. V., & Ludlow, L. H. (1989). A cross cultural study of test anxiety. *Journal of Cross Cultural Psychology, 20,* 178–190.

Hampe, E., Noble, H., Miller, L. C., & Barrett, O. L. (1973). Phobic children one and two years posttreatment. *Journal of Abnormal Psychology, 82,* 446–453.

Harris, B. (1979). Whatever happened to Little Albert? *American Psychologist, 34,* 151–160.

Harris, E. L., Noyes, R., Crowe, R., & Chaudhry, D. R. (1983). Family study of agoraphobia. *Archives of General Psychiatry, 35,* 1057–1059.

Hayward, C., Killen, J. D., Hammer, L. D., Litt, I. F., Wilson, D. M., Simmonds, B., & Taylor, C. B. (1992). Pubertal stage and panic attack history in sixth- and seventh-grade girls. *American Journal of Psychiatry, 149,* 1239–1243.

Hebb, D. O. (1946). On the nature of fear. *Psychological Review, 53,* 259–276.

Hebb, D. O. (1955). Drives and the conceptual nervous system. *Psychological Review, 62,* 243–254.

Hibbs, E. D., & Jensen, P. S. (in press). *Psychosocial treatment research of child and adolescent disorders.* Washington, DC: American Psychological Association Press.

Hinshaw, S. P. (1992). Externalizing behavior problems and academic underachievement in childhood and adolescence: Causal relationships and underlying mechanisms. *Psychological Bulletin, 111,* 127–155.

Hirshfeld, D. R., Rosenbaum, J. F., Biederman, J., Bolduc, E. A., Faraone, S. V., Snidman, N., Reznick, J. S., & Kagan, J. (1992). Stable behavioral inhibition and its association with anxiety disorders. *Journal of the American Academy of Child and Adolescent Psychiatry, 31,* 103–111.

Hodges, K., McKnew, D., Cytryn, L., Stern, L., & Kline, J. (1982). The Child Assessment Schedule (CAS) diagnostic interview: A report on the reliability and validity. *Journal of the American Academy of Child Psychiatry, 21,* 486–473.

Hope, D. A. (Ed.). (in press). *Nebraska Symposium on Motivation: Integrated views of motivation and emotion* (Vol. 43). Lincoln: University of Nebraska Press.

Izard, C. E., & Beuchler, S. (1979). Emotion expressions and personality integration in infancy. In C. E. Izard (Ed.), *Emotions in personality and psychopathology* (pp. 447–472). New York: Plenum Press.

Johnson, J. H., & McCutcheon, S. M. (1980). Assessing life stress in older children and adolescents: Preliminary findings with the Life Events Checklist. In I. G. Sarason & C. D. Speilberger (Eds.), *Stress and anxiety* (Vol. 7). Washington, DC: Hemisphere Press.

Jones, M. C. (1924a). The elimination of children's fears. *Journal of Experimental Psychology, 1,* 383–390.

Jones, M. C. (1924b). A laboratory study of fear: The case of Peter. *Pedagogical Seminar, 31,* 308–315.

Kagan, J. (1982). Heart rate and heart rate variability as signs of a temperamental dimension in infants. In C. E. Izard (Ed.), *Measuring emotions in infants and children* (pp. 38–66). Cambridge, UK: Cambridge University Press.

Kagan, J. (1989). Temperamental contributions to social behavior. *American Psychologist, 44,* 668–674.

Kagan, J., Reznick, J. S., & Gibbons, J. (1989). Inhibited and uninhibited types of children. *Child Development, 60,* 838–845.

Kagan, J., Reznick, J. S., & Snidman, N. (1987). The physiology and psychology of behavioral inhibition. *Child Development, 58,* 1459–1473.

Kagan, J., Reznick, J. S., & Snidman, N. (1988). Biological bases of childhood shyness. *Science, 240,* 167–171.

Karno, M., Golding, J. M., Sorenson, S. B., & Burnam, M. A. (1988). The epidemiology of obsessive-compulsive disorder in five U.S. communities. *Archives of General Psychiatry, 45,* 1094–1099.

Kashani, J. H., & Orvaschel, H. (1988). Anxiety disorders in midadolescence: A community sample. *American Journal of Psychiatry, 145,* 960–964.

Kashani, J. H., Orvaschel, H., Rosenberg, T. K., & Reid, J. C. (1989). Psychopathology in a community sample of children and adolescents: A developmental perspective. *Journal of the American Academy of Child and Adolescent Psychiatry, 28,* 701–706.

Kashani, J. H., Vaidya, A. F., Soltys, S. M., Dandoy, A. C., Katz, L. M., & Reid, J. C. (1990). Correlates of anxiety in psychiatrically hospitalized children and their parents. *American Journal of Psychiatry, 147,* 319–323.

Kearney, C. A. (1995). School refusal behavior. In A. R. Eisen, C. A. Kearney, & C. A. Schaefer (Eds.), *Clinical handbook of anxiety disorders in children and adolescents.* Northvale, NJ: Jason Aronson.

Kearney, C. A., & Allan, W. D. (1995). Panic disorder with or without agoraphobia. In A. R. Eisen, C. A. Kearney, & C. A. Schaefer (Eds.), *Clinical handbook of anxiety disorders in children and adolescents.* Northvale, NJ: Jason Aronson.

Kearney, C. A., Eisen, A. E., & Schaefer, C. A. (1995). General issues underlying the diagnosis and treatment of child and adolescent anxiety disorders. In A. R. Eisen, C. A. Kearney, & C. A. Schaefer (Eds.), *Clinical handbook of anxiety disorders in children and adolescents.* Northvale, NJ: Jason Aronson.

Kearney, C. A., Eisen, A. E., & Silverman, W. K. (1995). The legend and myth of school phobia. *School Psychology Quarterly, 10,* 65–85.

Kearney, C. A., & Silverman, W. K. (1990). A preliminary analysis of a functional model of assessment and treatment of school refusal behavior. *Behavior Modification, 14,* 340–366.

Kearney, C. A., & Silverman, W. K. (1992). Let's not push the "panic" button: A critical analysis of panic and panic disorder in adolescents. *Clinical Psychology Review, 12,* 293–305.

Kearney, C. A., & Silverman, W. K. (1993). Measuring the function of school refusal behavior: The School Refusal

Assessment Scale. *Journal of Clinical Child Psychology,* 22, 85–96.

Kearney, C. A., & Silverman, W. K. (1996). *The evolution and reconciliation of taxonomic strategies for school refusal behavior.* Manuscript submitted for publication.

Keller, M. B., & Baker, L. A. (1992). The clinical course of panic disorder and depression. *Journal of Clinical Psychiatry,* 53(Suppl. 3), 5–8.

Keller, M. B., Lavori, P., Wunder, J., Beardslee, W. R., Schwartz, C. E., & Roth, J. (1992). Chronic course of anxiety disorders in children and adolescents. *Journal of the American Academy of Child and Adolescent Psychiatry,* 31, 595–599.

Kendall, P. C. (1992). Childhood coping: Avoiding a lifetime of anxiety. *Behavioural Change,* 9, 1–8.

Kendall, P. C. (1994). Treating anxiety disorders in children: Results of a randomized clinical trial. *Journal of Consulting and Clinical Psychology,* 62, 100–110.

Kendall, P. C., Chansky, T. E., Kane, M. T., Kim, R., Kortlander, E., Ronan, K., Sessa, F., & Siqueland, L. (1992). *Anxiety disorders in youth: Cognitive-behavioral interventions.* New York: Macmillan.

Kendall, P. C., Kane, M., Howard, B., & Siqueland, L. (1990). *Cognitive behavioral therapy for anxious children: Treatment manual.* (Available from Philip C. Kendall, Department of Psychology, Temple University, Philadelphia, PA 19122.)

Kendler, K. S., Neale, M. C., Kessler, R. C., Heath, A. C., & Eaves, L. J. (1992). Major depression and generalized anxiety disorder: Same genes, (partly) different environments? *Archives of General Psychiatry,* 49, 716–722.

Kessler, R. C., McGonagle, K., Zhao, S., Nelson, C. B., Hughes, M., Eshleman, S., Wittchen, H.-U., & Kendler, K. S. (1994). Lifetime and 12-month prevalence of DSM-III-R psychiatric disorders in the United States. *Archives of General Psychiatry,* 51, 8–19.

King, N. J. (1993). Simple and social phobias. In T. H. Ollendick & R. J. Prinz (Eds.), *Advances in clinical child psychology* (Vol. 15, pp. 305–341). New York: Plenum Press.

King, N. J., Hamilton, D. I., & Ollendick, T. H. (1988). *Children's phobias: A behavioural perspective.* Chichester, UK: Wiley.

King, N. J., Ollendick, T. H., & Gullone, E. (1991). Negative affectivity in children and adolescents: Relations between anxiety and depression. *Clinical Psychology Review,* 11, 441–459.

Lapouse, R., & Monk, M. A. (1958). An epidemiologic study of behavior characteristics in children. *American Journal of Public Health,* 48, 1134–1144.

Lapouse, R., & Monk, M. A. (1959). Fears and worries in a representative sample of children. *American Journal of Orthopsychiatry,* 29, 803–818.

Last, C. G. (1989). Anxiety disorders of childhood or adolescence. In C. G. Last & M. Hersen (Eds.), *Handbook of child psychiatric diagnosis* (pp. 156–169). New York: Wiley.

Last, C. G. (1991). Somatic complaints in anxiety disordered children. *Journal of Anxiety Disorders,* 5, 125–138.

Last, C. G., & Francis, G. (1988). School phobia. In B. B. Lahey & A. E. Kazdin (Eds.), *Advances in clinical child psychology* (Vol. 11, pp. 193–222). New York: Plenum Press.

Last, C. G., Francis, G., Hersen, M., Kazdin, A. E., & Strauss, C. C. (1987). Separation anxiety and school phobia: A comparison using DSM-III criteria. *American Journal of Psychiatry,* 144, 653–657.

Last, C. G., Francis, G., & Strauss, C. C. (1989). Assessing fears in anxiety-disordered children with the Revised Fear Survey Schedule for Children (FSSC-R). *Journal of Clinical Child Psychology,* 18, 137–141.

Last, C. G., Hersen, M., Kazdin, A. E., Finkelstein, R., & Strauss, C. C. (1987). Comparison of DSM-III separation anxiety and overanxious disorders: Demographic characteristics and patterns of comorbidity. *Journal of the American Academy of Child and Adolescent Psychiatry,* 26, 527–531.

Last, C. G., Hersen, M., Kazdin, A., Orvaschel, H., & Perrin, S. (1991). Anxiety disorders in children and their families. *Archives of General Psychiatry,* 48, 928–934.

Last, C. G., & Perrin, S. (1993). Anxiety disorders in African-American and white children. *Journal of Abnormal Child Psychology,* 21, 153–164.

Last, C. G., Perrin, S., Hersen, M., & Kazdin, A. E. (1992). DSM-III-R anxiety disorders in children: Sociodemographic and clinical characteristics. *Journal of the American Academy of Child and Adolescent Psychiatry,* 31, 1070–1076.

Last, C. G., Perrin, S., Hersen, M., & Kazdin, A. E. (1995). *A prospective study of childhood anxiety-disorders.* Manuscript submitted for publication.

Last, C. G., & Strauss, C. C. (1989a). Panic disorder in children and adolescents. *Journal of Anxiety Disorders,* 3, 87–95.

Last, C. G., & Strauss, C. C. (1989b). Obsessive–compulsive disorder in childhood. *Journal of Anxiety Disorders,* 3, 295–302.

Last, C. G., & Strauss, C. C. (1990). School refusal in anxiety-disordered children and adolescents. *Journal of the American Academy of Child and Adolescent Psychiatry,* 29, 31–35.

Last, C. G., Strauss, C. C., & Francis, G. (1987). Comorbidity among childhood anxiety disorders. *Journal of Nervous and Mental Disease,* 175, 726–730.

Leonard, H. L., Goldberger, E. L., Rapoport, J. L., Cheslow, D. L., & Swedo, S. E. (1990). Childhood rituals: Normal development or obsessive compulsive symptoms? *Journal of the American Academy of Child and Adolescent Psychiatry,* 29, 17–23.

Leonard, H. L., & Rapoport, J. (1991). Obsessive–compulsive disorder. In J. M. Wiener (Ed.), *Textbook of child and adolescent psychiatry* (pp. 323–329). Washington, DC: American Psychiatric Press.

Leonard, H. L., Swedo, S., Lenane, M. C., Rettew, D. C., Hamburger, S. D., Bartko, J. J., & Rapoport, J. L. (1993). A 2- to 7-year follow-up study of 54 obsessive–compulsive children and adolescents. *Archives of General Psychiatry,* 50, 429–439.

Lewinsohn, P. M., Hops, H., Roberts, R. E., Seeley, J. R., & Andrews, J. A. (1993). Adolescent psychopathology: I. Prevalence and incidence of depression and other DSM-III-R disorders in high school students. *Journal of Abnormal Psychology,* 102, 133–144.

Liddell, A., & Lyons, M. (1978). Thunderstorm phobias. *Behaviour Research and Therapy,* 16, 306–308.

Lillienfeld, S. O., Waldman, I. D., & Israel, A. C. (1994). A critical examination of the use of the term and concept of *comorbidity* in psychopathology research. *Clinical Psychology: Science and Practice,* 1, 71–83.

Livingston, R., Taylor, J. L., & Crawford, S. L. (1988). A study of somatic complaints and psychiatric diagnosis in children. *Journal of the American Academy of Child and Adolescent Psychiatry,* 27, 185–187.

Lo, W. H. (1967). A follow-up study of obsessional neurotics in Hong Kong. *British Journal of Psychiatry, 113,* 823–832.

Macaulay, J. L., & Kleinknecht, R. A. (1989). Panic and panic attacks in adolescents. *Journal of Anxiety Disorders, 3,* 221–241.

MacFarlane, J., Allen, L., & Hoznik, M. (1954). *A developmental study of the behavior problems of normal children between twenty-one months and fourteen years.* Berkeley: University of California Press.

Manassis, K., & Kalman, E. (1990). Anorexia resulting from fear of vomiting in four adolescent girls. *Canadian Journal of Psychiatry, 35,* 548–550.

March, J. S. (Ed.). (1995). *Anxiety disorders in children and adolescents.* New York: Guilford Press.

March, J. S., Leonard, H. L., & Swedo, S. E. (1995). Obsessive–compulsive disorder. In J. S. March (Ed.), *Anxiety disorders in children and adolescents* (pp. 251–275). New York: Guilford Press.

March, J. S., Mulle, K., & Herbel, B. (1994). Behavioral psychotherapy for children and adolescents with obsessive-compulsive disorder: An open trial of a new protocol driven treatment package. *Journal of the American Academy of Child and Adolescent Psychiatry, 33,* 333–341.

Marks, I. M. (1988). Blood-injury phobia: A review. *American Journal of Psychiatry, 145,* 1207–1213.

Marks, I. M., & Gelder, M. G. (1966). Different ages of onset in varieties of phobia. *American Journal of Psychiatry, 123,* 218–221.

Masten, A. S., Best, K. M., & Garmezy, N. (1991). Resilience and development: Contributions from the study of children who overcome adversity. *Development and Psychopathology, 2,* 425–444.

McGee, R., Fehan, M., Williams, S., Partridge, F., Silva, P. A., & Kelly, J. (1990). DSM-III disorders in a large sample of adolescents. *Journal of the American Academy of Child and Adolescent Psychiatry, 29,* 611–619.

Messer, S. C., & Beidel, D. C. (1994). Psychosocial correlates of childhood anxiety disorders. *Journal of the American Academy of Child and Adolescent Psychiatry, 33,* 975–983.

Miller, L. C. (1983). Fears and anxieties in children. In C. E. Walker & M. D. Roberts (Eds.), *Handbook of clinical child psychology* (pp. 337–380). New York: Wiley.

Miller, L. C., Barrett, C. L., Hampe, E., & Noble, H. (1972). Factor structure of childhood fears. *Journal of Consulting and Clinical Psychology, 39,* 264–268.

Mineka, S. (1985). Animal models of anxiety-based disorders: Their usefulness and limitations. In A. H. Tuma & J. D. Maser (Eds.), *Anxiety and the anxiety disorders* (pp. 199–244). Hillsdale, NJ: Erlbaum.

Mineka, S., Gunnar, M., & Champoux, M. (1986). Control and early socioemotional development: Infant rhesus monkeys reared in controllable versus uncontrollable environments. *Child Development, 57,* 1241–1256.

Mineka, S., & Zinbarg, R. (in press). Conditioning and ethological models of anxiety disorders. In D. A. Hope (Ed.), *Nebraska symposium on motivation: Integrated views of motivation and emotion* (Vol. 43). Lincoln: University of Nebraska Press.

Moras, K., & Barlow, D. H. (1992). Dimensional approaches to diagnosis and the problem of anxiety and depression. In W. Fiegenbaum, A. Ehlers, J. Margraf, & I. Florin (Eds.), *Perspectives and promises of clinical psychology* (pp. 23–37). New York: Plenum Press.

Moreau, D., & Follett, C. (1993). Panic disorder in children and adolescents. *Child and Adolescent Psychiatric Clinics of North America, 2,* 581–602.

Moreau, D., & Weissman, M. M. (1992). Panic disorder in children and adolescents: A review. *American Journal of Psychiatry, 149,* 1306–1314.

Moreau, D., Weissman, M. M., & Warner, V. (1989). Panic disorder in children at high risk for depression. *American Journal of Psychiatry, 146,* 1059–1060.

Neal, A. M., Lilly, R. S., & Zakis, S. (1993). What are African American children afraid of? A preliminary study. *Journal of Anxiety Disorders, 7,* 129–139.

Neal, A. M., & Turner, S. M. (1991). Anxiety disorders research with African Americans: Current status. *Psychological Bulletin, 109,* 400–410.

Nelles, W. B., & Barlow, D. H. (1988). Do children panic? *Clinical Psychology Review, 8,* 359–372.

Nolen-Hoeksema, S. (1987). Sex differences in unipolar depression. *Psychological Bulletin, 101,* 259–282.

Noyes, R., Crowe, J., Harris, E. L., Hamra, B. J., McChesney, C. M., & Chaudhry, D. R. (1986). Relationship between panic disorder and agoraphobia: A family study. *Archives of General Psychiatry, 43,* 227–232.

Ollendick, T. H. (1979). Fear reduction techniques with children. In M. Hersen, R. M. Eisler, & P. M. Miller (Eds.), *Progress in behavior modification* (Vol. 8, pp. 127–168). New York: Academic Press.

Ollendick, T. H. (1983a). Fear in children and adolescents: Normative data. *Behaviour Research and Therapy, 23,* 465–467.

Ollendick, T. H. (1983b). Reliability and validity of the Revised Fear Survey Schedule for Children (FSSC-R). *Behaviour Research and Therapy, 21,* 685–692.

Ollendick, T. H. (1995). Cognitive-behavioral treatment of panic disorder with agoraphobia in adolescents: A multiple baseline design analysis. *Behavior Therapy, 26,* 517–531.

Ollendick, T. H., & Huntzinger, R. M. (1990). Separation anxiety disorder in childhood. In M. Hersen & C. G. Last (Eds.), *Handbook of child and adult psychopathology: A longitudinal perspective* (pp. 133–149). New York: Pergamon Press.

Ollendick, T. H., & King, N. J. (1991). Origins of childhood fears: An evaluation of Rachman's theory of fear acquisition. *Behaviour Research and Therapy, 29,* 117–123.

Ollendick, T. H., Matson, J., & Helsel, W. J. (1985). Fears in children and adolescents: Normative data. *Behaviour Research and Therapy, 23,* 465–467.

Ollendick, T. H., Mattis, S. G., & King, N. J. (1994). Panic in children and adolescents: A review. *Journal of Child Psychology and Psychiatry, 35,* 113–134.

Ollendick, T. H., & Mayer, J. A. (1984). School phobia. In S. M. Turner (Ed.), *Behavioral theories and treatment of anxiety* (pp. 367–411). New York: Plenum Press.

Orvaschel, H. (1988). Structured and semistructured interviews for children. In C. J. Kestenbaum & D. T. Williams (Eds.), *Handbook of clinical assessment of children and adolescents* (Vol. 1, pp. 31–42). New York: New York University Press.

Orvaschel, H., & Weissman, M. M. (1986). Epidemiology of anxiety disorders in children: A review. In R. Gittelman (Ed.), *Anxiety disorders in children* (pp. 58–72). New York: Guilford Press.

Öst, L-G. (1987). Age of onset of different phobias. *Journal of Abnormal Psychology, 96,* 223–229.

Parker, G. (1979). Parental characteristics in relation to depressive disorders. *British Journal of Psychiatry, 134,* 138–147.

Parker, G. (1981). Parental representation of patients with anxiety neurosis. *Acta Psychiatrica Scandinavica, 63,* 33–36.

Parker, G. (1983). *Parental overprotection: A risk factor in psychosocial development.* New York: Grune & Stratton.

Perrin, S., & Last, C. G. (1995). Dealing with comorbidity. In A. R. Eisen, C. A. Kearney, & C. A. Schaefer (Eds.), *Clinical handbook of anxiety disorders in children and adolescents* (pp. 412–435). Northvale, NJ: Jason Aronson.

Phillips, L., Draguns, J. G., & Bartlett, D. P. (1975). Classification of behavior disorders. In N. Hobbs (Ed.), *Issues in the classification of children.* San Francisco: Jossey-Bass.

Pollack, M. H., Otto, M. W., Rosenbaum, J. F., & Sachs, G. S. (1992). Personality disorders in patients with panic disorder: Association with childhood anxiety disorders, early trauma, comorbidity, and chronicity. *Comprehensive Psychiatry, 33,* 78–83.

Rapoport, J. L., Elkins, R., Langer, D. H., Sceery, W., Buchsbaum, M. S., Gillin, J. C., Murphy, D. L., Zahn, T. P., Lake, R., Ludlow, C., & Mendelson, W. (1981). Childhood obsessive–compulsive disorder. *American Journal of Psychiatry, 138,* 1545–1554.

Reznick, J. S. (Ed.). (1989). *Perspectives on behavioral inhibition.* Chicago: University of Chicago Press.

Riddle, M. A., Scahill, L., King, R., Hardin, M., Towbin, K. E., Ort, S. I., Leckman, J. F., & Cohen, D. J. (1990). Obsessive compulsive disorder in children and adolescents: Phenomenology and family history. *Journal of the American Academy of Child and Adolescent Psychiatry, 29,* 766–772.

Rosenbaum, J. F., Biederman, J., Bolduc, E. A., Hirshfeld, D. R., Faraone, S. V., & Kagan, J. (1992). Comorbidity of parental anxiety disorders as risk for childhood-onset anxiety in inhibited children. *American Journal of Psychiatry, 149,* 475–481.

Rosenbaum, J. F., Biederman, J., Gersten, M., Hirshfeld, D. R., Meminger, S. R., Herman, J. B., Kagan, J., Reznick, J. S., & Snidman, N. (1988). Behavioral inhibition in children of parents with panic disorder and agoraphobia: A controlled study. *Archives of General Psychiatry, 45,* 463–470.

Rosenbaum, J. F., Biederman, J., Hirshfeld, D. R., Bolduc, E. A., & Chaloff, J. (1991). Behavioral inhibition in children: A possible precursor to panic disorder or social phobia. *Journal of Clinical Psychiatry, 52*(Suppl. 5), 5–9.

Rosenbaum, J. F., Biederman, J., Hirshfeld, D. R., Bolduc, E. A., Faraone, S. V., Kagan, J., Snidman, N., & Reznick, J. S. (1991). Further evidence of an association between behavioral inhibition and anxiety disorders: Results from a family study of children from a non-clinical sample. *Journal of Psychiatric Research, 25,* 49–65.

Rutter, M., Tizard, J., & Whitmore, K. (Eds.). (1970). *Education, health and behaviour.* London: Longmans.

Rutter, M., & Tuma, A. H. (1988). Diagnosis and classification: Some outstanding issues. In M. Rutter, A. H. Tuma, & I. S. Lann (Eds.), *Assessment and diagnosis in child psychopathology* (pp. 437–452). New York: Guilford Press.

Sarason, S. B., Davidson, K. S., Lightfall, F. F., Waite, R. R., & Ruebush, B. K. (1960). *Anxiety in elementary school children.* New York: Wiley.

Scherer, M. W., & Nakamura, C. Y. (1968). A fear survey schedule for children (FSS-FC): A factor analytic comparison with manifest anxiety (CMAS). *Behaviour Research and Therapy, 6,* 173–182.

Sheehan, D. V., Sheehan, K. E., & Minichiello, W. E. (1981). Age of onset of phobic disorders: A reevaluation. *Comprehensive Psychiatry, 22,* 544–553.

Silove, D., Parker, G., Hadzi-Pavlovic, D., Manicavasagar, V., & Blaszczynski, A. (1991). Parental representations of patients with panic disorder and generalized anxiety disorder. *British Journal of Psychiatry, 159,* 835–841.

Silverman, W. K. (1991). *The Anxiety Disorders Interview Schedule for Children: Child and parent versions.* Albany, NY: Graywind Publications.

Silverman, W. K., Cerny, J. A., & Nelles, W. B. (1986). The familial influence in anxiety disorders: Studies on the offspring of patients with anxiety disorders. In B. B. Lahey & A. E. Kazdin (Eds.), *Advances in clinical child psychology.* New York: Plenum Press.

Silverman, W. K., Cerny, J. A., Nelles, W. B., & Burke, A. E. (1988). Behavior problems in children of parents with anxiety disorders. *Journal of the American Academy of Child and Adolescent Psychiatry, 27,* 779–784.

Silverman, W. K., & Ginsburg, G. S. (1995). Specific phobia and generalized anxiety disorder. In J. S. March (Ed.), *Anxiety disorders in children and adolescents* (pp. 151–180). New York: Guilford Press.

Silverman, W. K., LaGreca, A., & Wasserstein, S. (1995). What do children worry about? Worries and their relation to anxiety. *Child Development, 66,* 671–686.

Silverman, W. K., & Rabian, B. (1993). Simple phobias. *Child and Adolescent Psychiatric Clinics of North America, 2,* 603–622.

Solyom, L., Silberfeld, M., & Solyom, C. (1976). Maternal overprotection in the aetiology of agoraphobia. *Canadian Psychiatric Association Journal, 21,* 109–113.

Spielberger, C. D. (1973). *Manual for the State–Trait Anxiety Inventory for Children.* Palo Alto, CA: Consulting Psychologists Press.

Spielberger, C. D., & Diaz-Guerrero, R. (Eds.). (1986). *Cross cultural anxiety* (Vol. 3). Washington, DC: Hemisphere/Harper & Row.

Spielberger, C. D., Diaz-Guerrero, R., & Strelau, J. (Eds.). (1990). *Cross cultural anxiety* (Vol. 4). Washington, DC: Hemisphere/Harper & Row.

Sroufe, L. A. (1979). The coherence of individual development. *American Psychologist, 34,* 134–141.

Sroufe, L. A. (1990). Considering the normal and abnormal together: The essence of developmental psychopathology. *Development and psychopathology, 2,* 335–347.

Strauss, C. C. (1990). Anxiety disorders of childhood and adolescence. *School Psychology Review, 19,* 142–157.

Strauss, C. C., Frame, C., & Forehand, R. (1987). Psychosocial impairment associated with anxiety in children. *Journal of Clinical Child Psychology, 16,* 235–239.

Strauss, C. C., & Last, C. G. (1993). Social and simple phobias in children. *Journal of Anxiety Disorders, 7,* 141–152.

Strauss, C. C., Last, C. G., Hersen, M., & Kazdin, A. E. (1988). Association between anxiety and depression in children and adolescents with anxiety disorders. *Journal of Abnormal Child Psychology, 16,* 57–68.

Strauss, C. C., Lease, C. A., Last, C. G., & Francis, G. (1988). Overanxious disorder: An examination of developmental differences. *Journal of Abnormal Child Psychology, 16,* 433–443.

Suomi, S. J. (1984). The development of affect in rhesus monkeys. In N. Fox & R. Davidson (Eds.), *The psychobiology of affective development.* Hillsdale, NJ: Erlbaum.

Suomi, S. J. (1986). Anxiety-like disorders in young nonhuman primates. In R. Gittelman (Ed.), *Anxiety disorders in childhood* (pp. 1–23). New York: Guilford Press.

Swedo, S. E., Rapoport, J. L., Leonard, H., Lenane, M., & Cheslow, D. (1989). Obsessive–compulsive disorder in children and adolescents: Clinical phenomenology of 70

consecutive cases. *Archives of General Psychiatry, 46,* 335–341.

Thyer, B. A., Neese, R. M., Cameron, O. G., & Curtis, G. C. (1985). Agoraphobia: A test of the separation anxiety hypothesis. *Behaviour Research and Therapy, 23,* 75–78.

Thyer, B. A., Neese, R. M., Curtis, G. C., & Cameron, O. G. (1986). Panic disorder: A test of the separation anxiety hypothesis. *Behaviour Research and Therapy, 24,* 209–211.

Thyer, B. A., Parrish, R. T., Curtis, G. C., Nesse, R. M., & Cameron, O. G. (1985). Ages of onset of DSM-III anxiety disorders. *Comprehensive Psychiatry, 26,* 113–122.

Torgersen, S. (1983). Genetic factors in anxiety disorders. *Archives of General Psychiatry, 40,* 1085–1089.

Tuma, J. (1989). Mental health services for children: The state of the art. *American Psychologist, 44,* 188–199.

Turner, S. M., Beidel, D. C., & Costello, A. (1987). Psychopathology in the offspring of anxiety disorders patients. *Journal of Consulting and Clinical Psychology, 55,* 229–235.

Valez, C. N., Johnson, J., & Cohen, P. (1989). A longitudinal analysis of selected risk factors for childhood psychopathology. *Journal of the American Academy of Child and Adolescent Psychiatry, 28,* 861–864.

Valleni-Basile, L. A., Garrison, C. Z., Jackson, K. L., Waller, J. L., McKeown, R. E., Addy, C. L., & Cuffe, S. P. (1994). Frequency of obsessive–compulsive disorder in a community sample of young adolescents. *Journal of the American Academy of Child and Adolescent Psychiatry, 33,* 782–791.

van der Molen, G. M., van den Hout, M. A., van Dieren, A. C., & Greiz, E. (1989). Childhood separation anxiety and adult-onset panic disorders. *Journal of Anxiety Disorders, 3,* 97–106.

Vasey, M. W. (1993). Development and cognition in childhood anxiety: The example of worry. In T. H. Ollendick & R. Prinz (Eds.), *Advances in clinical child psychology* (Vol. 15, pp. 1–39). New York: Plenum Press.

Vasey, M. W. (1995). Social anxiety disorders. In A. R. Eisen, C. A. Kearney, & C. A. Schaefer (Eds.), *Clinical handbook of anxiety disorders in children and adolescents* (pp. 131–168). Northvale, NJ: Jason Aronson.

Vasey, M. W., Crnic, K. A., & Carter, W. G. (1994). Worry in childhood: A developmental perspective. *Cognitive Therapy and Research, 18,* 529–549.

Verhulst, F. C., & Akkerhuis, G. W. (1988). Persistence and change in behavioral and emotional problems reported by parents of children aged 4–14. *Acta Psychiatrica Scandinavia [Suppl.], 339,* 77.

Verhulst, F. C., Akkerhuis, G. W., & Althaus, M. (1985). Mental health in Dutch children II: The prevalence of psychiatric disorder and the relationship between measures. *Acta Psychiatrica Scandinavia [Suppl.], 324,* 72.

Vitiello, A. B., Behar, D., Wolfson, S., & Delaney, M. A. (1987). Panic disorder in prepubertal children (letter). *American Journal of Psychiatry, 144,* 525–526.

Vitiello, A. B., Behar, D., Wolfson, S., & McLeer, S. V. (1990). Diagnosis of panic disorder in prepubertal children. *Journal of the American Academy of Child and Adolescent Psychiatry, 29,* 782–784.

Warren, R., & Zgourides, G. (1988). Panic attacks in high school students: Implications for prevention and intervention. *Phobia Practice and Research Journal, 1,* 97–113.

Watson, D., & Clark, L. A. (1984). Negative affectivity: The disposition to experience negative emotional states. *Psychological Bulletin, 96,* 465–490.

Watson, J. B., & Rayner, P. (1920). Conditioned emotional reactions. *Journal of Experimental Psychology, 3,* 1–14.

Weisz, J. R., Suwanlert, S., Chaiyasit, W., Weiss, B., Achenbach, T. M., & Walter, B. R. (1987). Epidemiology of behavioral and emotional problems among Thai and American children. *Journal of the American Academy of Child and Adolescent Psychiatry, 26,* 890–897.

Werry, J. S., & Quay, H. C. (1971). The prevalence of behavior symptoms in younger elementary school children. *American Journal of Orthopsychiatry, 41,* 136–143.

Whitaker, A., Johnson, J., Shaffer, D., Rapoport, J., Kalikow, K., Walsh, B. T., Davies, M., Braiman, S., & Dolinsky, A. (1990). Uncommon troubles in young people: Prevalence estimates of selected psychiatric disorders in a nonreferred adolescent population. *Archives of General Psychiatry, 47,* 487–496.

Wilson, D. J., Chibaiwa, D., Majoni, C., Masukume, C., & Nkoma, E. (1990). Reliability and factorial validity of the Revised Children's Manifest Anxiety Scale in Zimbabwe. *Personality and Individual Differences, 11,* 365–369.

Wolff, R. (1989). Obsessive–compulsive disorder. In C. G. Last & M. Hersen (Eds.), *Handbook of child psychiatric diagnosis* (pp. 191–208). New York: Wiley.

World Health Organization. (1992). *International statistical classification of diseases and related health problems* (10th ed.). Geneva, Switzerland: Author.

World Health Organization. (1993). *The ICD-10 classification of mental and behavioural disorders: Diagnostic criteria for research.* Geneva, Switzerland: Author.

Zohar, A. H., Ratzoni, G., Pauls, D. L., Apter, A., Bleich, A., Kron, S., Rappaport, M., Weizman, A., & Cohen, D. J. (1992). An epidemiological study of obsessive-compulsive disorder and related disorders in Israeli adolescents. *Journal of the American Academy of Child and Adolescent Psychiatry, 31,* 1057–1061.

Childhood Posttraumatic Stress Disorder

Kenneth E. Fletcher

The unpredictable nature of many catastrophic events makes it difficult to determine the number of children each year who are exposed to traumatic events. Between 6% and 7% of the United States population is exposed annually to extreme stressors that range from natural disasters to driving accidents to crime to acts of terrorism (Norris, 1988; cited in Ursano, Fullerton, & McCaughey, 1994). Many of the victims of these disasters are children. The health and well-being of hundreds of thousands of American children is placed in jeopardy each year by floods (Earls, Smith, Reich, & Jung, 1988; Green et al., 1991), fires (Jones & Ribbe, 1991; McFarlane, 1987a), tornadoes (Bloch, Silber, & Perry, 1956), war (Saigh, 1985), life-threatening illnesses (Nir, 1985), interparental conflict and domestic violence (Emery, 1982; Wolfe, Zak, & Wilson, 1986), and shootings at school (Pynoos et al., 1987; Schwarz & Kowalski, 1991a), to name but a few of the possible calamities that can befall children.

Each year in the United States alone approximately 33,000 children under 15 years of age are hospitalized for severe burns (Garmezy & Rutter, 1985), as many as 100,000 children may be kidnapped (Lewis, 1978), and between 150,000 and 200,000 new incidents of child sexual abuse are reported (Finkelhor & Hotaling, 1984). Clearly, a good many children can be expected to encounter hazardous circumstances at least once before their childhood ends. In fact, 39% of one sample of young urban adults reported that

they had been exposed to at least one traumatic experience in their first 20 to 25 years of life (Breslau, Davis, Andreski, & Peterson, 1991).

Over the past 10 to 15 years, it has become increasingly clear that exposure to traumatic events in childhood can have dire and long-lasting consequences, not only for traumatized children but for society as well. Green (1985) has suggested that "failure to master the trauma of childhood creates a continual need to repeat and reenact them during adult life" (p. 146), and others who have studied the subject agree (Gold, 1986; Pynoos & Eth, 1985). There is evidence that the experience of childhood trauma is linked to later drug abuse, juvenile delinquency, and criminal behavior (Burgess, Hartman, & McCormack, 1987). Abused children may be more inclined than nonabused children to grow up to be abusing parents (Frederick, 1985a; Green, 1985). Childhood trauma also appears to be implicated in debilitating adult anxiety disorders (Faravelli, Webb, Ambonetti, Fonnesu, & Sessarego, 1985), dissociative experiences (Chu & Dill, 1990), borderline personality (Herman, Perry, & van der Kolk, 1989), multiple personality (Kluft, 1985), and adult psychiatric status in general (Carmen, Rieker, & Mills, 1984).

Unfortunately, the predominant view as late as 10 years ago was that children are generally little affected by the worst of experiences, and then not for very long (Bloch et al., 1956; Burt, 1943; Coromina, 1943; A. Freud & Burlingham,

1943; Garmezy & Rutter, 1985; Harrison, Davenport, & McDermott, 1967; Rigamer, 1986). This view prevailed despite evidence from other observers—and sometimes even from supporters of the dominant view (e.g., Burt, 1943)—that children respond to severe stress with behaviors that would today be recognized as symptomatic of posttraumatic stress (Brander, 1943; Dunsdon, 1941; Lacey, 1972; Terr, 1979). This chapter reviews the literature on children's responses to traumatic circumstances in the light of current research on the subject. First, as preparation for this discussion, the evolution of the concept of posttraumatic stress must briefly be considered.

EVOLUTION OF THE CONCEPT OF POSTTRAUMATIC STRESS

The notion that traumatic events can lead to psychological disturbance is not a new idea. Odysseus, by Homer's account, suffered from flashbacks (vivid reliving of the traumatic experience) and survivor's guilt (guilt over having survived when others did not) after fighting in the Trojan War (Figley, 1993). During the Civil War, combat-related stress reactions were recognized, but they were referred to as "nostalgia" (Ursano et al., 1994) or "melancholia" (Figley, 1993). Posttraumatic stress reactions have been discussed in the literature under a variety of names over the course of the past century (Foa, Steketee, & Rothbaum, 1989), names such as nervous shock (Page, 1885), shell shock (Myers, 1940), physioneurosis (Kardiner, 1941), traumatophobia (Rado, 1942), and war neurosis (Grinker & Spiegel, 1945). Regardless of the name used, these accounts have reported similar reactions among victims of catastrophic events: increased fearfulness and anxiety, fear of repetition of the stressful events, increased arousal and hypervigilance for other potentially threatening events, uncontrollable remembering of the original stressful events, efforts to forget about those events, avoidance of reminders of the events, social withdrawal, and a flattening of affect that sometimes leads to a sense of numbness. These symptoms still represent the core symptoms of posttraumatic stress disorder (PTSD) listed in current psychiatric taxonomies, such as the fourth edition of the *Diagnostic and Statistical Manual of Mental Disorders* (DSM-IV; American Psychiatric Association, 1994; see Table 6.1) and the *ICD-10 Classification of Mental and Behavioural Disorders: Diagnostic Criteria for Research* (ICD-10; World Health Organization, 1993; see Table 6.2).

The current diagnostic category of posttraumatic stress disorder represents a relatively recent conceptualization of traumatic stress reactions. PTSD was first described in 1980 in the third edition of the *Diagnostic and Statistical Manual of Mental Disorders* (DSM-III; American Psychiatric Association). The concept of PTSD at that time represented a radical departure from earlier conceptions of typical stress reactions.

Stress Reactions Prior to DSM-III

Traditional Psychoanalytic Conceptualization

Prior to DSM-III, the predominant view of traumatic stress reactions was based on the traditional psychoanalytic explanation. Freud argued that traumatization occurs when the ego's "stimulus barrier" is overwhelmed by a flood of unmanageable stimuli from external stressors. The breaking of the stimulus barrier disrupts the organism's functioning (Freud, 1920/1953; Brett, 1993; Wilson, 1994). In general, the removal of the external stressor is expected to lead to quick restoration of the organism's functioning. However, Freud did note that unmanageable stimuli can at times become so extreme as to overpower the individual's coping mechanisms, which leads to a sense of overwhelming helplessness. At this point the individual is thought to regress and begin resorting to a primitive defense, the repetition compulsion, in an attempt to gain mastery over the traumatic experiences by compulsively repeating them in dreams, memories, and reenactments (Freud, 1939/1953). When symptoms do not abate with time and distance from the trauma, the traditional psychoanalytic explanation is that current stress has revived infantile conflicts, which are the real cause of "traumatic neuroses" (Brett, 1993). In this way, traditional psychoanalytic theory ascribes enduring traumatic reactions to premorbid characteristics of the victim rather than to the threatening characteristics of the stressor.

DSM-I

The predominance of the psychoanalytic view of traumatic reactions was reflected in the first edition of the American Psychiatric Association's

TABLE 6.1. DSM-IV Diagnostic Criteria for Posttraumatic Stress Disorder

A. The person has been exposed to a traumatic event in which both of the following were present:

  (1) the person experienced, witnessed, or was confronted with an event or events that involved actual or threatened death or serious injury, or a threat to the physical integrity of self or others, and

  (2) the person's response involved intense fear, helplessness, or horror. **Note**: In children, this may be expressed instead by disorganized or agitated behavior.

B. The traumatic event is persistently reexperienced in one (or more) of the following ways:

  (1) recurrent and intrusive distressing recollections of the event, including images, thoughts, or perceptions. **Note**: In young children, repetitive play may occur in which themes or aspects of the trauma are expressed.

  (2) recurrent distressing dreams of the event. **Note**: In children, there may be frightening dreams without recognizable content.

  (3) acting or feeling as if the traumatic event were recurring (includes a sense of reliving the experience, illusions, hallucinations, and dissociative flashback episodes, including those that occur on awakening or when intoxicated). **Note**: In young children, trauma-specific reenactment may occur.

  (4) intense psychological distress at exposure to internal or external cues that symbolize or resemble an aspect of the traumatic event

  (5) physiological reactivity on exposure to internal or external cues that symbolize or resemble an aspect of the traumatic event

C. Persistent avoidance of stimuli associated with the trauma and numbing of general responsiveness (not present before the trauma), as indicated by three (or more) of the following:

  (1) efforts to avoid thoughts, feelings, or conversations associated with the trauma

  (2) efforts to avoid activities, places, or people that arouse recollections of the trauma

  (3) inability to recall an important aspect of the trauma

  (4) markedly diminished interest or participation in significant activities

  (5) feelings of detachment or estrangement from others

  (6) restricted range of affect (e.g., unable to have loving feelings)

  (7) sense of a foreshortened future (e.g., does not expect to have a career, marriage, children, or a normal life span)

D. Persistent symptoms of increased arousal (not present before the trauma), as indicated by two (or more) of the following:

  (1) difficulty falling or staying asleep

  (2) irritability or outbursts of anger

  (3) difficulty concentrating

  (4) hypervigilance

  (5) exaggerated startle response

E. Duration of the disturbance (symptoms in Criteria B, C, and D) is more than 1 month.

F. The disturbance causes clinically significant distress or impairment in social, occupational, or other important areas of functioning.

Specify if:
  Acute: if duration of symptoms is less than 3 months
  Chronic: if duration of symptoms is 3 months or more

Specify if:
  With Delayed Onset: if onset of symptoms is at least 6 months after the stressor

Associated descriptive features and mental disorders. Individuals with Posttraumatic Stress Disorder may describe painful guilt feelings about surviving when others did not survive or about the things they had to do to survive. Phobic avoidance of situations or activities that resemble or symbolize the original trauma may interfere with interpersonal relationships. . . . The following associated constellation of symptoms may occur and are more commonly seen in association with an interpersonal stressor (e.g., childhood sexual or physical abuse, domestic battering, being taken hostage, incarceration as a prisoner of war or in a concentration camp, torture): impaired affect modulation; self-destructive and impulsive behavior; dissociative symptoms; somatic complaints; feelings of ineffectiveness, shame, despair, or hopelessness; feeling permanently damaged; a loss of previously sustained beliefs; hostility; social withdrawal; feeling constantly threatened; impaired relationships with others; or a change from the individual's previous personality characteristics.

There may be increased risk of Panic Disorder, Agoraphobia, Obsessive–Compulsive Disorder, Social Phobia, Specific Phobia, Major Depressive Disorder, Somatization Disorder, and Substance-Related Disorders. It is not known to what extent these disorders precede or follow the onset of Posttraumatic Stress Disorder.

Age-specific features. In younger children, distressing dreams of the event may, within several weeks, change into generalized nightmares of monsters, of rescuing others, or of threats to self or others. Young children usually do not have the sense that they are reliving the past; rather, the reliving of the trauma may occur through repetitive play (e.g., a child who was involved in a serious automobile accident repeatedly reenacts car crashes with toy cars). Because it may be difficult for children to report diminished interest in significant activities and constriction of affect, these symptoms should be carefully evaluated with reports from parents, teachers, and other observers. In children, the sense of a foreshortened future may be evidence by the belief that life will be too short to include becoming an adult. There may also be "omen formation"—that is, belief in an ability to foresee future untoward events. Children may also exhibit various physical symptoms, such as stomachaches and headaches.

Note. From American Psychiatric Association (1994, pp. 425, 426, 427–428). Copyright 1994 by the American Psychiatric Association. Reprinted by permission.

TABLE 6.2. ICD-10 Diagnostic Criteria for Posttraumatic Stress Disorder

A. The patient must have been exposed to a stressful event or situation (either short- or long-lasting) of exceptionally threatening or catastrophic nature, which would be likely to cause pervasive distress in almost anyone.

B. There must be persistent remembering or "reliving" of the stressor in intrusive "flashbacks", vivid memories, or recurring dreams, or in experiencing distress when exposed to circumstances resembling or associated with the stressor.

C. The patient must exhibit an actual or preferred avoidance of circumstances resembling or associated with the stressor, which was not present before exposure to the stressor.

D. Either of the following must be present:

   (1) inability to recall, either partially or completely, some important aspects of the period of exposure to the stressor;

   (2) persistent symptoms of increased psychological sensitivity and arousal (not present before exposure to the stressor), shown by any two of the following:

     (a) difficulty in falling or staying asleep;
     (b) irritability or outbursts of anger;
     (c) difficulty in concentrating;
     (d) hypervigilance;
     (e) exaggerated startle response.

E. Criteria B, C, and D must all be met within 6 months of the stressful event or of the end of a period of stress. (For some purposes, onset delayed more than 6 months may be included, but this should be clearly specified.)

[In a small proportion of patients the condition may show a chronic course over many years and a transition to an enduring personality change.]

Note. From World Health Organization (1993, pp. 99–100). Copyright 1993 by the World Health Organization. Reprinted by permission.

Diagnostic and Statistical Manual of Mental Disorders (DSM-I) in 1952. The DSM-I classification of reactions to traumatic stress was termed gross stress reaction (GSR), a transient situational personality disorder. This classification was intended to cover acute responses to "intolerable stress" that "clear rapidly" when treated promptly, unless the condition progresses to a more chronic, "neurotic" disorder.

DSM-II

By the time the second edition of the *Diagnostic and Statistical Manual of Mental Disorders* (DSM-II; American Psychiatric Association) was published in 1968, the definition of traumatic stress responses had undergone a puzzling regression. The gross stress reaction of DSM-I was reclassified in the second edition as adjustment reaction of adult life, a condition about which DSM-II was strangely silent. This condition was defined only by three inadequate examples; no discussion of the symptomatology was included (Wilson, 1994). It may not be a coincidence that DSM-II was published at the height of the Vietnam War, at a time when both the military and the federal government argued vehemently against the possibility of long-term adverse psychological consequences to participation in the war.

PTSD in DSM-III and Beyond

The political debate about posttraumatic responses to the Vietnam experience lasted over a decade. During that time, several mental health professionals began collecting case histories and research data on posttraumatic reactions to a variety of extremely stressful events—the Vietnam War (Figley, 1978), Hiroshima (Lifton, 1967), the Holocaust (Ettinger, 1961), and other disasters (Gleser, Green, & Winget, 1981). The data collected eventually led to the codification of posttraumatic stress disorder in DSM-III (American Psychiatric Association, 1980; Blank, 1993; Scurfield, 1993).

DSM-III

The diagnostic definition of PTSD in DSM-III was ground-breaking for several reasons (Wilson, 1994). One innovation was the clustering of symptoms into four criteria that became the foundation of the definition of PTSD in all later editions. The first criterion of DSM-III, criterion A, may have represented the most radical change from the previously predominant conceptualization of traumatic stress responses. For a diagnosis of PTSD to be considered, criterion A required that an individual be exposed to "a recognizable

stressor that would be expected to evoke significant symptoms of distress in almost all individuals." This requirement implied that, contrary to previous formulations of stress reactions, PTSD was to be considered a normal reaction to abnormal circumstances. In line with this position, DSM-III indicated that the intensity and scope of an individual's reactions can be expected to be directly related to the intensity and duration of the individual's exposure to the stressor. Moreover, removing the stressor was no longer taken as a guarantee that symptoms would abate. DSM-III explicitly stated that symptoms might last indefinitely. Thus, with the publication of the DSM-III definition of PTSD, traumatic stress reactions were no longer to be considered the result of the weakened nature of the victim but rather caused by the unusually threatening nature of the stressor.

DSM-IV

The original description of PTSD contained in DSM-III has been refined in subsequent editions, but the current conceptualization contained in DSM-IV (American Psychiatric Association, 1994) is not as radically different from the definition given in DSM-III as that definition was different from earlier versions. According to the current definition of PTSD contained in DSM-IV (see Table 6.1), victims of traumatic stress tend to experience unbidden dreams, memories, feelings, and behaviors that are reminiscent of the original traumatic experience (criterion B). Victims tend to lose all sense of security, begin to anticipate further trouble, and become overaroused and easily startled (criterion D). In an attempt to modulate the overwhelming feelings evoked by the recurring memories of the trauma, victims often make an effort to avoid all thoughts and reminders of the trauma, and they may also try to "turn off" their feelings, leading to flat affect, a sense of emotional numbness, and social withdrawal (criterion C).

Alternative Definitions of PTSD

ICD-10

An alternative to the DSM-IV diagnostic description of PTSD is offered by the *ICD-10 Classification of Mental and Behavioural Disorders: Clinical Descriptions and Diagnostic Guidelines* (World Health Organization, 1992), and the *ICD-10 Classification of Mental and Behavioural Disorders: Diagnostic Criteria for Research* (World Health

Organization, 1993). On first view, the ICD-10 diagnostic criteria for research (see Table 6.2) appear quite similar to those of DSM-IV (see Table 6.1). Both classification systems require exposure to some extreme stressor that could be expected to distress nearly anyone (DSM-IV criterion A), followed by symptoms of reexperiencing the traumatic event (DSM-IV criterion B), avoidance of reminders of the event (DSM-IV criterion C), and overarousal (DSM-IV criterion D). However, although the two definitions of PTSD share many similarities, there are important differences.

Different Symptom Requirements

The ICD-10 diagnostic criteria for research (World Health Organization, 1993) require only one example each of reexperiencing, avoidance, and overarousal, whereas DSM-IV requires one symptom of reexperiencing, three of avoidance or numbing, and two of overarousal. This difference between the two diagnostic classification systems is enlarged upon in ICD-10 clinical descriptions and diagnostic guidelines (World Health Organization, 1992), which note:

> In addition to evidence of trauma, there must be a repetitive, intrusive recollection or reenactment of the event in memories, daytime imagery, or dreams. Conspicuous emotional detachment, numbing of feeling, and avoidance of stimuli that might arouse recollection of the trauma are often present but are *not essential* for the diagnosis. The autonomic disturbances, mood disorder, and behavioural abnormalities all contribute to the diagnosis but are *not of prime importance.* (pp. 148–149; emphasis added)

Thus, according to ICD-10 clinical diagnostic criteria, only exposure to traumatic events and symptoms of unwanted reexperiencing of those events are required for a clinical diagnosis of PTSD. Symptoms of avoidance and of overarousal are required only when defining groups for research according to ICD-10 criteria.

Different Duration Requirements

ICD-10 notes that most symptoms occur within 6 months of the stressful experience. DSM-IV, on the other hand, simply requires that symptom duration be longer than 1 month. Moreover, according to DSM-IV, onset of symptoms 6 or more months after exposure to the stressor is indicative of delayed PTSD. The validity of

delayed onset as a subtype of PTSD, however, has been questioned by Keane, Scott, Chavoya, Lamparski, and Fairbank (1985), who argue that symptoms may worsen with time, which can give the impression of delayed onset.

Age-Specific Symptomatology

One important difference between the two taxonomies is that age-specific manifestations of symptoms are described in DSM-IV (see Table 6.1), but not in ICD-10 (see Table 6.2). DSM-IV notes that children may express their feelings of fear, helplessness, and horror through "disorganized or agitated behavior." It also suggests that young children may recurrently and intrusively reexperience their traumatic experience by repetitively playing out "themes or aspects of the trauma," a practice often referred to as posttraumatic play. Repetitive dreams about the traumatic experiences may manifest in children as "frightening dreams without recognizable content." Young children might also relive their experience by reenacting specific aspects of it afterwards. These and other age-specific reactions are discussed in more detail below.

Other Alternative Definitions

Other sources also question current DSM-IV criteria for PTSD. Some argue, for example, that the requirement of three symptoms of denial or avoidance may be too restrictive (Green, 1993a), particularly because it can be more difficult to assess symptoms of denial and numbing in children than in adults (Schwarz & Kowalski, 1991b). It has furthermore been argued that the symptom lists for PTSD in DSM-IV and ICD-10 may not be inclusive enough (Keane, 1993), especially when the reactions of children are considered (Armsworth & Holaday, 1993). Others question the utility of any diagnostic criteria. They argue that it might be more fruitful to study PTSD as a continuous variable rather than a dichotomous one, as required by both DSM-IV and ICD-10 (Keane, 1993).

HISTORICAL OVERVIEW OF THE STUDY OF CHILDREN'S STRESS REACTIONS

The stress reactions of adults have been more thoroughly studied than have those of children.

Some of the earliest accounts of children's stress reactions originated during World War II (Brander, 1943; Burt, 1943; Coromina, 1943; Dunsdon, 1941; A. Freud & Burlingham, 1943). However, these accounts remained relatively infrequent during the war and came to be made with even less frequency during the first 25 to 30 years after the war's end. Research on children's reactions to traumatic events did not begin in earnest until the publication of DSM-III in 1980, and children's reactions were not specifically mentioned in DSM until the revised third edition, DSM-III-R, was published in 1987 (American Psychiatric Association).

Early Evidence

The first detailed evidence of child-specific posttraumatic reactions began to appear in the 1970s and 1980s, primarily from anecdotal sources (Benedek, 1985; Eth & Pynoos, 1985; Frederick, 1985a, 1986; Galante & Foa, 1986; Gislason & Call, 1982; Lacey, 1972; Newman, 1976; Rigamer, 1986; Senior, Gladstone, & Narcombe, 1982; Terr, 1979, 1981a, 1981b, 1983a, 1983b, 1985a, 1985b). Very few attempts were made in the 1970s to assess children's posttraumatic distress systematically (Elmer, 1977; Milgram & Milgram, 1976; Milne, 1977; Ziv & Israeli, 1973), and these studies tended to assess only general outcomes, such as anxiety, rather than PTSD-specific symptomatology. Few reports at this time considered comparison groups, and those that did did not always choose appropriate comparison groups. Perhaps as a consequence of all of these factors, the collective results of these studies were contradictory and generally inconclusive.

The Children of Chowchilla

The culmination of the early anecdotal literature can be found in the work of Terr (1979, 1983b, 1991), who has written extensively about the responses of school children in Chowchilla, California, to a 1976 kidnapping and subsequent 27-hour imprisonment, buried underground. Terr (1979) conducted detailed interviews with 23 of the 26 kidnapped children (6 boys and 17 girls, between the ages of 5 and 14 years) within 6 to 10 months after the kidnapping. Her report was among the first to provide counts of the children's various traumatic responses. Terr was also among the first to analyze the responses of children to traumatic events in terms of contemporary con-

ceptions of what she herself referred to as "post-traumatic symptomatology" (1979).

Terr realized that many of the responses found in the children of Chowchilla were strikingly similar to those found in traumatized adults. Like adults, for example, the children reexperienced their kidnapping in dreams, and like adults, the children avoided thoughts and reminders of their kidnapping. On the other hand, the children also reacted in child-specific ways. Unlike adults, for instance, the Chowchilla children did not appear to hallucinate or have flashback experiences of reliving the experience, nor did they exhibit any signs of affective numbing. In contrast with the tendency of traumatized adults to forget important aspects of their traumatic experience, no Chowchilla child, even 4 years after the event, forgot anything about the kidnapping (Terr, 1983b).

Children tended to relive their trauma through behavioral reenactments of significant parts of the experience, by retelling of the event, and in trauma-inspired play, wherein children played kidnapping or bus-driving games. The children of Chowchilla also suffered from misperceptions and/or hallucinations during and after the kidnapping, declining school performance, dreams of personal death, anniversary reactions (that is, anniversaries of the kidnapping triggered increased symptomatology), pessimism about the future, and omen formation (the belief that events that occurred before the trauma foretold its occurrence). The children's fears seemed to become progressively generalized over time, too, changing from fears associated specifically with kidnapping to more general fears of everyday events.

Children's Reactions to an Australian Bushfire

More systematic research began to appear in the 1980s (Blom, 1986; Burgess, Hartman, McCausland, & Powers, 1984; Burke, Borus, Burns, Millstein, & Beasley, 1982; Elizur & Kaffman, 1982; Gomes-Schwartz, Horowitz, & Sauzier, 1985; Ollendick & Hoffman, 1982; Saigh, 1985; Sirles, Smith, & Kusama, 1989; Stiffman, 1989). Despite the increased sophistication of the research, however, most studies remained primarily descriptive, lacked appropriate control or comparison groups, and depended upon reports from adults (parents or teachers) rather than the children themselves.

Furthermore, either nonstandardized assessments were used, or standardized measures were used that were designed to assess general conditions, such as anxiety, depression, fear, or self-esteem, rather than PTSD-specific responses. Despite these limitations, the overall results of these studies, combined with anecdotal observations, provided substantial support for the notion that children can respond to traumatic experiences in a manner similar to that of traumatized adults.

The research by McFarlane (1987a; McFarlane, Policansky, & Irwin, 1987) into the psychological impact of a 1983 Australian bushfire on 808 children (427 boys and 381 girls) ages 8 to 12 is one of the best examples of the research of this period. One advantage of this study was its large sample size. Another advantage of the study was the existence of an equally large age- and sex-matched comparison group of 734 children from schools unaffected by the bushfire. Furthermore, assessments were repeated over several time periods: at 2 months postdisaster, at 8 months, and at 26 months.

The results of McFarlane's research were mixed. Two months postdisaster, parents in the fire zone indicated their children were no more antisocial, restless, angry, neurotic, phobic, or somatic than children in the comparison group. At the same time, however, teachers rated these children as *less* antisocial, neurotic, distractable, and unpopular liars than children in the comparison group. McFarlane et al. (1987) suggest that these results might be due, in part, to a subdued and obedient attitude in the aftermath of the fire among children exposed to the fire. The authors also suggest that parents of exposed children might have underreported these behaviors in their children because the parents' own posttraumatic responses interfered with their ability to attend to their children's responses.

After 8 months, parents viewed their traumatized children as more angry, neurotic, phobic, and somatic, and teachers saw them as more neurotic and distractable than the comparison children. At 26 months, parents said their children were still more angry and phobic than children in the comparison group, but teachers saw no differences between the two groups of children. School performance, however, dropped for fire victims, and their school absenteeism increased. Separation from parents in the aftermath of the fire was associated with children's posttraumatic responses, as were maternal preoccupations with the fire, and changed family functioning.

Unfortunately, as noted above, the results of the McFarlane study were diluted by important methodological limitations. For example, although the children's reactions were assessed using standardized measures (Rutter & Graham, 1967; Rutter, Tizard, & Whitmore, 1970), these measured only general behavioral problems and did not directly measure posttraumatic symptomatology, a problem noted by the authors themselves (McFarlane et al., 1987, p. 737). McFarlane (1987a) did ask about specific symptoms of posttraumatic stress at 8 months and at 26 months, but only four symptoms were assessed: having dreams or nightmares about the fire, playing games or painting pictures about the fire, getting upset at reminders, and talking about the fire. Over half of the children (53% at 8 months and 57% at 26 months) were reported by parents to have one or more of these behaviors. Parents reported that 8 months after they were exposed to the bushfire, 35% of the children still got upset at reminders, and after 26 months, the proportion increased to 46%. Forty-three percent of exposed children were reported to talk about their traumatic experiences after 8 months, whereas 36% did so after 26 months. Fewer parents reported that their children played games related to the fire (13% after 8 months and 10% after 26 months), or that their children dreamed about the fire (13% after 8 months and 18% after 26 months). The comparison group does not appear to have been administered the PTSD items, perhaps because of the direct reference to exposure to the fire in those questions, and as a consequence, the incidence rates for the four PTSD symptoms were not compared with rates in the comparison children.

Another difficulty with this study was its reliance on parent and teacher reports. This difficulty was compounded by the fact that parent and teacher reports generally did not agree. Teachers, for example, both at 8 and 26 months after the fire, reported fewer than 30% of the children exposed to the bushfire displayed one or more of the PTSD symptoms. Parents, on the other hand, reported that more than 50% of the children had at least one symptom at both time periods.

School Shooting

Despite the limitations imposed on childhood trauma research by such factors as the unpredictability of catastrophic events, the reluctance of victims and their families to discuss their traumatic experiences, and difficulties defining and recruiting comparison groups, research has become increasingly rigorous since the mid-1980s (Bradburn, 1991; Clarke, Sack, & Goff, 1993; Deblinger, McLeer, Atkins, Ralphe, & Foa, 1989; Earls et al., 1988; Famularo, Kinscherff, & Fenton, 1990; Green et al., 1991; Jones & Ribbe, 1991; Kinzie, Sack, Angell, Manson, & Rath, 1986; Kiser, Heston, Millsap, & Pruitt, 1991; Malmquist, 1986; McLeer, Deblinger, Henry, & Orvaschel, 1992; Payton & Krocker-Tuskman, 1988; Pynoos & Nader, 1988; Realmuto et al., 1992; Saigh, 1989, 1991; Schwarz & Kowalski, 1991a, 1991b). Studies in the past 7 or 8 years have attempted to assess specific PTSD symptomatology, and many of them have used newly developed standardized measures. Larger sample sizes are becoming more common as well. Furthermore, an increasing number of studies have begun comparing symptomatology of traumatized children with that of nontraumatized children.

One of the first and best of these more rigorous research studies was conducted by Pynoos and his colleagues (1987), who used a modified version of Frederick's (1985b) adult PTSD Reaction Index (PTSD-RI) to interview 159 school children after a sniper fired repeatedly into their school's playground over a period of several hours, killing one child and one passerby, and wounding 13 children. The 53 children who had been at school during the attack reported higher incidence of all PTSD symptoms—except fear of recurrence of the event and feelings of guilt—than did the 106 children who had not been at school that day. A dose effect was also demonstrated, with those closer to the shooting evidencing greater symptomatology.

When the children's answers to the 16 PTSD-RI interview questions were factor analyzed, three factors that accounted for 50% of the variance were extracted. The first factor encompassed symptoms of two DSM-IV criteria: criterion B, reexperiencing the trauma; and criterion C, avoidance of reminders of the trauma or affective numbing. The second factor was defined by symptoms of the DSM-IV criterion D, overarousal: fears of recurrence; jumpiness and exaggerated startle response; and upset or made to feel afraid by thoughts of the shooting. The final factor included other symptoms of overarousal: sleep disturbance and difficulty concentrating. Feelings of guilt did not meet the criterion for inclusion in any factor. Items in the first and third factors were always present among children with severe reactions, and

they were least likely to be found among children with mild or no reactions. These results provide firm support for the application of DSM-IV criteria for PTSD to traumatized children.

Fourteen months after the school shooting, 100 of the 159 school shooting children originally interviewed by Pynoos et al. (1987) were reinterviewed with similar results (Nader, Pynoos, Fairbanks, & Frederick, 1990). Proximity to the shooting scene continued to be closely related to the severity of response. Fourteen months postdisaster, 19 children who had been on the playground during the sniper attack remained more symptomatic than 81 children who had not been on the playground. PTSD symptomatology at 14 months was strongly associated with the intensity of the child's original reaction to the shooting. The majority of the children who had been on the playground during the shooting still reported being afraid and being upset when thinking about the shooting. They continued to report more intrusive thoughts about the shooting, more fear of a recurrence of the incident, and more jumpiness, sleep disturbance, and somatic complaints than children who had not been on the playground that day. Their distress was increased by the expectations—of themselves as well as of others—that they should already have recovered, now that more than a year had passed since the shooting.

PREVALENCE OF POSTTRAUMATIC STRESS RESPONSES IN CHILDREN

Epidemiology

In the aftermath of Hurricane Hugo, the largest sample of children exposed to a single stressor yet to be systematically assessed for the extent and severity of specific DSM-III-R PTSD symptomatology was gathered (Lonigan, Shannon, Taylor, Finch, & Sallee, 1994; Shannon, Lonigan, Finch, & Taylor, 1994). Three months postdisaster 5,687 children between the ages of 9 and 19 years reported on their experiences during and after the hurricane. Fifty-one percent of the children were girls; 67.3% were white; 25.8%, African-American; 3.6%, Asian; and 1.4%, Hispanic. PTSD was assessed using the PTSD-RI (Frederick, 1985b; Pynoos et al., 1987), which was modified to allow conservative judgments to be drawn about DSM-III-R caseness for PTSD[1]. Overall, 5.4% of the children (308) met criteria A through D of DSM-III-R for PTSD. These are essentially the same

criteria required by DSM-IV. More girls (6.9%) than boys (3.8%) met all of these criteria for PTSD. No significant differences emerged as a function of race (African-Americans, 6.3%; non-African-Americans, 5.1%). School-aged children (ages 9 to 12 years) were more likely to meet all PTSD criteria (9.2%) than were older children (4.2% of those between 13 and 15 years, and 3.1% of those between 16 and 19 years).

Meta-Analysis

DSM-IV Criteria

Most research to date confirms the general conclusion that the diagnostic symptom clusters of DSM-IV apply to traumatized children of all ages, from preschool through adolescence, as well as they do to traumatized adults. The symptom incidence rates summarized in Table 6.3 indicate that an average 36% of children exposed to traumatic events are diagnosed with PTSD (based on 2,697 children from 34 samples; Fletcher, 1994); whereas, an average 24% of traumatized adults are diagnosed with PTSD (based on 3,495 adults from five samples reported on in den Velde et al., 1993; Kilpatrick & Resnick, 1993; and Smith & North, 1993). Similar results were found in a unique study of the reactions of both children (5 to 14 years old) and adults to the same event, a school shooting (Schwarz and Kowalski, 1991a, 1991b). Using a modified form of the PTSD-RI (Pynoos et al., 1987), the researchers found that children were at least as likely as adults to be diagnosed with PTSD. Using a moderate rating method, 27% of children versus 19% of adults, met DSM-III-R criteria for PTSD—not a significant difference.

On average, incidence rates for all DSM-IV symptoms of PTSD among traumatized children are higher than 20% (see Table 6.3), with the exception of a pessimistic outlook on the future (16%) and an inability to remember parts of the trauma (12%). Seven of the 11 highest ranked DSM-IV symptoms (excluding rates based on 50 or fewer children) for children of all ages are symptoms of criterion B, reexperiencing the trauma: feeling or showing distress at reminders of the trauma (51%); reenactment of significant parts of the event, through gestures, actions, or sounds (40%); feeling as if the event were being relived (39%); intrusive memories of the events (34%); bad dreams about the events (31%); trauma-specific fears (31%); and talking exces-

TABLE 6.3. Incidence Rates of Posttraumatic Stress Responses among Children and Adults

Symptoms	Average incidence rate				
	Children[a]				Adults[b]
	All ages	Preschool	School	Teen	
DSM-IV criteria and symptoms					
B. Reexperiencing (one required)	88%		92%		44%
B1. Intrusive memories	34%		46%	64%	45%
B1. Posttraumatic Play	23%	39%	14%		
B1. Daydream about the event	48%°		26%°		
B1. Talkative about the event	31%		31%		
B2. Bad dreams	31%	69%°°	23%	30%°	36%
B3. Reliving the event	39%		40%	40%°	29%
B3. Reenactment of the event	40%°°		54%°		
B4. Reminders are distressing	51%	89%°	42%	50%°	26%
B. Trauma-specific fears	31%	31%	35%	18%	45%
B5. Somatic complaints	23%	15%	37%	16%°	45%
C. Avoidance/numbness (three required)	46%		30%°°		31%
C. Numbness	47%	65%°	44%	62%°	23%
C1. Tries to forget about the event	24%		25%	46%°	46%
C2. Avoids reminders	32%	81%°	36%	32%°	33%
C3. Unable to recall parts of event	12%		0%°	36%°	27%
C4. Loss of interest in activities	36%		42%	32%°	28%
C5./C6. Detached or withdrawn	25%	30%	33%	24%°°	34%
C7. Pessimistic about the future	16%		35%	8%°	61%
D. Overarousal (two required)	66%		55%°°		43%
D1. Difficulty sleeping	29%	27%°	32%	28%°°	52%
D2. Irritability	23%	28%	14%	16%	29%
D3. Difficulty concentrating	41%	19%°	57%	20%°°	41%
D4. Hypervigilant	25%	24%°	34%	44%°	27%
D5. Exaggerated startle response	28%		37%	32%°	38%
Diagnosis of PTSD	36%	39%°°	33%	27%	24%
Associated symptoms or diagnoses					
Generalized anxiety	39%	57%	52%	14%°	38%
Separation anxiety	23%	36%	16%	4%	
Panic	8%		19%°°	0%°	18%
Depression	25%	34%°°	22%	22%°	14%
Guilt	43%		33%		15%
Regressive behavior	13%	17%	11%	4%	
Aggressive or antisocial behavior	18%	30%	12%	4%	35%
Low self-esteem	34%		53%°		
Dissociative response	48%°°		49%°	48%°	16%
Self-destructive behavior	9%	1%°°	15%°		
Eating problems	7%		14%		
Omen formation	26%		30%°°		
Warped time perspective	4%		4%		
Sleepwalking	1%		1%		
Adjustment disorder	20%		14%°°		
ADHD	13%		34%°°		

Note. Percentages based on total $n \geq 100$ unless otherwise noted.
[a]Data from Fletcher (1994). Preschool = < 7; school = 6–12; teen = 12+.
[b]Data from Crocq et al. (1993); den Velde et al. (1993); Harel, Kahana, & Wilson (1993); Kilpatrick & Resnick (1993); Smith & North (1993); Weisaeth & Eitinger (1993).
°n = 11–49; °°n = 50–99.

sively about the events (31%). Also included among the 11 symptoms with the highest incidence rates in Table 6.3 are three symptoms of the DSM-IV avoidance/numbing criterion: affective numbing (47%); loss of interest in previously important activities (36%); avoidance of reminders of the events (32%). One symptom of the DSM-IV overarousal criterion is included among the 11 most frequently reported childhood symptoms: difficulty concentrating (41%).

Associated Symptoms

Several clinicians and researchers have suggested that traumatized children are likely to present with other symptomatic responses in addition to those included in DSM-IV and ICD-10. Incidence rates for 14 of these possible associated symptoms are listed in Table 6.3. Half of these rates are higher than 20%: dissociative response (48%), guilt (43%), generalized anxiety or fears (39%), low self-esteem (34%), omen formation (26%), depression (25%), and separation anxiety (23%). The least likely associated symptoms to be observed among traumatized children are self-destructive behavior (9%), panic attacks (8%), eating problems (7%), a warped time perspective (4%), and sleepwalking (1%).

It is important to remember that the above incidence rates ignore the potential mediating and moderating influences of other factors on these rates. Thus, for example, disregarding any factor other than exposure to a traumatic event, aggressive or antisocial behavior is observed in traumatized children, on average, 18% of the time. Regressive behavior is observed 13% of the time. However, if these rates are viewed in terms of the age of the children, we find that both aggressive or antisocial behavior and regressive behavior occur most frequently among preschoolers and that the incidence of each kind of behavior decreases with age (see Table 6.3). The influence of such factors as age and type of stressor on symptom incidence rates is discussed in more detail in later sections of this chapter.

Associated Disorders

Alternative and comorbid diagnoses among traumatized children have yet to be studied in any depth. Two examples of alternative diagnoses have received some attention, however: adjustment disorder and attention-deficit disorder

(ADD). Overall, the average incidence rates of these diagnoses are 20% for adjustment disorder and 13% for ADD (see Table 6.3). At the moment it is unclear whether reported difficulties of children with concentration, hyperactivity, and oppositional behavior are the consequences of traumatic experiences or are symptoms of preexisting disorders such as ADD or oppositional disorder. This may be particularly true when the traumatic experience is of a protracted or physically abusive nature. In such cases, it is possible, as Famularo et al. (1992) point out, that the "difficult" behaviors associated with these diagnoses may have played a role in provoking physical abuse and that any similar symptoms stemming from the PTSD represent an overlap with a preexisting condition.

DEVELOPMENTAL COURSE AND PROGNOSIS

Too few prospective follow-up studies have been conducted to allow a close examination of the developmental course and prognosis of childhood PTSD. For the most part, findings from follow-up studies of children's responses to single-occurrence, nonabusive stressors have been inconsistent, with some investigators finding decreased incidence of symptoms over time (Blom, 1986; Green et al., 1991, 1994) and others finding either consistently high levels of symptoms over time (Nader et al., 1990; Pynoos et al., 1987; Terr, 1979, 1983b) or an increased incidence (McFarlane, 1987a; McFarlane et al., 1987). One long-term follow-up study found that 17 years after the Buffalo Creek dam collapse, among survivors who had been children at the time of the dam's collapse (Green et al., 1991), PTSD diagnosis fell from 32% 2 years after the flood to 7% 17 years later, suggesting that exposure to single-occurrence, nonabusive stressors is not likely to have long-term consequences for most children. On the other hand, time does not seem to make much of a difference when repeated, multiple, or abusive stressors are concerned, with incidence rates uniformly high regardless of the amount of time that had elapsed since the children had last been exposed to the stressors (Elizur & Kaffman, 1982; Kinzie et al., 1986; Kinzie, Sack, Angell, Clarke, & Ben, 1989; Mannarino, Cohen, Smith, & Moore-Motily, 1991; Stuber, Nader, Yasuda, Pynoos, & Cohen, 1991). In fact, retrospective studies of adults who

were victims of childhood sexual abuse, indicate that symptomatology can persist well into adulthood (Beitchman et al., 1992; Cahill, Llewelyn, & Pearson, 1991).

THE CONTEXT OF PTSD: A WORKING MODEL

Not everyone exposed to events "outside the range of usual human experience and that would be markedly distressing to almost everyone" (criterion A, DSM-III-R, American Psychiatric Association, 1987) reacts to the experience with symptoms of traumatic stress. DSM-IV reports that prevalence rates for PTSD among people exposed to traumatic events range from 3% to 58% (p. 426; American Psychiatric Association, 1994), and, as noted earlier, incidence rates for PTSD average 36% among children exposed to traumatic events and 24% among adults (see Table 6.3). This hardly amounts to a one-to-one correspondence between exposure to terrible circumstances and the subsequent development of PTSD. Individual reactions to disaster and catastrophe differ even among people who have been exposed to the same traumatic events.

In order to gain a more complete understanding of the etiology of PTSD, the contribution of other factors besides the traumatic experience itself must also be considered. Figure 6.1 illustrates one approach to delineating the process whereby multiple factors are considered to contribute to the development of PTSD. The model depicted in Figure 6.1 is a working model, created in part to facilitate this chapter's discussion of childhood PTSD. Similar models, however, have been suggested by others (Green, Wilson, & Lindy, 1985; Ursano et al., 1994). The factors considered important to the etiology of PTSD in the working model in Figure 6.1 include, in addition to the traumatic characteristics of the stressful event itself (its nature, cause, severity, duration, etc.), other factors such as a child's cognitive, emotional, psychobiological, and behavioral responses to the traumatic event; characteristics of the victim (biological vulnerabilities, age, gender, developmental stage, coping skills, etc.); and characteristics of the social environment (family support and cohesion, socioeconomic status, community support, etc.). The model of the context for the development

of PTSD, as delineated in Figure 6.1, will serve as a framework for the following discussion of the factors that current research indicates can contribute to the etiology of posttraumatic stress disorder in children.

THE TRAUMATIC EVENT

Although PTSD can not be diagnosed unless someone has first been exposed to a traumatic event, this criterion may be the least understood of the DSM-IV diagnostic criteria for PTSD. Unfortunately, there are presently few guidelines for systematically defining the type of events that are to be considered "outside the range of usual human experience and that would be markedly distressing to almost anyone" (DSM-III-R; American Psychiatric Association, 1987). The current version of criterion A in DSM-IV (American Psychiatric Association, 1994) attempts to define traumatic events more narrowly as those that involve "actual or threatened death or serious injury, or a threat to the physical integrity of self or others" (p. 427; see Table 6.1). However, events that qualify as traumatic according to DSM-IV standards can still vary greatly from one another. Reports have been made, for instance, of the reactions of children to such diverse traumatic events as earthquakes (Bradburn, 1991), hurricanes (Lonigan et al., 1994), floods (Earls et al., 1988), lightening strikes (Dollinger, 1985), fires (Jones & Ribbe, 1991), dog bites to the face followed by surgery (Gislason & Call, 1982), extensive burns to the body followed by years of corrective surgery (Stoddard, Norman, & Murphy, 1989), bone marrow transplantation (Stuber et al., 1991), kidnapping (Terr, 1979), child snatching (Terr, 1983a), accidents involving death or injury (Blom, 1986), school shootings (Schwarz & Kowalski, 1991a), witnessing sexual assaults on a parent (Pynoos & Nader, 1988), witnessing parental homicide (Malmquist, 1986), war (Saigh, 1989), life in a concentration camp (Kinzie et al., 1986), domestic violence (Jouriles, Murphy, & O'Leary, 1989), physical abuse (Adam, Everett, & O'Neal, 1992), and sexual abuse (Gomes-Schwartz, Horowitz, Cardelli, & Sauzier, 1990). Differences clearly exist among such diverse types of traumatic events, differences that are likely to contribute to the course of each child's individual posttraumatic reaction to those events. The ability to delineate these

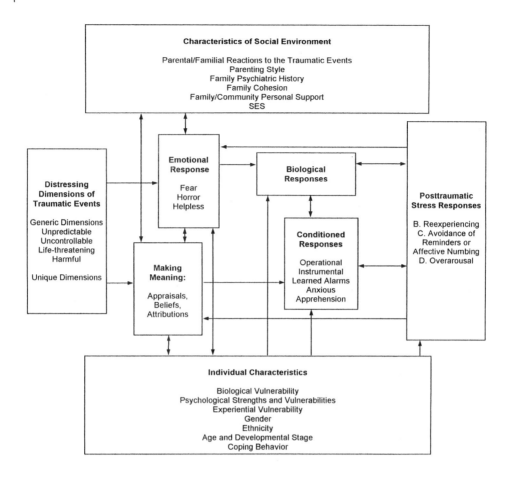

FIGURE 6.1. A working model of the context for the development of childhood posttraumatic stress disorder.

differences would presumably allow us to improve our understanding of the relationship between the kind of stressful experience and the resulting type of reaction.

Stressful Dimensions of Events

Inherent Stressfulness of Events

One approach to categorizing stressful events attempts to rank events according to their inherent stressfulness. Milgram (1989), for instance, has suggested that the following categories represent increasing degrees of stressfulness: upsetting, even painful, but not life-threatening events (e.g., breaking an arm); severe family disruptions (e.g., divorce); family misfortune (e.g., death through illness); personal misfortune (e.g., abuse); catastrophic group misfortune associated with natural disasters; and, catastrophic

group misfortune associated with man-made disasters. There are several problems with this approach to categorizing stressful events. One problem is that predefined categories and stressful events are not always easy to match up. It is difficult to understand where, for example, the witnessing of domestic violence would fit in Milgram's typology. Another limitation of this approach is that it ultimately relies on subjective judgments of the amount of stressfulness associated with each category. Not everyone, for example, would rate abuse as a less stressful experience than exposure to a natural experience, as seems to be implied by Milgram's typology.

Generic Stressful Dimensions of Events

Another approach to the categorization of stressful events proposes to shift the focus away from

a priori categories of events ranked by their purported inherent levels of stressfulness, to characteristics or dimensions of events that are thought to increase their stressfulness (e.g., Green et al., 1985; Green, 1993b). From this perspective, the more an event can be characterized by different traumatizing dimensions, the more stressful it can be considered to be. DSM-IV (American Psychiatric Association, 1994; see Table 6.1) lists several dimensions that are clearly associated with the increased stressfulness of any event: death, injury, or possible loss of physical integrity. The sudden occurrence and unexpectedness of events is another dimension thought to contribute to the stressfulness of events. Proximity to traumatic events has also been found to be associated with higher levels of posttraumatic stress. Children who were on the playground during a sniper attack, for instance, displayed a greater incidence of PTSD symptomatology than did children inside the school but not on the playground, and children at school, whether on the playground or not, displayed higher rates than children not at school that day (Nader et al., 1990; Pynoos et al., 1987; Pynoos & Nader, 1989).

Other dimensions of events that appear to be associated with increased traumatization have been documented in the literature. Traumatic events that are ongoing or chronic lead to different, and generally more severe, outcomes than do nonabusive events of short duration (as discussed below and in Famularo et al., 1990; Green, 1985; Kiser et al., 1988; Stiffman, 1989; Terr, 1991). Events that are perceived as uncontrollable (by children and/or by their parents) appear to lead to worse stress reactions afterwards (Weigel, Wertlieb, & Felstein, 1989). The more personal the impact of the traumatic events, the worse a child's reactions. For instance, children who were exposed to more damage to their homes in Hurricane Hugo were also more likely to have symptoms of PTSD afterwards (Shannon et al., 1994). Separations from the family during a crisis can have devastating consequences (Crawshaw, 1963; Faravelli et al., 1985; Frances & Petti, 1984; A. Freud & Burlingham, 1943; Friedman & Linn, 1957; van der Kolk, 1987; Yule & Williams, 1990). Social stigmatization of victims can also worsen reactions to traumatic events (Ayalon, 1982; Frederick, 1986; Nir, 1985). Many of the dimensions of stressors that have been suggested by the literature to be associated with increased stressfulness of events are listed in Table 6.4.[2]

Unique Stressful Dimensions of Events

The generic dimensions discussed above are those that might be found in nearly all stressful events. It is important to remember, however, that every traumatic event can be characterized not only by generic dimensions of distress but also by its own uniquely stressful dimensions. Child cancer patients, for instance, are more likely than victims of other traumatic events to experience feelings of estrangement and social isolation resulting in part from the stigma of their disease and in part from the side effects of therapy (e.g., loss of hair, prolonged absences from school; Nir, 1985). Children in war-torn countries may be more likely to have their social development inhibited, due partly to the greater sanctioning of violence in their social environment and partly

TABLE 6.4. Generic Distressing Dimensions of Traumatic Events for Children

General experience

Death, especially of someone related to the child or that the child knows

Injury, especially of the child or someone the child knows

Suddenness and unexpectedness of the events

Perceived uncontrollability of the events

Duration and frequency of exposure to the events

The events were among a series of different stressors experienced

The events are liable to recur

The source of the events was man rather than nature

Adverse consequences of the events are long lasting

Adverse consequences of the events are irreversible

Personal impact on the child

Child was impacted directly rather than as part of a group experience

Child perceived the events as a personal threat

Child was a primary victim rather than a secondary victim (one who is not the immediate target of the stressor, such as children of holocaust victims or Vietnam veterans)

Child experienced subjective loss as a consequence of the events (such as the loss of a pet)

Events involved moral conflicts for the child

Stigmatization is associated with exposure to the events

Impact on the child's family and home

Child perceived the events as a threat to family or friends

The event originated within the family

Child was dislocated from the home

Child was separated from parents or family

to their fear of others (Arroyo & Eth, 1985; Ayalon, 1982; Kinzie et al., 1986). Although uniquely stressful dimensions are not discussed any further in this chapter, their contribution to the development of PTSD in children to traumatic events should always be considered (see Figure 6.1).

Responses to Two Types of Stressors

Average incidence rates of DSM-IV PTSD symptoms, and associated symptoms, are listed in Table 6.5 according to a two-part classification of traumatic events that is based on a tripartite typology suggested by Terr (1991). A two-part, rather than tripartite, classification was necessitated because of limitations imposed by the available empirical literature; however, as the following discussion demonstrates, even this simple typology is capable of illustrating the differential impact that the type of stressor can have on a child's traumatic stress reactions. The two categories of stressor referred to in Table 6.5 are defined as follows: (1) acute, nonabusive stressors, which encompass traumatic events—other than physical or sexual abuse—that occur only once (disasters such as floods, fires, transportation accidents, etc.); and (2) chronic or abusive stressors, which encompass ongoing or multiple stressors (such as war, chronic illness, repeated surgeries, etc.) and/or incidents of physical or sexual abuse, whether of single or repeated occurrence.

Stress Reactions That Are Similar for Both Acute, Nonabusive, and Chronic or Abusive Stressors

Some stress reactions appear likely to be observed among children regardless of the type of stressor involved. The incidence rates in Table 6.5 (disregarding those responses whose rates are based on sample sizes of less than 50 children), for example, indicate that regardless of the type of stressor involved, trauma-specific fears are equally likely to develop (30% for acute, nonabusive stressors and 33% for chronic and/or abusive stressors), as are difficulties sleeping (29% for acute and 30% for chronic stressors), aggressive or antisocial behavior (17% for acute and 20% for chronic stressors), and eating problems (5% for acute and 8% for chronic stressors). Victims of both types of stressors are also equally likely to be diagnosed with PTSD (36% each).

Symptoms Observed More Frequently after Exposure to Chronic or Abusive Stressors

Incidence rates of most of the symptoms associated with PTSD listed in Table 6.5 differ according to the type of stressor involved. Quite a few symptoms, for instance, seem more likely to be observed among child victims of chronic or abusive stressors than among child victims of acute, nonabusive stressors. Children exposed to chronic or abusive stressors more often meet the DSM-IV criterion C of three or more symptoms of avoidance or numbing: 54% versus 30%. Victims of chronic or abusive stressors respond more frequently than do victims of acute, nonabusive stressors by actively avoiding reminders of the traumatic events (57% vs. 22%), numbing of affect (56% vs. 42%), actively trying to forget about the events (55% vs. 17%), and engaging in regressive behavior (22% vs. 6%). Child victims of chronic or abusive stressors are also more often distressed by reminders of their experiences (74% vs. 51%). They avoid reminders so much that they are more likely than victims of acute, nonabusive stressors to reexperience their traumas in bad dreams (61% vs. 23%). Children exposed to enduring or abusive stressors are more likely to meet the DSM-IV criterion D of two symptoms of overarousal (71% vs. 55%), too. Arousal in victims of chronic or abusive stress is revealed more often by symptoms of exaggerated startle response (48% vs. 24%) and general irritability (35% vs. 20%). Negative affect is also more closely associated with chronic or abusive stress: feelings of guilt (59% vs. 32%), a pessimistic attitude toward the future (35% vs. 12%), and depression (28% vs. 10%).

Inappropriate Sexual Behavior and Posttraumatic Play

Inappropriate sexual behavior may be the most frequently reported symptom of sexual abuse (Kendall-Tackett, Williams, & Finkelhor, 1993). Such behavior would appear to be an example of a trauma-specific symptom; however, some researchers have suggested that inappropriate sexual behaviors among sexually abused children might be considered a form of posttraumatic play. The incidence rates for posttraumatic play included in Table 6.5 for chronic or abusive stressors are based on this premise, in which case rates are higher (40%) than they are for nonsexualized posttraumatic play among children exposed to acute, nonabusive stressors (13%).

TABLE 6.5. Incidence Rates of Children's Posttraumatic Stress Responses to Acute, Nonabusive Stressors and to Chronic or Abusive Stressors

Symptoms	Type of stressor	
	Acute, nonabusive	Chronic or abusive
<u>DSM-IV criteria and symptoms</u>		
B. Reexperiencing (one required)	92%°°	86%
B1. Intrusive memories	38%	27%
B1. Posttraumatic Play	13%	40%
B1. Daydream about the event	26%°	
B1. Talkative about the event	31%	
B2. Bad dreams	23%	61%
B3. Reliving the event	30%	67%°
B3. Reenactment of the event	54%°	33%°
B4. Reminders are distressing	51%	74%°°
B. Trauma-specific fears	30%	33%
B5. Somatic complaints	31%	15%
C. Avoidance/numbness (three required)	30%°°	54%
C. Numbness	42%	56%
C1. Tries to forget about the event	17%	55%
C2. Avoids reminders	22%	57%
C3. Unable to recall parts of event	9%	34%°
C4. Loss of interest in activities	42%	29%
C5./C6. Detached or withdrawn	40%	14%
C7. Pessimistic about the future	12%	35%°°
D. Overarousal (two required)	55%°°	71%
D1. Difficulty sleeping	29%	30%
D2. Irritability	20%	35%
D3. Difficulty concentrating	52%	24%
D4. Hypervigilant	31%	15%
D5. Exaggerated startle response	24%	48%
<u>Diagnosis of PTSD</u>	36%	36%
<u>Associated symptoms or diagnoses</u>		
Generalized anxiety	55%	26%
Separation anxiety	45%	35%
Panic	35%°	6%
Depression	10%	28%
Guilt	32%	59%°°
Regressive behavior	6%	22%
Aggressive or antisocial behavior	17%	20%
Low self-esteem		34%
Dissociative response	31%°	100%°
Self-destructive behavior		9%
Eating problems	5%	8%
Omen formation	30%°°	0%°
Warped time perspective	13%	0%°
Sleepwalking	1%	3%°
Adjustment disorder	16%°	21%
ADHD	22%°	11%

Note. Percentages based on total $n \geq 100$ unless otherwise noted. Data from Fletcher (1994).
°n = 11–49; °°n = 50–99.

Symptoms Observed More Frequently after Exposure to Acute, Nonabusive Stressors

Some symptoms of PTSD seem to be more likely to be observed among victims of acute, nonabusive stressors than among victims of chronic or abusive stressors. Most of these differences, as might be expected, seem to be related either to the chronicity of the event or its abusive nature. Victims of chronic stressors, for example, are forced over time to come to some kind of accommodation with their traumas. As discussed above, many of the victims of chronic or abusive stressors seem to accomplish this by avoiding reminders, numbing of affect, and resorting to denial or dissociation. Victims of single-occurrence stressors, on the other hand, are not forced to come to terms with the traumatic disruption of their lives in the way that victims of more enduring stressors seem to be. Victims of acute, nonabusive stressors, in fact, appear to have a more difficult time putting the experience out of their minds. Thus, victims of acute, nonabusive stressors more frequently report intrusive memories (38% vs. 27%; see Table 6.5). Less frequent avoidance of reminders of the traumatic events coupled with more frequent occurrence of intrusive memories might be associated with greater incidence of hypervigilance (31% vs. 15%) when acute rather than chronic stressors are involved. Victims of acute, nonabusive stressors are in general more likely to report symptoms of anxiety: ranging from generalized anxiety (55% vs. 26%) to difficulties concentrating (52% vs. 24%) to separation anxiety (45% vs. 35%). They are also more likely to suffer from somatic complaints (31% vs. 15%), show decreased interest in previously important activities (42% vs. 29%), and become socially withdrawn (40% vs. 14%).

EMOTIONAL REACTIONS

In order for PTSD to be diagnosed, DSM-IV (American Psychiatric Association, 1994; Table 6.1) requires that an emotional reaction of horror, fear, or helplessness accompany exposure to traumatic circumstances. Few studies have actually assessed children's emotional reactions, however. Many children exposed to traumatic events do report feelings of distress (39%, on average; Fletcher, 1994). Children's emotional reactions to Hurricane Hugo were found to be associated with the level of symptomatology afterwards (Shannon et al., 1994). Children who reported feeling sad, worried, scared, alone, or angry during the hurricane, were

most likely to display the full range of PTSD symptomatology. In fact, children's emotional reactions during the hurricane were more strongly associated with PTSD than was the actual damage sustained by children's households as a consequence of the hurricane. These results suggest that children's emotional responses to traumatic events are closely related to the children's later stress responses, an important proposition that deserves further study.

MAKING MEANING: APPRAISALS, BELIEFS, AND ATTRIBUTIONS

The association between exposure to a traumatic event and extreme emotional response is usually mediated by an assessment of the meaning of the traumatic event. Feelings of horror and fear follow upon appraisals of the potential threat and harmfulness of traumatic events. Feelings of helplessness and hopelessness develop after exposure to events that call into question a person's basic assumptions about the essential predictability, controllability, safety and security of everyday life. This indirect path from trauma to emotional response via assessment of the meaning of the event is illustrated in Figure 6.1 by an arrow from traumatic event to assessment of meaning, followed by an arrow from meaning to emotional response.

Several theorists have suggested that posttraumatic responses represent a victim's attempt to accommodate to and assimilate experiences that challenge the victim's whole world view (e.g., Chemtob, Roitblat, Hamada, Carlson, & Twentyman, 1988; Epstein, 1990; Foa et al., 1989; Horowitz, 1976a, 1976b; Janoff-Bulman, 1989; McCann & Pearlman, 1990a, 1990b; Norris & Kaniasty, 1991). Before Freud published his conceptualization of traumatic stress, Janet (van der Kolk, Brown, & van der Hart, 1989) suggested that thoughts and memories of traumatic events intrusively recurred to victims because they were too emotionally threatening to be integrated into the victim's existing memory system. In Janet's view, traumatic memories split off from normal memory and become dissociated from normal consciousness, but they continue to have an unconscious impact on the individual's feelings and behavior. Similarly, Horowitz (1976a, 1976b) has argued that traumatic events represent information that is unacceptable to the victim's conceptual system and, therefore, is not capable of being integrated into the system, but at the same time the conceptual system is compelled some-

how to process this unacceptable information. Coming to terms with traumatic experience may require restructuring one's conceptual system to allow the traumatic experience to be accommodated to and then assimilated into a restructured understanding of the world and one's place in it (Epstein, 1990).

Appraisals

Appraisals are evaluations people make about the importance and meaning of events in terms of their own personal health and safety (Lazarus & Folkman, 1984). Foa et al. (1989) suggest that theories of cognitive appraisal must be considered in addition to a strictly behavioral approach when one is attempting to explain PTSD symptomatology. Peterson and Seligman (1983), for example, have attempted to apply the theory of learned helplessness to an understanding of victimization, suggesting that victims must appraise aversive situations as inescapable and unpredictable before a sense of helplessness can develop. Some theorists (Chemtob et al., 1988; Foa et al., 1989) have proposed that fear structures are created in a person's cognitive network after exposure to particularly aversive events. Fear structures are "programs for escape or avoidance behavior" (Foa et al., 1989, p. 166) that encompass at least three different kinds of information: information about the aversive situation, interpretative information about the meaning of the situation, and procedures for responding to the situation.

In the model of the context for the development of PTSD illustrated in Figure 6.1, appraisals are considered to mediate a child's emotional reactions to traumatic events. If an event is not perceived as threatening by a child, for instance, feelings of fear do not arise, and neither do symptoms of PTSD. Children younger than 8 years and 5 months who lived at Three Mile Island, for example, were unable to recognize the danger that the nuclear accident posed to them and their families, and, perhaps as a consequence, their concerns about the consequences of the nuclear accident were "vague and undifferentiated" (Handford et al., 1986, p. 351).

Beliefs

Some theorists (Epstein, 1990; Janoff-Bulman, 1989; McCann & Pearlman, 1990a, 1990b; Norris & Kaniasty, 1991) contend that stressful events become traumatic when they shatter certain basic beliefs that people normally assume about themselves and the world in which they live. Stressors can be traumatic if they pose overwhelming threats to a person's beliefs about the safety and security of the world, the certainty, orderliness, predictability, and controllability of the world, the person's sense of mastery and general self-esteem, or the trustworthiness of important others. An association has been found between PTSD symptomatology and such basic beliefs held by adults exposed to combat in Vietnam (Fletcher, 1988) and violent crime (Norris & Kaniasty, 1991). Few studies of children's beliefs have been made to date. Sexually abused children, however, have been found to report that they believe that the world is a dangerous place in which to live, that it is not responsive to their control, and that adults are not worthy of trust (Wolfe, Gentile, & Wolfe, 1989; Wolfe, Gentile, Michienzi, Sas, & Wolfe, 1991).

Foreshortened Future

One belief or attitude that has been assessed among children with some frequency is the so-called "sense of foreshortened future." This is a pessimistic attitude about the future, a belief that one's life can end at any moment, and that therefore the future can be neither anticipated nor planned for. Terr (1991) has suggested that a negative attitude about the future would be relatively prevalent regardless of the type of stressor encountered. Contrary to Terr's hypothesis, however, a pessimistic attitude about the future does not seem to be as prevalent among children exposed to acute, nonabusive stressors (12% on average—see Table 6.5; Green et al., 1991; Jones & Ribbe, 1991; Schwarz & Kowalski, 1991a; Terr, 1979) as it is among children exposed to more extreme chronic or abusive stressors (35% on average; Kinzie et al., 1986; Kiser et al., 1988; Zamvil, Wechsler, Frank, & Docherty, 1991). This illustrates the differential impact stressor characteristics can have on beliefs.

Attributions

Attribution theory is founded on the assumption that people try to make sense of their experience (Veronen & Kilpatrick, 1983). Explanations for unpredictable, uncontrollable, and aversive events can be attributed either to internal or external causes, to stable or unstable conditions over time, and either to specific or more global conditions (Abramson, Seligman, & Teasdale, 1978). Guilt or self-blame (an internal attribution of cause) has been found to be associated with children's trau-

matic experiences (see Tables 3 and 5; Kinzie et al., 1986; Pynoos et al., 1987; Realmuto et al., 1992; Schwarz & Kowalski, 1991a; Wolfe et al., 1989, 1991). Internal causal attributions for negative experiences made by adolescents involved in a ship disaster have been found to be related to greater PTSD symptomatology 1 year after the disaster (Joseph, Brewin, Yule, & Williams, 1993). A pessimistic attitude about the future (discussed above) is an example of an attribution of continued (stable) insecurity and safety into the future. Global attributions of causality (all adults are untrustworthy versus just the adult who abused is untrustworthy) also seem to be associated with traumatization, at least in sexually abused children (Wolfe et al., 1989, 1991).

BIOLOGICAL CHANGES

Some psychobiological models of PTSD argue that exposure to extreme stressors produces changes in various neurochemicals or endogenous opioids (Krystal et al., 1989; van der Kolk, Boyd, Krystal, & Greenberg, 1984). One psychobiological model proposes that "exposure to inescapable shock increases norepinephrine turnover, increases plasma catecholamine levels, depletes brain norepinephrine, and increases 3-methoxy-4-hydroxyphenylglycol (MHPG) production. . . . In addition, brain dopamine and serotonin are decreased, and acetylcholine is increased" (van der Kolk et al., 1984, p.126). There is some tentative evidence that such changes are associated with extreme stress in adults (Kosten, Mason, Giller, Ostroff, & Harkness, 1987; Yehuda, Southwick, Giller, Ma, & Mason, 1992) and in adolescents (De Bellis, Lefter, Trickett, & Putnam, 1994). These biological changes, however, do not appear to be necessarily trauma-specific. Increased catecholamine secretion, for instance, has been found both after tennis and after sexual intercourse (Rose, 1980).

Kolb (1987) has proposed a model of PTSD which suggests that, in addition to possible changes in neurochemical activity after traumatization, changes in neuronal pathways may occur as well. This has led him to speculate that children may be more likely than most adults to develop PTSD because their neuronal pathways are not developed enough to accommodate to the neurochemical reactions to trauma (Kolb, 1987). Possible neurological changes due to traumatic experiences have yet to be studied among either adults or children.

CONDITIONED RESPONSES

Cognitive-behaviorists note that many aspects of PTSD symptomatology can be explained by various models of learning, including traditional stimulus–response theories (Keane, Fairbank, Caddell, Zimering, & Bender, 1985; Foa et al., 1989) and more recently devised information-processing and cognitive-network models (Foa et al., 1989; Pittman, 1988; Yates & Nasby, 1993). Mowrer's (1960) two-factor theory of learning, for example, has been used to explain how victims of extreme stressors become aversively conditioned to a wide variety of cues (Keane, Fairbank et al., 1985). Both classical and instrumental conditioning are considered to come into play. First, previously neutral stimuli become associated with extremely stressful events, and the neutral stimuli assume aversive properties as a consequence. The previously unconditioned stimulus (UCS) becomes a conditioned stimulus (CS) for fear responses. Pairing the newly conditioned stimulus with a new neutral stimulus can also make the neutral stimulus aversive, through the process of higher-order conditioning. The process of stimulus generalization also helps increase the number and variety of aversive stimuli by making other stimuli that are similar to already aversive stimuli aversive as well. The second stage of this process occurs when a traumatized individual learns to respond to aversive situations with avoidance or withdrawal, which can lead to a decrease in anxiety. In this way, Mowrer's two-factor theory provides a means of explaining the acquisition of fear and avoidance responses. The theory, however, has been criticized for its inability to account for symptoms of reexperiencing and overarousal (Foa et al., 1989; Mineka, 1979; Jones & Barlow, 1990).

Learned Alarms

Jones and Barlow (1990) have suggested that symptoms of reexperiencing and overarousal can be accounted for by conditioned responses to internal or external cues that have become associated with traumatic experiences. Fearful responses to the original traumatic events are considered "true alarms," and the conditioned responses to cues associated with the original events are considered "learned alarms."

> True alarms are regarded as a fear response that occurs when an individual is faced with a life-threatening event, particularly a severe one . . . Learned

alarms are seen as conditioned responses to either interoceptive or external cues. . . . PTSD . . . may reflect in part the conditioning that occurs upon activation of true alarms (i.e., evocation of fear and accompanying increases in a variety of physiological response systems that would support escape [flight] behavior under life threatening conditions). Such a response is adaptive in situations such as combat or rape and is a protective mechanism often necessary for survival. . . . For patients with PTSD in response to single or repeated true alarms, fear likely has become associated with both internal and external cues associated with the initial event. (Jones & Barlow, 1990, pp. 318–319)

The consistent finding that the severity of the stressor is associated with PTSD symptomatology suggests that extreme stressors serve as true alarms. The tendency of trauma victims to react strongly to both external and internal cues related to the original trauma suggests that learned alarms play a large role in the etiology of PTSD as well.

Anxious Apprehension and Reexperiencing

According to Jones and Barlow (1990),

the crucial step to pathology is the development of anxious apprehension about learned alarms. It is only this process, with its strong cognitive components such as distorted processing of information along with marked negative affect, that can account for the downward spiral of symptomatology associated with PTSD. This downward spiral would include the unremitting re-experiencing of learned alarms and associated traumatic memories, as well as the pattern of affective instability associated with alternate numbing and exacerbation of negative emotions and the occasional delayed emotional experience of PTSD symptomatology. (p. 319)

From this view, learned alarms lead to anxious apprehension and reexperiencing of the traumatic experience. This is perhaps especially likely to be the case the less predictable and uncontrollable the circumstances surrounding the traumatic experience are perceived to be.

Thus, if the vulnerabilities described above line up correctly, an individual will experience the overwhelming true alarm and subsequent learned alarms as unpredictable, uncontrollable aversive events. The individual will react to these events with

chronic overarousal and additional cognitive symptoms of hypervigilance to trauma-related cues . . . accompanied by attention narrowing. . . . Since the original alarm contained strong arousal based components, the existing chronic overarousal combined with a hypervigilance to arousal that might signal the beginning of a future alarm would insure a succession of learned alarms and associated traumatic memories. (Jones & Barlow, 1990, p. 319)

The aversiveness can become emotionally overwhelming, which leads to avoidance of cues associated with the trauma. Unfortunately, due to the processes of stimulus generalization and higher-order conditioning described above, associated cues can be difficult to avoid. As a consequence, traumatized individuals become inclined to withdraw from the world, numb their affective responses, and sometimes resort to dissociation. However, they are rarely able to avoid intrusive memories of their traumatic experiences for long. As a result, the characteristic phasing found in PTSD begins—between reexperiencing and avoiding trauma-related memories and cues.

INDIVIDUAL CHARACTERISTICS

A child's stress reactions can be moderated at any stage of the process illustrated in Figure 6.1 by characteristics of both the individual child and the child's social environment. The meaning of the traumatic experience, for instance, will vary according to the capacity of the individual and his or her social environment to make sense of it. Similarly, a child's emotional repertoire can affect his or her capacity for emotional response. These and other moderating influences of the characteristics of the individual child and his or her social environment are considered in more detail below.

Biological Vulnerability

Family and twin studies have provided some evidence of familial predispositions to anxiety disorders (Jones & Barlow, 1990). However, only a few studies have explored the association between PTSD in adults and family psychiatric history, and none has done so for children. Davidson, Swartz, Storck, Krishnan, and Hammett (1985) found that "sixty-six percent of [adult] PTSD probands gave a family history positive for psychiatric illness" (p. 91), compared to 79% of

relatives of adult depressed probands and 93% for adult generalized anxiety disorder (GAD) probands. Foy, Resnick, Sipprelle, and Carroll (1987) found that 48% of one sample of Vietnam combat veterans with PTSD, and 71% of another sample, had family histories of psychopathology. On the other hand, these authors also found that 38% of combat veterans without PTSD in one sample, and 50% in the other, also had histories of psychopathology in the family. Support for a biological predisposition to PTSD is therefore only tentative at this point.

Genetic Components: Temperament and Intelligence

Jones and Barlow (1990) "postulate that the genetic component may be a predisposition to a diffuse stress responsivity reflected as chronic autonomic overarousal or noradrenergic lability" (p. 314), and they argue that research indicating differences in resting heart rate between combat veterans with PTSD and nonmilitary controls provides some evidence for this position. Evidence from the literature on resiliency among children exposed to extreme stressors indicates that temperament plays an important role in a child's ability to adapt successfully to stress (Wertlieb, Weigel, Springer, & Feldstein, 1987). Werner and Smith (1982) found that resilient children were more likely to be characterized as outgoing, positive in mood, and adaptable to change as infants. Wyman, Cowen, Work, and Parker (1991) found that among fourth- to sixth-grade children exposed to four or more stressors in their life, stress-resilient children were more likely to have been perceived by their parents as easy-going rather than difficult as infants. Higher intelligence may also mitigate some of the effects of traumatic stress (Masten et al., 1988; Werner & Smith, 1982).

Psychological Strengths and Vulnerabilities

Self-Efficacy and Locus of Control

Because traumatic experiences are often characterized as unpredictable and uncontrollable events, issues surrounding personal control often emerge among traumatized individuals. It has been suggested that personal experience of mastery, self-efficacy, or control in aversive situations prior to a traumatic experience can attenuate the negative effects of such experience (Bandura,

Taylor, Williams, Mefford, & Barchas, 1985; Foa et al., 1989; Foa, Zinbarg, & Rothbaum, 1992; Luthar, 1991; Miller, 1979; Mineka, 1979; Mineka & Kihlstrom, 1978; Weigel et al., 1989). Rotter (1966) has argued that individuals can be characterized according to whether or not they believe they have control over their environment. Those who believe they have control are said to exercise an internal locus of control. Those who consider themselves controlled by the environment, on the other hand, are said to have an external locus of control. Moran and Eckenrode (1992) found that female adolescent victims of maltreatment who demonstrated external locus of control and low self-esteem reported the highest levels of depression; whereas those with an internal locus of control and high self-esteem reported levels of depression that were close to levels of control subjects with similar personality profiles. Unfortunately, it is not clear whether these associations are due to predisposing personality characteristics, or if they are the outcome of exposure to extreme stressors that are outside the control of the individuals involved. One prospective study of factors that ameliorate risk in children (Seifer, Sameroff, Baldwin, & Baldwin, 1992), found that low external locus of control and unknown or undifferentiated locus of control (Connell, 1985; Peterson & Seligman, 1983), but not high internal locus of control, were associated with positive changes in functioning from 4 to 13 years of age, a finding that replicated earlier results reported by Weigel et al. (1989).

History of Psychiatric Problems

It is possible that a history of emotional or psychiatric problems can potentiate adverse posttraumatic stress responses. Prior developmental and psychiatric problems, for example, have been found to be associated with more behavioral problems and greater depression among sexually abused children (Mannarino, Cohen, & Berman, 1994). Earls et al. (1988) found that children most likely to be adversely affected 1 year after a disastrous flood were those with preexisting disorders. Shannon et al. (1994) found a positive association between trait anxiety and posttraumatic stress symptomatology among children exposed to Hurricane Hugo, leading them to suggest that a pretrauma history of anxiety may contribute to vulnerability to traumatic experiences. On the other hand, McLeer, Deblinger, Atkins, Foa, and Ralphe (1988) found no significant association between symptomatology and trait anxiety when

sexual abuse was involved. The difference, of course, may result from the greater traumatization associated with sexual abuse. A tendency to low trait anxiety might be less helpful in moderating a child's reactions to the more overwhelming experience of sexual abuse.

Experiential Vulnerability

Considerable evidence has accumulated that a history of stressful life events is associated with higher levels of PTSD in children when they are later exposed to traumatic stressors (Conte & Schuerman, 1987; Einbender & Friedrich, 1989; Kiser et al., 1988; Mannarino et al., 1994; Seifer et al., 1992; Wolfe, Jaffe, Wilson, & Zak, 1985). Early stressful experiences need not always sensitize a child to later trauma, however. How the child reacts to early stress experiences may be more important to the development of PTSD than exposure to such experiences (Rutter, 1983). As discussed previously, past experience of mastering threatening experiences may help steel the child against later traumatization from stressful circumstances. Weigel et al. (1989), for example, found that perceptions of control served to moderate the effects of exposure to stressful events among school-aged children.

Gender Differences

Few empirical studies have considered gender differences in children's responses to traumatic experiences. What little evidence exists is contradictory and inconclusive. Rutter (1983) has suggested that boys may be more vulnerable to stress than girls, but he was summarizing exposure to stressors that today would generally be considered less than traumatizing (such as hospitalization of the child, birth of a sibling, and divorce). Milgram and Milgram (1976) did find that 6 months after the Yom Kippur War, fifth- and sixth-grade boys in Israel reported higher levels of anxiety than did girls. Other, more recent studies, however, have not found boys more often symptomatic than girls. Some, in fact, have found higher incidence of PTSD among girls. Two years after the Buffalo Creek dam collapse, Green et al. (1991) found that among children between the ages of 2 and 15 years who had been exposed to the disaster, girls were more likely than boys to be rated as symptomatic of PTSD (44% of 87 girls vs. 30% of 92 boys were diagnosed with PTSD). The girls of Buffalo Creek were especially susceptible to symptoms of denial. Among

school-aged and adolescent children exposed to Hurricane Hugo, girls also reported higher levels of PTSD symptomatology than did boys (7% of 2,900 girls vs. 4% of 2,787 boys) (Shannon et al., 1994; Lonigan et al., 1994). Girls in this study were also more likely to report being distressed by the hurricane, feeling upset by thoughts of the hurricane, fearing its recurrence, isolating themselves, avoiding reminders of the hurricane, avoiding feelings about it, affective numbing, increased startle response, somatic complaints, and feelings of guilt (Shannon et al., 1994). A higher incidence of PTSD has also been found among girls exposed to sexual or physical abuse (46% of 13 girls vs. 24% of 49 boys) (Adam et al., 1992).

Some researchers have found no gender differences in reaction to traumatic events (Earls et al., 1988; McFarlane, 1987a). Nader et al. (1990; Pynoos et al., 1987) found no gender differences in reactions to a school sniper attack. Blom (1986) observed no striking differences between boys and girls in reaction to a fatal school accident. Shannon et al. (1994) found little or no differences between boys and girls exposed to Hurricane Hugo in the incidence of sleep problems, pessimistic outlook on the future, risky behavior, bad dreams, or intrusive imagery.

On the whole, however, there do appear to be gender-related differences in the incidence of some posttraumatic stress reactions. Jaffe, Wolfe, Wilson, and Zak (1986) reported the items on the Child Behavior Checklist (Achenbach & Edelbrock, 1981) that differentiated girls and boys of violent families from children of nonviolent families. Their results suggest that girls may react (at least to violence in the home) primarily with internalizing behavior problems (e.g., clinging, worrying, sullenness), whereas boys react with both internalizing and externalizing behavior problems (e.g., arguing, hyperactivity, cruelty, impulsivity, hot temper). Similar results were obtained by Kiser et al. (1988) who found that sexually abused girls between the ages of 2 and 6 years tended to feel sad and depressed, whereas sexually abused boys the same age tended to act enraged and aggressive. Blom (1986) found that after a school accident boys showed more sleep disturbances, fighting, and fears; whereas, girls showed more startle reactions, asked more questions, and appeared to think about the disaster more often than boys.

The time of assessment may also make a difference in gender-related symptomatology. Sexually abused preschool boys tended to withdraw

immediately after their abuse was revealed, whereas girls were more withdrawn a year later (Kiser et al., 1988). Five months after a disastrous New England blizzard and flood, preschool boys were reportedly more anxious than girls (Burke et al., 1982), but 10 months after the disaster, girls were observed to be more anxious (Burke, Moccia, Borus, & Burns, 1986). Blom (1986) noted that boys seemed to take longer to recover after a school accident.

Ethnic and Cultural Variations

Reactions to Acute, Nonabusive Stressors

Perhaps because of the difficulty of recruiting large enough samples of traumatized children of any background, investigation of ethnic and cultural variations in children's posttraumatic responses has been slow to develop (DeJong, Emmett, & Hervada, 1982; Frederick, 1988; Hjern, Angel, & Höjer, 1991; Lindholm & Willey, 1986; Pierce & Pierce, 1984). The largest study with the best methodology that has looked at the issue concerned an acute, nonabusive stressor, Hurricane Hugo (Shannon et al., 1994). The majority of the 5,687 9-year to 19-year-old children studied were white (67.3%); 25.8% were African-American; 3.6% were Asian; 1.4% were Hispanic; and 1.9% were "other minority." Because of the small numbers of non-African-American minorities in this sample, the researchers chose to analyze differences among three ethnic groups: whites, African-Americans, and non-African-American minorities. Even after statistically controlling for severity of the traumatic experience and levels of trait anxiety, African-American children reported symptoms related to each criterion A through D of DSM-III-R in greater proportions than the other children. Nevertheless, there was no significant difference between the proportions of African-American (6.3%) and non-African-American children (5.1%) who met the core criteria for PTSD, A through D.

Reactions to Chronic or Abusive Stressors

Sexual Abuse

Rao, DiClemente, and Ponton (1992) compared the medical records of 69 Asian children, 80 African-American children, 80 Hispanic children, and 80 Caucasian children who had been referred to a clinic for sexual abuse. The four ethnic groups differed on several potentially important demographic variables. The Asian and Hispanic children tended to be older than the African-American and Caucasian children when they were referred to the sexual abuse clinic, even though the groups did not differ in the amount of time elapsed between last episode and presentation at the clinic. Asians were most likely to be living with both parents at the time of evaluation, African-Americans were the least likely to be living with both parents, and Caucasians and Hispanics were in between the two extremes. Asians were also less than half as likely as the other children to be living in a single-parent family. On the other hand, Asian primary caretakers were half as likely as primary caretakers of the other groups to spontaneously report their child's abuse to authorities. Asian primary caretakers were also the least likely to believe their child's report of abuse. The most extreme forms of sexual abuse (vaginal or anal penetration) were less likely to have occurred among Asians (36.4%) and Caucasians (36.4%) than among Hispanics (50.0%) and African-Americans (58.4%).

Ethnic/Cultural Differences in Four Symptoms

Sexual acting out was least likely to be found among Asians (1.4% vs. 15.0% among African-Americans, 17.5% among Caucasians, and 13.8% among Hispanics). Asian children were also the least likely to display anger (8.7% vs. 21.3% among African-Americans, 22.5% among Caucasians, and 20.0% among Hispanics). Urinary symptoms were least frequently observed among Asian children (2.9%) and most frequently among Caucasian children (17.5%), with African-Americans (10.0%) and Hispanics (6.3%) in between the two extremes. Suicidal ideation or attempts, on the other hand, occurred most frequently among Asians (21.7% vs. 11.3% among African-Americans, 15.0% among Caucasians, and 10.0% among Hispanics).

War and Concentration Camps

Kinzie and his colleagues (Kinzie et al., 1986, 1989) assessed symptoms of PTSD among young Cambodian refugees living in the United States who had lived in concentration camps during the Pol Pot regime when they were of school age. Of 40 children (25 boys and 15 girls), 46.5% (19) met DSM-III-R criteria for PTSD 5 to 6 years after leaving the camps (Kinzie et al., 1989). Three

years later, 48% (13) of the 27 young Cambodians who took part in a follow-up study also met criteria for PTSD (Kinzie et al., 1989), with 8 of them meeting criteria at both time periods. Avoidant behaviors were the most commonly reported symptoms, which (according to the authors of the study) may have reflected, in part, a cultural tendency to cope by passively accepting adversity. The incidence of depressive disorders was also high at both time periods (53% at time one and 41% at time two), and its presence was strongly associated with the presence of PTSD. Fifteen percent of the children reported entertaining suicidal thoughts. Few incidents of antisocial or acting-out behaviors were observed. The children viewed school positively, an attitude that may have been due to their cultural value of scholarship. Those children living with a family member appeared to function better than did others living without a family member at time one (Kinzie et al., 1986) but not at follow-up 3 years later (Kinzie et al., 1989).

In another study of PTSD among 46 Cambodian refugees (36 male and 10 female refugees) in the United States 10 years after their traumatization as children and adolescents under the Pol Pot regime (Realmuto et al., 1992), 37% met DSM-III-R criteria for PTSD. Many more missed meeting the criteria because they displayed too few symptoms of overarousal. PTSD symptomatology was not significantly associated with depressive mood, anxiety, or dissociation in this sample of young people aged 12 to 23 years old.

On the whole, regardless of ethnicity, non-Caucasian children exposed to any type of stressor present with incidence rates of PTSD that are similar to rates among traumatized white children from the United States. African-American children may present with the most severe symptomatology of any ethnic background when exposed to acute, nonabusive stressors. Cultural differences become more complex when chronic or abusive stressors are involved. However, much more study of cross-cultural differences in response to traumatic experience is required before any definite conclusions can be drawn concerning the differential impact of trauma on children of different cultural backgrounds.

Developmental Differences

Although most research to date confirms that the diagnostic symptom clusters of DSM-IV apply as well to traumatized children of all ages, from preschool through adolescence, as they do to traumatized adults, the manifestation of posttraumatic stress responses in children may differ according to the child's age and level of development. Not only may symptomatology of children differ from that of adults, but it may also differ among children of different ages. A child's age and level of cognitive, emotional, and social development can significantly impact on each stage in the development of PTSD, as illustrated in Figure 6.1. Preschool children, for example, may be less capable than school-aged and adolescent children of appraising a technological disaster as threatening (Green et al., 1991; Handford et al., 1986). Even the assessment of posttraumatic stress reactions in children younger than 4 years old presents its own particular set of challenges (Scheeringa, Zeanah, Drell, & Larrieu, 1995). The emotional repertoire of younger children may be more limited than that of older children, too (Cicchetti, 1989; Cole & Putnam, 1992). Young children's previous experience with stressful events, especially with mastering such events, is also likely to be more limited than is the case for older children (Rutter, 1983), and as a consequence, the coping options available to younger children are probably more limited than those available to older children (Rossman, 1992). The younger a child, the more likely are his or her traumatic reactions to depend upon the traumatic reactions of others, especially parents (Cornely & Bromet, 1986; Famularo, Fenton, Kinscherff, Ayoub, & Barnum, 1994; McFarlane, 1987b).

The incidence rates for symptoms of PTSD listed in Table 6.3 provide a general indication of the kinds of differences in symptom presentation that might be found among adults and among children of three different age groups: preschoolers (approximately 6 years or younger), school-aged children (5–13 years of age), and adolescents (12 or 13 years and older). Unfortunately, most of the rates for preschoolers and adolescents in Table 6.3 are based on small samples of children. The following discussion of the influence of age and developmental stage on the etiology of PTSD will therefore frequently focus more on the differences between adults and children of all ages than on differences among the three age groups of children.

Reactions to Overwhelming Stimuli: Developmental Differences

Although theorists have only recently begun to apply developmental theory to the understanding of children's posttraumatic stress reactions

(Cicchetti, 1989; Cole & Putnam, 1992; Fish-Murray, Koby, & van der Kolk, 1987; Kagan, 1983; Maccoby, 1983; Pynoos & Eth, 1985; Rutter, 1983), several relevant principles have emerged from the literature. For example, because younger children have less control over their own physiological and emotional functioning than do older children, distressing events are more likely to overwhelm them and lead to disorganized behavior than is the case for older children (American Psychiatric Association, 1994; Cicchetti, 1989; Cole & Putnam, 1992; Maccoby, 1983; Pynoos & Eth, 1985). Traumatized children certainly seem more likely to be distressed by reminders of traumatic events (51% for all ages; Table 6.3) than are traumatized adults (26%). Furthermore, regressive behaviors—indicative of feelings of being overwhelmed—appear to be reported on average most frequently among preschoolers (17%; see Table 6.3), less frequently among school-aged children (11%), and least frequently among adolescents (4%). Affective numbing may be another reaction to feelings of being overwhelmed and helpless, which would help explain the greater incidence of numbing among traumatized children of all ages (47%; see Table 6.3) than among traumatized adults (23%).

The use of dissociation as a coping mechanism is thought to begin at about 2 years of age and to decline with age (Cole & Putnam, 1992). Children of all ages certainly appear to present with dissociative responses more frequently (48%; see Table 6.3) than do adults (16%), although this difference in incidence rates may be due to the small samples used to estimate children's rates combined with a more liberal definition of dissociation used to estimate children's rates. Nevertheless, in the light of developmental theory (Cole & Putnam, 1992), incidence rates as high as those in Table 6.3 do suggest that children's dissociative responses to trauma are worthy of closer study than they have so far received.

Social Development, Growth of Identity, and Traumatic Reactions

Preschoolers, by necessity, rely a great deal on parental support in times of stress (Pynoos & Eth, 1985). A child's dependence on parental support decreases with age, as the possibility of peer support develops during the school years, and as self-reliance increases during adolescence (Cole & Putnam, 1992; Pynoos & Eth, 1985; Rossman, 1992). This developmental progression is re-flected in a decrease with age in the incidence of separation anxiety after traumatization: from 36% among traumatized preschoolers to 16% among school-aged children to 4% among adolescents (see Table 6.3). Similarly, Rossman (1992) found that children aged 6 to 7 years were more likely to seek caregiver assistance in times of distress than were children aged 8 to 12 years. Rossman suggests that the older children's decreased dependence on caregiver assistance is a consequence of the child's growing use of social comparison during school years in conjunction with the child's growing awareness of the negative implications that dependence on adults has on evaluations of self-competence that also begin to emerge at this time (Cole & Putnam, 1992; Maccoby, 1983). At the same time, the egocentricity of younger children (Piaget & Inhelder, 1969) can lead them to feel more responsible for their traumatic experiences than is the actual case. This might contribute to a greater incidence of guilt feelings among traumatized children (43%; see Table 6.3) than among traumatized adults (15%).

Cognitive Development and Reactions to Stress

Before children attain the Piagetian stage of operational thinking between the ages of 7 and 11, their understanding of the world depends more on fantasy and play than is later the case (Fish-Murray et al., 1987; Piaget & Inhelder, 1969; Rossman, 1992). As a consequence, preschoolers appear likely to try to come to terms with traumatic experience by engaging in posttraumatic play more frequently (39%; see Table 6.3) than do school-aged children (14%). Younger children's memory may also be more visually and perceptually oriented rather than linguistically oriented (Fish-Murray et al., 1987; Pynoos & Eth, 1985). This could imbue their reexperiences of traumatic events with a more vivid quality than the reexperiences of adults, which may be reflected in the higher incidence among children of feelings of reliving the traumatic events (39% vs. 29% among adults).

As a result of the greater flexibility of the cognitive systems of adults (Fish-Murray et al., 1987; Pynoos & Eth, 1985), they may be more able than children to distance themselves from their reexperiences and view them as memories rather than actual experiences. Traumatized adults do, on average, report intrusive memories more fre-

quently (45%; see Table 6.3) than do traumatized children (34%). Cognitive development may provide older children and adults with more control over their thoughts as well, and, thus, even though traumatized children may try to avoid reminders of their traumatic experiences as frequently (32%; see Table 6.3) as do traumatized adults (33%), adults try more often to forget about their traumas (46%) than do children (24%). Moreover, adults appear to succeed at forgetting parts of their traumatic experiences more often (27%; see Table 6.3) than do children (12%).

Adolescents and adults are also better able than younger children to appreciate the threat of traumatic events, and as a consequence, they appear to have a greater understanding of their own increased vulnerability (Pynoos & Eth, 1985). This would help explain the higher incidence of trauma-specific fears among traumatized adults (45%; see Table 6.3) than among traumatized children (31%). It would also help account for the much greater pessimism about the future expressed by adults (61%) than by children (16%). The consequent anxiety and overarousal could also contribute to a greater incidence of startle response in adults than in children (38% vs. 28%; see Table 6.3), as well as a greater incidence of panic in adults (18% vs. 8%).

Coping Behavior

Researchers have only recently begun to investigate systematically the coping processes of children exposed to traumatic experiences (Ayalon, 1982; Compas, 1987; Curry & Russ, 1985; Maccoby, 1983; Murphy & Moriarty, 1976; Rutter, 1983; Wertlieb, Weigel, & Feldstein, 1987). Wertlieb, Weigel, and Feldstein (1987) have identified children's coping behaviors that (1) focus on the self, environment or others, (2) serve to problem solve or manage emotion, or (3) are examples of the following coping styles: information seeking, support seeking, direct action, inhibition of action, or intrapsychic coping. Coping styles and strategies appear to be closely associated with age and developmental stage (Compas, 1987). In this regard, Rossman (1992) found age and gender differences in children's use of several strategies to regulate their emotional reactions to stressful situations. The use of self-calming behaviors (e.g., try to calm oneself and relax when feeling bad) decreased with age, as did the use of self-distraction or avoidance behaviors (e.g., read a book to take one's mind off a bad thing). Children

6 or 7 years old were more likely than children 8 to 12 years old to seek refuge in a caregiver (e.g., get a parent to help). Girls were more likely than boys to seek out a caregiver and to make use of peers (e.g., play with a friend). Distress behaviors (e.g., cry or bite nails) were used more by girls at all ages, too, whereas boys' use of distress behaviors declined with age. On the other hand, girls' use of anger declined with age, whereas its use by boys declined between the ages of 8 to 9 years only to increase again from 10 to 12 years. These studies represent only a first step toward the understanding of a child's ability to cope with stressful experiences. It is especially unfortunate that no data are currently available on the impact coping behaviors might have on the development and course of PTSD in children.

SOCIAL CHARACTERISTICS

Social Support

As noted earlier, the reaction of a child to trauma is often closely related to the reactions of the child's parents or other important adults, especially the mother (Bloch et al., 1956; Burke et al., 1986; Crawshaw, 1963; Famularo et al., 1994; A. Freud & Burlingham, 1943; Gislason & Call, 1982; Harrison et al., 1967; McFarlane, 1987b; Newman, 1976; Silber, Perry, & Bloch, 1958), although this need not always be the case (Handford et al., 1986). Parents' reactions may be especially important for younger children (Crawshaw, 1963; A. Freud & Burlingham, 1943; Holahan & Moos, 1987; Pynoos & Eth, 1985; Sugar, 1989). Stress-resilient children have been found to have close, positive relationships with their caregivers and to receive more support from both within and outside of the family (Holahan & Moos, 1987; Seifer et al., 1992; Werner & Smith, 1982; Wyman et al., 1991, 1992). Sexually abused children who receive support from their mothers fare better after disclosure than do those whose mothers express disbelief or negative emotions toward their children (Conte & Schuerman, 1987; Everson, Hunter, Runyan, Edelsohn, & Coulter, 1989; Kendall-Tackett et al., 1993).

Parenting Style

A child's sense of competence and self-reliance appears to be encouraged, in part, by a flexible (Baumrind, 1971), warm, caring, and attentive

parenting style (Maccoby & Martin, 1983). Rigid, coercive parenting, on the other hand, appears to reduce a child's sense of self-competence and self-esteem (Slater & Power, 1987). Children whose parents provide positive, nurturant care and set limits in a constructive manner tend to be more stress resilient than those whose parents are more rigid and less warm in their caregiving (Wyman et al., 1991, 1992).

Family Discord versus Cohesion

Evidence is beginning to accumulate that family conflict (prior to, during, or after exposure to trauma) is associated with more severe symptoms of PTSD in children. Nir (1985) observed that parental discord can have a detrimental effect on children diagnosed with cancer. Stress-resilient children appear to come from more stable family environments than do less resilient children (Seifer et al., 1992; Wyman et al., 1991, 1992). The strongest predictor of PTSD symptomatology among children who lived through the Buffalo Creek flood was the parents' level of functioning and the home atmosphere (Green et al., 1991). Several writers have commented upon and documented the greater risk of psychosocial impairment among children from violent families as compared to children from nonviolent families (Arroyo & Eth, 1985; Burgess et al., 1987; Jaffe et al., 1986; Walker & Greene, 1987; Wolfe et al., 1985, 1986). The act of witnessing family violence has been found, in and of itself, to be associated with conduct problems, emotional problems, and deficits in social competence (Emery, 1982; Fantuzzo et al., 1991; Hughes, Parkinson, & Vargo, 1989; Jouriles et al., 1989; Kiser et al., 1988; Martinez & Richters, 1993; Rosenberg & Giberson, 1991).

Other Characteristics of the Social Environment

Additional characteristics of the social environment are likely to contribute to the development of PTSD after traumatization. The level of family stress, the mobility of the family, and the psychiatric history of the family, for instance, have all been found to influence a child's stress reactions (Anthony, 1986; Bloch et al., 1956; Felner, Gillespie, & Smith, 1985; Green, 1983; Livingston, 1987; Masten et al., 1988; Nir, 1985; Silber et al., 1958; Sugar, 1989). Felner et al. (1985) suggest that the composition of the family also

may contribute to a child's reaction to trauma in that children from single-parent families or reconstituted families may be more vulnerable than others.

Financial difficulties, too, have been found to be associated with symptoms of PTSD or general distress in children (Arroyo & Eth, 1985; Burgess et al., 1987; Elmer, 1977; Felner et al., 1985; Livingston, 1987; Lonigan et al., 1994; Masten et al., 1988; Sansonnet-Hayden, Haley, Marriage, & Fine, 1987; Shannon et al., 1994). Low socioeconomic status (SES), in fact, may increase a child's chance of being exposed to traumatic events in the first place, especially violence in the community as well as in the home. Symptoms of PTSD have been observed in child witnesses to, and victims of, community violence (Martinez & Richter, 1993).

CURRENT ISSUES AND FUTURE DIRECTIONS

It should be clear by this point that the last decade and a half of research on childhood traumatic stress reactions has demonstrated that children exposed to traumatic events can and do react in a manner very similar to that of traumatized adults. A substantial proportion of traumatized children, regardless of their age, exhibit behaviors symptomatic of the "core" DSM-IV symptoms of posttraumatic stress disorder: reexperiencing the traumatic experience, avoidance of reminders of the experience or affective numbing, and overarousal. Furthermore, children have often been observed to respond to traumatic events with additional symptoms such as guilt, depression, and generalized anxiety that are also associated with PTSD in adults.

It should be equally clear at this point that our current understanding of childhood posttraumatic stress disorder is far from complete. Future research must examine the etiology of childhood PTSD within a context that considers the impact of factors other than simply exposure to traumatic events. Sufficient data are currently available to indicate that differences among stressful events themselves need to be considered more carefully in the future. Other factors that might influence the development of childhood PTSD are less well understood. We know next to nothing, for example, about how children make meaning out of their traumatic experience, nor do we know much

about how their emotional reaction to trauma affects their posttraumatic reactions. Physiological responses to childhood trauma are also little understood at the moment. Current research does provides enough evidence to tell us that we need to know more about the impact on PTSD of personal characteristics such as gender, age, ethnicity, psychiatric history, sense of mastery, temperament, and coping skills. Less is known at the moment about how the characteristics of the child's social environment influence the development of PTSD.

Our contemporary understanding of childhood PTSD also rests on shaky methodological grounds. Better designed research is required to shore up our present understanding. Larger samples are required. More comparisons must be made between the reactions of traumatized children and *comparable* nontraumatized children. Reports, based on standardized assessment tools that ask PTSD-specific questions,[3] must be gathered from multiple sources, including the children themselves. Assessments of potentially important symptoms other than those included in the DSM-IV diagnostic criteria should also be gathered (Armsworth & Holaday, 1993). Similarly, comorbid conditions deserve closer study.

In the final analysis, we have only just begun to grasp the process whereby exposure to traumatic events leads to PTSD in children. We know that children's symptoms of PTSD often look strikingly similar to those of adults. We know, too, that children frequently manifest PTSD symptomatology in an age-specific manner. This knowledge represents a substantial gain in our understanding of childhood PTSD over the past decade and a half. Our accomplishments in this area should not allow us to become complacent, however. There is still much to learn about childhood PTSD. It is unclear, for example, why some children do not develop PTSD after exposure to traumatic events. The answer to that question could provide important clues about the kinds of treatment that would be most efficacious for those children who do develop PTSD, which is another topic about which little is currently known. Because traumatic experience can seriously disrupt a child's development and lead to difficult problems later in life, it is incumbent upon us to seek a better understanding, based on firm methodological grounds, of the context within which childhood PTSD develops.

NOTES

1. The PTSD-RI was not designed to allow DSM criteria to be assessed or a PTSD diagnosis to be made. Modifying the scale to allow this to be done can be problematic. One problem is related to the method used to dichotomize the five-point Likert ratings scales used for each question on the PTSD-RI. One approach is to rate a symptom as present if that symptom is rated with one of the two highest ratings on the Likert scale. Another approach rates a symptom as present if any of the three highest ratings is marked on the scale. Estimates of incidence rates of PTSD diagnosis will obviously differ according to which of these two approaches is chosen, with the first approach producing lower estimates (as demonstrated by Schwarz & Kowalski, 1991b). Shannon et al. (1994) and Lonigan et al. (1994) applied the first, more conservative approach.

2. Rating stressful events on each of the enumerated dimensions would allow for detailed comparisons between many kinds of events. A scale for assessing these dimensions in stressful events, the Dimensions of Stressful Events (DOSE) Scale, is available from the author.

3. A child's version of the Clinician-Administered PTSD Scale for Children (CAPS-C; Nader, Kriegler, Blake, & Pynoos, 1993) is a structured interview currently being tested. Four instruments that also are currently being tested are available from the author: a Childhood PTSD Interview suitable for paraprofessionals, a parent's version of the interview, a child's self-report (the When Bad Things Happen Scale) suitable for children with third-grade reading level and above, and a Parent's Report of the Child's Reactions to Stress paper-and-pencil scale.

REFERENCES

Abramson, L. Y., Seligman, M. E. P., & Teasdale, J. D. (1978). Learned helplessness in humans: Critique and reformulation. *Journal of Abnormal Psychology, 87*, 49–94.

Achenbach, T., & Edelbrock, C. S. (1981). Behavior problems and competencies reported by parents of normal and disturbed children aged four through sixteen. *Monographs of the Society for Research in Child Development, 46*(1, Serial No. 188).

Adam, B. S., Everett, B. L., & O'Neal, E. (1992). PTSD in physically and sexually abused psychiatrically hospitalized children. *Child Psychiatry and Human Development, 23*, 3–8.

American Psychiatric Association. (1952). *Diagnostic and statistical manual of mental disorders*. Washington, DC: Author.

American Psychiatric Association. (1968). *Diagnostic and statistical manual of mental disorders* (2nd ed.). Washington, DC: Author.

American Psychiatric Association. (1980). *Diagnostic and statistical manual of mental disorders* (3rd ed.). Washington, DC: Author.

American Psychiatric Association. (1987). *Diagnostic and statistical manual of mental disorders* (3rd ed. rev.). Washington, DC: Author.

American Psychiatric Association. (1994). *Diagnostic and statistical manual of mental disorders* (4th ed.). Washington, DC: Author.

Anthony, E. J. (1986). Terrorizing attacks on children by psychotic parents. *Journal of the American Academy of Child Psychiatry, 25,* 326–335.

Armsworth, M. W., & Holaday, M. (1993). The effects of psychological trauma on children and adolescents. *Journal of Counseling and Development, 72,* 49–56.

Arroyo, W., & Eth, S. (1985). Children traumatized by Central American warfare. In S. Eth & R. S. Pynoos (Eds.), *Post-traumatic stress disorder in children* (pp. 103–120). Washington, DC: American Psychiatric Press.

Ayalon, O. (1982). Children as hostages. *The Practitioner, 226,* 1773–1781.

Bandura, A., Taylor, C. B., Williams, S. L., Mefford, I. N., & Barchas, J. D. (1985). Catecholamine secretion as a function of perceived coping self-efficacy. *Journal of Consulting and Clinical Psychology, 53,* 406–415.

Baumrind, D. (1971). Current patterns of parental authority. *Developmental Psychology, 4,* 1–101.

Beitchman, J. H., Zucker, K. J., Hood, J. E., DaCosta, G. A., Akman, D., & Cassavia, E. (1992). A review of the long-term effects of child sexual abuse. *Child Abuse and Neglect, 16,* 101–118.

Benedek, E. P. (1985). Children and psychic trauma: A brief review of contemporary thinking. In S. Eth & R. S. Pynoos (Eds.), *Post-traumatic stress disorder in children* (pp. 3–16). Washington, DC: American Psychiatric Press.

Blank, A. S., Jr. (1993). Vet centers: A new paradigm in delivery of services of traumatic stress. In J. P. Wilson & B. Raphael (Eds.), *International handbook of traumatic stress syndromes* (pp. 915–923). New York: Plenum Press.

Bloch, D. A., Silber, E., & Perry, S. E. (1956). Some factors in the emotional reaction of children to disaster. *American Journal of Psychiatry, 113,* 416–422.

Blom, G. E. (1986). A school disaster—intervention and research aspects. *Journal of the American Academy of Child Psychiatry, 25,* 336–345.

Bradburn, I. S. (1991). After the earth shook: Children's stress symptoms 6–8 months after a disaster. *Advances in Behavior Research and Therapy, 13,* 173–179.

Brander, T. (1943). Psychiatric observations among Finnish children during the Russo-Finnish War of 1939–1940. *Nervous Child, 2,* 313–319.

Breslau, N., Davis, G. C., Andreski, P., & Peterson, E. (1991). Traumatic events and posttraumatic stress disorder in an urban population of young adults. *Archives of General Psychiatry, 48,* 216–222.

Brett, E. A. (1993). Psychoanalytic contributions to a theory of traumatic stress. In J. P. Wilson & B. Raphael (Eds.), *International handbook of traumatic stress syndromes* (pp. 61–68). New York: Plenum Press.

Burgess, A. W., Hartman, C. R., McCausland, M. P., & Powers, P. (1984). Response patterns in children and adolescents exploited through sex rings and pornography. *American Journal of Psychiatry, 141,* 656–662.

Burgess, A. W., Hartman, C. R., & McCormack, A. (1987). Abused to abuser: Antecedents of socially deviant behaviors. *American Journal of Psychiatry, 144,* 1431–1436.

Burke, J. D., Borus, J. F., Burns, B. J., Millstein, K. H., & Beasley, M. C. (1982). Changes in children's behavior after a natural disaster. *American Journal of Psychiatry, 139,* 1010–1014.

Burke, J. D., Jr., Moccia, P., Borus, J. F., & Burns, B. J. (1986). Emotional distress in fifth-grade children ten months after a natural disaster. *Journal of the American Academy of Child Psychiatry, 25,* 536–541.

Burt, C. (1943). War neuroses in British children. *Nervous Child, 2,* 324–337.

Cahill, C., Llewelyn, S. P., & Pearson, C. (1991). Long-term effects of sexual abuse which occurred in childhood: A review. *British Journal of Clinical Psychology, 30,* 117–130.

Carmen, E., Rieker, P. P., & Mills, T. (1984). Victims of violence and psychiatric illness. *American Journal of Psychiatry, 141,* 378–383.

Chemtob, C., Roitblat, H. C., Hamada, R. S., Carlson, J. G., & Twentyman, C. T. (1988). A cognitive action theory of post-traumatic stress disorder. *Journal of Anxiety Disorders, 2,* 253–275.

Chu, J. A., & Dill, D. L. (1990). Dissociative symptoms in relation to childhood physical and sexual abuse. *American Journal of Psychiatry, 147,* 887–892.

Cicchetti, D. (1989). How research on child maltreatment has informed the study of child development: Perspectives from developmental psychopathology. In D. Cicchetti & V. Carlson (Eds.), *Maltreatment: Theory and research on the causes and consequences of child abuse and neglect* (pp. 377–431). New York: Cambridge University Press.

Clarke, G., Sack, W. H., & Goff, B. (1993). Three forms of stress in Cambodian adolescent refugees. *Journal of Abnormal Child Psychology, 21,* 65–77.

Cole, P. M., & Putnam, F. W. (1992). Effect of incest on self and social functioning: A developmental psychopathology perspective. *Journal of Consulting and Clinical Psychology, 60,* 174–184.

Compas, B. E. (1987). Coping with stress during childhood and adolescence. *Psychological Bulletin, 101,* 393–403.

Connell, J. P. (1985). A new multidimensional measure of children's perceptions of control. *Child Development, 56,* 1018–1041.

Conte, J. R., & Schuerman, J. R. (1987). Factors associated with an increased impact of child sexual abuse. *Child Abuse and Neglect, 11,* 201–211.

Cornely, P., & Bromet, E. (1986). Prevalence of behavior problems in three-year-old children living near three mile island: A comparative analysis. *Journal of Child Psychology and Psychiatry, 27,* 489–498.

Coromina, J. (1943). Repercussions of the war on children as observed during the Spanish Civil War. *Nervous Child, 2,* 320–323.

Crawshaw, R. (1963). Reactions to a disaster. *Archives of General Psychiatry, 9,* 157–162.

Crocq, M., Macher, J., Barros-Beck, J., Rosenberg, S. J., & Duval, F. (1993). Posttraumatic stress disorder in World War II prisoners of war from Alsace-Lorraine who survived captivity in the USSR. In J. P. Wilson & B. Raphael (Eds.), *International handbook of traumatic stress syndromes* (pp. 253–261). New York: Plenum Press.

Curry, S. L., & Russ, S. W. (1985). Identifying coping strategies in children. *Journal of Clinical Child Psychology, 14,* 61–69.

Davidson, J., Swartz, M., Storck, M., Krishnan, R. R., & Hammett, E. (1985). A diagnostic and family study of posttraumatic stress disorder. *American Journal of Psychiatry, 142,* 90–93.

De Bellis, M. D., Lefter, L., Trickett, P. K., & Putnam, F. W., Jr. (1994). Urinary catecholamine excretion in

sexually abused girls. *Journal of the American Academy of Child and Adolescent Psychiatry, 33,* 320–327.

Deblinger, E., McLeer, S. V., Atkins, M. S., Ralphe, D., & Foa, E. (1989). Post-traumatic stress in sexually abused, physically abused, and nonabused children. *Child Abuse and Neglect, 13,* 403–408.

DeJong, A. R., Emmett, G. A., & Hervada, A. R. (1982). Sexual abuse of children: Sex-, race-, and age-dependent variations. *American Journal of Diseases of Children, 136,* 129–134.

den Velde, W. O., Falger, P. R. J., Hovens, J. E., de Groen, J. H. M., Lasschuit, L. J., Van Duijn, H., & Schouten, E. G. W. (1993). Posttraumatic stress disorder in Dutch resistance veterans from World War II. In J. P. Wilson & B. Raphael (Eds.), *International handbook of traumatic stress syndromes* (pp. 219–230). New York: Plenum Press.

Dollinger, S. J. (1985). Lightning-strike disaster among children. *British Journal of Medical Psychology, 58,* 375–383.

Dunsdon, M. I. (1941). A psychologist's contribution to air raid problems. *Mental Health, 2,* 37–41.

Earls, F., Smith, E., Reich, W., & Jung, K. G. (1988). Investigating psychopathological consequences of a disaster in children: A pilot study incorporating a structured diagnostic interview. *Journal of the American Academy of Child and Adolescent Psychiatry, 27,* 90–95.

Einbender, A. J., & Friedrich, W. N. (1989). Psychological functioning and behavior of sexually abused girls. *Journal of Consulting and Clinical Psychology, 57,* 155–157.

Elizur, E., & Kaffman, M. (1982). Children's bereavement reactions following death of the father: II. *Journal of the American Academy of Child Psychiatry, 21,* 474–480.

Elmer, E. (1977). A follow-up study of traumatized children. *Pediatrics, 59,* 273–279.

Emery, R. E. (1982). Interpersonal conflict and the children of discord and divorce. *Psychological Bulletin, 92,* 310–330.

Epstein, S. (1990). The self-concept, the traumatic neurosis, and the structure of personality. In D. Ozer, J. M. Healey, Jr., & A. J. Stewart (Eds.), *Perspectives on personality* (Vol. 3, pp. 63–98). Greenwich, CT: JAI Press.

Eth, S., & Pynoos, R. S. (Eds.). (1985). *Post-traumatic stress disorder in children.* Washington, DC: American Psychiatric Press.

Ettinger, L. (1961). Pathology of the concentration camp syndrome. *Archives of General Psychiatry, 5,* 371–379.

Everson, M. D., Hunter, W. M., Runyan, D. K., Edelsohn, G. A., & Coulter, M. L. (1989). Maternal support following disclosure of incest. *American Journal of Orthopsychiatry, 59,* 197–207.

Famularo, R., Fenton, T., Kinscherff, R., Ayoub, C., & Barnum, R. (1994). Maternal and child posttraumatic stress disorder in cases of child maltreatment. *Child Abuse and Neglect, 18,* 27–36.

Famularo, R., Kinscherff, R., & Fenton, T. (1990). Symptom differences in acute and chronic presentation of childhood post-traumatic stress disorder. *Child Abuse and Neglect, 14,* 439–444.

Fantuzzo, J. W., DePaola, L. M., Lambert, L., Martino, T., Anderson, G., & Sutton S. (1991). Effects of interparental violence on the psychological adjustment and competence of young children. *Journal of Consulting and Clinical Psychology, 59,* 258–265.

Faravelli, C., Webb, T., Ambonetti, A., Fonnesu, F., & Sessarego, A. (1985). Prevalence of traumatic early life events in 31 agoraphobic patients with panic attacks. *American Journal of Psychiatry, 142,* 1493–1494.

Felner, R. D., Gillespie, J. F., & Smith, R. (1985). Risk and vulnerability in childhood: A reappraisal. *Journal of Clinical Child Psychology, 14,* 2–4.

Figley, C. R. (Ed.). (1978). *Stress disorder among Vietnam veterans.* New York: Brunner/Mazel.

Figley, C. R. (1993). Foreword. In J. P. Wilson & B. Raphael (Eds.), *International handbook of traumatic stress syndromes* (pp. xvii–xx). New York: Plenum Press.

Finkelhor, D., & Hotaling, G. T. (1984). Sexual abuse in national incidence study of child abuse and neglect: An appraisal. *Child Abuse and Neglect, 8,* 23–32.

Fish-Murray, C. C., Koby, E. V., & van der Kolk, B. A. (1987). Evolving ideas: The effect of abuse on children's thought. In B. A. van der Kolk (Ed.), *Psychological trauma* (pp. 89–110). Washington, DC: American Psychiatric Press.

Fletcher, K. E. (1988). Belief systems, exposure to stress, and post-traumatic stress disorder in Vietnam veterans. Doctoral dissertation, University of Massachusetts at Amherst. Dissertation Abstracts International, 49, 1981B.

Fletcher, K. E. (1994). *What we know about children's posttraumatic stress responses: A meta-analysis of the empirical literature.* Unpublished manuscript, University of Massachusetts Medical Center, Worcester, MA.

Foa, E. B., Steketee, G., & Rothbaum, B. O. (1989). Behavioral/cognitive conceptualizations of post-traumatic stress disorder. *Behavior Therapy, 20,* 155–176.

Foa, E. B., Zinbarg, R., & Rothbaum, B. O. (1992). Uncontrollability and unpredictability in post-traumatic stress disorder: An animal model. *Psychological Bulletin, 112,* 218–238.

Foy, D. W., Resnick, H. S., Sipprelle, R. C., & Carroll, E. M. (1987). Premilitary, military, and postmilitary factors in the development of combat-related stress disorders. *The Behavior Therapist, 10,* 3–9.

Frances, A., & Petti, T. A. (1984). Boy with seriously ill mother manifests somatic complaints, withdrawal, disabling fears. *Hospital and Community Psychiatry, 35,* 439–440.

Frederick, C. J. (1985a). Children traumatized by catastrophic situations. In S. Eth & R. S. Pynoos (Eds.), *Post-traumatic stress disorder in children* (pp. 73–99). Washington, DC: American Psychiatric Press.

Frederick, C. J. (1985b). Selected foci in the spectrum of posttraumatic stress disorders. In J. Laube & S. A. Murphy (Eds.), *Perspectives on disaster recovery* (pp. 110–130). East Norwalk, CT: Appleton-Century-Crofts.

Frederick, C. J. (1986). Post-traumatic stress disorder and child molestation. In A. W. Burgess & C. R. Hartman (Eds.), *Sexual exploitation of patients by health professionals* (pp. 133–142). New York: Praeger.

Frederick, C. J. (1988). Minority status and adolescent depression and/or suicide. In A. R. Stiffman & R. A. Feldman (Eds.), *Advances in adolescent mental health: Depression and suicide* (Vol. 3, pp. 159–169). Greenwich, CT: JAI Press.

Freud, A., & Burlingham, D. T. (1943). *War and children.* Westport, CT: Greenwood Press.

Freud, S. (1920). *Beyond the pleasure principle.* In J. Strachey (Ed. and Trans.), *The standard edition of the complete works of Sigmund Freud* (Vol. 18, pp. 7–64). London: Hogarth Press, 1953.

Freud, S. (1939). *Moses and monotheism.* In J. Strachey (Ed. and Trans.), *The standard edition of the complete works of Sigmund Freud* (Vol. 23, pp. 7–56). London: Hogarth Press, 1953.

Friedman, P., & Linn, L. (1957). Some psychiatric notes on the Andrea Doria disaster. *American Journal of Psychiatry, 14,* 426–432.

Galante, R., & Foa, D. (1986). An epidemiological study of psychic trauma and treatment effectiveness for children after a natural disaster. *Journal of the American Academy of Child Psychiatry, 25,* 357–363.

Garmezy, N., & Rutter, M. (1985). Acute reactions to stress. In M. Rutter & L. Hersov (Eds.), *Child and adolescent psychiatry: Modern approaches* (2nd ed., pp. 152–176). Oxford, UK: Blackwell.

Gislason, I. L., & Call, J. D. (1982). Dog bite in infancy: Trauma and personality development. *Journal of the American Academy of Child Psychiatry, 21,* 203–207.

Gleser, G., Green, B. L., & Winget, C. (1981). *Prolonged psychological effects of disaster: A study of Buffalo Creek.* New York: Academic Press.

Gold, E. R. (1986). Long-term effects of sexual victimization in childhood: An attributional approach. *Journal of Consulting and Clinical Psychology, 54,* 471–475.

Gomes-Schwartz, B., Horowitz, J. M., Cardarelli, A. P., & Sauzier, M. (1990). The aftermath of child sexual abuse: 18 months later. In B. Gomes-Schwartz, J. M. Horowitz, & A. P. Cardarelli (Eds.), *Child sexual abuse: The initial effects* (pp. 132–152). Newbury Park, CA: Sage.

Gomes-Schwartz, B., Horowitz, J. M., & Sauzier, M. (1985). Severity of emotional distress among sexually abused preschool, school-age, and adolescent children. *Hospital and Community Psychiatry, 36,* 503–508.

Green, A. H. (1983). Child abuse: Dimension of psychological trauma in abused children. *Journal of the American Academy of Child Psychiatry, 22,* 231–237.

Green, A. H. (1985). Children traumatized by physical abuse. In S. Eth & R. S. Pynoos (Eds.), *Post-traumatic stress disorder in children* (pp. 135–154). Washington, DC: American Psychiatric Press.

Green, B. L. (1993a). Disasters and posttraumatic stress disorder. In J. R. T. Davidson & E. B. Foa (Eds.), *Posttraumatic stress disorder: DSM-IV and beyond* (pp. 75–97). Washington, DC: American Psychiatric Association.

Green, B. L. (1993b). Identifying survivors at risk: Trauma and stressors across events. In J. P. Wilson & B. Raphael (Eds.), *International handbook of traumatic stress syndromes* (pp. 135–144). New York: Plenum Press.

Green, B. L., Grace, M. C., Vary, M. G., Kramer, T. L., Gleser, G. C., & Leonard, A. C. (1994). Children of disaster in the second decade: A 17-year follow-up of Buffalo Creek survivors. *Journal of the American Academy of Child and Adolescent Psychiatry, 33,* 71–79.

Green, B. L., Korol, M., Grace, M. C., Vary, M. G., Leonard, A. C., Gleser, G. C., & Smitson-Cohen, S. (1991). Children and disaster: Age, gender, and parental effects on PTSD symptoms. *Journal of the American Academy of Child and Adolescent Psychiatry, 30,* 945–951.

Green, B. L., Wilson, J. P., & Lindy, J. D. (1985). Conceptualizing post-traumatic stress disorder: A psychosocial framework. In C. R. Figley (Ed.), *Trauma and its wake* (Vol. 1, pp. 53–69). New York: Brunner/Mazel.

Grinker, R. R., & Spiegel, J. P. (1945). *Men under stress.* Philadelphia: Blakiston.

Handford, H., Mayes, S. D., Mattison, R. E., Humphrey, F. J., Bagnoto, S., Bixler, E. O., & Kales, J. D. (1986). Child and parent reaction to the Three Mile Island nuclear accident. *Journal of the American Academy of Child Psychiatry, 25,* 346–356.

Harel, Z., Kahana, B., & Wilson, J. P. (1993). War and remembrance: The legacy of Pearl Harbor. In J. P. Wilson & B. Raphael (Eds.), *International handbook of traumatic stress syndromes* (pp. 263–274). New York: Plenum Press.

Harrison, S. I., Davenport, C. W., & McDermott, J. F. (1967). Children's reactions to bereavements: Adult confusions and misperceptions. *Archives of General Psychiatry, 17,* 593–597.

Herman, J. L., Perry, J. C., & van der Kolk, B. A. (1989). Childhood trauma in borderline personality disorder. *American Journal of Psychiatry, 146,* 490–495.

Hjern, A., Angel, B., & Höjer, B. (1991). Persecution and behavior: A report from Chile. *Child Abuse and Neglect, 15,* 239–248.

Holahan, C. J., & Moos, R. H. (1987). Risk, resistance, and psychological distress: A longitudinal analysis with adults and children. *Journal of Abnormal Psychology, 96,* 3–13.

Horowitz, M. (1976a). *Stress response syndromes.* New York: Jason Aronson.

Horowitz, M. J. (1976b). Psychological response to serious life events. In V. Hamilton & D. M. Warburton (Eds.), *Human stress and cognition* (pp. 235–263). New York: Wiley.

Hughes, H. M., Parkinson, D., & Vargo, M. (1989). Witnessing spouse abuse and experiencing physical abuse: A "double whammy"? *Journal of Family Violence, 4,* 197–209.

Jaffe, P., Wolfe, D., Wilson, S. K., & Zak, L. (1986). Family violence and child adjustment: A comparative analysis of girls' and boys' behavioral symptoms. *American Journal of Psychiatry, 143,* 74–77.

Janoff-Bulman, R. (1989). Assumptive worlds and the stress of traumatic events: Applications of the schema construct. *Social Cognition, 7,* 113–136.

Jones, J. C., & Barlow, D. H. (1990). The etiology of posttraumatic stress disorder. *Clinical Psychology Review, 10,* 299–328.

Jones, R. T., & Ribbe, D. P. (1991). Child, adolescent, and adult victims of residential fire: Psychological consequences. *Behavior Modification, 15,* 560–580.

Joseph, S. A., Brewin, C. R., Yule, W., & Williams, R. (1993). Causal attributions and post-traumatic stress in adolescents. *Journal of Child Psychology and Psychiatry, 34,* 247–253.

Jouriles, E. N., Murphy, C. M., & O'Leary, D. (1989). Interspousal aggression, marital discord, and child problems. *Journal of Consulting and Clinical Psychology, 57,* 453–455.

Kagan, J. (1983). Stress and coping in early development. In N. Garmezy & M. Rutter (Eds.), *Stress, coping, and development in children* (pp. 191–216). New York: McGraw-Hill.

Kardiner, A. (1941). *The traumatic neuroses of war.* New York: Hoeber.

Keane, T. M. (1993). Symptomatology of Vietnam veterans with posttraumatic stress disorder. In J. R. T. Davidson & E. B. Foa (Eds.), *Posttraumatic stress disorder: DSM-IV and beyond* (pp. 99–111). Washington, DC: American Psychiatric Association.

Keane, T. M., Fairbank, J. A., Caddell, J. M., Zimering, R. T., & Bender, M. E. (1985). A behavioral approach to assessing and treating post-traumatic stress disorder in Vietnam veterans. In C. R. Figley (Ed.), *Trauma and its wake* (Vol. 1, pp. 257–294). New York: Brunner/Mazel.

Keane, T. M., Scott, W. O., Chavoya, G. A., Lamparski, D. M., & Fairbank, J. A. (1985). Social support in Vietnam

veterans: A comparative analysis. *Journal of Consulting and Clinical Psychology, 53,* 95–102.

Kendall-Tackett, K. A., Williams, L. M., & Finkelhor, D. (1993). Impact of sexual abuse on children: A review and synthesis of recent empirical studies. *Psychological Bulletin, 113,* 164–180.

Kilpatrick, D., & Resnick, H. (1993). PTSD associated with exposure to criminal victimization in clinical and community populations. In J. Davidson & E. Foa (Eds.), *Posttraumatic stress disorder in review: Recent research and future directions* (pp. 113–143). Washington, DC: American Psychiatric Press.

Kinzie, J. D., Sack, W. H., Angell, R. H., Clarke, G., & Ben, R. (1989). A three-year follow-up of Cambodian young people traumatized as children. *Journal of the American Academy of Child and Adolescent Psychiatry, 28,* 501–504.

Kinzie, J. D., Sack, W. H., Angell, R. H., Manson, S., & Rath, B. (1986). The psychiatric effects of massive trauma on Cambodian children: I. The children. *Journal of the American Academy of Child Psychiatry, 25,* 370–376.

Kiser, L. J., Ackerman, B. J., Brown, E., Edwards, N. B., McColgan, E., Pugh, R., & Pruitt, D. B. (1988). Post-traumatic stress disorder in young children: A reaction to purported sexual abuse. *Journal of the American Academy of Child and Adolescent Psychiatry, 27,* 645–649.

Kiser, L. J., Heston, J., Millsap, P. A., & Pruitt, D. B. (1991). Physical and sexual abuse in childhood: Relationship with post-traumatic stress disorder. *Journal of the Academy of Child and Adolescent Psychiatry, 30,* 776–783.

Kluft, R. P. (1985). *Childhood antecedents of multiple personality.* Washington, DC: American Psychiatric Press.

Kolb, L. C. (1987). A neuropsychological hypothesis explaining posttraumatic stress disorders. *American Journal of Psychiatry, 144,* 989–995.

Kosten, T. R., Mason, J. W., Giller, E. L., Ostroff, R. B., & Harkness, L. (1987). Sustained urinary norepinephrine and epinephrine elevation in posttraumatic stress disorder. *Psychoneuroendocrinology, 12,* 13–20.

Krystal, J. H., Kosten, T. R., Southwick, S., Mason, J. W., Perry, B. D., & Giller, E. L. (1989). Neurobiological aspects of PTSD: Review of clinical and preclinical studies. *Behavior Therapy, 20,* 177–198.

Lacey, G. N. (1972). Observations on Aberfan. *Journal of Psychosomatic Research, 16,* 257–260.

Lazarus, R. S., & Folkman, S. (1984). *Stress, appraisal and coping.* New York: Springer.

Lewis, K. (1978). On reducing the child snatching syndrome. *Children Today, 7,* 19–35.

Lifton, R. J. (1967). *Death in life: Survivors of Hiroshima.* New York: Random House.

Lindholm, K. J., & Willey, R. (1986). Ethnic differences in child abuse and sexual abuse. *Hispanic Journal of Behavioral Sciences, 8,* 111–125.

Livingston, R. (1987). Sexually and physically abused children. *Journal of the American Academy of Child and Adolescent Psychiatry, 26,* 413–415.

Lonigan, C. J., Shannon, M. P., Taylor, C. M., Finch, A. J., Jr., & Sallee, F. R. (1994). Children exposed to disaster: Risk factors for the development of post-traumatic symptomatology. *Journal of the American Academy of Child and Adolescent Psychiatry, 33,* 94–105.

Luthar, S. S. (1991). Vulnerability and resilience: A study of high risk adolescents. *Child Development, 62,* 600–616.

Maccoby, E. E. (1983). Social-emotional development and response to stressors. In N. Garmezy & M. Rutter (Eds.), *Stress, coping, and development in children* (pp. 217–234). New York: McGraw-Hill.

Maccoby, E. E., & Martin, J. A. (1983). Socialization in the context of the family: Parent–child interaction. In P. H. Mussen (Series Ed.) & E. M. Hetherington (Vol. Ed.), *Handbook of child psychology: Vol. 4. Socialization, personality, and social development* (pp. 1–102). New York: Wiley.

Malmquist, C. P. (1986). Children who witness parental murder: Posttraumatic aspects. *Journal of the American Academy of Child Psychiatry, 25,* 320–325.

Mannarino, A. P., Cohen, J. A., & Berman, S. R. (1994). The relationship between preabuse factors and psychological symptomatology in sexually abused girls. *Child Abuse and Neglect, 18,* 63–71.

Mannarino, A. P., Cohen, J. A., Smith, J. A., & Moore-Motily, S. (1991). Six- and twelve-month follow-up of sexually abused girls. *Journal of Interpersonal Violence, 6,* 494–511.

Martinez, P., & Richters, J. E. (1993). The NIMH community violence project: II. Children's distress symptoms associated with violence exposure. *Psychiatry, 56,* 22–35.

Masten, A. S., Garmezy, N., Tellegen, A., Pellegrini, D. S., Larkin, K., & Larsen, A. (1988). Competence and stress in school children: The moderating effects of individual and family qualities. *Journal of Child Psychology and Psychiatry, 29,* 745–764.

McCann, I. L., & Pearlman, L. A. (1990a). *Through a glass darkly: Understanding and treating the adult trauma survivor through constructivist self-development theory.* New York: Brunner/Mazel.

McCann, I. L., & Pearlman, L. A. (1990b). Vicarious traumatization: A framework for understanding the psychological effects of working with victims. *Journal of Traumatic Stress, 3,* 131–149.

McFarlane, A. C. (1987a). Posttraumatic phenomena in a longitudinal study of children following a natural disaster. *Journal of the American Academy of Child and Adolescent Psychiatry, 26,* 764–769.

McFarlane, A. C. (1987b). Family functioning and overprotection following a natural disaster: The longitudinal effects of post-traumatic morbidity. *Australian and New Zealand Journal of Psychiatry, 21,* 210–218.

McFarlane, A. C., Policansky, S., & Irwin, C. P. (1987). A longitudinal study of the psychological morbidity in children due to a natural disaster. *Psychological Medicine, 17,* 727–738.

McLeer, S. V., Deblinger, E., Atkins, M. S., Foa, E. B., & Ralphe, D. L. (1988). Post-traumatic stress disorder in sexually abused children. *Journal of the American Academy of Child and Adolescent Psychiatry, 27,* 650–654.

McLeer, S. V., Deblinger, E., Henry, D., & Orvaschel, H. (1992). Sexually abused children at high risk for post-traumatic stress disorder. *Journal of the American Academy of Child and Adolescent Psychiatry, 31,* 875–879.

Milgram, N. A. (1989). Children under stress. In T. H. Ollendick & M. Hersen (Eds.), *Handbook of child psychopathology* (2nd ed., pp. 399–415). New York: Plenum Press.

Milgram, R. M., & Milgram, N. A. (1976). The effect of the Yom Kippur War on anxiety level in Israeli children. *Journal of Psychology, 94,* 107–113.

Miller, S. M. (1979). Controllability and human stress: Method, evidence, and theory. *Behaviour Research and Therapy, 17,* 287–304.

Milne, G. (1977). Cyclone Tracy: II. The effects on Darwin children. *Australian Psychologist, 12,* 55–62.

Mineka, S. (1979). The role of fear in theories of avoidance learning, flooding, and extinction. *Psychological Bulletin, 86*, 985–1010.

Mineka, S. M., & Kihlstrom, J. F. (1978). Unpredictable and uncontrollable events: A new perspective on experimental neurosis. *Journal of Abnormal Psychology, 87*, 256–271.

Moran, P. B., & Eckenrode, J. (1992). Protective personality characteristics among adolescent victims of maltreatment. *Child Abuse and Neglect, 16*, 743–754.

Mowrer, O. H. (1960). *Learning theory and behavior.* New York: Wiley.

Murphy, L. B., & Moriarty, A. E. (1976). *Vulnerability, coping, and growth.* New Haven, CT: Yale University Press.

Myers, C. S. (1940). *Shell shock in France, 1914–18.* Cambridge, UK: Cambridge University Press.

Nader, K., Kriegler, J. A., Blake, D. D., & Pynoos, R. S. (1993). *Clinician-administered PTSD scale for children (CAPS-C).* Unpublished manuscript, UCLA Neuropsychiatric Institute and Hospital and the National Center for PTSD.

Nader, K., Pynoos, R., Fairbanks, L., & Frederick, C. (1990). Children's PTSD reactions one year after a sniper attack at their school. *American Journal of Psychiatry, 147*, 1526–1530.

Newman, C. J. (1976). Children of disaster: Clinical observations at Buffalo Creek. *American Journal of Psychiatry, 133*, 306–312.

Nir, Y. (1985). Post-traumatic stress disorder in children with cancer. In S. Eth & R. S. Pynoos (Eds.), *Post-traumatic stress disorder in children* (pp. 123–132). Washington, DC: American Psychiatric Press.

Norris, F. H. (1988). *Toward establishing a database for the prospective study of traumatic stress.* Paper presented at the National Institute of Mental Health Workshop: Traumatic stress: Defining terms and instruments, Uniformed Services University of the Health Sciences, Bethesda, MD.

Norris, F. H., & Kaniasty, K. (1991). The psychological experience of crime: A test of the mediating role of beliefs in explaining the distress of victims. *Journal of Social and Clinical Psychology, 10*, 239–261.

Ollendick, D. G., & Hoffman, M. (1982). Assessment of psychological reactions in disaster victims. *Journal of Community Psychology, 10*, 157–167.

Page, H. (1885). *Injuries of the spine and spinal cord without apparent mechanical lesion.* London: J. & A. Churchill.

Payton, J. B., & Krocker-Tuskman, M. (1988). Children's reactions to loss of a parent through violence. *Journal of the American Academy of Child and Adolescent Psychiatry, 27*, 563–566.

Peterson, C., & Seligman (1983). Learned helplessness and victimization. *Journal of Social Issues, 2*, 103–116.

Piaget, J., & Inhelder, B. (1969). *The psychology of the child.* New York: Basic Books.

Pierce, L. H., & Pierce, R. L. (1984). Race as a factor in the sexual abuse of children. *Social Work Research Abstracts, 20*, 9–14.

Pittman, R. K. (1988). Post-traumatic stress disorder, conditioning, and network theory. *Psychiatric Annual, 18*, 182–189.

Pynoos, R. S., & Eth, S. (1985). Developmental perspective on psychic trauma in childhood. In C. R. Figley (Ed.), *Trauma and its wake* (Vol. 1, pp. 36–52). New York: Brunner/Mazel.

Pynoos, R. S., Frederick, C., Nader, K., Arroyo, W., Steinberg, A., Eth, S., Nunez, F., & Fairbanks, L. (1987).

Life threat and posttraumatic stress in school-age children. *Archives of General Psychiatry, 44*, 1057–1063.

Pynoos, R. S., & Nader, K. (1988). Children who witness the sexual assaults of their mothers. *Journal of the American Academy of Child and Adolescent Psychiatry, 27*, 567–572.

Pynoos, R. S., & Nader, K. (1989). Children's memory and proximity to violence. *Journal of the American Academy of Child and Adolescent Psychiatry, 28*, 236–241.

Rado, S. (1942). Pathodynamics and treatment of war neurosis (traumatophobia). *Psychosomatic Medicine, 42*, 363–368.

Rao, K., DiClemente, R. J., & Ponton, L. E. (1992). Child sexual abuse of Asians compared with other populations. *Journal of the American Academy of Child and Adolescent Psychiatry, 31*, 880–886.

Realmuto, G. M., Masten, A., Carole, L. F., Hubbard, J., Groteluschen, A., & Chhun, B. (1992). Adolescent survivors of massive childhood trauma in Cambodia: Life events and current symptoms. *Journal of Traumatic Stress, 4*, 589–599.

Rigamer, E. F. (1986). Psychological management of children in a national crisis. *Journal of the American Academy of Child Psychiatry, 25*, 364–369.

Rose, R. M. (1980). Endocrine responses to stressful psychological events. *Psychiatric Clinics of North America, 2*, 53–71

Rosenberg, M. S., & Giberson, R. S. (1991). The child witness of family violence. In R. T. Ammerman & M. Hersen (Eds.), *Case studies in family violence* (pp. 231–253). New York: Plenum Press.

Rossman, B. B. R. (1992). School-age children's perceptions of coping with distress: Strategies for emotion regulation and the moderation of adjustment. *Journal of Child Psychology and Psychiatry, 33*, 1373–1397.

Rotter, J. B. (1966). Generalized expectancies and internal versus external control of reinforcement. *Psychological Monograph, 80*, 1–28.

Rutter, M. (1983). Stress, coping, and development: Some issues and questions. In N. Garmezy & M. Rutter (Eds.), *Stress, coping, and development in children* (pp. 1–41). New York: McGraw-Hill.

Rutter, M., & Graham, P. (1967). A children's behaviour questionnaire for completion by teachers: Preliminary findings. *Journal of Child Psychology and Psychiatry, 8*, 1–11.

Rutter, M., Tizard, J., & Whitmore, K. (1970). *Education, health, and behavior.* London: Longman.

Saigh, P. A. (1985). Adolescent anxiety following varying degrees of war exposure. *Journal of Clinical Child Psychology, 14*, 311–314.

Saigh, P. A. (1989). The development and validation of the children's posttraumatic stress disorder inventory. *International Journal of Special Education, 4*, 75–84.

Saigh, P. A. (1991). The development of posttraumatic stress disorder following four different types of traumatization. *Behaviour Research and Therapy, 29*, 213–216.

Sansonnet-Hayden, H., Haley, G., Marriage, K., & Fine, S. (1987). Sexual abuse and psychopathology in hospitalized adolescents. *Journal of the American Academy of Child and Adolescent Psychiatry, 26*, 753–757.

Scheeringa, M. S., Zeanah, C. H., Drell, M. J., & Larrieu, J. A. (1995). Two approaches to the diagnosis of posttraumatic stress disorder in infancy and early childhood. *Journal of the American Academy of Child and Adolescent Psychiatry, 34*, 191–200.

Schwarz, E. D., & Kowalski, J. M. (1991a). Malignant memories: PTSD in children and adults after a school

shooting. *Journal of the American Academy of Child and Adolescent Psychiatry, 30,* 936–944.

Schwarz, E. D., & Kowalski, J. M. (1991b). Posttraumatic stress disorder after a school shooting: Effects of symptom threshold selection and diagnosis by *DSM-III, DSM-III-R,* or proposed *DSM-IV. American Journal of Psychiatry, 148,* 592–597.

Scurfield, R. M. (1993). Posttraumatic stress disorder in Vietnam veterans. In J. P. Wilson & B. Raphael (Eds.), *International handbook of traumatic stress syndromes* (pp. 285–295). New York: Plenum Press.

Seifer, R., Sameroff, A. J., Baldwin, C. P., & Baldwin, A. (1992). Child and family factors that ameliorate risk between 4 and 13 years of age. *Journal of the Academy of Child and Adolescent Psychiatry, 31,* 893–903.

Senior, N., Gladstone, T., & Narcombe, B. (1982). Child snatching: A case report. *Journal of the American Academy of Child Psychiatry, 21,* 893–903.

Shannon, M. P., Lonigan, C. J., Finch, A. J., Jr., & Taylor, C. M. (1994). Children exposed to disaster: I. Epidemiology of post-traumatic symptoms and symptom profiles. *Journal of the American Academy of Child and Adolescent Psychiatry, 33,* 80–93.

Silber, E., Perry, S. E., & Bloch, D. A. (1958). Patterns of parent–child interaction in disaster. *Psychiatry, 21,* 159–167.

Sirles, E. A., Smith, J. A., & Kusama, H. (1989). Psychiatric status of intrafamilial child sexual abuse victims. *Journal of the American Academy of Child and Adolescent Psychiatry, 28,* 225–229.

Slater, M. A., & Power, T. G. (1987). Multidimensional assessment of parenting in single-parent families. In J. P. Vincent (Ed.), *Advances in family intervention, assessment and theory* (Vol.4, pp. 197–228). New York: JAI Press.

Smith, E. M., & North, C. S. (1993). Posttraumatic stress disorder in natural disasters and technological accidents. In J. P. Wilson & B. Raphael (Eds.), *International handbook of traumatic stress syndromes* (pp. 405–419). New York: Plenum Press.

Stiffman, A. R. (1989). Physical and sexual abuse in runaway youths. *Child Abuse and Neglect, 13,* 417–426.

Stoddard, F. J., Norman, D. K., & Murphy, J. M. (1989). A diagnostic outcome study of children and adolescents with severe burns. *The Journal of Trauma, 29,* 471–477.

Stuber, M. L., Nader, K., Yasuda, P., Pynoos, R. S., & Cohen, S. (1991). Stress response after pediatric bone marrow transplantation: Preliminary results of a prospective longitudinal study. *Journal of the American Academy of Child and Adolescent Psychiatry, 30,* 952–957.

Sugar, M. (1989). Children in disaster: An overview. *Child Psychiatry and Human Development, 19,* 163–179.

Terr, L. C. (1979). Children of Chowchilla: A study of psychic trauma. *The Psychoanalytic Study of the Child, 34,* 552–623.

Terr, L. C. (1981a). "Forbidden Games": Post-traumatic child's play. *Journal of the American Academy of Child Psychiatry, 20,* 741–760.

Terr, L. C. (1981b). Psychic trauma in children: Observations following the Chowchilla school-bus kidnapping. *American Journal of Psychiatry, 138,* 14–19.

Terr, L. C. (1983a). Child snatching: A new epidemic of an ancient malady. *Pediatrics, 103,* 151–156.

Terr, L. C. (1983b). Chowchilla revisited: The effects of psychic trauma four years after a school-bus kidnapping. *American Journal of Psychiatry, 140,* 1543–1550.

Terr, L. C. (1985a). Children traumatized in small groups. In S. Eth & R. S. Pynoos (Eds.), *Post-traumatic stress disorder in children* (pp. 47–70). Washington, DC: American Psychiatric Press.

Terr, L. C. (1985b). Psychic trauma in children and adolescents. *Psychiatric Clinics of North America, 8,* 815–835.

Terr, L. C. (1991). Childhood traumas: An outline and overview. *American Journal of Psychiatry, 148,* 10–20.

Ursano, R. J., Fullerton, C. S., & McCaughey, B. G. (1994). Trauma and disaster. In R. J. Ursano, B. G. McCaughey, & C. S. Fullerton (Eds.), *Individual and community responses to trauma and disaster* (pp. 3–27). New York: Cambridge University Press.

van der Kolk, B. A. (1987). The separation cry and the trauma response: Developmental issues in the psychobiology of attachment and separation. In B. A. van der Kolk (Ed.), *Psychological trauma* (pp. 31–62). Washington, DC: American Psychiatric Press.

van der Kolk, B. A., Boyd, H., Krystal, J., & Greenberg, M. (1984). Post-traumatic stress disorder as a biologically based disorder: Implications of the animal model of inescapable shock. In B. A. van der Kolk (Ed.), *Post-traumatic stress disorder: Psychological and biological sequelae* (pp. 124–134). Washington, DC: American Psychiatric Press.

van der Kolk, B. A., Brown, P., & van der Hart, O. (1989). Pierre Janet on posttraumatic stress. *Journal of Traumatic Stress, 2,* 365–378.

Veronen, L. J., & Kilpatrick, D. G. (1983). Stress management for rape victims. In D. Meichenbaum & M. E. Jaremko (Eds.), *Stress reduction and prevention* (pp. 341–374). New York: Plenum Press.

Walker, L. S., & Greene, J. W. (1987). Negative life events, psychosocial resources, and psychophysiological symptoms in adolescents. *Journal of Clinical Child Psychology, 16,* 29–36.

Weisaeth, L., & Eitinger, L. (1993). Posttraumatic stress phenomena: Common themes across wars, disasters, and traumatic events. In J. P. Wilson & B. Raphael (Eds.), *International handbook of traumatic stress syndromes* (pp. 69–77). New York: Plenum Press.

Weigel, C., Wertlieb, D., & Feldstein, M. (1989). Perceptions of control, competence, and contingency as influences on the stress-behavior symptom relation in school-age children. *Journal of Personality and Social Psychology, 56,* 456–464.

Werner, E. E., & Smith, R. S. (1982). Vulnerable but invincible: A longitudinal study of resilient children and youth. New York: McGraw-Hill.

Wertlieb, D., Weigel, C., & Feldstein, M. (1987). Measuring children's coping. *American Journal of Orthopsychiatry, 57,* 548–560.

Wertlieb, D., Weigel, C., Springer, T., & Feldstein, M. (1987). Temperament as a moderator of children's stressful experiences. *American Journal of Orthopsychiatry, 57,* 234–245.

Wilson, J. P. (1994). The historical evolution of PTSD diagnostic criteria: From Freud to DSM-IV. *Journal of Traumatic Stress, 7,* 681–698.

Wolfe, D. A., Jaffe, P., Wilson, S. K., & Zak, L. (1985). Children of battered women: The relation of child behavior to family violence and maternal stress. *Journal of Consulting and Clinical Psychology, 53,* 657–665.

Wolfe, D. A., Zak, L., & Wilson, S. (1986). Child witnesses to violence between parents: Critical issues in behavioral and social adjustment. *Journal of Abnormal Child Psychology, 14,* 95–104.

Wolfe, V. V., Gentile, C., Michienzi, T., Sas, L., & Wolfe, D. (1991). The Children's Impact of Traumatic Events

Scale: A measure of post-sexual-abuse PTSD symptoms. *Behavioral Assessment, 13,* 359–383.

Wolfe, V. V., Gentile, C., & Wolfe, D. A. (1989). The impact of sexual abuse on children: A PTSD formulation. *Behavior Therapy, 20,* 215–228.

World Health Organization. (1992). *ICD-10 classification of mental and behavioural disorders: Clinical descriptions and diagnostic guidelines.* Geneva, Switzerland: Author.

World Health Organization. (1993). *ICD-10 classification of mental and behavioural disorders: Diagnostic criteria for research.* Geneva, Switzerland: Author.

Wyman, P. A., Cowen, E. L., Work, W. C., & Parker, G. R. (1991). Developmental and family milieu correlates of resilience in urban children who have experienced major life stress. *American Journal of Community Psychology, 19,* 405–426.

Wyman, P. A., Cowen, E. L., Work, W. C., Raoof, A., Gribble, P. A., Parker, G. R., & Wannon, M. (1992). Interviews with children who experienced major life stress: Family and child attributes that predict resilient outcomes. *Journal of the American Academy of Child and Adolescent Psychiatry, 31,* 904–910.

Yates, J. L., & Nasby, W. (1993). Dissociation, affect, and network models of memory: An integrative proposal. *Journal of Traumatic Stress, 6,* 305–326.

Yehuda, R., Southwick, S., Giller, E. L., Ma, X., & Mason, J. W. (1992). Urinary catecholamine excretion and severity of PTSD symptoms in Vietnam combat veterans. *Journal of Nervous and Mental Disorders, 180,* 321–325.

Yule, W., & Williams, R. M. (1990). Post-traumatic stress reactions in children. *Journal of Traumatic Stress, 3,* 279–295.

Zamvil, L. S., Wechsler, V., Frank, A., & Docherty, J. P. (1991). *Posttraumatic stress disorder in hospitalized children and adolescents.* Unpublished manuscript, Nashua Brookside Hospital, Nashua, NH.

Ziv, A., & Israeli, R. (1973). Effects of bombardment on the manifest anxiety level of children living in kibbutzim. *Journal of Consulting and Clinical Psychology, 40,* 287–291.

Social Withdrawal

Kenneth H. Rubin
Shannon L. Stewart

This chapter concerns a topic unlike most that appear in this volume. Although social withdrawal and other forms of social dysfunction characterize many clinical disorders, social withdrawal, in and of itself, is not a clinically defined behavioral, social, or emotional disorder in childhood. Instead, to some researchers, the expression of social withdrawal reflects particular temperament and/or personality characteristics or traits (e.g., Kagan, 1989). To others, withdrawal is viewed as a behavioral index of the child's isolation or rejection by the peer group (Rubin, LeMare, & Lollis, 1990). Still yet others believe that social withdrawal in childhood, depending on the age at which it is observed, reflects the lack of a social approach motive and a preference for object manipulation and construction over interpersonal exchange (Asendorpf, 1990a, 1993). And finally, there are those who believe that social withdrawal *is* linked to psychological maladaptation in that it represents a behavioral expression of internalized thoughts and feelings of social anxiety, loneliness, insecurity, and even depression (Rubin, Chen, & Hymel, 1993; Rubin, Hymel, & Mills, 1989). In short, as the reader may quickly surmise, social withdrawal is an extremely slippery construct that has defied precise meaning and understanding. As such, it becomes immediately evident why there has not been general agreement among traditionally trained clinical psychologists concerning the relevance and significance of social withdrawal vis-à-vis the development and expression of psychologically abnormal emotions, thoughts, and behaviors in childhood.

Given the heretofore slippery nature of the phenomenon, a central purpose of this chapter is to provide some definitional clarity for social withdrawal. This is especially important because it would appear as if social withdrawal has many "faces" (Rubin, 1982a; Rubin & Mills, 1988) and that the many different forms of social solitude typically expressed in childhood carry with them different psychological functions and meanings (Coplan, Rubin, Fox, Calkins, & Stewart, 1994). To make matters all the more confusing, the expression of different forms of solitude appears to have different meanings, not only at different points in childhood, but also within different social contexts and cultures (e.g., Hymel, Rubin, Rowden, & LeMare, 1990; Chen, Rubin, & Sun, 1992).

A second purpose of this chapter is to examine factors that may lead to the consistent display of social withdrawal during childhood. Third, we consider the correlates and predictive consequences of social withdrawal. These latter two goals are accomplished by referring to a developmental framework within which pathways to and from social withdrawal are described (see also Rubin et al., 1990; Rubin, Hymel, Mills, & Rose-Krasnor, 1991; Rubin & Lollis, 1988).

Having outlined the goals of this chapter, we

turn now to providing a rationale for including a chapter on social withdrawal in a volume concerned with child psychopathology. Perhaps the best way to begin is to provide the reader with a sense of the intrapersonal, felt significance of being socially withdrawn. The letter that follows was one of many that arrived in the office of the first author shortly after a description of his program of longitudinal research was carried by the newspaper wire services in Canada.

> I am taking the liberty of writing to you regarding an article in the newspaper last evening entitled "Socially Withdrawn Children Studied." I am now 51 years of age but definitely can identify with the children described in the article. I just wish—oh how I wish, that in-depth studies were done regarding the severity of the problem in my formative years.
>
> I have been employed for 27 years in the same position (stenographer), but my personality problem has been a detriment to me in my adult years. I recall one instance in my third year of grade school [when] my teacher approached me after recess with the enquiry "have you no one to play with—I have noticed you standing by yourself at recess for several days now." I recall replying and LYING—"yes I've friends." The teacher was observant, and I give her credit for this. However, I wish, oh how I wish, something had been done about my isolation at the tender age of 7 or 8. It has been a long, lonely road.
>
> Again my apologies for taking the liberty of writing, but [I] am so happy, so very, very happy, that help is in store for the self-isolated child.
>
> Thank you for listening to me.

This letter, as well as many others that have been received in response to media coverage of our research program, have brought to us a "real-world" sense of what it means to be socially withdrawn. It has also motivated us better to understand why social withdrawal, its meaning, its origins, its concomitants, and its consequences have been relatively ignored by clinical child psychologists. We begin this chapter with a substantive discussion, not of social withdrawal, but rather of the significance of peer engagement and peer relationships for normal growth and development. By addressing issues pertaining to the significance of peer interaction, we can illustrate, rather sharply, the experiences and benefits that the socially withdrawn child fails to accrue.

THE SIGNIFICANCE OF PEER INTERACTION FOR NORMAL DEVELOPMENT

Theoretical statements about the etiology and psychological significance of social withdrawal proved practically nonexistent until the late 1980s. Instead, those searching for a theoretical raison d'être for their research had to rely on the writings of cognitive and personality developmentalists vis-à-vis the significance of peer interaction for normal social, emotional, and cognitive growth. One familiar source was Jean Piaget who described the young, preoperational child as being cognitively egocentric and unable to comprehend the thoughts, feelings, and visual perspectives of others (Piaget, 1926, 1932). Like Piaget, contemporary researchers agree that social perspective-taking increases and egocentric thought wanes with age from early childhood to adolescence (e.g., Selman, 1980). Furthermore, it is now commonly accepted that knowing about children's abilities to (1) understand others' perspectives, intentions, and emotions, and (2) consider the consequences of their social behaviors for themselves and for others can help explain the behavioral expression of adaptive and maladaptive social behaviors (e.g., Dodge, 1986; Rubin & Rose-Krasnor, 1992; Selman, 1985).

If egocentrism and the inability to perspective-take does help to explain, in part, the expression of incompetent social behavior, how then does egocentrism wane? According to Piaget (1928), the major vehicle for the developmental decline of egocentrism was peer interaction. Within the more-or-less egalitarian peer system, children experience opportunities to examine conflicting ideas and explanations, to negotiate and discuss multiple perspectives, to decide to compromise with or to reject the notions held by peers. Consequently, children become able to generate ideas, social conceptions, and information-gathering skills regarding human psychological processes (Flavell, 1970). Put another way, children's social cognitions were posited to be actualized by their social interactions; and, in true dialectic fashion, these cognitions influence children's subsequent social behaviors.

Empirical support for these notions began to emerge in the 1970s when researchers demonstrated links between peer interaction, perspective-taking skills, and the development of socially adaptive and maladaptive behavior. For example,

evidence for the relation between peer interaction and the development of social cognition was derived from experimental demonstrations that peer exchange, conversations, and interactions produced *intrapersonal* cognitive conflict and a subsequent decline of egocentered thinking (e.g., Damon, 1977; Doise, Mugny, & Perret-Clermont, 1975). Evidence for association among the *inability* to perspective-take, the demonstration of *maladaptive* social behavior, and the experience of qualitatively poor peer relationships was also drawn from experimental work published in the 1970s (e.g., Chandler, 1973). Furthermore, researchers demonstrated that perspective-taking skills could be improved through peer interactive experiences, particularly those experiences that involved role play or socio-dramatic play. In turn, such improvement led to increases in prosocial behavior (Iannotti, 1978) and to decreases in aggressive behavior (Chandler, 1973).

Given the brief review offered above, it appears reasonable to conclude that peer interaction influences the development of social cognition and, ultimately, the expression of competent social behavior in the peer group. Peer interaction also allows children to understand the rules and norms of their peer subcultures. It is this understanding of norms and of normative performance levels that engenders, in the child, an ability to evaluate her/his own competency levels against the perceived standards of the peer group. Thus, in addition to facilitating the development of social cognition, peer interaction enables the child to make self-evaluative judgments and to understand the self in relation to significant others.

This latter view concerning self-definition and identity was addressed almost 60 years ago in the writings of George Herbert Mead (1934). He suggested that exchanges among peers, whether experienced during cooperative or competitive activity, or during conflict or friendly discussion, enabled children to understand the self as both a subject and an object. Understanding that the self could be an object of others' perspectives gradually evolved into the conceptualization of a "generalized other" or an organized and coordinated perspective of the "social" group. In turn, recognition of the "generalized other" led to the emergence of an organized sense of self.

Finally, the personality theorist Harry Stack Sullivan (1953) has served as an impetus for much current research concerning the significance of children's peer interactions. Sullivan suggested that the foundations of mutual respect, cooperation, and interpersonal sensitivity derived initially from children's peer and friendship relationships. Sullivan specifically emphasized the importance of chumships, or special relationships, for the emergence of these concepts. Thus, once understanding the concepts of equality, mutuality, and reciprocity was acquired from chums, these concepts could be applied more generally to other, less special, peer relationships.

From the theoretical perspectives outlined above, it seems clear that peer interaction is essential for normal social–cognitive and socioemotional development. There is now substantial empirical support for these theoretical premises (see Hartup, 1992; Rubin & Coplan, 1992, for reviews). The study of social withdrawal is necessarily implicated in this arena of study given that one must ask about the psychological adaptation of children who do not interact with peers as often as is the norm for their age group. *Regardless* of the reasons for nonsocial behavior, it seems likely that the proponents of the view that peer interaction plays a causal role in normal growth and development would express concern for the child who fails to interact, at a normal rate, with peers.

DEFINING SOCIAL WITHDRAWAL IN CHILDHOOD

The child who does not interact at a normal rate with peers is often referred to as "socially withdrawn." Similarly, the child who is observed or rated by others to spend more than an average amount of time alone is referred to as "socially withdrawn." Moreover, it has been commonplace, in the past decade, to use the terms "social withdrawal," "social isolation," "inhibition," and "shyness" interchangeably to describe the behavioral expression of solitude (Rubin & Asendorpf, 1993). Although these constructs may be interrelated statistically and linked conceptually, they carry with them different psychological meanings. In this chapter, we distinguish between these terms in the following manner.

"Inhibition" refers to the disposition to be wary and fearful when encountering novel situations. "Shyness" refers to inhibition in response to novel *social* situations. "Social isolation" refers to the expression of solitary behavior that results from

peer rejection. Finally, "social withdrawal" refers to the consistent (across situations and over time) display of solitary behavior when encountering familiar and/or unfamiliar peers. Social withdrawal, therefore, can be construed as isolating oneself *from* the peer group; social isolation indicates isolation *by* the peer group.

To further complicate matters, we noted earlier that there may be different motivations underlying withdrawal from the company of peers. For example, some children are more object-than person-oriented and thus prefer solitude to social activity. These children have been characterized as having a low social approach motive but not necessarily a high avoidance motive (Asendorpf, 1990a, 1990b, 1991). During the preschool period, when such children play alone, they are observed to engage in exploratory or constructive play (labeled "solitary–passive play"; Rubin, 1982b). Other children may wish to engage in social interaction but for some reason are compelled to avoid it. These children appear socially motivated, but for reasons to be noted later, they are wary, socially anxious, and fearful (Rubin & Asendorpf, 1993). During the preschool period, when such children play alone, they are observed to engage in unoccupied or onlooker behavior (labeled "reticence"; Coplan et al., 1994). In both cases, social solitude may be displayed consistently over time and across contexts.

Regardless of motivational tendencies, however, it would seem reasonable to suggest that refraining from peer interaction precludes children from taking advantage of the benefits of peer interchange described above. Thus, social withdrawal, regardless of motivational underpinnings, has been postulated to bring with it a number of developmental costs. Whether or not this conclusion is valid remains to be tested. Nevertheless, in the section that follows, we review the relevant literature on clinical diagnosis and assessment and describe what the potential "costs" of social withdrawal may be. As the reader will note, however, there do appear to be different clinical diagnoses associated with the varying forms of solitary behavior described above.

CLINICAL DIAGNOSIS AND ASSESSMENT OF SOCIAL WITHDRAWAL

Having defined the phenomenon of social withdrawal, having described the significance of peer interaction for normal growth and development, and having inferred that a lack of peer interaction should give pause for concern, it should not be surprising that the term "social withdrawal" is found in almost every textbook or review chapter on abnormal or clinical child psychology (e.g., Achenbach, 1982; Achenbach & Edelbrock, 1978; Quay & Werry, 1986; Rutter & Garmezy, 1983). It is also found on most standardized assessments of abnormal socioemotional development (e.g., Achenbach & Edelbrock, 1981). The phenomenon is cited consistently as evidence for an "overcontrolled disorder" (e.g., Lewis & Miller, 1990) or an internalizing problem (Achenbach & Edelbrock, 1981). In source after source, social withdrawal is contrasted with aggression as one of the two most consistently identified major dimensions of disturbed behavior in childhood (e.g., Moskowitz, Schwartzman, & Ledingham, 1985; Parker & Asher, 1987).

Despite the apparent clinical significance of social withdrawal, the phenomenon is not well represented in *formal* diagnostic categories of childhood psychological disturbance. In the section that follows, we provide an initial outline of the connections between social withdrawal, inhibition, and shyness and categories of psychological difficulty.

THE RELATION OF SOCIAL WITHDRAWAL TO OTHER DIAGNOSTIC CATEGORIES

Although social withdrawal is not a clinically defined entity per se, social withdrawal and related forms of social dysfunction characterize a number of clinical disorders of childhood and adulthood as specified by the fourth edition of the *Diagnostic and Statistical Manual of Mental Disorders* (DSM-IV; American Psychiatric Association, 1994) and the *ICD-10 Classification of Mental and Behavioural Disorders* (ICD-10; World Health Organization, 1993). These range from the severe forms of social disturbance that characterize children with autistic disorder to social withdrawal that may accompany episodic depression, social avoidance associated with anxieties, and even to long-term patterns of non-interaction characteristic of personality disorders. In Tables 7.1 and 7.2 are listed relevant diagnoses from DSM-IV and ICD-10.

Social withdrawal has long been a salient symptom distinguishing normal from abnormal popu-

TABLE 7.1. DSM-IV Diagnostic Categories That Include Social Withdrawal as a Symptom

Separation anxiety disorder

Many of the symptoms, such as sadness, excessive worrying, *social withdrawal,* and somatic complaints, may emerge as a part of fear of separation from those with whom the child is attached. The anxiety is focused around separation from major attachment figures rather than on contact with unfamiliar individuals.

Reactive attachment disorder
of infancy or early childhood

This disorder reflects disturbed social relatedness in most contexts, beginning at the age of 5 years. There are two types of attachment disorder—inhibited and disinhibited. The former is characterized by the child failing to initiate and respond to most social interactions is a developmentally appropriate way. The child is excessively inhibited, hypervigilant (e.g., frozen watchfulness, avoidance, resistant to comfort). The latter type is characterized by indiscriminate sociability or a lack of selectivity in the choice of attachment figures.

Autistic disorder

The essential features of autistic disorder are the presence of markedly abnormal or impaired development in social interaction and communication. There is gross impairment in the ability to make peer friendships (e.g., little interest in making peer friendships) and a restricted repertoire of interests and hobbies. There may be a lack of spontaneous seeking to share enjoyment and interests with others. There also may be a lack of varied, spontaneous, make-believe play or social imitative play appropriate to the developmental level of the child.

Social phobia (social anxiety disorder)

The avoidant behavior interferes with usual social activities or relationships with others. This occurs when the person is exposed to possible scrutiny by others and fears that something embarrassing/humiliating will happen. The phobic situations are avoided, or endured with intense anxiety. This avoidance behavior interferes with usual social activities or relationships with others.

Adjustment disorder with withdrawal

The essential feature of this disorder is a maladaptive reaction to an identifiable psychosocial stressor(s) that occurs within 3 months after the onset of the stressor and has persisted for no longer than 6 months. Impairment in occupational (including school) functioning or in usual social activities and relationships with others. This category is used when the predominant manifestation is *social withdrawal* without significantly depressed or anxious mood.

Major depression and dysthymia (depressive neurosis)

Depressed mood is present. Feelings of worthlessness, *social withdrawal,* hopelessness, appetite disturbances, sleeping problems, poor concentration, and low self-esteem are present in both disorders. The symptoms cause clinically significant distress or impairment in occupational, social, or other important areas of functioning.

Avoidant personality disorder

The features characterizing this disorder includes low self-esteem, fear of negative evaluation from others, and a pervasive behavioral, emotional, and cognitive avoidance of social interaction. Individuals tend to be *socially withdrawn* and reticent in spite of a strong desire for affection, acceptance and friendships. They tend to be lonely, intensely shy, and insecure. This diagnosis is made if there is an excessive reduction from contact with unfamiliar people. This reduction is severe enough to interfere with social functioning in peer relationships.

Schizoid personality disorder

Clinical features of this disorder include a reserved, *socially withdrawn* and seclusive interpersonal style. People with this disorder do not desire or enjoy close relationships. These individuals tend to be excessive introverts, who appear indifferent to praise or criticism of others, emotional coldness, detachment and flattened affectivity.

Note. Adapted from American Psychiatric Association (1994). Copyright 1994 by the American Psychiatric Association. Adapted by permission.

---

lations. For example, Lerner, Inui, Trupin, and Douglas (1985) reported that during the preschool period (3 to 5 years), the most frequent behavioral difficulty reported by teachers was social withdrawal. This was especially the case for girls. Eleven years later, Lerner et al. (1985) found that those children who had moderate or severe behavioral problems at preschool age had a twofold greater chance of developing a specific psychiatric disorder than children who did not earlier evidence psychological difficulties. These results are suggestive of the possibility that social withdrawal may be a "risk" factor for the later development of psychiatric problems. And although social withdrawal has not been a primary focus of psychiatric inquiry, it is known that peer rejec-

TABLE 7.2. ICD-10 Diagnostic Categories That Include Social Withdrawal as a Symptom

Elective mutism (F94.0)

"There is demonstrable evidence of a consistent failure to speak in specific social situations in which the child would be expected to speak (e.g., in school) despite speaking in other situations" (p. 166).

Autism (F84.0)

"Qualitative abnormalities in reciprocal social interaction are manifest in at least two of the following areas: . . . failure to develop . . . peer relationships that involve a mutual sharing of interests, activities, and emotions; . . . lack of socio-emotional reciprocity as shown by . . . weak integration of social, emotional, and communicative behaviours" (p. 148).

Simple schizophrenia (F20.6)

"There is slow but progressive development, over a period of at least 1 year, of . . . a significant and consistent change in the overall quality of some aspect of personal behaviour, manifest as loss of drive and interests, aimlessness, idleness, a self-absorbed attitude, and *social withdrawal*" (p. 68; emphasis added).

Reactive attachment disorder of childhood (F94.1)

"The child exhibits strongly contradictory or ambivalent social responses that extend across social situations. . . . Emotional disturbance is shown by lack of emotional responsiveness, *withdrawal* reactions, aggressive responses to the child's own or other's distress, and/or fearful hypervigilance" (p. 166; emphasis added).

Schizoid personality disorder (F60.1)

"Display of emotional coldness, detachment, or flattened affectivity; limited capacity to express either warm, tender feelings or anger toward others; an appearance of indifference to either praise or criticism; . . . consistent choice of solitary activities" (p. 125; emphasis added).

Acute stress reaction—severe (F43.02)

"The patient must have been exposed to an exceptional mental or physical stressor. . . . Exposure to the stressor is followed by an immediate onset of symptoms. . . . *Withdrawal* from expected social interaction. . . . Uncontrollable and excessive grief" (pp. 98–99; emphasis added).

Social phobias (F40.1)

"Marked fear of being the focus of attention, or fear of behaving in a way that will be embarrassing or humiliating. . . . These fears are manifested in social situations, such as eating or speaking in public; encountering known individuals in public or entering or enduring small group situations (e.g., parties,

meetings, classrooms). . . . Significant emotional distress is caused by the symptoms or by the avoidance, and the individual recognizes that these are excessive or unreasonable" (pp. 92–93).

Dysthymia (F34.1)

"There must be a period of at least 2 years of constant or constantly recurring depressed mood. . . . During at least some of the periods of depression at least three of the following should be present: reduced energy or activity; insomnia; loss of self-confidence or feelings of inadequacy; difficulty in concentration; . . . frequent tearfulness; . . . feeling of hopelessness or despair; . . . pessimism about the future or brooding over the past; *social withdrawal*; reduced talkativeness" (pp. 88–89; emphasis added).

Cyclothymia (F34.0)

"There must be a period of at least 2 years of instability of mood involving several periods of both depression and hypomania. . . . During at least some of the periods of depression at least three of the following should be present: reduced energy or activity; insomnia; loss of self-confidence or feelings of inadequacy; difficulty in concentration; *social withdrawal;* reduced talkativeness; pessimism about the future or brooding over the past" (p. 87; emphasis added).

Separation anxiety disorder of childhood (F93.0)

"Unrealistic and persistent worry about possible harm befalling major attachment figures or about the loss of such figures. . . . Excessive, recurrent distress in anticipation of, during, or immediately following separation from a major attachment figure (as shown by: anxiety, crying, tantrums; persistent reluctance to go away from home; excessive need to talk with parents; . . . apathy, or social withdrawal)" (pp. 162–163; emphasis added).

Phobic anxiety disorder of childhood (F93.1)

"The individual manifests a persistent or recurrent fear (phobia) that is developmentally phase-appropriate (or was so at the time of onset) but that is abnormal in degree and is associated with significant social impairment" (p. 163).

Social anxiety disorder of childhood (F93.2)

"Persistent anxiety in social situations in which the child is exposed to unfamiliar people, including peers, is manifested by socially avoidant behaviour. . . . There is significant interference with social (including peer) relationships, which are consequently restricted; when new or forced situations are experienced, they cause marked distress and discomfort as manifested by crying, lack of spontaneous speech, or *withdrawal* from the social situation" (pp. 163–164; emphasis added).

TABLE 7.2 (*continued*)

Generalized anxiety disorder of childhood (F93.8)	Anxious (avoidant) personality disorder (F60.6)
"Extensive anxiety and worry occur on at least half of the total number of days over a period of at least 6 months. . . . The multiple anxieties and worries occur across at least two situations, activities, contexts, or circumstances. . . . The anxiety, worry, or physical symptoms cause clinically significant distress or impairment in social, occupational, or other important areas of functioning" (p. 165).	"Persistent and pervasive feelings of tension and apprehension; belief that one is socially inept, personally unappealing, or inferior to others; excessive preoccupation with being criticized or rejected in social situations; . . . restrictions in lifestyle because of need for physical security; avoidance of social and occupational activities that involve significant interpersonal contact, because of fear of criticism, disapproval, or rejection" (p. 128).

Note. From World Health Organization (1993). Copyright 1993 by the World Health Organization. Reprinted by permission.

tion and deficient peer interactions, of which social withdrawal is a significant correlate and predictor (e.g., Hymel et al., 1990; Rubin et al., 1993) are common features of a number of child psychiatric disorders (Dodge, 1989).

Furthermore, behavioral inhibition, which may be a dispositional precursor of social withdrawal, appears to be associated with the development and display of anxiety disorders and depression. In the section that follows, behavioral inhibition as a developmental "risk factor" will be discussed. Subsequently, the exhibition of social withdrawal as a diagnostic criterion or associated symptom will be addressed.

Behavioral Inhibition and Anxiety and Phobic Disorders

As noted above, "behavioral inhibition" to the unfamiliar is a temperamental construct reflecting the tendency to be fearful and anxious during the toddler years and socially wary and withdrawn in unfamiliar situations during the early school-age years (Garcia Coll, Kagan, & Reznick, 1984; Kagan, 1989; Kagan, Reznick, Snidman, Gibbons, & Johnson, 1988; Reznick et al., 1986). It has been suggested that behavioral inhibition is a marker of anxiety proneness. Research by Kagan and colleagues demonstrates that behavioral inhibition is associated with exaggerated autonomic responses to novelty. For instance, a positive relation exists between cortisol production in saliva and the demonstration of extremely inhibited behavior (Kagan, Reznick, & Snidman, 1988). Moreover, exaggerated autonomic responses to novelty are associated with psychological problems of an internalizing nature such as anxiety (e.g., McBurnett et al., 1991).

To the extent that physiological mechanisms may be transmitted genetically, it is of significance to note that behavioral inhibition is highly prevalent in the nonpatient offspring of parents with panic disorder and agoraphobia. Specifically, Rosenbaum and colleagues (1988) reported a significantly higher risk for behavioral inhibition in children of parents who were in treatment for panic disorder and agoraphobia with or without comorbid major depressive disorder compared to children of parents without panic disorder, agoraphobia, or major depressive disorder.

Heritability aside, it is entirely possible that exposure to a parent's symptoms of anxiety will induce children to remain cautious, fearful, and inhibited in situations evoking uncertainty. Parents may provide models of social avoidance and may have difficulty encouraging exploratory and risk-taking behaviors in their children. Retrospective reports suggest that adults with anxiety disorders (e.g., phobias) recall their parents as having been more protective than controls (Arrindell, Emmelkamp, Monsma, & Brilman, 1983; Parker, 1983). Furthermore, parental protective behavior may be associated with parental anxiety (Parker & Lipscombe, 1981). Specifically, mothers of children who display anxiety disorders (e.g., separation anxiety disorder, school phobia) are typically described as overprotective, promoting dependencies, and inhibiting autonomy (Messer & Beidel, 1994).

Regardless of the derivation of social inhibition (this topic is discussed, at greater length, below), it is the case that the *consistent* display of wariness in the face of social novelty, from infancy through early childhood, is predictive of anxiety disorders and phobic disorders in midchildhood (Hirshfeld et al., 1992). And, behaviorally inhibited children evidence higher rates of phobic disorders than

uninhibited children (Biederman et al., 1993). Biederman and colleagues also reported that behaviorally inhibited children have significantly higher rates of multiple anxiety disorders (avoidant disorder, separation anxiety disorder, and agoraphobia; e.g., Rosenbaum et al., 1988) than uninhibited children. They further reported a developmental progression of an anxiety diathesis from early childhood into the later years from overanxious, phobic, and avoidant disorders to separation anxiety disorders and agoraphobia.

In summary, there appears to be growing evidence that behavioral inhibition, a potential precursor to the frequent demonstration of social withdrawal, is associated contemporaneously and predictively with indices of anxiety and phobic disorders. In the following section, we discuss specific diagnostic categories (e.g., anxiety, depression, schizophrenia, personality disorders) and the empirical evidence extant supporting their relation to social withdrawal.

Social Withdrawal and Anxiety Disorders

Anxiety disorders are the most common disorders of childhood (Costello, 1989; Kashani & Orvaschel, 1988; McGee et al., 1990). It has been suggested that anxiety interferes with social interaction thereby causing the avoidance of social situations. Whatever it is that induces the fearful or anxious response to social stimuli, it is the case that the response gives rise to the instrumental behavior of social withdrawal and avoidance. Avoidance of others serves to reduce visceral arousal. As such, social withdrawal and avoidance are reinforced and enhance the probability of its recurrence (Barrios & O'Dell, 1989).

It is not surprising to find that anxiety-disordered children are often described as socially withdrawn. In fact, to the lay public, the terms "social withdrawal and avoidance" readily conjure up images of anxiety-disordered children. The relation between withdrawal and anxiety may best be described as dialectic in nature. Although anxiety is reflected in the frequent withdrawal from, and avoidance of, peer interaction, it is also the case that social withdrawal and avoidance interfere with the normal development of social skills (see relevant discussion below). This lack of social skills serves to reinforce social anxiety and to foster the development and strengthening of negative self-appraisals and negative self-esteem

(Rubin et al., 1990). Thus, a dialectical and cyclical relationship comes to exist between the anxiety and its behavioral expression, social withdrawal.

Interestingly, empirical associations are found between heightened social anxiety and (1) problematic peer relationships (LaGreca, Dandes, Wick, Shaw, & Stone, 1988; Panella & Henggeler, 1986), and (2) negative self evaluations and esteem (Messer & Beidel, 1994). Anxious children tend to be less well liked than nonanxious children (Hymel, & Franke, 1985; Strauss, Frame, & Forehand, 1987), and teachers have reported anxious students to be teased more frequently than others (Edelbrock, 1984). Similarly, socially withdrawn children have poor peer relationships (Boivin, Thomassin, & Alain, 1989; French, 1990; Hymel et al., 1990; Rubin et al., 1993), and they view themselves in negative lights (e.g., Hymel, Bowker, & Woody, 1993). And, socially withdrawn children play less dominant roles and are teased more often when interacting with peers (Olweus, 1993; Rubin, 1985).

Social Withdrawal and Depression

Depression, like anxiety, is an index of internalizing disorders in childhood. And like anxiety, measures of depression tend to cluster statistically and conceptually with independent assessments of negative self-appraisals and esteem, loneliness, peer rejection, and social withdrawal (Bell-Dolan, Reaven, & Peterson, 1993; Jacobsen, Lahey, & Strauss, 1983; Rubin & Asendorpf, 1993). Furthermore, many researchers have documented statistically significant relationships among peer rejection, loneliness, and rejection, although it is noteworthy that the subgroup identified as most problematic in this regard comprises rejected socially withdrawn or timid children (Asher & Wheeler, 1985; Blechman, Tinsley, Carella, & McEnroe, 1985; Cole & Carpentieri, 1990; Rubin et al., 1993; Rubin & Mills, 1988; Vosk, Forehand, Parker, & Richard, 1982). And, as is the case for social withdrawal, greater submissiveness, inappropriate assertiveness, and negative self-esteem have been associated with depression (e.g., Altman & Gotlib, 1988; Kennedy, Spence, & Hensley, 1989; Wierzbicki & McCabe, 1988).

Social withdrawal, as exhibited by individuals suffering from depression, may have a different functional value from that served by withdrawal in the face of anxiety (especially socially induced anxi-

ety). Specifically, social withdrawal may evoke expressions of sympathy, interest, and social overtures from others. Yet, the manner in which depressed children initiate support seeking may actually cause others to withdraw from and reject them (Mullins, Peterson, Wonderlick, & Reaven, 1986; Peterson, Mullins, & Ridley-Johnson, 1985).

Finally, social withdrawal not only correlates with childhood depression, it also predicts it. For example, Bell-Dolan, Reaven, and Peterson (1993) examined the relation between childhood depression and social functioning in fourth and sixth graders. Six social functioning factors (negative social behavior, social withdrawal, other-rated social competence, self-rated social competence, social activity and accuracy of self-evaluated social competence) were used to predict depression. Results indicated that social withdrawal predicted depression as reported by both peers and teachers, and low social activity predicted self-rated depression. Additionally, Rubin (1993) has recently reported a predictive link between adolescent depression and the earlier consistent display of social withdrawal.

Social Withdrawal and Schizophrenia

It has been argued that children who display both aggressive and withdrawn behavior are at high risk for later developing psychopathology. For example, it has been found that hostile withdrawal, or withdrawn behavior in conjunction with aggression, is a more powerful indicator of peer rejection and serious, long-term adjustment problems than either aggression or social withdrawal alone (Landau & Millich, 1985; Ledingham, 1981; Schwartzman, Ledingham, & Serbin, 1985). Furthermore, social withdrawal, in combination with aggression, has been reported to distinguish preschizophrenic children from controls (Bower, Shellhammer, & Daily, 1960; Watt, Stolorow, Lubensky, & McClelland, 1970) and has been found to increase the probability of later schizophrenia over that of either dimension alone (Michael, Morris, & Soroker, 1957).

Clinical child psychologists have long placed significant emphasis on the pathological implications of social isolation vis-à-vis schizophrenia (Wickman, 1928). Early retrospective studies of schizophrenic populations demonstrated that preschizophrenic adolescents were isolated and reclusive as children (Pollack, Woerner, Goodman, & Greenberg, 1966; Stabenau & Pollin, 1969). However,

the retrospective nature of these studies renders the data suspect. In a more methodologically sound study, Bower et al. (1960) interviewed teachers of adolescents who were later identified as schizophrenic or normal. The teachers were unaware of the psychological status of their students, and were asked about the adjustment of the subjects when they were in high school. The preschizophrenic group was described as shy and rejected by their peers. Others have reported similarly that preschizophrenic groups are isolated and alienated from their peers (e.g., Flemming & Ricks, 1969). Nevertheless, the follow-back nature of all the aforementioned studies prohibits any firm conclusions regarding the extent to which social withdrawal may reflect or predict schizophrenia.

Indeed, follow-forward methodological designs indicate little support for a significant association between schizophrenia and social withdrawal. For example, Michael et al. (1957) found that the incidence of schizophrenia among a withdrawn group was no greater than among the general population. Moreover, methodological issues muddy the picture. In several studies (e.g., Ledingham, 1981; Schwartzman et al. 1985), researchers have argued that aggressive–withdrawn children share characteristics with schizophrenic adolescents and adults. They further suggest that an aggression–withdrawal characterization of children should raise a "red flag" in determining preschizophrenic status. It should be noted, however, that in most of this research (e.g., Ledingham, 1981; Schwartzman et al., 1985), these preschizophrenic, aggressive–withdrawn groups are identified by a peer and teacher nomination technique (the Pupil Evaluation Inventory [Pekarik, Prinz, Liebert, Weintraub, & Neale, 1976]) which confuses items describing being *isolated from peers* (social withdrawal) with *isolation by peers*. Rubin and Mills (1988) have argued that the "isolation by peers" items used to characterize "withdrawn–aggressive" children cluster as highly on statistical factors denoting aggression as on factors denoting sensitivity, anxiety, and withdrawal from peers. Hence, it would behoove researchers to examine the relation between social withdrawal–aggression and the subsequent development of schizophrenia with a "cleaner," conceptually sound index of social withdrawal. As such, we must conclude, at this time, that no clear relation exists, either contemporaneously or predictively, between social withdrawal (as defined herein) and schizophrenia.

Social Withdrawal and Personality Disorders

Social withdrawal is particularly significant as an index of psychopathology when categories of *adult* personality disorders are considered. A DSM-IV diagnosis of personality disorder is made when an individual's inflexible, long-lasting behavior pattern or personality style causes important problems in social situations, in his or her career, or when it results in a high level of personal distress (American Psychiatric Association, 1994; Clark, Vorhies, & McEwan, 1994; Widiger, Trull, Clarkin, Sanderson, & Costa, 1994). Key symptomatology reflective of specific personality disorders incorporates many characteristics seen in childhood—specifically, timidity, seclusiveness, social withdrawal, and avoidance of social interaction.

From the outset, it is important to note, that it is unknown whether indices of social withdrawal or inhibition in childhood are conceptually and empirically analogous to these same behavioral indices in later life. Similarly, it is not yet known whether the underlying motivations for these behaviors are the same. For example, some extremely withdrawn elementary school-aged children are "loners" because they are fearful and socially anxious; others are "loners" because they are more object- than person-oriented (Asendorpf, 1990a, 1990b, 1991). Nonetheless, it is interesting that these different motivations for social approach and avoidance discussed in the child personality literature may reflect vulnerabilities for particular adult personality disorders, specifically, schizoid and avoidant disorders.

For example, individuals with "schizoid personality disorder" are reserved, socially withdrawn, and seclusive (American Psychiatric Association, 1994; Joseph, 1992; Siever, 1981; Turkal, 1990). They prefer solitary work activities and hobbies, and they lack warm, close relationships. These individuals have a profound defect in the ability to form social relationships (Millon, 1987). They are excessive introverts, particularly characterized by low warmth, low positive emotionality, and lack of gregariousness (Widiger et al., 1994). Not only do they have few relationships with others, but they also seem to have little desire for them (O'Brien, Trestman, & Siever, 1993). In addition, they often have poor social skills, lack a sense of humor, and seem detached from their environment. Emotionally, they appear flat, restricted, and cold, with little observable hostility when angry (American Psychiatric Association, 1994; Widiger et al., 1994).

Conversely, adult "avoidant personality disorder" is characterized by low self-esteem, fear of negative evaluation, and a pervasive behavioral, emotional, and cognitive avoidance of social interaction (American Psychiatric Association, 1994; Millon, 1981). Key traits associated with this disorder include reticence in social relationships, avoidance of activities that require interpersonal contact, being overly sensitive to criticism, and fear of showing visible signs of anxiety in public (Stone, 1993). Individuals diagnosed with this particular personality disorder express a desire for affection, acceptance, and friendship; yet frequently, they have few friends and share little intimacy with anyone. Fear of rejection plays a key role in distancing them from personal attachments. These avoidant individuals fail to enter into relationships unless the prospective partner provides unusually strong guarantees of uncritical acceptance (Millon, 1981; Millon & Everly, 1985).

Individuals with avoidant personality disorders are typically described as timid and withdrawn (Pilkonis, 1984; Turkal, 1990; Widiger, Frances, Spitzer, & Williams, 1988; Widiger et al., 1994). Hypervigilance tends to be their major coping mechanism. In addition, their nervousness often results in making companions uncomfortable; this may lead to rejection or the damaging of the quality of ongoing relationships (Millon, 1981; Millon & Everly, 1985; Turkal, 1990; Widiger et al., 1994). Avoidant individuals also cope by restricting the range of impinging environmental stimuli; hence, they retreat from novel social experiences. This retreat inhibits the development of social self-efficacy for dealing with interpersonal situations (Costa & McCrae, 1985). Individuals diagnosed with avoidant personalities differ from those diagnosed with schizoid personality disorders in that those in the latter group appear to be motivated to establish social relationships, whereas the those in the former group appear disinterested in so doing.

Summary

In summary, social withdrawal has been implicated on several diagnostic categories of adult personality disturbance. Furthermore, social withdrawal is viewed as symptomatic of anxiety disorders, phobic disorders, and depression in childhood and adolescence. Given the review

offered above, and the information provided in Tables 7.1 and 7.2, it may be that the forms of solitude and the motivations underlying these behavioral expressions vary from one disturbance to another. Thus, we urge developmental and clinical researchers to address these possibilities in their future research agendas. Furthermore, we believe it timely to begin research programs directed to examining the etiology and developmental course of social withdrawal in childhood. To this end, we next describe a developmental model in which the causes, concomitants, and consequences of social withdrawal in childhood are described. Given the different meanings of solitude in childhood (as described above), the model presented below allows for a conceptual intertwining of its various forms.

THE DEVELOPMENTAL COURSE OF SOCIAL WITHDRAWAL IN CHILDHOOD

In keeping with the goals of developmental psychopathology (Sroufe & Rutter, 1984), we have recently described a conceptual model of the origins and course of social withdrawal in childhood. This developmental model has been published in several sources (e.g., Rubin et al., 1990; Rubin, Hymel, et al., 1991; Rubin, Stewart, & Chen, 1995; Rubin & Mills, 1992); nevertheless, with an ever increasing relevant knowledge base, conceptual revisions to this developmental model are continuously being applied.

We begin our description of the pathway to the ontogeny of a profile of social withdrawal with newborns who may be biologically predisposed to have a low threshold for arousal when confronted with social (or nonsocial) stimulation and novelty. Such "hyperarousability" may make these babies extremely difficult to soothe and comfort. We propose that under some circumstances, parents may find such dispositional characteristics aversive and difficult to deal with. For example, under conditions of stress and strain, parents may react to easily aroused and wary babies with hostility, insensitivity, lack of affection, nonresponsivity, and/or neglect. Parental insensitivity and unresponsiveness, in concert with the child's dispositional characteristic of a low threshold for arousal and an inability to be easily soothed (hereafter referred to as "emotion dysregulation"; Rubin, Coplan, Fox, & Calkins, 1995), are posited to predict the development of

an insecure parent–infant attachment relationship. Thus, an interplay of endogenous, socialization, and early relationship factors, as they coexist under an "umbrella" of negative setting conditions such as stress and the lack of familial support, is suggested to lead to a sense of felt insecurity.

It is important to note, that we believe the emotion-dysregulated infant will prove a significant challenge to parents who are experiencing stress in their lives. For example, a lack of financial resources may create feelings of frustration, anger, and helplessness that can be translated into less than optimal childrearing styles, especially if the infant is perceived to be "difficult." Parents who are financially distressed are less nurturant, involved, child-centered, and consistent with their children than their less-stressed counterparts (Elder, Van Nguyen, & Caspi, 1985; Patterson, 1983, 1986). "Spousal discord and marital dissatisfaction" are also stressors that may impede a sensitive response to children, especially temperamentally difficult infants. As with economic stress, spousal discord has been associated with insensitive, unresponsive parenting behaviors (Emery, 1982; Jouriles et al., 1991). And finally, "parental psychopathology," is a stressor that has been found to be related to the production of unresponsive, insensitive parenting styles. For example, maternal depression is associated with a lack of parental involvement, responsivity, spontaneity, and emotional support in childrearing (Downey & Coyne, 1990; Kochanska, Kuczynski, & Maguire, 1989; Zahn-Waxler et al., 1988). Given that depression is associated with maternal feelings of hopelessness and helplessness (Gurland, Yorkston, Frank, & Stone, 1967), the pattern of parenting behaviors noted above would not be surprising if the infant was perceived to be emotionally dysregulated.

It is important to note, however, that the effects of stress on parenting behaviors can be moderated, or buffered, by the availability of "social support" (Cohen & Wills, 1985; Compas, 1987; Crnic, Ragozin, Greenberg, Robinson, & Basham, 1983). It has been argued that supportive social networks may be sources of emotional and affective strength and of information that enhance feelings of competence in coping with stresses, including those concerned with parenting. In summary, we propose that an emotion-dysregulated infant reared by unresponsive parents in a "high stress/low support" environment will develop an insecure attachment rela-

tionship with his or her primary caregiver. This proposition is ripe for study; it has yet to be subjected to empirical inquiry.

We also propose that the dispositional characteristics of the baby, in concert with feelings of insecurity, guide her or him onto a trajectory to behavioral inhibition. The consistent expression of inhibition precludes these children from realizing the positive outcomes associated with social exploration and peer play. Thus, we predict a developmental sequence in which an inhibited, fearful, insecure child withdraws from his or her social world of peers, fails to develop those skills derived from peer interaction and, because of this, becomes increasingly anxious and isolated from the peer group.

As noted above, social reticence or withdrawal becomes increasingly salient to the peer group with age (Younger & Boyko, 1987). This deviation from age-appropriate social norms is associated with the establishment of peer rejection; for example, by the mid-to-late years of childhood, social withdrawal and anxiety are as strongly correlated with peer rejection and unpopularity as is aggression (French, 1988; Rubin, Hymel, & Mills, 1989; Rubin et al., 1993).

Reticence to explore and play cooperatively in their social environments is postulated to result in the development of an impoverished style of interpersonal negotiation skills. These children may make few attempts to direct the behaviors of peers, and when they do, it is likely that they will be met by peer rebuff (Rubin & Rose-Krasnor, 1992; Stewart & Rubin, 1995). One outcome of social interactive failure and peer rejection is likely to be the development of negative self-perceptions of social skills and relationships (Hymel, Bowker, & Woody, 1993; Lapa, Rubin, Booth, & Rose-Krasnor, 1994). And, sensing the child's difficulties and perceived helplessness, his or her parents may try to direct their child's social behaviors in a power-assertive fashion by *telling* the child how to act or what to do, or by actually solving the child's interpersonal dilemmas for him or her. We propose that such an overcontrolling, overinvolved parenting style serves to maintain and exacerbate the socially withdrawn child's inter- and intrapersonal difficulties.

To reiterate, we propose that social incompetence of an overcontrolled, withdrawn nature may be the product of "inhibited" temperament, of insecure parent–child relationships, of overdirective, overprotective parenting, of family stress, and most likely of the joint interactions

among "all of the above." The suggested outcomes of such a constellation of factors are the development of (1) negative feelings and thoughts about the self, (2) social anxiety, and, (3) loneliness. If the establishment and maintenance of close interpersonal relationships are considered significant objectives that have not been met, another outcome may be depression.

It is very important to note that we do not consider infant dispositional characteristics to lead, necessarily, to the the pathway described above. A fearful, wary inhibited temperament may be "deflected" to a pathway toward the development of social competence by responsive and sensitive caregiving and by a relatively stress-free environment. And, on the other hand, an inhibited, emotionally dysregulated temperament does not necessarily produce an incompetent, internalizing behavioral style. Parental overcontrol and overinvolvement, especially when accompanied by familial stress and a lack of social support, can deflect the temperamentally easy-going infant to a pathway of internalizing difficulties. Of course, these latter statements must be accepted within the context of supposition; data do not exist that address the assumptions just described.

Finally, the developmental pathway we offer represents a useful heuristic for the study of the etiology of social withdrawal in childhood. It is also suggestive of the indirect and direct ways that dispositional characteristics, parent–child relationships, parenting styles, and familial stress may contribute to the development and maintenance of social withdrawal and its concomitants and outcomes.

In summary, our developmental model begins with the suggestion that individual differences in temperament set the stage for particular parental reactions that aid in the induction of (1) an insecure parent–child attachment relationship, and (2) a socially wary and withdrawn behavioral style. In turn, felt insecurity and behavioral wariness and solitude in social settings become associated with, and reflective and predictive of, markers of socioemotional maladaptation in childhood. We consider below the empirical support for these possibilities.

Etiological Perspectives on Social Withdrawal

Why and how is it that children come to be socially withdrawn? Kagan and colleagues (e.g., Kagan, 1989; Kagan, Reznick, & Snidman, 1988)

have argued that the pathway to social withdrawal begins with a dispositional, or temperamental, trait now widely recognized as "behavioral inhibition." To Kagan and collaborators, some children are genetically "hard-wired" with a physiology that biases them to be cautious, timid, and wary in unfamiliar social and nonsocial situations. These "inhibited" children differ from their uninhibited counterparts in ways that imply variability in the threshold of excitability of the amygdala and its projections to the cortex, hypothalamus, sympathetic nervous system, corpus striatum, and central gray (Kagan, 1989).

Kagan has identified two dimensions of infant behavior predictive of later fearful and anxious behavior in children: (1) frequency of motor activity, and (2) the display of negative affect. According to Kagan and Snidman (1991), the combined and consistent expression of infant motor arousal and negative affect is a function of elevated excitability in areas of the limbic system thought to be involved in fear responses. Infants who are easily and negatively aroused motorically and emotionally are likely to display behavioral inhibition as toddlers (Kagan & Snidman, 1991).

Consistent with Kagan's argument that there is a *physiological* basis to social wariness and inhibition is the research of Fox and colleagues (e.g., Fox & Calkins, 1993). These researchers begin by noting that adults exhibiting right frontal EEG asymmetries are more likely to express negative affect and to rate emotional stimuli as negative (Jones & Fox, 1992). Moreover, adults diagnosed with unipolar depression, even in remission, are more likely to display right frontal EEG asymmetry compared to controls (Henriques & Davidson, 1990, 1991). Drawing from the adult literature on the psychophysiological underpinnings of emotion dysregulation, Fox and his collaborators have demonstrated that infants exhibiting right frontal EEG asymmetries are more likely to cry to maternal separation and display signs of negative affect and fear of novelty (Davidson & Fox, 1989; Fox, Bell, & Jones, 1992). Moreover, stable patterns of right frontal EEG asymmetries in infants predict temperamental fearfulness and behavioral inhibition in young children. For example, Calkins, Fox, and Marshall (in press) recorded brain electrical activity of children at 9, 14, and 24 months and found that infants who displayed a pattern of stable right frontal EEG asymmetry across this 15-month period were more fearful, anxious, compliant, and behaviorally inhibited as toddlers than other in-

fants. Additionally, Fox, Calkins, and Bell (in press) have reported that negative reactivity and right frontal EEG asymmetry in response to mild stress predict the display of toddler inhibition.

The physiological data presented above provide evidence to suggest that unique patterns of brain electrical activity may reflect increased arousal of particular brain centers involved in the expression of fear and anxiety (LeDoux, 1989) and appear to reflect a particular underlying temperamental type. The functional role of hemispheric asymmetries in the regulation of emotion may be understood in terms of an underlying motivational basis for emotional behavior, specifically along the approach–withdrawal continuum. Infants exhibiting greater relative right frontal asymmetry are more likely to withdraw from mild stress. Infants exhibiting the opposite pattern of activation are more likely to approach. It is argued that these patterns of frontal activation represent a dispositional characteristic underlying behavioral, temperamental responses to the environment. Further consistent with the findings of Kagan is the report that infants who exhibit extreme degrees of motor arousal and negative affect in response to novelty display greater relative right frontal EEG activation and are likely to be fearful and inhibited as toddlers (Calkins, Fox, & Marshall, in press).

Behaviorally inhibited toddlers demonstrate extreme wariness in the face of novel stimulation. When faced with novel objects or unfamiliar adults, they tend to remain in close proximity to their mothers, fail to explore or approach the novel stimuli (even upon request), and evidence behavioral signs of fear and anxiety. Inhibited toddlers display greater reactivity in the sympathetic nervous system, greater muscle tension and higher levels of salivary cortisol compared to uninhibited children (Reznick et al., 1986). Moreover, these children display elevated resting heart rates (Fox, 1989), higher basal cortisol readings and greater pupil dilation (Kagan, Reznick, & Snidman, 1987). When these children are followed into elementary school, their behavioral and physiological profiles remain constant (Kagan, Reznick, Snidman, et al., 1988), suggesting that there are stable physiological patterns corresponding with the behavioral expression of inhibition.

It is important to note that the research referred to above pertains to the expression of behavioral inhibition and shyness, or wary, timid, and withdrawn behavior in the face of *novel* so-

cial and nonsocial circumstances. Whether or not shyness and behavioral inhibition are empirically related to social withdrawal, defined earlier as the lack of peer interaction in both unfamiliar and *familiar* settings, is relatively unknown. Conceptually, such links can and do make sense; it remains to be seen whether these associations can be substantiated empirically.

Noteworthy is the fact that theorists who argue strongly for underlying biological components to the expression of social wariness and shyness do not generally suggest negative outcomes of a psychopathological nature for extremely shy or socially wary children. And, these theorists have not typically provided a strong account for how environmental circumstances may influence and modify these biologically based traits. Yet, in other relevant theories, causal connections have been made between experiential, familial factors and the development of socially wary and withdrawn behaviors. We review one such theory below.

Attachment Relationships

Attachment theorists have posited that the parent–infant attachment relationship results in the child's developing an internal working model of the self in relation to others (Bowlby, 1973). This internal working model allows the child to feel secure, confident, and self-assured when introduced to novel settings; this sense of "felt security" fosters the child's active exploration of the social environment (Sroufe, 1983). In turn, exploration of the social milieu allows the child to address a number of significant "other-directed" questions such as "What are the properties of this other person?"; "What is she or he like?"; "What can and does she or he do?" (Rubin, 1993). Once these exploratory questions are answered, the child can begin to address "self-directed" questions such as "What can I do with this person?" Thus, felt security is viewed as a central construct in socioemotional development. It enhances social exploration, and exploration results in interactive peer play (Rubin, Fein, & Vandenberg, 1983). Peer play, in turn, plays a significant role in the development of social competence (Rubin & Rose-Krasnor, 1992; Rubin, Stewart, & Chen, 1995).

Children who develop insecure internal working models of social relationships, on the other hand, come to view the world as unpredictable, comfortless, and unresponsive (Sroufe, 1983). This insecure internal representation may lead some children to "shrink from their social worlds" while others "do battle" with theirs (Bowlby, 1973, p. 208). That subgroup of insecurely attached young children who refrain from exploring their social environments have typically been classified as "anxious–resistant" or "C" babies (e.g., Goldberg, 1990). It has been suggested that the "C" baby's lack of exploration eventually impedes social-peer play and, thus, interferes with the development of social competence. In novel settings, these infants maintain close proximity to the attachment figure. And, when the attachment figure (usually the mother) leaves the paradigmatic "Strange Situation" for short period of time, "C" babies become disturbingly unsettled. Upon reunion with the attachment figure, these infants show angry, resistant behavior interspersed with attachment behavior (proximity and contact seeking, e.g., Greenspan & Lieberman, 1988).

This particular classification of insecure attachment is contrasted with that of "A" or "anxious–avoidant" infants. "A" babies tend to explore appropriately in novel settings and do not remain within arm's length of the attachment figure. Indeed, they appear unsettlingly comfortable away from the attachment figure. Upon separation, these babies do not appear upset and they are likely to continue playing. Upon reunion, they actively snub or avoid the attachment figure.

In conclusion, there presently exist a number of theories and research programs addressing issues pertaining to the etiology of social withdrawal in childhood. We describe below how these theories, and the research supportive of them, can be drawn together to explain the developmental course of social withdrawal.

Linking Temperament and Attachment

As noted above, some newborns may be biologically predisposed to have a low threshold for the arousal of negative emotionality (e.g., Kagan, Reznick, & Snidman, 1988; Miyake, Chen, & Campos, 1985). This temperamental trait may be a generally aversive stimulus and may make these babies extremely difficult for their parents to soothe and comfort (Kagan, Reznick, Clarke, Snidman, & Garcia-Coll, 1984). Thus, in our developmental model, we suggest that an interplay of endogenous, socialization, and early relationship factors will lead to a sense of felt insecurity. And, we posit further that the internal working models of insecurely attached, temperamentally inhibited children may lead them onto a developmental trajectory to social withdrawal.

Support for our speculations about the relations between temperament and attachment derives from several recent sources. Differences in irritability or reactivity in the neonatal period predict insecure attachment status (Miyake et al., 1985). Meta-analyses have indicated that the temperamental characteristic, "proneness to distress," predicts the resistant behavior that defines, in part, insecure attachment status of the "C" variety (Goldsmith & Alansky, 1987). It is possible that irritability or proneness to distress presents as a significant stressor to parents, and, as such, influences the quality of mother–infant interactions and the quality of the attachment relationship (Izard, Haynes, Chisholm, & Baak, 1991). Thus, the temperamental construct, "emotionality" (which comprises irritability and proneness to distress) may well lay the basis for the development of qualitatively insecure attachment relationships. Support for this contention stems from the research of Izard and colleagues (Izard et al., 1991) who found that infant emotionality, as well as infant resting-state cardiac activity (a physiological index of emotionality and emotion regulation) predicted, independently and significantly, insecure attachment status.

More specific evidence for a connection between infant temperament and insecure attachment status of a "C" nature derives from several recent sources. First, Thompson, Connell, and Bridges (1988) have reported that infant proneness to fear predicts distress to maternal separation. Such distress is usually allied with a "C" classification in the traditional attachment paradigm (Belsky & Rovine, 1987). The strongest support for a wariness–attachment link, however, stems from research demonstrating that infants who are dispositionally reactive to mildly stressful, novel social events are more likely to be classified as insecurely attached "C" (anxious–resistant) babies than are their less reactive counterparts (Calkins & Fox, 1992; Fox & Calkins, 1993).

Attachment, Inhibition, and Social Withdrawal

The social behaviors of toddlers and preschoolers who have an insecure "C"-type attachment history are thought to be guided largely by fear of rejection. Conceptually, psychologists have predicted that when these insecurely attached children are placed in group settings with peers, they should attempt to avoid rejection through the demonstration of passive, adult-dependent

behavior and withdrawal from social interaction (Renken, Egeland, Marvinney, Mangelsdorf, & Sroufe, 1989; Sroufe & Waters, 1977). Empirically, support for these conjectures derives from data indicating that anxious–resistant ("C") infants are more whiny, easily frustrated, and socially inhibited at 2 years of age than their secure ("B") counterparts (Fox & Calkins, 1993; Matas, Arend, & Sroufe, 1978). Anxious–resistant "C" babies also tend to be less skilled in peer interaction as toddlers and to be rated by their teachers as more dependent, helpless, tense, and fearful than their secure counterparts (Pastor, 1981).

Finally, Erickson, Sroufe, and Egeland (1985) have reported that "C" babies lack confidence and assertiveness at 4 years. At 7 years, they are observed to be socially withdrawn (Renken et al., 1989). Additional support for both predictive and contemporaneous connections between insecure attachment and indices of social withdrawal are found in recent studies by Rubin, Booth, Rose-Krasnor, and Mills (1995), and Booth, Rose-Krasnor, McKinnon, and Rubin (1994).

Toddler Inhibition, Social Reticence, and Withdrawal in the Early and Middle Years of Childhood

Having developed a psychological profile of behavioral inhibition and insecure attachment status, we suggest that such children may preclude themselves from the opportunities and outcomes associated with social exploration and peer play. As noted above, insecurity of attachment does appear to be associated predictively and contemporaneously with inhibition and social withdrawal.

Inhibition during the toddler period, which is arguably a dispositional variable (Kagan, 1989), has also been tied empirically to behavioral outcomes in early and midchildhood. First, investigators have demonstrated consistently that inhibited toddlers are likely to remain inhibited in the early and middle years of childhood (e.g., Broberg, Lamb, & Hwang, 1990; Kagan, Gibbons, Johnson, Reznick, & Snidman, 1990; Kochanska & Radke-Yarrow, 1992; Reznick et al., 1986; Sanson, Pedlow, Cann, Prior, & Oberklaid, in press). Notably, Kochanska, and Radke-Yarrow (1992) reported that *social*, but not nonsocial inhibition in toddlerhood predicted shy, inhibited behavior at 5 years when children played with an unfamiliar peer. Similarly, when inhibited toddlers were observed again at 7.5 years of age in a

group of unfamiliar peers, they were observed to be more distant from and less likely to converse with their playmates (Kagan & Snidman, 1991). And Calkins, Fox, Rubin, Coplan, and Stewart (1994) recently reported that extremely inhibited toddlers, when observed during free play in tetrads of unfamiliar peers, displayed more behavioral reticence than their uninhibited counterparts. Importantly, these latter researchers revealed that the traditional index of toddler inhibition did *not* predict the frequent display of solitary-constructive and -exploratory play (passive solitude; Rubin, 1982a). Given that reticence (unoccupied and onlooker activity) as assessed in toddlerhood, shares with behavioral inhibition a high association with indices of anxiety, and given that passive-solitude is unassociated with markers of maladaptation in early childhood, these data suggest that the developmental trajectory for behavioral inhibition is in the direction of maladaption. Indeed, Calkins et al. (1994) reported that toddler inhibition predicted parental ratings of internalizing difficulties at age 4 years; and, Coplan and Rubin (1993) indicated that extremely reticent, but not extremely passive–withdrawn preschoolers have higher-than-average internalizing problems.

It is important to note that in each of the studies described thus far, early inhibition has been linked predictively to frequent demonstrations of inhibition and reticence in *unfamiliar* peer settings. This is a significant shortcoming of the research extant given that it is social withdrawal among *familiar* children that appears most developmentally problematic (Asendorpf, 1993; Rubin & Mills, 1988; Rubin, Hymel, & Mills, 1989). Nevertheless, recent work by Calkins et al. (1994) and Coplan and Rubin (1993) does provide initial support for predictive and contemporaneous links between observed behavioral inhibition and reticence and assessments of internalizing problems in early childhood.

In summary, both behavioral inhibition and insecurity of attachment are predictive of, and contemporaneously associated with, frequent demonstrations of reticent behavior among unfamiliar peers. There is only limited support for a connection between each of the aforementioned constructs and social withdrawal in childhood. It remains our contention that the developmental origins of social withdrawal, and the internalizing disorders that it reflects, stem, in part, from the "conspiracy" between behavioral inhibition and insecure attachment; we await the products of future research for supportive evidence.

Developmental Course

Thus far, we have examined etiological factors associated with the development of social withdrawal in childhood. We turn now to an examination of the correlates and consequences of withdrawal once it has been established as characteristic of the child's social repertoire. In the developmental model we have described elsewhere (Rubin et al., 1990; Rubin, Hymel, et al., 1991; Rubin & Mills, 1992), we argue that reticence to explore novel, out-of-home settings impedes (1) possibilities of establishing normal social relationships; (2) the experience of normal social interactive play behaviors; and (3) the development of those social and cognitive skills that are supposedly encouraged by peer relationships and social play. Thus, we predict a developmental sequence in which a socially inhibited, fearful, insecure child withdraws from the social world of peers, fails to develop those skills derived from peer interaction and, because of this, becomes increasingly anxious and isolated from the peer group (Rubin et al., 1990; Rubin, Hymel, et al., 1991; Rubin & Lollis, 1988). We have also surmised that the recognition of social failure elicits thoughts and feelings of negative self-regard. These thoughts and feelings are continuously reinforced as the child develops an inadequate social repertoire to interact with and relate positively to peers.

Drawing from research on children's perceptions of their peers' social behaviors, we have also posited that social withdrawal becomes more salient to the peer group with increasing age (Younger & Boyko, 1987; Younger & Daniels, 1992; Younger, Gentile, & Burgess, 1993). Given that deviation from age-normative social behavior is associated with the establishment of negative peer reputations, we have predicted that by the mid-to-late years of childhood, social withdrawal and social anxiety become strongly associated with peer rejection and unpopularity. And finally, we argue that the constellation of social withdrawal, social failure, negative self-regard, and peer rejection conspire in an insidious fashion to maintain and predict psychological problems of an internalizing nature such as loneliness, depression, and feelings of insecurity in the peer group and family (Rubin, 1993).

The most extensive examination of the developmental course of social withdrawal emanates from the Waterloo Longitudinal Project (WLP), an ongoing study of an unselected sample of public school-attending children. In this study, ob-

served social withdrawal, as defined above, has been shown to be relatively stable from ages 5 to 9 years (Rubin, 1993; Rubin & Both, 1989). And peer assessments of withdrawal have resulted in significant intercorrelations (all $p < .001$) between ages 7 to 10 years. When a categorical approach was taken to identify extreme groups of socially withdrawn children, the WLP revealed that across any 2-year period, from ages 5 to 11 years, approximately two-thirds of identified socially withdrawn children maintain their status (Rubin, 1993; Rubin et al., 1993). This latter finding supports the contention of Kagan and colleagues (e.g., Kagan, 1989) who argue that the developmental continuity of inhibition is strongest when the longitudinal sample is composed of children who represent behavioral extremes.

The relative stability reported in the WLP also bolsters previous findings concerning the long-term stability of social withdrawal (Bronson, 1966; Kagan & Moss, 1962; Moskowitz et al., 1985; Olweus, 1980). Although these studies vary considerably in time spans covered, developmental periods involved, and measures employed, they show quite consistently that social withdrawal tends to persist across time.

The stability data described above are informative insofar as the prediction of solitary behavior is concerned. However, in our developmental model, we argue that social withdrawal reflects and predicts a negative quality of socioemotional life. The developmental course we have predicted for social withdrawal has received a good deal of support in recent years. It is now known, for example, that during the preschool and early elementary school years, socially withdrawn children are less able to comprehend the perspectives of others (LeMare & Rubin, 1987) and are more likely than their more sociable age-mates to be adult-dependent and unassertive when faced with interpersonal dilemmas (Rubin, 1982b, 1985; Rubin, Daniels-Beirness, & Bream, 1984). When they do attempt to assert themselves and attempt to gain compliance from their peers, these children are more likely than their more sociable counterparts to be rebuffed (Rubin & Krasnor, 1986). Indeed, noncompliance to the requests of socially withdrawn children increases with age from early to middle childhood (Stewart & Rubin, 1995). And importantly, among socially withdrawn children, the production of peer-directed requests become increasingly less assertive with age (Stewart & Rubin, 1995).

These latter findings are important for at least two reasons. First, the consistent and growing experience of failure in response to social initiatives suggests that the socially withdrawn child undergoes regular doses of rejection during peer interaction. And second, it is likely that the experience of peer noncompliance carries with it negative emotional and cognitive burdens. For example, in the face of consistent peer noncompliance, socially withdrawn children, unlike normal children, may begin to attribute their interactive failures to internal, stable causes. Such an interpretation would be consistent with research demonstrating that some children perceive their social successes as unstable and externally caused and their social failures as stable and internally caused (Goetz & Dweck, 1980; Hymel & Franke, 1985). In the WLP, extremely withdrawn children *were* found to interpret social failure as caused by internal, stable causes (Rubin & Krasnor, 1986). Taken together, the experience of peer rebuff and the attribution of peer noncompliance to internal, dispositional causes suggests a feedback loop, whereby the initially fearful and withdrawn youngster comes to believe that her or his social failures are dispositionally based, and these beliefs are strengthened by the increasing failure of her/his social initiatives. Ultimately, the behavioral reaction of the child is to withdraw further from the peer milieu.

Consistent with these negative attributions is the finding that socially withdrawn children, from about 7 years onward, have negative self-perceptions of their social skills and social relationships (Asendorpf & van Aken, 1994; Boivin et al., 1989; Hymel et al., 1990, 1993; Morison & Masten, 1991; Parkhurst & Asher, 1992; Rubin, 1985; Rubin et al., 1993; Rubin, Hymel, & Mills, 1989; Rubin & Mills, 1988). And, indeed, with increasing age, social withdrawal becomes accompanied by feelings of loneliness and depression (Asendorpf, 1993; Hymel et al., 1993; Rubin et al., 1993; Rubin & Mills, 1988).

Finally, as noted in the model, we have suggested that socially withdrawn children, when they become a salient and deviant subgroup, become rejected and isolated by their peers. Given the reality of peer rebuff during interactional encounters, it is not surprising that this postulate has been confirmed in numerous studies. Thus, observational and peer assessments of social withdrawal have consistently been associated with sociometric measures of rejection (e.g., French, 1988, 1990; Hymel & Rubin, 1985; Ollendick, Greene, Weist, & Oswald, 1990; Rubin et al., 1993; Rubin, Hymel, LeMare, & Rowden, 1989).

In summary, it would appear that many of the propositions we have offered in our developmental model have been confirmed. Social withdrawal in childhood *is* accompanied by intra- and interpersonal liabilities. By definition, socially withdrawn children do not interact as often as normal for their age cohort. Thus, they make it difficult for themselves to master the skills derived from peer interactional experiences that appear necessary for "survival" in the peer group. The costs accompanying social withdrawal include being unassertive and unable to gain peer compliance; being rejected by peers; thinking poorly of one's social competence and relationships; feeling poorly about the self and expressing loneliness. In short, social withdrawal can clearly be taken as a "warning flag" identifying a child as having social and emotional problems of an internalizing nature. Next we examine whether social withdrawal in the *familiar* peer group can predict subsequent psychological difficulties.

Social Withdrawal as a Predictor of Maladaptation

The most extensive study of the predictive consequences of social withdrawal in childhood has been the WLP (see Rubin, 1993, for a review). In the first "cuts" of data analyses, it was found that observed passive withdrawal in kindergarten predicted self-reported feelings of depression, and general self-worth, as well as teacher-rated anxiety at age 11 years. Similar predictive correlations were found for observed passive withdrawal at age 7 years (Hymel et al., 1990; Rubin & Mills, 1988). These findings are noteworthy because it would appear as if solitary play that is of a benign nature when observed during play sessions involving unfamiliar peers (*passive solitude* or solitary-constructive and -exploratory activity), carries with it a very different meaning when observed among *familiar* peers.

Given that social withdrawal, as defined earlier, is contemporaneously associated with intrapersonal difficulties, and thus may be considered a behavioral reflection of these difficulties (anxiety, negative self-perceptions of social competence and relationships, loneliness; e.g., Hymel et al., 1993; Rubin, 1993), it seemed reasonable, in the WLP, to examine how well the *constellation* of passive withdrawal, anxiety, and negative self-perceptions of social competence could predict subsequent socioemotional difficulty. Data analyses revealed that the aggregate described above, as assessed at

7 years, predicted measures of depression, loneliness, and anxiety at 11 years (Rubin & Mills, 1988). It appears, then, that anxiety and withdrawal, in concert with negative thoughts about the self, ultimately predict negative affect—most notably internalized feelings of loneliness and depression.

In addition, the most recent reports from the Waterloo Longitudinal study, Rubin (1993; Rubin, Chen, McDougall, Bowker, & McKinnon, 1995) indicated that a composite of observed social withdrawal and peer- and teacher-assessed passive withdrawal at age 7 years predicted adolescent (age 14 years) negative self-esteem, loneliness, and feelings of a *lack* of integration and involvement in the family and peer group. This latter measure was construed as an assessment of felt security within the family and peer group in the teen years. Furthermore, a composite of peer- and teacher-assessed passive withdrawal at age 11 years predicted negative self-perceptions of social competence, loneliness, and feelings of a *lack* of integration and involvement in the family and peer group (Rubin, 1993; Rubin, Chen, et al., 1995). Thus, once again, the data supported the premises of the earlier described developmental model.

The findings of the WLP have been augmented in recent reports from other studies. For example, Renshaw and Brown (1993) found that passive withdrawal at ages 9 to 12 years predicted loneliness assessed 1 year later. Also, Ollendick et al. (1990) reported that socially withdrawn 10-year-old children were more likely to be perceived by peers as withdrawn and anxious, more disliked by peers, and more likely to have dropped out of school than their well-adjusted counterparts 5 years later. And Morison and Masten (1991) indicated that children perceived by peers as withdrawn and isolated in middle childhood were more likely to think negatively of their social competencies and relationships in adolescence.

Summary

In the present review we have demonstrated that social withdrawal (1) is stable; (2) is associated concurrently, from early through late childhood, with measures conceptually reflective of felt insecurity, negative self-perceptions, dependency, and social deference, and (3) in concert with indices of negative self-appraisal, is significantly predictive of internalizing difficulties in early adolescence and the early teen period.

Most samples described in our review have comprised unselected school-attending groups of

children. Furthermore, the "outcomes" of social withdrawal have not typically involved clinical assessments. This leaves open the question of whether clinically assessed psychological disturbance can be predicted from earlier indices of social withdrawal and its concomitants. In one of the only published attempts to address this issue, Rubin (1993) administered the Child Depression Inventory (CDI; Kovacs, 1980) to the 11-year-olds participating in the WLP. Those whose CDI scores were one standard deviation or more above the mean for their age group were identified. The children so identified constituted the top 8% of children in terms of CDI scores (these children's CDI scores were above the clinical cutoff for depression). These children were then compared with their nondepressed schoolmates on indices of social and emotional well-being that had been assessed when they were 7 years of age. Follow-back discriminant function analyses indicated that these children could not be distinguished from their normal counterparts on the basis of their popularity among peers at age 7 years. Furthermore, they were neither observed to be more aggressive in their free play, nor rated by their teachers as more hostile and aggressive. The depressed children could be distinguished from their normal counterparts, however, on the basis of observed social withdrawal, peer assessments of social withdrawal, and self-reported negative self-perceptions of social competence. These results serve to support the developmental model proposed by Rubin and colleagues in which social withdrawal is described as a risk factor for the development of internalizing disorders (e.g., Rubin & Mills, 1991). Nevertheless, despite this initial support for the model, it is clear that further longitudinal research is necessary before social withdrawal can be implicated causally in the development of maladaptation in adolescence and adulthood.

THE PARENTS OF SOCIALLY WITHDRAWN CHILDREN

We have heretofore described etiological factors that may be responsible for the development of a socially withdrawn behavioral style in childhood—factors such as the child's dispositional characteristics and the quality of the parent–child relationship. We have also described the correlates and predictive consequences of social withdrawal in childhood. Thus far, we have suggested that parents play a role in determining the course

of social withdrawal in very early childhood. For example, mothers of insecurely attached "C" babies who appear to be on a trajectory to social withdrawal are more overinvolved and overcontrolling than mothers of securely attached babies (Erickson et al., 1985). Although this may be the case, it would be rather naive to believe that once the child develops a given behavioral style, her or his peer group and the self-system take over and insidiously conspire to maintain and exacerbate the problems associated with social withdrawal. While it *is* the case that socially withdrawn children become (1) increasingly salient to, and rejected by, peers with age, and (2) develop increasingly negative self-perceptions of their skills and relationships with age, it is also probable that the exigencies of being withdrawn filter back to the child's relationships and style of interaction with her or his parents. It is also likely that parents recognize the social insecurities and anxieties of their socially withdrawn children and respond in some fashion. In our developmental model we have proposed the following scenario.

Given reticence to explore their environments, socially withdrawn children demonstrate difficulties in getting social "jobs" done or social problems ameliorated (Rubin & Rose-Krasnor, 1992; Stewart & Rubin, 1995). Sensing their child's difficulties and perceived helplessness, some parents may try to support their children directly either by manipulating their child's social behaviors in a power-assertive, highly directive fashion (e.g., telling the child how to act or what to do) or by actually intervening and taking over for the child (e.g., intervening during object disputes; inviting a potential playmate to the home). For socially fearful and withdrawn children, the experience of parental overcontrol is likely to maintain or exacerbate rather than ameliorate their difficulties. Parental overdirectiveness will not allow the child to solve interpersonal problems on his or her own. It will also prevent the development of a belief system of social self-efficacy; and it likely perpetuates feelings of insecurity within and outside of the family.

The scenario offered above is just that; it is a relatively untested set of suppositions. Although an association between overcontrolling, overprotective, and overinvolved socialization strategies and social withdrawal in childhood has long been posited, it has seldom been directly investigated (e.g., Brunk & Henggeler, 1984; Hetherington & Martin, 1986). In the section that follows, we review the relevant literature extant.

Parenting Beliefs and Social Withdrawal in Childhood

In this chapter and elsewhere, we have argued that once an inhibited behavioral style is established, parents may sense the child's anxieties and insecurities and seek to help the child's mastery of the environment through authoritarian direction or by actually solving the child's interpersonal and intrapersonal problems for her or him. This possibility has been addressed in a recent series of studies by Rubin, Mills, and colleagues. Rubin and Mills begin with the notion that parenting behaviors are determined, in part, by parents' ideas about child behavior and development (Mills & Rubin, 1990, 1992, 1993a, 1993b; Rubin & Mills, 1992; Rubin, Mills, & Rose-Krasnor, 1989). Previous research has provided support for the notion that parents' behaviors are guided by (1) their values (Emmerich, 1969; Stolz, 1967); (2) their beliefs about how children develop and how quickly they develop (e.g., Dix & Grusec, 1985; Goodnow, Knight, & Cashmore, 1985); (3) the methods they believe can promote optimal development (e.g., Maccoby & Martin, 1983); and (4) their attributions for the causes of their children's behaviors (e.g., Bugental & Shennum, 1984; Dix, Ruble, & Zambarano, 1989; Grusec & Kuczynski, 1980). To this end, parents' thoughts and feelings may indirectly affect children's social development by guiding parental behaviors. These behaviors include not only the anticipatory or "proactive strategies" parents use to promote competent social behaviors, but also the "reactive strategies" they use to modify or eliminate unskilled and unacceptable behaviors in their children.

If the way parents think affects their sensitivity, and if their sensitivity contributes to the children's socioemotional development, then it is quite possible that parents of socially withdrawn children differ from other parents in their patterns of cognition. This possibility has been addressed in a series of studies by Rubin, Mills, and colleagues. For example, in one study, Rubin, Mills, and Rose-Krasnor (1989) asked mothers of preschoolers to rate how important they felt it was for their children to develop a number of representative social skills (e.g., how to make friends), to what they attributed the development of these social skills (e.g., child-centered dispositional causes versus external direct and indirect causes), and what they might do to aid in the development of such skills. In addition, the children were

observed during classroom free play. Those preschoolers whose mothers indicated that the attainment of social skills was relatively unimportant were observed to cry more often when attempting to meet their social goals and to experience less social problem-solving success; these latter results are much like those reported in studies of the social problem-solving behaviors of socially withdrawn children (Rubin & Krasnor, 1986; Stewart & Rubin, 1995). The children of mothers who believed that social skills emanated primarily from temperamental or dispositional factors were less socially assertive and successful during their peer exchanges. These children were also rated by teachers as anxious, fearful, and withdrawn. Finally, mothers who indicated that they would use high-power assertive strategies to socialize social skills (e.g., overcontrolling behaviors such as using force, coercion, and strong commands) had children who were more likely to seek help from others, especially adults, and to use nonassertive social strategies to meet their own social goals. These children were also rated by their teachers as fearful, withdrawn, and anxious.

In a second study, Rubin and Mills (1990) used behavioral observations and teacher ratings to identify preschool children who were extremely anxious and withdrawn. The mothers of these children were compared with those of average children concerning their beliefs about the development of social skills and social withdrawal. Mothers were asked to rank, in order of importance, the most likely influences on the acquisition of a series of social skills (e.g., getting acquainted with someone new, resolving peer conflicts, getting accepted into an ongoing play group of unfamiliar peers, persuading other children to do what one wants). For each of the four social skills, mothers of anxious–withdrawn children placed significantly more importance on directive teaching than did the mothers of the average children.

Rubin and Mills (1990) also presented the mothers of anxious–withdrawn children with stories describing hypothetical incidents in which their own child behaved consistently in a socially withdrawn fashion. Following each story, mothers were asked how they would feel if their own child consistently acted this way, what attributions they would make about the causes of the behavior, and what they thought they would do to modify the behavior. The mothers of anxious–withdrawn children were more likely than mothers of average children to prefer using coercive

strategies (e.g., directives) and less likely to prefer low-power strategies (e.g., redirecting the child) and indirect-no responses (e.g., seeking information from others, arranging opportunities for peer interaction, not responding) in reaction to their children's demonstration of socially withdrawn behavior.

Mothers of anxious–withdrawn children were also more likely than mothers of average children to attribute the consistent display of social withdrawal to dispositional sources. Moreover, they expressed less puzzlement and more anger, disappointment, embarrassment, and guilt about their children's displays of withdrawal than did mothers of average children.

Together, the findings of these studies paint a consistent picture of mothers whose preschool children are socially withdrawn. The facts that these mothers placed greater importance on a directive approach to teaching social skills than did mothers of average children and were more likely to choose controlling strategies for dealing with unskilled social behaviors suggest that children with internalizing difficulties tend to have mothers who may be overinvolved. The causal attributions and emotional reactions of these mothers are also indicative of overinvolvement, and they provide some tentative insights about why they may be overinvolved. These mothers were not only less tolerant of unskilled social behaviors than the other mothers, but they also felt more angry, disappointed, guilty, and embarrassed about these behaviors, and they were more inclined to blame them on a trait in their child. This constellation of emotions and attributions suggests that mothers of overcontrolled, withdrawn, preschool-aged children may be highly prone to regard their child as an extension of themselves and therefore to consider their child's behavior as if it were their own. Moreover, the negative feelings reported by these mothers suggests that this overinvolvement has negative undercurrents. This dynamic is reminiscent of the pattern of anxious, overprotective parenting that has previously been linked to internalizing difficulties in children (Levy, 1943; Parker, 1983).

While, in many ways, these data are consistent with the belief that socially withdrawn children are overcontrolled by their parents (e.g., Hetherington & Martin, 1986), it is important to remember that the data described above concern maternal beliefs, not behaviors; moreover, the studies described were of mothers of socially withdrawn preschoolers. Whether the belief patterns described above extend to maternal behaviors or to mothers of older children is relatively unknown.

Relevant to the issues noted above is a recent study that does suggest developmental change in maternal beliefs with regard to social withdrawal. Interestingly, these observations appear to change with the increasing age of the withdrawn child. Thus, for example, Mills and Rubin (1993b) found that mothers of extremely anxious and withdrawn elementary school-aged children (5 to 9 years) described their affective reactions to social withdrawal as involving less surprise and puzzlement than mothers of normal children. These data are themselves unsurprising given the stability of withdrawal from the early to the middle years of childhood. Moreover, although mothers of withdrawn elementary schoolers continued to attribute withdrawal to internal, personality traits in their children, they did *not* suggest that they would react to displays of withdrawal in a power-assertive manner (Mills & Rubin, 1993b). Perhaps these beliefs reflect parents' growing assumptions that dispositionally based behaviors become more difficult to change as children grow older; as such, it makes little sense to continue to use direct means to control or change their children's withdrawn behavioral styles.

In summary, parental beliefs and cognitions reflect an intricate mix of causes and consequences of children's social behaviors. It may be that mothers of socially withdrawn preschool-aged children are anxious and internalizing themselves and transmit these problems to their children through an overinvolved pattern of parenting that creates a sense of felt insecurity. Indeed, it is the case that preschool-aged children of depressed mothers exhibit significantly more inhibited and anxious–withdrawn forms of play with both familiar and unfamiliar playmates than do children of nondepressed mothers (Kochanska, 1991; Rubin, Both, Zahn-Waxler, Cummings, & Wilkinson, 1991; Welner, Welner, McCrary, & Leonard, 1977).

It may also be that mothers are very empathic with their children's hyperreactivity and extreme wariness; empathy may result in the demonstration of well-meant overcontrol and overinvolvement. This reaction to their child's social characteristics may produce a mixture of defensive reactions (e.g., downplaying the importance of social skills) and negative emotions. Thus, it would appear as if children's social withdrawal may be a function of the interplay between

maternal and child characteristics and the dialectic processes that are produced therein. Clearly, however, further *developmental* study of the relations between patterns of parenting and patterns of socioemotional adjustment is needed in order to gain a better understanding of this interplay (see for example, Mills & Rubin, 1993b). Furthermore, the possibility of a genetic link between parental psychopathology and children's anxious–withdrawn behavioral patterns should not be discounted in future research.

Parenting Behaviors and Social Withdrawal in Childhood

If parents' cognitions about the development of social competence and withdrawal influence their behaviors, then it would seem natural to expect that the socialization practices of parents whose children are withdrawn differ from those of parents whose children are socially competent and "normal." Two basic dimensions of parenting have been studied in this regard—"warmth/responsiveness" and "control/demandingness" (Baumrind, 1971; Maccoby & Martin, 1983). The dimension of warmth/responsiveness refers to an "affective continuum" of parenting ranging from warm and sensitive behavior to cold or hostile behavior. The dimension of control/demandingness deals with issues of "power assertion." At one end of the continuum is the frequent use of restrictive demands and high control; at the opposite end of the continuum is frequent lack of supervision and low control. The interaction of the two continua constitutes a fourfold scheme that includes (1) "authoritative parenting" (high warmth, high control), (2) "authoritarian parenting" (low warmth, high control), (3) "indulgent/permissive parenting" (high warmth, low control), and (4) "indifferent/uninvolved" parenting (low warmth, low control) (Baumrind, 1971).

Researchers have shown that children of *authoritative* parents are socially responsible and competent, friendly and cooperative with peers, and generally happy (Baumrind, 1967, 1971). This parenting style has been found to correlate contemporaneously and predictively with measures of moral reasoning and prosocial behavior in children, self-esteem (Hoffman, 1970; Yarrow, Waxler, & Scott, 1971), and academic achievement (Steinberg, Lamborn, Dornbusch, & Darling, 1992). In contrast, Baumrind (1967) found that the parents of socially anxious, unhappy children who were insecure in the company of peers

were more likely to demonstrate *authoritarian* socialization behaviors than the parents of more socially competent children. Relatedly, MacDonald and Parke (1984) found that boys perceived by teachers as socially withdrawn, hesitant, and as spectators in the company of peers had fathers who were highly directive and less engaging and physically playful in their interactions with their sons. Their mothers were described as being less likely than mothers of nonwithdrawn sons to engage them in verbal exchange and interaction. The findings were less clear-cut for socially withdrawn daughters. In general, however, the researchers reported that during parent–child play, the parents of socially withdrawn children were less spontaneous, playful, and affectively positive than parents of more sociable children.

Researchers have also reported that children's social timidity and withdrawal is associated with parental *overprotection* (Eisenberg, 1958; Kagan & Moss, 1962; Martin, 1975; Olweus, 1993; Parker, 1983). Overprotective parents tend to restrict their child's behavior and actively encourage dependency. For example, overprotective parents encourage their children to maintain close proximity to them, and they do not reinforce risk-taking behaviors and active exploration in unfamiliar situations. And, Hinde, Tamplin, and Barrett (1993) have reported that preschoolers who are often observed to be alone in school make and receive frequent initiations with their mothers. These data suggest that the influence between parenting and social withdrawal is bidirectional. In the study of Hinde et al. (1993), the interaction sequences between mothers and their children were described as brief, suggesting dependency bids on the part of the children and protectiveness and oversolicitation on the part of the mothers.

In summary, the literature extant suggests that shy, withdrawn children have parents who are highly power assertive and controlling. It may be that parental control places constraints on exploration and independence; this may preclude the development of social competence. Restrictive control may also deprive the child of opportunities to interact with peers. Thus, it is not surprising that socially withdrawn children are the recipients of parental overcontrol and overprotection.

It is extremely important to indicate that the findings just described stem from very few data bases. And, the children in the studies described varied widely with regard to age. Furthermore, the contexts within which parents of socially with-

drawn children display overcontrol and overprotection have not been well specified. Thus, at this point in time, it must be admitted that the socialization correlates and causes of social withdrawal are not well known. Clearly, this is an avenue of research that will garner some much required attention in the coming years.

EPIDEMIOLOGICAL FACTORS ASSOCIATED WITH SOCIAL WITHDRAWAL

Sex Differences and Social Withdrawal

In a longitudinal study conducted by Morison and Masten (1991), not only did the authors report that social withdrawal was a risk factor for the later development of psychological difficulties, but they also indicated that the risk of being socially withdrawn may differ depending on the child's sex. Withdrawn–isolated boys had more difficulties in adolescence than withdrawn–isolated girls. For example, boys reported less perceived athletic ability and lower self-esteem.

The long-term implications of being "shy" have been reported by Caspi, Elder, and Bem (1988). These researchers reported that boys rated by teachers as shy–withdrawn at ages 8 to 10 years were "off-time" in their age-specific adaptations to adulthood. For example, shy–withdrawn men were delayed, relative to the norm, in marrying, becoming a parent, and establishing stable careers. These delays appeared to have serious implications for adjustment in adulthood. Thus, shyness-withdrawal in men predicted delayed entry into a career, which in turn, predicted occupational instability. Those men who were shy and withdrawn as children and who were off-time in establishing a stable career were also identified as at risk for divorce and separation in adulthood. On the other hand, Caspi and colleagues found that shy-withdrawn females displayed no ill-effects of their behavioral style. They could best be described as "on-time" with regard to adult role-transitions, and as adults, they led prototypical "feminine" lives of marriage and homemaking. Morison and Masten (1991) likewise found limited evidence that withdrawn–isolated girls were at risk for subsequent difficulties. Given that Caspi's data on child shyness were collected in the middle of the 20th century, it remains to be seen how socially wary females, growing up in the latter decades of this century, fare in terms of life-course adaptations to the workplace and to the establishment and maintenance of normal adult relationships.

Although Morison and Masten (1991) focused on peer nominations of social isolation and withdrawal, and Caspi et al. (1988) centered on teacher ratings of shyness, the two studies suggest differential risk status for boys and girls who may experience social wariness and fearfulness in the company of peers. The results of these longitudinal reports have been supported in a number of recent studies. For example, Rubin et al. (1993) found that extremely withdrawn (as rated by peers) 11-year-old boys, but not girls, described themselves as more lonely and as having poorer social skills than a comparison group of average boys. And both Stevenson-Hinde (1989) and Engfer (1993) have reported that the parents of inhibited–withdrawn toddler and preschool-aged *girls* are warm, responsive, and sensitive. For boys the relations are in the opposite direction; parents of withdrawn young boys are cold, less affectionate, and less responsive than parents of average children (see also Radke-Yarrow, Richters, & Wilson, 1988; Stevenson-Hinde & Hinde, 1986). Furthermore, insecurely attached ("C" status) *boys,* but not girls, are more likely than their secure counterparts to display passive–withdrawn behaviors in early and midchildhood (Renken et al., 1989). Although it is difficult to ascertain whether dispositional factors led to different parental responses, or whether different parenting behavior led to different social behavioral profiles for boys versus girls, the bottom line is that passive, inhibited, withdrawn boys experience different socialization histories and different developmental outcomes than their female counterparts. And, as the present review indicates, it may be that withdrawn boys may be at particular risk for the development of socioemotional maladaptation.

Culture and Social Withdrawal

Thus far, we have described the developmental course, the concomitants, and the factors that influence the consistent demonstration of social withdrawal throughout childhood. We have also described some initial work that bears on the possibility of sex differences in the course of inhibition, shyness, and withdrawal. Another important epidemiological factor is cultural variation. Almost every study described above has emanated from research laboratories in the Western or developed world—countries such as Australia (Sanson, Pedlow, Cann, Prior, & Oberklaid, in

press), Canada (e.g., Rubin, 1993), England (Hinde et al., 1993), Germany (Asendorpf, 1993), Norway (Olweus, 1993), Sweden (Broberg et al., 1990), and the United States (Kagan, 1989). It is well known, however, that the evaluation of social behavior (e.g., withdrawal, inhibition) is influenced by cultural values and social conventions (Gresham, 1986). Thus, adults view children's behaviors as normal or not from the perspective of cultural norms and values; and, whether or not parents seek professional help for their children is likely to be partially determined by cultural beliefs, values, perceptions, and norms.

Adults' judgments about children's clinical problems differ markedly as a function of their cultural context. Prevailing social attitudes and values may help set thresholds for concerns about problematic child behaviors, emotions, and thoughts. For example, Weisz, Suwanlert, Chaiyasit, and Weiss (1988) compared the judgments of Thai and American parents, teachers, and clinical psychologists about two children, one with overcontrolled problems (e.g., shyness, fear) and one with undercontrolled problems (e.g., disobedience, fighting). Compared to Americans, Thais rated problems of both types as less serious, less worrisome, less likely to reflect personality traits, and more likely to improve with time. Cross-national differences in perceived seriousness were more pronounced for parents and teachers than for psychologists, suggesting that professional backgrounds and higher education may mitigate the effects of national belief systems.

In Western cultures, passive, reticent behavior is viewed negatively by parents and peers alike. As noted above, individuals who display such overt behavior are considered socially immature, fearful, and dependent (Morison & Masten, 1991; Rubin et al., 1993). Unlike Western cultures, however, children in China are encouraged to be dependent, cautious, self-restrained, and behaviorally inhibited (Ho, 1986; Ho & Kang, 1984). Such behaviors are generally considered indices of accomplishment, mastery, and maturity (Feng, 1962; King & Bond, 1985). Similarly, shy, reticent, and quiet children are described as good and well behaved. Researchers have consistently revealed that Chinese children, adolescents, and adults are more inhibited, anxious, and sensitive than their North American counterparts (Chan & Eysenck, 1981; Gong, 1984; Watrous & Hsu, 1963). Sensitive, cautious, and inhibited behavior in children is highly praised and encouraged (Ho, 1986; Ho & Kang, 1984) and has been positively associated with competent and prosocial behavior and with peer acceptance (Chen, Rubin, & Li, 1995; Chen et al., 1992). These latter results suggest that the cultural milieu and societal values may have a differential effect on the perception and treatment of wary, fearful, and withdrawn behaviors. And given that the majority of the world's inhabitants do not reside in Western countries, the studies just described bear careful note. It would appear as if the definitions of normalcy and psychological disorder described in the vast majority of texts may be culture-specific ones. Assuredly this is an issue that will require further examination, not only for the study of social withdrawal, but also for most other supposed behavioral anomalies in childhood. Relatedly, it would seem in the best interests of the psychological community of scholars not to generalize to other cultures our own culture-specific theories of the development of psychopathology.

FUTURE DIRECTIONS

In this chapter, we have reviewed the literature concerning social withdrawal in childhood. We began by providing the reader with a raison d'être for considering social withdrawal a relevant topic for a volume on child psychopathology. In so doing, we defined the phenomenon of interest and distinguished it from variables with which it is often confused, for example, inhibition, shyness, and isolation–rejection. Throughout the review was a guiding developmental model. The "gift" of the model was its provision of a framework for the material reviewed. Furthermore, it clearly specified areas that require future study.

The study of the developmental course of social withdrawal has garnered an enormous amount of attention in the past decade. A glance at the dates of the cited material in this chapter will attest to this fact. Much of the relevant work has been directed to establishing the contemporaneous and predictive correlates of social withdrawal at different points in childhood and adolescence. However, the few longitudinal studies that exist in this regard must necessarily be replicated and/or extended if one is to consider seriously that social withdrawal must be viewed as a risk factor for the development of psychopathology. Admittedly, the data extant do support this contention, but they are not conclusive.

Although we have suggested a number of etio-

logical factors that conspire to produce a socially withdrawn profile in childhood, it is important to note that the supportive data derive from very few developmental laboratories. Again, further replication work is necessary. The extent to which dispositional factors interact with parenting styles and parent–child relationships to predict the consistent display of socially withdrawn behavior in familiar peer contexts needs to be established. And, as alluded to in our review, the extent to which the developmental course of social withdrawal is similar for boys and girls requires serious attention.

Finally, what we know about the developmental course of social withdrawal is constrained by the cultures in which we have studied the phenomenon. The large majority of the published literature is derived from studies conducted in North America and Western Europe. Thus, virtually nothing is known about the developmental significance of social withdrawal in non-Western cultures. Clearly, cross-cultural work should be added to the research agendum.

The bottom line is that a review of the literature on social withdrawal in childhood does seem to have a place in this volume. The data do suggest that the quality of life for the socially withdrawn child is less than pleasant. Withdrawn children are socially deferent, anxious, lonely, and insecure in the company of peers. They fail to exhibit age-appropriate interpersonal problem-solving skills and tend to believe themselves to be deficient in social skills and social relationships. Withdrawn children are also rejected by peers. These characteristics do not auger well for these socially withdrawn children; whether or not the constellation of these factors leads inexorably to the development of psychopathology, or is associated contemporaneously with clinically defined disorders is, as yet, unknown. This leaves a good deal of room within which researchers can carve some personal territory.

REFERENCES

Achenbach, T. M. (1982). *Developmental psychopathology*. New York: Plenum Press.

Achenbach, T. M., & Edelbrock, C. (1978). The classification of child psychopathology: A review and analysis of empirical efforts. *Psychological Bulletin, 85*, 1275–1301.

Achenbach, T. M., & Edelbrock, C. (1981). Behavioral problems and competencies reported by parents of normal and disturbed children aged four through sixteen. *Monographs of the Society for Research in Child Development, 46* (Serial No. 188), 1–82.

Altman, E. O., & Gotlieb, I. H. (1988). The social behavior of depressed children: An observational study. *Journal of Abnormal Child Psychology, 16*, 29–44.

American Psychiatric Association. (1994). *Diagnostic and statistical manual of mental disorders* (4th ed.). Washington, DC: Author.

Arrindell, W. A., Emmelkamp, P. M. G., Monsma, A., & Brilman, E. (1983). The role of perceived parental rearing practices in the aetiology of phobic disorders: A controlled study. *British Journal of Psychiatry, 143*, 183–187.

Asendorpf, J. B. (1990a). Beyond social withdrawal: Shyness, unsociability, and peer avoidance. *Human Development, 33*, 250–259.

Asendorpf, J. B. (1990b). The development of inhibition during childhood: Evidence for situational specificity and a two-factor model. *Developmental Psychology, 26*, 721–730.

Asendorpf, J. B. (1991). Development of inhibited children's coping with unfamiliarity. *Child Development, 62*, 1460–1474.

Asendorpf, J. B. (1993). Beyond temperament: A two-factorial coping model of the development of inhibition during childhood. In K. H. Rubin & J. B. Asendorpf (Eds.), *Social withdrawal, inhibition and shyness in childhood* (pp. 265–289). Hillsdale, NJ: Erlbaum.

Asendorpf, J. B., & van Aken, M. A. G. (1994). Traits and relationship status: Stranger versus peer group inhibition and test intelligence versus peer group confidence as early predictors of later self-esteem. *Child Development, 65*, 1786–1798.

Asher, S. R., & Wheeler, V. A. (1985). Children's loneliness: A comparison of rejected and neglected peer status. *Journal of Consulting and Clinical Psychology, 53*, 500–505.

Barrios, B. A., & O'Dell, S. L. (1989). Fears and anxieties. In E. J. Mash & R. A. Barkley (Eds.), *Treatment of childhood disorders* (pp. 167–221). New York: Guilford Press.

Baumrind, D. (1967). Child care practices anteceding three patterns of preschool behavior. *Genetic Psychology Monographs, 76*, 43–88.

Baumrind, D. (1971). Current patterns of parental authority. *Developmental Psychology Monographs, 4*.

Bell-Dolan, D., Reaven, N. M., & Peterson, L. (1993). Depression and social functioning: A multidimensional study of the linkages. *Journal of Clinical Child Psychology, 22*, 306–315.

Belsky, J., & Rovine, M. (1987). Temperament and attachment security in the strange situation: An empirical rapprochement. *Child Development, 58*, 787–795.

Biederman, J., Rosenbaum, J. F., Bolduc-Murphy, E. A., Faraone, S. V., Chaloff, J., Hirshfeld, D. R., & Kagan, J. (1993). A 3-year follow-up of children with and without behavioral inhibition. *Journal of the American Academy of Child and Adolescent Psychiatry, 32*, 814–821.

Blechman, E. A., Tinsley, B., Carella, E. T., & McEnroe, M. J. (1985). Childhood competence and behaviour problems. *Journal of Abnormal Psychology, 94*, 70–77.

Boivin, M., Thomassin, L., & Alain, M. (1989). Peer rejection and self-perceptions among early elementary school children: Aggressive rejectees. In B. H. Schneider, G. Attili, J. Nadel, & R. P. Weissberg (Eds.), *Social competence in developmental perspective* (pp. 392–393). Dordrecht, The Netherlands: Kluwer.

Booth, C. L., Rose-Krasnor, L., McKinnon, J., & Rubin, K. H. (1994). Predicting social adjustment in middle childhood: The role of preschool attachment security and maternal style. *Social Development, 3*, 189–204.

Bower, E. M., Shellhammer, T. A., & Daily, J. M. (1960).

School characteristics of male adolescents who later became schizophrenic. *American Journal of Orthopsychiatry, 30,* 712–729.

Bowlby, J. (1973). *Attachment and loss: Vol. 1. Attachment.* New York: Basic Books.

Broberg, A., Lamb, M. E., & Hwang, P. (1990). Inhibition: Its stability and correlates in sixteen-to-forty-month-old children. *Child Development, 61,* 1153–1163.

Bronson, W. C. (1966). Central orientations: A study of behavior organization from childhood to adolescence. *Child Development, 37,* 125–155.

Brunk, M. A., & Henggeler, S. W. (1984). Child influences on adult controls: An experimental investigation. *Developmental Psychology, 20,* 1074–1081.

Bugental, D. B., & Shennun, W. A. (1984). "Difficult" children as elicitors and targets of adult communication patterns: An attributional-behavioral transactional analysis. *Monographs of the Society for Research in Child Development, 49* (Serial No. 205).

Calkins, S. D., & Fox, N. A. (1992). The relations among infant temperament, security of attachment and behavioral inhibition at 24 months. *Child Development, 63,* 1456–1472.

Calkins, S. D., Fox, N., & Marshall, T. (in press). Behavioral and physiological antecedents of inhibition in infancy. *Child Development.*

Calkins, S. D., Fox, N. A., Rubin, K. H., Coplan, R. J., & Stewart, S. (1994). *Longitudinal outcomes of behavioral inhibition: Implications for behavior in a peer setting.* Unpublished manuscript, University of Maryland.

Caspi, A., Elder, G. H., & Bem, D. J. (1988). Moving away from the world: Life-course patterns of shy children. *Developmental Psychology, 24,* 824–831.

Chan, J., & Eysenck, S. B. G. (1981, August). *National differences in personality: Hong Kong and England.* Paper presented at the joint IACCP–ICP Asian Regional Meeting, National Taiwan University, Taipei, Taiwan.

Chandler, M. (1973). Egocentrism and anti-social behavior: The assessment and training of social perspective-taking skills. *Developmental Psychology, 9,* 326–332.

Chen, X., Rubin, K. H., & Li, B. (1995). Social and school adjustment of shy and aggressive children in China. *Development and Psychopathology, 7,* 337–349.

Chen, X., Rubin, K. H., & Sun, Y. (1992). Social reputation and peer relationships in Chinese children: A cross-cultural study. *Child Development, 63,* 1336–1343.

Clark, L. A., Vorhies, L., & McEwan, J. L. (1994). Personality disorder symptomatology from the five-factor model perspective. In P. T. Costa & T. A. Widiger (Eds.), *Personality disorders and the five-factor model of personality* (pp. 41–56). Washington, DC: American Psychological Association.

Cohen, S., & Wills, T. A. (1985). Stress, social support and the buffering hypothesis. *Psychological Bulletin, 98,* 310–357.

Cole, D. A., & Carpentieri, S. (1990). Social status and the comorbidity of child depression and conduct disorder. *Journal of Consulting and Clinical Psychology, 58,* 748–757.

Compas, B. E. (1987). Coping with stress during childhood and adolescence. *Psychological Bulletin, 101,* 393–403.

Coplan, R. J., & Rubin, K. H. (1993, July). *Multiple forms of non-social play in preschoolers: Reticent, solitary-passive, and solitary-active behaviors.* Paper presented at the 12th biennial meeting of the International Society for the Study of Behavioral Development, Recife, Brazil.

Coplan, R. J., Rubin, K. H., Fox, N. A., Calkins, S. D., & Stewart, S. L. (1994). Being alone, playing alone, and acting alone: Distinguishing among reticence, and passive- and active-solitude in young children. *Child Development, 65,* 129–137.

Costa, P. T., Jr., & McCrae, R. R. (1985). *The NEO Personality Inventory manual.* Odessa, FL: Psychological Assessment Resources.

Costello, E. J. (1989). Child psychiatric disorders and their correlates: A primary care paediatric sample. *Journal of the American Academy of Child and Adolescent Psychiatry, 28,* 851–855.

Crnic, K. A., Ragozen, A. S., Greenberg, M. T., Robinson, M. M., & Basham, R. B. (1983). Social interaction and developmental competence of pre-term and full term infants during the first year of life. *Child Development, 54,* 1199–1210.

Damon, W. (1977). *The social world of the child.* San Francisco: Jossey-Bass.

Davidson, R., & Fox, N. (1989). Frontal brain asymmetry predicts infants' response to maternal separation. *Journal of Abnormal Psychology, 98,* 127–131.

Dix, T. H., & Grusec, J. E. (1985). Parent attribution processes in the socialization of children. In I. E. Sigel (Ed.), *Parental belief systems: The psychological consequences for children* (pp. 201–233). Hillsdale, NJ: Erlbaum.

Dix, T. H., Ruble, D. N., & Zambarano, R. J. (1989). Mothers' implicit theories of discipline: Child effects and the attribution process. *Child Development, 60,* 1373–1391.

Dodge, K. A. (1986). A social information processing model of social competence in children. In M. Perlmutter (Ed.), *Minnesota Symposia on Child Psychology, Vol, 18. Cognitive perspectives on children's social and behavioral development* (pp. 77–125). Hillsdale, NJ: Erlbaum.

Dodge, K. A. (1989). Problems in social relationships. In E. Mash & R. Barkley (Eds.), *Treatment of childhood disorders* (pp. 222–244). New York: Guilford Press.

Doise, W., Mugny, G., & Perret-Clermont, A. (1975). Social interaction and the development of cognitive operations. *European Journal of Social Psychology, 5,* 367–383.

Downey, G., & Coyne, J. C. (1990). Children of depressed parents: An integrative review. *Psychological Bulletin, 108,* 50–76.

Edelbrock, C. (1984). Developmental considerations. In T. Ollendick & M. Hersen (Eds.), *Child behavioral assessment: Principles and procedures* (pp. 20–37). New York: Pergamon Press.

Eisenberg, L. (1958). School phobia: A study of the communication of anxiety. *American Journal of Psychiatry, 114,* 712–718.

Elder, G. H., Jr., Van Nguyen, T., & Caspi, A. (1985). Linking family hardship to children's lives. *Child Development, 56,* 361–375.

Emery, R. (1982). Interparental conflict and the children of discord and divorce. *Psychological Bulletin, 92,* 310–330.

Emmerich, W. (1969). The parental role: A functional-cognitive approach. *Monographs of the Society for Research in Child Development, 34* (8, Serial No. 132).

Engfer, A. (1993). Antecedents and consequences of shyness in boys and girls: A 6 year longitudinal study. In K. H. Rubin & J. Asendorpf (Eds.), *Social withdrawal, inhibition, and shyness in childhood* (pp. 49–80). Hillsdale, NJ: Erlbaum.

Erickson, M. F., Sroufe, L. A., & Egeland, B. (1985). The relationship between quality of attachment and behavior problems in preschool in a high risk sample. In I. Bretherton & E. Waters (Eds.), *Growing points of attach-*

ment theory and research. *Monographs of the Society for Research in Child Development, 50* (1–2, Serial No. 209), pp. 147–166.

Feng, Y. L. (1962). *The spirit of Chinese philosophy* (Translated by E. R. Hughes). London: Routledge & Kegan Paul.

Flavell, J. H. (1970). Concept development. In P. H. Mussen (Ed.), *Carmichael's manual of child psychology* (Vol. 1, pp. 983–1060). New York: Wiley.

Flemming, P., & Ricks, D. F. (1969). Emotions of children before schizophrenia and before character disorder. In M. Roff & D. F. Ricks (Eds.), *Life history research in psychopathology.* Minneapolis: University of Minnesota Press.

Fox, N. (1989). Psychophysiological correlates of emotional reactivity during the first year of life. *Developmental Psychology, 25,* 364–372.

Fox, N., Bell, M., & Jones, N. (1992). Individual differences in response to stress and cerebral asymmetry. *Developmental Neuropsychology, 8,* 161.

Fox, N., & Calkins, S. (1993). Relations between temperament, attachment, and behavioral inhibition: Two possible pathways to extroversion and social withdrawal. In K. H. Rubin & J. Asendorpf (Eds.), *Social withdrawal, inhibition, and shyness in childhood.* Hillsdale, NJ: Erlbaum.

Fox, N. A., Calkins, S. D., & Bell, M. A. (in press). Neural plasticity and development in the first year of life: Evidence from cognitive and socio-emotional domains of research. *Development and Psychopathology.*

French, D. C. (1988). Heterogeneity of peer rejected boys: Aggressive and nonaggressive subtypes. *Child Development, 59,* 976–985.

French, D. C. (1990). Heterogeneity of peer rejected girls. *Child Development, 61,* 2028–2031.

Garcia Coll, C., Kagan, J., & Reznick, J. S. (1984). Behavioral inhibition in young children. *Child Development, 55,* 1005–1019.

Goetz, T., & Dweck, C. (1980). Learned helplessness in social situations. *Journal of Personality and Social Psychology, 39,* 246–255.

Goldberg, S. (1990). Attachment in infants at risk: Theory, research and practice. *Infant and Young Children, 2,* 11–20.

Goldsmith, H. H., & Alansky, J. A. (1987). Maternal and infant temperamental predictors of attachment: A meta-analytic review. *Journal of Consulting and Clinical Psychology, 55,* 805–816.

Gong, Y. (1984). Use of the Eysenck Personality Questionnaire in China. *Personality and Individual Differences, 5,* 431–438.

Goodnow, J. J., Knight, R., & Cashmore, J. (1985). Adult social cognition: Implications of parents' ideas for approaches to development. In M. Perlmutter (Ed.), *Cognitive perspectives and behavioral development. Vol. 18: The Minnesota Symposia on Child Psychology* (pp. 287–329). Hillsdale, NJ: Erlbaum.

Greenspan, S. I., & Lieberman, A. F. (1988). In J. Belsky & T. Nezworski (Eds.), *Clinical implications of attachment* (pp. 387–424). Hillsdale, NJ: Erlbaum.

Gresham, F. M. (1986). Conceptual issues in the assessment of social competence in children. In P. S. Strain, M. J. Guralnick, & H. M. Walker (Eds.), *Children's social behavior: Development, assessment and modification* (pp. 143–179). New York: Academic Press.

Grusec, J. E., & Kuczynski, L. (1980). Directions of effect in socialization: A comparison of the parents' vs. the child's behavior as determinants of disciplinary techniques. *Developmental Psychology, 16,* 1–9.

Gurland, B., Yorkston, N., Frank, L., & Stone, A. (1967). The structured and scaled interview to assess maladjustment. In *Biometric research* [Mimeographed booklet]. New York: Wiley.

Hartup, W. W. (1992). Peer relations in early and middle childhood. In V. B. Van Hasselt & M. Hersen (Eds.), *Handbook of social development: A lifespan perspective.* New York: Plenum Press.

Henriques, J., & Davidson, R. (1990). Regional brain electrical asymmetries discriminate between previously depressed and healthy control subjects. *Journal of Abnormal Psychology, 99,* 22–31.

Henriques, J., & Davidson, R. (1991). Left frontal hypoactivation in depression. *Journal of Abnormal Psychology, 100,* 535–545.

Hetherington, E. M., & Martin, B. (1986). Family factors and psychopathology in children. In H. Quay & J. S. Werry (Eds.), *Psychopathological disorders of childhood* (3rd ed., pp. 332–390). New York: Wiley.

Hinde, R. A., Tamplin, A., & Barrett, J. (1993). Social isolation of 4 year olds. *British Journal of Child Psychology, 11,* 211–236.

Hirshfeld, D. R., Rosenbaum, J. F., Biederman, J., Bolduc, E. A., Faraone, S. V., Snidman, N., Reznick, J. S., & Kagan, J. (1992). Stable behavioral inhibition and its association with anxiety disorder. *Journal of the American Academy of Child and Adolescent Psychiatry, 31,* 103–111.

Ho, D. Y. F. (1986). Chinese pattern of socialization: A critical review. In M. H. Bond (Ed.), *The psychology of Chinese people.* New York: Oxford University Press.

Ho, D. Y. F., & Kang, T. K. (1984). Intergenerational comparisons of child rearing attitudes and practices in Hong Kong. *Developmental Psychology, 20,* 1004–1016.

Hoffman, M. L. (1970). Moral development. In P. H. Mussen (Ed.), *Handbook of child psychology* (Vol. 2). New York: Wiley.

Hymel, S., Bowker, A., & Woody, E. (1993). Aggressive versus withdrawn unpopular children: Variations in peer and self-perceptions in multiple domains. *Child Development, 64,* 879–896.

Hymel, S., & Franke, S. (1985). Children's peer relations: Assessing self-perceptions. In B. H. Schneider, K. H. Rubin, & J. E. Ledingham (Eds.), *Children's peer relations: Issues in assessment and intervention* (pp. 75–91). New York: Springer-Verlag.

Hymel, S., & Rubin, K. H. (1985). Children with peer relationship and social skills problems: Conceptual, methodological, and developmental issues. In G. J. Whitehurst (Ed.), *Annals of child development* (Vol. 2, pp. 251–297). Greenwich, CT: JAI Press.

Hymel, S., Rubin, K. H., Rowden, L., & LeMare, L. (1990). A longitudinal study of sociometric status in middle and late childhood. *Child Development, 61,* 2004–2121.

Hymel, S., Woody, E., & Bowker, A. (1993). Social withdrawal in childhood: Considering the child's perspective. In K. H. Rubin & J. B. Asendorpf (Eds.), *Social withdrawal, inhibition and shyness in childhood* (pp. 237–262). Hillsdale, NJ: Erlbaum.

Iannotti, R. (1978). Effects of role-taking experiences on role-taking, empathy, altruism and aggression. *Developmental Psychology, 14,* 119–124.

Izard, C. E., Haynes, O. M., Chisholm, Y., & Baak, K. (1991). Emotional determinants of infant–mother attachment. *Child Development, 62,* 906–917.

Jacobsen, R. H., Lahey, B. B., & Strauss, C. C. (1983). Correlates of depressed mood in normal children. *Journal of Abnormal Child Psychology, 11,* 29–40.

Jones, N., & Fox, N. (1992). Electroencephalogram asymmetry during emotionally evocative films and its relation to positive and negative affectivity. *Brain and Cognition, 20,* 280–299.

Joseph, L. (1992). *Character structure and the organization of the self.* New York: Columbia University Press.

Jouriles, E. N., Murphy, C. M., Farris, A. M., Smith, D. A., Richters, J. E., & Waters, E. (1991). Marital adjustment, parental disagreements about child rearing and behavior problems in boys: Increasing the specificity of the marital assessment. *Child Development, 62,* 1424–1433.

Kagan, J. (1989). Temperamental contributions to social behavior. *American Psychologist, 44,* 668–674.

Kagan, J., Gibbons, J. L., Johnson, M. O., Reznick, J. S., & Snidman, N. (1990). A temperamental disposition to the state of uncertainty. In J. Rolf, A. F. Masten, D. Cicchetti, K. H. Nuechterlein, & S. Weintraub (Eds.), *Risk and protective factors in the development of psychopathology* (pp. 164–178). New York: Cambridge University Press.

Kagan, J., & Moss, H. A. (1962). *Birth to maturity: A study of psychological development.* New York: Wiley.

Kagan, J., Reznick, J. S., Clarke, C., Snidman, N., & Garcia-Coll, C. (1984). Behavioral inhibition to the unfamiliar. *Child Development, 55,* 2212–2225.

Kagan, J., Reznick, J. S., & Snidman, N. (1987). The physiology and psychology of behavioral inhibition in children. *Child Development, 58,* 1459–1473.

Kagan, J., Reznick, J. S., & Snidman, N. (1988). Biological bases of childhood shyness. *Science, 240,* 167–171.

Kagan, J., Reznick, J. S., Snidman, N., Gibbons, J., & Johnson, M. O. (1988). Childhood derivatives of inhibition and lack of inhibition to the unfamiliar. *Child Development, 59,* 1580–1589.

Kagan, J., & Snidman, N. (1991). Infant predictors of inhibited and uninhibited profiles. *Psychological Science, 2,* 40–44.

Kashani, J. H., & Orvaschel, H. (1988). Anxiety disorders in mid-adolescence: A community sample. *American Journal of Psychiatry, 145,* 960–964.

Kennedy, E., Spence, S. H., & Hensley, R. (1989). An examination of the relationship between childhood depression and social competence amongst primary school children. *Journal of Child Psychology and Psychiatry, 30,* 561–573.

King, A. Y. C., & Bond, M. H. (1985). The confucian paradigm of man: A sociological view. In W. S. Tseng & D. Y. H. Wu (Eds.), *Chinese culture and mental health.* New York: Academic Press.

Kochanska, G. (1991). Patterns of inhibition to the unfamiliar in children of normal and affectively ill mothers. *Child Development, 62,* 250–263.

Kochanska, G., Kuczynski, L., & Maguire, L. (1989). Impact of diagnosed depression and self-reported mood on mothers' control strategies: A longitudinal study. *Journal of Child Psychology and Psychiatry, 17,* 493–511.

Kochanska, G., & Radke-Yarrow, M. (1992). Inhibition in toddlerhood and the dynamics of the child's interaction with an unfamiliar peer at age five. *Child Development, 63,* 325–335.

Kovacs, M. (1980). Rating scales to assess depression in school-aged children. *Acta Paedopsychiatria, 46,* 305–315.

La Greca, A. M., Dandes, S. K., Wick, P., Shaw, K., & Stone, W. L. (1988). Development of the Social Anxiety Scale for Children: Reliability and concurrent validity. *Journal of Clinical Child Psychology, 17,* 84–91.

Landau, S., & Millich, R. (1985). Social status of aggressive and aggressive/withdrawn boys: A replication across age and method. *Journal of Consulting and Clinical Psychology, 53,* 141.

Lapa, L. M., Rubin, K. H., Booth, C. L., & Rose-Krasnor, L. (1994, June). *The social problem solving skills of children with low self perceptions.* Paper presented at the 13th biennial meetings of the International Society for the Study of Behavioral Development, Amsterdam, The Netherlands.

Ledingham, J. E. (1981). Developmental patterns of aggressive and withdrawn behaviour in childhood: A possible method for identifying preschizophrenics. *Journal of Abnormal Child Psychology, 9,* 1–22.

LeDoux, J. (1989). Cognitive-emotional interactions in the brain. *Cognition and Emotion, 4,* 267–274.

LeMare, L., & Rubin, K. H. (1987). Perspective-taking and peer interactions: Structural and developmental analyses. *Child Development, 58,* 306–315.

Lerner, J. A., Inui, T. S., Trupin, E. W., & Douglas, E. (1985). Preschool behavior can predict future psychiatric disorders. *Journal of the American Academy of Child Psychiatry, 24,* 42–48

Levy, D. M. (1943). *Maternal overprotectiveness.* New York: Columbia University.

Lewis, M., & Miller, S. M. (Eds.). (1990). *Handbook of developmental psychopathology.* New York: Plenum Press.

Maccoby, E. E., & Martin, J. A. (1983). Socialization in the context of the family: Parent–child interaction. In P. H. Mussen (Series Ed.) & E. M. Hetherington (Vol. Ed.), *Handbook of child psychology: Vol 4. Socialization, personality, and social development* (pp. 1–102). New York: Wiley.

MacDonald, K., & Parke, R. D. (1984). Bridging the gap: Parent–child play interaction and peer interactive competence. *Child Development, 55,* 1265–1277.

Martin, B. (1975). Parent–child relations. In F. Horowitz (Ed.), *Review of child development research* (pp. 463–540). Chicago: University of Chicago Press.

Matas, L., Arend, R. A., & Sroufe, L. A. (1978). The continuity of adaptation in the second year: Relationship between quality of attachment and later competence. *Child Development, 49,* 547–556.

McBurnett, K., Lahey, B. B., Frick, P. J., Risch, C., Loeber, R., Hart, E. L., Christ, M. A. G., & Hanson, K. S. (1991). Anxiety, inhibition, and conduct disorder in children: II. Relation to salivary control. *Journal of the American Academy of Child and Adolescent Psychiatry, 30,* 192–196.

McGee, R., Feehan, M., Williams, S., Partridge, F., Silva, P. A., & Kelly, J. (1990). DSM-III disorders in a large sample of adolescents. *Journal of the American Academy of Child and Adolescent Psychiatry, 29,* 611–619.

Mead, G. (1934). *Mind, self and society.* Chicago: University of Chicago Press.

Messer, S. C., & Beidel, D. C. (1994). Psychosocial correlates of childhood anxiety disorders. *Journal of the American Academy of Child and Adolescent Psychiatry, 33,* 975–983.

Michael, C. M., Morris, D. P., & Soroker, E. (1957). Follow-up studies of shy, withdrawn children: Evaluation of later adjustment. *American Journal of Orthopsychiatry, 24,* 743–755.

Millon, T. (1981). *Disorders of personality: DSM-III, Axis II.* New York: Wiley.

Millon, T. (1987). *Manual for the MCMI II.* Minneapolis, MN: National Computer Systems.

Millon, T., & Everly, G. S. (1985). *Personality and its disorders: A biological learning approach*. New York: Wiley.

Mills, R. S. L., & Rubin, K. H. (1990). Parental beliefs about problematic social behaviors in early childhood. *Child Development, 61,* 138–151.

Mills, R. S. L., & Rubin, K. H. (1992). A longitudinal study of maternal beliefs about children's social behavior. *Merrill-Palmer Quarterly, 38,* 494–512.

Mills, R. S. L., & Rubin, K. H. (1993a). Parental ideas as influences on children's social competence. In S. Duck (Ed.), *Learning about relationships* (pp. 98–117). Newbury Park, CA: Sage.

Mills, R. S. L., & Rubin, K. H. (1993b). Socialization factors in the development of social withdrawal. In K. H. Rubin & J. Asendorpf (Eds.), *Social withdrawal, inhibition and shyness in childhood*. Hillsdale, NJ: Erlbaum.

Miyake, K., Chen, S., & Campos, J. (1985). Infant temperament, mother's mode of interactions, and attachment in Japan: An interim report. In I. Bretherton & E. Waters (Eds.), *Growing points of attachment theory and research. Monographs of the Society for Research in Child Development, 50* (1–2, Serial No. 209), pp. 276–297.

Morison, P., & Masten, A. (1991). Peer reputation in middle childhood as a predictor of adaptation in adolescence: A seven year follow-up. *Child Development, 62,* 991–1007.

Moskowitz, D. S., Schwartzman, A. E., & Ledingham, J. E. (1985). Stability and change in aggression and withdrawal in middle childhood and early adolescence. *Journal of Abnormal Psychology, 94,* 30–41.

Mullins, L. L., Peterson, L., Wonderlich, S. A., & Reaven, N. (1986). The influence of depression in childhood on the social responses and perceptions of adults. *Journal of Clinical Child Psychology, 15,* 233–240.

O'Brien, M. M., Trestman, R. L., & Siever, L. J. (1993). Cluster A personality disorders. In D. L. Dunner (Ed.), *Current psychiatric therapy* (pp. 65–82). Philadelphia: Harcourt Brace Jovanovich.

Ollendick, T. H., Greene, R. W., Weist, M. D., & Oswald, D. P. (1990). The predictive validity of teacher nominations: A five-year follow-up of at risk youth. *Journal of Abnormal Child Psychology, 18,* 699–713.

Olweus, D. (1980). Familial and temperamental determinants of aggressive behavior in adolescent boys: A causal analysis. *Developmental Psychology, 16,* 644–660.

Olweus, D. (1993). Victimization by peers: Antecedents and long-term outcomes. In K. H. Rubin & J. B. Asendorpf (Eds.), *Social withdrawal, inhibition and shyness in childhood* (pp. 315–341). Hillsdale, NJ: Erlbaum.

Panella, D., & Henggeler, S. W. (1986). Peer interaction, conduct disordered, anxious withdrawn and well black adolescents. *Journal of Abnormal Child Psychology, 14,* 1–11.

Parker, G. (1983). *Parental overprotection: A risk factor in psychosocial development*. New York: Grune & Stratton.

Parker, G., & Lipscombe, P. (1981). Influences and maternal overprotectiveness. *British Journal of Psychiatry, 138,* 215–235.

Parker, J. G., & Asher, S. R. (1987). Peer relations and later personal adjustment: Are low-accepting children at risk? *Psychological Bulletin, 102,* 357–389.

Parkhurst, J. T., & Asher, S. R. (1992). Peer rejection in middle school: Subgroup differences in behavior, loneliness, and interpersonal concerns. *Developmental Psychology, 28,* 231–241.

Pastor, D. L. (1981). The quality of mother–infant attachment and its relationship to toddler's initial sociability with peers. *Developmental Psychology, 17,* 323–335.

Patterson, G. R. (1983). Stress: A change agent for family process. In N. Garmezy & M. Rutter (Eds.), *Stress, coping, and development in children* (pp. 235–264). New York: McGraw-Hill.

Patterson, G. R. (1986). Maternal rejection: Determinant or product for deviant child behavior? In W. Hartup & Z. Rubin (Eds.), *Relationships and development*. Hillsdale, NJ: Erlbaum.

Pekarik, E. G., Prinz, R. J., Liebert, D. E., Weintraub, S., & Neale, J. (1976). The Pupil Evaluation Inventory: A sociometric technique for assessing children's social behavior. *Journal of Abnormal Child Psychology, 4,* 83–97.

Peterson, L., Mullins, L., & Ridley-Johnson, R. (1985). Childhood depression: Peer reactions to depression and life stress. *Journal of Abnormal Child Psychology, 13,* 597–610.

Piaget, J. (1926). *The language and thought of the child*. London: Routledge & Kegan Paul.

Piaget, J. (1928). *Judgement and reasoning in the child*. London: Routledge & Kegan Paul.

Piaget, J. (1932). *Six psychological studies*. New York: Random House.

Pilkonis, P. A. (1984). Avoidant and schizoid personality disorders. In H. E. Adams & P. B. Sutker (Eds.), *Comprehensive handbook of psychopathology* (pp. 479–494). New York: Plenum Press.

Pollack, M., Woerner, M. G., Goodman, W., & Greenberg, J. W. (1966). Childhood development patterns of hospitalized adult schizophrenics and nonschizophrenic patients and their siblings. *American Journal of Orthopsychiatry, 36,* 492–509.

Quay, H., & Werry, J. (Eds.). (1986). *Psychopathological disorders of childhood* (2nd ed.). New York: Wiley.

Radke-Yarrow, M., Richters, J., & Wilson, W. E. (1988). Child development in a network of relationships. In R. A. Hinde & J. Stevenson-Hinde (Eds.), *Relationships within families: Mutual influences* (pp. 48–67). Oxford, UK: Clarendon Press.

Renken, B., Egeland, B., Marvinney, D., Mangelsdorf, S., & Sroufe, L. (1989). Early childhood antecedents of aggression and passive-withdrawal in early elementary school. *Journal of Personality, 57,* 257–281

Renshaw, P. D., & Brown, P. J. (1993). Loneliness in middle childhood: Concurrent and longitudinal predictors. *Child Development, 64,* 1271–1284.

Reznick, J. S., Kagan, J., Snidman, N., Gersten, M., Baak, K., & Rosenberg, A. (1986). Inhibited and uninhibited behavior: A follow-up study. *Child Development, 57,* 660–680.

Rosenbaum, J. F., Biederman, J., Gersten, M., Hirshfeld, D., Menninger, S., Herman, J., & Kagan, J. (1988). Behavioral inhibition in children of parents with panic disorder and agoraphobia: A controlled study. *Archives of General Psychiatry, 52,* 5–9.

Rubin, K. H. (1982a). Non-social play in preschoolers: Necessary evil? *Child Development, 53,* 651–657.

Rubin, K. H. (1982b). Social and cognitive developmental characteristics of young isolate, normal, and sociable children. In K. H. Rubin & H. S. Ross (Eds.), *Peer relationships and social skills in childhood* (pp. 353–374). New York: Springer-Verlag.

Rubin, K. H. (1985). Socially withdrawn children: An "at risk" population? In B. H. Schneider, K. H. Rubin, &

J. E. Ledingham (Eds.), *Children's peer relations: Issues in assessment and intervention* (pp. 125–139). New York: Springer-Verlag.

Rubin, K. H. (1993). The Waterloo Longitudinal Project: Correlates and consequences of social withdrawal from childhood to adolescence. In K. H. Rubin & J. Asendorpf (Eds.), *Social withdrawal, inhibition and shyness in childhood* (pp. 291–314). Hillsdale, NJ: Erlbaum.

Rubin, K. H., & Asendorpf, J. (Eds.). (1993). *Social withdrawal inhibition, and shyness in childhood.* Hillsdale, NJ: Erlbaum.

Rubin, K. H., Booth, C., Rose-Krasnor, L., & Mills, R. S. L. (1995). Family relationships, peer relationships and social development: Conceptual and empirical analyses. In S. Shulman (Ed.), *Close relationships and socio-emotional development* (pp. 63–94). New York: Ablex.

Rubin, K. H., & Both, L. (1989). Iris pigmentation and sociability in childhood. A reexamination. *Developmental Psychobiology, 22,* 717–726.

Rubin, K. H., Both, L., Zahn-Waxler, E. C., Cummings, M., & Wilkinson, M. (1991). Dyadic play behaviors of children of well and depressed mothers. *Development and Psychopathology, 3,* 243–251.

Rubin, K. H., Chen, X., & Hymel, S. (1993). The socioemotional characteristics of extremely aggressive and extremely withdrawn children. *Merrill-Palmer Quarterly, 39,* 518–534.

Rubin, K. H., Chen, X., McDougall, P., Bowker, A., & McKinnon, J. (1995). Predicting adolescent maladaptation from indices of psychological overcontrol in childhood. *Development and Psychopathology, 7,* 751–764.

Rubin, K. H., & Coplan, R. (1992). Peer relationships in childhood. In M. Bornstein & M. Lamb (Eds.), *Developmental psychology: An advanced textbook* (pp. 519–578). Hillsdale, NJ: Erlbaum.

Rubin, K. H., Coplan, R. J., Fox, N. A., & Calkins, S. D. (1995). Emotionality, emotion regulation, and preschoolers' social adaptation. *Development and Psychopathology, 7,* 49–62.

Rubin, K. H., Daniels-Beirness, T., & Bream, L. (1984). Social isolation and social problem solving: A longitudinal study. *Journal of Consulting and Clinical Psychology, 52,* 17–25.

Rubin, K. H., Fein, G., & Vandenberg, B. (1983). Play. In P. H. Mussen (Series Ed.) & E. M. Hetherington (Vol. Ed.), *Handbook of child psychology: Vol. 4. Socialization, personality, and social development* (pp. 693–774). New York: Wiley.

Rubin, K. H., Hymel, S., LeMare, L., & Rowden, L. (1989). Children experiencing social difficulties: Sociometric neglect reconsidered. *Canadian Journal of Behavioral Science, 21,* 94–111.

Rubin, K. H., Hymel, S., & Mills, R. S. L. (1989). Sociability and social withdrawal in childhood: Stability and outcomes. *Journal of Personality, 57,* 237–255.

Rubin, K. H., Hymel, S., Mills, R., & Rose-Krasnor, L. (1991). Conceptualizing different pathways to and from social isolation in childhood. In D. Cicchetti & S. Toth (Eds.), *The Rochester symposium on developmental psychopathology: Vol. 2. Internalizing and externalizing expressions of dysfunction* (pp. 91–122). Hillsdale, NJ: Erlbaum.

Rubin, K. H., & Krasnor, L. R. (1986). Social cognitive and social behavioral perspectives on problem-solving. In M. Perlmutter (Ed.), *Minnesota symposia on child psychology* (Vol. 18, pp. 1–68). Hillsdale, NJ: Erlbaum.

Rubin, K. H., LeMare, L. J., & Lollis, S. (1990). Social withdrawal in childhood: Developmental pathways to rejection. In S. R. Asher & J. D. Coie (Eds.), *Peer rejection in childhood* (pp. 217–249). New York: Cambridge University Press.

Rubin, K. H., & Lollis, S. (1988). Peer relationships, social skills, and infant attachment: A continuity model. In J. Belsky & T. Nezworski (Eds.), *Clinical implications of attachment* (pp. 167–221). Hillsdale, NJ: Erlbaum.

Rubin, K. H., & Mills, R. S. L. (1988). The many faces of social isolation in childhood. *Journal of Consulting and Clinical Psychology, 56,* 916–924.

Rubin, K. H., & Mills, R. S. L. (1990). Maternal beliefs about adaptive and maladaptive social behaviors in normal, aggressive, and withdrawn preschoolers. *Journal of Abnormal Child Psychology, 18,* 419–435.

Rubin, K. H., & Mills, R. S. L. (1991). Conceptualizing developmental pathways to internalizing disorders in childhood. *Canadian Journal of Behavioral Science, 23,* 300–317.

Rubin K. H., & Mills, R. S. L. (1992). Parent's thoughts about children's socially adaptive and maladaptive behaviors: Stability, change and individual differences. In I. Sigel, J . Goodnow, & A. McGillicuddy-deLisi (Eds.), *Parental belief systems* (2nd ed., pp. 41–68). Hillsdale, NJ: Erlbaum.

Rubin, K. H., Mills, R. S. L., & Rose-Krasnor, L. (1989). Maternal beliefs and children's social competence. In B. Schneider, G. Attili, J. Nadel, & R. Weissberg (Eds.), *Social competence in developmental perspective* (pp. 313–331). Dordrecht: Kluwer International.

Rubin, K. H., & Rose-Krasnor, L. (1992). Interpersonal problem-solving and social competence in children. In V. B. van Hasselt & M. Hersen (Eds.), *Handbook of social development: A lifespan perspective* (pp. 283–324). New York: Plenum Press.

Rubin, K. H., & Stewart, S. L., & Chen, X. (1995). Parents of aggressive and withdrawn children. In M. Bornstein (Ed.), *Handbook of parenting* (Vol. 1, pp. 255–284). Hillsdale, NJ: Erlbaum.

Rutter, M., & Garmezy, N. (1983). Developmental psychopathology. In P. H. Mussen (Series Ed.) & E. M. Hetherington (Vol. Ed.), *Handbook of child psychology: Vol. 4. Socialization, personality and social development* (pp. 775–911). New York: Wiley.

Sanson, A., Pedlow, R., Cann, W., Prior, M., & Oberklaid, F. (in press). Shyness ratings: Stability and correlates of early childhood. *International Journal of Behavioral Development.*

Schwartzman, A. E., Ledingham, J. E., & Serbin, L. (1985). Identification of children at risk for adult schizophrenia: A longitudinal study. *International Review of Applied Psychology, 34,* 363–380.

Selman, R. L. (1980). *The growth of interpersonal understanding.* New York: Cambridge University Press.

Selman, R. L. (1985). The use of interpersonal negotiation strategies and communicative competencies: A clinical-developmental exploration in a pair of troubled early adolescents. In R. A. Hinde, A. Perret-Clermont, & J. Stevenson-Hinde (Eds.), *Social relationships and cognitive development* (pp. 208–232). Oxford, UK: Clarendon Press.

Siever, L. J. (1981). Schizoid and schizotypal personality disorders. In J. R. Lion (Ed.), *Personality disorders: Diagnosis and management* (pp. 32–64). Baltimore: Williams & Wilkins.

Sroufe, L. A. (1983). Infant–caregiver attachment and patterns of adaptation in preschool: Roots of maladaptation

and competence. In M. Perlmutter (Ed.), *Minnesota symposia on child psychology* (Vol. 16). Hillsdale, NJ: Erlbaum.

Sroufe, L. A., & Rutter, M. (1984). The domain of developmental psychopathology. *Child Development, 55*, 17–29.

Sroufe, L. A., & Waters, E. (1977). Heart rate as a convergent measure in clinical and developmental research. *Merrill-Palmer Quarterly, 23*, 3–25.

Stabenau, J., & Pollin, R. (1969). Experimental differences for schizophrenics as compared to their non-schizophrenic siblings: Twin and family studies. In M. Roff & D. Ricks (Eds.), *Life history research in psychopathology*. Minneapolis: University of Minnesota Press.

Steinberg, L., Lamborn, S. D., Dornbusch, S. M., & Darling, N. (1992). Impact of parenting practices on adolescent achievement: Authoritative parenting, school involvement and encouragement to succeed. *Child Development, 63*, 1266–1281.

Stevenson-Hinde, J. (1989). Behavioral inhibition: Issues of context. In J. S. Reznick (Ed.), *Perspectives on behavioral inhibition* (pp. 125–138). Chicago: University of Chicago Press.

Stevenson-Hinde, J., & Hinde, R. A. (1986). Changes in associations between characteristics and interactions. In R. Plomin & J. Dunn (Eds.), *The study of temperament: Changes, continuities, and challenges* (pp. 115–129). Hillsdale, NJ: Erlbaum.

Stewart, S. L., & Rubin, K. H. (1995). The social problem-solving skills of anxious-withdrawn children. *Development and Psychopathology, 7*, 323–336.

Stolz, L. M. (1967). *Influences on parent behavior*. Stanford, CA: Stanford University Press.

Stone, M. H. (1993). Cluster C personality disorders. In D. L. Dunner (Ed.), *Current psychiatric therapy* (pp. 441–416). Philadelphia: Harcourt Brace Jovanovich.

Strauss, C. C., Frame, C. L., & Forehand, R. (1987). Psychosocial impairment associated with anxiety in children. *Journal of Clinical Child Psychology, 16*, 235–239.

Sullivan, H. S. (1953). *The interpersonal theory of psychiatry*. New York: Norton.

Thompson, R. A., Connell, J., & Bridges, L. J. (1988). Temperament, emotional and social interactive behavior in the strange situation: An analysis of attachment functioning. *Child Development, 59*, 1102–1110.

Turkal, I. D. (1990). *The personality disorders. A psychological approach to clinical management*. New York: Pergamon Press.

Vosk, B., Forehand, R., Parker, J. B., & Richard, K. (1982). A multimethod comparison of popular and unpopular children. *Developmental Psychology, 18*, 571–575.

Watrous, B. G., & Hsu, F. L. K. (1963). A thematic apperception test study of Chinese, Hindu and American college students. In F. L. K. Hsu (Ed.), *Clan, caste, and club* (pp. 263–311). New York: Van Nostrand.

Watt, N. F., Stolorow, R. D., Lubensky, A. W., & McClelland, D. C. (1970). School adjustment and behaviour of children hospitalized for schizophrenia as adults. *American Journal of Orthopsychiatry, 40*, 637–657.

Weisz, J. R., Suwanlert, S., Chaiyasit, W., & Weiss, B. (1988). Thai and American perspectives on over- and under-controlled child behavior problems: Exploring the threshold model among parents, teachers, and psychologists. *Journal of Consulting and Clinical Psychology, 56*, 601–609.

Welner, Z., Welner, A., McCrary, M. D., & Leonard, M. A. (1977). Psychopathology in children with depression: A controlled study. *Journal of Nervous and Mental Disease, 164*, 408–413.

Wickman, E. K. (1928). *Children's behavior and teacher's attitudes*. New York: Commonwealth Fund.

Widiger, T. A., Frances, A. J., Spitzer, R. L., & Williams, J. B. W. (1988). The DSM-III-R personality disorders: An overview. *American Journal of Psychiatry, 145*, 786–795.

Widiger, T. A., Trull, T. J., Clarkin, J. F., Sanderson, C., & Costa, P. T. (1994). A description of the DSM-III-R and DSM-IV personality disorders with the five-factor model of personality. In P. T. Costa & T. A. Widiger (Eds.), *Personality disorders and the five-factor model of personality* (pp. 41–56). Washington, DC: American Psychological Association.

Wierzbicki, M., & McCabe, M. (1988). Social skills and subsequent depressive symptomatology in children. *Journal of Clinical Child Psychology, 17*, 203–208.

World Health Organization. (1993). *The ICD-10 classification of mental and behavioural disorders*. Geneva, Switzerland: Author.

Yarrow, M. R., Waxler, C. Z., & Scott, P. M. (1971). Child effects on adult behavior. *Developmental Psychology, 5*, 300–311.

Younger, A. J., & Boyko, K. A. (1987). Aggression and withdrawal as social schemas underlying children's peer perceptions. *Child Development, 58*, 1094–1100.

Younger, A. J., & Daniels, T. (1992). Children's reasons for nominating their peers as withdrawn: Passive withdrawal versus active isolation. *Developmental Psychology, 28*, 955–960.

Younger, A. J., Gentile, C., & Burgess, K. (1993). Children's perceptions of social withdrawal: Changes across age. In K. H. Rubin & J. B. Asendorpf (Eds.), *Social withdrawal, inhibition and shyness in childhood* (pp. 215–235). Hillsdale, NJ: Erlbaum.

Zahn-Waxler, C., Mayfield, A., Radke-Yarrow, M., McKnew, D. H., Cytryn, L., & Davenport, D. (1988). A follow-up investigation of offspring of parents with bipolar disorder. *American Journal of Psychiatry, 145*, 506–509.

IV

DEVELOPMENTAL AND LEARNING DISORDERS

Autistic Disorder

Laura Grofer Klinger
Geraldine Dawson

Autism is one of the pervasive developmental disorders, which are characterized by an impairment in the development of reciprocal social and communication skills, abnormal language development, and a restricted repertoire of behaviors and interests. It is the fact that autism seriously affects multiple domains that makes it such a challenging disorder to understand and to treat. When writing about her 2-year-old daughter with autism, Catherine Maurice (1993) described how autism affected all aspects of her daughter's development:

> It wasn't just that she didn't understand language. She didn't seem to be aware of her surroundings. She wasn't figuring out how her world worked, learning about keys that fit into doors, lamps that turned off because you pressed a switch, milk that lived in the refrigerator. . . . If she was focusing on anything, it was on minute particles of dust or hair that she now picked up from the rug, to study with intense concentration. Worse she didn't seem to be picking up anyone's feelings. (pp. 32–33)

HISTORICAL CONTEXT

The term "autism" was coined by Bleuler in 1911 to describe individuals with schizophrenia who had a loss of contact with reality (Bleuler, 1911/1950). In the early 1940s, two men, Leo Kanner (1943) and Hans Asperger (1944/1991), independently described childhood disorders involving impaired social relationships, abnormal language, and restricted and repetitive interests. They believed that these children had a similar loss of contact with reality described by Bleuler without the concomitant diagnosis of schizophrenia.

In his initial report, Kanner presented case studies of 11 children whom he described as having an "extreme autistic aloneness" (p. 242). He noted that these children had an "inability to relate themselves in the ordinary way to people and situations from the beginning of life" (p. 242). In addition, he wrote that the syndrome led to language deviance characterized by delayed acquisition, echolalia, occasional mutism, pronoun reversals, and literalness. Finally Kanner described these children as having an "obsessive desire for the maintenance of sameness" (p. 245) characterized by the development of elaborate routines and rituals. Because of their good rote memory and their normal physical appearance, Kanner concluded that these children were capable of achieving normal cognitive abilities.

In 1944, Asperger described a similar, but less severely impaired, group of four children. He diagnosed these children as having a personality disorder that he termed "autistic psychopathy." Asperger believed that the disorder was present from the second year of life and was characterized by an essential disturbance in the ability to form "a lively relationship with the whole environment" (Asperger, 1944/1991). Similar to Kanner, Asperger described difficulties in social interaction including eye contact, affective expression, and

conversational abilities. In contrast to Kanner's report, Asperger wrote about children who developed good language abilities by the time they entered school and oftentimes spoke pedantically like adults. Despite good vocabularies and grammatical abilities, these children were impaired in their conversational skills and had unusual use of the volume, tone, and flow of speech. Asperger commented on the high level of original thought displayed by these children and their tendency to become excessively preoccupied with a singular topic of interest.

Historically, it was believed that parents of children with autism were overly intellectual, coldhearted, and had a limited interest in other people including their spouses and children (Kanner, 1943; Bettelheim, 1967). Bettelheim (1967) proposed that in response to rejecting parents, children with autism withdrew from social interaction and became self-sufficient. Until the mid-1970s, treatment regimes involved helping parents, usually mothers, to become less rejecting of their children. However, these initial hypotheses regarding the etiology of autism were not supported by empirical research conducted in the 1970s and 1980s. McAdoo and DeMyer (1978) and Koegel, Schreibman, O'Neill, and Burke (1983) administered the Minnesota Multiphasic Personality Inventory to parents of children with autism. These parents scored within the normal range on all of the personality measures. Additionally, parents of children with autism and parents of children without disabilities reported similar levels of marital satisfaction and family cohesion.

Bernard Rimland (1964) and Eric Schopler (Schopler & Reichler, 1971) were among the first researchers to argue against the theory that parents were responsible for their children's autism. Rimland proposed that the disorder was due to a neurological impairment. Schopler suggested that rather than treating the parents, the role of therapists was to involve parents as part of the treatment team working with their children.

DESCRIPTION OF THE DISORDER

Core Symptoms

Despite over 50 years of research by disciplines ranging from psychology to neuroanatomy, the cause of autism remains a mystery, and there continues to be much debate about which symptoms are considered to be "core" to defining the disorder. During the first few years of life, social, affective, communicative, and cognitive development are intrinsically linked and any impairment in one area is likely to have negative consequences on the development of all the other areas as well. This connection between early developing abilities has made it difficult, if not impossible, to ascertain whether autism results from a basic impairment in any one specific area. It is likely that there is no single primary deficit in autism, but rather a group of deficits affecting social, affective, linguistic, and cognitive development. Although we review each ability separately, it is important for the reader to realize that each of these abilities does not develop in isolation.

Social Abilities

Traditionally, autism has been considered to result from a primary deficit in socioemotional development that prevents children from interacting normally with others. In normal development, the abilities to form an attachment relationship, imitate another person, share a focus of attention with another person, understand another person's emotions, and engage in pretend play are all early-developing social skills. In autism, these social skills appear to be specifically impaired. However, recent research has revealed that these impairments may not be caused by an inability or complete lack of desire to interact with other people, but rather may be due to impairments in understanding and responding to social information (cf. Dawson, 1991). The literature suggesting impairments in each of these early-developing social/emotional abilities is reviewed below.

Attachment

It was originally assumed that children with autism fail to bond with their parents. Some even suggested that they are not able to discriminate between familiar and unfamiliar adults (Cohen, Paul, & Volkmar, 1987). However, empirical evidence suggests that children with autism do show differential responses to their caregivers compared to unfamiliar adults. Sigman and her colleagues (Sigman & Mundy, 1989; Sigman & Ungerer, 1984a) found that preschool-aged children with autism directed more social behaviors and proximity seeking toward their caregivers than to strangers following a brief separation.

Recent research has examined the quality of the attachment relationship between children with autism and their caregivers. Attachment quality is traditionally measured using Ainsworth's Strange Situation Paradigm in which a 12- to 18-month-old child experiences a series of separation and reunion episodes with the caregiver and a stranger (Ainsworth, Blehar, Waters, & Wall, 1978). Secure attachment is demonstrated by the child's preference for social interaction with the mother compared to a stranger as observed by the child's ability to use the mother as a secure base for exploration and seeking comfort from the mother when distressed. Approximately 65% of normally developing, middle-class American toddlers are classified as having a secure attachment relationship with their caregivers (Ainsworth, 1983). Capps, Sigman, and Mundy (1994) reported that all of the children with autism in their sample were classified as having an insecure attachment quality. Specifically, children with autism exhibited disoriented and disorganized behaviors directed toward their mothers. However, when the repetitive motor movements that are typically exhibited by individuals with autism were ignored (e.g., flapping, rocking, spinning), 40% of the children in their sample could be classified as being securely attached. Similarly, 50% of the children assessed by Rogers, Ozonoff, and Maslin-Cole (1993) were classified as having a secure attachment to their mothers. Thus, secure attachment quality in autism approaches the rates seen in normally developing populations. Taken together, these findings suggest that autism does not result from a global impairment in the ability to form attachments. Instead, autism may result from a specific impairment in the ability to understand and respond to social information (Rogers et al., 1993; Sigman & Mundy, 1989).

Social Imitation

Through early interactions involving mutual imitation, infants are able to understand the relationship between themselves and other people (Meltzoff & Gopnik, 1993; Stern, 1985). In normal development, imitation skills are present shortly after birth (Field, Woodson, Greenberg, & Cohen, 1982; Meltzoff & Moore, 1977). However, young children with autism have specific impairments in their ability to imitate the movements of others (Curcio, 1978; Dawson & Adams, 1984; DeMyer et al., 1972; Sigman & Ungerer;

1984b). DeMyer et al. (1972) reported that children with autism were impaired, relative to mental-age-matched controls, in both imitation of body movements and actions on objects. Dawson and Adams (1984) reported that although children with autism varied in their imitative abilities, overall their imitation skills were more impaired than other sensorimotor abilities such as object permanence. Imitation skills were positively correlated with social responsiveness, free play, and language. Based on this research, several investigators (e.g., Dawson, 1991; Rogers & Pennington, 1991; Meltzoff & Gopnik, 1993) have hypothesized that a failure to imitate may be a fundamental deficit in autism, interfering with the development of reciprocity, joint attention, and understanding of emotional states.

Loveland et al. (1994) reported that 8- to 26-year-old individuals with autism could imitate facial expressions as well as mental-age-matched children with Down syndrome. However, she noted that persons with autism showed an increased number of bizarre and mechanical expressions while attempting to imitate the examiner's facial expressions. Loveland et al. (1994) suggested that these unusual facial expressions may represent a subtle type of imitation impairment that is present in older, more advanced individuals with autism. Smith and Bryson (1994) proposed that imitation delays in autism may result from an inability to perceive and represent events (body movements and actions with objects). They argued that a basic representation impairment could lead to difficulties representing the actions of others in a form that could be translated into actions of the self. Indeed Loveland's findings that older individuals with autism are capable of imitation, but undergo a series of bizarre facial expressions in the process, suggest that these individuals may continue to have problems translating the representation of another person into actions of the self.

Joint Attention and Orienting

Another mechanism by which infants gain an understanding of social information is through the use of nonverbal behaviors such as eye contact and gesture to share a focus of attention with another person. These early-developing joint attention skills are considered important precursors to the development of spoken language (Bruner, 1975; Sugarman, 1984). Between 6 and 9 months of age, normally developing infants learn to share

attention by looking between an object and caregiver (Walden & Ogan, 1988). Later, between 9 and 12 months of age, infants learn that they can also share attention through the use of gesture (Hannan, 1987). Infants can both direct another's attention, through gestures such as pointing, and can follow the gestures of others.

Children with autism have impairments in their ability to use gaze and gesture as a means of sharing their attention with others (Mundy, Sigman, Ungerer, & Sherman, 1986; Wetherby & Prutting, 1984). Mundy et al. (1986) reported that deficits in referential looking correctly diagnosed 94% of the children with autism in a group of preschool-aged autistic children and mentally retarded children. Mundy, Sigman, and Kasari (1994) found that the extent of impairment in joint attention behaviors seems to be related to intellectual ability. In their study, preschool-aged children with both autism and mental retardation (IQ below 60) showed specific impairments in both gestural and referential-looking–joint attention behaviors. In contrast, relatively high-functioning young children with autism (IQ above 60) showed specific impairments in gestural joint attention abilities but not referential-looking abilities. Other forms of nonverbal communication, including requesting and turn-taking behaviors, have also been found to be impaired in children with autism (McEvoy, Rogers, & Pennington, 1993; Mundy et al., 1994). It is unclear whether joint attention impairments are specifically impaired in autism or whether they represent an instance of more globalized deficits in nonverbal communication skills.

In a study of home videotapes of toddler's first birthday parties, Osterling and Dawson (1994) found that, in addition to showing deficits in joint attention, toddlers with autism often failed to orient to social stimuli (faces, speech) in their environments. Dawson, Meltzoff, and Osterling (1995) recently assessed experimentally whether, compared to developmentally matched children with Down syndrome, children with autism fail to orient visually to naturally occurring social stimuli. It was found that children with autism more frequently failed to orient to both social stimuli (name calling, clapping) and nonsocial stimuli (rattle, jack-in-the-box), but this failure was much more extreme for social stimuli. These results suggest that children with autism exhibit a basic orienting impairment, especially for social stimuli. Such a failure may contribute to their deficits in joint attention.

Emotion Perception and Expression

Hobson (1989) proposed that individuals with autism have a core deficit in the perception and understanding of other people's emotions. Weeks and Hobson (1987) reported that children with autism sorted a group of photographs according to the type of hat being worn rather than by facial expression. In contrast, chronological and verbal-IQ-matched children with retardation sorted on the basis of facial expression rather than type of hat. These findings suggest that children with autism may be insensitive to other people's facial expressions of emotion. Hobson, Ouston, and Lee (1988) found that adolescents and young adults with autism were more impaired on a task assessing cross-modal perception of emotional stimuli (e.g., matching photographs of facial expressions with audio recordings of emotionally expressive voices) than they were on cross-modal perception tasks that did not involve emotional stimuli (e.g., matching photographs of people walking on different surfaces with corresponding audio recordings). However, Ozonoff, Pennington, and Rogers (1990) reported contradictory findings. They found that children with autism have a global impairment in cross-modal perception that is not specific to understanding emotional expressions.

Kasari, Sigman, Yirmiya, and Mundy (1993) reported that children with autism display unusual emotional expressions. In their study, children with autism were more likely to display negative affect and unusual blends of affective expressions. In contrast, Dawson, Hill, Spencer, Galpert, and Watson (1990) found that children with autism did not differ from receptive-language, age-matched, normally developing children in the frequency or duration of smiles during a face-to-face interaction with their mothers. However, children with autism were much less likely to combine smiles with eye contact and were less likely to smile in response to their mother's smiles. Dawson et al. (1990) suggested that children with autism have a specific impairment in their ability to engage in affective sharing experiences with another person.

Loveland et al. (1994) reported that producing affective expressions upon request is more difficult for persons with autism than persons with Down syndrome with similar chronological age, mental age, and IQ scores. In this study, individuals with autism could perform rote copying of facial expressions but had difficulty generating facial

expressions without a model. However, this does not necessarily mean that individuals with autism are unable to produce spontaneous facial expressions, but, rather, they may have difficulty matching the verbal label to the corresponding emotional expression. As in the emotion perception literature, these findings are suggestive of a possible cross-modal impairment underlying difficulties in the production of emotional expressions.

Symbolic Play

An important precursor to language development is the ability to engage in symbolic representation through pretend play. Normally, symbolic play gradually emerges between 12 and 22 months of age with the majority of children achieving symbolic play by approximately 20 months of age (Riguet, Taylor, Benaroya, & Klein, 1981; Ungerer & Sigman, 1984). Symbolic play involves attributing animate characteristics to inanimate objects (e.g., pretending that a doll can speak) and using one object as if it were another (e.g., pretending that a block is a piece of fruit). Children with autism show impaired symbolic-play skills relative to what would be expected by their language abilities (Riguet et al., 1981; Ungerer, 1989; Wing, 1978). Some higher-functioning children with autism do show "stereotyped pretend play" characterized by mechanical play that is repetitive in nature, but they fail to show more flexible play with rich, elaborate themes (Wing, 1978). The most significant impairments in children with autism have been observed in their ability to attribute animate characteristics to inanimate objects (Ungerer, 1989).

Language Abilities

Given the significant impairments in early-developing abilities that are considered to be precursors to language development (i.e., joint attention, symbolic play), it is not surprising that children with autism have significantly delayed and deviant language development. Approximately 50% of individuals with autism remain mute throughout their lives (Rutter, 1978). Mundy, Sigman, and Kasari (1990) found that those children who developed gestural, nonverbal joint attention behaviors were more likely to develop language.

Those individuals with autism who do eventually learn to speak have deviant language, characterized by immediate or delayed echolalia (e.g.,

verbatim repetition of previously heard words or phrases), abnormal prosody (e.g., atypical rhythm, stress, intonation, and loudness) and pronoun reversal (e.g., use of "you" instead of "I" when referring to the self) (Cantwell, Baker, Rutter, & Mawhood, 1989; Kanner, 1943). Approximately 85% of children with autism who develop speech show immediate or delayed echolalia (Schuler & Prizant, 1985). Prizant and Rydell (1984) demonstrated that echolalia has many different communicative functions including requesting, self-regulation, protesting, and affirmation. They suggested that echolalia should be viewed as an effort to communicate rather than as meaningless utterances. Lee, Hobson, and Chiat (1994) examined pronoun usage among adolescents with autism and reported the tendency to refer to the examiner by name rather than "you," and to themselves by name rather than "I" or "me." Additionally, those individuals who used personal pronouns tended to refer to themselves as "I" rather than "me." These findings suggest that although difficulties with personal pronouns may become less pronounced over time, they continue to exist throughout the lifespan.

Language impairments in autism are most pronounced in the pragmatic, or social, aspects of language use (see Tager-Flusberg, 1989, for a review). Conversations by persons with autism are characterized by the use of irrelevant detail in conversations (e.g., providing dates and ages when discussing a particular event or person), perseveration on a particular topic of conversation, inappropriate shifts to a new topic, and the ignoring of conversational initiations introduced by another person (Eales, 1993). Eales (1993) argued that these pragmatic impairments were due to impairments in understanding the intentions of another person during conversations. Tager-Flusberg (1993) hypothesized that persons with autism do not understand the speaker–listener discourse rules in conversations. Specifically, they have difficulty understanding that others have a different perspective than their own. As a result, they show unusual language such as abnormal pronoun use (e.g., saying "You want candy" when meaning "I want candy") and impairments in their use of questions and statements (e.g., saying "Want cracker?" instead of stating "I want a cracker").

In addition to pragmatic impairments, individuals with autism typically have difficulty in the semantic aspects of language. In a longitudinal

study comparing preschool-aged children with autism to a group of children with Down syndrome matched on expressive language age and chronological age, Tager-Flusberg (1989, 1993) reported that children with autism were not specifically impaired in their articulation abilities or acquisition of language structures (i.e., syntax and grammar). However, they were impaired in how effectively they used the language skills that they had acquired. For example, although both groups used words in a variety of different ways and contexts (e.g., use of nouns, verbs, adjectives, etc.), the children with autism showed less variety in their choice of terms within each category. They do not appear to utilize the vocabulary that they have developed. Additionally, the children with autism did not use their language to provide new information during a conversation or to elicit new information through the use of "wh-" questions (Tager-Flusberg, 1993). They seem to be lacking the curiosity necessary to utilize these types of information-gathering language skills (Koegel & Koegel, 1995).

In the area of language comprehension, persons with autism have been described as concrete and literal. They seem to have more difficulty understanding other people's language than they do learning the language structures necessary to produce language (Rapin, in press). For example, Paul, Fischer, and Cohen (1988) reported that children with autism tended to rely on syntax rather than semantic content in their comprehension of language (e.g., relying on a word when determining the meaning of a sentence).

Kurita (1985) reported that 37% of a sample of 261 Japanese children lost meaningful speech prior to 30 months of age. Although there is little research examining speech loss in autism, clinical lore supports this finding, that a small but significant portion of parents report that their children's language development was normal (i.e., use of single words or short two- to three-word sentences) and then regressed between 24 and 30 months of age.

Cognitive Abilities

It has been estimated that between 76% and 89% of children with autism have impaired intellectual abilities as indicated by IQ scores below 70 (Bryson, Clark, & Smith, 1988; Steffenburg & Gillberg, 1986). DeMyer and colleagues reported that intellectual abilities in autism appear to be stable after 5 years of age and are predictive of later aca-

demic and work achievement (DeMyer et al., 1974). More recently, Lord and Schopler (1989) reported good stability and predictability for intelligence and developmental quotients in a group of children followed from preschool to school years, even for children assessed at 3 years or under. However, there was one important caveat to their study: Half of the children under 3 years who received scores in the moderate/severe range of mental retardation showed significant gains by the school years. Although most of these children continued to show intellectual impairments, the delays were not as severe as the initial assessment indicated. It is likely that the focus on social behaviors (smiling, attention to another person, imitation) in the assessment of children under 3 years contributed to the lower initial scores.

Individuals with autism tend to display a specific pattern of intellectual abilities, performing better on nonverbal visual–spatial tasks than verbal tasks (Happe, 1995; Lockyer & Rutter, 1970). As a result, persons with autism tend to have higher performance IQ scores than verbal IQ scores. Although the majority of individuals with autism have some degree of mental retardation, it is important to note that some persons with autism have average or above-average intellectual abilities. These individuals without intellectual impairment are often underdiagnosed (Tsai, 1992).

Researchers have attempted to determine whether an underlying cognitive impairment can explain some of the social, affective, and communicative impairments observed in individuals with autism. Over the last few years, research has focused on four different areas of possible cognitive impairments in autism: categorization (Klinger & Dawson, 1995), memory (Bachevalier, 1994), theory of mind (Baron-Cohen, Leslie, & Frith, 1985), and executive function (Ozonoff, 1995a). A brief review of each of these different areas follows.

Categorization

Categorization is a mental process that allows individuals to form concepts and then understand new information based on these previously formed concepts. For example, once a child has developed the concept of "dog," he or she can categorize a new example (e.g., a dachshund) as belonging to the "dog" category. Research on normal development indicates that categorization can occur through several different processes. Using a rule-based approach, children learn to categorize by

memorizing a set of necessary and sufficient features (e.g., all squares have four equal sides joined by 90° angles). However, the majority of natural categories cannot be defined by a list of necessary and sufficient criteria (see Smith & Medin, 1981, for a review of this theory). An alternative categorization process involves abstracting a single best example (a prototype) from experiences with different category members (Posner & Keele, 1968, 1970). New examples are compared to this abstract summary image or prototype.

Previous categorization studies have found that children with autism are able to form concepts (e.g., color, shapes, function) and can categorize new objects based on these concepts (Tager-Flusberg, 1985a, 1985b; Ungerer & Sigman, 1987). However, Klinger and Dawson (1995) proposed that although individuals with autism may be able to categorize information, the process they use may be impaired. Specifically, they found that, compared to children with normal development, children with autism and children with mental retardation categorized using a rule-based approach (e.g., "all dogs have long noses") but were unable to categorize when no rule or combination of rules defined category membership. That is, they did not appear to use a prototype or summary representation approach to categorization. More research is needed to determine whether this impairment is specific to autism or is common among all individuals with developmental disabilities. A deficit in the formation of prototypes would be an impairment in basic information processing and may help to explain why individuals with autism have difficulty processing social information. Because social information is inherently unpredictable and variable in nature, it is less easily categorized using a strict rule-based approach (Dawson & Lewy, 1989).

Memory

Several investigators have proposed that autism shares some similarity with an amnesic syndrome that results from combined damage to the hippocampus and amygdala (Bachevalier, 1994; Boucher, 1981; Boucher & Warrington, 1976; DeLong, 1992). There is evidence of memory impairments in individuals with autism (e.g., Ameli, Courchesne, Lincoln, Kaufman, & Grillon, 1988; Boucher & Warrington, 1976; Minshew & Goldstein, 1993). There is much inconsistency across studies and much variability within studies across subjects. Although the pattern of deficits in autism does not fit a classic amnesic profile, there are some similarities between the pattern of memory deficits in the two syndromes. In classic amnesia, one expects to find (1) intact short-term memory and impaired long-term memory; (2) generally impaired long-term free recall and impaired recognition of newly acquired material; (3) impaired paired associate learning; and (4) intact or improved cued recall. In autism, both short-term and long-term memory have been found to be impaired, with the exception of auditory rote memory, which is not necessarily impaired. There is some evidence of impaired long-term free recall and recognition, but great variability exists across subjects. Paired associate learning has not been found to be impaired in high-functioning individuals with autism. Persons with autism do benefit from cues in recall tests, however. Thus, there is some evidence to suggest that autism may involve subtle dysfunction of the hippocampus and amygdala that results in memory abnormalities that are similar, but not identical, to those found in classical amnesia. Bachevalier (1994) has hypothesized that memory deficits specific to the hippocampus may occur only in the subgroup of individuals with autism who are mentally retarded.

Theory of Mind

The ability to understand that other people have beliefs, desires, and intentions that are different from one's own (i.e., a "theory of mind") emerges gradually from infancy and is firmly established by the age of 3 to 4 years (see Wellman, 1993, for a review). Baron-Cohen et al. (1985) hypothesized that children with autism have a specific impairment in their development of a theory of mind. Such an impairment in meta-representation would explain the difficulties that children with autism have in social understanding and communication. In their seminal study, Baron-Cohen et al. (1985) compared theory-of-mind abilities in children with autism, Down syndrome, and normal development. Children watched a puppet show in which a character, Sally, placed a toy in one location (e.g., a basket) and then left the room. While Sally was out of the room, the toy was moved to a different location (e.g., a box) by another puppet. Children were asked where Sally would look for the toy upon her return. In order to answer correctly (e.g., that Sally would look in the basket), children needed to understand that the puppet, Sally, had a belief that was different from their own. In this

study, the majority of children with normal development and Down syndrome answered the question correctly (85% and 86% of the time, respectively). In contrast only 20% of the children with autism were able to predict the beliefs of others. In a later study, Baron-Cohen (1989) reported that the 20% of children with autism who could successfully attribute a belief state to another person were impaired in more complex theory-of-mind tasks (e.g., predicting what one person thinks another person is thinking). Thus, even those children who were able to understand another person's theory of mind at the level of a normally developing 4-year-old child were unable to show the level of understanding usually obtained by 7 years of age.

In a recent longitudinal study, Ozonoff and McEvoy (1994) followed a group of nonretarded adolescents with autism over a 3-year time period. As a group, persons with autism did not exhibit an increase in theory-of-mind abilities over the 3-year period. These results confirmed Baron-Cohen's (1989) finding that there may be a ceiling on theory-of-mind development in autism, and they are supportive of the hypothesis presented by Burack (1992) that theory-of-mind abilities may be deviant rather than simply delayed in persons with autism. Interestingly, both verbal mental age and verbal IQ were significantly correlated with success on theory-of-mind tasks. Ozonoff and McEvoy (1994) concluded that verbal comprehension may be a prerequisite to successful performance on theory-of-mind tasks.

Certain prelinguistic deficits may contribute to later theory-of-mind impairments, including joint attention skills (Mundy & Sigman, 1989; Mundy, Sigman, & Kasari, 1993) and imitation skills (Meltzoff & Gopnik, 1993). Mundy and Sigman (1989) hypothesized that during the first year of life, infants' shared experiences with caregivers promote the development of early joint attention skills. Beginning in the third to fourth year of life, this ability to share attention promotes the understanding of another person's beliefs or intentions. Similarly, Meltzoff and Gopnik (1993) argued that early imitative games between infant and caregiver during the first year of life provide the infant with a tutorial in sharing and predicting human behavior. Meltzoff and Gopnik described these interactions as providing the child with a kind of "primer in common-sense psychology" in which the child learns about the effects of his or her behavior on another person. They argued that this information is necessary for the development of a theory of mind.

Executive Function

A number of researchers have documented that persons with autism have a core deficit in their ability to perform executive-function tasks (Ozonoff, 1995a; Ozonoff & McEvoy, 1994; Ozonoff, Pennington, & Rogers, 1991; Ozonoff, Strayer, McMahon, & Filloux, 1994; Prior & Hoffmann, 1990; Rumsey & Hamburger, 1988). Executive functions are cognitive functions thought to involve the ability to maintain an appropriate problem-solving set in order to attain a future goal. These functions include planning, impulse control, inhibition of irrelevant responses, and working memory. Ozonoff et al. (1991) found that a group of nonretarded children and adolescents with autism were less successful on two different executive-function tasks (the Tower of Hanoi and the Wisconsin Card Sorting Test) than a chronological age- and IQ-matched, learning-disabled control group. After 3 years, Ozonoff and McEvoy (1994) conducted a follow-up study with this same group of subjects. They reported that whereas the learning-disabled control group showed improvements on the executive-function tasks, the autistic group did not show any improvement with development. These findings support the notion that executive-function impairments may represent a life-long deficit in autism.

McEvoy et al. (1993) studied preschoolers with autism and reported impairments on an executive-function task measuring spatial reversal. In the spatial reversal task, children were asked to find a piece of candy that was hidden under one of two cups. After finding the candy in the same location for four consecutive trials, the hiding place was switched, and children were required to inhibit and shift the prepotent response that had been created over the previous four trials. Compared to developmentally delayed children matched on chronological age and a group of younger normally developing children matched on verbal ability, the children with autism displayed more perseverative responses (i.e., continuing to choose the cup that had been correct on previous trials). Performance on this spatial reversal task correlated significantly with measures of joint attention and social interaction. These data suggest that impaired executive-function abilities may be related to the core social impairments observed in autism.

Although it is possible that deficits in executive function are universally found in persons with autism, such deficits certainly are not specific to autism. Impairments on executive-function tasks have been reported in other disorders including schizophrenia and attention-deficit/hyperactivity disorder (see Pennington & Welsh, in press, for a review of executive-function impairments in these disorders). Recently, Ozonoff (1995b) suggested that the cognitive flexibility component rather than the inhibition component of executive function may be specifically impaired in autism.

Repetitive Behaviors and Interests

Children with autism often engage in abnormal, ritualistic behaviors. Volkmar, Cohen, and Paul (1986) reported parental ratings of stereotyped motor behaviors in a sample of 50 children with a diagnosis of autism. Parents overwhelmingly rated their children as being overactive (85%). The most commonly reported motor stereotypies were rocking (65%), toe-walking (57%), arm, hand, or finger flapping (52%), and whirling (50%). These repetitive motor movements tend to occur more often in younger and lower-functioning children with autism (Wing, 1988; Wing & Gould, 1979). More elaborate routines are observed in children with less severe levels of retardation. Elaborate routines can include a complex series of motor movements, repeated rearranging or ordering of toys, and insistence on following the same sequence of events during everyday activities such as driving routes, dressing routines, and food preferences. Intense, perseverative, circumscribed interests are common in higher-functioning individuals with autism (Wing, 1988). These perseverative interests usually involve memorization of facts about a specific topic (e.g., the solar system, weather, U.S. presidents).

Related Symptoms

Several behavioral problems including self-injurious behavior, sleep disturbance, eating disturbance, and anxiety symptoms often occur in persons with autism.

Self-Injurious Behaviors

Behaviors such as head-banging, finger- or hand-biting, head-slapping, and hair-pulling have been observed in persons with autism. When frustrated, persons with autism often have no verbal means of communicating their feelings and, as a result, may engage in self-injurious behaviors as a means of expressing their frustration (Donnellan, Mirenda, Mesaros, & Fassbender, 1984). Bartak and Rutter (1976) reported that self-injurious behavior was more likely to occur in mentally retarded autistic children than nonretarded autistic children. Thus, self-injurious behavior may be a function of retardation rather than the diagnosis of autism.

Sleep Disturbances

It is not uncommon for persons with autism to require less sleep than other family members, and parents often report that their children awake frequently during the night. Ruth Sullivan (1992) described her son, Joseph, at 2 years of age as being extremely hyperactive. She wrote: "It was as though his idle was stuck at rocket speed. He slept an average of three to four hours a night and screamed for the rest" (p. 247). Although comments like these are common from parents, there is little research documenting sleep disturbances in autism.

Eating Disturbances

Eating disturbances are also frequently reported by parents, yet there is little research in this area. Eating disturbances are characterized by unusual food preferences. Oftentimes, food preferences are determined by the texture of the food. For example, Powell, Hecimovic, and Christensen (1992) described a young man with autism who preferred foods with a soft texture: "He only eats steamed vegetables with a side dish of butterscotch pudding and half a banana for dinner" (p. 193). Additionally, some persons with autism develop rituals at mealtimes. For example, a 5-year-old boy whom we know will only eat peanut butter sandwiches if a particular type of peanut butter and a particular type of jam are used. In addition, he insists that the pieces be cut into triangular shapes and the crust removed.

Abnormal Fears and Response to Sensory Stimuli

Persons with autism often exhibit fearful responses to common everyday objects. Clinically, we have seen children with fears of the vacuum cleaner, particular television commercials, eleva-

tors, blacktop, and clothing. These fears can cause many problems in daily living situations. The child who was afraid of blacktop refused to walk across parking lots, streets, and the school playground. Often, these unusual fears appear related to abnormal sensory responses (Ornitz, 1989).

Children with autism often fail to respond to some sounds, such as their name being called, and overreact to other sounds such as a siren in the distance. This lack of response to some sounds leads many parents of children with autism to believe that their children have hearing impairments. Similarly, individuals with autism often seem insensitive to pain, but at the same time they may have a hypersensitivity to clothing touching their skin. Ornitz (1989) proposed that these disturbances result from an impaired ability to modulate sensory information that is manifested by both under- and overreactivity and is present in all sensory systems.

DEFINITIONAL AND DIAGNOSTIC ISSUES

As yet, there are no biological markers or medical tests for autism. Therefore, the diagnosis of autism is based on behavioral symptomatology. As our understanding of autism has improved, the behavioral symptoms necessary for a diagnosis of autism have changed. Currently, both major diagnostic systems—the *Diagnostic and Statistical Manual of Mental Disorders,* fourth edition (DSM-IV; American Psychiatric Association, 1994) and the *International Classification of Diseases,* 10th edition (ICD-10; World Health Organization, 1992)—use identical criteria. This represents a major revision in the diagnostic systems and allows for consistency in diagnosis across a wide variety of mental health care providers.

DSM-IV includes autistic disorder under the category of pervasive developmental disorders (American Psychiatric Association, 1994). Similarly, ICD-10 includes childhood autism as a type of pervasive developmental disorder (World Health Organization, 1992). Pervasive developmental disorders are characterized by severe and pervasive impairments in several areas of functioning including reciprocal social interaction skills, communication skills, and the presence of stereotyped behaviors, interests, and activities. Autism is the most prevalent of these disorders and includes impairments in all of the above areas. Additionally, the onset of autism must be present by 3 years of age. Table 8.1 lists DSM-IV diagnostic criteria for autistic disorder.

Diagnostic Instruments

The diagnosis of autism should be based on multiple sources of information including parent interviews and behavioral observations. Within the last 10 years, several instruments have been developed to aid in the diagnostic process. A few of these measures will be reviewed to give the reader a broad overview of the types of instruments that are available for use. This is by no means a complete list.

The Childhood Autism Rating Scale (CARS; Schopler, Reichler, De Vellis, & Daly, 1980; Schopler, Reichler, & Renner, 1988) is a behavior rating scale that can be completed by the child's teacher, parent, or therapist. The child's behavior in 15 different areas (e.g., social relatedness, nonverbal communication, verbal communication) is rated on a four-point scale ranging from age-appropriate behavior to severely abnormal behavior. Diagnostic classifications are made by adding up the scores for the 15 different areas. When compared to expert clinical judgments based on interviews with parents and their child, the CARS demonstrates good criterion validity ($r = .80$). An advantage of this behavioral rating scale is that it can be completed by a variety of different individuals who are familiar with the child and does not require a structured observational period.

The Autism Diagnostic Observation Schedule (ADOS; Lord et al., 1989) is a standardized semistructured play session that allows the examiner to observe communicative and social behaviors that are associated with autism. The examiner administers eight different tasks designed to assess the child's turn-taking, play, verbal, and nonverbal abilities. The ADOS is appropriate for use with children from 6 to 18 years of age with a mental age of at least 3 years. The ADOS requires 20 to 30 minutes to administer. A diagnosis is made based on scoring an algorithm that is consistent with a draft version of the current ICD-10 criteria. Criterion validity for the ADOS is adequate for the social and communication domains, but when the restricted repetitive interests domain is included, criterion validity is diminished. Overall, the ADOS correctly classified only 17 out of 40 children with previous diagnoses of autism based on clinical judgment (Lord et al., 1989). Parent information regarding restricted repetitive interests may be necessary along with

TABLE 8.1. DSM-IV Diagnostic Criteria for Autistic Disorder

A. A total of six (or more) items from (1), (2), and (3), with at least two from (1), and one each from (2) and (3):

  (1) qualitative impairment in social interaction, as manifested by at least two of the following:

   (a) marked impairment in the use of multiple nonverbal behaviors such as eye-to-eye gaze, facial expression, body postures, and gestures to regulate social interaction
   (b) failure to develop peer relationships appropriate to developmental level
   (c) a lack of spontaneous seeking to share enjoyment, interests, or achievements with other people (e.g., by a lack of showing, bringing, or pointing out objects of interest)
   (d) lack of social or emotional reciprocity

  (2) qualitative impairments in communication as manifested by at least one of the following:

   (a) delay in, or total lack of, the development of spoken language (not accompanied by an attempt to compensate through alternative modes of communication such as gesture or mime)
   (b) in individuals with adequate speech, marked impairment in the ability to initiate or sustain a conversation with others
   (c) stereotyped and repetitive use of language or idiosyncratic language

   (d) lack of varied, spontaneous make-believe play or social imitative play appropriate to developmental level

  (3) restricted repetitive and stereotyped patterns of behavior, interests, and activities, as manifested by at least one of the following:

   (a) encompassing preoccupation with one or more stereotyped and restricted patterns of interest that is abnormal in either intensity or focus
   (b) apparently inflexible adherence to specific, nonfunctional routines or rituals
   (c) stereotyped and repetitive motor mannerisms (e.g., hand or finger flapping or twisting, or complex whole-body movements)
   (d) persistent preoccupation with parts of objects

B. Delays or abnormal functioning in at least one of the following areas, with onset prior to age 3 years: (1) social interaction, (2) language as used in social communication, (3) symbolic or imaginative play.

C. The disturbance is not better accounted for by Rett's Disorder or Childhood Disintegrative Disorder.

Note. From American Psychiatric Association (1994, pp. 70–71). Copyright 1994 by the American Psychiatric Association. Reprinted by permission.

the behavioral observations from the ADOS. With parent information, approximately 37 out of 40 children with autism were correctly diagnosed. The benefit of the ADOS is that it provides a brief semistructured observational format that focuses on behaviors associated with autism.

The Parent Interview for Autism (PIA; Stone & Hogan, 1993) is a structured interview for gathering information from the parents of children under the age of 6 years. Parents are asked to rate the frequency of behaviors associated with autism on a five point scale ranging from never to almost always. The interview contains 118 items and requires 30 to 45 minutes to administer. The main use of the interview is to elicit clinically relevant information because cutoff scores for the diagnostic classification of autism are not provided. However, the total score on the PIA is moderately correlated with the CARS ($r = .42$) and with *Diagnostic and Statistical Manual of Mental Disorders*, third edition, revised (DSM-III-R; American Psychiatric Association, 1987) diagnoses ($r =$

.49). One benefit of the PIA is that it allows the examiner to gain a perspective across time and different contexts in the child's life.

The Autism Diagnostic Interview—Revised (ADI-R; Lord, Rutter, & Le Couteur, 1994) is a standardized, semistructured parent interview that can be used to assess children and adults with a mental age of 18 months and up. The interview lasts approximately 1½ hours for a child who is 3 to 4 years old and longer for an older child or adult. Caregivers are asked to describe their children's past and current behaviors with a focus on the behaviors observed during their children's preschool years. A diagnosis is made based on scoring an algorithm that is consistent with DSM-IV (American Psychiatric Association, 1994) and ICD-10 (World Health Organization, 1992) criteria. The ADI-R has good criterion validity with 24 out of 25 clinically diagnosed autistic children meeting criteria for autism on the ADI-R (Lord et al., 1994). Twenty-three out of 25 mentally retarded children without autism were diagnosed

accurately by the ADI-R. The two children who were inaccurately classified as having autism were 3 years old and nonverbal. Although the ADI-R requires a lengthy interview, to date it is the instrument that is the most consistent with our current diagnostic criteria.

Other Pervasive Developmental Disorders

Beginning with the publication of DSM-IV and ICD-10, several other pervasive developmental disorders have been differentiated from autism. These disorders include Asperger disorder, Rett disorder, childhood-onset disintegrative disorder, and pervasive developmental disorder, not otherwise specified. Each of these syndromes is reviewed briefly.

Asperger Disorder

Asperger (1944/1991) described a group of children with symptoms resembling Kanner autism but without mental retardation or significant language delay. However, only within the last 5 to 10 years have researchers focused on Asperger syndrome as a distinct disorder. Tantum (1988) described the person with Asperger syndrome as "intelligent, a fluent but original language user, clumsy, an assiduous pursuer of idiosyncratic interests, and cut off from others by a subtle but pervasive oddity which obtrudes in every social situation" (p. 246). There is relatively little research on Asperger syndrome, and the majority of published studies have not used consistent diagnostic criteria. Thus, it is difficult to make any definitive statements about the disorder. In general, researchers have agreed that the diagnosis of Asperger syndrome usually involves relatively intact intellectual and formal language functioning accompanied by the impairments in reciprocal social interaction that are associated with autism (Gillberg, 1989; Szatmari, Tuff, Finlayson, & Bartolucci, 1989; Tantum, 1988). Additionally, Asperger syndrome individuals have been characterized as having idiosyncratic interests that often are appropriate in content but always unusual in their intensity (Gillberg, 1989; Tantum, 1988). Finally, several researchers have noted increased motor clumsiness among some individuals with Asperger syndrome (Gillberg, 1989; Tantum, 1988).

DSM-IV and ICD-10 define Asperger disorder as involving a severe and sustained impairment in social interaction along with the development of restricted, repetitive behaviors and interests. In contrast to autistic disorder, DSM-IV and ICD-10 stipulate that individuals with Asperger disorder may not display clinically significant delays in language (e.g., single words must be used by age 2 years, and communicative phrases must be used by age 3 years), cognitive functioning, or adaptive behavior. If DSM-IV criteria are met for autistic disorder, a diagnosis of Asperger disorder cannot be given.

There continues to be considerable controversy about whether Asperger disorder represents a distinct clinical disorder or whether autistic disorder and Asperger disorder are both part of a single autism spectrum disorder. Szatmari, Tuff, et al. (1989) reported that a group of nonretarded individuals with autism showed more social and communication impairments and motor stereotypies than a group of individuals diagnosed with Asperger syndrome. There were no differences between the groups in their insistence on following routines or engaging in ritualistic behavior. Although these results support the notion that Asperger syndrome may represent a less severe form of autism, there were no differences in cognitive performance on a neuropsychological battery of tests. In contrast, Ozonoff, Rogers, and Pennington (1991) found that individuals with Asperger syndrome performed better on theory-of-mind and executive-function tasks than high-functioning individuals with autism.

Rett Disorder

Rett syndrome is a progressive neurological disorder that begins within the first few years of life (see Van Acker, 1991, for a review of the research). To date, this syndrome has only been reported to occur in females. DSM-IV and ICD-10 define Rett disorder as involving a period of normal development for at least 5 months followed by the loss of previously acquired skills. Degeneration occurs in five different areas. First, although girls with Rett disorder have a normal head circumference at birth, they show a deceleration of head growth between 5 and 48 months of age. Second, Rett disorder involves a loss of purposeful hand movements between 5 and 30 months of age and the subsequent development of characteristic stereotyped movements such as hand-wringing and hand-washing. Third, a loss of social engagement occurs that resembles the so-

cial difficulties present in autism. Fourth, Rett disorder is characterized by a poorly coordinated gait. Finally, Rett disorder involves severely impaired language development and is usually accompanied by severe or profound retardation. In a review of the literature, Van Acker (1991) noted the presence of associated symptoms including facial grimacing, teeth grinding, and breathing problems (e.g., hyperventilation, breath holding, and air swallowing).

Childhood Disintegrative Disorder

Childhood disintegrative disorder, also known as Heller syndrome, is characterized by an autistic-like condition that develops following at least a 2-year period of normal development (see Volkmar, 1992, for a review). DSM-IV criteria define childhood disintegrative disorder as a clinically significant loss of previously acquired skills before the age of 10 years in at least two of the following areas: expressive or receptive language, social skills or adaptive behaviors, bowel or bladder control, play, and motor skills. Prior to this loss of skills, the child must exhibit age-appropriate social, communicative, and play skills. Following this disintegrative period, the disorder is not distinguishable from autism. ICD-10 criteria are identical except that onset before 10 years of age is not stipulated.

In a review of the literature, Volkmar (1992) reported that the mean age of onset is 3.36 years with onset ranging from 1.2 to 9 years. He argued that this disorder is not simply a form of autism that is recognized later in life. In his study, children with autism that were not recognized as being delayed until after 2 years of age had developed limited speech and showed intact cognitive skills that tended to delay recognition of the autism. In contrast, the children diagnosed with childhood disintegrative disorder demonstrated a significant loss of previously acquired skills, and the majority had severe retardation. The majority of children reported in the literature (19 of 29 cases) spoke clearly in sentences prior to the onset of the disorder. Thus, childhood disintegrative disorder appears to represent a distinct disorder.

Atypical Autism/Pervasive Developmental Disorder, Not Otherwise Specified

ICD-10 includes a diagnosis of atypical autism for children who exhibit the symptoms of autism after the age of 3 years or for children who show autistic symptomatology but do not have impair-ments in all three of the areas required for a diagnosis of autism (social interaction, communication, repetitive behaviors or interests). DSM-IV includes a similar category but uses the label of pervasive developmental disorder, not otherwise specified.

Differential Diagnosis

Mental Retardation

Pervasive developmental disorders are defined in terms of behavior that is deviant in relation to mental age. Thus, although a majority of children with autism are retarded, the fact that at least a quarter of children with autism have normal intellectual ability indicates that autism and mental retardation are distinct disorders. Compared to children with mental retardation of a comparable developmental level, children with autism display specific impairments in joint attention, motor imitation, symbolic play, and theory-of-mind abilities. Simple motor stereotypies including self-injurious behaviors are observed both in children with autism and mental retardation and appear to be a function of mental age rather than diagnosis (Wing, 1978).

Developmental Language Disorders

The differential diagnosis between autism and developmental language disorders (e.g., expressive and mixed receptive–expressive language disorders; phonological disorder) may be difficult, especially in young children. However, Bartak, Rutter, and Cox (1975) and Cantwell et al. (1989) have documented that there are differences between these two disorders in terms of the type of language abnormalities, nonverbal communication, and social skills. Children with autism and developmental language disorder have similar delays in babbling, language acquisition, mean length of utterance, and grammatical complexity. However, children with autism show more deviant language development, including echolalia, pronoun reversal, stereotyped utterances, and metaphorical language. Also, children with autism are less likely to engage in spontaneous "chatting" conversation. Although articulation disorders are not common in verbal children with autism, children with developmental language disorders almost always show difficulties in articulation (Bishop, 1992). Compared to children with developmental language disorder, children with

autism show significantly more impairments in nonverbal communication including gesture and symbolic play (Bartak et al., 1975). Parents reported that approximately 57% of children with developmental language disorders used gesture at home, whereas only 11% of children with autism were reported to use gesture. Both children with autism and developmental language disorder show delayed symbolic play development. Riguet et al. (1981) reported that symbolic play in children with autism is more delayed than would be expected by their delayed language development. Children with autism also show more difficulty in social interactions including more gaze aversion, less group play, and more difficulty adapting to new situations (Bartak et al., 1975).

Childhood Schizophrenia

Autism and childhood schizophrenia are considered separate disorders (see J. R. Asarnow & R. F. Asarnow, Chapter 9, this volume). In his original description of autism, Kanner (1943) made the following distinction between the two disorders: "While the schizophrenic tries to solve his problem by stepping out of a world of which he has been a part and with which he has been in touch, our children gradually compromise by extending cautious feelers into a world in which they have been total strangers from the beginning" (p. 249).

Although both disorders are characterized by abnormal social interaction, childhood schizophrenia is differentiated from autism by a later age of onset (i.e., it rarely occurs prior to 7 years), less impaired intellectual abilities, the presence of hallucinations and delusions, and the tendency to experience periods of remission and relapse (Green et al., 1984; Kolvin, 1971; Rutter, 1978). Although the disorders are considered distinct, Petty, Ornitz, Michelman, and Zimmerman (1984) described three cases of children with diagnoses of autism who later received diagnoses of schizophrenia. Volkmar and Cohen (1991) reviewed case records of 163 adolescents and adults with histories of autism and reported only one concomitant diagnosis of schizophrenia. Thus, the rate of schizophrenia among individuals with autism is approximately 0.6%, which is comparable to the rate of schizophrenia in the general population.

DEVELOPMENTAL COURSE AND PROGNOSIS

Overall, the existing studies suggest that the prognosis for individuals with autism is poor with respect to academic achievement and independent living abilities. These studies pertain to individuals who probably have not received intensive early intervention, however. For many of those who do receive such intervention, the long-term prognosis may be more positive (see discussion below on early intervention).

There have been two recent studies examining outcome in a heterogeneous group of individuals with autism. Gillberg and Steffenburg (1987) conducted a population-based follow-up study of 23 young adults who had been diagnosed as having autism in childhood. At follow-up, 48% of individuals in this study were severely handicapped with no or limited independent living abilities. Seventeen percent had made social and educational progress, but only one individual was described as leading a normal social life with satisfactory employment.

Kobayashi, Murata, and Yoshinaga (1992) conducted a large-scale follow-up study of 197 young adults with autism who had received therapeutic services during their childhood years. Their outcome data were much more positive than the Gillberg and Steffenburg results, but overall the prognosis was poor. Kobayashi et al. (1992) reported that 27% of the individuals in their sample had achieved social independence (i.e., they were employed) or had a good chance for social independence (i.e., they were students at college or a technical school). The remaining 73% of their sample continued to need considerable supervision and were not employed. Only two individuals were living independently in an apartment. Approximately 47% of these young adults with autism had achieved a sufficient language ability that allowed them to communicate verbally with others.

Both Gillberg and Steffenburg (1987) and Kobayashi et al. (1992) noted that a significant percentage (31–57%) of individuals with autism showed a deterioration or aggravation of symptoms during adolescence. This deterioration was characterized by increased hyperactivity, aggression, ritualistic behavior and a loss of previously acquired language skills. Although some adolescents showed this deterioration concomitant with the onset of seizures, it was difficult to determine what precipitated the deterioration in the majority of

cases. Interestingly, Kobayashi et al. (1992) reported that adolescence could also be a period of positive change. Approximately 43% of parents in their study reported that their children showed remarkable improvements during adolescence.

Across a number of studies, the two best predictors of favorable outcome in autism are average intellectual abilities (e.g., IQ greater than 69) and the development of some communicative speech prior to 5 years of age (Gillberg & Steffenburg, 1987; Kobayashi et al., 1992; Szatmari, Bartolucci, Bremner, Bond, & Rich, 1989; Venter, Lord, & Schopler, 1992). Two recent studies have examined outcome in individuals with average intellectual abilities. Szatmari, Bartolucci, et al. (1989) followed a group of 16 high-functioning children diagnosed with autism into young adulthood. Although the majority of these individuals continued to have persistent social impairments, 50% of the sample had completed or were attending college and were engaged in full-time employment. Thirty-one percent were living independently. One person was married, and three additional individuals were participating in regular dating relationships.

Venter et al. (1992) conducted a follow-up study of a group of 58 high-functioning adolescents and young adults with autism. In comparison to similar follow-up studies conducted 20 years ago (Bartak & Rutter, 1976; Rutter & Bartak, 1973), Venter et al. (1992) reported higher levels of academic achievement including reading comprehension and arithmetic abilities. The authors suggest that improved academic abilities may be due to laws requiring education and treatment opportunities for all autistic children that were not available in the past. On average, the individuals in this study did not obtain academic abilities commensurate with their intellectual abilities; reading abilities were at the 8-year-old level, and mathematical abilities were limited to addition, subtraction, and simple multiplication. Also, their results were less optimistic in terms of social independence than the results reported by Szatmari, Bartolucci, et al. (1989). Venter et al. (1992) reported that only 27% of individuals over the age of 18 were employed at the time of follow-up, and only one man had completed a college degree.

Recent studies suggest that higher IQ, communicative language before age 5 years, and special education services are all associated with a better prognosis. As the diagnosis of autism can be made earlier than previously thought (e.g., by 2 to 3 years of age), it will be possible to implement more early interventions focusing on the development of communicative skills prior to entrance into elementary school.

EPIDEMIOLOGY: PREVALENCE AND INCIDENCE

Autism is a rare disorder. Historically, autism has been reported to occur in four to five cases per 10,000 persons (Lotter, 1966; Wing & Gould, 1979). However more recent research utilizing broader diagnostic criteria has produced higher prevalence rates ranging from 7 to 13 cases per 10,000 (Bryson et al., 1988; Steffenburg & Gillberg, 1986; Sugiyama & Abe, 1989). This increased prevalence rate is presumably due to a combination of broader diagnostic criteria as well as improved awareness and recognition of the disorder.

Sex Differences

Autism occurs more frequently in male individuals with approximately three or four males for every one female with autism (Bryson et al., 1988; Steffenburg & Gillberg, 1986; Volkmar, Szatmari, & Sparrow, 1993). Several researchers have reported that females with autism tend to receive lower scores on both verbal and nonverbal measures of intelligence (Bryson et al., 1988; Konstantareas, Homatidis, & Busch, 1989; Steffenburg & Gillberg, 1986; Volkmar et al., 1993). In a recent study, Volkmar et al. (1993) found that in their sample there were proportionately more females with autism in the severely retarded range (IQ below 35), and males with autism were 8.8 times more likely to have normal intellectual ability.

There have been conflicting reports about whether males and females differ in terms of severity of autistic symptomatology. Konstantareas and colleagues (1989) reported that girls with autism showed more severe autistic symptomatology including more impaired social relationships, increased inappropriate body use, more disturbed auditory sensitivity, and poorer nonverbal communication. However, these differences disappeared when intellectual differences between males and females were taken into account. More recently, McLennan, Lord, and Schopler (1993) reported that among a group of high-functioning persons

with autism (IQ greater than 60), parents rated males as more severely autistic than females, especially prior to 5 years of age. Taken together, these studies suggest that females with autism tend to be more severely retarded and thus have increased symptoms associated with autism. However, females with autism who do not have any retardation may be less impaired than males without retardation. This is an interesting area that will need to be further researched.

Social Class

Kanner's original sample consisted primarily of professional families from upper-class backgrounds (Kanner, 1943). As a result, clinicians initially believed that autism was caused by cold, rejecting parents from wealthy families (Bettelheim, 1967). However, it is believed that earlier reports of increased rates of autism in families with upper socioeconomic status resulted from the fact that these families were most able to afford treatment services for their children. Empirical research has revealed that the social class distribution of families with autistic children is similar to the distribution of social class within the general population (Schopler, Andrews, & Strupp, 1979; Steffenburg & Gillberg, 1986; Wing & Gould, 1979).

Cultural Factors

Autism is known to affect individuals throughout the world. Epidemiological research has been conducted in Canada (Bryson et al., 1988), England (Wing & Gould, 1979), France (Cialdella & Mamelle, 1989), Sweden (Steffenburg & Gillberg, 1986), Japan (Sugiyama & Abe, 1989), and Hong Kong (Chung, Luk, & Lee, 1990). Recently, brief reports from Eastern Europe including Russia (Lebedinskaya & Nikolskaya, 1993) and Croatia (Bujas-Petkovic, 1993) have been published. Across all of these studies, there is remarkable consistency in reports of prevalence, intellectual abilities, gender differences, and social class factors associated with autism.

ETIOLOGY

Genetic Factors

The results of both family and twin studies suggest that genetic factors play a role in the etiology of autism and other pervasive developmen-

tal disorders. Across several epidemiological studies, the pooled frequency of autism in siblings of autistic children was approximately 3% (Smalley, Asarnow, & Spence, 1988). This is approximately 50 times greater than the prevalence of autism in the general population. If the entire range of pervasive developmental disorders are examined, the prevalence rate in siblings is even higher, approximately 5% (Szatmari et al., 1993). Three epidemiological same-sex twin studies have reported concordance rates for monozygotic twins ranging from 36% to 91% (Folstein & Rutter, 1977; Rutter et al., 1990; Steffenburg et al., 1989). There was not a single pair of dizygotic twins concordant for autism in any of these studies. These data are strongly suggestive of a genetic transmission for at least some cases of autism.

Rutter and colleagues (Bolton & Rutter, 1990; Folstein & Rutter, 1977; Rutter et al., 1990) have suggested that a broader phenotype of cognitive and social impairments may aggregate in families with an autistic child. Indeed, Folstein and Rutter (1977) and Rutter et al. (1990) reported an 82% to 86% concordance rate of cognitive abnormalities in monozygotic twins with an autistic proband and a 9% to 10% concordance rate of general cognitive impairments in dizygotic twins with an autistic proband. Cognitive impairments (e.g., developmental disorders of speech, language, or reading) have been reported in approximately 15% to 25% of siblings of autistic children (Baird & August, 1985; Bartak et al., 1975; Bolton & Rutter, 1990). Bolton and Rutter (1990) reported that 12% of siblings of autistic children showed impairments in reciprocal social interaction compared to no siblings of Down syndrome children.

In a recent study, Szatmari et al. (1993) examined social, communicative, and cognitive abilities in siblings of children with pervasive developmental disorders compared to siblings of children with either Down syndrome or low birth weight. They excluded siblings with any type of pervasive developmental disorder other than autism (e.g., Asperger syndrome and PDD-NOS). Contrary to previous findings, they did not find an increased rate of cognitive or social problems in siblings. The authors suggested that previous studies indicating a high rate of impairments in siblings may have failed to exclude siblings with pervasive developmental disorders other than autism. Although, pervasive developmental disorders do appear to be genetically determined in some families, the question of whether there is a phenotypic transmission of cognitive, linguistic,

and social impairments that may take the form of autism needs further investigation.

Several specific genetic disorders, including fragile X syndrome, phenylketonuria (PKU), and tuberous sclerosis, have been associated with autism (see Folstein & Rutter, 1987, for a review of the research). The relationship between fragile X syndrome and autism has been studied extensively. Data pooled from a number of studies indicate that the fragile X anomaly is found in approximately 8% of individuals with autism (Smalley et al., 1988). This rate is equivalent to the rate of fragile X syndrome in mentally retarded males and suggests that the fragile X gene is associated more with mental retardation than autism per se. Similarly, the rates of other genetic disorders such as phenylketonuria and tuberous sclerosis are quite low and cannot fully account for the cause of autism.

Prenatal and Perinatal Complications

Numerous researchers have examined the relationship between pre- and perinatal complications and autism. In a review of the literature, Tsai (1987) concluded that increased maternal age (greater than 35 years), bleeding after the first trimester, use of prescription medication, and meconium in the amniotic fluid were seen more frequently in children with autism compared to siblings or normally developing control children. However, these findings were not supported by Lord, Mulloy, Wendelboe, and Schopler (1991) in their study of high-functioning (IQ greater than 50) children with autism. In this study, there was a slight increase in the rate of prenatal difficulties in children with autism compared to their siblings, but this increase was not as large as indicated by previous research. The only two factors that were more common in children with autism were gestational age greater than 42 weeks and the tendency of the child with autism to be either first-born or fourth- or later-born. Taken together, these results suggest that pre- and perinatal complications may be more associated with mental retardation than with autism per se.

BIOLOGICAL BASIS OF AUTISM

Biochemical Findings

No specific biochemical markers for autism have been identified. Researchers have examined serotonin, dopamine, norepinephrine, and brain opioids in individuals with autism, but they have found inconsistent results (see Volkmar and Anderson, 1989, for a review of the research). The lack of consistent results possibly stems from methodological differences in whether peripheral or central levels of neurotransmitter were measured, from the lack of careful control for level of mental retardation, and from the relatively small samples that have been studied. It is important for additional work to continue in this area to isolate possible biochemical markers. A brief review of the research findings to date is provided below.

Serotonin

The neurotransmitter serotonin has been linked to the behavioral–physiological processes of sleep, pain and sensory perception, motor function, appetite, learning, and memory (Volkmar & Anderson, 1989). The most consistent biochemical finding related to autism has been that between 30% and 50% of individuals with autism are hyperserotonemic; that is, their peripheral blood platelet levels are in the upper 5% of levels found in the normal population (Geller, Ritvo, Freeman, & Yuwiler, 1982; Schain & Freedman, 1961). Research examining the mechanism for hyperserotonemia has indicated that there may be an increased level of platelet uptake or platelet storage of serotonin (Katsui, Okuda, Usuda, & Koizumi, 1986; Rotman, Caplan, & Szekely, 1980). The link between increased serotonin and the behavioral symptoms of autism are unknown. A multicenter study of fenfluramine, a stimulant medication that reduces systemic levels of serotonin, yielded inconclusive results. Overall, fenfluramine was not found to have a consistent effect on IQ, social responsiveness, or communication skills, but it may be effective in reducing hyperactivity in some children with autism (du Verglas, Banks, & Guyer, 1988). However, mentally retarded nonautistic individuals have also been reported to have elevated levels of serotonin (Anderson & Hoshino, 1987). Thus, hyperserotonemia may be related to mental retardation rather than autism per se.

Dopamine

The neurotransmitter dopamine has been linked to the presence of stereotyped and repetitive behaviors. Major tranquilizers that decrease dopamine levels by blocking dopamine receptors tend

to decrease stereotyped behaviors in persons with autism (Mikkelsen, 1982). Conversely, stimulant medications that increase dopamine levels have been associated with increased stereotyped behavior in persons with autism (Mikkelsen, 1982). Theoretically, increased levels of dopamine may play a role in the stereotyped behavior observed in autism. This theory was supported by the Garreau et al. (1980) finding that persons with autism have elevated urinary levels of homovanillic acid (HVA), a metabolite of dopamine. However, studies of cerebrospinal fluid levels of HVA have not consistently reported elevations. Research on levels of HVA in persons with autism has failed to differentiate between persons with autism and persons with other psychiatric impairments (Gillberg, Svennerholm, & Hamilton-Hellberg, 1983; Young, Kavanagh, Anderson, Shaywitz, & Cohen, 1982). That is, elevated dopamine levels may be indicative of psychotic disorders in general rather than be specific to autism.

Norepinephrine

Norepinephrine, a neurotransmitter and a hormone, is influential in respiratory and cardiac function, attention, arousal, memory, anxiety, and movement (Volkmar & Anderson, 1989). Because of the increased arousal and anxiety symptoms associated with autism, there has been considerable interest in the possible link between autism and an elevation of norepinephrine. However, research examining peripheral and central amounts of norepinephrine and its metabolite, 3-methoxy-4-hydroxyphenylglycol (MHPG), has not found consistent evidence in support of abnormal levels of norepinephrine in persons with autism (Gillberg et al., 1983; Young et al., 1981).

Endogenous Opioids

Endogenous opioid peptides (endorphins) have been implicated in the regulation of pain perception, social and emotional behaviors, and motor activity (Panksepp & Sahley, 1987). Self-injurious behaviors have been associated with increased levels of endogenous opioids that decrease pain sensitivity (Sandman et al., 1983). Based on this finding, Panksepp and colleagues (Panksepp, 1979; Panksepp & Sahley, 1987) proposed that self-injurious behaviors as well as social and cognitive impairment in autism may be linked to an elevation in endogenous opioids. However, there is little empirical evidence directly supporting elevated

endogenous opioids in autism (Panksepp & Sahley, 1987). Support for the endorphin theory of autism comes from clinical evidence that opiate agonists (e.g., naltrexone and naloxone) reduce self-injurious behaviors in some persons with autism (Campbell, Overall, Small, & Sokol, 1989; Walters, Barrett, Feinstein, Mercurio, & Hole, 1990). However, in a recent double-blind, placebo-controlled study with a group of 41 autistic children, Campbell et al. (1993) reported that naltrexone did not have any effect on the core symptoms of autism. Self-injurious behaviors decreased, but not significantly. Hyperactivity was the only symptom that was significantly reduced by naltrexone. Further research is needed to verify whether there is a relationship between autism and elevated endogenous opioids.

Neuroanatomical Findings

Several promising findings have recently been reported by researchers examining possible neuroanatomical abnormalities in autism. These findings are from studies using magnetic resonance imaging and brain autopsies, as well as from animal models of autism. Although few of these findings have been replicated, the majority are pointing toward developmental malformations during early brain development in persons with autism.

Magnetic Resonance Imaging

Courchesne and colleagues (Courchesne, Yeung-Courchesne, Press, Hesselink, & Jernigan, 1988) conducted magnetic resonance imaging (MRI) scans on 18 persons with autism ranging in age from 6 to 30 years. They reported that, compared to a group of nonautistic persons with normal MRI scans, 14 of the individuals with autism displayed hypoplasia of cerebellar vermal lobules VI and VII. Eleven of the persons with autism who had diminished cerebellum size had intellectual abilities within the average range. Therefore, cerebellar hypoplasia does not appear to be associated with mental retardation. Additionally, no abnormalities were evident in the pons or the midbrain, suggesting that cerebellar hypoplasia is not associated with anatomical abnormalities of the major input and output pathways to the cerebellum (Hsu, Yeung-Courchesne, Courchesne, & Press, 1991). The authors speculated that cerebellar hypoplasia may result from maldevelopment within the cerebellum rather than an atrophy following a period of normal development.

If neural output from the cerebellum is damaged as a result of this maldevelopment, there may be subsequent abnormal development and functioning in neuronal systems that are directly connected to the cerebellum including systems regulating attention, sensory modulation, autonomic activity, and motor and behavior initiation (Courchesne et al., 1988). These systems have been implicated in the etiology of autism. Although promising, these results have not been consistently replicated (Garber & Ritvo, 1992; Kleiman, Neff, & Rosman, 1992).

Other researchers have documented an enlargement of the fourth ventricle in autism (Gaffney, Kuperman, Tsai, Minchin, & Hassanein, 1987). However, recent studies have not confirmed this result (Garber & Ritvo, 1992; Kleiman et al., 1992).

Several studies have used MRI scans to examine malformations in the cerebral cortex of individuals with autism. Piven et al. (1990) reported cortical malformations in seven of their 13 high-functioning autistic subjects. These abnormalities included polymicrogyria, macrogyria, and schizencephaly and were located in a variety of different brain locations in both hemispheres. The authors believed that these malformations resulted from a defect in the migration of neurons to the cerebral cortex during the first 6 months of prenatal development. Courchesne, Press, and Yeung-Courchesne (1993) noted more localized malformations in their study of 21 persons with autism. They reported reduced volume in the parietal lobes (e.g., cortical volume loss and thinning of the corpus callosum) in nine (43%) of their subjects. These abnormalities could result from either early-onset developmental malformations or from late-onset progressive atrophy. While intriguing, neither of these results have been replicated, and further research is needed to determine whether cortical abnormalities are associated with autism.

Autopsy Studies

Consistent with abnormal cerebellum development, postmortem studies have revealed Purkinje and granule cell loss in the neocerebellum (Bauman & Kemper, 1985; Ritvo et al., 1986). Increased cell-packing density in limbic structures (e.g., the hippocampus and amygdala) have also been noted (Bauman & Kemper, 1988). Thus far, autopsy studies support an abnormality in subcortical structures and have not found any abnormalities in the cerebral cortex in autism.

Animal Models

Bachevalier (1991, 1994) proposed an animal model for childhood autism, purporting that monkeys with lesions in the medial temporal lobe (e.g., the amygdala and hippocampus) show autistic-like behaviors including failure to develop normal social relationships, blank facial expressions, poor body language, lack of eye contact, and motor stereotypies.Interestingly, when specific lesions were made in either the amygdala or the hippocampus, persistent disturbances in social interactions were only noted in the monkeys with lesions in the amygdala (Bachevalier, 1994). However, the most severe autistic-like behaviors were observed in monkeys with combined damage to both the amygdala and hippocampus. This finding suggests that less severe forms of autism may result from damage to the amygdala, whereas more severe forms of autism including mental retardation may require damage to both the amygdala and the hippocampus. This anatomical model is supported by previous research findings of subcortical anatomic abnormalities in autism. Importantly, this model explains the relationship between subcortical abnormalities and behaviors observed in autism and distinguishes between severe and mild forms of autism.

Positron Emission Tomography Studies

Studies using positron emission tomography (PET) to examine brain function have found hyper- or hypofrontality, atypical asymmetries in the frontal and temporal lobes and basal ganglia, and lowered correlations between activity in the frontal and other brain regions (Buchsbaum et al., 1992; DeVolder, Bol, Michel, Congneau, & Goffinet, 1987; George, Costa, Kouris, Ring, & Ell, 1992; Rumsey et al., 1985). Taken together, the evidence gathered thus far suggests that autistic persons suffer from dysfunction of a complex brain system involving the frontal lobe and functionally related cortical and subcortical structures.

Cortical Electroencephalographic Findings

Quantitative Electroencephalographic Analyses

Several studies have examined patterns of brain activity in individuals with autism using quantitative electroencephalographic (EEG) analyses.

Two studies examined brain activity during the administration of cognitive tasks (Dawson, Warrenburg, & Fuller, 1982, 1983). These studies found that, as compared to chronological age-matched, normally developing controls, individuals with autism showed atypical patterns of hemispheric activation during language and motor imitation tasks, characterized by greater right than left hemisphere activation. Two additional studies examined patterns of brain activity in children with autism during an alert, resting state. Cantor, Thatcher, Hrybyk, and Kaye (1986) found that children with autism showed less inter- and intra-hemispheric asymmetry than either normally developing or mentally retarded children, a finding that these authors interpreted as diminished cortical differentiation in autism. More recently, in a study using EEG to measure brain activity in groups of autistic and developmentally matched normal children, Dawson and her colleagues (Dawson, Klinger, Panagiotides, Lewy, & Castelloe, 1995) found that children with autism exhibited reduced EEG power in the frontal and temporal regions, but not in the parietal region. Differences were more prominent in the left than the right hemisphere.

Event-Related Potential Studies

Event-related potential (ERP) studies in autism have examined neural activity in response to a variety of discrete stimuli. The P3 component of the ERP is considered to be a measure of attention to novel, unpredictable stimuli. Across several studies, individuals with autism have been shown to display a reduced P3 component of the ERP (Courchesne, Lincoln, Kilman, & Galambos, 1985; Dawson, Finley, Phillips, Galpert, & Lewy, 1988; Novick, Kurtzberg, & Vaughn, 1979; Novick, Vaughn, Kurtzberg, & Simson, 1980). The question of whether the reduced P3 is more apparent for certain stimuli (e.g., social) versus other stimuli has not been addressed. Persons with autism show a larger P3 response to novel (rare) stimuli than to background (frequent) stimuli, suggesting that although the P3 is reduced, this does not indicate that persons with autism are unable to detect novel stimuli (Courchesne, 1987; Dawson et al., 1988).

Consistent with his hypothesis of an impaired attention mechanism in persons with autism, Courchesne and colleagues (Courchesne et al., 1994) reported abnormal ERPs in persons with autism during an attention-shifting paradigm. Subjects were required to shift attention from one sensory modality to another following the detection of a target stimulus. Compared to normally developing individuals, persons with autism exhibited significantly reduced ERP responses following the detection of a cue to shift attention.

NEUROPSYCHOLOGICAL PERSPECTIVES

Neuropsychological studies of individuals with autism have been conducted for well over a decade, and quite a lot is known about the neuropsychology of autism. Table 8.2 provides a summary of the neuropsychological findings in autism. Two general conclusions can be derived from these findings: First, individuals with autism show impairments in a wide range of domains, including attention, memory, language, and executive functions. Thus, it is probable that brain dysfunction in autism involves a distributed brain system rather than one specific brain locus. Second, in every domain, except perhaps executive functions, impairments are not found across the board. Instead, in most domains, some functions are spared. These findings suggest that autism is restricted to dysfunction of some brain systems and not others.

Another interesting finding to emerge from the neuropsychological literature is the great deal of heterogeneity that exists in certain domains. Whereas virtually all, if not all, individuals with autism have impairments in executive functions associated with the prefrontal cortex, large individual differences exist in the domains of memory and language (and perhaps, attention). In the area of language, for example, approximately 50% of individuals with autism remain mute, whereas others have only mild language difficulties. In the area of memory, lower-functioning individuals show a pattern of memory deficits that is similar, although not identical, to persons with amnesia who have damage to subcortical brain structures (amygdala and hippocampus). Namely, they show difficulties in acquiring new information, yes/no recognition, and other aspects of declarative memory while having relatively intact nondeclarative memory abilities (e.g., discrimination learning and operant conditioning) (Barth & Fein, 1995). Higher-functioning individuals, on the other hand, have much more subtle memory impairments that are more likely to be associated

TABLE 8.2. Neuropsychological Findings in Autism

Domain	Impaired function	Spared function
Intelligence	Verbal, abstract, sequential	Visuospatial organization
Attention	Orienting Shifting/disengaging Selective attention	Sustained attention
Memory		
High functioning	Mild long-term memory, especially complex information	Paired associate learning
	Strategies for encoding complex information	Auditory rote memory
	Sequential, abstract information	Cued recall
Low functioning	Short- and long-term memory Declarative memory	Discrimination learning Operant learning
Language		
High functioning	Pragmatics Prosody Comprehension of complex verbal information	Phonology Syntax
Low functioning	Severe expressive and receptive language (e.g., mutism)	
Executive functions	Working memory Inhibition Planning/organization Flexibility/set shifting	

with higher cortical functions. Such impairments include mild long-term memory impairments for complex, meaningful material and poor strategies for encoding complex material (Ameli et al., 1988; Minshew & Goldstein, 1993).

Another important finding is that, for virtually all domains tested, persons with autism have more difficulty processing social information, as compared to nonsocial information (cf., Dawson, 1991; Dawson et al., 1995). For example, persons with autism are much less likely to orient to social than nonsocial stimuli, they have more difficulty imitating body actions than toy actions, they have more difficulty with the social aspects of language (pragmatics) than the more formal aspects (syntax), and so on. These findings have led some investigators to question whether autism involves a dysfunction of a brain system that is specialized for social cognition.

Animal studies (e.g., Bachevalier, 1994) and brain damage literature (e.g., Damasio, 1994) have led some investigators to suggest that there indeed exists a brain system specialized for social cognition (limbic system). As eloquently described in a recent book by Damasio (1994) and

in the writings of Brothers and Ring (1993), the amygdala and hippocampus and the adjacent cortical brain regions seem very likely candidates for such a system. For example, the amygdala has been shown to be sensitive to the perception of body movements and cross-modal associations, both of which are critical for motor imitation (Nahm, Tranel, Damasio, & Damasio, 1993). Based on a clinical case involving bilateral lesion of the amygdala (Adolphs, Tranel, Damasio, & Damasio, 1994), it has been shown that this brain structure is specialized for the perception of emotion. In addition to the amygdala and adjacent cortical regions, the entire medial temporal lobe, including the hippocampus, and aspects of the frontal lobe (e.g., orbital frontal region) are likely to be part of a brain system specialized for social cognition (Damasio, 1994).

Based on an animal model of autism, Bachevalier (1994) has proposed that individuals with extensive involvement of this system, including dysfunction of both the hippocampus and amygdala, will show more severe memory and social impairments than those with selective damage of only the amygdala. In fact, Barth and Fein (1995)

document distinct memory profiles in low- versus high-functioning individuals with autism. Low-functioning, but not high-functioning, children with autism had difficulty compared to matched controls on a visual recognition memory task sensitive to hippocampal/amygdala damage.

Other evidence supporting the existence of at least two, if not three, subgroups of persons with autism is accumulating. Rapin (in press) found evidence of discontinuity in functioning levels of a large sample of children with pervasive developmental disorder and concluded that there exists two distinct subgroups. Based on a large-scale epidemiological study, Wing and Gould (1979) proposed that there are three subgroups of autism. Focusing on variations in social behavior, Wing and Gould (1979) characterized the three groups as (1) aloof/withdrawn, (2) passive, and (3) actively social-but-odd. Castelloe and Dawson (1993) validated this subgroup classification system by demonstrating the existence of clusters of cognitive, language, and social symptoms as predicted by Wing and Gould (1979). In addition, Dawson et al. (1995) found that children classified as passive versus active-but-odd showed distinct patterns of EEG activity.

In summary, the neuropsychological evidence suggests that autism involves a distributed brain system that is specialized for social cognition. In particular, the medial temporal lobe and orbital frontal region are receiving increasing attention as a possible neural substrate for autism. Furthermore, large-scale studies have suggested the possibility of distinct subgroups of autism that have been hypothesized to differ in the extent and degree of limbic system dysfunction.

FUTURE DIRECTIONS

Early Diagnosis

Parents of children with autism often report that they were concerned about their child's development prior to one year of age and expressed this concern to their pediatrician by 18 months of age (Siegel, Pilner, Eschler, & Elliot, 1988). However, on average, a diagnosis of autism is not given until 4 years of age (Siegel et al., 1988). Recent research has focused on the recognition and diagnosis of autism in the first few years of life. Osterling and Dawson (1994) analyzed home videotapes of first birthday parties of children who

later received a diagnosis of autism. Compared to normally developing one-year-old children, children with autism showed significantly fewer social and joint attention behaviors including: pointing, showing an object to another person, looking at the face of another person, and orienting to their name being called. Ninety-one percent of the children who later received a diagnosis of autism could be correctly diagnosed at 1 year of age based on these behaviors. Interestingly, self-stimulatory behaviors did not differentiate between autistic and normally developing one-year-old children. Stone and Hogan (1993) suggested that ritualized behaviors including the need for routine and sameness may emerge later in the course of autism and may be more apparent in older children compared to younger ones. Thus, symptoms of autism are present from the first year of life, and early social behaviors seem to be the best indicators of a later diagnosis of autism. It is likely that detection of autism during the first 2 years of life will be possible in the very near future. As early detection becomes more likely, investigators will increasingly focus on the development of methods for early intervention, as discussed below.

Early Intervention

It is commonly believed that early diagnosis is essential because it allows for earlier intervention and therefore a better prognosis for individuals with pervasive developmental disorders. With the advent of better diagnostic instruments and a better ability to recognize autism within the first 2 years of life, there will be a greater demand for interventions designed for toddlers and preschoolers. Indeed, it is becoming increasingly more common for the authors to receive phone calls requesting diagnostic and treatment services for children as young as 20 months of age. Because of the devastating nature of the disorder, parents have shown a willingness to try any possible treatment approach, and research needs to be conducted that critically examines the effectiveness of different research programs and provides parents with a checklist of the most important components of early-intervention programs.

In a review of eight different university-based intervention programs for children with autism in the United States, Dawson and Osterling (in press) reported that the majority of these intervention programs have demonstrated effectiveness as mea-

sured by approximately 50% of children who received intervention services being placed in regular education elementary school classrooms (Anderson, Campbell, & Cannon, 1994; Handleman & Harris, 1994; Lord & Schopler, 1994; Lovaas, 1987; McClannahan & Krantz, 1994; McGee, Daly, & Jacobs, 1994; Rogers & DiLalla, 1991; Strain & Cordisco, 1994). Across these programs, IQ score improvements ranging from 19 to 30 points were noted, with an average IQ gain of 23 points. Investigators did not report whether a positive response to intervention was related to specific child characteristics, such as IQ or language ability. It should be noted, however, that the average full-scale IQ of children participating in the programs fell in the moderately mentally retarded range and that all children scored in the mentally retarded range (70 or below) at the beginning of intervention. Thus, despite having autism and considerable mental delay, approximately half of the children responded very positively to early intervention, and all children reportedly made substantial gains.

Dawson and Osterling (in press) identified several elements that were common to early-intervention programs for children with autism, which are listed below:

1. A curriculum that focused on the areas of attention and compliance, motor imitation, communication, appropriate use of toys, and social skills.
2. The need for highly structured teaching environments with a low student-to-staff ratio.
3. Systematic strategies for generalizing newly acquired skills to a wide range of situations.
4. Need for predictability and routine in the daily schedule.
5. A functional approach to problem behaviors (Donnellan et al., 1984).
6. A focus on skills needed for successful transitions from the early-intervention program to the regular preschool or kindergarten classroom.
7. A high level of family involvement.

Dawson and Osterling (in press) argued that there is a serious gap between the state of our knowledge of early-intervention methods for children with autism and the methods actually used in most public school systems. They proposed that one of the most important goals for researchers in the field of autism is to become more effective communicators of our current knowledge to parents, teachers, and other service providers.

CONCLUSIONS

The past decade has witnessed substantial progress in our understanding and treatment of young children with autism. In particular, important strides have been made in the areas of early identification, description of early social characteristics, and early-intervention methods.

In addition, neuropsychological studies have increased our understanding of the wide range of impairments shown by individuals with autism and yielded evidence of distinct subgroups that may have different neuropsychological profiles. Development of neuropsychological tests that are appropriate for very young children with autism are very likely to yield new insights into the neuropsychology of autism. When combined with our ability to detect autism at an early age, subgroup identification may lead to more individualized treatment strategies.

Genetic studies are under way, and it is expected that our understanding of the genetic basis of autism will increase in the near future, especially in light of more sophisticated genetic methods, such as linkage analysis. In addition, techniques for measuring brain anatomy and brain function, including functional MRI and improved PET methods, hold promise for increasing our understanding of the neurological basis of this disorder.

ACKNOWLEDGMENTS

We wish to thank Sarah Sirbasku and Beverly Thorn for their helpful comments on earlier versions of this chapter. Also, we would like to thank the children with autism and their families who have eagerly participated in research and provided the clinical insights that we have described in this chapter.

REFERENCES

Adolphs, R., Tranel, D., Damasio, H., & Damasio, A. (1994). Impaired recognition of emotion in facial expressions following bilateral damage to the human amygdala. *Nature, 372,* 669–672.

Ainsworth, M. D. (1983). Patterns of infant–mother attachment as related to maternal care: Their early history and

their contribution to continuity. In D. Magnusson & V. Allen (Eds.), *Human development: An interactional perspective* (pp. 35–55). New York: Academic Press.

Ainsworth, M. D., Blehar, M. D., Waters, E., & Wall, S. (1978). *Patterns of attachment: A psychological study of the strange situation.* Hillsdale, NJ: Erlbaum.

Ameli, R., Courchesne, E., Lincoln, A., Kaufman, A. S., & Grillon, C. (1988). Visual memory processes in high-functioning individuals with autism. *Journal of Autism and Developmental Disorders, 18,* 601–615.

American Psychiatric Association. (1987). *Diagnostic and statistical manual of mental disorders* (3rd ed., rev.). Washington, DC: Author.

American Psychiatric Association. (1994). *Diagnostic and statistical manual of mental disorders* (4th ed.). Washington, DC: Author.

Anderson, G. M., & Hoshino, Y. (1987). Neurochemical studies of autism. In D. J. Cohen & A. Donnellan (Eds.), *Handbook of autism and pervasive developmental disorders* (pp. 166–191). New York: Wiley.

Anderson, S. R., Campbell, S., & Cannon, B. O. (1994). The May Center for early childhood education. In S. Harris & J. Handleman (Eds.), *Preschool education programs for children with autism* (pp. 15–36). Austin, TX: Pro-ed.

Asperger, H. (1991). "Autistic psychopathy" in childhood. In U. Frith (Ed. and Trans.), *Autism and Asperger syndrome* (pp. 37–92). Cambridge, UK: Cambridge University Press. (Original work published 1944)

Bachevalier, J. (1991). An animal model for childhood autism: Memory loss and socioemotional disturbances following neonatal damage to the limbic system in monkeys. In C. A. Tamminga & S. C. Schulz (Eds.), *Advances in neuropsychiatry and psychopharmacology: Vol. 1. Schizophrenia research* (pp. 129–140). New York: Raven Press.

Bachevalier, J. (1994). Medial temporal lobe structures and autism: A review of clinical and experimental findings. *Neuropsychologia, 32,* 627–648.

Baird, T. D., & August, G. J. (1985). Familial heterogeneity in infantile autism. *Journal of Autism and Developmental Disorders, 15,* 315–321.

Baron-Cohen, S. (1989). The autistic child's theory of mind: A case of specific developmental delay. *Journal of Child Psychology and Psychiatry, 30,* 285–297.

Baron-Cohen, S., Leslie, A. M., & Frith, U. (1985). Does the autistic child have a "theory of mind"? *Cognition, 21,* 37–46.

Bartak, L., & Rutter, M. (1976). Differences between mentally retarded and normally intelligent autistic children. *Journal of Autism and Childhood Schizophrenia, 6,* 109–120.

Bartak, L., Rutter, M. L., & Cox, A. (1975). A comparative study of infantile autism and specific developmental language disorder: I. The children. *British Journal of Psychiatry, 126,* 127–145.

Barth, C., & Fein, D. (1995). Delayed match to sample performance in autistic children. *Developmental Neuropsychology, 11*(1), 53–59.

Bauman, M., & Kemper, T. (1985). Histoanatomic observations of the brain in early infantile autism. *Neurology, 35,* 866–874.

Bauman, M., & Kemper, T. (1988). Limbic and cerebellar abnormalities: Consistent findings in infantile autism. *Journal of Neuropathology and Experimental Neurology, 47,* 369.

Bettelheim, B. (1967). *The empty fortress: Infantile autism and the birth of self.* New York: Free Press.

Bishop, D. V. (1992). The underlying nature of specific language impairment. *Journal of Child Psychology and Psychiatry, 33,* 3–66.

Bleuler, E. (1950). *Dementia praecox or a group within the schizophrenias* (J. Zinkin, Trans.). New York: International Universities Press. (Original work published in 1911)

Bolton, P., & Rutter, M. (1990). Genetic influences in autism. *International Review of Psychiatry, 2,* 67–80.

Boucher, J. (1981). Immediate free recall in early childhood autism: Another point of behavioral similarity with amnesic syndrome. *British Journal of Psychology, 72,* 211–215.

Boucher, J., & Warrington, E. K. (1976). Memory deficits in early infantile autism: Some similarities to the amnesic syndrome. *British Journal of Psychology, 67,* 73–87.

Brothers, L., & Ring, B. (1993). Mesial temporal neurons in the macaque monkey with responses selective for aspects of social stimuli. *Behavioral Brain Research, 57,* 53–61.

Bruner, J. (1975). From communication to language: A psychological perspective. *Cognition, 3,* 255–287.

Bryson, S. E., Clark, B. S., & Smith, I. M. (1988). First report of a Canadian epidemiological study of autistic syndromes. *Journal of Child Psychology and Psychiatry, 29,* 433–445.

Buchsbaum, M. S., Siegel, B. V., Wu, J. C., Hazlett, E., Sicotte, N., Haier, R., Tanguay, P., Asarnow, R., Cadorette, T., Donoghue, D., Lagunas-Solar, M., Lott, I., Paek, J., & Sabalesky, D. (1992). Attention and performance in autism and regional brain metabolic rate assessed by positron emission tomography. *Journal of Autism and Developmental Disorders, 22,* 115–126.

Bujas-Petkovic, Z. (1993). The three-dimensional modeling ability of a boy with autism [Letter to the editor]. *Journal of Autism and Developmental Disorders, 23,* 569–571.

Burack, J. A. (1992). Debate and argument: Clarifying developmental issues in the study of autism. *Journal of Child Psychology and Psychiatry, 33,* 617–621.

Campbell, M., Anderson, L. T., Small, A. M., Adams, P., Gonzalez, N. M., & Ernst, M. (1993). Naltrexone in autistic children: Behavioral symptoms and attentional learning. *Journal of the American Academy of Child and Adolescent Psychiatry, 32,* 1283–1291.

Campbell, M., Overall, J. E., Small, A. M., & Sokol, M. S. (1989). Naltrexone in autistic children: An acute open dose range tolerance trial. *Journal of the American Academy of Child and Adolescent Psychiatry, 28,* 200–206.

Cantor, D. S., Thatcher, R. W., Hrybyk, M., & Kaye, H. (1986). Computerized EEG analyses of autistic children. *Journal of Autism and Developmental Disorders, 16,* 169–188.

Cantwell, D. P., Baker, L., Rutter, M., & Mawhood, L. (1989). Infantile autism and developmental receptive dysphasia: A comparative follow-up into middle childhood. *Journal of Autism and Developmental Disorders, 19,* 19–31.

Capps, L., Sigman, M., & Mundy, P. (1994). Attachment security in children with autism. *Development and Psychopathology, 6,* 249–261.

Castelloe, P., & Dawson, G. (1993). Subclassification of children with autism and pervasive developmental disorder: A questionnaire based on Wing's subgrouping scheme. *Journal of Autism and Developmental Disorders, 23,* 229–241.

Chung, S. Y., Luk, S. L., & Lee, P. W. H. (1990). A follow-up study of infantile autism in Hong Kong. *Journal of Autism and Developmental Disorders, 20,* 221–232.

Cialdella, P., & Mamelle, N. (1989). An epidemiological study of infantile autism in a French department (Rhone): A research note. *Journal of Child Psychology and Psychiatry, 30,* 165–175.

Cohen, D. J., Paul, R., & Volkmar, F. R. (1987). Issues in the classification of pervasive developmental disorders and associated conditions. In D. J. Cohen, A. M. Donnellan, & R. Paul (Eds.), *Handbook of autism and pervasive developmental disorders* (pp. 221–243). New York: Wiley.

Courchesne, E. (1987). A neurophysiological view of autism. In E. Schopler & G. B. Mesibov (Eds.), *Neurobiological issues in autism* (pp. 285–324). New York: Plenum Press.

Courchesne, E., Lincoln, A. J., Kilman, B. A., & Galambos, R. (1985). Event-related brain potential correlates of the processing of novel visual and auditory information in autism. *Journal of Autism and Developmental Disorders, 15,* 55–75.

Courchesne, E., Press, G. A., & Yeung-Courchesne, R. (1993). Parietal lobe abnormalities detected with magnetic resonance in patients with infantile autism. *American Journal of Roentgenology, 160,* 387–393.

Courchesne, E., Townsend, J. P., Akshoomoff, N. A., Yeung-Courchesne, R., Press, G. A., Murakami, J. W., Lincoln, A. J., James, H. E., Saitoh, O., Egaas, B., Haas, R. H., & Schreibman, L. (1994). A new finding: Impairment in shifting attention in autistic and cerebellar patients. In H. Broman & J. Grafman (Eds.), *Atypical cognitive deficits in developmental disorders: Implications for brain function* (pp. 101–137). Hillsdale, NJ: Erlbaum.

Courchesne, E., Yeung-Courchesne, R., Press, G. A., Hesselink, J. R., & Jernigan, T. L. (1988). Hypoplasia of cerebellar vermal lobules VI and VII in autism. *New England Journal of Medicine, 318,* 1349–1354.

Curcio, F. (1978). Sensorimotor functioning and communication in mute autistic children. *Journal of Autism and Childhood Schizophrenia, 2,* 264–287.

Damasio, A. R. (1994). *Descartes' error: Emotion, reason, and the human brain.* New York: G. P. Putnam.

Dawson, G. (1991). A psychobiological perspective on the early socio-emotional development of children with autism. In D. Cicchetti & S. L. Toth (Eds.), *Rochester Symposium on Developmental Psychopathology* (Vol. 3, pp. 207–234). Rochester, NY: University of Rochester Press.

Dawson, G., & Adams, A. (1984). Imitation and social responsiveness in autistic children. *Journal of Abnormal Child Psychology, 12,* 209–225.

Dawson, G., Finley, C., Phillips, S., Galpert, L., & Lewy, A. (1988). Reduced P3 amplitude of the event-related potential: Its relationship to language ability in autism. *Journal of Autism and Developmental Disorders, 18,* 493–504.

Dawson, G., Hill, D., Spencer, A., Galpert, L., & Watson, L. (1990). Affective exchanges between young autistic children and their mothers. *Journal of Abnormal Child Psychology, 18,* 335–345.

Dawson, G., Klinger, L. G., Panagiotides, H., Lewy, A., & Castelloe, P. (1995). Subgroups of autistic children based on social behavior display distinct patterns of brain activity. *Journal of Abnormal Child Psychology, 23,* 569–583.

Dawson, G., & Lewy, A. (1989). Arousal, attention, and the socioemotional impairments of individuals with autism. In G. Dawson (Ed.), *Autism: Nature, diagnosis, and treatment* (pp. 49–74). New York: Guilford Press.

Dawson, G., Meltzoff, A. N., & Osterling, J. (1995, March). *Autistic children fail to orient to naturally occurring social stimuli.* Poster presented at the biennial meeting of the Society for Research in Child Development, Indianapolis, IN.

Dawson, G., & Osterling, J. (in press). Early intervention in autism: Effectiveness and common elements of current approaches. In M. J. Guralnick (Ed.), *The effectiveness of early intervention: Second generation research.* Baltimore: Brookes.

Dawson, G., Warrenburg, S., & Fuller, P. (1982). Cerebral laterization in individuals diagnosed as autistic in early childhood. *Brain and Language, 15,* 353–368.

Dawson, G., Warrenburg, S., & Fuller, P. (1983). Hemisphere functioning and motor imitation in autistic persons. *Brain and Cognition, 2,* 346–354.

DeLong, G. R. (1992). Autism, amnesia, hippocampus, and learning. *Neuroscience Behavior Review, 16,* 63–70.

DeMyer, M. K., Alpern, G., Barton, S., DeMyer, W. E., Churchill, D. W., Hingtgen, N. J., Bryson, C. Q., Pontius, W., & Kimberlin, C. (1972). Imitation in autistic, early schizophrenic, and nonpsychotic subnormal children. *Journal of Autism and Childhood Schizophrenia, 2,* 264–287.

DeMyer, M. K., Barton, S., Alpern, G., Kimberlin, C., Allen, J., Yang, E., & Steele, R. (1974). The measured intelligence of autistic children. *Journal of Autism and Childhood Schizophrenia, 4,* 42–60.

DeVolder, A., Bol, A., Michel, C., Congneau, M., & Goffinet, A. M. (1987). Brain glucose metabolism in children with the autistic syndrome: Positron tomography analysis. *Brain Development, 9,* 581–587.

Donnellan, A. M., Mirenda, P. L., Mesaros, R. A., & Fassbender, L. L. (1984). Analyzing the communicative functions of aberrant behavior. *Journal of the Association for Persons with Severe Handicaps, 9,* 201–212.

du Verglas, G., Banks, S. R., & Guyer, K. E. (1988). Clinical effects of fenfluramine on children with autism: A review of the research. *Journal of Autism and Developmental Disorders, 18,* 297–308.

Eales, M. J. (1993). Pragmatic impairments in adults with childhood diagnoses of autism or developmental receptive language disorder. *Journal of Autism and Developmental Disorders, 23,* 593–617.

Field, T. M., Woodson, R., Greenberg, R., & Cohen, D. (1982). Discrimination and imitation of facial expressions by neonates. *Science, 218,* 179–181.

Folstein, S., & Rutter, M. (1977). Infantile autism: A genetic study of 21 twin pairs. *Journal of Child Psychology and Psychiatry, 18,* 297–321.

Folstein, S., & Rutter, M. (1987). Autism: Familial aggregation and genetic implications. In E. Schopler and G. Mesibov (Eds.), *Neurobiological issues in autism* (pp. 83–105). New York: Plenum Press.

Gaffney, G. R., Kuperman, S., Tsai, L. Y., Minchin, S., & Hassanein, K. M. (1987). Midsagittal magnetic resonance imaging of autism. *British Journal of Psychiatry, 151,* 831–833.

Garber, H. J., & Ritvo, E. R. (1992). Magnetic resonance imaging of the posterior fossa in autistic adults. *American Journal of Psychiatry, 149,* 245–247.

Garreau, B., Barthelemy, C., Domenech, J., Sauvage, D., Num, J. P., Lelord, G., & Callaway, E. (1980). Disturbances in dopamine metabolism in autistic children: Results of clinical tests and urinary dosages of homovanillic acid (HVA). *Acta Psychiatrica Belgica, 80,* 249–265.

Geller, E., Ritvo, E. R., Freeman, B. J., & Yuwiler, A. (1982). Preliminary observations on the effect of fenfluramine on blood serotonin and symptoms in three autistic boys. *New England Journal of Medicine, 307,* 165–167.

George, M. S., Costa, D. C., Kouris, K., Ring, H. A., & Ell, P. J. (1992). Cerebral blood flow abnormalities in adults with infantile autism. *Journal of Nervous and Mental Disease, 180,* 413–417.

Gillberg, C. (1989). Asperger syndrome in 23 Swedish children. *Developmental Medicine and Child Neurology, 21,* 520–531.

Gillberg, C., & Steffenburg, S. (1987). Outcome and prognostic factors in infantile autism and similar conditions: A population-based study of 46 cases followed through puberty. *Journal of Autism and Developmental Disorders, 17,* 273–287.

Gillberg, C., Svennerholm, L., & Hamilton-Hellberg, C. (1983). Childhood psychosis and monoamine metabolites in spinal fluid. *Journal of Autism and Developmental Disorders, 13,* 383–396.

Green, W. H., Campbell, M., Hardesty, A. S., Grega, D. M., Padron-Gayol, M., Shell, J., & Erlenmeyer-Kimling, I. (1984). A comparison of schizophrenia and autistic children. *Journal of the American Academy of Child Psychiatry, 23,* 399–409.

Handleman, J., & Harris, S. (1994). The Douglass Developmental Disabilities Center. In S. Harris & J. Handleman (Eds.), *Preschool education programs for children with autism* (pp. 71–86). Austin, TX: Pro-ed.

Hannan, T. (1987). A cross-sequential assessment of the occurrences of pointing in 3- to 12-month-old human infants. *Infant Behavior and Development, 10,* 11–22.

Happe, F. (1995, March). *Wechsler IQ profile and theory of mind in autism.* Poster presented at the biennial meeting of the Society for Research in Child Development, Indianapolis, IN.

Hobson, R. P. (1989). Beyond cognition: A theory of autism. In G. Dawson (Ed.), *Autism: Nature, diagnosis, and treatment* (pp. 22–48). New York: Guilford Press.

Hobson, R. P., Ouston, J., & Lee, A. (1988). Emotion recognition in autism: Coordinating faces and voices. *Psychological Medicine, 18,* 911–923.

Hsu, M., Yeung-Courchesne, R., Courchesne, E., & Press, G. A. (1991). Absence of magnetic resonance imaging evidence of pontine abnormality in infantile autism. *Archives of Neurology, 48,* 1160–1163.

Kanner, L. (1943). Autistic disturbances of affective contact. *Nervous Child, 2,* 217–250.

Kasari, C., Sigman, M., Yirmiya, N., & Mundy P. (1993). Affective development and communication in children with autism. In A. P. Kaiser & D. B. Gray (Eds.), *Enhancing children's communication: Research foundations for intervention* (pp. 201–222). Baltimore: Brookes.

Katsui, T., Okuda, M., Usuda, S., & Koizumi, T. (1986). Kinetics of ^{3}H-serotonin uptake by platelets in infantile autism and developmental language disorder (including five pairs of twins). *Journal of Autism and Developmental Disorders, 16,* 69–76.

Kleiman, M. D., Neff, S., & Rosman, N. P. (1992). The brain in infantile autism: Are posterior fossa structures abnormal? *Neurology, 42,* 753–760.

Klinger, L. G., & Dawson, G. (1995). A fresh look at categorization abilities in persons with autism. In E. Schopler and G. Mesibov (Eds.), *Learning and cognition in autism* (pp. 119–136). New York: Plenum Press.

Kobayashi, R., Murata, T., & Yoshinaga, K. (1992). A follow-up study of 201 children with autism in Kyushu and Yamaguchi areas, Japan. *Journal of Autism and Developmental Disorders, 22,* 395–411.

Koegel, L. K., & Koegel, R. L. (1995). Motivating communication in children with autism. In E. Schopler and G. Mesibov (Eds.), *Learning and cognition in autism* (pp. 73–87). New York: Plenum Press.

Koegel, R. L., Schreibman, L., O'Neill, R. E., & Burke, J. C. (1983). The personality and family-interaction characteristics of parents of autistic children. *Journal of Consulting and Clinical Psychology, 51,* 683–692.

Kolvin, I. (1971). Psychoses in childhood: A comparative study. In M. Rutter (Ed.), *Infantile autism: Concepts, characteristics, and treatment.* Edinburgh: Churchill Livingstone.

Konstantareas, M. M., Homatidis, S., & Busch, J. (1989). Cognitive, communication, and social differences between autistic boys and girls. *Journal of Applied Developmental Psychology, 10,* 411–424.

Kurita, H. (1985). Infantile autism with speech loss before the age of thirty months. *Journal of the American Academy of Child Psychiatry, 24,* 191–196.

Lebedinskaya, K. S., & Nikolskaya, O. S. (1993). Brief report: Analysis of autism and its treatment in modern Russian defectology. *Journal of Autism and Developmental Disorders, 23,* 675–679.

Lee, A., Hobson, R. P., & Chiat, S. (1994). I, you, me, and autism: An experimental study. *Journal of Autism and Developmental Disorders, 24,* 155–176.

Lockyer, L., & Rutter, M. (1970). A five to fifteen year follow-up study of infantile psychosis: IV. Patterns of cognitive ability. *British Journal of Social and Clinical Psychology, 9,* 152–163.

Lord, C., Mulloy, C., Wendelboe, M., & Schopler, E. (1991). Pre- and perinatal factors in high-functioning females and males with autism. *Journal of Autism and Developmental Disorders, 21,* 197–209.

Lord, C., Rutter, M., Goode, S., Heemsbergen, J., Jordan, H., Mawhood, L., & Schopler, E. (1989). Autism diagnostic observation schedule: A standardized observation of communicative and social behavior. *Journal of Autism and Developmental Disorders, 19,* 185–212.

Lord, C., Rutter, M., & Le Couteur, A. (1994). Autism diagnostic interview-revised: A revised version of a diagnostic interview for caregivers of individuals with possible pervasive developmental disorders. *Journal of Autism and Developmental Disorders, 24,* 659–685.

Lord, C., & Schopler, E. (1989). The role of age at assessment, developmental level, and test in the stability of intelligence scores in young autistic children. *Journal of Autism and Developmental Disorders, 19,* 483–499.

Lord, C., & Schopler, E. (1994). TEACCH services for preschool children. In S. Harris & J. Handleman (Eds.), *Preschool education programs for children with autism* (pp. 87–106). Austin, TX: Pro-ed.

Lotter, V. (1966). Epidemiology of autistic conditions in young children: I. Prevalence. *Social Psychiatry, 1,* 124–137.

Lovaas, I. (1987). Behavioral treatment and normal educational and intellectual functioning in young autistic children. *Journal of Consulting and Clinical Psychology, 55,* 3–9.

Loveland, K. A., Tunali-Kotoski, B., Pearson, D. A., Brelsford, K. A., Ortegon, J., & Chen, R. (1994). Imitation and expression of facial affect in autism. *Development and Psychopathology, 6,* 433–444.

Maurice, C. (1993). *Let me hear your voice: A family's triumph over autism.* New York: Fawcett Columbine.

McAdoo, W. G., & DeMyer, M. K. (1978). Personality characteristics of parents. In M. Rutter & E. Schopler

(Eds.), *Autism: A reappraisal of concepts and treatment* (pp. 251–267). New York: Plenum Press.

McClannahan, L., & Krantz, P. (1994). The Princeton Child Development Institute. In S. Harris & J. Handleman (Eds.), *Preschool education programs for children with autism* (pp. 107–126). Austin, TX: Pro-ed.

McEvoy, R. E., Rogers, S. J., & Pennington, B. F. (1993). Executive function and social communication deficits in young autistic children. *Journal of Child Psychology and Psychiatry, 34,* 563–578.

McGee, G., Daly, T., & Jacobs, H. A. (1994). The Walden preschool. In S. Harris & J. Handleman (Eds.), *Preschool education programs for children with autism* (pp. 127–152). Austin, TX: Pro-ed.

McLennan, J. D., Lord, C., & Schopler, E. (1993). Sex differences in higher functioning people with autism. *Journal of Autism and Developmental Disorders, 23,* 217–227.

Meltzoff, A. N., & Gopnik, A. (1993). The role of imitation in understanding persons and developing a theory of mind. In S. Baron-Cohen, H. Tager-Flusberg, & D. J. Cohen (Eds.), *Understanding other minds: Perspectives from autism* (pp. 335–366). Oxford, UK: Oxford University Press.

Meltzoff, A. N., & Moore, M. K. (1977). Imitation of facial and manual gestures by human neonates. *Science, 198,* 75–78.

Mikkelsen, E. (1982). Efficacy of neuroleptic medication in pervasive developmental disorders of childhood. *Schizophrenia Bulletin, 8,* 320–328.

Minshew, N. J., & Goldstein, G. (1993). Is autism an amnesic disorder?: Evidence from the California Verbal Learning Test. *Neuropsychology, 7,* 1–8.

Mundy, P., & Sigman, M. (1989). The theoretical implications of joint-attention deficits in autism. *Development and Psychopathology, 1,* 173–183.

Mundy, P., Sigman, M., & Kasari, C. (1990). A longitudinal study of joint attention and language development in autistic children. *Journal of Autism and Developmental Disorders, 20,* 115–128.

Mundy, P., Sigman, M., & Kasari, C. (1993). The theory of mind and joint-attention deficits in autism. In S. Baron-Cohen, H. Tager-Flusberg, & D. J. Cohen (Eds.), *Understanding other minds: Perspectives from autism* (pp. 181–203). Oxford, UK: Oxford University Press.

Mundy, P., Sigman, M., & Kasari, C. (1994). Joint attention, developmental level, and symptom presentation in autism. *Development and Psychopathology, 6,* 389–401.

Mundy, P., Sigman, M., Ungerer, J., & Sherman, T. (1986). Defining the social deficits of autism: The contribution of nonverbal communication measures. *Journal of Child Psychology and Psychiatry, 27,* 657–669.

Nahm, F. K., Tranel, D., Damasio, H., & Damasio, A. R. (1993). Cross-modal associations and the human amygdala. *Neuropsychologia, 31,* 727–744.

Novick, B., Kurtzberg, D., & Vaughn, H. G. (1979). An electrophysiologic indication of defective information storage in childhood autism. *Psychiatry Research, 1,* 101–108.

Novick, B., Vaughn, H. G., Kurtzberg, D., & Simson, R. (1980). An electrophysiological indication of auditory processing defects in autism. *Psychiatry Research, 3,* 107–114.

Ornitz, E. M. (1989). Autism at the interface between sensory and information processing. In G. Dawson (Ed.), *Autism: Nature, diagnosis, and treatment* (pp. 174–207). New York: Guilford Press.

Osterling, J., & Dawson, G. (1994). Early recognition of children with autism: A study of first birthday home videotapes. *Journal of Autism and Developmental Disorders, 24,* 247–257.

Ozonoff, S. (1995a). Executive function impairments in autism. In E. Schopler & G. Mesibov (Eds.), *Learning and cognition in autism* (pp. 199–220). New York: Plenum Press.

Ozonoff, S. (1995b, March). *Flexibility and inhibition deficits in autism: The information processing approach.* Paper presented at the biennial meeting of the Society for Research in Child Development, Indianapolis, IN.

Ozonoff, S., & McEvoy, R. (1994). A longitudinal study of executive function and theory of mind development in autism. *Development and Psychopathology, 6,* 415–431.

Ozonoff, S., Pennington, B. F., & Rogers, S. J. (1990). Are there specific emotion perception deficits in young autistic children? *Journal of Child Psychology and Psychiatry, 31,* 343–361.

Ozonoff, S., Pennington, B. F., & Rogers, S. J. (1991). Executive function deficits in high-functioning autistic individuals: Relationship to theory of mind. *Journal of Child Psychology and Psychiatry, 32,* 1081–1105.

Ozonoff, S., Rogers, S. J., & Pennington, B. F. (1991). Asperger's syndrome: Evidence of an empirical distinction from high-functioning autism. *Journal of Child Psychology and Psychiatry, 32,* 1107–1122.

Ozonoff, S., Strayer, D. L., McMahon, W. M., & Filloux, F. (1994). Executive function abilities in autism and tourette syndrome: An information processing approach. *Journal of Child Psychology and Psychiatry, 35,* 1015–1032.

Panksepp, J. (1979). A neurochemical theory of autism. *Trends in Neuroscience, 2,* 174–177.

Panksepp, J., & Sahley, T. L. (1987). Possible brain opioid involvement in disrupted social intent and language development of autism. In E. Schopler & G. B. Mesibov (Eds.), *Neurobiological issues in autism* (pp. 357–372). New York: Plenum Press.

Paul, R., Fischer, M. L., & Cohen, D. J. (1988). Brief report: Sentence comprehension strategies in children with autism and specific language disorders. *Journal of Autism and Developmental Disorders, 18,* 669–677.

Pennington, B. F., & Welsh, M. (in press). Neuropsychology and developmental psychopathology. In D. Cicchetti & D. J. Cohen (Eds.), *Handbook of developmental psychopathology.* Cambridge, UK: Cambridge University Press.

Petty, L. K., Ornitz, E. M., Michelman, J. D., & Zimmerman, E. G. (1984). Autistic children who become schizophrenic. *Archives of General Psychiatry, 41,* 129–135.

Piven, J., Berthier, M. L., Starkstein, S. E., Nehme, E., Pearlson, G., & Folstein, S. (1990). Magnetic resonance imaging evidence for a defect of cerebral cortical development in autism. *American Journal of Psychiatry, 147,* 734–739.

Posner, M. I., & Keele, S. W. (1968). On the genesis of abstract ideas. *Journal of Experimental Psychology, 77,* 353–363.

Posner, M. I., & Keele, S. W. (1970). Retention of abstract ideas. *Journal of Experimental Psychology, 83,* 304–308.

Powell, T. H., Hecimovic, A., & Christensen, L. (1992). Meeting the unique needs of families. In D. E. Berkell (Ed.), *Autism: Identification, education, and treatment* (pp. 187–224). Hillsdale, NJ: Erlbaum.

Prior, M., & Hoffmann, W. (1990). Brief report: Neuropsychological testing of autistic children through an exploration with frontal lobe tests. *Journal of Autism and Developmental Disorders, 20,* 581–590.

Prizant, B. M., & Rydell, P. J. (1984). An analysis of the functions of delayed echolalia in autistic children. *Journal of Speech and Hearing Research, 27,* 183–192.

Rapin, I. (in press). *Preschool children with inadequate communication: Developmental language disorder, autism, and low IQ.* (Clinics in Developmental Medicine, No. 139). London: Mac Keith Press.

Riguet, C., Taylor, N., Benaroya, S., & Klein, L. (1981). Symbolic play in autistic, Down's, and normal children of equivalent mental age. *Journal of Autism and Developmental Disorders, 11,* 439–448.

Rimland, B. (1964). *Infantile autism: The syndrome and its implications for a neural theory of behavior.* New York: Appleton-Century-Crofts.

Ritvo, E. R., Freeman, B. J., Scheibel, A. B., Duong, T., Robinson, H., Guthrie, D., & Ritvo, A. (1986). Lower purkinje cell counts in the cerebella of four autistic subjects: Initial findings of the UCLA–NSAC autopsy research report. *American Journal of Psychiatry, 143,* 862–866.

Rogers, S. J., & DiLalla, D. L. (1991). A comparative study of the effects of a developmentally based instructional model on young children with autism and young children with other disorders of behavior and development. *Topics in Early Childhood Special Education: Emerging Trends for Child Behavior Disorders, 11,* 29–47.

Rogers, S. J., Ozonoff, S., & Maslin-Cole, C. (1993). Developmental aspects of attachment behavior in young children with pervasive developmental disorders. *Journal of the American Academy of Child and Adolescent Psychiatry, 32,* 1274–1282.

Rogers, S. J., & Pennington, B. F. (1991). A theoretical approach to deficits in infantile autism. *Development and Psychopathology, 3,* 137–162.

Rotman, A., Caplan, R., & Szekely, G. A. (1980). Platelet uptake of serotonin in psychotic children. *Psychopharmacology, 67,* 245–248.

Rumsey, J., Duara, R., Grady, C., Rapoport, J. L., Margolin, R. A., Rapoport, S. I., & Cutler, N. R. (1985). Brain metabolism in autism: Resting cerebral glucose utilization rates as measured with positron emission tomography. *Archives of General Psychiatry, 42,* 448–455.

Rumsey, J., & Hamburger, S. (1988). Neuropsychological findings in high-functioning men with infantile autism, residual state. *Journal of Clinical and Experimental Neuropsychology, 10,* 201–221.

Rutter, M. (1978). Diagnosis and definition. In M. Rutter & E. Schopler (Eds.), *Autism: A reappraisal of concepts and treatment* (pp. 1–25). New York: Plenum Press.

Rutter, M., & Bartak, L. (1973). Special educational treatment of autistic children: A comparative study: II. Follow-up findings and implications for services. *Journal of Child Psychology and Psychiatry, 14,* 241–270.

Rutter, M., Macdonald, H., Le Couteur, A., Harrington, R., Bolton, P., & Bailey, A. (1990). Genetic factors in child psychiatric disorders: II. Empirical findings. *Journal of Child Psychology and Psychiatry, 31,* 39–83.

Sandman, C. A., Data, P. C., Barron, J., Hoehler, F. K., Williams, C., & Swanson, J. M. (1983). Naloxone attenuates self-abusive behavior in developmentally disabled clients. *Applied Research in Mental Retardation, 4,* 5–11.

Schain, R. J., & Freedman, D. (1961). Studies on 5-hydroxyindole metabolism in autistic and other mentally retarded children. *Journal of Pediatrics, 58,* 315–320.

Schopler, E., Andrews, C. E., & Strupp, K. (1979). Do autistic children come from upper middle-class parents? *Journal of Autism and Developmental Disorders, 9,* 139–152.

Schopler, E., & Reichler, R. (1971). Parents as co-therapists in the treatment of psychotic children. *Journal of Autism and Childhood Schizophrenia, 1,* 87–102.

Schopler, E., Reichler, R., De Vellis, R., & Daly, K. (1980). Toward objective classification of childhood autism: Childhood Autism Rating Scale (CARS). *Journal of Autism and Developmental Disorders, 10,* 91–103.

Schopler, E., Reichler, R., & Renner, B. (1988). *The Childhood Autism Rating Scale (CARS).* Los Angeles: Western Psychological.

Schuler, A., & Prizant, B. (1985). Echolalia. In E. Schopler & G. Mesibov (Eds.), *Communication problems in autism* (pp. 163–184). New York: Plenum Press.

Siegel, B., Pilner, C., Eschler, J., & Elliott, G. R. (1988). How children with autism are diagnosed: Difficulties in identification of children with multiple developmental delays. *Developmental and Behavioral Pediatrics, 9,* 199–204.

Sigman, M., & Mundy P. (1989). Social attachments in autistic children. *Journal of the American Academy of Child and Adolescent Psychiatry, 28,* 74–81.

Sigman, M., & Ungerer, J. A. (1984a). Attachment behaviors in autistic children. *Journal of Autism and Developmental Disorders, 14,* 231–244.

Sigman, M., & Ungerer, J. A. (1984b). Cognitive and language skills in autistic, mentally retarded, and normal children. *Developmental Psychology, 20,* 293–302.

Smalley, S. L., Asarnow, R. F., & Spence, A. (1988). Autism and genetics: A decade of research. *Archives of General Psychiatry, 45,* 953–961.

Smith, I. M., & Bryson, S. E. (1994). Imitation and action in autism: A critical review. *Psychology Bulletin, 116,* 259–273.

Smith, E. E., & Medin, D. L. (1981). *Categories and concepts.* Cambridge, MA: Harvard University Press.

Stern, D. N. (1985). *The interpersonal world of the infant.* New York: Basic Books.

Steffenburg, S., & Gillberg, C. (1986). Autism and autistic-like conditions in Swedish rural and urban areas: A population study. *British Journal of Psychiatry, 149,* 81–87.

Steffenburg, S., Gillberg, C., Hellgren, L., Andersson, L., Gillberg, I. C., Jakobsson, G., & Bohman, M. (1989). A twin study of autism in Denmark, Finland, Iceland, Norway, and Sweden. *Journal of Child Psychology and Psychiatry, 30,* 405–416.

Stone, W. L., & Hogan, K. L. (1993). A structured parent interview for identifying young children with autism. *Journal of Autism and Developmental Disorders, 23,* 639–652.

Strain, P. S., & Cordisco, L. K. (1994). LEAP preschool. In S. Harris & J. Handleman (Eds.), *Preschool education programs for children with autism* (pp. 225–244). Austin, TX: Pro-ed.

Sugarman, S. (1984). The development of preverbal communication. In R. Schiefelbusch & J. Pickar (Eds.), *The acquisition of communicative competence* (pp. 23–67). Baltimore: University Park Press.

Sugiyama, T., & Abe, T. (1989). The prevalence of autism in Nagoya, Japan: A total population study. *Journal of Autism and Developmental Disorders, 19,* 87–96.

Sullivan, R. C. (1992). Parent essays: Rain man and Joseph. In E. Schopler & G. Mesibov (Eds.), *High-functioning individuals with autism* (pp. 243–250). New York: Plenum Press.

Szatmari, P., Bartolucci, G., Bremner, R., Bond, S., & Rich, S. (1989). A follow-up study of high-functioning autistic children. *Journal of Autism and Developmental Disorders, 19,* 213–225.

Szatmari, P., Jones, M. B., Tuff, L., Bartolucci, G., Fisman, S., & Mahoney, W. (1993). Lack of cognitive impairment in first-degree relatives of children with pervasive

developmental disorders. *Journal of the American Academy of Child and Adolescent Psychiatry, 32,* 1264–1273.

Szatmari, P., Tuff, L., Finlayson, M. A., & Bartolucci, G. (1989). Asperger's syndrome and autism: Neurocognitive aspects. *Journal of the American Academy of Child and Adolescent Psychiatry, 29,* 130–136.

Tager-Flusberg, H. (1985a). Basic level and superordinate level categorization in autistic, mentally retarded and normal children. *Journal of Experimental Child Psychology, 40,* 450–469.

Tager-Flusberg, H. (1985b). The conceptual basis for referential word meaning in children with autism. *Child Development, 56,* 1167–1178.

Tager-Flusberg, H. (1989). A psycholinguistic perspective on language development in the autistic child. In G. Dawson (Ed.), *Autism: Nature, diagnosis, and treatment* (pp. 92–115). New York: Guilford Press.

Tager-Flusberg, H. (1993). What language reveals about the understanding of minds in children with autism. In S. Baron-Cohen, H. Tager-Flusberg, & D. J. Cohen (Eds.), *Understanding other minds: Perspectives from autism* (pp. 138–157). Oxford, UK: Oxford University Press.

Tager-Flusberg, H., Calkins, S., Nolin, T., Baumberger, T., Anderson, M., & Chadwick-Dias, A. (1990). A longitudinal study of language acquisition in autistic and Down syndrome children. *Journal of Autism and Developmental Disorders, 20,* 1–21.

Tantum, D. (1988). Annotation: Asperger's syndrome. *Journal of Child Psychology and Psychiatry, 29,* 245–255.

Tsai, L. (1987). Pre-, peri-, and neonatal factors in autism. In E. Schopler & G. Mesibov (Eds.), *Neurobiological issues in autism* (pp. 179–189). New York: Plenum Press.

Tsai, L. (1992). Diagnostic issues in high-functioning autism. In E. Schopler & G. Mesibov (Eds.), *High-functioning individuals with autism* (pp. 11–40). New York: Plenum Press.

Ungerer, J. (1989). The early development of autistic children: Implications for defining primary deficits. In G. Dawson (Ed.), *Autism: Nature, diagnosis, and treatment,* (pp. 75–91). New York: Guilford Press.

Ungerer, J., & Sigman, M. (1984). The relation of play and sensorimotor behavior to language in the second year. *Child Development, 55,* 1448–1455.

Ungerer, J., & Sigman, M. (1987). Categorization skills and receptive language development in autistic children. *Journal of Autism and Developmental Disorders, 17,* 3–16.

Van Acker, R. (1991). Rett syndrome: A review of current knowledge. *Journal of Autism and Developmental Disorders, 21,* 381–406.

Venter, A., Lord, C., & Schopler, E. (1992). A follow-up study of high-functioning autistic children. *Journal of Child Psychology and Psychiatry, 33,* 489–507.

Volkmar, F. R. (1992). Childhood disintegrative disorder: Issues for DSM-IV. *Journal of Autism and Developmental Disorders, 22,* 625–642.

Volkmar, F. R., & Anderson, G. M. (1989). Neurochemical perspectives on infantile autism. In G. Dawson (Ed.), *Autism: Nature, diagnosis, and treatment* (pp. 208–224). New York: Guilford Press.

Volkmar, F. R., & Cohen, D. J. (1991). Comorbid association of autism and schizophrenia. *American Journal of Psychiatry, 148,* 1705–1707.

Volkmar, F. R., Cohen, D. J., & Paul, R. (1986). An evaluation of DSM-III criteria for infantile autism. *Journal of the American Academy of Child Psychiatry, 25,* 190–197.

Volkmar, F. R., Szatmari, P., & Sparrow, S. S. (1993). Sex differences in pervasive developmental disorders. *Journal of Autism and Developmental Disorders, 23,* 579–591.

Walden, T., & Ogan, T. (1988). The development of social referencing. *Child Development, 59,* 1230–1240.

Walters, A. S., Barrett, R. P., Feinstein, C., Mercurio, A., & Hole, W. T. (1990). A case report of naltrexone treatment of self-injury and social withdrawal in autism. *Journal of Autism and Developmental Disorders, 20,* 169–176.

Weeks, S. J., & Hobson, R. P. (1987). The salience of facial expression for autistic children. *Journal of Child Psychology and Psychiatry, 28,* 137–152.

Wellman, H. M. (1993). Early understanding of mind: The normal case. In S. Baron-Cohen, H. Tager-Flusberg, & D. J. Cohen (Eds.), *Understanding other minds: Perspectives from autism* (pp. 10–39). Oxford, UK: Oxford University Press.

Wetherby, A., & Prutting, C. (1984). Profiles of communicative and cognitive-social abilities in autistic children. *Journal of Speech and Hearing Research, 27,* 364–377.

Wing, L. (1978). Social, behavioral, and cognitive characteristics: An epidemiological approach. In M. Rutter & E. Schopler (Eds.), *Autism: A reappraisal of concepts and treatment* (pp. 27–46). New York, Plenum Press.

Wing, L. (1988). The continuum of autistic characteristics. In E. Schopler & G. Mesibov (Eds.), *Diagnosis and assessment in autism* (pp. 91–110). New York: Plenum Press.

Wing, L., & Gould, J. (1979). Severe impairments of social interaction and associated abnormalities in children: Epidemiology and classification. *Journal of Autism and Developmental Disorders, 9,* 11–29.

World Health Organization. (1992). *International classification of diseases* (10th ed.). Geneva, Switzerland: Author.

Young, J. G., Cohen, D. J., Kavanagh, M. E., Landis, H. D., Shaywitz, B. A., & Maas, J. W. (1981). Cerebrospinal fluid, plasma, and urinary MHPG in children. *Life Sciences, 28,* 2837–2845.

Young, J. G., Kavanagh, M. E., Anderson, G. M., Shaywitz, B. A., & Cohen, D. J. (1982). Clinical neurochemistry of autism and associated disorders. *Journal of Autism and Developmental Disorders, 12,* 147–165.

Childhood-Onset Schizophrenia

Joan Rosenbaum Asarnow
Robert F. Asarnow

This chapter focuses on schizophrenia with childhood onset. Schizophrenia is a psychotic disorder, or group of disorders, characterized by the presence of one or more of a series of key symptoms such as bizarre delusions, mood incongruent hallucinations, thought disorder, grossly disorganized or catatonic behavior, flat or grossly inappropriate affect, and significant impairment and/or deterioration. Consider, for example, the following description of a young girl with schizophrenia.

> Mary had always been a very shy child. At times, she would become mute, had severe difficulties making friends, was frequently oppositional, and had occasional enuresis. By the time she reached roughly 10 years of age, Mary showed academic difficulties in addition to continuing social isolation. She became depressed, felt that the devil was trying to make her do bad things, believed that her teacher was trying to hurt her, and became preoccupied with germs. Her behavior became increasingly disorganized, she talked of killing herself, appeared disheveled, and ran in front of a moving car in an apparent suicide attempt.
>
> This episode precipitated an inpatient psychiatric evaluation where Mary continued to show bizarre behavior. She lapsed into periods of intense anxiety and had one episode of uncontrolled screaming. At times she would stare blankly into space and was frequently mute. Although Mary's functioning improved during hospitalization and she returned to her family, throughout her childhood and adolescent years she was tormented by fears, hallucinations, the belief that others were out to get her, and occasional bouts of depression often accompanied by suicide attempts. She continued to be socially isolated, withdrawn, and to perform poorly at school. At age 17, after several brief inpatient hospitalizations, Mary was admitted to a state hospital where she remained until the age of 19. During this period her affect was increasingly flat, and her psychotic symptoms persisted. One week after discharge from the hospital, Mary went into her room, locked the door, and overdosed on her medications. She was found dead the next morning.

This girl's story underscores several features of early-onset schizophrenia. First, schizophrenia does occur in children, although most cases of schizophrenia have their onsets in late adolescence or early adulthood. Second, children with schizophrenia frequently continue to struggle with schizophrenic symptoms during adolescence and adulthood. Third, because childhood is a period when crucial psychosocial competencies are developing, early-onset schizophrenia has a powerful impact on developing academic and social competence. Finally, Mary's battle with schizophrenia underscores the pain and morbidity associated with this illness.

This chapter reviews the literature on childhood-onset schizophrenia. Research conducted

after the introduction of the ninth edition of the *International Classification of Diseases* (ICD-9; World Health Organization, 1978) and the third edition of the *Diagnostic and Statistical Manual of Mental Disorders* (DSM-III; American Psychiatric Association, 1980) is emphasized. DSM-III and ICD-9 endorsed the practice of using the same criteria to diagnose schizophrenia in children and adults. Prior to that time, the construct of childhood-onset schizophrenia was used to denote a relatively heterogeneous group of children with adult-type schizophrenia, autism, and other psychotic conditions. This made comparisons with the adult literature difficult and complicated cross-study comparisons because of variations in the proportion of various subtypes of "childhood schizophrenics" across studies. Several excellent reviews are available of the earlier pre-DSM-III and ICD-9 literature (Beitchman, 1985; Cantor, 1988; Fish, 1977; Fish & Ritvo, 1979; McClellan & Werry, 1992; Prior & Werry, 1986; Rutter, 1972; Tanguay & Asarnow, 1985).

Renewed interest in childhood-onset schizophrenia has been stimulated by several factors. First, research suggesting that childhood-onset schizophrenia may be a more severe and familial variant of the disorder has stimulated the hope that etiological pathways and the biological substrate for the disorder may be more clearly discernable in childhood- as opposed to later-onset schizophrenia (R. Asarnow & Asarnow, 1994; J. Asarnow, Asarnow, Hornstein, & Russell, 1991; Fish, 1977; Kallman & Roth, 1956). Second, because of their youth, findings with schizophrenic children are less likely to be confounded by factors such as neuroleptic treatment, institutionalization, and years of dysfunction. Third, the emergence of "developmental psychopathology" as a scientific discipline in conjunction with the findings yielded by studies of children at risk for schizophrenia have stimulated interest in developmental questions such as the impact of age of onset on the development of schizophrenia (for review, see J. Asarnow, 1988; Nuechterlein, 1986; Zeitlin, 1986, 1990). Finally, advances in child assessment techniques have provided systematic and reliable assessment of schizophrenic symptoms and syndromes.

BRIEF HISTORICAL CONTEXT

As noted above, the 20th century has witnessed major changes in the criteria employed to diagnose schizophrenia in childhood. Two leading factors contributed to the changes in diagnostic criteria. First, in the 1930s child psychiatry began to emerge as a medical subspecialty. Early child psychiatrists, when confronted with the broad group of psychotic children who presented clinically, began to question whether these children were suffering from developmentally earlier manifestations of the adult form of schizophrenia. Second, this period was characterized by multiple shifts in the definition of schizophrenia as the field addressed the still unresolved problem of defining the boundaries of schizophrenia (Kendler et al., 1993).

Cases of childhood psychosis, in the absence of apparent organic brain disease, have been reported for at least 200 years (Walk, 1964). Contemporaneous with the description of various psychotic symptoms in adult psychiatry, descriptions of psychotic symptoms in children began to appear in the psychiatric literature. For example, describing what would later be called a functional psychosis in a child, Conolly (1861–1862) noted:

> The occasional existence of a disordered state of mental faculties in children, not depending on any temporary condition of an inflammatory kind, or on recognized chronic disease, and not on the result of accident, and more resembling mania than imbecility, does not seem to have been noticed even by medical practitioners until somewhat recently and certainly has not attracted particular attention. (p. 395)

Early in the 20th century, De Sanctis (1906) described a group of children presenting with an illness which he termed "dementia praecosissima," which he likened to Kraepelin's dementia praecox. Kraepelin (1919) and Bleuler (1911/1950) observed that dementia praecox could begin during childhood. Further, Kraepelin (1919) noted that because of difficulties in identifying the point of time when the disease begins, it is likely that only the most severe cases of schizophrenia are identified in children.

Prior to the 1930s, schizophrenia was diagnosed in children using standards similar to those applied with adult patients (Fish & Ritvo, 1979). However, beginning in the 1930s, child psychiatry began to emerge as a medical subspecialty. Child psychiatrists saw children with a broad range of conditions and varying levels of retardation. These conditions included mental retardation, organic brain syndromes, developmental disabilities, infantile autism, and childhood-onset forms of schizophrenia.

Early child psychiatrists struggled with the question of how best to diagnose and classify this broad range of children. Recognition that schizophrenic symptoms might be expressed somewhat differently in children, in conjunction with efforts to classify the broad range of psychotic children, led to the emergence of the construct of "childhood schizophrenia" in American child psychiatry.

Thus, paralleling the numerous shifts in the concept of "schizophrenia" in adult psychiatry, the term "childhood schizophrenia" began to be used to describe a relatively heterogeneous group of children with profound early-onset impairments. Complicating matters further, during the 1930s, operational definitions and specific diagnostic criteria were not generally used. Instead, samples were characterized using brief case descriptions or a list of major symptoms (see Fish & Ritvo, 1979).

The broad construct of "childhood schizophrenia" included children who today would receive *Diagnostic and Statistical Manual of Mental Disorders,* fourth edition (DSM-IV; American Psychiatric Association, 1994) diagnoses of autistic disorder, pervasive developmental disorder (PDD), schizophrenia, and psychotic disorder not otherwise specified. This contributed to considerable variability in the criteria that different clinicians used to define the category. Moreover, the breadth of the construct resulted in considerable heterogeneity among children grouped under the broad rubric of "childhood schizophrenia" and associated differences in the characteristics of "childhood schizophrenics" studied in various clinical centers. To illustrate, Potter (1933) offered the following criteria for making a diagnosis of schizophrenia in the prepubertal child.

1. A generalized retraction of interest from the environment.
2. Dereistic thinking,[1] feeling and acting.
3. Disturbances of thought, manifest through blocking, symbolization, condensation, perseveration, incoherence and diminution sometimes to the extent of mutism.
4. Defect in emotional rapport.
5. Diminution, rigidity and distortion of affect.
6. Alterations of behavior with either an increase of motility leading to incessant activity, or a diminution of motility, leading to complete immobility or bizarre behavior with a tendency to perseveration or stereotypy. (p. 1254)

Compared to current DSM-IV criteria, Potter's criteria would likely include a broader group of

children including those with DSM-IV-defined schizophrenia, schizotypal personality disorder, and some children with PDD and autism (see Klinger & Dawson, Chapter 8, this volume). Interestingly, a 30-year follow-up of Potter's cases revealed that most of these children showed schizophrenia in adulthood, as defined in the early 1960s (Bennett and Klein, 1966).

In contrast, the nine criteria for "schizophrenic syndrome of childhood" proposed by the British working party (Creak, 1964) were more similar to the current criteria for autism and PDD. To complicate matters further, Kanner's descriptions of "early infantile autism" overlapped with other clinicians' descriptions of "childhood schizophrenia." Kanner (1949) concluded:

1. Early infantile autism is a well-defined syndrome which an experienced observer has little difficulty in recognizing in the course of the first two years of the life of the patient.
2. The basic nature of its manifestations is so intimately related to the basic nature of childhood schizophrenia as to be indistinguishable from it, especially from the cases with insidious onset. . . .
4. Early infantile autism may, therefore, be looked upon as the earliest possible manifestation of childhood schizophrenia. As such, because of the age at the time of the withdrawal, it presents a clinical picture which has certain characteristics of its own, both at the start and in the course of later development. I have tried to do justice to this by including the discussion of early infantile autism in the schizophrenia chapter of the rewritten edition of my textbook of Child Psychiatry (published in 1948), at the same time acknowledging its special features by dealing with it under a special subheading.
5. I do not believe that there is any likelihood that early infantile autism will at any future time have to be separated from the schizophrenias, as was the case with Heller's disease.
6. Nosologically, therefore, the great importance of the group which I have described as early infantile autism lies in the correction of the impression that a comparatively normal period of adjustment must precede the development of schizophrenia. It also confirms the observation, made of late by many authors, that childhood schizophrenia is not so rare as was believed as recently as twenty years ago. (pp. 419–420)

In the late 1940s and 1950s, many disturbed children were given a diagnosis of schizophrenia

who would be considered by current standards to show only questionable borderline or no psychotic symptoms. This contributed to even greater heterogeneity among children classified as schizophrenic.

Bender's (1956) concept of schizophrenia, for example, included young children who were mute and retarded, whose symptoms would be viewed as autistic, and children with complex speech problems similar to those described by Potter. Bender distinguished between two groups of schizophrenic children on the basis of age at onset: (1) a "pseudo-defective group," similar to Kanner's early infantile autistics, where the onset was under age 2 years, and (2) "schizophrenic" children with later onsets who were described as showing more neurotic, paranoid, and sociopathic symptoms. Many of the second later-onset group were followed into adulthood and showed schizophrenia as defined in that period (Fish & Ritvo, 1979, p. 269).

The DSM-II (American Psychiatric Association, 1968) concept of "childhood schizophrenia" reflects the influences of Kanner and Bender:

This category is for cases in which schizophrenic symptoms appear before puberty. The condition may be manifested by autistic, atypical, and withdrawn behavior; failure to develop identity separate from the mother's; and general unevenness, gross immaturity and inadequacy in development. These developmental defects may result in mental retardation, which should also be diagnosed. (This category is for use in the United States and does not appear in ICD-8. It is equivalent to "Schizophrenic reaction, childhood type" in DSM-I.) (p. 35)

Kolvin's classic studies of psychotic children (Kolvin, Ounsted, Humphrey, & McNay, 1971) contributed to a major shift in the conceptualization of schizophrenia in children. Kolvin and colleagues (1971) identified a group of children with late-onset psychosis (onset between 5 and 15 years of age) who, like adults with schizophrenia, were characterized by hallucinations, delusions, and formal thought disorder. Alternatively, children with infantile psychosis (onset prior to 3 years of age) showed autistic symptoms but not the characteristic schizophrenic symptoms seen in the late-onset group.

These data were complemented by the finding of Rutter, Greenfeld, and Lockyer (1967) that autistic children followed into adulthood did not show schizophrenic symptoms. Rutter (1972) concluded:

Childhood schizophrenia has tended to be used as a generic term to include an astonishingly heterogeneous mixture of disorders with little in common other than their severity, chronicity, and occurrence in childhood. To add to the difficulty, the term has been employed in widely divergent ways by different psychiatrists. Some make the diagnosis very frequently, others do so quite rarely. A host of different syndromes have been included in the general category of "childhood schizophrenia"—infantile autism, the atypical child, symbiotic psychosis, dementia praecosissima, dementia infantilis, schizophrenic syndrome of childhood, pseudo-psychopathic schizophrenia, and latent schizophrenia to name but a few. In addition, a collection of eponyms have been attached to different conditions—Kanner, Mahler, and Heller, for example, all have syndromes named after them. The diagnostic situation can only be described as chaotic. Clinicians from different centers use the same term to mean different conditions and different terms to mean the same condition. We must conclude that the term "childhood schizophrenia" has outlived its usefulness. (p. 315)

DSM-III, DSM-III-R, and DSM-IV (as well as ICD-9 and ICD-10) represent a shift toward pre-1930 diagnostic practices. Schizophrenia in children is diagnosed using the same criteria applied with adults, allowing for minor differences in the manifestations of symptoms during childhood.

DESCRIPTION OF THE DISORDER

Whereas the definition of schizophrenia in DSM-III marked a sharp narrowing of the concept, there have been relatively few changes in diagnostic criteria between DSM-III, DSM-III-R (American Psychiatric Association, 1987), and DSM-IV. Table 9.1 summarizes the diagnostic criteria listed in DSM-IV.

Core Symptoms

As shown in Table 9.1, DSM-IV criteria for schizophrenia specify: (1) The minimal duration of characteristic psychotic symptoms, with the requirement that characteristic psychotic symptoms be present for a significant portion of the time during a 1-month period (or less if successfully treated), and (2) the core symptoms of schizophrenia, namely characteristic delusions, hallucinations, formal thought disorder, grossly

disorganized behavior, and negative symptoms (flat affect and anhedonia). As indicated in Table 9.1, some core symptoms, such as bizarre delusions and characteristic hallucinations, are sufficient by themselves to meet the active symptom (A) criterion. Alternatively, other symptoms such as disorganized speech and negative symptoms, are weighted less heavily, and two or more of these symptoms are required to meet the active symptom (A) criterion. DSM-IV criteria also require a deterioration in functioning or failure to achieve the expected level of social development (criterion B). The boundaries between schizophrenia, mood disorder, schizoaffective disorder, organic disorders, substance use, and autism are also specified (criteria D, E, and F). The duration of disturbance (6 months), prodromal features, and residual features are defined.

Results from several independent studies, all of which feature the use of operational diagnostic criteria to derive clinical diagnoses, provide compelling evidence that schizophrenia can be reliably diagnosed in children using the same criteria used with adults (for review, see Werry, 1992).

Related Symptoms

Schizophrenic children often present with a number of other symptoms and problems. Common symptoms reported among samples of children with schizophrenia include depression, oppositional behavior, conduct problems, and suicidal tendencies (see R. Asarnow et al., 1994; Russell, 1994; Russell, Bott, & Sammons, 1989).

In considering the data on related symptoms, however, it is important to note that childhood-onset schizophrenia typically presents with insidious, as opposed to acute onset. Although some children experience acute onsets of schizophrenia, the majority of children appear to have been chronically impaired or to show insidious onset patterns (J. Asarnow & Ben-Meir, 1987; Fish, 1977; Gordon, Frazier, et al., 1994; Green et al., 1984; Kolvin, 1971; for review, Werry, 1992). This frequent combination of insidious onset and premorbid impairments complicates precise identification of the point of onset of the disorder, as well as interpretation of "premorbid" or "comorbid" symptoms. How, for example, should one interpret the frequent presentation of symptoms of attention-deficit/hyperactivity disorder (ADHD) prior to and during schizophrenic episodes? Should the ADHD be viewed as a precursor state, early manifestation of the schizophrenic illness, or as a co-occurring condition? Future work is needed to address these issues.

DEFINITIONAL AND DIAGNOSTIC ISSUES

Developmental Issues

DSM-III, DSM-III-R, and DSM-IV employ comparable diagnostic criteria across age. This would appear to facilitate comparisons of child-, adolescent-, and adult-onset cases as well as analyses of continuities between childhood and

---

TABLE 9.1. Summary of DSM-IV Criteria for Schizophrenia

A. *Characteristic symptoms:* Two or more of the symptoms listed below must be present for a significant portion of time during a 1-month period (or less if successfully treated):

   (1) delusions[a]
   (2) hallucinations[a]
   (3) disorganized speech (e.g., frequent derailment or incoherence)
   (4) grossly disorganized or catatonic behavior
   (5) negative symptoms, i.e., affective flattening, alogia, or avolition

B. Social/occupational dysfunction.

C. *Duration:* Continuous signs of disturbance for at least 6 months.

D. Disorder not attributable to Mood Disorder or Schizoaffective Disorder.

E. Disorder not due to substance use or general medical condition.

F. If there is a history of Pervasive Developmental Disorder, an additional diagnosis of Schizophrenia is given only if prominent delusions or hallucinations are also present for at least a month (or less if successfully treated).

Note. Adapted from American Psychiatric Association (1994, pp. 285–286). Copyright 1994 by the American Psychiatric Association. Adapted by permission.
[a]Only one Criterion A symptom is required if delusions are bizarre or hallucinations consist of a running commentary on the person's behavior or thoughts, or two or more conversing voices.

adulthood. However, it is also possible that distinct developmental differences exist in the expression of the disorder. Indeed, current data suggest that hallucinations, delusions, and formal thought disorder are rare or difficult to diagnose prior to 7 years of age (for review, see Caplan, 1994). The use of the same criteria across different ages may mask developmental trends. Further, the use of criteria that are not adjusted to account for developmental trends will likely result in the exclusion of some children who show early signs of the syndrome but who develop full-blown, adult-type schizophrenia at a developmentally later stage (Fish, 1977, 1987).

Diagnosticians also confront age-specific problems in deriving diagnoses. For example, distinguishing between pathological symptoms such as delusions and imaginative fantasies typical during childhood can present diagnostic dilemmas. Because young children have more immature language and cognitive development, there are also frequent limitations in children's abilities to describe their experiences. (For review, see Cantor, 1988; Edgell & Kolvin, 1972; Garralda, 1984a, 1984b; Russell, 1994.)

The Boundaries of the Schizophrenia Spectrum

Further work is needed to clarify the boundaries of the schizophrenia spectrum in childhood. For example, Gordon, Frazier, et al. (1994) have identified a group of children whom they have labeled "multidimensionally impaired" (MDI). These children are described as presenting with multiple early impairments in cognitive and social functioning and falling closest to the DSM-IV criteria for borderline personality disorder. However, Gordon, Frazier, et al. (1994) note that some researchers might diagnose schizophrenia in these MDI children because they also show core schizophrenic symptoms.

Another example of the difficulties defining schizophrenia in early-onset cases is provided by the relatively consistent observation across follow-up studies that a subgroup of children and adolescents diagnosed as schizophrenic when evaluated at the time of their first episodes were found to present with bipolar or schizoaffective disorders when evaluated over the course of several years of follow-up (J. Asarnow, Tompson, & Goldstein, 1994; Eggers, 1989; Werry, McClellan, & Chard, 1991; Zeitlin, 1986). This under-scores the need for longitudinal diagnostic evaluations in both research and clinical practice.

EPIDEMIOLOGY

Prevalence/Incidence

Most cases of schizophrenia have their onsets during late adolescence and early adulthood (Bleuler, 1911/1950; Kraepelin, 1919; Riecher et al., 1991; Remschmidt, 1993; Weinberger, 1987). Schizophrenia is relatively rare in childhood and increases in frequency with adolescence (Beitchman, 1985; Burd & Kerbeshian, 1987; Remschmidt, 1993). Kraepelin (1919) estimated that at least 3.5% of cases of dementia praecox had onsets prior to 10 years of age, with another 2.7% of cases developing between 10 and 15 years. Similarly, Bleuler (1911/1950) and Lutz (1937) projected that between 0.5% and 1% of schizophrenic cases had onsets before 10 years of age, with 4% of schizophrenic psychoses beginning prior to age 15 years.

The relative rarity of schizophrenia with childhood onset has resulted in limited epidemiological data on rates of schizophrenia in the general population. Results from a recent study conducted in North Dakota suggest a prevalence rate for DSM-III-defined schizophrenia of 0.19 per 10,000 children between 2 and 12 years of age (Burd & Kerbeshian, 1987), and Remschmidt, Schulz, Martin, Warnke, and Trott (1994) have suggested that roughly 1 child in 10,000 can be expected to develop schizophrenia. Because rates of a disorder may vary across communities with different characteristics (e.g., rural vs. urban, ethnicity), these prevalence figures must be viewed as highly tentative until more representative data become available.

Sex Differences

Consistent with the adult literature documenting a predominance of males among early-onset cases (Riecher et al., 1991), extant literature suggests an excess of males among childhood-onset cases (Green, Padron-Gayol, Hardesty, & Bassiri, 1992; Kallman & Roth, 1956; Remschmidt et al., 1994; Russell et al., 1989; Volkmar, Cohen, Hoshino, Rende, & Rhea, 1988; for review, see McClellan & Werry, 1992; Werry, 1992). The ratio of males to females appears to become more even in ado-

lescence (Remschmidt et al., 1994). It has been suggested that the excess of males to females in younger age groups may reflect a biological vulnerability in young males similar to that seen in their higher rates of neurological disorders (Fish & Ritvo, 1979; Lewine, 1988). This apparent variation in the age-of-onset distributions for males and females could also reflect etiological differences across gender (e.g., greater vulnerability to viral infection in one gender).

Social Class Factors

Epidemiological studies of adult schizophrenia have indicated an excess of schizophrenic cases among lower socioeconomic groups (see Dohrenwend, Shrout, Link, & Skodol, 1987). It remains unclear, however, whether the association between schizophrenia and social class is a consequence of the disorder such that individuals suffering with the illness drift to lower socioeconomic levels due to the social dysfunction associated with the illness, or alternatively, whether this association reflects causal factors. With respect to childhood-onset schizophrenia, results have been equivocal across studies. Extant studies have also employed clinic patients with associated referral biases, underscoring the need for further research to clarify this issue (for review, see Werry, 1992).

Cultural Variations

Results from the World Health Organization (WHO) Collaborative Study on Determinants of Outcome of Severe Mental Disorders (Sartorius, Jablensky, Emberg, Leff, & Gulbinat, 1987) indicate highly similar symptom profiles and incidence rates for schizophrenia across different countries and cultures. The WHO study employed carefully developed transculturally standardized diagnostic instruments and included individuals between 15 and 54 years of age. Thus, although some adolescents were included in this sample, the majority of the sample were adults. Epidemiological studies with child and adolescent populations are needed to determine whether similar patterns will be detected among younger age groups. Another finding from the WHO study that merits examination with younger samples is the more favorable course and outcomes observed among patients in "developing" as opposed to "developed" countries (Leff et al., 1991; Sartorius et al., 1987). The more favorable

outcome among individuals in developing countries was evident on measures of both clinical symptoms (e.g., remission, number of episodes) and measures of social functioning.

THEORETICAL FRAMEWORK

Most current etiological models of schizophrenia adopt a vulnerability–stress model. This framework has proven useful as a general guide to research because it emphasizes the joint contribution of genetic predisposition and stressful life events to the development and recurrence of schizophrenia (see for example, Nuechterlein, 1987; Zubin & Spring, 1977). These multifactorial models that emphasize interactions among biology, behavior, and environments have generally replaced single-factor models that posited constitutional or environmental "causes" of schizophrenia. This shift toward multifactorial transactional models was stimulated by research underscoring the likely complexity and diversity of the etiological pathways to schizophrenia. For example, as shown in the vulnerability–stress model of childhood-onset schizophrenia presented as Figure 9.1, genetic risk factors are hypothesized to lead to central nervous system dysfunction and impairments in attention and information processing. These individual characteristics are thought to interact with environmental stressors and protective factors to influence the likelihood that any individual will develop schizophrenia at various developmental stages.

As is discussed in the sections on etiological factors that follow, the general vulnerability–stress model lacks specificity as to the indices of vulnerability or stress that are relevant to the disorder. Thus, the vulnerability–stress model is generally offered as a heuristic device for integrating existing knowledge and organizing research rather than as a formal hypotheticodeductive system. Three central constructs that are emphasized across various vulnerability–stress models are as follows:

"Vulnerability factors" refer to characteristics that predispose an individual to develop the disorder and are assumed to be present in individuals at risk for the disorder and to comprise an enduring characteristic of individuals who suffer from schizophrenic episodes. Both constitutional and environmental vulnerability factors have been posited such as genetic factors, central nervous system damage resulting from obstetrical

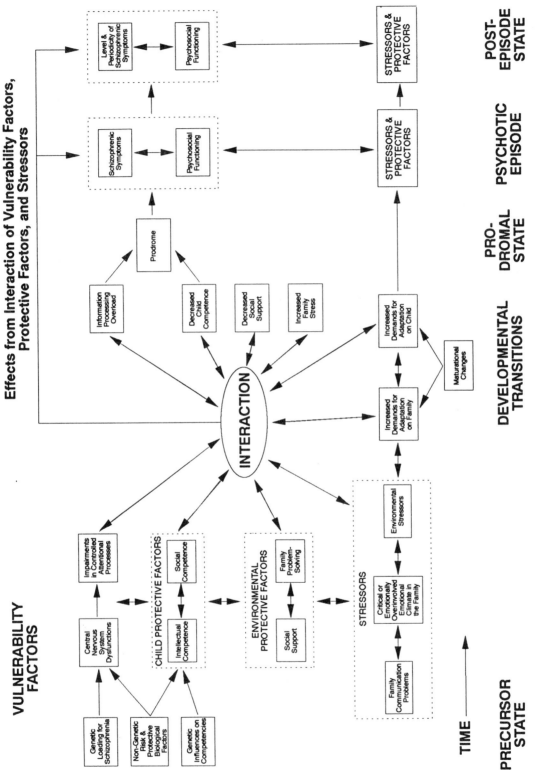

FIGURE 9.1. Vulnerability–stress model of childhood-onset schizophrenia.

and birth complications, inadequate learning opportunities, and exposure to deviant family communication patterns. Some vulnerability factors may be specific to schizophrenia, whereas others may be associated with general risk for psychiatric disorder. Turning to Figure 9.1, whereas genetic loading for schizophrenia might represent a specific risk factor for schizophrenia, malnutrition might represent a nongenetic, biological factor that might be associated with increased risk for psychiatric disorder in general.

"Stressors" are hypothesized to lead to an increased likelihood of a schizophrenic episode. Stressors may include major life events such as death of a parent, as well as more chronic stressors, strains, and hassles. Major life-change events that were acute at one point in time (e.g., death of a parent) may also become more chronic as time progresses (e.g., living in a home with a bereaved parent).

"Protective factors" refer to characteristics of the individual or environment that are associated with a reduced risk of an episode among individuals who are at risk. Possible protective factors that have been suggested in the literature include intelligence, social support, social competence, and healthy family communication (see J. Asarnow & Goldstein, 1986). Because you have to determine if an individual is truly at risk before you can evaluate whether he or she has been protected from an illness, it is often difficult to identify protective factors. However, if one could identify a "true" and modifiable protective factor, this would have major implications for the development of primary and secondary prevention strategies.

Hypotheses concerning the ways in which vulnerability factors, stressors, and protective factors interact vary across models. Whereas some models postulate additive relationships in which posited factors are presumed to act relatively independently, transactional models emphasize person-by-environment interactions over time. Transactional models, thus, focus on the question of how genetically transmitted predispositions are expressed at various developmental stages and interact with care-giving environments to determine whether individuals develop schizophrenia as well as their levels of psychosocial functioning. (For more extensive discussion, see R. Asarnow, Asarnow, & Strandberg, 1989; J. Asarnow & Goldstein, 1986; Nuechterlein, 1987; and Sameroff, 1990.)

Figure 9.1, which depicts a multifactorial vulnerability–stress model of childhood-onset schizophrenia (R. Asarnow et al., 1989), is an example of a transactional model. Variations in symptomatic behavior and psychosocial functioning are hypothesized to result from the interaction between enduring psychobiological vulnerabilities, environmental and biological stressors, and the moderating effects of individual competencies and individual and family coping responses. The model posits that a predisposition to schizophrenia is genetically transmitted. However, schizophrenic episodes are hypothesized to occur only among vulnerable individuals who are exposed to certain levels and types of stressors. Individuals with the greatest loading on vulnerability factors, the least effective coping responses and competencies, and the greatest exposure to stress are viewed as most likely to develop schizophrenic episodes and to have the most malignant outcomes. Alternatively, lower loadings on vulnerability factors, more effective coping responses and competencies, and lower levels of stress exposure are hypothesized to lead to more favorable outcomes.

Similar to other models proposed for adult schizophrenia (e.g., see Nuechterlein, 1987), the model presented in Figure 9.1 emphasizes developmental pathways by following a time line from left to right beginning with genetic predisposition and progressing to precursor states, developmental transitions, prodromal states, psychotic episodes, and postpsychotic states. Schizophrenic episodes as well as postpsychotic states are conceptualized as including clinical symptoms and levels of social adaptation and school functioning.

Based on the existing literature, the model attempts to specify some hypotheses regarding measures that may serve as personal vulnerability factors, significant stressors, and protective factors that may mitigate the effects of vulnerabilities and/or stressors. The literature with respect to these measures is reviewed in subsequent sections of this chapter.

ETIOLOGIES

Despite the increased complexity of current theoretical frameworks and the major advances in our knowledge about schizophrenia, the causes of this illness (or set of illnesses) are still unknown. With respect to childhood-onset cases, efforts to understand etiology must further address the fact that children suffering from schizophrenia are clearly atypical among the larger group of schizo-

phrenic patients by virtue of their early onset. Four major hypotheses have been offered to account for the atypical early onset among childhood cases:

1. Childhood-onset schizophrenia represents a particularly severe and chronic form of the illness, with the very early childhood onset reflecting a more severe biological disposition to the illness (Fish, 1977).
2. Childhood- and later-onset schizophrenia represent different illnesses.
3. The atypically early-onset characteristic of childhood cases is associated with the presence of potentiating factors, such as severe psychosocial and/or biological stressors.
4. Childhood onset has no particular etiological significance; thus childhood-onset cases represent cases at the early end of the age of onset distribution, and early- and later-onset schizophrenia represent the same illness or illnesses with similar levels of clinical and etiological heterogeneity.

In the sections below, we review extant evidence with respect to major types of etiological factors in the context of these hypotheses regarding the significance of childhood onset.

Biological Factors

Increasing support for the view that schizophrenia is a primary brain disease has been stimulated by numerous studies documenting central nervous system dysfunction among schizophrenics as well as the dramatic improvements in outcome associated with neuroleptic medication (Weinberger, 1987). As Weinberger (1987) points out, however, two important facts need to be addressed in any attempt to understand the nature of the central nervous system dysfunction in schizophrenia. First, there is no unitary brain lesion found in all schizophrenic patients. Second, the brain lesions found in some schizophrenic patients are not unique or specific to schizophrenia "because other disorders that are associated with pathology in similar brain areas usually do not present as schizophrenia" (Weinberger, 1987, p. 661).

The Neurodevelopmental Model

In an elegant analysis, Weinberger (1987, p. 660) proposed a "neurodevelopmental model" of

schizophrenia to account for the following three "inescapable clinical 'facts' about schizophrenia": (1) most cases of schizophrenia have their onsets in late adolescence or early adulthood; (2) stress has been found to be associated with both onset and relapse; and (3) neuroleptic medications have dramatically improved outcome in many patients (1987, p. 660). As proposed by Weinberger, the neurodevelopmental model suggests that the neuropathology in schizophrenia involves a fixed brain lesion involving the limbic system and prefrontal cortex that occurs early in life, substantially prior to the onset of psychotic symptoms, and is "clinically silent" until a certain level of normal maturation is complete among the neural systems mediating the schizophrenic psychosis. The role of stress in precipitating clinical symptoms is proposed to be associated with normal maturational features of dopaminergic neural systems, specifically dopaminergic mechanisms involved in the activation of the prefrontal cortex. These mechanisms may comprise a key part of normal responses to stress. Consequently, the clinical decompensation often seen following stress among individuals with schizophrenia may reflect a breakdown in the normal physiological response to stress (Weinberger, 1987).

Despite the fact that childhood- and early adolescent-onset schizophrenia are atypical by virtue of the early onset, several findings are consistent with aspects of Weinberger's neurodevelopmental model. First, the view that schizophrenia is a neurodevelopmental disorder associated with early-occurring neural pathology derives some support from accumulating data demonstrating that children with schizophrenia tend to manifest neurobehavioral, behavioral, and social impairments well in advance of the first onset of psychotic symptoms. For example, retrospective studies of children with schizophrenia (Watkins, Asarnow, & Tanguay, 1988) have revealed that during infancy and early childhood their language acquisition is slow (particularly for expressive language), and gross-motor functioning is impaired. Somewhat later there are impairments in fine-motor coordination. These neurobehavioral impairments may be early manifestations of the brain lesions posited by neurodevelopmental models. As noted above, in the neurodevelopmental model hypothesized, brain lesions are thought to be "clinically silent" at early developmental stages. Results from studies of schizophrenic children, as well as studies of children at risk for schizophrenia, suggest that the lesions

may be silent only in the sense that they do not immediately produce active psychotic symptoms (e.g., Walker, Savoie, & Davis, 1994; Watkins et al., 1988; J. Asarnow, 1988, for review). It is worth noting that expressive language and motor skills are subserved by structures in the frontal lobes. It is these areas where many of the early brain lesions are also found (Weinberger, 1987).

Difficulties with social behavior have also been noted in the early childhood histories of children who developed schizophrenia. Notably, Watkins et al. (1988) found that these children were characterized as showing a lack of social responsiveness during infancy, and problems with extreme mood lability, inappropriate clinging, and unexplained rage reactions during early childhood. Further, J. Asarnow, Tompson, and Goldstein (1994) found that children with schizophrenia were characterized by lower levels of premorbid adjustment than were a comparison group of children with major depression. Children with schizophrenia showed particularly poor levels of premorbid functioning in the areas of peer relationships, scholastic performance, school adaptation, and interests.

The Dopamine Hypothesis

The hypothesis that dopamine is involved in the pathogenesis of schizophrenia in adults is supported by several sources of evidence (see Carlsson, 1987). Most notably, the efficacy of phenothiazines and related drugs in controlling psychotic symptoms is correlated with the extent to which they block dopaminergic transmission. Alternatively, drugs such as amphetamine or L-dopa that produce excessive release of dopamine have been found to be associated with the intensification of psychotic disorders. As Carlsson (1987) points out, however, it may "be more appropriate to speak of a dopamine hypothesis of psychosis" as opposed to schizophrenia because these drugs appear to affect psychotic conditions other than schizophrenia, and some patients with schizophrenia show a poor response to pharmacological treatment (p. 223).

Advances in basic knowledge regarding dopaminergic systems have underscored the complexity of dopaminergic mechanisms and suggested multiple alternative hypotheses concerning the nature of the dysfunction in schizophrenia. For example, problems could arise because of dopaminergic hyperfunction, an imbalance between dopaminergic systems and other systems, or a variety of subtle dopaminergic dysfunctions (Carlsson, 1987). Dopaminergic neurons, however, "play a crucial role in the modulation of mental, motor, endocrine and autonomic functions and appear to be involved in the functional integration of recent cortical with older subcortical functions" (Carlsson, 1987, p. 233).

The Evidence on Biological Factors

To date there are relatively few brain imaging, morphological, or neurochemical studies of childhood-onset schizophrenia. However, the premise that childhood-onset schizophrenia, similar to adult schizophrenia, will be characterized by evidence of neural pathology is supported by the limited extant evidence. Casanova, Carosella, and Kleinman (1990) found brainstem abnormalities in the autopsied material of a man who died at age 22 years and had his first onset of schizophrenia at about 10 years of age. Specific findings included central chromatolysis of neurons and mild gliosis in a restricted distribution of the brainstem and thalamus, and cell loss and cytoarchitectural disruption in the frontal lobes, prepyriform cortex, and entorhinal region. Casanova et al. (1990) suggest that these findings may reflect a "chronic derangement in the function of neurons of the rostral brainstem tegmental area and medial thalamus with secondary involvement of their terminal projection sites" (p. 313).

Highlighting the likelihood that diverse indicators of CNS dysfunction will be identified among schizophrenic children, Woody, Bolyard, Eisenhauer, and Altschuler (1987) found that a CT scan and MRI conducted on a 10-year-old boy with schizophrenia revealed dilated lateral, third, and fourth ventricles and an enlarged cisterna magna with left cerebellar atrophy or hypoplasia. Early magnetic resonance imagery (MRI) and positron emission tomography (PET) scan results from the National Institute of Mental Health (NIMH) group suggest increased size of the left ventricular horn in some patients, as well as some abnormalities in glucose metabolism (Gordon, Frazier, et al., 1994). Hendren, Hodde-Vargas, Vagras, Orrison, and Dell (1991) reported that a subgroup of children with "schizophrenia" identified within a larger sample of psychiatrically disturbed children also had enlarged left ventricular horns, and Schulz et al. (1983) described ventriculomegaly in adolescents with schizophrenia. Thus, similar to findings with adult schizophrenia, the very limited findings with childhood-

onset cases underscore both the high probability of central nervous system anomalies, as well as the likelihood of diverse neurological and anatomic findings in childhood-onset schizophrenia.

Adopting another approach to clarifying the nature of hypothesized central nervous system dysfunctions, R. Asarnow and colleagues (R. Asarnow et al., 1994) have used a series of neuropsychological and experimental tasks to link behavioral findings to putative CNS dysfunctions based on data from patients with focal neuropathology and/or studies of brain electrical activity. A strong finding to emerge from this research is that schizophrenic children show some of the same difficulties with attention and information processing that have been identified in adult schizophrenia. Specifically, R. Asarnow and colleagues (R. Asarnow, Granholm, & Sherman, 1991; R. Asarnow & Sherman, 1984) have established that schizophrenic children show impairments on the span of apprehension task. This task requires the child to identify a target stimulus (either a T or F) shown briefly (for 50 milliseconds) on a screen embedded in an array of other letters. When required to process larger arrays of visual information (5 and 10 letters vs. 1 and 3 letters), schizophrenic children performed more poorly than children with attention-deficit disorder and normal controls. The slope of the function relating the probability of target detection to array size is also steeper in schizophrenic children, suggesting that the performance of schizophrenic children is more disrupted by increasing the amount of information that the child has to process. Further, event-related potential (ERP) data recorded during performance of the span of apprehension task indicate similar patterns of brain activity for both adults and children with schizophrenia (Strandburg, Marsh, Brown, Asarnow, & Guthrie, 1994). Both child- and adult-onset schizophrenics produce less endogenous negative activity, as compared to age-matched normal controls, which may reflect limitations in the amount of processing resources available to carry out cognitive processing (R. Asarnow et al., 1994; Strandburg et al., 1994).

Thus, consistent with the hypothesis that schizophrenia in children and adults is associated with similar disease processes and dysfunctions, children with schizophrenia demonstrate an attention/information-processing deficit that has been shown to characterize schizophrenic adults. This deficit also shows some specificity to childhood-onset schizophrenia when compared to attention-deficit/hyperactivity disorder, another childhood-onset disorder associated with attentional impairment. These findings assume particular significance when considered in relation to other research documenting that impairments on the span of apprehension task (1) remain relatively stable across changes in clinical state and characterize adult schizophrenic patients during periods of remission as well as during periods of disturbance, (2) show some specificity to schizophrenia in adults, and (3) show some degree of genetic influence (for review, R. Asarnow et al., 1991).

In a series of studies, R. Asarnow and colleagues (R. Asarnow et al., 1994) have also analyzed the task demands and/or experimental conditions that are associated with the greatest and least neuropsychological impairment in children with schizophrenia. Results to date indicate the following:

1. Schizophrenic children do not show impairments relative to normal controls on tasks assessing reception and comprehension of auditory stimuli, but they do show impaired performance when required to attend to, remember, and respond to sequences of verbal and nonverbal stimuli that make extensive demands on processing capacity.

2. Children with schizophrenia show impairments on tests of visual perception, but only when memory demands are added to the task such that the child is required to hold the sample stimulus in short-term memory prior to responding.

3. Impairments in visual–motor coordination and fine-motor speed were found using the dominant hand, nondominant hand, and both hands.

4. Similar to schizophrenic adults, children with schizophrenia show impairments in executive functions such as allocating attention as assessed on tests such as the Wisconsin Card Sorting Test (Grant & Berg, 1981) that require subjects to sort cards varying along multiple dimensions into categories based on a sorting principle that the subject must discover.

5. Providing task-appropriate strategies or information to schizophrenic children sometimes paradoxically impairs performance. Rather than pointing to unilateral brain disease, this pattern of results suggests that schizophrenic children have difficulties on tasks that make extensive demands on information-processing resources regardless of the hemisphere that subserves the function(s) assessed by the task. If this hypoth-

esis proves correct, the search for a CNS substrate for schizophrenia will likely involve examination of the CNS structures involved in recruiting and allocating resources and the dynamic interaction between these structures. (See R. Asarnow et al., 1994 for a fuller discussion of these issues.)

Genetic Factors

Similar to a number of genetically transmitted disorders where early onset of disorder is associated with a heavy genetic loading for the disease, there are some early data suggesting a twofold increase in the aggregation of schizophrenic disorders among the first-degree relatives of children with schizophrenia, as compared to adults with schizophrenia (Fish, 1977; Kallman & Roth, 1956; Kolvin, 1971). Additionally, Kallman and Roth (1956) reported uncorrected concordance rates of 88.2% and 22.9% respectively for monozygotic and dizygotic twins in the only major study of twins of schizophrenic probands with onsets prior to 15 years of age. Adult schizophrenia also clustered in the families of childhood-onset cases, providing support for the view of similar genetic mechanisms. Based on these data, Rosenthal (1970) suggested that preadolescent schizophrenia may represent a more virulent form of adult schizophrenia with virtually complete penetrance.

In considering these early data, however, it should be noted that these early studies did not include modern features such as blind assessments of relatives that minimize the risk of biased diagnoses arising from knowledge of the proband's diagnostic status, control groups, structured diagnostic assessments, and operational diagnostic criteria. Consequently, results from early studies require confirmation using more stringent experimental procedures.

Early results from one ongoing study (R. Asarnow, 1993) that employed blind diagnoses, control groups, and personal interviews using structured diagnostic procedures provide some tentative support of the prior findings. Although very early results from this study suggest a very high rate of schizophrenia among relatives of childhood-onset schizophrenics, results based on the full sample are needed.

Interestingly, the ongoing NIMH study of childhood-onset schizophrenia has identified one case with a translocation (Gordon, Krasnewich, et al., 1994). This finding is interesting in relation to the literature indicating a variety of different cytogenetic anomalies among schizophrenic adults (for review, see De Lisi & Lovett, 1991). The translocation identified was an apparently balanced one involving chromosomes 1 and 7 [46,XY,t(1;7)(p22;q22)].

Environmental Stressors

The available data suggest that childhood-onset schizophrenia is a familial disorder. However, the observation that concordance rates for monozygotic twins are substantially less than 100% indicates that nongenetic factors also influence the likelihood that an individual will develop schizophrenia. Because the presence of psychiatric illness in a parent is likely to be associated with impaired parental role functioning, it is also likely that there are complex interactions between familial psychiatric disorder and environmental factors. Further, if as expected with adult schizophrenia, considerable genetic and etiological heterogeneity is identified in childhood-onset schizophrenia, some forms of the disorder may prove to be more closely linked to environmental stress than others.

Pregnancy and birth complications comprise one environmental factor that has been implicated as a potential etiological factor in schizophrenia. The difficulties in differentiating between the effects of child and environmental characteristics, however, are highlighted by Cantor's (1988) finding that although comparable rates of birth complications were observed among her "schizophrenic" and control samples, a higher rate of "perinatal instability" was observed for schizophrenic male subjects as compared to control male subjects. The category of "perinatal instability" included difficulties such as cyanotic episodes that could reflect vulnerability in the infant, thus highlighting the possibility that some children may be more vulnerable to prenatal and/or perinatal complications. However, data indicating high rates of perinatal difficulties among adults with schizophrenia (for review, see McNeil, 1988) as well as among high-risk children (of schizophrenic parents) who developed schizophrenia (Cannon, Barr, & Mednick, 1991; Parnas et al., 1982), highlight the need for further examination of pregnancy and birth complications among cases of childhood-onset schizophrenia.

Recent data highlighting possible links between schizophrenia and prenatal exposure to viral infection further underscore the possible etiological role of such early environmental stressors. Notably, Mednick, Machon, Huttunen, and

Bonett (1988) reported an elevated rate of adult schizophrenia among individuals who were exposed to a severe Type A2 influenza epidemic during their second trimester of gestation. Increased risk for schizophrenia was not found among individuals exposed to the epidemic during the first and third trimesters of gestation, suggesting that it is the *timing* of the stressor during a *critical period of gestation* that is associated with the increased risk for schizophrenia. Given the likely etiological heterogeneity of schizophrenia, Cannon et al. (1991) have suggested that "teratogenic agents such as viruses may be responsible for the fetal neural disturbances leading to schizophrenia in *some* cases" (p. 13).

Interested readers are referred to Fish and Ritvo (1979) for a review of the earlier literature and Cannon et al. (1991) for a review of the high-risk literature.

Psychosocial Stress

The role of psychosocial stress in the etiology of schizophrenia is clearest in studies of high-risk samples where the illness has not yet developed, because the occurrence of the schizophrenic illness is associated with significant psychosocial stress in families. Unfortunately, because childhood-onset schizophrenia is relatively rare, very few cases of childhood-onset schizophrenia have been described in the literature on children at-risk for schizophrenia. However, Fish did describe two cases of childhood-onset schizophrenia, both independently diagnosed at 10 years of age (for review, see Fish, 1987). Although this represents a very small sample, it merits note that these were the only children in the sample who were identified as having histories of physical abuse. These two children were also reared by schizophrenic mothers and had the most severe signs of neurointegrative disorder, or what Fish has termed "pandysmaturation," which is defined as a pattern of transient lags and disorganization of gross-motor and/or visual–motor development in conjunction with lags in physical growth. These descriptions highlight the likely interactions between genetic and environmental factors in the development of many schizophrenic children.

Kallman and Roth (1956) examined the home environments of siblings and dizygotic twins of probands with childhood-onset schizophrenia. Disturbed rearing environments were somewhat more likely to be associated with schizophrenia-spectrum outcomes but were also found in cases with healthy outcomes. Whereas roughly 82% of the homes of twins and siblings diagnosed as schizoid or schizophrenic were classified as "inadequate" based on the presence of at least one disturbed or inadequate parent, economic distress, or broken homes, 64.8% of all twins and siblings classified as "normal" also came from homes classified as "inadequate." The high level of difficulties described in these home environments may be associated, however, with the fact that all of these homes contained a child with schizophrenia.

J. Asarnow and colleagues (for review, see J. Asarnow, Tompson, & Goldstein, 1994) have conducted a series of studies aimed at describing the environments of schizophrenic children and children with schizotypal personality disorder (SPD). Although SPD is controversial in childhood, links between schizophrenia and SPD are suggested by research indicating elevated rates of SPD among the biological relatives of schizophrenics (for review, see Kendler, 1988), as well as by high-risk research suggesting that schizotypal symptoms such as social isolation and signs of thought disturbance may be early precursors of schizophrenia (for review, see J. Asarnow, 1988). By including children with SPD in our studies, we sought to examine the broader schizophrenia spectrum and possibly evaluate predictors of the onset of schizophrenia among a group of children hypothesized to be at risk for full-blown schizophrenic disorders.

Our work has addressed two general questions: (1) Are the family attributes that have been found to be associated with the onset and course of adult schizophrenia also observed in families of children with schizophrenia-spectrum disorders? (2) Are there specific family environmental attributes that are associated with schizophrenia-spectrum disorders in childhood and less common in families of children with other psychiatric disorders and families of children with no evidence of psychiatric disorder? Recognizing that both parents and children contribute to the quality of family interaction, we have assessed both parent and child behaviors.

Communication quality was assessed using a measure of communication deviance (CD; Jones, 1977; Singer & Wynne, 1965). Typically, CD is assessed using projective tests such as the Thematic Apperception Test (TAT) or Rorschach and is conceptualized as an interpersonal manifestation of thought and attentional disturbance. Prior research has demonstrated that parents of adult

schizophrenics tend to show higher levels of CD as compared to parents of patients with other disorders and parents of normal controls. Additionally, Goldstein (1987) found an increased risk for adult schizophrenia-spectrum disorders among disturbed but nonschizophrenic adolescents whose parents scored high on the CD measure. Similar to these findings for adult schizophrenia, J. Asarnow, Goldstein, and Ben-Meir (1988) observed that parents of schizophrenic and SPD children were more likely to score high on CD (assessed on the TAT) than were parents of children with depressive disorders (J. Asarnow et al., 1988). Schizophrenic and SPD children from high-CD families showed the most severe impairments and the poorest attentional functioning, as indexed by the freedom from distractibility factor of the Wechsler Intelligence Scale for Children—Revised (WISC-R) (based on scores from the arithmetic, digit span, and coding subtests). This suggests that CD in parents may be associated with a particularly severe form of childhood schizophrenia-spectrum disorder or, perhaps, may be associated with family interactional processes that exacerbate the severity of dysfunction. CD was also found among some parents of depressed children, but CD was not associated with differences in the severity of impairment or attentional functioning in depressed children, suggesting that the CD construct may have particular significance for the development of schizophrenic disorders.

The clinical and etiological significance of the CD findings merit exploration. One hypothesis that has been offered is that the high rate of CD identified among parents may be associated with the stress of living with a severely disturbed schizophrenic child. Alternatively, it has been suggested that high CD may be a marker of subclinical or full-blown psychopathology in a relative. Goldstein et al. (1992), however, did not find a significant association between high CD and the presence of diagnosable psychiatric disorder among parents of adults with schizophrenia.

Another construct examined by J. Asarnow and colleagues is the affective quality of parent–child interactions. Observational measures of direct parent–child interaction, as well as the expressed emotion (EE) measure (which is obtained in the child's absence) were used. The EE measure assesses critical and emotionally overinvolved attitudes of the parent toward the child. Numerous studies have shown that EE is a strong predictor of outcome among schizophrenic adults (for review, see Leff, 1991; Leff & Vaughn, 1985), and Goldstein (1987) reported that measures of EE obtained during adolescence were associated with an increased risk of schizophrenia-spectrum disorders in young adulthood.

In contrast to results with adult schizophrenia, rates of EE using the Five Minute Speech Sample index were relatively low among parents of children with schizophrenia-spectrum disorders (23% vs. 44% in the most comparable adult sample) and did not differ significantly from rates of EE in a normal comparison group (Asarnow, Tompson, Hamilton, Goldstein, & Guthrie, 1994). High EE ratings among parents of children with schizophrenia-spectrum disorders tended to result from high scores on the criticism dimension rather than emotional overinvolvement. Interestingly, high EE was significantly more frequent among parents of depressed children as compared to children with schizophrenia-spectrum disorders or normal controls, a finding that is consistent with other reports indicating high rates of EE among parents of children with other nonschizophrenic disorders (Hibbs et al., 1991; Stubbe, Zahner, Goldstein, & Leckman, 1993).

On an interaction task in which parents and children attempted to resolve an affectively charged family problem, however, parents of children with schizophrenia-spectrum disorders were more likely to express harsh criticism toward the child than were parents of normal controls, or parents of depressed children (Hamilton, 1991). This again underscores the likely impact of children's behavior on the behavior of their parents.

In summary, results of studies of the family environments of children with schizophrenia-spectrum disorders underscore the stress and distress experienced by many of these families. Future research is needed to clarify the impact of family stress on the course of childhood-onset schizophrenia and SPD, and to clarify associations among family–genetic and family–environmental variables.

COMMON COMORBIDITIES

One observation that has received clear documentation is that many schizophrenic children meet criteria for comorbid diagnoses. Despite uncertainties regarding how the presence of a comorbid condition should be viewed in the context of a schizophrenic diagnosis, investigators

who have used semistructured diagnostic interviews have tended to report high rates of codiagnoses among schizophrenic children. To illustrate, Russell et al. (1989) found that 68% of their sample of schizophrenic children met criteria for another diagnosis. The most common codiagnoses were conduct/oppositional disorder (31%) and atypical depression or dysthymic disorder (37%). This high rate of depression codiagnoses, coupled with reports that some cases initially presenting as schizophrenic meet criteria for bipolar or schizoaffective disorders at follow-up (Eggers, 1989; Werry et al., 1991; Zeitlin, 1986), underscores the limitations of cross-sectional diagnoses based on evaluations conducted at a single point in time. In this context, it is important to recall that the boundaries of the schizophrenia spectrum are not resolved, and some forms of schizoaffective disorder appear to be closely linked to schizophrenia (Kendler, 1988; Kendler et al., 1993).

Given earlier controversies regarding the association between autism and schizophrenia, it merits note that there does not appear to be an elevated risk of schizophrenia among samples of children with autism or PDD (Burd & Kerbeshian, 1987; Volkmar & Cohen, 1991), although there is occasional overlap between autistic and schizophrenic syndromes and symptoms over time (e.g., Petty, Ornitz, Michelman, & Zimmerman, 1984). These data reinforce the importance of distinguishing between autistic and schizophrenic syndromes.

CURRENT ISSUES

Pharmacological Treatment

There is an urgent need for additional research focusing on the efficacy of pharmacological treatments for schizophrenic children. Despite the widespread use of neuroleptics in treating schizophrenic children and the serious and sometimes toxic side effects that can develop (see, J. Asarnow et al., 1991), there are very few controlled drug treatment trials.

Spencer, Kaftantaris, Padron-Gayol, Rosenberg, and Campbell (1992) used a double-blind, crossover design to investigate the effects of haloperidol, as compared to placebo. The sample included 16 children between 5 and 12 years of age meeting DSM-III-R criteria for schizophrenia. Reductions in psychotic symptoms were observed

using doses of haloperidol ranging from 0.5 to 3.5 mg/day. (See also Spencer & Campbell, 1994.)

Recent reports also suggest that clozapine may prove useful in the treatment of child and adolescent schizophrenia. Remschmidt et al. (1994) reported improvements in schizophrenic symptoms after clozapine treatment among 75.6% (31 of 41) adolescents with schizophrenia who had failed to respond to conventional neuroleptic treatment. Mozes et al. (1994) also described successful clozapine trials in four children with schizophrenia. Additionally, Gordon, Frazier, et al. (1994) reported preliminary results from the ongoing NIMH double-blind trial comparing the effects of clozapine and haloperidol in a group of adolescents with childhood onsets of schizophrenia. The effects of clozapine plus placebo are compared with the effects of haloperidol plus benztropin administered over a 6–week period. Although the early results from the NIMH trial must be viewed as tentative, early results from this ongoing trial suggest reductions in psychotic symptoms and few side effects among a small sample of adolescents receiving clozapine treatment. Additional research is needed to clarify further the relative efficacy of alternative medications as well as various side effects and complications.

Psychosocial Treatment

Although the literature contains rich clinical descriptions of psychosocial treatment strategies for children with schizophrenia (e.g., Campbell, 1978; Cantor, 1988; Fish, 1968; McClellan & Werry, 1992; Remschmidt et al., 1994), recent searches revealed no controlled trials of psychosocial interventions (J. Asarnow, 1994; Caplan, 1994). While medications may control psychotic symptoms for some children with schizophrenia, the need to supplement pharmacological treatment with special school programs, social skills training, family treatment, case management, and rehabilitation services is generally recognized in clinical practice. Recent advances in psychosocial treatments for adults with schizophrenia may also have applicability for children and teenagers (see for example, Falloon et al., 1985; Bellack & Mueser, 1984; Leff, Kuipers, Berkowitz, & Sturgeon, 1985; Liberman et al., 1993). Behavioral family treatment emphasizing training in communication and problem-solving skills and social skills training emphasizing instruction and practice in skills such as maintaining appropriate

eye contact and initiating conversations would seem to have particular promise. Systematic evaluation of alternative psychosocial treatment strategies is clearly needed.

Outcome and Prognostic Factors

Despite the crucial importance of data on longitudinal course and prognostic factors for providing optimal clinical care and establishing the validity of psychiatric syndromes, there are limited data on the course of childhood-onset schizophrenia. The time needed to complete longitudinal studies has also resulted in most of current outcome data deriving from samples collected during the pre-DSM-III period when more modern assessment and diagnostic procedures were not available. With this caveat, we review results from three studies of early-onset schizophrenia and one comprehensive case record study of children receiving psychiatric care both during childhood and as adults (Zeitlin, 1986). Three of these four studies based initial diagnoses on case record information (Werry et al., 1991; Eggers, 1989; Zeitlin, 1986).

Congruous with pre-DSM-III data suggesting poor prognosis for childhood-onset schizophrenia (for review, Fish & Ritvo, 1979), Werry et al. (1991) describe remission (defined as an absence of subsequent schizophrenic episodes) in only 3% of their sample over a 1- to 16-year follow-up interval (mean follow-up interval of roughly 5 years). Ninety percent of the sample showed chronic schizophrenia or two or more schizophrenic episodes. Thirteen percent of their sample had died, although it was unclear whether these deaths represented suicides, delusion-driven accidents, or other kinds of accidental deaths. Seventeen percent of the sample were in school full-time or had full-time employment, and the average level of general adaptive functioning (GAF) was 40 reflecting a relatively severe level of impairment (major impairment in several areas or some impairment in reality testing or communication). Ninety percent of the sample were receiving neuroleptic treatment. Outcome may have appeared particularly poor for this sample because subjects were classified as schizophrenic based on outcome as opposed to admission diagnoses (Werry et al., 1991). This was due to the observation that bipolar affective disorder was frequently misdiagnosed initially as schizophrenia.

Eggers (1989) report on 57 patients diagnosed as schizophrenic prior to 14 years of age suggests a more favorable outcome. At a follow-up evaluation 6 years to 40 years later (mean = 16 years), cases with schizophrenia and schizoaffective psychoses were analyzed separately. Among the schizophrenic cases, 27% were described as in remission, 24% were described as showing slight defect, and 49% were described as showing severe defect. Because cultural differences may influence outcome, it is important to note that the Werry et al. (1991; Werry & McClellan, 1992; Werry, McClellan, Andrews, & Ham, 1994) study was conducted in New Zealand, and the Eggers (1978, 1989) study was conducted in Germany.

Follow-up data from our California sample of schizophrenic children seen originally between 7 and 14 years of age (J. Asarnow, Tompson, & Goldstein, 1994) are more consistent with the outcomes observed in the Eggers (1989) sample. Over the course of a 2- to 7-year follow-up, 61% of our sample showed continuing schizophrenia as the children progressed through adolescence, and 67% showed continuing schizophrenia or schizoaffective disorder. There was also considerable variability in global adjustment, with 56% of the sample showing improvement in functioning over the course of the follow-up and the other 44% showing minimal improvement or deteriorating course. Twenty-eight percent of the sample were classified as showing good outcomes, based on global assessment scores of 60 or above at the final follow-up, indicating relatively good psychosocial adjustment.

Variability in outcome is also suggested by Zeitlin's (1986) case record study conducted in England. Half of the cases (four of eight) diagnosed with schizophrenia between 8 and 15 years of age received schizophrenic diagnoses as adults, and the other half received other adult diagnoses (manic–depressive, $n = 3$; unspecified personality disorder with questions regarding possible schizophrenia, $n = 1$). Less variability was apparent if children were characterized based on the presence versus absence of psychosis. Ninety percent of children diagnosed with psychosis in childhood (9 of 10) presented with psychoses as young adults. Eight of these 10 children (80%) were identified with schizophrenia as children, and the other two were diagnosed with manic depression as children. Interestingly, acute onsets and depressed mood were more common among schizophrenic children receiving adult diagnoses

of affective psychoses, as compared to schizophrenic children diagnosed with schizophrenia as adults. These data point to considerable continuity for psychotic disorder between childhood and adulthood. However, these data also underscore both the difficulties one encounters when differentiating between schizophrenic and affective psychoses and the potential utility of using clinical features, such as onset patterns and depressed mood, to identify subgroups of children who may prove to show less heterogeneity in outcome and possibly treatment response.

Werry and McClellan (1992) and Eggers (1989) examined predictors of outcome. Results differed somewhat depending on the outcome criterion (e.g., symptoms, social functioning), but abnormal premorbid adjustment predicted poor outcome in both samples. Additionally, impairment after first admission was a predictor of outcome in the Werry and McClellan (1992) sample. Thus, having a poor level of adjustment prior to the onset of schizophrenia, as well as a high level of impairment following the first admission for the illness, was associated with poorer outcome.

FUTURE DIRECTIONS

Major advances in our understanding of childhood-onset schizophrenia have been achieved since the 1930s. Notably, we currently have clear evidence that schizophrenia with childhood onset can be reliably diagnosed using the same criteria employed with adults and that childhood-onset schizophrenia continues into adult life in many cases. Extant research further indicates similarities in the characteristics and performance patterns of children and adults with schizophrenia on a variety of measures tapping such diverse dimensions as attention and information processing, thought disorder, treatment response, outcome, and family patterns. However, similar to findings with adults, considerable within-group variability is also observed among children with schizophrenia, underscoring the need to clarify the degree of clinical and etiological heterogeneity among children suffering from schizophrenia. Finally, there appear to be important differences between childhood- and later-onset schizophrenia. In addition to the atypical, early onset characteristic of childhood-onset cases, current findings suggest that these children may be characterized by particularly poor premorbid adjustment, higher rates of insidious as opposed to acute onsets, and possibly poorer outcome.

The progress that has been achieved to date has allowed us to better treat and understand this devastating illness. Current data (1) support the view of schizophrenia as a primary brain disease with complex etiological pathways involving biological, environmental, and cultural factors, (2) provide tentative support for the view that childhood-onset cases may represent a particularly severe variant of schizophrenia in which etiological pathways and the biological substrate for the disorder may be more clearly discernable, and (3) suggest that, similar to adult schizophrenia, childhood-onset schizophrenia also shows some degree of heterogeneity. As outlined in this chapter, future research is needed to clarify the causes, consequences, treatment, and prevention of schizophrenic disorders in children.

ACKNOWLEDGMENTS

Preparation of this chapter was facilitated by National Institute of Mental Health Grant Nos. MH46981–02 and MH45112–02.

NOTE

1. "Mental activity in which fantasy runs on unhampered by logic and experience" (*Dorland's Illustrated Medical Dictionary*, 1985, p. 360).

REFERENCES

American Psychiatric Association, Committee on Nomenclature and Statistics. (1968). *Diagnostic and statistical manual of mental disorders* (2nd ed.). Washington, DC: Author.

American Psychiatric Association. (1980). *Diagnostic and statistical manual of mental disorders* (3rd ed.). Washington, DC: Author.

American Psychiatric Association. (1987). *Diagnostic and statistical manual of mental disorders* (3rd ed., rev.). Washington, DC: Author.

American Psychiatric Association. (1994). *Diagnostic and statistical manual of mental disorders* (4th ed.). Washington, DC: Author.

Asarnow, J. R. (1988). Children at risk for schizophrenia: Converging lines of evidence. *Schizophrenia Bulletin*, 14(4), 613–631.

Asarnow, J. R. (1994). Annotation: Childhood-onset schizophrenia. *Journal of Child Psychology and Psychiatry, 35*, 1345–1371.

Asarnow, J. R., Asarnow, R. F., Hornstein, N., & Russell, A. T. (1991). Childhood-onset schizophrenia: Developmental perspectives on schizophrenic disorders. In E. F. Walker (Ed.), *Schizophrenia: A life course developmental perspective* (pp. 95–122). New York: Academic Press.

Asarnow, J. R., & Ben-Meir, S. (1987). Children with schizophrenia spectrum and depressive disorders: A comparative study of onset patterns, premorbid adjustment, and severity of dysfunction. *Journal of Child Psychology and Psychiatry, 29,* 477–488.

Asarnow, J. R., & Goldstein, M. J. (1986). Schizophrenia during adolescence and early adulthood: A developmental perspective. *Clinical Psychology Review, 6,* 211–235.

Asarnow, J. R., Goldstein, M. J., & Ben-Meir, S. (1988). Parental communication deviance in childhood onset schizophrenia spectrum and depressive disorders. *Journal of Child Psychology and Psychiatry, 29,* 825–838.

Asarnow, J. R., Tompson, M. C., Hamilton, E., Goldstein, M. J., & Guthrie, D. (1994). Family expressed emotion, childhood-onset depression, and childhood-onset schizophrenia spectrum disorders: Is expressed emotion a nonspecific correlate of child psychopathology or a specific risk factor for depression? *Journal of Abnormal Child Psychology, 22,* 129–146.

Asarnow, J. R., Tompson, M., & Goldstein, M. J. (1994). Childhood-onset schizophrenia: A follow-up study. *Schizophrenia Bulletin, 20,* 599–618.

Asarnow, R. F. (1993, February). *Cognitive and physiological measures in childhood schizophrenia.* Paper presented at the annual meeting of the Society for Research in Child and Adolescent Psychopathology, Santa Fe, NM.

Asarnow, R. F., Asamen, J., Granholm, E., Sherman, T., Watkins, J., & Williams, M. (1994). Cognitive/neuropsychological studies of children with a schizophrenic disorder. *Schizophrenia Bulletin, 20,* 647–670.

Asarnow, R. F., & Asarnow, J. R. (1994). Childhood-onset schizophrenia (Editors' introduction). *Schizophrenia Bulletin, 20,* 591–598.

Asarnow, R. F., Asarnow, J. R., & Strandberg, R. (1989). Schizophrenia: A developmental perspective. In D. Cicchetti (Ed.), *The emergence of a discipline: Rochester Symposium of Developmental Psychopathology* (pp. 189–219). Hillsdale, NJ: Erlbaum.

Asarnow, R. F., Granholm, E., & Sherman, T. (1991). Span of apprehension in schizophrenia. In S. R. Steinhauer, J. H. Gruzelier, & J. Zubin (Eds.) *Handbook of schizophrenia, Vol. 5: Neuropsychology, psychophysiology and information processing* (pp. 335–370). Amsterdam: Elsevier.

Asarnow, R. F., & Sherman, T. (1984). Studies of visual information processing in schizophrenic children. *Child Development, 55,* 249–261.

Beitchman, J. H. (1985). Childhood schizophrenia: A review and comparison with adult-onset schizophrenia. *Psychiatric Clinics of North America, 8,* 793–814.

Bellack, A. S., & Mueser, K. T. (1984). A comprehensive treatment program for schizophrenia and chronic mental illness. *Community Mental Health Journal, 22,* 175–189.

Bender, L. (1956). Schizophrenia in childhood—its recognition, description and treatment. *American Journal of Orthopsychiatry, 26,* 499–506.

Bennett, S., & Klein, H. R. (1966). Childhood schizophrenia: 30 years later. *American Journal of Psychiatry, 122,* 1121–1124.

Bleuler, E. (1950). *Dementia praecox or the group of schizophrenias* (J. Zinkin, Trans.). New York: International Universities Press. (Original work published in German 1911)

Burd, L., & Kerbeshian, J. (1987). A North Dakota prevalence study of schizophrenia presenting in childhood. *Journal of the American Academy of Child and Adolescent Psychiatry, 26,* 347–350.

Campbell, M. (1978). Use of drug treatment in infantile autism and childhood schizophrenia: A review. In M. A. Lipton, A. DiMascio, & K. F. Killam (Eds.), *Psychopharmacology: A generation of progress* (pp. 1451–1462). New York: Raven Press.

Cannon, T. D., Barr, C. E., & Mednick, S. A. (1991). Genetic and perinatal factors in the etiology of schizophrenia. In E. F. Walker (Ed.), *Schizophrenia: A life course developmental perspective* (pp. 9–31). New York: Academic Press.

Cantor, S. (1988). *Childhood schizophrenia.* New York: Guilford Press.

Caplan, R. (1994). Communication deficits in childhood schizophrenia spectrum disorders. *Schizophrenia Bulletin, 20,* 671–684.

Carlsson, A. (1987). The dopamine hypothesis of schizophrenia 20 years later. In H. Hafner, W. F. Gattaz, & W. Janzarik (Eds.), *Search for the causes of schizophrenia* (Vol. I, pp. 223–235). Berlin: Springer-Verlag.

Casanova, M. F., Carosella, N., & Kleinman, J. E. (1990). Neuropathological findings in a suspected case of childhood schizophrenia. *Journal of Neuropsychiatry and Clinical Neurosciences, 2,* 313–319.

Conolly, J. (1861–1862). Juvenile insanity. *American Journal of Insanity, 18,* 395–403.

Creak, M. (1964). Schizophrenia syndrome in childhood: Further progress report of a working party. *Developmental Medicine and Child Neurology, 6,* 530–535.

DeLisi, L. E., & Lovett, M. (1991). The reverse genetic approach to the etiology of schizophrenia. In H. Hafner & W. F. Gattaz (Eds.), *Search for the causes of schizophrenia* (Vol. 2, pp. 144–170). Heidelberg: Springer-Verlag.

De Sanctis, S. (1906). Sopra alcuna varieta della demenza precoce. *Rivista Sperimentale di Freniatria e Medicina Legale delle Alienazioni Mentale,* pp. 141–165.

Dohrenwend, B. P., Shrout, P. E., Link, B. G., & Skodol, A. E. (1987). Social and psychological risk factors for episodes of schizophrenia. In H. Hafner, W. F. Gattaz, & W. Janzarik (Eds.), *Search for the causes of schizophrenia* (Vol. I, pp. 275–296). Berlin: Springer-Verlag.

Dorland's Illustrated Medical Dictionary (26th ed.). (1985). Philadelphia: W. B. Saunders.

Edgell, H. G., & Kolvin, I. (1972). Childhood hallucinations. *Journal of Child Psychology and Psychiatry, 13,* 279–287.

Eggers, C. (1978). Course and prognosis in childhood schizophrenia. *Journal of Autism and Childhood Schizophrenia, 8,* 21–36.

Eggers, C. (1989). Schizoaffective disorders in childhood: A follow-up study. *Journal of Autism and Developmental Disorders, 19,* 327–342.

Falloon, I. R. H., Boyd, J. L., McGill, C. W., et al. (1985). Family management in the prevention of morbidity of schizophrenia: Clinical outcome of a two year longitudinal study. *Archives of General Psychiatry, 42,* 887–896.

Fish, B. (1968). Methodology in child psychopharmacology. In D. H. Efron, J. O. Cole, J. Levine, & J. R. Wittenborn (Eds.), *Psychopharmacology: Review of progress* (Public Health Service Pub. No. 1836, pp. 989–1001). Washington, DC: U.S. Government Printing Office.

Fish, B. (1977). Neurobiological antecedents of schizophrenia in children: Evidence for an inherited congenital

neurointegrative deficit. *Archives of General Psychiatry, 34,* 1297–1313.

Fish, B. (1987). Infant predictors of the longitudinal course of schizophrenic development. *Schizophrenia Bulletin, 13,* 395–410.

Fish, B., & Ritvo, E. R. (1979). Psychoses of childhood. In J. D. Noshpitz (Ed.), *Basic handbook of child psychiatry: Vol. 2* (pp. 249–304). New York: Basic Books.

Garralda, M. E. (1984a). Hallucinations in children with conduct and emotional disorders: I. The clinical phenomena. *Psychological Medicine, 14,* 589–596.

Garralda, M. E. (1984b). Psychotic children with hallucinations. *British Journal of Psychiatry, 145,* 74–77.

Goldstein, M. J. (1987). The UCLA High Risk Project. *Schizophrenia Bulletin, 13,* 505–514.

Goldstein, M. J., Talovic, S. A., Nuechterlein, K. H., Fogelson, D. L., Subotnick, K., & Asarnow, R. (1992). Family interaction versus individual psychopathology: Do they indicate the same processes in the families of schizophrenics? *British Journal of Psychiatry, 161,* 97–102.

Gordon, C. T., Frazier, J. A., McKenna, K., Giedd, J., Zametkin, A., Zahn, T., Hommer, D., Hong, W., Kaysen, D., Albus, K. E., & Rapoport, J. L. (1994). Childhood-onset schizophrenia: An NIMH study in progress. *Schizophrenia Bulletin, 20,* 697–712.

Gordon, C. T., Krasnewich, D., White, B., Lenane, M., & Rapoport, J. L. (1994). Translocation involving chromosomes 1 and 7 in a boy with childhood-onset schizophrenia. *Journal of Autism and Developmental Disorders, 24,* 537–545.

Grant, D. A., & Berg, E. A. (1981). *Wisconsin Card Sorting Test.* Odessa, FL: Psychological Assessment Resources.

Green, W., Campbell, M., Hardesty, A., Grega, D., Padron-Gayol, M., Shell, J., & Erlenmeyer-Kimling, L. (1984). A comparison of schizophrenic and autistic children. *Journal of the American Academy of Child Psychiatry, 23,* 399–409.

Green, W., Padron-Gayol, M., Hardesty, A. S., & Bassiri, M. (1992). Schizophrenia with childhood onset: A phenomenological study of 38 cases. *Journal of the American Academy of Child and Adolescent Psychiatry, 35,* 968–976.

Hamilton, E. B. (1991). *Interactional styles in families of children with depressive disorders, schizophrenia spectrum disorders and normal controls.* Unpublished doctoral dissertation, University of California, Los Angeles.

Hendren, R. L., Hodde-Vargas, M. S., Vargas, L. A., Orrison, W. W., & Dell, L. (1991). Magnetic resonance imaging of severely disturbed children: A Preliminary study. *Journal of the American Academy of Child and Adolescent Psychiatry, 30,* 466–470.

Hibbs, E. D., Hamburger, S. D., Lenane, M., Rapoport, J. L., Kreusi, M. J. P., Keysor, C. S., & Goldstein, M. J. (1991). Determinants of expressed emotion in families of disturbed and normal children. *Journal of Child Psychology and Psychiatry, 32,* 757–770.

Jones, J. E. (1977). Patterns of transactional style deviance in the TAT's of parents of schizophrenics. *Family Process, 16,* 327–337.

Kallman, F. J., & Roth, B. (1956). Genetic aspects of pre-adolescent schizophrenia. *American Journal of Psychiatry, 112,* 599–606.

Kanner, L. (1949). Problems of nosology and psychodynamics of early infantile autism. *American Journal of Orthopsychiatry, 19,* 416–426.

Kendler, K. S. (1988). The genetics of schizophrenia: An overview. In M. T. Tsuang & J. C. Simpson (Eds.), *Handbook of schizophrenia: Vol. 3. Nosology, epidemiology and genetics of schizophrenia* (pp. 437–462). Amsterdam: Elsevier.

Kendler, K. S., McGuire, M., Gruenberg, A. M., O'Hare, A., Spellman, M., & Walsh, D. (1993). The Roscommon Family Study: I. Methods, diagnosis of probands, and risk of schizophrenia in relatives. *Archives of General Psychiatry, 50,* 527–540.

Kolvin, I. (1971). Psychoses in childhood—a comparative study. In M. Rutter (Ed.), *Infantile autism: Concepts, characteristics and treatment* (pp. 7–26). Edinburgh: Churchill Livingstone.

Kolvin, I., Ounsted, C., Humphrey, M., & McNay, A. (1971). The phenomenology of childhood psychoses. *British Journal of Psychiatry, 118,* 385–395.

Kraepelin, E. (1919). *Dementia praecox and paraphrenia* (R. M. Barclay, Trans.; from the 8th German ed. of the *Textbook of psychiatry*). Edinburgh: Livingstone.

Kraepelin, E. (1971). *Dementia praecox and paraphrenia.* (R. M. Barclay, Trans.; G. M. Robertson, Ed.). Huntington, NY: Robert E. Krieger. (Original work published in German 1919)

Lachar, D. (1982). *Personality Inventory for Children(PIC): Revised format manual supplement.* Los Angeles: Western Psychological Services.

Leff, J. (1991). Interaction of environment and personality in the course of schizophrenia. In H. Hafner & W. F. Gattaz (Eds.), *Search for the causes of schizophrenia* (Vol. II, pp. 94–108). Berlin: Springer-Verlag.

Leff, J. P., Kuipers, L., Berkowitz, R., & Sturgeon, D. (1985). A controlled trial of social intervention in the families of schizophrenic patients: Two year follow-up. *British Journal of Psychiatry, 146,* 594–600.

Leff, J., Sartorius, N., Jablensky, A., Anker, M., Korten, A., Gulbinat, W., & Ernberg, G. (1991). The International Pilot Study of Schizophrenia: Five-year follow-up of findings. In H. Hafner & W. F. Gattaz (Eds.), *Search for the causes of schizophrenia* (Vol. II, pp. 57–66). Berlin: Springer-Verlag.

Leff, J., & Vaughn, C. (1985). *Expressed emotion in families: Its significance for mental illness.* New York: Guilford Press.

Lewine, R. R. J. (1988). Gender in schizophrenia. In M. T. Tsuang & J. C. Simpson (Eds.), *Handbook of schizophrenic: Vol. 3. Nosology, epidemiology and genetics of schizophrenia* (pp. 379–397). Amsterdam: Elsevier.

Liberman, R. P., Wallace, C., Blackwell, G., Eckman, T., Vaccaro, J., & Kuehnel, T. (1993). Innovations in skills training for the seriously mentally ill: The UCLA Social and Independent Living Skills Modules. *Innovations and Research, 2,* 43–60.

Lutz, J. (1937). Dementia praecox in infants and children. *Schweizer Archiv für Neurologie und Psychiatrie, 39,* 335–372.

McClellan, J. M., & Werry, J. S. (1992). Schizophrenia. *Psychiatric Clincs of North America, 15,* 131–148.

McKenna, K., Gordon, C. T., & Rapoport, J. L. (1993, February). *Phenomenology and neurobiology of prepubertal onset schizophrenia.* Paper presented at the annual meeting of the Society for Research in Child and Adolescent Psychopathology. Santa Fe, NM.

McNeil, T. F. (1988). Obstetric factors and perinatal injuries. In M. T. Tsuang & J. C. Simpson (Eds.), *Handbook of schizophrenia: Vol. 3. Nosology, epidemiology and genetics* (pp. 319–344). New York: Elsevier.

Mednick, S. A., Machon, R. A., Huttunen, M. O., & Bonett, D. (1988). Adult schizophrenia following prenatal exposure to an influenza epidemic. *Archives of General Psychiatry, 45,* 189–192.

Mozes, T., Toren, P., Chernauzan, N., Mester, R., Yoran-Hegesh, R., Blumensohn, R., & Weizman, A. (1994). Clozapine treatment in very early onset schizophrenia. *Journal of the American Academy of Child and Adolescent Psychiatry, 33,* 65–70.

National Institute of Mental Health. (1992). *The NIMH Diagnostic Interview Schedule for Children.* Rockville, MD: Author.

Nuechterlein, K. H. (1986). Annotation: Childhood precursors of adult schizophrenia. *Journal of Child Psychology and Psychiatry, 27,* 133–144.

Nuechterlein, K. H. (1987). Vulnerability models for schizophrenia: State of the art. In H. Hafner, W. F. Gattaz, & W. Janzarik (Eds.), *Search for the causes of schizophrenia* (Vol. I, pp. 297–316). Berlin: Springer-Verlag.

Parnas, J., Schulsinger, F., Teasdale, T. W., Schulsinger, H., Feldman, P. M., & Mednick, S. A. (1982). Perinatal complications and clinical outcome within the schizophrenia spectrum. *British Journal of Psychiatry, 140,* 416–420.

Petty, L. P., Ornitz, E. M., Michelman, J. D., & Zimmerman, E. G. (1984). Autistic children who become schizophrenic. *Archives of General Psychiatry, 41,* 129–135.

Potter, H. W. (1933). Schizophrenia in children. *American Journal of Psychiatry, 12,* 1253–1270.

Prior, M., & Werry, J. S. (1986). Autism, schizophrenia, and allied disorders. In H. C. Quay & J. S. Werry (Eds.), *Psychopathological disorders of childhood* (3rd ed., pp. 156–210). New York: Wiley.

Remschmidt, H. (1993). Schizophrenic psychoses in children and adolescents. *Triangle, 32,* 15–24.

Remschmidt, H. E., Schulz, E., Martin, M., Warnke, A., & Trott, G. (1994). Childhood-onset schizophrenia: History of the concept and recent studies. *Schizophrenia Bulletin, 20,* 727–746.

Riecher, A., Maurer, K., Loffler, W., Fatkenheuer, B., An Der Heiden, W., Munk-Jorgensen, P., Stromgren, E., & Hafner, H. (1991). Gender differences in age at onset and course of schizophrenic disorders. A contribution to the understanding of the disease? In H. Hafner & W. F. Gattaz (Eds.), *Search for the causes of schizophrenia* (Vol. II, pp. 14–33). Berlin: Springer-Verlag.

Rosenthal, D. (1970). *Genetic theory and abnormal behavior.* New York: McGraw-Hill.

Russell, A. T. (1994). The clinical presentation of childhood-onset schizophrenia. *Schizophrenia Bulletin, 20,* 631–646.

Russell, A. T., Bott, L., & Sammons, C. (1989). The phenomenology of schizophrenia occurring in childhood. *Journal of the American Academy of Child and Adolescent Psychiatry, 28,* 399–407.

Rutter, M. (1972). Childhood schizophrenia reconsidered. *Journal of Autism and Childhood Schizophrenia, 2,* 315–337.

Rutter, M., Greenfeld, D., & Lockyer, L. (1967). A five to fifteen year follow-up study of infantile psychosis II. Social and behavioral outcome. *British Journal of Psychiatry, 113,* 1183–1199.

Sameroff, A. J. (1990). *Prevention of developmental psychopathology using the transactional model: Perspectives on host, risk agent, and environment interactions.* Paper presented at the first National Conference on Prevention Research, National Institute of Mental Health, Bethesda, MD.

Sartorius, N., Jablensky, A., Ernberg, G., Leff, J., & Gulbinat, W. (1987). Course of schizophrenia in different countries: Some results of a WHO International Comparative 5-Year Follow-up Study. In H. Hafner, W. F. Gattaz, & W. Janzarik (Eds.), *Search for the causes of schizophrenia* (Vol. I, pp. 107–113). Berlin: Springer-Verlag.

Schulz, S. C., Koller, M. M., Kishore, P. R., Hamer, R. M., Gehl, J. J. & Friedel, R. O. (1983) Ventricular enlargement in teenage patients with schizophrenia spectrum disorder. *American Journal of Psychiatry, 140,* 1592–1595.

Singer, M. T., & Wynne, L. C. (1965). Thought disorder and family relations of schizophrenics. IV. Results and implications. *Archives of General Psychiatry, 12,* 201–209.

Spencer, E. K., & Campbell, M. (1994). Schizophrenic children: Diagnosis, phenomenology and pharmacotherapy. *Schizophrenia Bulletin, 20,* 713–726.

Spencer, E. K., Kaftantaris, V., Padron-Gayol, M., Rosenberg, C., & Campbell, M. (1992). Haloperidol in schizophrenic children: Early findings from a study in progress. *Psychopharmacology Bulletin, 28,* 183–186.

Strandburg, R. J., Marsh, J. T., Brown, W. S., Asarnow, R. F., & Guthrie, D. (1994). Information processing deficits across childhood- and adult-onset schizophrenia: ERP correlates. *Schizophrenia Bulletin, 20,* 685–696.

Stubbe, D. E., Zahner, G., Goldstein, M. J., & Leckman, J. F. (1993). Diagnostic specificity of a brief measure of expressed emotion: A community study of children. *Journal of Child Psychology and Psychiatry, 34,* 139–154.

Tanguay, P. E., & Asarnow, R. F. (1985). Schizophrenia in children. In A. J. Solnit, D. J. Cohen, & J. E. Schowalter (Eds.), *Psychiatry: Vol. 2. Child psychiatry* (pp. 1–10). Philadelphia: J. B. Lippincott.

Tompson, M. C., Asarnow, J. R., Goldstein, M. J., & Miklowitz, D. J. (1990). Thought disorder and communication problems in children with schizophrenia spectrum and depressive disorders and their parents. *Journal of Clinical Child Psychology, 19,* 159–168.

Volkmar, F. R., & Cohen, D. J. (1991). Comorbid association of autism and schizophrenia. *American Journal of Psychiatry, 148,* 1705–1707.

Volkmar, F. R., Cohen, D. J., Hoshino, Y., Rende, R. D., & Rhea, P. (1988). Phenomenology and classification of the childhood psychoses. *Psychological Medicine, 18,* 191–201.

Walk, A. (1964). The pre-history of child psychiatry. *British Journal of Psychiatry, 110,* 754–767.

Walker, E. F., Savoie, T., & Davis, D. (1994). Neuromotor precursors of schizophrenia. *Schizophrenia Bulletin, 20,* 441–451.

Watkins, J. M., Asarnow, R. F., & Tanguay, P. (1988). Symptom development in childhood onset schizophrenia. *Journal of Child Psychology and Psychiatry, 29,* 865–878.

Weinberger, D. R. (1987). Implications of normal brain development for the pathogenesis of schizophrenia. *Archives of General Psychiatry, 44,* 660–669.

Werry, J. S. (1992). Child and adolescent (early onset) schizophrenia: A review in light of DSM-III-R. *Journal of Autism and Developmental Disorders, 22,* 601–624.

Werry, J. S., & McClellan, J. M. (1992). Predicting outcome in child and adolescent (early onset) schizophrenia and bipolar disorder. *Journal of the American Academy of Child and Adolescent Psychiatry, 31,* 147–150.

Werry, J. S., McClellan, J. M., Andrews, L. K., & Ham, M. (1994). Clinical features and outcome of child and adolescent schizophrenia. *Schizophrenia Bulletin, 20,* 619–630.

Werry, J. S., McClellan, J. M., & Chard, L. (1991). Childhood and adolescent schizophrenia, bipolar, and schizoaffective disorders: A clinical and outcome study. *Journal of the American Academy of Child and Adolescent Psychiatry, 30,* 457–465.

Woody, R. C., Bolyard, K., Eisenhauer, G., & Altschuler, L. (1987). CT scan and MRI findings in a child with schizophrenia. *Journal of Child Neurology, 2,* 105–110.

World Health Organization. (1978). *International statistical classification of diseases and related health problems* (9th ed.). Geneva, Switzerland: Author.

World Health Organization. (1992). *ICD-10 classification of mental and behavioral disorders: Diagnostic criteria for research.* Geneva, Switzerland: Author.

Zeitlin, H. (1986). The natural history of psychiatric disorder in children. *Institute of Psychiatry Maudsley Monograph, 29.* Oxford, UK: Oxford University Press.

Zeitlin, H. (1990). Annotation: Current interests in child–adult psychopathological continuities. *Journal of Child Psychology and Psychiatry, 31,* 671–679.

Zubin, J., Spring, B. (1977). Vulnerability—a new view of schizophrenia. *Journal of Abnormal Psychology, 86,* 103–126.

Mental Retardation

Robert M. Hodapp
Elisabeth M. Dykens

Mental retardation has historically been an area of intense interest to scientists, practitioners, and policymakers. Today as well, scientists are making important new discoveries, fostering hope that certain forms of mental retardation might be eliminated over the next few decades. Practitioners are excited by the participation of persons with mental retardation into the "mainstream," where these individuals are increasingly being treated as fully participating members of their societies. Policymakers, too, have contributed to this new era, passing laws that mandate educational and service rights, as well as an end to discrimination in employment and other areas.

To get a feel for just how far persons with retardation have advanced, some brief history is useful. Like the disciplines of social work, education, nursing, and medicine, the field of mental retardation essentially began in the mid-1800s (Scheerenberger, 1983). In the early 1850s, Samuel Gridley Howe founded the first public and Harvey Wilbur the first private training schools for persons with mental retardation in the United States. Quickly thereafter, facilities were started throughout the country; by 1890, 20 of these facilities had been opened, in 15 states (Haskell, 1944). As originally operated, these facilities served as warm, humane "substitute families" for persons with retardation. These facilities—and the professionals who ran them—opened the way for the field's modern service delivery system.

In 1876, these training school directors met to form a society that was later to become the American Association on Mental Retardation (AAMR), the main professional organization in the mental retardation field (Scheerenberger, 1983). Through its two journals, the *American Journal on Mental Retardation* and *Mental Retardation,* the AAMR has long promoted research, intervention, and social policy efforts on behalf of persons with mental retardation. As we describe below, the AAMR remains involved in many social and scientific debates.

In both earlier and present times, mental retardation has been a multidisciplinary field, touching on numerous professions and perspectives that relate to individuals with retardation. In all these disciplines, research has been prominent, much of it related to new applications from the psychological and biological sciences. Such applications began early on, including Goddard's (1913a) studies employing the new Binet–Simon tests to examine residents at the Vineland (New Jersey) Training School in the years directly after the tests had been developed in France. Such "translations" of new developments to the mentally retarded population have always been a hallmark of the scientific study of mental retardation.

At the same time as the field of mental retardation featured service, institutional, and scientific advances, many dark days have also occurred. Particularly important have been the many scandals and abuses first discovered in the 1960s (Blatt & Kaplan, 1966). In essence, the home-like training schools of the late 19th century often became the inhumane warehouses of the mid-20th cen-

tury. Although less widespread, abuses have occurred in science and social policy as well, especially with regard to the "science" of eugenics (Dugdale, 1910; Goddard, 1913b) and the sterilization laws passed in California and other states during the 1920s (see Davies & Ecob, 1959).

This mixture of advances and abuses leads to the current situation, which can best be described as monumental advances amidst monumental controversies. Advances have arisen as we learn the causes, consequences, and cures (or at least management) of mental retardation, and most of this knowledge has occurred over the past 30 to 40 years. It is startling to realize, for example, that the chromosomal cause of the most common genetic form of mental retardation—Down syndrome—was only discovered in 1959 (Lejeune, Gautier, & Turpin, 1959), or that the genetic basis of the second most common genetic form of mental retardation—fragile X syndrome—was only understood in the late 1960s and early 1970s (see Dykens, Hodapp, & Leckman, 1994). Several hundred genetic causes of mental retardation have now been identified, and treatments for many seem likely over the next few decades. Similar advances have occurred in the biochemistry, psychology, and psychiatry of mental retardation.

But if the 1990s are exciting times in mental retardation, so too are they contentious times. Debates continue as to what should be the appropriate definition of mental retardation, what is the appropriate role of professionals as opposed to consumers (i.e., persons with retardation), and how the field should best study many aspects of behavior in persons with retardation. Such issues pit well-meaning persons against one another in ways that threaten progress.

This chapter describes the many issues present in mental retardation. Although we express our opinions, our attempt throughout is to overview "the state of the art" in the field of mental retardation. Such concerns run from definitional and diagnostic issues, to how one performs research, to how best one serves or supports persons with mental retardation.

WHAT IS MENTAL RETARDATION?

Core Features

When asked to describe a person with mental retardation, most people would probably speak of a person with Down syndrome, probably a boy.

Some mention might be made that the problem first appears in childhood, and that the child learns at a slower rate, has deficient cognitive-mental processes, and is below normal in intelligence. Furthermore, most adults clearly differentiate mental retardation from mental illness, where people talk of emotional instability, erratic behavior, and tenseness or anxiety (Caruso & Hodapp, 1988).

Although partially accurate, mental retardation is a much more complex phenomenon. For example, persons with mental retardation vary widely in their levels of functioning, in their abilities to function in school or at work, and in the degree to which they have concomitant emotional, physical, or medical conditions. The causes of mental retardation are also numerous, from the many genetic disorders, to other pre-, peri-, and postnatal problems and insults.

At present, three major features are thought to characterize persons with mental retardation. First, these individuals have subnormal intellectual functioning. Defined as IQ scores below a certain level, this criterion highlights the intellectual nature of mental retardation. But intellectual deficits do not exist in a vacuum. A second important feature of mental retardation therefore involves deficits in adaptive behavior, or the ability to perform "daily activities required for personal and social self-sufficiency" (Sparrow, Balla, & Cicchetti, 1984, p. 6). Such abilities involve communicating one's needs to others, performing daily living skills such as eating, dressing, grooming, and toileting, and being socialized to follow rules and to work and play with others. A third feature of mental retardation is that it begins early in life. Deficiencies caused by adult-onset degenerative diseases such as Alzheimer disease or adult-onset head trauma are not considered to be mental retardation.

Levels of Functioning

Lowered intelligence, impaired adaptive behaviors, and childhood onset give a basic sense of mental retardation, but these common features hide the wide variation within the retarded population. For this reason, researchers have long described persons with mental retardation by their degree of intellectual impairment. This classification system designates persons with retardation as mildly, moderately, severely, or profoundly retarded.

"Mild mental retardation" (IQ 55–70) constitutes the largest group of persons with mental

retardation, possibly as many as 90% of all persons with retardation (American Psychiatric Association, 1994). These individuals appear similar to nonretarded individuals and often blend into the nonretarded population in the years before and after formal schooling. As adults, some of these individuals hold jobs, marry, raise families, and are indistinguishable from nonretarded people—they may simply appear slow or need extra help in negotiating life's problems and tasks. More persons with mild mental retardation come from minority and low socioeconomic (SES) backgrounds than would be expected from their numbers in the general population (Hodapp, 1995a). This so-called "overrepresentation" of minority group members has been used to criticize measures of intelligence (see Reynolds & Brown, 1984), as well as to highlight the importance of both environmental–cultural (Ogbu, 1994) and genetic (Jensen, 1969) influences.

"Moderate mental retardation" (IQ 40–54), the second most common level of impairment, refers to those individuals who are more impaired intellectually and adaptively. More of these individuals are diagnosed as having mental retardation during the preschool years. Many individuals with moderate mental retardation show one or more clear organic causes for their mental retardation. For example, many persons with Down syndrome and with fragile X syndrome are at moderate levels of mental retardation. Although some persons with moderate retardation require few supportive services, most continue to require some help throughout life. In a study by Ross, Begab, Dondis, Giampiccolo and Meyers (1985), for example, 20% of persons with IQs from 40 to 49 lived independently, whereas 60% were considered dependent and 20% totally dependent on others. In a similar way, some of these individuals hold jobs in the outside workforce as unskilled laborers, and others work in supervised workshop programs.

"Severe mental retardation" (IQ 25–39) refers to persons with more severe impairments. The majority of these individuals suffer from one or more organic causes of mental retardation. Many persons with severe mental retardation show concurrent physical or ambulatory problems, while others have respiratory, heart, or other co-occurring conditions. Most persons with severe mental retardation require some special assistance throughout their lives. Many live in supervised group homes or small regional facilities, and most work in either workshop or "preworkshop" settings.

"Profound mental retardation" (IQ below 25 or 20) involves persons with the most severe levels of intellectual and adaptive impairments. These persons generally learn only the rudiments of communicative skills, and intensive training is required to teach basic eating, grooming, toileting, and dressing behaviors. Persons with profound mental retardation require life-long care and assistance. Almost all show organic causes for their retardation, and many have severe co-occurring conditions that sometimes lead to death during childhood or early adulthood. Some persons with profound mental retardation can perform preworkshop tasks, and most live in supervised group homes or small, specialized facilities.

Situational and Contextual Issues

Core features and levels of impairment highlight several issues that further complicate the picture of mental retardation. The first of these issues involves "social system factors." As noted above, persons with mild mental retardation are often not diagnosed in the preschool years (Gruenberg, 1964). These individuals often become known to psychologists and social service workers during the school years.

Several reasons account for the school-based rise in the numbers of children considered to have mild mental retardation. Obviously, schools emphasize cognitive skills; when children are required to read, write, or perform arithmetic and other school subjects, their cognitive deficiencies become apparent. Their abilities are further challenged in junior high and high school, when more complex intellectual and academic tasks are required.

In addition, teachers have extensive experience in dealing with children of a particular age. Whereas a parent may not realize that the child is behind intellectually relative to age-mates, a primary or secondary school teacher has seen hundreds of 1st-, 4th-, or 10th-grade children. That teacher can identify and refer for testing children who have problems associated with mild mental retardation. Testing often substantiates the teacher's concerns, leading to remedial actions and decisions by school personnel and parents.

Again after the school years, persons with mild mental retardation often blend back into the

larger population. Although studies vary wildly in their prevalence rates based on when, where, and how the study was conducted (see Kiely & Lubin, 1991, for a discussion of epidemiology in mental retardation), such studies generally show low rates of mental retardation during the preschool years, gradual increases until a peak in early adolescence, then gradual declines in the adult years. For the most part, this higher prevalence rate during the school years is due to the mildly retarded population; individuals with mild retardation are most likely to be identified and diagnosed only during the school years (cf. Zigler & Hodapp, 1986).

In this sense, mental retardation is a social phenomenon that is influenced by schools and other social systems. Special educators even refer to "system identified" retarded samples, or persons with retardation who are identified through the school system as opposed to by parents or physicians. Others decry the so-called "6-hour retarded child," the child who is considered to be mildly retarded while attending school, but not after school hours (or years). How system factors relate to mental retardation is a difficult, if not unresolvable, issue.

A second important complication involves the "overrepresentation" of minority and low-SES children within the retarded population (Artiles & Trent, 1994). Such overrepresentation seems due to the lower average IQ scores of African-American and other minority groups, as well as to the generally lower scores of persons from lower-SES groups. Indeed, if minority or low-SES groups show an average IQ of, say 90 or 85, then their entire "IQ curve" has been shifted to the left; many more individuals from these groups will therefore fall below IQ 70, assuming that these groups also show standard deviations of approximately 15 points (i.e., as in the general population). Historically, such concern led the AAMR to change the intellectual criterion from below IQ 85 to below IQ 70 from 1961 to 1973 (Grossman, 1973). In addition, all definitions from the 1970s on have advocated the use of adaptive behavior as a central feature of mental retardation. The idea has been to ensure that persons with mental retardation truly do show intellectual and adaptive deficits. Yet even with these changes, the overrepresentation of minority and low-SES children continues, particularly among those children with mild mental retardation (MacMillan, Gresham, & Siperstein, 1993).

DEFINITIONAL AND DIAGNOSTIC ISSUES

Definitions in mental retardation are complicated by the presence of two different professional groups that produce definitional and classificatory manuals. The first, the American Psychiatric Association (1994), considers mental retardation as the first of its "developmental disorders." As noted in DSM-IV, mental retardation and personality disorders are listed along a separate axis to ensure "that consideration will be given to the possible presence of personality disorder and mental retardation that might otherwise be overlooked when attention is directed to the usually more florid Axis I disorders" (American Psychiatric Association, 1994, p. 26).

The other main diagnostic and classification criteria are those presented by the AAMR. The AAMR has produced diagnostic manuals or revisions in 1959, 1961, 1973, 1977, and 1983 (see Grossman, 1983). In late 1992, the AAMR produced a revised definition of mental retardation (American Association on Mental Retardation, 1992). This "new" definition proposes sweeping definitional and classificatory changes from the organization's earlier manuals. We first describe the 1983 AAMR and DSM-III-R (American Psychiatric Association, 1987) definitions, then the new AAMR definition. We end our discussion with DSM-IV and ICD-10 (World Health Organization, 1992) definitions.

DSM-III-R and 1983 AAMR Definitions

The criteria for a diagnosis of mental retardation promulgated in DSM-III-R are nearly identical to that provided in the AAMR's 1983 classification manual (Grossman, 1983). According to both manuals, mental retardation is characterized by three essential features: "(1) significantly subaverage general intellectual functioning, accompanied by (2) significant deficits or impairments in adaptive functioning, with (3) onset before the age of 18" (American Psychiatric Association, 1987, p. 28).

Both the old AAMR and DSM-III-R criteria further specify the first two factors. "Significantly subaverage general intellectual functioning" is defined as an IQ score of 70 or below on the WISC-R, Stanford–Binet, K-ABC, or other individually administered psychometric test of intelligence. Deficits in adaptive behavior are defined

as deficient functioning on the Vineland Adaptive Behavior Scales (Sparrow et al., 1984) or other adaptive behavior scales. Lacking psychometric measures of adaptive behavior, ". . . clinical judgment of general adaptation alone, the person's age and cultural background being taken into consideration, may suffice" (American Psychiatric Association, 1987, p. 29).

1992 AAMR Definition

On the surface, the new AAMR definition (AAMR, 1992) appears similar to DSM-III-R and 1983 AAMR definitions. The definition reads as follows:

> Mental retardation refers to substantial limitations in present functioning. It is characterized by significantly subaverage intellectual functioning, existing concurrently with related limitations in two or more of the following applicable adaptive skill areas: communication, self-care, home living, social skills, community use, self-direction, health and safety, functional academics, leisure, and work. Mental retardation manifests before age 18. (AMR, 1992, p. 1)

In further specifying each of these criteria, the new AAMR definition notes that "significantly subaverage" is equivalent to "IQ standard scores of approximately 70 or 75 and below" (p. 5). Although the exact meaning of this phrase remains unclear, most mental retardation researchers (e.g., MacMillan et al., 1993) have concluded that the new definition essentially changes the IQ criteria from IQ below 70 to IQ below 75.

Similarly, the new AAMR definition also gives increasing weight to adaptive behavior. As opposed to general adaptive behavior deficits, the new AAMR definition proposes 10 areas of adaptive behavior; the criteria for mental retardation is satisfied when the individual shows deficits in two or more of these 10 adaptive areas.

A third change in the AAMR definition involves levels of impairment. In an effort to conceptualize mental retardation more as an interaction between the person and the environment, the new AAMR definition discards the categories of mental retardation based on levels of impairment; according to this system, individuals should no longer be considered to have mild, moderate, severe, or profound mental retardation. Instead, individuals are categorized in terms of their need for supportive services. Supportive services are specified as intermittent, limited, extensive, and pervasive; these levels of support are to be listed in each area of adaptive skills (AAMR, 1992, pp. 31–33).

DSM-IV and ICD-10 Definitions

In contrast to earlier times, when the AAMR and American Psychiatric Association definitions were virtually identical, the American Psychiatric Association (1994) was faced with a difficult decision when providing its definition of mental retardation in DSM-IV. AAMR's definitional manual was published in late 1992, and even before its publication, the definition received harsh reviews (e.g., Jacobsen & Mulick, 1992). Much of the criticism concerned the effects on practice—on diagnosis and classification—brought about by the new AAMR definition. The critics decried the "political correctness" of the new AAMR definition, noting that adherence to the new system might have many negative, unintended consequences. Should the American Psychiatric Association make definitional changes in line with the new, but controversial, AAMR definition, or should it keep the definition more or less unchanged from DSM-III-R?

The resulting diagnostic criteria are in many ways a compromise. The DSM-IV definition proposes the following three criteria of mental retardation:

A. Significantly subaverage intellectual functioning: an IQ of approximately 70 or below on an individually administered IQ test. . . .
B. Concurrent deficits or impairment in present adaptive functioning (i.e., the person's effectiveness in meeting the standards expected for his or her age by his or her cultural group) in at least two of the following skill areas: communication, self-care, home living, social/interpersonal skills, use of community resources, self-direction, functional academic skills, work, leisure, health, and safety.
C. Onset is before age 18 years. (American Psychiatric Association, 1994, p. 46)

Thus, DSM-IV retains the old AAMR definition's IQ 70 criterion; the "approximately" refers to the small errors that occur in estimating any person's "true IQ" from a single testing (allowing the examiner some small leeway). At the same time, the DSM-IV system adopts the new AAMR adaptive criteria of deficits in 2 of 11 adaptive

domains—DSM-IV appears to consider as separate "health" and "safety," thus producing 11, as opposed to 10, adaptive domains (the 1992 AAMR definition combines the two). In addition, DSM-IV provides codes based on the "degree of severity reflecting level of intellectual impairment" (American Psychiatric Association, 1994, p. 46), the mild, moderate, severe, and profound levels of mental retardation historically discussed in the mental retardation field.

The recent publication of ICD-10 (World Health Organization, 1992) follows the older definitional criteria, those established in the 1983 AAMR and DSM-III-R definitions (Grossman, 1983). Although ICD-10 emphasizes that intelligence may not be a single entity, it nonetheless notes that IQ scores below 70 constitute functioning in the mentally retarded range. Adaptive behavior deficits are also included among the diagnostic criteria, although the authors of ICD-10 do not advocate deficits in 2 of 10 (or 11) adaptive domains. In addition, ICD-10 adopts the levels of impairment classification, although its IQ ranges differ slightly from those generally used in America. Thus, ICD-10 considers as mild mental retardation IQs from 50 to 69; moderate retardation IQs from 35 to 49; severe retardation IQs from 20 to 34; and profound retardation IQs below 20.

Most notably, however, ICD-10 appears interested in a definition of mental retardation that will hold cross-culturally. Unfortunately, the mental retardation field is not as advanced as fields studying other areas of psychopathology. Few measures of adaptive behavior have been normed across cultures, and even IQ tests have yet to be normed in many countries. As a result, ICD-10 notes that "only general guidance can be given here about the most appropriate methods of assessment to use" (World Health Organization, 1992, p. 140). See Table 10.1 for a comparison of the four main definitions of mental retardation.

Overview of the Definition of Mental Retardation

Of all the definitions of mental retardation, the AAMR 1992 definition has generated the most controversy. Much of this debate has centered on the IQ criterion. Most mental retardation workers feel that a change to "IQ standard scores of approximately 70 or 75 and below . . ." effectively

TABLE 10.1. Comparing the Main Definitions of Mental Retardation

Definition	IQ	Adaptive
AAMR (Grossman, 1983)	"IQ 70 and below on standardized tests of intelligence" (can extend to IQ 75 "depending on the reliability of the intelligence test used")	"Significant limitations in meeting standards of maturation, learning, personal independence and/or social responsibility that are expected for his or her age level and cultural group, as determined by clinical assessment and, usually, standardized scales"
AAMR (1992)	"IQ standard scores of approximately 70 or 75 and below"	"Limitations in two or more of the following applicable skill areas" (10 listed; see text)
DSM-IV	IQ standard scores of "approximately 70"	"Concurrent deficits or impairments in present adaptive functioning . . . in at least two of the following areas" (11 listed, see text)
ICD-10	IQ standard scores of 69 or less "based on global assessments of ability" . . . "IQ levels given are provided as a guide"	"Diminished social competence" (no domains listed, but "within most European and North American cultures, the Vineland Social Maturity Scale is recommended for use, if judged appropriate")

changes the IQ criterion to IQs below 75. Although a 5-point increase may seem small, the Gaussian (or bell-curve) nature of the IQ distribution makes particularly important this "high-end" change in the definition of mental retardation. MacMillan et al. (1993) note that "Small shifts in the upper limit have substantial consequences for the percentage of the population eligible to be diagnosed with mental retardation (Reschly, 1992). *Twice as many people are eligible* when the cutoff is 'IQ 75 and below' as when it is 'IQ 70 and below'" (p. 327; emphasis in original).

In a similar way, many critics have derided the changes in the adaptive behavior criterion. The AAMR definition proposes 10 areas of adaptive behavior, including such rarely tested areas as leisure, health and safety, community use, and self-direction. But factor analytic studies of adaptive behavior have consistently revealed from two to seven factors of adaptive behavior, with a single primary factor accounting for most of the variance (Harrison, 1987; McGrew & Bruininks, 1989). It thus seems inappropriate to test 10 (or 11) areas when little empirical support suggests that the construct has 10 separate domains.

A further problem is the absence of formal, psychometrically sound measures for several of these domains. For such areas as leisure, health and safety, and use of community resources, for example, it is unclear exactly how (or with which instrument) these domains are to be measured. The new AAMR definition allows for clinical judgment to be used in these cases. In fairness, all other diagnostic manuals—including DSM-III-R (American Psychiatric Association, 1987) and the 1983 AAMR (Grossman, 1983)—allow the use of clinical judgment in the evaluation of adaptive deficiencies, but problems associated with clinical judgment would seem exacerbated when there are so many domains. Making things more difficult are the findings that many of these domains are not independent, and that many are new to clinicians and other social service personnel.

A final issue concerns the levels of impairment. In the 1992 AAMR definition, the authors have disposed of mild, moderate, severe, and profound mental retardation in favor of four levels of environmental supports (intermittent, limited, extensive, and pervasive). The desire was to change the concept of mental retardation from an inherent characteristic of the individual to an interaction between the individual and the services needed by that individual. In this way, the "problem" of mental retardation is shared by the individual and that individual's environments.

Although well intentioned, the effects of such a change remain unclear. Researchers and clinicians have long used levels of retardation as a way to characterize the individual's level of impairment. Such levels of intellectual impairment are sometimes, but not always, related to needed levels of support. Whereas persons with IQs in the moderate, severe, and profound range almost always need some supports, those with mild retardation vary widely in their adaptive abilities. For example, in their study of special education students as adults, Ross et al. (1985) found that, whereas 64% of persons with mild mental retardation functioned independently, 24% and 12% were either partially or totally dependent on others, even though they were at identical intellectual levels. The move away from level of impairment to levels of support thus generates unnecessary confusion. At least among researchers, it seems unlikely that this change will be followed (Gresham, MacMillan, & Siperstein, 1995; Hodapp, 1995a).

In reviewing the many definitions of mental retardation and their effects, we agree with many of the criticisms of the new AAMR definition. For both clinicians and researchers, the new AAMR definition's lack of attention to basic psychometric issues is troubling (Gresham et al., 1995). Many critics (e.g., Jacobsen & Mulick, 1992; MacMillan et al., 1993) predict that, if the new AAMR definition is followed, it will lead to an increase in the size of the mentally retarded population, greater numbers of incorrect diagnoses, and increases in overrepresentation of several minority groups. Jacobsen and Mulick (1993) have even convinced the American Psychological Association's Division 33—the psychology division interested in mental retardation—to adopt its own definition. This definition promises to be closer to the DSM-III-R, 1983 AAMR, DSM-IV, and ICD-10 definitions. Given that so many professionals and groups criticize the 1992 AAMR definition, its fate remains in doubt.

DEVELOPMENTAL COURSE AND PROGNOSIS

As noted earlier, DSM-IV (American Psychiatric Association, 1994) considers mental retardation as a disorder that begins in childhood and persists in relatively stable form into adulthood. Al-

though in general this characterization is accurate, several qualifications are necessary.

Stability of IQ

The first issue involves the stability of intelligence as measured by IQ tests. In general, IQ tests do not predict later IQ when given in the infancy years. For example, the correlation is essentially 0 between Bayley Developmental Quotient scores (i.e., "infant IQs") when children are 1 year of age and IQ scores when children are 12 years old (Vernon, 1979). Yet by the time children are 4 years of age, the correlation with IQ 12 years later is .77; similar correlations—ranging from .70 to .90—occur when children are tested during middle to late childhood or adulthood, then again 6 or 12 years later.

In children with retardation, the picture is somewhat different in that even the youngest infants show IQ stability, particularly at the lower IQ levels. Infants who score below IQ 50 on the Bayley test are likely to continue to have low IQs in their childhood and adult years (Maisto & German, 1986). Similarly, in a 5-year longitudinal study of children who had mild to moderate delays at age 3 years, Bernheimer and Keogh (1988) found very high correlations (.70 to .90) of early to later IQ. From a mean IQ of 67.1 at age 3 years, these children showed a mean IQ of 70.3 when tested 6 years later. Similarly, in a study of educable retarded children tested at 4-year intervals, Silverstein (1982) also found high stability in average IQ, from 65.7 at age 11 years to 64.0 at age 14 years. Such stability continues on into adulthood. In the sole study of this issue, Ross et al. (1985) examined adults who had been in special education classes as children 35 years earlier. These researchers concluded that IQ scores "showed no meaningful increase over some 35 years" (p. 69).

But group stability over time does not imply that the IQ stays constant for every single individual. Many studies have found that individual IQs can change up or down and that most changes occur for children at or just above the mild mental retardation range (e.g., Goodman & Cameron, 1978). As a result, many persons who test in the mildly retarded range on first testing will show slightly higher IQs on second testing, thereby making it unclear who should and should not be diagnosed with mental retardation. Such IQ changes are not as often observed for children with moderate, severe, and profound retardation.

As Bernheimer and Keogh (1988) note, "the predictive validity of developmental tests is related to level of performance early on, with less reliable prediction for the children within the higher developmental quotient range" (p. 541).

Type of Retardation

A second issue affecting the stability of IQ concerns the child's type of mental retardation. Although we discuss this issue in more detail below, children with different types of mental retardation vary in their trajectories of intellectual development as they get older. Children with Down syndrome decrease in IQ over time; these children continue to develop in intelligence, but they do so at slower and slower rates throughout the childhood years (see Hodapp & Zigler, 1990, for a review).

A similar problem occurs in fragile X syndrome, but only in the late middle childhood or teen years. Thus, boys with fragile X syndrome show steady or near-steady IQs until approximately 10 to 15 years of age, at which point their development slows considerably (Dykens et al., 1989; Hodapp et al., 1990). In fragile X syndrome, these slowings appear to be "age-related"; that is, fragile X boys of whatever IQ show these slowings during the 10- to 15-year age period, suggesting some link to pubertal development. Whatever the reason for such slowings, fragile X and Down syndromes show that the specific type of mental retardation may affect rates of intellectual development as children get older.

Although less often examined, trajectories of adaptive behavior may also change based on the child's type of mental retardation. Dykens, Hodapp, and Evans (1994) have recently found that the Vineland adaptive behavior age-equivalent scores of children with Down syndrome "plateau" during the middle childhood years. Similar to findings for IQ (Gibson, 1966) and grammatical development (Fowler, 1988), Down syndrome children as a group seem to make few advances in adaptive behavior between the ages of approximately 7 and 11 years, even as development occurs before and after these times. In fragile X syndrome, the early teen years again seem implicated in the slowing of development. Dykens, Hodapp, Ort, and Leckman (1993) found that boys with fragile X syndrome slowed in adaptive levels in the early teen years, even after they had been developing steadily (albeit at a slowed pace) until that time.

Mental retardation is, then, a relatively stable condition from childhood into adulthood, but a condition that is affected by the child's level of impairment and type of retardation. In addition, certain intensive early intervention programs—such as that mounted by the Abecedarian Project (Ramey & Ramey, 1992)—have been shown to boost IQ scores by approximately 10 to 15 points, although more family-centered, less "IQ-oriented" interventions seem more effective in promoting school and postschool achievement (e.g., Seitz, 1992). For many reasons, then, one's IQ score is not perfectly stable. Given that IQ is not perfectly stable, some individuals will go into and out of the retardation category. More IQ instability seems to occur among persons with mild mental retardation; persons with more severe levels of retardation show higher test–retest stability in IQ over the childhood and adulthood years. In addition, certain types of mental retardation show slowings or plateaus in intellectual and adaptive development, leading to greater impairments as these children get older.

EPIDEMIOLOGY

Prevalence

Depending on where one draws IQ and adaptive cutoff scores, the numbers of persons with mental retardation will vary widely. But even with a stable IQ criterion of IQ 70 and below, the number of persons with mental retardation is open to debate. The standard view is that approximately 3% of the population has mental retardation. This 3% number is derived from adding the 2.28% of people with IQs two or more standard deviations below the population mean (i.e., below 70 given a normal, bell-curve of intelligence) to some "extra" persons who will be described below. But this standard view makes several assumptions that seem, on the surface, unacceptable. Jane Mercer (1973), a main proponent for a prevalence rate of only 1%, describes these four assumptions.

1. *IQ as sole criterion of mental retardation.* A 3% prevalence rate implies that IQ is the sole criterion of mental retardation. But in all recent definitions of mental retardation, adaptive behavior is also highlighted. Terms such as "accompanied by significant limitations in adaptive functioning" (American Psychiatric Association, 1994,

p. 39) are common, highlighting that intellectual deficits, by themselves, constitute only one of the diagnostic criteria. But adaptive behavior and IQ levels are not synonomous, particularly at mild levels of mental retardation. Especially for persons with mild mental retardation, some individuals will show below 70 IQ and have adaptive deficits, whereas others will show below 70 IQs and not have adaptive deficits. To the extent that IQ and adaptive behavior are not correlated, fewer and fewer children will be both intellectually and adaptively impaired.

2. *IQ stability.* Although IQ scores are relatively stable after infancy and for lower-IQ children, mildly retarded persons will often show increases from one testing to another. Such IQ changes seem more likely among children with mild mental retardation. As in the discussion of IQ as the sole criteria of mental retardation, the instability of IQ—particularly its likelihood of "regressing to the population mean" (i.e., to go up) on second testings—makes it likely that fewer persons are diagnosed with mental retardation.

3. *System issues.* A third issue relates to diagnostic practices. The "school-based" nature of diagnosis—again with children in the mild range of mental retardation—means that fewer children are identified during the preschool and afterschool years. Again, prevalence rates are affected.

4. *Life expectancy.* A final issue relates to death rates. Particularly at the lowest levels of functioning, death occurs at earlier ages. Earlier deaths occur especially in persons with profound mental retardation, particularly when these individuals have ambulatory or respiratory problems (Eyman & Miller, 1978). Several specific etiologies of mental retardation also seem prone to earlier deaths; witness Down syndrome (Pueschel, 1987)—with its high prevalence of heart, respiratory, leukemia, and early-onset Alzheimer disease—and Prader-Willi Syndrome (another genetic disorder of mental retardation)—with its extreme obesity (Cassidy, 1992).

As a result of these four factors, the prevalence rates of mental retardation are generally below 3%. DSM-IV estimates the prevalence rate at "approximately 1%." Although this rate may be slightly low, a 3% rate seems too high. In the few studies so far, rates around 2% have often been found (Zigler & Hodapp, 1986), particularly when studies have examined every person in a town or region, as opposed to only those persons

diagnosed through clinics, schools, or other social-service systems. All of these numbers are suspect, however, and seem particularly influenced by the diagnostic and case-finding procedures employed in a particular study.

In contrast to the prevalence rates of mental retardation overall, more precise numbers are available for more severe levels of mental retardation. Many studies have shown that 0.4% of the population has moderate, severe, and profound mental retardation, or IQs below 50 or 55 (Abramowicz & Richardson, 1975). Because mental retardation at these levels is less influenced by issues such as how diagnoses are made, IQ stability, or the relationship of IQ to adaptive behavior, 0.4% seems an accurate percentage of persons with more severe mental retardation. How many additional people fall in the upper ranges of mental retardation seems debatable, but the total number of persons with retardation is most probably between 1% and 3% of the entire population.

Sex Differences

More male than female individuals are found in the mentally retarded population (American Psychiatric Association, 1994). Some of the overabundance of boys results from particular sex-linked disorders, and the most prevalent of these disorders is fragile X syndrome (Dykens, Hodapp, & Leckman, 1994). Fragile X syndrome is a recently discovered disorder that is now recognized as the second most common genetic disorder (after Down syndrome) and the most common hereditary disorder. That is, unlike Down syndrome, fragile X syndrome is passed down from one generation to the next.

Although the gene for fragile X syndrome (the FMR-1 gene) is located on the X chromosome, this syndrome does not follow a traditional X-linked inheritance pattern. About one-third to one-half of the females who carry and transmit the disorder are themselves affected with a variant of the syndrome, showing mild to moderate cognitive or emotional involvements. Further, about 20% of males with the FMR-1 gene transmit the disorder but are themselves unaffected. Peculiarities of the FMR-1 gene account for some of this variable expression in males and females. Overall, though, more boys than girls are affected with fragile X syndrome. Partly because of the prevalence of fragile X syndrome and other X-linked disorders, more males than females have mental retardation.

Social Class and Ethnic Factors

As mentioned above, mental retardation is more prevalent among children who are of lower SES and who are from minority groups. Like many findings in mental retardation, however, the tie of mental retardation to low SES and minority status is found primarily in children with mild mental retardation; children at more severe levels of mental retardation appear to occur about equally in different racial and economic groups.

This relationship of mild mental retardation and parental SES—and its highly correlated measure, parental IQ—is found in a classic study by Reed and Reed (1965). Studying several generations of families in Minnesota, Reed and Reed found that children from low IQ parents tended to themselves have lower IQs, whereas children from higher IQ parents generally had higher IQs. In a more recent study, Broman, Nichols, Shaughnessy, and Kennedy (1987) first divided socioeconomic status (SES) into the lowest 25% (SES Group 1), the middle 50% (SES Group 2), and the highest 25% (SES Group 3). For both white and African-American children, a clear relationship was found between the child's SES level and mild mental retardation as measured at 7 years (see Broman et al., 1987, Table 3.1). For the white sample, 3.34% of children from SES Group 1 had mild mental retardation, whereas only 1.31% and 0.30% of children from SES Groups 2 and 3 showed mild mental retardation. For the African-American sample, the numbers were even more extreme: 7.75% of children in SES Group 1 showed mild mental retardation, whereas rates of mild mental retardation were only 3.59% and 1.19% in SES Groups 2 and 3. Both genetic and environmental factors probably account for such findings, but there does seem to be a reasonably strong relationship between parental SES and IQ levels and children's IQs (particularly within the mild ranges of mental retardation).

The issue of mild mental retardation's association with race is more complicated. In many studies, average IQ levels for the African-American population are lower than those found in the white population. As a result, more African-American children would be expected to be among the mildly retarded group; this indeed has been the general finding (MacMillan et al., 1993). Again, many environmental and cultural factors are involved, as is the possibility that tests may be biased in favor of children from white, middle-

class backgrounds. Concern over minority over-representation partly led to the AAMR's change in the IQ criterion from IQ 85 to IQ 70 in its 1973 manual (Grossman, 1973). The idea was that children with retardation should show significant intellectual deficits that co-occur with the children's problems in adaptive behavior.

In recent years, many school and mental retardation professionals have deemphasized even further the importance of IQ in diagnostic decisions. California has gone furthest in this regard, mainly as a result of a well-known case against the San Francisco school system. In this case, *Larry P. v. Wilson Riles* (1979), parent advocates joined professionals such as Jane Mercer in arguing that African-American children were being unfairly placed in special education classes on the basis of IQ test results. The plaintiffs further argued that IQ tests were biased against African-American children and that the use of these tests was the main reason for the overrepresentation of minority children in special education programs. Other professionals argued strongly against such sweeping generalizations. They noted that, considered alone, lower average IQ scores do not constitute evidence that tests are biased against minority-group children. Furthermore, these professionals questioned whether IQ tests were the major reason why minorities are overrepresented in special education classes, especially given that most children are not tested with psychometric instruments until they have already failed in school (Lambert, 1981). In spite of these arguments, the presiding judge in the *Larry P.* case, Judge Peckham, ruled for the plaintiffs, holding that IQ tests were biased and should not be used in placement decisions for minority-group children. California school systems now prohibit IQ tests in decisions to place minority-group children in special education classes.

Regardless of one's views of the correctness of Judge Peckham's ruling, the *Larry P.* decision has produced several changes in diagnostic practice in California. Lambert (1981) notes that the judge's decision has led to fewer diagnoses of mild mental retardation in California's school systems; whereas 35,110 children were diagnosed as educable mentally retarded (the school term for mild retardation) in the 1973–1974 school year, only 19,370 were diagnosed as educable mentally retarded in 1977–1978. Furthermore, Prasse and Reschly (1986) note that school psychologists now give greater weight to tests of intellectual processing and of adaptive behavior. Ironically, the decision has not affected overrepresentation rates

per se. Taylor (1990) notes that minority overrepresentation continues among the mildly retarded school population, particularly among California's African-American children (MacMillan, Hendrick, & Watkins, 1988). Minority and SES factors in mild mental retardation remain difficult and unresolved.

THEORETICAL FRAMEWORKS

As with any population, different theoretical perspectives have been used to conceptualize individuals with mental retardation. We detail below several aspects of developmental approaches and then briefly discuss a few other prominent perspectives. Table 10.2 highlights the major theoretical approaches.

Developmental Approaches

Some of the greatest developmental thinkers of the 20th century have been interested in mental retardation. Werner (1941) examined children with retardation in his early work at the Wayne State Training School outside of Detroit, Piaget and Inhelder (1947; also Inhelder, 1943/1968) examined thinking in children with retardation, and Vygotsky (Reiber & Carton, 1993) started the entire field of "defectology" in the Soviet Union during the late 1920s (Hodapp & Zigler, 1995).

But a full-fledged "developmental approach" to mental retardation only began in the late 1960s. At that time, Zigler (1969) applied the sequences and structures found in nonretarded children to children with mental retardation. Zigler's focus was mainly on children with "familial mental retardation," that is, children showing no obvious organic insult that caused their mental retardation. In recent years, however, developmental approaches have included newer work on families and other ecologies in which children develop (Hodapp, Burack, & Zigler, 1990) and have been applied to children with Down syndrome (Cicchetti & Beeghly, 1990), fragile X syndrome (Dykens, Hodapp, & Leckman, 1994), and other mental retardation conditions. We now discuss three issues in these expanded approaches: sequences, cross-domain relations, and families.

Sequences

The most salient aspect of all developmental approaches concerns sequences of development. In

TABLE 10.2. Theoretical Frameworks Used in Mental Retardation

Framework	Main characteristics	Implications in mental retardation
Developmental Child issues	Use of normal development to inform us about mental retardation populations Similar sequence and structure hypotheses Two-group approach and revisions	Sequences used in curriculum; identifies important prerequisites and domains of development; mentally retarded populations tell us about nonretarded development; focus on development in persons with different types of mental retardation
Family issues	Family systems reactions to offspring with mental retardation Double ABCX model Stress–coping emphases	Interventions with all members and subsystems of families; identification of stressors, and ameliorating factors
Ecocultural	Relation of culture and disability Familial reactions based on cultural norms and expectations	Helps determine culturally sensitive interventions
Social role	Person with retardation plays a role in a social system Emphasis on system relations to person with mental retardation	Highlights effects of school, social service, and other institutions; questions professional practice
Behaviorist	Behaviors due to history of environmental rewards, punishments Emphasis on how changes in environment lead to improved performance	Successfully teaches lowest functioning individuals self-help skills; decreases maladaptive behaviors; teaches parents techniques to control behavior and teach new behaviors

Zigler's (1969) original approach, he proposed the "similar sequence hypothesis," the idea that children with mental retardation (particularly those with familial mental retardation) would proceed, in order, through the various cognitive sequences found in nonretarded children's development. Children with retardation were predicted to proceed from sensorimotor, to preoperational, to concrete operational, to formal operational thought, and to proceed in order even through the substages of sensorimotor (e.g., Dunst, 1980) and other Piagetian stages. Whenever children without retardation proceeded in invariant order, children with retardation too should traverse an identical sequence.

With very few exceptions, the similar sequence hypothesis has held true for children with retardation. Across many Piagetian and other cognitive and linguistic sequences, children with retardation—like nonretarded children—have been found to develop in the same sequences. Such sequential development has been found in examinations of several sensorimotor concepts, affective responding, identity and equivalence conser-

vation, seriation, transitivity, moral reasoning, comparison processes, time, space, relative thinking, role taking, mental imagery, geometric concepts, and classification and class inclusion (for a review of these studies, see Weisz & Zigler, 1979).

Furthermore, such similar sequences occurred for children with familial and with various organic forms of mental retardation. In Down syndrome, for example, Cicchetti and Mans-Wagener (1987), Dunst (1990), and others have noted that sensorimotor developments of children with Down syndrome occur in identical order to sensorimotor development in nonretarded children. Children with Down syndrome also show similar, identically ordered developments in such areas as symbolic play (Beeghly, Weiss-Perry, & Cicchetti, 1990) and language (Fowler, 1988).

Cross-Domain Relations

The second tenet of Zigler's original developmental formulation concerned the so-called "similar structure hypothesis," that children with retardation have the same organization of intelligence as

do nonretarded children. Hypothesized most directly for children with familial mental retardation, the similar structure hypothesis predicts that these children should perform similarly to nonretarded children when matched on overall mental age (MA) or other indices of overall mental functioning. Thus, children with and without mental retardation who have the same mental age should perform equally on attentional, linguistic, information-processing, vocabulary, or other cognitive or linguistic tasks. Having no single "defect" or deficit causing their impaired intellectual functioning, children with familial mental retardation, like all groups of children, should demonstrate even or flat profiles from one domain to another.

For the most part, the similar structure hypothesis has been supported, at least when children have familial mental retardation (Weisz, Yeates, & Zigler, 1982). These children may have some slight deficits in memory and learning set formation compared to MA-matched, nonretarded children (Weiss, Weisz, & Bromfield, 1986), but the reasons for such possible deficits are unclear. Children with familial mental retardation may indeed have deficits in memory, learning set formation, or information-processing skills (Mundy & Kasari, 1990); conversely, these children's relatively poor performance may result from the trouble these children have staying motivated to perform what are often boring, repetitive tasks (Weisz, 1990). Yet these children perform similarly to MA-matched, nonretarded children on Piagetian tasks, making the entire issue less clear-cut.

The picture for children with organic mental retardation is much clearer. Over many studies, children with organic mental retardation perform worse than do nonretarded, MA-matched children (Weisz et al., 1982). In contrast to children with familial mental retardation, then, these children do appear to have one or more specific areas of deficit.

But researchers now realize that organic mental retardation is not a single entity, that children with different etiologies differ in their behaviors. For example, children with Down syndrome demonstrate particular deficits in linguistic grammar relative to their abilities in other areas (Fowler, 1990). Boys with fragile X syndrome perform reasonably well on holistic, gestalt-like tasks and tasks tapping learned knowledge (i.e., achievement tasks). In contrast, these boys are particularly weak in sequential (or bit-by-bit) processing, either compared to their own abilities in other areas (Dykens, Hodapp, & Leckman, 1987)

or to children with Down syndrome of the same MAs (Hodapp et al., 1993).

The most startling etiology-based findings involve Williams syndrome. Williams syndrome is a rare disorder in which children have a particular, "elfin-like" facial appearance; these children are often talkative and outgoing (Udwin, Yule, & Martin, 1987). Recently, Bellugi, Wang, and Jernigan (1994) have noted that many of these children show particular, high-level abilities in language and language-like tasks compared to MA-matched retarded or nonretarded children. These children show vocabulary levels that are several years ahead of overall MAs (Bellugi, Marks, Bihrle, & Sabo, 1988), and they can tell stories with high-level grammar, as well as with sound effects and other storytelling devices (Reilly, Klima, & Bellugi, 1990). Consider the storytelling and language skills of two representative children, one with Williams syndrome and one with Down syndrome. The children are of the same chronological ages, mental ages, and IQs, and are responding to a picture-book story about a boy and a dog who lose and then find their pet frog (Reilly, Klima, & Bellugi, 1991, p. 377):

> [Williams syndrome child] Once upon a time there was this boy who had a dog and a frog. And it was night time. And there was a . . . bowl. And the boy and the dog looked in the . . . looked in the bowl. Then, it was nighttime and time for the boy to go to bed. But, as the boy and the dog were sleeping the frog climbed out. And, when it was morning [whispers] "The frog was gone."
>
> [Down syndrome child] He looks in the bowl. He . . . sleep. Then the frog got away. He looked in the bowl . . . and it empty.

Two lessons arise from behavior in different organic syndromes of mental retardation. First, contrary to Piaget's views of horizontally organized stages of development, both nonretarded and retarded children show unevenness from one developmental domain to the next. Such findings support Fodor's (1983) proposals that many domains (specifically language) are "modular," having little contact and interaction with other domains. Similarly, Gardner (1983) hypothesizes independent development in linguistic, musical, logicomathematical, spatial, bodily kinesthetic, and personal domains.

Findings from Williams syndrome and from exceptional individual children (e.g., Curtiss, 1977; Yamada, 1990) support such modular views

of children's functioning. A child's levels of grammatical functioning can be widely discrepant from levels of overall cognitive development. Why or how these dissociations develop remains unclear, but the previous view that development is "all of a piece" (i.e., showing equivalent levels in different domains) seems incorrect.

A second lesson involves the realization that children with different forms of mental retardation differ in their behavioral functioning. So far, specific types of mental retardation show different strengths and weaknesses in certain cognitive, linguistic, or adaptive skills (Hodapp & Dykens, 1994); some disorders show high susceptibilities to particular types of psychopathology (Dykens, 1995). Future research may need to emphasize the various *types* of mental retardation, as opposed to a single, all-encompassing entity of "mental retardation" per se.

Families and Ecologies

The past few years have seen a renewed interest in the families of children with mental retardation (e.g., Krauss, Simeonsson, & Ramey, 1989). Three major themes characterize this work.

New Perspectives

Family researchers have recently changed from "pathology-oriented" to "stress-and-coping-oriented" perspectives when examining families of children with mental retardation. To provide a flavor of this change, consider how in prior years many studies examined mothers and fathers to see if they were more likely to be depressed or to suffer from other forms of psychopathology. Solnit and Stark (1961) noted how parents "mourn" the loss of the idealized (i.e., normal) infant; Drotar, Baskiewicz, Irvin, Kennell, and Klaus (1975) proposed three stages of maternal mourning (shock, depression–anger, emotional reorganization); and Gath (1977) noted that parents of children with Down syndrome were more likely to divorce. Even siblings were examined for the extent to which they suffered "role tensions" (Farber, 1959) and psychopathology (Lobato, 1983) compared to siblings of nonretarded children (see Hodapp, 1995b).

In recent years, the perspective has shifted from psychopathology to stress and coping. Using this perspective, researchers conceptualize the child as an "extra stressor" in the family system (e.g., Crnic, Friedrich, & Greenberg, 1983).

As with all stressors, families and individual family members can be affected, sometimes negatively. But positive effects can also occur, as when a couple is brought closer together through caring for a difficult child.

Most importantly, the stress–coping perspective identifies factors that help parents cope. For example, among families raising a child with retardation, those who are more affluent cope better than poorer families (Farber, 1970), two-parent families cope better than single-parent families (Beckman, 1983), and women in better marriages cope better than those in more conflicted marriages (Beckman, 1983; Friedrich, 1979). Though such findings may not be surprising, they do show the effects of various supports for families raising the child with disabilities.

In addition, supports that help mothers may not help fathers. Mothers request more social–emotional support, information about the child's condition, and help in child care (Bailey, Blasco, & Simeonsson, 1992), whereas fathers are more concerned about the financial costs of raising the child with retardation (Price-Bonham & Addison, 1978). Krauss (1993) finds that mothers are especially concerned about the "personal" costs of raising the child with retardation (such things as changes in their relationship with their husbands, role restrictions, etc.), whereas fathers report more stress related to the child's temperament and their relationship to the child (such as feelings of being close to and reinforced by the child). In addition, mothers are helped by supportive social networks, whereas fathers cope better when extended social networks provide a minimum amount of criticism (Frey, Greenberg, & Fewell, 1989). Thus, mothers and fathers may differ in how they understand the child with retardation, which aspects of raising the child are stressful, and which factors best alleviate stress.

New Models

Just as researchers have changed from pathological to stress–coping perspectives, so too have they developed new models to understand families of children with retardation. One of the most influential of these models is the "Double ABCX" model (Minnes, 1988). The Double ABCX model states that the crisis (or "X") of raising a child with retardation is a function of the specific characteristics of the child (the "stressor event," or A), mediated by the family's internal and external resources (B) and by the family's perceptions of

the child (C). But this ABCX is not static: the child develops, familial resources may change, and so too may familial perceptions. Thus, the "Double" of the Double ABCX model.

The Double ABCX model is a useful general framework to examine families of children with retardation. Consider, for example, the "developmental" aspects of familial reactions. Mothers of children with mental retardation have long been thought to undergo a "mourning process" in response to their child with handicaps (Solnit & Stark, 1961). Based on this mourning model, researchers developed "stage models" of maternal mourning (cf. Blacher, 1984), emphasizing the time-bound nature of maternal reactions.

Recently, however, we have come to realize that mothers do not undergo one, single reaction to parenting their child with retardation, but that many reactions occur, at many times over the child's life. Wikler (1986) finds that mothers report extra stress when the child is entering puberty (11–15 years) and again when the child enters adulthood (20–21 years); others find a "pile-up" of stressors as the child gets older (Minnes, 1988). To worsen matters, parents often have smaller social networks (Kazak & Marvin, 1984) and make less use of formal support services as the child gets older (Suelzle & Keenan, 1981). Thus, changes in the child and in the parents' perceptions of the child—A (child) and C (perceptions) in the Double ABCX model—affect parental and familial adaptation.

New Attention to Etiology

Children with different forms of mental retardation may differ in their behavior (Hodapp & Dykens, 1991), and such differences may also affect family functioning. Specifically, it appears that families of children with Down syndrome are more often cohesive and harmonious (Mink, Nihira, & Meyers, 1983); these mothers also experience less stress and have larger and more satisfying social support networks (Goldberg, Marcovitch, MacGregor, & Lojkasek, 1986). Such differences occur even years later, when researchers compare adaptation in families of middle-aged adults with Down syndrome versus with other disorders. Seltzer, Krauss, and Tsunematsu (1993) find that, compared to mothers of middle-aged individuals with other forms of mental retardation, mothers of middle-aged adults with Down syndrome report less conflicted family environments, more satisfaction with their

social supports, and less stress and burden associated with caregiving.

Exactly why such "etiology-based" familial patterns appear is unknown. Hodapp and Dykens (1994) hypothesize that differences may relate to child characteristics such as degree and type of psychopathology (or degree of impairment, personality, or other child characteristic), but other possibilities cannot be ruled out. Specifically, Seltzer et al. (1993) note that Down syndrome is a common, well-known, and well-researched syndrome, with large and active parent organizations. As a result, parents may feel less isolated and more supported. Whatever the reason, the child's etiology of retardation—or something related—seems differentially to affect family functioning in children with different forms of mental retardation.

Other Important Theoretical Orientations

Ecocultural Perspectives

Following from anthropological and cross-cultural work with nonretarded children (Super & Harkness, 1986), several researchers have examined the "developmental niche" filled by the child with retardation. Much of this work centers around the meaning of the child to the family and how parental goals for the child fit with parental goals for themselves, for other family members, and for the family as a whole.

For example, Gallimore, Weisner, Kaufman, and Bernheimer (1989) note the "accommodations" made by different families of children with retardation. Some families set up the entire family system to ensure that the child with retardation receives maximal intellectual stimulation. In contrast, other families were much more concerned with the other, nonretarded children. For these families, the child with retardation was not felt to need extra stimulation, and more family-oriented goals were emphasized. In both cases, family routines and the behaviors of each family member were aligned with the family's goals, as was the meaning of "success" to each family.

Social Role Theory

Following from the social system perspective of mental retardation, the child with retardation is seen by many as merely fulfilling a societal role. Indeed, to some (e.g., Mercer, 1992), the "social"

nature of retardation is emphasized by the recent decrease in diagnoses of mild mental retardation.

Along with the rise in social role perspectives on retardation has been the view that the field is undergoing a "support revolution" (Schwartz, 1992). Some claim that developmental and biomedical orientations toward retardation have been replaced by this new support paradigm, which emphasizes the supports a given individual needs in order to play an age-appropriate role in the society. Although attempts to provide better, more individualized services are beneficial, the effect of other changes seems unclear. For instance, many segments of AAMR are now demanding representation of consumers—persons with mental retardation—on all boards, committees, and review panels. Such changes may not necessarily ensure adequate representation or input for all persons with mental retardation.

Behavioral Techniques

Following from the writings of Skinner (1968), Foxx and Azrin (1974), and others, behavioral techniques have been successfully used in three different ways. First, behavior modification techniques have been effective in training adaptive behaviors to persons with mental retardation. Such behaviors as grooming, toileting, eating, and dressing have all been taught to individuals at the profound and severe levels of retardation. Behavioral techniques have also been successfully employed to stop maladaptive behaviors such as hurting others or oneself. Overall, the record of behavioral training for adaptive or maladaptive behaviors has been impressive (Matson, 1990).

Second, behavioral techniques have been very helpful for parents. Parents of very impaired or difficult-to-control children are often at a loss as to how to proceed. In many cases, the behaviorist's clear schedules of rewards and punishments have helped parents elicit adaptive as opposed to maladaptive behaviors. Similarly, parents have been taught how to model desired behaviors, to break down complex tasks into smaller components, and to "chain together" these components (Baker, 1989).

A third area of behavioral success involves vocational and prevocational training and work. Using behavioral techniques to teach skills and token economies to keep workers on task, many persons with retardation can now work successfully in supported work environments (Wehman, Sale, & Parent, 1992). Again, many of these individuals are very impaired, whereas others had shown maladaptive behaviors that previously made it impossible for them to produce in a job setting.

ETIOLOGIES

Mental retardation results from many different causes. Some of these causes occur prenatally, as in all of the genetic disorders and accidents in utero. Other types of retardation are caused by perinatal insults, such things as prematurity or anoxia at birth. Still other types of mental retardation occur as a result of meningitis, head trauma, or other "after-birth insults." In addition to the many different types of retardation that have one or more specific causes, many—perhaps the majority—of persons have mental retardation with no obvious pre-, peri-, or postnatal cause.

How to make sense of these many different etiologies? Historically, researchers have postulated what has come to be called the "two-group approach" to mental retardation. We briefly overview this approach, then describe recent advances in behavioral knowledge, particularly concerning persons with different genetic disorders of mental retardation.

Two-Group Approach

Mental retardation workers have historically described two distinct groups of persons with mental retardation (Zigler, 1967, 1969). The first group demonstrates a clear organic cause for their mental retardation; the second group shows retardation with no clear organic cause. This distinction between "organic" and "familial" forms of mental retardation has characterized mental retardation work throughout the 20th century (cf. Burack, 1990). Table 10.3 shows the two-group approach.

To begin with the familial group, these individuals represent what is probably the single biggest mystery in mental retardation. Comprising slightly over one-half of all retarded persons, these individuals show no cause for their retardation. Some researchers feel that persons with familial mental retardation do indeed have slight, hard-to-detect neurological problems that cause their lowered levels of intelligence (Baumeister & MacLean, 1979). Others feel that these persons form the lower end of a Gaussian, bell-shaped curve of intelligence (e.g., Zigler, 1967).

TABLE 10.3. The Two-Group Approach to Mental Retardation

	Organic	Cultural–familial
Definition	Individual shows a clear organic cause of mental retardation	Individual shows no obvious cause of retardation; sometimes other family member is also retarded.
Characteristics	More prevalent at moderate, severe, and profound mental retardation	More prevalent in mild mental retardation
	Equal or near-equal rates across all ethnic and SES levels	Higher rates within minority groups and low SES groups
	More often associated with other physical disabilities	Few associated physical or medical disabilities
Causes[a]	Prenatal (genetic disorders, accidents in utero)	Polygenic (i.e., parents of low IQ)
	Perinatal (prematurity, anoxia)	Environmentally deprived
	Postnatal (head trauma, meningitis)	Undetected organic conditions

[a]Causes are suspected for cultural–familial mental retardation.

Still others feel that environmental deficits, or overstimulation, may cause familial mental retardation. Such different views of what causes this form of mental retardation are most clearly seen in the many different names for this disorder: familial mental retardation has been called familial, cultural–familial, and sociocultural–familial mental retardation; retardation due to environmental deprivation; and nonorganic or nonspecific mental retardation. The appropriate name, like the appropriate cause, is open to debate.

Regardless of cause, persons with familial mental retardation are predominantly at the mild levels of retardation. As such, these are the individuals who blend into the larger population before and after the school years and who are more likely to be minorities and of low SES. In addition, these individuals are much more likely to come from impoverished backgrounds and from parents who are themselves low in intelligence. Thus, the many controversies surrounding definition and supportive services are all present in discussions of familial mental retardation (Hodapp, 1994).

Persons in the second group, those with organic mental retardation, demonstrate one or more clear causes of their mental retardation. Such causes can occur pre-, peri-, or postnatally, but a clear cause of retardation is present. In 1983, Grossman noted that there were over 200 organic causes of mental retardation (including all types), but mainly as a result of the discovery of new genetic causes every year, there are now over 1,000 different organic forms (Moser, 1992). Table 10.4 presents several of the more prominent genetic forms of mental retardation.

Although persons with certain organic conditions (e.g., Prader–Willi syndrome) can be found at mild levels of mental retardation, most persons with organic mental retardation are more severely impaired. Reviewing across several studies, Zigler and Hodapp (1986) found that a median of 77% of individuals with IQs in the moderate-to-profound mental retardation range showed organic etiologies, whereas only 23% of individuals with IQs below 50 or 55 (depending on the study) showed no clear reason for their retardation. In contrast, 61% of individuals in the mild mental retardation range showed no clear cause of their retardation; only 39% showed specific, identified etiological conditions.

Similarly, compared to predictions from a normal or Gaussian curve of intelligence, there are too many persons with severe and profound mental retardation. This excess of individuals at the lower ranges of intelligence constitutes the "extra" persons who make up the hypothesized 3% prevalence rate of mental retardation discussed above (Dingman & Tarjan, 1960). This excess is assumed to occur because of the many individuals who have organic forms of mental retardation.

Differentiating Organic Mental Retardation

As noted above, researchers are increasingly realizing that persons with different forms of organic mental retardation differ behaviorally (Burack, Hodapp, & Zigler, 1988). For example, many boys with fragile X syndrome show cognitive profiles and trajectories that differ from children with Down syndrome. Striking differences also occur in psychopathology between etiological groups (see "Dual Diagnosis," below). Variable profiles, trajectories, and psychopathology highlight that it is overly simplistic to speak of "organic mental retardation" as if it were a single entity.

A better understanding of each particular syndrome's characteristic behaviors, or "behavioral phenotype," also helps refine both the timing and type of intervention efforts (e.g., Hodapp & Dykens, 1991). In fragile X syndrome, for example, trajectories of IQ and adaptive behaviors underscore the importance of early intervention, and the syndrome's characteristic cognitive profile has led to a host of specific educational recommendations (see Dykens, Hodapp, & Leckman, 1994, for a review). Detailed descriptions of behavioral phenotypes also help screen high-risk samples.

Behavioral research on genetic etiologies is also critical given recent revolutionary advances in molecular genetics. Technological advances in the so-called "new genetics" bring forth a demand for improved research that links genes to behavior. For example, much of the variable and puzzling behavioral phenotype in fragile X syndrome is attributed to the degree of expansion—the actual amount of extra genetic material—of the FMR-1 gene. This type of genotype–phenotype work furthers knowledge of gene function and may ultimately lead to innovative gene therapies (Anderson, 1994).

Despite the renewed importance of syndromic behavior, most researchers interested in the behavior of persons with mental retardation classify groups according to level of impairment. Thus, psychologists and special educators often compare children with mild mental retardation versus those with severe or profound retardation; these workers rarely consider the causes of the child's retardation. In contrast, geneticists, pediatricians, and psychiatrists generally classify by etiology. These researchers examine persons with Down syndrome, fragile X syndrome, or other causes of mental retardation.

We have described these orientations as two, rarely overlapping "cultures" of behavioral research in mental retardation (Hodapp & Dykens, 1994). Both cultures study the behavior of persons with mental retardation, yet they differ in their technical languages, expertises, and journals. As a result, many workers in the genetic tradition do not often use sophisticated behavioral measures or apply their findings to pertinent issues in the wider mental retardation field. Conversely, many behavioral researchers are unaware of revolutionary advances in genetics and ignore the effects of etiology on their research designs

TABLE 10.4. Prominent Genetic Forms of Mental Retardation

Disorder	Genetics	Prevalence	Prominent behavioral features
Down syndrome	95% involve trisomy 21	1–1.5/1,000 live births	Moderate mental retardation; slowing rate of development as child gets older; social strengths; weaknesses in grammar and speech.
Fragile X syndrome	Fragile site on X chromosome	0.73–0.92/1,000 live births	Moderate mental retardation; more males than females; for males, strength in simultaneous processing, weakness in sequential processing, slowed development from puberty; hyperactivity and autistic-like behaviors.
Prader–Willi syndrome	2/3 involve deletions on chromosome 15; remainder involve maternal disomy on 15	1/15,000 live births	Mild mental retardation; proneness to obesity, food foraging, and preoccupations; stubbornness and obsessive–compulsive behaviors.

TABLE 10.5. The "Two Cultures" of Behavioral Research in Mental Retardation

Level of impairment-based	Etiology-based
Main characteristics	
Group by degree of disability	Group by etiology
Less regard for genetic etiology	De-emphasize degree of disability
Professions (with some overlap)	
Behavioral psychologists	Geneticists
Special educators	Genetic counselors
Clinical psychologists	Child psychiatrists
Social workers	Pediatricians
	Psychiatrists
Strengths	
Advances in behavioral measurement	Advances in molecular genetics
Weaknesses	
Often less aware of advances in genetics and molecular genetics	Often less sophisticated in behavioral measurement
Often less appreciation for impact of genetic etiology on research or intervention	Often less application of findings to pertinent issues in larger mental retardation field

and findings. The main features of these two cultures are summarized in Table 10.5.

The challenges of bridging these two cultures include problems in understanding each side's different technical languages, in assessing the impact of mental retardation versus genetic status, and in accounting for between-syndrome similarities and differences (Hodapp & Dykens, 1994). More specific definitional and measurement issues inherent in phenotype research have also been outlined (Dykens, 1995). The issue of "dual diagnosis"—described below—also exemplifies this need for "cross-cultural" collaborations and more genetically informed research.

DUAL DIAGNOSIS

Early interests in psychopathology and mental retardation waned in the 1920s and were revisited in the late 1960s (Menolascino, 1970). Since that time, remarkable strides have been made in developing appropriate maladaptive behavior rating scales (Aman, 1991), identifying advantages and limitations of psychiatric nosology in this population (Sovner, 1986), and using research to fine-tune pharmacological and behavioral treatments (Menolascino & Fleisher, 1993). These accomplishments have helped in under-

standing the degree to which children with mental retardation can be "dually diagnosed," that is, have both mental retardation and (other) psychiatric disorders.

As a result of these advances, we now know that children with mental retardation show the full range of psychiatric disorders. Relative to nonretarded children, children with mental retardation often show more problems with anxiety, depression, withdrawal, conduct-disordered behaviors, aggression, and self-injury, and they are also more apt to be diagnosed with autism (Cullinan, Epstein, Matson, & Rosemier, 1984; Dekry & Ehly, 1981; Volkmar, Burack, & Cohen, 1990).

In addition to showing most types of psychopathology, children with mental retardation, compared to their nonretarded peers, display psychiatric disorders or behavioral and emotional problems at very high rates (Matson & Frame, 1986). Estimates of dual diagnoses among these children range from 10% (Jacobson, 1982) to 50% (Richardson, Katz, Koller, McLaren, & Rubinstein, 1979; Rutter, Tizard, Yule, Graham, & Whitmore, 1976). Although these estimates vary widely, they do indicate that psychiatric disorders are common among children with mental retardation.

Understanding dual diagnosis is complicated by several major problems. First, studies vary

widely in their methodologies. Some studies examine entire populations of persons with retardation, whereas others limit their examinations to clinic-based samples. Different approaches are used for assessing pathology, such as behavioral checklists, psychiatric nosology, or focusing on just one type of problem (e.g., psychoses or phobias). Such differences among studies make problematic any general, overall statements about dual diagnosis.

A second issue involves the "goodness of fit" between standard psychiatric nosology and persons with mental retardation (Sovner, 1986). Many psychiatric categories do not easily relate to persons with retardation. For example, certain problems seem quite common in children with mental retardation, including temper tantrums, aggression, hyperactivity and diminished responsiveness to others (Jacobson, 1982). While many of these behaviors can be quite severe and warrant intensive intervention, they may or may not be symptomatic of psychiatric illness. In addition, many children and adults with mental retardation have particular difficulty labeling and expressing internal states (Glick, in press; Jacobson, 1990). As a result, clinicians may have particular difficulty accurately diagnosing "internalizing" psychiatric disorders such as depression or anxiety in persons with mental retardation.

Even when professionals receive information from other informants, difficult issues arise. For example, checklists and diagnoses require judgments from parents, teachers, or clinicians as to when certain behaviors should be labeled as maladaptive or deviant. Some behaviors—such as hallucinations or delusions—are clearly deviant regardless of the person's chronological or mental age. Other behaviors or emotions, however, may be quite consistent with a person's mental age, yet are deviant from chronological age expectations. The 15-year-old with a mental age of 2 or 3 years may show fantasy–reality blurrings typical of "normal" preschoolers, or he or she may exhibit "terrible two" tantrums that reflect "normal" bids for increased separation and autonomy. Consideration of mental age versus chronological age expectations is thus an important aspect of making accurate diagnoses in this population.

These problems have recently been addressed by work that specifically examines psychopathology in retarded populations. Dosen and Gielen (1993) have proposed alternative diagnostic criteria for features such as depression, and behavioral checklists are increasingly being normed on mentally retarded versus "normal" children (e.g.,

Reiss, 1990). Such efforts allow for a better "fit" of psychopathology and mental retardation in the dual-diagnosis field.

But other advances are also needed. Researchers have yet to consider the effects of etiology on any of the dual-diagnosis prevalence rates or on other key findings emanating from the dual-diagnosis movement. As noted above, this lack of attention to etiology seems associated with the "level-of-impairment" research bias in the larger mental retardation field. Yet many genetic syndromes do show salient patterns of maladaptive behavior and psychopathology. Three syndromes exemplify such syndrome-specific psychiatric and behavioral features.

Fragile X Syndrome

Fragile X syndrome results in a spectrum of learning and emotional problems in both males and carrier females. Many individuals with the syndrome show characteristic cognitive profiles, as well as hyperactivity and attention deficits (see Dykens, Hodapp, & Leckman, 1994, for a review). Females are only rarely affected with mental retardation, whereas males are apt to be moderately affected, especially in the postpubertal years. These males may also manifest perseverative speech and behaviors, stereotypies, and tactile defensiveness.

Early case reports noted several fragile X boys who met DSM-III criteria for autism (August & Lockhart, 1984; Meryash, Szymanski, & Gerald, 1982). Many researchers were excited by the hypothesis that fragile X was a common genetic cause of autistic disorder. Indeed, certain fragile X behaviors seemed to be classically autistic, including delayed and echolalic speech, stereotypies, withdrawal, and poor eye contact. Based on these behaviors, a flurry of research linked the disorders by identifying the prevalence of autistic disorder in fragile X males, and by screening autistic males for the fragile X marker (see Dykens, Hodapp, & Leckman, 1994, for a review).

Only after careful, in-depth studies of the behaviors shown by fragile X males was it discovered that most of these males relate to others and are attached to their caregivers. Unlike early estimates, current estimates suggest that only about 5% of fragile X males have autistic disorder. Instead of autism per se, the majority of these males are better described along a continuum of social anxiety and oddities, shyness, and mutual gaze aversion (Bregman, Leckman, & Ort, 1988;

Cohen, Veitze, Sudhalter, Jenkins, & Brown, 1991; Reiss & Freund, 1990).

Many affected females can also be placed on this continuum, and some (carrier) mothers also show increased depressive vulnerabilities relative to mothers of non-fragile X developmentally delayed children (Freund, Reiss, Hagerman, & Vinogradov, 1992). As previously stated, the degree of involvement in males and females can now be attributed, in part, to the degree of expansion of the FMR-1 gene. This link highlights the need for future work to correlate aspects of the FMR-1 gene to behavior.

Prader-Willi Syndrome

First identified in 1956 (Prader, Labhart, & Willi, 1956), Prader–Willi syndrome is now known to be caused in one of several ways. Most cases of Prader–Willi syndrome are attributed to a paternally inherited deletion, or missing piece, on chromosome 15. But about 30% of cases are caused by a maternal disomy, or when both chromosomes of the 15th pair come from the mother. In either case, genetic information is missing from the father. It is not yet known how these two causes of the syndrome might differentially affect behavior.

Developmentally, Prader–Willi syndrome shows at least two distinct phases. Infants show hypotonia, feeding and sucking problems, and developmental delay. In striking contrast to this "failure to thrive" period, phase two begins between 2 to 6 years and is characterized by hyperphagia, food preoccupations, and food-seeking (Holm et al., 1993). Without proper dietary management, persons with the syndrome often become obese.

Maladaptive behaviors may also change as these children develop. Young children are typically described as pleasant, friendly, and affectionate (Cassidy, 1992). Although these features do not necessarily disappear, the beginning of hyperphagia is associated with the onset or worsening of many maladaptive behaviors. These problems include temper tantrums, stubbornness, lability, depression, argumentativeness, and highly repetitive thoughts and behaviors such as skin-picking, food preoccupations, and getting "stuck" on ideas. Indeed, Dykens, Leckman, and Cassidy (1995) recently found that as many as 50–60% of children and adults with Prader–Willi syndrome may meet DSM-IV criteria for obsessive–compulsive disorder; this rate is many times higher than the 2–3% commonly found in mentally retarded populations.

Other key aspects of maladaptive behavior also remain unknown. Children, for example, seem to show increases in maladaptive behavior with age, whereas adults may show a more variable course (Dykens, Hodapp, Walsh, & Nash, 1992a; Dykens & Cassidy, in press). Weight does not appear related to intelligence (Dykens, Hodapp, Walsh, & Nash, 1992b), yet it may be associated with psychopathology. Curiously, Dykens and Cassidy (in press) note that confused thinking, delusions, hallucinations, anxiety, fearfulness, and sadness appear more common in thinner as opposed to heavier individuals; such findings may lead to a wider emphasis in interventions on issues other than the individual's weight loss. Other issues remain unexplored, for example the relationship between behavior problems and genetic status (e.g., paternal deletion vs. maternal disomy).

Smith-Magenis Syndrome

This newly discovered syndrome involves a deletion on chromosome 17 (Smith et al., 1986). Many individuals with Smith–Magenis syndrome show distinctive features such as significant sleep disorders and self-abuse involving pulling out fingernails or toenails and inserting foreign objects into bodily orifices (Greenberg et al., 1991). When excited or happy, many persons with the syndrome show a highly unusual "upper body spasmodic squeeze," or self-hug, that can occur up to 100 times an hour (Finucane, Konar, Haas-Givler, Kurtz, & Scott, 1994).

It appears, then, that fragile X, Prader–Willi, and Smith–Magenis syndromes have distinct maladaptive behaviors, yet there are far too many syndromes to presume that each syndrome shows unique psychopathology. Indeed, even though these three syndromes share certain maladaptive behaviors such as "perseveration," persons with each syndrome may perseverate in different ways (e.g., on odd preoccupations in fragile X, food in Prader–Willi, and "self-hugging" in Smith–Magenis). Future phenotypic research will need to identify how syndromes are "the same but different" (Dykens, 1995). Clearly, considerable work remains in each of the three syndromes presented, as well as in hundreds of lesser-known syndromes. This work needs to better describe maladaptive behavior and psychiatric illness within syndromes, refine treatment, and assess the "percentage of variance" attributed to general mental retardation versus to specific genetic status (Dykens, 1995).

Compared to earlier times, researchers and clinicians have advanced greatly in their understanding of dually diagnosed persons. Many of these advances involve views of psychopathology that are specifically related to persons with mental retardation. But other advances are also needed. Traditionally, the dual diagnosis movement has not been etiologically based, leaving unanswered critical issues regarding syndrome-specific psychopathology, treatment, and outcome, as well as potential new understandings of gene–behavior relationships.

CURRENT ISSUES AND FUTURE DIRECTIONS

Although many issues pervade mental retardation, five deserve special notice. Working toward the solution of each will help advance the field of mental retardation for many years to come.

Defining Mental Retardation

The AAMR's new 1992 definition is probably mental retardation's "hottest" current debate. By changing from a definition of below-70 IQ and adaptive deficits to one focusing on IQ "below 70 or 75" and deficits in 2 of 10 adaptive domains, the new definition may affect the number and characteristics of the retarded population. The definition has been strongly criticized by some researchers (e.g., Jacobsen & Mulick, 1992, 1993; MacMillan et al., 1993), even as it is strongly defended by others (Reiss, 1994). Professional groups such as the American Psychological Association's Division 33 (the main mental retardation division) have rejected the definition and are even planning to issue their own "official" definition (Jacobsen & Mulick, 1993). Other professional groups have rejected parts of the new definition, as in the American Psychiatric Association's (1994) adoption of 2 of 11 adaptive domains, while keeping the IQ criterion at 70. On the state level as well, controversy abounds among policymakers and clinicians. Led by psychologists and psychiatrists, some states (e.g., Connecticut) have chosen not to follow the new definition. Others undoubtedly will adopt the new definition.

The debate over the new definition also highlights mental retardation's many constituencies. Mental retardation concerns many different people: the affected individuals themselves, families and advocates, policymakers, special educators, social workers, physicians, group home and other mental retardation workers, geneticists and genetic counselors, psychologists, and psychiatrists. All benefit from a standard definition of mental retardation, from a definition that different professions—each with its unique perspectives and approaches—can apply to a common population to be studied and served.

Improving Service Delivery

Equally challenging are issues of service delivery. These issues mostly pertain to schools and residences. On the whole, great strides in service delivery have been made over the past 20 to 30 years. Persons with mental retardation now enjoy the right to a public school education, and, in many cases, this schooling occurs in the same classrooms as with nonretarded age mates. Many children with retardation benefit from such contacts and experiences. In the postschool years, persons with mental retardation enjoy residential opportunities such as individual or small apartments and group homes. Such homes allow adults with retardation to become part of their communities, to live among and interact with nonretarded peers. Such progress in "normalized" schooling and living settings would have been unheard of only three decades ago.

Yet some retardation workers are concerned about exactly how normalization has been implemented. Zigler, Hodapp, and Edison (1990) note that there has often been more concern with where a person with retardation lives or is educated than what happens within that setting. They decry the overemphasis on a "social address model" in mental retardation, on the single issue of the setting in which interactions occur. Instead, these authors note, we should pay more attention to what occurs *within* every setting, while providing a continuum of high-quality services for every person with retardation, no matter one's age, etiology, or degree of impairment. This issue, and the interplay between what should—philosophically—be the best environment for a particular person and what is—empirically—the best environment, promise to remain difficult research and policy problems in the years to come.

Joining the Two Cultures of Behavioral Research

A third issue involves the two cultures of behavioral research in mental retardation. Compared to the numerous advances in genetics, we know

relatively little about the behaviors associated with many different genetic disorders. Indeed, the two cultures of mental retardation remain divided.

But in order to research and intervene with persons with mental retardation, we must link psychologists, special educators, and others interested in behavior to geneticists, psychiatrists, and others interested in etiology. As noted above, researchers are discovering that specific etiological groups differ in their behavior one from another. With new genetic techniques and advances, gene–behavior linkages will become increasingly possible and precise. In short, if progress in behavioral research is to continue, the two cultures of mental retardation research must join together.

Describing Psychopathology

A fourth, related issue concerns psychopathology. For many years, parents, advocates, and even researchers were loathe to examine the tie between mental retardation and psychopathology. More recently, we have begun to realize that persons with retardation often do have various psychopathological conditions.

Again, a joining of different fields seems necessary. It will not be enough simply to apply diagnoses—or even checklists—derived from nonretarded populations and apply them to persons with retardation. More attention will need to be given to how retardation and issues within retarded populations complicate the dual diagnosis issue (Dykens, 1994). A joining of different professionals and different perspectives seems mandatory if we are ever to truly understand and intervene with persons who show both mental retardation and psychopathological conditions.

Changing Populations with Mental Retardation

Although it is currently unclear if future years will bring greater or lesser numbers of persons with retardation, it does appear certain that the composition of that population will change dramatically. Already on the horizon are new discoveries that will lead to more precise genetic diagnoses in utero for many different genetic disorders. Similarly, gene therapies may someday cure many disorders, or at least greatly alleviate their effects.

But other forces may lead to greater numbers of persons with retardation. The ability of newborn intensive care units to save neonates below 1,000 grams (who are at higher risk for retardation), the rise in pediatric AIDS, the epidemic of babies suffering from their mother's drug abuse—all would seem to increase mental retardation prevalence rates in the years to come. Already we are seeing the effects of fetal alcohol syndrome; Streissguth et al. (1991) note that these children have lower IQs (mean = 68), often show attention-deficit disorder (ADD) and other attentional problems, and have difficulties in school and later life. The effects of crack cocaine are less clear: although the early reports on these children are not showing lower IQs, these children do appear more distractible and prone to behavioral disorganization (Griffith, Azuma, & Chasnoff, 1994; although see also Richardson & Day, 1994). It remains unclear whether crack babies will grow up to have higher-than-normal risks for mental retardation. Reviewing these issues, Baumeister, Kupstas, and Klindworth (1991) have spoken of "the new morbidity," a mental retardation population that may differ radically from retarded populations of earlier years.

We return, then, to the idea that mental retardation is a field of monumental advances amidst monumental controversies. The advances involve characterizations of development, attention to etiology, and new research in genetics, psychopathology, and many other areas. But the controversies also deserve mention, as definitional, service delivery, and "cultural" issues threaten to divide the mental retardation field. Given an uncertain future in all of these areas, and a changing, possibly growing, population, only time will tell how well we advance in understanding and helping individuals with mental retardation.

REFERENCES

Abramowicz, H. K., & Richardson, S. (1975). Epidemiology of severe mental retardation in children: Community studies. *American Journal of Mental Deficiency, 80,* 18–39.

Aman, M. G. (1991). *Assessing psychopathology and behavior problems in persons with mental retardation: A review of available instruments.* Rockville, MD: U.S. Department of Health and Human Services.

American Association on Mental Retardation. (1992). *Mental retardation: Definition, classification, and systems of supports.* Washington, DC: Author.

American Psychiatric Association. (1987). *Diagnostic and statistical manual* (3rd ed., rev.). Washington, DC: Author.

American Psychiatric Association. (1994). *Diagnostic and statistical manual* (4th ed.). Washington, DC: Author.

Anderson, W. F. (1994). Gene therapy for genetic disorder. *Human Gene Therapy, 5,* 281–282.

Artiles, A. J., & Trent, S. C. (1994). Overrepresentation of minority students in special education: A continuing debate. *Journal of Special Education, 27,* 410–437.

August, G. J., & Lockhart, L. H. (1984). Familial autism and the fragile X chromosome. *Journal of Autism and Developmental Disorders, 14,* 197–204.

Bailey, D., Blasco, P., & Simeonsson, R. (1992). Needs expressed by mothers and fathers of young children with disabilities. *American Journal on Mental Retardation, 97,* 1–10.

Baker, B. (1989). *Parent training and developmental disabilities.* Washington, DC: American Association on Mental Retardation.

Baumeister, A. A., Kupstas, F. D., & Klindworth, L. M. (1991). The new morbidity: A national plan of action. *American Behavioral Scientist, 34,* 468–500.

Baumeister, A., & MacLean, W. (1979). Brain damage and mental retardation. In N. R. Ellis (Ed.), *Handbook of mental deficiency: Psychological theory and research* (2nd ed., pp. 197–230). Hillsdale, NJ: Erlbaum.

Beckman, P. (1983). Influence of selected child characteristics on stress in families of handicapped children. *American Journal of Mental Deficiency, 88,* 150–156.

Beeghly, M., Weiss-Perry, M., & Cicchetti, D. (1990). Beyond sensorimotor functioning: Early cognitive development and play development of children with Down syndrome. In D. Cicchetti & M. Beeghly (Eds.), *Children with Down syndrome: A developmental approach* (pp. 329–368). New York: Cambridge University Press.

Bellugi, U., Marks, S., Bihrle, A., & Sabo, H. (1988). Dissociation between language and cognitive functions in Williams syndrome. In D. Bishop & K. Mogford (Eds.), *Language development in exceptional circumstances* (pp. 177–189). London: Churchill Livingstone.

Bellugi, U., Wang, P., & Jernigan, T. (1994). Williams syndrome: An unusual neuropsychological profile. In S. H. Broman & J. Grafman (Eds.), *Atypical cognitive deficits in developmental disorders* (pp. 23–56). Hillsdale, NJ: Erlbaum

Bernheimer, C., & Keogh, B. (1988). Stability of cognitive performance of children with developmental delays. *American Journal of Mental Deficiency, 92,* 539–542.

Blacher, J. (1984). Sequential stages of parental adjustment to the birth of the child with handicaps: Fact or artifact? *Mental Retardation, 22,* 55–68.

Blatt, B., & Kaplan, F. (1966). *Christmas in purgatory.* Boston: Allyn & Bacon.

Bregman, J. D., Leckman, J. F., & Ort, S. I. (1988). Fragile X syndrome: Genetic predisposition to psychopathology. *Journal of Autism and Developmental Disorders, 18,* 343–354.

Broman, S., Nichols, P. L., Shaughnessy, P., & Kennedy, W. (1987). *Retardation in young children: A developmental study of cognitive deficit.* Hillsdale, NJ: Erlbaum.

Burack, J. A. (1990). Differentiating mental retardation: The two-group approach and beyond. In R. M. Hodapp, J. A. Burack, & E. Zigler (Eds.), *Issues in the developmental approach to mental retardation* (pp. 27–48). New York: Cambridge University Press.

Burack, J. A., Hodapp, R. M., & Zigler, E. (1988). Issues in the classification of mental retardation: Differentiating among organic etiologies. *Journal of Child Psychology and Psychiatry, 29,* 765–779.

Caruso, D. R., & Hodapp, R. M. (1988). Perceptions of mental retardation and mental illness. *American Journal on Mental Retardation, 93,* 118–124.

Cassidy, S. B. (1984). Prader–Willi syndrome. *Current Problems in Pediatrics, 14,* 1–55.

Cassidy, S. B. (Ed.).(1992). *Prader–Willi syndrome and other chromosome 15q deletion disorders.* New York: Springer-Verlag.

Cicchetti, D., & Beeghly, M. (Eds.). (1990). *Children with Down syndrome: A developmental approach.* New York: Cambridge University Press.

Cicchetti, D., & Mans-Wagener, L. (1987). Sequences, stages, and structures in the organization of cognitive development in infants with Down syndrome. In I. Uzgiris & J. McV. Hunt (Eds.), *Infant performance and experience: New findings with the Ordinal Scales* (pp. 281–310). Urbana, IL: University of Illinois Press.

Cohen, I. L., Vietze, P. M., Sudhalter, V., Jenkins, E. C., & Brown, W. T. (1991). Effects of age and communication level of eye contact in fragile X males and non-fragile X autistic males. *American Journal of Medical Genetics, 38,* 498–502.

Crnic, K., Friedrich, W., & Greenberg, M. (1983). Adaptation of families with mental retardation: A model of stress, coping, and family ecology. *American Journal of Mental Deficiency, 88,* 125–138.

Cullinan, D., Epstein, M. H., Matson, J. L., & Rosemier, R. A. (1984). Behavior problems of mentally retarded and nonretarded adolescent pupils. *School Psychology Review, 13,* 381–384.

Curtiss, S. (1977). *Genie: A psycholinguistic study of a modern-day "wild child."* New York: Academic Press.

Davies, S. P., & Ecob, K. C. (1959). The challenge to the schools. In S. P. Davies (Ed.), *The mentally retarded in society* (pp. 173–192). New York: Columbia University Press.

Dekry, S. J., & Ehly, S. W. (1981). Factor/cluster classification of profiles from Personality Inventory for Children in a school setting. *Psychological Reports, 48,* 843–846.

Dingman, H. F., & Tarjan, G. (1960). Mental retardation and the normal distribution curve. *American Journal of Mental Deficiency, 64,* 991–994.

Dosen, A. & Gielen, J. M. (1993). Depression in persons with mental retardation: Assessment and diagnosis. In R. J. Fletcher & A. Dosen (Ed.), *Mental health aspects of mental retardation: Progress in assessment and treatment* (pp.70–97). New York: Lexington Books.

Drotar, D., Baskiewicz, A., Irvin, N., Kennell, J., & Klaus, M. (1975). The adaptation of parents to the birth of an infant with congenital malformation: A hypothetical model. *Pediatrics, 56,* 710–717.

Dugdale, R. L. (1910). *The Jukes: A study in crime, pauperism, disease, and heredity.* New York: Putnam.

Dunst, C. J. (1980). *A clinical and educational manual for use with the Uzgiris and Hunt Scales of Infant Psychological Development.* Baltimore: University Park Press.

Dunst, C. J. (1990). Sensorimotor development of infants with Down syndrome. In D. Cicchetti & M. Beeghly (Eds.), *Children with Down syndrome: A developmental approach* (pp. 180–230). New York: Cambridge University Press.

Dykens, E. M. (1995). Measuring behavioral phenotypes: Provocations from the "new genetics." *American Journal on Mental Retardation, 99,* 522–532.

Dykens, E. M., & Cassidy, S. B. (in press). Correlates of maladaptive behavior in children and adults with Prader–Willi syndrome. *American Journal of Medical Genetics*.

Dykens, E. M., Hodapp, R. M., & Evans, D. W. (1994). Profiles and development of adaptive behavior in males with fragile X syndrome. *Journal of Autism and Developmental Disorders, 23*, 135–145.

Dykens, E. M., Hodapp, R. M., & Leckman, J. F. (1987). Strengths and weaknesses in the intellectual functioning of males with fragile X syndrome. *American Journal of Mental Deficiency, 92*, 234–236.

Dykens, E. M., Hodapp, R. M., & Leckman, J. F. (1994). *Behavior and development in fragile X syndrome. Sage Series on Developmental Clinical Psychology and Psychiatry (No. 28)*. Newbury Park, CA: Sage.

Dykens, E. M., Hodapp, R. M., Ort, S. I., Finucane, B., Shapiro, L., & Leckman, J. F. (1989). The trajectory of cognitive development in males with fragile X syndrome. *Journal of the American Academy of Child and Adolescent Psychiatry, 28*, 422–426.

Dykens, E. M., Hodapp, R. M., Ort, S. I., & Leckman, J. F. (1993). Trajectory of adaptive behavior in males with fragile X syndrome. *Journal of Autism and Developmental Disorders, 23*, 135–145.

Dykens, E. M., Hodapp, R. M., Walsh. K., & Nash, L. J. (1992a). Adaptive and maladaptive behavior in Prader–Willi syndrome. *Journal of the American Academy of Child and Adolescent Psychiatry, 31*, 1131–1136.

Dykens, E. M., Hodapp, R. M., Walsh, K., & Nash. L. J. (1992b). Profiles, correlates and trajectories of intelligence in Prader–Willi syndrome. *Journal of the American Academy of Child and Adolescent Psychiatry, 31*, 1125–1130.

Eyman, R. K., & Miller, C. A. (1978). A demographic overview of severe and profound mental retardation. In C. E. Meyers (Ed.), *Quality of life in severely and profoundly mentally retarded people* (pp. ix–xii). Washington, DC: American Association on Mental Retardation.

Farber, B. (1959). The effects of the severely retarded child on the family system. *Monographs of the Society for Research in Child Development, 24*, No. 2.

Farber, B. (1970). Notes on sociological knowledge about families with mentally retarded children. In M. Schreiber (Ed.), *Social work and mental retardation* (pp. 118–124). New York: John Day.

Finucane, B. M., Konar, D., Haas-Givler, B., Kurtz, M., & Scott, C. I. (1994). The spasmodic upper body squeeze: A characteristic behavior in Smith–Magenis syndrome. *Developmental Medicine and Child Neurology, 36*, 78–83.

Fodor, J. (1983). *Modularity of mind: An essay on faculty psychology*. Cambridge, MA: MIT Press.

Fowler, A. (1988). Determinants of rate of language growth in children with Down syndrome. In L. Nadel (Ed.), *The psychobiology of Down syndrome* (pp. 217–245). Cambridge, MA: MIT Press.

Fowler, A. (1990). The development of language structure in children with Down syndrome. In D. Cicchetti & M. Beeghly (Eds.), *Children with Down syndrome: A developmental approach* (pp. 302–328). New York: Cambridge University Press.

Foxx, R. M., & Azrin, N. H. (1974). *Toilet training the retarded: A rapid program for day and nighttime independent toileting*. Champaign, IL: Research Press.

Freund, L., Reiss, A. L., Hagerman, R. J., & Vinogradov, S. (1992). Chromosome fragility and psychopathology in obligate female carriers of the fragile X syndrome. *Archives of General Psychiatry, 49*, 54–60.

Frey, K., Greenberg, M., & Fewell, R. (1989). Stress and coping among parents of handicapped children: A multidimensional perspective. *American Journal on Mental Retardation, 94*, 240–249.

Friedrich, W. N. (1979). Predictors of coping behavior of mothers of handicapped children. *Journal of Consulting and Clinical Psychology, 47*, 1140–1141.

Gallimore, R., Weisner, T., Kaufman, S., & Bernheimer, L. (1989). The social construction of eco-cultural niches: Family accommodation of developmentally delayed children. *American Journal of Mental Retardation, 94*, 216–230.

Gardner, H. (1983). *Frames of mind*. New York: Basic Books.

Gath, A. (1977). The impact of an abnormal child upon the parents. *British Journal of Psychiatry, 130*, 405–410.

Gath, A. (1978). *Down's syndrome and the family: The early years*. New York: Academic Press.

Gibson, D. (1966). Early developmental staging as a prophesy index in Down's syndrome. *American Journal of Mental Deficiency, 70*, 825–828.

Glick, M. (in press). A developmental approach to psychopathology in people with mild mental retardation. In J. A. Burack, R. M. Hodapp, & E. Zigler (Eds.), *Handbook of mental retardation and development*. New York: Cambridge University Press.

Goddard, H. H. (1913a). The improvability of feeble-minded children. *Journal of Psycho-Aesthenics, 17*, 121–126.

Goddard, H. H. (1913b). *The Kallikak family: A study in the heredity of feeble-mindedness*. New York: Macmillan.

Goldberg, S., Marcovitch, S., MacGregor, D., & Lojkasek, M. (1986). Family responses to developmentally delayed preschoolers: Etiology and the father's role. *American Journal on Mental Retardation, 90*, 610–617.

Goodman, J. F., & Cameron, J. (1978). The meaning of IQ constancy in young retarded children. *Journal of Genetic Psychology, 132*, 109–119.

Greenberg, F., Guzzetta, V., Oca-Luna, R. M., Magenis, R. E., Smith, A. E., Richter, S. F., Kondo, I., Dobyns, W. B., Patel, P. I., & Lupisiki, J. R. (1991). Molecular analysis of the Smith–Magenis syndrome: A possible contiguous-gene syndrome associated with del(17)(p11.2). *American Journal of Human Genetics, 49*, 1207–1218.

Gresham, F. M., MacMillan, D. L., & Siperstein, G. N. (1995). Critical analysis of the 1992 AAMR definition: Implications for school psychology. *School Psychology Quarterly, 10*, 1–19.

Griffith, D. R., Azuma, S. D., & Chasnoff, I. J. (1994). Three-year outcome of children exposed prenatally to drugs. *Journal of the American Academy of Child and Adolescent Psychiatry, 33*, 20–27.

Grossman, H. (1973). *Manual on terminology and classification in mental retardation (Special Publications Series, No. 2)*. Washington, DC: American Association on Mental Deficiency.

Grossman, H. (Ed.). (1983). *Classification in mental retardation* (3rd rev.). Washington, DC: American Association of Mental Deficiency.

Gruenberg, E. (1964). Epidemiology. In H. A. Stevens & R. Heber (Eds.), *Mental retardation* (pp. 255–285). Chicago: University of Chicago Press.

Harrison, P. (1987). Research with adaptive behavior scales. *Journal of Special Education, 21*, 37–68.

Haskell, P. H. (1944). Mental deficiency over a hundred years. *American Journal of Psychiatry, 100*, 107–118.

Hodapp, R. M. (1994). Cultural-familial mental retardation. In R. Sternberg (Ed.), *Encyclopedia of intelligence* (pp. 711–717). New York: Macmillan.

Hodapp, R. M. (1995a). Definitions in mental retardation: Effects on research, practice, and perceptions. *School Psychology Quarterly, 10,* 24–28.

Hodapp, R. M. (1995b). Parenting children with Down syndrome and other types of mental retardation. In M. Bornstein (Ed.), *Handbook of parenting: Vol. 1. How children influence parents* (pp. 233–253). Hillsdale, NJ: Erlbaum.

Hodapp, R. M., Burack, J. A., & Zigler, E. (Eds.). (1990). *Issues in the developmental approach to mental retardation.* New York: Cambridge University Press.

Hodapp, R. M., & Dykens, E. M. (1991). Toward an etiology-specific strategy of early intervention with handicapped children. In K. Marfo (Ed.), *Early intervention in transition* (pp. 41–60). New York: Praeger.

Hodapp, R. M., & Dykens, E. M. (1994). The two cultures of behavioral research in mental retardation. *American Journal on Mental Retardation, 97,* 675–687.

Hodapp, R. M., Dykens, E. M., Hagerman, R., Schreiner, R., Lachiewicz, A., & Leckman, J. F. (1990). Developmental implications of changing trajectories of IQ in males with fragile X syndrome. *Journal of the American Academy of Child and Adolescent Psychiatry, 29,* 214–219.

Hodapp, R. M., Leckman, J. F., Dykens, E. M., Sparrow, S., Zelinsky, D., & Ort, S. I. (1993). K-ABC profiles in children with fragile X syndrome, Down syndrome, and nonspecific mental retardation. *American Journal on Mental Retardation, 97,* 39–46.

Hodapp, R. M., & Zigler, E. (1990). Applying the developmental perspective to individuals with Down syndrome. In D. Cicchetti & M. Beeghly (Eds.), *Children with Down syndrome: A developmental approach* (pp. 1–28). New York: Cambridge University Press.

Hodapp, R. M., & Zigler, E. (1995). Past, present, and future issues in the developmental approach to mental retardation. In D. Cicchetti & D. Cohen (Eds.), *Manual of developmental psychopathology* (pp. 299–331). New York: Wiley.

Holm, V. A., Cassidy, S. B., Butler, M. G., Hanchett, J. M., Greenswag, L. R., Whitman, L., & Greenberg, F. (1993). Prader–Willi syndrome: Consensus diagnostic criteria. *Pediatrics, 91,* 398–402.

Inhelder, B. (1968). *The diagnosis of reasoning in the mentally retarded* (W. B. Stephens, Trans.). New York: John Day Company. (Original work published in French 1943)

Jacobson, J. W. (1982). Problem behavior and psychiatric impairment within a developmentally delayed population: I. behavior frequency. *Applied Research in Mental Retardation. 3,* 121–139.

Jacobson, J. W. (1990). Do some mental disorders occur less frequently among persons with mental retardation? *American Journal on Mental Retardation, 94,* 596–602.

Jacobsen, J. W., & Mulick, J. (1992). A new definition of mental retardation or a new definition of practice? *Psychology in Mental Retardation and Developmental Disabilities, 18,* 9–14.

Jacobsen, J., & Mulick, J. (1993). Walkn' the walk: APA takes a step forward in professional practice. *Psychology in Mental Retardation and Developmental Disabilities, 19,* 4–8.

Jensen, A. R. (1969). How much can we boost IQ and scholastic achievement? *Harvard Educational Review, 39,* 1–123.

Kazak, A., & Marvin, R. (1984). Differences, difficulties, and adaptation: Stress and social networks in families with a handicapped child. *Family Relations, 33,* 67–77.

Kiely, M., & Lubin, R. A. (1991). Epidemiological methods. In J. L. Matson & J. A. Mulick (Eds.), *Handbook of mental retardation* (2nd ed., pp. 586–602). New York: Pergamon Press.

Krauss, M. W. (1993). Child-related and parenting stress: Similarities and differences between mothers and fathers of children with disabilities. *American Journal on Mental Retardation, 97,* 393–404.

Krauss, M. W., Simeonsson, R., & Ramey, S. L. (Eds.). (1989). Special issue on research on families. *American Journal on Mental Retardation, 94*(Whole No. 3).

Lambert, N. M. (1981). Psychological evidence in *Larry P. v. Wilson Riles*: An evaluation by a witness for the defense. *American Psychologist, 36,* 937–952.

Larry P. v. Wilson Riles, Civil Action No. C-71–2270 343F. (1979). Supp. 1306 (Northern District, California).

Lejeune, J., Gautier, M., & Turpin, R. (1959). Etudes des chromosomes somatiques de neuf enfants mongoliens. *Comptes Rendus de l'Academie les Sciences, 48,* 1721.

Lobato, D. (1983). Siblings of handicapped children: A review. *Journal of Autism and Developmental Disorders, 13,* 347–364.

MacMillan, D. L., Gresham, F. M., & Siperstein, G. N. (1993). Conceptual and psychometric concerns about the 1992 AAMR definition of mental retardation. *American Journal on Mental Retardation, 98,* 325–335.

MacMillan, D. L., Hendrick, I. G., & Watkins, A. (1988). Impact of *Diana, Larry P.,* and P. L. 94–142 on minority students. *Exceptional Children, 54,* 24–30.

Maisto, A. A., & German, M. L. (1986). Reliability, predictive validity, and interrelationships of early assessment indices used with developmentally delayed infants and children. *Journal of Clinical Child Psychology, 15,* 327–332.

Matson, J. (Ed.). (1990). *Handbook of behavior modification with the mentally retarded.* New York: Plenum Press.

Matson, J. L., & Frame, C. L. (1986). *Psychopathology among mentally retarded children and adolescents.* Beverly Hills, CA: Sage.

McGrew, K., & Bruininks, R. (1989). Factor structure of adaptive behavior. *School Psychology Review, 18,* 64–81.

Menolascino, F. J. (Ed.). (1970). *Psychiatric approaches to mental retardation.* New York: Basic Books.

Menolascino, F. J., & Fleisher, M. H. (1993). Mental health care in persons with mental retardation: Past, present and future. In R. J. Fletcher & A. Dosen (Eds.), *Mental health aspects of mental retardation: Progress in assessment and treatment* (pp. 18–41). New York: Lexington Books.

Mercer, J. (1973). *Labeling the mentally retarded: Clinical and social systems perspectives on mental retardation.* Berkeley: University of California Press.

Mercer, J. (1992). The impact of changing paradigms of disability on mental retardation in the year 2000. In L. Rowitz (Ed.), *Mental retardation in the year 2000* (pp. 15–38). New York: Springer-Verlag.

Meryash, D. L., Szymanski, L. S., & Gerald, P. (1982). Infantile autism associated with the fragile X syndrome. *Journal of Autism and Developmental Disorders, 12,* 295–296.

Mink, I., Nihira, C., & Meyers, C. (1983). Taxonomy of family life styles: I. Homes with TMR children. *American Journal of Mental Deficiency, 87,* 484–497.

Minnes, P. (1988). Family stress associated with a developmentally handicapped child. *International Review of Research on Mental Retardation, 15,* 195–226.

Moser, H. (1992). Prevention of mental retardation (genetics). In L. Rowitz (Ed.), *Mental retardation in the year 2000.* New York: Springer-Verlag.

Mundy, P., & Kasari, C. (1990). The similar-structure hypothesis and differential rate of development in mental retardation. In R. M. Hodapp, J. A. Burack, & E. Zigler (Eds.), *Issues in the developmental approach to mental retardation* (pp. 71–92). New York: Cambridge University Press.

Ogbu, J. (1994). Culture and intelligence. In R. J. Sternberg (Ed.), *Encyclopedia of human intelligence* (pp. 328–338). New York: Macmillan.

Piaget, J., & Inhelder, B. (1947). Diagnosis of mental operations and theory of intelligence. *American Journal of Mental Deficiency, 51,* 401–406.

Prader, A., Labhart, A., & Willi, H. (1956). Ein Syndrom von Adipositas, Kleinwuchs, Kryptorchismus and Oligophrenie nach myotonieartigem Zustand in Neugeborenenalter. *Schweizerische Medizinishe Wochenschrift, 86,* 1260.

Prasse, D. P., & Reschly, D. J. (1986). *Larry P.*: A case of segregation, testing, or program efficacy? *Exceptional Children, 52,* 333–346.

Price-Bonham, S., & Addison, S. (1978). Families and mentally retarded children: Emphasis on the father. *The Family Coordinator, 27,* 221–230.

Pueschel, S. (1987). Health concerns in persons with Down syndrome. In S. Pueschel, C. Tingey, J. Rynders, A. Crocker, & D. Crutcher (Eds.), *New perspectives on Down syndrome* (pp. 113–133). Baltimore: Brookes.

Ramey, C., & Ramey, S. L. (1992). Effective early intervention. *Mental Retardation, 30,* 337–345.

Reed, E. W., & Reed, S. C. (1965). *Mental retardation: A family study.* Philadelphia: W. B. Saunders.

Reiber, R. W., & Carton, A. S. (Eds.). (1993). *The fundamentals of defectology.* Vol. 2. *The collected works of L. S. Vygotsky* (J. Knox & C. B. Stephens, Trans.). New York: Plenum Press.

Reid, D. H., Wilson, P. G., & Faw, G. D. (1991). Teaching self-help skills. In J. L. Matson & J. A. Mulick (Eds.), *Handbook of mental retardation* (2nd ed., pp. 436–450). New York: Pergamon Press.

Reilly, J. S., Klima, E., & Bellugi, U. (1990). Once more with feeling: Affect and language in atypical populations. *Development and Psychopathology, 2,* 367–391.

Reiss, A. L., & Freund, L. (1990). Fragile X syndrome, DSM-III-R and autism. *Journal of the American Academy of Child and Adolescent Psychiatry, 29,* 885–891.

Reiss, S. (1990). *Reiss Scales for Children's Dual Diagnosis.* Orland Park, IL: International Diagnostic Systems.

Reiss, S. (1994). Issues in defining mental retardation. *American Journal on Mental Retardation, 99,* 1–7.

Reschly, D. J. (1992). Mental retardation: Conceptual foundations, definitional criteria, and diagnostic operations. In S. R. Hynd & R. E. Mattison (Eds.), *Assessment and diagnosis of child and adolescent psychiatric disorders, Vol. II, Developmental disorders* (pp. 23–67). Hillsdale, NJ: Erlbaum.

Reynolds, C. R., & Brown, R. T. (1984). *Perspectives on bias in mental testing.* New York: Wiley.

Richardson, G. A., & Day, N. L. (1994). Detrimental effects of prenatal cocaine exposure: Illusion or reality? *Journal of the American Academy of Child and Adolescent Psychiatry, 33,* 28–34.

Richardson, S. A., Katz, M., Koller, H., McLaren, J., & Rubinstein, B. (1979). Some characteristics of a population of mentally retarded young adults in a British city: A basis for estimating some service needs. *Journal of Mental Deficiency Research, 23,* 275–285.

Ross, R. T., Begab, M. J., Dondis, E. H., Giampiccolo, J., & Meyers, C. E. (1985). *Lives of the retarded: A forty-year follow-up study.* Stanford, CA: Stanford University Press.

Rutter, M., Tizard, J., Yule, W., Graham, P., & Whitmore, K. (1976). Research report: Isle of Wight studies, 1964–1974. *Psychological Medicine, 6,* 313–332.

Scheerenberger, R. C. (1983). *A history of mental retardation.* Baltimore: Brookes.

Schwartz, D. (1992). *Crossing the river: Creating a conceptual revolution in community and disability.* Cambridge, MA: Brookline Books.

Seitz, V. (1992). Intervention programs for impoverished children: A comparison of educational and family support programs. *Annals of Child Development, 7,* 73–103.

Seltzer, M., Krauss, M. W., & Tsunematsu, N. (1993). Adults with Down syndrome and their aging mothers: Diagnostic group differences. *American Journal on Mental Deficiency, 97,* 496–508.

Silverstein, A. B. (1982). Note on the constancy of IQ. *American Journal of Mental Deficiency, 87,* 227–228.

Skinner, B. F. (1968). *The technology of teaching.* New York: Appleton-Century-Crofts.

Smith, A. C. M., McGavran, L., Robinson, J., Waldstein, G., Macfarlane, J., Zonona, J., Reiss, J., Lahr, M., Allen, L., & Magenis, E. (1986). Interstitial deletion of (17) (p11.2p11.2) in nine patients. *American Journal of Medical Genetics, 24,* 393–414.

Solnit, A., & Stark, M. (1961). Mourning and the birth of the defective child. *Psychoanalytic Study of the Child, 16,* 523–537.

Sovner, R. (1986). Limiting factors in the use of DSM-III criteria with mentally ill/mentally retarded persons. *Psychopharmacology Bulletin, 22,* 1055–1059.

Sparrow, S. S., Balla, D. A., & Cicchetti, D. V. (1984). *Vineland Adaptive Behavior Scales.* Circle Pines, MN: American Guidance Service.

Streissguth, A. P., Aase, J. M., Clarren, S. K., Randels, S. P., LaDue, R. A., & Smith, D. F. (1991). Fetal Alcohol Syndrome in adolescents and adults. *Journal of the American Medical Association, 265,* 1961–1967.

Suelzle, M., & Keenan, V. (1981). Changes in family support networks over the life cycle of mentally retarded persons. *American Journal of Mental Deficiency, 58,* 267–274.

Super, C., & Harkness, S. (1986). The developmental niche: A conceptualization at the interface of child and culture. *International Journal of Behavioral Development, 9,* 545–569.

Taylor, R. L. (1990). The *Larry P.* decision a decade later: Problems and future directions. *Mental Retardation, 28*(1), iii–vi.

Udwin, O., Yule, W., & Martin, N. (1987). Cognitive abilities and behavioral characteristics of children with idiopathic infantile hypercalcaemia. *Journal of Child Psychology and Psychiatry, 28,* 297–309.

Vernon, P. (1979). *Intelligence: Heredity and environment.* San Francisco: W. H. Freeman.

Volkmar, F. R., Burack, J. A., & Cohen, D. J. (1990). Deviance and developmental approaches in the study of autism. In R. M. Hodapp, J. A. Burack, & E. Zigler (Eds.), *Issues in the developmental approach to mental retardation* (pp. 246–271). New York: Cambridge University Press.

Wehman, P., Sale, P., & Parent, W. S. (Eds.). (1992). *Supported employment: Strategies for integration of work-*

ers with disabilities. Boston: Andover Medical Publishers.

Weiss, B., Weisz, J. R., & Bromfield, R. (1986). Performance of retarded and nonretarded persons on information-processing tasks: Further tests of the similar structure hypothesis. Psychological Bulletin, 100, 157–175.

Weisz, J. R. (1990). Cultural-familial mental retardation: A developmental perspective on cognitive performance and "helpless" behavior. In R. M. Hodapp, J. A. Burack, & E. Zigler (Eds.), Issues in the developmental approach to mental retardation (pp. 137–168). New York: Cambridge University Press.

Wiesz, J. R., Yeates, K., & Zigler, E. (1982). Piagetian evidence and the developmental-difference controversy. In E. Zigler & D. Balla (Eds.), Mental retardation: The developmental-difference controversy (pp. 213–276). Hillsdale, NJ: Erlbaum.

Weisz, J. R., & Zigler, E. (1979). Cognitive development in retarded and nonretarded persons: Piagetian tests of the similar sequence hypothesis. Psychological Bulletin, 86, 831–851.

Werner, H. (1941). Psychological processes investigating deficiencies in learning. American Journal of Mental Deficiency, 43, 233–235.

Wikler, L. (1986). Periodic stresses in families of mentally retarded children: An exploratory study. American Journal of Mental Deficiency, 90, 703–706.

World Health Organization. (1992). The ICD-10 classification of mental and behavioural disorders. Geneva: Author.

Yamada, J. E. (1990). Laura: A case for the modularity of language. Cambridge, MA: MIT Press.

Zigler, E. (1967). Familial mental retardation: A continuing dilemma. Science, 155, 292–298.

Zigler, E. (1969). Developmental versus difference theories of retardation and the problem of motivation. American Journal of Mental Deficiency, 73, 536–556.

Zigler, E., & Hodapp, R. M. (1986). Understanding mental retardation. New York: Cambridge University Press.

Zigler, E., Hodapp, R. M., & Edison, M. (1990). From theory to practice in the care and education of retarded individuals. American Journal on Mental Retardation, 95, 1–12.

Learning Disabilities

G. Reid Lyon

Since its recognition as a federally designated handicapping condition in 1968, the field of learning disabilities (LD) now represents approximately one-half of all children receiving special education services nationally (U.S. Department of Education, 1989). At the same time, it remains one of the least understood and most debated disabling conditions that affect children. Indeed, even a cursory perusal of the literature relevant to the history and current status of LD reveals that the field has been, and continues to be, beset by pervasive and, at times, contentious disagreements about the definition of the disorder, diagnostic criteria, assessment practices, treatment procedures, and educational policies (Lyon, 1987, 1995; Lyon & Moats, 1988, 1993; Lyon, Gray, Kavanagh, & Krasnegor, 1993; Moats & Lyon, 1993).

A number of influences have contributed to these disagreements which, in turn, have produced difficulties in building a generalizable body of scientific and clinical knowledge relevant to LD and in establishing reliable and valid diagnostic criteria (Lyon, 1985a, 1987). Although some progress has been made during the last decade in establishing more precise definitions and a theoretically based classification system for LD (see Lyon et al., 1993), one must clearly understand these historical influences and their impact on current diagnostic and treatment practices for children with LD if one is to obtain a genuine comprehension of the field.

Within this context, the next section of this chapter reviews briefly the historical events that have molded the general field of learning disabilities into its present form. Subsequent sections will address in detail the core features of specific types of LD. The reader should note at this point that LD is not a homogeneous disorder. In fact, learning disabilities, by definition, refer to deficits in one or more of several domains including reading disorders, mathematics disorders, disorders of written expression, and receptive (listening) and expressive (speaking) language disorders. Since each of these types of LD is characterized by its own distinct definitional and diagnostic issues, as well as its own issues associated with heterogeneity, each is covered separately in the following sections. Thus, for each type of LD, a review of critical background information, constructs, and research and clinical trends is provided. More specifically, a review of each major learning disability is organized to address (1) unique historical issues related to each disability; (2) a review of current definitional and diagnostic issues confronting the specific type of disability; (3) the developmental course, prognosis, and epidemiology of the disability; (4) the major theoretical frameworks that currently guide research and practice in each area of disability; and (5) a review of the etiological mechanisms and comorbidities hypothesized to cause and/or contribute to the specific type of LD. The chapter concludes with a brief review of current issues and a look toward the future.

HISTORY OF THE FIELD

General Historical Influences

A number of sources are available that provide overarching reviews of the field's scientific, social, and political history and development to include those by Coles (1987), Doris (1993), Fletcher and Morris (1986), Hallahan and Cruickshank (1973), Kavale and Forness (1985), Kavanagh and Truss (1988), Myers and Hammill (1990), Morrison and Siegel (1991), and Torgesen (1991). These are well-rounded and scholarly works that trace the origins of the field in a comprehensive and detailed fashion, and they should be consulted if one desires a more complete understanding of the construct of learning disabilities from a historical perspective. In general, the majority of these commentaries indicate that the field of learning disabilities developed in response to two major needs.

First, the field is linked closely with the historical need to understand individual differences in learning and performance among children and adults who displayed *specific* deficits in using spoken or written language while maintaining integrity in general intellectual functioning. This unexpected pattern of strengths and *specific* weaknesses in learning was first noted and studied by physicians, thus giving the field its historical biomedical orientation. Second, the LD movement developed as an applied field of special education driven by social and political forces and in response to the need to provide services to youngsters whose learning characteristics were not being adequately addressed by the educational system. Each of these historical contexts is reviewed briefly.

Learning Disabilities and the Study of Individual Differences

Gall's Influence

As Torgesen (1991) and Mann (1979) have pointed out, interest in the causes and outcomes of inter- and intraindividual differences in cognition and learning can be traced to early Greek civilization. However, the first work that had clear relevance to today's conceptualizations of LD was conducted by Gall in the context of his work on disorders of spoken language in the early 19th century (Wiederholt, 1974). In describing the characteristics of one patient with brain damage, Gall recorded the following:

> In consequence of an attack of apoplexy, a soldier found it impossible to express in spoken language his feelings and ideas. His face bore no signs of a deranged intellect. His mind (esprit) found the answer to questions addressed to him and he carried out all he was told to do; shown an armchair and asked if he knew what it was, he answered by seating himself in it. He could not articulate on the spot a word pronounced for him to repeat; but a few moments later the word escaped from his lips as if voluntarily. . . . It was not his tongue which was embarrassed; for he moved it with great agility and could pronounce quite well a large number of isolated words. His memory was not at fault, for he signified his anger at being unable to express himself concerning many things which he wished to communicate. It was the faculty of speech alone which was abolished. (cited in Head, 1926, p. 11)

The relevance of Gall's observations to present conceptualizations of LD has been summarized recently by Hammill (1993). According to Hammill, Gall noted that some of his patients could not speak but could produce thoughts in writing, thus manifesting a pattern of relative strengths and weaknesses in oral and written language. In addition, Gall established that such patterns of strengths and weaknesses were a function of brain damage and that brain damage could selectively impair one particular language capability but not affect others. Thus the clinical roots for the present day observation that children with LD manifest "specific" or "modular" deficits rather than pervasive or "generalized" deficits were established. Finally, Gall argued that it was essential to rule out other handicapping conditions, such as mental retardation or deafness, that could impair the patient's performance. Within this context, the origins for the "exclusion" component of current day definitions of learning disabilities are evident.

The Influence of Early Medicine

A number of other medical professionals also began to observe and report on patients demonstrating intraindividual strengths and weaknesses that included specific deficits in linguistic, reading, and cognitive abilities. For example, Broca (1863, 1865) provided important observations

that have served to build the foundation of the "specificity" hypothesis in learning disabilities. Broca (1865) reported that expressive aphasia or the inability to speak resulted from selective (rather than diffuse) lesions to the anterior aspect of the left hemisphere primarily localized in the second frontal convolution. The effects of a lesion to this area of the brain were highly consistent in right-handed individuals, and *did not* appear to effect receptive language ability (listening) or other nonlanguage functions (e.g., visual perception, spatial awareness, etc.). In a similar vein, Wernicke (1894) introduced the concept of a disconnection syndrome when he predicted that the aphasic syndrome termed conduction aphasia could result from a disconnection of the receptive (sensory) speech area from the motor speech zone by a punctate lesion in the left hemisphere. Wernicke's observations have also been relevant to theory building in LD, since he reported that a complex function such as receptive language could be impaired within an individual who did not display other significant cognitive or linguistic dysfunctions. Thus the concept of intraindividual differences in information processing was born more than a century ago primarily via observations and clinical studies with adults with specific brain damage.

In the latter 1800s and early 1900s, an additional series of cases of unexpected cognitive and linguistic difficulties within the context of normal functioning were reported. For example, Kussmaul (1877) described a patient who was unable to read despite having intact intellectual and perceptual skills. Additional reports by Hinshelwood (1895, 1900, 1917), Jackson (1906), Morgan (1896) and others (Bastian, 1898; Clairborne, 1906; Stephenson, 1905) distinguished a specific type of learning deficit characterized by an inability to read against a background of normal intelligence and adequate opportunity to learn. For example, Hinshelwood (1917) described one 10-year-old youngster as follows:

> The boy had been at school three years and had got on well with every subject except reading. He was apparently a bright and in every respect an intelligent boy. He had been learning music for a year and had made good progress in it. . . . In all departments of his studies where the instruction was oral he had made good progress, showing that his auditory memory was good. . . . He performs simple sums quite correctly, and his progress in arithmetic has been regarded as quite satisfactory. He has no dif-

ficulty in learning to write. His visual acuity is good. (pp. 46–47)

Thus, by the beginning of the 20th century, evidence from several sources contributed to a set of observations that defined a unique type of learning difficulty in adults *and* children, specific, rather than general in presentation, and distinct from disorders associated with sensory handicaps and subaverage general intelligence. As Hynd and Willis (1988) have summarized, the most salient and reliable observations included the following: (1) the children had some form of congenital learning problem; (2) more male than female children were affected; (3) the disorder was heterogeneous with respect to the specific pattern and the severity of deficits; (4) the disorder may be related to a developmental process affecting primarily left hemisphere central language processes; and, (5) normal classroom instruction was not adequate in meeting the children's educational needs. More recent evidence has supported some of these observations, but many have not been validated as is made evident in later discussions.

Orton's Influence

During the 1920s, Samuel Orton, extended the study of reading disabilities with clinical studies designed to test the hypothesis that reading deficits were a function of a delay or failure of the left cerebral hemisphere to establish dominance for language functions. According to Orton (1928), reading-disabled children tended to reverse letters such as b/d and p/q and words such as saw/was and not/ton because of the lack of left hemispheric dominance for the processing of linguistic symbols.

As Torgesen (1991) has pointed out, neither Orton's theory of reading disability nor his observation that reversals were symptomatic of the disorder have stood the test of time. However, Orton's (1928, 1937) writings were highly influential in stimulating research, mobilizing teacher and parent groups to bring attention to reading and learning disorders that had a deleterious impact on a child's academic, behavioral, and social development, and on the development of instructional techniques for teaching reading-disabled children. Moreover, Orton's influence on present day conceptualizations of learning disabilities can be seen indirectly in his early attempts to classify within the same conceptual and etiological framework, a *range* of language and

motor disabilities in addition to a reading disability (Doris, 1993). More specifically, in 1937 Orton reported a number of cases of children of average to above-average intelligence who manifested (1) developmental alexia, or difficulty learning to read, (2) developmental agraphia, or significant difficulty in learning to write, (3) developmental word deafness, or a specific deficit in verbal understanding within a context of normal auditory acuity, (4) developmental motor aphasia, or motor speech delay, (5) abnormal clumsiness, and (6) stuttering. Orton (1937) was the first to stress that reading disability was a problem manifested at the symbolic level, appeared to be related to cerebral dysfunction rather than a neurological defect as postulated by Hinshelwood, and unexpectedly, did not co-occur with low intelligence.

The Influence of Strauss and Werner

Whereas Orton's contributions are linked primarily to the development of scientific and clinical interest in reading disabilities or dyslexia, it was the work of Strauss and Werner (1943) and their colleagues (Strauss & Lehtinen, 1947) during the period after World War II that led directly to the emergence of the more general category of learning disabilities as a formally recognized field (Doris, 1993; Torgesen, 1991). Strauss and Werner's influence grew out of research with children with mental retardation. They were particularly interested in comparing the behavior of children whose retardation was associated with known brain damage with children whose retardation was not associated with neurological impairment but, rather, was familial in nature. Strauss and Lehtinen (1947) reported that mentally retarded children with brain injury manifested difficulties on tasks assessing figure–ground perception, attention, and concept formation, whereas non-brain-damaged mentally retarded children performed in a manner similar to children who were not retarded. Within the context of these studies, Strauss' group also had the opportunity to study children who were not retarded but who displayed learning difficulties. From these studies, the concept of "minimal brain damage" was introduced via conclusions such as the following:

When no mental retardation exists, the presence of psychological disturbances can be discovered by the use of some of our qualitative tests for perceptual and cognitive disturbances. Although the . . . [other] criteria may be negative, whereas the behavior of

the child in question resembles that characteristic for brain injury, and even though the performances of the child on our tests are not strongly indicative of brain injury, it may still be reasonable to consider a diagnosis of brain injury. (Strauss & Lehtinen, 1947, p. 112)

Most students of the history of learning disabilities agree that Strauss and his colleagues had a profound influence on the development of the field (Doris, 1993; Hallahan & Cruickshank, 1973; Kavale & Forness, 1985). In summarizing the work of Strauss, Torgesen (1991, p. 12) pointed out that three concepts emerged from his work that served to provide a rationale for the development of the field of LD separate from other fields of education. These three concepts are:

1. Individual differences in learning should be understood by examining the different ways that children approached learning tasks (the processes that aided or interfered with learning).
2. Educational procedures should be tailored to patterns of processing strengths and weaknesses in the individual child.
3. Children with deficient learning processes might be helped to learn normally if those processes were strengthened, or if teaching methods that did not stress weak areas could be developed.

Likewise, Kavale and Forness (1985) have reported that the research and writings of Strauss and his colleagues had a significant influence on the development of the LD paradigm—but through ideas that were more theoretical than those summarized by Torgesen (1991). The ideas included the following:

1. The locus of the LD was within the affected individual and thus represented a medical (disease) model.
2. LD is associated with (or caused by) neurological dysfunction.
3. The academic problems observed in children with LD are related to psychological processing deficits, most notably in the perceptual–motor domain.
4. The academic failure of children with LD occurs despite the presence of normal intelligence—that is, there is a discrepancy between IQ (average or above) and academic achievement (subaverage).

5. LD cannot primarily be due to other handicapping conditions.

Although the work of Strauss and his colleagues was indeed critical to the development of the LD paradigm, empirical support for their hypotheses concerning minimal brain damage without mental retardation has not accrued over the past 50 years (Fletcher & Morris, 1986; Kavale & Forness, 1985; Lyon & Moats, 1988). Despite this current lack of validation for their postulates, Strauss and Werner's writings had a tremendous impact on the thinking and careers of several behavioral scientists who, in the 1950s and 1960s, were studying children who failed to learn in school despite having normal intelligence.

The Influence of Cruickshank, Myklebust, Johnson, and Kirk

Foremost among the behavioral scientists involved in the early conceptualization and study of learning disabilities were William Cruickshank, Helmer Myklebust, Doris Johnson, and Samuel Kirk, all of whom propelled the field away from a focus on etiology toward an emphasis on learner characteristics and educational interventions to address learning deficits. For example, Cruickshank and his colleagues (Cruickshank, Bice, & Wallin, 1957; Cruickshank, Bentzen, Ratzburg, & Tannenhauser, 1961) were instrumental in studying and recommending modifications in classroom environments to reduce stimuli hypothesized to be distracting for children with learning and attention deficits. Likewise, Helmer Myklebust and Doris Johnson, working at Northwestern University, conducted numerous studies of the effects of different types of language and perceptual deficits on academic and social learning in children and were among the first to develop well-designed intervention procedures for the remediation of disabilities in skills related to school learning (Johnson & Myklebust, 1967). However, it was Samuel Kirk who had the greatest influence on the formal recognition of learning disabilities as a handicapping condition. In fact, it was Kirk who proposed the term learning disabilities in a 1963 conference devoted to exploring problems of perceptually handicapped children. Kirk (1963) stated:

I have used the term "learning disabilities" to describe a group of children who have disorders in the development of language, speech, reading and associated communication skills needed for social interaction. In this group, I do not include children who have sensory handicaps such as blindness, because we have methods of managing and training the deaf and blind, I also excluded from this group children who have generalized mental retardation. (pp. 2–3)

Thus, by 1963, the new field of LD had received its formal designation as a handicapping condition based largely on the arguments of Kirk and others that children with LD were indeed different with respect to learning characteristics than children with mental retardation or emotional disturbance, that these learning characteristics resulted from intrinsic (i.e., neurobiological) rather than environmental factors, and that children with LD required specialized educational interventions. What is interesting is that the field received its initial momentum on the strength of advocacy rather than on the basis of objective hypothesis-driven scientific study, the latter largely taking place within the past decade.

Learning Disabilities as an Applied Field Molded by Social and Political Forces

As has been noted, the creation of the applied special education category of LD in the 1960s reflected a belief by behavioral scientists, educators, and parents that some children had learning handicaps that were not being addressed effectively by extant educational practices (Zigmond, 1993). More specifically, prior to the mid-1960s, children who displayed unusual learning characteristics in the context of average to above average intelligence were disenfranchised from formal special education services because their cognitive and educational characteristics did not correspond to any recognized categories of disability. This disenfranchisement successfully stimulated a socially and politically based advocacy movement designed to protect children from being underserved by our educational system (Lyon & Moats, 1993; Moats & Lyon, 1993).

The fact that LD was initially and formally identified as a handicapping condition on the basis of advocacy rather than systematic scientific inquiry is certainly not uncommon in either educational or public health domains. In fact, in the United States, the majority of scientific advances are typically stimulated by vocal critics of the educational or medical status quo. It is rare that a psychological condition, disease, or educational problem is afforded attention until political forces are mobilized by parents, patients, or victims expressing their concerns about their quality of life

to their elected officials. Clearly, this was the case in the field of learning disabilities where parents and child advocates successfully lobbied Congress to enact legislation in 1970 via the Education of the Handicapped Act (P.L. 91–230) that authorized research and training programs to address the needs of children with specific learning disabilities (Doris, 1993).

The diagnostic concept of learning disabilities gained significant momentum during the 1960s and 1970s. As Zigmond (1993) has explained, the proliferation of children diagnosed as LD during these two decades was related to multiple factors. First, the label of "learning disabled" was not a stigmatizing one. Parents and teachers were certainly more comfortable with the term than with etiologically based labels such as brain injured, minimal brain dysfunction, and perceptually handicapped. Second, receiving a diagnosis of LD did not imply low intelligence, behavioral difficulties, or sensory handicaps. Quite the contrary, children with LD manifested difficulties in learning *despite* having average to above-average intelligence and intact hearing, vision, and emotional status. The fact that the youngster with LD displayed robust intelligence gave parents and teachers hope that difficulties in learning to read, write, calculate, or reason mathematically could be surmounted if only the right set of instructional conditions and settings could be identified.

Summary

Learning disabilities as an applied field of special education came into prominence primarily because the diagnostic concept made intuitive sense to clinicians, parents, and teachers. The concept represented an array of difficulties in learning that could not be explained by subaverage intellectual functioning, a lack of opportunity to learn, psychopathology, or sensory deficits. In a sense, the disorder became legitimized and codified in public law more for what it was not than what it was.

The field of learning disabilities emerged from a genuine social and educational need and currently remains a diagnostic practice that is viable in clinical practice, law, and policy. Historically, parents and other advocates for children with learning disabilities have successfully negotiated a diagnostic category subsuming educational problems as a means to educational protection (Keogh, 1993; Lyon & Moats, 1993; Martin, 1993; Zigmond, 1993).

It has only been within the last 15 years that serious and systematic research efforts have been deployed toward the task of understanding the causes, developmental course, treatment conditions, and the long-term outcomes of LD from a scientific perspective. Unfortunately, to date, many of these efforts have not led to more precise definitions and scientific understanding of learning disabilities and their educational, linguistic, genetic, physiological, and neurophysiological correlates. On the positive side, within the past 5 years, we have begun to identify specific influences and reasons why research in LD has not produced knowledge fundamental to definition, diagnosis, developmental course, and treatment. A brief overview of these influences can serve as a reminder that unless we understand and address these historical and methodological issues, our ability to define, classify, and treat LD in an efficacious manner will be limited.

SPECIFIC IMPEDIMENTS TO RESEARCH IN LEARNING DISABILITIES

There are many influences that historically and currently contribute to difficulties in validating the learning disabilities construct. As mentioned earlier, a few of the more important ones are reviewed here.

Youth of the Field

The field's limitations as a clinical science can be related to its brief tenure as a recognized category of disability (Lyon, 1987, 1994a, 1994b). The formal category of LD as a federally designated condition has been in existence only since 1968 (Moats & Lyon, 1993), Thus, there has not been time to collect and consolidate the necessary observations under experimental conditions that could lead to a better understanding of the critical diagnostic markers and treatment interventions that have a known probability of success.

Theoretical and Conceptual Heterogeneity

Many different theoretical and conceptual views are offered to explain LD, and these views clearly reflect the multidisciplinary nature of the field (Lyon, 1995a; Moats & Lyon, 1993; Torgesen, 1993). Learning disabilities are considered the legitimate concern of many disciplines and professions, including psychology, education, neurology, neuropsychology, psychiatry, speech and

language pathology, and optometry, to name a few. Each of these professions has focused on different aspects of the child or adult with LD, so that there exist highly divergent ideas and frequently contentious disagreements about the importance of etiology, diagnostic methods, intervention methods, and professional roles and responsibilities (Torgesen, 1991, 1993). Unfortunately, from the perspective of developing a valid definition and classification system for LD, such variation in views and beliefs results in differences in the numbers of children (and adults) identified and differences in how phenotypic characteristics are measured and characterized. In turn, conducting research on samples of individuals with putative LD who vary widely in diagnostic and demographic characteristics provides little opportunity for the replication and generalization of clinical and empirical findings—the cornerstones of scientific inquiry.

Limitations in Measurement Practices

Many diagnostic and treatment decisions about individuals with LD have been based on technically inadequate tests and measures. Recent comprehensive reviews of instruments used to diagnose oral language, reading, mathematics, and written language deficits do not meet criteria for adequate norms, reliability, and validity (Lyon, 1994a). As importantly, the valid assessment of change over time, and change as a function of treatment, is very difficult to accomplish at present because few instruments have the scaling properties necessary to satisfy conditions for the measurement of individual growth curves (Francis, Shaywitz, Steubing, Shaywitz, & Fletcher, 1994; B. Shaywitz & Shaywitz, 1994).

Limitations in Experimental Design and Criteria for Diagnosis

The study of individuals identified a priori as LD by school or clinic criteria within the context of "single-shot" investigations or cross-sectional designs has significantly hampered efforts to develop a valid definition and classification system for LD (a point that will be discussed in detail shortly). It has been pointed out many times that schools and clinics lack consistency in the way in which LD is diagnosed. A child can literally be "cured" of an LD condition or have a diagnosis changed from mental retardation to LD simply by moving across state boundaries or even by changing schools within the same community (Lyon et al., 1993; Lyon, 1994b; Moats & Lyon, 1993). Such variability in sample characteristics prohibits replication and generalization of findings—a severe impediment to the development of any clinical science. Moreover, "single-shot" investigations that compare children achieving normally with children with LD on one or more dependent variables of interest at one point in time ignore the developmental nature of learning and change over time, and how such change interacts with information processing characteristics, teacher characteristics, response to different treatment interventions, and classroom settings and climates (Lyon, 1987, in press-b). As such, information relevant to the developmental course of LD and how children may display different characteristics at different points in time remains limited.

Problems in Establishing a Valid Definition and Classification System

By far the most significant and persistent problem impeding progress in the field of LD has been the difficulty in establishing a precise *inclusionary* definition and *theoretically based classification system* that can provide: (1) a framework for the identification of different types of LD; and (2) a framework for recognizing distinctions and interrelationships (comorbidities) between LD and other learning and behavioral disorders to include attention deficit disorders (ADD), mental retardation, general academic underachievement, and the psychopathologies (Fletcher & Morris, 1986; Lyon & Moats, 1993; Lyon et al., 1993; Morris, 1988, 1993). At present, the field continues to construct and utilize vague, ambiguous, *exclusionary,* and nonvalidated definitions of LD that attempt to cluster together extremely heterogeneous subgroups of disorders. Consider the past and current *general* definitions, which serve to frame diagnostic and eligibility criteria.

The Education for All Handicapped Children Act (P.L. 94–142) incorporated the following definition, originally proposed by the National Advisory Committee on Handicapped Children (1968):

> The term specific learning disability means a disorder in one or more of the basic psychological processes involved in understanding or in using language, spoken or written, which may manifest itself in an imperfect ability to listen, speak, read, write, spell, or do mathematical calculations. The term

includes such conditions as perceptual handicaps, brain injury, minimal brain dysfunction, dyslexia, and developmental aphasia. Such terms do not include children who have learning difficulties which are primarily the result of visual, hearing, or motor handicaps, of mental retardation, of emotional disturbance, or of environmental, cultural, or economic disadvantage. (U.S. Office of Education, 1977, p. 65083)

Unfortunately, this definition is virtually useless with respect to providing clinicians and researchers objective guidelines and criteria for distinguishing individuals with LD from those with other primary handicaps or generalized learning difficulties. Indeed, many papers have been written criticizing the use of this vague definition in driving diagnostic and educational practices (e.g., Fletcher & Morris, 1986; Kavale & Forness, 1985; Kavale & Nye, 1981; Lyon, 1987, 1994a, 1994b; Lyon et al., 1993; Moats & Lyon, 1993; Senf, 1981, 1986, 1987; Ysseldyke & Algozzine, 1983).

As Torgesen (1991) has pointed out, this definition has at least four major problems that renders it ineffective:

1. It does not indicate clearly enough that learning disabilities are a heterogeneous group of disorders.
2. It fails to recognize that learning disabilities frequently persist and are manifest in adults as well as children.
3. It does not clearly specify that, whatever the cause of learning disabilities, the "final common path" is inherent alterations in the way information is processed.
4. It does not adequately recognize that persons with other handicapping or environmental limitations may have a learning disability *concurrently* with these conditions.

Recent formal attempts to tighten the general definition of LD have not fared appreciably better (Moats & Lyon, 1993), as can be seen in the revised definition produced by the National Joint Committee on Learning Disabilities (NJCLD, 1988) (see Hammill, 1993; Hammill, Leigh, McNutt, & Larsen, 1981). This version states the following:

Learning disabilities is a general term that refers to a heterogeneous group of disorders manifested by significant difficulty in the acquisition and use of listening, speaking, reading, writing, reasoning, or mathematical abilities. These disorders are intrinsic to the individual, presumed to be due to central nervous system dysfunction, and may occur across the life span. Problems in self-regulatory behavior, social perception, and social interaction may exist with learning disabilities but do not by themselves constitute a learning disability. Although learning disabilities may occur concomitantly with other handicapping conditions (for example, sensory impairment, mental retardation, social and emotional disturbance) or with extrinsic influences (such as cultural differences, insufficient or inappropriate instruction, they are not the result of these conditions or influences. (p. 1)

While the NJCLD revised definition addresses the issues of heterogeneity, persistence, intrinsic etiology, and comorbidity discussed by Torgesen (1991), it continues to reflect a vague and ambiguous description of multiple and heterogeneous disorders. In essence, the definition, as it is stated at this time, cannot be easily operationalized or empirically validated. Thus to date, most definitions of LD still do not provide clinicians, teachers, and researchers with useful information to enhance communication or improve predictions. Given this state of the field, many scholars have called for a moratorium on the development of broad definitions (at least for research purposes) and advocate a definition that only addresses learning disabilities defined in terms of coherent and operational domains.

For example, Stanovich (1993) argued the following point:

Scientific investigations of some generically defined entity called "learning disability" simply make little sense given what we already know about heterogeneity across various learning domains. Research investigations must define groups specifically in terms of the domain of deficit (reading disability, arithmetic disability). The extent of co-occurrence of these dysfunctions then becomes an empirical question, not something decided a priori by definition practices. (p. 273)

It should be noted that both the fourth edition of the *Diagnostic and Statistical Manual of Mental Disorders* (DSM-IV; American Psychiatric Association, 1994) and the *ICD-10 Classification of Mental and Behavioural Disorders* (ICD-10; World Health Organization, 1992) have, in fact, defined classified and coded learning disorders and

specific developmental disorders of scholastic skills into specific domains of deficit. For example, DSM-IV (1994) subdivides communication disorders (listening and speaking in the language of educational definitions) into expressive language disorder (Code 315.31), mixed receptive–expressive language disorder (Code 315.31), and phonological disorder (Code 315.39). DSM-IV provides criteria for the diagnosis of reading disorder (Code 315.00), while ICD-10 provides identification criteria under the term specific reading disorder (F81.0). DSM-IV and ICD-10 refer to disabilities in mathematics as mathematics disorder (Code 315.1) and specific disorder of arithmetical skills (Code F81.2), respectively. Finally, disabilities involving written language skills are classified and coded by DSM-IV as a disorder of written expression (Code 315.2) and by ICD-10 as a specific spelling disorder (Code F81.1).

However, regardless of whether one approaches the task of defining learning disabilities in a general fashion as has been traditionally done at the federal level, or one seeks to define domain-specific learning disabilities such as reading disability, as advocated by Stanovich (1993), the American Psychiatric Association (1994), and the World Health Organization (1992), the definitional process must be informed by, and constructed within, a classification system that ultimately has communicative and predictive power. The logic underlying the development of such a classification system is that identification, diagnosis, treatment, and prognosis cannot be addressed effectively until the heterogeneity across and within domain-specific learning disabilities is accounted for and subgroups and subtypes are delineated that are theoretically meaningful, reliable, and valid.

More specifically, in developing such a classification system, one must ensure that the resulting nosology be (1) theory driven (Fletcher & Morris, 1986; Kavale & Forness, 1985; Lyon, 1985b, 1987; Skinner, 1981); (2) based on variables that have theoretical relevance and adequate psychometric properties (Blashfield, 1993; Fletcher, Francis, Rourke, Shaywitz, & Shaywitz, 1993; Lyon & Risucci, 1989; Morris, 1993); (3) developed on nonreferred samples within the context of prospective, longitudinal studies (Fletcher et al., 1993; Francis et al., 1994; Lyon, 1987, 1994a, 1994b; B. Shaywitz & Shaywitz, 1994); (4) replicable and internally valid (Blashfield & Draguns, 1976; Morris, 1993; Skinner, 1981); and (5) externally valid and useful for

precise description of subject attributes, prediction, and clinical practice (Lyon, 1985b; Lyon & Flynn, 1991; Lyon & Moats, 1988; Lyon, Moats, & Flynn, 1989).

As B. Shaywitz and Shaywitz (1994) have eloquently pointed out, "The decisions emanating from a classification influence how an entity is defined, and consequently, who is selected and identified as having a particular disorder" (p. 2). If the factors guiding classification decisions do not adhere to the criteria cited above also and become explicit in their usage, heterogeneity will continue to confuse the definitional and diagnostic process in the field of learning disabilities. As a result, children with LD will continue to be defined in different ways and identified by different sets of criteria. As such, generalization and replication of research or clinical findings will be impossible.

Problems with the Concept of Discrepancy

As pointed out earlier, a fundamental historical assumption underlying the construct of LD is that the academic difficulties manifested by individuals with learning disabilities are *unexpected*, given the discrepancy between their relatively robust intellectual capabilities, opportunities to learn, and freedom from social disadvantage or emotional handicap (as specified in the exclusionary criteria of most definitions) and their reading, written language and/or math performance. The assumption of "unexpected underachievement" as reflected in an aptitude–achievement discrepancy (typically assessed using intelligence tests) is based on the premise that individuals who display such a discrepancy are indeed different from individuals who do not (i.e., "slow learners") with respect to phenotypic variables, such as information processing characteristics or response to intervention, and genotypic variables such as differences in the heritability of the disorder or its neurophysiological signature (Lyon, 1988).

However recent studies of reading development and disorders among children with LD and pervasively underachieving children cast doubt on the utility and validity of the notion of discrepancy (see Lyon, 1995b; Siegel, 1988a, 1988b, 1989, 1990, 1991, 1992). More specifically, Fletcher et al. (1994) and Stanovich and Siegel (1994) have clearly demonstrated, at least in the area of dyslexia, that discrepancies between IQ and reading achievement are meaningless in that

discrepant and nondiscrepant poor readers *do not* differ on measures of information processing, genetic variables, response to instruction, or neurophysiological markers. These particular findings, which will be addressed in detail in the section devoted to learning disabilities in reading, do not obviate the possibility that "unexpected underachievement" is, in fact, a cardinal sign of LD, but the data clearly demonstrate that the practice of assessing IQ–achievement to determine unexpected underachievement (at least in reading) is invalid. It is possible that comparisons between intellectual functioning and performance in different achievement domains may have relevance as a secondary characteristic that predicts response to intervention, level of self-concept, or long-term outcomes (Lyon, 1989, 1995b).

Limited Knowledge Relevant to Cultural and Ethnic Factors

Although all current definitions of learning disabilities state that learning deficits encompassed by the disorder cannot be attributed to cultural factors (including race and ethnicity), limited information exists regarding how race, ethnicity, and cultural background might influence school learning, in general, and the expression of different types of LD, in particular. However, it is encouraging to note that work being conducted by Frank Wood and his colleagues (Wood, Felton, Flowers, & Naylor, 1991) has begun to shed light on these issues. In a longitudinal study of specific learning (reading) disabilities within a random sample of 485 children selected in the first grade and followed through the third grade (55% caucasian, 45% African-American), Wood et al. (1991) found that the effects of race were, in fact, important as well as highly complicated. For example, at the first-grade level, race did not appear to be an influential variable in reading development once vocabulary ability was accounted for. That is, once a child's age and level of vocabulary development were known, race did not provide any additional predictive power to forecasting first-grade reading scores. However, by the end of the third grade, race had become a significant predictive factor ($p = .001$) even when the most powerful predictors—first-grade reading scores—were also in the prediction equation. Specifically, by the end of the third grade, African-American youngsters were having significantly greater difficulties learning to read.

In attempting to understand this race effect, Wood and his group assessed a number of additional demographic factors to include parental marital status, parental education, parental status as a welfare recipient, SES, the number of books in the home, and occupational status. Their findings were clear. The presence of any or all of these demographic variables in the prediction equation "did not remove the race effect from its potency as an independent predictor of third-grade reading" (Wood et al., 1991, p. 9).

In continuing to explore this systematic bias of race vis-à-vis the development of reading abilities, Frank Wood (personal communication, March 1993) has hypothesized that African-American youngsters may be penalized by particular teaching methods that are used to develop reading skills. More specifically, during this longitudinal study, the majority of children (caucasian and African-American) were taught reading via a "whole-language" curriculum that deemphasized decoding and word recognition strategies and emphasized the use of context to infer meaning from text. Unfortunately, as Wood notes (personal communication, March 1993) the nature of African-American children's dialect may interact negatively with any reading approach that does not explicitly emphasize specific sound–symbol relationships. Wood has continued this longitudinal study into the fifth grade and has found that African-American children's reading difficulties become more severe with age. Because of these findings, the National Institute of Child Health and Human Development (NICHD) within the National Institutes of Health (NIH) has provided additional support for these studies to be continued through the high school years and to be replicated with a new sample of first-grade children.

It is clear from these emerging data that some aspects of race and culture can influence the development of reading abilities, even though such a bias or disadvantage is not reflected in referral patterns. Obviously, continued systematic study will be required to fully understand these phenomena.

Summary

A number of factors have impeded efforts within the general field of learning disabilities to establish a valid definition and classification system. However, substantial progress is being made in a number of domain-specific areas such as reading and language, with less progress in the areas

of mathematics and written language. With this as background, the next sections of this chapter address learning disabilities in oral language (primarily phonology), reading, written language, and mathematics. For each specific type of learning disability, the most current findings with respect to definition, developmental course, prognosis, epidemiology, theoretical frameworks, and etiologies will be presented.

SPECIFIC LEARNING DISABILITIES IN ORAL LANGUAGE

Historical Underpinnings

Deficits in oral language (broadly termed listening and speaking in extant definitions) and their relationship to the field of learning disabilities were discussed briefly in the first sections of this chapter. Keeping in mind that the fundamental clinical manifestation of learning disabilities from a historical perspective is *unexpected under-acheivement,* we recall that in the 1800s, it was Gall who observed patients who could produce thoughts in writing but could not produce expressive language, demonstrating an unexpected dissociation between listening, speaking, and writing (Hammill, 1993; Torgesen, 1991). In a more contemporary time frame, the work of Samuel Kirk and his associates (Kirk & Kirk, 1971; Kirk, McCarthy, & Kirk, 1968) stands out as a major contributor to the realization that language development and disorders were not only critical to learning, but they could negatively affect the development of different academic abilities. Within this context, Kirk, McCarthy, and Kirk (1968) developed the Illinois Test of Psycholinguistic Abilities to assess relative strengths and weaknesses in receptive and expressive language and to use the data to design prescriptive remedial education programs. While Kirk's diagnostic and intervention concepts have not yet stood the test of time (Newcomer & Hammill, 1976), he clearly made explicit the fact that children could display unexpected patterns of strengths and weaknesses in linguistic abilities and the need to consider oral language development as a significant prerequisite to academic learning. Similar contributions in this regard were made by Berry and Eisenson (1956), Myklebust (1954), Johnson and Myklebust (1967), and de Hirsh, Jansky, and Langsford (1965). For comprehensive reviews of

the early history in the area of oral language and learning disabilities, the reader is referred to Gerber (1993).

Definitions and Diagnostic Criteria

Both the National Advisory Committee on Handicapped Children (NACHC) definition of learning disabilities (1968) and the NJCLD (1988) definition reference the terms listening and speaking disorders in their respective texts. Moreover, the NACHC definition states that "Specific learning disability means a disorder in one or more of the basic psychological processes involved in using language . . ." (p. 65083). Unfortunately, neither the NACHC nor the NJCLD definition provides specific inclusionary criteria for diagnosis.

DSM-IV (American Psychiatric Association, 1994) also addresses oral language disorders under the major heading of communication disorders, which are partitioned into expressive language disorder, mixed receptive/expressive language disorder, phonological disorder (articulation disorder), and stuttering and communication disorder not otherwise specified. Stuttering and nonspecified communication disorders are not covered in this chapter as they are not routinely considered within the diagnostic net of LD. Table 11.1 displays DSM-IV (American Psychiatric Association, 1994) diagnostic criteria for expressive language disorder, mixed receptive/expressive language disorder, and phonological disorder.

As with the majority of definitions used to describe different types of LD, the NACHC, NJCLD, and DSM-IV definitions for expressive, receptive, and phonological language disorders have not been internally or externally validated. Even though the DSM-IV definitions provide inclusionary criteria (Table 11.1), it is not yet known whether such criteria (i.e., discrepancy between nonverbal IQ and expressive or receptive language test scores) differentiate among different disorders or differentiate between different types within a specific disorder.

Relationship of Developmental Language Disorders to Learning Disabilities

Several issues must be addressed when one is analyzing the place of oral language disorders in a discussion of learning disabilities. At the outset,

TABLE 11.1. DSM-IV Diagnostic Criteria for Language Disorders Related to Learning Disabilities

Expressive Language Disorder

A. The scores obtained from standardized individually administered measures of expressive language development are substantially below those obtained from standardized measures of both nonverbal intellectual capacity and receptive language development. The disturbance may be manifest clinically by symptoms that include having a markedly limited vocabulary, making errors in tense, or having difficulty recalling words or producing sentences with developmentally appropriate length or complexity.

B. The difficulties with expressive language interfere with academic or occupational achievement or with social communication.

C. Criteria are not met for Mixed Receptive–Expressive Language Disorder or a Pervasive Developmental Disorder.

D. If Mental Retardation, a speech–motor or sensory deficit or environmental deprivation is present, the language difficulties are in excess of those usually associated with these problems.

Mixed Receptive–Expressive Language Disorder

A. The scores obtained from a battery of standardized individually administered measures of both receptive and expressive language development are substantially below those obtained from standardized measures of nonverbal intellectual capacity. Symptoms include those for Expressive Language Disorder as well as difficulty understanding words, sentences, or specific types of words, such as spatial terms.

B. The difficulties with receptive and expressive language significantly interfere with academic or occupational achievement or with social communication.

C. Criteria are not met for a pervasive Developmental Disorder.

D. If Mental Retardation, a speech–motor or sensory deficit, or environmental deprivation is present, the language difficulties are in excess of those usually associated with these problems.

Phonological Disorder

A. Failure to use developmentally expected speech sounds that are appropriate for age and dialect (e.g., errors in sound production, use, representation, or organization such as, but not limited to, substitutions of one sound for another [use of /t/ for target /k/ sound] or omissions of sounds such as final consonants).

B. The difficulties in speech sound production interfere with academic or occupational achievement or with social communication.

C. If Mental Retardation, a speech–motor or sensory deficit, or environmental deprivation is present, the language difficulties are in excess of those usually associated with these problems.

Note. From American Psychiatric Association (1994, pp. 58, 60, 61, 63). Copyright 1994 by the American Psychiatric Association. Reprinted by permission.

it should be noted that the terms used in the NACHC, NJCLD, and DSM-IV definitions to describe subsets or components of language (with the exception of phonology) are vague, ambiguous, and typically lead to multiple interpretations by clinicians and researchers. Clearly the terms listening and speaking, as noted in the NACHC and NJCLD definitions, reflect conceptualizations of language that are far too broad and imprecise to provide a foundation for the measurement and assessment of linguistic capabilities (Moats, 1994). If one is to do justice to the complex area of oral language development and its relationship to the learning of other symbol systems (i.e., reading, spelling, written language),

then the domain itself should, at the least, be subdivided into linguistic competence, which refers to a child's knowledge of phonological rules, morphological rules, semantic rules, syntactic rules, and pragmatic language functions (Moats, 1994). Linguistic performance, on the other hand, refers to how the individual deploys the component rule systems in communication and thought (Gerber, 1993).

Second, disorders of receptive and expressive language, which are also ambiguous and imprecise terms, clearly vary in severity and presentation. In general, children who display language delays, severe language comprehension deficits, and marked deficits in the use of syntactic and

morphosyntactic rules are first seen by speech and language pathologists where diagnosis and treatment plans are formulated. The point to be made here is that developmental language disorders constitute an extremely complex and large domain of study that can occur outside of the diagnostic net used for learning disabilities, whereas more subtle linguistic deficits co-occur with different types of LD. The one major area of oral language competence and performance that is clearly related to learning disabilities, and in particular to reading, is phonology, which will be discussed in detail in this section and the section "Specific Learning Disabilities in Reading," below. The decision to focus on the relationship between phonological development and learning disabilities should not imply that semantics, syntax, morphology, and pragmatics are not also critically related to some types of LD. They are. However, space limitations do not allow for an in-depth discussion of these rule systems, how and when they develop, and how they influence cognitive and academic development. As such, the reader is referred to Gerber (1993), Tallal (1988), and Wiig and Semmel (1976) for comprehensive reviews of these issues.

Phonological Processing and Learning Disabilities

It is clear that the majority of children and adults with LD manifest their greatest difficulties in language-based activities related to learning to read and spell (Lyon, 1985a, 1985b). As mentioned earlier, while developmental reading disorders will be addressed in greater detail in the next section, it is important to point out that deficits in phonology appear to be the major culprit in impeding reading development in children with learning disabilities (Catts, 1986; Kamhi & Catts, 1989). By definition, phonology refers to the linguistic rule system that contains the inventory of speech sounds that occur in the language and the rules for combining the sounds into meaningful units. Phonological processing refers to the use of phonological information, especially the sound structure of one's oral language in processing written and oral information (Jorm & Share, 1983; Wagner & Torgesen, 1987; Wagner, Torgesen, Laughon, Simmons, & Rashotte, 1993). Speech sounds, or phonemes, are described by their phonetic properties, such as their manner or place of articulation, and their acoustic features

or patterns of sound waves (Gerber, 1993). Phonemes having the same features are clustered together into classes of consonant or vowel sounds, voiced or unvoiced sounds, and oral or nasal sounds, and so forth (see Table 11.1 for diagnostic criteria for expressive phonological disorders).

Phonology and Learning to Read and Spell

In the English language, which is an alphabetic language containing 44 phonemes, the unit characters (letters) that children learn to read and spell are keyed to the phonological structure of words (Liberman & Shankweiler, 1979). Thus, the child's primary task in the early development of reading and spelling is to develop the realization that speech can be segmented into phonemes and that these phonemes represent printed forms (Blachman, 1991; Liberman, 1971; Lyon, 1995b). However, as Blachman (1991) has pointed out, this awareness that words can be divided into the smallest discernible segments of sound is a very difficult task for many children. The difficulty lies in large part in the fact that speech, unlike writing, "does not consist of separate phonemes" produced one after another "in a row over time" (Blachman, 1991; Gleitman & Rosen, 1973, p. 460). Instead the sounds are coarticulated (overlapped with one another) to permit rapid communication of speech, rather than sound by sound pronunciation. This property of coarticulation, critical for speech, but possibly harmful to the beginning reader and speller, is explained by Liberman and Shankweiler (1991) as follows:

> The advantageous result of . . . coarticulation of speech sounds is that speech can proceed at a satisfactory pace—at a pace indeed at which it can be understood (Liberman, Cooper, Shankweiler, & Studdert-Kennedy, 1967). Can you imagine trying to understand speech if it were spelled out to you letter by painful letter? So coarticulation is certainly advantageous for the perception of speech. But a further result of coarticulation, and a much less advantageous one for the would-be reader, is that there is, inevitably, no neat correspondence between the underlying phonological structure and the sound that comes to the ears. Thus, though the word "bag," for example, has three phonological units, and correspondingly three letters in print, it has only one pulse of sound: The three elements of

the underlying phonological structure—the three phonemes (/b/ /a/ /g/)—have been thoroughly overlapped (coarticulated) into the one beginning sound—"bag. . . ."

[Beginning readers] can understand, and properly take advantage of, the fact that the printed word *bag* has three letters, only if they are aware that the spoken word *"bag,"* with which they are already quite familiar, is divisible into three segments. They will probably not know that spontaneously, because as we have said, there is only one segment of sound, not three, and because the processes of speech perception that recover the phonological structure are automatic and quite unconscious. (pp. 5–6)

Thus, the awareness of the phonological structure of the English language, the way in which phonological awareness makes possible the reading of new words, and the automatic and fluent recognition of known words are critical language skills necessary for basic reading, reading comprehension, spelling, and written expression (Shankweiler & Liberman, 1989). In addition to serving as a prerequisite for basic reading skills, phonological processing also appears highly related to expressive language development. For example, Kamhi, Catts, Mauer, Apel, and Gentry (1988) attempted to identify whether different types of phonological processing deficits were related to deficits in oral and written language (reading). In essence, the Kamhi group found similar phonological deficits in both groups, with the only difference being that the group with expressive language disorders manifested more severe phonological processing difficulties. Kamhi et al. (1988) speculated that the greater severity observed in children with expressive language impairment may be attributed to a more specific deficit in speech programming abilities.

Although the relationship of phonological processing to written language domains will be explicated in the section of this chapter addressing "Specific Learning Disabilities in Reading," we review the development of phonological awareness in the young child now. In addition, diagnostic tasks useful in the assessment of phonological awareness are also addressed.

The Development of Phonological Awareness

Liberman, Shankweiler, Fisher, and Carter (1974) conducted a number of studies to identify the developmental trajectories of young children's ability to identify the number of segments in spoken utterances and syllables. Using a game-like procedure, Liberman and her associates required 4-, 5-, and 6-year-old children to indicate the number of syllables and phonemes in a series of test utterances by tapping a wooden dowel on a table. At age 4 years, none of the children could segment by phoneme, although nearly half could segment by syllable. The ability to segment syllables into their respective phonemes did not appear until age 5 years, and even then only a fifth of the children could accomplish the task. On the other hand, approximately half of the 5-year-olds could segment multisyllabic words into syllables. By age 6 years, 70% of the children succeeded in the phoneme segmentation task, and 90% were successful in the syllable task.

More recent studies by Ball and Blachman (1988), Blachman (1991), and Bradley and Bryant (1983) suggest that approximately 80% of children have mastered the ability to segment words and syllables into their constituent phonemes by the time they reach 7 years of age. Unfortunately, studies conducted by Francis et al. (1994), Fletcher et al. (1994), and B. Shaywitz and Shaywitz (1994) strongly indicate that at least 15% to 20% of young children continue to have difficulty understanding the alphabetic principle underlying the ability to segment words and syllables into phonemes, and not surprisingly, approximately the same percentage of children manifest difficulties in learning to read.

Epidemiology

Phonological deficits are common among children with LD, and particularly among those children who display reading and spelling deficits. Approximately 20% of children in the United States manifest difficulties in the development of basic reading skills (S. Shaywitz, Escobar, Shaywitz, Fletcher, & Makuch, 1992), and approximately 80% to 90% of these disabled readers have deficits in phonological processing (Fletcher et al., 1994). As will be noted in the discussion of developmental reading disorders, the gender ratio among individuals with phonological deficits is not different than the gender ratio within the population as a whole (DeFries & Gillis, 1991; Felton & Brown, 1991; S. Shaywitz, Shaywitz, Fletcher, & Escobar, 1990; Wood & Felton, 1994), although more male than female individuals have been reported to display

a greater frequency of syntactic and pragmatic language deficits and more severe impairments in general language development (Montgomery, Windsor, & Stark, 1991).

There is some evidence that deficits in phonological awareness may occur more frequently in populations that use nonstandard English. Frank Wood (personal communication, March 1993) has reported that the dialect of African-American children may interact with their ability to apply phonological rules to the decoding and rapid reading of words. More specifically, Wood has found that although African-American youngsters read at the same grade level as caucasian children at the beginning of the first grade, marked declines in reading are noted for the African-American children by the third grade, with severe declines by the fifth grade. As mentioned earlier, Wood (1995) attributes these declines to a negative relationship between the youngster's dialectical characteristics and the context-based reading program (whole language) used in the schools where the children were studied.

Etiological Bases for Phonological Deficits

Neurobiological Factors

There is converging evidence from anatomical microstructure studies, gross morphology studies, and neuroimaging studies that deficits in phonology, particularly those deficits in phonological awareness and segmentation that interfere with reading development, are related to anomalous organization of neural tissue and processing systems subserved within the posterior left hemisphere, particularly in the region of the perisylvian fissure (Lyon, in press-a). For instance, regional blood flow studies (rCBF) indicate that poor performance on tasks demanding phonological awareness is associated with less activation than normal in the left temporal region with atypically increased activation in the region of the angular gyrus (Wood, 1990; Wood et al., 1991). Neuroimaging studies employing positron emission tomography (PET) (Gross-Glenn et al., 1986) and structural magnetic resonance imaging (MRI) (Filipek & Kennedy, 1991; Lubs et al., 1991) have led to similar findings. These neuroimaging data should be interpreted with caution at this time, given that the majority of studies have been conducted with heterogeneous groups of adults whose developmental histories are typically unknown. On the other hand, the data strongly suggest a neurobiological correlate for phonological deficits that involves aberrant processing in posterior left hemisphere systems, an observation that agrees with clinical observations and lesion studies (Lyon, in press-a; Rumsey, in press).

Genetic Factors

There is increasing evidence from behavioral genetic studies that deficits in phonological processing abilities are heritable. For example, Lewis (1990) found that siblings of children with severe phonological disorders manifested significantly poorer performance than siblings of nonimpaired children on several measures of phonological abilities (rhyming, elision, segmentation). Out of 20 families of children with severe phonological disorders, four families demonstrated a high incidence of speech–language problems over three consecutive generations. Not surprisingly, given the previous discussion of the critical role phonology plays in learning to read, those family members displaying linguistic phonological deficits manifested a significantly higher rate of reading disorders.

In a series of twin studies designed to assess the relative contributions of phonological and orthographic processes to word recognition skill, Olson and his colleagues (DeFries, Olson, Pennington, & Smith, 1991; Olson, 1985; Olson, Wise, Conners, Rack, & Fulker, 1989; Olson, Forsberg, Wise, & Rack, 1994) have reported that deficits on phonological coding tasks are significantly heritable, whereas deficits in orthographic skills are more highly related to environmental factors.

Common Comorbidities

Comorbidities are a frequently encountered problem in learning disabilities, and understanding the causal bases that link two or more co-occurring disorders in the same individual is critical because different explanations may have implications for developmental theory and clinical practice (Pennington, Groisser, & Welsh, 1993). In a broad sense, there are compelling data that indicate that learning disabilities, no matter what specific type, manifest social adjustment problems in addition to their academic deficits (Hazel & Shumaker, 1988). Bruck (1986), in her review of the literature related to social and emotional adjustment, concluded that children with LD were more likely to exhibit increased levels

of anxiety, withdrawal, depression, and low self-esteem compared to their nonhandicapped peers. Social-skill deficits have been found to exist at significantly high rates among children with LD (see Gresham, 1986, and Hazel & Schumaker, 1988, for comprehensive reviews). In general, social-skill deficits include difficulties interacting with people in an appropriate fashion (e.g., lack of knowledge of how to greet people, how to make friends, how to engage in playground games, or a failure to use knowledge of such skills in these situations). Although all children with LD do not exhibit social-skills deficits, there are certain common characteristics among those who do. For example, Bruck (1986) reported that the severity of the LD is positively related to the number and severity of social-skills deficits that are manifested by the child. Moreover, the sex of the child appears to be another factor, with evidence suggesting that female LD children are more likely to have social adjustment problems than male LD children (also see Bruck, 1985).

Comorbidities between specific language disorders and social–emotional disorders have also been identified. For example, Cantwell, Baker, and Mattison (1980) reported the results of a comprehensive psychiatric evaluation of 100 consecutive cases of children with speech and language seen in a community clinic. Psychiatric assessment of this cohort indicated the presence of a psychiatric disorder, according to DSM-III criteria, in at least 50% of the group. It should be noted that included in the types of psychiatric disorder were deficits in reading and mathematics as well as attention-deficit disorder. It was reported that children with speech articulation problems, without co-occurring language deficits, had the lowest prevalence of psychiatric morbidity, whereas youngsters with speech and language disorders or language disorders alone were most at risk for DSM-III diagnoses.

In an even more specific vein, there is a wealth of evidence that deficits in phonology clearly co-occur with deficits in reading decoding and word recognition skills (Lyon, 1995b; Vellutino & Scanlon, 1987) and that the relationship is, in fact, a causal one, with phonological deficits impeding the acquisition of reading skills (Wagner, 1988; Wagner & Torgesen, 1987). Indeed, as addressed earlier, the nature of the English orthography and its alphabetic characteristics must rely heavily on those linguistic abilities that allow the reader to parse words into their constituent sounds (pho-

nemes). A lack of awareness of this "alphabetic principle" leads to slow and inaccurate decoding and word recognition (Liberman, Shankweiler, & Liberman, 1989; Lundborg, Olofsson, & Wall, 1980; Mann, 1984).

Summary

The preceding sections addressing oral language deficits and LD have focused on the nature of phonological linguistic abilities, with an emphasis on their theoretical underpinnings, their developmental course, their assessment, their epidemiology, their etiology, and their co-occurrence and causal role in reading and spelling disabilities. Clearly, deficits in other language domains that include semantics, syntax, and pragmatics are also influential in the phenotypic expression of learning disabilities. Readers interested in a comprehensive review of these linguistic areas and how they influence reading comprehension, written expression, mathematics, and social behavior are referred to Gerber (1993).

SPECIFIC LEARNING DISABILITIES IN READING

Historical Underpinnings

Of all the learning disabilities, the area of reading disabilities has the richest clinical and experimental history (Lyon, 1995b; Lyon & Chhabra, in press). Many sources are available that provide fine-grained analyses of the history of reading disability (Coles, 1987; Doris, 1993; Kavale & Forness, 1985; Wiederholt, 1974), and these sources should be consulted for a comprehensive review. For the purposes of this chapter however, it is important to point out that difficulties in learning to read in the presence of intellectual strength and integrity in other academic skills have been observed and recorded for at least a century. Consider the following observations of a 14-year-old boy made by Morgan in 1896:

> I then asked him to read me a sentence out of an easy child's book without spelling the words. The result was curious. He did not read a single word correctly, with the exception of "and," "the," "of," "that," etc; the other words seemed to be quite unknown to him, and he could not even make an attempt to pronounce them. . . . He multiplied 749

by 876 quickly and easily. . . . I may add that the boy is bright and of average intelligence in conversation. . . . The schoolmaster who has taught him for some years says that he would be the smartest lad in school if the instruction were entirely oral. (p. 1378)

A critically important historical figure in the development of research and clinical interest in reading disability was Samuel Orton who studied children with unexpected reading failure over a 10-year period. In 1937, Orton published an explanation for reading disability that stressed that the disorder did not result from localized brain damage as proposed by Hinshelwood (1917) but, rather, could be attributed to a failure or a delay in establishing dominance for language in the left hemisphere of the brain. Orton's theory of reading disability also predicted that children's inefficient reading was related to the tendency to reverse and transpose letters and words prompting him to coin the label "Strephosymbolia" (twisted symbols) (Orton, 1937). Although Orton's specific neurological theories were never validated (Liberman, Shankweiler, Orlando, Harris, & Bell-Berti, 1971; Torgesen, 1991), his work stimulated much research and clinical activity in the development of remediation and treatment methods for reading disability. Orton's contributions to the intervention area eventually led to the founding of the Orton Dyslexia Society in 1949. Of some importance here is that the term "dyslexia" began to be used frequently in clinical and educational communities, and to this date, it is frequently used synonymously with the terms reading disability, reading disorder, and LD in reading.

Definitions and Diagnostic Criteria

Both the NACHC Definition and the NJCLD definition (discussed earlier) make only a passing reference to learning disabilities in reading. The Office of Education (USOE; 1977) has helped to operationalize the identification of learning disabilities in reading by developing criteria (Section 121a.541) that delineate the reading domain into (1) basic reading skills, which include decoding and word recognition abilities, and (2) reading comprehension skills, which include the ability to derive meaning from print. The USOE criteria also specified that learning disabilities in basic reading skills or reading comprehension could be identified only if a severe discrepancy existed between a child's intellectual ability and his or her reading abilities as assessed by standardized intelligence and achievement measures (USOE, 1977).

The DSM-IV (American Psychiatric Association, 1994) definition and criteria for reading disorder specify that the condition is marked by subaverage reading ability in the presence of average to above-average intelligence. In addition, a diagnosis of reading disorder should adhere to the three major criteria cited in Table 11.2.

The criteria presented in Table 11.2 show that the core issue in the diagnosis of reading disability is the degree to which an individual's reading accuracy, reading speed, or reading comprehension differs from chronological age or measured intelligence. It is important for the reader to note again that the concept of "discrepancy" as reflected in these criteria is a problematic one and not validated at the present time (Lyon, 1995a, 1995b; Lyon et al., 1993). This issue is explored in detail in the next section.

In contrast to the definitions and criteria discussed thus far, the *ICD-10 Classification of Mental and Behavioural Disorders: Diagnostic Criteria for Research* (World Health Organization, 1993) provides diagnostic criteria for research with individuals with specific reading disorder (Table 11.3) and a separate set of guidelines for clinical descriptions and clinical guidelines for diagnoses. Table 11.3 depicts the major diagnostic criteria for specific reading disorder if one wishes to conduct research with individuals who display deficits in this area. Readers are encour-

TABLE 11.2. DSM-IV Diagnostic Criteria for Reading Disorder

A. Reading Achievement, as measured by individually administered standardized tests of reading accuracy or comprehension, is substantially below that expected given the person's chronological age, measured intelligence, and age-appropriate education.	B. The disturbance in Criterion A significantly interferes with academic achievement or activities of daily living that require reading skills.
	C. If a sensory deficit is present, the reading difficulties are in excess of those usually associated with it.

Note. From American Psychiatric Association (1994, p. 50). Copyright 1994 by the American Psychiatric Association. Reprinted by permission.

TABLE 11.3. ICD-10 Diagnostic Criteria for Specific Reading Disorder

A. Either of the following must be present:

(1) a score on reading accuracy and/or comprehension that is at least 2 standard errors of prediction below the level expected on the basis of the child's chronological age and general intelligence, with both reading skills and IQ assessed on an individually administered test standardized for the child's culture and educational system;

(2) a history of serious reading difficulties, or test scores that met criterion A(1) at an earlier age, plus a score on a spelling test that is at least 2 standard errors of prediction below the level expected on the basis of the child's chronological age and IQ.

B. The disturbance in criterion A significantly interferes with academic achievement or activities of daily living that require reading skills.

C. The disorder is not the direct result of a defect in visual or hearing acuity, or of a neurological disorder.

D. School experiences are within the average expectable range (i.e., there have been no extreme inadequacies in educational experiences).

E. *Most commonly used exclusion clause.* IQ is below 70 on an individually administered standardized test.

Note. From World Health Organization (1993, p. 144). Copyright 1993 by the World Health Organization. Reprinted by permission.

aged to peruse the ICD-10 clinical descriptions for an elaboration of the characteristics of reading disorders.

The publication of diagnostic criteria for research purposes coupled with an extended discussion of clinical characteristics and manifestations across different developmental epochs reflect an impressive attempt to aid in the standardization of sampling procedures for the study of individuals with LD (Morris et al., 1994). In addition, ICD-10's *Clinical Descriptions and Diagnostic Guidelines* (World Health Organization, 1992) provide useful information related to possible predictors of reading disorder as well as commonly observed comorbidities.

By comparison, the World Federation of Neurology (Rutter 1978, p. 12) is general to the point of being vague. This definition refers to learning disabilities in reading as "specific developmental dyslexia" and defines it as follows: "a disorder manifested by difficulty in learning to read despite conventional instruction, adequate intelligence, and sociocultural opportunity. It is dependent upon fundamental cognitive disabilities which are frequently of constitutional origin."

The Validity of Discrepancy as a Diagnostic Criterion

As alluded to earlier in the section identifying specific impediments to research in LD, a basic assumption underlying current definitions and diagnostic practices for LD in reading (reading disability, dyslexia) is that LD readers manifest a significant discrepancy between their potential,

as reflected in IQ scores, and their reading abilities, as assessed by achievement measures (Lyon, 1987, 1995b). Tacitly ingrained within this assumption are the notions that: (1) that poor readers with average or above-average IQs are cognitively and neurologically different from poor readers with low IQs (i.e., IQ scores that matched their reading scores); (2) LD readers can be reliably differentiated from nondisabled readers and "slow-learning" or nondiscrepant children on a variety of nonreading cognitive tasks; (3) LD readers, in contrast to "slow learners" can attain levels of achievement commensurate with their IQ if they are assessed and taught properly (Lyon, 1987; Lyon & Moats, 1988). However, the concept of discrepancy as a diagnostic marker and the assumptions that derive from it stand on shaky empirical, conceptual, and logical grounds.

To review, all professional and legal definitions of LD in reading highlight the same salient feature—that is, the child with a reading disability manifests an "unexpected" difficulty in decoding, word recognition, or comprehension that is not predicted by general intellectual competence (Lyon, 1995b). However, as authorities have noted (Fletcher et al., 1994; Stanovich & Siegel, 1994), the concept of discrepancy and the definitions that employ it as a diagnostic criterion have never been empirically validated. To do this, one would have to demonstrate that the reading difficulties of LD children with reading disabilities and high IQ (discrepant readers) are different from those characterizing children with reading disabilities and low aptitude (nondiscrepant readers) (Pennington, Gilger, Olson, & DeFries,

1992). It has only been within the past 6 years that studies designed to assess differences between discrepant and nondiscrepant readers have been carried out. Unfortunately, without exception, such studies do not support the use of IQ–reading achievement discrepancy criteria in the identification of reading disabilities (see Fletcher, 1992, for comprehensive coverage of these studies).

For example, a series of studies by B. Shaywitz and his associates (Fletcher et al., 1994; Fletcher, Francis, Rourke, Shaywitz, & Shaywitz, 1992; B. Shaywitz, Fletcher, Holahan, & Shaywitz, 1992) have not supported the use of discrepancy-based definitions for LD in reading. In 1992, B. Shaywitz and his group reported the results of a longitudinal study where a group of poor readers diagnosed according to a discrepancy criterion were compared with a group of poor readers matched for level of reading deficit without a discrepancy with IQ. Given that the investigation had followed a longitudinal cohort from kindergarten through the fifth grade, a number of comparisons could be made over time between the two poor-reader groups as well as a normal-reader group. B. Shaywitz et al. (1992) found no differences between the poor-reader groups on measures of tests of linguistic function, dexterity, visual perception, and teacher's assessment of learning and behavior at any time point within the developmental trajectory. The investigation also indicated that as many as 75% of children meeting criteria for discrepancy were also identified as low achieving.

In a more recent study, Fletcher et al. (1994) compared LD children with reading disabilities identified according to a discrepancy criterion with a group of nondiscrepant poor readers on nine cognitive variables related to reading proficiency. The groups did not differ with respect to performance on visual, vocabulary, memory, or phonological measures. In addition, measures of phonological awareness were the most robust indicators of differences between children with impaired reading and children without impaired reading, *regardless* of how reading disability was defined. Finally, Stanovich and his colleagues (Stanovich, 1993; Stanovich & Siegel, 1994) have obtained compelling data that show no differences between discrepant LD readers and nondiscrepant, "garden-variety," poor readers on measures of word recognition skills, phonology, and orthography. The discrepant and nondiscrepant groups were found to differ on tasks assessing memory and arithmetic. In summarizing their findings, Stanovich and Siegel (1994) stated:

Neither the phenotypic nor genotypic indicators of poor reading are correlated in any reliable way with IQ discrepancy. If there is a special group of children with reading disabilities who are behaviorally, cognitively, genetically, or neurologically different, it is becoming increasingly unlikely that they can be easily identified by using IQ discrepancy as a proxy for the genetic and neurological differences themselves. Thus, the basic assumption that underlies decades of classification in research and educational practice regarding reading disabilities (LD in reading) is becoming increasingly untenable. (p. 48)

Some Caveats with Respect to Discrepancy

The converging evidence reviewed here indicates clearly that IQ-achievement discrepancies are invalid diagnostic markers for LD in basic reading skills. A discrepancy simply does not differentiate a poor reader with average to above-average intelligence from a poor reader whose intelligence is commensurate with his or her low reading ability. On the other hand, it is important to keep in mind that all the studies reviewed used single-word reading or word recognition as the measure of reading disability and ability. It remains to be seen whether differences exist between discrepant and nondiscrepant readers on measures of reading comprehension or response to instruction (Lyon, 1989, 1995b; Moats & Lyon, 1993). Moreover, as Stanovich (1993) has pointed out, the lack of validity demonstrated for IQ-achievement discrepancies in the diagnosis of LD in reading does not obviate the conceptual notion that LD individuals' poor academic performance can be characterized as "unexpected." The critical task will be to identify the most valid predictor of one's potential to read. Whereas the best predictor does not appear to be IQ, preliminary data suggest measures of listening comprehension as a possible candidate (Stanovich, 1991).

Categorical versus Dimensional Definitions and Models of Learning Disabilities in Reading

As S. Shaywitz, Fletcher, and Shaywitz (1994) have pointed out, LD in reading, dyslexia, or specific reading retardation (used synonymously) have been viewed as a "specific *categorical* entity that affects a small, circumscribed group of children, that is invariable over time" (p. 3). Moreover, the categorical view holds that more male than female individuals are affected with the dis-

order, that the specific type of reading deficits observed is qualitatively different from that of other poor readers with lower aptitudes for reading, and that a discontinuity exists between the distribution for specific reading disability and the reading disabilities associated with lower cognitive potential (the hypothesized "hump" at the tail of the reading distribution; Rutter & Yule, 1975).

However, in the past several years, a numbers of studies have not supported the Rutter and Yule (1975) hypothesis of a bimodally distinct reading distribution characterized by a "hump" at the tail of the reading distribution (Fletcher & Morris, 1986; Olson, Kliegel, Davidson, & Foltz, 1985; Share, Jorm, MacLean, & Matthews, 1984; Silva, McGee, & Williams, 1985; Stanovich, 1988). In the most convincing study to date to refute the bimodality hypothesis, B. Shaywitz et al. (1992) used data from their Connecticut Longitudinal Study to ascertain whether a categorical or dimensional definition and model best described LD in reading or dyslexia. The Shaywitz group hypothesized that reading ability follows a normal distribution, with reading disability at the lower end of the continuum. Using Rutter and Yule's (1975) criteria, reading disability was defined in terms of a discrepancy score representing the difference between the actual reading achievement and the achievement predicted on the basis of intelligence. B. Shaywitz et al. (1992) obtained empirical evidence to support Stanovich's (1988) findings that LD in reading or dyslexia occurs along a continuum that blends imperceptibly with normal reading ability. The results clearly indicated that no distinct cut-off point is available to clearly distinguish LD readers from slow learners, or from normal readers. These findings support a revision in the current definitional model for LD in reading (dyslexia) in that the data support a shift from a categorical model to one that considers LD in reading to be similar to hypertension and other biological disorders that occur along a continuum (S. Shaywitz et al., 1994). Moreover, these findings indicate that LD in reading is not an all-or-none phenomenon but, rather, occurs in degrees. These results are in line with the data showing no differences between discrepant and nondiscrepant poor readers, and suggest that many more children may be affected with LD in reading than previously thought. The impact of these findings on clinical diagnostic practices and public policy could be substantial. For example, although limited resources may necessitate imposition of cut-off points for the provision of special education services, it must be recognized that such cut-off points are arbitrary and that many children in need of specialized interventions may be denied help (Lyon, 1995b; S. Shaywitz et al., 1994).

Characteristics, Theories, and Proposed Etiologies

As could be expected given the continuous and heterogeneous distribution of reading behaviors associated with reading ability and disability (S. Shaywitz, Shaywitz, Schnell, & Towle, 1988), both single-causal and multiple-causal theories have been advanced to represent the nature and etiologies of reading disorders. In the area of LD in reading, the phenotypic characteristics of the disorder are intimately interwoven with known and hypothesized causes of such characteristics. As such, this section is organized to review the most frequent types of reading deficits observed in LD readers. Following this discussion, issues associated with single- versus multiple-causal theories and models for these reading deficits are summarized. Then, etiological theories and models that presently have the greatest amount of empirical support are analyzed.

The Core Reading Deficits Manifested by LD Readers

The major academic deficits characterizing children with LD in reading are difficulties in decoding and the ability to read single words (Olson et al., 1994; Perfetti, 1985; Stanovich, 1986). While this statement may appear at odds with those who argue that reading comprehension skills reflect the most salient abilities in reading development (Goodman, 1969, 1986; Smith, 1971), we must consider that comprehension is dependent upon one's ability to decode rapidly and recognize single words in an automatic and fluent manner. Stanovich (1994) places the substantial importance of word recognition vis-à-vis reading comprehension within the following perspective: "Reading for meaning [comprehension] is greatly hindered when children are having too much trouble with word recognition. When word recognition processes demand too much cognitive capacity, fewer cognitive resources are left to allocate to higher-level processes of text integration and comprehension" (p. 281).

In essence then, the core academic deficit in reading disability involves a failure to rapidly, ac-

curately, and automatically read single words. This paramount importance given to single-word reading is based on the finding that word recognition is a prerequisite to understanding what is read (Olson et al., 1994; Vellutino, 1987; Vellutino, Scanlon, & Tanzman, 1994). This is primarily because slow and labored decoding and recognition of single words requires substantial effort and detracts from the child's ability to retain what has been communicated in a sentence, much less a paragraph or a passage (Lyon, 1995b).

The relatively greater importance of word recognition skills over reading comprehension flies in the face of theories and models of reading that hold that the ability to use contextual information to predict upcoming words is the cornerstone of fluent reading (Goodman, 1969; Smith, 1971). However, work conducted by a number of investigators (Bruck, 1988; Leu, DeGroff, & Simmons, 1986; Nicholson, 1991; Perfetti, 1985; Stanovich, 1980; Stanovich, West, & Feeman, 1981; West & Stanovich, 1978) has demonstrated that less-skilled readers were more likely to depend upon text for word recognition; highly skilled readers did not rely on contextual information for decoding or single-word reading, since their word recognition processes were so rapid and automatic (Stanovich, 1994).

Given the converging evidence documenting the importance of word recognition, it is not surprising that the ability to read single words accurately and fluently has been the most frequently selected research target in the study of LD in reading (dyslexia). Again, this is not to diminish the role of reading comprehension as an academic and cognitive skill to be taught and acquired. However, word recognition is not only a prerequisite behavior to comprehension, it is a more narrowly circumscribed behavior and is not related to numerous nonreading factors typically associated with comprehension (Wood et al., 1991). Therefore, it offers a more precise developmental variable for study. With the dependent variable thus identified, there continues to be some debate about the nonreading factor(s) (i.e., linguistic, perceptual, temporal processing speed) that account(s) for deficits in single-word reading. Two different perspectives continue to exist. One school of thought is that deficits in the ability to read single words rapidly and automatically are referable to multiple factors, thus giving rise to hypothesized subtypes of reading disabilities. The second, and more influential school of thought, proposes that deficits in word recognition are primarily associated with, or caused by one primary nonreading factor (i.e., phonological awareness). Each view is discussed in turn.

Multiple Etiologies and Subtypes of Reading Disabilities

It has been increasingly recognized over the past 25 years that learning disabilities, in general, are composed of multiple *subgroups* reflecting the fact that some LD children manifest reading deficits, whereas others have difficulties in oral language, or written expression, and/or mathematics (Blashfield, 1993; Feagans, Short, & Meltzer, 1991; Fletcher, Francis, Rourke, Shaywitz, & Shaywitz, 1993; Fletcher & Morris, 1986; Hooper & Willis, 1989; Lyon & Risucci, 1989; Morris, 1993; Newby & Lyon, 1991; Rourke, 1985; Speece, 1993). Obviously comorbidities can exist between and among these general conditions. It has also been hypothesized that a number of *subtypes* exist within the LD reader population and can be identified on the basis of how their members perform on measures of cognitive–linguistic, perceptual, memory span, and achievement skills (Bakker, 1988; Boder, 1973; Doehring & Hoshko, 1977; Fisk & Rourke, 1979; Lovett, 1984; Lyon, 1985a, 1985b, 1987; Lyon & Flynn, 1989, 1991; Lyon, Rietta, Watson, Porch, & Rhodes, 1981; Lyon, Stewart, & Freedman, 1982; Lyon & Watson, 1981; Mattis, French, & Rapin, 1975; Petrauskas & Rourke, 1979; Satz & Morris, 1981).

The argument for the existence of subtypes in the LD reader population has been based on the practical observation that even though LD readers may appear very similar with respect to their reading deficits (i.e., word recognition deficits), they may differ significantly in the development of skills that are correlated with basic reading development (Lyon, 1985a). Thus, even within well-defined samples of LD readers, there is large within-sample variance. This degree of heterogeneity suggests that not all children read poorly for the same reasons nor respond equally well to the same treatment interventions (Newby & Lyon, 1991). This observation may explain, in part, why LD readers have been reported to differ from controls on so many variables related to reading (Rourke, 1978).

The literature on subtyping reading disabilities is voluminous (Tables 11.4 and 11.5) comprising over 100 classification studies since 1963, and the

TABLE 11.4. Clinical–Inferential Learning Disability Subtyping Models

Classification models	Subtypes	Classification models	Subtypes
Achievement models		Neurolinguistic models	
Boder (1970)	Dysphonetic dyslexia Dyseidetic dyslexia Alexic dyslexia (mixed)	Marshall & Newcombe (1973)	Visual dyslexia Surface dyslexia Deep dyslexia
Rourke & Finlayson (1978)	Reading/spelling deficits Arithmetic deficits Reading/spelling/arithmetic deficits	Denckla (1981)	Anomic disorder Anomic disorder with repetition deficits Dysphonemic sequencing disorder
Sweeney & Rourke (1978)	Phonetic spelling deficits Dysphonetic spelling deficits		Verbal memory disorder Mixed language disorder Right hemisyndrome with mixed language disorder
Mitterer (1982)	Recoding readers Whole-word readers		
Thomson (1982)	Auditory–linguistic deficits Visual–spatial deficits	Marshall (1984)	Surface dyslexia Direct dyslexia
Frith (1983)	Phonological spelling deficits Lexical spelling deficits		Phonological dyslexia
Lovett (1984)	Reading accuracy disabled Reading rate disabled	Combined models	
Lennox & Siegel (1988)	Reading disabled Arithmetic disabled	Nelson & Warrington (1974)	Reading–spelling deficits Spelling deficits
Siegel & Ryan (1988)	Reading deficits Writing–arithmetic deficits Attention deficits	Vernon (1979)	Deficits in analyzing visual shapes Deficits in analyzing whole words into phonemes
Neurocognitive models			Deficits in the acquisition of grapheme–phoneme associations
Kinsbourne & Warrington (1963)	Language retarded Gerstmann		Deficits in grasping irregularities in grapheme–phoneme association and complex orthography
Johnson & Myklebust (1967)	Audiophonic dyslexia Visuospatial dyslexia		Deficits in grouping single words into phrases and sentences
Mattis, French, & Rapin (1975)	Language disordered Articulatory and graphomotor dyscoordination Visual–perceptual	Decker & DeFries (1981)	Spatial reasoning and reading deficits Coding speed and reading deficits
Myklebust (1978)	Auditory-processing deficits Visual-processing deficits Language impaired Intersensory integration		Mixed deficits Normal pattern with low reading achievement
Bakker (1979)	P-type dyslexia L-type dyslexia		
Wilson & Risucci (1986)	Expressive deficits Receptive deficits Memory and retrieval deficits Global deficits No deficits		

Note. Adapted from Hooper & Willis (1989). Copyright 1989 by Springer-Verlag New York, Inc. Adapted by permission.

TABLE 11.5. Empirical Learning Disability Subtyping Models

Classification models	Technique	Subtypes
Achievement models		
Satz & Morris (1981)	Cluster analysis	2 Learning problem groups (undescribed); 7 normal groups
Van der Vlugt & Satz (1985)	Cluster analysis	5 Learning problem groups (undescribed); 4 normal groups
DeLucca, Del Dotto, & Rourke (1987)	Cluster analysis	Mild deficits in tactile perception and aspects of expressive language, short-term memory, attention Deficits in tactile problem solving, visual–motor speed, language Mild deficits in psychomotor skills, finger localization, conceptual flexibility Deficits in retrieval, organization, visual manipulation, conceptual flexibility, finger graphesthesias, spelling, math
Johnston, Fennell, & Satz (1987)	Cluster analysis	Learning disabled—nonspecific Specific reading disability 4 normal groups
Neurocognitive models		
Fisk & Rourke (1979)	Q-type factor analysis	Auditory-verbal deficits, impaired tactile perception Motor, auditory–verbal processing deficits Auditory–verbal, memory, tactile perception deficits (not seen in 9-to 10-year-olds)
Petrauskas & Rourke (1979)	Cluster analysis	Language deficits Linguistic, sequencing, finger localization deficits Normals
Lyon & Watson (1981)	Cluster analysis	Language comprehension, memory, sound blending, visual–spatial deficits Language comprehension, auditory memory, visual–motor deficits Aphasic Excessive, receptive language deficits Visuoperceptive deficits Normal pattern with low reading skills
Satz & Morris (1981)	Cluster analysis	Global language deficits Specific language deficits Visual–perceptual deficits Mixed deficits Unexpected (normal profile with low reading skills)
Lyon, Stewart, & Freedman (1982)	Cluster analysis	Normal pattern Linguistic deficits Visual–spatial, visual–motor deficits Auditory comprehension, selected visual–perceptual deficits Mixed deficits
Joschko & Rourke (1985)	5 clustering procedures	Younger group (ages 6 to 8 years) Poor general perception, motor, academic deficits

TABLE 11.5 (continued)

Classification models	Technique	Subtypes
		Poor auditory perception, sequencing, academics
		Older group (ages 9 to 14 years)
		Poor auditory perception
		Poor tactile and auditory perception; motor and academic deficits
McKinney, Short, & Feagans (1985)	Cluster analysis	Linguistic deficits Mixed—severe visual–perceptual, mild linguistic deficits Mixed—mild visual, linguistic deficits Normal pattern, low coding 2 normal patterns
Snow, Cohen, & Holliman (1985)	Cluster analysis	Global deficits Attention deficits Language deficits Mild language deficits 2 normal groups
Van der Vlugt & Satz (1985)	Cluster analysis	Severe global language deficits Selective language, perceptual deficits Mild global language deficits Severe global language, selective perceptual–motor deficits Global visual–perceptual–motor deficits Normal
Morris, Blashfield, & Satz (1986)	Cluster analysis	Deficient verbal skills with poor achievement, more active, emotionally reactive, increasing strengths in visual–perceptual–motor skills with age Increasing deficits in verbal–conceptual skills, below-average achievement Below-average achievement, familial component Normal, above-average achievement Normal
Shinn-Strieker (1986)	Cluster analysis	Dysphonetic Dyseidetic Mixed
Neurolinguistic models		
Aram & Nation (1975)	Q-type factor analysis	Repetition strengths Nonspecific formulation–repetition deficits Generalized low performance Phonological comprehension–formulation–repetition deficits Formulation deficits
Feagans & Appelbaum (1986)	Cluster analysis	Intact syntax Intact semantic Hyperverbal Intact narrative Superior narrative Superior syntax and semantic

(continued)

TABLE 11.5 (*continued*)

Classification models	Technique	Subtypes
Combined models		
Doehring & Hoshko (1977)	Q-type factor analysis	Linguistic deficits Phonological deficits Intersensory integration deficits Visual–perceptual deficits
Doehring, Hoshko, & Bryans (1979)	Q-type factor analysis	Linguistic deficits Phonological deficits
Thompson, Hicks, & Wilsher (1980)	Q-type factor analysis	Auditory–perceptual deficits Sequencing deficits General written language deficits Specific verbal deficits Coding deficits Visual–spatial deficits Labeling deficits
Doehring, Trites, Patel, & Fiedorowicz (1981)	Q-type factor analysis	Type O reading disability Type A reading disability Type S reading disability
Watson, Goldgar, & Ryschon (1983)	Cluster analysis	Language disabled Visual processing deficit Minimal deficits
Meacham & Fisher (1984)	Q-type factor analysis	Reading disabled Language disabled
Snow & Hynd (1985b)	Q-type factor analysis	Expressive and receptive language deficits with impaired academics Reading and spelling deficits Expressive and receptive language deficits, tactile perception problems Borderline to low-average IQ, variable adaptive behavior, no achievement or processing discrepancy
Speece (1987)	Cluster analysis	Short-term memory deficit Speed of recoding deficit Mild recoding/attention deficit Mild encoding/severe recoding deficit Marginal performance Mild memory/recoding deficit
Snow & Desch (1988)	Cluster analysis	Congenital anomalies Developmental delays Neurological dysfunction Neurological dysfunction–encephalitic subgroup Normal profile
Watson & Goldgar (1988)	Cluster analysis	Auditory processing deficits Auditory short-term memory, auditory and visual processing deficits Language deficits Auditory short-term memory and visual processing deficits

Note. Adapted from Hooper & Willis (1989). Copyright 1989 by Springer-Verlag New York, Inc. Adapted by permission.

reader is referred to Hooper and Willis (1989) and Newby and Lyon (1991) for comprehensive reviews of this literature. For the purposes of this chapter, two subtype research programs are reviewed: one that focuses on rational grouping of LD readers into subtypes on the basis of clinical observations and/or theories related to LD (Lovett, Ransby, & Barron, 1988) (see Table 11.4 for additional examples); and a second approach that exemplifies the use of empirical multivariate statistical methods to identify homogeneous subtypes of LD readers (Lyon, 1983, 1985a; Lyon et al., 1981) (see Table 11.5 for additional examples).

Rational Subtyping Methods

As an example of a rational (clinical) subtyping research program, Lovett (1984, 1987) proposed two subtypes of reading disability based on the theory that word recognition develops in three successive phases. The three phases are related to response accuracy in identifying printed words, automatic recognition without the need to "sound-out" words, followed by developmentally appropriate maximum speed as components of the reading process become consolidated in memory. Children who fail at the first phase are identified as "accuracy disabled," and those who achieve age-appropriate word recognition but are markedly deficient in the second or third phase are termed "rate disabled." The greatest strength of the Lovett subtype research program is its extensive external validation (Newby & Lyon, 1991). In a study of the two subtypes (rate-disabled versus accuracy-disabled subtype) and a normal sample matched on word recognition ability to the rate-disabled group, accuracy-disabled readers were deficient in a wide array of oral and written language areas external to the specific reading behaviors used to identify subtype members. On the other hand, rate-disabled readers' deficiencies were more restricted to deficient connected text reading and spelling (Lovett, 1987). Reading comprehension was impaired on all measures for the accuracy-disabled group and was highly correlated with word recognition skill, but the rate-disabled group was impaired on only some comprehension measures. Two additional subtype-treatment interaction studies (Lovett et al., 1988; Lovett, Ransby, Hardwick, & Johns, 1989) found some differences between accuracy- and rate-disabled groups on contextual reading, whereas word recognition improved for both groups.

Lovett's program is founded on explicit developmental reading theory, illustrates methodological robustness, and offers detailed, thoughtful alternative explanations for the complex external validation findings (Newby & Lyon, 1991). Important treatment-outcome findings are muted somewhat by clinically minimal reading gains on standardized measures in spite of statistically significant results and by the lack of significant subtype × treatment interactions (Lyon & Flynn, 1989).

Additional examples of clinical subtyping studies from achievement, neurocognitive, neurolinguistic and combined models are presented in Table 11.4.

Empirical Subtyping Methods

In a series of studies employing multivariate cluster analytic methods, Lyon and his colleagues (Lyon, 1983, 1985a, 1985b; Lyon et al., 1981, 1982; Lyon & Watson, 1981) identified six subtypes of older LD readers (11- to 12-year-old children) and five subtypes of younger LD readers (6- to 9-year-old children) on measures assessing linguistic skills, visual-perceptual skills, and memory-span abilities. The theoretical viewpoint guiding this subtype research was based on Luria's (1966, 1973) observations that reading ability is a complex behavior effected by means of a complex functional system of cooperating zones of the cerebral cortex and subcortical structures. Within the context of this theoretical framework, it could be hypothesized that a deficit in any one or several zones of the functional system could impede the acquisition of fluent reading behavior. The identification of multiple subtypes within both age cohorts suggested the possibility that several different types of LD readers exist, each characterized by different patterns of neuropsychological subskills relevant to reading acquisition.

Follow-up subtype-by-treatment interaction studies using both age samples (Lyon 1985a, 1985b) only partially supported the independence of the subtypes with respect to response to treatment. It was found, however, that subtypes characterized at both age levels by significant deficits in blending sounds, rapid naming, and memory span did not respond to intervention methods employing synthetic phonics procedures. Rather, members of this linguistic-deficit subtype first had to learn phonetically regular words by sight, and then learn the internal pho-

nological structure using the whole word as a meaningful semantic context. Again, this was true for both younger and older disabled readers within the linguistic-deficit subtype.

In summary, multiple causal models of LD in reading have been tested primarily through the use of rationale/clinical-inferential methods or through the application of multivariate statistical approaches. During the past decade, criteria for the reliability and validity of these complex subtype models have been proposed (Lyon & Flynn, 1989, 1991), and applied with some success (Newby & Lyon, 1991). An integrated analysis of several prominent reading-disability subtype systems that have been intensively investigated in recent years suggests some areas of convergence in the literature (Hooper & Willis, 1989). In particular, memory span, phonological, and orthographic processing in reading appear to be central in defining subtypes. Although a dichotomy of auditory–linguistic versus visuospatial reading disability subtypes has been commonly proposed, this division has not been effectively validated (Newby & Lyon, 1991). More recently, the field has been moving from a search for discrete subtypes toward a dimensional view of individual differences in reading development (S. Shaywitz et al., 1992). For reference, Table 11.5 presents numerous examples of empirical subtyping studies derived from achievement, neurocognitive, neurolinguistic, and combined classification models.

Single Causal Theories and Models of Reading Disabilities

In contrast to the view that word-recognition deficits can have multiple independent causes, a substantial body of evidence has accrued over the past 10 years that suggests that phonological processing deficits are the single, core etiological factor in reading disability (Stanovich, 1993) (see earlier discussion on phonological development and processing in "Phonology and Learning to Read and Spell"). The theoretical and experimental evidence for a phonological processing deficit as an explanation for LD in reading derives centrally from the work of Isabelle Liberman and her associates at the Haskins Laboratories (Brady & Shankweiler, 1991; Liberman, 1971; Shankweiler & Liberman, 1989). According to the phonological deficit theory, children with LD in reading display particular difficulties acquiring fluent word-identification skills. Such children have

great difficulty in learning to apply the "alphabetic principle" to take advantage of grapheme–phoneme correspondences in reading unfamiliar words (Torgesen, 1993). As Frith (1985) has pointed out, LD children with this key phonological deficit are often unable to attain alphabetic reading skills.

A review of the recent literature shows that LD readers with core deficits in phonological processing have difficulty segmenting phonemes, retrieving the names for common objects, letters, and the like, storing phonological codes in short-term memory, categorizing phonemes, and producing some speech sounds (Bruck & Treiman, 1990; Fletcher et al., 1994; Kamhi & Catts, 1989; Lieberman, Meskill, Chatillion, & Shupack, 1985; Lyon, 1995b; Mann, 1986; Pennington, 1986; Perfetti, 1985; Pratt & Brady, 1986; Snowling, 1987; Stanovich, 1993; Stanovich & Siegel, 1994; Torgesen, 1993; Vellutino et al., 1994; Wagner & Torgesen, 1987). As Stanovich (1993) has also pointed out, there is increasing evidence that the linkage between phonological processing ability and reading development is a casual one, and this view is supported by a number of recent studies (Adams, 1990; Ball & Blachman, 1991; Blachman, 1991; Bradley & Bryant, 1985; Lundberg, Frost, & Peterson, 1988; Stanovich, 1986, 1988; Treiman & Baron, 1983; Wagner & Torgesen, 1987; Vellutino & Scanlon, 1987).

While substantial support exists for a causal role of deficient phonological processing in reading disabilities, the unitary nature of the phonological deficit is challenged by data that suggests that some LD readers have difficulties accessing the lexicon on a visual/orthographic basis (Lyon, 1995b; Stanovich, 1992, 1993; Stanovich & West, 1989). Further, Lovegrove and his associates (Lovegrove, Martin, & Slaghuis, 1986; Martin & Lovegrove, 1988) have adduced evidence that suggests a visually based reading disability, although the data remain somewhat controversial (Hulme, 1988). In addition, other candidate linguistic and visual processes have been implicate in reading disabilities. For example, Wolf and her associates (Bowers & Wolf, 1993; Wolf, 1986, 1991; Wolf, Bally, & Morris, 1986; Wolf, Michael, & Ovrut, 1990) argue that reading deficits can also be caused by impairments in precise timing processes underlying rapid retrieval of names for visual symbols (visual naming-speed [VNS] deficits). According to Bowers and Wolf (1993), children with both VNS deficits and phonological deficits are the poorest readers, but children with

either deficit alone are significantly less capable in reading than youngsters who are phonologically adept and are rapid namers.

At present however, the clear weight of the evidence indicates that the ability to read and comprehend depends on rapid and automatic recognition and decoding of single words, and slow and inaccurate decoding are the best predictors of difficulties in reading comprehension. In turn, the ability to decode single words accurately and fluently is dependent on the ability to segment words and syllables into abstract constituent sound units (phonemes). Based on the extant data, one can conclude that for the majority of LD readers, deficits in phonological processing reflect the core deficit in reading disabilities.

The Developmental Course of LD in Reading

Reading disabilities reflect a persistent deficit rather than a developmental lag in linguistic and reading skills (Francis et al., 1994; Lyon, 1994b). Longitudinal studies show that of the children who are reading disabled in the third grade, 74% remain disabled in the ninth grade (Fletcher et al., 1993; Francis et al., 1994; Lyon, 1994; S. Shaywitz et al., 1992). Clearly these data reflect a pessimistic outcome for LD youngsters who have difficulties learning to read. However, at least three factors could be responsible for the lack of progress made by LD readers. First, because most diagnostic criteria continue to require the use of a discrepancy between IQ and reading achievement in the eligibility process, many children are not identified until the third grade—the point at which their achievement has suffered enough to demonstrate the required discrepancy between the ostensible predictor (IQ) and reading skills. As Fletcher (1992) has pointed out, initiating intervention after a child has failed for 2 to 3 years does not bode favorably for realistic gains in reading. Second, it has not yet been established which teaching interventions are most efficacious for LD readers. In addition, many of the children followed in the longitudinal studies described above were provided several different types of interventions without knowing how each intervention interacted with the next. Given this lack of systematic program planning and teaching, it is not surprising that only 20% to 25% of children make gains in reading. Unfortunately, those who did improve their reading ability were children with the least severe forms of reading disability (S. Shaywitz et al., 1992). Third, it is quite possible that the motivation to learn to read diminishes with time given the extreme effort that many disabled readers put into the learning process without success resulting in protracted periods of failure.

Epidemiology

Reading disabilities affect at least 10 million children, or approximately 1 child in 5 (S. Shaywitz et al., 1992). This figure reflects an increase over previous estimates primarily because it reflects the finding that children with and without IQ–achievement discrepancies (see "Validity of IQ–Achievement Discrepancies") are similar with respect to severity levels, etiology, and language characteristics. While schools identify approximately four times as many boys as girls as reading disabled, longitudinal and epidemiological studies show that approximately as many girls are affected as boys (DeFries et al., 1991; Lubs et al., 1991; Lyon, 1994b; S. Shaywitz et al., 1990). In the S. Shaywitz et al. (1990) epidemiological study of reading disabilities the male:female ratio was found to be 1.2:1.

Etiology of Phonologically Based Reading Disability

As noted earlier in the section "Etiological Bases for Phonological Deficits," the same neurobiological and genetic factors are linked to reading deficiency as well. This would be expected given the substantial role played by phonological abilities in the developmental reading process. To review briefly, the locus of brain dysfunction hypothesized to be responsible for phonologically based reading disorders is in the left temporal region of the brain (Lyon, 1995a). One research team has hypothesized that the particular anomalies in this area of cortex arise early in development and most likely cause the phonological processing deficit leading to LD in reading (Galaburda, 1988).

Substantial evidence derived from studies of reading-disabled twins indicates that the brain anomalies described above are related to genetic transmission. DeFries and his colleagues (Cardon et al., 1994; Defries et al., 1991; Olson et al., 1989) have further found that deficits in phonological awareness are highly heritable and that there appears to be a quantitative trait locus on chro-

mosome 6 predisposing children to LD in reading.

Common Comorbidities

Disorders of reading often co-occur with disorders of attention (ADHD, ADD) (Barkley, 1990; Shelton & Barkley, 1994), but the two disorders are distinct and separable (Lyon, 1994a, 1994b; Wood et al., 1991). As pointed out earlier in the section "Specific Learning Disabilities in Reading," reading disabilities are consistently associated with deficits in phonological awareness, whereas the effects of ADHD/ADD on cognitive functioning are variable with primary deficits noted in rote verbal learning and memory. Further, ADHD/ADD appears relatively unrelated to phonological awareness tasks (Wood et al., 1991).

A number of authors have reported that LD children with reading disabilities present with co-occurring social-emotional difficulties (Bryan, Donahue, Pearl, & Sturm, 1981; Tallal, 1988). A majority of such social–emotional difficulties appear, in some clinical studies, to be secondary to difficulties learning to read. For example, of the 93 adults in a learning-disabilities clinic population, the majority of whom displayed reading problems, 36% had received counseling or psychotherapy for low self-esteem, social isolation, anxiety, depression, and frustration (Johnson & Blalock, 1987). Likewise, others (Bruck, 1986; Cooley & Ayres, 1988; Paris & Okla, 1989) have reported that many of the emotional problems displayed by LD readers reflect adjustment difficulties resulting from labeling or academic failure. These findings point out the significant need to identify and intervene early with those children who are at risk for reading failure, given the substantial social and emotional consequences that can occur if the disability is not remediated.

Summary

A number of significant new findings relevant to LD in reading have been discussed in this section. Given the importance of these findings, selected discoveries critical for diagnosis, research, and clinical practice are summarized here. For an in depth review of these findings the reader is referred to Lyon (1995a, 1995b).

- One in five children is affected by deficits in reading.
- Reading disability reflects a persistent deficit rather than a developmental lag.
- LD readers differ from one another and from normal readers along a continuous distribution and do not aggregate together in a distinct "hump" at the tail of the distribution as previously thought.
- The gender ratio among disabled readers is no different than the gender ratio within the population as a whole.
- Accurate and fluent reading ability is dependent upon rapid and automatic recognition and decoding of words. Therefore, reading disability is best studied at the single-word level.
- Slow and inaccurate decoding and recognition of single words is a robust predictor of deficient reading comprehension.
- The etiological basis for LD readers' deficient word recognition and decoding skills appears to be a specific deficit in phonological processing. This deficit appears to be heritable and is further characterized by a distinct neurophysiological signature in the left temporal (perisylvian) region of the cortex.
- Phonological deficits appear to impede the development of basic reading abilities (decoding and word recognition) irrespective of the level of general intelligence. Poor readers, with and without IQ–reading achievement discrepancies, demonstrate impairments in the ability to segment words and syllables into abstract constituent phonemes.
- Disorders of attention and reading disability often co-occur, but the two disorders are distinct and separable.
- Intervention programs that capitalize on "code-emphasis" methodologies are superior to meaning-based, "whole-language" approaches.

Given the reliability of these findings across research programs (see Lyon, 1995b), the Orton Dyslexia Society Research Committee has constructed a new definition of dyslexia that reduces the exclusionary language inherent in all definitions of LD and dyslexia and defines dyslexia using the most current and valid research evidence available at this time. The definition is as follows:

Dyslexia is one of several distinct learning disabilities. It is a specific language-based disorder of constitutional origin characterized by difficulties in single

word decoding, usually reflecting insufficient phonological processing abilities. These difficulties in single word decoding are often unexpected in relation to age and other cognitive and academic abilities; they are not the result of generalized developmental disability or sensory impairment. Dyslexia is manifest by variable difficulty with different forms of language, often including, in addition to problems reading, a conspicuous problem with acquiring proficiency in writing and spelling. (Lyon, 1995b)

The construction of this new definition provides a good example of how research can inform both policy and practice. Note that in contrast to the definitions of learning disabilities, developmental reading disorder, and dyslexia previously discussed, the Orton Research Committee definition is composed of specific data-based inclusionary statements that can be operationalized.

SPECIFIC LEARNING DISABILITIES IN WRITTEN EXPRESSION

Historical Underpinnings

Disorders in the writing process have been discussed since the 1960s (Hooper et al., 1994), and over a century ago, Ogle (1867) used the term agraphia to describe the relationship between aphasia and agraphia, although he noted that the two disorders were dissociable. In the first half of the 20th century, Goldstein (1948), Head (1926), and others applied clinical observation and case-study methodology to explore the association and dissociation between written and oral expression. According to Hooper et al. (1994), much of the research related to disorders of written expression and agraphia continues to employ case-study methodology and, in the main, continues to rely on the study of individuals with acquired brain damage.

It has only been within the past decade that the study of disorders of written expression has risen above its status as "a poor relative of aphasia" (Shallice, 1988). For example, Wong (1991) argued that deficits in written expression are clinically important, since they are frequently associated with reading disorders and/or are governed by similar metacognitive processes to include planning, self-monitoring, self-evaluation, and self-modification. As Hooper et al. (1994) have pointed out, these more recent perspectives have contributed to an understanding that written expression and its disorders are multidimensional in nature and require detailed definition. Hooper et al. (1994) have also reported that, in the past decade, writing has been conceptualized as a complex problem-solving process reflecting the writer's declarative knowledge, procedural knowledge, and conditional knowledge, all of which is subserved by a network of neuropsychological factors, personality factors, and other conditions to include teacher–student relationships, amount of writing instruction, and the teacher's knowledge of the writing process. Within this context, declarative knowledge refers to the specific writing and spelling subskills that the learner has acquired, whereas procedural knowledge refers to the learner's competence in using such knowledge while writing for meaning.

Definitions and Diagnostic Criteria

A review of the available definitions for disorders of written expression reveals that the complexity and multidimensionality of the disorder are not reflected appropriately in any formal characterization or definition. This statement is based on the observation that there are literally no clear operational definitions of written language expression that address all components of the written language domain (see Berninger, 1994a, for a discussion of these issues). Emergent research on written language indicates that most, if not all, children with learning disabilities have problems with at least one component of writing, whether it is handwriting, spelling, written syntax, vocabulary, or written discourse (Hooper et al., 1994). No current definition identifies and defines these components in any objective or operational manner.

Perusal of the NACHC, NJCLD, and DSM-IV definitions indicates that none of them provide comprehensive and operational coverage for the diagnosis of written expression. For example, both the NACHC and NJCLD definitions, discussed above in "Problems in Establishing a Valid Definition and Classification System" refer to writing and spelling in vague and ambiguous terms that are not useful to researchers, clinicians, and teachers (see definitions on pp. 396–397). In addition, even though the NACHC definition, which was codified into Public Law 94–142, introduces the term "spelling" in the definition, most current and state guidelines for learning disabilities (with the exception of ICD-10) do not include spelling as a recognized area of dis-

ability (Moats, 1994). DSM-IV (American Psychiatric Association, 1994) continues to conceptualize developmental expressive writing disorders using vague terms that cannot be operationalized and treats the disorder as a unitary construct labeled disorder of written language (see Table 11.6).

Given the criteria presented in Table 11.6, one would be hard pressed to characterize accurately a group of children diagnosed using this highly ambiguous definition. In fact, conducting research with samples of children identified on the basis of criteria in the NACHC, NJCLD, and DSM-IV definitions discussed would result in substantially heterogeneous groups and difficulty in replicating and generalizing results.

In contrast to providing criteria for the classification of written language disorders, ICD-10 (World Health Organization, 1992) limits the identification of writing disorders to deficits in spelling under specific spelling disorder. The diagnostic guidelines are presented in Table 11.7.

Perusal of ICD-10 clinical descriptions and diagnostic guidelines (World Health Organization, 1992) indicates that the main feature of a specific spelling disorder is an impairment in the development of spelling skills in the *absence* of a history of reading problems. By dissociating spelling and reading deficits, ICD-10 provides the most circumscribed description of a writing deficit when compared to all the other definitions and guidelines reviewed thus far. Unfortunately, the isola-

TABLE 11.6. DSM-IV Diagnostic Criteria for Disorder of Written Expression

A. Writing skills, as measured by individually administered standardized tests (or functional assessments of writing skills), are substantially below that expected given the person's chronological age, measured intelligence, and age-appropriate education.

B. The disturbance in Criterion A significantly interferes with academic achievement or activities of daily living that require the composition of written texts (e.g., writing grammatically correct sentences and organized paragraphs).

C. If a sensory deficit is present, the difficulties in writing skills are in excess of those usually associated with it.

Note. From American Psychiatric Association (1994, p. 53). Copyright 1994 by the American Psychiatric Association. Reprinted by permission.

TABLE 11.7. ICD-10 Diagnostic Criteria for Specific Spelling Disorder

A. The score on a standardized spelling test is at least 2 standard errors of prediction below the level expected on the basis of the child's chronological age and general intelligence.

B. Scores on reading accuracy and comprehension and on arithmetic are within normal range (± 2 standard deviations from the mean).

C. There is no history of significant reading difficulties.

D. School experience is within the average expectable range (i.e., there have been no extreme inadequacies in educational experiences).

E. Spelling difficulties have been present from the early stages of learning to spell.

F. The disturbance described in criterion A significantly interferes with academic achievement or activities of daily living that require spelling skills.

G. *Most commonly used exclusion clause*: IQ is below 70 on an individually administered standardized test.

Note. From World Health Organization (1993, pp. 145–146). Copyright 1993 by the World Health Organization. Reprinted by permission.

tion of spelling as a major disorder leaves unattended the critical aspects of writing that are as or more important than spelling to include written language formulation, organization, thematic maturity, and the like (Berninger, 1994b).

While a number of authorities in this area have offered strategies to bolster definitions of disorders in written language (Graham, Harris, & MacCarthur, 1990; Graham, Harris, McArthur, & Schwartz, 1991; Gregg, 1991), the major criterion for this category continues to depend on the use of IQ-achievement discrepancy models (Hooper et al., 1994). As pointed out repeatedly in this chapter and elsewhere (Kavale, 1987), discrepancy models are most likely invalid and serve more to confuse diagnostic issues than to clarify them.

Characteristics, Theories, and Proposed Etiologies

Characteristics

Despite continued difficulties in establishing exact criteria for disorders of written expression and

in developing reliable and valid measures of the multiple processes involved in writing, a good deal of work has been completed on describing the characteristics of good and poor writers. For instance, several investigators (Bereiter, 1980; Berninger, 1994a, 1994b; Hays & Flower, 1980; Hooper et al., 1994) report that good writers are goal directed; they understand the purpose of the writing assignment; they have, or they develop, a good knowledge of the topic prior to writing; they generate more ideas and use significant numbers of transitional ties; they produce a more cohesive text and flow of ideas; and they continuously monitor their written products for correctness of spelling and grammar.

On the other hand, Hooper et al. (1994) and others (Englert, 1990; Graham & Harris, 1987) report that LD writers demonstrate deficits in deploying strategies during production of written text and also have problems in actually generating text. When compared to "good" writers, LD writers produce shorter and less interesting essays, produce poorly organized text at the sentence and paragraph levels, and are less likely to review spelling, punctuation, grammar, or the body of their text to increase clarity (Hooper et al., 1994).

Theoretical Models for Written Language Expression

A comprehensive review of several theoretical models of written language expression is presented by Hooper and his colleagues (Hooper et al., 1994) and by Berninger (1994b). Because of space constraints, only the theoretical model proposed by Ellis (1982) is reviewed here. According to Ellis, the writing process is described as a series of transformations between different types of representations, with the representations being stored in temporary form in a series of memory buffers. Ellis' framework is dependent on a recall hierarchy that distinguishes between graphemes (abstract letters), allographs (concrete letter formations), and graphic–motor patterns. When content information reaches the latter stage of the hierarchy, neuromotor execution can occur. In the Ellis theoretical model, different types of written language difficulties are hypothesized to correspond to deficits in different memory buffers. For example, letter transformations are assumed to occur when one is retrieving information from the graphic buffer, while letter substitutions are attributed to deficits in the graphic–motor buffer. As Hooper et al. (1994) points out, although the Ellis model makes a comprehensive case for different types of memory necessary for written language, other variables (e.g., neuropsychological) are excluded. Alternative theoretical models have been proposed by Abbot and Berninger (1993), Berninger (1994b), Hays and Flower (1980), and Roeltgen (1985).

Developmental Predictors of Written Expression

Over 25 years ago, Johnson and Myklebust (1967) presented a developmental model of language learning that posited that the ability to write is dependent upon adequate development in listening, speaking, and reading. In a series of more current studies, Berninger and her associates (Berninger, 1994a, 1994b; Berninger & Hart, 1993; Berninger et al., 1992) have reported that automaticity in the production of alphabet letters, rapid coding of orthographic information, and speed of sequential finger movements were the best predictors of handwriting and composition skills. Spelling abilities were predicted by orthographic–phonological mappings and visual–motor integration (although see Lindamood, 1994, and Moats, 1994, for alternative predictions). Berninger, Mizokawa, and Bragg (1991) have also suggested that neuropsychological, linguistic, and higher cognitive constraints may be recursive throughout the development of the writing process but that each of these constraints may exert relatively more influence at different points in the developmental process (Hooper et al., 1994).

Epidemiology

As Hooper et al. (1994) have pointed out, few epidemiological studies of disorders in written expression have been carried out. Likewise, the American Psychiatric Association (1994) explains that the prevalence for disorders of written language are difficult to establish because "many studies focus on the prevalence of Learning Disorders in general without careful separation into specific disorders of reading, mathematics, or written expression. Disorder of Written Expression is rare when not associated with other Learning Disorders" (p. 51).

Basso, Taborelli, and Vignolo (1978) reported that acquired disorders of written expression occurred infrequently at a rate of approximately 1 in every 250 subjects. However, given the high

rate of developmental language disorders in the general population (8% to 15%) and the significantly high rate of disorders in basic reading skills (15% to 20% of the general population), one could predict that written language disorders affect at least 10% of the school-age population.

Berninger and Fuller (1992) reported that more boys than girls display written language deficits when level of achievement was used as the comparison variable, but there were no gender differences when IQ–achievement criteria were used. Hooper et al. (1994) studied 30% of a middle school population that included an equal number of boys and girls and an equal number of whites and nonwhites. Of the children studied, approximately 34% to 47% fell greater than 1 standard deviation below the mean on subtests of the test of written language (Hammill & Larsen, 1988). Nonwhites evidenced spontaneous writing problems at a ratio of nearly 2:1, and boys showed a greater rate of impairment approximating a rate of 1.5:1. Clearly, both the amount and accuracy of epidemiological data are lacking, particularly in comparison to studies of oral language and reading. However, with the development of objective criteria for the assessment of components of written language, this trend should shift in the future (see Berninger, 1994b).

Etiology of Written Language Disorders

The multivariate nature of the developmental writing process suggests that disorders in written language can be referable to multiple etiologies spanning biological, genetic, psychosocial, and environmental causes. Indeed, consider that in order to express thoughts in writing, one must first formulate the idea, sequence relevant points in appropriate order, ensure that the written output is syntactically and grammatically correct, spell individual words correctly, and express the words, sentences, and passages in a legible manner via the graphomotor system.

Given this multidimensional nature of the writing process, multiple causal models for deficits in writing are the rule. For example, Gregg (1991) reported that a variety of language-based deficits in phonology and word retrieval could impair several aspects of the writing task, as could deficits in visual–spatial skills, and executive functions to include organization, planning, and evaluating. Similarly, Roeltgen (1985) has proposed that

deficits in linguistic, visual–spatial, and motor systems can interfere with the developmental writing process in distinct ways.

In addition to cognitive, linguistic, and neuropsychological etiologies, it is clear that the way in which children are taught (or not taught) to write can influence their development (Lyon, Vaasen, & Toomey, 1989; Nolen, McCutchen, & Berninger, 1990). The complexity of written language expression and its dependence on multiple correlated factors (e.g., language ability, reading ability, visual–motor skills) require that teachers understand not only the developmental conditions necessary for writing, but the content and the declarative and procedural aspects of the writing process itself. In many cases, teachers have simply not been provided with in-depth training in these areas.

Common Comorbidities

Given the complexity of the writing process and the fact that it is the last language domain to develop in children (Johnson & Myklebust, 1967; Hooper et al., 1994), it should not be surprising that deficits in written expression can co-occur with deficits in oral language, reading, and mathematics. However, as Berninger (1994a) has pointed out, the relationship between these symbol systems is by no means invariant. For example, Abbott and Berninger (1993) found that written expression could not be explained just by oral expression; receptive written language ability always contributed uniquely to expressive written language ability. In addition, the widely held view that deficits in written expression invariably co-occur with reading disorders is not substantiated. More specifically, Berninger et al. (1991) and Berninger and Hart (1992, 1993) have demonstrated that reading and writing systems can be dissociated. Some children have reading problems but not writing problems and other children have writing problems but not reading problems. As expected, many, but not all, disabled writers manifest deficits in reading.

Berninger and Abbott (1994) have found that LD children with written expression problems frequently also present with deficits in attention, executive functions, and motivation. Hooper et al. (1994) also reported that impaired writing can lead to a lack of motivation, conduct problems, or a tendency to withdraw. Hooper's group hypothesizes that difficulties producing appropriate

writing products in the classroom have the potential to result in daily embarrassment or humiliation in school. In order to cope with these negative factors, LD children with writing deficits may attempt to avoid writing tasks by engaging in inappropriate behavior.

Summary

In contrast to our current understanding of oral language and reading disorders among LD children, little is known about the etiology, developmental course, prognosis, and treatment for disorders of written expression. As Hooper et al. (1994) point out, the area of written expression requires systematic longitudinal study to increase our knowledge of possible predictors and precursors to the continuum of written language competence. In addition, an emphasis must be placed on the design of multivariate studies and the use of growth curve analyses to develop comprehensive models of written language expression, map developmental trajectories, conduct syndrome analyses, and design efficacious treatment programs (Berninger, 1994b).

SPECIFIC LEARNING DISABILITIES IN MATHEMATICS

Historical Underpinnings

Deficits in math among LD individuals have not been extensively reported in the historical literature. In general, clinicians and researchers have paid less attention to children and adults with math difficulties, possibly because illiteracy has been considered to be more of a problem to society than math deficiency (Fleishner, 1994). Given this limited historical context, Keller and Sutton (1991) have argued for a research emphasis on math abilities and performance of individuals with LD. Clearly this suggestion is warranted given that achievement in math for students in the United States has declined steadily over the past 25 years (Alexander & James, 1987). Although this trend downward cannot be entirely attributed to learning disabilities, LD is certainly a large source of the underachievement.

Definitions and Diagnostic Criteria

All current definitions of LD acknowledge that impairment in the ability to learn math should be considered as one of the major disorders subsumed within the category if certain inclusionary and exclusionary conditions are to be met. The NACHC (1968) definition adopted by the USOE (1977) refers to disabilities in mathematical calculations, whereas the NJCLD (1988) definition of LD refers to significant difficulties in math abilities (see earlier discussion of NACHC and NJCLD definitions).

DSM-IV (American Psychiatric Association, 1994) refers to deficits in math via the term mathematics disorder and provides a number of criteria to be used in the diagnostic process (see Table 11.8).

As with specific spelling disorder, ICD-10 (World Health Organization, 1992) provides research criteria for the identification of individuals with deficits in a highly specific domain termed specific disorder of arithmetical skills (see Table 11.9).

Similar to the criteria presented for disorders of spelling, Table 11.9 indicates that the diagnosis of disorders of arithmetical skills is appropriate when such weaknesses occur against a background of normal reading and spelling development. Again, this level of specificity via dissociation with other commonly occurring learning disorders has both positive and negative implications. While the definition is circumscribed sufficiently to permit replication and generalization of research findings, limiting the math domain to basic computational skills ignores the very important aspects of arithmetic reasoning and problem solving.

Thus definitions of LD in math, like definitions

TABLE 11.8. DSM-IV Diagnostic Criteria for Mathematics Disorder

A. Mathematical ability, as measured by individually administered standardized tests is substantially below that expected given the person's chronological age, measured intelligence, and age-appropriate education.

B. The disturbance in Criterion A significantly interferes with academic achievement or activities of daily living that require mathematical ability.

C. If a sensory deficit is present, the difficulties in mathematical ability are in excess of those usually associated with it.

Note. From American Psychiatric Association (1994, p. 51). Copyright 1994 by the American Psychiatric Association. Reprinted by permission.

TABLE 11.9. ICD-10 Diagnostic Criteria for Specific Disorder of Arithmetical Skills

A. The score on a standardized arithmetic test is at least 2 standard errors of prediction below the level expected on the basis of the child's chronological age and general intelligence.

B. Scores on reading accuracy and comprehension and on spelling are within normal range (± 2 standard deviations from the mean).

C. There is no history of significant reading or spelling difficulties.

D. School experience is within the average expectable range (i.e., there have been no extreme inadequacies in educational experiences).

E. Arithmetical difficulties have been present from the early stages of learning arithmetic.

F. The disturbance described in criterion A significantly interferes with academic achievement or activities of daily living that require arithmetical skills.

G. *Most commonly used exclusion clause*: IQ is below 70 on an individually adminstered standardized test.

Note. From World Health Organization (1993, p. 146). Copyright 1993 by the World Health Organization. Reprinted by permission.

of LD in oral language, reading, and written expression, are based upon assumptions of normal or above-average ability to learn (as assessed by IQ measures), normal sensory function, adequate educational opportunity, and absence of developmental disorders and emotional disturbance. Like all other existing definitions of LD except the definition of dyslexia provided by the Orton Dyslexia Research Committee (see Lyon, 1995b), the definitions, with the exception of the ICD-10 definition, are vague and cannot be operationalized at this time.

Because of this persistent vagueness and/or parochial nature of the quality of extant definitions, no clear objective standards have been established by which to judge the presence or absence of a learning disability in math. Adding to this dilemma is the fact that learning disabilities in math, developmental arithmetic disorder, math disabilities, and specific math disabilities are typically broad terms used for a variety of impairments in math skills. In addition, as Fleishner (1994) has pointed out, in some cases the term

math learning disability has been used synonymously with the term dyscalculia, to denote *specific* (as opposed to generalized) deficits in calculation or mathematical thinking. In these situations, there is often the assumption that oral language, reading, and writing are intact (i.e., see World Health Organization, 1992, and Strang & Rourke, 1985). However, as is discussed in the section "Common Comorbidities," math deficits are frequently associated with other learning disabilities (Fleishner, 1994).

Characteristics, Theories, and Proposed Etiologies

Characteristics

In general, children who manifest LD in math typically display deficits in arithmetic calculation and/or math reasoning abilities. Historically, characteristics in math were described under the term developmental dyscalculia, which refers to the failure to develop arithmetic competence (Novick & Arnold, 1988, p. 132). Classification of the characteristics of LD in math, or dyscalculia, was first initiated by Kosc (1974) who identified the following six subtypes:

1. *Verbal dyscalculia*—an inability to name mathematical amounts, numbers, terms, symbols, and relationships.
2. *Practognostic dyscalculia*—an inability to enumerate, compare, and mathematically manipulate objects, either pictured or real.
3. *Lexical dyscalculia*—a disorder in reading mathematical symbols.
4. *Graphical dyscalculia*—a disability in writing mathematical symbols.
5. *Ideognostical dyscalculia*—a disorder in understanding mathematical concepts and in performing calculations mentally.
6. *Operational dyscalculia*—a disability in performing computational operations.

Kosc (1974) hypothesized that these variants of math disability were a function of a congenital structural disorder of cortical regions of the brain involved in math abilities. To date, however, that has been no evidence to suggest that these subtypes are either distinct or their deficiencies are associated with specific cortical regions. It is clear from Kosc's (1974) description of the characteristics of each type, that children diagnosed with LD in math today would most likely manifest

difficulties similar to those observed in ideognostical dyscalculia and/or operational dyscalculia.

More recent attempts to characterize the population of children who manifest LD in math have been made by Rourke and his associates. For example, Rourke and Finlayson (1978) Rourke and Strang (1978), and Ozols and Rourke (1988) identified different patterns of performance on verbal–auditory and visual–spatial skills of LD children who either: (1) had low achievement on all subtests of the Wide Range Achievement Test (WRAT); (2) had low achievement in reading and spelling, but not in arithmetic; and (3) had low achievement in arithmetic relative to reading and spelling scores. In the main, those children with low arithmetic performance relative to reading and spelling, demonstrated high scores on auditory–verbal measures, with low scores on visual–perceptual and visual–spatial measures. These same patterns of performance have now been identified for children ranging from 7 to 14 years of age (Keller & Sutton, 1991). Rourke's data clearly support the long-held belief that deficits on arithmetic calculation tasks or math reasoning tasks are highly associated with deficiencies in visual–perceptual, visual–spatial domains (Novick & Arnold, 1988; Rourke, 1985).

Other subtyping schemes have been proposed by Nolan, Hammeke, and Barkley (1983), Spreen and Haaf (1986), and Ackerman, Anhalt, and Dykman (1986). The Nolan et al. (1983) and Ackerman et al. (1986) investigations did not show subtype differences in shape or severity of patterns of performance. However, Spreen and Haaf (1986) adduced data supporting a distinct arithmetic subtype, thus lending some support to Rourke's (1985) hypothesis.

In a more general vein, it is known that achievement in math is related to other attributes in addition to visual–spatial and visual–perceptual ability. For example, Aiken (1971) found clear relationships between math achievement and general intelligence and verbal ability. In addition, Kulm (1980) reported strong correlations between math performance and affective characteristics such as attitude, interest, and anxiety.

Theories and Etiologies of LD in Math

A number of neuropsychological theories of math disabilities are directly tied to an etiological focus. For example, Novick and Arnold (1988) hypothesized that neuropsychological deficits in posterior right hemisphere regions are highly associated with deficits in comprehension and production of written math because of the high loading on visual–spatial capabilities. Conversely, the performance of math reasoning tasks appears more related to those posterior secondary and tertiary cortical regions that subserve linguistic comprehension and the analysis of relationships among ideas. This particular set of theoretical hypotheses is not notably different from that proposed by Luria (1973).

Gaddes (1985) and Novick and Arnold (1988) have argued that children who display difficulties in doing rapid calculations, conceptualizing abstract information, and solving problems have neuropsychological deficits that are referable to deficiencies in the frontal lobes. Gaddes (1985) implicated deficits in the temporal lobes in children who display poor auditory–verbal memory for math. The reader is referred to Gaddes (1985), Keller and Sutton (1991), and Novick and Arnold (1988) for comprehensive reviews of the literature related to neuropsychological theories and proposed etiologies. It would be safe to say at this time, however, that both neuropsychological and cognitive theories of math performance are in their emerging stages.

Many clinicians and researchers believe that the most significant etiological factor in disabilities in math relates to poor teaching. Russell and Ginsburg (1984) found that teachers were not adequately prepared in math principles themselves, much less in how to teach them. This finding was replicated by Lyon et al. (1989) in studies of both classroom teachers and special educators. Carnine (1991) and Russell and Ginsburg (1984) have also found that math textbooks are frequently confusing for LD and achieving students alike. In his evaluation of math textbooks, Carnine (1991) concluded that textbook organization and coverage almost ensured that teachers had to teach too many math concepts in a rapid and superficial manner. As such, students do not have the time and practice to attain mastery of the concepts, procedures, or algorithms that are introduced.

Epidemiology

As Fleishner (1994) has pointed out, efforts to establish the prevalence of math learning disabilities have produced similar estimates. For example, Badian and Ghublikian (1983), Kosc (1974), McKinney and Feagans (1984), and Norman and Zigmond (1980) have all reported that

approximately 6% of school-age children have some form of LD in math. Children with LD in math can be identified early in schooling, and their difficulties tend to persist through adolescence (Cawley & Miller, 1989). A number of studies have also found gender differences in math performance and achievement (see Stanley, Brody, Dauber, Lupowski, & Benbow, 1987), although the direction and source of the differences is not clear (Fleishner, 1994).

Common Comorbidities

Fleishner (1994) has reported that math learning disabilities often co-occur with deficits in reading, writing, and/or spoken language. She and others make the point however that when comorbidity occurs to this degree, LD in math should not be construed to be a selective impairment but, rather, a feature of a generalized problem in learning (Feagans & McKinney, 1981; Fleishner & Frank, 1979). However, B. Shaywitz, Shaywitz, and Fletcher (1992) have found in their classification studies that children who manifest specific LD in math are likely also to display more disorders of attention than children with reading or writing deficits.

During the past 15 years, Rourke and his colleagues (Casey, Rourke, & Picard, 1991; Rourke, 1987, 1988, 1989, 1995) have been attempting to identify the features of the syndrome of nonverbal learning disabilities (NLD). Within this process, these investigators have uncovered a replicable set of features that appear to co-occur with deficiencies in mechanical arithmetic. Specifically, the NLD syndrome, in addition to being characterized by math deficiencies, is marked by bilateral tactile deficits (more observable on the left side of the body), bilateral psychomotor coordination deficiencies (more observable on the left side), deficiencies in visual–spatial–organizational abilities, deficits in nonverbal problem solving and concept formation, well-developed verbal capabilities, difficulties in adapting to novel and complex situations, significant deficits in social perception and social interaction skills, and a tendency to communicate in a rote repetitive manner (see Rourke, 1995, for a comprehensive discussion of these features). Although still in an early stage of development, the NLD syndrome model has significant implications for addressing the neuropsychological basis for deficits in math and comorbidities that may be useful in predicting accuracy of diagnosis and response to treatment.

Summary

As with the review of learning disabilities in written language, solid research in LD in math is just beginning to emerge. A major difficulty in diagnosing math learning disabilities is that learning math concepts is, more than any other content area, tied closely to the teacher's knowledge and the way the concepts are presented. It is clear however that approximately 6% of school-aged children demonstrate some form of math deficit that cannot be attributed to sociocultural factors, poor instruction, low intelligence, or substantial comorbidity. Recent research applied to pure math disabilities (Rourke, 1989) holds promise in explicating neuropsychological and cognitive factors associated with this type of learning disability.

CONCLUSIONS

This chapter has attempted to provide a review of the most recent research related to LD in children. Within this context, it can be clearly noted that the most productive research in LD has been carried out in the language and reading areas and particularly in the study of the relationship between specific linguistic skills such as phonological processing and word recognition abilities. Substantial gaps continue to exist in our knowledge of written language and math disabilities, particularly with respect to their etiologies, developmental course, and treatment.

A major advance that has occurred within the past decade in learning disabilities research has been the emphasis on conducting prospective, longitudinal studies to develop valid classification systems and definitions. This approach to classification and definition does not assume an a priori identification of children with LD but, rather, requires the identification of large representative cohorts of preschool children who are followed for a period of at least 5 years. During this period, the children are administered a number of theoretically and conceptually grounded measures of cognitive, linguistic, academic, neurophysiological, and attentional skills at intervals of 6 months or 1 year. By conducting studies of these unselected samples, problems associated with school-identified and clinic-referred samples are controlled, and the emergence of abilities, disabilities, and comorbidities can be operationally defined and classified. Clearly with this type of methodology, substantial progress has been made in the classification and definition of LD in read-

ing. These findings should provide a stable context for additional epidemiological studies on various other LDs (written language, math) and allow better data to be gathered on their prevalence, developmental course, and response to various interventions.

Certainly one research direction of the future lies in the design and conduct of intervention studies for all types of LD. Historically, little emphasis has been placed on understanding which specific types of interventions or combination of interventions are most efficacious for well-defined groups of children with LD. This trend is changing, with major new treatment initiatives being sponsored by the National Institute of Child Health and Human Development (Lyon, 1995a). As the data from these and new studies accrue, relationships among cognitive, neuropsychological, linguistic, and behavioral attributes and response to treatment will be possible. Given these data, the selection of particular treatment methodologies for particular children will be possible.

REFERENCES

Abbott, R. D., & Berninger, V. W. (1993). Structural equation modelling of relationships among developmental skills and writing skills in primary- and intermediate-grade writers. *Journal of Educational Psychology, 85*, 478–508.

Ackerman, P. T., Anhalt, J. M., & Dykman, R. A. (1986). Arithmetic automatization failure in children with attention and reading disorders: Associations and sequelae. *Journal of Learning Disabilities, 19*, 222–232.

Adams, M. J. (1990). *Beginning to read: Thinking and learning about print.* Cambridge, MA: MIT Press.

Aiken, L. R. (1971). Intellective variables and mathematics achievement: Directions for research. *Journal of School Psychology, 9*, 201–212.

Alexander, L., & James, H. T. (1987). *The nation's report card.* Cambridge, MA: National Academy of Education.

American Psychiatric Association. (1994). *Diagnostic and statistical manual of mental disorders* (4th ed.). Washington, DC: Author.

Aram, D. M., & Nation, J. E. (1975). Patterns of language behavior in children with developmental language disorders. *Journal of Speech and Hearing Research, 18*, 229–241.

Badian, N. A., & Ghublikian, M. (1983). The personal-social characteristics of children with poor mathematical computation skills. *Journal of Learning Disabilities, 16*, 154–157.

Bakker, D. J. (1979). Perceptual asymmetries and reading proficiency. In M. Bortner (Ed.), *Cognitive growth and development* (pp. 134–152). New York: Brunner/Mazel.

Bakker, D. J. (1988, July). *Neuropsychological treatment of dyslexia subtypes.* Paper presented at symposium "Subtyping in Developmental Dyslexia" at the 11th European conference of the International Neuropsychological Society, Lahti, Finland.

Ball, E. W., & Blachman, B. A. (1988). Phoneme segmentation training: Effect on reading readiness. *Annals of Dyslexia, 38*, 208–225.

Ball, E. W., & Blachman, B. A. (1991). Does phoneme awareness training in kindergarten make a difference in early word recognition and developmental spelling? *Reading Research Quarterly, 26*, 49–66.

Barkley, R. A. (1990). *Attention-deficit hyperactivity disorder: A handbook for diagnosis and treatment.* New York: Guilford Press.

Basso, A., Taborelli, A., & Vignolo, L. A. (1978). Dissociated disorders of speaking and writing in aphasia. *Journal of Neurology, Neurosurgery, and Psychiatry, 41*, 556–563.

Bastian, H. C. (1898). *Aphasia and other speech defects.* London: H. K. Lewis.

Bereiter, C. (1980). Toward a developmental theory of writing. In L. W. Gregg & E. R. Steinberg (Eds.), *Cognitive processes in writing* (pp. 73–93). Hillsdale, NJ: Erlbaum.

Berninger, V. W. (1994a). Future directions for research on writing disabilities: Integrating endogenous and exogenous variables. In G. R. Lyon (Ed.), *Frames of reference for the assessment of learning disabilities: New views on measurement issues* (pp. 419–439). Baltimore: Brookes.

Berninger, V. W. (1994b). *Reading and writing acquisition: A developmental neuropsychological perspective.* Madison, WI: Brown & Benchmark.

Berninger, V. W., & Abbott, R. D. (1994). Redefining learning disabilities: Moving beyond aptitude–achievement discrepancies to failure to respond to validated treatment protocols. In G. R. Lyon (Ed.), *Frames of reference for the assessment of learning disabilities: New views on measurement issues* (pp. 163–184). Baltimore: Brookes.

Berninger, V. W., & Fuller, F. (1992). Gender differences in orthographic, verbal, and compositional fluency: Implications for assessing writing disabilities in primary grade children. *Journal of School Psychology, 30*, 363–382.

Berninger, V. W., & Hart, T. (1992). A developmental neuropsychological perspective for reading and writing acquisition. *Educational Psychologist, 27*, 415–434.

Berninger, V. W., & Hart, T. (1993). From research to clinical assessment of reading and writing disorders: The unit of analysis problem. In R. M. Joshi & C. K. Leong (Eds.), *Reading disabilities: Diagnosis and component processes* (pp. 33–61). Dordrecht, The Netherlands: Kluver Academic.

Berninger, V. W., Mizokowa, D. T., & Bragg, R. (1991). Theory-based diagnosis and remediation of writing disabilities. *Journal of School Psychology, 29*, 57–79.

Berninger, V. W., Yates, C., Cartwright, A., Ruthberg, J., Remy, E., & Abbott, R. (1992). Lower-level developmental skills in beginning writing. *Reading and Writing: An Interdisciplinary Journal, 4*, 257–280.

Berry, M. F., & Eisenson, J. (1956). *Speech disorders: Principles and practices of therapy.* New York: Appleton-Century-Crofts.

Blachman, B. A. (1991). Getting ready to read. In J. F. Kavanagh (Ed.), *The language continuum: From infancy to literacy* (pp. 41–62). Parkton, MD: York Press.

Blashfield, R. K. (1993). Models of classification as related to a taxonomy of learning disabilities. In G. R. Lyon, D. B. Gray, J. F. Kavanagh, & N. A. Krasnegor (Eds.), *Better understanding learning disabilities: New views from research and their implications for education and public policies* (pp. 17–26). Baltimore: Brookes.

Blashfield, R. K., & Draguns, J. G. (1976). Towards a taxonomy of psychopathology. The purposes of psychiatric classification. *British Journal of Psychiatry, 129*, 574–583.

Boder, E. (1970). Developmental dyslexia: A new diagnostic approach based on the identification of three subtypes. *The Journal of School Health, 40*, 289–290.

Boder, E. (1973). Developmental dyslexia: A diagnostic approach based on three atypical reading–spelling patterns. *Developmental Medicine and Child Neurology, 15*, 663–687.

Bowers, P., & Wolf, M. (1993). Theoretical links among naming speed, precise timing mechanisms, and orthographic skill in dyslexia. *Reading and Writing, 5,* 69–86.

Bradley, L., & Bryant, P. (1983). Categorizing sounds and learning to read. *Nature, 30,* 419–421.

Bradley, L., & Bryant, P. (1985). *Rhyme and reason in reading and spelling.* Ann Arbor: University of Michigan Press.

Brady, S. A., & Shankweiler, D. P. (Eds.). (1991). *Phonological processes in literacy.* Hillsdale, NJ: Erlbaum.

Broca, P. P. (1863). Localisation des fonctions cérébrales: Siège du langage articule. *Bulletin de la Société d'Anthropoligie de Paris, 4,* 200–203.

Broca, P. P. (1865). Sur la siège du faculté de langage articule. *Bulletin de la Société d'Anthropoligie de Paris, 6,* 377–393.

Bruck, M. (1985). The adult functioning of children with specific learning disabilities. In I. Sigel (Ed.), *Advances in applied developmental psychology* (Vol. 1, pp. 91–129). Norwood, NJ: Apex.

Bruck, M. (1986). Social and emotional adjustments of learning disabled children: A review of the issues. In S. J. Ceci (Ed.), *Handbook of cognitive, social and neuropsychological aspects of learning disabilities* (pp. 361–380). Hillsdale, NJ: Erlbaum.

Bruck, M. (1988). The word-recognition and spelling of dyslexic children. *Reading Research Quarterly, 23,* 51–69.

Bruck, M., & Treiman, R. (1990). Phonological awareness and spelling in normal children and dyslexics: The case of initial consonant clusters. *Journal of Experimental Child Psychology, 50,* 156–178.

Bryan, T. H., Donahue, M., Pearl, T., & Sturm, C. (1981). Learning disabled conversational skills—the T.V. talk show. *Learning Disabilities Quarterly, 4,* 250–259.

Cantwell, D. P., Baker, L., & Mattison, R. E. (1980). Factors associated with the development of psychiatric disorder in children with speech and language retardation. *Archives of General Psychiatry, 37,* 423–426.

Cardon, L. R., Smith, S. D., Fulker, D. W., Kimberling, W. J., Pennington, B. F., & DeFries, J. C. (1994). Quantitative trait locus for reading disability on chormosome 6. *Science, 268,* 276–279.

Carnine, D. (1991). Reforming mathematics instruction: The role of curriculum materials. *Journal of Behavioral Education, 1,* 37–57.

Casey, J. E., Rourke, B. P., & Picard, E. M. (1991). Syndrome of nonverbal learning disabilities: Age differences in neuropsychological, academic, and socioemotional function. *Development and Psychopathology, 3,* 331–347.

Catts. W. (1986). Speech production//phonological deficits in reading-disordered children. *Journal of Learning Disabilities, 19,* 504–508.

Cawley, J. F., & Miller, J. H. (1989). Cross-sectional comparisons of the mathematical performance of children with learning disabilities: Are we on the right track toward comprehensive programming? *Journal of Learning Disabilities, 22,* 250–259.

Clairborne, J. H. (1906). Types of congenital symbol amblyopia. *Journal of the American Medical Association, 47,* 1813–1816.

Coles, G. (1987). *The learning mystique: A critical look at learning disabilities.* New York: Pantheon Press.

Cooley, E. J., & Ayers, R. R. (1988). Self-concept and success–failure attributions of nonhandicapped students and students with learning disabilities. *Journal of Learning Disabilities, 21,* 174–178.

Cruickshank, W. M., Bentzen, F. A., Ratzburg, F. H., & Tannenhauser, M. T. (1961). *A teaching method for brain-injured and hyperactive children.* Syracuse, NY: Syracuse University Press.

Cruickshank, W. M., Bice, H. V., & Wallen, N. E. (1957). *Perception and cerebral palsy.* Syracuse, NY: Syracuse University Press.

Decker, S. N., & DeFries, J. C. (1981). Cognitive ability profiles in families of reading-disabled children. *Developmental Medicine and Child Neurology, 23,* 217–227.

DeFries, J. C., & Gillis, J. J. (1991). Etiology of reading deficits in learning disabilities: Quantitative genetic analyses. In J. E. Obrzut & G. W. Hynd (Eds.), *Neuropsychological foundations of learning disabilities: A handbook of issues, methods, and practice* (pp. 29–48). San Diego: Academic Press.

DeFries, J. C., Olson, R. K., Pennington, B. F., & Smith, S. D. (1991). Colorado reading project: An update. In D. Duane & D. Gray (Eds.), *The reading brain: The biological basis of dyslexia* (pp. 53–87). Parkton, MD: York Press.

de Hirsch, K., Jansky, J., & Langsford, W. (1965). *Predicting reading failure.* New York: Harper & Row.

DeLucca, J., Del Dotto, J., & Rourke, B. P. (1987). Subtypes of arithmetic disabled children: A neuropsychological taxonomic approach. *Journal of Clinical and Experimental Neuropsychology, 9,* 26.

Doehring, D. G., & Hoshko, I. M. (1977). Classification of reading problems by the Q-technique of factor analysis. *Cortex, 13,* 281–294.

Doehring, D. G., Hoshko, I. M., & Bryans, B. N. (1979). Statistical classification of children with reading problems. *Journal of Clinical Neuropsychology, 1,* 5–16.

Doehring, D. G., Trites, R. L., Patel, P. G., & Fiedorowicz, A. M. (1981). *Reading disabilities: The interaction or reading, language, and neuropsychological deficits.* New York: Academic Press.

Doris, J. L. (1993). Defining learning disabilities: A history of the search for consensus. In G. R. Lyon, D. B Gray, J. F. Kavanagh, & N. A. Krasnegor (Eds.), *Better understanding learning disabilities: New Views from research and their implications for education and public policies* (pp. 97–116). Baltimore: Brookes.

Ellis, A. W. (1982). Spelling and writing (and reading and speaking). In W. W. Ellis (Ed.), *Normality and pathology in cognitive functions* (pp. 113–146). London: Academic Press.

Englert, C. S. (1990). Unraveling the mysteries of writing through strategy instruction. In T. E. Scruggs & B. Y. L. Wong (Eds.), *Intervention research in learning disabilities* (pp. 220–262). New York: Springer-Verlag.

Feagans, L., & Appelbaum, M. I. (1986). Language subtypes and their validation in learning disabled children. *Journal of Educational Psychology, 78,* 358–364.

Feagans, L., & McKinney, J. D. (1981). The pattern of exceptionality across domains in learning disabled children. *Journal of Applied Developmental Psychology, 1,* 313–328.

Feagans, L., Short, E., & Meltzer, L. (1991). *Subtypes of learning disabilities.* Hillsdale, NJ: Erlbaum.

Felton, R. H., & Brown, I. S. (1991). Neuropsychological prediction of reading disabilities. In J. E. Obrzut & G. W.

Hynd (Eds.), *Neuropsychological foundations of learning disabilities: A handbook of issues, methods, and practice* (pp. 387–410). New York: Academic Press.

Filipek, P., & Kennedy, D. (1991). Magnetic resonance imaging: Its role in developmental disorders. In D. D. Duane & D. B. Gray (Eds.), *The reading brain: The biological basis of dyslexia* (133–160). Parkton, MD: York Press.

Fisk, J. L., & Rourke, B. P. (1979). Identification of subtypes of learning disabled children at three age levels: A neuropsychological multivariate approach. *Journal of Clinical Neuropsychology, 1,* 289–310.

Fleishner, J. E. (1994). Diagnosis and assessment of mathematics learning disabilities. In G. R. Lyon (Ed.), *Frames of reference for the assessment of learning disabilities: New views on measurement issues* (pp. 441–458). Baltimore: Brookes.

Fleishner, J. E., & Frank, B. (1979). Visual-spatial ability and mathematics achievement in learning disabled and normal boys. *Focus on Learning Problems in Mathematics, 1,* 7–22.

Fletcher, J. M. (1992). The validity of distinguishing children with language and learning disabilities according to discrepancies with IQ: Introduction to the special series. *Journal of Learning Disabilities, 25,* 546–548.

Fletcher, J. M., Francis, D. J., Rourke, B. P., Shaywitz, S. E., & Shaywitz, B. A. (1992). The validity of discrepancy-based definitions of reading disabilities. *Journal of Learning Disabilities, 25,* 55–61.

Fletcher, J. M., Francis, D. J., Rourke, B. P., Shaywitz, S. E., & Shaywitz, B. A. (1993). Classification of learning disabilities: Relationships with other childhood disorders. In G. R. Lyon, D. B. Gray, J. F. Kavanagh, & N. A. Krasnegor (Eds.), *Better understanding learning disabilities: New views from research and their implications for education and public policies* (pp. 27–56). Baltimore: Brookes.

Fletcher, J. M., & Morris, R. (1986). Classification of disabled learners: Beyond exclusionary definitions. In S. J. Cici (Ed.), *Handbook of cognitive, social, and neuropsychological aspects of learning disabilities* (pp. 55–80). Hillsdale, NJ: Erlbaum.

Fletcher, J. M., Shaywitz, S. E., Shankweiler, D., Katz, L., Liberman, I. Y., Steubing, K. K., Francis, D. J., Fowler, A. F., & Shaywitz, B. A. (1994). Cognitive profiles of reading disability: Comparisons of discrepancy and low achievement definitions. *Journal of Educational Psychology, 86,* 6–23.

Francis, D. J., Shaywitz, S. E., Steubing, K. K., Shaywitz, B. A., & Fletcher, J. M. (1994). Measurement of change: Assessing behavior over time and within a developmental context. In G. R. Lyon (Ed.), *Frames of reference for the assessment of learning disabilities: New views on measurement issues* (pp. 29–58). Baltimore: Brookes.

Frith, U. (1985). Beneath the surface of developmental dyslexia. In K. Patterson, J. Marshall, & M. Colheart (Eds.), *Surface dyslexia* (pp. 301–330). London: Erlbaum.

Gaddes, W. H. (1985). *Learning disabilities and brain function: A neuropsychological approach.* New York: Springer-Verlag.

Galaburda, A. M. (1988). The pathogenesis of childhood dyslexia. In F. Plum (Ed.), *Language, communication, and the brain* (pp. 22–64). New York: Raven Press.

Gerber, A. (1993). *Language-related learning disabilities: Their nature and treatment.* Baltimore: Brookes.

Gleitman, L. R., & Rosen, P. (1973). Teaching reading by use of a syllabary. *Reading Research Quarterly, 8,* 447–483.

Goldstein, K. (1948). *Language and language disorders.* New York: Grune & Stratton.

Goodman, K. (1986). *What's whole about whole language?* Portsmouth, NH: Heinemann.

Goodman, K. S. (1969). Words and morphemes in reading. In K. S. Goodman & J. Fleming (Eds.), *Psycholinguistics and the teaching of reading* (pp. 3–36). Newark, DE: International Reading Association.

Graham, S., & Harris, K. (1987). Improving composition skills of inefficient learners with self-instructional strategy training. *Topics in Language Disorders, 7,* 67–77.

Graham, S., Harris, K., & MacArthur, C. (1990). [Learning disabled and normally achieving students' knowledge of the writing process]. Unpublished raw data.

Graham, S., Harris, K., MacArthur, C., & Schwartz, S. (1991). Writing and writing instruction with students with learning disabilities: A review of a program of research. *Learning Disability Quarterly, 14,* 89–114.

Gregg, N. (1991). Disorders of written expression. In A. Bain, L. Bailet, & L. Moats (Eds.), *Written language disorders: Theory into practice* (pp. 65–97). Austin, TX: Pro-ed.

Gresham, F. M. (1986). Conceptual issues in the assessment of social competence in children. In P. Strain, M. Guralink, & H. Walker (Eds.), *Children's social behavior: Development, assessment, and modification* (pp. 143–186). New York: Academic Press.

Gross-Glenn, K., Duara, R., Yoshii, F., Baker, W., Chen, Y., Apicella, A., Boothe, T., & Lubs, H. (1986). PET-scan studies during reading in dyslexic and non-dyslexic adults. *Society for Neuroscience Abstracts, 12,* 1364.

Hallahan, D. P., & Cruickshank, W. M. (1973). *Psychoeducational foundations of learning disabilities.* Englewood Cliffs, NJ: Prentice-Hall.

Hammill, D. D. (1993). A brief look at the learning disabilities movement in the United States. *Journal of Learning Disabilities, 26,* 295–310.

Hammill, D. D., & Larsen, S. (1988). *Test of written language—Revised.* Austin, TX: Pro-ed.

Hammill, D. D., Leigh, J., McNutt, G., & Larsen, S. (1981). A new definition of learning disabilities. *Journal of Learning Disabilities, 4,* 336–342.

Hays, J. R., & Flower, L. S. (1980). Identifying the organization of the writing process. In L. W. Gregg & E. R. Steinberg (Eds.), *Cognitive processes in writing* (pp. 3–30). Hillsdale, NJ: Erlbaum.

Hazel, S., & Shumaker, J. B. (1988). Social skills and learning disabilities: Recommendations for future research. In J. F. Kavanagh & T. Truss (Eds.), *Learning disabilities: Proceedings of the national conference* (pp. 293–344). Parkton, MD: York Press.

Head, H. (1926). *Aphasia and kindred disorders of speech.* London: Cambridge University Press.

Hinshelwood, J. (1895). Word-blindness and visual memory. *Lancet, 2,* 1564–1570.

Hinshelwood, J. (1900). Congenital word-blindness. *Lancet, 1,* 1506–1508.

Hinshelwood, J. (1917). *Congenital word-blindness.* London: H. K. Lewis.

Hooper, S. R., Montgomery, J., Swartz, C., Reed, M., Sandler, A., Levine, M., & Watson, T. (1994). Measurement of written language expression. In G. R. Lyon (Ed.), *Frames of reference for the assessment of learning disabilities: New views on measurement issues* (pp. 375–418). Baltimore: Brookes.

Hooper, S. R., Montgomery, J., Swartz, C., Reed, M., Sand-

ler, A., Levine, M., Watson, T., & Wasileski, T. (1994). Measurement of written language. In G. R. Lyon (Ed.), *Frames of reference for the assessment of learning disabilities: New views on measurement issues* (pp. 375–418). Baltimore: Brookes.

Hooper, S. R., & Willis, W. G. (1989). *Learning disability subtyping: Neuropsychological foundations, conceptual models, and issues in clinical differentiation.* New York: Springer-Verlag.

Hulme, C. (1988). The implausibility of low-level visual deficits as a cause of children's reading difficulties. *Cognitive Neuropsychology, 5,* 369–374.

Hynd, G. W., & Willis, W. G. (1988). *Pediatric neuropsychology.* Orlando, FL: Grune & Stratton.

Jackson, E. (1906). Developmental alexia. *American Journal of Medical Science, 131,* 843–849.

Johnson, D. J., & Blalock, J. (Eds.). (1987). *Adults with learning disabilities.* Orlando, FL: Grune & Stratton.

Johnson, D. J., & Myklebust, H. (1967). *Learning disabilities: Educational principles and practices.* New York: Grune & Stratton.

Jorm, A. F., & Share, D. L. (1983). Phonological reading and acquisition. *Applied Psycholinguistics, 4,* 103–147.

Joschko, M., & Rourke, B. P. (1985). Neuropsychological subtypes of learning-disabled children who exhibit the ACID pattern on the WISC. In B. P. Rourke (Ed.), *Neuropsychology of learning disabilities: Essentials of subtype analysis* (pp. 65–88). New York: Guilford Press.

Kamhi, A. G., & Catts, H. W. (1989). *Reading disabilities: A developmental language perspective.* Boston: College-Hill Press.

Kamhi, A. G., Catts, H. W., Mauer, D., Apel, K., & Gentry, B. F. (1988). Phonological and spatial processing abilities in language- and reading-impaired children. *Journal of Learning Disabilities, 53,* 316–327.

Kavale, K. (1987). Theoretical issues surrounding severe discrepancy. *Learning Disabilities Research, 3,* 12–20.

Kavale, K., & Forness, S. (1985). *The science of learning disabilities.* San Diego, CA: College-Hill Press.

Kavale, K. A., & Nye, C. (1981). Identification criteria for learning disabilities: A survey of the research literature. *Learning Disability Quarterly, 4,* 383–388.

Kavanagh, J. F., & Truss, T. J. (Eds.). (1988). *Learning disabilities: Proceedings of the national conference.* Parkton, MD: York Press.

Keller, C. E., & Sutton, J. P. (1991). Specific mathematics disorders In J. E. Obrzut & G. W. Hynd (Eds.), *Neuropsychological foundations of learning disabilities: A handbook of issues, methods, and practice* (pp. 549–572). New York: Academic Press.

Keogh, B. K. (1993). Linking purpose and practice: Social/political and developmental perspectives on classification. In G. R. Lyon, D. B. Gray, J. F. Kavanagh, & N. A. Krasnegor (Eds.), *Better understanding learning disabilities: New views from research and their implications for education and public policies* (pp. 311–324). Baltimore: Brookes.

Kinsbourne, M., & Warrington, E. K. (1963). Developmental factors in reading and writing backwardness. *British Journal of Psychology, 54,* 145–146.

Kirk, S. A. (1963). Behavioral diagnosis and remediation of learning disabilities. *Conference Exploring Problems of the Perceptually Handicapped Child, 1,* 1–23.

Kirk, S. A., & Kirk, W. D. (1971). *Psycholinguistic learning disabilities: Diagnosis and remediation.* Chicago: University of Chicago Press.

Kirk, S. A., McCarthy, J. J., & Kirk, W. D. (1968). *Illinois Test of Psycholinguistic Abilities.* Urbana, IL: University of Illinois Press.

Kosc, L. (1974). Developmental dyscalculia. *Journal of Learning Disabilities, 7,* 164–177.

Kulm, G. (1980). Research on mathematics attitudes. In R. J. Shumway (Ed.), *Research in mathematics education* (pp. 356–387). Reston, VA: National Council of Teachers of Mathematics.

Kussmaul, A. (1877). Disturbance of speech. *Cyclopedia of Practical Medicine, 14,* 581–875.

Lennox, C., & Siegel, L. (1988). Visual and phonetic spellers in subtypes of children with learning disabilities. *Journal of Experimental and Clinical Neuropsychology, 10,* 91.

Leu, D. J., DeGroff, L., & Simmons, H. D. (1986). Predictable texts and interactive-compensatory hypotheses: Evaluating individual differences in reading ability, context use, and comprehension. *Journal of Educational Psychology, 78,* 347–352.

Lewis, B. A. (1990). Familial phonological disorders: Four pedigrees. *Journal of Speech and Hearing Disorders, 55,* 160–170.

Liberman, A. M., Cooper, F. S., Shankweiler, D., & Studdert-Kennedy, M. (1967). Perception of the speech code. *Psychological Review, 74,* 431–461.

Liberman, I. Y. (1971). Basic research in speech and lateralization of language. *Bulletin of the Orton Society, 21,* 72–87.

Liberman, I. Y., & Shankweiler, D. (1979). Speech, the alphabet, and teaching to read. In L. B. Resnick & P. A. Weaver (Eds.), *Theory and practice in early reading* (Vol. 2, pp. 109–134). Hillsdale, NJ: Erlbaum.

Liberman, I. Y., & Shankweiler, D. (1991). Phonology and beginning reading: A tutorial. In L. Rieben & C. A. Perfetti (Eds.), *Learning to read: Basic research and its implications* (pp. 46–73). Hillsdale, NJ: Erlbaum.

Liberman, I. Y., Shankweiler, D., Fischer, F. W., & Carter, B. (1974). Explicit syllable and phoneme segmentation in the young child. *Journal of Experimental Child Psychology, 18,* 201–212.

Liberman, I. Y., Shankweiler, D., & Liberman, A. (1989). The alphabetic principle and learning to read. In D. Shankweiler & I. Y. Liberman (Eds.), *Phonology and reading disability: Solving the reading puzzle* (pp. 1–34). Ann Arbor: University of Michigan Press.

Liberman, I. Y., Shankweiler, D., Orlando, C., Harris, K. S., & Bell-Berti, F. (1971). Letter confusions and reversals of sequence in the beginning reader: Implications for Orton's theory of developmental dyslexia. *Cortex, 7,* 127–142.

Lieberman, P., Meskill, R. H., Chatillon, M., & Schupack, H. (1985). Phonetic speech perception deficits in dyslexia. *Journal of Speech and Hearing Research, 28,* 480–486.

Lindamood, P. C. (1994). Issues in researching the link between phonological awareness, learning disabilities, and spelling. In G. R. Lyon (Ed.), *Frames of reference for the assessment of learning disabilities: New views on measurement issues* (pp. 351–374). Baltimore: Brookes.

Lovegrove, W., Martin, F., & Slaghuis, W. (1986). A theoretical and experimental case for a visual deficit in specific reading disability. *Cognitive Neuropsychology, 3,* 225–267.

Lovett, M. W. (1984). A developmental perspective on reading dysfunction: Accuracy and rate criteria in the subtyping of dyslexic children. *Brain and Language, 22,* 67–91.

Lovett, M. W. (1987). A developmental approach to reading disability: Accuracy and speed criteria of normal and deficient reading skill. *Child Development, 58,* 234–260.

Lovett, M. W., Ransby, M. J., & Barron, R. W. (1988). Treatment, subtype, and word type effects in dyslexic children's response to remediation. *Brain and Language, 34,* 328–349.

Lovett, M. W., Ransby, M. J., Hardwick, N., & Johns, M. S. (1989). Can dyslexia be treated? Treatment-specific and generalized treatment effects in dyslexic children's response to remediation. *Brain and Language, 37,* 90–121.

Lubs, H., Duara, R., Levin, B., Jallad, B., Lubs, M. L., Rabin, M., Kushch, & Gross-Glenn, K. (1991). Dyslexia subtypes: Genetics, behavior, and brain imaging. In D. D. Duane & D. B. Gray (Eds.), *The reading brain: The biological basis of dyslexia* (pp. 89–118). Parkton, MD: York Press.

Lundberg, I., Frost, J., & Peterson, O. (1988). Effects of an extensive program for stimulating phonological awareness in preschool children. *Reading Research Quarterly, 23,* 263–284.

Lundberg, I., Olofsson, A., & Wall, S. (1980). Reading and spelling skills in the first school years, predicted from phoneme awareness skills in kindergarten. *Scandinavian Journal of Psychology, 21,* 159–173.

Luria, A. R. (1966). *Higher cortical functions in man.* New York: Basic Books.

Luria, A. R. (1973). *The working brain.* New York: Basic Books.

Lyon, G. R. (1983). Learning-disabled readers: Identification of subgroups. In H. R. Myklebust (Ed.), *Progress in learning disabilities* (Vol. 5, pp. 103–134). New York: Grune & Stratton.

Lyon, G. R. (1985a). Educational validation studies of learning disability subtypes. In B. P. Rourke (Ed.), *Neuropsychology of learning disabilities: Essentials of subtype analysis* (pp. 228–256). New York: Guilford Press.

Lyon, G. R. (1985b). Identification and remediation of learning disability subtypes: Preliminary findings. *Learning Disability Focus, 1,* 21–35.

Lyon, G. R. (1987). Learning disabilities research: False starts and broken promises. In S. Vaughn & C. Bos (Eds.), *Research in learning disabilities: Issues and future directions* (pp. 69–85). San Diego, CA: College-Hill Press.

Lyon, G. R. (1988). The concept of severe discrepancy in the diagnosis of learning disabilities: Theoretical, developmental, psychometric, and educational implications. *Learning Disabilities Research, 3,* 1, 9–11.

Lyon, G. R. (1989). IQ is irrelevant to the definition of learning disabilities: A position in search of logic and data. *Journal of Learning Disabilities, 22,* 504–512.

Lyon, G. R. (Ed.).(1994a). *Frames of reference for the assessment of learning disabilities: New views on measurement issues.* Baltimore, MD: Brookes.

Lyon, G. R. (1994b). Critical issues in the measurement of learning disabilities. In G. R. Lyon (Ed.), *Frames of reference for the assessment of learning disabilities: New views on measurement issues* (pp. 3–13). Baltimore: Brookes.

Lyon, G. R. (1995a). Research initiatives and discoveries in learning disabilities. *Journal of Child Neurology, 10,* 120–126.

Lyon, G. R. (1995b). Toward a definition of dyslexia. *Annals of Dyslexia, 45,* 3–27.

Lyon, G. R. (in press-a). Foundations of neuroanatomy and neuropsychology. In G. R. Lyon & J. Rumsey (Eds.), *Neuroimaging: A window to the neurological foundations of learning and behavior.* Baltimore: Brookes.

Lyon, G. R. (in press-b). Methodological issues and strategies for assessing developmental change and evaluating response to instruction. In D. L. Speece & B. K. Keogh (Eds.), Research on classroom ecologies: Implications for children with learning disabilities. Mahweh, NJ: Erlbaum.

Lyon, G. R., & Chhabra, V. (in press). The current state of science and the future of specific reading disability. *Mental Retardation and Developmental Disabilities Research Reviews.*

Lyon, G. R., & Flynn, J. M. (1989). Educational validation studies with subtypes of learning disabled readers. In B. P. Rourke (Ed.), *Neuropsychological validation of learning disability subtypes* (pp. 243–242). New York: Guilford Press.

Lyon, G. R., & Flynn, J. M. (1991). Assessing subtypes of learning disabilities. In H. L. Swanson (Ed.), *Handbook on the assessment of learning disabilities: Theory, research, and practice* (pp. 59–74). Austin, TX: Pro-ed.

Lyon, G. R., Gray, D. B., Kavanagh, J. F., & Krasnegor, N. A. (Eds.). (1993). *Better understanding learning disabilities: New views from research and their implications for education and public policies.* Baltimore: Brookes.

Lyon, G. R., & Moats, L. C. (1988). Critical issues in the instruction of the learning disabled. *Journal of Consulting and Clinical Psychology, 56,* 830–835.

Lyon, G. R., & Moats, L. C. (1993). An examination of research in learning disabilities: Past practices and future directions. In G. R. Lyon, D. B. Gray, J. F. Kavanagh, & N. A. Krasnegor (Eds.), *Better understanding learning disabilities: New views from research and their implications for education and public policies* (pp. 1–14). Baltimore: Brookes.

Lyon, G. R., Moats, L. C., & Flynn, J. M. (1989). From assessment to treatment: Linkages to interventions with children. In M. Tramontana & S. Hooper (Eds.), *Issues in child neuropsychology: From assessment to treatment* (pp. 133–144). New York: Plenum Press.

Lyon, G. R., Rietta, S., Watson, B., Porch, B., & Rhodes, J. (1981). Selected linguistic and perceptual abilities of empirically derived subgroups of learning disabled readers. *Journal of School Psychology, 19,* 152–166.

Lyon, G. R., & Risucci, D. (1989). Classification of learning disabilities. In K. A. Kavale (Ed.), *Learning disabilities: State of the art and practice* (pp. 40–70). San Diego, CA: College-Hill Press.

Lyon, G. R., Stewart, N., & Freedman, D. (1982). Neuropsychological characteristics of empirically derived subgroups of learning disabled readers. *Journal of Clinical Neuropsychology, 4,* 343–365.

Lyon, G. R., Vaasen, M., & Toomey, F. (1989). Teachers' perceptions of their undergraduate and graduate preparation. *Teacher Education and Special Education, 12,* 164–169.

Lyon, G. R., & Watson, B. (1981). Empirically derived subgroups of learning disabled readers: Diagnostic characteristics. *Journal of Learning Disabilities, 14,* 256–261.

Mann, L. (1979). *On the trail of process.* New York: Grune & Stratton.

Mann, V. A. (1984). Longitudinal prediction and prevention of early reading difficulty. *Annals of Dyslexia, 34,* 117–136.

Mann, V. A. (1986). Why some children encounter reading problems: The contribution of difficulties with language processing and linguistic sophistication to early reading disability. In J. K. Torgesen & B. Y. Wong (Eds.), *Psychological and educational perspectives on learning disabilities* (pp. 133–159). New York: Academic Press.

Marshall, J. C. (1984). Toward a rational taxonomy of the developmental dyslexias. In R. N. Malatesha & H. A. Whitaker (Eds.), *Dyslexia: A global issue* (pp. 45–58). The Hague: Nijhoff.

Marshall, J. C., & Newcombe, F. (1973). Patterns of paralexia: A psycholinguistic approach. *Journal of Psycholinguistic Research, 2,* 175–197.

Martin, E. W. (1993). Learning disabilities and public policy: Myths and outcomes. In G. R. Lyon, D. B. Gray, J. F. Kavanagh, & N. A. Krasnegor (Eds.), *Better understanding learning disabilities: New views from research and their implications for education and public policies* (pp. 27–56). Baltimore: Brookes.

Martin, F., & Lovegrove, W. (1988). Uniform and field flicker in control and specifically-disabled readers. *Perception, 17,* 203–214.

Mattis, S., French, J. H., & Rapin, I. (1975). Dyslexia in children and adults: Three independent neuropsychological syndromes. *Developmental Medicine and Child Neurology, 17,* 150–163.

McKinney, J. D., & Feagans, L. (1984). Academic and behavioral characteristics: Longitudinal studies of learning disabled children and average achievers. *Learning Disability Quarterly, 7,* 251–265.

McKinney, J. D., Short, E. J., & Feagans, L. (1985). Academic consequences of perceptual-linguistic subtypes of learning disabled children. *Learning Disabilities Quarterly, 1,* 6–17.

Meacham, M. L., & Fisher, G. L. (1984). The identification and stability of subtypes of disabled readers. *International Journal of Clinical Neuropsychology, 4,* 269–274.

Mitterer, J. O. (1982). There are at least two kinds of poor readers: Whole word readers and recoding poor readers. *Canadian Journal of Psychology, 36,* 445–461.

Moats, L. C. (1994). The missing foundation in teacher education: Knowledge of the structure of spoken and written language. *Annals of Dyslexia, 44,* 81–102.

Moats, L. C., & Lyon, G. R. (1993). Learning disabilities in the United States: Advocacy, science, and the future of the field. *Journal of Learning Disabilities, 26,* 282–294.

Montgomery, J. W., Windsor, J., & Stark, R. E. (1991). Specific speech and language disorders. In J. E. Obrzut & G. W. Hynd (Eds.), *Neuropsychological foundations of learning disabilities: A handbook of issues, methods, and practice* (pp. 573–601). New York: Academic Press.

Morgan, W. P. (1896). A case of congenital word blindness. *British Medical Journal, 2,* 1378.

Morris, R. (1988). Classification of learning disabilities: Old problems and new approaches. *Journal of Consulting and Clinical Psychology, 56,* 789–794.

Morris, R. (1993). Issues in empirical versus clinical identification of learning disabilities. In G. R. Lyon, D. B. Gray, J. F. Kavanagh, & N. A. Krasnegor (Eds.), *Better understanding learning disabilities: New views from research and their implications for education and public policies* (pp. 73–94). Baltimore: Brookes.

Morris, R., Blashfield, R., & Satz, P. (1986). Developmental classification of reading-disabled children. *Journal of Clinical and Experimental Neuropsychology, 8,* 371–392.

Morris, R., Lyon, G. R., Alexander, D., Gray, D., Kavanagh, J., Rourke, B., & Swanson, H. (1994). Proposed guidelines and criteria for describing samples of persons with learning disabilities. *Learning Disabilities Quarterly, 17,* 106–109.

Morrison, S. R., & Siegel, L. S. (1991). Learning disabilities: A critical review of definitional and assessment issues. In J. E. Obrzut & G. W. Hynd (Eds.), *Neuropsychological foundations of learning disabilities: A handbook of issues, methods, and practice* (pp. 79–98). New York: Academic Press.

Myers, P., & Hammill, D. D. (1990). *Learning disabilities.* Austin, TX: Pro-ed.

Myklebust, H. R. (1954). *Auditory disorders in children: A manual for differential diagnosis.* New York: Grune & Stratton.

Myklebust, H. R. (1978). Toward a science of dyslexiology. In H. R. Myklebust (Ed.), *Progress in learning disabilities* (Vol. 4, pp. 1–39). New York: Grune & Stratton.

National Advisory Committee on Handicapped Children (NACHC). (1968). *Special education for handicapped children* (First annual report). Washington, DC: U.S. Department of Health, Education, and Welfare.

National Joint Committee on Learning Disabilities. (1988, April). [Letter from NJCLD to member organizations]. Austin, TX: NJCLD.

Nelson, H. E., & Warrington, E. K. (1974). Developmental spelling retardation and its relation to other cognitive abilities. *British Journal of Psychology, 65,* 265–274.

Newby, R. F., & Lyon, G. R. (1991). Neuropsychological subtypes of learning disabilities. In J. E. Obrzut & G. W. Hynd (Eds.), *Neuropsychological foundations of learning disabilities: A handbook of issues, methods, and practice* (pp. 355–385). New York: Academic Press.

Newcomer, P., & Hammill, D. D. (1976). *Psycholinguistics in the schools.* Columbus, OH: Merrill.

Nicholson, T. (1991). Do children read words better in contexts or in lists? A classic study revisited. *Journal of Educational Psychology, 83,* 444–450.

Nolan, D. R., Hammeke, T. A., & Barkley, R. A. (1983). A comparison of the patterns of the neuropsychological performance in two groups of learning disabled children. *Journal of Clinical Child Psychology, 12,* 22–27.

Nolen, P., McCutchen, D., & Berninger, V. (1990). Ensuring tomorrow's literacy: A shared responsibility. *Journal of Teacher Education, 41,* 63–72.

Norman, C. A., & Zigmond, N. (1980). Characteristics of children labeled and served as learning disabled in school systems affiliated with Child Service Demonstration Centers. *Journal of Learning Disabilities, 13,* 542–547.

Novick, B. Z., & Arnold, M. M. (1988). *Fundamentals of clinical child neuropsychology.* Philadelphia: Grune & Stratton.

Ogle, J. W. (1867). Aphasia and agraphia. *Report of the Medical Research Council of Saint George's Hospital, 2,* 83–122.

Olson, R. K. (1985). Disabled reading processes and cognitive profiles. In D. B. Gray & J. F. Kavanagh (Eds.), *Biobehavioral measures of dyslexia* (pp. 215–244). Parkton, MD: York Press.

Olson, R. K., Forsberg, H., Wise, B., & Rack, J. (1994). Measurement of word recognition, orthographic, and phonological skills. In G. R. Lyon (Ed.), *Frames of reference for the assessment of learning disabilities* (pp. 243–278). Baltimore: Brookes.

Olson, R. K., Kliegel, R., Davidson, B. J., & Foltz, G. (1985). Individual and developmental differences in reading disability. In G. E. MacKinnon & T. G. Waller (Eds.), *Reading research: Advances in theory and practice* (pp. 1–64). New York: Academic Press.

Olson, R. K., Wise, B., Connors, F., Rack, J., & Fulker, D. (1989). Specific deficits in component reading and language skills: Genetic and environmental influences. *Journal of Learning Disabilities, 22,* 239–248.

Orton, S. (1928). Specific reading disability—strephosymbolia. *Journal of the American Medical Association, 90,* 1095–1099.

Orton, S. (1937). *Reading, writing and speech problems in children: A presentation of certain types of disorders in the development of the language faculty.* New York: Norton.

Ozols, E. J., & Rourke, B. P. (1988). Characteristics of young learning-disabled children classified according to patterns of academic achievement: Auditory-perceptual and visual-perceptual abilities. *Journal of Clinical Child Psychology, 17,* 44–52.

Paris, S., & Ika, E. R. (1989). Strategies for comprehending text and coping with reading disabilities. *Learning Disabilities Quarterly, 12,* 32–42.

Pennington, B. F. (1986). Issues in the diagnosis and phenotype analysis of dyslexia: Implications for family studies. In S. D. Smith (Ed.), *Genetics and learning disabilities* (pp. 69–96). Bristol, PA: College-Hill Press.

Pennington, B. F., Gilger, J. W., Olson, R. K., & DeFries, J. C. (1992). The external validity of age- versus IQ-discrepancy definitions of reading disability: Lessons from a twin study. *Journal of Learning Disability, 25,* 562–573.

Pennington, B. F., Groisser, D., & Welsh, M. (1993). Contrasting cognitive deficits in attention deficit hyperactivity disorder versus reading disability. *Developmental Psychology, 29,* 511–523.

Perfetti, C. A. (1985). *Reading ability.* New York: Oxford University Press.

Petrauskas, R., & Rourke, B. P. (1979). Identification of subgroups of retarded readers: A neuropsychological multivariate approach. *Journal of Clinical Neuropsychology, 1,* 17–37.

Pratt, A. C., & Brady, S. (1988). Relation of phonological awareness to reading disability in children and adults. *Journal of Educational Psychology, 80,* 319–323.

Roeltgen, D. (1985). Agraphia. In K. M. Heilman & E. Valenstein (Eds.), *Clinical neuropsychology* (pp. 75–96). New York: Oxford University Press.

Rourke, B. P. (1978). Neuropsychological research in reading retardation: A review. In A. L. Benton & D. Pearl (Eds.), *Dyslexia: An appraisal of current knowledge* (pp. 240–278). New York: Oxford University Press.

Rourke, B. P. (Ed.). (1985). *Neuropsychology of learning disabilities: Essentials of subtype analysis.* New York: Guilford Press.

Rourke, B. P. (1987). Syndrome of nonverbal learning disabilities: The final common pathway of white-matter disease/dysfunction. *Clinical Neuropsychologist, 1,* 209–234.

Rourke, B. P. (1988). The syndrome of nonverbal learning disabilities: Developmental manifestations in neurological disease, disorder, and dysfunction. *Clinical Neuropsychologist, 2,* 293–330.

Rourke, B. P. (1989). *Nonverbal learning disabilities: The syndrome and the model.* New York: Guilford Press.

Rourke, B. P. (Ed.). (1995). *Syndrome of nonverbal learning disabilities: Neurodevelopmental manifestations.* New York: Guilford Press.

Rourke, B. P., & Finlayson, M. A. J. (1978). Neuropsychological significance of variations in patterns of academic performance: Verbal and visual-spatial abilities. *Journal of Pediatric Psychology, 3,* 62–66.

Rourke, B. P., & Strang J. D. (1978). Neuropsychological significance of variations in patterns of academic performance: Motor, psychomotor, and tactile perception abilities. *Journal of Pediatric Psychology, 3,* 212–225.

Rumsey, J. M. (in press). The neuroimaging of developmental dyslexia: A review and conceptualization. In G. R. Lyon & J. M. Rumsey (Eds.), *Neuroimaging: A window to the neurological foundations of learning and behavior in children.* Baltimore: Brookes.

Russell, R., & Ginsburg, H. P. (1984). Cognitive analysis of children's mathematics difficulties. *Cognition and Instruction, 1,* 217–247.

Rutter, M. (1978). Dyslexia. In A. L. Benton & D. Pearl (Eds.), *Dyslexia: An appraisal of current knowledge* (pp. 3–23). New York: Oxford University Press.

Rutter, M., & Yule W. (1975). The concept of specific reading retardation. *Journal of Child Psychology and Psychiatry, 16,* 181–197.

Satz, P., & Morris, R. (1981). Learning disability subtypes: A review. In F. J. Pirozzolo & M. C. Wittrock (Eds.), *Neuropsychological and cognitive processes in reading* (pp. 109–141). New York: Academic Press.

Senf, G. M. (1981). Issues surrounding the diagnosis of learning disabilities: Child handicap versus failure of the child–school interaction. In T. R. Kratochwill (Ed.), *Advances in school psychology* (Vol. 1, pp. 126–142). Hillsdale, NJ: Erlbaum.

Senf, G. M. (1986). LD research in sociological and scientific perspective. In J. K. Torgesen & B. Y. Wong (Eds.), *Psychological and educational perspectives on learning disabilities* (pp. 27–53). New York: Academic Press.

Senf, G. M. (1987). Learning disabilities as sociological sponge: Wiping up life's spills. In S. Vaughn & C. Bos (Eds.), *Research in learning disabilities: Issues and future directions* (pp. 87–101). Boston: Little, Brown.

Shallice, T. (1988). *From neuropsychology to mental structure.* New York: Cambridge University Press.

Shallice, T., & Warrington, E. (1980). Single and multiple component central dyslexic syndromes. In M. Colheart, K. Patterson, & J. Marshall (Eds.), *Deep dyslexia* (pp. 119–145). London: Routledge & Kegan Paul.

Shankweiler, D., & Liberman, I. Y. (Eds.). (1989). *Phonology and reading disability: Solving the reading puzzle.* Ann Arbor: University of Michigan Press.

Share, D. J., Jorm, A. F., MacLean, R., & Matthews, R. (1984). Sources of individual differences in reading achievement. *Journal of Educational Psychology, 76,* 466–477.

Shaywitz, B. A., Fletcher, J. M., Holahan, J. M., & Shaywitz, S. E. (1992). Discrepancy compared to low achievement definitions of reading disability: Results of the Connecticut longitudinal study. *Journal of Learning Disabilities, 25,* 639–648.

Shaywitz, B. A., & Shaywitz, S. E. (1994). Measuring and analyzing change. In G. R. Lyon (Ed.), *Frames of reference for the assessment of learning disabilities: New views on measurement issues* (pp. 29–58). Baltimore: Brookes.

Shaywitz, B. A., Shaywitz, S. E., & Fletcher, J. M. (1992). The Yale Center for the study of learning disabilities. *Learning Disabilities, 3,* 1–12.

Shaywitz, S. E., Escobar, M. D., Shaywitz, B. A., Fletcher, J. M., & Makuch, R. (1992). Evidence that dyslexia may represent the lower tail of a normal distribution of reading ability. *New England Journal of Medicine, 326,* 145–150.

Shaywitz, S. E., Fletcher, J. M., & Shaywitz, B. A. (1994). Issues in the definition and classification of attention deficit disorder. *Topics in Language Disorders, 14,* 1–25.

Shaywitz, S. E., Shaywitz, B. A., Fletcher, J. M., & Escobar, M. D. (1990). Prevalence of reading disability in boys and girls: Results of the Connecticut longitudinal study. *Journal of the American Medical Association, 264,* 998–1002.

Shaywitz, S. E., Shaywitz, B. A., Schnell, C., & Towle, V. R. (1988). Concurrent and predictive validity of the Yale Children's Inventory: An instrument to assess children with attentional deficits and learning disabilities. *Pediatrics, 81,* 562–571.

Shelton, T. L., & Barkley, R. A. (1994). Critical issues in the assessment of attention deficit disorders in children. *Topics in Language Disorders, 14,* 26–41.

Shinn-Strieker, T. (1986). Patterns of cognitive style in normal and handicapped children. *Journal of Learning Disabilities, 19,* 572–576.

Siegel, L. S. (1988a). Evidence that IQ scores are irrelevant to the definition and analysis of reading disability. *Canadian Journal of Psychology, 42,* 202–215.

Siegel, L. S. (1988b). Definitional and theoretical issues and research on learning disabilities. *Journal of Learning Disabilities, 21,* 264–266.

Siegel, L. S. (1989). IQ is irrelevant to the definition of learning disabilities. *Journal of Learning Disabilities, 22,* 469–478.

Siegel, L. S. (1990). IQ and learning disabilities: RIP. In H. L. Swanson & B. Keogh (Eds.), *Learning disabilities: Theoretical and research issues* (pp. 111–128). Hillsdale NJ: Erlbaum.

Siegel, L. S. (1991, July). *Phonological processing, working memory, and syntactic awareness as determinates of reading skill.* Paper presented at the International Conference on Memory, Lancaster, UK.

Siegel, L. S. (1992). An evaluation of the discrepancy definition of dyslexia. *Journal of Learning Disabilities, 25,* 618–629.

Siegel, L. S., & Ryan, E. (1988). Working memory in subtypes of learning disabled children. *Journal of Clinical and Experimental Neuropsychology, 10,* 55.

Silva, P. A., McGee, R., & Williams, S. (1985). Some characteristics of 9-year-old boys with general reading backwardness or specific reading retardation. *Journal of Child Psychology and Psychiatry, 26,* 407–421.

Skiner, H. (1981). Toward the integration of classification theory and methods. *Journal of Abnormal Psychology, 90,* 68–87.

Smith, F. (1971). *Understanding reading: A psycholinguistic analysis of reading and learning to read.* New York: Holt, Rinehart, & Winston.

Snow, J. H., Cohen, M., & Holliman, W. B. (1985). Learning disability subgroups using cluster analysis of the WISC-R. *Journal of Psychoeducational Assessment, 4,* 391–397.

Snow, J. H., & Desch, L. W. (1988). Learning disorder subgroups based on medical, developmental, and growth variables [Abstract]. *Journal of Clinical and Experimental Neuropsychology, 10,* 55–56.

Snow, J. H., & Hynd, G. W. (1985). A multivariate investigation of the Luria–Nebraska Neuropsychological Battery—Children's Revision with learning-disabled children. *Journal of Psychoeducational Assessment, 3,* 101–109.

Snowling, M. J. (1987). *Dyslexia.* Oxford, UK: Basil Blackwell.

Speece, D. L. (1987). Information processing subtypes of learning disabled readers. *Learning Disability Research, 2,* 91–102.

Speece, D. L. (1993). Broadening the scope of classification research. In G. R. Lyon, D. B. Gray, J. F. Kavanagh, & N. A. Krasnegor (Eds.), *Better understanding learning disabilities: New views from research and their implications for education and public policies* (pp. 57–72). Baltimore: Brookes.

Spreen, O., & Haaf, R. G. (1986). Empirically derived learning disability subtypes: A replication attempt and longitudinal patterns over 15 years. *Journal of Learning Disabilities, 19,* 170–180.

Stanley, J. C., Brody, L. E., Dauber, S. L., Lupowski, A. E., & Benbow, C. P. (1987). *Sex differences in cognitive abilities and achievements.* A symposium presentation at the annual meeting of the American Educational Research Association, Washington, DC.

Stanovich, K. E. (1980). Toward an interactive–compensatory model of individual differences in the development of reading fluency. *Reading Research Quarterly, 16,* 32–71.

Stanovich, K. E. (1986). Matthew effects in reading: Some consequences of individuals differences in the acquisition of literacy. *Reading Research Quarterly, 21,* 360–407.

Stanovich, K. E. (1988). Explaining the differences between the dyslexic and the garden-variety poor reader: The phonological-core variable difference model. *Journal of Learning Disabilities, 21,* 590–612.

Stanovich, K. E. (1991). Word recognition: Changing perspectives. In M. L. Kamil, P. Mosenthal, & P. D. Pearson (Eds.), *Handbook of reading research* (Vol. 2, pp. 418–452). New York: Longman.

Stanovich, K. E. (1992). Seculations on the causes and consequences of individual differences in early reading acquisition. In P. Gough, L. Ehri, & R. Treiman (Eds.), *Reading acquisition* (pp. 307–342). Hillsdale, NJ: Erlbaum.

Stanovich, K. E. (1993). The construct validity of discrepancy definitions of reading disability. In G. R. Lyon, D. B. Gray, J. F. Kavanagh, & N. A. Krasnegor (Eds.), *Better understanding learning disabilities: New views on research and their implications for education and public policies* (pp. 273–307). Baltimore: Brookes.

Stanovich, K. E. (1994). Romance and reality. *The Reading Teacher, 47,* 280–291.

Stanovich, K. E., & Siegel, L. S. (1994). Phenotypic performance profile of children with reading disabilities: A regression-based test of the phonological-core variable-difference model. *Journal of Educational Psychology, 86,* 24–53.

Stanovich, K. E., & West, R. F. (1989). Exposure to print and orthographic processing. *Reading Research Quarterly, 24,* 402–433.

Stanovich, K. E., West, R. F., & Feeman, D. J. (1981). A longitudinal study of sentence context effects in second-grade children: Tests of an interactive-compensatory model. *Journal of Experimental Child Psychology, 32,* 185–199.

Stephenson, S. (1905). Six cases of congenital word blindness affecting three generations of one family. *Opthalmoscope, 5,* 482–484.

Strang, J. D., & Rourke, B. P. (1985). Arithmetic disability subtypes: The neuropsychological significance of specific arithmetic impairment in childhood. In B. P. Rourke (Ed.), *Neuropsychology of learning disabilities: Essentials of subtype analysis.* New York: Guilford Press.

Strauss, A. A., & Lehtinen, L. E. (1947). *Psychopathology and education of the brain-injured child: Vol. II. Progress in theory and clinic.* New York: Grune & Stratton.

Strauss, A. A., & Werner, H. (1943). Comparative psychopathology of the brain-injured child and the traumatic brain-injured adult. *American Journal of Psychiatry, 19,* 835–838.

Sweeney, J. E., & Rourke, B. P. (1978). Neuropsychological significance of phonetically accurate and phonetically inaccurate spelling errors of younger and older retarded spellers. *Brain and Language, 6,* 212–225.

Tallal, P. (1988). Developmental language disorders. In J. F. Kavanagh & T. Truss (Eds.), *Learning disabilities: Proceedings of the national conference* (pp. 181–272). Parkton, MD: York Press.

Thompson, M. E. (1982). *Developmental dyslexia: Its nature, assessment, and remediation.* London, UK: Edward Arnold.

Thompson, M. E., Hicks, C., & Wilsher, C. (1980). *Specific written language difficulty in children: A clinical and factorial approach.* Unpublished manuscript, University of Aston.

Torgesen, J. K. (1991). Learning disabilities: Historical and conceptual issues. In B. Y. L. Wong (Ed.), *Learning about learning disabilities* (pp. 3–39). New York: Academic Press.

Torgesen, J. K. (1993). Variations on theory in learning disabilities. In G. R. Lyon, D. B. Gray, J. F. Kavanagh, & N. A. Krasnegor (Eds.), *Better understanding learning disabilities: New views from research and their implications for education and public policies* (pp. 27–56). Baltimore: Brookes.

Treiman, R., & Baron, J. (1983). Phonemic-analysis training helps children benefit from spelling-sound rules. *Memory and Cognition, 11,* 382–389.

U.S. Department of Education. (1989). *To assure the free appropriate public education of all handicapped children: Eleventh report to congress on the implementation of the Education of the Handicapped Act.* Washington, DC: Author.

U.S. Office of Education. (1977). Definition and criteria for defining students as learning disabled. *Federal Register, 42*(259), 65083.

Van Der Vlugt, H. & Satz, P. (1985). Subgroups and subtypes of learning-disabled and normal children: A cross-cultural comparison. In B. P. Rourke (Ed.), *Neuropsychology of learning disabilities: Essentials of subtype analysis* (pp. 212–227). New York: Guilford Press.

Vellutino, F. R. (1987). Dyslexia. *Scientific American, 256,* 34–41.

Vellutino, F. R., & Scanlon, D. M. (1987). Linguistic coding and reading ability. In S. Rosenberg (Ed.), *Advances in applied psycholinguistics* (pp. 33–197). Hillsdale, NJ: Erlbaum.

Vellutino, F. R., Scanlon, D. M., & Tanzman, M. S. (1994). Components of reading ability: Issues and problems in operationalizing word identification, phonological coding, and orthographic coding. In G. R. Lyon (Ed.), *Frames of reference for the assessment of learning disabilities: New views on measurement issues* (pp. 279–329). Baltimore: Brookes.

Vernon, M. D. (1979). Variability in reading retardation. *British Journal of Psychology, 70,* 7–16.

Wagner, R. K. (1988). Causal relationships between the development of phonological-processing abilities and the acquisition of reading skills: A meta-analysis. *Merrill-Palmer Quarterly, 34,* 261–279.

Wagner, R. K., & Torgesen, J. K. (1987). The nature of phonological processing and its causal role in the acquisition of reading skills. *Psychological Bulletin, 101,* 192–212.

Wagner, R. K., Torgesen, J. K., Laughon, P., Simmons, K., & Rashotte, C. A. (1993). Development of young readers' phonological processing abilities. *Journal of Educational Psychology, 85,* 83–103.

Watson, B. U., & Goldgar, D. E. (1988). Evaluation of a typology of reading disability. *Journal of Clinical and Experimental Neuropsychology, 10,* 432–450.

Watson, B. U., Goldgar, D. E., & Ryschon, K. L. (1983). Subtypes of reading disability. *Journal of Clinical Neuropsychology, 5,* 377–399.

Wernicke, C. (1894). Grundriss der Psychiatrie. *Psychophysiologische Eindeitung.* Wiesbaden, Germany.

West, R. F., & Stanovich, K. E. (1978). Automatic contextual facilitation in readers of three ages. *Child Development, 49,* 717–727.

Wiederholt, J. L. (1974). Historical perspectives on the education of the learning disabled. In L. Mann & D. A. Sabatino (Eds.), *The second review of special education* (pp. 103–152). Austin TX: Pro-ed.

Wiig, E. H., & Semel, E. M. (1976). *Language disabilities in children and adolescents.* Columbus, OH: Merrill.

Wilson, B. C., & Risucci, D. A. (1986). A model for clinical-quantitative classification: Generation I. Application to language-disordered preschool children. *Brain and Language, 27,* 281–309.

Wolf, M. (1986). Rapid alternating stimulus naming in the developmental dyslexias. *Brain and Language, 29,* 360–379.

Wolf, M. (1991). Naming speed and reading: The contribution of the cognitive neurosciences. *Reading Research Quarterly, 26,* 123–141.

Wolf, M., Bally, H., & Morris, R. (1986). Automaticity, retrieval processes, and reading: A longitudinal study in average and impaired readers. *Child Development, ,57,* 988–1005.

Wolf, M., Michel, G., & Ovrut, M. (1990). Rate variables and automatized naming in developmental dyslexia. *Brain and Language, 39,* 556–575.

Wong, B. Y. L. (1991). *Learning about learning disabilities.* New York: Academic Press.

Wood, F. B. (1990). Functional neuroimaging in neurobehavioral research. In A. A. Boulton, G. B. Baker, & M. Hiscock (Eds.), *Neuromethods, Vol. 17, Neuropsychology* (pp. 65–89). Clifton, NJ: Humana Press.

Wood, F. B, & Felton, R. H. (1994). Separate linguistic and attentional factors in the development of reading. *Topics in Language Disorders, 14,* 42–57.

Wood, F. B, Felton, R. H., Flowers, L., & Naylor, C. (1991). Neurobehavioral definition of dyslexia. In D. D. Duane & D. B. Gray (Eds.), *The reading Brain: The biological basis of dyslexia* (pp. 1–26). Parkton, MD: York Press.

World Health Organization. (1992). *The ICD-10 classification of mental and behavioral disorders: Clinical descriptions and diagnostic guidelines.* Geneva, Switzerland: Author.

World Health Organization. (1993). *The ICD-10 classification of mental and behavioral disorders: Diagnostic criteria for research.* Geneva, Switzerland: Author.

Ysseldyke, J. E., & Algozzine, b. (1983). LD or not LD? That's not the question. *Journal of Learning Disabilities, 16,* 29–31.

Zigmond, N. (1993). Learning disabilities from an educational perspective. In G. R. Lyon, D. B. Gray., J. F. Kavanagh, & N. A. Krasnegor (Eds.), *Better understanding learning disabilities: New views from research and their implications for education and public policies* (pp. 27–56). Baltimore: Brookes.

Tic Disorders

David W. Evans
Robert A. King
James F. Leckman

Tic disorders are transient or chronic conditions that are often associated with difficulties in self-esteem, family life, peer acceptance, and school or job performance. In their most severe form, tics can be incessant and disabling. Many individuals with tics also experience a broad range of behavioral difficulties including disinhibited speech or conduct, impulsivity, heightened perceptual awareness, distractibility, motoric hyperactivity, and a full range of obsessive–compulsive symptoms (Leckman & Cohen, 1988). Professional opinion remains divided on how broadly to conceive the spectrum of maladaptive behaviors associated with chronic tic disorders. This controversy is driven in part by the genuine frustration that parents and educators encounter when they attempt to divide an individual child's repertoire of problem behaviors into those that are "tic-related" and those that are not.

This perplexing array of symptoms has called forth a broad range of explanations typically reflecting the perspective of the observer and the zeitgeist of the era. For example, Sprenger's (1489) account of a priest who sporadically thrust out his tongue and yelled out uncontrollably is presented in the context of demonic possession. Four centuries later, Itard (1825), Gilles de la Tourette (1885), and Guinon (1886, 1887) saw these same symptoms as involuntary movements, distinguishable from chorea, and the product of "neuropathic heredity." The possible pathogenic role of more epigenetic psychological forces came

to the fore early in this century (Meige & Feindel, 1907) and culminated in a range of psychoanalytic explanations (Mahler, Luke, & Daltroff, 1945). Fueled by advances in psychopharmacology, genetics, and the neurosciences, the past several decades have witnessed efforts to deepen our understanding of the biological vulnerabilities as well as the specific environmental and psychological forces that shape the course and impact of these disorders (Cohen, Detlor, Shaywitz, & Leckman, 1982; Leckman et al., 1992).

In this chapter, a brief discussion of the phenomenology, nosology, natural history, and epidemiology of chronic tic disorders precedes the presentation of a biopsychosocial model of the pathogenesis. An effort is made to expand earlier versions of this model including a consideration of the individual's immediate psychosocial environment. Much of the discussion focuses on individuals with the most severe form of chronic tic disorder, commonly referred to as Gilles de la Tourette syndrome (TS).

DEFINITIONS

Tics

Tics are sudden, repetitive, nonrhythmic motor movements or phonic productions (Leckman & Cohen, 1988). Generally speaking, motor and phonic tics can be characterized along several

dimensions: their location or verbal content, frequency, complexity (how elaborate are they?), and their forcefulness or loudness. Examples of simple motor tics are eye blinking, nose wrinkling, facial grimacing, shoulder shrugging, or head jerking. Although more sustained dystonic tics may occur, most motor tics are sudden and abrupt, usually lasting less than 1 second. Complex motor tics appear more purposeful and elaborate, sometimes involving several body parts that are moved in a ritualistic, orchestrated manner (Cohen, 1990). These can include touching objects or oneself, bending of the whole body, and obscene gesturing (copropraxia). Vocal or phonic tics include *simple* vocalizations such as throat clearing, grunting, barking or sniffing, or *complex* vocalizations/sounds such as uttering syllables, whole words or phrases, which may include obscenities blurted out in an abrupt and explosive manner (coprolalia) (see Table 12.1).

The number, distribution, frequency, and intensity (forcefulness or loudness) of tics can fluctuate greatly over time. They typically occur in bout-like episodes that are intensified by stress and fatigue over the course of a day. Tics can be voluntarily suppressed for brief periods (seconds to minutes). They also wax and wane in severity over weeks to months. This changeable array of symptoms can be quite confusing, exasperating, and frightening to parents, teachers, and peers. When tics occur particularly in the context of comorbid conditions such as attention-deficit/hyperactivity disorder (ADHD) and/or obsessive–compulsive disorder (OCD), the boundaries between and among tics, impulsive behavior, and compulsions can be obscure. The impact of the tics can be magnified by parental censure, punitive responses in the classroom, and ostracism on the playground.

Premonitory Sensory Urges

Recent years have seen an appreciation for the sensations that precede or accompany tics (Scahill, Leckman, & Marek, 1995). Although children often describe their tics as being completely involuntary and occurring without warning, most adolescents and adults report intense, discrete sensory urges that precede and are relieved by tics (Leckman, Walker, & Cohen, 1993). These premonitory urges may also be accompanied by less focal sensations of a general heightened tension in the body. Typically efforts to suppress tics intensify the urge to tic (Scahill et al., 1995), and

TABLE 12.1. Examples of Motor and Phonic Tics

Simple motor tics

Eye blinking, eye movements, grimacing, nose twitching, mouth movements, lip pouting, head jerks, shoulder shrugs, arms jerks, abdominal tensing, kicks, finger movements, jaw snaps, tooth clicking, rapid jerking of any part of the body

Complex motor tics

Sustained "looks," facial gestures, biting, touching objects or self, throwing, banging, thrusting arms, gestures with hands, gyrating and bending, dystonic postures, copropraxia (obscene gestures)

Simple phonic tics

Throat clearing, coughing, sniffling, spitting, screeching, barking, grunting, growling, gurgling, clacking, hissing, sucking, and innumerable other sounds

Complex phonic tics

Syllables, words, phrases, statements such as "shut up," "stop that," "oh, okay," "I've got to," "okay, honey," "what makes me do this?" "how about it," or "now you've seen it"; speech atypicalities (unusual rhythms, tone, accents, intensity of speech); echo phenomenon (immediate repetition of one's own or another's words or phrases); and coprolalia (obscene, inappropriate, and aggressive words and statements)

some individuals with TS report that the tic is actually performed to relax the premonitory urge. Sensory phenomena occur in approximately 50% to 80% of children with TS, with estimates ranging from 8% (E. Shapiro, Shapiro, Young, & Feinberg, 1988) to as high as 96% (Lang, 1991). Of those subjects who report premonitory urges, roughly 80% characterize the urge as a physical sensation and are able to identify a specific site on the body. Common loci of the premonitory urge include the shoulders, the hands, abdomen, and throat (Leckman et al., 1993; Figure 12.1). These urges can sometimes be more troublesome than the tics themselves (Cohen & Leckman, 1992) and are a source of distraction that can contribute to the self-perception of being "weak" for the inability to resist these unwanted urges.

NOSOLOGY

Tourette syndrome is often conceptualized as a hyperkinetic "movement disorder" to be distinguished from a variety of other conditions includ-

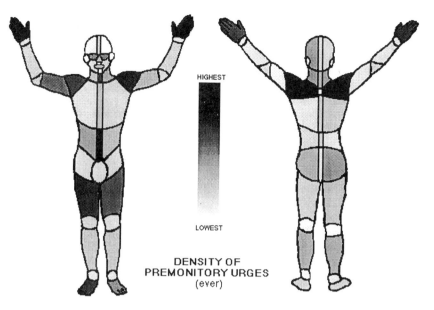

HIGHEST

LOWEST

DENSITY OF PREMONITORY URGES
(ever)

FIGURE 12.1. Body diagram of loci of premonitory urges.

ing myoclonus, chorea, hemiballismus, dystonia, athetosis, and seizures (Jankovic, 1992). Others view TS and tic disorders as conditions with the potential to affect sensory, perceptual, emotional, and cognitive domains, as well as motor function. These investigators may be more conscious of the troublesome nosological boundaries between TS, OCD, and ADHD, and the intrapsychic impact of these symptoms.

The fourth edition of the *Diagnostic and Statistical Manual of Mental Disorders* (DSM-IV; American Psychiatric Association, 1994) as well as the World Health Organization's *International Classification of Diseases* (ICD-10; World Health Organization, 1992, 1993) distinguish between four subtypes of tic disorders: Tourette disorder, transient tic disorder, chronic motor or vocal tic disorder, and tic disorder not otherwise specified. A diagnosis of tic disorder requires the exclusion of several other kinds of "uncontrollable" movements, especially those associated with Wilson disease, Sydenham chorea, or Huntington disease, as well as neuroleptic-induced dyskinesias grouped under the category of medication-induced movement disorder not otherwise specified (American Psychiatric Association, 1994).

Body-rocking and other rhythmic, stereotyped movements that are sometimes present in autism or severe mental retardation (Berkson, 1983) re-

semble complex motor tics. Such stereotypies differ fundamentally from tics in that tics are abrupt jerking movements, and they are by definition not rhythmic. Also, the nature of the stereotypies of mentally retarded or autistic children is obscured by cognitive and linguistic impairment that precludes an assessment of the degree of volition in their movements. Thus any similarities in the subjective experiences of tiqueurs and these more pervasively impaired individuals remain unknown.

Tics are usually distinguishable from compulsions, such as repetitive hand washing or checking behaviors typical of OCD. Whereas compulsions are typically preceded by anxious, obsessive worries, they are only rarely preceded by premonitory urges (Leckman et al., 1993; Leckman, Walker, Goodman, Pauls, & Cohen, 1994). Certain compulsive touching of objects or of self, or "evening-up" behaviors (such as needing to rub the left hand on a door after the right hand accidentally grazed the door, so as to make the contact "even" on both sides) are common among children with TS, and they are not easily distinguished from complex tics.

Tourette syndrome and chronic tic disorder are differentially classified by DSM-IV and ICD-10 based on pervasiveness of symptomatology. In TS, both motor and phonic tics must be present, whereas chronic tic disorder may consist of either motor or vocal tics. Transient tic disorder is more

common than either TS or chronic tic disorder and consists of motor or vocal tics that do not persist for longer than 12 consecutive months (American Psychiatric Association, 1994; see Tables 12.2, 12.3, and 12.4).

One important difference between DSM-IV and ICD-10 criteria lies in the DSM-IV stipulation that the tics must cause "marked distress or significant impairment" in order for a diagnosis to be conferred. An individual may then display a full range of tics yet not meet all diagnostic criteria for TS because of a lack of distress or marked impairment in adaptive functioning. This may pose problems for researchers faced with defining inclusion and exclusion criteria for their studies. Problems of reliability in research studies that occur because of the variety of possible interpretations as to what qualifies as sufficient subjective distress may further complicate research. It is also likely that those individuals with comorbid mood or anxiety disorders may be more likely to report symptoms of psychological distress, thereby increasing the rate of TS diagnoses in these comorbid samples.

NATURAL HISTORY

The age of onset of tics typically falls between 2 to 14 years (Bruun, 1988; Jagger et al., 1982), with a modal age of onset of 5 to 7 years. The first tics are usually simple motor movements of cranial or facial muscle groups—most commonly those involving the eye (E. Shapiro et al., 1988)—such as forceful eye blinking or eye rolling. Facial grimacing, lip biting, or mouth movements are also common. These types of tics are those most commonly seen (in 74% of cases, according to E. Shapiro et al., 1988) within the early weeks of the onset of TS. Early phonic tics might include repetitive throat clearing, sniffing, or coughing (Leckman et al., 1988; see Figure 12.2).

The exact course of TS is difficult to predict. There is often a progression from simple to more complex tics, and from caudal to more rostral motor groups (Leckman et al., 1988). Only rarely does a child go from being tic-free one day into TS with its full expression of complex motor and phonic tics the next (Leckman & Cohen, 1994). It is also rare to find complex vocal tics, such as coprolalia, in the absence of simpler vocal or motor tics. For those children with comorbid attention and hyperactivity problems (see below), ADHD symptoms are often first apparent in the preschool years and may precede the onset of tics

TABLE 12.2. DSM-IV Diagnostic Criteria for Tourette Syndrome

A. Both multiple motor and one or more vocal tics have been present at some time during the illness, although not necessarily concurrently. (A *tic* is a sudden, rapid, recurrent nonrhythmic, stereotyped motor movement or vocalization.)

B. The tics occur many times a day (usually in bouts) nearly every day or intermittently throughout a period of more than 1 year, and during this period there was never a tic-free period of more than 3 consecutive months.

C. The disturbance causes marked distress or significant impairment in social, occupational, or other important areas of functioning.

D. The onset is before age 18 years.

E. The disturbance is not due to the direct physiological effects of a substance (e.g., stimulants) or a general medical condition (e.g., Huntington disease or postviral encephalitis).

Note. From American Psychiatric Association (1994, p. 103). Copyright 1994 by the American Psychiatric Association. Reprinted by permission.

by as much as 3 years (Comings & Comings, 1993; Robertson, Trimble, & Lees, 1988).

The first tics associated with TS may be transient, lasting only for a period of a few weeks before they go into a full (but temporary) remission. In other instances the tics may wane but not completely disappear, or they can become more florid and prominent (Leckman et al., 1992). Over time, other tics such as head jerking or shoulder shrugging often emerge. As many as 69% of all TS patients eventually develop complex tics of larger muscle groups such as arms, legs, or abdominal tensing (E. Shapiro et al., 1988). Habits such as "needing" to touch, tap, or rub objects or other people are also common.

More rarely, these later-developing complex motor symptoms can include copropraxia (obscene gestures) or self-abusive behaviors such as head-banging; lip, tongue or cheek biting; self-punching (Nee, Caine, Polinsky, Eldridge, & Ebert, 1980; A. Shapiro, Shapiro, Bruun, & Sweet, 1978; Robertson, 1992; Van Wort, Jutkowitz, Rosenbaum, & Bowers, 1976); and even enucleation (plucking out one's eye) or tooth self-extractions (Robertson, 1992).

Vocal tics generally have a later age of onset than motor tics, usually appearing between 9 to

TABLE 12.3. ICD-10 Diagnostic Guidelines for Tic Disorders

F95 Tic disorders definition

The predominant manifestation in these syndromes is some form of tic. A tic is an involuntary, rapid, recurrent, non-rhythmic motor movement (usually involving circumscribed muscle groups), or vocal production, that is of sudden onset and serves no apparent purpose. Tics tend to be experienced as irresistible but they can usually be suppressed for varying periods of time. Both motor and vocal tics may be classified as either simple or complex, although the boundaries are not well defined. Common simple motor tics include eye-blinking, neck-jerking, shoulder-shrugging, and facial grimacing. Common simple vocal tics include throat-clearing, barking, sniffing, and hissing. Common complex tics include hitting one's self, jumping, and hopping. Common complex vocal tics include the repetition of particular words, and sometimes the use of socially unacceptable (often obscene) words (coprolalia), and the repetition of one's own sounds or words (palilalia).

F95.0 Transient tic disorder

Meets the general criteria for a tic disorder, but tics do not persist for longer than 12 months. This is the commonest form of tic and is most frequent about the age of 4 or 5 years; the tics usually take the form of eye-blinking, facial grimacing, or head-jerking. In some cases the tics occur as a single episode but in other cases there are remissions and relapses over a period of months.

F95.1 Chronic motor or vocal tic disorder

Meets the criteria for a tic disorder, in which there are motor or vocal tics (but not both); tics may be either single or multiple (but usually multiple), and last for more than one year.

F95.2 Combined vocal and multiple motor tic disorder [de la Tourette's syndrome]

A form of tic disorder in which there are, or have been, multiple motor tics and one or more vocal tics, although these need not have occurred concurrently. Onset is almost always in childhood or adolescence. A history of motor tics before development of vocal tics is common; the symptoms frequently worsen during adolescence, and it is common for the disorder to persist into adult life.

The vocal tics are often multiple with explosive repetitive vocalizations, throat clearing, and grunting, and there may be the use of obscene words or phrases. Sometimes there is associated gestural echopraxia, which also may be of an obscene nature (copropraxia). As with motor tics, the vocal tics may be voluntarily suppressed for short periods, be exacerbated by stress, and disappear during sleep.

F95.9 Tic disorder, unspecified

A non-recommended residual category for a disorder that fulfils the general criteria for a tic disorder but in which the specific subcategory is not specified or in which the features do not fulfil the criteria for F95.0, F95.1 or F95.2.

Note. From World Health Organization (1992, pp. 282–283, 284). Copyright 1992 by the World Health Organization. Reprinted by permission.

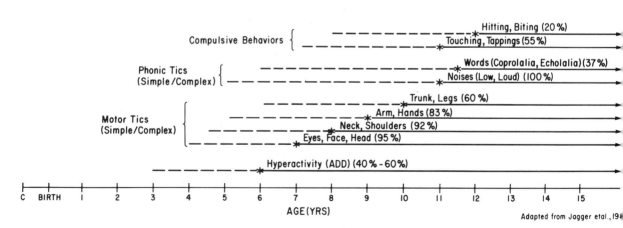

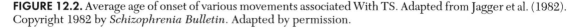

FIGURE 12.2. Average age of onset of various movements associated With TS. Adapted from Jagger et al. (1982). Copyright 1982 by *Schizophrenia Bulletin.* Adapted by permission.

TABLE 12.4. ICD-10 Research Diagnostic Criteria for Tic Disorders

F95 Tic disorders

Note: A tic is an involuntary, sudden, rapid, recurrent, non-rhythmic, stereotyped motor movement or vocalization.

F95.0   Transient tic disorder

A. Single or multiple motor or vocal tic(s) or both occur many times a day, on most days, over a period of at least 4 weeks.

B. Duration of the disorder is 12 months or less.

C. There is no history of Tourette syndrome, and the disorder is not the result of physical conditions or side-effects of medication.

D. Onset is before the age of 18 years.

F95.1   Chronic motor and vocal tic disorder

A. Motor or vocal tics, but not both, occur many times per day, on most days, over a period of at least 12 months.

B. No period of remission during that year lasts longer than 2 months.

C. There is no history of Tourette syndrome, and the disorder is not the result of physical conditions or side-effects of medication.

D. Onset is before the age of 18 years.

F95.2   Combined vocal and multiple motor tic disorder [de la Tourette's syndrome]

A. Multiple motor tics and one or more vocal tics have been present at some time during the disorder, but not necessarily concurrently.

B. The frequency of tics must be many times a day, nearly every day, for more than 1 year, with no period of remission during that year lasting longer than 2 months.

C. Onset is before the age of 18 years.

F95.9   Tic disorder, unspecified

A non-recommended residual category for a disorder that fulfils the general criteria for a tic disorder but in which the specific subcategory is not specified or in which the features do not fulfil the criteria for F95.0, F95.1, or F95.2.

Note. From World Health Organization (1993, pp. 167–168). Copyright 1993 by the World Health Organization. Reprinted by permission.

12 years of age (Bruun, 1988; Comings & Comings, 1985). For the vast majority of children with TS, the first vocal tics to present are simple tics such as throat clearing, sniffing, grunting, and/or animal or bird noises. Elaborate and complex vocal symptoms occur more rarely. Echolalia (echoing the last word or phrase uttered by another person) or palilalia (repeating one's own last syllable, word, or phrase) are thought to be present in approximately 17% of TS patients. Sudden changes in rate, pitch, or rhythm of speech and coprolalia are also relatively rare, and when present do not emerge until the early teen years (E. Shapiro, Shapiro, Young, & Feinberg, 1988; see Table 12.1).

Some children can describe premonitory sensory phenomena early in the course of their tic symptoms, but most do not. The premonitory urges typically appear by 9 or 10 years of age (Leckman et al., 1993). The reasons for this developmental lag are not clear. It may be that the appearance of premonitory urges reflects intrinsic maturational or pathogenic factors that simply are not present before a given age. Alternatively, the ability to identify or report premonitory urges may require a certain level of cognitive, self-reflective, and descriptive abilities. The increased awareness of such urges over time may also be the result of repeated efforts to resist, suppress, or understand the tics (Scahill et al., 1995). This level of thought would seem to reflect cognitive abilities that are not typically present in young children, but ones that emerge later in childhood and adolescence. Alternatively, these sensations and perceptions may be present from early on, but the younger child is simply unaware or not able to articulate them.

Whenever the tics appear, they disrupt the existing way of life, giving the child a sense of not being fully in control. The symptoms can be discomforting for everyone until they are understood better and placed in a more benign perspective.

The natural history of TS, then, generally is one of fluctuation throughout childhood and gradual attenuation by late adolescence (Cohen & Leckman, 1994; Bruun & Budman, 1992; Comings & Comings, 1987). In a study following 136 TS children from 5 to 15 years of age, Bruun (1988) found that initially 59% of these children were considered to have milder forms of the dis-

order, whereas at follow-up, 91% fell into milder categories. Fifty-two percent of these subjects reported that their tics had decreased spontaneously (Bruun, 1988; Bruun & Budman, 1992). With decreases in tic symptoms, related problems of social impairment may decrease as well, although some research (Singer & Rosenberg, 1989) suggests that older children with TS (12- to 16-year-olds) may exhibit more concomitant psychological symptoms (i.e., obsessive–compulsive symptoms) than do younger patients.

Not surprisingly, the psychological outcome of TS in late adolescence may be related to a number of factors including parental and peer support and the ability to maintain an overall positive outlook during the earlier and more severe phases of the disorder. Even when TS symptoms persist into adulthood many individuals live a relatively happy and successful life. As with many chronic disorders, critical determinants of outcome may include level of social support (parents, teachers, and peers), intelligence, personality, presence or absence of comorbid conditions, and access to appropriate medical and educational services. The impact of these variables on the later development of TS children remains to be fully explored in the TS population.

COMORBIDITY

Tourette syndrome and other chronic tic disorders are often accompanied by maladaptive behavioral patterns that meet criteria for other childhood disorders in addition to TS. Nearly 50% of all children with TS meet criteria for diagnoses of OCD, ADHD, anxiety disorders, or learning disabilities (Cohen, Friedhoff, Leckman, & Chase, 1992). Such concomitant problems are often the reason for initial referrals (Walk-up, Scahill, & Riddle, 1995). Few population-based epidemiological studies have been conducted to establish unbiased rates of comorbidity (Apter et al., 1993). Twin and family genetic studies however, lend some insight into the relationship between tic disorders and these comorbid conditions. Although the following discussion focuses just on ADHD, learning disabilities, and OCD, some investigators have suggested that TS is etiologically related to a number of other conditions including conduct disorder (Modolfsky, Tullis, & Lamon, 1974), anxiety disorder, alcoholism, bipolar disorder, agoraphobia, or eating disorders (Comings & Comings, 1984, 1987, 1993), as well as autism (Burd & Kerbeshian, 1985), migraine headaches (Barabas, Matthews, & Ferrari, 1984a), and dissociative states (night terrors, sleepwalking) (Barabas, Matthews, & Ferrari, 1984b). A definitive exploration of these putative associations lies beyond the scope of this review and requires additional population-based epidemiological studies.

Attention-Deficit/Hyperactivity Disorder

Among clinic samples, 40% to 50% of children who develop tics have a history of impulsivity, high activity level, and inattentiveness (Cohen et al., 1992; Comings & Comings, 1987; Robertson et al., 1988). These symptoms may worsen upon the onset of the tics because of the increases in frustration that are brought about by yet another array of uncontrollable behaviors. In many cases, the attention deficit associated with tics causes greater disruption to social and academic functioning than do the tics themselves (Dykens et al., 1990; Stokes, Bawden, Camfield, Backman, & Dooley, 1991).

The nature of the etiological relationship between TS and ADHD remains unclear with some investigators suggesting that the two disorders are alternate expressions of the same underlying vulnerability (Comings & Comings, 1987), whereas others suggest that severe TS may exacerbate ADHD symptoms (Pauls, Leckman, & Cohen, 1993; Randolph, Hyde, Gold, Goldberg, & Weinberger, 1993). The majority of the evidence that links TS and ADHD is derived from clinic-referred samples (see Walkup et al., 1995). The only population-based study, however, with its low rate of ADHD (12%) (Apter et al., 1993) appears to be more consistent with the presence of an ascertainment bias in clinic referrals such that children with both disorders are more likely to be referred for treatment than children with only one of these two conditions (Berkson, 1946).

Learning Disabilities

Learning disabilities are relatively common among clinic-referred TS cases (Comings, 1990; Dykens et al., 1990; Pauls et al., 1993). Tourette syndrome children have been found to demonstrate more reading and mathematics problems than children without TS (Burd, Kaufman, & Kerbeshian, 1992; Comings, 1990). The limited twin and family genetic data do not support the view that any par-

ticular form of learning disability is etiologically related to TS, however (Pauls et al., 1993).

Obsessive–Compulsive Disorder

In both clinical and population-based samples, OCD is among the most common comorbidities associated with TS, occurring in about 30% to 40% of TS patients (Apter et al., 1993; Frankel et al., 1986; Green & Pitman, 1986; Peterson, Leckman, & Cohen, 1995; Leonard, Lenane, et al., 1992; Yaryura-Tobias, Neziroglu, Howard, & Fuller, 1983). Obsessive–compulsive disorder is characterized by intrusive thoughts (obsessions) and/or compulsive, rule-governed, repetitive behaviors. A wide range of OC symptoms may be seen in TS patients including: violent, sexual, and religious obsessions and checking and hoarding behaviors (Leckman et al., 1994). Obsessions of contamination and the accompanying compulsive hand-washing that are relatively common in OCD are less often seen in the OC repertoire of children with TS (Leckman et al., 1992). Compulsive behaviors in OCD differ from complex motor tics, in that compulsions—again, such as hand washing—tend to be more purposeful, more elaborate, and often occur in response to some obsession (contamination, in this case). As mentioned earlier in this chapter, complex tics may be difficult to distinguish from compulsions, as in the compulsive need to touch a particular object again and again (King & Noshpitz, 1991; Leonard, Swedo, et al., 1992). Other compulsive rituals include retracing steps, ordering or arranging objects, repeated checking, and counting. Twin and family genetic studies have suggested that TS and OC symptoms may be alternate and somewhat gender-specific expressions of the same underlying vulnerability (Pauls, Raymond, Stevenson, & Leckman, 1991).

NEUROPSYCHOLOGICAL CORRELATES

Neuropsychological studies of TS subjects have reported deficits in the domains of fine motor dexterity, visuomotor and spatial skills, and executive functioning (Bornstein, 1990; Bornstein & Yang, 1991; Denckla et al., 1991). Other investigators have focused on the impulsivity of many TS subjects and their difficulties in editing their intention (Baron-Cohen et al., 1994). Related weaknesses in attention, sensory perception, and mathematics have also been reported (Incagnoli & Kane, 1982; Joschko & Rourke, 1982; Randolph et al., 1993). Tourette syndrome patients may show a reduction in the normally occurring asymmetry on a series of lateralizing neuropsychological tests (Yazgan, Peterson, Wexler, & Leckman, in press).

Greater clarity of these neuropsychological aspects of TS will emerge from studies of subjects free of neuropsychopharmacological agents and nonreferred subjects. Controlling for comorbid conditions using dimensional measures of ADHD and OCD symptoms may also help delineate those neuropsychological features that closely correlate with motor or phonic tic severity as opposed to symptoms of ADHD or OCD (Dykens et al., 1990).

PARENTAL, PEER, AND SELF-ACCEPTANCE

The visible and apparent nature of tics predictably influences how the child with TS perceives her- or himself and how she or he is viewed by others in the course of social interactions. This is an area of research in which few empirical studies exist, but one that is nonetheless important for advancing our understanding of the subjective experiences of children with tic disorders.

Parents and Family

Among the many risks to the psychological well-being of the young child with tics are the social environment and parental attitudes toward the child and his or her disorder. As with all disorders, there is some risk of parental misunderstanding, fear, distress, or perhaps a heightened sense of the child's fragility. The ADHD symptoms that often precede the onset of tics may also strain these early parent–child interactions. The parent may develop a sense of the child as defiant or out of control, such that when tic symptoms begin, the parent may regard this as just another manifestation of the child's failure to regulate his or her own behavior. These interactions may hinder the social–emotional well-being of the child and interfere with a sense of self-worth and social competency, and yet these elements remain virtually unexplored in the literature on TS and other movement disorders (Cohen, 1990).

A transactional approach to parent–child interaction (Sameroff & Chandler, 1975; Bell, 1968)

is an appropriate model for understanding TS. Once the child begins to manifest TS symptoms, a wheel is set into motion that may strongly influence the course of tics as well as the child's overall psychosocial adjustment. Punishment or continual criticism for having tics induces additional stress and anxiety in a child who may already be inclined to self-reproach. Such chastising may increase the child's subjective distress over the presence of tics and, in turn, exacerbate the severity of tics, thus perpetuating a cycle of potentially maladaptive parent–child interactions (Carter & Pauls, 1991; Carter, Pauls, Leckman, & Cohen, 1994). Indeed such a maladaptive cycle of interaction may be set into motion long before the onset of TS symptoms. A genetic predisposition for developing TS combined with particular parental attitudes may set the stage for a less-than-optimal outcome.

"Goodness-of-fit" (Thomas & Chess, 1977) between the TS child and his or her environment is a crucial element in the development of the disorder itself and related psychosocial factors. Certain family environments may accommodate the child with tics better than others. An overly rigid or authoritarian parenting style may serve only to heighten the subjective toll of tics for the child. On the other hand, the child whose TS is accompanied by ADHD may benefit from a parenting style that maintains a structured home environment with consistent and developmentally appropriate expectations and consequences without becoming overly reactive.

Parents may also experience their own sense of blame or guilt regarding the possible origins of their child's tic behavior (Scahill, Ort, & Hardin, 1993). When parents realize that stress or anxiety may exacerbate tics, they may take measures to protect their child from stressful or challenging situations—even those that are the fabric of normal child development (Scahill et al., 1993). Protecting the child against undue stress while at the same time fostering a sense of independence are among the many challenges facing the parent of the TS child.

School Environment

Parents of children with TS sometimes express a concern as to how to serve their child academically without exposing the child to undue social stress. Tics (and related comorbid symptoms) not only interfere with the child's concentration and classroom participation but also disrupt the class milieu for teachers and students. Prior to the onset of tics, many children with TS have attentional difficulties and/or uneven patterns of cognitive abilities that may interfere with academic achievement and adaptation to the classroom environment. Because some tics may be regarded as deliberately provocative or oppositional behavior, it is important that teachers (and parents) realize that tics are not the act of defiance that they may appear to be. Educating school staff and classmates is a delicate but necessary task to help prevent alienation and to ensure the child's academic and social progress. Schools, teachers, and peers will vary in their willingness and ability to tolerate and support the child with tics. Thus "goodness-of-fit" applies not only to the parent–child interaction but also to school and larger community.

Peers

Three studies have directly addressed the social world of children with TS. Children with TS were rated by their peers as being lower on all indices of the Pupil Evaluation Inventory, suggesting that children with TS are viewed as both more aggressive, more withdrawn, and less popular than their sex-matched classmates (Stokes et al., 1991). These sociometric peer ratings were associated with higher levels of internalizing and externalizing symptomatology as assessed by teachers, but they were unrelated to the TS children's current degree of tic severity. Similarly, Dykens et al. (1990) found that children with TS (especially those with ADHD symptoms) demonstrate relative weaknesses in socialization compared to other areas of adaptive behavior. In a study of Japanese adolescents and adults, TS patients and their families (Nomura, Kita, & Segawa, 1992) reported that 85% of family members believed that others' awareness of an individual's tics was emotionally upsetting for the patient with TS. Yet no studies report the distress that young children with TS experience in the face of social scrutiny or peer rejection.

Longitudinal research is needed in order to understand the long-term effects of (perceived) social deficits of the child with TS. Few will argue that peer rejection and an early sense of social incompetence do not auger well for forging ahead to adolescence with a sense of confidence and social competence. The development of the self in a social context has not been adequately studied in the TS population, however, and promises to add to our understanding of the psychosocial world of children with TS and other chronic disorders.

Self-Acceptance, Self-Esteem, and Self-Concept

Because the self-concept changes throughout development, the child's subjective experiences of his or her tics will depend on the child's age or developmental status. For example, we do not generally think of the young child as being particularly introspective or self-aware. Thus the presence of tics in a 2-year-old will not likely affect his or her self-concept in the same way that tics affect self-concept of an adolescent. Before the point where formal self-reflection is present, children—even infants—possess a self-knowledge in the way of sensory perceptions (Butterworth, 1990; Gibson, 1966, 1979) that allows them to recognize themselves in mirror images, or in the face of contingent or delayed video feedback (Bertenthal & Fisher, 1978; Lewis & Brooks-Gunn, 1979). It is possible that these sensory perceptions would be experienced differently for the child with TS, whose movements are not wholly "in synch" with his or her intentions or anticipations. The sequelae of these early self-perceptions on later development present an open field of study and one that may benefit from the study of TS, where a dyssynchrony between actions and motives is prominent, particularly early in the course of the disease when the premonitory sensory urges are a less salient feature.

Many theorists in developmental psychology point to the age of 7 or 8 years as the time when children begin to form a coherent self-concept—a cognitive representation of self, founded on reflective self-awareness (Butterworth, 1990; Harter, 1983). It is also at this time, probably not coincidentally, when children begin to compare themselves with peers thereby enabling them to assess their own strengths and weaknesses in various domains (Harter, 1983) and the similarities and dissimilarities between themselves and their peers. In the school-age years, a sense of isolation caused by peer rejection is a risk factor to social-emotional well-being. The TS child's trepidation regarding his or her social presentation adds further to a picture of the TS child as an outcast.

As the child approaches adolescence, new risk and protective factors appear. Adolescence brings new cognitive abilities that allow the teenager to reason more abstractly, yet it may also pave the way for greater self-deprecation and decreases in self-esteem (Elkind, 1967; Zigler & Glick, 1986). In adolescence, social relationships generally take on a more intimate quality. One's physical self becomes inextricably linked to areas such as romantic relationships and an overall sense of self-esteem (Evans, Brody, & Noam, 1995). The negative impact of tics in an already too self-conscious adolescent is easily imagined; if a facial blemish is seen as a social catastrophe, prominent tics can put the adolescent at a still greater risk for depression and low self-esteem in this vulnerable period of development.

Another aspect of the adolescent self is the ability to perceive the self as composed of many separate aspects. Adolescents who report greater self-complexity (a perception of the self as multifaceted) report lower levels of depression and higher self-esteem (Evans, 1994; Evans et al., 1995). The adolescent with tics may be hindered in achieving this sense of self-complexity. Tics follow him or her wherever he or she goes, affecting friendships, romantic prospects, identity as a pupil or athlete. Whether these emerging social spheres can represent new areas of vulnerability to hostile scrutiny and peer rejection, or constitute new opportunities for acceptance and affiliation, depends on both the adolescent's self-perception and the level of empathy and understanding of his or her peers.

The adolescent's task is to weave a line of continuity through the various aspects of the personality, which means both integrating and differentiating contradictory self-aspects (Erikson, 1968). This may be more difficult for the adolescent with TS. More subtle aspects of tic behavior may be adopted as personality characteristics. A sense of self as spontaneous or uninhibited may be integrated into a picture of the overall self as a way of gaining—perhaps for the first time—a sense of control and meaning to the tic behaviors, rather than merely being a victim of them.

EPIDEMIOLOGY

Only a few decades ago, the literature on TS was limited to isolated case studies, and TS was thought to be an extremely rare disorder. Prevalence estimates vary widely and depend on the nature of the populations studied, methodological approaches, and diagnostic criteria (Leckman & Cohen, 1994). Estimates of the frequency of tic disorders include figures from 2.9 per 10,000 (Caine et al., 1987), 4.5 per 10,000 (Apter et al., 1993), 5.9 per 10,000 (Burd, Kerbeshian, Wikenheiser, & Fisher, 1986) to as high as 59 per 10,000

(Comings, Himes, & Comings, 1990). Tics are most commonly reported between the ages of 7 to 11 years with fewer adults than children identified as exhibiting tics or tic disorders (Leckman & Cohen, 1991). Tics and tic disorders occur much more frequently in male than female individuals, with a reported sex ratio of up to 9:1 (Burd et al., 1986).

Studies of more broadly defined and milder forms of tics yield much higher estimates. In the United States, parent surveys indicate that as many as 18% of boys and 11% of girls exhibit "tics, twitches or nervous movements" (Achenbach & Edelbrock, 1981). In a study of 10- and 11-year-olds in the United Kingdom, this figure is 5.9% (Rutter & Hemming, 1970), and roughly 10% of Dutch parents report that their children engage in such behaviors (Verhulst, Akkerhuis, & Althaus, 1985). This relatively high prevalence rate of tic-like movements in the general population calls for a closer look at tics as normal developmental phenomena. With as many as 18% of all children exhibiting some "nervous" movements or tic-like behavior at some time (Achenbach & Edelbrock, 1981), much may be learned about the nature of tics by studying the general population. Since our knowledge of the presence of tics in the general population of children is based on parental responses to a single global question, many issues remain open for study. Issues such as the frequency, intensity, duration, locus of the movement, subjective distress caused by the movements or sounds, age of onset, and whether these more mild tics demonstrate the characteristic waxing and waning course are as yet all unexplored issues, and they promise to inform our understanding of the causes and developmental correlates of tic behavior in the general population and in individuals with tic disorders. Unbiased estimates of comorbidity also require such population-based studies.

MODEL OF PATHOGENESIS

TS has been proposed as a model disorder for studying gene–environment interactions in the course of central nervous system development (Cohen et al., 1982; Leckman et al., 1992; Cohen & Leckman, 1994). Recent advances in the study of TS have led to a proposed model of pathogenesis that involves four areas: phenomenology and natural history, genetic factors, epigenetic and environmental factors, and neurobiological substrates (Leckman et al., 1992) (see Figure 12.3).

This model proposes that the expression of TS first requires a *genetic predisposition* to the disorder. Once thought to be the result of a single autosomal gene, it is more likely that there may be one or more genes of major effect, with other modifying genes of lesser effect. These genes acting alone or in concert, at one or more points in the course of CNS development, influence both the microenvironment of the cells in which they are expressed and the developing *neurobiological substrate*. This substrate likely includes corticostriatothalamocortical (CSTC) circuits that channel and subchannel information concerning motor planning and the monitoring of motor function. This substrate may also include other closely related circuits that process cognitive and emotive information and circuits in the central limbic continuum that regulate stress sensitivity and influence the activity of the CSTC circuits. Over the course of development, the resulting clinical phenotype is further modified by the effects of *specific epigenetic or environmental factors* (Leckman et al., 1992). Some of these factors have been identified and the crucial importance of events early in CNS development have been firmly established. These epigenetic and environmental risk and protective factors also have the potential to alter the microenvironment of cells (and therefore alter the expression of the vulnerability genes at a later point in development) and to influence the developing neurobiological substrate. The *clinical phenotype* can in turn alter the mix of risk and protective factors leading to reciprocal changes in phenotype.

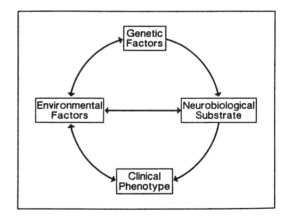

FIGURE 12.3. Model of pathogenesis of Tourette syndrome.

Following is a brief outline on the current developments in each of the areas representing the components of the model of pathogenesis.

Genetic Factors

In his original article, Gilles de la Tourette (1885) suggested a familial transmission of TS. Several twin and family studies confirm that the first-degree relatives of probands with TS have an increased prevalence of tic disorders compared to normal controls (Eldridge, Sweet, Lake, Ziegler, & Shapiro, 1977; Kidd, Prusoff, & Cohen, 1980; Kidd & Pauls, 1982; Nee et al., 1980; Pauls, Cohen, Heimbuch, Detlor, & Kidd, 1981; A. Shapiro & Shapiro, 1982). Some forms of OCD may also represent an alternate phenotypic expression of the TS vulnerability gene(s) (Pauls et al., 1991).

Various modes of genetic transmission of TS have been proposed, including recessive (Nee et al., 1980), dominant (Pauls & Leckman, 1986; Eapen, Pauls, & Robertson, 1993), and polygenic models (A. Shapiro et al., 1978). Segregation analyses indicate that the vertical transmission of TS and the other affected phenotypes is most consistent with an autosomal dominant mode of transmission (Comings, Comings, Devor, & Cloninger, 1984; Eapen et al., 1993; Pauls & Leckman, 1986; Price, Pauls, & Caine, 1984). As mentioned earlier, TS appears more frequently in male than in female probands (as high as 9:1 ratio; E. Shapiro et al., 1988), yet there is no evidence for a sex-linked genetic transmission of TS. Indeed, the recent studies performed on dizygotic versus monozygotic twins give further support to the hypothesis of an autosomal (non-sex-linked) dominant transmission. The concordance rate for monozygotic twin pairs is 50% to 60% for TS and 77% to 90% if other chronic tic disorders are included. The concordance rate for dizygotic twin pairs is lower—8% concordance for TS and 22% if chronic motor tic disorder is included in the affected phenotype (Hyde, Aaronson, Randolph, Rickler, & Weinberger, 1992; Price, Kidd, Cohen, Pauls, & Leckman, 1985; Walkup et al., 1988). If OCD is also included among the affected phenotypes, the concordance for dizygotic twins could be as high 30% to 35%.

The identification of large multigenerational families has facilitated genetic linkage studies (Kurlan et al., 1986). Genetic linkage studies have examined more than 90% of the autosomal genome thus far without identifying a chromosomal location for the putative TS gene or genes (Pauls et al., 1991; Pakstis et al., 1991). Exclusion of the entire genome would pose a major (fatal) challenge to the view that a single autosomal gene is responsible for the vulnerability to TS. As a consequence, a new round of studies are under way using nonparametric techniques, such as affected sib pair designs, to test various candidate genes and to identify chromosomal regions shared by common descent across distantly related TS cases.

Recent research suggests that individuals with TS have a greater-than-chance probability of having bilineal familial history of tics (Kurlan, Eapen, Stern, McDermott, & Robertson, 1994)—that is, both maternal and paternal families have a history of some form of the disorder, including certain types of OCD. While it is not surprising that two families with a history of TS have a greater likelihood of producing offspring with some form of the disorder, it is interesting that individuals with family histories of TS may mate with each other more often than would be expected by chance. Whether homozygosity at specific loci is associated with more severe outcomes remains to be determined.

The reasons for this assortative mating process are not clear. Individuals who have been exposed to TS through family members may have a greater tolerance for TS symptomatology. Certain TS-related personality features, such as OC traits, may similarly be viewed as desirable, or at least less nondesirable, traits in the process of selecting a mate.

Epigenetic and Environmental Risk and Protective Factors

Despite a clear genetic component, environmental factors greatly influence the phenotypic expression as evidenced by discrepancies in observed symptom severity between MZ twins (twins sharing identical genetic endowment). Pre- and perinatal nutritional and hormonal environments are thought to be particularly important in the phenotypic variation of the TS gene (Leckman & Peterson, 1993). Among MZ twins discordant in tic severity, the twin with the lower birth weight generally manifests more severe tic symptomatology, with the difference in symptom severity being proportionate to the differences in their birth weights (Hyde et al., 1992; Leckman et al., 1987). In these studies, the birth weight of the TS probands were within the normal range. This

points to the power of studying genetically homogenous MZ pairs to evaluate potential risk and/or protective factors. Children with tics generally have more complications *in utero* than controls (Pasamanick & Kawi, 1956; Santangelo et al., 1994). Although it is possible that some of these difficulties are a consequence of the individual's genetic vulnerability, the alternative view that the nutritional (based on blood flow to the developing brain) and hormonal milieu of the developing central nervous system critically shape the neurobiological systems that will later mediate the expression of tic-, ADHD-, and OC-related symptoms seems intuitively more attractive especially given the MZ twin data. Sex-specific hormones and maternal stress during pregnancy may be important determinants of later tic severity (Leckman et al., 1990; Leckman & Peterson, 1993; Peterson et al., 1995). The normal testosterone surges that occur in males during in utero brain development and in the first year of life may also contribute to later tic severity in those who are genetically predisposed to the disorder. Subjective reports of maternal stress during pregnancy also correlate with later symptom severity as do self-reported nausea and vomiting in the first trimester (Leckman et al., 1990).

Other epigenetic factors involved in the development of TS and tic disorders may include chronic or intermittent psychosocial stressors in postnatal life. Tics are often exacerbated by anxiety, upset, or excitement (Surwillo, Shafii, & Barrett, 1978), and it is possible that chronic stressors attendant on having a tic disorder (e.g., ridicule, embarrassment) may increase tic symptoms. Short-term increases in tic frequency have also been noted in some individuals in response to thermal variations, with tics increasing as room temperature is increased (Lombroso, Mack, Scahill, King, & Leckman, 1992). Whether these intramorbid factors also act at an earlier point in development to influence the pathogenesis of TS and related conditions is unclear, although it presents an attractive possibility (Leckman et al., 1988).

Recent research has focused on autoimmune and neurological sequelae of streptococcal infection including Sydenham chorea, and potentially tics, obsessions and/or compulsions (Kiessling, Marcotte, & Culpepper, 1993; March, Swedo, & Leonard, 1992; Swedo et al., 1989). However, some caution is warranted in the interpretation of these findings given the widespread prevalence of putative antineuronal antibodies in the sera of normal children and the apparent lack of specificity of these antibodies to specific brain regions.

Typically these epigenetic and environmental risk factors have each been studied in virtual isolation of each other. It will be important to conduct controlled studies so that the independent effects of each variable can be determined. But the complex interaction among factors in the pathogenesis of TS necessitates a look at these multiple factors as having a synergistic relationship. For example, how the psychosocial risk factors work in concert with various pre- and perinatal factors in the pathogenesis of TS requires further study.

Neurobiological Substrates

Speculation concerning the neurobiological substrates of TS has typically focused on the role of midbrain dopaminergic systems and their projections to CSTC circuits believed to play a role in planning and monitoring motor activity (Albin, Young, & Penny, 1989; Leckman et al., 1992). The involvement of the CSTC circuits is supported by (1) anecdotal reports of neuropathological changes in the striatum (Balthasar, 1957; Richardson, 1982); (2) the ameliorative effect on tic symptoms of neurosurgical lesions to the ventral and intralaminar thalamic nuclei (Leckman et al., 1993); (3) volumetric magnetic resonance imaging (MRI) studies showing alterations in the normal asymmetry of the basal ganglia (Peterson et al., 1993; Singer et al., 1993); (4) positron emission tomography (PET) studies showing decreased regional metabolic activity in the frontal, cingulate, and insular cortex of TS patients (Braun et al., 1993); and (5) imaging studies documenting a reduced midsagittal cross-sectional area of the corpus callosum (Peterson et al., 1994). Some of the neuropsychological data (reviewed above) are also consistent with these findings, particularly those showing a reduction in the normally occurring asymmetry on a series of lateralizing tests (Yazgan et al., in press).

Central dopaminergic systems have been repeatedly implicated in the pathobiology of TS. Pharmacological data include marked tic reductions during treatment with haloperidol, pimozide, and other neuroleptics (E. Shapiro et al., 1989), as well as following the administration of agents that either reduce dopamine synthesis (Jankovic, Glaze, & Frost, 1984; Sweet, Bruun, Shapiro, & Shapiro, 1976) or activate dopamine autoreceptors (Feinberg and Carroll, 1979). Conversely, increased tics have been reported in

some, but not all, TS patients following withdrawal of neuroleptics and following exposure to agents that increase central dopaminergic activity such as L-dopa and central nervous system stimulants (Denckla, Bemporad, & McKay, 1976; Erenberg, Cruse, & Rathner, 1985; Klawans, Nausieda, Goetz, Tanner, & Weiner, 1982; Sverd, Gladow, & Paolicelli, 1989). The finding in postmortem and neuro-imaging studies of an increase (number or affinity) of the dopamine transporters in the striatum (Singer, Hahn, & Moran, 1991) also supports this conclusion (Malison et al., 1994; Wong et al., 1994).

Other investigators have focused attention on the potential role of the mesolimbic dopamine system and its projections to structures within the central limbic continuum: amygdala, septum, hippocampal formation, hypothalamus, ventral tegmental area (VTA), and the periaqueductal gray matter, as well as structures within the anteriormost CSTC circuits including the entorhinal cortex and the nucleus accumbens (Alexander, Delong, & Strick, 1986; Devinsky, 1983; Nauta, 1972; Nauta & Haymaker, 1969; Nieuwenhuys, Voodg, & van Huijzen, 1988). Evidence supporting the involvement of these circuits in TS include: elevated CSF concentrations of corticotropin releasing factor (CRF) and norepinephrine (Chappell et al., 1993; Leckman et al., 1995); evidence of heightened responsivity to stress (Jagger et al., 1982) (such as stress of lumbar puncture; see Chappell et al., 1994) as well as heat (Lombroso et al., 1992). Evidence of reduced prepulse inhibition of the startle response (Castellanos et al., 1993; Smith & Lees, 1989; Swerdlow, Caine, Braff, & Geyer, 1992) and disrupted sleep patterns (Allen, Singer, Brown, & Salam, 1992; Barabas et al., 1984b; Glaze, Frost, & Jankovic, 1983; Mendelson, Caine, Goyer, Ebert, & Gillin, 1980) provides further support for the involvement of these structures. Hypotheses concerning the role of gonadal steroid hormones and central nervous system sexual dimorphisms in the pathobiology also point to the possible involvement of limbic structures and midbrain dopaminergic centers (Leckman & Scahill, 1990; Peterson et al., 1993).

This convergent evidence as to the possible neurobiological substrates of TS is consistent with the ability of certain risk and protective factors to alter the laterality of neuronal systems and reset stress-sensitive hormonal and neurochemical circuits (Leckman & Peterson, 1993). These sites also offer a wealth of potential candidate genes that might be examined using the latest nonparametric genetic techniques.

CONCLUSIONS

This chapter gives an overview of TS in the context of a model of pathogenesis that integrates genetic, neurobiological, psychological and environmental influences. The role of the self in the context of social, emotional, and cognitive development is highlighted from a developmental framework and presented as a key element in the pathogenesis of TS. Future refinements to the model of pathogenesis presented here will necessarily include a closer examination of the precise mechanisms by which the various elements in this model interrelate with each other. Data from animal models will likely make important contributions, e.g., in elucidating the role of maternal stress during pregnancy as establishing enduring changes in stress responsivity in adult animals.

Advances in the study of genetics, neurochemistry, and brain structure and function have contributed to our understanding of the nature and causes of TS. Yet many issues remain unresolved. The exact gene or genes for TS have yet to be identified. Such a discovery holds a potential key in the treatment of TS and promises a fuller understanding to how genes work to transmit both normal and pathological aspects of human behavior. Genetics has also the complex task of elucidating the extent to which comorbid conditions represent possible phenotypic variants of a common genotype. A broader issue of the nature of the reciprocal relationship between genes and the neurochemical microenvironment of the brain may be understood better through research on TS and other disorders.

Epidemiological studies give some sense of the incidence and prevalence of TS. Here too, discrepant findings leave many questions unanswered. Definition and classification are fundamental elements of this area of research; a consensus as to the definition of "tic" and tic disorder remains a prerequisite for future epidemiological and genetic advances. The continuities and discontinuities between pathological tic symptoms and more subtle, normative tic-like habits need clarification. The fact that many children during their development exhibit some degree of tics is a clue that the study of normative development will yield insights to the pathological ex-

tremes of our behavior. Researchers must then work toward precise definition and classification systems, while at the same time keeping sight of the possible similarities between TS, other movement disorders, and normal development.

Advances in genetics and the developmental neurosciences have set the stage for a deeper understanding of the biological factors that mediate the expression of TS and related disorders. Knowledge in these areas is vital to the development of somatic and psychopharmacological treatment, yet other issues are also pressing on the TS research agenda including: the development of cognitive-behavioral approaches to the treatment of TS and related disorders (Azrin & Nunn, 1973; Azrin & Peterson, 1988, 1990); and a deeper understanding of the social deficits associated with TS (Dykens et al., 1990; Stokes et al., 1991). Are these social deficits an inevitable feature of the syndrome or are they simply the product of chronic peer rejection?

In the face of the complexity of the genetics and neurobiology of TS, it is crucial to keep in mind that the individual with TS has a unique self. Advances in the physical sciences must be met with efforts to understand the phenomenology, subjective experiences and social world of the child with TS. This includes parent–child interactions, the development of peer relationships, and the development of a sense of self as a competent and valued member of a classroom, family, or circle of friends. The social environment poses some uncertainty for the child with TS. Yet the social environment has a capacity to foster other aspects of the child that lie beyond his or her uncontrolled movements. Educating those around the child as to the myths and facts of TS will reveal an image of the child with TS as a whole person. An informed, empathic understanding of the child with TS will in turn facilitate his or her adaptive passage through the vicissitudes of development.

ACKNOWLEDGMENTS

This work is supported in part by Grant Nos. MH48351, MH44843, and MH30929 from the National Institute of Mental Health, and by Grant Nos. NS16648, HD03008, RR06022, and RR00125 from the National Institutes of Health, the Tourette Syndrome Association, and the Gatepost Foundation. Portions of this chapter appeared in Leckman et al. (1992), Peterson et al. (1995), and Leckman and Cohen (1995). The authors thank Mr. Lawrence Scahill and Dr. Daniel M. Tucker for their insightful comments, and Ms. Amy Vitale for editing a draft of this chapter.

REFERENCES

Achenbach, T. M., & Edelbrock, C. (1981). Behavioral problems and competencies reported by parents of normal and disturbed children aged four through sixteen. *Monographs of the Society for Research in Child Development, 46.*

Albin, R. L., Young, A. B., & Penny, J. B. (1989). The functional anatomy of basal ganglia disorders. *Trends in Neuroscience, 12,* 366–375.

Alexander, G. E., Delong, M. R., & Strick, P. L. (1986). Parallel organization of functionally segregated circuits linking basal ganglia and cortex. *Annual Review of Neuroscience, 9,* 357–381.

Allen, R. P., Singer, H. S., Brown, J. E., & Salam, M. M. (1992). Sleep disorders in Tourette syndrome: A primary or unrelated problem? *Pediatric Neurology, 8,* 275–280.

American Psychiatric Association. (1994). *Diagnostic and statistical manual of mental disorders* (4th ed.). Washington, DC: Author.

Apter, A., Pauls, D., Bleich, A., Zohar, A., Kron, S., Ratzoni, G., Dycian, A., Kotler, M., Weizman, A., Gadot, N., & Cohen, D. J. (1993). An epidemiological study of Tourette's syndrome in Israel. *Archives of General Psychiatry, 50,* 734–738.

Azrin, N. H., & Nunn, R. G. (1973). Habit reversal: A method of eliminating nervous habits and tics. *Behaviour Research and Therapy, 11,* 619–628.

Azrin, N. H., & Peterson, A. L. (1988). Habit reversal for the treatment of Tourette syndrome. *Behaviour Research and Therapy, 26,* 347–351.

Azrin, N. H., & Peterson, A. L. (1990). Treatment of Tourette syndrome by habit reversal: A waiting-list control group comparison. *Behavior Therapy, 21,* 305–318.

Balthasar, K. (1957). Uber das anatomische substrar der generalisieten tic-krankeit (maladie des tics, Gilles de la Tourette): Entwicklungshemmung des corpus striatum. *Archiv für Psychiatrie und Zeitschrift für die Gesamte Neurologie, 195,* 531–549.

Barabas, G., Matthews, W. S., & Ferrari, M. (1984a). Disorders of arousal in Gilles de la Tourette's syndrome. *Neurology, 34,* 815–817.

Barabas, G., Matthews, W. S., & Ferrari, M. (1984b). Somnabulism in children with Tourette syndrome. *Developmental Medicine and Child Neurology, 26,* 457–460.

Baron-Cohen, S., Cross, P., Crowson, M., & Robertson, M. (1994). Can children with Gilles de la Tourette syndrome edit their intentions? *Psychological Medicine, 24,* 29–40.

Bell, R. Q. (1968). A reinterpretation of the direction of effects in studies of socialization. *Psychological Review, 75,* 81–95.

Berkson, G. (1983). Repetitive stereotyped behaviors. *American Journal of Mental Retardation, 88,* 239–246.

Berkson, J. B. (1946). Limitations of the application of fourfold table analyses to hospital data. *Biometrics, 2,* 47–51.

Bertenthal, B. I., & Fisher, K. W. (1978). Development of self-recognition in the infant. *Developmental Psychology, 14,* 44–50.

Bornstein, R. A. (1990). Neuropsychological performance in children with Tourette's syndrome. *Psychiatry Research, 33,* 73–81.

Bornstein, R. A., & Yang, V. (1991). Neuropsychological performance in medicated and unmedicated patients with Tourette's disorder. *American Journal of Psychiatry, 148,* 468–471.

Braun, A. R., Stoetter, B., Randolph, C., Hsiao, H. K., Vladar, K., Gernert, J., Carson, R. E., Herscovitch, P., & Chase, T. N. (1993). The functional neuroanatomy of Tourette's syndrome: An FDG-PET study; I. Regional changes in cerebral glucose metabolism differentiating patients and controls. *Neuropsychopharmacology, 9,* 277–291.

Bruun, R. D. (1988). The natural history of Tourette's syndrome. In D. J. Cohen, R. D. Bruun, & J. F. Leckman (Eds.), *Tourette's syndrome and tic disorders* (pp. 21–39). New York: Wiley.

Bruun, R. D., & Budman, C. L. (1992). The natural history of Tourette syndrome. In T. N. Chase, A. J. Friedhoff, & D. J. Cohen (Eds.), *Advances in Neurology* (Vol. 58, pp. 1–6). New York: Raven Press.

Burd, L., Kaufman, D. W., & Kerbeshian, J. (1992). Tourette syndrome and learning disabilities. *Journal of Learning Disabilities, 25,* 598–604.

Burd, L., & Kerbeshian, J. (1985). Tourette syndrome, atypical pervasive developmental disorder and Ganser syndrome in a 15 year-old visually impaired, mentally retarded boy. *Canadian Journal of Psychiatry, 30,* 74–76.

Burd, L., Kerbeshian, J., Wilkenheiser, M., & Fisher, W. (1986). Prevalence of Gilles de la Tourette syndrome in North Dakota adults. *American Journal of Psychiatry, 143,* 787.

Butterworth, G. (1990). Self-perception in infancy. In D. Cicchetti & M. Beeghly (Eds.), *The self in transition: Infancy to childhood* (pp. 119–137). Chicago: University of Chicago Press.

Caine, E. D., McBride, M. C., Chiverton, P., Bamford, K. A., Rediess, S., & Shiao, S. (1987). Tourette syndrome in Monroe County school children. *Neurology, 38,* 472–475.

Carter, A., & Pauls, D. (1991). Preliminary results of a prospective study of Tourette's syndrome. *Psychiatric Genetics, 2,* 26–27.

Carter, A., Pauls, D., Leckman, J. F., & Cohen, D. J. (1994). A prospective longitudinal study of Gilles de la Tourette's syndrome. *Journal of the American Academy of Child and Adolescent Psychiatry, 33,* 377–385.

Castellanos, F. X., Fine, E. J., Kaysen, D. L., Kozuch, P. L., Hamburger, S. D., & Rapoport, J. L. (1993). Sensorimotor gaiting in boys with Tourette's syndrome (TS) and attention deficit hyperactivity disorder (ADHD). *Society for Neuroscience Abstracts, 19,* 991.

Chappell, P., Leckman, J. F., Goodman, W., Bissette, G., Pauls, D., Anderson, G. M., Riddle, M., Scahill, L., McDougle, C., & Cohen, D. J. (1993, December 12–17). *Elevated CSF corticotropin-releasing factor in Tourette syndrome: Comparison to obsessive–compulsive disorder and normal controls.* Paper presented at the 32nd annual meeting of the American College of Neuropsychopharmacology, Honolulu, HI.

Chappell, P., Leckman, J. F., Pauls, D., & Cohen, D. J. (1990). Biochemical and genetic studies of Tourette's syndrome: Implications for treatment and future research. In S. Deutsch, A. Weiszman, & R. Weizman (Eds.), *Application of basic neuroscience to child psychiatry* (pp. 241–260). New York: Plenum Medical.

Chappell, P., Riddle, M. A., Anderson, G. M., Scahill, L. D., Hardin, M. T., Walker, D. E., Cohen, D. J., & Leckman, J. F. (1994). Enhanced stress responsivity of Tourette syndrome patients undergoing lumbar puncture. *Biological Psychiatry, 36,* 35–43.

Cohen, D. J. (1990). *Tourette's syndrome: Developmental psychopathology of a model neuropsychiatric disorder of childhood.* Strecker Monograph Series, Pennsylvania Hospital.

Cohen, D. J., Detlor, J., Shaywitz, B. A., & Leckman, J. F. (1982). Interaction of biological and psychological factors in the natural history of Tourette syndrome: A paradigm for childhood neuropsychiatric disorders. In A. J. Friedhoff & T. N. Chase (Eds.), *Advances in neurology* (Vol. 35, pp. 31–40). New York: Raven Press.

Cohen, D. J., Friedhoff, A. J., Leckman, J. F., & Chase, T. N. (1992). Tourette syndrome: Extending basic research to clinical care, the clinical phenotype and natural history. In T. N. Chase, A. J. Friedhoff & D. J. Cohen (Eds.), *Tourette syndrome: Neurobiology, genetics and treatment* (pp. 341–362). New York: Raven Press.

Cohen, A., & Leckman, J. F. (1992). Sensory phenomena associated with Gilles de la Tourette's syndrome. *Journal of Clinical Psychiatry, 53,* 319–323.

Cohen, D. J., & Leckman, J. F. (1994). Developmental psychopathology and neurobiology of Tourette's syndrome. *Journal of the American Academy of Child and Adolescent Psychiatry, 33,* 2–15.

Comings, D. E. (1990). *Tourette syndrome and human behavior.* Duarte, CA: Hope Press.

Comings, D. E., & Comings, B. E. (1984). Tourette syndrome and attention deficit disorder with hyperactivity— are they genetically related? *Journal of the American Academy of Child Psychiatry, 23,* 138–144.

Comings, D. E., & Comings, B. E. (1985). Tourette syndrome: Clinical and psychological aspects of 250 cases. *American Journal of Human Genetics, 37,* 435–450.

Comings, D. E., & Comings, B. E. (1987). Hereditary agoraphobia and obsessive–compulsive behavior in relatives of patients with Gilles de la Tourette's syndrome. *British Journal of Psychiatry, 151,* 195–199.

Comings, D. E., & Comings, B. E. (1993). Co-morbid behavioral disorders. In R. Kurlan (Ed.), *Handbook of Tourette's syndrome and related tic and behavioral disorders* (pp. 111–147). New York: Marcel Dekker.

Comings, D. E., Comings, B. E., Devor, E. J., & Cloninger, C. R. (1984). Detection of the major gene for Gilles de la Tourette syndrome. *American Journal of Human Genetics, 36,* 586–600.

Comings, D. E., Himes, J. A., & Comings, B. G. (1990). An epidemiological study of Tourette syndrome in a single school district. *Journal of Clinical Psychiatry, 51,* 463–469.

Denckla, M. B., Bemporad, J. R., & McKay, M. C. (1976). Tics following methylphenidate administration: A report of 20 cases. *Journal of the American Medical Association, 235,* 1379–1381.

Denckla, M. B., Harris, E. L., Aylward, E. H., Singer, H. S., Reiss, A. L., Reader, M. J., Bryan, R. N., & Chase, T. N. (1991). Executive functions and volume of the basal ganglia in children with Tourette's syndrome and attention deficit hyperactivity disorder. *Annals of Neurology, 30,* 476.

Devinsky, O. (1983). Neuroanatomy of Gilles de la Tourette's syndrome: Possible midbrain involvement. *Archives of Neurology, 40,* 508–513.

Dykens, E. M., Leckman, J. F., Riddle, M. A., Hardin, M. T., Schwartz, S., & Cohen, D. J. (1990). Intellectual, academic, and adaptive functioning of Tourette syndrome children with and without attention deficit disorder. *Journal of Abnormal Child Psychology, 18,* 607–614.

Eapen, V., Pauls, D., & Robertson, M. M. (1993). Evidence for autosomal dominant transmission in Tourette's syndrome: United Kingdom Cohort Study. *British Journal of Psychiatry, 162,* 593–596.

Eldridge, R., Sweet, R., Lake, C. R., Ziegler, M., & Shapiro, A. K. (1977). Gilles de la Tourette's syndrome: Clinical genetic, physiologic, and biochemical aspects in 21 selected families. *Neurology, 27,* 115–124.

Elkind, D. (1967). Egocentrism in adolescence. *Child Development, 8,* 1025–1034.

Erenberg, G., Cruse, R. P., & Rothner, A. D. (1985). Tourette's syndrome: Effects of stimulant drugs. *Neurology, 35,* 1346–1348.

Erikson, E. H. (1968). *Identity, youth and crisis.* New York: Norton.

Evans, D. W. (1994). Self-complexity and its relation to development, symptomatology and self-perception during adolescence. *Child Psychiatry and Human Development, 24*(3), 173–182.

Evans, D. W., Brody, L., & Noam, G. (1995). Self-perceptions of adolescents with and without mood disorders: Content and structure. *Journal of Child Psychology and Psychiatry and Allied Disciplines, 36*(8), 1337–1351.

Feinberg, M., & Carroll, B. J. (1979). Effects of dopamine agonists and antagonists in Tourette's disease. *Archives of General Psychiatry, 36,* 979–985.

Frankel, M., Cummings, J., Robertson, M., Trimble, M., Hill, M., & Benson, D. (1986). Obsessions and compulsions in Tourette's syndrome. *Neurology, 37,* 378–382.

Gibson, J. J. (1966). *The senses considered as perceptual systems.* Boston: Houghton-Mifflin.

Gibson, J. J. (1979). *An ecological approach to visual perception.* Boston: Houghton-Mifflin.

Gilles de la Tourette, G. (1885). Etude sur une affection nerveuse caractisée par de l'incoordination motrice accompagnée d'echolalie et de coprolalie. *Archives of Neurology, 9,* 158.

Glaze, D. G., Frost, J. D., & Jankovic, J. (1983). Sleep in Gilles de la Tourette's syndrome: Disorder of arousal. *Neurology, 33,* 586–592.

Green, R., & Pitman, R. (1986). Tourette syndrome and obsessive-compulsive disorder. In M. A. Kline, L. Baer, & W. O. Minichiello (Eds.), *Obsessive–compulsive disorders: Theory, and management* (pp. 147–164). Littleton, MA: PSGP.

Guinon, G. (1886). Sur la maladie des tics convulsifs. *Revue Médicine, 6,* 50–80.

Guinon, G. (1887). Tics convulsifs et hystérie. *Revue de Médicine, 7,* 509–519.

Harter, S. (1983). Developmental perspective on the self-system. In P. Mussen (Ed.), *Handbook of child psychology* (pp. 275–385). New York: Wiley.

Hyde, T. M., Aaronson, B. A., Randolph, C., Rickler, K. C., & Weinberger, D. R. (1992). Relation of birthweight to the phenotypic expression of Gilles de la Tourette's syndrome in monozygotic twins. *Neurology, 42,* 652–658.

Incagnoli, T., & Kane, R. (1982). Neuropsychological functioning in Tourette syndrome. In A. J. Friedhoff & T. N. Chase (Eds.), *Advances in neurology* (Vol. 35, pp. 305–309). New York: Raven Press.

Itard, J. M. G. (1825). Memoires sur quelques fonctions involuntaires des appareils de la locomotion de la prehension et de la voix. *Archives of General Medicine, 8,* 385.

Jagger, J., Prusoff, B. A., Cohen, D. J., Kidd, K. K., Carbonari, C. M., & John, K. (1982). The epidemiology of Tourette's syndrome. *Schizophrenia Bulletin, 8*(2), 267–278.

Jankovic, J. (1992). Diagnosis and classification of tics and Tourette syndrome. In T. N. Chase, A. J. Friedhoff, & D. J. Cohen (Eds.), *Advances in neurology* (Vol. 58, pp. 7–14). New York: Raven Press.

Jankovic, J., Glaze, D. G., & Frost, J. D. (1984). Effect of tetrabenazine on tics and sleep of Gilles de la Tourette's syndrome. *Neurology, 34,* 688–692.

Joschko, M., & Rourke, B. P. (1982). Neuropsychological dimensions of Tourette syndrome: Test–retest stability and implications for intervention. In A. J. Friedhoff & T. N. Chase (Eds.), *Advances in neurology: Gilles de la Tourette syndrome* (Vol. 35, pp. 297–304). New York: Raven Press.

Kidd, K. K., & Pauls, D. (1982). Genetic hypotheses for Tourette syndrome. In A. J. Friedhoff & T. N. Chase (Eds.), *Advances in neurology* (Vol. 35, pp. 243–249). New York: Raven Press.

Kidd, K. K., Prusoff, B. A., & Cohen, D. J. (1980). The familial pattern of Tourette syndrome. *Archives of General Psychiatry, 37,* 1366–1339.

Kiessling, L. S., Marcotte, A. C., & Culpepper, L. (1993). Antineuronal antibodies: Tics and obsessive–compulsive symptoms. *Journal of Developmental and Behavioral Pediatrics, 14,* 281–282.

King, R., & Noshpitz, J. (1991). *Pathways of growth: Essentials of child psychiatry—psychopathology* (Vol. 2). New York: Wiley.

Klawans, H. L., Nausieda, P. A., Goetz, C. C., Tanner, C. M., & Weiner, W. J. (1982). Tourette-like symptoms following chronic neuroleptic therapy. In A. J. Friedhoff & T. N. Chase (Eds.), *Advances in neurology* (Vol. 35, pp. 415–418). New York: Raven Press.

Kurlan, R., Behr, J., Medved, L., Shoulson, I., Pauls, D., Kidd, J. R., & Kidd, K. (1986). Familial Tourette's syndrome: Report of a large pedigree and potential for linkage analysis. *Neurology, 36,* 772–776.

Kurlan, R., Eapen, V., Stern, J., McDermott, M., & Robertson, M. M. (1994). Bilineal transmission in Tourette syndrome families. *Neurology, 44,* 2336–2342.

Kurlan, R., Lichter, D., & Hewitt, D. (1989). Sensory tics in Tourette syndrome. *Neurology, 39,* 731–734.

Lang, A. (1991). Patient perception of tics and other movement disorders. *Neurology, 41,* 223–228.

Leckman, J. F., & Cohen, D. J. (1988). Descriptive and diagnostic classification of tic disorders. In D. J. Cohen, R. D. Bruun, & J. F. Leckman (Eds.), *Tourette's syndrome and tic disorders.* New York: Wiley.

Leckman, J. F., & Cohen, D. J. (1991). Tic disorders. In M. Lewis (Ed.), *Handbook of child and adolescent psychiatry: A comprehensive textbook* (pp. 613–621). Baltimore: Williams & Wilkins.

Leckman, J. F., & Cohen, D. J. (1994). Tic disorders. In M. Rutter, L. Hersov, & E. Taylor (Eds.), *Child and adolescent psychiatry* (pp. 455–466). Oxford: Blackwell Scientific Publishers.

Leckman, J. F., Cohen, D. J., Price, A., Riddle, M., Mindera, R., Anderson, G., & Pauls, D. (1988). The pathogenesis of Tourette syndrome. In A. B. Shah, N. S. Shah, & A. Donald (Eds.), *Movement disorders* (pp. 257–272). New York: Plenum Press.

Leckman, J. F., Dolnansky, E. S., Hardin, M. T., Clubb, M., Walkup, J. T., Stevenson, J., & Pauls, D. L. (1990). Perinatal factors in the expression of Tourette's syndrome: An exploratory study. *Journal of the American Academy of Child and Adolescent Psychiatry, 29,* 220–226.

Leckman, J. F., Grice, D., Barr, L., de Vries, A., Martin, C., Cohen, D. J., McDougle, C. J., Goodman, W. K., & Ras-

mussen, S. A. (1995). Tic-related versus non-tic-related obsessive-compulsive disorder. *Anxiety, 1,* 208–215.

Leckman, J. F., Pauls, D., Peterson, B., Riddle, M., Anderson, G., & Cohen, D. J. (1992). Pathogenesis of Tourette syndrome: Clues from the clinical phenotype and natural history. In T. N. Chase, A. J. Friedhoff, & D. J. Cohen (Eds.), *Advances in neurology* (Vol. 58, pp. 15–24). New York: Raven Press.

Leckman, J. F., & Peterson, B. (1993). The pathogenesis of Tourette's syndrome: Role of epigenetic factors active in early CNS development. *Biological Psychiatry, 34,* 425–427.

Leckman, J. F., Price, R. A., Walkup, J. T., Ort, S. I., Pauls, D., & Cohen, D. J. (1987). Birthweights of monozygotic twins discordant for Tourette's syndrome. *Archives of General Psychiatry, 44,* 100.

Leckman, J. F., & Scahill, L. (1990). Possible exacerbation of tics by androgenic steroids. *New England Journal of Medicine, 322,* 1647.

Leckman, J. F., Walker, D. E., & Cohen, D. J. (1993). Premonitory urges in Tourette syndrome. *American Journal of Psychiatry, 150,* 98–102.

Leckman, J. F., Walker, D., Goodman, W., Pauls, D., & Cohen, D. J. (1994). Just right perceptions in obsessive behavior in Tourette's syndrome. *American Journal of Psychiatry, 151,* 675–680.

Leonard, H. L., Lenane, M. C., Swedo, S., Rettew, D. C., Gershon, E. S., & Rapoport, J. (1992). Tics and Tourette syndrome: A 2- to 7-year follow-up of 54 obsessive–compulsive children. *American Journal of Psychiatry, 149,* 1244–1251.

Leonard, H. L., Swedo, S. E., Rapoport, J. L., Rickler, K. C., Topol, D., Lee, S., & Rettew, D. (1992). Tourette syndrome and obsessive–compulsive disorder. In T. N. Chase, A. J. Friedhoff, & D. J. Cohen (Eds.), *Advances in neurology* (Vol. 58, pp. 83–93). New York: Raven Press.

Lewis, M., & Brooks-Gunn, J. (1979). *Social cognition and the acquisition of self.* New York: Plenum Press.

Lombroso, P. J., Mack, G., Scahill, L., King, R., & Leckman, J. F. (1992). Exacerbation of Tourette's syndrome associated with thermal stress: A family study. *Neurology, 41,* 1984–1987.

Mahler, S. M., Luke, J. A., & Daltroff, W. (1945). Clinical and follow-up study of the tic syndrome in children. *American Journal of Orthopsychiatry, 15,* 631–647.

Malison, R. T., Vessotskie, J. M., Kung, M. P., McElgin, W., Romaniello, G., et al. (1994). SPECT imaging of striatal dopamine transporters in non-human primate with N-[(*E*)-3-iodopropen-2-yl]-2B-carbomethoxy-3B-(4-chlorophenyl) tropane ([123I]IPT). *Journal of Nuclear Medicine.*

March, J. S., Swedo, S. E., & Leonard, H. (1992). *New developments in obsessive–compulsive disorder.* Paper presented at the annual meeting of the American Academy of Child and Adolescent Psychiatry.

Meige, H., & Feindel, E. (1907). *Tics and their treatment* (S. A. K. Wilson, Trans. & Ed.). New York: William Wood.

Mendelson, W. B., Caine, E. D., Goyer, P., Ebert, M., & Gillen, J. C. (1980). Sleep in Tourette syndrome. *Biological Psychiatry, 15,* 339–343.

Modolfsky, H., Tullis, C., & Lamon, R. (1974). Multiple tic syndrome (Gilles de la Tourette's syndrome). *Journal of Nervous and Mental Disorders, 159,* 282–292.

Nauta, W. J. H. (1972). The central visceromotor system: A general survey. In C. C. Hockman (Ed.), *Limbic system mechanics and autonomic function* (pp. 21–38). Springfield, IL: Charles C. Thomas.

Nauta, W. J. H., & Haymaker, W. (1969). Hypothalamic nuclei and fiber connections. In W. Haymaker, E. Anderson, & W. J. H. Nauta (Eds.), *The hypothalamus* (pp. 136–209). Springfield, IL: Charles C. Thomas.

Nee, L. E., Caine, E. D., Polinsky, R. J., Eldridge, R., & Ebert, M. H. (1980). Gilles de la Tourette syndrome: Clinical and family study of 50 cases. *Annals of Neurology, 7,* 41–49.

Neiuwenhuys, R., Voogd, J., & van Huijzen, C. (1988). *The human central nervous system: A synopsis and atlas.* New York: Springer-Verlag.

Nomura, Y., Kita, M., & Segawa, M. (1992). Social adaptation of Tourette syndrome families in Japan. In T. N. Chase, A. J. Friedhoff, & D. J. Cohen (Eds.), *Advances in neurology* (Vol. 58, pp. 323–332). New York: Raven Press.

Pakstis, A., Heutink, P., Pauls, D., Kurlan, R., van de Wetering, B. J. M., Leckman, J. F., Sandkuyl, L. A., Kidd., J. R., Breedveld, G. J., Castiglione, C. M., Weber, J., Sparkes, R. S., Cohen, D. J., Kidd, K. K., & Oostra, B. A. (1991). Progress in the search for genetic linkage with Tourette syndrome: An exclusion map covering more than 50% of the autosomal genome. *American Journal of Human Genetics, 48,* 281–294.

Pasamanick, B., & Kawi, A. (1956). A study of the association of prenatal and perinatal factors in the development of tics in children. *Journal of Pediatrics, 48,* 596.

Pauls, D., Cohen, D. J., Heimbuch, R., Detlor, J., & Kidd, K. K. (1981). Familial pattern and transmission of Gilles de la Tourette's syndrome and multiple tics. *Archives of General Psychiatry, 38,* 1091–1093.

Pauls, D., & Leckman, J. F. (1986). The inheritance of Gilles de la Tourette's syndrome and associated behaviors: Evidence for autosomal dominant transmission. *New England Journal Medicine, 315(16),* 993–997.

Pauls, D., Leckman, J. F., & Cohen, D. J. (1993). Familial relationship between Gilles de la Tourette syndrome, attention deficit disorder, learning disabilities, speech disorders and stuttering. *Journal of the American Academy of Child and Adolescent Psychiatry, 32,* 1044–1050.

Pauls, D., Raymond, C., Stevenson, J., & Leckman, J. F. (1991). A family study of Gilles de la Tourette syndrome. *American Journal of Human Genetics, 48,* 154–163.

Peterson, B., Leckman J. F., & Cohen, D. J. (1995). Tourette's syndrome: A genetically predisposed and an environmentally specified developmental psychopathology. In D. Cicchetti & D. J. Cohen (Eds.), *Manual of developmental psychopathology* (pp. 213–242). New York: Wiley.

Peterson, B., Leckman, J. F., Duncan, J. S., Wetzles, R., Riddle, M. A., Hardin, M. T., & Cohen, D. J. (1994). Corpus callosum morphology from magnetic resonance images in Tourette syndrome. *Psychiatry Research: Neuroimaging, 55,* 85–99.

Peterson, B., Riddle, M., Cohen, D. J., Katz, L., Smith, J. C., Hardin, M. T., & Leckman, J. F. (1993). Reduced basal ganglia volumes in Tourette's syndrome using 3-dimensional reconstruction techniques from magnetic resonance images. *Neurology, 43,* 941–949.

Price, R. A., Kidd, K. K., Cohen, D. J., Pauls, D., & Leckman, J. F. (1985). A twin study of Tourette's syndrome. *Archives of General Psychiatry, 42,* 815–820.

Price, R. A., Pauls, D., & Caine, E. D. (1984). Pedigree and segregation analysis of clinically defined subgroups of Tourette syndrome. *American Journal of Human Genetics, 36(4: Suppl),* 178S.

Randolph, C., Hyde, T. M., Gold, J. M., Goldberg, T. E., & Weinberger, D. R. (1993). Tourette's syndrome in monozygotic twins. Relationship of tic severity to neuro-

psycholigical function. *Archives of Neurology, 50,* 725–728.

Richardson, E. P. (1982). Neuropathological studies of Tourette syndrome. In A. J. Friedhoff & T. N. Chase (Eds.), *Gilles de la Tourette syndrome* (pp. 83–87). New York: Raven Press.

Robertson, M. M. (1992). Self-injurious behavior in Tourette syndrome. In T. N. Chase, A. J. Friedhoff, & D. J. Cohen (Eds.), *Advances in neurology* (Vol. 58). New York: Raven Press.

Robertson, M. M., Trimble, M. R., & Lees, A. J. (1988). The psychopathology of the Gilles de la Tourette's syndrome. *British Journal of Psychiatry, 152,* 383–390.

Rutter, M., & Hemming, M. (1970). Individual items of deviant behavior. In M. Rutter, J. Tizard, & K. Whitmore (Eds.), *Education Health and Behavior* (pp. 202–232). London: Longman.

Sameroff, A., & Chandler, M. (1975). Reproductive risk and the continuum of caretaking casualty. In F. D. Horowitz, M. Hetherington, S. Scarr-Salapatek, & G. Siegel (Eds.), *Review of child development research* (Vol. 4, pp. 187–244). Chicago: University of Chicago Press.

Santangelo, S., Pauls, D., Goldstein, J., Faraone, V., Tsuang, M. T., & Leckman, J. F. (1994). Tourette's syndrome: What are the influences of gender and co-morbid obsessive--compulsive disorder? *Journal of the American Academy of Child and Adolescent Psychiatry, 33,* 795–804.

Scahill, L., Leckman, J. F., & Marek, K. L. (1995). Sensory phenomena in Tourette syndrome. In W. J. Weiner & A. E. Lang (Eds.), *Advances in neurology* (Vol. 65, pp. 273–280). New York: Raven Press.

Scahill, L., Ort, S. I., & Hardin, M. T. (1993). Tourette's syndrome. Part II: Contemporary approaches to assessment and treatment. *Archives of Psychiatric Nursing, 7,* 209–216.

Shapiro, A. K., & Shapiro, E. (1982). Tourette syndrome: History and present status. In A. J. Friedhoff & T. N. Chase (Eds.), *Advance in neurology* (Vol. 35). New York: Raven Press.

Shapiro, A. K., Shapiro, E. S., Bruun, R. D., & Sweet, R. (1978). *Gilles de la Tourette's syndrome.* New York: Raven Press.

Shapiro, E. S., Shapiro, A. K., Fulop, G., Hubbard, M., Mandeli, J., Nordlie, J., & Phillips, R. A. (1989). Controlled study of haloperidol, pimozide, and placebo for the treatment of Gilles de la Tourette's syndrome. *Archives of General Psychiatry, 46,* 722–730.

Shapiro, E. S., Shapiro, A. K., Young J. G., & Feinberg, T. E. (1988). *Gilles de la Tourette Syndrome.* New York: Raven Press.

Singer, H. S., Hahn, I.-H., & Moran, T. M. (1991). Abnormal dopamine uptake sites in portmortem striatum from patients with Tourette's syndrome. *Annals of Neurology, 30,* 558–562.

Singer, H. S., Reiss, A. L., Brown, J., Aylward, E. H., Shih, B., Chee, E., Harris, E. L., Reader, M. J., Chase, G. A., Bryan, N., & Denckla, M. B. (1993). Volumetric MRI changes in basal ganglia of children with Tourette syndrome. *Neurology, 43,* 950–956.

Singer, H. S., & Rosenberg, L. A. (1989). The development of behavioral and emotional problems in Tourette's syndrome. *Pediatric Neurology, 5,* 41–44.

Smith, S. J. M., & Lees, A. J. (1989). Abnormalities of the blink reflex in Gilles de la Tourette syndrome. *Journal of Neurology, Neurosurgery, and Psychiatry, 52,* 895–898.

Sprenger, J. (1948). *Malleus maleficarum* (M. Summers, Trans.). London: Pushkin. (Original work published 1489)

Stokes, A., Bawden, H. N., Camfield, P. R., Backman, J. E., & Dooley, J. M. (1991). Peer problems in Tourette disorder. *Pediatrics, 87,* 936–942.

Surwillo, W., Shafii, M., & Barrett, C. (1978). Gilles de la Tourette's syndrome. *Journal of Nervous and Mental Disease, 166,* 812–816.

Sverd, J., Gladow, K. D., & Paolicelli, L. M. (1989). Methylphenidate treatment of attention-deficit hyperactivity disorder in boys with Tourette syndrome. *Journal of the American Academy of Child and Adolescent Psychiatry, 28,* 574–579.

Swedo, S., Rapoport, J. L., Cheslow, D., Leonard, H., Ayoub, E. M., Hosier, D. M., & Wald, E. R. (1989). High prevalence of obsessive–compulsive symptoms in patients with Sydenham's chorea. *American Journal of Psychiatry, 146,* 246–249.

Sweet, R. D., Bruun, R., Shapiro, E., & Shapiro, A. K. (1976). Presynaptic catecholamine antagonists as treatment for Tourette syndrome: Effects of alpha-methyl-*para*-tyrosine and tetrabenazine. *Archives of General Psychiatry, 31,* 857–861.

Swerdlow, N. R., Caine, S. B., Braff, D. L., & Geyer, M. A. (1992). The neural substrates of sensorimotor gaiting of the startle reflex: A review of recent findings and their implications. *Journal of Psychopharmacology, 6,* 176–190.

Thomas, A., & Chess, S. (1977). *Temperament and development.* New York: Brunner/Mazel.

Van Wort, M. H., Jutkowitz, R., Rosenbaum, D., & Bowers, M. B. (1976). Gilles de la Tourette's syndrome: Biomedical approaches. In M. D. Yahr (Ed.), *The basal ganglia* (pp. 459–465). New York: Raven Press.

Verhulst, F. C., Akkerhuiss, G. W., & Althaus, M. (1985). Mental health in Dutch children: (1) A cross-cultural comparison. *Acta Psychiatrica Scandinavica, 72*(Suppl.), 323.

Walkup, J. T., Leckman, J. F., Price, R. A., Harden, M. T., Ort S., & Cohen, D. J. (1988). The relationship between Tourette's syndrome and obsessive–compulsive disorder: A twin study. *Psychopharmacology Bulletin, 24,* 375–379.

Walkup, J. T., Scahill, L., & Riddle, M. A. (1995). Disruptive behavior, hyperactivity and learning disabilities in children with Tourette's syndrome. In W. J. Weiner & A. E. Lang (Eds.), *Advances in neurology* (Vol. 65, pp. 259–272). New York: Raven Press.

Wong, D. F., Singer, H., Marenco, S., Brown, J., Yung, B., Yokoi, F., Chan, B., Mathews, W., Musachio, J., & Dannals, R. F. (1994). Dopamine transporter reuptake sites measured by [C11] WIN 35, 428 PET imaging are elevated in Tourette syndrome patients. *Journal of Nuclear Medicine, 35*(Suppl. 5), 130P.

World Health Organization. (1992). *The ICD-10 classification of mental and behavioural disorders: Clinical descriptions and diagnostic guidelines.* Geneva, Switzerland: Author.

World Health Organization. (1993). *The ICD-10 classification of mental and behavioural disorders: Diagnostic criteria for research.* Geneva, Switzerland: Author.

Yaryura-Tobias, J., Neziroglu, F., Howard, S., & Fuller, B. (1983). Gilles de la Tourette's syndrome. In *Obsessive—compulsive disorders: Pathogenesis—diagnosis—treatment.* New York: Marcel Dekker.

Yazgan, Y., Peterson, B., Wexler, B. E., & Leckman, J. F. (in press). Functional correlates of basal ganglia alterations in Tourette's syndrome. *Biological Psychiatry.*

Zigler, E., & Glick, M. (1986). *A developmental approach to adult psychopathology.* New York: Wiley.

V

INFANTS AND CHILDREN AT RISK FOR DISORDER

Disorder and Risk for Disorder during Infancy and Toddlerhood

Karlen Lyons-Ruth
Charles H. Zeanah
Diane Benoit

Sameroff (1992) recently declared that the study of behavior in context was the most significant advance in developmental research in the past 25 years. This is no surprise to those who study, observe, or treat infants and young children, all of whom must be impressed again and again with the extraordinary importance of context for infant development. Nevertheless, this observation also underscores a major challenge of attempting to conceptualize disorders of infancy. A series of questions challenges our efforts to define disorders of infancy. Can infants be diagnosed as having within-the-person psychiatric disorders or are their symptoms relationship specific? To what degree should the caregiving contexts of infants' development be considered an integral part of a relationship disorder as opposed to an associated feature of individual disordered behavior? Are disturbed behaviors in infants indicative of disorder per se, or do they merely indicate risk for subsequent disorder? To what degree are we to take into account here and now suffering, or must we also demonstrate links between infant developmental disturbances and subsequent disorders? How we answer these questions may lead us in different directions.

There are, in fact, two major and quite different traditions in infant mental health regarding how to conceptualize psychiatric disturbances in young children. These approaches make different assumptions about disturbances and seem likely to direct efforts at intervention differently, as well.

One tradition, which has dominated research in developmental psychology and developmental psychopathology, suggests that infants may be considered as having a number of specific risk and/or protective factors that increase or decrease the probability that they will develop a given disorder in later childhood. These risk and protective factors may be either biological (intrinsic) or social (contextual) or both. Much of contemporary research has been devoted to detecting early "markers" of subsequent disorder, with the aim of delineating developmental pathways or trajectories of at-risk infants.

Another tradition, which has more clinical than empirical roots, suggests that infants may have formal psychiatric disorders, even in the first 3 years of life. Research in support of this tradition is only beginning to appear, and there is much work to be done to test some of the assertions that have been made. Nonetheless, this approach to disorders of infancy appears to have widespread support (Minde & Minde, 1986; Minde, 1995; Zeanah, 1993; Zero to Three/National Center for Clinical Infant Programs, 1994).

The plan for this chapter is to first consider some of the conceptual controversies regarding

relational versus individual approaches to diagnostic classification issues, which emerge with particular clarity in the study of disorders of infancy. Current competing approaches to diagnosis in infancy are discussed. Research relevant to the definition and correlates of the various particular "disorders" of infancy are then reviewed, including common clinical problems not yet represented in the fourth edition of the *Diagnostic and Statistical Manual of Mental Disorders* (DSM-IV; American Psychiatric Association, 1994) such as colic or regulatory disorders. In the final section, longitudinal developmental research exploring both infant behavioral constellations and family characteristics that may constitute risk factors, precursors, or prodromal forms of later childhood disorders is selectively reviewed. Three particularly active areas of current research are considered, including studies of the intergenerational transmission of patterns of relational behavior, research exploring the context and correlates of disorganized/disoriented infant attachment behaviors, and recent studies of early predictors of aggressive behavior disorders.

DIAGNOSTIC CLASSIFICATION IN INFANCY

The clinical tradition of examining disorders of infancy requires us to consider some of the special challenges of diagnostic classification relevant to this age group. Emde, Bingham, and Harmon (1993) have suggested that these challenges include the multidisciplinary nature of infant mental health, the developmental perspective inherent in infant mental health, the multigenerational focus of problems, and the prevention orientation of the field. These features complicate the diagnostic process in infancy, but the failure to include such features may also be responsible in part for the widespread dissatisfaction among clinicians with the approach to disorders of infancy taken by standard nosologies (Zeanah, 1993).

DSM-IV and Disorders of Infancy

Disorders of infancy described in DSM-IV (American Psychiatric Association, 1994) (see Table 13.1) are limited in both number and scope, and with few exceptions, they use the same criteria for children less than 3 years that they use for children older than 3 years. Thus, they fail to take into account possible developmental differ-

TABLE 13.1. Psychiatric Disorders of the First 3 Years: DSM-IV

Axis I: Primary diagnosis
    Feeding and Eating Disorders of Infancy or Early Childhood
        Pica
        Rumination Disorder
        Feeding Disorder
    Reactive Attachment Disorder of Infancy or Early Childhood
    Pervasive Developmental Disorders
        Autistic Disorder
        Rett's Disorder
        Childhood Disintegrative Disorder (after age 2)
    Problems Related to Abuse or Neglect
        Physical Abuse of Child
        Sexual Abuse of Child
        Neglect of Child
    Relational Problems
        Parent–Child Relational Problem

Note. Axis I diagnostic categories particularly relevant to infants and toddlers appearing in American Psychiatric Association (1994).

ences in symptom picture, the implications of rapid developmental change over the first 3 years of life, and the likelihood of symptoms or syndromes specific to this developmental period.

Zero to Three and Disorders of Infancy

In response to these issues, a task force of Zero to Three/National Center for Clinical Infant Programs began meeting a number of years ago for the purpose of developing a classificatory scheme for disorders apparent in the first 3 years of life. Chaired initially by Stanley Greenspan, and later by Serena Wieder, this group included a number of influential figures in infant mental health who met regularly to formulate approaches to the problem. This effort resulted in the recent publication of a manual (Zero to Three/National Center for Clinical Infant Programs, 1994) delineating criteria intended to capture the clinical phenomenology of disorders of infancy (see Table 13.2).

This scheme describes seven specific disorders believed to occur in infants and young children and provides criteria for diagnosing them. In addition, it adopts the multiaxial approach to diagnosis similar to that of DSM (American Psychiatric Association, 1980, 1987, 1994) although its axes are somewhat different. Axis I comprises one or more of the disorders listed in Table 13.2.

TABLE 13.2. Proposed Diagnostic Classification: 0–3

Axis I: Primary diagnosis
   Disorders of Relating and Communicating
     Multisystem Developmental Disorder
   Regulatory Disorders
   Eating Behavior Disorder
   Sleep Behavior Disorder
   Traumatic Stress Disorder
   Disorders of Affect
     Anxiety Disorders
     Mood Disorders
     Mixed Disorder of Emotional Expressiveness
     Gender Identity Disorder
     Reactive Attachment Disorder
   Adjustment Disorder
Axis II: Relationship Disorder Classification
   Perturbation
   Disturbance
   Disorder
Axis III: Other Medical and Developmental
   Conditions
Axis IV: Psychosocial Stressors
Axis V: Functional Emotional Developmental Level

Note. Diagnostic system proposed in Zero to Three/National Center for Clinical Infant Programs (1994).

Axis II comprises a classification of relationship disorders, that is, a relationship with a caregiver that is so disturbed as to constitute a disorder. Nevertheless, the relationship disorder is believed to exist between caregiver and infant rather than within the infant. Types of disordered relationships defined include overinvolved, underinvolved, anxious/tense, angry/hostile, abusive, and mixed. In this classificatory system, a relationship disorder may occur with or without an Axis I disorder and vice versa.

Axes III and IV are quite similar to their DSM-IV counterparts. Axis III includes physical, neurological, or developmental problems not considered elsewhere. These may or may not be related to the Axis I or Axis II diagnoses. Axis IV comprises a rating of psychosocial stressors. Axis V is used to describe the infant's functional emotional level. A Parent–Infant Relationship Global Assessment Scale (PIRGAS) is also included in an appendix for the purpose of rating the level of relationship adaptation or disturbance. Ratings range from well adapted through perturbed, disturbed, disordered, to frankly dangerous. Only if the relationship is determined to be disordered or dangerously impaired using this scale does an Axis II classification apply.

It remains to be seen how useful the approach of the Zero to Three system will prove to be.

There are almost no reliability or validity data about the criteria for any of the disorders included. Nevertheless, there is clear merit in proposing a system that can be evaluated formally. The view of the Task Force is that this represents a significant advance for the field precisely for that reason.

On the other hand, there are already some problems apparent with the system. For example, clearer boundaries need to be delineated between related but different types of disorders, and issues of comorbidity need to be addressed. When, for example, an infant exhibits difficulty in regulating emotions, both disorders of affect and regulatory disorders might be considered. Also, at times, there is a lack of clarity in specifying rules for decision making in using the criteria to make a diagnosis. These are typical problems characterizing new nosologies, however, and the hope of the Zero to Three Task Force was to stimulate much needed research.

Other Diagnostic Issues

With both DSM-IV and Zero to Three diagnostic systems, there is an implicit acceptance of the traditional biomedical model of a categorical typology of disorders. Nevertheless, we might reasonably ask whether a continuous or dimensional approach to psychopathology of infancy may have important advantages over a categorical or disorder approach, as some have suggested (Rutter, 1994). Some have advocated a continuous approach to diagnosis with older children as well, although there is considerable controversy about this (Quay, 1986).

Another issue to be considered is whether disorders of infancy are better conceptualized as within-the-individual or as between infants and their primary caregivers. Sameroff and Emde (1989) have suggested that with a few notable exceptions, such as autistic spectrum disorder, most disorders of early infancy are relationship disorders rather than individual disorders. Anchoring their approach in disturbances in the infant–caregiver relationship, and particularly, in the caregiver's regulatory function for the infant, they defined different levels of disturbance (relationship perturbations, disturbances, and disorders) and provided some preliminary ideas about diagnosis (Anders, 1989). The Zero to Three Task Force has made two efforts to incorporate an approach to relationship difficulties. First, they have included an axis of relationship disorders,

although the types of disordered relationships described in the Zero to Three system are quite different than those proposed by Sameroff and Emde (1989). Second, they included PIRGAS, which was developed specifically from Sameroff and Emde's (1989) proposed continuum of relationship difficulties. An infant may be diagnosed as having an Axis I disorder or an Axis II disorder or both. Nevertheless, data about the reliability and validity of PIRGAS are still pending. The question remains whether it is possible or desirable to accommodate such divergent views about the nature of developmental disturbances in the same classificatory system.

In summary, extant systems of classifying disorders of infancy are preliminary in the case of Zero to Three and underdeveloped in the case of DSM-IV. An attempt to validate the classification systems and the specific criteria included for various disorders is a necessary next step. For the discussion that follows, we have selected for review common problems seen by infant mental health clinicians. We begin with problems commonly believed to be more biologically rooted, such as regulatory disorders and colic, and conclude with disorders believed to be more experientially rooted, such as posttraumatic stress disorder and attachment disorder. Between these two poles of the spectrum are disorders believed to have more variable or mixed contributions from individual differences in central nervous system functioning and psychological experiences. Throughout the discussion we emphasize the ongoing importance of contextual factors, and especially the primary caregiving relationship, on the expression and experience of disorders throughout this spectrum.

REGULATORY DISORDERS

As discussed in the opening section on diagnostic issues during infancy, several common problems encountered during infancy are not included in DSM-IV. Given the frequency of presentation of these problems and the controversies surrounding infant diagnosis, they also are reviewed below.

Description of Disorder

Regulatory disorders were first described by Greenspan and Lourie (1981). They are characterized by "difficulties in regulating physiological, sensory, attentional, and motor or affective processes, and in organizing a calm, alert, or affectively positive state" (Greenspan & Wieder, 1993, p. 282).

Clinically, infants with regulatory disorders are behaviorally (or temperamentally) difficult. They may present with an inability to regulate sleep–wake cycles, mood, and self-soothing, or with difficulties such as irritability, feeding problems, colic, hypersensitivities to stimulation, and a lack of cuddliness (DeGangi & Greenspan, 1988). Most of these difficulties are believed to reflect, or be associated with problems in sensory, sensorimotor, or processing capacities that may include impaired reactivity to auditory, visual, tactile, gustatory, vestibular stimulation, olfactive, temperature, motor tone, motor planning skills, fine motor skills, and capacity to discriminate or integrate auditory–verbal or visual–spatial stimuli (Greenspan & Wieder, 1993).

Diagnostic Considerations

Although regulatory disorders are not included in the diagnostic nomenclature of DSM-IV, Greenspan and Wieder (1993) have described six types of regulatory disorders, each including specific diagnostic criteria: Type I (hypersensitive type), Type II (underreactive type), Type III (active/aggressive type), Type IV (mixed type), Type V (sleeping difficulties), and Type VI (eating difficulties).

Greenspan and Wieder (1993) suggest that regulatory disorders may affect one or more areas of development and range in severity from mild to severe. In the most severe regulatory disorders, physiological or state repertoires are affected. For example, infants may have irregular breathing, startles, gagging, and so forth. In the mildest regulatory disorders, infants may exhibit sleep, eating, or elimination problems. Between these two extremes of severity, other difficulties may be found in the area of (1) gross and fine motor activity (e.g., abnormal tonus or posture, jerky or limp movements, poor motor planning); (2) attentional organization (e.g., driven or perseverating on small details); or (3) affective organization, including predominant affective tone, range, and modulation of affective experiences.

Regulatory disorders are diagnosed only in infants older than 6 months because transient difficulties with self-regulation (e.g., sleep problems) are common in young infants and resolve spontaneously by 5 to 6 months of age (DeGangi, Craft, & Castellan, 1991). Further, in order for a

diagnosis of regulatory disorder to be made, both behavioral and constitutional maturational elements must be present, and the difficulties in sensory, sensorimotor, or processing capacities must affect daily adaptation and relationships (DeGangi, Craft, & Castellan, 1991; Greenspan & Wieder, 1993).

Developmental Course and Prognosis

There is no documented adult equivalent of regulatory disorder. To date, only one study (DeGangi, Porges, Sickel, & Greenspan, 1993) has examined the natural history and prognosis of regulatory disorders. In this follow-up study, 9 out of 11 infants with a regulatory disorder diagnosed at ages 8 to 10 months (and 13 out of 24 controls) were followed for 4 years. Findings from this study showed that eight of the nine regulatory-disordered children had developmental, sensorimotor, and/or emotional and behavioral problems at 4 years of age. In addition, there were significant group differences on measures of cognitive abilities, attention span and activity level, emotional maturity, motor maturity, and tactile sensitivity between preschoolers without regulatory disorders and those with regulatory disorders (in the expected direction). The authors concluded that if left untreated, regulatory disorders and the associated behavioral difficulties may persist.

Epidemiology

The incidence and prevalence rates of regulatory disorders have not yet been established. However, regulatory disorders are believed to be rare (DeGangi, Craft, & Castellan, 1991). To the best of our knowledge, only one sample of 11 infants with regulatory disorders has been described. In that sample, there was an overrepresentation of male subjects (10 out of 11 subjects were male children) (DeGangi, Craft, & Castellan, 1991). No information is yet available on either social-class factors or cultural variations of regulatory disorders.

Etiology

Although the etiology of regulatory disorders is unclear (Greenspan & Wieder, 1993), dysfunctions in the autonomic nervous system have been hypothesized. In support of this hypothesis, DeGangi and her colleagues (DeGangi, DiPietro, Greenspan, & Porges, 1991) found that some physiological responses relating to vagal tone

(heart period and cardiac vagal tone) differentiated 8- to 11-month-old infants with regulatory disorders ($n = 11$) and infants without regulatory disorders ($n = 24$). Specifically, infants with regulatory disorders tended to have higher baseline vagal tone and showed inconsistent vagal reactivity (i.e., heterogeneous response to sensory and cognitive tasks). These findings suggest that infants with regulatory disorders may have autonomic (parasympathetic) hyperirritability caused by defective central neural programs and mediated via neurotransmitters through the vagus nerve (DeGangi, DiPietro, et al., 1991; Porges, 1991). No genetic etiological contributor has yet been hypothesized for the disorder.

DeGangi (1991) examined possible environmental factors, especially caregiving environment, that might contribute to regulatory disorders. Her group found that, compared to mothers of infants without regulatory disorders, mothers of infants with regulatory disorders showed less contingent responses, less physical proximity, and more flat affect during play interactions. Parents of infants with regulatory disorders also have more negative perceptions of their infant than parents of infants without regulatory disorders (DeGangi et al., 1993). Although findings from these studies do not point directly to an environmental etiology for regulatory disorders, they suggest that the quality of the caregiving environment may contribute to the improvement or perpetuation of some regulatory disorders.

Future Directions

More research is necessary to validate this diagnostic entity and to determine the prevalence, developmental course, and prognosis of the disorder. More research is also needed to examine the relative contributions of both the autonomic nervous system and the caregiving environment to regulatory disorders. The relationship between sleeping and feeding disorders and regulatory disorders should be explored as well. Finally, future research should examine prevention and treatment issues.

COLIC

Although colic is not a DSM-IV diagnosis, it is a common problem during infancy. Because colic is often viewed as a form of excessive crying, it is useful to review normal patterns of crying during infancy. In his landmark study of 80 mothers

who kept detailed diaries of their infants' daily patterns of crying for 3 months, Brazelton (1962) found that in normal, healthy infants, the duration of crying increases progressively from birth to 6 weeks of age. By 6 weeks old, normal infants reach a peak of crying with approximately 2 hours and 45 minutes of crying per day. By 12 weeks old, the average duration of crying decreases to approximately 1 hour per day. Brazelton also found that normal crying patterns tend to cluster around the evening hours, beginning at 3 weeks, peaking at 6 weeks, and gradually disappearing by 12 weeks. Barr and his colleagues (Barr, Kramer, Pless, Boisjoly, & Leduc, 1989), found that the amount of crying over 24 hours or by period of day was not affected by method of feeding (breast vs. bottle).

Description of Disorder

Lester et al. (1990) described the physical and behavioral signs of colic as including facial grimacing, flexed elbows, clenched fists, drawn up or stiff and extended knees, tense and distended abdomen, tightly closed or widely opened eyes, arched back, red face, cold feet, brief breath-holding episodes, increased bowel sounds, and gas. Associated features of colic include spasms in the gastrointestinal tract. These spasms are believed to be secondary to the colic rather than causing the colic (Lester, Boukydis, Garcia-Coll, & Hole, 1990). Infants with colic are more likely to have or develop difficult temperament than noncolicky infants even after the colic has ended (Carey, 1972; Lester et al., 1990; Weissbluth, Christoffel, & Davis, 1984; Weissbluth, Davis, & Poncher, 1984). Sleep problems have been found in infants with colic (Stahlberg & Savilahti, 1986; Weissbluth, 1987; Weissbluth, Christoffel, & Davis, 1984; Weissbluth, Davis, & Poncher, 1984). In fact, Weissbluth suggests that colic reflects a disturbance of the sleep–wake control mechanisms, suggesting an underlying autonomic imbalance and providing some support for Greenspan and Wieder's (1993) view that colic may represent one manifestation of a child's difficulty in self-regulation.

Diagnostic Considerations

Several attempts have been made to provide empirical definitions for normal crying (Brazelton, 1962), excessive crying, and colic in infancy (Barr, Rotman, Yaremko, Leduc, & Francoeur, 1992; Lester et al., 1990; Wessel, Cobb, Jackson, Harris, & Detwilet, 1954). However, there is no universally accepted definition of colic. In fact, many clinicians and researchers use colic and excessive crying interchangeably, or view colic as an extreme form of the normal crying activity in infants (Barr, 1990; Brazelton, 1990). However, Lester and colleagues (1990) distinguish colic from excessive crying, based on empirical evidence suggesting that the cry characteristics of colicky infants differ from those of noncolicky infants.

Wessel and colleagues (1954) have provided the most widely used definition of colic, also known as the "rule of 3" in which colic is defined as crying or fussing (paroxysmal onset) occurring for more than 3 hours per day, 3 days per week, and for 3 weeks occurring in otherwise healthy infants during the first 3 to 4 months of life.

Lester et al. (1990) define colic as a syndrome consisting of four major characteristics: (1) paroxysmal onset; (2) distinctive high-pitched pain cry; (3) physical signs associated with hypertonia (described above); and (4) inconsolability. Their definition is based on empirical findings. Further, Lester and his group have extensively studied the cry characteristics of infants with colic (see next section, below).

Barr and his colleagues (1992) argue that infants with colic could be classified in two groups, based on their symptomatology: (1) the "Wessel colic" in which mothers reported the symptomatology originally described by Wessel et al. (1954); and (2) the "non-Wessel colic" in which mothers reported crying and fussing periods less than 3 days per week. Barr and his colleagues report that "maternal measures of total daily crying/fussing duration, crying/fussing bout length, and infant temperament and objective analyses of facial activity showed a consistent pattern of differences in which Wessel's colic infants differed from both non-Wessel's colic and control infants, who in turn did not differ from each other" (p. 14). Mothers in both groups of colic infants characterized their infants' cries following feeds as being more "sick sounding."

Developmental Course and Prognosis

Little is known about the sequelae of colic (Lester et al., 1990). No mortality or serious morbidity associated with colic has been documented. Colic continues to be perceived by clinicians as a transitory phenomenon that spontaneously improves after the first 4 to 6 months of life. There is no known adult equivalent of the disorder.

Epidemiology

Because of the absence of universally accepted definitions of excessive crying and colic, incidence and prevalence estimates vary greatly. Nonetheless, colic (or excessive crying) is a frequent problem, estimated to affect 20% to 25% of normal healthy infants during the first 6 months of life. Given its frequency and the associated stress on the families (Brazelton, 1990; Carey, 1990; Lester et al., 1990), it is surprising that no definition has yet been developed. However, Lester et al. (1990) argue that the incidence and prevalence rate estimates ranging from 8% to 40% (Asnes & Mones, 1982; Brazelton, 1990; Carey, 1984; Forsyth, McCarthy, & Leventhal, 1985; Hewson, Oberklaid, & Menahem, 1987; Hide, 1982; Lester et al., 1990; Meyer & Thaler, 1972; Paradise, 1966; Pinyerd & Zipf, 1989; Wessel et al., 1954) may overestimate the "true" incidence and prevalence rates of colic as they probably reflect the incidence and prevalence rates for both excessive crying and colic. Lester et al. (1990) argue that true colic probably affects 8% to 10% of infants, whereas excessive crying is more common.

The incidence rates of colic are similar for term and age-corrected preterm infants (Meyer & Thaler, 1972; Pierce, 1948). Controlled studies have shown that there is no difference in the prevalence of colic between infants who are breastfed and infants who are bottle-fed (Forsyth et al., 1985; Illingworth, 1954; Paradise, 1966; Stahlberg, 1984). There are no documented sex differences or social-class factors, although some cultural variations in crying have been documented (e.g., Barr, 1990).

Etiology

Little is known about the etiology and pathophysiology of colic. Several potential causes of colic have been studied, but findings from these studies remain inconclusive. A distinction between "intrinsic" (or biological) and "extrinsic" (or environmental) causes of colic has been made (Asnes & Mones, 1982; Illingworth, 1985).

Suspected *intrinsic* causes of colic include food allergy (in particular to cow's milk protein), hypertonia secondary to gastrointestinal contractions, immaturity of the gastrointestinal tract, and progesterone deficiency. Suspected *extrinsic* causes of colic include maternal anxiety, personality factors, inappropriate handling, mother–infant relationship, tobacco smoking, and inadequate feeding (see Lester et al., 1990, for a review). For example, mothers of infants with excessive crying have been described as depressed (Brazelton, 1962; White, 1936), exhausted (Jones & Verduyn, 1983; Menahem, 1978), and angry (Waldman & Sarsgard, 1983), and providing fewer positive responses to their infants than controls (Shaver, 1979; Shaw, 1977). Because of inconclusive evidence from research on etiology and pathophysiology, some researchers and clinicians view colic as the final common pathway between various intrinsic and extrinsic factors (Carey, 1984; Hewson et al., 1987).

Lester and his colleagues (Lester, 1987; Lester & Boukydis, 1991; Lester et al., 1990) argue that colic might be caused by an imbalance in the autonomic (interplay between the sympathetic and parasympathetic) nervous system. They base their argument in part on their findings related to the specific acoustic characteristics of the cry of infants with colic. Indeed, they argue that the vagal complex (cranial nerves IX to XII) and the phrenic and thoracic nerves control the acoustic characteristics of the cry, in addition to influencing some of the muscles of the larynx (Lester, 1987; Lester & Boukydis, 1991). Some infants may experience sympathetic dominance, which triggers the sudden onset of crying, the high-pitched pain cry, and hypertonia characteristic of colic. Lester et al. (1990) argue that infants with colic have lower thresholds of reactivity that can be traced to the hypothalamic–limbic circuits that initiate the cry (Lester & Boukydis, 1991) and that result in higher levels of motor arousal to stimulation (hypertonia). Lester and his colleagues argue that because of the diminished parasympathetic inhibition, the infant with colic lacks regulatory capacities for self-soothing, cannot be soothed by the caregiver, and is thus difficult to console.

Lester et al. (1990) also found that the cry characteristics of infants with colic differ from those of infants without colic. Lester and his group studied a group of 16 term and preterm infants between the ages of 1 and 4 months who met the criteria for excessive crying (as defined by crying for at least 3 hours per day, 3 days per week, and for 3 weeks) and colic [as defined by (1) paroxysmal or sudden onset of cry; (2) distinctive high-pitched pain cry; (3) physical signs associated with hypertonia; and (4) inconsolability]. The acoustic characteristics of the cries of 16 infants with colic were compared to those of a group of infants without colic, matched for age, prematurity,

medical illness, and socioeconomic status. Findings showed that the cries of infants with colic had a 25% higher-pitched cry, a 30% greater pitch variability, and more than twice the turbulence or disphonation than the cries of the control infants. In that study, mothers of infants with colic rated the cries of their infants as more urgent, more piercing, more grating, and more arousing than did mothers in the control group.

Future Directions

The absence of a standard definition and accepted diagnostic criteria for colic has hampered research on colic, including its etiology, pathophysiology, and management (Lester et al., 1990). As a first step, Lester and his colleagues (1990) recommend differentiating colic and excessive crying. Other areas in need of research include the contribution of parental characteristics, including quality of caregiving, to the onset and/or perpetuation of colic.

FAILURE TO THRIVE

Description of Disorder

Although there is no universally accepted definition of failure to thrive (FTT) or feeding disorder (see below), FTT is an Axis I diagnosis in DSM-IV under "feeding disorder of infancy or early childhood." Considerable heterogeneity exists with respect to characteristics of infants with FTT, their caregivers, their family and social circumstances (see Benoit, 1993a, 1993b, for reviews).

Infants with FTT

Because of their state of malnutrition, infants with FTT often look cachectic, are prone to recurrent infections and show a decreased ability to recover from them. They are often developmentally delayed and may exhibit unusual postures. Infants with FTT may look depressed, withdrawn, sad, apathetic, wary, or hypervigilant, irritable, and angry.

Caregivers of Infants with FTT

Mothers of infants with FTT have been described (both in controlled and noncontrolled studies) as exhibiting a wide variety of clinical problems such as affective disorders, substance abuse, and personality disorder (e.g., Crittenden, 1987; Polan et al., 1991). However, conflicting findings continue to surround this area of research (see Benoit, 1993a, 1993b, for reviews). In their controlled study of maternal attachment characteristics, Benoit and colleagues (Benoit, Zeanah, & Barton, 1989) found that, compared to their matched counterparts, mothers of infants with FTT were more likely to be classified as insecure with respect to attachment (using the Adult Attachment Interview; George, Kaplan, & Main, 1985). The findings of Benoit et al. suggest that compared to their matched counterparts, mothers of infants with FTT are either more passive, confused, and intensely angry when discussing past and current attachment relationships, or else they dismiss attachment relationships as unimportant and noninfluential. Such patterns of responses are usually characterized by insensitive caregiving (van IJzendoorn, 1995).

Family, Caregiving, and Social Characteristics of Infants with FTT

Several controlled (Crittenden, 1987; Valenzuela, 1990) and noncontrolled (Drotar et al., 1985; Gordon & Jameson, 1979) studies have documented increased rates of insecure attachment between infants with FTT and their mothers. Further, Chatoor (1989) reports that compared to matched controls, infants with FTT interact with their mothers in ways characterized by more conflict, less dyadic reciprocity, more struggle for control, and more negative affect (e.g., anger, sadness, frustration). In fact, mothers of children with FTT used more rough, abrupt, and controlling interactions, fewer positive vocalizations, and more criticism or threats when interacting with their FTT infants and were generally less responsive and more intrusive than the control mothers (Chatoor, Egan, Getson, Menvielle, & O'Donnell, 1987; Berkowitz & Senter, 1987; Finlon et al., 1985).

To date, most studies on FTT have reported that infants with FTT generally have a late birth order in a two-parent family (Benoit et al., 1989; Crittenden, 1987; Shapiro, Fraiberg, & Adelson, 1976) with three to four children close in age (Benoit et al., 1989; Drotar et al., 1985; Kerr, Bogues, & Kerr, 1978; Shaheen, Alexander, Truskowsky, & Barbero, 1968). Controlled studies have documented various family and marital problems (Benoit et al., 1989; Crittenden, 1987;

Mitchell, Gorrell, & Greenberg, 1980) including inadequate housing, frequent moves, poverty, unemployment, substance abuse, violence, and social isolation (Altemeier, O'Connor, Sherrod, Yeager, & Vietze, 1985; Benoit et al., 1989; Bruenlin, Desay, Stone, & Swilley, 1983; Crittenden, 1987; Drotar et al., 1985; Glaser, Heagarty, Bullard, & Pivchik, 1968; Kotelchuck & Newberger, 1983; Leonard, Rhymes, & Solnit, 1966; Rathbun, 1985), and child maltreatment (Crittenden, 1987; Hufton & Oates, 1977; Oates, Peacok, & Forrest, 1985).

Diagnostic Considerations

Several attempts at classifications (e.g., DSM-IV; World Health Organization, 1993 [ICD-10]; Chatoor, Dickson, Schaefer, & Egan, 1985; Dahl & Sundelin, 1986; Woolston, 1983, 1985) have failed to use operationalized diagnostic criteria to cover the spectrum of feeding disorders and FTT and to distinguish between feeding disorders and FTT. Although FTT and feeding disorder may coexist, there are no data documenting the frequency of association (Drotar, 1985). Despite these problems, a common definition of FTT includes weight below the fifth percentile for age on standardized growth charts and/or deceleration in the rate of weight gain from birth to the present of at least two standard deviations on standard growth charts.

Developmental Course and Prognosis

Several factors are associated with the outcome and prognosis of FTT. The shorter the duration of FTT before diagnosis and the greater the initial growth velocity with treatment, the more favorable the outcome, both from a physical and nutritional point of view. Clearly, the areas of developmental course and outcome of FTT have been understudied and should be the foci of future research.

Epidemiology

FTT is estimated to affect 1% to 5% of infants admitted to hospital and 4% to 14% of infants seen in ambulatory care settings. Male and female infants are equally affected. By definition, all FTT infants share a serious underlying medical ("organic") problem: malnutrition. Only 16% to 30% of FTT children have organic problems (in addition to malnutrition) severe enough to explain their growth failure (Berwick, Levy, & Kleiner-

man, 1982). FTT is overrepresented in high-risk samples from lower socioeconomic status (Frank & Zeisel, 1988; Mitchell et al., 1980).

Etiology

Many etiological factors have been suggested and reflect the apparent heterogeneity of FTT. The common denominator in all cases of FTT is that the infant is not receiving an adequate amount of calories to meet nutritional and caloric needs. There are many possible reasons why the infant with FTT is not receiving an adequate number of calories. Such reasons may, of course, include a variety of underlying medical problems that increase the caloric/nutritional needs of the child (e.g., some hypermetabolic states, malabsorption). No genetic contributor per se has been identified as causing FTT or eating disorders. However, some genetic disorders (e.g., inborn errors of metabolism, cystic fibrosis) have been associated with FTT. Importantly, not all children with genetic or metabolic disorders have FTT. Other possible etiological factors may include a disordered caregiver–infant relationship, various forms of infant maltreatment, and various family problems (see Benoit, 1993a, 1993b, for reviews).

Despite warnings that the traditional use of "organic" versus "nonorganic" (or environmental) etiological dichotomy is misleading (Berwick et al., 1982; Casey, 1988; Woolston, 1985), it is still widely used in clinical settings. A "mixed" etiology (i.e., both organic and nonorganic factors simultaneously present and likely contributing to the onset and/or perpetuation of FTT) can be found in 15% to 35% of FTT infants (Berwick et al., 1982; Casey, Worthman, & Nelson, 1984; Singer, 1986). As stated earlier, only 16% to 30% of FTT children have organic diseases severe enough to explain their growth failure (Berwick et al., 1982). There has been recent impetus to examine simultaneously both organic and nonorganic contributors to FTT (Bithoney & Dubowitz, 1985; Casey, 1988).

Future Directions

The lack of a universally accepted definition of FTT and a validated classification system continues to hamper research in this area. In fact, research in the field is characterized by inconsistencies in diagnostic criteria, small case series or individual case reports, noncontrolled samples, retrospective and nonrandomized trial designs fail-

ing to use standardized assessments, and paucity of treatment data (Benoit, 1993a). Future research should address the shortcomings of prior research.

OTHER FEEDING DISORDERS

Description of Disorder

Rumination Disorder

This disorder (see Benoit, 1993a, for a review) consists of repeated voluntary regurgitation of food, followed by rechewing and reswallowing the food in a state of relaxation, self-absorption, and pleasure. The age of onset is usually between 3 to 12 months of age. The condition is usually self-limited. Complications of rumination disorder may include malnutrition/failure to thrive, dehydration, gastric problems, and a 25% mortality. Boys are affected five times more often than girls. Rumination disorder is rare. Two types of rumination disorder have been described: (1) psychogenic (with a younger age of onset and associated significant disturbances or inadequacies in the caregiving environment); and (2) self-stimulation (with a later age of onset and associated mental retardation in the affected child).

Pica

Pica (see Benoit, 1993a, for a review) is the repeated ingestion of nonnutritive substances such as clay, dirt, sand, stones, pebbles, hair, feces, and many other substances. The ingestion of nonnutritive substances must have been occurring for at least 1 month in order for a diagnosis of pica to be made. Pica usually appears during the second year of life and often remits spontaneously during early childhood. Children with mental retardation and autism are affected more frequently than children without these problems. Possible "physical" etiological factors have been identified, such as deficiencies in iron, calcium, and zinc. Other possible etiological or associated factors include poverty, child maltreatment, parental psychopathology, lack of stimulation, and family disorganization.

Importantly, modern medical technology now contributes to the survival of infants with complex medical problems who would not have survived several years ago. These infants' survival is often contingent upon prolonged periods of tube feeding. Several reports suggest that infants who are tube fed are at risk for developing severe feeding difficulties (e.g., extreme food selectivity, conditioned avoidance or "food phobia") when oral feeds are introduced (Blackman & Nelson, 1985, 1987; Geertsma, Hyams, Pelletier, & Reiter, 1985; Levy, Winters, & Heird, 1980; Linscheid, Tarnowski, Rasnake, & Brams, 1987; Palmer, Thompson, & Linscheid, 1975). The traumatic oral experiences related to medical treatment (e.g., suctioning, repeated insertion of nasogastric or endotracheal tubes) that many of these children experience, or episodes of choking and gagging on food or medicine may lead to pervasive problems with refusal of solids and fluids. Because many of these infants are tube-fed, they may not suffer from FTT even though they often have severe feeding disorders. Also, because of the traumatic nature of their earlier oral experiences, these children have been described as suffering from a "posttraumatic eating disorder" (Chatoor, Conley, & Dickson, 1988).

Diagnostic Considerations

The field of feeding disorders in infancy and early childhood is plagued with the same kinds of definitional, diagnostic, and classification problems described in the FTT section. Research is needed to document the frequency of association between FTT and other feeding disorders.

Developmental Course and Prognosis

Marchi and Cohen (1990) followed a sample of over 800 children over a 10-year period (from early-middle childhood to late childhood–adolescence). They found that feeding problems in young children were stable over time. Maladaptive eating behavior and pica in early childhood were a significant risk for bulimia nervosa in 9- to 18-year-old children and young adolescents, whereas picky eating and "digestive problems" were risk factors for later anorexia nervosa. Findings from this study suggest that eating problems in infancy and early childhood may persist into later childhood and adolescence. More research is needed to determine whether eating problems in infancy and early childhood are also risk factors for eating disorders in adulthood.

Epidemiology

Feeding disorders are believed to affect 6% to 35% of young children (Jenkins, Bax, & Hart, 1980;

Palmer & Horn, 1978; Richman, 1981). However, because FTT and feeding disorder have often been used interchangeably in the literature and because there is no universally accepted definition of either FTT or feeding disorder, it is impossible to determine the accurate incidence or prevalence rates of particular types of disorder.

Future Directions

As with other problems of infancy and early childhood, the lack of a standard definition and accepted diagnostic criteria for feeding disorder, in addition to the lack of distinction between feeding disorder and FTT, have hampered research on infant feeding disorders. Future research should address issues of definition, etiology, pathophysiology, prevention, and treatment. Possible factors contributing to the onset and/or perpetuation of feeding disorders (e.g., parental characteristics, quality of the caregiving environment and parent–infant relationship) should also be systematically examined.

SLEEP DISORDERS

Description of Disorder

Although the sleep problems seen among infants and toddlers are not represented in DSM-IV, sleep problems during the first 3 years of life represent one of the most common pediatric problems. As Sadeh and Anders (1993) argue, familiarity with normal sleep states, diurnal organization (sleep-wake cycle), and ultradian organization (REM–NREM cycle) is useful to understand sleep disorders occurring during infancy and early childhood (see Anders, 1975, and Anders, Carskadon, & Dement, 1980, for reviews). The most common sleep disturbances in infants include problems with settling at bedtime and night waking. The most common sleep disorders in preschool and school-aged children are parasomnias (or disturbances of the NREM sleep) and include night terrors, sleepwalking, sleeptalking, and certain types of enuresis (see Anders et al., 1980, for a review).

Diagnostic Considerations

Richman (1981) provided one set of operational criteria for diagnosing sleep disorder in infants and young children. These include (1) waking three or more times per night; (2) waking for more than 20 minutes during the night; (3) being taken into the parents' bed; or (4) refusing to go to sleep at bedtime or requiring parental presence to fall asleep. These symptoms must have been present for at least 3 months consecutively and for 5 nights per week or more.

Developmental Course and Prognosis

A majority of infants and toddlers with sleep problems will no longer have sleep problems when they reach the preschool years. In fact, reports suggest that about 14% of 3-year-olds and about 8% of 4-year-olds have sleep problems (Jenkins et al., 1980; Richman, 1981; Richman, Stevenson, & Graham, 1982). To our knowledge, there are no longitudinal studies that have examined the developmental course of sleep disorders from infancy into adulthood.

Epidemiology

It is estimated that 15% to 30% of infants and toddlers have sleep problems, including resisting going to bed and/or settling down to sleep or night waking (Lozoff, Wolf, & Davis, 1985; Richman, 1981). No gender differences have been identified with respect to night waking (Paret, 1983). No known social-class factors are associated with sleep problems in infancy and early childhood. However, an association between breastfeeding and sleep problems in infancy has been reported (Carey, 1974; Paret, 1983). There are cultural variations and individual family differences in sleeping habits and routines (e.g., some families and cultures have adults and children sleep in close proximity, whereas others isolate children from adults during sleep).

Etiology

Transient sleep difficulties may be associated with physical illness (e.g., ear infection, cold) or pain from teething during the first 2 years of life. Stress, maturational factors, and temperament have repeatedly been related to sleep state organization. As discussed above, some clinicians and researchers view sleep disorders as a manifestation of an underlying regulatory disorder (Greenspan & Wieder, 1993). No genetic determinant of sleep problems has been identified.

Environmental factors (specifically, the caregiving environment, e.g., parent–child relationship disturbances) have been identified as contributing

to the onset and/or perpetuation of sleep problems in infancy and toddlerhood (e.g., Benoit, Zeanah, Boucher, & Minde, 1992; Bernal, 1973; Paret, 1983). For instance, Paret (1983) examined the home interactions between 34 first-time mothers and their 9-month-old infants during the day, obtained sleep diaries from the mothers, and videotaped the infant through the night (with a camera placed over the baby's crib before the baby went to sleep). Eleven infants were "night wakers," and 23 were "night sleepers" as defined by maternal report of sleep problem, the mean number of awakenings over 5 nights, and duration of the longest sleep period, and independent analysis of videotaped night-time behavior. Paret found that, compared to their matched counterparts, night wakers were held or touched by their mother more often and for longer periods during the day. Paret argues that, compared to their matched counterparts, mothers of night wakers might have more difficulty tolerating or encouraging independence in their infants (e.g., weaning) or letting the child find his or her own ways to soothe himself back to sleep (by the use of thumbsucking or transitional object).

In addition, Benoit et al. (1992) found that, compared to their matched counterparts ($n = 21$), mothers of toddlers with sleep problems ($n = 20$) were significantly more insecure with respect to attachment than mothers of toddlers without sleep problems. These findings suggest that some mothers of toddlers with severe sleep problems are more insensitive in reading their toddler's cues and signals of distress and in responding to them. The types of insensitivity associated with maternal insecurity in the attachment literature include rejection and inconsistency.

Future Directions

Future research might examine factors within the sleep-disordered infant and the caregiving environment that might contribute to the onset and perpetuation of sleep problems. Research on prevention and outcome of sleep problems during infancy is also necessary.

POSTTRAUMATIC STRESS DISORDER

Description of Disorder

Posttraumatic stress disorders (PTSD) include symptom clusters of reexperiencing the traumatic event, avoidance of reminders, numbing of responsiveness, and increased arousal as central features (American Psychiatric Association, 1994; Fletcher, Chapter 6, this volume). These types of symptoms have been noted in both children (Pynoos, 1990; Terr, 1990) and adults (Davidson & Fairbank, 1993), but some have questioned whether criteria developed to describe a disorder in adults can be effectively applied to young children even if the disorder occurs in them (Zeanah, 1994). Notable in this regard, is that the field tests of DSM-IV criteria for PTSD were conducted exclusively with adults.

Diagnostic Considerations

Drell, Siegel, and Gaensbauer (1993), based on a thorough review of the salient developmental literature, concluded that infants are capable of remembering events, including traumatic ones, from the first few months of life. Further, they asserted that PTSD can and does occur in infants. In support of this assertion, a number of the symptoms and signs of PTSD have been described in case reports of young children traumatized by their exposure to violence or other terrifying experiences (Goodwin, 1985; MacLean, 1977; Pruett, 1979; Sugar, 1992; Terr, 1990; Zeanah & Burk, 1984). Nevertheless, it has not been clear whether traumatized infants actually meet criteria for posttraumatic stress disorder.

A recent study evaluated the usefulness of DSM-IV criteria for diagnosing PTSD in children less than 48 months old (Scheeringa, Zeanah, Drell, & Larrieu, 1995). The investigators identified 20 cases of traumatized young children (mean age 24 months) that contained sufficient data about symptoms to make ratings possible. Each of the children had experienced a severe trauma, such as an attack by an animal, abuse, or had witnessed the murder of a parent, and each had been evaluated by a mental health professional prior to age 48 months.

Results of this study were provocative. Despite the fact that most of the traumatized infants had signs and symptoms similar to what has been described in older children and adults, in none of the 20 cases did infants meet sufficient criteria for a diagnosis of PTSD. A number of the criteria were noted to be developmentally inappropriate because they required cognitive and communicative skills not yet available to infants. In fact, 9 of 19 of the criteria in DSM-IV require individuals to report on their subjective experiences during or after the traumas occurred.

Scheeringa et al. (1995) then developed an alternative set of criteria based upon DSM-IV criteria and clinical experiences with traumatized infants. These criteria were developed to be more behaviorally anchored and developmentally appropriate for young children because so many DSM-IV criteria require reporting on subjective experiences. Some of the alternative criteria were modifications of DSM-IV criteria: play reenactment rather than intrusive thoughts, and social withdrawal and play constriction rather than detachment and estrangement. Other criteria were new items, such as aggressive behavior and separation protest that developed after the traumatic experience. Using 12 new cases of traumatized infants (mean age 24 months), the investigators then evaluated an alternative set of criteria and compared them to DSM-IV criteria. Using DSM-IV criteria, only one severely traumatized infant could be diagnosed with PTSD. Using the alternative criteria, 8 of the 12 traumatized infants met criteria for PTSD. In addition, interrater reliabilities among four untrained raters were unacceptably low for DSM-IV criteria (mean κ for all items = .50) but much better for the alternative criteria (mean κ for all items = .67). Because each of the cases involved a young child who had experienced a severe trauma, the investigators concluded that PTSD occurs in infancy, but the criteria require modification because of important developmental differences.

Developmental Course and Prognosis

Many other important questions about individual differences in PTSD remain to be explored. In a preliminary effort to address these questions, Scheeringa and Zeanah (in press) analyzed the symptom pictures and other infant and trauma characteristics in 32 cases. Specifically, they explored the effects of gender, acute versus repeated traumas, witnessing violence versus directly experiencing a trauma, and age at time of trauma (younger or older than 18 months) on symptom clusters of reexperiencing the trauma, avoiding reminders/numbing of responsiveness, hyperarousal, new fears and aggression, and overall severity of posttraumatic symptomatology. Results of this exploratory investigation are described below.

Physically and sexually abused young children also have been noted to develop posttraumatic symptoms, although in many of these cases the trauma may not have been a single, discrete event but rather a series of traumatic events or even an enduring circumstance. In examining the effects of acute versus chronic trauma, it was found that infants who had suffered acute traumas were more severely affected overall and had more symptoms of reexperiencing the traumatic event than infants who had experienced a chronic trauma. This should not suggest that acute traumas are more injurious than chronic traumas but only that the symptom picture differs in the two instances. Some have suggested, for example, that the effects of chronic traumas may be more apparent in long-term effects on personality or other developmental domains rather than on acute symptomatology (Zero to Three/National Center for Clinical Infant Programs, 1994).

Another important consideration concerns age at the time of the trauma and its effects on traumatic memories. Terr (1988) suggested, based on her clinical experiences, that infants experiencing traumas occurring prior to 28 months are less likely to have "full verbal recollection" (p. 103) than older infants. Nevertheless, other case reports strongly suggest that verbal recollection may be available at least from the latter part of the second year of life (Sugar, 1992). From a developmental perspective, a change might be expected after 18 months, given the well-known qualitative advance in symbolic representation that occurs around this time (Kagan, 1981; Stern, 1985). With this in mind, Scheeringa and Zeanah (in press) found that infants older than 18 months were likely to have significantly more reexperiencing symptoms than infants younger than 18 months. This finding makes sense given that reexperiencing symptoms probably require fairly developed capacities for symbolic functioning. Nevertheless, it is also clear that some infants less than 18 months of age are capable of later representing the catastrophic traumatic events symbolically in vivid detail (see Gaensbauer, Chatoor, Drell, Siegel, & Zeanah, 1995). How and if implicit traumatic memories become transformed later into explicit memories are fascinating questions for developmental investigators.

Increasingly, questions have been raised about the harmful effects on children of witnessing traumatic events rather than experiencing them directly (Osofsky, 1995). Here, of course, cognitive immaturity may serve a protective function for infants in the first year of life, who have a limited ability to understand and to anticipate threat, danger, and even loss. By the second year and third years, however, one might expect increased vulnerability to the witnessing of violence. Indeed, many case reports of infants with posttrau-

matic symptoms involve witnessing the injury or death of others rather than directly experiencing injury oneself (Bevin, 1993; Drell et al., 1993; Gaensbauer et al., 1995; Hendriks, Black, & Kaplan, 1993; Osofsky, 1994; Pruett, 1979; Schetky, 1978; Terr, 1990; Zeanah & Burk, 1984). Scheeringa and Zeanah (in press) found that infants who had witnessed violent traumas rather than experienced them directly were likely to exhibit more symptoms of hyperarousal. Also, they found that infants whose caregiver was threatened in the traumatic event were significantly more symptomatic than infants whose caregiver was not.

Data about the long-term adaptation of traumatized young children are quite limited. Nevertheless, Terr (1990) has suggested that effects are likely to be far-reaching, and some case reports provide support for that assertion (Pruett, 1979; Terr, 1990). Factors that may be related to outcome, including gender, age at exposure, comprehension of danger, premorbid functioning, and available support, should be addressed in future research. Most clinicians seem to agree that the nature of supports available in the posttraumatic environment is likely to be crucial for facilitating adaptation (Pruett, 1979; Zeanah & Burk, 1984; Drell et al., 1993; Pynoos & Eth, 1985).

REACTIVE ATTACHMENT DISORDER

Description of Disorder

Despite concerns about clinical disorders of attachment in the scientific literature dating back to the turn of the century, clinical disorders of attachment first appeared in official psychiatric nomenclatures only in 1980, with the publication of DSM-III (American Psychiatric Association, 1980). Criteria describing these disorders were revised substantially in DSM-III-R (American Psychiatric Association, 1987), but only minor changes were made subsequently in DSM-IV (American Psychiatric Association, 1994). Although controversies abound about the specific characteristics of this group of disorders, there is a general consensus that the disorders describe symptom pictures unaccounted for by other disorders (Rutter, 1994; Volkmar, in press; Zeanah & Emde, 1994).

What has emerged in the classification system is a description of disorders that involve a persistent disturbance in the child's social relatedness that begins before age 5 years and that extends across social situations. Attachment disorders in DSM-IV must be distinguished from pervasive developmental disorders. DSM-IV nosology also ties these disorders etiologically to parental abuse/neglect or to extremes of caregiving, such as children raised in institutions.

There are two distinct types of reactive attachment disorder outlined in DSM-IV, an inhibited and a disinhibited type (see Table 13.3). In the first, ambivalent, inhibited, unresponsive, and/or hypervigilant social responses are characteristic. In the other type, the infant exhibits indiscriminate oversociability, a failure to show selective attachments, a relative lack of selectivity in the persons from whom comfort is sought, and poorly modulated social interactions with unfamiliar persons across a range of social situations.

Curiously, despite hundreds of studies of attachment in developmental research in the past 15 years, there has been not even one study of clinical disorders of attachment in that same time span. Although many insecurely attached infants may meet criteria for attachment disorders, no investigation has explored disturbed attachment behaviors and relationships from the standpoint of clinical criteria. Given this paucity of research, it seems reasonable to ask how the criteria for these disorders were derived.

Zeanah and Emde (1994) suggested that two major data bases have informed the criteria for attachment disorders in the DSM-IV. First, the social behaviors of maltreated children, documented in a number of investigations during the past 15 years, have contributed to the criteria for the inhibited type of disorder, describing a withdrawn, unresponsive, or ambivalent child who seeks comfort in deviant ways (Gaensbauer & Sands, 1979; George & Main, 1979; Main & George, 1985; Mueller & Silverman, 1989; Powell, Low, & Speers, 1987). Second, research on young children raised in institutions (Skeels, 1966; Provence & Lipton, 1962; Tizard & Hodges, 1978; Tizard & Rees, 1974, 1975) has influenced both the criteria for the withdrawn and unresponsive type of attachment disorder and the criteria for the disinhibited and indiscriminately social type of attachment disorder. In the Tizard and Rees (1975) investigation, for example, 8 of 26 children institutionalized from birth were emotionally withdrawn and bizarre, being largely unresponsive to anyone. Another 10 of the 26 institutionalized children were noted on evaluation at age 4½ years to have superficial attachments to staff members,

TABLE 13.3. Reactive Attachment Disorder

Inhibited type	Disinhibited type
Excessively inhibited *or* Hypervigilant *or* Highly ambivalent and contradictory responses	Absence of selective attachments shown by: Excessive familiarity with strangers *or* Lack of selectivity in choice of attachment figures

Both types

Present in most social contexts
Must begin before age 5
Not a result of mental retardation or PDD
Occurs in context of pathological care *or* repeated changes of primary caregiver

with attention-seeking, clinginess, and overfriendly behavior with strangers being notable social characteristics.

Diagnostic Considerations

The DSM approach to attachment disorders has been criticized for a number of reasons (Zeanah, Mammen, & Lieberman, 1993; Zeanah, 1996). Discussions of some of the major controversies are important because in order to understand the scope of the disorders, their course and prognosis and response to treatment, it will be necessary to have a better consensus than currently exists about the nature of the disorders themselves. Three of the major criticisms are reviewed below.

First, by defining attachment disorders in terms of generally aberrant social relatedness, the criteria ignore attachment behaviors to caregivers specifically, which have been well-operationalized, as discussed in more detail in the next section. As written, the criteria for disorders of attachment primarily describe children who, as a result of extreme maltreatment or deprivation, have not developed attachments to caregiving adults. The criteria would be enhanced if they focused more specifically on the child's attachment–exploration balance in relation to specific caregivers and use of the attachment figure as a secure base and a safe haven. This would bring the guidelines more in line with our current understanding of the functioning of the attachment system and avoid the confusion introduced by diffusing the features of the disorder to broad indices of social functioning.

Second, attachment, whether disordered or not, may be expressed differentially in different

relationships. It is possible to define a disorder within an individual even if its expression is not cross-contextual. Given the large number of studies documenting that an infant's attachment to different caregivers may be different (Fox, Kimmerly, & Schafer, 1991), the insistence on a similar expression of symptoms across different relationships serves further to reduce the focus on attachment in attachment disorders. The requirement that disordered attachment be present across social contexts should be dropped in recognition of these data.

Third, the criteria used to describe attachment disorders in DSM-IV more properly define maltreatment syndromes than attachment disorders. In recognition of this fact, Zero to Three (1994), which models its definition on DSM-IV, calls the disorder "reactive attachment deprivation/maltreatment disorder of infancy and early childhood" (pp. 29–30). This is reflected in the data bases used to derive the criteria as well as the explicit (DSM-IV) emphasis on maltreatment. Because of this emphasis, the clinical usefulness of the criteria is diminished by the narrowness of the population to whom they can be applied. By incorporating research findings and definitions from basic developmental research, it is possible to modify the criteria and to describe the clinical features of a larger group of children who are in stable but disordered attachment relationships (Zeanah et al., 1993).

Some efforts have been made to develop criteria that are compatible with the findings of developmental attachment research. Most recently, Lieberman and Zeanah (1995) proposed a typology that included three major types of attachment disorders: disorders of nonattachment, disordered attachment (secure-base distortions), and disrupted attachment disorder (unresolved grief following loss of attachment figure). This typology is described more completely elsewhere (Lieberman & Zeanah, 1995) but is reviewed briefly below.

Disorders of nonattachment are diagnosed when the child, who has a mental age of at least 10 months, has no preferred attachment figure. There is a withdrawn, inhibited subtype and an indiscriminately social subtype. These disorders are similar to the DSM-IV descriptions of reactive attachment disorders.

Disordered attachments are distortions in the child's use of the caregiver as a secure base from which to explore the world and a safe haven to which to return in times of danger. What is char-

acteristic of secure-base distortions is that the symptomatic behaviors are relationship-specific and confined to the disordered attachment relationship. If the young child is clingy and inhibited about exploring, an attachment disorder with inhibition is suggested. Conversely, if the child ventures away from the caregiver too easily without checking back even in times of danger and exhibits a pattern of reckless and dangerous behavior, then an attachment disorder with self-endangerment may be suggested. Finally, if the attachment relationship is inverted so that the child cares for or worries about the emotional and physical well-being of the attachment figure to a developmentally inappropriate degree, then disordered attachment with role reversal may be considered.

Disrupted attachment disorder describes the grief responses of young children who lose their major attachment figure. These reactions were originally described by the work of Robertson and Robertson (1989) with children separated from their parents. Because of the central importance of the attachment figure in the first 3 years of life, the loss of an attachment figure at this time may be qualitatively different than if the loss occurs at other points in the life cycle. Indeed, there is evidence that loss before age 5 years places the child at increased risk for subsequent psychopathology (Brown, Harris, & Bifulco, 1986).

Developmental Course and Prognosis

There are no direct data available about the course of disorders of attachment. Nevertheless, data about the consequences of insecure attachment in infancy and about children raised in institutions converge to suggest that attachment difficulties in infancy are likely to be related to a number of subsequent problems. These include relatively profound effects in the areas of social competence, intermediate effects on behavior problems, and few if any effects in the cognitive domain (Zeanah & Emde, 1994). Thus, it is clear that the quality of early attachment relationships is important to subsequent adaptation (see also the section that follows) and that significant disruptions in the infant's access to a relatively small number of emotionally available caregivers in the first few years of life is associated with serious deviation in social relationships.

Still, it is unclear what happens to children experiencing clinical disorders of attachment in infancy at later points in development. Research

on the sequelae of insecure attachments in infancy discussed in the section of this chapter, "Aggressive Behavior Disorders," points to disruptive behavior disorders as one important outcome, but internalizing disorders also need to be explored.

Future Directions

The lack of data about the validity of attachment disorders, however defined, is a major problem for the field. All validity data salient to the classificatory schemes of attachment disorders are indirect. The effort to validate criteria for attachment disorders should be a top research priority. As a part of that effort, these disorders must be distinguished from other types of psychiatric disorders that affect young children. The question of when insecure attachment behaviors become problematic enough to warrant the designation of disorder will be particularly important to establish and will depend on an adequate body of research on prognosis as well as on the concurrent symptom picture.

It is already clear that thinking about attachment disorders can be greatly enhanced by drawing on the rich body of longitudinal data available from developmental attachment research (Zeanah, 1996; Zeanah & Emde, 1994). It seems likely that such an integration will be useful to both clinicians and to investigators. The remainder of the chapter reviews recent prospective longitudinal work on the intergenerational family context of risk for disorder, with a particular emphasis on new findings in the attachment literature.

INFANCY, FAMILY CONTEXT, AND RISK FOR LATER DISORDER

Because of the unique location of infancy at the beginning of the developmental process, infant clinicians and researchers have a special charge to maintain an orientation toward prevention of mental disorder as well as treatment of existing conditions. As longitudinal research increasingly makes clear, family factors that substantially increase the risk of the child "suffering death, pain, disability, or an important loss of freedom" (American Psychiatric Association, 1994, p. xxi) associated with mental disorder are beginning to be traced back to the infancy or prebirth periods, before the child herself may be symptomatic. Because of the rapidity of developmental changes

characteristic of the early years, family factors may also be more stable predictors of later child status than particular infant symptoms, although this remains an important question for research. The relatively recent application of sophisticated longitudinal research methods to the study of child psychopathology now offers the potential to delineate predictable relations in how family factors and child factors interrelate and produce identifiable developmental trajectories over time (e.g., Egeland, Pianta, & O'Brien, 1993; Elder, Caspi, & Downey, 1986; Lyons-Ruth, Alpern, & Repacholi, 1993).

Prospective longitudinal studies from the early years of life are a particularly powerful methodology for exploring whether there are identifiable distal (nonpsychological) or proximal (family-process-related) risk conditions or early precursor forms of child behavior that contribute to the development of a deviant trajectory over time. Because of the dramatic cognitive and behavioral reorganizations that take place during the first 4 years of life, early behavioral maladaption at either the child or family level may have little surface similarity to forms of individual or family psychopathology exhibited later in development and may not initially be recognized as an important precursor, prodrome, or disorder of infancy. For example, certain forms of child caregiving toward the parent or odd behaviors in the presence of the parent, such as those being described in current attachment studies, may gain significance as indicators of infant disorder if they are shown to be systematically related to later serious psychopathology. Thus, studies of infant diagnostic groupings in concert with more broadly based community studies of high-risk groups will be important to the evolution of the knowledge base in infant and child psychopathology. The past two decades of infancy research have also been distinctive in maintaining a concentrated research focus on relationships, exploring how to conceptualize and assess parent–infant relationships at both a behavioral and a representational level. A focus on understanding the role and patterning of relationships is critical to a complete understanding of emotional disorder. However, the study of family relationships has been relatively neglected in recent psychopathology research because of the methodological and conceptual challenges inherent in directly observing relational behavior.

While there has been a relative dearth of systematic research on diagnostically defined disorders of infancy, a sophisticated research literature exists delineating family contextual features evident before or during infancy that are associated with infant or child maladaption. In this section, three particularly active areas of infant-oriented longitudinal work relevant to exploring the developmental trajectories leading to childhood psychopathology will be reviewed. These include research on intergenerational transmission of relational behavior, research on the context and correlates of disorganized/disoriented infant attachment behaviors, and research on early predictors of aggressive behavior disorders.

Intergenerational Transmission of Relational Behavior

Researchers from a variety of traditions have been demonstrating that the caregiving patterns established in relation to the infant are not only stable over time in many respects but have roots in the adaptation of the parent *prior* to the birth of the child, as reviewed below. One clear implication of this literature is that parental developmental history and psychological structure make a contribution to the shaping of the child's relational behavior and need to be understood in their own right if the complex interplay between parent and child contributions to deviant pathways is to be understood.

A number of earlier studies have documented univariate prediction from single prenatal variables (e.g., unplanned pregnancy) to aspects of subsequent parenting and have found associations between parent's childhood experience (e.g., abuse) and aspects of later parental and marital relationships (for review, see Belsky & Pensky, 1988). However, recent infancy work has been more sophisticated in using multimethod, prospective longitudinal designs and searching for mediating processes that might explain how prenatal adaptation and/or parents' childhood experiences influence the early parent–child relationship. For example, Heinecke, Diskin, Ramsey-Klee, and Oates (1986) followed 46 families from midpregnancy until infant age 2 years and found that the child's modulation of aggression at age 2 years was predicted by a path model that included both direct and indirect effects of three of the four prebirth parental variables assessed. The three variables that influenced child aggression directly were prebirth husband–wife adaptation, maternal competence, and maternal MMPI warmth scores. In contrast, maternal pre-

birth IQ scores did not contribute to the prediction of child aggression modulation but did predict 2-year-old attention and verbal expressiveness. Mother's prebirth characteristics such as maternal adaptation, competence, and warmth also contributed to the child's aggression modulation indirectly because prebirth characteristics were in turn related to mother's higher responsiveness to infant needs at 1, 3, 6, 12, and 24 months of age, with responsiveness, in turn, related to decreased infant fretting over the first 2 years of life and increased aggression modulation at age 2 years.

In a second study, Cox et al. (1985) found that prebirth maternal characteristics predicted 41% of the variance in positive quality of mother–infant interaction at 3 months of age. However, in this study the maternal prebirth characteristics included an interview measure of the quality of parenting received in the family of origin, as well as prenatal marital competence (assessed both through interview and observational measures) and individual psychological health based on 10 standardized measures. Unexpectedly, the family-of-origin reports, in particular mothers' parents' intrusiveness and hostility, were much stronger predictors of mothers' parenting than the marital and psychological health variables, and the latter variables accounted for no further variance after family-of-origin variables were entered. The strength of prediction from the family-of-origin measure was surprising because both the marital competence measure and the individual psychological health measure were based on a variety of more comprehensive and well-validated instruments.

However, the particular power of family-of-origin interview assessments has been replicated in other multivariate studies. For example, in a particularly comprehensive study of determinants of parenting over the first year, Belsky, Hertzog, and Rovine (1986) gathered data on the contributions of prebirth maternal personality and marital adjustment, quality of care in family of origin, maternal social network contact assessed at 3 and 9 months, and infant temperament assessed at 3 and 9 months. They evaluated how well this set of measures predicted a composite measure of mother–infant interaction observed in the home at 1, 3, and 9 months of infant age. Belsky and colleagues had expected to find that effects of mother's family history on her parenting would be mediated through current personality variables, and such a mediated path did occur.

However, as Belsky and colleagues (1986) noted, "The most important contradiction [to the hypothesized model] . . . involved the direct and unmediated effect of developmental history on maternal interaction with the infant" (p. 188). The variance accounted for by the direct effect of mother's family history outweighed the mediated effects, not only on maternal involvement with the infant but also on social network and marital quality, and the family-of-origin assessment made the greatest overall contribution of any variable to the prediction of parenting.

While all of the above studies involved middle-income, low-risk samples, similar findings have also emerged from a multivariate longitudinal study of infants from high-social-risk, impoverished families, half of whom were referred for clinical infant services. Lyons-Ruth (1992) explored the degree of prediction of parenting at 18 months available from the mother's report of her family history as well as from 10 measures of the mother's current life circumstances, including extent of maternal depressive symptoms, sex and birth order of the infant, single parenthood, age at birth of first child, welfare status, family income, educational level, ethnicity, and number of children under 6 years. It was anticipated that influences of family history on parenting would be mediated through influences on the mother's current depressive symptoms, marital status, number of children and age of first childbearing. However, these mediated effects of childhood history were overshadowed by the large direct effects of mother's childhood experiences on her own behavior toward her child, with the childhood experience measure accounting for more overall variance in parenting (27%) than all other risk factors. In response to these accumulated findings, Lyons-Ruth concluded that implicit representations of strategies of interaction and emotion regulation in intimate relationships may be developed in early family relationships and reaccessed directly as parents establish a relationship with their infant.

Although not focused on infancy per se, the most impressive demonstration of intergenerational continuity in parenting has come from Elder and colleagues' longitudinal study using the Berkeley Guidance Study Archives (Elder et al., 1986). In this longitudinal study begun in 1928, four generations have been studied over time, encompassing grandparents, parents, children, and grandchildren, so that measures of childhood experience were obtained *prospectively*, rather

than by retrospective report as in the above studies. They found that personality measures, marital conflict, and parenting styles tended to be correlated within families across generations, and these correlated parental qualities were in turn related to child behavior. Parents who displayed conflicted, unstable personalities also experienced marital tension and displayed irritable, explosive behavior toward their children. Their children, in turn, displayed irritable, explosive behavior both in childhood and adulthood. However, if unstable personality and marital conflict did not find expression in punitive parental behavior toward children, intergenerational transmission did not occur. Thus, adult behavior in both marital and parenting roles was foreshadowed by the adult's directly observed childhood behavior and relationships.

Recent research guided by attachment theory is also underscoring the power of assessments that explore parents' childhood experiences by demonstrating the strong associations between scores on the Adult Attachment Interview (AAI; George et al., 1985), which is administered before the child's birth, and infant attachment behavior assessed at 1 year of age (see below). The AAI was developed to explore the implicit mental representations or "internal working models" that parents have formed of their own early attachment-related experiences. The scoring of the AAI has been revolutionary, however, in enabling investigators to go beyond a focus on the objective content of early experience and beyond a reliance on the adult's conscious reporting and evaluation of their experiences to a focus on the underlying forms of discourse and cognition through which those experiences are presented. The coherence of the parent's discourse about childhood experiences, as assessed through coding principles based on Grice's four maxims for coherent discourse (Grice, 1975), has been demonstrated to predict sensitive parental behavior toward the infant and secure infant attachment behavior toward the parent as reviewed below. One can also identify three qualitatively distinct patterns of less coherent discourse, identified by the pervasiveness of processes of distortion, including tendencies either to augment or to downplay more negative or painful attachment-oriented memories. Thus, the implicit, rather than conscious, organization is assessed, giving us a vital window onto defensive strategies and their relationship to parental behavior and intergenerational transmission (Main & Goldwyn, in press). A summary description of the

interview and its coding procedures can be found in van IJzendoorn and Bakermans-Kranenburg (1996).

In recent studies, the AAI has shown good test–retest stability (Bakermans-Kranenburg & van IJzendoorn, 1993; Benoit & Parker, 1994; Sagi et al., 1994) and discriminant validity (Waters et al., 1993) as well as independence from IQ, verbal ability and general personality measures (see van IJzendoorn, 1995, for review). Thus, the AAI appears to be a valid and reliable instrument with the potential to enhance considerably the study of representational processes underlying parenting behavior as well as to predict aspects of child behavior.

In several prospective studies, parental attachment classification assessed before the birth of the first child was found to predict the infant's attachment classification 1 year later, with 70% agreement between three-category maternal and infant classification systems. Prediction from fathers to infants was somewhat lower (Benoit & Parker, 1994; Fonagy, Steele, & Steele, 1991; Radojevic, 1992; Steele & Steele, in press; Ward & Carlson, 1995). In a recent meta-analysis of 18 studies, including both prospective and concurrent designs, van IJzendoorn (1995) confirmed a 75% correspondence rate between secure versus insecure mother and child attachment classifications, with an overall effect size of .47 (see next section for definitions of secure and insecure attachment patterns). Van IJzendoorn also evaluated the relationship between parental AAI classification and parental sensitive responsiveness toward the infant, because sensitive parental behavior is hypothesized to mediate the relationship between parent and infant attachment classifications. For 10 studies, the effect size was .34 in the expected direction. As van IJzendoorn points out, this effect size indicates that parental interactive behavior (as currently assessed) is not accounting for all the correspondence between parent and infant attachment classification, so that other factors such as genetic resemblance may also play a role in the obtained correspondences.

In a subsequent series of meta-analyses, van IJzendoorn and Bakermans-Kranenburg (1996) have shown that AAI classifications of fathers, nondisturbed adolescents, and adults from other Western countries display similar distributions to those of nondisturbed mothers, with 58% of adults in the world-wide literature classified in the autonomous (secure attachment) category. In contrast, in five available studies ($n=148$), moth-

ers of young children with psychiatric problems (sleep disorders, failure to thrive, conduct problems) show a highly deviant distribution of attachment classifications, with only 14% of parents in the autonomous group. This distribution is similar to that of adults with psychiatric diagnoses themselves, among whom 12% are classified as autonomous. The extent of the deviation in attachment classifications among parents of clinic-referred children is striking given the outpatient nature of the samples. The possibility that the child's problem behavior negatively influenced the coherence of the parent's discourse concerning his or her own earlier attachment experiences seems unlikely. For example, earlier meta-analytic findings have shown that serious infant medical problems during the first year (congenital heart problems, extreme prematurity, cystic fibrosis, retardation) did *not* result in lowered proportions of secure infant attachment classifications. In contrast, serious parental psychiatric problems substantially altered the proportion of secure infant classifications (van IJzendoorn, Goldberg, Kroonenberg, & Frenkel, 1992). Thus, most parents may be able to compensate even for severe deviations in the infant's behavior and development, although infants are not similarly able to compensate for parental disturbance.

Work documenting conditions of *discontinuity* from childhood experience to later parenting is also beginning to emerge, with several studies indicating that a supportive marriage may buffer women from the detrimental effects of difficult childhood experiences (Belsky, Youngblade, & Pensky, 1989; Quinton, Rutter, & Liddle, 1984). Why some women can make such supportive matches and others do not remains a question for investigation, however. Recent studies suggest that a positive relationship with another adult in childhood and/or a positive therapeutic relationship in adulthood may alter the process of intergenerational transmission (Egeland, Jacobvitz, & Sroufe, 1988). Other studies point to a role for positive peer relationships in childhood (Lyons-Ruth, 1992; Quinton, Pickles, Maughan, & Rutter, 1993) and for physical attractiveness (Belsky, Youngblade, & Pensky, 1989; Elder, Van Nguyen, & Caspi, 1985) in leading to more positive parenting behavior by adults with difficult childhoods. Studies of adult patterns of attachment are also pointing to sizable subgroups of parents who exhibit secure adult patterns of attachment despite difficult or traumatic childhood relationships (Grossmann, Fremmer-Bombik, Rudolph,

& Grossman, 1988; Jacobvitz, Goldetsky, & Hazen, 1933). A reliable body of work on processes related to changes in adult attachment patterns has not yet emerged, however.

The continuity being demonstrated in patterns of relational behavior across generations is undoubtedly influenced by complex interactions between genetic and behavioral processes. Recent well-controlled research indicates that genetic diathesis and rearing conditions interact, often in unexpected ways, to produce complex social behavior (e.g., Arcus, Gardner, & Anderson, 1992; Suomi, 1987; Suomi & Champeaux, 1992). Given the lack of power of current behavioral genetic designs to assess gene–environment interactions reliably (e.g., Wahlsten, 1991), we will need to continue to treat family interactive behavior as a complex product of both inherited and acquired tendencies. These studies of the intergenerational transmission of relational patterns indicate that finely meshed, complementary patterns of parent and infant behavior, accompanied by detailed parental "internal models" of relationships, operate at an influential interface in this transmission process, continue to be viable contenders for causal influence on development, and must be included in our models of pathways to childhood emotional disorder.

Disorganized/Disoriented Attachment Patterns and Infant Risk

These findings on the intergenerational transmission of relational patterns have both grown out of and increased interest in further understanding how the infant organizes patterns of relational behavior within particular caregiving contexts. One influential research tradition that is now exploring the interface between normal and disturbed behavior in infancy is that of attachment studies. This literature began by exploring the organization of infant attachment behavior in normal samples, but it has more recently begun to document the occurrence of disorganized/disoriented forms of infant behavior in disturbed family contexts. The emerging data on the context and correlates of disorganized/disoriented infant behavior are creating interest in these behaviors as possible symptoms of current disorder or as precursor forms or risk factors for later clinical disorders. In this section we review what is known about the infant context of disorganized attachment behaviors, and in the section that follows, we link this literature with what is known

about the early family context of aggressive behavior disorders.

As defined initially by John Bowlby (1969), the term *attachment* does not refer to all aspects of the parent–infant relationship. Instead, the attachment behavioral system includes those infant behaviors that are activated by stress and that have as a goal the reinstating of a sense of security, usually best achieved in infancy by close physical contact or proximity with a familiar caregiver. The complementary parental caregiving system theoretically encompasses the reciprocal set of parental behaviors that monitor infant safety and distress and cooperate with the infant's attachment behaviors to promote optimal regulation of infant security. Parental behaviors such as teaching, limit-setting, and playing are less central to the attachment function than more general aspects of parental availability and sensitive responsiveness to infant signals. Because the attachment behavioral system is a system activated by experienced stress, attachment behaviors may not be evident in familiar, low-stress environments, so the assessment paradigm of choice has involved two brief separations in an unfamiliar setting (Ainsworth et al., 1978).

From 1970 to 1985, investigators focused on replicating and extending the original discovery of Ainsworth and colleagues (Ainsworth, Blehar, Waters, & Wall, 1978) that three organized patterns of infant behavior toward the caregiver were identifiable at 1 year of age in response to the mild stress generated by brief separations from the parent in an unfamiliar laboratory setting (termed the "strange situation" assessment). These behavioral profiles were termed secure, avoidant, and ambivalent attachment patterns. From 1985 to the present, as attachment researchers increasingly began to study high-risk families and clinical samples, it became apparent that the behaviors of some infants did not fit any of the three behavioral patterns common among low-risk cohorts, leading Main and Solomon (1990) to develop coding criteria for a fourth infant attachment category, labeled disorganized/disoriented (*D*) attachment behavior. During the first wave of attachment research, secure, avoidant, and ambivalent patterns of infant behavior were empirically related to both current and prior differences in maternal caregiving behavior observed at home, with mothers of infants classified "secure" rated more sensitive and responsive than mothers of infants in the other two groups (Ainsworth et al., 1978). A series of subsequent studies demonstrated that infants displaying secure patterns of attachment behavior also exhibited more positive social behaviors toward both parents and peers throughout the preschool years (for reviews see Lyons-Ruth, 1991; Sroufe, 1988). Approximately 65% of infants studied worldwide up to 1985 displayed a secure pattern of behavior, with an additional 20% displaying an avoidant pattern. Fewer infants, 10% to 15%, displayed ambivalent patterns, particularly in middle-income samples (van IJzendoorn & Kroonenberg, 1988). See Table 13.4 for post-1985 data.

Because an understanding of the organized attachment patterns displayed in relatively undisturbed family settings is important to the interpretation of disorganized forms of attachment behavior, these organized attachment patterns will be described first and are summarized in Table 13.4. Briefly, infants who display a secure pattern of attachment behavior are likely to protest separation from a caregiver in an unfamiliar place by 12 months of age. This protest often includes distress, disruption of play, and rejection of comforting by an unfamiliar adult. When the caregiver returns, the infant greets her warmly and with minimal avoidance or ambivalence, or if distressed, seeks physical contact with her, calms quickly, and returns to play and exploration. Main (1990) describes secure infants as maintaining a stance, or strategy, of open communication of both positive and negative affect.

Infants in the ambivalent group display behavior characterized by distress at the caregiver's absence and contact-seeking at her return, mixed with direct or displaced anger, resistance to contact, and a failure to be fully comforted and return to play. Several studies have found mothers of ambivalent infants to be less consistently available during the first year (for review see Cassidy & Berlin, 1994). Main (1990) characterizes the underlying organized strategy among this group as one of heightening signals of anger and distress with the presumed goal of eliciting a response from a less responsive caregiver.

Infants in the avoidant group do not show protest or distress to the caregiver's departure. Instead, they displace their attention away from her exit, explore actively, and are friendly to the unfamiliar adult in the room. This behavior often appears quite positive and autonomous. However, when the caregiver returns, infants in this group displace attention away from her entrance, fail to greet her, and initially move away if she approaches them. Numerous laboratories have

TABLE 13.4. Organized Patterns of Attachment Behavior during Infancy

Secure strategy	Avoidant strategy	Ambivalent strategy
Open communication of affect	Restricted communication of affect	Heightened communication of affect
May or may not be distressed at separation	Little display of distress	Heightened distress
Positive greeting or contact seeking	Avoidance of contact	Anger and contact seeking combined
Soothing effective if distressed	Displacement of attention	Failure of soothing
Few avoidant or ambivalent behaviors	Displacement of anger	Possible heightened passivity/helplessness
Low cortisol secretion	Higher cortisol secretion	(No cortisol data)
55% incidence	23% incidence	8% incidence
Organized strategy	Organized strategy	Organized strategy

documented a relationship between infant avoidance and mothers' suppressed anger, lack of tenderness in touching and holding, insensitive intrusiveness, and rejection of attachment behavior (Belsky, Rovine, & Taylor, 1984; Grossmann, Grossmann, Spangler, Suess, & Unzner, 1985; Lyons-Ruth, Connell, Zoll, & Stahl, 1987; Main, Tomasini, & Tolan, 1979; Matas, Arend, & Sroufe, 1978). Main (1990) characterizes the underlying organized strategy of avoidant infants as one of restricting the communication of anger and distress by displacing attention onto the inanimate environment, away from cues that might intensify the desire to seek comfort from a parent who rejects attachment behavior. In support of this interpretation, Spangler and Grossmann (1993) demonstrated that avoidant infants and secure infants exhibited equivalent heart rate increases during separation in the laboratory, even though secure infants were significantly more likely to signal their distress. In addition, the heart rates of avoidant infants remained elevated while they were apparently attending to play objects, whereas the heart rates of secure infants decreased while they were attending to objects, as expected. In addition, there was a strong trend toward elevated cortisol levels among avoidant infants 30 minutes after the separation assessment, an elevation that was not seen among secure infants. (Ambivalent infants were not studied.)

Four sources of evidence indicate that infant attachment patterns are not primarily dispositional traits but have their origins in patterns of relationship developed with a particular caregiver:

1. The attachment strategy shown with one parent is not strongly associated with the attachment pattern shown to the other parent (Fox et al., 1991; Grossmann, Grossmann, Huber, & Wartner, 1981; Main & Weston, 1981).

2. In 70% of cases, the infant attachment strategy shown to the primary caregiver is predictable from the caregiver's state of mind with regard to attachment issues assessed prior to the birth of the infant, as noted earlier.

3. The attachment strategy displayed toward the primary caregiver is more predictive of later social adaptation than strategies shown toward other caregivers (Main, Kaplan, & Cassidy, 1985; Main & Weston, 1981; Suess, Grossmann, & Sroufe, 1992), even when the primary caregiver is not biologically related (Oppenheim, Sagi, & Lamb, 1988).

4. Various measures of infant temperament have predicted distress to separation but have not predicted whether the distressed or nondistressed behavior pattern is classified secure or insecure (Belsky & Rovine, 1987; Vaughn, Lefever, Seifer, & Barglow, 1989).

Other scattered relationships between temperament and aspects of attachment behavior have appeared in the literature but have not yielded a replicated and clearly interpretable body of data (Bates, Maslin, & Frankel, 1985; Calkins & Fox, 1992; Crockenberg, 1981; Crockenberg & McClusky, 1986; Grossmann et al., 1985; Miyake, Chen, & Campos, 1985).

The consistency and organization characterizing avoidant and ambivalent, as well as secure, attachment patterns set them apart from disorganized/disoriented attachment behavior. The term "disorganized/disoriented" refers to the apparent lack of a consistent strategy for organizing responses to the need for comfort and security when the individual is under stress. The term does *not* refer to mental disorganization or to behavioral disorganization more generally, although other infant correlates of disorganized attachment behavior are only beginning to be explored. Although approximately 15% of infants in two-parent, middle-class families display disorganized attachment behavior, the incidence of disorganized behavior increases under attachment-relevant family risk conditions such as child maltreatment, maternal alcohol consumption, maternal depression, adolescent parenthood, or multiproblem family status, with estimates ranging from 24% among infants of middle-income depressed mothers (DeMulder & Radke-Yarrow, 1991) to 62% among low-income depressed mothers (Lyons-Ruth, Connell, Grunebaum, & Botein, 1990) to a high of 82% among maltreated infants (Carlson, Cicchetti, Barnett, & Brannwald, 1989; see Lyons-Ruth, Repacholi, McCleod, & Silva, 1991, for review).

Infants who show *D* behavior do not consistently manage distress and approach tendencies by avoidance and displacement, as in the avoidant attachment pattern, nor do they consistently voice their distress at separation and actively seek contact when their mothers return, as usually occurs in the secure or ambivalent patterns. The particular forms and combinations of disorganized behaviors tend to be fairly idiosyncratic from child to child, but they include apprehensive, helpless or depressed behaviors or expressions, unexpected alternations of approach and avoidance toward the attachment figure, or other conflict behaviors, such as prolonged freezing or stilling, or slowed "underwater" movements, as summarized in Table 13.5 (see Main & Solomon, 1990, for a full description of coding system). Often the outlines of a "best-fitting" or "forced" secure, avoidant, or ambivalent strategy can also be discerned in the context of the infant's disorganized attachment behavior and is coded as a secondary strategy, yielding designations such as "disorganized–secure" or "disorganized–avoidant."

In support of the view that infant disorganized attachment behavior constitutes the least adaptive behavior pattern, Spangler and Grossmann

(1993) demonstrated that disorganized infants exhibited significantly greater heart rate elevation during the strange situation assessment than secure or avoidant infants (ambivalent infants were not studied), even though overt distress was similar among disorganized and secure infants. In addition, cortisol levels assessed 30 minutes after the assessment remained significantly elevated among infants with disorganized strategies compared to infants with secure strategies, whereas cortisol levels of avoidant infants were intermediate in value. Spangler and Grossmann (1993) interpret these data as consistent with animal data indicating that the adrenocortical system is only activated when adequate behavioral strategies cannot be applied.

During the Adult Attachment Interview, parents of infants exhibiting disorganized attachment behavior have been found to display lapses of monitoring of reasoning or discourse in discussing childhood experiences of loss or trauma (see van IJzendoorn, 1995), leading Main and Goldwyn (in press) to characterize them as Unresolved with respect to those experiences. Van IJzendoorn (1995), in his meta-analysis, reports an overall association of .31 between the Unresolved classification of mother's AAI and infant disorganized attachment behavior. However, the relationship between the parent's unresolved status on the AAI and disorganized infant attachment

TABLE 13.5. Indices of Disorganization and Disorientation in Presence of Parent

1. Sequential display of contradictory behavior patterns, such as strong attachment behavior followed by avoidance or disorientation

2. Simultaneous display of contradictory behavior patterns, such as strong avoidance with strong contact seeking, distress or anger

3. Undirected, misdirected, incomplete, and interrupted movements and expressions

4. Stereotypies, asymmetrical movements, mistimed movements, and anomalous postures

5. Freezing, stilling, or "slow-motion" movements and expressions

6. Direct indices of apprehension regarding the parent

7. Direct indices of disorganization or disorientation in presence of parent, such as disoriented wandering, confused or dazed expressions, or multiple, rapid changes of affect

Note. See Main & Solomon (1990) for complete descriptions.

status has been explored primarily in nonclinical samples. Recent studies indicate that AAI interview protocols of adults in clinical samples are often placed in rare and less well-described AAI coding categories (e.g., Cannot Classify or Overwhelmed by Trauma) in addition to or in place of categorization in the Unresolved group (Holtzworth-Munroe, Hutchinson, & Stuart, 1994; Patrick, Hobson, Castle, Howard, & Maughn, 1994). Therefore, further description is needed of parental states of mind regarding attachment in high-risk cohorts and their relationship to infant behavior.

Main and Hesse (1990) have hypothesized that disorganization of infant attachment strategies results from parental unresolved fear which is then transmitted through behavior that is either frightened or frightening. Such parental behavior should place the infant in an unresolvable paradox since the parent's presence would both heighten the infant's fear and need for soothing contact *and* make such contact fear-arousing rather than comforting. Studies of frightened or frightening parental behavior have not yet been conducted, however. In indirect support of the role of fear in the genesis of disorganization, Lyons-Ruth and Block (1993) have demonstrated that disorganized infant attachment strategies (especially those that combined avoidance with disorganization) occurred predominantly in the context of maternal childhood experiences of family violence or abuse but not in maternal childhood experiences of neglect alone. In addition, overall severity of maternal childhood trauma was significantly related to maternal withdrawal from interaction with the infant, whereas severity of childhood physical abuse was related both to withdrawal and to increased hostile and intrusive maternal interaction with the infant. Thus, both maternal hostility and infant disorganization occurred in the context of fear-provoking maternal childhood experience.

Studies directly exploring the caregiving behaviors of parents of disorganized infants are slowly beginning to accumulate. Main et al. (1985), studying middle-income families, reported that mothers of disorganized infants as well as mothers of avoidant infants exhibited low fluency and balance in discourse with the same children at age 6 years, with mothers of disorganized infants particularly dysfluent (see also Strage & Main, 1985). Spieker and Booth (1988) also found that mothers of disorganized infants differed from mothers of secure infants in having lower adult conversational skills and less positive perceptions of their infants' temperaments. Bronfman (1993) has recently found that mothers of infants with disorganized strategies can be discriminated from mothers of infants with organized strategies in the total number of atypical interactive behaviors displayed with the infant during the Strange Situation assessment at 18 months. Affective communication errors, in which the mother either displays confusing cues to the infant (e.g., extends arms toward infant while backing away) or doesn't respond appropriately to clear infant cues (e.g., ignores infant's outstretched arms) were especially strongly related to infant disorganized behavior. Both the mother's tendency to misread or miscommunicate to her infant and the infant's display of a disorganized strategy were associated with increased infant distress at home, but not with increased anger or resistance at home (Lyons-Ruth, Bronfman, & Parsons, 1994).

Hann, Castino, Jarosinski, and Britton (1991), studying 67 infants and their impoverished adolescent mothers, reported that disorganized attachment status at 13 months was significantly related to the form of conflict negotiation between mother and child at 20 months. Toddlers who had displayed disorganized–avoidant or disorganized–ambivalent attachment patterns at 13 months were significantly more likely than other toddlers to initiate conflict with their mothers by aggressive behavior. Among these dyads, child-initiated conflicts were unlikely to be resolved, while aggressive conflict behavior initiated by the mother was significantly more likely to be resolved. This imbalance in maternal and child outcomes observed among disorganized dyads contrasted with the more balanced patterns of maternal and child outcomes observed among organized secure or insecure dyads. Mothers of disorganized toddlers were also observed to initiate more interaction but to agree less frequently with their children's initiatives, in comparison to organized dyads. Disorganized toddlers showed the lowest frequency of social initiatives and tended to show more refusals of their mothers' initiatives. Mothers of disorganized toddlers also showed less affection than other mothers. The overall picture that emerged was one of interactive imbalance, mutual rejection of overtures, and increased aggressive conflict tactics by the child by 20 months of age.

Lyons-Ruth et al. (1991) also reported that disorganized infant attachment behavior accounted for variance in infant mental development scores at 18 months, independent of variance related to maternal behavior and maternal IQ (Lyons-Ruth et al., 1991). Infant physical development quotients were not lowered, producing a pattern of "mental lag" or disparity between mental and performance scores, which occurred almost exclusively among a subset of disorganized infants. This link between disorganized attachment strategies and less effective cognitive functioning has also been demonstrated in an Icelandic cohort followed from ages 7 to 17 years (Jacobsen, Edelstein, & Hoffman, 1994). Lyons-Ruth et al. (1991) also found that most of the infants who became disorganized in their attachment behavior by 18 months had displayed organized attachment strategies at 12 months. This suggests that the inclusion of attachment assessments after 12 months of age will be particularly important in studies of high-risk populations (see also Beckwith & Rodning, 1991; Renken, Egeland, Marvinney, Mangelsdorf, & Sroufe, 1989).

As disorganized infants and toddlers make the transition into the preschool years, a developmental reorganization apparently occurs for many of these children, with the signs of conflict, apprehension, or helplessness characteristic of disorganized attachment strategies in infancy becoming augmented or replaced by various forms of controlling behavior toward the parent, including caregiving behavior, directing and organizing behavior, or coercive behavior. This developmental transition toward a reversal of roles with the parent has been reported in two 6-year-old follow-up studies of middle-income samples that used the 6-year-old attachment classification system developed by Main and Cassidy (1988) (Main et al., 1985; Wartner, Grossmann, Fremmer-Bombik, & Suess, 1994). Additional longitudinal studies investigating this shift in behavioral organization are needed, however, particularly among high-risk or clinically referred infants. For example, Cicchetti and Barnett (1991) found that the disorganized behaviors seen in infancy were still more prominent than controlling patterns among maltreated children from 30 to 48 months of age.

In summary, disorganized infant attachment behaviors are emerging as potential indexes of a relational disorder of infancy since they are often characterized by signs of conflict and disphoria and show an increased incidence in contexts marked by current parental disorder and caregiving disturbances, by past parental histories of loss or trauma, by increased infant distress, and by increased physiological indices of unmodulated infant stress. As currently described, however, these behaviors are subtle, need considerable training to identify reliably, and include a wide range of infant presentations that make them difficult to use clinically. The diversity of behavioral presentations also raises the possibility that a number of subgroups may exist within the overall category, with different implications for current disorder or later prognosis (e.g., Lyons-Ruth et al., 1991). However, the established reliability and emerging concurrent validity of these infant behaviors mandate continued research to distill the most powerfully predictive and clinically usable indicators of disorganized attachment status and integrate them into current diagnostic thinking. New data on the longitudinal prediction of aggressive behavior from early assessments of attachment status and family context, which are reviewed next, further underscore this conclusion.

Aggressive Behavior Disorders and Risk Factors during Infancy

The research literatures on conduct disorder and antisocial personality disorder have long pointed to the early onset of aggressive behavior disorders among a substantial subgroup of cases identified in adolescence or adulthood (e.g., Hinshaw & Anderson, Chapter 3, this volume; Olweus, 1980). Recent work is now beginning to identify predictors of childhood aggressive disorders evident during the first 3 years of life (see Lyons-Ruth, 1996, for review). The literature on childhood correlates of conduct disorder indicates that compared to children with ADHD, families of conduct-disordered children have particularly elevated scores on measures of family adversity (Blanz, Schmidt, & Esser, 1991), as well as higher rates of diagnosable disorder, including antisocial personality, major depression and substance abuse (Biederman, Munir, & Knee, 1987; Lahey, Russo, Walker, & Piacentini, 1989). Even more well-documented is the relationship between harsh and ineffective parental discipline and aggressive behavior problems, a relationship now documented as early as 2 and 3 years of age (e.g., Campbell, 1991).

Patterson and Bank (1989) have shown that parental dispositions placing the family at risk for

initiation of coercive cycles of interaction included parental lack of social skills, parental antisocial trait (self-reported aggression and motor vehicle violations) and parent-reported child difficult temperament. These variables were substantially correlated and predicted variance primarily among single-parent families. Work by Dodge and others has further established that both aggressive boys and their mothers tend to attribute hostile intentions to others in ambiguous situations, with mothers of aggressive children attributing child misbehavior more to negative personality dimensions and endorsing more forceful disciplinary responses, and children of mothers who make hostile attributions displaying more aggression (Dix & Lochman, 1990; Dodge, Pettit, McClaskey, & Brown, 1986; Pettit, Dodge, & Brown, 1988). Another robust finding has been the documentation of a verbal IQ deficit of about 8 points or ½ standard deviation among conduct-disordered children, compared both to non-deviant peers and to the conduct-disordered child's own nonverbal scores (see Moffitt, 1993).

Infant research is now indicating that all of these correlates of disorder may be evident and predictive of later aggression during the first 18 months of life, before the onset of coercive cycles of interaction. Egeland et al. (1993), studying a large low-income cohort, (before the discovery of the disorganized form of infant attachment behavior), demonstrated that maternal intrusive control, observed when children were 6 months old, predicted insecure infant attachment behavior at 12 months of age, negative, noncompliant, and hyperactive behavior at age 3½ years, and elevated teacher ratings of both internalizing and externalizing problems in first grade. When assessed in infancy, intrusive mothers reported more anxiety and suspiciousness, displayed less appreciation of the need for reciprocity with the child and were unlikely to be living with a partner. In a later follow-up, both insecure infant attachment and maternal hostility at age 3½ years predicted first- through third-grade teacher-rated aggression.

Lyons-Ruth et al. (1993) following a cohort of 64 low-income families from infancy, evaluated prediction of later hostile–aggressive behavior in the classroom from several summary variables in infancy, including mother–child interaction, attachment, and other demographic and social risk factors. Results indicated that maternal psychosocial problems, particularly the presence of chronic depressive symptoms, and disorganized infant attachment behavior made additive contributions to the prediction of child hostile–aggressive behavior in kindergarten (see also Alpern & Lyons-Ruth, 1993). Looking backward, preschoolers with highly hostile behavior were six times more likely to have been classified as disorganized in their attachment relationships in infancy than to have been classified secure, with 71% of hostile children in the disorganized group in infancy compared to 33% of nonhostile children. Predicting forward, if the mother had psychosocial problems *and* the attachment relationship was disorganized, a majority of infants (56%) exhibited highly hostile behavior in kindergarten, compared to 5% of low-income children with neither risk factor. Further regression analyses indicated that the predictive effect of maternal psychosocial problems was mediated through the increased hostile–intrusive behavior shown by such mothers in interaction with their infants at home at 18 months.

In a school-aged follow-up of this cohort, Lyons-Ruth, Easterbrooks, and Cibelli (1994) found that a deviant level of externalizing behavior at school at age 7 years was correctly predicted in 87% of cases from infancy assessments. Disorganized attachment behavior in infancy predicted externalizing behavior at age 7 years but only if the child had also displayed lowered mental development scores in infancy on the Bayley Scales. Predicting forward, 50% of the disorganized/low-mental-development infants displayed deviant levels of externalizing symptoms at age 7 years, compared to 5% of other infants. Predicting backward, 83% of deviant children were in the disorganized/low-mental-development group at 18 months of age compared to only 13% of nondeviant children. In contrast, performance scores of deviant children were not lowered in comparison to other children. Mothers of deviant children had slightly *higher* verbal scores than mothers of nondeviant children.

In the same cohort, internalizing symptoms at age 7 years were predicted by avoidant rather than disorganized attachment strategies in infancy and by high levels of maternal depressive symptoms before age 5 years, but only maternal depressive symptoms predicted internalizing symptoms at clinical levels. Children who displayed both disorganized and avoidant behavior in infancy (classified disorganized–avoidant) exhibited elevated levels of both internalizing and externalizing symptoms at age 7 years. In addition, among children displaying disorganized strategies in infancy, 50%

were rated by teachers as showing very poor adaptation to the school environment, compared to 20% of children whose infant attachment strategies were organized.

Hubbs-Tait and colleagues (1991) following up the low-income, adolescent-mother sample of Hann et al. (1991), also found that externalizing behavior at 4½ was predicted by disorganized attachment classification at 13 months. The association was only evident among girls, but the absence of findings among boys may have stemmed from the high rate of selective attrition among disorganized boys (Hubbs-Tait et al., 1991).

All of the above studies used teacher or parent rating scales rather than DSM-III-R diagnostic criteria to define aggressive or externalizing behavior. However, a similar pattern of findings relating disorganized/controlling attachment patterns (the preschool equivalent of the infant disorganized classification) to aggressive behavior disorders has also emerged in two cross-sectional studies of 4- to 5-year-old clinic-referred children, one of which used DSM-III-R criteria for defining ODD (Greenberg, Speltz, DeKlyen, & Endriga, 1991; Speltz, Greenberg, & DeKlyen, 1990). In both studies, oppositional children were significantly more likely to display insecure attachment patterns, with a majority of oppositional children (67% and 58% in each study respectively) exhibiting disorganized/controlling attachment behaviors. Oppositional children were also more likely to show separation distress, and teachers rated oppositional children higher on both internalizing and externalizing behaviors in preschool. Mothers of oppositional children were also more likely to be classified insecure on the Adult Attachment Interview, with a majority of clinic mothers in the Unresolved category (the adult counterpart of the disorganized/controlling classification).

This body of infant studies on early predictors of childhood aggression considerably broadens and deepens our view of the developmental pathways leading to conduct problems. This literature identifies many of the same correlates of child aggression evident in the literature on school-aged children, such as poor parental social skills, intrusive and rejecting parental behavior, single parenthood, and child verbal deficits, but it reveals that these correlates are evident in infancy before infants are old enough to engage in coercive parent–child cycles. This literature also indicates that the child's coercive behavior is likely to be preceded by serious dis-turbances in the security of the attachment relationship established with the primary caregiver in infancy. Finally, the literature suggests substantial phenotypic discontinuity in the presentation of to-be aggressive children from infancy to school age, with the disorganization in infancy characterized by indicators of conflict, apprehension, helplessness, and distress rather than by coercive behavior per se. Attachment theory would interpret these behaviors as responses to dysfunction in the infant's primary attachment relationships that leave the infant unable to develop an organized relational strategy for regulating arousal.

This accumulated literature also indicates that a D dyadic relationship in infancy, in which both parent and infant display identifiable deviations in attachment organization, is gaining research validity both as a disorder of infancy (as well as a deviation in caregiving) and as a potential precursor or prodromal form of later childhood psychopathology. Whether D early attachment relationships create risk primarily for early-onset aggressive behavior or whether this relational dysfunction creates a broader diathesis for childhood psychopathology more generally needs further research. The finding of Lyons-Ruth, Easterbrooks, and Cibelli (1994) that 50% of 7-year-olds classified disorganized in infancy were later rated by teachers as showing very poor adaptation to school suggests a broader vulnerability among these children than was captured by the symptom scales alone.

SUMMARY AND CONCLUSIONS

The body of infant research reviewed here has implications for our conception of childhood disorder more generally. First, this literature points up the need for a longitudinal–developmental conception of childhood psychopathology, since both internalizing and externalizing symptoms appear to be more related to early precursors or risk factors than previously thought. Second, this literature converges with the broader clinical literature in pointing to the importance of the biological and social regulation available in the family context as one mediator of childhood psychopathology (see Downey & Coyne, 1990; Ledingham, 1990, for reviews). Longitudinal research from infancy has constituted particularly fertile ground for the development of sophisticated theoretical and research approaches to the assessment of relational

processes between parents and children, including the implicit representational processes that guide behavior in intimate relationships. As noted earlier, case-control studies of infant disorders such as feeding disorders, sleep disorders, and regulatory disorders have implicated both current parent–child interactional problems and problematic parental attachment histories as correlates of child disorder. This literature presses us to extend more sophisticated relational assessments to the study of psychopathology, including a more comprehensive view of parental affect and behavior toward the child, increased information about parental relationship histories and their derived implicit representational models for guiding caregiving behavior, and increased study of the intergenerational transmission of particular patterns of relating. Finally, the infancy literature, as well as the larger developmental and clinical research literatures, is pressing us to reexamine our tradition of individually oriented, diagnostic criteria and assessment practices to move toward more systematic assessment of family context and relational behavior. Current diagnostic criteria are inconsistent in emphasizing relational behavior as intrinsic to some disorders (e.g., externalizing disorders and character disorders) but not others (e.g., most internalizing disorders). Infant research is urging us toward a more systematic and developmental view of implicit representation, affect, and relational behavior as inextricably linked expressions of interpersonal relational systems with potentially intergenerational trajectories. These accumulated insights into family relational systems will need to be integrated with work in behavioral genetics, child temperament, and psychophysiology to better understand how genetic diathesis and temperamental or regulatory qualities of the individual interact with the quality of biopsychological regulation provided in the family system to produce developmental trajectories culminating in psychological disorder (e.g., Arcus et al., 1992; Calkins & Fox, 1992; Hirshfeld et al., 1992).

REFERENCES

Ainsworth, M. D. S., Blehar, M. C., Waters, E., & Wall, S. (1978). *Patterns of attachment: A psychological study of the Strange Situation.* Hillsdale, NJ: Erlbaum.

Alpern, L., & Lyons-Ruth, K. (1993). Preschool children at social risk: Chronicity and timing of maternal depressive symptoms and child behavior problems at school and at home. *Development and Psychopathology, 5,* 371–387.

Altemeier, W. A. III, O'Connor, S., Sherrod, K. B., Yeager, T. D., & Vietze, P. M. (1985). A strategy for managing nonorganic failure to thrive based on a prospective study of antecedents. In D. Drotar (Ed.), *New directions in failure to thrive: Implications for research and practice* (pp. 211–222). New York: Plenum Press.

American Psychiatric Association. (1980). *Diagnostic and statistical manual of mental disorders* (3rd ed.). Washington, DC: Author.

American Psychiatric Association. (1987). *Diagnostic and statistical manual of mental disorders* (3rd ed., rev.). Washington, DC: Author.

American Psychiatric Association. (1994). *Diagnostic and statistical manual of mental disorders* (4th ed.). Washington, DC: Author.

Anders, T. F. (1975). Maturation of sleep patterns in the newborn infant. *Advances in Sleep Research, 2,* 43–66.

Anders, T. F. (1989). Clinical syndromes, relationship disturbances and their assessment. In A. J. Sameroff & R. N. Emde (Eds.), *Relationship disturbances in early childhood* (pp. 125–144). New York: Basic Books.

Anders, T. F., Carskadon, M. A., & Dement, W. C. (1980). Sleep and sleepiness in children and adolescents. *Pediatric Clinics of North America, 27,* 29–43.

Arcus, D., Gardner, S., & Anderson, C. (1992, May). *Infant reactivity, maternal style, and the development of inhibited and uninhibited behavioral profiles.* Paper presented in a Symposium on Temperament and Environment at the Biennial Meeting of the International Society for Infant Studies, Miami, FL.

Asnes, R. S., & Mones, R. L. (1982). Infantile colic: A review. *Journal of Developmental and Behavioral Pediatrics, 4*(1), 57–62.

Bakermans-Kranenburg, M. J., & van IJzendoorn, M. H. (1993). A psychometric study of the Adult Attachment Interview: Reliability and discriminant validity. *Developmental Psychology, 29,* 870–880.

Barr, R. G. (1990). The "colic" enigma: Prolonged episodes of a normal predisposition to cry. *Infant Mental Health Journal, 11,* 340–348.

Barr, R. G., Kramer, M. S., Pless, I. B., Boisjoly, C., & Leduc, D. (1989). Feeding and temperament as determinants of early infant cry/fuss behavior. *Pediatrics, 84,* 514–521.

Barr, R. G., Rotman, A., Yaremko, J., Leduc, D., & Francoeur, T. E. (1992). The crying of infants with colic: A controlled empirical description. *Pediatrics, 90,* 14–21.

Bates, J. E., Maslin, C. A., & Frankel, K. A. (1985). Attachment security, mother-child interaction, and temperament as predictors of behavior-problem ratings at age three years. In I. Bretherton & E. Waters (Eds.), *Growing points of attachment theory and research. Monographs of the Society for Research in Child Development, 50* (1–2, Serial No. 209), 167–193.

Beckwith, L., & Rodning, C. (1991, April). Stability and correlates of attachment classifications from 13 to 36 months in a sample of preterm infants. In R. S. Marvin & J. Cassidy (Chairs), *Attachment during the preschool years: Examination of a new measure.* Symposium conducted at the biennial meeting of the Society for Research in Child Development, Seattle.

Belsky, J., Hertzog, C., & Rovine, M. (1986). Causal analyses of multiple determinants of parenting: Empirical and methodological advances. In M. Lamb, A. Brown, & B. Rogoff (Eds.), *Advances in developmental psychology* (Vol. 4, pp. 153–202). Hillsdale, NJ: Erlbaum.

Belsky, J., & Pensky, E. (1988). Developmental history, personality, and family relationships: Toward an emergent

family system. In R. A. Hinde & J. Stevenson-Hinde (Eds.), *Relationships within families: Mutual influences* (pp. 193–217). New York: Oxford University Press.

Belsky, J., & Rovine, M. (1987). Temperament and attachment security in the Strange Situation: An empirical rapprochement. *Child Development, 58,* 787–795.

Belsky, J., Rovine, M., & Taylor, D. (1984). The Pennsylvania infant and family development project III. The origins of individual differences in infant–mother attachment: Maternal and infant contributions. *Child Development, 55,* 718–728.

Belsky, J., Youngblade, L., & Pensky, E. (1989). Childrearing history, marital quality, and maternal affect: Intergenerational transmission in a low-risk sample. *Developmental Psychopathology, 1,* 291–304.

Benoit, D. (1993a). Failure to thrive and feeding disorders. In C. H. Zeanah (Ed.), *Handbook of infant mental health* (pp. 317–331). New York: Guilford Press.

Benoit, D. (1993b). Phenomenology and treatment of failure to thrive. *Child and Adolescent Psychiatric Clinics of North America (Eating and Growth Disorders), 2,* 61–73.

Benoit, D., & Parker K. (1994). Stability and transmission of attachment across three generations. *Child Development, 65,* 1444–1456.

Benoit, D., Zeanah, C. H., & Barton, L. M. (1989). Maternal attachment disturbances in failure to thrive. *Infant Mental Health Journal, 10,* 185–202.

Benoit, D., Zeanah, C. H., Boucher, C., & Minde, K. K. (1992). Sleep disorders in early childhood: Association with insecure maternal attachment. *Journal of the American Academy of Child & Adolescent Psychiatry, 31,* 86–93.

Berkowitz, C. D., & Senter, S. A. (1987). Characteristics of mother–infant interactions in nonorganic failure to thrive. *Journal of Family Practice, 25,* 377–381.

Bernal, J. (1973). Night waking in infants during the first 14 months. *Developmental Medicine and Child Neurology, 14,* 362–372.

Berwick, D. M., Levy, J. C., & Kleinerman, R. (1982). Failure to thrive: Diagnostic yield of hospitalization. *Archives of Disease in Childhood, 57,* 347–351.

Bevin, T. (1993). Violent deaths of both parents: Case of Marty, age two-and-a-half. In N. B. Webb (Ed.), *Helping bereaved children* (pp. 156–168). New York: Guilford Press.

Biederman, J., Munir, K., & Knee, D. (1987). Conduct and oppositional disorder in clinically referred children with attention deficit disorder: A controlled family study. *Journal of the American Academy of Child and Adolescent Psychiatry, 26,* 724–727.

Bithoney, W. G., & Dubowitz, H. (1985). Organic concomitants of nonorganic failure to thrive: Implications for research. In D. Drotar (Ed.), *New directions in failure to thrive: Implications for research and practice* (pp. 47–68). New York: Plenum Press.

Blackman, J. A., & Nelson, C. L. A. (1985). Reinstituting oral feedings in children fed by gastrostomy tube. *Clinical Pediatrics, 24,* 434–438.

Blackman, J. A., & Nelson, C. L. A. (1987). Rapid introduction of oral feedings to tube-fed patients. *Journal of Developmental and Behavioral Pediatrics, 8*(2), 63–67.

Blanz, B., Schmidt, M. H., & Esser, G. (1991). Familial adversities and child psychiatric disorder. *Journal of Child Psychology and Psychiatry, 32,* 939–950.

Bowlby, J. (1969). *Attachment and loss: Vol. 1. Attachment.* New York: Basic Books.

Brazelton, T. B. (1962). Crying in infancy. *Pediatrics, 29,* 579–588.

Brazelton, T. B. (1990). Crying and colic. *Infant Mental Health Journal, 11,* 349–356.

Bronfman, E. T. (1993). *The relation between maternal behavior ratings and disorganized attachment status in eighteen month old at-risk infants.* Doctoral dissertation, Boston College, Boston, MA.

Brown, G. W., Harris, T. O., & Bifulco, A. (1986). Long-term effects of early loss of a parent. In M. Rutter, C. E. Izard, & P. B. Read (Eds.), *Depression in young people* (pp. 251–296). New York: Guilford Press.

Bruenlin, D. C., Desay, V. J., Stone, M. E., & Swilley, J. (1983). Failure to thrive with no organic etiology: A critical review. *International Journal of Eating Disorders, 2,* 25–49.

Calkins, S., & Fox, N. (1992). The relations among infant temperament, security of attachment, and behavioral inhibition at twenty-four months. *Child Development, 63,* 1456–1472.

Campbell, S. B. (1991). Longitudinal studies of active and aggressive preschoolers: Individual differences in early behavior and in outcome. In D. Cicchetti & S. L. Toth (Eds.), *Internalizing and externalizing expression of dysfunction, Rochester Symposium on Developmental Psychopathology* (Vol. 2, pp. 57–89). Hillsdale, NJ: Erlbaum.

Carey, W. B. (1972). Clinical applications in infant temperament measurements. *Journal of Pediatrics, 81,* 823–828.

Carey, W. B. (1974). Night waking and temperament in infancy. *Journal of Pediatrics, 84,* 756–758.

Carey, W. B. (1984). "Colic"—Primary excessive crying as an infant–environment interaction. *Pediatric Clinics of North America, 31*(5), 993–1005.

Carey, W. B. (1990). Infantile colic: A pediatric practitioner–researcher's point of view. *Infant Mental Health Journal, 11,* 334–339.

Carlson, V., Cicchetti, D., Barnett, D., & Braunwald, K. (1989). Disorganized/disoriented attachment relationships in maltreated infants. *Developmental Psychology, 25*(4), 525–531.

Casey, P. H. (1988). Failure-to-thrive: Transitional perspective. *Journal of Developmental and Behavioral Pediatrics, 8,* 37–38.

Casey, P. H., Worthman, B., & Nelson, J. Y. (1984). Management of children with failure to thrive in a rural ambulatory setting: Epidemiology and growth outcome. *Clinical Pediatrics, 23*(6), 325–330.

Cassidy, J., & Berlin, L. J. (1994). The insecure/ambivalent pattern of attachment: Theory and research. *Child Development, 65,* 971–991.

Chatoor, I. (1989). Infantile anorexia nervosa: A developmental disorder of separation and individuation. *Journal of the American Academy of Psychoanalysis, 17*(1), 43–64.

Chatoor, I., Conley, C., & Dickson, L. (1988). Food refusal after an incident of choking: A posttraumatic eating disorder. *Journal of the American Academy of Child and Adolescent Psychiatry, 27,* 105–110.

Chatoor, I., Dickson, L., Schaefer, S., & Egan, J. (1985). A developmental classification of feeding disorders associated with failure to thrive: Diagnosis and treatment. In D. Drotar (Ed.), *New directions in failure to thrive: Implications for research and practice* (pp. 235–258). New York: Plenum Press.

Chatoor, I., Egan, J., Getson, P., Menvielle, E., & O'Donnell, R. (1987). Mother–infant interactions in infantile

anorexia nervosa. *Journal of the American Academy of Child and Adolescent Psychiatry, 27*(5), 535–540.

Cicchetti D., & Barnett, D. (1991). Attachment organization in maltreated preschoolers. *Development and Psychopathology, 3,* 397–411.

Cox, M. J., Owen, M. T., Lewis, J. M., Riedel, C., Scalf-McIver, L., & Suster, A. (1985). Intergenerational influences on the parent-infant relationship in the transition to parenthood. *Journal of Family Issues, 6,* 543–564.

Crittenden, P. M. (1987). Non-organic failure to thrive: Deprivation or distortion? *Infant Mental Health Journal, 8,* 51–64.

Crockenberg, S. B. (1981). Infant irritability, mother responsiveness, and social support influences on the security of infant–mother attachment. *Child Development, 52,* 857–865.

Crockenberg, S. B., & McCluskey, K. (1986). Change in maternal behavior during the baby's first year of life. *Child Development, 57,* 746–753.

Dahl, M., & Sundelin, C. (1986). Early feeding problems in an affluent society—I. Categories and clinical signs. *Acta Paediatrica Scandinavica, 75,* 370–379.

Davidson, J. R., & Fairbank, J. A. (1993). The epidemiology of posttraumatic stress disorder. In J. R. Davidson & E. B. Foa (Eds.), *Posttraumatic stress disorder: DSM-IV and beyond* (pp. 147–169). Washington, DC: American Psychiatric Association Press.

DeGangi, G. A. (1991). Assessment of sensory, emotional, and attentional problems in regulatory disordered infants: Part 1. *Infants and Young Children, 3,* 1–8.

DeGangi, G. A., Craft, P., & Castellan, J. (1991). Treatment of sensory, emotional, and attentional problems in regulatory disordered infants: Part 2. *Infants and Young Children, 3,* 9–19.

DeGangi, G. A., DiPietro, J. A., Greenspan, S. I., & Porges, S. W. (1991). Psychophysiological characteristics of the regulatory disordered infant. *Infant Behavior and Development, 14,* 37–50.

DeGangi, G. A., & Greenspan, S. I. (1988). The development of sensory functioning in infants. *Physical and Occupational Therapy in Pediatrics, 8*(3), 21–33.

DeGangi, G. A., Porges, S. W., Sickel, R. Z., & Greenspan, S. I. (1993). Four-year follow-up of a sample of regulatory disordered infants. *Infant Mental Health Journal, 14,* 330–343.

DeMulder, E. K., & Radke-Yarrow, M. (1991). Attachment with affectively ill and well mothers: Concurrent behavioral correlates. *Development and Psychopathology, 3,* 227–242.

Dix, T. H., & Lochman, J. E. (1990). Social cognition and negative reactions to children: A comparison of mothers of aggressive and nonaggressive boys. *Journal of Social and Clinical Psychology, 9,* 418–438.

Dodge, K. A., Pettit, G. S., McClaskey, C. L., & Brown, M. M. (1986). Social competence in children. *Monographs of the Society for Research in Child Development, 51*(2, Serial No. 213).

Downey, G., & Coyne, J. C. (1990). Children of depressed parents: An integrative review. *Psychological Bulletin, 108,* 50–76.

Drell, M. J., Siegel, C. H., & Gaensbauer, T. J. (1993). Posttraumatic stress disorder. In C. H. Zeanah (Ed.), *Handbook of infant mental health* (pp. 291–304). New York: Guilford Press.

Drotar, D. (1985). Failure to thrive and preventive mental health: Diagnostic and therapeutic implications. In D. Drotar (Ed.), *New directions in failure to thrive: Impli-*

cations for research and practice (pp. 27–44). New York: Plenum Press.

Drotar, D., Malone, C. A., Devost, L., Brickell, C., Mantz-Clumpner,L., Negray, J., Wallace, M., Waychik, J., Wyatt, B., Eckerle, D., Bush, L., Finlon, M. A., ElAmin, D., Nowak, M., Satola, J., & Pallotta, J. (1985). Early preventive interventions in failure to thrive: Methods and early outcome. In D. Drotar (Ed.), *New directions in failure to thrive: Implications for research and practice* (pp. 119–138). New York: Plenum Press.

Egeland, B., Jacobvitz, D., & Sroufe, L. A. (1988). Breaking the cycle of abuse. *Child Development, 59,* 1080–1088.

Egeland, B., Pianta, R., & O'Brien, M. A. (1993). Maternal intrusiveness in infancy and child maladaptation in early school years. *Development and Psychopathology, 5,* 359–370.

Elder, G., Caspi, A., & Downey, G. (1986). Problem behavior and family relationships: Life course and intergenerational themes. In A. Sorensen, F. Weinert, & L. Sherrod (Eds.), *Human development: Interdisciplinary perspectives* (pp. 293–340). Hillsdale, NJ: Erlbaum.

Elder, G., Van Nguyen, T., & Caspi, A. (1985). Linking family hardships to children's lives. *Child Development, 56,* 361–375.

Emde, R. N., Bingham, R. D., & Harmon, R. J. (1993). Classification and the diagnostic process in infancy. In C. H. Zeanah (Ed.), *Handbook of infant mental health* (pp. 225–235). New York: Guilford Press.

Ferber, R. (1985). *Solving your child's sleep problems.* New York: Simon & Schuster.

Finlon, M. A., Drotar, D., Satola, J., Pallotta, J., Wyatt, B., & El-Amin, D. (1985). Home observation of parent-child transaction in failure to thrive. In D. Drotar (Ed.), *New directions in failure to thrive: Implications for research and practice* (pp. 177–190). New York: Plenum Press.

Fonagy, P., Steele, H., & Steele, M. (1991). Maternal representations of attachment during pregnancy predict the organization of infant-mother attachment at one year of age. *Child Development, 62,* 891–905.

Forsyth, B. W. C., McCarthy, P. L., & Leventhal, J. M. (1985). Problems of early infancy, formula changes, and mothers' beliefs about their infants. *Journal of Pediatrics, 106,* 1012–1017.

Fox, N. A., Kimmerly, N. L., & Schafer, W. D. (1991). Attachment to mother/attachment to father: A meta-analysis with emphasis on the role of temperament. *Child Development, 62,* 210–225.

Frank, D. A., & Ziesel, S. H. (1988). Failure to thrive. *Pediatric Clinics of North America, 35*(6), 1187–1206.

Gaensbauer, T. J. (1982). The differentiation of discrete affects: A case report. *Psychoanalytic Study of the Child, 37,* 29–66.

Gaensbauer, T. J., Chatoor, I., Drell, M., Siegel, D., & Zeanah, C. H. (1995). Traumatic loss in a one-year-old girl. *Journal of the American Academy of Child and Adolescent Psychiatry, 34,* 94–102.

Gaensbauer, T. J., & Sands, M. (1979). Distorted affective communications in abused/neglected infants and their potential impact on caregivers. *Journal of the American Academy of Child Psychiatry, 18,* 236–250.

Geertsma, M. A., Hyams, J. S., Pelletier, J. M., & Reiter, S. (1985). Feeding resistance after parental hyperalimentation. *American Journal of Diseases of Children, 139,* 255–256.

George, C., Kaplan, N., & Main, M. (1985). *Adult Attachment Interview.* Unpublished manuscript, University of California, Berkeley CA.

George, C., & Main, M. (1979). Social interactions in young abused children: Approach, avoidance, and aggression. *Child Development, 50,* 306–318.

Glaser, H. H., Heagarty, M. C., Bullard, D. M., & Pivchik, E. C. (1968). Physical and psychological development of children with early failure to thrive. *Journal of Pediatrics, 73,* 690–698.

Goodwin, J. (1985). Post-traumatic symptoms in incest victims. In S. Eth, & R. S. Pynoos (Eds.), *Post-traumatic stress disorder in children* (pp. 157–168). Washington, DC: American Psychiatric Association.

Gordon, A. H., & Jameson, J. C. (1979). Infant–mother attachment in patients with nonorganic failure to thrive syndrome. *Journal of the American Academy of Child Psychiatry, 18,* 251–259.

Greenberg, M. T., Speltz, M. L., DeKlyen, M., & Endriga, M. C. (1991). Attachment security in preschoolers with and without externalizing problems: A replication. *Development and Psychopathology, 3,* 413–430.

Greenspan, S. I., & Lourie, R. I. (1981). Developmental structuralist approach to the classification of adaptive and pathologic personality organizations: Applications to infancy and early childhood. *American Journal of Psychiatry, 138,* 725–735.

Greenspan, S. I., & Wieder, S. (1993). Regulatory disorders. In C. H. Zeanah (Ed.), *Handbook of infant mental health* (pp. 280–290). New York: Guilford Press.

Grice, H. P. (1975). Logic and conversation. In D. Davidson & G. Harman (Eds.), *The logic of grammar* (pp. 64–153). Encino, CA: Dickinson.

Grossmann, K., Fremmer-Bombik, E., Rudolph, J., & Grossmann, K. (1988). Maternal attachment representations as related to patterns of infant–mother attachment and maternal care during the first year. In R. Hinde & J. Stevenson-Hinde (Eds.), *Relationships within families: Maternal influences* (pp. 241–260). Oxford, UK: Oxford University Press.

Grossmann, K. E., Grossmann, K., Huber, F., & Wartner, U. (1981). German children's behavior towards their mothers at 12 months and their fathers at 18 months in Ainsworth's Strange Situation. *International Journal of Behavioral Development, 4,* 157–181.

Grossmann, K., Grossmann, K. E., Spangler, G., Suess, G., & Unzner, L. (1985). Maternal sensitivity and newborn's orientation responses as related to quality of attachment in northern Germany. *Monographs of the Society for Research in Child Development, 50*(1–2, Serial No. 209), 233–256.

Hann, D. M., Castino, R. J., Jarosinski, J., & Britton, H. (1991, April). Relating mother–toddler negotiation patterns to infant attachment and maternal depression with an adolescent mother sample. Paper presented at J. Osofsky & L. Hubbs-Tait (Chairs), *Consequences of adolescent parenting: Predicting behavior problems in toddlers and preschoolers.* Symposium conducted at the biennial meeting of the Society for Research in Child Development, Seattle, WA.

Heinecke, C. M., Diskin, S. D., Ramsey-Klee, D. M., & Oates, D. S. (1986). Pre- and postbirth antecedents of 2-year-old attention, capacity for relationships, and verbal expressiveness. *Developmental Psychology, 22,* 777–787.

Hendriks, J. H., Black, D., & Kaplan, T. (1993). *When father kills mother: Guiding children through trauma and grief* (pp. 95–96, 112–115). London: Routledge.

Hewson, P., Oberklaid, F., & Menahem, S. (1987). Infant colic, distress, and crying. *Clinical Pediatrics, 26*(2), 69–75.

Hide, D. W. (1982). Prevalence of infant colic. *Archives of Disease in Childhood, 47,* 559–566.

Hirshfeld, D. R., Rosenbaum, J. F., Biederman, J., Bolduc, E. A., Faraone, S. V., Snidman, N., Reznick, J. S., & Kagan, J. (1992). Stable behavioral inhibition and its association with anxiety disorder. *Journal of the American Academy of Child and Adolescent Psychiatry, 31,* 103–111.

Holtzworth-Munroe, A., Hutchinson, G., & Stuart, G. L. (1994). *Comparing the working models of attachment of violent and nonviolent husbands.* Manuscript submitted for publication.

Hubbs-Tait, L., Eberhart-Wright, A., Ware, L., Osofsky, J., Yockey, W., & Fusco, J. (1991, April). Maternal depression and infant attachment: Behavior problems at 54 months in children of adolescent mothers. Paper presented at J. Osofsky & L. Hubbs-Tait (Chairs), *Consequences of adolescent parenting: Predicting behavior problems in toddlers and preschoolers.* Symposium conducted at the biennial meeting of the Society for Research in Child Development, Seattle, WA.

Hufton, I., & Oates, K. (1977). Nonorganic failure to thrive: A long-term follow-up. *Pediatrics, 59,* 73–77.

Illingworth, R. S. (1954). "Three months' colic." *Archives of Disease in Childhood, 29,* 165–174.

Illingworth, R. S. (1985). Infantile colic revisited. *Archives of Disease in Childhood, 60,* 981–985.

Jacobsen, T., Edelstein, W., & Hoffman, V. (1994). A longitudinal study of the relation between representations of attachment in childhood and cognitive functioning in childhood and adolescence. *Developmental Psychology, 30,* 112–124.

Jacobvitz, D., Goldetsky, G., & Hazen, N. (1993, March). Romantic and caregiving relationships in "earned-secure" adults. Paper presented at P. Costanzo (Chair), *Mental representations of relationships: Intergenerational and temporal continuity?* Symposium conducted at the Biennial meeting of the Society for Research in Child Development, New Orleans, LA.

Jenkins, S., Bax, M., & Hart, H. (1980). Behaviour problems in pre-school children. *Journal of Child Psychology and Psychiatry, 21,* 5–17.

Jones, D. P. H., & Verduyn, D. M. (1983). Behavioral management of sleep problems. *Archives of Disease in Childhood, 58,* 442–444.

Kagan, J. (1981). *The second year: The emergence of self-awareness.* Cambridge, MA: Harvard University Press.

Kerr, M., Bogues, J., & Kerr, D. (1978). Psychosocial functioning of mothers of malnourished children. *Pediatrics, 62,* 778–784.

Kotelchuck, M., & Newberger, E. H. (1983). Failure to thrive: A controlled study of familial characteristics. *Journal of the American Academy of Child and Adolescent Psychiatry, 22*(4), 322–328.

Lahey, B. B., Russo, M. F., Walker, J. L., & Piacentini, J. C. (1989). Personality characteristics of the mothers of children with disruptive behaviour disorders. *Journal of Consulting and Clinical Psychology, 57,* 512–515.

Ledingham, J. (1990). Recent developments in high risk research. In B. Lahey & A. Kazdin (Eds.), *Advances in clinical child psychology* (Vol. 13, pp. 91–137). New York: Plenum Press.

Leonard, M. F., Rhymes, J. P., & Solnit, A. J. (1966). Failure to thrive: A family problem. *American Journal of Diseases in Children, 111,* 600–612.

Lester, B. M. (1987). Prediction of developmental outcome from acoustic cry analysis in term and preterm infants. *Pediatrics, 80,* 529–534.

Lester, B. M., & Boukydis, C. F. Z. (1991). No language but a cry. In H. Papousek (Ed.), *Origin and development of non-verbal communication*. New York: Cambridge University Press.

Lester, B. M., Boukydis, C. F. Z., Garcia-Coll, C. T., & Hole, W. T. (1990). Colic for developmentalists. *Infant Mental Health Journal, 11,* 321–333.

Levy, J. S., Winters, R. W., & Heird, W. (1980). Total parenteral nutrition in pediatric patients. *Pediatrics, 2,* 99–106.

Lieberman, A. F., & Zeanah, C. H. (1995). Disorders of attachment in infancy. In K. Minde (Ed.), *Infant psychiatry, child psychiatric clinics of North America* (pp. 571–588). Philadelphia: W. B. Saunders.

Linscheid, T. R., Tarnowski, K. J., Rasnake, L. K., & Brams, J. S. (1987). Behavioral treatment of food refusal in a child with short-gut syndrome. *Journal of Pediatric Psychology, 12*(5), 451–459.

Lozoff, B., Wolf, A. W., & Davis, N. S. (1985). Sleep problems seen in pediatric practice. *Pediatrics, 75,* 477–483.

Lyons-Ruth, K. (1991). Rapprochement or approchement: Mahler's theory reconsidered from the vantage point of recent research on early attachment relationships. *Psychoanalytic Psychology, 8*(1), 1–23.

Lyons-Ruth, K. (1992). Maternal depressive symptoms, disorganized infant–mother attachment relationships and hostile-aggressive behavior in the preschool classroom: A prospective longitudinal view from infancy to age five. In D. Cicchetti & S. Toth (Eds.), *Developmental perspectives on depression* (pp. 131–169). Rochester, NY: University of Rochester Press.

Lyons-Ruth, K. (1996). Attachment relationships among children with aggressive behavior problems: The role of disorganized early attachment patterns. *Journal of Consulting and Clinical Psychology* [Special section on attachment and psychopathology], *64,* 64–73.

Lyons-Ruth, K., Alpern, L., & Repacholi, B. (1993). Disorganized infant attachment classification and maternal psychosocial problems as predictors of hostile-aggressive behavior in the preschool classroom. *Child Development, 64,* 572–585.

Lyons-Ruth, K., & Block, D. (1993). The disturbed caregiving system: Conceptualizing the impact of childhood trauma on maternal caregiving behavior during infancy. Paper presented at J. Solomon (Chair), *Defining the caregiving system.* Symposium conducted at the biennial meeting of the Society for Research in Child Development, New Orleans, LA.

Lyons-Ruth, K., Bronfman, E., & Parsons, E. (1994). *Atypical maternal behavior and disorganized infant attachment strategies.* Manuscript submitted for publication.

Lyons-Ruth, K., Connell, D. B., Grunebaum, H., & Botein, S. (1990). Disorganized attachment behavior in infancy: Short-term stability, maternal correlates, and the prediction of aggression in kindergarten. *Development and Psychopathology, 3,* 377–396.

Lyons-Ruth, K., Connell, D. B., Zoll, D., & Stahl, J. (1987). Infants at social risk: Relations among infant maltreatment, maternal behavior, and infant attachment behavior. *Developmental Psychology, 23,* 223–232.

Lyons-Ruth, K., Easterbrooks, M. A., & Cibelli, C. (1994). Disorganized attachment strategies and mental lag in infancy: Prediction of externalizing problems at age seven. Manuscript submitted for publication.

Lyons-Ruth, K., Repacholi, B., McLeod, S., & Silva, E. (1991). Disorganized attachment behavior in infancy: Short-term

stability, maternal and infant correlates, and risk-related subtypes. *Development and Psychopathology, 3,* 377–396.

MacLean, G. (1977). Psychic trauma and traumatic neurosis: Play therapy with a four-year-old boy. *Canadian Psychiatric Association Journal, 22*(2), 71–75.

Main, M. (1990). Cross-cultural studies of attachment organization: Recent studies, changing methodologies, and the concept of conditional strategies. *Human Development, 33,* 48–61.

Main, M., & Cassidy, J. (1988). Categories of response to reunion with the parent at age six: Predictable from infant attachment classifications and stable over a one-month period. *Developmental Psychology, 24,* 415–426.

Main, M., & George, C. (1985). Responses of abused and disadvantaged toddlers to distress: A study in the day care setting. *Developmental Psychology, 21,* 407–412.

Main, M., & Goldwyn, R. (in press). Adult attachment rating and classification systems. In M. Main (Ed.), *A typology of human attachment organization assessed in discourse, drawings, and interviews.* New York: Cambridge University Press.

Main, M., & Hesse, E. (1990). Parents' unresolved traumatic experiences are related to infant disorganized attachment status: Is frightened and/or frightening parental behavior the linking mechanism? In M. Greenberg, D. Cicchetti, & E. M. Cummings (Eds.), *Attachment in the preschool years: Theory, research and intervention* (pp. 161–184). Chicago: University of Chicago Press.

Main, M., Kaplan, N., & Cassidy, J. (1985). Security in infancy, childhood and adulthood: A move to the level of representation. In I. Bretherton & E. Waters (Eds.), *Growing points of attachment theory and research. Monographs of the Society for Research in Child Development, 50*(1–2, Serial No. 209), 66–104.

Main, M., & Solomon, J. (1990). Procedures for identifying infants as disorganized/disoriented during the Ainsworth Strange Situation. In M. Greenberg, D. Cicchetti, & E. M. Cummings (Eds.), *Attachment in the preschool years: Theory, research and intervention* (pp. 121–160). Chicago: University of Chicago Press.

Main, M., Tomasini, L., & Tolan, W. (1979). Differences among mothers of infants judged to differ in security of attachment. *Developmental Psychology, 15,* 472–473.

Main, M., & Weston, D. R. (1981). The quality of the toddler's relationship to mother and to father: Related to conflict behavior and the readiness to establish new relationships. *Child Development, 52,* 932–940.

Marchi, M., & Cohen, P. (1990). Early childhood eating behaviors and adolescent eating disorder. *Journal of the American Academy of Child and Adolescent Psychiatry, 29,* 112–117.

Matas, L., Arend, R. A., & Sroufe, L. A. (1978). Continuity of adaptation in the second year: The relationship between quality of attachment and later competence. *Child Development, 49,* 547–556.

Menahem, S. (1978). The crying baby—Why colic? *Australian Family Physician, 7,* 1262–1266.

Meyer, J. E., & Thaler, M. (1972). Colic in low birthweight infants. *American Journal of Diseases in Childhood, 122,* 25–27.

Minde, K. K. (1995). Infant psychiatry. In M. Lewis (Consulting Ed.), *Child and adolescent clinics of North America* (pp. 571–588). Philadelphia: W. B. Saunders.

Minde, K. K., & Minde, R. (1986). *Infant psychiatry: An introductory textbook.* London: Sage.

Mitchell, W. G., Gorrell, R. W., & Greenberg, R. A. (1980). Failure-to-thrive: A study in primary care setting—Epidemiology and follow-up. *Pediatrics, 65,* 971–977.

Miyake, K., Chen, S., & Campos, J. (1985). Infant temperament, mother's mode of interaction, and attachment in Japan: An interim report. In I. Bretherton & E. Waters (Eds.), *Growing points of attachment theory and research. Monographs of the Society for Research in Child Development, 50*(1–2, Serial No. 209), 276–297.

Moffitt, T. E. (1993). Adolescence-limited and life-course-persistent antisocial behavior: A developmental taxonomy. *Psychological Review, 100*(4), 674–701.

Mueller, E., & Silverman, N. (1989). Peer relations in maltreated children. In D. Cicchetti & V. Carlson (Eds.), *Child maltreatment: Theory and research on the causes and consequences of child abuse and neglect* (pp. 529–578). Cambridge, UK: Cambridge University Press.

Oates, R. K., Peacok, A., & Forrest, D. (1985). Long-term effects of nonorganic failure to thrive. *Pediatrics, 75,* 36–40.

Olweus, D. (1980). Familial and temperamental determinants of aggressive behavior in adolescent boys: A causal analysis. *Developmental Psychology, 16,* 644–660.

Oppenheim, D., Sagi, A., & Lamb, M. (1988). Infant–adult attachments on the kibbutz and their relation to socioemotional development four years later. *Developmental Psychology, 24,* 427–433.

Osofsky, J. D. (Ed.). (1994). Hurt, healing and hope: Caring for infants and toddlers in violent environments. Arlington, VA: Zero to Three.

Osofsky, J. D. (1995). The effects of exposure to violence on young children. *American Psychologist, 50,* 782–788.

Palmer, S., & Horn, S. (1978). Feeding problems in children. In S. Palmer & S. Ekvall (Eds.), *Pediatric nutrition in developmental disorders* (pp. 107–129). Springfield, IL: Charles C. Thomas.

Palmer, S., Thompson, R. J., & Linscheid, T. R. (1975). Applied behavior analysis in the treatment of childhood feeding disorders. *Developmental Medicine and Child Neurology, 17,* 333–339.

Paradise, J. L. (1966). Maternal and other factors in the etiology of infantile colic. *Journal of the American Medical Association, 197,* 191–199.

Paret, I. (1983). Night waking and its relation to mother–infant interaction in nine-month-old infants. In J. D. Call & E. Galenson (Eds.), *Frontiers of infant psychiatry* (Vol. I, pp. 171–177). New York: Basic Books.

Patrick, M., Hobson, R. P., Castle, D., Howard, R., & Maughn, B. (1994). Personality disorder and the mental representation of early social experience. *Development and Psychopathology, 6,* 375–388.

Patterson, G. R., & Bank, L. (1989). Some amplifying mechanisms for pathologic processes in families. In M. R. Gunnar & E. Thelen (Eds.), *Systems and development: The Minnesota symposia on child psychology* (Vol. 22, pp. 16–20). Hillsdale, NJ: Erlbaum.

Pettit, G. S., Dodge, K. A., & Brown, M. M. (1988). Early family experience, social problem solving patterns and children's social competence. *Child Development, 59,* 107–120.

Pierce, P. (1948). Delayed onset of "three months colic" in premature infants. *American Journal of Diseases in Childhood, 75,* 190–192.

Pinyerd, B. J., & Zipf, W. B. (1989). Colic: Idiopathic, excessive infant crying. *Journal of Pediatric Nursing, 4,* 147–161.

Polan, H. J., Leon, A., Kaplan, M. D., Kessler, D. B., Stern, D. N., & Ward, M. J. (1991). Disturbances of affect expression in failure to thrive. *Journal of the American Academy of Child and Adolescent Psychiatry, 30,* 897–903.

Porges, S. W. (1991). Vagal tone: A mediator of affect. In J. A. Garber & K. A. Dodge (Eds.), *The development of affect regulation and dysregulation.* New York: Cambridge University Press.

Powell, G. F., Low, J. F., & Speers, M. A. (1987). Behavior as a diagnostic aid in failure to thrive. *Journal of Developmental and Behavioral Pediatrics, 8,* 18–24.

Provence, S., & Lipton, R. C. (1962). *Infants reared in institutions.* New York: International Universities Press.

Pruett, K. D. (1979). Home treatment for two infants who witnessed their mother's murder. *Journal of the American Academy of Child and Adolescent Psychiatry, 18,* 647–657.

Pynoos, R. S. (1990). Post-traumatic stress disorder in children and adolescents. In B. Garfinkel, G. Carlson, & E. Weller (Eds.), *Psychiatric disorders in children and adolescents* (pp. 48–63). Philadelphia: W. B. Saunders.

Pynoos, R. S., & Eth, S. (1985). Children traumatized by witnessing acts of personal violence: Homicide, rape or suicide behavior. In S. Eth & R. S. Pynoos (Eds.), *Post-traumatic stress disorder in children.* Washington, DC: American Psychiatric Association.

Quay, H. (1986). Classification. In H. C. Quay & J. S. Werry (Eds.), *Psychopathological disorders of childhood* (pp. 1–34), New York: Wiley.

Quinton, D., Pickles, A., Maughan, B., & Rutter, M. (1993). Partners, peers and pathways: Assortative pairing and continuities in conduct disorder. *Development and Psychopathology, 5*(4), 763–783.

Quinton, D., Rutter, M., & Liddle, C. (1984). Institutional rearing, parenting difficulties, and marital support. *Psychological Medicine, 14,* 107–124.

Radojevic, M. (1992, July). Predicting quality of infant attachment to father at 15 months from pre-natal paternal representations of attachment: An Australian contribution. Paper presented at the XXV International Congress of Psychology, Brussels.

Rathbun, J. M. (1985). Issues in the treatment of emotional and behavioral disturbances in failure to thrive. In D. Drotar (Ed.), *New directions in failure to thrive: Implications for research and practice* (pp. 311–314). New York: Plenum Press.

Renken, B., Egeland, B., Marvinney, D., Mangelsdorf, S., & Sroufe, L. A. (1989). Early childhood antecedents of aggression and passive-withdrawal in early elementary school. *Journal of Personality, 57,* 257–281.

Richman, N. (1981). A community survey of the characteristics of the 1–2-year-olds with sleep disruptions. *Journal of the American Academy of Child Psychiatry, 20,* 281–291.

Richman, N., Stevenson, J., & Graham, P. J. (1982). *Preschool to school. A behavioral study.* New York: Academic Press.

Robertson, J., & Robertson, J. (1989). *Separation and the very young.* London: Free Association Books.

Rutter, M. (1994, July). *Clinical implications of attachment concepts: Retrospect and prospect.* Paper presented as the Bowlby Memorial Lecture at the 13th International Congress, International Association of Child and Adolescent Psychiatry and Allied Professions, San Francisco.

Sadeh, A., & Anders, T. F. (1993). Sleep disorders. In C. H. Zeanah (Ed.), *Handbook of infant mental health* (pp. 305–316). New York: Guilford Press.

Sagi, A., van IJzendoorn, M., Scharf, M., Koren-Karie, N., Joels, T., & Mayseless, O. (1994). Stability and discriminant validity of the Adult Attachment Interview: A psychometric study in young Israeli adults. *Developmental Psychology, 30,* 771–777.

Sameroff, A. (1992). Systems, development and early intervention: A commentary. In J. Shonkoff, P. Hauser-Cram, M. W. Krauss, & C. C. Upshur, Development of infants with disabilities and their families. *Monographs of the Society for Research in Child Development, 57* (6, Serial No. 230), 154–163.

Sameroff, A., & Emde, R. N. (1989). *Relationship disturbances in early childhood.* New York: Basic Books.

Scheeringa, M. & Zeanah, C. H. (in press). Symptom differences in traumatized infants and young children. *Infant Mental Health Journal.*

Scheeringa, M., Zeanah, C. H., Drell, M., & Larrieu, J. (1995). Two approaches to the diagnosis of post-traumatic stress disorder in infancy and early childhood. *Journal of the American Academy of Child and Adolescent Psychiatry, 34,* 191–200.

Schetky, D. H. (1978). Preschoolers' responses to murder of their mothers by their fathers: A study of four cases. *Bulletin of the American Academy of Psychiatry and the Law, 6,* 45–57.

Shaheen, E., Alexander, D., Truskowsky, M., & Barbero, G. J. (1968). Failure to thrive: A retrospective profile. *Clinical Pediatrics, 7,* 255–261.

Shapiro, W., Fraiberg, S., & Adelson, E. (1976). Infant–parent psychotherapy on behalf of a child in a critical nutritional state. *Psychoanalytic Study of the Child, 31,* 461–491.

Shaver, B. A. (1979). Maternal personality and early adaptation as related to infantile colic. In P. Shereslefsky & L. J. Yarrow (Eds.), *Psychological aspects of a first pregnancy and early postnatal adaptation* (pp. 209–215). New York: Raven Press.

Shaw, C. A. (1977). A comparison of the patterns of mother–baby interaction for a group of crying, irritable babies and a group of more amenable babies. *Child: Care, Health, and Development, 3,* 1–2.

Singer, L. (1986). Long-term hospitalization of failure-to-thrive infants: Developmental outcome at three years. *Child Abuse and Neglect, 10,* 479–486.

Skeels, H. M. (1966). Adult status of children with contrasting early life experiences. *Monographs of the Society for Research in Child Development, 31*(Serial No. 105).

Spangler, G., & Grossmann, K. E. (1993). Biobehavioral organization in securely and insecurely attached infants. *Child Development, 64,* 1439–1450.

Speltz, M. L., Greenberg, M. T., & DeKlyen, M. (1990). Attachment in preschoolers with disruptive behavior: A comparison of clinic-referred and nonproblem children. *Development and Psychopathology, 2,* 31–46.

Spieker, S. J., & Booth, C. (1988). Maternal antecedents of attachment quality. In J. Belsky & T. Nezworski (Eds.), *Clinical implications of attachment* (pp. 300–323). Hillsdale, NJ: Erlbaum.

Sroufe, L. A. (1988). The role of infant–caregiver attachment in development. In J. Belsky & T. Nezworski (Eds.), *Clinical implications of attachment* (pp. 18–38). Hillsdale, NJ: Erlbaum.

Stahlberg, M. R. (1984). Infantile colic: Occurrence and risk factors. *European Journal of Pediatrics, 143,* 108–111.

Stahlberg, M. R., & Savilahti, E. (1986). Infantile colic and feeding. *Archives of Disease in Childhood, 61,* 1232–1233.

Steele, H., & Steele, M. (in press). Intergenerational patterns of attachment. In D. Perlman & K. Bartholomew (Eds.), *Advances in personal relationships series* (Vol. 5). London: Kingsley.

Stern, D. N. (1985). *The interpersonal world of the infant: A view from psychoanalysis and developmental psychology.* New York: Basic Books.

Strage, A., & Main, M. (1985, April). *Attachment and parent-child discourse patterns.* Paper presented at M. Main (Chair), *Attachment: A move to the level of representation.* Symposium conducted at the biennial meeting of the Society for Research in Child Development, Toronto.

Suess, G. J., Grossmann, K. E., & Sroufe, L. A. (1992). Effects of infant attachment to mother and father on quality of adaptation to preschool: From dyadic to individual organization of self. *International Journal of Behavioral Development, 15,* 43–65.

Sugar, M. (1992). Toddlers' traumatic memories. *Infant Mental Health Journal, 13,* 245–251.

Suomi, S. J. (1987). Genetic and maternal contributions to individual differences in rhesus monkey biobehavioral development. In N. Krasnegor (Ed.), *Perinatal development: A psychological perspective* (pp. 397–419). New York: Academic Press.

Suomi, S. J., & Champeaux, M. (1992, May). *Genetic and environmental influences on rhesus monkey biobehavioral development: A cross-fostering study.* Paper presented in a Symposium on Temperament and Environment at the Biennial Meeting of the International Society for Infant Studies, Miami.

Terr, L. C. (1988). What happens to early memories of trauma? A study of twenty children under age five at the time of documented traumatic events. *Journal of The American Academy of Child and Adolescent Psychiatry, 27,* 96–104.

Terr, L. C. (1990). *Too scared to cry.* New York: Harper & Row.

Tizard, B., & Hodges, J. (1978). The effect of early institutional rearing on the development of eight-year-old children. *Journal of Child Psychology, Psychiatry, and Allied Disciplines, 19,* 99–118.

Tizard, B., & Rees, J. (1974). A comparison of the effects of adoption, restoration to the natural mother, and continued institutionalization on the cognitive development of four-year-old children. *Journal of Child Psychology, Psychiatry, and Allied Disciplines, 16,* 61–73.

Tizard, B., & Rees, J. (1975). The effect of early institutional rearing on the behaviour problems and affectional relationships of four-year-old children. *Journal of Child Psychology, Psychiatry, and Allied Disciplines, 16,* 61–73.

Valenzuela, M. (1990). Attachment in chronically underweight young children. *Child Development, 61,* 1984–1996.

van IJzendoorn, M. (1995). Adult attachment representations, parental responsiveness, and infant attachment: A meta-analysis on the predictive validity of the Adult Attachment Interview. *Psychological Bulletin, 117,* 387–403.

van IJzendoorn, M., & Bakermans-Kranenburg, M. J. (1996). Attachment representations in mothers, fathers, adolescents, and clinical groups: A meta-analytic search for normative data. *Journal of Consulting and Clinical Psychology, 64,* 8–21.

van IJzendoorn, M., Goldberg, S., Kroonenberg, P. M., & Frenkel, O. J. (1992). The relative effects of maternal and

child problems on the quality of attachment: A meta-analysis of attachment in clinical samples. *Child Development, 63,* 840–858.

van IJzendoorn, M., & Kroonenberg, P. (1988). Cross-cultural patterns of attachment: A meta-analysis of the strange situation. *Child Development, 59,* 147–156.

Vaughn, B. E., Lefever, G. B., Seifer, R., & Barglow, P. (1989). Attachment behavior, attachment security, and temperament during infancy. *Child Development, 60,* 728–737.

Volkmar, F. (in press). Reactive attachment disorders: Issues for DSM-IV. In A. Frances (Ed.), *DSM-IV source book.* Washington, DC: American Psychiatric Association.

Wahlsten, D. (1991). Insensitivity of the analysis of variance to heredity–environment interaction. *Behavior and Brain Sciences, 13,* 109–161.

Waldman, W. H., & Sarsgard, E. (1983). Helping parents to cope with colic. *Pediatric Basics, 33,* 12–14.

Ward, M. J., & Carlson, E. A. (1995). Associations among adult attachment representations, maternal sensitivity, and infant–mother attachment in a sample of adolescent mothers. *Child Development, 66,* 69–79.

Wartner, U. G., Grossmann, K., Fremmer-Bombik, E., & Suess, G. (1994). Attachment patterns at age six in south Germany: Predictability from infancy and implications for preschool behavior. *Child Development, 65,* 1014–1027.

Waters, E., Crowell, J., Treboux, D., O'Connor, E., Posado, G., & Golby, B. (1993, March). *Discriminant validity of the Adult Attachment Interview.* Poster presented at the 60th Meeting of the Society for Research in Child Development, New Orleans, LA.

Weissbluth, M. (1987). Sleep and the colicky infant. In C. Guilleminault (Ed.), *Sleep and its disorders in children* (pp. 129–140). New York: Raven Press.

Weissbluth, M., Christoffel, K. K., & Davis, T. (1984). Treatment of infantile colic with dicyclomine hydrochloride. *Journal of Pediatrics, 194,* 951–955.

Weissbluth, M., Davis, T., & Poncher, J. (1984). Night waking in 4- to 8-month-old infants. *Journal of Pediatrics, 104,* 477–480.

Wessel, M. A., Cobb, J. C., Jackson, E. B., Harris, G. S., &

Detwilet, A. C. (1954). Paroxysmal fussing in infancy, sometimes called "colic." *Pediatrics, 14,* 421–434.

White, P. J. (1936). The classification and treatment of infantile colic. *Medical Clinics of North America, 20,* 511–525.

Woolston, J. L. (1983). Eating disorders in infancy and early childhood. *Journal of the American Academy of Child and Adolescent Psychiatry, 22*(2), 114–121.

Woolston, J. L. (1985). The current challenge in failure to thrive syndrome research. In D. Drotar (Ed.), *New directions in failure to thrive: Implications for research and practice* (pp. 225–235). New York: Plenum Press.

World Health Organization. (1993). *The ICD-10 classification of mental and behavioural disorders: Clinical description and diagnostic guidelines.* Geneva, Switzerland: Author.

Zeanah, C. H. (Ed.). (1993). *Handbook of infant mental health.* New York: Guilford Press.

Zeanah, C. H. (1994). Assessment and treatment of infants exposed to violence. In J. Osofsky & E. Fenichel (Eds.), *Hurt, healing and hope* (pp. 29–37). Arlington, VA: Zero to Three.

Zeanah, C. H. (1996). A reconceptualization of clinical disorders of attachment. *Journal of Consulting and Clinical Psychology, 64,* 42–52.

Zeanah, C. H., & Burk, G. S. (1984). A young child who witnessed her mother's murder: Therapeutic and legal considerations. *American Journal of Psychotherapy, 38,* 132–145.

Zeanah, C. H., & Emde, R. N. (1994). Attachment disorders in infancy. In M. Rutter, L. Hersov, & E. Taylor (Eds.), *Child and adolescent psychiatry: Modern approaches* (pp. 490–504). Oxford, UK: Blackwell.

Zeanah, C. H., Mammen, O., & Lieberman, A. (1993). Disorders of attachment. In C. H. Zeanah (Ed.), *Handbook of infant mental health* (pp. 332–349). New York: Guilford Press.

Zero to Three/National Center for Clinical Infant Programs. (1994). *Diagnostic classification of mental health and developmental disorders of infancy and early childhood.* Arlington, VA: Author.

Child Maltreatment

Christine Wekerle
David A. Wolfe

Child maltreatment is a tragedy—one of human error and human circumstances. At its most basic level, child maltreatment denotes parenting failure—a failure to protect the child from harm and a failure to provide the positive aspects of a parent–child relationship that can foster development. The responsibility for this failure is shared not only by the individual parents for not adequately providing for their child, but by society as well, for not adequately providing families with supports and safety nets when their parenting falters. Whereas child characteristics no doubt play a factor in parental abuse (Wolfe, 1987), the child is never responsible for being abused (deYoung & Lowry, 1992); the abusive action is an adult action.

Child maltreatment has been typically categorized into neglect, physical abuse, psychological (or "emotional") abuse, and sexual abuse, although it is generally believed that the various types of child abuse often overlap and rarely occur in isolation (Wolfe & McGee, 1994). Although neglect is the most prevalent form of maltreatment (49% of children; U.S. Department of Health and Human Services [USDHHS], 1994), it is the least well researched, highlighting a curious fact that greater attention is paid to acute, dramatic, and observable acts rather than to those that are more insidious, persistent, and common (Finkelhor & Dziuba-Leatherman, 1995). Multiple forms of abuse affecting the same individual have been documented (Pianta, Egeland, & Erickson, 1989; Westen, Ludolph, Misle, Ruffins, & Block, 1990; Wolfe & McGee, 1994) and perhaps are the "norm" rather than the exception. Moreover, a widely endorsed view is that psychological abuse is implicated in all types of maltreatment and thus may be a critical factor in accounting for negative developmental sequelae (McGee & Wolfe, 1991; National Research Council, 1993). For example, psychological abuse is a very common concomitant to both physical abuse and neglect, especially in referred samples (Claussen & Crittenden, 1991). At the most basic level, the dependency of children sets the stage for their greater vulnerability to a wide range of victimization experiences (Finkelhor & Dziuba-Leatherman, 1995). Given our limited empirical knowledge about the differential outcomes of various types of abuse, however, a focus on the common developmental issues shared by all forms of child maltreatment may be most parsimonious at this stage of inquiry.

One purpose of this chapter is to highlight the common ground shared by different forms of maltreatment. Importantly, maltreatment occurs in a relational context. Whether a parent or other caregiver is the perpetrator, this relational context provides significant emotional weight to the abuse experience. A further common core of child maltreatment is violence, which creates a situation of trauma within a relational context (Herman, 1992; Terr, 1991). Thus, a posttraumatic stress response is one important conceptualization of

how child maltreatment affects the individual's developmental course.

Because maltreated children have to adapt in major ways to violent and unpredictable experiences and environments, their seemingly "disturbed" developmental abilities and behavior patterns are often considered a central feature of how children respond to the trauma of violence (Herman, 1992; Terr, 1991). From the child's perspective, the violence in physically abusive homes can be traumatizing because of its seemingly unpredictable, overwhelming, nonsensical, and unfair nature. The violence in homes of incest victims can be traumatizing because of intimidation by a powerful adult, the physical pain of sexual assault, as well as the pervading threat of harm and death to the child, their family, friends, pets, and even of the perpetrator (Conte, 1992). The violence of neglect, although not as visible, can be traumatizing as a function of the parent's disregard of basic childcare and the violation of a child's dependency status, which may involve a parent's vehement refusal to provide for the child as well as a passive withholding of love and affection. Are parents who physically desert their child any less violent in terms of child injuries and exposure to danger than parents who lock their children in a room, assault their child sexually, or injure their child physically? The violence of child maltreatment, therefore, is expressed in many different ways, all of which repudiate, revoke, distort, or infringe on the child's basic human rights (Hart & Brassard, 1987).

To examine the context of this violence, one needs to consider societal, cultural, and socioeconomic factors, as well as those closest to the child's social world—the parent–child relationship and the entire family. Accordingly, child maltreatment may be viewed as a "relational psychopathology" resulting from a "poor fit" of the parent, child, and environment (Cicchetti & Olsen, 1990). Given the context of violence, the common denominator of maltreatment necessarily becomes an interpersonal one that includes the parent–child relationship as well as the entire family. The parents' failure to provide nurturant, sensitive, available, and supportive caregiving may be a fundamental feature across all forms of maltreatment (Friedrich, 1990), and it may be a link to future developmental problems or recurring violence across generations. For example, prospective research suggests that unresponsive and insensitive maternal care during infancy may be associated with later sexual victimization when

the child is between 4 and 6 years of age (Erickson, Egeland, & Pianta, 1989).

From a developmental psychopathology viewpoint, a breakdown in the formation of a secure parent–child attachment relationship creates a core disturbance in the ability of abused children to form future healthy relationships (Cicchetti, 1990; Sroufe & Fleeson, 1986). Alexander (1992) proposes that insecure infant and child attachments to either the mother or father may set the stage for abuse because poor attachment fosters common themes: rejection, role reversals, fear, and the parent's own unresolved trauma. It is important to note that such disturbances in the parent–child relationship are not a matter of absolutes, because virtually all children will form some type of attachment with their caregiver (Ainsworth, 1980).

The orientation of this chapter is weighted toward the importance of the parent–child relational context of child maltreatment, which provides a comprehensive understanding of the symptom presentations of abused children, the developmental impact of different forms of abuse, and theoretical underpinnings. Child physical abuse, neglect, and sexual abuse are described separately to highlight unique and overlapping dimensions relating to developmental consequences, presenting symptoms, and theory. An overview is first provided of the "traumatized child," because this general concept applies to the maltreated child in important ways. Child maltreatment is then discussed broadly in terms of its negative influence on child development. Because the study of how maltreatment specifically disrupts development is recent and much of the work is unfolding, salient issues across the principle domains of development (physical, cognitive, socioemotional) are presented along with emerging empirical data. Epidemiology, theoretical perspectives, and etiologies are discussed in reference to each form of maltreatment.

HISTORICAL CONTEXT

Acts ranging from extreme parental indifference and neglect to physical and sexual abuse of children have, in all likelihood, been commonplace throughout history (Radbill, 1968). For centuries, the implicit societal viewpoint that children are the exclusive property and responsibility of their parents was undaunted by any countermovement

to seek more humane treatment for children who suffered from improper care. However, public awareness and concerns became fomented by descriptions of the "battered child syndrome" in the early 1960s (Kempe, Silverman, Steele, Droegenmueller, & Silver, 1962), leading to the drafting of model child-abuse legislation and mandatory reporting laws. Such laws required, for the first time, that anyone who comes into contact with children as part of their professional responsibilities (e.g., teachers, doctors, school bus drivers) must report any suspicion of child abuse to official child protection authorities or police. Not until the passage of the first Child Abuse and Neglect Treatment Act in 1974, however, were funds earmarked for research on the causes and effects of this malady.

For the problem of maltreatment to be identified and responded to by the public and by government agencies, the most visible and shocking aspects of its physical trauma were dramatized and publicized. The problem had gone unnoticed for so long because children have few rights to begin with and even fewer courses of action to take if maltreated. Moreover, many parental actions that we term "abuse" today (e.g., using a belt to beat a child; using degrading or embarrassing forms of punishment) were widely accepted and used to a greater or lesser extent during previous generations. However, public awareness took a major upswing in response to the widespread media attention being paid to severely injured and mistreated children, which set the stage for public outcry over such discoveries and public demand to seek answers to such tragic events (Wolfe, 1987).

Despite the well-known fact that child abuse has existed in many different forms throughout history, efforts to address this injustice through education and intervention have begun only very recently (see Wekerle & Wolfe, 1993; and Wolfe & Wekerle, 1993, for reviews of prevention and treatment efforts). Like so many other major social issues over the past century, child abuse became the focus of concern mainly because of the "crisis" atmosphere that resulted from mandatory reporting laws and more careful investigations (U.S. Advisory Board on Child Abuse and Neglect, 1990). The "child protection movement," which began in the 1930s and 1940s primarily in response to the need for alternative care for orphans and unwanted children, responded to growing public awareness to seek alternative care and protection for children deemed to be at risk of harm. Con-

currently, a backlash of criticism and disagreement as to the causes of maltreatment surfaced, due in part to the confusing array of suspected factors. Debate arose, on the basis of polarized social, political, and empirical viewpoints, as to whom to blame, punish, or rehabilitate (see, e.g., Gelles, 1973; Gil, 1970; Light, 1973).

Thus, over the past three decades it was not uncommon for the media and professionals alike to present child abuse as an extremely deviant, malicious act that could only be committed by a disturbed individual (Wolfe, 1991). In the section on definition to follow, we show that these viewpoints have been largely replaced by more realistic and service-minded definitions of maltreatment that place such behavior along a continuum of parental responses to children that range from appropriate and child-focused responses to harsh and exploitative ones.

COSTS OF CHILD MALTREATMENT TO SOCIETY

The seriousness of child maltreatment can be translated into economic costs as well. According to 1991 estimates by the General Accounting Office (GAO; cited in National Research Council, 1993), the services required for children in the United States who have been abused or neglected, including medical care, family counseling, foster care, and specialized education, cost more than $500 million annually. Furthermore, the GAO provides three estimates of the long-term costs of operating services to control or assist some proportion of those individuals who have been abused: (1) assuming a 20% delinquency rate among adolescent abuse victims that would require an average of 2 years in a correctional institution, the public cost of their incarceration would be more than $14.8 million; (2) if 1% of severely abused children suffer permanent disabilities, the annual cost of community services (estimated at $13/day) for treatment increases by 1.1 million; (3) the future lost productivity of severely abused children is estimated to be between $658 million and $1.3 billion annually, if impairments limit their potential earnings by only 5% to 10%. Although shocking, these figures reflect only the economic burden of maltreatment. They probably underestimate the costs significantly, because they do not include health costs, educational costs, or costs to the victim across his or her lifespan.

DEFINITIONAL ISSUES IN CHILD MALTREATMENT

The existence of an adequate definition of child abuse and neglect is essential for research on its etiology and course and is central to the entire system of detection, prevention, and service delivery to problem families. Communities must identify those children and families in need of help while simultaneously educating all community members in the currently acceptable and unacceptable forms of child rearing. However, despite public outcry and disdain for child maltreatment, efforts to define child abuse and neglect have been fraught with controversy and shortcomings. This controversy exists, in part, because the nature of child maltreatment does not lend itself to clear definitions that apply to each new situation without considerable discretion (McGee & Wolfe, 1991).

Thinking and responding to the diverse problem of child abuse has often left both professionals and the public in a hiatus regarding what is acceptable and what is unacceptable treatment of children by caregivers. Consequently, actions to counteract this problem have reverberated in response to public sentiment, highly publicized cases, new legislation, and promising treatment methods. Both legal definitions and research definitions of physical abuse, in particular, have made considerable effort to define in greater detail the types of physical evidence that constitute abuse, the behavioral signs that indicate an abused child, and the pervasive and longstanding psychological and developmental consequences of inadequate (i.e., abusive, neglectful, inappropriate) childrearing (e.g., Cicchetti, 1990; Mash & Wolfe, 1991).

These gains notwithstanding, different definitions of maltreatment have emerged over the past 20 years, primarily as a function of the particular purpose of an organization, government legislation, community agency, or researcher. Municipalities and states, for example, often adopt a definition that focuses largely on evidentiary criteria to prosecute or act on behalf of the child, whereas treatment providers may weigh other discretionary criteria more heavily in determining what they consider to be an act of abuse or neglect. Sexual abuse, by and large, is the exception to this ambiguity: whereas acts of physical discipline, for example, might be construed as "abusive" or "non-abusive" by different agencies, acts of a sexual nature toward a child are more definitive and universally taboo (Finkelhor, 1984).

Classification of Maltreatment

Four categories of maltreatment (physical abuse, sexual abuse, neglect, and psychological abuse) have emerged as separate issues for study of incidence and etiology. This approach has revealed both important similarities (e.g., the developmental consequences to the child), as well as important differences (e.g., the predatory, exploitative aspect of much of sexual abuse). However, several difficulties remain in terms of defining such behavior (summarized from a review by the National Research Council, 1993):

- There is generally a lack of consensus as to what constitutes dangerous or unacceptable childrearing practices.
- Uncertainty exists as to whether to define maltreatment on the basis of adult characteristics or behavior, the effects on the child, the environmental causes, or some combination of these factors.
- The definition of a particular behavior may vary due to the somewhat competing purposes of various settings or organizations, such as scientific, legal, or clinical.
- The definition of maltreatment may vary as a function of the child's age, gender, relationship to offender, and so forth.
- Uncertainty exists as to whether or not maltreatment is a discrete phenomenon (i.e., a "category") or falls along a dimension or continuum that includes a broader spectrum of typical behavior of parents, for example (see Wolfe, 1991).

General Definitions of Maltreatment

The Child Abuse Prevention and Treatment Act of 1984 defines child abuse and neglect as:

> The physical or mental injury, sexual abuse or exploitation, negligent treatment, or maltreatment of a child under the age of eighteen, or the age specified by the child protection law of the State in question, by a person (including any employee of a residential facility or any staff person providing out-of-home care) who is responsible for the child's welfare under circumstances which indicate that the child's health or welfare is harmed or threatened thereby, as determined in regulations prescribed by the Secretary.

This definition was expanded in 1988 to indicate that the behavior had to be avoidable and

nonaccidental. This general definition, moreover, separates abuse into two categories: (1) moderate injury or impairment not requiring professional treatment but remaining observable for a minimum of 48 hours; and (2) serious injury or impairment involving a life-threatening condition, long-term impairment of physical capacities, or treatment to avoid such impairments.

Based on these general criteria, acts considered to define "physical abuse" usually include scalding, beatings with an object, severe physical punishment, slapping, punching, and kicking; acts defining "neglect" include deficiencies in caretaker obligations, such as educational, supervisory, shelter and safety, medical, physical, or emotional needs of the child, as well as physical abandonment; acts defining "sexual abuse" include touching (fondling) of the breasts or genital areas of the child (or having the child perform acts on the adult), vaginal or anal intercourse, exposure to indecent acts, sexual rituals, or involvement in child pornography. The offender, in the case of sexual abuse in particular, may include other children or adolescents (usually considered to have an age differential of more than 5 years, such as a babysitter) and other adults in addition to the primary caregivers (e.g., teachers, coaches, strangers) (Finkelhor & Browne, 1988).

A widely cited definition of psychological abuse or maltreatment was offered by Garbarino, Guttman, and Seeley (1986) and further clarified by Brassard, Germain, and Hart (1987):

> Psychological maltreatment of children and youth consists of acts of commission and omission which are judged on a basis of a combination of community standards and professional expertise to be psychologically damaging. Such acts are committed by individuals, singly or collectively, who by their characteristics (e.g., age, status, knowledge, organizational form) are in a position of differential power that renders a child vulnerable. Such acts damage immediately or ultimately the behavioral, cognitive, affective, or physical functioning of the child. Examples of psychological maltreatment include acts of rejecting, terrorizing, isolation, exploiting, and missocializing. (Hart & Brassard, 1987, p. 6)

Although this definition is problematic, the term clearly implies that much more is at stake than physical injuries alone in terms of what may define harsh parental treatment and its diverse impact on the child. Whereas in physical abuse the primary casualty is considered the physical injuries to the child victim, psychological abuse carries such nonphysical (and often intangible) injuries as assaults on self-esteem, self-concept, and social competence (Garbarino et al., 1986).

DESCRIPTION OF CHILD MALTREATMENT

This section discusses symptoms of trauma, in reference to posttraumatic stress disorder (PTSD) (American Psychiatric Association, 1994). Many of these trauma-related symptoms emerge throughout our presentation of each type of maltreatment, and therefore a knowledge of the general effects of trauma is germane to understanding the child's psychological profile. Subsequently, symptom presentations across specific types of abuse are discussed to identify the range in symptomatology and to highlight abuse-specific as well as overlapping symptoms.

Immediate and Prolonged Effects of Childhood Trauma

A prominent model for understanding the immediate and enduring effects of childhood abuse is contained within the framework of PTSD (see also Fletcher, Chapter 6, this volume). As defined by DSM-IV (American Psychiatric Association, 1994), PTSD entails (1) a recognizable stressor, plus a specified number of symptoms in the areas of (2) reexperiencing the trauma, (3) avoidance of trauma-related stimuli, and (4) increased arousal/anxiety. DSM-IV defines exposure to an extreme traumatic stressor as involving personal experience of an event, witnessing an event, or learning about an event affecting a family member or close associate. Applied to child maltreatment, PTSD could therefore arise from direct participation in the abuse, witnessing abuse, and/or learning about familial abuse. The stress response is further divided into acute (i.e., symptoms less than 3 months), chronic (i.e., symptoms 3 months or longer), and delayed onset (i.e., 6 months beyond the traumatic event).

A traumatic event can be reexperienced in a variety of ways, commonly with recurrent and intrusive recollections of the event, distressing dreams of the event, or a sense of reliving the event (e.g., dissociative flashback episode). Reexperiencing symptoms may involve bodily sensations as well as mental imagery. Intrusions occur spontaneously and involuntarily and can be

stimulated by seemingly minor connections. DSM-IV identifies that intense psychological distress and physiological reactivity to internal or external trauma cues may occur as reexperiencing symptoms.

It has been reported that children typically manifest reexperiencing symptoms in the form of nightmares specific to the trauma, behavioral reenactment of the event, or traumatic play, which can have an obsessional, driven quality (Lipovsky, 1991). DSM-IV specifically notes that children may display more generalized reexperiencing, as in a frightening dream, without recognizable content. The compulsion to repeat the trauma can be regarded as a means of accommodation to, and ultimate integration of, the anxiety-provoking abuse event whereby a feeling and sense of efficacy and power can be restored (Herman, 1992). However, there is an emotional cost to reliving the trauma, given the intensity of distressing affect and consequent threat to and burden on coping.

The second PTSD symptom class pertains to persistent avoidance of stimuli linked to the trauma and the numbing of general responsiveness. These include: efforts to avoid internal (thoughts, feelings) or external cues associated with the trauma, impaired recall of an important aspect of the trauma, diminished interest in significant activities, feelings of estrangement from others, constricted affect, and a sense of a foreshortened future. Events may continue to register in awareness, but with alterations in the perceptual processes, including affective detachment ("emotional anesthesia") that is akin to a hypnotic trance (Herman, 1992). With such numbing, time sense may be changed as in slow motion, and there may be a sense of the unreal, either as if events were part of a bad dream (derealization) or as if events were occurring outside of oneself or one's body, as unreal or unfamiliar (depersonalization). DSM-IV notes that the ability to feel emotions associated with intimacy, tenderness, and sexuality may be especially reduced.

The third class of symptoms marks the occurrence of increased arousal and anxiety that were not present before the trauma. Symptoms may include hypervigilance, an exaggerated startle response, irritability or angry outbursts, difficulty concentrating or completing tasks, and sleep problems which may result from recurrent nightmares.

Although not part of formal criteria, DSM-IV lists associated features of PTSD, especially following from an interpersonal stressor such as childhood sexual or physical abuse. These include: impaired affect modulation, self-destructive and impulsive behavior, dissociative symptoms, psychosomatic complaints, feelings of ineffectiveness, shame, despair, or hopelessness, feeling permanently damaged, a loss of previously sustained beliefs, hostility, social withdrawal, feeling constantly threatened, impaired relationships with others, or a change in personality characteristics. Children may also exhibit physical symptoms, such as stomachaches and headaches.

Importantly, Terr (1991) emphasizes that some of these PTSD symptoms (e.g., rage, blunted or flat affect, self-hypnosis, dissociation, aggressive acting out) may be conceptualized by mental health professionals as conduct disorders, attention-deficit disorders, depression, or dissociative disorders, instead of a fundamental PTSD disorder. As an adult, the PTSD sufferer has an increased risk for panic disorder, agoraphobia, obsessive-compulsive disorder, and substance-related disorders (American Psychiatric Association, 1994).

Terr (1991) identifies a Type I and Type II PTSD, with Type I denoting a response to a single traumatic event and Type II denoting a response to multiple or chronic trauma. A mixed Type I/Type II pattern can occur in cases of sudden, shocking deaths and accident. Four symptoms are common to both types of PTSD: (1) reexperiencing of the trauma through visualization or other sense modes; (2) repetitive behaviors denoting a reenacting of the trauma events; (3) trauma-specific fears; and (4) changed attitudes about people, life, and the future. With respect to the latter, Terr notes that a rethinking of life can occur, as evident in a sense of a limited future (e.g., the belief in an early death, a focus on the here-and-now), a shattered sense of "invincibility" (e.g., people and the world as predatory), and a sense of isolation (e.g., "you can't count on anyone or anything to protect you").

Terr (1991) suggests that Type I PTSD is more common and less severely disruptive to functioning, largely because the child has experienced a one-time event usually followed by a restored sense of support by others. Symptoms specific to Type I PTSD include: (1) a full, detailed "etched-in" memory of the event, (2) "omens," or retrospective reworkings of the trauma, and (3) misperceptions of responsibility and blame. Terr advances that single-event trauma is retained in memory as a "whole," given the high level of detail and integration of accompanying events. As

such, such trauma may remain in "active" memory, thereby promoting cognitive processing of the event until existing schemas about self and others can be changed (Horowitz, 1986). One implication of this view is that the affective responses of hyperarousal (e.g., heightened arousal, anxiety) also remain while memory is active, although some perceptual distortion is thought to occur (e.g., missequencing of events). Finally, these memories are subjected to an ad-hoc appraisal process where some meaning is attached to the trauma, labeled by Terr as an "omen" signaling the need to process what has transpired.

Terr (1991) suggests that Type II, or chronic, trauma is characterized by more severe psychopathology, including personality disturbances. Specific Type II PTSD symptoms include: (1) denial and numbing, (2) self-hypnosis and dissociation, (3) rage, and (4) persistent sadness. Children fitting this Type II pattern do not complain or show awareness of these symptoms, despite the fact they may display a range of numbing-related symptoms such as significant forgetting of their childhood histories, a relative indifference to pain, lack of empathy, failure to acknowledge or to label feelings, feelings of invisibility, and avoidance of psychological intimacy. To illustrate this numbed personal stance, Terr includes the following description given by a 9-year-old, who had been sexually abused since age 6 by her older brother: "Sometimes now I find myself not feeling things. I don't feel sad or mad when I should be. I'm not afraid when I should be. I act silly and crazy a lot. The people at my school think I'm funny because of it" (p. 16).

To achieve this anaesthetized state, chronically traumatized children employ a range of techniques–self-calming, self-hypnosis, depersonalization, dissociation, repression (i.e., passive forgetting, usually where components are related to unconsciousness), and denial (refusal to acknowledge the external reality of something, even in the face of convincing evidence). However, this overall numbed pattern in Type II PTSD can be disrupted by intense rage felt by the child, directed toward others as well as to the self. Terr (1991) notes that dramatic fluctuations of active anger and extreme passivity (created in part by the child's fear of his or her own anger) may dominate the clinical picture. In fact, rage-driven reenactments may become so prevalent that aggressive behavior can become a habitual pattern.

Empirical support for the Type I and II distinction was found in a study comparing an acute versus chronic sample of sexually abused and physically abused children (Famularo, Kinscherff, & Fenton, 1990). Based on data from a PTSD symptom inventory, the acute group was more anxious and agitated (signifying hyperarousal), whereas the chronic group showed more depression and detachment (signifying numbing). Kiser, Heston, Millsap, and Pruitt (1991) also found two distinct symptom clusterings: 55% of physically and/or sexually abused children had PTSD, and the remaining children had more diffuse symptomatology (anxiety, depression, conduct problems). Further studies on the relationship between PTSD (and other psychiatric disorders) and child maltreatment are presented in the following sections.

The Physically Abused Child

Physical victimization of children can take many varied forms including acts experienced by the majority of children (e.g., physical punishment, sibling violence, peer assault) as well as acts experienced by a significant minority, such as physical abuse (Finkelhor & Dziuba-Leatherman, 1995). Physical abuse involves both minor and more severe injuries to the child, as well as a relatively rare form of abuse called Munchausen by proxy syndrome, in which a parent subjects a child to injury or painful medical procedures to seek attention from medical authorities. Moreover, indications of physical abuse and/or neglect should raise the question of sexual abuse, given the suspected overlap in incestuous families (Asher, 1988).

Despite the clinical profile of the abused child as exhibiting developmental deficiencies and adjustment problems, there has been little confirmation of the opinion that physical or emotional maltreatment leads to *particular developmental outcomes* for children across their lifespan (Ammerman, 1992; Fantuzzo, 1990; Wolfe, 1987). The reason for the lack of a linear relationship between physical abuse and particular developmental problems may be that abuse represents only the visible aspect of a very major disrupting influence in the child's ongoing development. Such disruptions are of such a pronounced and significant level that the child's behavioral, emotional, and social–cognitive dimensions of development are impaired to varying degrees (Aber & Cicchetti, 1984).

Physical Signs

Children who have been physically abused may present with a wide variety of external signs of physical injury, ranging from bruises, lacerations,

scars, and abrasions, to burns, sprains, or broken bones. Internal injuries may be present as well, such as head injury (from violent shaking or contact with a hard object), bone fractures, and intraabdominal injuries (e.g., ruptured liver or spleen). These physical manifestations represent only the more visible injuries to the child, however; as discussed below, their developmental progress is often impaired across several dimensions.

Cognitive Development

Not surprisingly, both the social–cognitive and the academic/intellectual development of physically abused children have been found to be delayed in comparison to their age mates. Social–cognitive development (i.e., the child's emerging view of the world and development of moral reasoning) is fostered by healthy parental guidance and control; it stands to reason, therefore, that because abused children have been raised in an atmosphere of power assertion and external control, their level of moral reasoning would be significantly below that of their nonabused peers. Typically, abusive parents fail to invoke in their children concern for the welfare of others, especially in a manner that the child will internalize and imitate.

Smetana, Kelly, and Twentyman (1984) illustrated the problems in moral reasoning experienced by abused and neglected children. These investigators compared 12 abused, 16 neglected, and 16 matched-control children of preschool age in their judgments regarding the dimensions of seriousness, deserved punishment, rule contingency (the permissibility of actions in the absence of rules), and generalizability of familiar moral and conventional nursery school transgressions (e.g., pictures depicting physical harm, psychological distress, and resource distribution). The results indicated that abused children considered transgressions entailing psychological distress to be more universally wrong for others (but not for themselves), whereas neglected children considered the unfair distribution of resources to be more universally wrong for themselves (but not for others). These findings are consistent with the type of maltreatment experienced by each of the two groups of children. It appears that abused children, as a function of their physical and psychological maltreatment, may have a heightened sensitivity to the intrinsic wrongness of such offenses (although further clarification is needed to understand the somewhat paradoxical relationship between this increased sensitivity and higher rates of aggression among abused children; see below).

Academic performance and language development are also often delayed among abused children (e.g., Appelbaum, 1977; Barahal, Waterman, & Martin, 1981; Erickson et al., 1989). For example, an average difference of approximately 20 IQ points was found in a comparison of abused and nonabused preschoolers on the Stanford–Binet Intelligence Scale and the Peabody Picture Vocabulary Test (Hoffman-Plotkin & Twentyman, 1984). Similar differences have been noted among school-aged samples of abused children as well. Salzinger, Kaplan, Pelcovitz, Samit, and Krieger (1984), comparing 30 abused children with 26 neglected and 48 nonmaltreated children on standard achievement tests and measures of classroom performance, found both the abused and neglected children to be 2 years below grade level in verbal and math abilities. Approximately one-third of the abused and neglected samples were failing one or more subjects and/or placed in a special classroom. Such delays are most likely due to the limited stimulation received in the home from parents who are overly concerned with the child's behavioral appearance and obedience, which impairs the child's need to explore, attempt new challenges, and to be exposed to a variety of cognitive and social stimuli. Moreover, punishment that involves verbal, emotional, and/or physical abuse is likely to suppress aspects of the child's interpersonal behavior (Parke & Slaby, 1983), which may partially account for the child's slowness in acquiring new cognitive and social skills.

Although physically abused children have difficulty performing well at academic tasks, there is no clear evidence that they are more likely than nonabused children to have a specific learning disability or, vice versa, that children with learning disabilities are more likely to be abused (Caplan & Dinardo, 1986). Also, because physically abused children resemble some of the behavior patterns of children diagnosed with attention-deficit/hyperactivity disorder (ADHD), investigators have considered a link between abuse and ADHD. One possible link would be the increased risk of harsh physical punishment toward children with ADHD, because of their more difficult and disruptive behavior. A comprehensive study of this possible connection was reported by Whitmore, Kramer, and Knutson (1993), based on the abuse histories and home environments of adult males who had been referred for ADHD-related problems and their nonreferred siblings. The findings indicated that the 14 ADHD children and their brothers did not

differ in their reports of physical punishment, discipline, parental rejection, positive contact, or their general impression of their home environments. These findings, moreover, were generally replicated in a larger sample of 70 probands, 29 brothers, and 22 former classmates. Based on these findings, the researchers conclude that ADHD per se does not appear to evoke excessively punitive parenting, although they caution that the child's ADHD patterns may interact with certain parental characteristics to increase the risk of child abuse.

Behavioral Development

The most notable behavioral sign appears to be heightened aggressivity and hostility toward others, especially authority figures, and angry outbursts, sometimes to minor provocation (Kolko, 1992; Wolfe, 1987). Maltreated children seem to be prone to engaging in power struggles and counteracting peer aggression with aggression or resistance, whereas nonmaltreated children tend to respond to aggression with distress (Howes & Eldredge, 1985). In addition, they may form a hostile attributional bias toward peers (i.e., presuming a peer means harm), which leads to an aggressive response. Physically abused children's pattern of approach–avoidance and avoidance behaviors toward a friendly adult and their aggressive response to adult caregivers was also shown by George and Main (1979), who suggest that control over interactions may be an important dimension for abused children.

Thus, a general consensus exists that physical maltreatment is associated with (but, of course, may not be the direct *cause* of) the child victim's more aggressive, resistant, and avoidant behavior with adults and peers (e.g., Fantuzzo, 1990; Shaw-Lamphear, 1985; Wolfe, 1987). The relationship between physical abuse and aggressivity may be mediated by impairments in the ongoing process of acquiring social knowledge, where adaptive social cognitive learning is hampered by the abusive social context (Shirk, 1988).

Another behavioral pattern among younger physically abused children has been labeled "compulsive compliance" (Crittenden & DiLalla, 1988). Compulsive compliance refers to a child's ready and quick compliance to significant adults, which occurs in the context of the child's general state of vigilance or watchfulness for adult cues. A child's compulsively compliant behavior may be accompanied by masked facial expressions, ambiguous affect, nonverbal–verbal incongruence,

and rote verbal responses. Such behavior seems to emerge in pace with the child's abstraction abilities, at about 12 months of age, concurring with the child's ability to form a stable mental representation of the caregiver. It has been suggested that abused infants learn to inhibit behaviors that have been associated with maternal anger (e.g., requests for attention, protests against intrusions) and that, in toddlerhood, such children may actively behave in a manner designed to please their mothers.

Crittenden and DiLalla (1988) found compulsive compliance to predominate in physically abused and abused/neglected children, in response to a controlling, hostile, and punitive parenting style. Such increases in compulsive compliance, as well as cooperative behavior, are most evident from ages 1 year through 2½ years among maltreated children, which contrasts with adequate-care children who usually display the normative independence-striving ("testing limits") behaviors expected of toddlers. Thus, while compulsive compliance may be adaptive in terms of reducing the risk of violence and increasing positive mother–child interactions during early childhood, such a style may impair the child's long-term development due to the denial of strongly felt emotions and the relegation of self-experience and self-direction to a lower priority. This early pattern may lead to inflexible strategies of behavior, with the consequence of reduced reciprocity in interactions (Crittenden, 1992).

Socioemotional Development

The above behavioral symptoms of aggressivity and excessive compliance can be understood in terms of the nature of the caregiver–child interactions, which provide a basis for the child's formation of an interpersonal style (Sroufe & Fleeson, 1986). The primary attachment relationship between the parent and child has been theoretically linked to the intergenerational transmission of abuse (e.g., Kaufman & Zigler, 1989), the failure of these children to form subsequent relationships with others (Erickson, Sroufe, & Egeland, 1985), and their vulnerability to additional developmental failures that rely to some extent on early attachment success (Aber & Allen, 1987). Indeed, the vast majority of maltreated infants form insecure attachments with their caregivers (70% to 100% across studies; Cicchetti, Toth, & Bush, 1988), suggesting the child's lack of confidence in the mother as an available and

responsive provider and the mother's difficulty in providing sensitive, nurturant, and responsive care.

In particular, physically abused children tend to display a pattern of avoidant behavior toward the mother when under stress (e.g., Crittenden, 1992; Egeland & Sroufe, 1981). Rather than make direct bids to the mother for assistance, support, and attention, the avoidant abused child will inhibit overt displays of negative affect to the caregiver, perhaps preoccupying him or herself with tasks (playing with toys). Such avoidance serves an adaptive function in reducing the likelihood of maternal rejection and angry interchanges that may lead to abuse, while still maintaining proximity to the mother (Crittenden, 1992). Although adaptive in the short term, such nonoptimal attachment may be most significant in terms of influencing a child's relationship formation with peers, future partners, and future offspring (Wolfe, 1991; Wolfe, Wekerle, Reitzel-Jaffe, & Lefebvre, 1995).

As abused children grow older, they are faced with another very important period of relationship development, this time with peers and other adults. During preschool and school ages, the children's initial manifestations of sensitivity to others' emotions and their early prosocial behavior become paramount. Because a positive bond or relationship between parent and child is an important component of such development among nonabused children, abused children would be expected to show problems in their understanding or acceptance of the emotions of others. Initial studies have indicated that abused children perform more poorly than nonabused controls on measures of affective and cognitive role taking, social sensitivity, and the ability to discriminate emotions in others (Barahal et al., 1981; Frodi & Smetana, 1984; Straker & Jacobson, 1981). A study involving 10 abused and 10 nonabused toddlers (Main & George, 1985) illustrates this lack of social sensitivity. No abused child ever exhibited a concerned response at witnessing the distress (e.g., crying, fearfulness) of another toddler, whereas the nonabused children responded with a concerned expression to one-third of the distress events. Abused children not only failed to show concern, they also actively responded to distress in others with *fear, physical attack, or anger*. Thus, abused children appear to bear a strong behavioral resemblance to their own abusive parents regarding their tendency to isolate themselves, to respond aggressively under a range of circumstances, and to respond with anger and aversion to the distress of others (Main & George, 1985).

Evidence of depressive symptomatology among maltreated children has grown considerably in recent years. Initial clinical observations of physically abused children had noted an elevated incidence of suicidal and self-destructive behavior, especially among inpatient or clinic-referred samples, as well as impairments in the expression of positive feelings or outlook (e.g., Deykin, Alpert, & McNamara, 1985; Green, 1978; Kazdin, Moser, Colbus, & Bell, 1985). The suspected parallel between maltreatment and depression stems from the belief that maltreating parents resemble affectively ill parents (e.g., adults suffering from manic–depression) in terms of disturbances in their attachment relationships and inappropriate or inconsistent parental stimulation and care during early childhood; moreover, studies of the development of the offspring of both groups of parents have shown strong consistencies in the development of these two groups of high-risk children (Kaufman, 1991).

Using a nonclinic sample and controlling for several critical background factors, Allen and Tarnowski (1989) compared 18 physically abused and 18 nonabused children (ages 7 to 13 years) on self-report measures of depression, hopelessness, self-esteem, and locus of control. After controlling for age, sex, race, gender, IQ, and socioeconomic status, these researchers found the abused children to score significantly higher on all measures relating to depression. In a related study, Stone (1993) classified a child guidance clinic sample of children into abused ($n = 45$) and nonabused ($n = 30$) on the basis of therapist information and ratings, and compared the samples on the basis of diagnoses of depression. Findings revealed a significant association between abuse and the diagnoses of major depressive episode (MDE) or dysthymia, with 12 abused children receiving a diagnosis of MDE and 9 diagnosed with dysthymia. A further breakdown of their sample according to the type of maltreatment (sexual, physical, neglect, and/or emotional), however, revealed that depression diagnoses appeared to be most reliably associated with emotional abuse.

Other studies have also found a tendency for physically abused and emotionally abused children to have a higher incidence of depressive symptoms, relative both to nonabused controls as well as neglected children (e.g., Kaufman, 1991; Toth, Manley, & Cicchetti, 1992). In one of the most complete studies of this issue to date, Toth et al.

(1992) compared physically abused (*n* = 46), neglected (*n* = 35), and nonmaltreated children (*n* = 72) using the several measures of depression and social adjustment (e.g., the Children's Depression Inventory [CDI]; Child Behavior Checklist [CBCL]). After controlling for age and cognitive functioning, their results indicated that the physical abuse group differed significantly from both the neglect and nonmaltreated samples, which did not differ from each other. Children from physically abusive homes also evidenced lower self-esteem than the nonmaltreated sample, with the neglect group falling in between (i.e., not differing significantly from) the abused and nonmaltreated samples on this dimension. In this study, 22% of the physically abused children met the criteria for clinical depression (based on CDI scores), which is comparable to the 18% reported by Kaufman (1991) in her sample of 56 maltreated children. Notably, only 6% of the comparison and 3% of the neglect samples of children met criteria for depression (Toth et al., 1992).

Munchausen by Proxy Syndrome

Baron von Munchausen was an 18th-century military mercenary who became famous for his wartime tales, suspected to be fabrications. As an adult disorder, Munchausen syndrome refers to an intentional fabrication of illness. As a form of child abuse, Munchausen by proxy syndrome (MBPS) refers to physical and psychological harm either through direct attack by the parent (which can be life-threatening) or as a function of being subjected to painful and numerous unnecessary medical assessment procedures. Although the disorder is more likely to involve the mother, the father may be a passive colluder and an uninvolved or absent parent (Schreier & Libow, 1993). Little is known of this form of abuse, however, and prevalence rates have not been determined. In a 1991 U.S. survey of 316 pediatric neurologists and gastroenterologists, 273 confirmed cases and 192 suspected cases were reported (Schreier & Libow, 1993).

Schreier and Libow (1993) compiled recent research on MBPS and found that MBPS varies widely in terms of symptom presentation. Clues to the problem are usually a pattern of unexpected symptoms in the child and chronic and varied child illness behaviors. An important clue to MBPS is when the child's symptoms improve or remit when removed from the MBPS parent's care. Overall, gastrointestinal symptoms and seizures tend to dominate the MBPS picture, although less serious symptoms can include asthma and allergies. Infants and preverbal children seem to be at greatest risk because intrusive, active induction of illness is most likely (e.g., active suffocation, diarrhea, vomiting, seizures). Older children tend to present with falsified reports or simulated symptoms (e.g., misrepresentation of medical history, contamination of laboratory specimens). Adolescents may become involved with validating their mother's fabrications or even in directly harming themselves.

The Neglected Child

Child neglect denotes deficiencies in caretaking obligations that harm the child's psychological and/or physical health (National Research Council, 1993). Neglecting behaviors can encompass educational, supervisory, medical, physical, and emotional domains. Although most drowning and near-drowning cases (bathtubs, pools) occur when children are unsupervised, these tend to be classified as accidental deaths and injury (some incidents may, however, constitute neglect; Mrazek, 1993). In children under the age of 2 years, the most prominent form of neglect is failure to thrive (National Research Council, 1993), which is discussed below (for a detailed discussion, see Lyons-Ruth, Zeanah, & Benoit, Chapter 13, this volume).

Physical Signs

Because child neglect is an act of omission rather than commission, there are usually fewer physical signs present. The one exception to this general finding is the occurrence of failure to thrive (FTT), a form of maltreatment related to a failure of the infant to gain weight due to inadequate caloric intake linked to poor caregiving (Benoit, 1993). FTT is considered to be a factor if a child gains weight with hospitalization, or if he or she gains weight after age 2 years, when children are better able to obtain food for themselves (Mrazek, 1993). FTT families tend to have children who are close in age, and siblings may have FTT, chronic illness, and other forms of abuse (Benoit, 1993).

Significant disruptions in the mother–child relationship seem to characterize FTT cases. If we consider controlled observational studies, FTT children and their mothers display more negative behavior and affect than control fami-

lies; FTT mothers show fewer positive behaviors and affect; and FTT mothers and their children show less contingent responsiveness and mutual behaviors (Benoit, 1993). Further, when relationship-specific measures are used, FTT mothers show unhealthy relationship patterns as compared to control mothers. Specifically, FTT mothers tend to dismiss the importance of relationships and have passive, confused, or intensely angry views about them (Benoit, Zeanah, & Barton, 1989). In a similar fashion, over 90% of FTT children are considered to show an insecure attachment to their mother, which compares to fewer than 50% of control children. This finding suggests that from the child's perspective, fear, anger, and anxiety characterize his or her relationship to the mother (Crittenden, 1987; Valenzuela, 1990). Thus, FTT children seem to have low confidence in the mother's availability and responsivity to their needs, and mothers show more aversive, less positive, and less contingent responsivity to their child.

Cognitive and Behavioral Development

Similar to physically abused children, neglected children tend to differ from nonabused children on measures of language ability and intelligence (Crouch & Milner, 1993), which persist from infancy through to school age (Erickson et al., 1989). Given the low level of educational input in the primary-care environment of neglected children, their cognitive and academic achievement has been found to be worse than other maltreated groups (Erickson et al., 1989).

Compared to physically abusive mothers, more neglecting mothers are found to be mentally retarded (e.g., Crittenden & DiLalla, 1988), which has implications for the ability of the caregiver to meet the developmental needs of the child. Accordingly, Crittenden and Ainsworth (1989) identify two main behavioral patterns in neglected children: undisciplined activity and extreme passivity. Because of the unresponsivity of neglecting parents, neglected children often adapt by turning more to their environment in an attempt to meet unmet physical, cognitive, and socioemotional needs. Given the lack of adult supervision and guidance, the neglected child's exploratory activity lacks structure, focus, and often safety. Crittenden and Ainsworth (1989) also make the association between hyperactive behavior that may be seen in neglected children and an understimulating environment. In observed interactions, neglected toddlers show little persistence and enthusiasm, much negative affect and noncompliance, and little positive affect, yet they were found to be highly reliant on their mothers. As preschoolers, these neglected children showed poor impulse control and were found to be highly dependent on teachers for support and nurturance (e.g., Erickson et al., 1989).

Socioemotional Development

Like physically abused children, most neglected children form insecure attachments with their caregivers (Crittenden, 1985, 1992; Egeland & Sroufe, 1981). Consequently, some neglected children never learn strategies for engaging adults and for independently exploring their environments (Crittenden & Ainsworth, 1989). For example, Crittenden and DiLalla (1988) found neglected children to be more passive in interactions with their mother than physically abused and abused-and-neglected groups; additionally, neglected children were found to become increasingly angry and resistant from the ages of 1 to 2½ years. In other words, passivity and noncompliance are independent dimensions seen in neglected children. Moreover, the passivity of neglected children often extends to their peer domain. Hoffman-Plotkin and Twentyman (1984) found that neglected children appeared to be more withdrawn in peer social interaction than either physically abused or control children. However, the extent to which such withdrawal indicates differences in psychological difficulties (e.g., depression, anxiety, repressed anger), motivation, cognitive/organizational abilities, or acquired social skills remains to be understood.

The Sexually Abused Child

Sexual abuse includes incest, sexual assault by a relative or stranger, exposure to indecent acts, sexual rituals, or involvement in child pornography (National Research Council, 1993). There is no uniform or "classic" symptom pattern for victims of sexual abuse, given the diverse characteristics in the nature of the sexual assault (intrafamilial vs. extrafamilial, number of perpetrators, type of abuse, duration of abuse, frequency of abuse, level of coercion and violence), along with individual differences in the child, the perpetrator, and the social context (Wolfe & Wolfe, 1988). Reviews by Finkelhor and colleagues (Finkelhor

& Browne, 1988; Kendall-Tackett, Williams, & Finkelhor, 1993) have found factors that relate to increased child distress include: longer duration/greater frequency of abuse, the use of force, penetration, and a closer relationship to the perpetrator. Further, Kendall-Tackett et al. (1993) report that about one third of sexually abused children show no symptoms and two-thirds show significant recovery during the first 12 to 18 months following the abuse, although researchers and clinicians acknowledge the possibility of delayed emergence of symptoms. Assessment of these symptoms is complicated by the fact that identification of child problem areas often relies on maternal report, which may be misleading due to the possible connection between maternal distress and elevated ratings of child maladjustment (Richters, 1992).

Reviews of the child sexual-abuse literature converge in identifying a range of common symptoms and adjustment disorders (e.g., Asher, 1988; Beitchman et al., 1992; Finkelhor & Browne, 1988; Hartman & Burgess, 1989; Kendall-Tackett et al., 1993; Mrazek & Mrazek, 1981; V. Wolfe & Wolfe, 1988). Sexual abuse is often related to specific symptoms of sexualized behavior, as well as clinical indications of aggression, depression, withdrawal, and anxiety. The range of symptoms can be meaningfully described in reference to (1) "acute symptoms" representing a primary stress response to the abuse trauma, and (2) "secondary symptoms" representing an accommodation and adaptation to the abuse experience. Research on the developmental and descriptive characteristics of sexually abused children is discussed below in reference to such acute and chronic symptoms.

It should be additionally noted that the characteristics of the sexually abused child cluster generally more toward trauma-related emotional and behavioral problems rather than toward cognitive/developmental delays and interpersonal conflict (as was more the case with physical abuse and neglect). These major differences in symptom presentation, in all likelihood, result from the fact that sexual abuse has less to do with parental caregiving, discipline, or stimulation but, instead, is an act related to breach of trust, exploitation, and deception. Whereas all three types of maltreatment share a common ground in relation to the abuse of power by an adult over a child, sexual abuse stands out from physical abuse and neglect in terms of these specific dynamics (further discussion of these issues emerges in the section on Theoretical Frameworks, below).

Acute Symptoms of Sexual Abuse

Many of the acute symptoms of sexual abuse resemble children's common reactions to stressors. Rather than being directly related to the sexual offense per se, such stress-related problems may be connected to related (but nonsexual) aspects of the abuse, such as other forms of abuse by adults (physical, emotional), victimization by peers (teasing, physical assaults), stressful living conditions (domestic violence, criminal activity, alcohol and substance abuse), and more subtle sexually abusive behaviors (exposure to sexual activity by adults, seductive parenting). Acute symptoms of onset of child sexual abuse can be best detected by those individuals who are most familiar with the child's level of functioning, because these symptoms represent a *change* in behavior and disruption of previous competencies (Hartman & Burgess, 1989). Parents, relatives, teachers, coaches, and friends of the child may note symptoms of distress across physical, psychological, and behavioral dimensions signifying that "something is different."

Acute *physical symptoms* or signs noted among child sexual-abuse victims include headaches, stomachaches, appetite changes, vomiting, sensitivity to touch in specific areas, genital complaints, and urinary tract infections. Gynecological problems in children, such as infections and perineal bruises and tears, are signs highly specific to sexual abuse (Asher, 1988). *Psychological symptoms* may further include: general and abuse-specific fears, emotional over- or underreactivity (increased anger, anxiety, fatigue, depression, passivity), difficulties focusing and sustaining attention, and withdrawal in interest and participation from usual activities. These symptoms of distress may be associated with a decline in school performance, in academics, behavior, and peer relations. *Behavioral symptoms* may include: regression to behaviors of earlier levels of development (bedwetting, eneuresis, encopresis, clinging, excessive crying, tantrums, fearfulness), sleeping problems and nightmares, self-destructive behaviors (self-injury, risk-taking behaviors), hyperactivity, truancy, running away from home, or pseudomaturity. As the child approaches adolescence, acting-out behaviors can include delinquency, drug use, promiscuity, and prostitution (Asher, 1988).

The most specific *behavioral signs* of sexual abuse are described as sexualized behaviors, which include persistent sexualized behavior with other children and/or with toys, excessive masturbation, age-inappropriate knowledge of sexual activity, and/or pronounced seductive or promiscuous behavior. Friedrich (1993), using a parent-report inventory tapping child sexual behavior, found a greater incidence of sexually related problems (e.g., "French kisses," "uses sexual words") among sexually abused preschool children (compared to the normative sample). Higher problem scores were related to abuse severity, number of perpetrators, the use of force, and a sexual family environment (exposure to nudity, witnessing parental sexual behavior). Such sexualized behaviors are more predominant among younger abused children, and are less often seen among latency-age children (given these children's increased awareness of social norms); however, sexualized behavior sometimes reemerges during adolescence as promiscuity, prostitution, or sexual aggression (Beitchman et al., 1992; Kendall-Tackett et al., 1993).

Secondary Symptoms of Sexual Abuse

Enduring symptoms of sexual abuse may be complicated by the disclosure and discovery process (Hartman & Burgess, 1989) and by the extended involvement of official agents (e.g., child protection, police, and court systems; Friedrich, 1990). In contrast to acute symptoms, a more identifiable clustering of secondary symptoms often appears along trauma-specific dimensions. Although sexually abused children often cannot be differentiated from their nonabused counterparts using traditional psychological measures (Berliner, 1991), "abuse-specific effects" have emerged when measures that are more sensitive to the trauma of abuse have been used. For example, abuse-specific fears (e.g., fear of being alone, fear of men) and idiosyncratic fears related to the specific abuse events (e.g., fear of the bathroom) may develop (Foa & Kozak, 1986; Terr, 1991; V. Wolfe, Gentile, & Wolfe, 1989).

Specific findings regarding these secondary symptoms have emerged among studies that have used measures that are more sensitive to the symptoms of chronic trauma or PTSD. For example, Kiser et al. (1988) found that all 10 children (aged 2–6 years) who had been subjected to ritualistic abuse in a daycare setting were displaying Type II PTSD. McLeer, Deblinger, Alkins, Foa, and Ralphe (1988) found that *Diagnostic and Statistical Manual of Mental Disorders,* third edition, revised (American Psychiatric Association, 1987; DSM-III-R) criteria for PTSD were met by almost half of their sample of school-aged sexually abused children in an outpatient setting, despite the fact that children scored within the normal range on standard psychological tests. Similarly, Wolfe, Sas, and Wekerle (1994) found no differences on standard measures of psychological functioning when looking at their full sample of 90 sexually abused (school-aged) children. However, they discovered that half the sample displayed a positive PTSD symptom cluster (based primarily on child self-report measures). When these PTSD-positive children were compared with the PTSD-negative subsample, it was evident that the abused children who showed PTSD-related problems also had the more elevated scores on traditional psychological measures of general fears, depression, anxiety, and abuse-specific fears. To date, therefore, these initial studies show the utility of using PTSD-sensitive measures in identifying some of the negative effects of childhood sexual abuse. Also, the relational context of abuse may be important in the development of PTSD; Alexander (1992) suggests that children with disorganized attachment (i.e., a lack of a clear strategy for achieving a felt sense of security with parental figures) may be most vulnerable to long-term PTSD symptoms.

The incidence of depressive symptomatology and diagnosis has been only recently explored in studies of sexually abused children, and findings have generally been less clear than studies involving physically abused children. Citing the relationship between adult survivors of childhood sexual abuse and clinical depression (see below), investigators have been attempting to identify those patterns of depression, lowered self-esteem, or cognitive distortion that may result from childhood sexual abuse and progress into adulthood.

Two studies of sexually abused girls are illustrative of the nature and features of depression among this population. Using a composite score based on the CBCL and the CDI, Koverola, Pound, Heger, and Lytle (1993) found that 67% of their sample of 39 girls could be classified as having symptoms matching the diagnosis of depression. These researchers also found life

events and IQ to be the strongest correlates of depression which, combined with family support and age at onset of abuse, accounted for 39% of the variance in depression scores in their sample. Wozencraft, Wagner, and Pellegrin (1991) administered the CDI to a sample of 65 sexually abused girls and reported that 28% scored above the 90th percentile (i.e., clinical cutoff) on this instrument. In addition, 42% were having some degree of suicidal ideation at the time of the evaluation. A noteworthy finding of this latter investigation was that the older victims, and those whose mothers were less supportive, were more likely to describe themselves as depressed. This latter finding of lower maternal support being associated with greater symptomatology has been seen in similar studies of sexually abused children (e.g., Sas, Hurley, Hattch, Malla, & Dick, 1993), suggesting the importance of this factor in the expression and course of children's adjustment and recovery. Additional factors such as the presence of PTSD (V. Wolfe et al., 1989; Wolfe et al., 1994) and the degree of disruption and stress (e.g., Friedrich, Urquiza, & Beilke, 1986) have also been shown to be associated with elevated behavioral and emotional problems among sexually abused girls, suggesting that the relationship between sexual abuse and depression may be mediated by a number of interrelated factors.

Hartman and Burgess (1989) describe five patterns of adaptation to sexual abuse that are most often shown by children, which summarizes much of the above descriptive information (notably, these patterns resemble the range of symptoms described in adulthood as well: adequate functioning, depression, sexual dysfunction, personality disorders, and severe personality disturbances and psychoses (e.g., Finkelhor & Browne, 1988; Herman, 1992).

1. *Integrated pattern* denotes the situation where the child clearly views the abuser as to blame and views criminal prosecution of the abuser positively. The child is able to talk about the event with some objectivity, has a future orientation, and shows evidence of making age-appropriate adjustments with family, peer, and school.

2. *Avoidant pattern* denotes the situation where the child does not acknowledge negative affect about the sexual abuse, tending to deny it, minimize it, or be unable to clearly articulate it. The child shows a here-and-now orientation and,

when not under stress, tends to act as if nothing had happened. However, under stress, a breakdown of avoidance behaviors may occur with depression and self-destructive behavior. It is speculated that with this pattern there is an underlying feeling of guilt and responsibility for the abuse by the child.

3. *Symptomatic pattern* denotes the situation where acute symptoms become chronic, with the child exhibiting anxiety. The child has a "past orientation" and may feel hopeless about the future. The child feels guilty and responsible for the abuse and may exhibit significant impairment in functioning in school and peer and family relations.

4. *Identification with the abuser* denotes the situation where the child has managed his or her anxiety through forming an identification with the perpetrator. The child's threatening demeanor is seen in the exploitation of others and antisocial behavior toward peers, school, and family. The child tends to minimize the negative effects of the abuse, may have maintained an emotional, social, and economic relationship with the abuser, and feels sorry or angry that the perpetrator was exposed. Substance abuse also tends to be present.

5. *Psychotic pattern* denotes the situation where the most profound symptoms are found, involving difficulties in distinguishing reality. Often the abuse is cognitively split off, such that it is buried in delusional symptoms and material. Regressive behavior and primitive, fixed, and sexualized thinking patterns are noted.

Table 14.1 presents a summary of the range of child characteristics associated with physical abuse, neglect, and sexual abuse, based on the above section.

DEVELOPMENTAL COURSE AND PROGNOSIS OF CHILD MALTREATMENT

Overview of the Developmental Consequences

Because child abuse is a private event as well as a personal invasion, it can have a wide range of impact on development. As noted, there is a trend toward conceptualizing various forms of child maltreatment as fundamentally involving trauma–

TABLE 14.1. Range of Child Characteristics Associated with Physical Abuse, Neglect, and Sexual Abuse

Dimension of development	Physical abuse	Neglect	Sexual abuse
Physical	Minor: Bruises, lacerations, abrasions. Major: Burns, brain damage, broken bones	Failure to thrive symptoms: Slowed growth, immature physical development	Physical symptoms: Headaches, stomach aches, appetite changes, vomiting; gynecological complaints
Cognitive	Mild delay in areas of cognitive and intellectual functioning; academic problems; difficulties in moral reasoning	Mild delay in areas of cognitive and intellectual functioning; academic problems; difficulties in moral reasoning	No evidence of cognitive impairment; self-blame; guilt
Behavioral	Aggressivity; peer problems; "compulsive compliance"	Passivity; "hyperactivity"	Fears, anxiety, PTSD-related symptoms; sleep problems
Socioemotional	Social incompetence; hostile intent attributions; difficulties in social sensitivity	Social incompetence; withdrawn, dependent; difficulties in social sensitivity	Symptoms of depression and low self-esteem; "sexualized" behavior; behaviors that accommodate to the abuse (e.g., passive compliance; no or delayed disclosure)

an external stressor to the child creating internal turmoil. Considering this view, Herman (1992) notes:

> The child trapped in an abusive environment is faced with formidable tasks of adaptation. She must find a way to preserve a sense of trust in people who are untrustworthy, safety in a situation that is unsafe, control in a situation that is terrifyingly unpredictable, power in a situation of helplessness. Unable to care for or protect herself, she must compensate for the failures of adult care and protection with the only means at her disposal, an immature system of psychological defenses. (p. 98)

The following review of empirical findings concerning the short- and long-range impact of maltreatment considers how such acts may interfere with development across several dimensions (i.e., physical, cognitive, socioemotional development) and over time.

Physical Development and Outcome

Physical Abuse and Neglect

Abuse and neglect violate the child at the basic, concrete level of physical autonomy and dignity (Hartman & Burgess, 1989). Physical abuse and neglect can result in child fatalities (e.g., an estimated 1,200 deaths in 1990, USDHHS, 1992). Infants are particularly vulnerable to serious head injury, which can follow from shaking an infant (Dykes, 1986). Physically abused children presenting to a psychiatric facility have been found to exhibit more mild neurological impairment and more serious and minor physical injury, as compared to their nonabused counterparts (Kolko, Moser, & Weldy, 1990). With respect to neglect, a myriad of physical health problems, limited growth, and increased complications arising from other health conditions (e.g., diabetes, allergies) have been linked to poor caregiving practices, although these subtle effects are often difficult to document. FTT children who have experienced extended malnutrition (>6 months of age) are at risk of not reaching their expected growth patterns for age and sex (Benoit, 1993).

Sexual Abuse

Negative effects to physical health specific to childhood sexual abuse include urinary tract problems, gynecological problems, elevated risk for sexually transmitted diseases (including AIDS), and elevated risk for pregnancy (National Research Council, 1993). Asher (1988) notes that the statistics for pregnancy due to incest are unclear given the range in sample characteristics (court-ordered vs. clinical), with some studies citing a pregnancy rate of about 20%. Early sexual victimization, moreover, has been linked to adolescent pregnancy (Gershenson et al., 1989). Adolescent pregnancy may have the functional effect of ending an incestuous relationship (Herman, 1981).

Disruptions to physical/sexual development can occur as a function of the emotional abuse within the sexual context. Finkelhor and Browne (1988) conceptualize this as "traumatic sexualization," referring to the process of the child's sexuality being shaped in developmentally inappropriate and interpersonally dysfunctional ways. It may be more prominent in situations where force was used, a sexual response was evoked from the child, and the child was enticed to participate. Traumatic sexualization may involve the child learning sexual behavior as a means to an end (gifts, privilege, affection, attention), or it may involve problematic emotional associations to sexual behavior (e.g., fear, disgust, shame, and confusion). This may translate into distorted views about the body and sexuality, in some cases leading to weight problems, eating disorders, poor physical health care, and physically self-destructive behaviors.

Studies of inappropriate sexual behavior among younger children suggest that about 35% of sexually abused preschoolers display such behavior (Friedrich, 1990). Although the findings are largely correlational, there is support for the notion that childhood sexual abuse heightens the risk of problems in sexual as well as general health. For example, a community survey of women visiting a family practice clinic showed childhood sexual abuse to be associated with a greater number of poor health indicators (overweight, heavier amount of smoking, earlier onset of smoking, more sexual partners, fewer Pap smears), gynecological problems (yeast infections, pelvic pain, pelvic inflammatory disease, pregnancy complications), breast disease, and higher scores on a somatization scale (Springs & Friedrich, 1992).

Cognitive Development and Outcome

One explanation for the diversity in symptom presentation and outcome of maltreated children is

the manner in which their harsh treatment is cognitively processed and, ultimately, understood. Hartman and Burgess (1989) note that when the first expression of acute symptoms by the child is not met by any substantive response, the child is "trapped" and must in some way encapsulate the abuse. The child's cognitive coping can be further challenged by rationales given by the offender about the abuse, such as abuse being discipline or love, abuse as a secret or private family matter, or abuse being the norm. Thus, the child must embark on creating some defensive structure that may involve cognitive vigilance or reality-mediating strategies such as dissociation, which can negatively affect social cognition and cognitive outcome.

Such cognitive readaptation does not occur in a vacuum but, rather, in a relational context. The extent to which the abuse is experienced as invasive, unfair, and wrong may depend on child factors (age, cognitive ability) as well as certain fundamental beliefs. Lerner (1980) proposes that a basic belief most children operate under is one of a "just world" where people get what they deserve and deserve what they get. However, the power of such basic beliefs to guide information processing may depend on the relational context. For example, abuse occurring in a fundamentally secure relational context may be experienced as more novel and, hence, more cognitively disrupting, thereby propelling the child to make cognitive shifts. Indirect evidence for this comes from reviews showing maternal support to function as a buffer for child sexual abuse (Kendall-Tackett & Finkelhor, 1993) and from studies showing decreased long-term negative sequelae when the adult survivor of child sexual abuse can identify some "meaning" for the abuse (Silver, Boon, & Stones, 1983). Self-blame may also serve a preventative function, i.e., knowing "better" what to do next time or how to prevent further abuse (Janoff-Bulman, 1979).

In contrast, abuse occurring in the context of a fundamentally insecure relational life, where everyday hassles may be seen as the child's fault, may foster the cognitive processing of abuse through attributions of characterological self-blame, lower self-efficacy, and feelings of guilt. Cognitive distortions (deYoung & Lowry, 1992) and disruption to a success-based orientation (Cicchetti et al., 1988) have been noted as salient relationship effects of many forms of maltreatment. As we consider below the additional disruptions to cognitive and socioemotional development, a relational context can be kept in mind,

although research has not yet tested such interaction effects specifically.

Cognitive Vigilance

As Herman (1992) discusses, hypervigilance includes not only constant scanning of the environment but also developing the ability to detect subtle variations to alert the child about possible abuse. Children can become quite adept at processing nonverbal communication such that facial, intonational, and body language cues signifying danger states (e.g., adult anger, sexual arousal, intoxication, or dissociation) seem to be automatically processed without much conscious awareness. Indeed, a child victim can learn to respond to danger signals because they have evoked a feeling of alarm within the child without his or her being able to label or identify such cues verbally. In other words, it appears that the "feeling state" is most accessible to the child (Herman, 1992). However, once alarmed, the abused child must make quiet efforts at escape, avoiding visible displays of agitation and instead effortfully attempting to be inconspicuous, avoiding the abuser if possible or placating or complying if necessary.

Although hypervigilance is a commonly described clinical phenomenon, empirical efforts have failed to substantiate maltreated children's superior sensitivity to other-cues (e.g., Frodi & Smetana, 1984). Some evidence, however, supports maltreated children's sensitivity to a particular class of affective cues—unresolved anger. Hennessy, Rabideau, Cicchetti, and Cummings (1994) report a study in which children with a history of maltreatment and exposure to domestic violence reported greater fear following videotaped presentations of interadult anger than did matched low-socioeconomic-status (SES) children who were exposed to domestic violence. However, this heightened emotional reaction occurred in the context of unresolved anger but not in the context of resolved anger, suggesting maltreated children are particularly sensitive to cues of conflict termination. These researchers suggest that placating behaviors often observed in maltreated children may represent fear-based attempts to calm or soothe angry parents so as to avoid becoming the receiver of parental aggression.

Dissociation

Dissociation denotes the situation of altering one's usual level of self-awareness in an effort to

escape an upsetting event or feeling (Trzepacz & Baker, 1993). It is a normal reaction to an emotionally overloaded situation, enacted in the service of self-preservation when neither resistance nor escape is possible (Herman, 1992). With dissociation, the child diverts attention away from the abuse, psychologically escaping from it. This process can include actively pretending to be somewhere or someone else, experiencing amnesia, and having the ability to "cut off" pain perception from parts of the body. The cognitive outcome of dissociation is a fragmentation of abuse-related information in memory, such that informational details may be separated from each other and from affective and physiological responses. This fragmentation can translate into patchy and disorganized event recall, seemingly illogical associations, and seemingly extreme affective reactions, such as extreme rage in reaction to relatively minor interpersonal "offenses." Thus, the trauma may lead to the experience of intense emotion without clear memory of an event or clear and vivid recall, accompanied in some instances by flat affect (Herman, 1992). For example, Hartman and Burgess (1989) cite Stoller's (1973) example of a patient's persistent delusion of a having a "rotting" brain eventually being connected to a childhood sexual assault occurring among rotting leaves.

Social Cognition and Behavioral Expression

Social cognition is an important dimension of development to consider because it offers one of the clearer explanatory links between maltreatment experiences and the child's subsequent social behavior. Domains of social cognition can include inferences about the thoughts, feelings, and intentions of others, as in person perception and causal attributions (Smetana & Kelly, 1989). For example, in the domain of affective cognitions, maltreated preschoolers have been found to have greater difficulties with affect recognition than their peers (e.g., Camras, Ribordy, Spaccarelli, & Stefani, 1986). This may be a function of a lower mastery of verbal expressiveness about inner feelings. To illustrate, Cicchetti and Beeghly (1987) found that maltreated toddlers used fewer "internal state" words (e.g., talking about the feelings and emotions of self and other–"ouch"; "I be good"; "You hurt my feelings") in interactions with their mothers than their nonmaltreated peers, and they spoke less often

about their negative internal states. Further, maltreated children produced fewer utterances about negative affect and about physiological states (hunger, thirst). These researchers suggest that inhibition of emotional language may be adaptive in the abusive environment, because otherwise its expression may function as a parental trigger for child abuse. That is, certain classes of children's affect, like distress, may be met with disapproval in maltreating families.

Alternatively, maltreating mothers may be poor models for children in their decoding abilities, perhaps overlabeling affects as negative. Cicchetti (1990) also found similarities in the level of emotional language of maltreated and insecurely attached children, which again emphasizes the relational context as a main teaching environment for the child about feeling states, labeling of emotions, and affective perspective taking. Indeed, Beeghly and Cicchetti (1994) clarify that toddlers at greatest risk for delayed internal state language were those maltreated children with insecure attachments, as compared to maltreated toddlers with secure attachment and comparison toddlers with insecure attachment. This suggests that maltreatment occurring within a generally problematic relational context is particularly toxic for young children's developing sociocommunicative abilities. Also, this finding identifies secure attachment as a protective factor for maltreated children's cognitive and socioemotional development.

Also of relevance to maltreatment is the manner in which abused children come to understand their abuser's behavior, especially in terms of attributions of causality and blame. Theoretically, more internal attributions of responsibility would be expected to be associated with negative outcome, depression in particular (Kaslow, Rehm, Pollack, & Siegel, 1988). Celano (1992) lists potential internal attributions about sexual abuse, wherein the child takes responsibility for failing to recognize the abuse, participation in the abuse, family reaction to disclosure, failing to avoid or control the abuse, any pleasure experienced, failing to protect siblings, and failing to protect oneself from the abuse. Although empirical tests of this assumption are limited, two recent studies suggest that internal attributions of blame are linked to greater maladjustment. For example, sexually abused children's endorsement of stable negative attributions about the abuse (V. Wolfe et al., 1989) and of guilt and self-blame items (Wolfe et al., 1994) were significant predictors of their degree of psychological distress. Further-

more, retrospective studies show that an attribution of self-blame about childhood sexual abuse is a strong predictor of negative emotional, relational, and sexual adjustment in adulthood (Wyatt & Newcomb, 1990). Self-blame/stigmatization for childhood victimization has also been found to account for about 40% of the variance across measures of adult global distress, depression, anxiety, interpersonal sensitivity, and self-esteem (Hazzard, 1993).

These studies converge in identifying self-blame as an important construct for understanding symptomatology in children after disclosure of abuse, as well as problems experienced by adult survivors. This conclusion raises the question as to whether self-blame may be an adaptive response during the abuse phase. Herman (1992) argues that the abused child's tendency to reinterpret the abuse functions to absolve parents of blame and responsibility, perhaps as a way to preserve the attachment relationship. A prominent way by which this is achieved is when the child denies the abuse in some manner—through minimalization, rationalization, suppression of thoughts, denial, and dissociative reactions—which absolves the abuser of responsibility for the abuse. In the process of denying the abuse, its meaning is changed from bad to "less bad," or even "good," an interpretation that may be conveyed directly to the child by others in her environment (i.e., positive benefits or rewards, experience of pleasure, etc.). This process of adaptive misperception of adult behavior and self-blame is not unique to abused children, however. It also differentiates preschool children who are anxiously attached from those who are securely attached to their caregivers, and such reactions are considered to be a strategy that serves attachment (Waters, Posada, Crowell, & Lay, 1993).

Studies of physically abused children and matched controls indicate that such children often take responsibility for parental punishments, believing them to be in response to their own bad behavior (Herzberger, Potts, & Dillon, 1981). However, physically abused children also hold a more negative view of their parents: they are also significantly more likely to perceive physical punishment to be due to their parent's mean character, which may lay the foundation for an attributional bias toward inferring negative and hostile intent. Physically abused children, for example, show a negative attributional bias with peers, which increases the likelihood of aggressive responding (Dodge, Bates, & Pettit, 1990).

Moreover, in contrast to nonabused children, abused children may be less able to inhibit their egocentrism during peer interactions, tending to overfocus on their own personal needs (Smetana & Kelly, 1989).

Thus, cognitive development among maltreated children may be altered by their experiences to such an extent that adaptational strategies, such as hypervigilance and dissociation, form to become a cognitive "style" that is highly responsive to signs of personal danger. When the environment changes (as when the child starts school), such strategies ipso facto are no longer as adaptive, making cognitive flexibility more challenging. Instead, these original strategies often lead to difficulties in appraising interactional events, such as potential misperceptions of hostile intent from peers and teachers (Dodge, Pettit, & Bates, 1994).

Cognitive Outcome

Given the wide range of cognitive adaptations and abuse characteristics, it is not surprising to find that physical abuse and neglect (Azar, Barnes, & Twentyman, 1988) and child sexual abuse (Einbender & Friedrich, 1989) are linked to cognitive impairments (see section on Social Cognition and Behavioral Expression, above). A specific cognitive deficit noted consistently for maltreated children is expressive language deficits (Beeghly & Cicchetti, 1994; Friedrich, Einbender, & Luecke, 1983; Vondra, Barnett, & Cicchetti, 1990), which in part may be related to the lower levels of sustained, positive, verbal interactions in maltreating families. Lower academic achievement is also found for maltreated children relative to controls (Eckenrode & Doris, 1991; Wolfe & Mosk, 1983). These findings are suggestive of global cognitive delay and language deficits among maltreated youngsters, which may be a function of the avoidance patterns learned in the home environment (i.e., not moving or talking too much) and the associated lack of stimulation of cognitive development (Green, 1983).

Recent studies continue to indicate the presence of abuse-related cognitive deficits. Eckenrode, Laird, and Doris (1993), controlling for welfare status, report that maltreated children obtained significantly lower reading and mathematics achievement scores than matched controls. Neglected children had the lowest achievement scores. Sexually abused children did not differ from controls on standardized tests or on

grades and frequency of grade retention. While sexual abuse may not be related to grades, it is related to poorer cognitive performance, as indicated by poorer teacher ratings of overall academic performance, being a competent learner (high task orientation, low learning problems), parent ratings of dissociation/distractibility, and greater school avoidance (e.g., absences, teacher ratings of shy–anxious) (Trickett, McBride-Chang, & Putnam, 1994). Such cognitive difficulties may be a long-term effect of maltreatment, which may not be evident until adolescence or adulthood. For example, a large-scale study of young adults found that a history of child neglect or physical abuse (but not sexual abuse) was associated with lower IQ and reading achievement, controlling for age, sex, race, and social class (Perez & Widom, 1994). In the aggregate, the emerging findings point to intellectual and achievement impairments that are indirectly associated with child maltreatment, especially neglect and physical abuse, due largely to features associated with poor caregiving and limited stimulation (Wolfe & Mosk, 1983). Additional research will be required to determine if differential effects on cognitive development resulting from a specific form of maltreatment are present.

One interpretation of the cognitive and academic difficulties of maltreated children posits that an impoverished environment, rather than specific aspects of child abuse, is largely responsible for these deficits. Nonabused siblings, for example, show poorer academic performance, relative to control families (Salzinger et al., 1984), and cognitive differences have not emerged in some studies comparing physically abused to neglected children (e.g., Hoffman-Plotkin & Twentyman, 1984). Maltreated children also do not differ from socioeconomically disadvantaged children on measures of cognitive abilities (Vondra et al., 1990). Although maltreated preschoolers displayed more immature play behavior (solitary vs. parallel and group play, less symbolic play, less sustained attention in play) than their nonabused counterparts, they did not show differences in intellectual functioning (Alessandri, 1991). As Eckenrode and Doris (1991) note, poorer school and cognitive performance may be a function of environmental factors, such as the discontinuity in education as a result of frequent moves, school transfers, suspensions, and tardiness.

Socioemotional Development and Outcome

Child abuse requires the child to make social and emotional adjustments that may compromise emotional development (Hartman & Burgess, 1989; Herman, 1992). Part of the abuser's intent is to achieve an accepting, even willing, victim. This process can entail the use of coercive strategies to ensure psychological control over the victim, including fear-based tactics (e.g., threatening greater harm to the child or others) and tactics aimed at destroying the child's sense of self (e.g., verbally denigrating the child). For many abused children, these abuser behaviors occur within (and sometimes contribute to) the context of an insecure attachment to parental figures (Aber & Allen, 1987). This attachment context is important to understanding the impact of child abuse, because the child's conceptualization of self and of others in relationships represents both a belief system and a relationship prototype (Waters et al., 1993). Thus, attachment provides one context for how the abuse event will be cognitively and emotionally processed. As seen from the preceding sections, the experience of child abuse can induce numerous negative feelings (i.e., shame, hostility, rage, depression, differentness) that are potentially damaging to the child's evolving sense of self, others, and affect regulation.

Conceptions of the Self

Finkelhor and Browne (1988) identify the sense of *powerlessness* accompanying child sexual abuse as being a salient component to the disruption of the self. This disempowerment refers to the process by which the child's will, desire, and sense of self-efficacy are thwarted and rebuked. In neglect, a child's personal power or self-efficacy is diminished by the child's low value and status as a recipient of adequate care. In child physical abuse, power is usurped from the child as a function of the invasion to her or his physical space and subjugation. Self-efficacy of the child is further diminished when the child's attempts to avoid or end the abuse meet with no or limited success. Thus, the emotional undercurrent to the self as a function of childhood abuse is one of disrespect, being valued only as an "object," and lack of self-determination. This real and felt powerlessness can result in a damaged sense of self, characterized by shame and doubt (Her-

man, 1992), with a poor sense of personal rights, entitlement and power (Hartman & Burgess, 1989).

Finkelhor and Browne (1988) also identify "stigmatization" as a dynamic process where negative connotations about the abuse experience are conveyed to the child and become incorporated into the child's self-image or self-esteem. Again, this process can be seen across all abuse types, whereby the child resorts to conceptualizing him- or herself as "bad" or deserving of the abuse experiences. Ironically, this strategy may instill a sense of hope, power, and meaning to some children: if the child views him- or herself as "bad," the parent can be more easily seen as "good;" that is, the child's "wrongful" behavior helps to explain the parent's reaction (Herman, 1992). Abused children's difficulties in handling their anger and rage further encourage a sense of self as bad. This sense of "inner badness" is so profoundly felt by the child victim that it often persists into adulthood. In the case of child sexual abuse, any positive feelings attached to the abuse or abuser (i.e., sexual stimulation, enjoyment of the abuser's special attention or rewards) may confirm feelings of personal blame and negative view of the self (Herman, 1992).

Physically abused and neglected children, compared to nonmaltreated controls, have also been described as showing lower self-esteem, based on measures of depression as well as clinical observations (Allen & Tarnowski, 1989; Kaufman & Cicchetti, 1989). For example, awareness of a negative or "bad" sense of self was inferred from findings in which maltreated toddlers responded to their mirror reflections with neutral or negative affect more often than controls (Schneider-Rosen & Cicchetti, 1991). Further, chronic negative self-esteem and a low sense of self-efficacy are reported clinically among sexual abuse survivors, although self-esteem is not a strong discriminator between samples of abused and nonabused adults (Kendall-Tackett et al., 1993).

The process of developing a conceptualization of the self as bad may involve psychological splitting, or a "dual self," where people and things (including the child him- or herself) are viewed in extreme and rigid categories (Trzepacz & Baker, 1993). Thus, a splitting into categories of good and bad may be present in the child. This splitting process can manifest as an alternation between idealization and denigration (a labile sense of self). Also, it can lead to a dual self characterized by a "disguised presentation" (Gelinas,

1983) of outward happiness, competence, and positive functioning, which stands in contrast to the inner sense of self as unhappy, incompetent, and dysfunctional. Herman (1992) explains that, paradoxically, the child victim of sexual abuse may become an empathic caretaker, an efficient housekeeper, an achiever (academically, in sports, etc.), and an overall model of social conformity. While the child's successful performance will undoubtedly be met with acceptance and positive regard from others outside the abusive environment, the child's ability to take credit for and appreciate these sentiments is limited by that child's sense of self as "bad." Indeed, such positive experiences can be felt as nonauthentic and invalid, since if others "really knew" him or her, they would shun and not praise the child. Thus, a dual sense of self can be engendered by the abuse experience: a "true bad" and a "false good." As a result, the child abuse victim cannot develop an integration of positive and negative aspects of the self and realistic self-appraisal (Cole & Puttnam, 1992). In the most extreme cases, these alternate views of the self form the core of alternate personalities (Herman, 1992).

Unfortunately, little empirical work has been done in relation to the construct of self. Two studies addressing the issue of self found that young, maltreated children inhibited negative affect (Cicchetti & Beeghly, 1987; Crittenden, 1988), with Crittenden (1988) noting some maltreated children displayed false positive affect. Moreover, difficulties in developing an integrated sense of self may not be limited to child maltreatment experience but may reflect more general attachment patterns. Cassidy (1988) gave preschoolers a puppet interview and story completion task to elicit their self-conceptualization. Whereas securely attached children tended to present a positive self-picture, often including less than perfect aspects, insecurely attached children tended either to present purely perfect self-responses, excessively negative self-statements, or no clear pattern of responses.

Conceptions of Others

Research suggests that sexual abuse involving fathers and stepfathers is experienced as more traumatic than that with nonrelated offenders (Finkelhor & Browne, 1988). Finkelhor and Browne (1988) discuss this in terms of the betrayal dynamic of sexual abuse perpetrated by trusted persons on whom the child was in some

way dependent. Betrayal also involves the degree to which the child feels his or her confidence was gained, even with strangers. Similarly, the dynamic of betrayal can be considered operative in physical abuse and neglect, because the perpetrator is someone in a position of trust. Thus, the developing child's interpersonal needs are compromised by intense and contradictory feelings of need for closeness and the fear of it (Dodge et al., 1994). For example, V. Wolfe et al. (1989) found that child sexual abuse victims tended to report that, in their belief system, sexual abuse is a pervasive phenomenon and that adults are generally exploitative of children.

Betrayal can translate into victim rage toward the abuser for the victimization and to the non-offending parent for a failure to protect or provide. Anger directed at the father and the mother (whether or not it is consciously expressed) may lead to difficulties establishing trusting, secure relationships with both male and female adults. Moreover, the previously noted process of cognitive splitting (i.e., extreme categorizations) can extend to conceptualizations of the "other," which can translate into seeing relationships in terms of black-and-white roles, such as "good–bad" or "abuser–victim" (Herman, 1992). Over the course of development, this process can further translate into interpersonal wariness, interpersonal idealization, labile interpersonal interactions, and indiscriminate interpersonal relationships.

The disruption in relatedness caused by child abuse can also lead to general interpersonal patterns of withdrawal/isolation and anxious clinging (Hartman & Burgess, 1989). For example, some physically abused children (Friedrich & Einbender, 1983) and neglected and sexually abused children (Friedrich, 1990) show indiscriminate affection seeking, readily engaging strangers in interaction. Similarly, Lynch and Cicchetti (1991) found physically abused and neglected children showed a high degree of proximity-seeking to mothers, teachers, and peers, suggesting their anxiety about closeness to others. In addition, maltreated children show a high preponderance of insecure attachment to their caregiver, in particular a disorganized mixture of approach and avoidance behaviors and a general disorientation (noncontextualized aggression, stereotyped behavior) toward their caregivers, as compared to nonmaltreated children (e.g., Carlson, Cicchetti, Barnett, & Braunwald, 1989; Schneider-Rosen, Braunwald, Carlson, & Cic-

chetti, 1985). On a projective story-telling task, maltreated children's responses were characterized by difficulty resolving relationship problems and negative interpersonal expectations more often than comparison children, even when controlling for family SES and child IQ (McCrone, Egeland, Kalkoske, & Carlson, 1994). Given the ambiguity of the social situations portrayed in the picture cards, it is suggested that children use their well-learned information about social relationships to formulate stories. For abused children, it is proposed that conceptualizations of themselves as unworthy and others as unavailable, rejecting, or exploitative may explain the preponderance of interpersonal difficulties noted in their projective stories.

Other disruptions to relatedness are noted in heightened antisocial behavior. For example, Walker, Downey, and Bergman (1989) found male and female children with a history of physical abuse showed significantly greater externalizing (aggressive acting-out) problems than their nonabused counterparts. Greater aggressiveness has been shown in physically abused children, as compared to those neglected (Kaufman & Cicchetti, 1989), and this aggressiveness extends into delinquency during adolescence (Hotaling, Straus, & Lincoln, 1990; Widom, 1989b). The increased aggressiveness of physically abused children may relate to their difficulties in empathizing and responding supportively to the distress of others (Kolko, 1992). As noted above, abused children are more likely than their nonabused counterparts to respond to peer distress in playground interactions with negative affect (e.g., fear, anger, physical attack) (Main & George, 1985). A recent study examined the relationship of type of abuse to social competence and behavior problems. Manley, Cicchetti, and Barnett (1994) found sexually abused children to be more socially competent than physically abused and neglected groups. Only the physical abuse group was found to differ from nonmaltreated comparison children on ratings of behavior problems.

An important conclusion relating to protective mechanisms affecting sexually abused children warrants a final comment in relation to the development of self: A main factor that mitigates the negative effects of sexual abuse is the experience of a positive relationship with the mother, as seen in maternal support and protective actions (Kendall-Tackett et al., 1993). Also, maternal warmth was found to be a stronger predictor of

adult adjustment than were several child sexual abuse variables (e.g., duration of abuse, number of incidents) (Peters, 1988). In their 3-year follow-up of a sample of 61 sexually abused children following their testifying in court, Sas et al. (1993) similarly found that perceived support by mothers was one of the most important mediators of sexually abused children's adjustment over time. Thus, researchers and clinicians concur that experiencing any trusting, supportive relationship appears to be a protective factor affecting maltreating children from diverse backgrounds and experiences (National Research Council, 1993).

Affect Regulation

A child's self-regulation of affect involves the ability to modulate, modify, redirect, and otherwise control his or her emotions, especially intense ones, in a way that facilitates adaptive functioning (Cicchetti, Ganiban, & Barnett, 1990). For abused children, affective issues seem in particular to involve difficulties with modulation, resulting in experiencing affective extremes and the more fundamental difficulty of lack of awareness of body states or physiological responses (Herman, 1992). Modulation difficulties can be seen in extreme depressive reactions and intense angry outbursts. For example, Kaufman (1991) reported a high number of maltreated children met psychiatric diagnostic criteria for depressive disorders (18% of the sample were diagnosed with major depression; 25% of the sample with dysthymia; see following discussion). Both modulation difficulties and lack of awareness of feelings can be seen in self-injurious behaviors. One study found that physically abused children were less able to identify appropriate feelings and were less advanced in describing the precipitants of emotions than nonabused children, although these differences were not significant when IQ was taken into account (Barahal et al., 1981).

Difficulties with affect regulation may lead to maladaptive and self-destructive behaviors in an attempt to manage the painful affect. For example, Herman (1992), based on her clinical observations, suspects that child self-injurious behavior may be a pathological form of self-soothing, replacing intolerable psychological pain with physical pain. She postulates that a compulsion to self-mutilate is preceded by a strong dissociative state, tends to develop before puberty, and is often a source of shame and is practiced in secret. Other maladaptive attempts at negative af-

fect regulation among maltreated children and adult survivors include: purging and vomiting, compulsive sexual behavior, compulsive risk-taking or exposure to danger, and alcohol and drug use (Beitchman et al., 1992).

The Family Context

A pattern of compromise and undervaluing of children within the family can be seen across all three types of abuse, in which a common factor is the family climate of domination and abuse of power. Thus, the child's experience of helplessness may stem from the fact that the child is powerless in changing his or her home environment or the abuse itself. Similarly, the climate of domination seems to extend to the social isolation of the family; the social life of the child can be restricted as a result of the need to keep the home situation out of public view. Friedrich (1990) comments on the family context of abuse, particularly recurrent abuse, as one of insensitive, marginal parenting, although some parents and children may "perform" as superficially appropriate in interactions (Crittenden, 1988). Interactional studies of maltreating families have generally supported this view, indicating the parent–child dyad to be characterized by a lower level of verbal communication, especially positive verbalizations (Aragona & Eyberg, 1981; Burgess & Conger, 1978), deviant affective displays, such as a constricted range of affect and affective lability (Gaensbauer, Mrazek, & Harmon, 1980), and a lack of behavioral synchrony, such as maternal intrusiveness or nonresponsiveness (Crittenden & Bonvillian, 1984; Crittenden, 1988). Perhaps more difficult to capture in traditional behavioral coding systems, however, is the climate of domination and abuse of power that has been clinically noted with abusive families.

Childhood maltreatment often occurs in the context of multiproblem homes where poverty, parental psychopathology, parental alcoholism, and family dysfunction have a major influence on child development (National Research Council, 1993). For example, socioeconomic disadvantage, marital distress, domestic violence, and family conflict seem to characterize many of the families presenting clinically for failure to thrive (Benoit, 1993). Peterson and Brown (1994), in a major review of accidental and nonaccidental child injuries, identify poverty, family chaos and unpredictability, household crowding, and frequent residence changes as being characteristic

of both unintentional child injury as well as child abuse and neglect cases, arguing that as the number of such stressors increase there is an amplification of the risk of multiple forms of maltreatment.

Such family dynamics may be important in explaining the range of psychological sequelae of abuse. Friedrich and Luecke (1988), for example, found that family conflict and cohesion were better predictors of the young child's internalizing and externalizing behavioral problems than the abuse characteristics per se. Similarly, low family adaptability and greater social isolation were predictive of poorer social adjustment in a college sample of sexual abuse survivors (Harter, Alexander, & Neimeyer, 1988). These accompanying stressors have led some researchers to conclude that abuse-specific effects are difficult to identify given the preponderance of marital conflict and parental psychopathology (Beitchman et al., 1992; Wolfe & Mosk, 1983). Similarly, Downey and Walker (1989) found parental psychopathology interacted with child maltreatment status to result in increased behavioral maladjustment, especially when significant parental psychological disturbance (e.g., schizophrenia) was also present.

Disorders in Adulthood

Although child maltreatment often poses major challenges to the child's cognitive, emotional, and behavioral coping strategies, many children and adolescents still remain capable of accomplishing major developmental milestones and become well-functioning adults. However, evidence from community sample studies attests to the clinical reality that childhood abuse can result in significant negative sequelae that persist into adulthood. For example, Finkelhor and Browne (1988) note that four survey studies that took into account the range of background diversity all found an association between childhood sexual abuse experiences and adult mental health impairment; however, they estimate that less than 20% of childhood sexual abuse survivors evidence serious psychopathology (e.g., diagnoses of major thought disorder or impaired function). Thus, although most abuse survivors can function adequately in later life, the lives of some can be fraught with serious psychological distress and disturbance. This conclusion is supported by the increasing awareness that many individuals insti-

tutionalized for mental illness have been sexually abused as children (Carmen, Rieker, & Mills, 1984; Scott, 1992). Some of the major forms of adult psychopathology or adjustment problems are described below.

Depression

Although childhood maltreatment has been speculated to be a risk factor for depression and self-destructive behavior, the need exists for prospective research to establish such a connection (National Research Council, 1993). In clinical studies, depression has been the most commonly reported effect of child sexual abuse (Briere & Runtz, 1991; Browne & Finkelhor, 1986). In particular, there is emerging evidence to indicate that chronic dysphoria seems to affect many survivors of child sexual abuse (Browne & Finkelhor, 1986) as well as those of physical abuse (Kolko, 1992). For example, in the case of childhood sexual abuse, Finkelhor and Browne (1988) cite two controlled studies of college populations that indicate childhood sexual abuse was related to elevated depressive symptomatology (compared to peers), suggesting that childhood sexual abuse places the individual at future risk for depression. A study of adolescent in-patients found major depression to be the most common diagnosis among those with a history of sexual abuse, although this diagnosis was equally common among the nonabused in-patient sample (Sansonnet-Hayden, Haley, Marriage, & Fine, 1987). Notably, the rate of suicide attempts and self-mutilating behavior is more elevated among sexual abuse survivors than matched controls (Hartman & Burgess, 1989). Such repetitive self-injury seems to be most prevalent when onset of sexual abuse occurred early in childhood (van der Kolk, Perry, & Herman, 1991).

Alcohol and Drug Use

Because avoidance strategies, such as emotional "numbing," often fail to reduce psychological pain, some traumatized individuals may be attracted to alcohol and drugs in an effort to obtain similar numbing effects (Herman, 1992). Other possible reasons for abusing substances include an effort to bolster self-esteem and to reduce feelings of isolation (National Research Council, 1993). Although the association between childhood sexual abuse and later drug and alcohol use has received

empirical support from controlled research (Finkelhor & Browne, 1988), such a connection has not been firmly established between physical abuse and neglect and alcohol and drug use (National Research Council, 1993).

Sexual Dysfunction

Sexual dysfunction may be an outcome particular to childhood sexual abuse. In their review of this research Finkelhor and Browne (1988) concluded that, compared to women with no early sexual abuse history, sexual abuse survivors show specific sexual dysfunction, including difficulties with arousal, vaginismus, flashbacks, as well as sex-related emotional problems (sexual guilt, sexual anxiety, low sexual self-esteem). A further robust finding is the increased risk for further repeated victimization among child sexual abuse victims, such as rape or domestic violence (Finkelhor & Browne, 1988; Kendall-Tackett et al., 1993; Russell, 1986). Due to a breach of the child's normal development of self-awareness and self-protection, he or she is less capable of identifying risk situations or persons or of knowing how to respond to unwanted sexual or physical attention (Wolfe, Wekerle, Reitzel-Jaffe, & Gough, 1995). Not surprisingly, a high prevalence of sexual abuse histories has been found among prostitutes as well (e.g., Silbert & Pines, 1981).

Personality Disorders

Borderline personality disorder (BPD) refers to a constellation of symptoms associated with affect regulation, impulse control, reality testing, and interpersonal relationships. Although BPD has often been found to be preceded by a history of sexual abuse (Briere & Runtz, 1991), it has increasingly been linked with chronic, severe, and pervasive psychological abuse, where parental abuse and love alternate unpredictably (Park, Imboden, Park, Hulse, & Unger, 1992). BPD symptoms have also been identified as overlapping with severe PTSD (Herman & van der Kolk, 1987; Briere & Runtz, 1991). In one of the few controlled studies of 36 adult women who had suffered different forms of early childhood trauma, Weaver and Clum (1993) found sexual abuse to be the only significant predictor of BPD, after controlling for physical abuse, family environment, and other diagnostic differences.

Eating Disorders

Patients diagnosed with eating disorders, such as anorexia and bulimia nervosa, have been found to have other indices of psychopathology as well as a history of childhood sexual abuse. Disorders such as depression, anxiety, alcohol problems, and personality disorders as noted above are particularly common comorbid features of patients who present with an eating disorder (Gleaves & Eberenz, 1993). For example, in a study of female psychiatric in-patients, those with a history of child sexual abuse were more likely to be diagnosed with BPD and eating disorder than those without a sexual abuse history (Lobell, 1992). Conceptually, bingeing or purging (i.e., eating disorder) and self-mutilation (i.e., borderline feature) have been considered to be maladaptive tension-reducing activities (Briere & Runtz, 1991) and maladaptive self-conceptualizations (Steiger, Leung, & Houle, 1992).

Antisocial and Abusive Behavior

Although most victims of abuse do not grow up to be adult perpetrators of violence, it has been estimated that approximately 30% do (Kaufman & Zigler, 1989). When this occurs, the victim is thought to have formed an identification with the childhood aggressor, either consciously or unconsciously reenacting sexual exploitation or physical abuse of children (Hartman & Burgess, 1989). In a review of the intergenerational transmission of violence, Widom (1989a) concluded that evidence supported an increased likelihood for perpetrating as a parent when childhood histories were positive for abuse. Further, history of physical abuse and neglect, but not sexual abuse, was predictive of arrests for violent crime; abuse history was associated with earlier mean age at first offense, higher frequency of offenses, and higher proportion of chronic offenders (Widom, 1989b).

The suspected association between physical abuse during childhood and violent and antisocial behavior during adolescence and adulthood is supported by retrospective studies of delinquent populations. For example, the most striking factor distinguishing violent from nonviolent delinquents is the amount of violence in the adolescent's past (Lewis, Pincus, & Glaser, 1979; Loeber, Weissman, & Reid, 1983; Tarter, Hegedus, Winsten, & Alterman, 1984). Tarter et al. (1984) dichotomized the crimes of delinquents

referred by juvenile court as assaultive or non-assaultive and discovered that 44% of the abused delinquents ($n = 27$) committed violent crimes, in comparison to 16% ($n = 74$) of the nonabused delinquents. A 40-year longitudinal study of 232 males from violent and nonviolent low-income families (McCord, 1979, 1983) similarly found that 22% of the abused ($n = 49$), 23% of the neglected ($n = 48$), and 50% of the rejected ($n = 34$) boys had been later convicted for serious juvenile crimes, such as theft, auto theft, burglary, or assault, compared to 11% ($n = 101$) of the boys from matched comparison families. These findings notwithstanding, the research into the long-term aftermath of abuse is in its infancy and suffers from methodological problems that limit any firm conclusions regarding antisocial behavior (Mash & Wolfe, 1991; Widom, 1989a).

EPIDEMIOLOGY

Prevalence/Incidence Rates of Maltreatment

The most recent prevalence figures from the U.S. Department of Health and Human Services, National Center on Child Abuse and Neglect (USDHHS, 1994), which gathers data on substantiated as well as unsubstantiated reports of maltreatment each year across the country, indicate that the rate of substantiated cases (which includes physical, sexual, emotional, and neglect) had increased overall from 14 per 1,000 to 16 per 1,000 children (these data were based on 34 states for the period 1990–1993). Moreover, during this same period, the rate of reporting had increased from 40 per 1,000 to 43 per 1,000 cases. An interesting trend in reporting appears to be emerging, based on these yearly data from the 1970s: From 1976 to 1992 the overall change in reporting has been a growth of 331%, up from an estimated 10 reports per 1,000 in 1976 to 43 per 1,000 in 1992.

Overall, 993,000 children were substantiated victims of maltreatment in 1992, with an estimated number of deaths ranging from 949 to 2,022 per year (USDHHS, 1994). Importantly, both the types and the characteristics of maltreatment have remained constant in recent years: Neglect continues to be the largest category, accounting for 49% (7.6 per 1,000 children) of all maltreatment reports. Physical abuse has remained constant at 23% (3.5 per 1,000), and sexual abuse at 14% (2.3 per 1,000). Sexual abuse reports and substantiated cases rose dramatically in the 1980s but have leveled off more recently. Another 5% of reports are listed as emotional abuse; 3% medical; and 9% "other" (these percentages exceed 100% due to overlap of some children in different categories).

Gender and Cultural Differences

In comparing the substantiated cases across the United States, it appears that age, not gender, is the most critical distinguishing feature of child victims of *neglect*—the number of victims rapidly decreases with increasing age for both male and female cases. Notably, for children under the age of 12, boys are more likely to be victims of *physical abuse*, but above age 12, girls are more likely to be physically abused. For *sexual abuse*, girls are clearly more likely to be victims, at all ages: The ratio of female to male victims for infants is 2:1; for school-aged children the ratio is approximately 3:1, and for adolescents approximately 6:1 female to male cases.

Racial characteristics of child victims by type of maltreatment were collected and analyzed by the state of New Jersey, which provides the best breakdown on these characteristics. These data revealed that 38% of physical abuse cases, 28% of sexual abuse cases, and 54% of neglect cases involved African-American victims, and 38% of physical abuse cases, 50% of sexual abuse cases, and 29% of neglect cases involved caucasian child victims. In contrast, the proportion of Hispanic children verified as maltreated in the state was more evenly distributed across each type of maltreatment (USDHHS, 1994).

Family Structure and Socioeconomic Differences

Offenders of child maltreatment are, by and large, related to the victim, and they are often one of the primary caregivers. For neglect, 69% of the perpetrators were female offenders, and 82% of perpetrators of sexual abuse were male offenders. In contrast, relatively equal proportions of male and female individuals were reported as the offenders of physical abuse (USDHHS, 1994).

Further data related to the nature and description of unsubstantiated, suspected, and substantiated reports of child maltreatment were recently analyzed by the Institute for the Prevention of Child Abuse in Toronto, based on the Ontario Incidence Study of Reported Child Abuse and

Neglect (OIS; Trocme, 1994). A sample of 2,950 family intake cases was randomly drawn from a total population of 53,000 open cases across Ontario in 1993. Two-thirds of the sample (1,898) were opened for investigation of suspected abuse or neglect, involving a total of 2,447 child investigations that were used for the estimates of incidence in the study. These data offer an interesting comparison to U.S. data as well as further insights into the associated characteristics of these families.

Highlights of this study point to several important features of the families who are most likely to be reported for maltreatment:

1. The investigated families were substantially younger compared to the average age of caregivers in Ontario, and 42% were led by single parents (more than three times the rate of single parents in the general population). The factor of poverty among such single-parent families, however, may be the issue placing them at higher risk (Gil, 1970).

2. Several risk factors associated with maltreatment reports also warrant attention: Alcohol abuse was a suspected problem in 13%, and drug abuse was a concern in 7% of investigations (with 70% overlap between the two).

3. Interparental violence was suspected in 17% of investigations (which corresponds to a recent Canadian survey indicating that 17% of women in the general population stated that, to the best of their knowledge, their fathers were violent toward their mothers (Statistics Canada, 1993).

4. At least 36% of investigated families depended on social assistance as their primary source of income. Not surprisingly, source of income was related to type of maltreatment: neglect was more prevalent among families dependent on social assistance than among those with full-time employment (43% vs. 13%). It should be further noted that this connection between child neglect and poverty was reported as well in the U.S. survey, where families with incomes under $15,000 were seven times more likely to be reported for child neglect than families with income over $15,000 (USDHHS, 1994).

Comparing the overall incidence in the United States to that of Canada indicates the United States has about double the rate of maltreatment (43/1,000 in United States vs. 21/1,000 in Canada). The difference can be accounted for primarily in rela-

tion to twice the number of neglect investigations in the United States, which may reflect the higher rates of poverty in the United States as well as the more limited social services, medical, and educational programs available to many U.S. families (Trocme, 1994). Moreover, the Ontario child welfare system deals with fewer and less serious cases of child maltreatment than does the U.S. system, according to the descriptive information provided to the state and provincial organizations in both countries (Trocme, 1994).

THEORETICAL FRAMEWORKS LINKING CHILD PSYCHOPATHOLOGY TO MALTREATMENT

Until recently, little theoretical effort had been expended toward understanding the short- and long-term impact of maltreatment on children's development, including the unique as well as the shared consequences of physical abuse, sexual abuse, neglect, psychological abuse, and children's exposure to marital violence. The impact of abuse on the child's development was first assumed to be invariably negative and disruptive, until researchers began to recognize that abuse does not affect each victim in a predictable or consistent fashion (Cicchetti & Rizley, 1981). Because some child victims display no major indications of psychopathology or personality disorder, either in child- or adulthood (Kaufman & Zigler, 1989), the impact of abuse cannot always be detected in terms of its negative or undesirable influences upon child development. Diverse outcomes are especially understandable when positive mediators of adjustment, such as supportive relatives or the child's coping abilities, are taken into consideration (Cicchetti & Rizley, 1981).

A further complication in understanding the effect of maltreatment on the child's development has been the recognition that such experiences may not constitute an event that is powerful enough to outweigh many other significant events occurring in the family. For example, abuse is often accompanied by major systemic influences which, in all probability, share the responsibility for disrupting the child's development. These influences include the more dramatic events, such as marital violence and separation of family members, as well as the mundane, yet influential, everyday activities that may be disturbing or maladaptive, such as impoverished

parent–child interactions, few teaching opportunities, and environmental interferences. It may be premature, on the basis of the research to date, to conclude that physical abuse is the sole or even primary contributing factor to the psychological problems noted among research samples of abused children. Such problems are most likely embedded in the nature of the parent–child relationship, and therefore the prevention of physical abuse per se may not correct the damaging effects of this relationship without additional effort being directed at the relationship itself. The *unique* impact that maltreatment has on child development may be difficult to separate from other family and environmental forces (Wolfe, 1987).

The significance of violence in the family on children's development can be further understood in terms of its connection to socialization failure of the family. Violence between adult partners or directed at children can have both *direct* and *indirect* effects on development that may not be clearly recognized until the role of the family and its context is acknowledged. Violence between family members and toward children, therefore, may not only impair children's ongoing development directly (e.g., in terms of increased aggression, delayed social–cognitive abilities, etc.); such events may further instigate stressful circumstances in the family that, in turn, contribute additional stress and disruption to the child's ongoing development and adaptation (e.g., separation and divorce, moves, school changes).

A principle implied by these developmental sequelae is that issues at one developmental period lay the groundwork for subsequent issues (Sroufe & Rutter, 1984). That is, the child who fails to develop interpersonal trust, receives little affection from others, and is governed by authoritarian rule (i.e., common characteristics of the abused child) has missed important socialization experiences that may interfere with adolescent and adult relationships. From the perspective of the child's psychological development, therefore, maltreatment signifies that *disruption* has likely occurred in critical areas of development, such as attachment, self-control, moral and social judgment, and others. It is these disruptions and deviations in socialization practices that may be primarily responsible for upsetting the child's normal developmental progress, resulting in visible signs of emotional and behavioral problems.

The following theories explaining the effects of maltreatment on children's development take into account developmental processes and how they might interact with the particular pattern and trauma of maltreatment. Two major theoretical perspectives are presented: (1) the childhood trauma model, and (2) developmental psychopathology (the influential traumagenic model of sexual abuse proposed by Finkelhor, 1988, was previously discussed). The particular developmental impact of either physical abuse, neglect, or sexual abuse is considered in relation to each theory whenever appropriate.

Childhood Trauma Model

The contributions of Horowitz (1986) and Foa and colleagues (e.g., Foa & Kozak, 1986; Foa, Steketee, & Rothbaum, 1989) are presented briefly in relation to the conceptualization of sexual abuse dynamics in particular. Theoretical concepts emerging from the study of the psychological processes underlying an individual's reaction to traumatic events provide further clarification of the nature of PTSD-related disorders or symptomatology.

Horowitz's (1986) model identifies posttraumatic stress as resulting from an individual's inability to integrate a traumatic event into an existing cognitive schema. Intrusions are viewed as a primary symptom; when mental representations of the trauma overwhelm one's coping ability, an inhibitory system develops to allow for slower assimilation of trauma information. The failure of this system is thought to lead to avoidance symptoms. In contrast, Foa's model proposes that phobic avoidance is a primary symptom, which occurs as a function of classically conditioned avoidance responses to environments where repeated trauma has occurred and/or where strongly held "core" beliefs are violated (e.g., expectations of safety). These viewpoints are not without criticism—differences in the features of the abuse, such as the presence of danger, violence, coercion vs. seduction, have not been adequately considered in the models to date (Finkelhor, 1988).

Two familiar psychological mechanisms may account for the manner in which a traumatic experience can result in an individual's long-term threat, demand, or response that continues well beyond the original stressor (Baum et al., 1990). The first of these mechanisms is explained by the process of "conditioning," or the manner by which traumatic episodes become associated with particular eliciting stimuli (e.g., odors, places, persons) and lead to maladaptive or atypical

reactions. Conditioning may play an important role in the formation of children's adjustment disorders because the repetitive acute episodes occur on an irregular basis, thus eliciting stress reactions in an unpredictable, chronic fashion. Perhaps the reason that some children's adjustment remains impaired over time (rather than extinguishing) can be partially explained by the fact that such conditioning episodes are more resistant to extinction because of their unpredictability and intensity (Wolfe & Jaffe, 1991). Child maltreatment symbolizes the myriad of opportunities a child may have to be exposed to aversive events, which in turn give rise to negative affect and escape/aggression. One would expect, on the basis of this explanation, that child victims of maltreatment (e.g., sexual abuse, physical abuse, exposure to wife assault) would share similar developmental problems and maladaptive behaviors.

In addition to conditioning, major and minor stressful life events (referred to as "secondary stressors") often occur as a result of the original traumatic event. Disclosure of sexual abuse, for example, gives rise to both immediate (e.g., change in living arrangements, arrest) as well as long-term (e.g., loss of self-esteem) events that also play a role in reducing an individual's coping resources relative to new demands. According to Baum et al. (1990), such secondary events may be sparked by intrusive imagery of the original traumatic event(s), in which the individual has recollections of the negative event in dreams or thoughts that serve to renew the potency of the original stimuli and create generalization to other, previously unrelated, events (e.g., fear of dating or sexual contact among adolescents who were sexually abused). These secondary stressors, bolstered by intrusive recollection of traumatic experiences, give rise to a chronic, stress-filled lifestyle that makes habituation to the original stressor(s) more difficult. The sources of such stress may be several steps removed from the original events themselves, such as when a child must cope with parental inconsistency, changes in family residence, sibling distress, and so forth that result from the aftermath of wife abuse, parental separation, or disclosure of sexual abuse.

When considered together, the reactions comprising posttraumatic stress disorder, the underlying process of conditioning, and the nature of trauma-related secondary events help to explain the wide-ranging adjustment difficulties of children who have been abused. The extent to which

problems emerge over time may be a function of a person-by-situation interaction in which the child's individual characteristics (e.g., coping, intelligence, information processing) interact with the nature of the stressor to determine whether or not he or she will reexperience the trauma and continue to respond ineffectively to stress (Baum et al., 1990).

Developmental Psychopathology

Clinicians and researchers have recognized that disturbances in the parent–child relationship or the family are widely implicated in children's developmental problems and psychopathology. Yet, maltreatment as a special instance of major parent–child conflict was seldom studied until the field of developmental psychopathology turned its attention toward these phenomena (Aber & Cicchetti, 1984). Using a developmental framework to explain how maltreatment may interfere with important developmental milestones has resulted in considerable advances in both clinical and research activity over the past decade.

Developmental psychopathology is one of the most comprehensive and well-supported theoretical structures in psychology (Cicchetti, 1989), and the theory lends itself readily to the study of child maltreatment. With its emphasis on the study of developing systems, this theory views normal development in terms of a series of interrelated physical, biological, and psychological competencies. Ipso facto, when there are prominent disturbances in the parent–child–environment transaction (as is the case with child maltreatment), the child will be at greater risk of failure in the development of stage-salient issues (Cicchetti et al., 1988). According to this organizational, developmental perspective, a child's failure at one stage of development (as a result of inadequate, insensitive caregiving) will lead to greater probability of failure in subsequent tasks or milestones, such as attachment, early self-recognition and differentiation, peer and social relations, and emotional functioning (Cicchetti et al., 1988; Sroufe & Fleeson, 1986). Such failure is clearly linked to the nature and role of the family—primarily the parent(s) or parent-figures —and the family context (e.g., socioeconomic disadvantage, excessive levels of stressful stimuli, limited social supports, etc.).

Therefore, to understand the effects of maltreatment on children's development, it is necessary to place their experiences in a broader context that

includes their perceived emotional climate of their families, their previous experiences with conflict and abuse, their interpretations of violence and maltreatment, and their available coping abilities and resources to countermand stress and inadequate caregiving (Wolfe & Jaffe, 1991). The implication of this view is that children from abusive families have experienced more than just violence; rather, they have experienced an entire family context that fails to provide appropriate developmental opportunities and is marked by disruptive events that affect development in both subtle and blatant ways. Because theoretical explanations presume that abuse interferes with ongoing development in a pervasive and damaging way, we should see converging evidence of adjustment problems across studies of related, but different, forms of maltreatment.

Cole and Puttnam (1992) provide a specific example of the application of developmental psychopathology to the study of sexual abuse. They argue that incest has a unique negative impact to domains of the self and related social functioning, thereby linking it to adult disorders that have self- and social impairments as core features (e.g., disorders of borderline personality, multiple personality disorder, somatization, eating, and substance use). These researchers consider the developmental stage at which abuse begins as influential in symptom structure. For example, school-aged children may be particularly vulnerable to guilt and shame, given their increased introspective abilities. A child's reaction to victimization at different developmental stages may also be modified by developmental changes in other domains—for example, attachment and pubescence, cognitive appraisal skills, and/or the forms of symptom expression specific to different stages of development (Finkelhor, 1994).

Another developmental view, presented by Alexander (1992), centers on the relational context of sexual abuse. Alexander proposes an insecure attachment of the victimized child to at least one primary caretaker, setting the stage for abuse and subsequent relationship-formation difficulties. The nature of the insecure attachment is further linked to long-term sequelae. For example, a childhood avoidant attachment would place the abuse survivor at risk for denial-based coping strategy and avoidance of abuse memories.

Recently, Spaccarelli (1994) has presented a related model in reference to child sexual abuse that emphasizes the reciprocal nature of interactions between the child and his or her environment, acknowledging individual differences in the child's coping with the series of stressors of sexual abuse (the abuse itself, abuse-related phenomenon, and the disclosure process) as being related to subsequent distress. Individual differences in children's responses to abuse are therefore seen as mediators of the abuse–symptomatology relationship. Specifically, negative cognitive appraisals (e.g., self-blame, perceptions of physical and mental damage) and less adaptive coping strategies (wishful thinking, cognitive avoidance) are viewed as predictive of poorer outcome. Social support, on the other hand, is considered to buffer the negative effects of abuse. Finally, various individual difference factors are seen as qualifying the effects of abuse, such as the child's age, intellectual ability, temperament, and so forth.

A persistent question being asked by developmental psychopathology theorists is: how does abuse during childhood affect the child's developing view of the world and him- or herself? Victims' lingering, negative evaluations of themselves, their families, and the world in general are often noted by clinicians, which led Peterson and Seligman (1983) to describe how the learned helplessness model and its reformulation might aid in understanding reactions to victimization that involve what they term "emotional numbing and maladaptive passivity." They propose that during traumatic episodes involving personal danger (such as abusive incidents) responding by the victim is futile. Such experiences, in turn, can result in learning an expectation of future helplessness, whereby the victim comes to believe that there is little that he or she can do to prevent or gain control over stressful situations. The result is the development of a passive response style in new situations, even though these new situations may not resemble the one that was originally encountered. Thus, an abused child may learn to attribute stressful, uncontrollable events to something about him- or herself as opposed to something about the situation or circumstances, which makes the child more prone to a loss of self-esteem. Similarly, if the child perceives the cause to be persistent across time (i.e., stable) versus transient (i.e., unstable), then he or she is more prone to *chronic* helplessness.

ETIOLOGY

There is now a well-established consensus that child maltreatment does not result from any

single risk factor or etiological process that provides a necessary or sufficient basis for such behavior (National Research Council, 1993). Current approaches to understanding these phenomena emphasize the combination of individual, family, environmental, and social-cultural risk factors that can result in increased risk of maltreatment, as well as the possible protective mechanisms that disrupt this etiological process. Accordingly, most models seeking to explain physical abuse and neglect, in particular, have focused their attention on the nature of the parent–child relationship and the factors that influence the normal formation of a healthy, child-focused relationship. Models of child sexual abuse, in contrast, have looked for evidence of deviant sexual histories of the adult offender as well as environmental and cultural risk factors that play a role in promoting the exploitation of children. Below are some of the major etiological factors that have been identified as part of this complex process.

Characteristics of the Adult and the Family Context

Physical Abuse and Neglect

The earliest, and very influential, theoretical viewpoint on child abuse and neglect firmly embraced the medical model: Child abuse was a deviant act, and therefore such offenders were themselves deviant or psychiatrically disturbed (Spinetta & Rigler, 1972). Accordingly, this viewpoint upholds the belief that abuse and neglect are symptomatic behavior indicative of a much more basic personality defect or disturbance. The early clinical descriptions of abusive parents by and large supported this view, emphasizing their multisituational aggressive behavior, isolation from family and friends, rigid and domineering personality style, impulsivity, and similar personality problems. The notion that a fundamental personality disorder could be responsible for physical abuse (in particular) was further advanced by reports that abusers often had a propensity for impulsive and/or antisocial acts that extended beyond the parenting role. According to this explanation, a parent may abuse his or her child because of unmet emotional needs that signify discontentment, anger, or irritability, an inability to balance the child's own needs and capabilities with parental expectations, or emotional scars from that parent's

own abusive or deprived family background that affects the parent's ability to care for his or her own offspring (Wolfe, 1987).

The role of psychopathology has been very influential in drafting child protection legislation and treatment, even though it places less emphasis on the many risk factors associated with parents labeled as abusive or neglectful, such as barriers to educational, housing, family support, medical assistance, daycare, employment, and so forth (Gelles, 1973). Moreover, research efforts aimed at distinguishing abusive from nonabusive parents on the basis of personality dimensions (e.g., self-esteem, mood, defense mechanisms, etc.) have been largely unsuccessful in showing that abusers suffered from an identifiable form of psychopathology or personality disturbance that distinguished them from parents with similar stressful circumstances (Gelles, 1973; Wolfe, 1985).

Although personality features alone cannot adequately explain this complicated phenomena, the psychopathology viewpoint still has value. The model essentially is an attempt to understand individual characteristics of abusive parents in relation to prior experience and current demands, although it places more emphasis on the parent than on any other person or event as the principal cause of the abuse and relegates situational variables to lesser importance. A more promising expansion of this model places a more specific focus on *psychological processes* that could account for behavioral differences, such as coping mechanisms or attributional styles, rather than more general psychiatric disturbance or behavioral symptoms. This expanded view is reflected in variations of social information-processing models, discussed below.

Information-processing models have recently been applied to parenting, in recognition of the cognitive demands inherent in the parenting process. These models focus on the internal processes in the parent, where child behavior A leads to parental behavior B. Typically, sequential stages of information processing are suggested, spanning parental attention to and perception of child behavior to the selection and implementation of a parental response. Four recent models focus on different abuse phenomena, with Crittenden's (1993) model centering on neglectful families and Bugental's (1993), Milner's (1993) and Strassberg and Dodge's (1995) models emphasizing physically abusive families. While Alexander's (1992) application of attachment theory

to child sexual abuse (discussed in "Developmental Psychology," above) may be categorized as a developmental model, it also represents how an individual's information-processing heuristics or social knowledge can structure the more "on-line" cognitive processes.

Crittenden (1993) argues that neglectful parenting could occur as a function of a range of information-processing deficits. "Neglect occurs when there is a pattern in which mental processing is aborted before appropriate and necessary parental behavior is undertaken" (p. 32). Specifically, a pattern of deficits could include perceptual and interpretive "misses" where the parent either did not perceive that the child was in need or, having accurately perceived a need, made an inaccurate interpretation. This pattern could include situations where child distress was misinterpreted (e.g., seeking attention) or was unrealistically interpreted, as in cases of overestimating the child's ability to care for him- or herself. Further deficits could occur at the response stage where the neglectful parent "knew" a response was required but could not develop a response strategy or, when a response was selected, failed to implement it. Thus, the neglectful parent is considered to have a systematic bias toward not perceiving, accurately interpreting, appropriately and effectively responding to child signals of need, as well as contextual signals (e.g., time since last meal, mealtime).

Crittenden suggests a variety of parental personal factors that make these information-processing deficits more likely, such as parental depression, mental retardation, preoccupation with meeting their own needs, a low sense of self-efficacy, and inappropriate belief systems (e.g., early child independence). Different patterns of neglectful families are suggested from this model. For example, the depressed or withdrawn neglectful parent may have a perceptual bias against processing affective information or may exclude from perception (primarily unconsciously) certain classes of stimuli, such as distress signals. This perceptual deficit is further linked to "higher-order" cognitive variables, such as a parent's internal models of relationships, developed from their own experiences of being parented (Bowlby, 1980). Thus, a neglectful parent who has learned as a child that he or she is powerless in eliciting loving and caring responses from adults may come to detach from distress signals in his or her own child as that parent him- or herself had to as a child, in an effort to avoid being overwhelmed by distress and maintain an attachment with the parent's own childhood caregiver.

Like Crittenden (1993), Bugental (1993) links information-processing deficits (in particular, a negative interpretive bias) to "higher-order" cognitive variables, such as stable, cognitive constructions about relationships, termed interpersonal schemas. Physically abusive parents are proposed to interact with a "threat-oriented" relationship prototype, such that they are sensitive to and expect possible challenges to their authority. As a consequence, these individuals are at an elevated risk for invoking aversive response strategies to defuse the perceived or feared power of others. Given the enduring and well-practiced nature of these schematic guides to information processing, aversive response strategies are rapidly and automatically accessed. Bugental centers on the power dynamics in abusive families, where parents attribute high levels of power to children, and children are indeed placed in a reversed, parenting role. This role reversal in turn leaves the child vulnerable to parental effort to "counterpower." In this regard, abusive parents will tend to see themselves as "victims" of aversive child behavior, perceived by the parent to be intentional and controllable by the child. Thus, parental aversiveness and abuse is seen as deriving from the parent having a threat-oriented schema of interpersonal relationships, which may have originated from the parent's own early relationship experiences.

Bugental (1993) also identifies a sequence of coping efforts by the cognitively threatened parent. For example, innocuous child actions, such as asking "why" questions, may be negatively interpreted as threatening the parent's position of power. Further, this individual child act is interpreted within a wider context of whether the parent has categorized the child as "easy" or "difficult," with greater perceived threat flowing from a child who is considered dispositionally problematic. In response to perceived threat from the child, Bugental suggests that superficially appropriate, positive parental responses may be attempted, which she labels "ingratiation." For example, the parent may at first be more pleading with the child. Bugental and Shennum (1984) showed that women with low power attribution interacted with unresponsive child confederates with exaggerated engagement efforts (e.g., exaggerated, insincere smiles, head tilts). However, if such an ingratiating style is unsuccessful with the child, the parent would be expected to switch

rapidly to more power-assertive strategies, including physical action. Given that aversive parental strategies do not sustain positive parent–child interactions, the groundwork is set for further escalation and coercive parent–child interactions.

Several empirical studies have supported aspects of Bugental's (1993) proposed model. Compared to controls, abusive mothers were found to display higher levels of negative affect with their children, even during neutral–positive interactions (Bugental, Blue, & Lewis, 1990), and the children of abusive parents show speech patterns indicative of escalating levels of stress during interactions with their parents (Bugental & Lin, 1991, as cited in Bugental, 1993). In an effort to control the stimulus of the child, Bugental and associates have observed adults "interacting" with a computer-simulated child, on a computer-based teaching task. For example, Bugental et al. (1993) found that women who were categorized as low-perceived control (based on responses to a parent attribution questionnaire) exhibited greater physiological arousal and negative affect to computer-simulated "unresponsive" child behaviors and minimal levels of arousal and negative affect with responsive children.

In the Strassberg and Dodge (1995) social information-processing perspective, emphasis is placed on cognitive constructs that guide the steps of information processing, labeled in this model as "data base." An individual's data base is defined as a memory store of knowledge structures that have developed through experience. For the mother, this would reflect knowledge garnered from her history of interaction with her child, as well as historical interactions of the mother with significant others (e.g., her childhood care experiences). This data base is proposed to act as an active filter for incoming information (e.g., child behavior), as a standard for making interpretations and accessing response options (e.g., usual parental response to a specific child behavior), and as a repertoire of responses from which to derive a response strategy. Compared to nonmaltreating mothers, abusive mothers are expected to utilize data bases containing more negative knowledge about the child. Given that such a negative cognitive set is guiding specific information-processing aspects, an abusive mother would be expected to have negative, aggression-prone perceptual, interpretive, and response biases. These authors advocate that data base influences have a perseverative quality, in that data base-inconsistent information will tend to be ignored or re(mis)interpreted. Thus, physically abusive mothers may bring into interactions with their children a variety of negatively valenced knowledge about children (e.g., unrealistically high expectations for normative behavior, overestimated frequencies of problem child behaviors) and about themselves as parents (e.g., belief that childrearing is very difficult, an orientation toward the self rather than toward the child).

Milner (1993) describes a social information-processing model of physical abusive parenting in which parental cognition is given a central role. This model is based on four primary etiological factors related to social information processing: (1) parental perception of child behavior, (2) interpretation, evaluation, and expectations of behavior, (3) information integration and response selection, and (4) response implementation and monitoring. Cognitive mediation is the crux of the social information-processing view: The cognitive activities at one or more of the first three stages are thought to mediate events at the latter behavioral response stage.

Abusive parents are thought to be less attentive to child behavior and, further, are considered to be "faulty discriminators." For example, the finding that abusive mothers are equally highly reactive to a crying and smiling infant (e.g., Frodi & Lamb, 1980) has been interpreted as suggesting the abusive parent perceives *the child* as an aversive stimulus, failing to perceive accurately the distinct features of child behavior. Further, Milner (1993) postulates that the personal "distress" of abusive mothers, from both child- and non-child-related events, decreases their perceptual abilities, such that greater inaccuracy in child-related perceptions results. Maternal depression in abusive mothers is cited as an important factor in accounting for a negative bias in abuse-relevant cognitive activities. For example, a lower threshold for perceived child misbehavior is suggested to be a function of depressive symptomatology.

The importance of parental perception of child behavior is indicated by Milner's proposing a direct path from perception to abusive parenting, via "automatic processing." That is, seeing a child's behavior as undesirable could initiate a rapid cognitive sequence that ends in abusive parental behavior. Automatic processing is believed to occur outside of conscious awareness, to involve low demands on attention and, because it is difficult to modify or suppress (especially under stress or threat), such processing generally

proceeds to completion. Hence, automatic processing would likely be invoked under the low-attention condition presumed present in abusive parents. Milner notes that such rapid processing could account for the nature of abusive behavior: immediate, rapid, and explosive parental reactions and a lack of consideration of mitigating details about the child. However, in considering the limited empirical literature, Milner notes that more evidence is needed to distinguish whether abusive parents (1) misperceive child behavior (stage 1 perceptual deficit) or (2) accurately perceive behavior but make different evaluations and interpretations (stage 2 interpretive deficit).

In accounting for abusive rather than aversive parental behavior, Milner (1993) places special emphasis on the negative evaluations of child behavior, particularly the parent's estimation of "wrongness." That is, an abusive parent would not only perceive child problem behavior and attribute responsibility and negative intent to the child, but would also evaluate the behavior as "very wrong" in order to justify severe parental disciplinary actions.

Overview of Parental Characteristics

Studies of abusive parents have supported the development of the cognitive-behavioral models presented above. In a review of studies comparing abusive and nonabusive parents on psychological variables, Wolfe (1987) concluded that, although physically abusive parents may not manifest any distinguishable personality or psychiatric disorders, they do exhibit behavioral differences and lifestyle patterns indicative of incompetence in the role of childrearing. In comparison to nonabusive parents, abusers are not as effective or successful in the parenting role, both in terms of teaching their children new behaviors as well as in controling child problem behavior. Abusive parents are less flexible in their choices of disciplinary techniques, and they often fail to match their choice of discipline to the child's misdeed and the situation. Their over-reliance on physical punishment as a control strategy, in combination with limited child-management skills, is intensified by their failure to develop social supports to alleviate stress and to assist in family problem solving. Empirical findings also suggest that both overcontrol (e.g., depression, physical complaints) and undercontrol (e.g., aggression, verbal abuse) behaviors and symptoms are possible reactions to, or precipitants of, child- and

family-mediated stress. Individual adult characteristics, such as low tolerance for stress, inappropriate or inadequate models or learning opportunities, and a poor repertoire of life skills may be important psychological processes that are involved in determining the expression of these stressful life events. Furthermore, it is highly probable that abusive parents' perceptions of adverse family and environmental conditions are exacerbated by their failure to use social supports and to develop social networks.

Emotional arousal and reactivity may also play a crucial role in the manifestation of abusive parenting. A pattern of arousal is presumed to develop over time as a function of more and more problems in the parent–child relationship. During everyday interactions, a parent may become conditioned to experience negative arousal and emotions in his or her responses. Such conditioning may occur over an extended or a very brief time period (i.e., gradually, such as during early parent–infant contact or struggles, or suddenly, such as during high stress periods in which the parent perceives the child to be purposefully misbehaving). The role of an arousal pattern in physical abuse has not been linked to any particular personality variables or situational events per se; rather, it appears to be an idiosyncratic pattern that emerges as a function of an individual's predisposition (e.g., exposure to violence as a child, emotional distress) and his or her learning experiences.

Neglectful parents, in contrast to physical and sexual abusers, have received far less attention (Drotar, 1992), perhaps because *omissions* of proper caretaking behaviors are more difficult to describe and detect. Hillson and Kuiper (1994), in their description of a stress and coping model of physical abuse and neglect, convincingly argue that neglectful caregivers engage in varying degress of behavioral disengagement (i.e., reducing one's efforts to remove, avoid, or cope with a stressor). Neglectful parents may also engage in activities aimed at distracting him or her from the current stressor (which they term "mental disengagement") in an effort to cope with stress. These depictions of neglectful parenting, framed within a stress and coping model, are generally consistent with the existing empirical evidence. For example, based primarily on clinical descriptions, neglectful parents are described as having more pronounced personality disorders (than comparable nonmaltreating parents), inadequate knowledge of child development and stimulation, and

chronic patterns of social isolation and/or deviant subculture identification (Gaines, Sandgrund, Green, & Power, 1978; Wolfe, 1985). In many other ways, however, the personality characteristics and lifestyle choices overlap considerably among these two forms of maltreatment.

From the above overview we can highlight three key elements that stand out as common etiological features concerning the parent's role in child abuse and neglect: (1) the manner in which the parent interacts with the child on an everyday basis (i.e., a greater proportion of negative than positive interactions and a lack of stimulation; Wolfe, 1985), (2) the frustration–aggression relationship that is learned by the parent in relation to childrearing, which accounts for the rapid and often uncontrollable escalation from annoyance to rage, and (3) the cognitive, social–informational processes that explain the distorted beliefs and attributions underlying a parent's actions. These dimensions provide considerable coverage of the known findings regarding the psychological processes associated with child abuse and neglect, although they admittedly do not focus on the more distal events that may shape the childrearing environment (e.g., poverty, stress, etc.). None of these psychological components is static or assumed to be inherent in the individual or family per se. Instead, social interactional, social information-processing and arousal-aggression processes are useful in explaining the constant changes in the behavior of family members in response to events within or outside of the family unit. Thus, child maltreatment can best be explained as the *result of an interaction* between the parent and child within a system that seldom provides alternative solutions (e.g., through exposure to appropriate parental models, education, and supports), or clear-cut restraints (e.g., laws, sanctions, and consequences) for the use of excessive force to resolve common childrearing conflicts (Wolfe, 1987).

Sexual Abuse

Despite the myth of the child sexual abuse perpetrator as a "dirty old man," research has shown pedophiles and incest offenders to be a heterogeneous group, with an undercurrent being the association of violence and aggression to sexual abuse (Hartman & Burgess, 1989). Perpetrators of sexual assaults on children are overwhelmingly male; data suggest that the majority of female offenders are usually in a coercive relationship with a male offender (Friedrich, 1990). Mother involvement spans the continuum from active participation and encouragement (considered to be very rare), to denying the abuse and siding with the offender (a minority of instances), to supporting the child's disclosure and terminating the partner relationship, although sometimes in an ambivalent or defensive manner (Salter, 1988).

Critical features in classifying perpetrators identified from the literature include offense factors, such as degree of violence used, emphasis on coercion versus seduction, relationship to the victim, and age of victim, as well as offender factors, such as level of education of the offender, preoffense social and occupational adjustment, criminal history, personality traits, and alcohol abuse (Hartman & Burgess, 1989). Personality features, on the other hand, are quite heterogeneous. Some sexual abusers of children are described as timid and unassertive, whereas others show a pattern of poor impulse control and domineering interpersonal style (Hall, 1992). Psychiatric profiles often indicate the presence of antisocial personality disorder among sexual offenders of children, although no accepted system of sexual offender classification has been established (National Research Council, 1993). Notably, a recent study of 246 male juvenile sex offenders (Becker, Kaplan, Tenke, & Tartaglini, 1991) reported that 42% of the subjects reported appreciable depressive symptomatology. Such symptoms, moreover, were higher related to the offender's own history of sexual or physical abuse.

Finkelhor (1984) identified the principal individual and situational conditions that foster sexual abuse of children. Four offender preconditions are proposed as necessary before a sexual assault of a child can occur: (1) the motivation to sexually abuse, (2) overcoming internal inhibitors, (3) overcoming external inhibitors, and (4) overcoming the child's resistance. These preconditions parallel the offending process identified by Sgroi (1982) where the child is first recruited and engaged, then induced into sexual interaction, following which secrecy is enforced. Finkelhor (1986) proposes that the first two conditions are necessary for abuse to occur, that is, the perpetrator must be inclined to abuse and uninhibited about it, which is consistent with the notion that the offender bears responsibility for the abuse.

The first precondition, the motivation to sexually abuse, pertains to the offender. It can be seen in the adult's sexual arousal to children, the blockage of appropriate outlets for sexual gratification (i.e., alternative sources are not available, less

readily available, or less satisfying), and the sexualization of unmet emotional needs. Such unmet emotional needs can include the need for power and control, narcissistic identification with the self as a young child, and unconscious reenactment of childhood trauma. These individual needs are considered to be fostered by societal practices such as the erotic portrayal of children in mainstream advertising and in pornography and the tolerance of male domination. Friedrich (1990) comments on a more general motivation for sexualizing behavior as shown by the sexualized family environments of some families that predate overt abuse. Such sexualization is defined as the presence of pornography, the lack of privatization of adult sexual activity, and the eroticization of normative child behavior (e.g., attention bids seen as "flirting").

The second precondition identifies that the perpetrator must overcome internal obstacles to sexually using children. These include inherent perpetrator characteristics such as impulsivity, mental retardation, psychosis and senility, lack of empathy for the child, as well as environmental factors as the use of alcohol, and the failure of incest inhibition in family dynamics. Society-level factors include the lack of deterrence due to weak criminal sanctions against offenders, the social and criminal consideration of alcohol as a mitigating factor in deviance, and the ideology of private family matters and the prerogative of parents, especially fathers, vis-à-vis their children. Friedrich (1990) notes that the perpetrator's efforts at establishing a relationship with the child (i.e., time alone, singling the child out as favored or "special") may also reduce offender internal inhibitors via a distortion of the caretaking role and blurring of interpersonal boundaries. Thus, the perpetrator may develop a sense of entitlement and privilege with a child and may come to distort his parental role (e.g., as sexually instructive), and/or there may be a role reversal where the child is deemed to be the caretaker for the adult's needs.

The third precondition considers the need to overcome external barriers to child sexual abuse. The most critical factor here is the failure of parental supervision and caretaking in enabling offender access to the child. Some of the factors in heightening a child's vulnerability to abuse include a mother who is absent, ill, overwhelmed, experiencing spousal abuse, not emotionally close to or protective of the child; lack of child supervision and monitoring; opportunities to be alone with the child (e.g., unusual sleeping or rooming conditions, babysitting, the child left unattended at play); marital dissatisfaction; socioeconomic disadvantage; and social isolation (Finkelhor, 1979, 1984). Prior to the overt sexual abuse, the child may be subjected to a "parentification" process, wherein parental role expectations (e.g., household duties, sibling care, etc.) are burdened on the child, forcing him or her to adopt a "pseudomaturity" (Friedrich, 1990). Some of the society-level variables include erosion of social networks and the lack of social supports to the mother, barriers to women's and children's rights, and the loss of ideology of family sanctity.

The fourth precondition involves overcoming the child's ability to resist abuse. An important factor here is the illusion of a trusting relationship (Sgroi, 1982), often where childcare is part of the perpetrator's responsibilities, as in the case of a biological or stepparent, coach, babysitter, religious leader, and so forth. Factors that make it more difficult for a child to rebuke abuse attempts include an emotionally vulnerable child (e.g., emotionally and/or physically deprived, compliant, or quiet child), the use of coercion and/or seduction, the child having witnessed parental conflict, the lack of education about sexual abuse, and the social powerlessness of children. For example, reasons for the response to adult male sexual overtures by male youths include a need for affection, a desire for money/gifts, pursuit of adventure, and sexual arousal/stimulation (Rossman, 1980). Methods used to lower the child's resistance include friendship, playing games, giving rewards (money, toys, cigarettes, etc.), having hobbies or interests appealing to the child, and using peer pressure (Budin & Johnson, 1989; Lanning, 1987). If such subtler methods are not successful, coercion and violence may be employed; these can also be deceptive to a child, as in the offender framing abuse as "discipline." Often, the actual sexual behavior takes place only after a period of "grooming" or gradual indoctrination into sexual activity (Conte, 1992), suggesting that many sex offenders are "sophisticated, calculating, and patient" (Singer, Hussey, & Strom, 1992, p. 884).

Child Risk Characteristics

Considerable research has been conducted into the possible role that the child victim might play in terms of his or her own abuse (Ammerman, 1992). Rather than "victim-blaming," however,

these studies seek to distinguish any characteristics a child might display that would place him or her "at-risk" of an adult becoming abusive, either physically or sexually. Certain child factors may increase the potential for abuse only in the presence of other important causal factors, such as those noted above. Both longitudinal and comparative studies, however, have failed to discern any child characteristics, such as age or gender, temperament, low birth weight, hyperactivity, or conduct problems that clearly increase the risk of maltreatment, once environmental and adult factors are controlled (National Research Council, 1993). However, child characteristics may play more of a role in the persistence of an abusive or neglectful relationship or the escalation of a high-risk relationship.

In the case of neglect, for example, the child's early feeding problems or irritability may place an increased strain on the parent's limited child-care ability, which sets in motion a pattern of caregiver withdrawal from the child and a concomitant escalation in the child's dependency needs and demandingness (Drotar, 1992). Similarly, the physically abused child may learn from an early age how to elicit attention from his or her parent through aversive means such as crying, hitting, clinging, and so forth, which escalate in intensity because of the parent's further decline in appropriate child management and stimulation. As shown by Patterson (1982), aggressive and disruptive children are at greater risk for harsh punitive reactions from their parents based on a process of reciprocal escalation in aversive exchanges between the parent and the child. That is, the child may do something that annoys the parent (e.g., hits a sibling), which results in scolding or punishment by the parent. With non-aggressive children, the probability that the child will continue with annoying behaviors is reduced by the parent's response; however, with aggressive children (and maltreated children who lack self-control and appropriate means of communication), the probability of continued and escalated coercion is actually increased by parental attempts at discipline (Patterson, 1982).

The *expectancies* that the parent and child develop over time on the basis of their ongoing relationship also play a role in the maintenance of abuse and neglect. The parent who experiences a difficult infant for several months learns to anticipate such problems before they actually surface. Similarly, the infant or toddler quickly learns to distinguish among different parental cues or behaviors that may lead to desired or unpleasant events. In healthy dyads, this process of learning what to expect of the other party is important for the development of a stable relationship built on expectations and awareness of the other's behavior. The development of the parent–child relationship may be impeded, however, as a result of contamination from previous conflict or distress that predominated during an earlier stage in the relationship (Wolfe, 1987).

CURRENT ISSUES AND FUTURE DIRECTIONS IN CHILD MALTREATMENT

The developmental implications for children who have been abused or neglected have been emphasized throughout this chapter, in an effort to establish the significance and interconnectedness of these events vis-à-vis developmental psychopathology and the perpetuation of violence. These different forms of violence and maltreatment, although multiply determined, share common causes and outcomes; most importantly, the formation of healthy relationships is significantly impaired (parenthetically, abusive families may represent only the most visible portion of this problem). This relational theme emerged throughout the review and discussion of physical abuse, neglect, and sexual abuse, and one of the prominent issues in the field is establishing adequate services and supports for families and children that may serve to strengthen the parent–child relationship and protect the child from exploitation and harm. In closing, we discuss some ideas pertaining to this current direction of early identification and prevention.

How can we improve our definitions and understanding of different forms of maltreatment? Defining child maltreatment in a manner that encompasses all of the social, methodological, and practical concerns poses a major challenge to research in this area. Typically, researchers have somewhat arbitrarily defined their groups of interest in a dichotomous manner, based on the most salient presenting characteristics of each child or family (e.g., evidence of physical abuse). However, this practice disguises other experiences these children may have had, resulting in a nonspecific categorization of maltreating families. Moreover, this common strategy treats each different type of maltreatment as singular

independent variables, when in reality such events often co-occur and are highly related (Lewis, Lovely, Yeager, & Femina, 1989). The categorical approach, therefore, fails to identify other relevant factors, such as other forms of maltreatment or family experiences, that can have a synergistic or unique impact on the child's development.

Researchers have also expressed dissatisfaction with current methodology in defining child maltreatment (Aber & Cicchetti, 1984; Cicchetti & Rizley, 1981; Mash & Wolfe, 1991; Wolfe & McGee, 1994). A categorization approach to defining forms of maltreatment obscures differences in the severity of abuse, and ignores the co-occurrence of many forms of maltreatment in the lives of children (McGee & Wolfe, 1991). Furthermore, recent studies have reported considerable overlap among the types of maltreatment experienced. For example, Lewis et al. (1989) reported that among their follow-up sample of 95 young adults previously incarcerated for violent and nonviolent crimes, 60% (*n* = 57) had been both abused and had witnessed extraordinary family violence. These findings indicate that unique or nonoverlapping forms of maltreatment are atypical.

Rather than considering maltreating experiences to be static or uniform, theories should take into consideration the assumption that such experiences can be attenuated or accentuated by the occurrence of new events. This approach would be in keeping with a developmental model that bases prediction of future adjustment on events other than trauma or negative experiences and allows for individual and systemic mediating factors (e.g., Belsky, Youngblade, & Pensky, 1989; Cicchetti & Lynch, 1993). In line with the suggestions of Kaufman, Jones, Stieglitz, Vitulano, and Mannarino (1994), multiple sources of data (e.g., parents, records, clinical observations) should be utilized whenever possible, and better efforts to describe the full nature of maltreatment experiences should become the norm for research in this area.

How are we currently responding to child maltreatment? The reduction or elimination of child maltreatment, sexual abuse, and related forms of family violence may be more readily achieved through a wide range of family support, education, and health promotion efforts (Wekerle & Wolfe, 1993). In contrast to the view that offenders can be identified and controlled, an inclusionary (prevention) perspective strives to raise the level of understanding and skill among the broadest section of the population. Building healthy relationships is the central theme associated with violence prevention and enhanced family functioning.

Recently, our understanding of the causes and the developmental course of violence against women and children has grown significantly, allowing prevention efforts to be generated from a reasonable knowledge base. For example, children with a history of family disruption and violence have been shown to be at an elevated risk of becoming victims or perpetrators of violence toward others, especially during mid- to late adolescence (Dutton, 1994; Widom, 1989, 1989a). Straus and Kantor (1994), using state records of offenses coupled with detailed histories of childrearing, contend that maltreatment experiences (including "milder" forms of corporal punishment) are the singlemost significant risk factor for subsequent relationship violence in adulthood. Thus, it is believed that abuse experiences in one's family of origin create a vulnerability for further victimization by others (especially among young women) as well as a propensity to use power and control as a means of resolving conflict (especially among young men) (Wolfe, Wekerle, Reitzel-Jaffe, & Gough, 1995). In addition to prior abuse experiences, the risk of becoming a victim or perpetrator of violence increases as a result of negative influences from peers (i.e., condoning violence), the absence of compensatory factors (such as success at school; a healthy relationship with siblings, friends, etc.), and the relative lack of alternative sources of information that serve to counteract existing biases, attitudes, and beliefs (Jessor, 1993).

Although child abuse prevention has been attempted at all three levels (i.e., tertiary, secondary, and primary), it has met with only varying degrees of success. Tertiary prevention studies with identified abusive parents have reported some degree of success at improving childrearing skills and knowledge of development, although limited follow-up data, evidence of recidivism, and high cost of delivery contribute to the inadequacy of this form of "prevention" (Wolfe & Wekerle, 1993). Secondary prevention efforts, which range from interventions with high-risk to low-risk parents and expectant parents, favor assisting parents and children at an earlier point in time. These wide-ranging strategies have shown considerable promise, especially when the intervention is matched closely to the needs of each family (Wekerle & Wolfe, 1993). Primary prevention of child abuse, the least studied approach, has largely focused on educational strategies

aimed at teaching high school-aged youth and young adults about parenthood, domestic violence, and general violence issues. Evaluations of such programs are limited, although initial results suggest that adolescents do acquire relevant information about parenting and exhibit attitudinal gains consistent with positive parenting (e.g., lower authoritarian attitudes) (Lewko, Carriere, Whissell, & Radford, 1986; Ritchett & Towns, 1980). Behavioral gains supporting the preventative nature of such programs vis-à-vis child-rearing ability have not been evaluated, however.

From these initial beginnings, child abuse prevention efforts have reorganized around the principle of building upon strengths and developing protective factors in an effort to deter violence (Helfer, 1982). This principle underscores the importance of the relational context to child abuse prevention. That is, learning to relate to others, especially intimates, in a respectful, non-violent manner is a crucial foundation for building a child abuse prevention strategy (Garbarino, Drew, Kostelny, & Pardo, 1992; Wekerle & Wolfe, 1993).

REFERENCES

Aber, J. L., & Allen, J. P. (1987). Effects of maltreatment on young children's socioemotional development: An attachment theory perspective. *Developmental Psychology*, 23, 406–414.

Aber, J. L., & Cicchetti, D. (1984). The socio-emotional development of maltreated children: An empirical and theoretical analysis. In H. Fitzgerald, B. Lester, & M. Yogman (Eds.), *Theory and research in behavioral pediatrics* (Vol. 2, pp. 147–205). New York: Plenum Press.

Ainsworth, M. D. S. (1980). Attachment and child abuse. In G. Gerbner, C. J. Ross, & E. Zigler (Eds.), *Child abuse: An agenda for action* (pp. 35–47). New York: Oxford University Press.

Alessandri, S. M. (1991). Play and social behavior in maltreated preschoolers. *Development and Psychopathology*, 3, 191–205.

Alexander, P. C. (1992). Application of attachment theory to the study of sexual abuse. *Journal of Consulting and Clinical Psychology*, 60, 185–195.

Allen, D. M., & Tarnowski, K. J. (1989). Depressive characteristics of physically abused children. *Journal of Abnormal Child Psychology*, 17, 1–11.

American Psychiatric Association. (1987). *Diagnostic and statistical manual of mental disorders* (3rd ed., rev.). Washington, DC: Author.

American Psychiatric Association. (1994). *Diagnostic and statistical manual of mental disorders* (4th ed.). Washington, DC: Author.

Ammerman, R. T. (1992). The role of the child in physical abuse: A reappraisal. *Violence and Victims*, 6, 87–101.

Appelbaum, A. S. (1977). Developmental retardation in infants as a concomitant of physical child abuse. *Journal of Abnormal Child Psychology*, 5, 417–423.

Aragona, J. A., & Eyberg, S. M. (1981). Neglected children: Mother's report of child behavior problems and observed verbal behaviors. *Child Development*, 52, 596–602.

Asher, S. J. (1988). The effects of childhood sexual abuse: A review of the issues and evidence. In L. Walker (Ed.), *Handbook on sexual abuse of children* (pp. 3–18). New York: Springer.

Azar, S. T., Barnes, K. T., & Twentyman, C. T. (1988). Developmental outcomes in abused children: Consequences of parental abuse or a more general breakdown in caregiver behavior? *Behavior Therapist*, 11, 27–32.

Barahal, R., Waterman, J., & Martin, H. P. (1981). The social cognitive development of abused children. *Journal of Consulting and Clinical Psychology*, 49, 508–516.

Baum, A., O'Keefe, M., & Davidson, L. (1990). The case of traumatic stress. *Journal of Applied Social Psychology*, 20, 1643–1654.

Becker, J. V., Kaplan, M. S., Tenke, C. E., & Tartaglini, A. (1991). The incidence of depressive symptomatology in juvenile sex offenders with a history of abuse. *Child Abuse and Neglect*, 15, 531–536.

Beeghly, M., & Cicchetti, D. (1994). Child maltreatment, attachment, and the self system: Emergence of an internal state lexicon in toddlers at high social risk. *Development and Psychopathology*, 6, 5–30.

Beitchman, J. H., Zucker, K. J., Hood, J. E., DaCosta, G. A., Akman, D., & Cassavia, E. (1992). A review of the long-term effects of child sexual abuse. *Child Abuse and Neglect*, 16, 101–118.

Belsky, J., Youngblade, L., & Pensky, E. (1989). Childrearing history, marital quality, and maternal affect: Intergenerational transmission in a low-risk sample. *Development and Psychopathology*, 1, 291–304.

Benoit, D. (1993). Failure to thrive and feeding disorders. In C. H. Zeanah, Jr. (Ed.), *Handbook of infant mental health* (pp. 317–331). New York: Guilford Press.

Benoit, D., Zeanah, C. H., & Barton, M. L. (1989). Maternal attachment disturbances in failure to thrive. *Infant Mental Health Journal*, 10, 185–202.

Berliner, L. (1991). Effects of sexual abuse on children. *Violence Update Newsletter*, 1, 1, 8, 10–11.

Bowlby, J. (1980). *Attachment and loss*. New York: Basic Books.

Brassard, M. R., Germain, R., & Hart, S. N. (Eds.). (1987). *The psychological maltreatment of children and youth*. New York: Pergamon.

Briere, J., & Runtz, M. (1991). The long-term effects of sexual abuse: A review and synthesis. *New Directions on Mental Health Services*, 51, 3–13.

Browne, A., & Finkelhor, D. (1986). Impact of child sexual abuse: A review of the research. *Psychological Bulletin*, 99, 66–77.

Budin, L. E., & Johnson, C. F. (1989). Sex abuse prevention programs: Offenders' attitudes about their efficacy. *Child Abuse and Neglect*, 13(1), 77–87.

Bugental, D. B. (1993). Communication in abusive relationships: Cognitive constructions of interpersonal power. *American Behavioral Scientist*, 36, 288–308.

Bugental, D. B., Blue, J., Cortez, V., Fleck, K., Kopeiken, H., Lewis, J. C., & Lyon, J. (1993). Social cognitions as organizers of autonomic and affective responses to social challenge. *Journal of Personality and Social Psychology*, 64, 94–103.

Bugental, D. B., Blue, J., & Lewis, J. (1990). Caregiver beliefs and dysphoric affect to difficult children. *Developmental Psychology*, 26, 631–638.

Bugental, D. B., & Shennum, W. A. (1984). "Difficult" chil-

dren as elicitors and targets of adult communication patterns: An attributional–behavioral transactional analysis. *Monographs of the Society for Research in Child Development, 49*(1, Serial No. 205), 1–79.

Burgess, R., & Conger, R. (1978). Family interaction in abusive, neglectful and normal families. *Child Development, 19,* 1163–1173.

Camras, L. A., Ribordy, S., Spaccarelli, S., & Stefani, R. (1986, August). *Emotion recognition and production by abused children and mothers.* Paper presented at the meeting of the American Psychological Association, Washington, DC.

Caplan, P. J., & Dinardo, L. (1986). Is there a relationship between child abuse and learning disability? *Canadian Journal of Behavioural Sciences, 18,* 367–380.

Carlson, V., Cicchetti, D., Barnett, D., & Braunwald, K. G. (1989). Finding order in disorganization: Lessons from research on maltreated infants' attachments to their children. In D. Cicchetti & V. Carlson (Eds.), *Child maltreatment: Theory and research on the causes and consequences of child abuse and neglect* (pp. 494–528). Cambridge, UK: Cambridge University Press.

Carmen, E. H., Rieker, P. P., & Mills, T. (1984). Victims of violence and psychiatric illness. *American Journal of Psychiatry, 141,* 378–383.

Cassidy, J. (1988). Child–mother attachment and the self in six year olds. *Child Development, 59,* 121–134.

Celano, M. P. (1992). A developmental model of victims' internal attributions of responsibility for sexual abuse. *Journal of Interpersonal Violence, 7,* 57–69.

Cicchetti, D. (1989). How research on child maltreatment has informed the study of child development: Perspectives from developmental psychopathology. In D. Cicchetti & V. Carlson (Eds.), *Child maltreatment: Theory and research on the causes and consequences of child abuse and neglect* (pp. 377–431). New York: Cambridge University Press.

Cicchetti, D. (1990). The organization and coherence of socioemotional, cognitive, and representational development: Illustrations through a developmental psychopathology perspective on Down syndrome and child maltreatment. In R. Thompson (Ed.), *Nebraska symposium on motivation: Vol. 36. Socioemotional development* (pp. 266–375). Lincoln: University of Nebraska Press.

Cicchetti, D., & Beeghly, M. (1987). Symbolic development in maltreated youngsters: An organizational perspective. *New Directions for Child Development, 36,* 5–29.

Cicchetti, D., Ganiban, J., & Barnett, D. (1990). Contributions from the study of high risk populations to understanding the development of emotion regulation. In K. Dodge & J. Garber (Eds.), *The development of emotion regulation* (pp. 1–54). New York: Cambridge University Press.

Cicchetti, D., & Lynch, M. (1993). Toward an ecological/transactional model of community violence and child maltreatment: Consequences for children's development. *Psychiatry, 56,* 96–118.

Cicchetti, D., & Olsen, K. (1990). The developmental psychopathology of child maltreatment. In M. Lewis & S. M. Miller (Eds.), *Handbook of developmental psychopathology* (pp. 261–279). New York: Plenum Press.

Cicchetti, D., & Rizley, R. (1981). Developmental perspectives on the etiology, intergenerational transmission, and sequelae of child maltreatment. In D. Cicchetti & R. Rizley (Eds.), *New directives for child development: Developmental perspectives on child maltreatment* (pp. 31–55). San Francisco: Jossey-Bass.

Cicchetti, D., Toth, S., & Bush, M. (1988). Developmental psychopathology and incompetence in childhood: Suggestions for intervention. In B. B. Lahey & A. E. Kazdin (Eds.), *Advances in clinical child psychology* (Vol. 11, pp. 1–77). New York: Plenum Press.

Claussen, A. K., & Crittenden, P. M. (1991). Physical and psychological maltreatment: Relations among types of maltreatment. *Child Abuse and Neglect, 15,* 5–18.

Cole, P. M., & Puttnam, F. W. (1992). Effect of incest on self and social functioning: A developmental psychopathology perspective. *Journal of Consulting and Clinical Psychology, 60,* 174–184.

Conte, J. R. (1992). Has this child been sexually abused? Dilemmas for the mental health professional who seeks the answer. *Criminal Justice and Behavior, 19,* 54–73.

Crittenden, P. M. (1985). Maltreated infants: Vulnerability and resilience. *Journal of Child Psychology and Psychiatry, 26,* 1299–1313.

Crittenden, P. M. (1987). Non-organic failure-to-thrive: Deprivation or distortion? *Infant Mental Health Journal, 8,* 51–64.

Crittenden, P. (1988). Relationships at risk. In J. Belsky & T. Nezworski (Eds.), *Clinical implications of attachment theory* (pp. 136–174). Hillsdale, NJ: Erlbaum.

Crittenden, P. M. (1992). Children's strategies for coping with adverse home environments: An interpretation using attachment theory. *Child Abuse and Neglect, 16,* 329–343.

Crittenden, P. M. (1993). An information-processing perspective on the behavior of neglectful parents. *Criminal Justice and Behavior, 20,* 27–48.

Crittenden, P. M., & Ainsworth, M. D. S. (1989). Child maltreatment and attachment theory. In D. Cicchetti & V. Carlson (Eds.), *Child maltreatment: Theory and research on the causes and consequences of child abuse and neglect* (pp. 432–463). Cambridge, UK: Cambridge University Press.

Crittenden, P. M., & Bonvillian, J. D. (1984). The relationship between maternal risk status and maternal sensitivity. *American Journal of Orthopsychiatry, 54,* 250–262.

Crittenden, P. M., & DiLalla, D. L. (1988). Compulsive compliance: The development of an inhibitory coping strategy in infancy. *Journal of Abnormal Child Psychology, 16,* 585–599.

Crouch, J. L., & Milner, J. S. (1993). Effects of child neglect on children. *Criminal Justice and Behavior, 20,* 49–65.

Deykin, E., Alpert, J., & McNamara, J. (1985). A pilot study of the effect of exposure to child abuse or neglect on adolescent suicidal behavior. *American Journal of Psychiatry, 142,* 1299–1303.

deYoung, M., & Lowry, J. A. (1992). Traumatic bonding: Clinical implications in incest. *Child Welfare, 71,* 165–175.

Dodge, K. A., Bates, J. E., & Pettit, G. S. (1990). Mechanisms in the cycle of violence. *Science, 250,* 1678–1682.

Dodge, K. A., Pettit, G. S., & Bates, J. E. (1994). Effects of physical maltreatment on the development of peer relations. *Development and Psychopathology, 6,* 43–55.

Downey, G., & Walker, E. (1989). Social cognition and adjustment in children at risk for psychopathology. *Developmental Psychology, 25*(5), 835–845.

Drotar, D. (1992). Prevention of neglect and nonorganic failure to thrive. In D. J. Willis, E. W. Holden, & M. Rosenberg (Eds.), *Prevention of child maltreatment: Developmental and ecological Perspectives* (pp. 115–149). New York: Wiley.

Dutton, D. *The domestic assault of women: Psychological and criminal justice perspectives.* Vancouver: University of British Columbia Press.

Dykes, L. (1986). The whiplash shaken infant syndrome: What has been learned? *Child Abuse and Neglect, 10,* 211–221.

Eckenrode, J., & Doris, J. (1991). *The academic effects of child abuse and neglect* (Progress report). Washington, DC: National Center for Child Abuse and Neglect.

Eckenrode, J., Laird, M., & Doris, J. (1993). School performance and disciplinary problems among abused and neglected children. *Developmental Psychology, 29,* 53–62.

Egeland, B., & Sroufe, A. (1981). Attachment and early maltreatment. *Child Development, 52,* 44–52.

Einbender, A. J., & Friedrich, W. N. (1989). Psychological functioning and behavior of sexually abused girls. *Journal of Consulting and Clinical Psychology, 57,* 155–157.

Erickson, M. F., Egeland, B., & Pianta, R. (1989). The effects of maltreatment on the development of young children. In D. Cicchetti & V. Carlson (Eds.), *Child maltreatment: Theory and research on the causes and consequences of child abuse and neglect* (pp. 647–684). New York: Cambridge University Press.

Erickson, M. F., Sroufe, L. A., & Egeland, B. (1985). The relationship between quality of attachment and behavior problems in preschool in a high-risk sample. In I. Bretherton & E. Waters (Eds.), *Growing points of attachment theory and research. Monographs of the Society for Research in Child Development, 50* (1–2, Serial No. 209), 147–168.

Famularo, R., Kinscherff, R., & Fenton, T. (1990). Symptom differences in acute and chronic presentation of childhood post-traumatic stress disorder. *Child Abuse and Neglect, 14,* 439–444.

Fantuzzo, J. W. (1990). Behavioral treatment of the victims of child abuse and neglect. *Behavior Modification, 14,* 316–339.

Finkelhor, D. (1979). *Sexually victimized children.* New York: Free Press.

Finkelhor, D. (1984). *Child sexual abuse: New theories and research.* New York: Free Press.

Finkelhor, D. (1986). Sexual abuse: Beyond the family system approach. In T. S. Trepper & M. J. Barrett (Eds.), *Treating incest: A multiple systems perspective* (pp. 53–65). New York: Haworth Press.

Finkelhor, D. (1988). The trauma of child sexual abuse: Two models. In G. E. Wyatt & G. J. Powell (Eds.), *Lasting effects of child sexual abuse* (pp. 61–82). Beverly Hills: Sage.

Finkelhor, D. (1994). *The victimization of children in a developmental perspective.* Unpublished manuscript, University of New Hampshire, Durham, NH.

Finkelhor, D., & Browne, A. (1988). Assessing the long-term impact of child sexual abuse: A review and conceptualization. In L. Walker (Ed.), *Handbook on sexual abuse of children* (pp. 55–71). New York: Springer.

Finkelhor, D., & Dziuba-Leatherman, J. (1995). Victimization prevention programs: A national survey of children's exposure and reactions. *Child Abuse and Neglect, 19*(2), 129–140.

Foa, E. B., & Kozak, M. J. (1986). Emotional processing of fear: Exposure to corrective information. *Psychological Bulletin, 99,* 20–35.

Foa, E., Steketee, G., & Rothbaum, B. O. (1989). Behavioral/cognitive conceptualizations of post-traumatic stress disorder. *Behavior Therapy, 20,* 155–176.

Friedrich, W. N. (1990). *Psychotherapy of sexually abused children and their families.* New York: Norton.

Friedrich, W. N. (1993). Sexual behavior in sexually abused children. *Violence Update, 3,* 1, 5, 7.

Friedrich, W. N., & Einbender, A. J. (1983). The abused child: A psychological review. *Journal of Consulting and Clinical Psychology, 12,* 244–256.

Friedrich, W. N., Einbender, A. J., & Luecke, W. J. (1983). Cognitive and behavioral characteristics of physically abused children. *Journal of Consulting and Clinical Psychology, 51,* 313–314.

Friedrich, W. N., & Luecke, W. J. (1988). Young school-age sexually aggressive children. *Professional Psychology Research and Practice, 19*(2), 155–164.

Friedrich, W. N., Urquiza, A. J., & Beilke, R. L. (1986). Behavior problems in sexually abused young children. *Journal of Pediatric Psychology, 11,* 47–57.

Frodi, A., & Lamb, M. (1980). Child abusers responses to infant smiles and cries. *Child Development, 51,* 238–241.

Frodi, A., & Smetana, J. (1984). Abused, neglected, and normal preschoolers' ability to discriminate emotions in others: The effects of IQ. *Child Abuse and Neglect, 8,* 459–465.

Gaensbauer, T. J., Mrazek, D. A., & Harmon, R. J. (1980). Emotional expression in abused and/or neglected infants. In N. Frude (Ed.), *Psychological approaches to child abuse* (pp. 120–135). London: Batsford.

Gaines, R., Sandgrund, A., Green, A. H., & Power, E. (1978). Etiological factors in child maltreatment: A multivariate study of abusing, neglecting, and normal mothers. *Journal of Abnormal Psychology, 87,* 531–541.

Garbarino, J., Drew, N., Kostelny, K., & Pardo, C. (1992). *Children in danger.* San Francisco: Jossey-Bass.

Garbarino, J., Guttman, E., & Seeley, J. (1986). *The psychologically battered child.* San Francisco: Jossey-Bass.

Gelinas, D. J. (1983). The persisting negative effects of incest. *Psychiatry, 46,* 312–332.

Gelles, R. J. (1973). Child abuse as psychopathology: A sociological critique and reformulation. *American Journal of Orthopsychiatry, 43,* 611–621.

George, C., & Main, M. (1979). Social interactions of young abused children: Approach, avoidance, and aggression. *Child Development, 50,* 306–318.

Gershenson, H. P., Musick, J. S., Ruch-Ross, H. S., Magee, V., Rubino, K. K., & Rosenberg, D. (1989). The prevalence of coercive sexual experience among teenage mothers. *Journal of Interpersonal Violence, 4,* 204–219.

Gil, D. G. (1970). *Violence against children: Physical child abuse in the United States.* Cambridge, MA: Harvard University Press.

Girshick, L. B. (1993). Teen dating violence. *Violence Update, 3,* 1–2, 4, 6.

Gleaves, D. H., & Eberenz, K. P. (1993). Eating disorders and additional psychopathology in women: The role of prior sexual abuse. *Journal of Child Sexual Abuse, 2,* 71–80.

Green, A. H. (1978). Self-destructive behavior in battered children. *American Journal of Psychiatry, 135,* 579–582.

Green, A. H. (1983). Dimensions of psychological trauma in abused children. *Journal of the American Association of Child Psychiatry, 22,* 231–237.

Hall, G. C. N. (1992). Sexual aggression against children: A conceptual perspective of etiology. *Criminal Justice and Behavior, 19,* 8–23.

Hart, S. N., & Brassard, M. R. (1987). A major threat to children's mental health: Psychological maltreatment. *American Psychologist, 42,* 160–165.

Harter, S., Alexander, P. C., & Neimeyer, R. A. (1988).

Long-term effects of incestuous child abuse in college women: Social adjustment, social cognition, and family characteristics. *Journal of Consulting and Clinical Psychology, 56*, 5–8.

Hartman C. R., & Burgess, A. W. (1989). Sexual abuse of children: Causes and consequences. In D. Cicchetti & V. Carlson (Eds.), *Child maltreatment: Theory and research on the causes and consequences of child abuse and neglect* (pp. 95–128). Cambridge, UK: Cambridge University Press.

Hazzard, A. (1993). Trauma-related beliefs as mediators of sexual abuse impact in adult women survivors: A pilot study. *Journal of Child Sexual Abuse, 2*, 55–69.

Helfer, R. E. (1982). A review of the literature on the prevention of child abuse and neglect. *Child Abuse and Neglect, 6*, 251–261.

Hennessy, K. D., Rabideau, G. J., Cicchetti, D., & Cummings, E. M. (1994). Responses of physically abused and nonabused children to different forms of interadult anger. *Child Development, 65*, 815–828.

Herman, J. L. (1981). *Father–daughter incest.* Cambridge, MA: Harvard University Press.

Herman, J. L. (1992). *Trauma and recovery: The aftermath of violence–from domestic abuse to political terror.* New York: Basic Books.

Herman, J. L., & van der Kolk, B. A. (1987). Traumatic antecedents of borderline personality disorder. In B. A. van der Kolk (Ed.), *Psychological trauma* (pp. 111–126). Washington, DC: American Psychiatric Press.

Herzberger, S. D., Potts, D. A., & Dillon, M. (1981). Abusive and nonabusive parental treatment from the child's perspective. *Journal of Consulting and Clinical Psychology, 49*, 81–90.

Hillson, J. M. C., & Kuiper, N. A. (1994). A stress and coping model of child maltreatment. *Clinical Psychology Review, 14*, 261–285.

Hoffman-Plotkin, D., & Twentyman, C. T. (1984). A multimodal assessment of behavioral and cognitive deficits in abused and neglected preschoolers. *Child Development, 55*, 794–802.

Horowitz, M. J. (1986). *Stress response syndromes* (2nd ed). Northvale, NJ: Jason Aronson.

Hotaling, G. T., Straus, M. A., & Lincoln, A. J. (1990). Intrafamily violence and crime and crime outside the family. In M. A. Straus & R. J. Gelles (Eds.), *Physical violence in American families: Risk factors and adaptations to violence in 8,145 families* (pp. 431–470). New Brunswick, NJ: Transaction.

Howes, C., & Eldredge, R. (1985). Responses of abused, neglected, and non-maltreated children to the behaviors of their peers. *Journal of Applied Developmental Psychology, 6*, 261–270.

Janoff-Bulman, R. (1979). Characterological versus behavioral self-blame: Inquiries into depression and rape. *Journal of Personality and Social Psychology, 37*, 1798–1809.

Jessor, R. (1993). Successful adolescent development among youth in high-risk settings. *American Psychologist, 48*, 117–126.

Kaslow, N. J., Rehm, L. P., Pollack, S. L., & Siegel, A. W. (1988). Attributional style and self-control behavior in depressed and non-depressed children and their parents. *Journal of Abnormal Child Psychology, 16*, 163–175.

Kaufman, J. (1991). Depressive disorders in maltreated children. *Journal of the American Academy of Child and Adolescent Psychiatry, 30*, 257–265.

Kaufman, J., & Cicchetti, D. (1989). The effects of maltreatment on school-aged children's socioemotional development: Assessments in a day-camp setting. *Developmental Psychology, 25*, 516–524.

Kaufman, J., Jones, B., Stieglitz, E., Vitulano, L., & Mannarino, A. P. (1994). The use of multiple informants to assess children's maltreatment experiences. *Journal of Family Violence, 9*, 227–248.

Kaufman, J., & Zigler, E. (1989). The intergenerational transmission of child abuse and the prospect of predicting future abusers. In D. Cicchetti & V. Carlson (Eds.), *Child maltreatment: Research and theory on the causes and consequences of child abuse and neglect* (pp. 129–150). New York: Cambridge University Press.

Kazdin, A. E., Moser, J., Colbus, D., & Bell, R. (1985). Depressive symptoms among physically abused and psychiatrically disturbed children. *Journal of Abnormal Psychology, 94*, 298–307.

Kempe, C. H., Silverman, F. N., Steele, B. F., Droegenmueller, W., & Silver, H. K. (1962). The battered child syndrome. *Journal of the American Medical Association, 181*, 17–24.

Kendall-Tackett, K. A., Williams, L. M., & Finkelhor, D. (1993). Impact of sexual abuse on children. *Psychological Bulletin, 113*, 164–180.

Kiser, L. J., Ackerman, B. J., Brown, E., Edwards, N. B., McColgan, E., Pugh, R., & Pruitt, D. B. (1988). Posttraumatic stress disorder in young children: A reaction to purported sexual abuse. *Journal of the American Academy of Child and Adolescent Psychiatry, 27*, 645–649.

Kiser, L. J., Heston, J., Millsap, P. A., & Pruitt, D. B. (1991). Physical and sexual abuse in childhood: Relationship with post-traumatic stress disorder. *Journal of the American Academy of Child and Adolescent Psychiatry, 30*, 776–783.

Kolko, D. J. (1992). Characteristics of child victims of physical violence: Research findings and clinical implications. *Journal of Interpersonal Violence, 7*, 244–276.

Kolko, D., Moser, J., & Weldy, S. (1990). Medical/health histories and physical evaluation of physically and sexually abused child psychiatric patents: A controlled study. *Journal of Family Violence, 5*, 249–266.

Koverola, C., Pound, J., Heger, A., & Lytle, C. (1993). Relationship of child sexual abuse to depression. *Child Abuse and Neglect, 17*, 393–400.

Lanning, K. (1987). *Child molesters: A behavioral analysis.* Arlington, VA: National Center for Missing and Exploited Children.

Lerner, M. J. (1980). *The belief in a just world.* New York: Plenum Press.

Lewis, D. O., Lovely, R., Yeager, C., & Femina, D. B. (1989). Toward a theory of the genesis of violence: A follow-up study of delinquents. *Journal of the American Academy of Child and Adolescent Psychiatry, 28*, 431–436.

Lewis, D. O., Pincus, J. H., & Glaser, G. H. (1979). Violent juvenile delinquents: Psychiatric, neurological, psychological, and abuse factors. *Journal of the American Academy of Child Psychiatry, 18*, 307–319.

Lewko, J., Carriere, R., Whissell, C., & Radford, J. (1986). *Final report of the study investigating the long-term effectiveness of the Parenting for Teens and Children Project.* Sudbury, Ontario: Centre for Research in Human Development, Laurentian University.

Light, R. (1973). Abused and neglected children in America:

A study of alternative policies. *Harvard Educational Review, 43,* 556–598.

Lipovsky, J. A. (1991). Post-traumatic stress disorder in children. *Family Community Health, 14,* 42–51.

Lobell, C. M. (1992). Relationship between childhood sexual abuse and borderline personality disorder in women psychiatric inpatients. *Journal of Child Sexual Abuse, 1,* 63–80.

Loeber, R., Weissman, W., & Reid, J. (1983). Family interactions of assaultive adolescents, stealers, and nondelinquents. *Journal of Abnormal Child Psychology, 11,* 1–14.

Lynch, M., & Cicchetti, D. (1991). Patterns of relatedness in maltreated and nonmaltreated children: Connections among multiple representational models. *Development and Psychopathology, 3,* 207–226.

Main, M., & George, C. (1985). Responses of abused and disadvantaged toddlers to distress in age mates: A study in the day care setting. *Developmental Psychology, 21,* 407–412.

Manly, J. T., Cicchetti, D., & Barnett, D. (1994). The impact of subtype, frequency, chronicity, and severity of child maltreatment on social competence and behavior problems. *Development and Psychopathology, 6,* 121–143.

Mash, E. J., & Wolfe, D. A. (1991). Methodological issues in research on physical child abuse. *Criminal Justice and Behavior, 18,* 8–29.

McCord, J. (1979). Some childrearing antecedents of criminal behavior in adult men. *Journal of Personality and Social Psychology, 37,* 1477–1486.

McCord, J. (1983). A forty year perspective on effects of child abuse and neglect. *Child Abuse and Neglect, 7,* 265–270.

McCrone, E. R., Egeland, B., Kalkoske, M., & Carlson, E. A. (1994). Relations between early maltreatment and mental representations of relationships assessed with projective storytelling in middle childhood. *Development and Psychopathology, 6,* 99–120.

McGee, R., & Wolfe, D. A. (1991). Psychological maltreatment: Towards an operational definition. *Development and Psychopathology, 3,* 3–18.

McLeer, S. V., Deblinger, E., Atkins, M. S., Foa, E. B., & Ralphe, D. L. (1988). Post-traumatic stress disorder in sexually abused children: A prospective study. *Journal of the American Academy of Child and Adolescent Psychiatry, 27,* 650–654.

Milner, J. S. (1993). Social information processing and physical child abuse. *Clinical Psychology Review, 13,* 275–294.

Mrazek, P. J. (1993). Maltreatment and infant development. In C. H. Zeanah, Jr. (Ed.), *Handbook of infant mental health* (pp. 159–170). New York: Guilford Press.

Mrazek, P., & Mrazek, D. (1981). The effects of child abuse: Methodological considerations. In P. Mrazek & C. H. Kempe (Eds.), *Sexually abused children and their families.* London: Pergamon.

National Research Council. (1993). *Understanding child abuse and neglect.* Washington, DC: National Academy Press.

Park, L. C., Imboden, J. B., Park, T. J., Hulse, S. H., & Unger, H. T. (1992). Giftedness and psychological abuse in borderline personality disorder: Their relevance to genesis and treatment. *Journal of Personality Disorders, 6,* 226–240.

Parke, R. D., & Slaby, R. G. (1983). The development of aggression. In E. M. Hetherington (Ed.), *Handbook of child psychopathology* (Vol. 4, pp. 547–641). New York: Wiley.

Patterson, G. R. (1982). *Coercive family process.* Eugene, OR: Castalia.

Perez, C. M., & Widom, C. S. (1994). Childhood victimization and long-term intellectual and academic outcomes. *Child Abuse and Neglect, 18,* 617–633.

Peters, S. D. (1988). Child sexual abuse and later psychological problems. In G. E. Wyatt & G. J. Powell (Eds.), *Lasting effects of child sexual abuse* (pp. 101–117). Newbury Park, CA: Sage.

Peterson, C., & Seligman, M. E. P. (1983). Learned helplessness and victimization. *Journal of Social Issues, 39,* 103–116.

Peterson, L., & Brown, D. (1994). Integrating child injury and abuse-neglect research: Common histories, etiologies, and solutions. *Psychological Bulletin, 116,* 293–315.

Pianta, R., Egeland, B., & Erickson, M. F. (1989). The antecedents of maltreatment: Results of the mother–child interaction research project. In D. Cicchetti & V. Carlson (Eds.), *Child maltreatment: Theory and research on the causes and consequences of child abuse and neglect* (pp. 203–253). New York: Cambridge University Press.

Radbill, S. X. (1968). A history of child abuse and infanticide. In R. E. Helfer & C. H. Kempe (Eds.), *The battered child* (pp. 3–17). Chicago: University of Chicago Press.

Richters, J. E. (1992). Depressed mothers as informants about their children: A critical review of the evidence for distortion. *Psychological Bulletin, 112,* 485–499.

Ritchett, D., & Towns, K. (1980, April). *Education for parenthood: Eighth graders change childrearing attitudes.* Paper presented at the annual meeting of the American Educational Research Association, Boston, MA.

Rossman, P. (1980). The pederasts. In L. G. Schultz (Ed.), *The sexual victimology of youth* (pp. 335–349). Springfield, IL: Charles C. Thomas.

Russell, D. E. H. (1986). *The secret trauma.* New York: Basic Books.

Salter, A. C. (1988). *Treating child sex offenders and victims: A practical guide.* Beverly Hills: Sage.

Salzinger, S., Kaplan, S., Pelcovitz, D., Samit, C., & Krieger, R. (1984). Parent and teacher assessment of children's behavior in child maltreating families. *Journal of the American Academy of Child Psychiatry, 23,* 458–464.

Sansonnet-Hayden, H., Haley, G., Marriage, K., & Fine, S. (1987). Sexual abuse and psychopathology in hospitalized adolescents. *Journal of the American Academy of Child and Adolescent Psychiatry, 26,* 753–757.

Sas, L., Hurley, P., Hatch, A., Malla, S., & Dick, T. (1993). *Three years after the verdict: A longitudinal study of the social and psychological adjustment of child witnesses referred to the child witness project.* Final report prepared for the Family Violence Prevention Division, Health and Welfare Canada (FVDS #4887–06–91–026).

Schneider-Rosen, K., Braunwald, K., Carlson, V., & Cicchetti, D. (1985). Current perspectives in attachment theory: Illustrations from the study of maltreated infants. *Monographs of the Society for Research in Child Development* (Vol. 50, Serial No. 209), pp. 194–210.

Schneider-Rosen, K., & Cicchetti, D. (1991). Early self-knowledge and emotional development: Visual self-recognition and affective reactions to mirror self-image in maltreated and nonmaltreated toddlers. *Developmental Psychology, 27,* 471–478.

Schreier, H. A., & Libow, J. A. (1993). *Hurting for love: Munchausen by proxy syndrome.* New York: Guilford Press.

Scott, K. D. (1992). Childhood sexual abuse: Impact on a community's mental health status. *Child Abuse and Neglect, 16*, 285–295.

Sgroi, S. M. (1982). *Handbook of clinical intervention in child sexual abuse.* Lexington, MA: Lexington Books.

Shaw-Lamphear, V. S. (1985). The impact of maltreatment on children's psychosocial adjustment: A review of the research. *Child Abuse and Neglect, 9*, 251–263.

Shirk, S. R. (1988). The interpersonal legacy of physical abuse of children. In M. Straus (Ed.), *Abuse and victimization across the lifespan* (pp. 57–81). Baltimore: Johns Hopkins Press.

Silbert, M. H., & Pines, A. M. (1981). Sexual child abuse as an antecedent to prostitution. *Child Abuse and Neglect, 5*, 407–411.

Silver, R., Boon, C., & Stones, M. (1983). Searching for meaning in misfortune: Making sense of incest. *Journal of Social Issues, 39*, 81–101.

Singer, M. I., Hussey, D. L., & Strom, K. J. (1992). Grooming the victim: An analysis of a perpetrator's seduction letter. *Child Abuse and Neglect, 16*(6), 877–886.

Smetana, J. G., & Kelly, M. (1989). Social cognition in maltreated children. In D. Cicchetti & V. Carlson (Eds.), *Child maltreatment: Theory and research on the causes and consequences of child abuse and neglect* (pp. 620–646). Cambridge, UK: Cambridge University Press.

Smetana, J., Kelly, M., & Twentyman, C. (1984). Abused, neglected, and nonmaltreated children's judgments of moral and social transgressions. *Child Development, 55*, 277–287.

Spaccarelli, S. (1994). Stress, appraisal, and coping in child sexual abuse: A theoretical and empirical review. *Psychological Bulletin, 116*, 340–362.

Spinetta, J. J., & Rigler, D. (1972). The child abusing parent: A psychological review. *Psychological Bulletin, 77*, 296–304.

Springs, F. E., & Friedrich, W. N. (1992). Health risk behaviors and medical sequelae of childhood sexual abuse. *Mayo Clinic Proceedings, 67*, 1–6.

Sroufe, L. A., & Fleeson, J. (1986). Attachment and the construction of relationships. In W. W. Hartup & Z. Rubin (Eds.), *Relationships and development* (pp. 51–71). Hillsdale, NJ: Erlbaum.

Sroufe, L. A., & Rutter, M. (1984). The domain of developmental psychopathology. *Child Development, 55*, 17–29.

Statistics Canada. (1993). *Violence against women survey.* Ottawa: Author.

Steiger, H., Leung, F. Y. K., & Houle, L. (1992). Relationships among borderline features, body dissatisfaction, and bulimic symptoms in nonclinical females. *Addictive Behaviors, 17*, 397–406.

Stoller, R. (1973). *Splitting: A case of female masculinity.* New York: Delta.

Stone, N. (1993). Parental abuse as a precursor to childhood onset depression and suicidality. *Child Psychiatry and Human Development, 24*, 13–24.

Straker, G., & Jacobson, R. S. (1981). Aggression, emotional maladjustment, and empathy in the abused child. *Developmental Psychology, 17*, 762–765.

Strassberg, Z., & Dodge, K. A. (1995). *Maternal physical abuse of the child: Social information processing perspective.* Unpublished manuscript, Department of Psychology, State University of New York at Stony Brook.

Straus, M. A., & Kantor, G. K. (1994). Corporal punishment of adolescents by parents: A risk factor in the epidemiol-

ogy of depression, suicide, alcohol abuse, child abuse, and wife beating. *Adolescence, 29*, 543–561.

Tarter, R. E., Hegedus, A. E., Winsten, N. E., & Alterman, A. I. (1984). Neuropsychological, personality, and familial characteristics of physically abused delinquents. *Journal of the American Academy of Child Psychiatry, 23*, 668–674.

Terr, L. C. (1991). Childhood traumas: An outline and overview. *American Journal of Psychiatry, 148*, 10–20.

Toth, S. L., Manly, J. T., & Cicchetti, D. (1992). Child maltreatment and vulnerability to depression. *Development and Psychopathology, 4*(1), 97–112.

Trickett, P. K., McBride-Chang, C., & Putnam, F. W. (1994). The classroom performance and behavior of sexually abused females. *Development and Psychopathology, 6*, 183–194.

Trocme, N. (1994). *Ontario incidence study of reported child abuse and neglect* (Final report). Toronto: The Institute for the Prevention of Child Abuse.

Trzepacz, P. T., & Baker, R. W. (1993). *The Psychiatric Mental Status Examination.* New York: Oxford University Press.

U.S. Advisory Board on Child Abuse and Neglect. (1990). *First report of the U.S. Advisory Board on Child Abuse and Neglect.* Washington, DC: U.S. Department of Health and Human Services/National Center on Child Abuse and Neglect.

U.S. Department of Health and Human Services. (1992). *National child abuse and neglect data system: Working paper 1, 1990 summary data component* (DHHS Pub. No. ACF 92–30361). Washington, DC: U.S. Government Printing Office.

U. S. Department of Health and Human Services, National Center on Child Abuse and Neglect. (1994). *Child maltreatment 1992: Reports from the states to the National Center on Child Abuse and Neglect.* Washington, DC: U.S. Government Printing Office.

Valenzuela, M. (1990). Attachment in chronically underweight young children. *Child Development, 61*, 1984–1996.

van der Kolk, B. A., Perry, C., & Herman, J. L. (1991). Childhood origins of self-destructive behavior. *American Journal of Psychiatry, 148*, 1665–1671.

Vondra, J. A., Barnett, D., & Cicchetti, D. (1990). Self-concept, motivation, and competence among preschoolers from maltreating and comparison families. *Child Abuse and Neglect, 14*, 525–540.

Walker, E., Downey, G., & Bergman, A. (1989). The effects of parental psychopathology and maltreatment on child behavior: A test of the diathesis–stress model. *Child Development, 60*, 15–24.

Waters, E., Posada, G., Crowell, J., & Lay, K. (1993). Is attachment theory ready to contribute to our understanding of disruptive behavior problems? *Development and Psychopathology, 5*, 215–224.

Weaver, T. L., & Clum, G. A. (1993). Early family environments and traumatic experiences associated with borderline personality disorder. *Journal of Consulting and Clinical Psychology, 61*, 1068–1075.

Wekerle, C., & Wolfe, D. A. (1993). Prevention of child physical abuse and neglect: Promising new directions. *Clinical Psychology Review, 13*, 501–540.

Westen, D., Ludolph, P., Misle, B., Ruffins, S., & Block, J. (1990). Physical and sexual abuse in adolescent girls with borderline personality disorders. *American Journal of Orthopsychiatry, 60*, 55–66.

Whitmore, E. A. W., Kramer, J. R., & Knutson, J. F. (1993). The association between punitive childhood experiences

and hyperactivity. *Child Abuse and Neglect, 17,* 357–366.

Widom, C. S. (1989a). Does violence beget violence? A critical examination of the literature. *Psychological Bulletin, 106,* 3–28.

Widom, C. S. (1989b). The cycle of violence. *Science, 244,* 160–165.

Wolfe, D. A. (1985). Child abusive parents: An empirical review and analysis. *Psychological Bulletin, 97,* 462–482.

Wolfe, D. A. (1987). *Child abuse: Implications for child development and psychopathology.* Newbury Park, CA: Sage.

Wolfe, D. A. (1991). *Preventing physical and emotional abuse of children.* New York: Guilford Press.

Wolfe, D. A., & Jaffe, P. (1991). Child abuse and family violence as determinants of child psychopathology. *Canadian Journal of Behavioral Science, 23,* 282–299.

Wolfe, D. A., & McGee, R. (1994). Child maltreatment and adolescent adjustment. *Development and Psychopathology, 6,* 165–181.

Wolfe, D. A., & Mosk, M. D. (1983). Behavioral comparisons of children from abusive and distressed families. *Journal of Consulting and Clinical Psychology, 51,* 702–708.

Wolfe, D. A., Sas, L., & Wekerle, C. (1994). Factors associated with the development of posttraumatic stress disorder among child victims of sexual abuse. *Child Abuse and Neglect, 18,* 37–50.

Wolfe, D. A., & Wekerle, C. (1993). Treatment strategies for child physical abuse and neglect: A critical progress report. *Clinical Psychology Review, 13,* 473–500.

Wolfe, D. A., Wekerle, C., Reitzel-Jaffe, D., & Gough, R. (1995). Strategies to address violence in the lives of high-risk youth. In E. Peled, P. G. Jaffe, & J. L. Edelson (Eds.), *Ending the cycle of violence: Community responses to children of battered women* (pp. 255–274). Newbury Park, CA: Sage.

Wolfe, D. A., Wekerle, C., Reitzel-Jaffe, D., & Lefebvre, L. (1995). *Factors associated with increased risk of gender-based violence among adolescents.* Manuscript submitted for publication.

Wolfe, V. V., Gentile, C., & Wolfe, D. A. (1989). The impact of sexual abuse on children: A PTSD formulation. *Behavior Therapy, 20,* 215–228.

Wolfe, V. V., & Wolfe, D. A. (1988). Sexual abuse of children. In E. J. Mash & L. G. Terdal (Eds.), *Behavioral assessment of childhood disorders* (2nd ed., pp. 670–714). New York: Guilford Press.

Wozencraft, T., Wagner, W., & Pellegrin, A. (1991). Depression and suicidal ideation in sexually abused children. *Child Abuse and Neglect, 15,* 505–511.

Wyatt, G. E., & Newcomb, M. (1990). Internal and external mediators of women's sexual abuse in childhood. *Journal of Consulting and Clinical Psychology, 58,* 758–767.

VI

HEALTH DISORDERS

Eating Disorders

G. Terence Wilson
Karen Heffernan
Carolyn M. D. Black

Eating disorders consist of severe disturbances in eating behavior, maladaptive and unhealthy efforts to control body weight, and abnormal attitudes about body weight and shape. The two most well-established eating disorders are anorexia nervosa and bulimia nervosa. The former is characterized by a refusal to maintain a normal body weight. The latter is characterized by recurrent episodes of binge eating and inappropriate behaviors designed to control body weight and shape such as self-induced vomiting or laxative misuse. Dysfunctional attitudes toward body weight and shape are a prominent feature of both disorders. Disorders that are closely related to anorexia nervosa and bulimia nervosa, but do not meet all of the formal diagnostic criteria, are classified as eating disorder not otherwise specified (EDNOS). A large number of the patients seen in clinical practice would receive the diagnosis of EDNOS. However, the different variations of eating disorders that are grouped within this category are not well-specified, and as a whole they have been relatively ignored in the clinical and research literature. The single exception, and perhaps the most common example of this category, is what the *Diagnostic and Statistical Manual of Mental Disorders,* fourth edition (DSM-IV) labels "binge-eating disorder" (BED) (American Psychiatric Association, 1994).

This disorder is characterized by recurrent binge eating in the absence of inappropriate weight-control behaviors as in bulimia nervosa. In this chapter, we focus on the three disorders of anorexia nervosa, bulimia nervosa, and binge eating disorder.

Anorexia nervosa has been identified as a psychiatric disorder for more than a century (Gull, 1873). What we know as bulimia nervosa was originally described by Russell in 1979 in England. Shortly thereafter "bulimia" was included as a disorder in the American Psychiatric Association's *Diagnostic and Statistical Manual of Mental Disorders,* third edition (DSM-III) in 1980. It is now widely accepted that bulimia nervosa emerged as a clinical disorder during the 1970s. This development can be seen in an analysis of referrals to prominent centers for the treatment of eating disorders in different countries (Fairburn, Hay, & Welch, 1993). In Toronto the referral rates for anorexia nervosa between 1975 and 1986 were relatively stable, but there was a noticeable increase in referral rates for bulimia nervosa. The same trend occurred in Wellington, New Zealand, where the annual referral rate for bulimia nervosa increased between 1977 and 1986 from 6 to 44 per 100,000 female persons aged 15 to 29 years, while those for anorexia nervosa did not change. In London, the annual

referral rates for bulimia nervosa increased between 1980 and 1989 from 2.8 to 10.1 per 10,000 female persons.

The alternative view is that the disorder had simply not previously come to the attention of mental health professionals. According to this line of reasoning, the disorder either had been overlooked or misdiagnosed by clinicians, or people only began seeking treatment in the 1970s. These possibilities seem implausible.

The inclusion of BED within the category of EDNOS in DSM-IV (American Psychiatric Association, 1994) was in response to reports of large numbers of patients who engaged in binge eating but who did not meet the diagnostic criteria for bulimia nervosa (Spitzer et al., 1992). Most patients with this disorder are overweight. In fact, Stunkard in 1959 had identified the problem of binge eating in obese patients in terms very similar to the current description of BED. But this problem was largely overlooked until recently. The reasons are probably twofold: First, views on the nature of obesity have changed over the past three decades. It is now seen as a chronic physical disorder under strong genetic control with identifiable biological causes (Stunkard, Harris, Pedersen, & McClearn, 1990). The rapid ascendancy of this genetic–biological perspective led to a relative decline in research on psychological or behavioral analyses of obesity that would have focused more attention on the behavior of binge eating. Second, the publication in 1980 of DSM-III (American Psychiatric Association, 1980) included "bulimia" as an eating disorder, a syndrome in which binge eating was the core feature. This resulted in attention being directed primarily toward normal-weight patients who both binged and purged, namely bulimia nervosa.

It is important to emphasize that obesity itself is neither a psychiatric disorder nor an eating disorder. Nonetheless, many mental health professionals continue to lump obesity, or what is sometimes called a "weight disorder," together with eating disorders. This serves only to stigmatize further obese people whose condition is better viewed as a complex metabolic disorder rather than simply a behavioral problem (Garner & Wooley, 1991; Wilson, 1993a). Obese individuals may develop eating disorders and a small fraction of patients with bulimia nervosa are obese. A much larger minority of obese patients engage in binge eating and receive the diagnosis of BED as we discuss below.

DEFINITIONAL AND DIAGNOSTIC ISSUES

Binge Eating

The terms "binge" and "binge eating" refer to a form of overeating that is a core feature of the eating disorders. Binge eating occurs across the weight spectrum and is one of the diagnostic criteria of anorexia nervosa (the binge-eating/purging subtype), bulimia nervosa, and BED. Yet the definition of binge eating has changed over successive versions of the American Psychiatric Association's *Diagnostic and Statistical Manual*. DSM-IV (American Psychiatric Association, 1994) defines binge eating as "characterized by both of the following: (1) eating, in a discrete period of time (e.g., within any 2-hour period), an amount of food that is definitely larger than most people would eat during a similar period of time and under similar circumstances; and (2) a sense of lack of control over eating during the episode (e.g., a feeling that one cannot stop eating or control what or how much one is eating).

The DSM-IV definition was adapted from the Eating Disorder Examination (EDE) (Fairburn & Cooper, 1993), a semistructured clinical interview that is the "gold standard" for assessing eating disorders. Research has shown that when the lay public use the word "binge" to describe their eating they are referring to the sense of loss of control and not the amount of food consumed (Beglin & Fairburn, 1992). Accordingly, it is most important that in any assessment of disordered eating both the assessor and the patient share the same, unambiguous meaning of the nature of a binge. Most self-report questionnaires simply refer to binge eating without providing an explicit definition, and for this reason they may provide misleading information concerning the presence and frequency of binge eating in respondents (Wilson, 1993b).

The most comprehensive and valid scheme for classifying binge eating and other forms of overeating is provided by the EDE. As shown in Figure 15.1, "objective bulimic episodes" are what the DSM-IV criteria term binge eating. "Subjective bulimic episodes" are similar, except that the amount of food eaten is not objectively large. The EDE terms "objective overeating" and "subjective overeating" describe parallel episodes of perceived overeating except that there is no loss of control. These different patterns of actual and

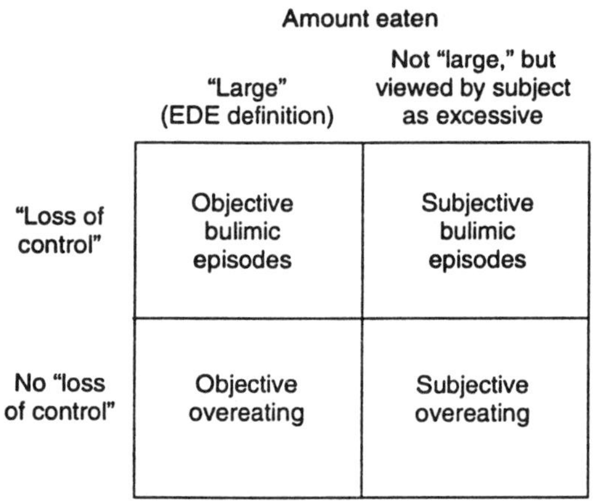

	Amount eaten	
	"Large" (EDE definition)	Not "large," but viewed by subject as excessive
"Loss of control"	Objective bulimic episodes	Subjective bulimic episodes
No "loss of control"	Objective overeating	Subjective overeating

FIGURE 15.1. The EDE scheme for classifying episodes of overeating.

ation, 1994) subdivides anorexia nervosa on the basis of the presence of binge eating and purging into a binge-eating/purging type in which there are regular episodes of binge eating or purging and a restricting type in which binge eating and purging do not occur regularly. The basis for this distinction is the evidence that, compared with the restricting group, those who regularly binge or purge tend to have stronger personal and family histories of obesity and higher rates of so-called impulsive behaviors, including stealing, drug misuse, deliberate self-harm, and lability of mood (Garner, 1993). The *International Classification of Disease,* 10th edition (ICD-10; World Health Organization, 1992) criteria (see Table 15.2) are similar to those of DSM-IV. Unlike the latter, the former do not provide subtypes.

perceived overeating are not mutually exclusive, and the data indicate that both patients with bulimia nervosa and those who are obese binge eaters engage in both objective and subjective bulimic episodes (Wilson, 1993b).

Anorexia Nervosa

DSM-IV criteria for anorexia nervosa are listed in Table 15.1. In contrast to previous diagnostic schemes, DSM-IV (American Psychiatric Associ-

Bulimia Nervosa

DSM-IV criteria, presented in Table 15.3, make some important changes from previous versions. The first is the definition of a "binge." As described above, to be classified as a "binge" an episode of overeating must involve both an objectively large amount of food, given the circumstances, and the sense of lack of control. The second is that DSM-IV subdivides bulimia nervosa into a "purging type," in which there is either regular self-induced vomiting or regular misuse

---

TABLE 15.1. DSM-IV Diagnostic Criteria for Anorexia Nervosa

A. Refusal to maintain body weight at or above a minimally normal weight for age and height (e.g., weight loss leading to maintenance of body weight less than 85% of that expected; or failure to make expected weight gain during period of growth, leading to body weight less than 85% of that expected).

B. Intense fear of gaining weight or becoming fat, even though underweight.

C. Disturbance in the way in which one's body weight or shape is experienced, undue influence of body weight or shape on self-evaluation, or denial of the seriousness of the current low body weight.

D. In postmenarcheal females, amenorrhea, i.e., the absence of at least three consecutive menstrual cycles. (A woman is considered to have amenorrhea if her periods occur only following hormone, e.g., estrogen, administration.)

Specify type:
 Restricting Type: during the current episode of Anorexia Nervosa, the person has not regularly engaged in binge-eating or purging behavior (i.e., self-induced vomiting or the misuse of laxatives, diuretics, or enemas)
 Binge-Eating/Purging Type: during the current episode of Anorexia Nervosa, the person has regularly engaged in binge-eating or purging behavior (i.e., self-induced vomiting or the misuse of laxatives, diuretics, or enemas)

Note. From American Psychiatric Association (1994, pp. 544–545). Copyright 1994 by the American Psychiatric Association. Reprinted by permission.

TABLE 15.2. ICD-10 Diagnostic Guidelines for Anorexia Nervosa

(A) Body weight is maintained at least 15% below that expected (either lost or never achieved), or Quetelet's body-mass index is 17.5 or less. Prepubertal patients may show failure to make the expected weight gain during the period of growth.

(B) The weight loss is self-induced by avoidance of "fattening foods." One or more of the following may also be present: self-induced vomiting; self-induced purging; excessive exercise; use of appetite suppressants and/or diuretics.

(C) There is body-image distortion in the form of a specific psychopathology whereby a dread of fatness persists as an intrusive, overvalued idea and the patient imposes a low weight threshold himself or herself.

(D) A widespread endocrine disorder involving the hypothalamic–pituitary–gonadal axis is manifest in women as amenorrhoea and in men as a loss of sexual interest and potency. (An apparent exception is the persistence of vaginal bleeds in anorexic women who are receiving replacement hormonal therapy, most commonly taken as a contraceptive pill.) There may also be elevated levels of growth hormone, raised levels of cortisol, changes in the peripheral metabolism of the thyroid hormone, and abnormalities of insulin secretion.

(E) If onset is prepubertal, the sequence of pubertal events is delayed or even arrested (growth ceases; in girls the breasts do not develop and there is a primary amenorrhoea; in boys the genitals remain juvenile). With recovery, puberty is often completed normally, but the menarche is late.

Note. From World Health Organization (1992, p. 117). Copyright 1992 by the World Health Organization. Reprinted by permission.

TABLE 15.3. DSM-IV Diagnostic Criteria for Bulimia Nervosa

A. Recurrent episodes of binge eating. An episode of binge eating is characterized by both of the following:
(1) eating, in a discrete period of time (e.g., within any 2-hour period), an amount of food that is definitely larger than most people would eat during a similar period of time and under similar circumstances
(2) a sense of lack of control over eating during the episode (e.g., a feeling that one cannot stop eating or control what or how much one is eating)

B. Recurrent inappropriate compensatory behavior in order to prevent weight gain, such as self-induced vomiting; misuse of laxatives, diuretics, enemas, or other medications; fasting; or excessive exercise.

C. The binge eating and inappropriate compensatory behaviors both occur, on average, at least twice a week for 3 months.

D. Self-evaluation is unduly influenced by body shape and weight.

E. The disturbance does not occur exclusively during episodes of Anorexia nervosa.

Specify type:
Purging Type: during the current episode of Bulimia Nervosa, the person has regularly engaged in self-induced vomiting or the misuse of laxatives, diuretics, or enemas
Nonpurging Type: during the current episode of Bulimia Nervosa, the person has used other inappropriate compensatory behaviors, such as fasting or excessive exercise, but has not regularly engaged in self-induced vomiting or the misuse of laxatives, diuretics, or enemas

Note. From American Psychiatric Association (1994, pp. 549–550). Copyright 1994 by the American Psychiatric Association. Reprinted by permission.

of laxatives or diuretics, and a "nonpurging type" in which such behavior is not present.

Finally, DSM-IV specifies that the individual does not currently meet diagnostic criteria for anorexia nervosa. This has the effect of restricting the diagnosis of bulimia nervosa to those of average or above-average weight. The main rea-son for allowing the diagnosis of anorexia nervosa to trump that of bulimia nervosa concerns therapeutic implications. In the former, but not the latter, there is the need for weight gain. Furthermore, the therapeutic outlook is quite different. Bulimia nervosa can be effectively treated in the majority of cases with good prospects for a full and lasting

recovery (Fairburn et al., 1995). Anorexia nervosa, however, remains a disorder that is resistant to successful long-term treatment (Hsu, 1990).

The DSM-IV requirement that a binge consist of a large amount of food is consistent with the findings of laboratory studies and self-reports of the caloric size of the binges of patients with bulimia nervosa. Nevertheless, several groups of investigators have challenged this definitional requirement, arguing that the amount of food consumed is not the cardinal characteristic of a binge. For example, Rosen, Leitenberg, Fisher, and Khazam (1986) found that one-third of their patients, who otherwise satisfied diagnostic criteria for bulimia nervosa, reported consuming fewer than 600 kcal per binge, with no relationship between the size of the self-reported binge and the accompanying anxiety. Similarly, Rossiter and Agras (1990) observed that a significant minority of their patients with bulimia nervosa reported binges of fewer than 500 kcal. However, both of these studies were restricted to relatively small samples of patients seen in treatment, and it is unclear whether or not the findings apply in general to individuals with bulimia nervosa. A recent epidemiological study by Fairburn and his colleagues in Oxford has addressed this important question (Hay, Fairburn, & Doll, 1994).

In a landmark investigation, Hay et al. (1994) studied a representative community-based sample of women between the ages of 16 and 35 years who met carefully assessed criteria for recurrent binge eating. Cluster analysis was then used to identify clinically meaningful subgroups from this sample based on current eating-disorder characteristics. Four subgroups emerged from this analysis yielding a solution that was reproducible and had satisfactory descriptive and construct validity. The first cluster showed a high frequency of self-induced vomiting and laxative misuse, high levels of dietary restraint, and marked concerns about body weight and shape. The second cluster resembled those in the first, reporting a high frequency of objective bulimic episodes (i.e., binge eating) but little purging. They did, however, show high levels of dietary restraint and concerns about body weight and shape. The third cluster had frequent subjective bulimic episodes and lower levels of purging, and the fourth was heterogeneous in nature.

Several very important implications for the diagnosis of eating disorders follow from this study. The first concerns the DSM-IV requirement that binges involve large amounts of food.

The first cluster closely resembles the purging subtype of bulimia nervosa according to DSM-IV but with one notable difference, namely, that the size of the binge-eating episodes was not necessarily large. This finding lends support to the view that amount of food consumed is not a critical feature of binge eating. To summarize, there are no data showing fundamental differences in the nature of binges, in associated psychopathology, or in predictive validity, as a function of the quantity of food consumed.

A second implication bears on the DSM-IV decision to subtype bulimia nervosa. The data are consistent with the DSM-IV practice of subtyping bulimia nervosa according to the presence or absence of purging, since the first two clusters may be regarded as subtypes of the same core disorder rather than being two separate disorders. This is because they differed mainly in terms of the severity of eating-disorder features rather than the presence or absence of the features themselves. The only significant qualitative difference between the two clusters was the presence or absence of purging. Support for keeping the distinction between the purging and non-purging types of bulimia nervosa rests on the finding of predictive validity—the two clusters differed in their outcomes at 1 year.

A second major population-based study failed to find any significant differences between individuals with bulimia nervosa who purged (self-induced vomiting or laxative abuse) and those who did not (Walters et al., 1993). This study compared 54 purgers with 69 nonpurgers identified from interviews with over 1,000 pairs of twins from the population-based Virginia twin registry. No differences between the two groups emerged on a variety of demographic, weight-related, or personality variables. Nor were there differences in associated psychiatric disorders. Both groups showed significant association with major depression, alcoholism, and anorexia nervosa. A unique strength of this study is that it examined twins, thereby allowing an analysis of genetic and nongenetic influences. Consistent with other evidence, Walters et al. (1993) found support for a genetic predisposition in bulimia nervosa, a finding we elaborate on below. But these data indicate that the presence of purging is not intrinsically part of this genetic predisposition. Walters et al. (1993) summarized their findings as follows:

> There was no significant association between MZ twins concordant for bulimia and purging. Purging

bulimics do not appear to have a greater threshold along a liability continuum than nonpurging bulimics, because the cotwin of a purger was not at increased risk for bulimia than the cotwin of a nonpurger. If purging bulimia required a higher threshold than nonpurging, then the relatives of purgers should be at increased risk for the disorder. (p. 271)

These findings are not necessarily inconsistent with those of Hay et al. (1994). Indeed, the latter argue for the existence of a core disorder of bulimia nervosa regardless of the presence of purging. Their conclusion that the subtyping of purgers and nonpurgers is warranted is based on their 1-year follow-up findings. Walters et al. (1993) did not include a test of the predictive validity of the distinction between purging and nonpurging.

The ICD-10 guidelines for bulimia nervosa (World Health Organization, 1992) are listed in Table 15.4. They are arguably inferior to DSM-IV criteria (American Psychiatric Association, 1994) on several counts. They fail to define binge eating operationally. No mention is made of loss of control, the importance of which we have detailed above. It is not always the case that patients set themselves weight goals that are "well below" premorbid weights that would be considered healthy. Although the guidelines refer to a "morbid dread of fatness," they do not specify the importance of weight and shape to the person's sense of self as do DSM-IV criteria, which were influenced by the EDE (Fairburn & Cooper, 1993).

Binge-Eating Disorder

DSM-IV (American Psychiatric Association, 1994) includes binge-eating disorder (BED) as an example within the general category of EDNOS and provides specific diagnostic criteria for BED in Appendix B (see Table 15.5). Individuals with this disorder engage in recurrent binge eating but do not meet the criteria for bulimia nervosa. For example, they do not regularly engage in purging (Marcus, 1993). BED criteria do not specify any weight range, but unlike bulimia nervosa, preliminary data clearly indicate that BED occurs predominantly in obese patients (Spitzer et al., 1992). Obese patients who binge are often referred to as "compulsive overeaters" in the clinical and popular literature. The literature has been marked by diagnostic variability and inconsistency in the identification of the obese binge eater. The common denominator across the different diagnostic schemes is the phenomenon of binge eating. Even here, however, there is inconsistency in how a binge is defined and questions about the validity of its assessment (Fairburn & Wilson, 1993).

The wisdom of identifying BED as a new diagnosis has been widely debated. Fairburn, Welch, and Hay (1993) have argued against its inclusion in DSM-IV on the following grounds. First, they contend that it is premature to single out this particular subgroup of EDNOS patients. As more research is conducted more useful or valid ways of classifying different subgroups of individuals with recurrent binge eating might emerge. Second, they point out that the two main studies on which the case for including BED as a new diagnosis was based (Spitzer et al., 1992; Spitzer, Yanovski, et al., 1993) used an unvalidated self-report questionnaire that could have yielded unreliable estimates of binge eating. Third, there is a problem of definitional overlap

---

TABLE 15.4. ICD-10 Diagnostic Guidelines for Bulimia Nervosa

(A) There is a persistent preoccupation with eating, and an irresistible craving for food; the patient succumbs to episodes of overeating in which large amounts of food are consumed in short periods of time.

(B) The patient attempts to counteract the "fattening" effects of food by one or more of the following: self-induced vomiting; purgative abuse, alternating periods of starvation; use of drugs such as appetite suppressants, thyroid preparations or diuretics. When bulimia occurs in diabetic patients they may choose to neglect their insulin treatment.

(C) The psychopathology consists of a morbid dread of fatness and the patient sets herself or himself a sharply defined weight threshold, well below the premorbid weight that constitutes the optimum or healthy weight in the opinion of the physician. There is often, but not always, a history of an earlier episode of anorexia nervosa, the interval between the two disorders ranging from a few months to several years. This earlier episode may have been fully expressed, or may have assumed a minor cryptic form with a moderate loss of weight and/or a transient phase of amenorrhoea.

Note. From World Health Organization (1992, p. 179). Copyright 1992 by the World Health Organization. Reprinted by permission.

TABLE 15.5. DSM-IV Research Criteria for Binge-Eating Disorder

A. Recurrent episodes of binge eating. An episode of binge eating is characterized by both of the following:

    (1) eating, in a discrete period of time (e.g., within any 2-hour period), an amount of food that is definitely larger than most people would eat in a similar period of time under similar circumstances

    (2) a sense of lack of control over eating during the episode (e.g., a feeling that one cannot stop eating or control what or how much one is eating)

B. The binge-eating episodes are associated with three (or more) of the following:

    (1) eating much more rapidly than normal

    (2) eating until feeling uncomfortably full

    (3) eating large amounts of food when not feeling physically hungry

    (4) eating alone because of being embarrassed by how much one is eating

    (5) feeling disgusted with oneself, depressed, or very guilty after overeating

C. Marked distress regarding binge eating is present.

D. The binge eating occurs, on average, at least 2 days a week for 6 months.

Note: The method of determining frequency differs from that used for Bulimia Nervosa; future research should address whether the preferred method of setting a frequency threshold is counting the number of days on which binges occur or counting the number of episodes of binge eating.

E. The binge eating is not associated with the regular use of inappropriate compensatory behaviors (e.g., purging, fasting, excessive exercise) and does not occur exclusively during the course of Anorexia Nervosa or Bulimia Nervosa.

Note. From American Psychiatric Association (1994, p. 731). Copyright 1994 by the American Psychiatric Association. Reprinted by permission.

between nonpurging bulimia nervosa and BED. Both engage in binge eating. The difference is that BED patients do not report strict dieting (fasting) or abnormal attitudes toward body weight and shape. Fairburn, Hay, et al. (1993) argue that this difference is a matter of degree. Because these features are difficult to measure, the risk of overlap is considerable.

In their response to Fairburn, Hay, et al. (1993), Spitzer, Stunkard, et al. (1993) concur that more attention needs to be devoted to specifying the nature of EDNOS. They contend, however, that carving out the diagnosis of BED is an important step in this direction. They also reject the charge of overlapping categories, pointing out that DSM-IV criteria for bulimia nervosa do not include "strict dieting" as an extreme form of weight control, only fasting. The latter, they maintain, provides a clear boundary for separating the two disorders.

Recent findings provide little support for designating BED as a new and separate diagnostic entity within the eating disorders. The epidemiological research of Hay et al. (1994) failed to find support for the existence of a distinctive diagnosis of binge-eating disorder as described by Spitzer et al. (1992). This disorder did not emerge

as a natural, empirically derived cluster. Subjects who met BED criteria were indistinguishable from those in cluster 2 who seem best characterized as showing the nonpurging form of bulimia nervosa. A second study in Germany compared patients with bulimia nervosa with those with BED and nonpurging obesity (Fichter, Quadflieg, & Brandl, 1993). The authors interpreted their results in a manner consistent with the conclusion of Hay et al. (1994), namely, that there is a core clinical disorder of bulimia nervosa with clinical subtypes (e.g., purging vs. nonpurging subgroups). As such, their results would not support the Spitzer et al. (1992) proposal.

The diagnostic criteria for all eating disorders that feature binge eating refer to recurrent episodes of binge eating. Treatment studies of bulimia nervosa have routinely measured outcome in terms of change in the frequency of discrete binge-eating episodes. With the recent attention devoted to the diagnosis of BED (see below), however, it has been suggested that assessment should focus on the number of days on which binge eating occurred rather than discrete episodes of binge eating. Consistent with this view, the proposed criteria in DSM-IV for binge-eating

disorder specify that "binge eating occurs, on average, at least 2 days a week for 6 months" (American Psychiatric Association, 1994, p. 731).

As noted in DSM-IV, the issue of assessing *episodes* versus *days* of binge eating remains to be explored. Rossiter, Agras, Telch, and Bruce (1992) found that compared with self-monitoring data, obese binge eaters recalled almost twice as many binge episodes. In contrast, patients' recall of the number of days on which binge eating occurred was similar to that obtained from self-recording in daily diaries. The investigators concluded that the number of days of binge eating provides a more accurate measure than discrete episodes.

CLINICAL CHARACTERISTICS

Anorexia Nervosa

Core Psychopathology

A central feature of the psychopathology of anorexia nervosa is its ego-syntonic nature. It is more common for patients to come to professional attention because of the concerns of family members over their extreme weight loss than to seek help themselves. Consequently, there is a marked resistance to change; unless physical or psychological symptoms resulting from starvation cause sufficient distress, the patient with anorexia nervosa cannot be persuaded that her intense fear of weight gain and her dangerously low weight are unreasonable. Weight loss signifies for her a triumph of self-discipline, upon which her self-esteem depends, and weight gain is felt to be intolerable. Even when weight loss is achieved, it is never enough—there is always reason to lose a few more pounds just to be on the safe side, and "insufficient" weight loss from one day to the next may generate panic.

The two subtypes of anorexia nervosa exhibit significantly different clinical characteristics. The restricting subtype are highly controlled, rigid, and often obsessive. The binge-eating/purging subtype alternate between periods of rigid control and impulsive behavior. The latter display significantly more psychopathology and are more likely to attempt suicide than the former.

Associated Psychopathology

Associated psychopathology is commonplace. We discuss this comorbidity below.

Medical Complications

Serious complications can emerge as a result of starvation and malnutrition in anorexia nervosa, beginning with the striking emaciation of these patients. Amenorrhea is invariably present in postmenarcheal patients, and other common physical signs include dry, sometimes yellowish skin (due to hypercarotenemia), lanugo (fine, downy hair) on the trunk, face and extremities, sensitivity to cold, hypotension, bradycardia, and other cardiovascular problems (Hsu, 1990).

Purging behaviors may result in enlarged salivary glands, erosion of dental enamel, and calluses on the dominant hand from repeated skin abrasion by teeth when using the hand to induce vomiting. More dangerously, chronic dehydration and electrolyte imbalance, particularly serum potassium depletion, may lead to hypokalemia, increasing the risk of both renal failure and cardiac arrhythmia. Osteopenia may also result from malnutrition and decreased estrogen secretion, and in early-onset anorexia nervosa there may be some retardation of bone growth, although with recovery this may be reversed by normal "catch-up" growth (Hsu, 1990). These potentially serious conditions make thorough medical assessment an essential part of treatment for anorexia nervosa.

Bulimia Nervosa

Core Psychopathology

The eating behavior of patients with bulimia nervosa has been studied directly under controlled laboratory conditions. Patients were instructed either to overeat or to eat normally on different occasions. Their eating was compared with that of control subjects free of any eating disorder who were tested under the same instructions. In studies by Walsh and his colleagues, the patients were also asked to rate how typical these different episodes of overeating were of an actual binge (Walsh, 1993). They found that patients with bulimia nervosa ate significantly larger amounts of food than normal control subjects when instructed to overeat. However, the bulimia nervosa patients did not differ from the normal controls in terms of relative percentages of macronutrients consumed. On average, patients consumed 47% of carbohydrates in their binge episode compared with 46% in the controls' episode of overeating. The comparable figures for fat were 40% and 39% respectively. These findings are consistent with those from other laboratories (Kaye et al., 1992).

The finding that patients with bulimia nervosa do not consume an abnormally large amount of carbohydrates during binges discredits the widespread myth that binge eating is caused by "carbohydrate craving." There is no empirical evidence to support this view, despite its continued popularity. Typical binge foods (desserts and snacks) tend to be sweet with high fat content.

As with anorexia nervosa, patients with bulimia nervosa show a cognitive style marked by rigid rules and absolutistic (all-or-nothing) thinking (Butow, Beumont, & Touyz, 1993). Patients view themselves as either completely in control or out of control; virtuous or indulgent. Food is either "good" or "bad."

Associated Psychopathology

Bulimia nervosa is associated with high rates of comorbid psychopathology, featuring depression, substance abuse, and personality disorders. This comorbidity is described below. Patients with bulimia nervosa are often stereotyped as disinhibited, impulsive people who not only lose control over food intake but also act out in other ways (e.g., substance abuse, sexual promiscuity). Some clinical findings indicate that some patients do have problems with impulse control (Lacey & Evans, 1986), but it is likely that they are a minority. Other clinical reports dispute this profile, showing low rates of acting-out behavior. More importantly, a community-based study of a random sample of individuals has shown that important risk factors for bulimia nervosa closely resemble clinical descriptions of the personality profile of restricting anorexics rather than the more impulsive binge-eating/purging subtype (Fairburn, 1994).

Medical Complications

Although the physical sequelae of bulimia nervosa can be serious, they are not nearly as severe as in anorexia nervosa, characterized as it is by dangerously low body weight. Common physical complaints include fatigue, headaches, puffy cheeks due to enlargement of the salivary glands, dental problems due to permanent erosion of teeth enamel, and finger calluses from stimulating the gag reflex to induce vomiting (Mitchell, Pomeroy, & Colon, 1990).

Electrolyte abnormalities, such as hypokalemia and hypochloremia, probably pose the most serious medical complication. Some patients ingest ipecac, a drug that may lead to cardiomyopathy, to force emesis. Excessive laxative abuse entails the risk of becoming dependent on laxatives and suffering severe constipation on withdrawal, or even permanent damage to the colon. For these reasons, it is important that any patient who purges (by whatever means) be medically screened and have blood tests to assess electrolyte status and any fluid imbalance.

Binge-Eating Disorder

Laboratory studies have shown that obese patients with BED consume significantly more food than obese nonbingers when instructed to binge or eat normally (Yanovski, Leet, et al., 1992). Consistent with the data from normal-weight bulimia nervosa patients, obese patients with BED do not consume more carbohydrates during binge meals. Rossiter et al. (1992) replicated this finding using self-monitoring of food records. Yanovski, Leet, et al. (1992) found that their obese BED patients consumed a greater percentage of calories as fat and a lesser percentage as protein during binge meals than patients without BED. Obese binge eaters are more likely than obese nonbingers to report a history of weight cycling (Spitzer et al., 1992) and to show more attitudinal disturbance concerning body weight and shape (Wilson, Nonas, & Rosenblum, 1993).

Patients with BED often have significant levels of associated psychopathology, as described in the section below on "Common Comorbidities." This is perhaps the most robust difference between obese binge eaters and nonbingers. However, the degree of associated psychopathology in patients with BED is typically less than in patients with bulimia nervosa (Fichter et al., 1993; Marcus, 1993).

DEVELOPMENTAL COURSE AND PROGNOSIS

Anorexia Nervosa

Anorexia nervosa typically strikes in adolescence, with evidence indicating bimodal points of onset at ages 14 and 18 years (American Psychiatric Association, 1994). The course and outcome are highly variable. Some individuals recover after a single episode. Others continue to show fluctuating patterns of restoration of normal weight and

relapse. This fluctuating course is often punctuated by periods of hospitalization when these individuals' weight sinks to dangerously low levels. Still others gain weight but continue to experience bulimia nervosa or EDNOS. Finally, a significant minority never recover, and it is estimated that as many as 10% of patients may die from suicide or the medical complications of the disorder (American Psychiatric Association, 1994). In contrast to the other eating disorders discussed in this chapter, there are no well-established treatments that have been shown to promote lasting weight gain and recovery in these patients.

Bulimia Nervosa

Bulimia nervosa usually begins in adolescence or early adulthood. In most people binge eating develops during or after a period of restrictive dieting (Hsu, 1990), a consistent finding in clinical samples that has implicated dieting in the etiology of the disorder as discussed below. Nevertheless, results from the largest and best-controlled study of risk factors for bulimia nervosa in the general population have revealed that dieting was not an antecedent of binge eating in almost 20% of cases (Fairburn, 1994). Purging typically follows the onset of binge eating.

DSM-IV states that the course of the disorder is chronic or intermittent, with periods of remission alternating with binge eating or purging (American Psychiatric Association, 1994). Based on findings from their naturalistic study of clinic patients, Keller, Herzog, Lavori, Brodburn, and Mahoney (1992) concluded that the course is characterized by "extraordinarily high rates of chronicity, relapse, recurrence, and psychosocial morbidity" (p. 7). Other treatment reports have described more successful outcomes (Johnson-Sabine, Reiss, & Dayson, 1992; Mitchell et al., 1989). All of these studies have significant methodological limitations, however.

The only prospective study of the long-term outcome of bulimia nervosa, using state-of-the-art assessment, has shown that outcome is significantly determined by the type of treatment (Fairburn et al., 1995). This study compared the 5-year outcome of patients from two controlled-outcome studies comparing behavior therapy (BT), cognitive-behavioral therapy (CBT), and focal psychotherapy (FPT). The BT group had done poorly; 86% were diagnosed as having an eating disorder according to the *Diagnostic and Statistical Manual of Mental Disorders,* third edition, revised (DSM-III-R; American Psychiatric Association, 1987). These patients had improved significantly at the end of the 5-month treatment program, but they relapsed within a year. This pattern is similar to that described by Keller et al. (1992) in their naturalistic study of clinical outcome.

In contrast, patients who had been treated with CBT or FPT had fared well. The majority had maintained the impressive improvement they had shown at a 1-year follow-up (Fairburn, Jones, Peveler, Hope, & O'Connor, 1993), showing little tendency to relapse. Two-thirds no longer could be diagnosed with an eating disorder. These findings strongly dispute the notion that bulimia nervosa is a particularly refractory disorder that is marked by inevitable relapse. Specific psychological therapies do enable patients to make lasting recovery from this otherwise chronic disorder.

Binge-Eating Disorder

At this point little is known about the course of recurrent binge eaters who do not meet criteria for bulimia nervosa. Clinical reports indicate that the course is chronic, characterized by episodic and unsuccessful attempts to control binge eating and lose weight. In marked contrast to bulimia nervosa, a large percentage of patients with binge-eating disorder report that binge eating precedes dieting (Wilson et al., 1993). The prognosis for BED is good. Initial studies have shown that both psychological and pharmacological treatments are effective in the short term (Agras, 1993; Marcus, 1993). Even if BED is successfully treated, however, obese patients show no lasting weight loss (Agras et al., 1994). Furthermore, the bulk of the evidence indicates that the presence of BED in obese patients does not predict response to weight loss (Wilson, 1993c). The majority of studies to date have failed to show the purported negative effects of binge eating (de Zwaan, Nutzinger, & Schoenbeck, 1992; Marcus et al., 1990; Schlundt et al., 1991; Telch & Agras, 1993; Yanovski & Sebring, 1994). Marcus, Wing, and Hopkins (1988) reported greater relapse in obese binge eaters at 6-month follow-up, but not posttreatment or at 12-month follow-up. The only two studies that have shown that binge eating affects posttreatment weight loss had methodological shortcomings (Beliard, Kirschenbaum, & Fitzgibbon, 1992; Keefe, Wyshogrod, Weinberger, & Agras, 1984). It must be concluded that

to date there is no reliable effect of binge eating on weight loss.

EPIDEMIOLOGY

Prevalence

Although definitive epidemiological data are not yet available, the prevalence of eating disorders appears to have risen over recent decades (Fairburn, Hay, et al., 1993). In a study of nine girl's schools in England, Crisp, Palmer and Kalucy (1976) found severe anorexia nervosa in 1/200 (0.5%) girls under age 16 years, and 1/100 (1.0%) among those over 16 years. Varying rates have been found, according to method of detection, but recent studies using strict criteria have yielded estimates of prevalence between 0.2% and 0.8% (Hoek, 1993; Hsu, 1990). This figure increases among higher socioeconomic groups (Hsu, 1990; Jones, Fox, Babigian, & Hutton, 1980) and may be as high as 5% to 7% among adolescent dance or modeling students, whose vocational context puts a high premium on weight control (Garner & Garfinkel, 1980; Szmuckler, Eisler, Gillis, & Hayward, 1985).

While prevalence rates for bulimia nervosa range from 1% to 4.5% (Hoek, 1993; Hsu, 1990), the most sophisticated of recent studies have been consistent in finding a rate of about 1% among adolescent and young adult women in the general population (Fairburn & Beglin, 1990). In a recent British study specifically of an adolescent population, 1,010 14- to 16-year-old female high school students were interviewed (Johnson-Sabine, Wood, Patton, Mann, & Wakeling, 1988). Using strict criteria equivalent to the current DSM-IV purging subtype of bulimia nervosa, this study reported a prevalence rate of 1%. As with anorexia nervosa, bulimia nervosa appears to be more common in higher socioeconomic groups. There also appear to be higher rates among women at college, with recent studies reporting prevalence rates of 3% to 4% (Drenowski, Yee, & Krahn, 1988; Striegel-Moore, Silberstein, Frensch, & Rodin, 1989), and there are indications that the condition may be on the increase.

In two large multisite studies based on a self-report questionnaire, Spitzer and his colleagues reported a rate of 30% of BED in obese patients seeking weight-control treatment and 2% in community samples (Spitzer et al., 1992). In an analysis of a sample of 243 woman from their commu-

nity-based study, Fairburn, Hay, et al. (1993) found that 4.1% reported objective bulimic episodes (binges) once a week on average, and 1.7% reported episodes twice a week. They concluded that "binge eating, as defined in DSM-IV, does not appear to be a common behavior even among the group thought to be most at risk (i.e., young women)" (p. 134). Confidence can be had in these findings because the subjects were a representative sample from the population, and binge eating was assessed using the EDE interview rather than an unvalidated self-report questionnaire. The data from the Fairburn, Hay, et al. (1993) study also confirm earlier reports that recurrent binge eating (or BED) is more common in obese individuals.

Two general points should be noted regarding prevalence of eating disorders. First, there appears to be an overrepresentation of eating disorders among those who not do respond to or cooperate with prevalence studies. In the Johnson-Sabine et al. (1988) study of adolescents, for example, there were no cases of anorexia nervosa detected in the sample, but there were at least two among those who declined to participate. This has been detected in other studies and would suggest that our current figures may be underestimating the true prevalence of eating disorders (Fairburn & Beglin, 1994). Second, since prevalence rates in most studies are given only for cases meeting full diagnostic criteria, these do not provide a full picture of the degree of subclinical or "partial" morbidity in the population. This is particularly pertinent for eating disorders given the widely held-view that these lie at the extreme end of a continuum that begins with "normative" weight concern, body dissatisfaction, and dieting (Hsu, 1990). These concerns and dieting behaviors, which are increasingly widespread among young adolescents, may contribute significantly to later onset of eating disorders.

Gender Differences

Eating disorders occur predominantly in female individuals, although cases do exist among male individuals. The proportion of male anorexia nervosa cases is between 4% and 8% (Fichter & Hoffman, 1990; Herzog, Norma, Gordon, & Pepose, 1984). In a recent study, which differentiated between full and "partial" cases of bulimia nervosa, King (1989) found that the combined prevalence of these was 0.5% among men, compared to 3.9% among women. Among male college students, the

prevalence of bulimia nervosa is estimated to be between 0.2% and 1% depending on the measures used. The best-controlled research establishes that bulimia nervosa is rare among men (Fairburn, Hay, et al., 1993). Although obese binge eaters are predominantly women, the proportion of men with this problem is greater than in normal-weight bulimia nervosa (Marcus, 1993).

Although relatively little research has been conducted with male individuals, Schneider and Agras (1987) conducted a matched comparison of male and female cases with bulimia nervosa and reported that men were not significantly different from women on psychometric eating disorder measures such as the EAT (Eating Attitudes Test; Garner, Olmstead, Bohr, & Garfinkel, 1982) and the EDI (Eating Disorders Inventory; Garner, Olmstead, & Polivy, 1983), although they did exhibit a tendency toward less food preoccupation and drive for thinness. Since eating disorders may be underdiagnosed among men to some extent, because of a perception of these as being "female problems," those who work with adolescents should be aware of their existence in young men. In particular, it should be noted that while male individuals in general are at lower risk for eating disorders, gay adolescents and young men may be significantly more vulnerable (Heffernan, 1994).

Athletes

Physical condition and build are closely tied to performance in most athletic activities. Consequently, both male and female athletes are likely to engage in weight-control behaviors and abnormal eating for the purpose of enhancing performance, especially in sports such as horse racing or wrestling that require the meeting of specific weight thresholds and those such as gymnastics that require low body weight.

However, as King (1989) notes, it is important "to distinguish between behaviors (no matter how extreme) aimed principally at maintaining a low weight for reasons such as vocation, and the central psychopathology of an eating disorder" (p. 25). Thus, the significance of such behaviors for the athlete is the key: If the behavior is engaged in strictly for instrumental reasons, does not persist during off-season when performance pressure is lessened, and is not accompanied by the overvalued ideas about the importance of weight for self-evaluation characteristic of patients with eating disorders, then it is not a clini-

cally diagnostic phenomenon (Wilson & Eldredge, 1992).

At the same time, there are features of athletic competition that may contribute to the development of disordered eating in certain individuals, such as those whose natural body weight or family history of overweight presents significant difficulties in meeting low ideal weights. Men are less likely to be among the minority of athletes who do go on to develop an eating disorder, since they are more likely to engage in weight-control behavior solely for instrumental purposes and less likely to experience weight and shape as important aspects of their self-evaluation than women (Wilson & Eldredge, 1992).

Cultural Variations

It has long been observed that rates of eating disorders are lower among non-Caucasian populations, but recent evidence suggests that the incidence may be increasing among African-Americans (Hsu, 1987) and also among immigrants to western cultures as they become acculturated (Hsu, 1990). For example, in a study of 369 female high school students at English-medium schools in Pakistan, Mumford, Whitehouse, and Choudry (1992) looked at 1-year prevalence and only found one case of bulimia nervosa. In a study of 204 Indian and Pakistani high school students living in England, there were seven cases, amounting to a prevalence rate of 3.4% (Mumford, Whitehouse, & Platts, 1991). Similarly, a study that compared Arab students at Cairo University with those at London University, found higher levels of disturbed eating attitudes among those in London (Nasser, 1986). Although this finding is based on a self-report questionnaire, which cannot be assumed to function in the same manner across different populations (Fairburn & Beglin, 1990), and we do not know the degree of acculturation of either the Arab or Indian students, it does suggest that acculturation may increase risk.

Eating disorders do occur in non-Western cultures such as Japan and Malaysia, with the same concentration among female individuals of upper socioeconomic status (Hsu, 1990), although the prevalence is not known. A prevalence rate of 1.1% for bulimia nervosa (American Psychiatric Association, 1987) was reported among 509 college freshmen (male and female cases) in China (Chun et al., 1992). The low prevalence rate of 0.64% for anorexia nervosa and bulimia (American Psy-

chiatric Association, 1987) combined, including partial syndromes, among 1,234 seventh- to 12th-graders (male and female cases) on the island of Sao Miguel, Portugal, is attributed by the authors to the absence of social pressure to control eating and weight (deAzevedo & Ferreira, 1992).

ETIOLOGY

Biological Mechanisms

The biological factors involved in eating disorders are numerous. Because of the complex nature of eating and the mechanisms behind it, research into the biological aspects of eating disorders has had to examine the effects of dieting on neurobiology and neuroendocrine systems in addition to identifying biological abnormalities in patients with eating disorders. Since eating behavior can effect changes in neurobiology and vice versa, determining causality has been a problem for researchers examining the biological bases of eating disorders. In many cases it has not yet been determined whether the biological abnormalities seen in patients with eating disorders are secondary to the disregulated eating behavior or whether they play a causal role. It is clear, however, that there are a number of neurochemical disturbances that are associated with both anorexia nervosa and bulimia nervosa.

Anorexia Nervosa

Abnormalities in both the noradrenergic and serotonergic systems have been identified in anorexia nervosa. The difficulties in studying neurochemical disturbances in anorexia nervosa are compounded by low body weight. Because of the interactive nature of neurobiology, diet, and weight, determining which states are causal is highly difficult.

In general, studies have consistently reported low levels of cerebrospinal fluid (CSF) norepinephrine and its metabolite, MHPG, in patients with anorexia nervosa (Fava, Copeland, Schweiger, & Herzog, 1989). In the early stages of weight gain, norepinephrine levels appear to return to normal. These results have generally been interpreted as indicating that low norepinephrine concentrations in anorexia nervosa are the result of low body weight. A few studies, however, indicate that anorexics may enter treatment with normal or even elevated levels of norepinephrine,

although these levels appear to drop within the first few weeks of treatment and dietary stabilization (Lesem, George, Kaye, Goldstein, & Jimerson, 1989). Again, with weight gain, norepinephrine levels returned to normal. Lesem et al. (1989) hypothesize that elevated levels of norepinephrine may be influenced by such factors as the stress of dieting and intense exercise and that medical, metabolic, and psychological stabilization contribute to the decrease in norepinephrine levels as opposed to weight alone.

Although weight gain appears to return norepinephrine levels to normal in the short term (Fava et al., 1989), one study (Kaye, Ebert, Raleigh, & Lake, 1984) found that anorexic patients who had maintained weight gain for an extended period of time (20 + 7 months) showed a 50% lower level of CSF norepinephrine than normal controls, indicating possible trait disturbances in the noradrenergic systems of patients with anorexia nervosa.

Studies examining serotonergic functioning in anorexic patients have been somewhat inconsistent. While some studies have found reduced CSF levels of the serotonin metabolite 5-HIAA (Kaye, Ebert, Gwirtsman, & Weiss, 1984; Kaye, Gwirtsman, George, Jimerson, & Ebert, 1988), other studies have found normal ranges in anorexics (Gerner et al., 1984). Kaye et al. (1988) have hypothesized that this difference may result from the fact that the subjects in the Gerner et al. study had begun gaining weight, since weight gain in patients with anorexia nervosa is associated with a normalization of CSF 5-HIAA levels (Kaye et al., 1988). Anorexics who have maintained weight at normal levels for at least 6 months have exhibited elevated CSF 5-HIAA levels in one study (Kaye, Gwirtsman, George, & Ebert, 1991), possibly indicating increased brain serotonin activity. While the reasons for this finding remain unclear, it does lend support to hypothesized serotonergic disturbances.

Bulimia Nervosa

Disturbances in both the noradrenergic and serotonergic systems have also been observed in bulimia nervosa. Both systems are involved in the regulation of eating behavior with norepinephrine activating feeding in general and serotonin inhibiting it. The bingeing behavior observed in bulimia nervosa is consistent with disregulation in either or both of these systems (Kaye & Weltzin, 1991).

Disturbances in the noradrenergic systems of patients with bulimia nervosa have been a consistent finding. Studies have found lower levels of the norepinephrine metabolite MHPG in patients with bulimia nervosa as compared to controls (Pirke, 1990), reduced plasma and CSF norepinephrine concentrations (Kaye & Weltzin, 1991; Kaye, Ballenger, et al., 1990; Kaye, Gwirtsman, et al., 1990), and increased adrenoreceptor capacity (Kaye & Weltzin, 1991; Pirke, 1990).

Despite the consistent findings of noradrenergic system disturbance, it is still not clear if the norepinephrine alterations cause bulimia nervosa or are a result of pathological eating behavior (Kaye & Weltzin, 1991; Pirke, 1990).

In addition to disturbances in the noradrenergic systems, patients with bulimia nervosa also exhibit abnormalities in serotonin function. Serotonin plays a major role in inhibition of feeding. Serotonin agonists tend to produce satiety and decrease food intake, while serotonin antagonists increase meal size. The role of serotonin in the regulation of hunger and satiety has led researchers to hypothesize that bingeing behavior in bulimia nervosa is influenced by hyposerotonergic function (Jimerson, Brandt, & Brewerton, 1988; Kaye & Weltzin, 1991).

A number of studies support the hypothesis that bulimics have decreased serotonin activity (Jimerson, Lesem, Kaye, Hegg, & Brewerton, 1990; Kaye & Weltzin, 1991; Pirke, 1990), while others have found no significant difference between patients with bulimia nervosa and controls in serotonin metabolite CSF levels (Jimerson, Lesem, Kaye, & Brewerton, 1992). Recent findings, however, indicate that bingeing frequency may inversely correlate with serotonin metabolite levels. In other words, as bingeing frequency increases, serotonin metabolite levels decrease (Jimerson et al., 1992). This finding may indicate that the failure to find serotonin differences in some studies may be related to a lack of severity of bulimic symptoms in subjects.

Further support for the role of serotonin in bulimia nervosa can be found in studies of the serotonin precursor tryptophan. Tryptophan directly influences brain serotonin levels with an increase in the amount of tryptophan transported into the brain producing an increase in brain serotonin content. Tryptophan and the other five large neutral amino acids (LNAA) are actively transported across the blood–brain barrier by a common transport system. The larger the ratio of plasma tryptophan to the other LNAAs, the more tryptophan is transported to the brain. Dietary intake affects brain serotonin levels via tryptophan. Meals that are protein rich decrease the tryptophan/LNAA ratio, while carbohydrate-rich meals, mediated by the effects of insulin, increase the ratio. Thus, low-carbohydrate diets will produce lower brain serotonin levels (Kaye & Weltzin, 1991; Pirke, 1990). This dietary effect has been supported empirically in healthy dieters (Cowen, Anderson, & Fairburn, 1992), and bulimic patients have been found to have an unusually large drop in the plasma tryptophan: LNAA ratio after eating a protein-rich meal (Broocks, Fichter, & Pirke, 1988). In testing the neurochemical effects of dieting, Cowen, Anderson, and Fairburn (1992) found that women appear to be more sensitive to the tryptophan-depleting effects of a low carbohydrate diet than men. This may indicate a possible mechanism by which dieting leads into eating disorders, especially since women are more prone to dieting behaviors than men.

Jimerson et al. (1992) have hypothesized that low serotonin turnover may contribute to impaired satiety in bulimics. Although low levels of presynaptic serotonin would usually result in a compensatory increase in postsynaptic receptors (Goodwin, Fairburn, & Cowen, 1988; Delgado, Charney, Price, Landis, & Henninger, 1989), Jimerson et al. (1992) have found that the expected upregulation in receptor sensitivity is missing. They propose that binge eating increases the tryptophan:LNAA ratio, thus temporarily increasing brain serotonin and forestalling the compensatory response. Whether the initial hyposerotonergic state is causal or secondary to dieting (via the mechanism described above), however, is still unclear. It is conceivable that if dieting is the causal determinant in changing brain serotonin levels, once pathological eating has begun, a self-main-taining cycle may be engaged.

Genetic Influences

Genetic influences in eating disorders have been considered for over a century (Strober, 1991), although research into this area is a relatively new phenomenon. Both family and twin studies point to a genetic component in the development of eating disorders: However, the exact role that genetics play in the development of bulimia nervosa and anorexia nervosa is still a subject of speculation.

Anorexia Nervosa

Evidence for the role of genetics in the etiology of anorexia nervosa comes from two main sources, family and twin studies. Family studies, which assess the degree to which eating disorders cluster within families, have demonstrated a strong tendency for rates of both anorexia nervosa and bulimia nervosa to be elevated in the families of anorexic probands as compared to controls (Strober, 1991, 1995). Family studies have yielded rates of 2.0% of relatives to 4.1% of female relatives of anorexic probands as diagnosable with anorexia nervosa (Gershon et al., 1983; Strober, Lampert, Morrell, Burroughs, & Jacobs, 1990). These rates are considerably higher than estimates of the prevalence of anorexia nervosa in the general population, which is thought to be under 1% (Strober, 1991). Although two studies have failed to find elevated rates of eating disorders in the families of eating-disorder probands, both studies suffered from such methodological shortcomings as small sample size and indirect assessment of eating disorders in family members (Strober, 1995). Overall, family studies seem to implicate some familial role in the transmission of eating disorders and raise the possibility of a genetic predisposition to anorexia nervosa.

While family studies are useful in determining if genetics can be considered as a possible etiological factor in the development of a psychiatric disorder, they do not allow for a separation of environmental and genetic factors. In order to address this issue and to separate out the role of a common environment, researchers often turn to the study of twin pairs. Twin studies, which compare concordance rates of disorders between monozygotic (MZ) and dizygotic (DZ) twins, allow for a separation of environmental and genetic components.

Studies of twin pairs have evidenced greater concordance rates for MZ twins as compared with DZ twins for anorexia nervosa, indicating that genetics probably play an etiological role in the development of the disorder. Discrepancies in concordance have ranged from 55% to 83% of MZ twins as compared with 7% to 27% for DZ twins, respectively (Strober, 1991).

Strober (1991, 1995) has hypothesized that the genetic predisposition in anorexia nervosa may be expressed through genotypic personality structures. Research and clinical observation have indicated that certain personality traits seem to cluster in patients with anorexia nervosa. Strober argues that such anorexic traits as obsessional tendencies, rigidity, emotional restraint, preference for the familiar, and poor adaptability to change leave the anorexic individual at a disadvantage when negotiating adolescence and puberty. Anorexic symptomatology is thus seen as a defensive adaptation designed to deal with the conflict between adolescence and a need for order and predictability.

Bulimia Nervosa

Family studies of bulimic probands have produced conflicting results. While one study found a 9.6% rate of risk of bulimia nervosa among the relatives of bulimic probands as compared to 3.5% for relatives of controls, another study failed to find elevated rates of bulimia nervosa among the relatives of bulimic probands (Strober, 1991). Given the methodological shortcomings of the latter study (described above, in "General Influences"), it seems reasonable at this point to infer familial aggregation in bulimia nervosa.

Three studies have examined concordance rates between MZ and DZ twins for bulimia nervosa. Two of these studies suffered from methodological weaknesses such as very small sample sizes and a lack of blind diagnosis (Strober, 1995). The third examined over 1,000 female twin pairs obtained from a population-based register (Walters et al., 1992), thereby ensuring a representative sample. Clinical diagnoses were based on blind reviews of interviews. Findings showed a significantly higher concordance for MZ versus DZ twins, and unique environmental and genetic factors were each found to account for roughly half of the variance in liability. Common family environment was not found to play an etiological role.

In general, although family studies have produced some conflicting results, findings do seem to implicate genetic factors in the formation of bulimia nervosa.

Childhood Experiences

A variety of personal and familial factors have been put forward as causes of eating disorders, but until recently, none has received much empirical support. Speculation about etiological factors has been based mainly on clinical samples. This is an important limitation, however, because patients seeking treatment may not be representative of a majority of people with the disorder.

A recent study by the Oxford group has remedied this and other methodological deficiencies in a study of the etiology of bulimia nervosa (Fairburn, 1994). Using a case-control design, these investigators recruited a representative community-based sample of 102 cases of bulimia nervosa, together with 204 individually matched normal controls and 102 psychiatric controls. The latter comprised mainly cases of depression. This psychiatric control group is needed to identify specific risk factors.

Underscoring the importance of basing etiological analyses on community-based rather than clinical samples, the Oxford study revealed that roughly 75% of their sample had never received treatment for bulimia nervosa. It seems clear that we know most about what seems to be only a small subset of individuals with eating disorders who seek treatment. Another distinguishing feature of this well-designed study was the use of state-of-the-art clinical interviews for screening and assessing the prevalence of bulimia nervosa and its possible risk factors.

Several important findings have emerged from this research. It is popularly believed that early sexual abuse is a cause of bulimia nervosa, although empirical support for this belief has been lacking. The Oxford study found that childhood sexual abuse occurred more frequently in both the bulimia nervosa and psychiatric control subjects than in the normal controls. In other words, childhood sexual abuse is a general risk for psychopathology, but not a specific risk factor for bulimia nervosa. A study by Pope, Mangweth, Negrao, Hudson, and Cordas (1994) of community-based samples of women with bulimia nervosa in the United States, Austria, and Brazil, used more refined methodology and definitions than some recent studies to rate both severity of reported childhood sexual abuse and its relationship to severity of bulimic, depressive, and associated symptoms. They failed to find higher rates of childhood sexual abuse in the bulimia nervosa cohorts than in comparable studies of women in the general populations of each country (no comparable study was available for the Brazilian cohort). Their results did not support the hypothesis that women with bulimia nervosa might show similar basic rates of abuse as the general population but higher rates of severe or prolonged abuse, and those who had experienced abuse did not display greater severity of bulimia nervosa or associated psychopathology than their nonabused counterparts. In summary, 84% to 91% of the women with bulimia nervosa in this combined sample did not report childhood sexual abuse prior to the onset of an eating disorder.

Among other childhood experiences examined in the Oxford epidemiological study, negative self-evaluation, perfectionism, and shyness were identified as specific risk factors with attributable risks of 11%, 13%, and 15% respectively. Attributable risk refers to that proportion of cases in the population under study that is attributable to the individual risk factor. The salient role of shyness is at odds with the common view that patients with bulimia nervosa (binge/purgers) are impulsive, disinhibited stimulus seekers. Indeed, they seem more akin to Strober's (1995), description of the phenotypic personality structure of restricting anorexics.

Personal and Family Weight History

Clinical reports have indicated that patients with bulimia nervosa commonly have a history of being overweight prior to onset and are also more likely to come from families in which parents are overweight (Garfinkel, Moldofsky, & Garner, 1980). The Oxford epidemiological study has confirmed this association. Both subject and parental obesity proved to be specific risk factors, with sizable attributable risks. Moreover, there is evidence of a linear dose–response effect—the greater the severity of the obesity, the stronger the risk factor. The significance of this association is strengthened by two additional findings. The first is that the only two predictors of outcome from a 5-year follow-up of the psychological treatment of bulimia nervosa were patients' premorbid and parental obesity (Fairburn et al., 1995). The second is that a report of a 10-year follow-up of the behavioral treatment of childhood obesity (children between the ages of 6 and 12 years) noted what seems to be an unusually high rate of occurrence of bulimia nervosa (6% in girls) (Epstein, Valoski, Wing, & McCurley, 1994; Wilson, 1994).

A likely explanation of this finding is that a tendency toward being overweight makes it more difficult for these women to achieve or maintain the thinness that is culturally valued and therefore drives them to engage in more extreme weight-control measures (e.g., rigid dieting) that puts them at greater risk for bulimia nervosa.

The role of a personal or familial history of being overweight is less clear for anorexia nervosa. There is evidence, however, of a higher pre-

valence of overweight parents among the binge eating/purging subtype of anorexia nervosa patients (DaCosta & Halmi, 1992).

Family History of Psychopathology

As we noted in "Genetic Influences," the familial transmission of anorexia nervosa and bulimia nervosa is well-documented (Strober, 1995). Evidence from clinical samples of patients has suggested that a family history of depression or substance abuse is a risk factor for bulimia nervosa. The Oxford study has confirmed this association. Parental alcohol or drug abuse was a specific risk factor in this community-based sample. This conclusion is strengthened by Strober's (1995) data showing that relatives of patients with bulimia nervosa or the binge eating/purging subtype of anorexia nervosa had a three-to fourfold increase in their lifetime of substance abuse disorders compared with relatives both of normal controls and relatives of the restricting subtype anorexics.

Gender and the Sociocultural Context

The eating disorders are dramatically gender related. Our contemporary western sociocultural context is thought to determine this differential risk in direct and indirect ways. While the ideal female weight has decreased over recent decades, the average weight of women, and the prevalence of eating disorders, in the population has increased (Striegel-Moore, Silberstein, & Rodin, 1986). It is argued that the socialization of girls to evaluate themselves in terms of their appearance lays the groundwork for the low self-esteem and negative body image that results when they cannot meet this ideal and for dieting and other efforts to close the gap that may lead to disordered eating.

Studies have shown that weight concern is endemic among adolescent girls. Estimates of the percentage who have been on diets range from 30% to 80% (Dwyer, Feldman, Seltzer, & Mayer, 1969; Rosen & Gross, 1987). Moreover, there is evidence that concerns about being fat, and attitudes similar to those of older adolescents regarding physical attractiveness, are to be found in children as young as 7 or 8 years (Hsu, 1990; Striegel-Moore et al., 1986). This influence appears to be mediated by a differential emphasis on appearance and weight among girls and women of higher socioeconomic status (Striegel-Moore

et al., 1986). In a study of a representative sample of 7,524 girls 12 to 17 years old, Dornbusch et al. (1984) found that, controlling for weight, girls in the higher SES groups wanted to be thinner more often than those in the lower SES groups.

This intensification of vulnerability to social norms of attractiveness within certain societal subgroups may explain to some degree why it is that these norms appear to have more harmful impact on some women than others. Striegel-Moore et al. (1986) suggest that those at greatest risk "should be those who have accepted and internalized most deeply the sociocultural mores about thinness and attractiveness" (p. 247), and that certain environments increase the likelihood of this. As mentioned above, such environments include boarding schools and colleges, where social contagion increases the vulnerability of young, mostly upper- to middle-class women who represent the classes most at risk.

Sociocultural norms regarding attractiveness may be said to influence girls and women through their sex-role identification. Women's social conduct is shaped by pervasive notions of what it is to be "feminine," to be perceived, and to perceive oneself, as possessing the characteristics associated with the female sex-role stereotype. Striegel-Moore (1993) argues that two aspects of our contemporary female sex-role stereotype have particular relevance to women's risk for eating disorders. First, beauty is a central aspect of "femininity"; girls learn early on that being "pretty" is what draws attention and praise from others, and girls in books and on television focus on their appearance while boys are playing and "doing." Small wonder that, as early as fourth grade, body build and self-esteem are correlated for girls but not for boys (Striegel-Moore et al., 1986). A second aspect is women's interpersonal orientation. According to contemporary psychology of women theorists, a woman's identity is organized as a "self-in-relation," and her self-worth is closely tied to the establishing and maintenance of close relationships (Jordan, Kaplan, Miller, Stiver, & Surrey, 1991; Miller, 1976). Thus, women's self-concept is interpersonally constructed: girls' self-descriptions at age 7 years have been found to be more based on the perceptions of others than are boys' self-descriptions (Striegel-Moore et al., 1986). Consequently, women are said to derive significant self-worth from other's opinions and approval of them; and in our culture, social approval is significantly related to physical attractiveness (Hatfield & Sprecher, 1985). Research has consistently shown

a significant correlation between self-esteem and feelings about one's body, especially in women, for whom it is significantly related to how they are evaluated by others (Hsu, 1990). A recent study found that even lesbians, who generally take a more critical stance toward sociocultural norms regarding women and female sex-role stereotypes, were not significantly different from heterosexual women in their attitudes about weight. Self-esteem was strongly related to feelings about one's body, and the prevalence of bulimia nervosa among lesbians was similar to that of heterosexual women (Heffernan, in press).

Given the socially constructed centrality of appearance and weight for girls and women, we need to ask next what it is about the passage through adolescence that amplifies its salience and contributes to the emergence of anorexia nervosa and bulimia nervosa specifically during this period.

Female Adolescent Development: Changes and Challenges

No single variable explains the onset of eating disorders, but research indicates that certain developmental transitions may help to explain the increased risk during adolescence.

Physical Maturation

While physical maturation for boys involves the development of muscle and lean tissue, girls experience weight gain in the form of increased fat tissue during this period, which moves them further away from the culture's lean physical ideal (Striegel-Moore et al., 1986). Onset of menarche and breast development also occur at this time and have been found to be associated with increased dieting among 7th- to 10th-graders, independent of age (Attie & Brooks-Gunn, 1989). Recent research has confirmed that early menarche is a specific risk factor for bulimia nervosa (Fairburn, 1994).

The task of integrating these changes into one's changing self-image, may be especially difficult for "early developers." In addition to earlier weight gain than peers, which may prompt dieting, adjustment problems may result from parents who react with concern to their daughter's early sexual maturation (Hsu, 1990), or alternatively, from increased freedom to engage in experiences for which she may not be sufficiently mature cognitively or emotionally to cope (Striegel-Moore, 1993).

Development of Intimate Relationships

Some adolescent women may also feel ill-prepared for initiation of adult sexual behaviors, and their anxiety may be heightened by parental unreadiness for this transition into womanhood in their daughter. The view that eating disorders represent phobic avoidance of adult sexuality (Crisp, 1980) has not been established empirically, however.

Development of Sense of Self

One of the psychosocial tasks of adolescence is the formation of one's own, coherent identity. Consistent with the characterizations of women's self-concept as interpersonally oriented, female adolescents have been found to be more self-conscious and concerned with how others view them than males are (Striegel-Moore et al., 1986). Identity deficits have long been a focus of theories regarding the development of eating disorders. Bruch (1973), for example, believed anorexia nervosa to involve underlying deficits of sense of self and autonomy, feelings of paralyzing ineffectiveness, emptiness and lack of emotional awareness; although there is a lack of data here, recent studies have found elevated levels of personal ineffectiveness, lack of interoceptive awareness, and interpersonal distrust (Garner, Olmstead, Polivy, & Garfinkel, 1984). Patton (1988) reported that social difficulties and introversion, which Hsu (1990) takes to indicate poor identity formation, among 1,010 high school girls were associated with eating disturbances at 1-year follow-up. Striegel-Moore's (1993) suggestion that girls whose identity is insecure, and who are concerned about how others view them, may focus on physical appearance as a concrete way to construct an identity, is persuasive.

Dieting

In a society that prescribes dieting for those who do not meet its prepubertal body ideal, those who are naturally heavier may be at increased risk for the consequences of repeated unsuccessful dieting. Several lines of evidence show that dieting is closely linked to the onset and maintenance of eating disorders.

Clinical reports indicate that virtually all patients have a history of dieting prior to the onset of binge eating (Pyle et al., 1990). Dieting here refers to rigid and unhealthy restriction of over-

all caloric intake, skipping meals, and excessive avoidance of specific foods in order to influence body weight and shape. Laboratory studies have shown that chronic dieting can predispose to disinhibition of dietary restraint in the face of the consumption of high calorie food. This phenomenon is known as the counterregulation effect and has been seen as an analogue of binge eating (Polivy & Herman, 1993). Studies have compared the amount of food eaten by dieters and nondieters after an actual or perceived high-calorie preload. Nondieters tend to regulate their eating so that those who have been given a preload eat less in a subsequent taste test than those who have not, but dieters either fail to regulate in this manner, or eat more following the preload. The same disinhibition appears to be triggered by negative emotional states, and there is also evidence that the effect is cognitively mediated: a dieter's belief that she has overeaten, or "blown it," may be sufficient to trigger counterregulation (Polivy & Herman, 1993). It should be noted, however, that the robustness of the counterregulation effect, and its relevance to binge eating, has been criticized (Charnock, 1989; Lowe, 1993).

A prospective study of 1,010 teenage girls in England found that 21% of those who had been dieting at the time of initial interview had developed an eating disorder by 1-year follow-up, compared to only 3% of nondieters (Patton, 1988). Other factors such as increased weight, dieting in the family and family psychological history, introversion, and social difficulties were also predictive, but the prospective nature of this study provides clear evidence that dieting, in the presence of other risk factors, may have a direct effect on the onset of an eating disorder. The Oxford study that we summarize here (Fairburn, 1994) focused on risk factors that operate before the development of behavioral precursors of bulimia nervosa. Persistent dieting was regarded as one such precursor, so it is excluded in the analyses of risk factors. But consistent with prior research on dieting as a risk factor, dieting was the initial characteristic of bulimia nervosa in the majority (80%) of cases.

How is it that dieting leads to overeating in this way? And how is it that this increases the risk for the development of an eating disorder? The answer may lie in the biological and psychological sequelae of dieting. Significant decreases in caloric intake result in reduced metabolic rate, so that weight loss is in fact impeded, setting the stage for a vicious cycle of increased dieting and

consequent vulnerability to binge eating. The psychological consequences of severe dietary restriction also contribute to this cycle, creating a sense of deprivation and increased vulnerability to loss of control; once control is "lost" and binge eating occurs, purging may be seen as a way to counteract the perceived effects of binge eating on weight gain, but it is invariably followed by disgust and self-recrimination, which prompts renewed vows of abstinence, and sets the stage for the whole cycle to begin again.

The role of dieting in the development of eating disorders is now widely accepted. Some clinicians have gone so far as to suggest that we should refer to "dieting disorders" rather than eating disorders. But the contribution of dieting must be placed in perspective. It is not a sufficient cause of eating disorders. A majority of young women in North America diet in order to influence body weight and shape. Yet only a small minority of women develop an eating disorder. Dieting is a risk factor, but a relatively weak one. Clearly, it must interact with some other biological or psychological vulnerabilities in precipitating an eating disorder.

Nor is dieting a necessary causal condition for the development of an eating disorder. Although clinicians rarely see a case of bulimia nervosa where dieting was not a proximal antecedent of the onset of binge eating, there are data showing that the disorder can develop in the absence of dieting. It is important to note that, in 20% of cases in the Oxford epidemiological study, dieting was not the initial feature of the development of bulimia nervosa (Fairburn, 1994).

Dieting is presumed to lead to loss of control and hence to binge eating. But this cannot explain the restrictor subtype of anorexia nervosa, those patients who do not binge despite near starvation. The mechanisms whereby these individuals successfully restrict food intake without loss of control remain unknown (Garner, 1993).

Finally, the role of dieting is less clear in BED in the obese than in the development of the binge-eating/purging subtype of anorexia nervosa and bulimia nervosa. In cases of the former, many and in some studies a majority, report having developed binge eating before dieting (Raymond, Mussell, Mitchell, de Zwaan, & Crosby, 1995; Wilson et al., 1993). Obese binge eaters show significantly less dietary restraint than patients with bulimia nervosa (Marcus, Smith, Santelli, & Kaye, 1992; Rossiter et al., 1992). Yanovski and Sebring (1994) found that obese binge eaters reported greater

average food intake than nonbingers on both a total (2,707 vs. 1,869 kcal/day) and weight-adjusted basis, with higher intake on nonbinge days. The latter pattern stands in marked contrast to bulimia nervosa patients. Furthermore, several studies have shown that obese binge eaters do not differ from obese nonbingers on the Cognitive Restraint subscale of the Stunkard and Messick (1985) Eating Inventory (EI) (Marcus et al., 1988; Rossiter et al., 1992; Wadden, Foster, Letizia, & Wilk, 1993). Lowe and Caputo (1991) found that scores on this measure were inversely related to binge eating in obese patients.

If binge eating is not a consequence of periodic breakdowns in overly restrictive dieting, what accounts for it? Clinical experience suggests that binge eating is a source of negative reinforcement. Patients commonly report that negative emotional states trigger eating episodes and that the binge eating serves to dampen the distress, at least in the short run. In this sense, binge eating does seem functionally equivalent to other maladaptive behaviors such as substance abuse.

Individual Personality Characteristics

Theorists since Bruch (1973) have described patients with anorexia nervosa as perfect and compliant children, lacking in an autonomous sense of self, for whom affective overcontrol and obsessiveness are an attempt to compensate for these core deficiencies (Crisp, 1980; Palazzoli, 1985). While these reports are largely anecdotal and often retrospective, they have consistently been a part of the clinical impressions of this population. Although objective studies are sparse, partly because of the difficulty of separating stable personality factors from those that result from the illness, Strober (1980) has found confirmation for greater conformity, obsessiveness, control of emotionality, lack of personal effectiveness and adaptation to the maturational challenges of adolescence, and need for social approval, among young women with anorexia nervosa.

We have mentioned that Strober (1995) views the genetic predisposition in anorexia nervosa as possibly expressed through a phenotypic personality structure. The personality characteristics he describes in the restricting and binge-eating/purging subtypes of eating disorders correspond somewhat to the Type I and Type II personality subgroups of alcoholics, described by Cloninger (1987). The extremes of emotional constraint, avoidance of intense or novel experience, and

focus on external validation of patients with restricting anorexia parallel the low novelty seeking, high harm avoidance, and high reward dependence of the Type I subtype. The stimulus seeking and affective lability of the binge-eating/purging subtype more resemble the high novelty seeking, low harm avoidance, and low reward dependence profile of the Type II.

Although Strober (1995) hypothesizes that anorexia nervosa may result from a phenotypic personality pattern that is ill-suited to the developmental challenges of adolescence, this diathesis is not in itself sufficient. Its particular behavioral expression in an individual depends upon interaction with environmental factors such as an emphasis on physical appearance in the family, or exposure to drinking.

While it appears that women with bulimia nervosa (and perhaps the binge-eating/purging subtype of anorexia) also have a high need for approval (Katzman & Wolchik, 1984), clinical impressions and correlational data suggest that they differ from anorexia nervosa patients in exhibiting greater affective instability and poor impulse control (Johnson & Connors, 1987). It is important to note, however, that while there seems to be some evidence that the binge-eating/purging subtype of anorexia nervosa may be associated with more severe personality problems (DaCosta & Halmi, 1992), there is no evidence to support the existence of a "bulimic" personality type. As Tobin (1993) notes, "given that dieting, binge eating, and even self-induced vomiting are normative in western culture . . . it is no surprise that the clinical presentation of bulimic symptoms occurs with every possible personality structure" (p. 301).

The Role of the Family

Families of daughters with anorexia nervosa have been portrayed as being concerned with external appearances, anxious to maintain a show of harmony and solidarity at the expense of open communication and expression of negative feelings, disinclined to acknowledge preferences and needs, and often speaking for one another as if they could read each other's minds (Bruch, 1973, 1978; Minuchin, Rosman, & Baker, 1978; Palazzoli, 1985; Stierlin & Weber, 1989).

In an early observational study, Minuchin and his colleagues (1978) identified five characteristic patterns of interaction in families of adolescents with anorexia nervosa: (1) enmeshment

characterizes families where members are over-involved with one another, and personal boundaries are easily crossed; (2) overprotectiveness hinders children's development of autonomous functioning; (3) rigidity causes families to feel threatened by changes that come with puberty and adolescence in their daughters; (4) conflict avoidance; and (5) poor conflict resolution also characterize these families. Minuchin and colleagues portrayed the daughter with anorexia nervosa as a "regulator" in the family system, over-involved in parental conflict as either the object of diverted conflict, or drawn into coalition with one parent against the other.

Despite the echoing of these characteristics in the family literature, reliable empirical data are fragmentary (Strober & Humphrey, 1987) and inconclusive (e.g., Calam, Waller, Slade, & Newton, 1990; Waller, Slade, & Calam, 1990). A recent study (Kog, Vandereycken, & Vertommen, 1985) that attempted to operationalize the patterns of Minuchin et al. (1978), found high levels of en-meshment in families of both anorexia nervosa and bulimia nervosa patients, but evidence for the other patterns was weak, and there was considerable variability in its small sample of families. More importantly, the lack of controlled prospective studies makes it difficult to distinguish whether these family characteristics are a cause or consequence of the eating disorder.

While it may not be possible to demonstrate relationships of causality, recent observational studies provide some correlational evidence for the existence of disturbed family interaction patterns. Using the Structural Analysis of Behavior (SASB; Benjamin, 1979), a self-report measure of interpersonal transactions and their intrapsychic representations, Humphrey (1987, 1989) has analyzed these patterns in families among various eating-disorder subgroups.

Humphrey (1989) used the SASB to discriminate bulimic–anorexic families (American Psychiatric Association, 1980) from control families. Coding of videotaped family discussions about the patient's separation from the family revealed a significantly higher incidence of "ignoring and walling off" and belittling behavior on the part of the parents. There was also a higher incidence of negative, contradictory communication, and less trusting, helping, and nurturing. In studies comparing the perceptions of daughters with normal-weight bulimia, bulimic anorexia, restricting anorexia, and normal controls, Humphrey (1987) found more overt distress, expression of hostility,

and impulsivity, more severe deficits in empathy, understanding, and nurturance, more blaming of each other by mothers and daughters, and more perception of fathers as controlling by resentful daughters with bulimia and bulimic anorexia, than those with restricting anorexia. The latter were more distressed than controls and reported double messages of affection and caring with enmeshment and neglect of daughter's needs for expression, but they tended to downplay these deficits, presenting a facade of what Humphrey calls "pseudo-mutuality," which may keep conflict less overt in these families compared to those of the daughters with bulimia.

Strober and Humphrey (1987) argue that such family environments impede healthy psychological development in teens with eating disorders. They suggest, for example, that bulimia may be partially mediated by self-efficacy and self-regulation deficits stemming from the family environment described above, which may create behavioral deficits in coping with negative affective states. However, it has yet to be shown that such dysfunctional interaction patterns are pathognomic of eating disorders, or that they can account for the occurrence of an eating disorder rather than any other symptomatic reaction. For now, their importance may lie in helping to explain how families may play a role in sustaining or reinforcing certain aspects of the disorders, which makes them an important dimension of the treatment of adolescents within a family system.

Finally, the family functions to some extent as a mediator of the sociocultural values described earlier. Striegel-Moore et al. (1986) hypothesize that risk may be increased if family members (particularly female ones) model weight preoccupation and dieting, if weight is a form of evaluation and thinness valued, and also if weight is believed to be something one can and should control. There are fewer studies of this more "ordinary" influence from the family, but Pike and Rodin (1991) found elevated scores on measures of disordered eating among girls whose mothers were more critical of their daughters' weight, compared to those whose mothers were accepting of their daughters' appearance. Along with Attie and Brooks-Gunn (1989), Pike and Rodin (1991) reported that mothers who diet are significantly more likely to have daughters who diet. In fact, both mothers and fathers on diets have been found to be significantly more likely to encourage dieting in their child, than parents who are not dieting (Striegel-Moore & Kearney-Cooke, in press).

The Oxford study (Fairburn, 1994) provides solid support for the influence of family dieting as a risk factor. The study further found that critical comments about patients' weight, shape, or eating, in addition to absence of, or tension during, family meals are specific factors that account for a sizable portion of risk for later bulimia nervosa. The study also reports that a number of more general aspects of parenting were surprisingly specific risk factors. These were frequent parental absence, underinvolvement, high expectations, criticism, and discord between parents. Thus, even though the possibility of recall bias in patients is acknowledged, this methodologically sophisticated study provides welcome empirical substantiation of family variables that have been implicated in previous theory and research on the etiology of bulimia nervosa.

COMMON COMORBIDITIES

Eating disorders co-occur with a number of other disorders, and lifetime prevalence studies indicate that individuals with eating disorders are likely to exhibit the symptoms of other psychological disorders throughout their lifetime. Although a number of theories have been proposed to link eating disorders and such disorders as depression and substance abuse via a common etiology, many such theories have been discredited (Kennedy & Garfinkel, 1992; Strober & Katz, 1987; Wilson, 1991). Thus, while eating disorders frequently co-occur and share specific features with other disorders, most findings indicate that they are a separate and distinct class of psychological disorders.

Anorexia Nervosa

Anorexia nervosa and substance abuse have been found to co-occur with prevalence rates of substance abuse in patients with anorexia nervosa ranging from 6.7% to 23% (Wilson, 1991). Although these numbers suggest a lower rate of substance abuse in anorexia nervosa as compared with bulimia nervosa, differences emerge depending on the subtype of anorexia nervosa studied. Findings have consistently reported significantly higher levels of substance abuse for the binge-eating/purging subtype as compared with the restricting subtype of anorexia nervosa (Wilson, 1991). For example, Laessle, Kittl, Fichter, Wittchen, and Pirke (1987) reported a 20%

rate of alcohol abuse or dependence in the binge-eating/purging subtype compared with 0% in the restricting subtype. Similarly, Jonas, Gold, Sweeney, and Pottash (1987) have reported finding a rate of 7% for anorexia nervosa bulimic subtype as compared to 2% restrictor subtype among a sample of 259 cocaine abusers.

Of all the anxiety disorders, obsessive–compulsive disorder (OCD) has been most frequently linked with anorexia nervosa. Obsessional tendencies in anorexia nervosa have been noticed by numerous observers and have been reported to predate the development of anorexia nervosa and to exist after weight restoration (Kaye, Weltzin, & Hsu, 1993). In a long-term follow-up study of anorexics, Toner, Garfinkel, and Garner (1988) reported finding that 26.7% of symptomatic anorexics, 38.5% of improved anorexics, and 36.8% of asymptomatic anorexics evidenced lifetime OCD; in addition, each group showed a prevalence rate of over 15% within the previous year. Among a sample of obsessive–compulsive patients, Rubenstein, Pigott, L'Heureux, Hill, and Murphy (1992) found that 9.7% met criteria for lifetime anorexia nervosa and that an additional 12.9% qualified for subthreshold lifetime anorexia nervosa. Similarly, Fahy, Osacar, and Marks (1993) reported finding a lifetime prevalence of anorexia nervosa in 11% of 105 normal-weight OCD patients.

Although a specific relationship between OCD and anorexia nervosa has been explored, anxiety disorders in general co-occur with anorexia nervosa. In their long-term follow-up study, Toner et al. (1988) found lifetime anxiety disorder rates to range from 47.4% to 73% in asymptomatic anorexics as compared to symptomatic anorexics respectively. Similarly, Halmi et al. (1991) found a lifetime anxiety disorder prevalence rate of 64.5 among a sample of 62 patients with a known history of anorexia nervosa. Prevalence rates among this sample varied as a function of current eating-disorder diagnosis.

The high rates of anxiety disorders in anorexia nervosa have been used to argue against a specific relationship between eating disorders and affective disorders (Fornari et al., 1992), although findings consistently show higher rates of depression as compared to anxiety disorders in anorexics (Fornari et al., 1992; Halmi et al., 1991; Herzog, Keller, Sacks, Yeh, & Lavori, 1992). Probably the most commonly cited comorbidity, depression, has been reported to co-occur with acute anorexia frequently, with prevalence rates ranging from 21% to 91% (Kaye et al., 1993). Problems with

interpretation of these findings, however, have been pointed out since many of the symptoms associated with starvation closely resemble those of depression (Kaye et al., 1993).

In an attempt to clarify the relationship between affective disorders and anorexia nervosa, some researchers have attempted to examine the rates of depression in anorexics after treatment. Toner et al. (1988) found no significant difference in the rates of affective disorders between symptomatic, improved, and asymptomatic anorexics for the year prior to assessment, indicating that the relationship between anorexia and affective disorders does extend beyond the secondary effects of starvation. Given the difficulty of differential diagnosis in emaciated individuals, however, Toner et al. (1988) caution that findings with regard to symptomatic subjects should be interpreted with caution. A number of studies have also examined rates of comorbidity between personality disorders and eating disorders. Although the effects of a co-occurring personality disorder in eating-disorder patients have not yet been firmly established, some evidence does suggest that such comorbidity may be associated with a poorer prognosis (Skodol et al., 1993). In general, although most studies find that personality disorders do co-occur with eating disorders, reported rates of personality disorders in eating-disorder samples range from 27% to 93% (Skodol et al. 1993). In an attempt to address some of the inconsistencies in the literature, Skodol et al. (1993) examined two populations of patients who were likely to have personality disorders. Patients with and without a lifetime history of eating disorders were then compared. Using conservative, consensus diagnosis, this study found personality disorders in 74% of those patients with a lifetime eating disorder as compared to 42% of those with no lifetime eating disorder. Anorexia nervosa was strongly associated with the Cluster C personality (avoidant, dependent, and obsessive–compulsive) disorders in general, and specifically with avoidant personality disorder.

Bulimia Nervosa

Many analogies have been drawn between bulimia nervosa and addictive disorders. On the surface, the pattern of bingeing exhibited by bulimics seems to share many features with substance abuse. Studies have, in fact, found that eating disorders and substance abuse co-occur to a degree greater than that predicted by chance.

Studies of normal-weight individuals with eating disorders consistently reveal significantly higher rates of past and present substance-abuse problems than in the general population, and lifetime prevalence rates of substance abuse in individuals with bulimia nervosa range from 9% to 55% (Wilson, 1991).

This apparent relationship between bulimia nervosa and substance abuse might simply reflect an increased tendency for persons with more than one problem to find their way into treatment. However, Kendler et al. (1991), in their examination of over 1,000 female twin pairs obtained from a population-based register, found that of the 123 subjects with bulimia nervosa, 15.5% had a lifetime diagnosis of alcoholism. These results indicate that bulimia nervosa and alcohol abuse co-occur even in the general population, and that earlier reports of co-occurrence are not simply a result of sample bias.

Even if a relationship between eating disorders and substance abuse does exist, there is the question of whether this association is a specific one. If eating disorders and substance abuse do occur together, then there should be a higher frequency of eating problems in individuals with substance-abuse problems. This association has been found. In the largest study, Higuchi, Suzuki, Yamada, Parrish, and Kono (1993) reported finding that 11% of female probands and 0.2% of male probands in a sample of 3,592 patients admitted for alcohol abuse or dependence also had an eating disorder. In another study, 29% of 259 consecutive callers to the National Cocaine Hotline were found also to meet DSM-III-R criteria for bulimia or bulimia and anorexia nervosa combined (Jonas et al., 1987).

Several explanations have been proposed to explain the possible relationship between eating disorders and substance abuse. Perhaps the most popular view is that a common genetic or biological vulnerability exists in some people, although its nature has yet to be determined. Another possible explanation is reciprocal reinforcement.

Laboratory studies with animals have demonstrated that limiting food quantities results in the animals consistently feeding themselves alcohol. Humans may also increase their drug and/or alcohol consumption when deprived of food. This may be particularly true of persons who have bulimia nervosa, since these individuals tend to eat very little between binges. Thus, self-imposed dietary restriction may have two major effects: First, it may increase the desirability of highly

palatable, binge foods and prompt binge eating; and second, it might increase the attractiveness of alternative reinforcers, such as alcohol and drugs, leading to abuse. An alternative proposal is that both binge eating and substance abuse are different expressions of some form of an underlying problem. At this point, a clear answer does not exist. Additional research will be needed to determine the link between eating disorders and substance abuse.

Anxiety disorders are also frequently found to co-occur with bulimia nervosa, although findings vary as to prevalence rates (Schwalberg, Barlow, Alger, & Howard, 1992). Laessle et al. (1987) reported finding at least one anxiety disorder in 56% of a sample of 39 patients with bulimia nervosa, and Hudson, Pope, Yurgelun-Todd, Jonas, and Frankenburg (1987) found a 43% rate of anxiety disorders among 70 patients. Herzog et al. (1992), however, only found anxiety disorders in 20% of a sample of 98 patients with bulimia nervosa. Rates of panic disorder among bulimics have been found to range from 2% to 41% (Schwalberg et al., 1992), and reported rates of OCD range from 3% to 80% (Mitchell, Specker, & de Zwaan, 1991). Lifetime prevalence rates of OCD of 43% have also been reported (Fornari et al., 1992). While fewer studies have examined the rates of eating disorders in patients with anxiety disorders, Rubenstein et al. (1992) found the lifetime prevalence of bulimia nervosa among a sample of patients with OCD to be 4.8% with an additional 11.3% of subjects showing subthreshold lifetime bulimia nervosa. Surprisingly, in this sample, rates of bulimia nervosa did not significantly differ between male and female subjects.

In an attempt to address the inconsistencies in the literature, Schwalberg and colleagues (1992) examined 20 bulimia nervosa patients, 20 social phobics, and 20 individuals with panic disorder for comorbidity between eating and anxiety disorders. Seventy-five percent of the bulimics assessed met DSM-III-R criteria for an additional diagnosis of one or more anxiety disorders; the most commonly diagnosed anxiety disorders in this population were generalized anxiety disorder and social phobia (Schwalberg et al., 1992). Elevated levels of eating disorders among anxiety-disorder subjects were not found, arguing against a simple relationship between eating disorders and anxiety disorders (Schwalberg et al., 1992). Given the range of findings regarding anxiety-disorder comorbidity prevalence rates among individuals with eating disorders, Schwalberg et al. (1992) caution that problems with differential diagnosis between anxiety disorders and eating disorders may lead to unreliability in studies examining such comorbidity.

Affective disorders and eating disorders have been commonly linked. Studies have found lifetime affective disorder prevalence rates among individuals with eating disorders ranging from 24% to 88% (Mitchell et al., 1991). Herzog et al. (1992) found that 50% of a sample of 98 bulimic patients met criteria at intake for at least one affective disorder with 63% being accounted for by major depression, and Fornari and colleagues (1992) reported that 52.4% of their bulimia nervosa sample met criteria for a lifetime major depressive disorder. Schwalberg et al. (1992), however, found no significant difference between the lifetime prevalence rates of affective disorders between individuals with bulimia nervosa, social phobia, or panic disorder, thus raising the possibility that the connection between affective disorders and eating disorders is nonspecific.

Although some recent studies indicate that affective disorders may be no more common among bulimia nervosa patients than are anxiety disorders (Fornari et al., 1992), a number of researchers have argued that affective disorders and eating disorders are linked by a causal mechanism (Mitchell et al., 1991; Strober & Katz, 1987); others, however, have challenged this idea (Mitchell et al., 1991; Strober & Katz, 1987). One recent study has shed some light on the relationship between depression and bulimia nervosa. In an analysis of the data generated by the twin study of 1,033 female twin pairs (described above), Walters et al. (1992) examined the role of unique environment and genetics in the development of bulimia nervosa and major depression. Unique environment refers to environmental factors that are unique for each individual in a twin pair. While unique environmental factors accounted for roughly half of the variation in both disorders, these factors were unrelated between the disorders. Thus, the unique environmental factors that contribute to bulimia nervosa are specific and do not appear to contribute to depression and vice versa. Genetic factors, which also accounted for roughly half of the variation in both disorders, however, did not appear to be as specific. The genetic liabilities of the two disorders were correlated at .46, suggesting that some genes are influential in both disorders. As a result, this study implies that there is some genetic overlap be-

tween the two disorders, although bulimia and depression are clearly not identical conditions, since a portion of the genetic factors and all of the unique environmental factors appear to be specific to each disorder.

A number of studies have examined the prevalence of personality disorders in bulimia nervosa. On the surface, it appears that binge eating may be indicative of a general impulsivity such as that associated with some personality disorders (Skodol et al., 1993). Studies examining the relationship between bulimia and borderline personality disorder, however, have produced inconsistent results with prevalence rates of borderline personality disorder ranging from as little as 2% to over 50% in patients with bulimia (Skodol et al., 1993). Overall, reported prevalence rates of personality disorders in individuals with bulimia range from 33% to 77% (Skodol et al., 1993).

Skodol et al. (1993) have reported findings regarding the relationship between bulimia nervosa and specific personality disorders. In their study, current and lifetime bulimia nervosa was found to be significantly associated with both schizotypal and borderline personality disorders. Avoidant personality disorder was associated with lifetime, but not current, bulimia. The strongest association between bulimia and a specific personality disorder was found with borderline personality disorder. Overall, bulimia nervosa was significantly associated with the Cluster B personality disorders (antisocial, borderline, histrionic, and narcissistic) in general, and lifetime bulimia was also associated with Cluster C disorders.

Binge-Eating Disorder

Studies have consistently shown significantly greater levels of psychopathology in obese binge eaters compared with obese nonbingers. Marcus et al. (1990) found that 60% of obese binge eaters had a history of at least one psychiatric disorder, as opposed to 28% of nonbingers. Schwalberg et al. (1992) found a 60% lifetime prevalence of affective disorder and a 70% lifetime rate of anxiety disorders in their sample of obese binge eaters (Hudson et al., 1987; Yanovski, Nelson, Dubbert, & Spitzer, 1992). Obese binge eaters and nonbingers do not appear to differ in frequency of alcohol use or abuse (Wilson, 1991). de Zwaan et al. (1994) found that binge-eating severity was significantly associated with ineffectiveness and perfectionism as measured by the Eating Disorder Inventory, as well as with poorer self-esteem

and greater impulsivity. In general, significant findings were from those subjects meeting criteria for BED and not from subjects who were bingeing at lower levels.

FUTURE DIRECTIONS

Diagnosis and Classification

The current diagnostic controversy is the status of BED. If nothing else, the publication in DSM-IV (American Psychiatric Association, 1994) of specific criteria for this disorder will stimulate research on the validity and utility of the proposed diagnosis. Recent research using sophisticated cluster analysis does not provide support for this diagnosis. But it is clear that there are many individuals who suffer from recurrent binge eating that goes beyond the diagnosis of bulimia nervosa. How best to conceptualize this recurrent binge eating, and its relationship to obesity, will be an important area of future investigation. More generally, the category of EDNOS as a whole requires elaboration and refinement. The hope is that modified diagnostic criteria for the eating disorders will emerge based more on controlled empirical research than has been the case in the past.

Etiology

The literature abounds with proposals for putative etiologies of eating disorders. In most instances, these are based on retrospective clinical reports or cross-sectional studies. We need the necessary prospective studies now to follow up on these leads and sort out cause from correlation and consequence. We know that dieting is a risk factor for anorexia nervosa and bulimia nervosa. Although a very common proximal antecedent of binge eating, it is neither necessary nor sufficient. There is perhaps no more important issue to pursue than to identify those factors with which dieting interacts in precipitating an eating disorder.

Prevention

There is considerable interest in developing programs that prevent eating disorders. Most proposals focus on intervening in elementary or middle school curricula (Shisslak, Crago, Neal, & Swain, 1987). The problem, however, is that we do not yet know enough about the causes of eat-

ing disorders, or even their risk factors, to design effective interventions. Dieting is often discussed as a possible target of preventive programs, but most young women in our society diet. Thus, a prevention program would have to be aimed somewhat indiscriminately at most girls. It is premature to rush into investing in costly prevention programs that have insufficient theoretical or empirical justification.

The preferred approach is to pursue research on risk factors so that we can identify those children or adolescents who are most vulnerable to the development of eating disorders. The Oxford case control study that we have highlighted in this chapter (Fairburn, 1994) provides a conceptual and methodological model in this regard. Once risk factors have been identified, they would ideally be followed up in subsequent prospective studies.

Treatment

Anorexia nervosa remains a disorder that is largely resistant to current therapies (Hsu, 1990). The picture is much brighter with respect to bulimia nervosa. Effective treatments have been developed that result in significant improvements in the majority of patients (Fairburn et al., 1995). Even here, however, the current treatments fail to benefit some patients and produce only modest effects in others (Wilson, 1993d). We need to develop more effective therapies for the full range of patients. Much the same applies to BED.

Continued research on etiology will likely lead to refinements in existing treatments. Ultimately, the treatment of eating disorders should follow logically from an improved understanding of their etiology and maintenance. Reciprocally, research on the mechanisms and outcome of different therapies may advance our understanding of the nature of these disorders. For example, Fairburn et al. (1995) found that interpersonal psychotherapy (IPT) was an effective treatment for bulimia nervosa, producing lasting improvement. What is striking is that this IPT explicitly avoided any focus on patients' eating behavior or attitudes about body weight and shape (Fairburn, 1994). Thus it is possible to overcome bulimia nervosa by concentrating only on current interpersonal issues. This treatment outcome suggests that interpersonal processes play an important role in the maintenance of bulimia nervosa. In similar fashion, possible differential effects of specific pharmacological and other psychological treatments that are currently under evaluation might provide clues for the understanding of all the eating disorders.

REFERENCES

Agras, W. S. (1993). Short-term psychological treatments for binge eating. In C. G. Fairburn & G. T. Wilson (Eds.), *Binge eating: Nature, assessment, and treatment* (pp. 270–286). New York: Guilford Press.

Agras, W. S., Telch, C. F., Arnow, B., Eldredge, K., Wilfley, D. E., Raeburn, S. D., Henderson, J., & Marnell, M. (1994). Weight loss, cognitive-behavioral, and desipramine treatments in binge eating disorder: An additive design. *Behavior Therapy, 25,* 225–238.

American Psychiatric Association. (1980). *Diagnostic and statistical manual of mental disorders* (3rd ed.). Washington, DC: Author.

American Psychiatric Association. (1987). *Diagnostic and statistical manual of mental disorders* (3rd ed., rev.). Washington, DC: Author.

American Psychiatric Association. (1994). *Diagnostic and statistical manual of mental disorders* (4th ed.). Washington, DC: Author.

Attie, I., & Brooks-Gunn, J. (1989). Development of eating problems in adolescent girls: A longitudinal study. *Developmental Psychology, 25,* 70–79.

Beglin, S. J., & Fairburn, C. G. (1992). Women who choose not to participate in surveys on eating disorders. *International Journal of Eating Disorders, 12,* 113–116.

Beliard, D., Kirschenbaum, D. S., & Fitzgibbon, M. L. (1992). Evaluation of an intensive weight control program using *a priori* criteria to determine outcome. *International Journal of Obesity, 16,* 1–13.

Benjamin, L. S. (1979). Use of structural analysis of social behavior (SASB) and Markov chains to study dyadic interactions. *Journal of Abnormal Psychology, 88,* 303–319.

Broocks, A., Fichter, M. M., & Pirke, K. M. (1988). Effects of test meals on insulin, glucose, plasma large neutral amino acids and norepinephrine in patients with bulimia nervosa. *Proceedings of 3rd International Conference on Eating Disorders,* p. 242.

Bruch, H. (1973). *Eating disorders: Obesity, anorexia nervosa, and the person within.* New York: Basic Books.

Bruch, H. (1978). *The golden cage: The enigma of anorexia nervosa.* New York: Basic Books.

Butow, P., Beumont, P., & Touyz, S. (1993). Cognitive processes in dieting disorders. *International Journal of Eating Disorders, 14,* 319–330.

Calam, R., Waller, G., Slade, P., & Newton, T. (1990). Eating disorders and perceived relationships with parents. *International Journal of Eating Disorders, 9,* 479–485.

Charnock, D. J. K. (1989). A comment on the role of dietary restraint in the development of bulimia nervosa. *British Journal of Clinical Psychology, 28,* 329–340.

Chun, Z. F., Mitchell, J. E., Li, K., Yu, W. M., Lan, Y. D., Jun,Z., Rong, Z. Y., Huan, Z. Z., Filice, G. A., Pomeroy, C., & Pyle, R. L. (1992). The prevalence of anorexia nervosa and bulimia nervosa among freshman medical college students in China. *International Journal of Eating Disorders, 12,* 209–214.

Cloninger, C. R. (1987). Neurogenetic adaptive mechanisms in alcoholism. *Science, 236,* 410–416.

Cowen, P. J., Anderson, I. M., & Fairburn, C. G. (1992). Neurochemical effects of dieting: Relevance to eating and affective disorders. In G. H. Anderson & S. H. Kennedy (Eds.), *The biology of feast and famine: Relevance to eating disorders* (pp. 269–284). New York: Academic Press.

Crisp, A. H. (1980). *Anorexia nervosa: Let me be.* London: Plenum Press.

Crisp, A. H., Palmer, R. L., & Kalucy, R. S. (1976). How common is anorexia nervosa? A prevalence study. *British Journal of Psychiatry, 128,* 549–554.

DaCosta, M., & Halmi, K. A. (1992). Classification of anorexia nervosa: Question of subtypes. *International Journal of Eating Disorders, 11,* 305–314.

deAzevedo, M. H., & Ferreira, C. P. (1992). Anorexia nervosa and bulimia: A prevalence study. *Acta Psychiatrica Scandinavica, 86,* 432–436.

Delgado, P. L., Charney, D. S., Price, L. H., Landis, H., & Henninger, G. R. (1989). Neuroendocrine and behavioral effects of dietary tryptophan restriction in healthy subjects. *Life Sciences, 45,* 2323–2332.

de Zwaan, M., Mitchell, J. E., Seim, H. C., Specker, S. M., Pyle, R. L., Raymond, N. C., & Crosby, R. B. (1994). Eating related and general psychopathology in obese females with binge eating disorder. *International Journal of Eating Disorders, 15,* 43–52.

de Zwaan, M., Nutzinger, D. O., & Schoenbeck, G. (1992). Binge eating in overweight women. *Comprehensive Psychiatry, 33,* 256–261.

Dornbusch, S. M., Carlsmith, J. M., Duncan, P. D., Gross, R. T., Martin, J. A., Ritter, P. L., & Siegel-Gorelick, B. (1984). Sexual maturation, social class, and the desire to be thin among adolescent females. *Developmental and Behavior Pediatrics, 5,* 308–314.

Drenowski, A., Yee, D. K., & Krahn, D. D. (1988). Bulimia in college women: Incidence and recovery rates. *American Journal of Psychiatry, 145,* 753–755.

Dwyer, J. T., Feldman, J. J., Seltzer, C. C., & Mayer, J. (1969). Body image in adolescents: Attitudes towards weight and perception of appearance. *The American Journal of Clinical Nutrition, 20,* 1045–1056.

Epstein, L. H., Valoski, A., Wing, R. R., & McCurley, J. (1994). Ten-year outcomes of behavioral family-based treatment for childhood obesity. *Health Psychology, 13,* 373–383.

Fahy, T. A., Osacar, A., & Marks, I. (1993). History of eating disorders in female patients with obsessive-compulsive disorder. *International Journal of Eating Disorders, 14,* 439–443.

Fairburn, C. G. (1994, May). *The aetiology of bulimia nervosa.* Paper presented at the Sixth International Conference on Eating Disorders, New York.

Fairburn, C. G., & Beglin, S. J. (1990). Studies of the epidemiology of bulimia nervosa. *American Journal of Psychiatry, 147,* 401–408.

Fairburn, C. G., & Beglin, S. J. (1994). The assessment of eating disorders: Interview or self-report questionnaire? *International Journal of Eating Disorders, 16,* 363–370.

Fairburn, C. G., & Cooper, P. J. (1993). The Eating Disorder Examination (12th ed.). In C. G. Fairburn & G. T. Wilson (Eds.), *Binge eating: Nature, assessment, and treatment* (pp. 317–360). New York: Guilford Press.

Fairburn, C. G., Hay, P. J., & Welch, S. L. (1993). Binge eating and bulimia nervosa: Distribution and determinants. In C. G. Fairburn & G. T. Wilson (Eds.), *Binge eating: Nature, assessment, and treatment* (pp. 123–143). New York: Guilford Press.

Fairburn, C. G., Jones, R., Peveler, R. C., Hope, R. A., & O'Connor, M. (1993). Psychotherapy and bulimia nervosa: The longer-term effects of interpersonal psychotherapy, behaviour therapy and cognitive behaviour therapy. *Archives of General Psychiatry, 50,* 419–428.

Fairburn, C. G., Norman, P. A., Welch, S. L., O'Connor, M. E., Doll, H. A., & Peveler, R. C. (1995). A prospective study of outcome in bulimia nervosa and the long-term effects of three psychological treatments. *Archives of General Psychiatry, 52,* 304–312.

Fairburn, C. G., Welch, S. L., & Hay, P. J. (1993). The classification of recurrent overeating: The "binge eating disorder" proposal. *International Journal of Eating Disorders, 13,* 155–160.

Fairburn, C. G., & Wilson, G. T. (Eds.). (1993). *Binge eating: Nature, assessment, and treatment.* New York: Guilford Press.

Fava, M., Copeland, P. M., Schweiger, U., & Herzog, D. B. (1989). Neurochemical abnormalities of anorexia nervosa and bulimia nervosa. *American Journal of Psychiatry, 146,* 963–971.

Fichter, M. M., & Hoffman, R. (1990). Bulimia (nervosa) in the male. In M. M. Fichter (Ed.), *Bulimia nervosa: Basic research, diagnosis and therapy* (pp. 99–111). New York: Wiley.

Fichter, M. M., Quadflieg, N., & Brandl, B. (1993). Recurring overeating: An empirical comparison of binge eating disorder, bulimia nervosa, and obesity. *International Journal of Eating Disorders, 14,* 1–16.

Fornari, V., Kaplan, M., Sandberg, D. E., Matthews, M., Skolnick, N., & Katz, J. L. (1992). Depressive and anxiety disorders in anorexia nervosa and bulimia nervosa. *International Journal of Eating Disorders, 12,* 21–29.

Garfinkel, P. E., Moldofsky, H., & Garner, D. (1980). The heterogeneity of anorexia nervosa: Bulimia as a distinct subgroup. *Archives of General Psychiatry, 37,* 1036–1040.

Garner, D. M. (1993). Binge eating in anorexia nervosa. In C. G. Fairburn & G. T. Wilson (Eds.), *Binge eating: Nature, assessment, and treatment* (pp. 50–76). New York: Guilford Press.

Garner, D. M., & Garfinkel, P. E. (1980). Sociocultural factors in the development of anorexia nervosa. *Psychological Medicine, 9,* 273–279.

Garner, D. M., Olmstead, M. A., Bohr, Y., & Garfinkel, P. E. (1982). The Eating Attitudes Test: Psychometric features and clinical correlates. *Psychological Medicine, 12,* 871–878.

Garner, D. M., Olmstead, M. A., & Polivy, J. (1983). Development and validation of a multidimensional eating disorder inventory for anorexia nervosa and bulimia nervosa. *International Journal of Eating Disorders, 2,* 15–34.

Garner, D. M., Olmstead, M. P., Polivy, J., & Garfinkel, P. E. (1984). Comparison between weight-preoccupied women and anorexia nervosa. *Psychosomatic Medicine, 14,* 255–266.

Garner, D. M., & Wooley, S. C. (1991). Confronting the failure of behavioral and dietary treatments for obesity. *Clinical Psychology Review, 11,* 729–780.

Gerner, R. H., Cohen, D. J., Fairbanks, L., Anderson, G. M., Young, J. G., Scheinin, M., Linnoila, M., Shaywitz, B. A., & Hare, T. A. (1984). CSF neurochemistry of women with anorexia nervosa and normal women. *American Journal of Psychiatry, 141,* 1441–1444.

Gershon, E. S., Hamovit, J. R., Schreiber, J. L., Dibble, E. D., Kaye, W., Nurnberger, J. I., Andersen, A., & Ebert, M. (1983). Anorexia nervosa and major affective disorders

associated in families: A preliminary report. In S. B. Guze, F. Earls, & J. E. Barrett (Eds.), *Childhood psychopathology and development* (pp. 279–299). New York: Raven Press.

Goodwin, G. M., Fairburn, C. G., & Cowen, P. J. (1988). The effects of dieting and weight loss on neuroendocrine responses to tryptophan, clonidine, and apomorphine in volunteers: Important implications for neuroendocrine investigations in depression. *Archives of General Psychiatry, 44,* 952–957.

Gull, W. W. (1873). Anorexia hysterica (apepsia hysteria). *British Medical Journal, 2,* 527.

Halmi, K. A., Eckert, E. & Marchi, P., Sampugnaro, V., Apple, R., & Cohen, J. (1991). Comorbidity of psychiatric diagnoses in anorexia nervosa. *Archives of General Psychiatry, 48,* 712–718.

Hatfield, E., & Sprecher, S. (1985). *Mirror, mirror: The importance of looks in everyday life.* New York: SUNY Press.

Hay, P. J., Fairburn, C. G., & Doll, H. A. (1994). *Towards the re-classification of bulimic eating disorders: A community-based cluster analytic study.* Unpublished manuscript, Oxford University, Oxford, UK.

Heffernan, K. (1994). Sexual orientation as a factor in risk for binge eating and bulimia nervosa: A review. *International Journal of Eating Disorders, 16,* 335–348.

Heffernan, K. (in press). Eating disorders and weight concern among lesbians. *International Journal of Eating Disorders.*

Herzog, D. B., Keller, M. B., & Sacks, N. R., Yeh, C. J., & Lavori, P. W. (1992). Psychiatric comorbidity in treatment-seeking anorexics and bulimics. *Journal of the American Academy of Child and Adolescent Psychiatry, 31,* 810–818.

Herzog, D. B., Norman, D. K., Gordon, C., & Pepose, M. (1984). Sexual conflict and eating disorders in 27 males. *American Journal of Psychiatry, 141,* 989–990.

Higuchi, S., Suzuki, K., Yamada, K., Parrish, K., & Kono, H. (1993). Alcoholics with eating disorders: Prevalence and clinical course, a study from Japan. *British Journal of Psychiatry, 162,* 403–406.

Hoek, H. W. (1993). Review of the epidemiological studies of eating disorders. *International Review of Psychiatry, 5,* 61–74.

Hsu, L. K. G. (1987). Are the eating disorders becoming more common in blacks? *International Journal of Eating disorders, 6,* 113–124,

Hsu, L. K. G. (1990). *Eating disorders.* New York: Guilford Press.

Hudson, J., Pope, H., & Yurgelun-Todd, D., Jonas, J. M., & Frankenburg, F. R. (1987). A controlled study of lifetime prevalence of affective and other psychiatric disorders in bulimic outpatients. *American Journal of Psychiatry, 144,* 1283–1287.

Humphrey, L. L. (1987). Comparison of bulimic–anorexic and non-distressed families using structural analysis of social behavior. *American Academy of Child and Adolescent Psychiatry, 26,* 248–255.

Humphrey, L. L. (1989). Observed family interactions among subtypes of eating disorders using structural analysis of social behavior. *Journal of Consulting and Clinical Psychology. 57,* 206–214.

Jimerson, D. C., Brandt, H. A., & Brewerton, T. D. (1988). Evidence for altered serotonin function in bulimia and anorexia nervosa: Behavioral implications. In K. M. Pirke, W. Vandereycken, & D. Ploog (Eds.), *Psychobiology of bulimia nervosa* (pp. 83–89). Berlin: Springer.

Jimerson, D. C., Lesem, M. D., Kaye, W. H., & Brewerton, T. D. (1992). Low serotonin and dopamine metabolite concentrations in cerebrospinal fluid from bulimic patients with frequent binge episodes. *Archives of General Psychiatry, 49,* 132–139.

Jimerson, D. C., Lesem, M. D., Kaye, W. H., Hegg, A. P., & Brewerton, T. D. (1990). Eating disorders and depression: Is there a serotonin connection? *Biological Psychiatry, 28,* 443–454.

Johnson, C., & Conners, M. E. (1987). Demographic and clinical characteristics. In E. Johnson & M. E. Conners (Eds.), *The etiology and treatment of bulimia nervosa: A biopsychosocial perspective* (pp. 31–60). New York: Basic Books.

Johnson-Sabine, E., Reiss, D., & Dayson, D. (1992). Bulimia nervosa: A 5 year follow-up study. *Psychological Medicine, 22,* 951–959.

Johnson-Sabine, E., Wood, K., Patton, G., Mann, A., & Wakeling, A. (1988). Abnormal eating attitudes in London schoolgirls—a prospective epidemiological study: Factors associated with abnormal response on screening questionnaires. *Psychological Medicine, 18,* 615–622.

Jonas, J. M., Gold, M. S., Sweeney, M. D., & Pottash, A. L. C. (1987). Eating disorders and cocaine abuse: A survey of 259 cocaine abusers. *Journal of Clinical Psychiatry, 48,* 47–50.

Jones, D. J., Fox, M. M., Babigian, H. M., & Hutton, H. E. (1980). Epidemiology of anorexia nervosa in Monroe County, New York: 1960–1979. *Psychosomatic Medicine, 42,* 551–558.

Jordan, J. V., Kaplan, A. G., Miller, J. B., Stiver, I. P., & Surrey, J. L. (1991). *Women's growth in connection: Writings from the Stone Center.* New York: Guilford Press.

Katzman, M. A., & Wolchik, S. S. (1984). Bulimia and binge eating in college women: A comparison of personality and behavioral characteristics. *Journal of Consulting and Clinical Psychology, 52,* 423–428.

Kaye, W. H., Ballenger, J. C., Lydiard, R. B., Stuart, G. W., Laraia, M. T., O'Neil, P., Fossey, M. D., Stevens, V., Lessers, S., & Hsu, G. (1990). CSF monoamine levels in normal-weight bulimia: Evidence for abnormal noradrenergic activity. *American Journal of Psychiatry, 147,* 225–229.

Kaye, W. H., Ebert, M. H., Gwirtsman, H. E., & Weiss, S. R. (1984). Differences in brain serotonergic metabolism between nonbulimic and bulimic patients with anorexia nervosa. *American Journal of Psychiatry, 141,* 1598–1601.

Kaye, W. H., Ebert, M. H., Raleigh, M., & Lake, R. (1984). Abnormalities in CNS monoamine metabolism in anorexia nervosa. *Archives of General Psychiatry, 41,* 350–355.

Kaye, W. H., Gwirtsman, H. E., George, D. T., & Ebert, M. H. (1991). Altered serotonin activity in anorexia nervosa after long-term weight restoration. *Archives of General Psychiatry, 48,* 556–562.

Kaye, W. H., Gwirtsman, H. E., George, D. T., Jimerson, D. C., & Ebert, M. H. (1988). CSF 5–HIAA concentrations in anorexia nervosa: Reduced values in underweight subjects normalize after weight gain. *Society of Biological Psychiatry, 23,* 102–105.

Kaye, W. H., Gwirtsman, H. E., George, D. T., Jimerson, D. C., Ebert, M. H., & Lake C. R. (1990). Disturbances of noradrenergic systems in normal-weight bulimia: Relationship to diet and menses. *Biological Psychiatry, 27,* 4–21.

Kaye, W. H. & Weltzin, T. E. (1991). Neurochemistry of bulimia nervosa. *Journal of Clinical Psychiatry, 52,* 617–622.

Kaye, W. H., Weltzin, T., & Hsu, L. K. G. (1993). Relationship between anorexia nervosa and obsessive compulsive behaviors. *Psychiatric Annals, 23,* 365–373.

Kaye, W. H., Weltzin, T. E., McKee, M., McConaha, C., Hansen, D., & Hsu, L. K. G. (1992). Laboratory assessment of feeding behavior in bulimia nervosa and healthy women: Methods for developing a human-feeding laboratory. *American Journal of Clinical Nutrition, 55,* 372–380.

Keefe, P. H., Wyshogrod, D., Weinberger, E., & Agras, W. S. (1984). Binge eating and outcome of behavioral treatment in obesity: A preliminary report. *Behaviour Research and Therapy, 22,* 319–321.

Keller, M. B., Herzog, D. B., Lavori, P. W., Bradburn, I. S., & Mahoney, E. M. (1992). The naturalistic history of bulimia nervosa: Extraordinarily high rates of chronicity, relapse, recurrence, and psychosocial morbidity. *International Journal of Eating Disorders, 12,* 1–9.

Kendler, K. S., MacLean, C., Neale, M., Kessler, R., Heath, A., & Eaves, L. (1991). The genetic epidemiology of bulimia nervosa. *American Journal of Psychiatry, 148,* 1627–1637.

Kennedy, S. H., & Garfinkel, P. E. (1992). Advances in diagnosis and treatment of anorexia nervosa and bulimia nervosa. *Canadian Journal of Psychiatry, 37,* 309–315.

King, M. B. (1989). Eating disorders in a general practice population: Prevalence, characteristics and follow-up at 12 to 18 months. *Psychological Medicine* (Suppl. 14).

Kog, E., Vandereycken, W., & Vertommen, H. (1985). Towards a verification of the psychosomatic family model: A pilot study of ten families with an anorexia/bulimia nervosa patient. *International Journal of Eating Disorders, 4,* 525–538.

Lacey, J. H., & Evans, C. D. (1986). The impulsivist: A multi-impulsive personality disorder. *British Journal of Addiction, 81,* 641–649.

Laessle, R. G., Kittl, S., Fichter, M., Wittchen, H. U., & Pirke, K. M. (1987). Major affective disorder in anorexia nervosa and bulimia: A descriptive diagnostic study. *British Journal of Psychiatry, 151,* 785–789.

Lesem, M. D., George, D. T., Kaye, W. H., Goldstein, D. S., & Jimerson, D. C. (1989). State-related changes in norepinephrine regulation in anorexia nervosa. *Biological Psychiatry, 25,* 509–512.

Lowe, M. R. (1993). The effects of dieting on eating behavior: A three-factor model. *Psychological Bulletin, 114,* 100–121.

Lowe, M. R., & Caputo, G. C. (1991). Binge eating in obesity: Toward the specification of predictors. *International Journal of Eating Disorders, 10,* 49–56.

Marcus, M. D. (1993). Binge eating in obesity. In C. F. Fairburn & G. T. Wilson (Eds.), *Binge eating: Nature, assessment, and treatment* (pp. 77–96). New York: Guilford Press.

Marcus, M. D., Smith, D. E., Santelli, R., & Kaye, W. (1992). Characterization of eating disordered behavior in obese binge eaters. *International Journal of Eating Disorders, 12,* 249–256.

Marcus, M. D., Wing, R. R., Ewing, L., Kern, E., Gooding, W., & McDermott, M. (1990). Psychiatric disorders among obese binge eaters. *International Journal of Eating Disorders, 9,* 69–77.

Marcus, M. D., Wing, R. R., & Hopkins, J. (1988). Obese binge eaters: Affect, cognitions, and response to behavioral weight control. *Journal of Consulting and Clinical Psychology, 56,* 433–439.

Miller, J. B. (1976). *Toward a new psychology of women.* Boston: Beacon Press.

Minuchin, S., Rosman, B. L., & Baker, L. (1978). *Psychosomatic families: Anorexia nervosa in context.* Cambridge, MA: Harvard University Press.

Mitchell, J., Pomeroy, C., & Colon, E. (1990). Medical complications in bulimia nervosa. In M. M. Fichter (Ed.), *Bulimia nervosa: Basic research, diagnosis and therapy* (pp. 99–111). New York: Wiley.

Mitchell, J. E., Pyle, R. L., Eckert, E. D., Hatsukami, D., Pomeroy, C., & Zimmerman, R. (1989). Response to alternative antidepressants in imipramine nonresponders with bulimia nervosa. *Journal of Clinical Psychopharmacology, 9,* 291–293.

Mitchell, J. E., Specker, S. M., & de Zwaan, M. (1991). Comorbidity and medical complications of bulimia nervosa. *Journal of Clinical Psychiatry, 52,* 13–20.

Mumford, D. B., Whitehouse, A. M., & Choudry, I. Y. (1992). Survey of eating disorders in English-medium schools in Lahore, Pakistan. *International Journal of Eating Disorders, 11,* 173–184.

Mumford, D. B., Whitehouse, A. M., & Platts, M. (1991). Sociocultural correlates of eating disorders among Asian schoolgirls in Bradford. *British Journal of Psychiatry, 158,* 222–228.

Nasser, M. (1986). Comparative study of the prevalence of abnormal eating attitudes among Arab females of both London and Cairo universities. *Psychological Medicine, 16,* 621–625.

Palazzoli, M. S. (1985). *Self-starvation: From the intrapsychic to transpersonal approach.* New York: Jason Aronson.

Patton, G. C. (1988). The spectrum of eating disorders in adolescence. *Journal of Psychosomatic Research, 32,* 579–584.

Pike, K. M., & Rodin, J. (1991). Mothers, daughters, and disordered eating. *Journal of Abnormal Psychology, 100,* 198–204.

Pirke, K. M. (1990). Central neurotransmitter disturbances in bulimia (nervosa). In M. M. Fichter (Ed.), *Bulimia nervosa: Basic research, diagnosis and therapy* (pp. 223–234). Chichester, UK: Wiley.

Polivy, J., & Herman, C. P. (1993). Etiology of binge eating: Psychological mechanisms. In C. G. Fairburn & G. T. Wilson (Eds.), *Binge eating: Nature, assessment, and treatment* (pp. 173–205). New York: Guilford Press.

Pope, H. G., Mangweth, B., Negrao, A. B., Hudson, J. I., & Cordas, T. A. (1994). Childhood sexual abuse and bulimia nervosa: A comparison of American, Austrian, and Brazilian women. *American Journal of Psychiatry, 151,* 732–737.

Pyle, R. L., Mitchell, J. E., Eckert, E. D., Hatsukami, D., Pomeroy, C., & Zimmerman, R. (1990). Maintenance treatment and 6-month outcome for bulimic patients who respond to initial treatment. *American Journal of Psychiatry, 147,* 871–875.

Raymond, N. C., Mussell, M. P., Mitchell, J. E., de Zwaan, M., & Crosby, R. D. (1995). An age-matched comparison of subjects with binge eating disorders and bulimia nervosa. *International Journal of Eating Disorders, 18,* 135–144.

Rosen, J. C., & Gross, J. (1987). The prevalence of weight reducing and weight gaining in adolescent girls and boys. *Health Psychology, 6,* 131–147.

Rosen, J. C., Leitenberg, H., Fisher, C., & Khazam, C. (1986). Binge-eating episodes in bulimia nervosa: The amount and type of food consumed. *International Journal of Eating Disorders, 5,* 255–257.

Rossiter, E. M., & Agras, W. S. (1990). An empirical test of the DSM-III-R definition of binge. *International Journal of Eating Disorders, 9,* 513–518.

Rossiter, E. M., Agras, W. S., Telch, C. F., & Bruce, B. (1992). The eating patterns of non-purging bulimic subjects. *International Journal of Eating Disorders, 11,* 111–120.

Rubenstein, C. S., Pigott, T. A., L'Heureux, F., Hill, J. L., & Murphy, D. L. (1992). A preliminary investigation of the lifetime prevalence of anorexia and bulimia nervosa in patients with obsessive compulsive disorder. *Journal of Clinical Psychiatry, 53,* 309–314.

Russell, G. (1979). Bulimia nervosa: An ominous variation of anorexia nervosa. *Psychological Medicine, 9,* 429–448.

Schlundt, D. G., Taylor, D., Hill, J. O., Sbrocco, T., Pope-Cordle, J., Kasser, T., & Arnold, D. (1991). A behavioral taxonomy of obese female participants in a weight-loss program. *American Journal of Clinical Nutrition, 53,* 1151–1158.

Schneider, J. A., & Agras, W. S. (1987). Bulimia in males: A matched comparison with females. *International Journal of Eating Disorders, 2,* 235–242.

Schwalberg, M. D., Barlow, D. H., Alger, S. A., & Howard, L. J. (1992). Comparison of bulimics, obese binge eaters, social phobics, and individuals with panic disorder on comorbidity across DSM-III-R anxiety disorders. *Journal of Abnormal Psychology, 101,* 675–681.

Shisslak, C., Crago, M., Neal, M. E., & Swain, B. (1987). Primary prevention of eating disorders. *Journal of Consulting and Clinical Psychology, 55,* 660–667.

Skodol, A. E., Oldham, J. M., Hyler, S. E., Kellman, H. D., Doidge, N., & Davies, M. (1993). Comorbidity of DSM-III-R eating disorders and personality disorders. *International Journal of Eating Disorders, 14,* 403–416.

Spitzer, R. L., Devlin, M., Walsh, B. T., Hasin, D., Wing, R., Marcus, M., Stunkard, A., Wadden, T., Yanovski, S., Agras, S., Mitchell, J., & Nonas, C. (1992). Binge eating disorder: A multisite field trial of the diagnostic criteria. *International Journal of Eating Disorders, 11,* 191–203.

Spitzer, R. L., Stunkard, A., Yanovski, S., Marcus, M. D., Wadden, R., Wing, R., Mitchell, J., & Hasin, D. (1993). Binge eating disorder should be included in DSM-IV: A reply to Fairburn et al.'s "The classification of recurrent overeating: The binge eating disorder proposal." *International Journal of Eating Disorders, 13,* 161–170.

Spitzer, R. L., Yanovski, S., Wadden, T., Wing, R., Marcus, M., Stunkard, A., Devlin, M., Mitchell, J., Hasin, D., & Horne, R. L. (1993). Binge eating disorder: Its further validation in a multisite study. *International Journal of Eating Disorders, 13,* 137–153.

Stierlin, H., & Weber, G. (1989). *Unlocking the family door: A systematic approach to the understanding and treatment of anorexia nervosa.* New York: Brunner/Mazel.

Striegel-Moore, R. H. (1993). Etiology of binge eating: A developmental perspective. In C. G. Fairburn & G. T. Wilson (Eds.), *Binge eating: Nature, assessment, and treatment* (pp. 144–172). New York: Guilford Press.

Striegel-Moore, R. H., & Kearney-Cooke, A. (in press). Exploring determinants and consequences of parents' attitudes about their children's physical appearance. *International Journal of Eating Disorders.*

Striegel-Moore, R. H., Silberstein, L. R., Frensch, P., & Rodin, J. (1989). A prospective study of disordered eating among college students. *International Journal of Eating Disorders, 8,* 499–509.

Striegel-Moore, R. H., Silberstein, L. R., & Rodin, J. (1986). Toward an understanding of risk factors for bulimia. *American Psychologist, 41,* 246–263.

Strober, M. (1980). Personality and symptomatological fea-tures in young, nonchronic anorexia nervosa patients. *Journal of Psychosomatic Research, 24,* 353–359.

Strober, M. (1991). Family-genetic studies of eating disorders. *Journal of Clinical Psychiatry, 52*(Suppl.), 9–12.

Strober, M. (1995). Family–genetic perspectives on anorexia nervosa and bulimia nervosa. In K. Brownell & C. G. Fairburn (Eds.), *Eating disorders and obesity: A comprehensive handbook* (pp. 212–218). New York: Guilford Press.

Strober, M., & Humphrey, L. L. (1987). Familial contributions to the etiology and course of anorexia nervosa and bulimia. *International Journal of Eating Disorders, 5,* 654–659.

Strober, M., & Katz, J. L. (1987). Do eating disorders and affective disorders share a common etiology? A dissenting opinion. *International Journal of Eating Disorders, 6,* 171–180.

Strober, M., Lampert, C., Morrell, W., Burroughs, J., & Jacobs, C. (1990). A controlled family study of anorexia nervosa: Evidence of familial aggregation and lack of shared transmission with affective disorders. *International Journal of Eating Disorders, 9,* 239–253.

Stunkard, A. J. (1959). The results of treatment for obesity. *Archives of Internal Medicine, 103,* 79–85.

Stunkard, A. J., Harris, J. R., Pedersen, N. L., & McClearn, G. E. (1990). The body-mass index of twins who have been reared apart. *New England Journal of Medicine, 322,* 1483–1487.

Stunkard, A. J., & Messick, S. (1985). The three-factor eating questionnaire to measure dietary restraint and hunger. *Journal of Psychosomatic Research, 29,* 71–83.

Szmuckler, G. I., Eisler, I., Gillis, C., & Hayward, M. E. (1985). The implications of anorexia nervosa in a ballet school. *Journal of Psychiatric Research, 19,* 177–181.

Telch, C. F., & Agras, W. S. (1993). The effects of a very low calorie diet on binge eating. *Behavior Therapy, 24,* 177–194.

Tobin, D. L. (1993). Psychodynamic psychotherapy and binge eating. In C. G. Fairburn & G. T. Wilson (Eds.), *Binge eating: Nature, assessment, and treatment* (pp. 287–313). New York: Guilford Press.

Toner, B. B., Garfinkel, P. E. & Garner, D. M. (1988). Affective and anxiety disorders in the long-term follow-up of anorexia nervosa. *International Journal of Psychiatry in Medicine, 18,* 357–364.

Wadden, T. A., Foster, G. D., & Letizia, K. A., & Wilk, J. E. (1993). Metabolic, anthropometric, and psychological characteristics of obese binge eaters. *International Journal of Eating Disorders, 14,* 17–26.

Waller, G., Slade, P., & Calam, R. (1990). Family adaptability and cohesion: Relation to eating attitudes. *International Journal of Eating Disorders, 9,* 225–228.

Walsh, B. T. (1993). Binge eating in bulimia nervosa. In C. F. Fairburn & G. T. Wilson (Eds.), *Binge eating: Nature, assessment, and treatment* (pp. 37–49). New York: Guilford Press.

Walters, E. E., Neale, M. C., Eaves, L. J., Health, A. C., Kessler, R. C., & Kendler, K. S. (1992). Bulimia nervosa and major depression: A study of common genetic and environmental factors. *Psychological Medicine, 22,* 617–622.

Walters, E. E., Neale, M. C., Eaves, L. J., Health, A. C., Kessler, R. C., & Kendler, K. S. (1993). Bulimia nervosa: A population-based study of purgers versus nonpurgers. *International Journal of Eating Disorders, 13,* 265–272.

Wilson, G. T. (1991). The addiction model of eating disor-

ders: A critical analysis. *Advances in Behavior Research and Therapy, 13,* 27–72.

Wilson, G. T. (1993a). Behavioral treatment of obesity: Thirty years and counting. *Advances in Behavior Research and Therapy, 16,* 31–75.

Wilson, G. T. (1993b). Assessment of binge eating. In C. G. Fairburn & G. T. Wilson (Eds.), *Binge eating: Nature, assessment, and treatment* (pp. 227–249). New York: Guilford Press.

Wilson, G. T. (1993c). *Behavioral and psychological predictors of treatment outcome in obesity.* Unpublished manuscript, Rutgers University, Piscataway, NJ.

Wilson, G. T. (1993d). Psychological and pharmacological treatments of bulimia nervosa: A research update. *Applied and Preventive Psychology: Current Scientific Perspectives, 2,* 35–42.

Wilson, G. T. (1994). Behavioral treatment of childhood obesity: Theoretical and practical implications. *Health Psychology, 13,* 371–372.

Wilson, G. T., & Eldredge, K. (1992). Pathology and development of eating disorders: Implications for athletes. In K. D. Brownell, J. Rodin, & J. H. Wilmore (Eds.), *Eat-ing, body weight, and performance in athletics: Disorders of modern society* (pp. 115–127). Philadelphia: Lea & Febiger.

Wilson, G. T., Nonas, C. A., & Rosenblum, G. (1993). Assessment of binge eating in obese patients. *International Journal of Eating Disorders, 13,* 25–33.

World Health Organization. (1992). *The ICD-10 classification of mental and behavioural disorders: Clinical descriptions and diagnostic guidelines.* Geneva, Switzerland: Author.

Yanovski, S. Z., Leet, M., Yanovski, J. A., Flood, M., Gold, P. W., Kissileff, H. R., & Walsh, B. T. (1992). Food selection and intake of obese women with binge eating disorder. *American Journal of Clinical Nutrition, 56,* 975–980.

Yanovski, S. Z., Nelson, J. E., Dubbert, B. K., & Spitzer, R. L. (1992). Binge eating disorder is associated with psychiatric comorbidity in the obese. *American Journal of Psychiatry, 150,* 1472–1479.

Yanovski, S. Z., & Sebring, N. G. (1992). Recorded food intake of obese women with binge eating disorder before and after weight loss. *International Journal of Eating Disorders, 15,* 135–150.

Health-Related Disorders

Cynthia Harbeck-Weber
Lizette Peterson

Over the last decade, the field of pediatric health disorders has "come of age" as a distinct area of specialization (Olson, Mullins, Gillman, & Chaney, 1994). This field is extremely diverse and includes tasks such as intervening with children who are primarily healthy to decrease their pain during injections, assist them in coping with the sequelae of unintentional injuries, and work to prevent later health disorders. The field also focuses on acute or chronically ill children, to improve their medication adherence, reduce their nonorganic pain, decrease their pseudoseizures, assist them in coping with chronic illness, and reduce the psychological sequelae of their health disorders. As can be seen from these varied activities, the area of health-related disorders ranges along a continuum of severity. Some of the problems discussed in this chapter are not truly "disorders" but may be conceptualized as medical stressors with which children and their parents must cope. These stressors, in turn, range along a continuum from mild stress that is experienced by a majority of the pediatric population (e.g., injections, minor injuries) to rare health problems that are life-threatening and include complicated, daily medical treatment (e.g., cystic fibrosis, open-heart surgery), to unintentional injuries that are currently the leading cause of death for children in this nation. Other disorders discussed in this chapter refer to forms of significant psycho-pathology in child patients such as somatization disorder and conversion disorder.

The field of childhood health disorders differs from childhood psychopathology in its emphasis on the interaction between physical well-being and psychology. Indeed, each of the disorders presented in this chapter has medical, psychological, and psychosocial components. Because of the importance of each component in the biopsychosocial model, the field of health disorders is truly an interdisciplinary field and requires teamwork among psychologists, physicians, nurses, occupational and physical therapists, dietitians, public health officials, educators, chaplains, and administrators.

In this chapter, an effort will be made to help the reader appreciate the diversity of this field and understand the particular challenges of working with children who have health-related disorders. In contrast to the other chapters in this book, this chapter provides an overview, rather than an in-depth examination of a particular disorder. We begin our discussion with an examination of the history of this diverse field.

HISTORICAL CONTEXT

Scientists have been interested in health-related disorders throughout the course of history. For

example, interest in somatoform disorders can be traced to 1900 B.C. when Egyptians recognized the existence of a syndrome in which physical symptoms were present in the absence of organic causes (Ford & Folks, 1985). Early cultures were also interested in the relationship between behavior and health and the prevention of disease. The earliest records of oriental, Islamic, Buddhist, Judaic, and Christian religions suggest an understanding of the relationship between personal habits (e.g., avoiding certain foods, moderating food and drink, good sleep habits) and good physical health (Matarazzo, 1984).

During the early part of this century, attention turned to psychodynamic theory, which was utilized to explain such diverse conditions as child abuse and neglect, enuresis and encopresis, and somatoform disorders. In the second half of the century, several developments greatly influenced the field of pediatric health disorders, including growth of the field of psychoneuroimmunology, advent of behavioral therapy, and increased understanding of the biopsychosocial model of health and disease.

The field of psychoneuroimmunology has been influential in helping scientists understand the link between psychological factors such as stress and coping style and biological systems such as the immune system. It is now widely accepted that a wide variety of stressors such as maternal separation, bereavement, restraint, and crowding affect the immune system (Maier, Watkins, & Fleshner, 1994). Psychological processes such as mood state and coping style may also affect the immune system. This relationship is bidirectional, as immune processes may also affect the central nervous system and behavior. For example, it has been hypothesized that the immune system may activate the central nervous system in such a way as to increase perceived pain, which therefore may result in behaviors to reduce the pain (Maier et al., 1994).

Similar to the development of psychoneuroimmunology, the advent of behavioral theory has had a strong influence on the field of health-related disorders. Operant conditioning models have been been utilized to teach children specific skills such as pill swallowing, glucose testing, and compliance with a medical regimen as well as to treat pain disorders and elimination disorders. Classical conditioning models have been utilized to understand and treat such conditions as anticipatory nausea and certain types of feeding disorders.

Although professionals have relied on behavioral models, recent writings in the pediatric field have increasingly emphasized a systems perspective (e.g., Hanson, 1992; Kazak, 1992; Mullins, Gillman, & Harbeck, 1992). Currently, the behavioral–systems model has gained popularity. This model retains the behavioral emphasis on thorough assessment, use of empirically based treatment approaches, and concern for treatment maintenance and generalization. In addition, this approach adds systems concepts such as inclusion of multiple levels of inquiry and intervention (e.g., biological, cognitive, affective, behavioral, family, community). Finally, the behavioral–systems model recognizes that patterns of interaction within a given system are not linear, but circular.

Currently, interest in health-related disorders remains high. Several organizations have been formed to promote interest and scientific inquiry in this field including the Society for Pediatric Psychology, Society of Behavioral Pediatrics, and Association for the Care of Children's Health. Numerous texts have been written that further our understanding of child health disorders and illustrate the richness of this field. Examples of these recent works (in order of publication date) include *Pediatric Psychology* (Roberts, 1986), *Handbook of Pediatric Psychology* (Routh, 1988), *The Pediatric Psychologist* (Peterson & Harbeck, 1988), *Stress and Coping in Child Health* (La Greca, Siegel, Wallander, & Walker, 1992), *The Sourcebook of Pediatric Psychology* (Olson et al., 1994), and the second edition of *Handbook of Pediatric Psychology* (Roberts, 1995).

As many of the above-listed texts illustrate, large strides have been made in our understanding of childhood health disorders. Researchers have improved the knowledge base describing the biological and psychological components of many chronic illnesses. Although much of the research in this area has been descriptive and has focused on increasing clinicians' understanding about health-related disorders, research on effective interventions and prevention programs is beginning. In addition, there has been a recent emphasis on theory-driven research in the last several years, with two entire issues of the 1992 *Journal of Pediatric Psychology* (Roberts, 1992a) devoted to the emphasis of research guided by formal theoretical frameworks.

As previously stated, one of the hallmarks of this field is the emphasis on the interface between physical well-being and psychological variables. In the next section, some examples of these health-related disorders are sampled.

CHILDHOOD HEALTH DISORDERS

Health-related disorders vary along numerous dimensions including severity, chronicity, predictability of illness course, degree of lifestyle changes required, presence of visible changes due to illness or treatment, and etiology. For the purposes of this chapter, we have divided child health-related problems into four categories based on etiology: (1) medical problems with a primary psychological etiology; (2) medical problems with a primary psychosocial etiology; (3) medical problems with a primary physiological etiology; and (4) distress due to medical procedures. It should be noted that these are not discrete categories; most health-related disorders have psychological, psychosocial, and medical components. Table 16.1 lists the relative contributions of each of these etiological factors for the disorders that are discussed in this chapter.

Medical Problems with a Primary Psychological Etiology

Somatoform Disorders

It is not uncommon for children and adolescents to present to the medical system with recurrent or persistent physical complaints, such as abdominal pain, dizziness, or headaches, for which an appropriate medical evaluation identifies no organic cause. Other children with known organic disease present with symptoms disproportionate to the symptoms expected from their particular illness. Treatment of these children and their families is extremely challenging for both medical and mental health professionals. Unlike most of the disorders described in this chapter, which have been viewed as outside the purview of traditional psychiatry and clinical psychology, the problems experienced by these children have been given psychiatric diagnostic labels.

In the *Diagnostic and Statistical Manual of Mental Disorders*, fourth edition (DSM-IV; American Psychiatric Association, 1994), and the *International Classification of Diseases*, 10th edition (ICD-10; World Health Organization, 1993) these heterogeneous disorders are grouped under the heading of somatoform disorders. Types of somatoform disorders included are somatization disorder, undifferentiated somatoform disorder, conversion disorder, pain disorder, hypochondriasis, body dysmorphic disorder, somatoform autonomic dysfunction, and somatoform disorder not otherwise specified (SDNOS). The essential feature in these disorders is the presence of physical symptoms in the absence of organic pathology or known physiological mechanisms. In addition, strong presumption of a psychological component to the symptom is required. Mullins, Olson, and Chaney (1992) recently reported that approximately 12% of children referred to a pediatric inpatient consultation service met the DSM-III-R (American Psychiatric Association, 1987) criteria for a somatoform disorder.

Somatization Disorder

Somatization disorder (SD), which is perhaps the most chronic of the somatoform disorders, is defined by a long history of multiple physical complaints that occur over a period of several years and result in treatment being sought or significant social, occupational, or other impairments. DSM-IV requires a minimum of eight symptoms from four categories, and ICD-10 requires a minimum of six symptoms from at least two separate physiological categories (see Table 16.2 for DSM-IV and ICD-10 diagnostic criteria).

TABLE 16.1. Etiologies of Health-Related Disorders

Hypothesized etiological factors	Psychological	Psychosocial	Physiological	Procedure-related distress
Somatoform disorders	P	S		
Elimination disorders	P	P	S	
Feeding disorders	S	P	S	
Adjustment disorder (major stressor is aspects of chronic illness)	S	S	P	S
Distress related to medical procedures	P	P		P

Note. P, primary etiology; S, secondary etiologies.

Somatization disorder is a chronic fluctuating condition that rarely totally remits and results in consumption of a disproportionate amount of health care resources by individuals with SD. Because these patients view themselves as seriously ill, their use of health care resources may be as high as nine times that of the general population (Smith, Monson, & Ray, 1986).

Unfortunately, most research on SD has been conducted with adults, and little information is available on children and adolescents. Adult studies suggest that prevalence rates vary widely, depending on the definitions used. For example, when full DSM-III criteria are used, the prevalence rate is very low; approximately 0.7% (Escobar, Golding, & Hough, 1987; Swartz, Blazer, George, Woodbury, & Manton, 1988). When subsyndromal forms of somatization are included (i.e., undifferentiated somatoform disorder), the prevalence rate increases to between 9% and 20% (Escobar, Rubio-Stipec, Canino, & Karno, 1989).

Somatization disorder is more common in female than male cohorts. The onset is typically during adolescence (Margo & Margo, 1994), and must occur before age 30, in order to meet DSM-IV criteria. Cultural factors are important in this disorder, as the symptom presentation may reflect cultural ideology. It should be noted that the criteria developed in DSM-IV are based on U.S. data and may not fully reflect this disorder in other cultures.

Treatment of SD is often complicated by comorbid psychiatric diagnoses. Estimates suggest that individuals with SD are also at high risk to develop major depression, generalized anxiety disorder, and phobic disorders (Brown, Golding, & Smith, 1990). For individuals with both SD and a depressive disorder, the SD typically preceded the mood disorder (Rief, Schaefer, Hiller, & Fichter, 1992). In addition to Axis I diagnoses, individuals with SD are also frequently diagnosed with personality disorders, with avoidance, paranoia, self-defeating, and obsessive–compulsive being the most commonly diagnosed personality disorders in this population (Rost, Akins, Brown, & Smith, 1992). As with many of the somatoform disorders, the etiology of SD is unclear. Researchers have speculated that SD is caused by somatic amplification, labile physiological reactions, distortions in somatic perception, high levels of somatic attention, suppression of emotions, and developmental and social factors (Kirmayer, Robbins, & Paris, 1994).

However, few of these factors have received consistent empirical support. Empirical work does suggest the importance of social and developmental factors, with the finding that emotional neglect followed by childhood illness may lead to SD (Craig, Boardman, Mills, Daly-Jones, & Drake, 1993). Correlational research suggests that high levels of unexplained somatic symptoms are related to high levels of somatic attention and emotional inhibition (Larson & Chastain, 1990; Pennebaker, 1982; Robbins & Kirmayer, 1991). In addition to these individuals' prior experience of illness and greater focus on illness symptoms, individuals with SD have difficulty accurately detecting their internal body cues (Gardner, Morrell, & Ostrowski, 1990). It is likely that a complex interaction of multiple factors accounts for SD. Clearly, more research is needed on this costly disorder.

Undifferentiated Somatoform Disorder

Similar to SD, the defining criteria of undifferentiated somatoform disorder includes the presentation of multiple physical complaints for which no organic cause can be found. This diagnosis is a residual category and is used for individuals with persistent somatic complaints (lasting a minimum of 6 months), who do not meet the criteria for SD (see Table 16.3). ICD-10 diagnosis of somatoform autonomic dysfunction (see Table 16.4) would likely be included under this diagnosis in the DSM-IV diagnostic system.

Some evidence suggests that multiple somatic complaints in childhood and adolescence may be a precursor for SD (Ernst et al., 1984; Routh & Ernst, 1984). Because a diagnosis of SD is highly unusual in prepubertal children due to the requirement that one of the individual's symptoms be a sexual symptom, a diagnosis of undifferentiated somatoform disorder is more likely to be made with a younger population. Unfortunately, little research exists in children with this diagnosis; however, it is hypothesized that the etiology is similar to that of SD. Undifferentiated somatoform disorder occurs most commonly in women of low socioeconomic status (American Psychiatric Association, 1994). In contrast to children who present with multiple physical complaints and are given a diagnosis of SD or undifferentiated somatization disorder, the children and adolescents to be considered in the next section present with more focal complaints.

TABLE 16.2. Criteria for Somatization Disorder

DSM-IV criteria	ICD-10 research criteria

A. A history of many physical complaints beginning before age 30 years that occur over a period of several years and result in treatment being sought or significant impairment in social, occupational, or other important areas of functioning.
 	
B. Each of the following criteria must have been met, with individual symptoms occurring at any time during the course of the disturbance:
  (1) *four pain symptoms:* a history of pain related to at least four different sites or functions (e.g., head, abdomen, back, joints, extremities, chest, rectum, during menstruation, during sexual intercourse, or during urination)
  (2) *two gastrointestinal symptoms:* a history of at least two gastro-intestinal symptoms other than pain (e.g., nausea, bloating, vomiting other than during pregnancy, diarrhea, or intolerance of several different foods)
  (3) *one sexual symptom:* a history of at least one sexual or reproductive symptom other than pain (e.g., sexual indifference, erectile or ejaculatory dysfunction, irregular menses, excessive menstrual bleeding, vomiting throughout pregnancy)
  (4) *one pseudoneurological symptom:* a history of at least one symptom or deficit suggesting a neurological condition not limited to pain (conversion symptoms such as impaired coordination or balance, paralysis or localized weakness, difficulty swallowing or lump in throat, aphonia, urinary retention, hallucinations, loss of touch or pain sensation, double vision, blindness, deafness, seizures; dissociative symptoms such as amnesia; or loss of consciousness other than fainting)
 	
C. Either (1) or (2):
  (1) after appropriate investigation, each of the symptoms in Criterion B cannot be fully explained by a known general medical condition or the direct effects of a substance (e.g., a drug of abuse, a medication)
  (2) when there is a related general medical condition, the physical complaints or resulting social or occupational impairment are in excess of what would be expected from the history, physical examination, or laboratory findings
 	
D. The symptoms are not intentionally produced or feigned (as in Factitious Disorder or Malingering).
	A. There must be a history of at least 2 years' complaints of multiple and variable physical symptoms that cannot be explained by any detectable physical disorders. (Any physical disorders that are known to be present do not explain the severity, extent, variety, and persistence of the physical complaints, or the associated social disability.) If some symptoms clearly due to autonomic arousal are present, they are not a major feature of the disorder in that they are not particularly persistent or distressing.
	
	B. Preoccupation with the symptoms causes persistent distress and leads the patient to seek repeated (three or more) consultations or sets of investigations with either primary care or specialist doctors. In the absence of medical services within either the financial or physical reach of the patient, there must be persistent self-medication or multiple consultations with local healers.
	
	C. There is persistent refusal to accept medical reassurance that there is no adequate physical cause for the physical symptoms. (Short-term acceptance of such reassurance, i.e., for a few weeks during or immediately after investigations, does not exclude this diagnosis.)
	
	D. There must be a total of six or more symptoms from the following list, with symptoms occurring in at least two separate groups:
	Gastrointestinal symptoms
	  (1) abdominal pain;
	  (2) nausea;
	  (3) feeling bloated or full of gas;
	  (4) bad taste in mouth, or excessively coated tongue;
	  (5) complaints of vomiting or regurgitation of food;
	  (6) complaints of frequent and loose bowel motions or discharge of fluids from anus;
	Cardiovascular symptoms
	  (7) breathlessness without exertion;
	  (8) chest pains;
	Genitourinary symptoms
	  (9) dysuria or complaints of frequency of micturition;
	  (10) unpleasant sensations in or around the genitals;
	  (11) complaints of unusual or copious vaginal discharge;
	Skin and pain symptoms
	  (12) blotchiness or discoloration of the skin;
	  (13) pain in the limbs, extremities, or joints;
	  (14) unpleasant numbness or tingling sensations.
	
	E. *Most commonly used exclusion clause.* Symptoms do not occur only during any of the schizophrenic or related disorders (F20–F29), any of the mood [affective] disorders (F30–F39), or panic disorder (F41.0).

Note. DSM-IV criteria from American Psychiatric Association (1994, pp. 449–450). Copyright 1994 by the American Psychiatric Association. Reprinted by permission. ICD-10 criteria from World Health Organization (1993, pp. 105–106). Copyright 1993 by the World Health Organization. Reprinted by permission.

TABLE 16.3. Criteria for Undifferentiated Somatoform Disorder

---

DSM-IV criteria

A. One or more physical complaints (e.g., fatigue, loss of appetite, gastrointestinal or urinary complaints).

B. Either (1) or (2):
   (1) after appropriate investigation, the symptoms cannot be fully explained by a known general medical condition or the direct effects of a substance (e.g., a drug of abuse, a medication)
   (2) when there is a related general medical condition, the physical complaints or resulting social or occupational impairment is in excess of what would be expected from the history, physical examination, or laboratory findings.

C. The symptoms cause clinically significant distress or impairment in social, occupational, or other important areas of functioning.

D. The duration of the disturbance is at least 6 months.

E. The disturbance is not better accounted for by another mental disorder (e.g., another Somatoform Disorder, Sexual Dysfunction, Mood Disorder, Anxiety Disorder, Sleep Disorder, or Psychotic Disorder).

F. The symptom is not intentionally produced or feigned (as in Factitious Disorder or Malingering).

ICD-10 research criteria

A. Criteria A, C, and E for somatization disorder (F45.0) are met, except that the duration of the disorder is at least 6 months.

B. One or both of criteria B and D for somatization disorder (F45.0) are incompletely filled.

Note. DSM-IV criteria from American Psychiatric Association (1994, pp. 451–452). Copyright 1994 by the American Psychiatric Association. Reprinted by permission. ICD-10 criteria from World Health Organization (1993, p. 106). Copyright 1993 by the World Health Organization. Reprinted by permission.

Conversion Disorder

The most common somatoform disorder seen in children is conversion disorder (Maloney, 1980; Mullins & Olson, 1990; Siegel & Barthel, 1986). The defining feature of a conversion disorder is the presence of unexplained symptoms or deficits affecting voluntary motor or sensory function that suggest the presence of a neurological or other general medical condition. These symptoms typically do not conform to known anatomical pathways and physiological mechanisms. A thorough medical evaluation with an absence of organic findings is required before a diagnosis of conversion disorder can be made (see Table 16.5 for full diagnostic criteria).

Reported rates of conversion disorder vary from 11/100,000 to 300/100,000 in general population samples and occur more frequently in women than men (American Psychiatric Association, 1994). According to DSM-IV, the onset of a conversion disorder generally occurs between late childhood and early adulthood. Although rarely seen in children below age 10 years, conversion symptoms in children below 10 years of age do occur, but these are usually limited to gait problems or seizures. The onset of symptoms in conversion disorder is acute, and symptoms typically remit within 2 weeks, with recurrence of symptoms in 20% to 25% of individuals. Spierings, Pels, Sijben, Gabreels, and Renier (1990) reported that of 69 children aged 6 to 17 years diagnosed with a conversion disorder, 72% reported improvement over time (only a portion of these children had received treatment), but 33% still had the same complaints. Although conversion disorder is perhaps the most common somatoform disorder in children, more research is needed on the etiology, prognosis, and treatment of this disorder.

For children who present with a primary symptom involving pain rather than neurological symptoms, a diagnosis of pain disorder is more appropriate. As is seen in the next section, several forms of chronic childhood illness are correctly labeled as pain disorder.

Pain Disorder

When an individual presents with a primary symptom of pain with no motor, sensory, or seizure symptoms, a diagnosis of pain disorder should be considered (see Table 16.6 for diagnostic criteria). In contrast to past DSM versions, DSM-IV (American Psychiatric Association, 1994) instructs clinicians to code pain disorder into one of the following three categories: (1) pain disorder associated with psychological factors, (2) pain disorder associated with both psychological factors and a general medical condition, and (3) pain disorder associated with a general medical condition. It should be noted that the last category, pain disorder associated with a general medical condition, is not considered a mental disorder and is coded on Axis III. This last category is further considered later in the chapter under the headings of "Medical Problems with Primary Physiological Etiology" and "Distress Due To Medical Procedures."

TABLE 16.4. ICD-10 Research Criteria for Somatoform Autonomic Dysfunction

A. Symptoms of autonomic arousal, such as palpitation, sweating, tremor, flushing, which are persistent and troublesome;

B. Additional subjective symptoms referred to a specific organ or system;

C. Preoccupation with and distress about the possibility of a serious (but often unspecified) disorder of the stated organ or system, which does not respond to repeated explanation and reassurance by doctors;

D. No evidence of a significant disturbance of structure or function of the stated system or organ.

A fifth character may be used to classify the individual disorders in this group, indicating the organ or system regarded by the patient as the origin of the symptoms:
    Heart and cardiovascular system
    Upper gastrointestinal tract
    Lower gastrointestinal tract
    Respiratory system
    Genitourinary system
    Other organ or system

Note. From World Health Organization (1993, pp. 107–108). Copyright 1993 by the World Health Organization. Adapted by permission.

Certain types of pains in the first category of pain disorder are referred to as "recurrent pain" in the pediatric literature. Recurrent pain syndromes typically involve frequently occurring episodes of headaches, abdominal pains, or limb pain that persist beyond a 3-month period. These pains occur in otherwise healthy children and are not symptomatic of an underlying physical disease requiring medical treatment (McGrath, 1990). Recurrent pain syndromes occur at strikingly high rates. In a study of 2,200 children aged 6 to 19 years, Oster (1972) reported that 14.4% experienced recurrent abdominal pain, 20.6% reported headache pain, and 15.5% experienced limb pains.

Of children with recurrent abdominal pain (RAP), less than 10% are found to have an organic illness (Apley, 1975). The incidence of RAP peaks between the ages of 9 and 12 years, and girls are affected more frequently than boys with a ratio of approximately 5:3 (Hodges & Burbach, 1991). In their longitudinal study, Apley and Hale (1973) reported that of children with recurrent abdominal pain, only one-third had lost all symptoms by adulthood. In another third of these children, the abdominal pains ceased but were replaced with other somatic symptoms. In the remaining third of the children, the abdominal pains continued, with the addition of other somatic symptoms.

In her review of the available research on recurrent headaches, McGrath (1990) summarized data suggesting that the average age of headache onset is approximately 7 years of age and that headache prevalence increases with age. Interestingly, although more young boys report headaches than girls, the trend reverses such that more adolescent girls suffer from headaches than do boys. Finally, recovery-rate estimates vary widely,

TABLE 16.5. DSM-IV Diagnostic Criteria for Conversion Disorder

A. One or more symptoms or deficits affecting voluntary motor or sensory function that suggest a neurological or other general medical condition.

B. Psychological factors are judged to be associated with the symptom or deficit because the initiation or exacerbation of the symptom or deficit is preceded by conflicts or other stressors.

C. The symptom or deficit is not intentionally produced or feigned (as in Factitious Disorder or Malingering).

D. The symptom or deficit cannot, after appropriate investigation, be fully explained by a general medical condition, or by the direct effects of a substance, or a culturally sanctioned behavior or experience.

E. The symptom or deficit causes clinically significant distress or impairment in social, occupational, or other important areas of functioning or warrants medical evaluation.

F. The symptom or deficit is not limited to pain or sexual dysfunction, does not occur exclusively during the course of Somatization Disorder, and is not better accounted for by another mental disorder.

Specify type of symptom or deficit:
    With Motor Symptom or Deficit
    With Sensory Symptom or Deficit
    With Seizures or Convulsions
    With Mixed Presentation

Note. From American Psychiatric Association (1994, p. 457). Copyright 1994 by the American Psychiatric Association. Reprinted by permission.

TABLE 16.6. Criteria for Pain Disorder

DSM-IV criteria

A. Pain in one or more anatomical sites is the predominant focus of the clinical presentation and is of sufficient severity to warrant clinical attention.

B. The pain causes clinically significant distress or impairment in social, occupational, or other important areas of functioning.

C. Psychological factors are judged to have an important role in the onset, severity, exacerbation, or maintenance of the pain.

D. The symptom or deficit is not intentionally produced or feigned (as in Factitious Disorder or Malingering).

E. The pain is not better accounted for by a Mood, Anxiety, or Psychotic Disorder and does not meet criteria for Dyspareunia.

Code as follows:
Pain Disorder Associated with Psychological Factors
Pain Disorder Associated with Both Psychological Factors and a General Medical Condition
Pain Disorder Associated with a General Medical Condition

ICD-10 research criteria

A. There is persistent severe and distressing pain (for at least 6 months, and continuously on most days), in any part of the body, which cannot be explained adequately by evidence of a physiological process or a physical disorder, and which is consistently the main focus of the patient's attention.

B. *Most commonly used exclusion clause.* This disorder does not occur in the presence of schizophrenia or related disorders (F20–F29), or only during any of the mood [affective] disorders (F30–F39), somatization disorder (F45.0), undifferentiated somatoform disorder (F45.1), or hypochondriacal disorder (F45.2).

Note. DSM-IV criteria from American Psychiatric Association (1994, pp. 461–462). Copyright 1994 by the American Psychiatric Association. Reprinted by permission. ICD-10 criteria from World Health Organization (1993, p. 108). Copyright 1993 by the World Health Organization. Reprinted by permission.

from 3% to 80%. In a 23-year follow-up of 73 school-aged children diagnosed with migraine headaches, Billie (1981) reported that over half of the original sample were symptom-free during adolescence and young adulthood. However, by age 30, 60% reported continued headache symptoms. It should be noted that similar to other somatoform disorders, few longitudinal studies on nonspecific pains have been conducted on children in North America, and therefore these data should be interpreted with caution.

Much of the research on recurrent pain syndromes has utilized a social learning framework. According to the social learning perspective, an individual's functioning can be explained in terms of "a continuous reciprocal interaction of personal and environmental determinants" (Bandura, 1977, pp. 11–12). Bandura theorized that children learn behaviors through observing models in their environment. Whether they imitate the behavior observed depends, in part, on the consequences experienced by the model. If a behavior is imitated, consequences given to the child for the behavior will determine if the child will repeat the imitated behavior. Several analogous studies assessing pain tolerance in adults support social learning theory. Craig (1983) reported that during studies of induced pain, healthy adults conformed to the behavior of tolerant or intolerant pain models in verbal reports of pain. In addition, exposure to different models of pain behavior influenced psychophysiological measures and correlates of pain. Although these analogous studies have not been conducted with children, anecdotal clinical reports and several empirical studies with children have utilized a social learning framework to examine the way in which familial and environmental factors influence children's pain.

For example, Osborne, Hatcher, and Richtsmeier (1989) compared a group of 20 parents and their children with recurrent unexplained pain and 20 children and their parents with recurrent pain secondary to sickle cell anemia to determine the presence of pain and illness models in the child's environment. The authors reported that when parent and child reports were combined, a pain model was identified for each child with recurrent unexplained pain. In contrast, less than half of the children with pain due to the sickle cell anemia identified a pain model. Routh and Ernst (1984) reported similar findings. They found that children with functional abdominal pain were more likely to identify a familial pain model than were children with abdominal pain due to organic causes. Several hypotheses for the link between familial pain models and pain experience have been suggested, including a genetic predisposition to somatic pain syndromes, social learning, and the family's emphasis on health and illness

issues (Peterson, Harbeck, Farmer, & Zink, 1991; Routh, Ernst, & Harper, 1988).

Hughes and Zimin (1978) reported that families of children with recurrent abdominal pain experience multiple illnesses and that parents are often preoccupied with health concerns. However, these suggestions that such families have a higher number of health-related events are only partially supported by empirical research. For example, Hodges, Kline, Barbero, and Flanery (1984) reported that both children with recurrent abdominal pain and children with behavior disorders experienced significantly more negative life events and stress than did healthy children. When looking at the type of stresses experienced, they found that children with recurrent abdominal pain were more likely to have experienced life events related to illness, hospitalization, and death than were children with behavior disorders. However, other studies have found no difference in the amount of illness-related events or life-event stress reported by children with recurrent pain and healthy children (McGrath, Goodman, Firestone, Shipman, & Peters, 1983; L. Walker & Greene, 1991; Wasserman, Whitington, & Rivara, 1988). One recent study suggests that the influence of negative life events on pain syndromes is moderated by a child's social competence (L. Walker, Garber, & Greene, 1994). In this section, we have discussed several forms of somatoform disorders, which clearly have a primary psychological etiology. The remaining disorders that are discussed in this section frequently have a primary behavioral etiology, but social and medical factors are also clearly important and contribute to the disorder.

Elimination Disorders

Studies suggest that toileting is a major concern for parents (Chamberlin, 1974; Mesibov, Schroeder, & Wesson, 1977), and when children do not learn toilet training as quickly as expected, the resulting problems may cause extreme stress for the family. Kempe and Helfer (1972) reported that incontinence was the second most commonly stated reason for nonaccidental injury to children (Kempe & Helfer, 1972). Although toilet training is a stressful process for many parents, few data-based programs for toilet training are available. In fact, since the early 1900s, suggestions for toilet training have swung like a pendulum from passive permissiveness to full systemic control (Luxem & Christophersen, 1994). Currently, the trend is to begin toilet training between the

second and third year. When toilet training is unsuccessful, two types of elimination disorders may result: enuresis and encopresis.

Enuresis

Enuresis refers to the involuntary discharge of urine. Three types of enuresis exist: Diurnal enuresis refers to wetting during the day; nocturnal enuresis refers to wetting during the night; and mixed enuresis includes both daytime and nighttime wetting. In order to be given a diagnosis of enuresis, both DSM-IV and ICD-10 require that the child's chronological and mental age be at least 5 years (see Table 16.7). In addition, the voiding of urine into bed or clothes must not be due exclusively to a general medical condition or the result of a diuretic. Although DSM-IV requires the urine voiding into bed or clothes to occur at least twice a week for 3 consecutive months, ICD-10 suggests that a frequency of twice a month for children under age 7 and once a month for children above age 7 warrants a diagnosis.

Reports estimate that in the United States, approximately 20% of 5-year-olds, 5% of 10-year-olds, and approximately 2% of 12- to 14-year-olds experience nocturnal enuresis (Oppel, Harper, & Rider, 1968; Perlmutter, 1985). Diurnal enuresis is less prevalent than nocturnal enuresis, with estimates suggesting that only 3% of 6-year-olds in Great Britain and Sweden experience diurnal enuresis (Blomfield & Douglas, 1956; Hallgren, 1956). If untreated, the spontaneous remission rate of enuresis is approximately 15% each year from ages 5 to 19 (Forsythe & Redmond, 1974). However, other reports suggest that the remission rate for girls may actually be much higher, with a spontaneous remission rate of 44% to 71% between the ages of 4 and 6 (Verhulst et al., 1985).

Several etiologies for enuresis have been proposed, including genetic causes, organic disorders, emotional factors, and impaired learning. Genetic factors appear to contribute significantly to enuresis. Bakwin (1973) observed a 68% concordance of enuresis for monozygotic twins and a 36% concordance rate for dyzygotic twins. He also reported that enuresis occurs among approximately 70% of children who have two parents with a history of enuresis. Although hereditary factors do appear to account for some of the prevalence of enuresis, no specific mechanism of this transmission has been documented, and environmental influences (e.g., family attitudes, training procedures) have not totally been ruled out (C. Walker, Milling, & Bonner, 1988).

TABLE 16.7. Criteria for Enuresis

DSM-IV criteria	ICD-10 research criteria
A. Repeated voiding of urine into bed or clothes (whether involuntary or intentional).	A. The child's chronological and mental age is at least 5 years.
B. The behavior is clinically significant as manifested by either a frequency of twice a week for at least 3 consecutive months or the presence of clinically significant distress or impairment in social, academic (occupational), or other important areas of functioning.	B. Involuntary or intentional voiding of urine into bed or clothes occurs at least twice a month in children aged under 7 years, and at least once a month in children aged 7 years or more.
C. Chronological age is at least 5 years (or equivalent developmental level).	C. The enuresis is not a consequence of epileptic attacks or of neurological incontinence, and not a direct consequence of structural abnormalities of the urinary tract or any other non-psychiatric medical condition.
D. The behavior is not due exclusively to the direct physiological effect of a substance (e.g., diuretic) or a general medical condition (e.g., diabetes, spina bifida, a seizure disorder).	D. There is no evidence of any other psychiatric disorder that meets the criteria for other ICD-10 categories.
Specify type: Nocturnal Only Diurnal Only Nocturnal and Diurnal	E. Duration of the disorder is at least 3 months. A fifth character may be used, if desired, for further specification: **F98.00 Nocturnal enuresis only** **F98.01 Diurnal enuresis only** **F98.02 Nocturnal and diurnal enuresis**

Note. DSM-IV criteria from American Psychiatric Association (1994, pp. 109–110). Copyright 1994 by the American Psychiatric Association. Reprinted by permission. ICD-10 criteria from World Health Organization (1993, p. 169). Copyright 1993 by the World Health Organization. Reprinted by permission.

Organic disorders that may contribute to incontinence include a variety of acquired and congenital lesions of the spinal cord, and anomalies of innervation of the bladder (Vaughan, McKay, & Behrman, 1979). These conditions may result in an inability to empty the bladder completely, or in decreased bladder capacity, both of which may result in dribbling and wetting. Other organic conditions that may cause incontinence include structural problems in the anatomy of the urogenital system, vaginal reflux, hormonal disturbances, and urinary tract infections (Schroeder & Gordon, 1991; C. Walker et al., 1988). Although children with these organic conditions will not meet DSM-IV or ICD-10 criteria for a diagnosis of enuresis, it is helpful if professionals are aware of these conditions and that an adequate assessment of organic etiology be included in the assessment of incontinence or enuresis.

Although most children with enuresis do not have emotional or behavioral problems, enuresis is more frequent in children who do have emotional disturbance (Shaffer, 1973). Stressful life events or family stress may contribute to enuresis by interfering with the process of being toilet trained, thus resulting in incomplete training and functional enuresis (C. Walker, Kenning, & Faust-Campanile, 1989). Although psychodynamic theorists have hypothesized that enuresis may reflect repressed conflicts or an expression of emotional needs, research has not supported these hypotheses (C. Walker et al., 1989).

Perhaps the theory that has received the most empirical support is learning theory. Learning theory posits that achieving bladder control requires a child to learn the complex skill of gaining control over the urination reflex. This reflex includes contraction of the detrusor muscle simultaneously with relaxation of the internal and external sphincter muscles. If the child does not learn to control the urination reflex completely, develops poor habits, or environmental contingencies interfere with learning, enuresis may result. Support for this theory comes from the numerous empirical studies that document strategies designed to help a child learn control over the urination reflex decrease the frequency of enuresis, with success rates of 70% to 90% (C. Walker et al., 1989). Similar to enuresis, learning theory may explain many of the cases of the next disorder examined, encopresis.

Encopresis

Both DSM-IV and ICD-10 describe encopresis as the passage of feces into places that are inappropriate and include both intentional and involuntary actions. In order to give the diagnosis of encopresis, both diagnostic systems require that the event occurs at least once per month, the child has a mental and chronological age of at least 4 years, and that no organic conditions exist that may fully explain the condition. Although DSM-IV only requires a duration of 3 months, ICD-10 requires a duration of 6 months (see Table 16.8).

Encopresis can be categorized as primary or secondary. Children with primary encopresis have reached age 4 without being continent for at least 1 year, whereas children with secondary encopresis have had at least 1 full year of being continent before the current episode of encopresis began. In addition to the primary/secondary distinction, three major categories of encopresis exist (Howe & Walker, 1992). The most common type of encopresis is retentive encopresis, which accounts for 80% to 95% of all encopretic cases (Christopherson & Rapoff, 1983;

Levine, 1975). Retentive encopresis occurs when a child becomes extremely constipated and fecal material leaks around the fecal obstruction into the underwear. The second type of encopresis includes chronic diarrhea and irritable bowel syndrome, which may be related to stress. The third and least common type of encopresis is manipulative soiling, during which the child intentionally soils in order to manipulate people in his or her environment.

The reported prevalence of encopresis ranges from 0.3% to 8%, depending on the definitions, settings, and age ranges examined (C. Walker et al., 1989). Encopretic referrals account for approximately 3% of outpatient pediatric clinic referrals (Abrahamian & Lloyd-Still, 1984), and 5.7% of referrals to psychiatric clinics (Olatawura, 1973). Encopresis is five to six times more common in boys than girls (Schroeder & Gordon, 1991). Finally, the frequency of encopresis decreases with age, with a spontaneous remission rate of about 28% per year (Schaefer, 1979).

The etiology of encopresis is similar to that of enuresis in that biological, psychological, and social factors are important. Several organic eti-

TABLE 16.8. Criteria for Encopresis

DSM-IV criteria	ICD-10 research criteria
A. Repeated passage of feces into inappropriate places (e.g., clothing or floor) whether involuntary or intentional.	A. The child passes feces in places that are inappropriate for the purpose (e.g., clothing, floor), either involuntarily or intentionally. (The disorder may involve overflow incontinence secondary to functional fecal retention.)
B. At least one such event a month for at least 3 months.	B. The child's chronological and mental age is at least 4 years.
C. Chronological age is at least 4 years (or equivalent developmental level).	C. There is at least one encopretic event per month.
D. The behavior is not due exclusively to the direct physiological effects of a substance (e.g., laxatives) or a general medical condition except through a mechanism involving constipation.	D. Duration of the disorder is at least 6 months.
	E. There is no organic condition that constitutes a sufficient cause for the encopretic events.
Code as follows: **With Constipation and Overflow Incontinence Without Constipation and Overflow Incontinence**	A fifth character may be used, if desired, for further specification: **F98.10 Failure to acquire bowel control** **F98.11 Adequate bowel control with normal feces deposited in inappropriate places** **F98.12 Soiling associated with excessively fluid feces(such as with retention with overflow)**

Note. DSM-IV criteria from American Psychiatric Association (1994, p. 107). Copyright 1994 by the American Psychiatric Association. Reprinted by permission. ICD-10 criteria from World Health Organization (1993, pp. 169–170). Copyright 1993 by the World Health Organization. Reprinted by permission.

ologies frequently contribute to the disorder; however, it should be noted again that if organic causes are the sole etiology of the incontinence, the disorder is not labeled encopresis. Organic disorders that may contribute to encopresis include anal lesions, structural neurological pathology, anorectal malformations, or Hirschsprung disease (Vaughan et al., 1979). Recent research by Loening-Baucke (1990) also suggests that up to 50% of children with chronic constipation and encopresis have abnormal defecation dynamics (i.e., they contract, rather than relax the external sphincter when they attempt to defecate.) They further report that these children respond well to biofeedback training, during which they are taught to appropriately relax the external sphincter muscle.

According to C. Walker et al. (1988), two major theoretical orientations describing the etiology of functional encopresis have been delineated. Historically, psychodynamic theorists have viewed encopresis as a symptom of an unconscious conflict (Lehman, 1944; Lifshitz & Chovers, 1972; Silber, 1969). Other theorists postulate that factors such as overly aggressive or early toilet training, family disturbance and stress, or the child's psychopathology contribute to the encopresis (e.g., Amsterdam, 1979; Fisher, 1979; Hersov, 1977; Knopf, 1979; Ringdahl, 1980). However, no empirical data exist to support these positions.

Several authors have investigated the relationship between encopresis and emotional problems. Abrahamian and Lloyd-Still (1984) reported that 20% of the encopretic children had significant psychological problems. They further stated that in a majority of the children, the psychological problems appeared to be a result from, rather than a cause of, the encopresis.

Learning models have been proposed to explain the development of encopresis, and they appear to fit especially well with children who have retentive encopresis. These models posit that the chronic constipation the child experiences interferes with the child's mastery of the toileting process. These children either have not acquired or are no longer able to perform the many skills required for successful toileting, including recognizing body cues, undressing, going into the bathroom, sitting on the toilet chair, and relaxing the appropriate muscles.

Finally, the type of encopresis labeled manipulative soiling may best be understood from an operant conditioning model (C. Walker et al., 1988). Children with manipulative soiling receive rewards (i.e., parental attention, school absence, etc.) for soiling behavior, and these reinforcements then increase the soiling behavior.

Treatment of encopresis usually includes both medical interventions (e.g., increased fluid and fiber intake) as well as behavioral interventions (e.g., rewards for appropriate toileting behavior, establishing a regular time for emptying the bowels, usually just after a meal). Successful intervention protocols can be found in Schroeder and Gordon (1991) and C. Walker et al. (1988).

Medical Problems with a Primary Psychosocial Etiology

Similar to problems discussed here in "Medical Problems with a Primary Psychological Etiolgy," medical problems with a psychosocial etiology typically do not have a primary organic etiology, but in contrast to topics described above, they are not primarily influenced by characteristics of the child. Instead, they are most often caused by an individual serving as caregiver to the child. Three types of medical problems with a primary psychosocial etiology are considered in this section including child abuse and neglect, Munchausen by proxy syndrome, and feeding disorders.

Child Abuse and Neglect

Child abuse and neglect refers to a number of events, both acute and chronic that "interact with the child's ongoing development to interrupt, alter, or impair his or her psychological development" (Wolfe, 1987, p. 10). Included in this definition are physical and sexual abuse, as well as emotional abuse and neglect (see Wekerle & Wolfe, Chapter 14, this volume). Recent estimates suggest that in 1990 there were more than 2.5 million cases of child maltreatment and over 1,200 child-abuse-related fatalities in the United States (National Committee for Prevention of Child Abuse, 1991). In the hospital setting, child abuse often presents as an organic illness or "accidental" injury. Recently, there has been compelling evidence that as many as half of child fatalities from birth to age 4 years ascribed in the past to unintentional injury may be due to clear physical abuse or neglect (Ewigman, Kivlahan, & Land, 1993). Special diagnostic skills are required to distinguish unintentional injury from abuse, and it may be impossible to determine when unintentional injury is due to neglect (Peterson

& Brown, 1994). In order to diagnose an injury due to abuse, physicians and other professionals need a thorough knowledge of the signs of particular types of abuse, knowledge about the effects of falls and other unintentional injuries, and the ability to question caretakers carefully about the injury etiology (Warner & Hansen, 1994). Unfortunately, for physicians as well as many other professionals, training in the diagnosis and treatment of child abuse has not kept pace with the needs for such expertise (Gallmeier & Bonner, 1992). Because general issues regarding child maltreatment are covered more fully in Chapter 14 (Wekerle & Wolfe, this volume), the remainder of this section focuses on specific types of abuse that masquerade as physical illness rather than injury, as these types of abuse are more likely to be diagnosed or treated by the pediatric psychologist.

Munchausen by Proxy Syndrome

According to Coury (1994), Munchausen by proxy syndrome (MBPS) is an unusual form of child abuse in which a parent or other primary caregiver brings harm to a child through induction of medical symptoms and encourages numerous unnecessary medical treatments. MBPS has been further delineated by Rosenberg (1987) as a syndrome cluster consisting of: (1) an illness in a child that is produced or simulated by a parent or primary caregiver, (2) persistent presentation of the child for medical assessment and treatment, often resulting in numerous medical procedures that bring further suffering to the child, (3) denial by the perpetrator of knowledge about the etiology of the child's illness, and (4) acute illness symptoms that remit when the child is separated from the caregiver. Examples of documented cases include poisoning (Chan, Salcedo, Atkins, & Ruley, 1986), adding blood to urine to mimic hematuria (Outwater, Lipnick, Luban, Ravenscroft, & Ruley, 1981), and physically induced apnea (Rosen et al., 1983). Incidence and prevalence data are largely unavailable, but what information does exist suggests that MBPS is extremely uncommon. However, Coury (1994) asserts that it is frequently misdiagnosed and may be more common than the literature suggests.

Information regarding the etiology and prognosis of MBPS is sketchy, because the existing literature appears predominantly as case studies. However, in an effort to discover patterns among MBPS cases, Kaufman (1990, 1994) reviewed descriptions of 117 MBPS cases to develop a proposed etiology of MBPS. According to Kaufman, offenders (who are typically mothers) often grow up in emotionally rejecting households where positive attention is typically reserved for times when external interventions are necessary (e.g., when the child is ill). The offender's initial contacts with the health care system may be positive and are perceived as extremely rewarding in comparison to her own rejecting family. Offenders may escalate their own complaints and engage in activities such as doctor shopping and may even become trained in the health care field. After having a child, the offender may discover during pediatric medical visits that she receives much positive attention and support for the care she gives her child with a "medical illness." One of the hallmarks of this condition is a parent who is having her own social support needs met by medical professionals and needs to create an illness in her child in order to avail herself of these relationships.

Feeding Disorders

Feeding disorders are examined under the heading "disorders with a primary psychosocial etiology" because the examples that are discussed have a primarily psychosocial origin. However, it should be noted at the outset that there are many types of feeding disorders, and these disorders vary along a continuum of medical etiology to psychosocial etiology. The term feeding disorders includes a variety of conditions characterized by insufficient or atypical food intake such as poor appetite, swallowing difficulties, selective food refusal, pica, and ruminative vomiting (Ginsberg, 1988; Palmer, Thompson, & Linscheid, 1975; Riordan, Iwata, Finney, Wohl, & Stanley, 1984; Woolston, 1985). Although feeding disorders were formerly divided into two groups labeled organic and nonorganic, researchers now acknowledge that there is much overlap between the two groups. Budd et al. (1992) divided their sample of children with feeding disorders into four descriptive groups: only organic, primarily organic, primarily nonorganic, and only nonorganic, and they reported that almost two thirds of the children had both organic and nonorganic characteristics.

Both DSM-IV and ICD-10 characterize feeding disorder of infancy or early childhood as a disturbance that includes a failure to eat adequately and failure to gain weight or significant loss of weight for at least one month. If an organic

disease (e.g., esophageal reflux) is present, it must not be sufficient to account for the failure to eat. Additional criteria include onset before the age of 6 years and no mental disorders that sufficiently account for the eating disturbance (see Table 16.9). In this section, we briefly consider two of many potential examples of feeding disorders; nonorganic failure to thrive, and feeding problems associated with children who have cystic fibrosis.

Nonorganic Failure to Thrive

Consistent with other types of feeding disorders, Nonorganic failure to thrive (NOFT) often presents to the medical system as an organically based problem. It usually presents in infancy. NOFT is defined as a severe growth deficiency, including weight for age at less than the 5th percentile and in which the growth deficiency is caused by psychosocial factors (Hammill et al., 1979; Homer & Ludwig, 1980). The incidence of NOFT is quite high. Research suggests that NOFT may account for approximately 1% of all hospital admissions and up to 5% of hospital admissions for young children (Berwick, 1980; Bruenlin, Desai, Stone, & Swilley, 1983; Homer & Ludwig, 1980; Sils, 1978). Consequences of NOFT are severe and include severe malnutrition, dehydration, rumination, and later behavioral and learning difficulties (Drotar, 1988).

When children with NOFT present to the medical system, they typically appear listless and withdrawn and often appear younger than their chronological age, both physically and behaviorally. According to Drotar and Sturm (1994), the family environment can influence the development of NOFT in three primary ways: (1) by limiting the availability of food and the child's caloric intake, (2) by restricting food allocation to the child, and (3) by contributing to maladaptive caregiver– child relationships that interfere with the child's behavioral feeding skills. In some cases, parents of children with NOFT may be too disturbed to care for their child, may have substance abuse problems, or may be unaware of the appropriate way to provide care (Roberts, 1986). Treatment of these children is wide ranging and often includes a behavioral–systems orientation, with an emphasis on behavioral programs to improve the feeding interaction between the child and caregiver (Linscheid, Budd, & Rasnake, 1995).

Feeding Disorders in Children with Cystic Fibrosis

Cystic fibrosis (CF) is a genetically inherited disease that affects the respiratory, gastrointestinal, and reproductive systems and leads to early death. Although the primary cause of death is

TABLE 16.9. Criteria for Feeding Disorder of Infancy or Early Childhood

DSM-IV criteria	ICD-10 research criteria
A. Feeding disturbance as manifested by persistent failure to eat adequately with significant failure to gain weight or significant loss of weight over at least 1 month.	A. There is persistent failure to eat adequately, or persistent rumination or regurgitation of food.
B. The disturbance is not due to an associated gastrointestinal or other general medical condition (e.g., esophageal reflux).	B. The child fails to gain weight, loses weight, or exhibits some other significant health problem over a period of at least 1 month. (In view of the frequency of transient eating difficulties, researchers may prefer a minimum duration of 3 months for some purposes.)
C. The disturbance is not better accounted for by another mental disorder (e.g., Rumination Disorder) or by lack of available food.	C. Onset of the disorder is before the age of 6 years.
D. The onset is before age 6 years.	D. The child exhibits no other mental or behavioural disorder in the ICD-10 classification (other than mental retardation, F70–F79).
	E. There is no evidence of organic disease sufficient to account for the failure to eat.

Note. DSM-IV criteria from American Psychiatric Association (1994, pp. 99–100). Copyright 1994 by the American Psychiatric Association. Reprinted by permission. ICD-10 criteria from World Health Organization (1993, p. 170). Copyright 1993 by the World Health Organization. Reprinted by permission.

severe pulmonary disease, malnutrition is highly correlated with pulmonary disease progression and early death (Gurwitz, Corey, Francis, Crozier, & Levison, 1979). Perhaps because of this correlation, CF programs have emphasized the prevention of malnutrition and promotion of normal growth and nutrition (Ramsey, Farrell, & Pencharz, 1992). This emphasis on nutrition is especially important because children with CF have a high required caloric intake. MacDonald, Holden, and Harris (1991) reported that the CF treatment recommendations suggest that children with CF consume 120% to 150% of the recommended daily allowance of energy for healthy children. This increased energy intake is required because of the increased energy demands caused by inadequate digestion, malabsorption of nutrients caused by pancreatic insufficiency, and chronic lung infections (Dodge, 1988).

This emphasis on nutrition has been hypothesized to contribute to psychosocial problems such as increased parental anxiety and child behavior problems at meals (McDonald et al., 1991). This hypothesis has been supported by data that suggest that mealtimes are the most commonly cited problem of parents of 2- to 5-year-old children with CF (Quittner, DiGirolamo, & Winslow, 1991). Perhaps because of their frustration and anxiety, a majority of parents of children with CF report using ineffective mealtime strategies such as coaxing and preparing a second meal if their child did not eat the first meal (Crist et al., 1994). These behaviors appear to inadvertently reward noneating behaviors, and parents of children with CF do report that their children have significantly more behavior problems at meals than healthy children, including excessively long meals, eating delays, and spitting out food (Crist, McDonnell, Beck, Gillespie, & Mathews, 1992). These behavior problems are significant, because they are clearly frustrating for parents and have been found to be related to caloric intake. Available reports suggest that although these children with CF are at increased risk to develop feeding disorders, their eating quickly improves when behavioral principles such as contingent attention for appropriate eating within a shorter time frame are utilized.

Medical Problems with a Primary Physiological Etiology

This section considers children and adolescents whose health disorder arises from an organic condition. In contrast to the disorders discussed in the first half of the chapter, many children and adolescents with primary organic disorders have adjustment problems or psychosocial sequelae that do not merit a DSM-IV diagnosis. Children with significant adjustment problems may be given a DSM-IV diagnosis of psychological factors affecting physical condition (see Table 16.10) or an adjustment disorder.

The prevalence of children with medical problems with a primary physiological etiology is actually quite high, with estimates ranging from less than 5% to over 30%. A recent study (Newacheck & Taylor, 1992) suggested that approximately 31% of children are affected by chronic health conditions, with the most common conditions being respiratory allergies, repeated ear infections, and asthma. Of children with chronic health conditions, approximately 66% have mild conditions, 29% have conditions of moderate severity that result in some restrictions or bother, and 5% have severe conditions that cause frequent bother and activity limitations.

As a result of advances in the biomedical sciences over the past several decades, children with serious health disorders are living much longer. As an example, the cure rate for childhood cancers has increased from approximately 20% in the 1950s to over 50% today, with the cure rate for certain types of cancer such as acute lymphoblastic leukemia over 80% (Cecalupo, 1994). Estimates suggest that by the year 2,000, 1 in every 1,000 young adults will be a survivor of childhood cancer. The lifespan expectancy for children with cystic fibrosis has also risen dramatically, with a median life expectancy of 28.3 years in 1994 (Cystic Fibrosis Foundation Patient Registry, 1995). Because of these improvements, much of the focus in pediatric centers is on helping children with medical disorders achieve an optimal quality of life.

Many researchers and clinicians have utilized a behavioral–systems approach to understand children's adaptation to chronic illness and other physical disorders. As previously mentioned, the behavioral–systems approach includes aspects of both a traditional behavioral orientation and a classic systems orientation. The behavioral–systems approach is most frequently seen in studies of adaptation to chronic illness or disability. Models of adaptation to illness are typically multifactorial and include disease and illness parameters (e.g., disease severity, time since diagnosis), socioeconomic variables, as well as external life

TABLE 16.10. DSM-IV Criteria for Psychological Factors Affecting Medical Condition

A. A general medical condition (coded on Axis III) is present.

B. Psychological factors adversely affect the general medical condition in one of the following ways:

  (1) the factors have influenced the course of the general medical condition as shown by a close temporal association between the psychological factors and the development or exacerbation of, or delayed recovery from, the general medical condition

  (2) the factors interfere with the treatment of the general medical condition

  (3) the factors constitute additional health risks for the individual

  (4) stress-related physiological responses precipitate or exacerbate symptoms of the general medical condition

Choose name based on the nature of the psychological factors (if more than one factor is present, indicate the most prominent):

  Mental Disorder Affecting . . . [Indicate the General Medical Condition] (e.g., an Axis I disorder such as Major Depressive Disorder delaying recovery from a myocardial infarction)

  Psychological Symptoms Affecting . . . [Indicate the General Medical Condition] (e.g., depressive symptoms delaying recovery from surgery; anxiety exacerbating asthma)

  Personality Traits or Coping Style Affecting . . . [Indicate the General Medical Condition] (e.g., pathological denial of the need for surgery in a patient with cancer; hostile, pressured behavior contributing to cardiovascular disease)

  Maladaptive Health Behaviors Affecting . . . [Indicate the General Medical Condition] (e.g., overeating; lack of exercise; unsafe sex)

  Stress-Related Physiological Response Affecting . . . [Indicate the General Medical Condition] (e.g., stress-related exacerbations of ulcer, hypertension, arrhythmia, or tension headache)

  Other or Unspecified Psychological Factors Affecting . . . [Indicate the General Medical Condition] (e.g., interpersonal, cultural, or religious factors)

Note. From American Psychiatric Association (1994, p. 678). Copyright 1994 by the American Psychiatric Association. Reprinted by permission.

stressors (Hanson, Henggeler, & Burghen, 1987; La Greca, 1988; Wallander et al., 1989). For example, when examining the adaptation of a child with diabetes, consideration must be given to biological factors such as metabolism, individual factors such as the child's understanding about his or her disease and treatment, the child's diabetes-relevant skills (e.g., correct blood glucose measurement), helpfulness of the child's coping strategies, and family factors such as level of family support and family stress. In addition, other systems must be considered such as the peer and school system's reaction to the child's need for treatment during school hours.

Historically, research on children with health problems has emphasized comparisons between physically ill and healthy children, including variables such as behavior problems, anxiety, depression, self-esteem, and symptoms of psychiatric dysfunction. A recent meta-analysis by Lavigne and Faier-Routman (1992) reviewed 87 studies of children's adjustment to physical disorders. Their review suggested that children with chronic physical disorders show an increased risk for overall

adjustment problems, with an elevated level of both internalizing (e.g., anxiety and depression) and externalizing symptoms (e.g., noncompliance, aggression). The mean change in effect sizes on overall psychological adjustment was approximately one-half of a standard deviation, and somewhat higher on studies making normative comparisons. In addition to type of comparison, level of risk also varied with informant, with higher rates of internalizing problems being noted by teachers than by parents. Although children with a chronic illness appear to experience an increased level of psychological adjustment difficulties, their adjustment is typically better than that of a sample referred to mental health clinics (Wallander, Varni, Babani, Banis, & Wilcox, 1988). Overall, these findings suggest that children with a chronic illness are *at risk* for development of more psychosocial problems than their healthy peers; however, few will evidence clinically significant problems or meet the criteria for a DSM-IV diagnosis of psychopathology.

Recently, many pediatric psychologists have abandoned this comparative paradigm and instead

have begun to interpret chronic illness as a stressor that will challenge a child's and family's available coping resources. Within this framework, much recent research has focused on identifying factors that promote successful adaptation to chronic illness. Factors that have been found to promote successful adaptation include demographic variables such as higher socioeconomic status (SES) and residence in a two-parent family (MacLean, Perrin, Gortmaker, & Pierre, 1992; Mulhern, Carpentieri, Shema, Stone, & Fairclough, 1993), illness variables such as low illness severity, little visible disfigurement, and low functional impairment (MacLean et al., 1992; Mulhern et al., 1993), individual factors such as perception of self-worth (Thompson, Gustafson, Hamlett, & Spock, 1992), and active coping (Gil, Williams, Thompson, & Kinney, 1991), and family factors including healthy parental adjustment (Barakat & Linney, 1992), low maternal anxiety (Thompson et al., 1992), positive sibling relationships (Hanson et al., 1992), and good family communication and conflict resolution skills (Wysocki, 1993).

Within the field of chronic illness, researchers are debating the advantages and disadvantages of using a noncategorical approach to the study of children with a chronic illness. Because many chronic illnesses have a low incidence rate, some authors advocate combining children with several illnesses into one sample (e.g., Wallander & Varni, 1992). This strategy is often used when examining global concepts such as overall psychological adjustment, self-esteem, and externalizing behavior problems. Other researchers have suggested that it is beneficial to study children with different illnesses separately because each chronic illness has its own set of challenges. For example, children with diabetes experience complex medical regimens, but they also have a relatively normal life expectancy. Children with cancer also experience a complex medical regimen, but they have the added challenges of significant side effects and a less predictable prognosis. In order to help the reader understand some of the specific challenges faced by children with chronic health disorders, diabetes mellitus and childhood cancer will be explored further. The discussion will focus on physical manifestations of the disease as well as special challenges faced by these children.

Diabetes Mellitus

Diabetes mellitus occurs in approximately one in 800 children and adolescents below 18 years of age, making it the most common endocrine disorder of childhood (Bennett, 1981). Insulin-dependent diabetes mellitus (IDDM) is usually diagnosed between the ages of 5 to 6 years or 11 to 13 years (Johnson, 1988). Diabetes mellitus is a chronic disorder in which the body is unable to adequately metabolize carbohydrates due to inadequate pancreatic release of and eventual inability to synthesize insulin. This absence of insulin results in a high level of glucose in the blood. Left untreated, acidosis can develop; if left untreated long enough, coma and death can ensue.

The treatment of IDDM involves establishing and maintaining a balance among the amount of food intake, exercise, and insulin intake. Adequate treatment therefore includes frequent daily testing of blood to assess the amount of glucose in the blood, a complex regimen of daily insulin injections, dietary restrictions, and close monitoring of food, exercise, stress, and illness. Children and adolescents must monitor their insulin levels carefully because too little insulin can result in a diabetic coma; too much insulin can result in an immediate insulin reaction called hypoglycemia, an emergency situation leading to coma. Hypoglycemic episodes are extremely unpleasant and include irritability, headaches, and shakiness. Factors that can upset the relationship between glucose and required insulin levels include illness, stress, and fluctuating levels of growth hormone. Stress has a direct influence on physical metabolic control and also has an indirect effect by lowering regimen adherence (Hanson et al., 1987).

A diagnosis of IDDM includes both long- and short-term consequences. Short-term consequences include the necessity for a regimen of monitoring glucose levels and a minimum of twice-daily insulin shots, as well as the potential for daily episodes of hypoglycemia. Long-term consequences if insulin regimens are not adhered to include vascular changes that can result in retinopathy, a leading cause of blindness in children, gangrene, and kidney failure.

Perhaps because of the significant consequences for children with poorly managed IDDM, researchers have spent much effort attempting to discover factors that promote regimen adherence and metabolic control. Regimen adherence and metabolic control are separate constructs with complex relationships (Johnson, 1990). Metabolic control is a biological/metabolic construct representing the degree to which the patient's glucose levels are maintained within the

normal range (80–120 mg/dl). Regimen adherence, on the other hand, refers to the degree to which the child follows the instructions given to him or her by the physician. It should be noted that regimen adherence is not a uniform construct (Geffken & Johnson, 1994); children are frequently compliant with certain aspects of diabetes care such as insulin injections, while they are much less compliant with other aspects such as glucose testing and foot care.

Factors associated with good regimen adherence and metabolic control include individual factors such as correct knowledge regarding the behaviors included in the diabetic regimen (Geffken & Johnson, 1994), beliefs that adherence is important (Brownlee-Duffeck et al., 1987), and adequate problem-solving skills (La Greca, 1988). Important systems-based factors include social support and family relationships. In one of the few truly systems-based investigations, Hanson, Henggeler, Harris, Burghen, and Moore (1989) confirmed previous findings that flexible family relations, high family cohesion, and high parental marital satisfaction were positively related to good metabolic control. However, these associations were attenuated with increased duration of the disease, such that the family factors were less predictive of metabolic control in children with longer disease duration. Future research would also benefit from this developmental framework to discover factors that are most likely to affect control in later stages of illness.

Childhood Cancer

Similar to IDDM, children with cancer face complicated medical treatment regimens. However, in contrast to children with IDDM, children with cancer often experience multiple school absences, significant side effects from their treatment, and an uncertain prognosis. Cancer occurs in approximately one out of 600 children prior to the age of 15, with acute lymphoblastic leukemia (ALL) being the most common cancer in childhood and accounting for 30% to 40% of all childhood cancers (Stehbens, 1988).

Treatment of ALL usually includes an intensive 2- to 3-year regimen of several phases including induction therapy to destroy the blast cells, central nervous system (CNS) prophylaxis, and maintenance chemotherapy. Frequent monitoring of the child's disease state is accomplished by blood value determinations, spinal taps, and bone marrow aspirations. Side effects of the treatment protocol are often considered worse than the disease itself (Katz, 1980) and may include nausea, pain, vomiting, diarrhea, dental complications, cataracts, growth impairment, endocrine abnormalities, sterility, future cancers, and neuropsychological effects (Stehbens, 1988). Much of the research on psychosocial aspects of pediatric cancer has included management of distress related to the multiple diagnostic procedures these children face. This research is covered in a later section of the chapter (see "Distress Caused by Medical Procedures"). A second area of research that is emerging is the study of child cancer patients' peer relationships.

Children with cancer experience multiple physical side effects from their treatment that put them at risk for psychosocial difficulties. These side effects include changes in appearance (e.g., loss of hair, weight gain due to steroid medication), increased fatigue, and a depressed immune system that often requires them to be away from friends and most family members. When children with ALL are in the induction phase of treatment, they may have hospital clinic visits three times per week, which necessitates many school absences.

In a longitudinal study of children with cancer, Noll and colleagues (Noll, Bukowski, Rogosch, LeRoy, & Kulkarni, 1990; Noll, LeRoy, Bukowski, Rogosch, & Kulkarni, 1991) reported that adolescents treated for cancer had a reputation as being more socially isolated than their peers but did not differ from matched control children in areas such as popularity or self-reports of loneliness and self-concept. However, teachers reported these children to be less sociable, less prone toward leadership, and more socially isolated and withdrawn.

For some children with cancer, a bone marrow transplant (BMT) holds the best prognosis for cure. The bone marrow transplant includes three stages. In the first stage, the conditioning stage, the patient receives high-dose systemic chemotherapy or radiation in order to destroy the patient's own bone marrow and weaken his or her immune system to prevent rejection of the donated bone marrow. The second phase is the actual bone marrow transplant, in which the marrow is transfused through an intravenous line. In the final stage, the posttransplant period, the new bone marrow gradually engrafts and begins producing mature granulocytes. Throughout this process, patients are required to remain in protective isolation. Isolation requires the patient to remain in his or her hospital room for the 3- to

10-week period of the BMT. Typically, the number of visitors is restricted, and these individuals must be clothed in a hospital gown, mask, head covering, and gloves each time they enter the patient's room.

For individuals in isolation, boredom and a sense of isolation may set in quickly. Although few data exist on the psychosocial effects of this isolation period, preliminary evidence suggests that adolescents (but not school-aged children) experience elevated levels of anxiety, as do the parents of children of all ages (Powazek, Goff, Schyving, & Paulson, 1978). In addition, preliminary evidence suggests that approximately 50% of these pediatric patients evidence significant adherence problems with the oral antibiotic medication regimen (Phipps, & DeCuir-Whalley, 1990), and many patients experience elevated internalizing behavior problems (Kronenberger et al., 1993). On a positive note, children who receive intensive psychosocial intervention such as regular play and visiting by staff appear to have no long-term negative effects of the isolation (Kellerman, Rigler, & Siegel, 1979).

With increasingly successful but aggressive diagnostic and therapeutic techniques to treat medical problems, current procedures may often be accompanied by extensive pain and anxiety. Coping with these procedures is considered in the next section.

Distress Caused by Medical Procedures

Distress due to medical procedures is caused by a variety of stressors, which influence healthy children, acutely ill children, and chronically ill children alike. Some of the stressors are relatively mild and time-limited ones, such as injections, and others are severe and life-threatening stressors, such as open-heart surgery. For certain stressors such as injections, venipunctures, and burn hydrotherapy, interventions are focused primarily on reducing a child's pain, anxiety, and overall distress. With other procedures, however, the child is anesthetized and thus feels little pain during the actual procedure. With procedures involving anesthesia during the procedure encounter phase, interventions typically emphasize reducing anticipatory anxiety and reducing pain after the event.

Venipunctures and Injections

Many children first experience injections at a very young age, and hopefully continue to receive necessary injections and dental restorations throughout their lifetime, thus making these procedures an almost universal experience of childhood. Research suggests that even young infants experience pain during an injection (Johnson & Strada, 1986), and their response changes as they grow older, such that 12- to 24-month-old infants cry for a shorter period than do younger infants, but they are more likely to orient toward the painful site (Craig, McMahon, Morison, & Zaskow, 1984). Although children's observed distress varies widely, children often report that venipunctures and injections are the most fear-provoking events in the hospital (Eland & Anderson, 1977; Poster, 1983).

In a study of over 800 children, Ross and Ross (1984) reported that almost all children interviewed stated that they prefer to have a parent present during medical procedures. However, data regarding the impact of parental presence during painful medical procedures is inconclusive. For example, Gross, Stern, Levin, Dale, and Wojnilower (1983) observed 24 children from 4 to 10 years of age. They reported that children whose mothers were not present during the injection procedure actually displayed less distress than children whose mothers were present. The authors suggested that an extinction paradigm explained their results. They hypothesized that children typically rely on parents to give comfort and protect from pain; however, in this situation the parents were unable to prevent the pain, and therefore an extinction burst in distress cues occurred. A similar finding was noted by Gonzalez et al. (1989) when they noted that the older children in their study (mean age of 5½ years) displayed less distress during an injection when their parent was absent. However, they noted that 86% of these children indicated that they would prefer their parents be with them during injection procedures. Shaw and Routh (1982) suggested that although children may inhibit distress cues in their parents' absence, this does not mean they feel less stressed. In other words, the child's expressions of anxiety may actually be adaptive. The influence of parental presence on distress during acute medical procedures is thus worth continued examination.

In their 1991 review, Blount, Davis, Powers, and Roberts suggested that parental behavior during the procedure may mediate the relationship between parental presence and child distress. One of the first studies to examine the impact of specific parental behaviors on children's

distress during procedures was conducted by Bush, Melamed, Sheras, and Greenbaum (1986). They reported that mothers who frequently utilized distraction and did not ignore their child typically had children who displayed low rates of distress and more prosocial behaviors prior to a medical procedure. Blount et al. (1989) utilized sequential analysis of the Child–Adult Medical Procedure Interaction Scale (CAMPIS) to examine the relationship between parental behaviors and children's reaction to an injection. They reported that adults' reassuring comments, apologies to the child, empathetic statements, and criticism of the child typically preceded child distress. Note that this does not mean that all of these parental responses cause child distress. The data may only suggest that parents recognize early signs of child distress but are not completely able to block them. In contrast, adult commands to the child to engage in coping procedures (i.e., "Take a deep breath now") and distracting talk were typically followed by and may have cued children's coping attempts.

Given these findings that some children appear more distressed when their parent is present and that certain parental behaviors elicit distress, preparation of parents as well as children appears extremely important. Some hospital preparation programs contain segments about coping with venipunctures and injections (e.g., Peterson & Shigetomi, 1981) and have found that including parents in the preparation program diminishes the child patient's distress.

In a study of children's perceptions about medical professionals, Ross (1988) reported that children preferred having medical professionals who were honest with them about the presence of pain and the duration of a painful event. In one of the few studies that examined medical professionals' behavior, Fernald and Corry (1981) reported that when laboratory technicians prepared children for a venipuncture in an empathic manner, the children displayed less distress than if they were prepared in a stern manner. Clinical observations suggest that there are immense inconsistencies in the preparatory techniques that laboratory technicians utilize, and further research in this area is needed.

Lumbar Punctures and Bone Marrow Aspirations

In addition to injections, children with chronic illnesses frequently experience invasive procedures such as lumbar punctures (i.e., spinal taps) and bone marrow aspirations (BMAs). For children with cancer, both lumbar punctures and BMAs are diagnostic procedures used to determine remission or relapse of the cancer. As such, these procedures are extremely anxiety provoking for both children and their parents. Even children who are too young to understand the implications of the tests can perceive the anxiety in their parents. Further, these procedures take place on the child's back, highlighting the child's sense of helplessness even to observe what is happening. During a lumbar puncture, a topical anesthetic is placed on the site, the child is asked to sit on the table in a fetal position, curled around a pillow, an anesthetic is injected, a needle is inserted into the spinal cord, and spinal fluid is drawn. For BMAs, children typically lie on their stomachs on a table, anesthetic is injected, and then a large needle is inserted into the iliac crest. Each procedure is relatively brief (5–15 minutes), but children sometimes have a long anticipatory phase in the clinic waiting room.

Naturalistic studies suggest that adults' reassurance, agitation, criticism, empathy, and giving control to the child were associated with increased child distress (Blount et al., 1989; Blount, Sturges, & Powers, 1990). Children's adaptive coping behaviors were associated with caregiver distractions of the child, attending to the child, and instructing the child in specific coping strategies. The coping strategies in these studies were phase specific such that distracting talk and humor were more often used during the anticipatory periods and deep breathing was more often used during the painful phases.

Burn Hydrotherapy

Although lumbar punctures and BMAs are painful for children, children with burn injuries likely experience a greater degree of pain and distress. Approximately 1 million children experience burn injuries yearly, and approximately 100,000 children and adolescents are hospitalized for treatment of their burns (Muir & Barclay, 1974; Silverstein & Lack, 1987). Children who have been burned experience extensive pain from the actual tissue damage as well as acute pain from the treatment regimen itself. The extent of the pain typically depends on the depth of the burn, with second-degree burns being more painful than first-degree burns. Third-degree burns are generally not particularly painful at first, because

sensory nerve endings have been destroyed. Because maintaining adequate respiration is essential to avoid complications such as pneumonia, physicians are hesitant to provide extensive medication for pain to burned children. For many children, the once- or twice-daily burn-dressing changes are the most aversive aspect of hospitalization. These dressing changes typically include unwrapping of the layers of gauze that protect the injury, debridement (scrubbing the burned area with gauze to remove dead tissue), hydrotherapy, application of topical antibacterial cream, and rewrapping the injury (Maron & Bush, 1991). In addition to the pain involved, children usually have the opportunity to see their wounds, which can be upsetting for young children.

Research on helping children cope with burn injuries suggests that strategies such as relaxation, deep breathing, and attending to positive stimuli such as cartoons decrease children's distress and increase their cooperation during hydrotherapy (Elliott & Olson, 1983). However, it appears that these strategies are only effective when a pediatric psychologist or other coach is present to cue the child to utilize the coping strategies.

The research that has been described in this recent section is oriented toward prevention as well as treatment. Prevention is clearly one of the most important activities of professionals working in the child health area. Whether it is the prevention of pain and distress from medical procedures, prevention of side effects resulting from nonadherence to a chronic illness regimen, or the prevention of illness and injury, much of the activity of pediatric psychologists, behavioral pediatricians, nurses, and others in this field can be conceptualized as prevention oriented. Although space constraints do not permit a thorough discussion of health-related prevention activities, a sampling of some prevention issues follows.

Prevention

Preparation for Surgery

Presurgery preparation programs often prepare children for several aspects of the hospitalization including venipunctures, preoperative injections, anesthesia induction, and postoperative pain. Multiple studies suggest the efficacy of surgery preparation programs. Two separate meta-analyses of preparation studies have indicated that the effect size for reduction of procedural distress as well as posthospital behavior problems was iden-

tical at .44 (Saile, Burgmeier, & Schmidt, 1988; Vernon & Thompson, 1993). The two types of preparation programs most often reported in the literature are modeling programs and stress-inoculation programs.

The first efforts to reduce distress associated with surgery focused on education and modeling techniques. Various presentation formats have been utilized including a film, slide presentation, individual presentation by a staff member, or group presentations. In one of the earliest studies, Melamed and Siegel (1975) compared the film *Ethan Has an Operation* with the control film *Living Things are Everywhere*. *Ethan Has an Operation* is a 7-minute film portraying a boy experiencing admission to a hospital, a blood test, presurgical injection, IV insertion, anesthesia induction, surgery recovery, and discharge from the hospital. The child narrates the story and shows realistic but adaptive behavioral reactions to all of these procedures. Children who were randomly assigned to view the *Ethan* film had lower palmar sweating before and after surgery, reported fewer hospital-related fears, and exhibited less behavioral distress as rated by observers uninformed as to the child's treatment group. Other studies have confirmed the efficacy of modeling presentations (e.g., Peterson, Schultheis, Ridley-Johnson, Miller, & Tracy, 1984; Twardosz, Weddle, Border, & Stevens, 1986).

A second strategy frequently utilized to prepare children for surgery typically includes a modeling component, but also includes segments that explicitly teach the child coping techniques for the upcoming medical stressor. One of the earliest studies that included coping techniques was conducted by Peterson and Shigetomi (1981). Children were randomly assigned to one of four groups: basic preparation using a puppet model, basic preparation plus the *Ethan Has an Operation* film, basic preparation plus training in three coping techniques (deep muscle relaxation, imagery, and self-instruction), or all three components. Ratings by parents, nurses, and uninformed observers suggested that children who received training in coping skills were less upset and more cooperative both before and after surgery than children who did not receive it. Zastowny, Kirschenbaum, and Meng (1986) reported similar findings in their study of modeling and preparation of coping skills. Similarly, the meta-analysis by Saile et al. (1988) suggests that cognitive-behavioral interventions have a larger effect size than modeling interventions.

After researchers had confirmed the efficacy of preparation programs, the next task was to determine which preparation programs were most effective for which children. A study by Rasnake and Linscheid (1989) clearly demonstrated that preparation programs that are matched to children's developmental needs are more effective than preparation programs that are too developmentally advanced. Findings from studies examining other factors such as children's prior medical experience, children's coping styles, and preparation timing are much less clear.

Although few studies have examined preparation programs with children having prior medical experience, recent studies in this area suggest that these children may respond differently to preparation programs than naive children (Lumley, 1987; Melamed, Dearborn, & Hermecz, 1983; Melamed & Siegel, 1980). Perhaps these children need a different style of preparation program. Children who report positive prior experiences and successful coping during previous hospital experiences may benefit from a "refresher course" style preparation. Children who report negative prior experience may require a more extensive preparation tailored specifically to their needs (Harbeck-Weber & McKee, 1995).

A second aspect of preparation programs that has been considered is the effect of children's coping styles on preparation efficacy. Schultheis, Peterson, and Selby (1987) reported that one of the most popular ways of categorizing coping in the literature has been to describe individuals as either "sensitizers" or "repressors." Sensitizers typically cope with a stressor during the anticipation phase by attempting to gather information about the stressor and familiarize themselves with the procedure they will undergo. Repressors are more likely to turn away from the stressor and cope by utilizing denial or distraction during anticipation. Although most studies documenting the existence of coping styles have been conducted with adults, emerging research suggests that the same sensitizer/repressor continuum exists in children (e.g., Field, Alpert, Vega-Lahr, Goldstein, & Perry, 1988; LaMontagne, 1984, 1987; Peterson & Toler, 1986; Siegel, 1981). These studies clearly indicate that children who cope with stressful medical situations by seeking out information during the anticipation phase have more adaptive responses to hospitalization and surgery than children who cope by avoiding information.

However, the relationship between coping styles and reaction to preparation programs is not as clear. Melamed and Siegel (1980) suggested that individuals who typically cope by denial may be upset by prehospital preparation programs. Onufrak and Melamed (cited in Melamed, 1992) examined this hypothesis and reported that children who preferred to avoid receiving information and had had previous negative hospital experience were more anxious after viewing the *Ethan* film than the other groups. Children who avoid information during the anticipation phase may be better prepared with coping techniques such as imagery and distraction that teach children to successfully block out threatening encounters with the medical procedures they must endure.

Although there are benefits, such as reduced costs and effort, associated with utilizing one preparation program for all children undergoing surgery at a particular hospital, the available research suggests that clinicians may need to abandon the concept that one preparation program will meet the needs of all children. Further research matching preparation programs to children's needs is indeed warranted.

Although surgery is not an uncommon event for children, experiencing injuries is an even more common event in childhood. Therefore, some pediatric researchers have focused on the prevention of injury, as seen in the next section.

Prevention of Injury

Each year, almost 40% of children experience an injury that results in medical attention or a missed day of school, and these injuries account for 20% of all pediatric hospital admissions (Guyer, 1989; Guyer & Ellers, 1990). In addition, injuries are the leading cause of death for children over 1 year of age (Rodriguez, 1990).

One method of categorizing injury-prevention attempts is by examining the targets of prevention (Peterson & Mori, 1985; Peterson, Zink, & Downing, 1993). Programs typically target the injury source, the caregiver, or the child. Programs targeting the injury source involve altering the hazard itself, rather than requiring children or caregivers to change their behavior. Examples of this type of prevention include the Poison Prevention Packaging Act (Walton, 1982) and the Refrigerator Safety Act (Robertson, 1983).

Although injury-prevention programs targeting the injury source are likely to be the most far-reaching of prevention programs, they are very rare (Peterson & Cook, 1994). Most involve leg-

islation that is exceptionally difficult to pass or rulings against the product from the Product Safety Commission, which are also difficult to achieve (Rivara, 1982). As an alternative, emphasis has been placed on targeting the behavior of the caregiver. Examples of these types of prevention programs include programs educating parents about the need to install smoke detectors (Gorman, Charney, Holtzman, & Roberts, 1985), the need to turn down water-heater thermostats (Thomas, Hassanein, & Christopherson, 1984), and laws mandating the use of automobile safety restraints. However, Peterson and Cook (1994) note that many of these programs have had disappointing results. It appears that strong contingencies for compliance (i.e., home inspections for smoke detectors) may be necessary for successful injury prevention.

The final target of many prevention programs is the child's behavior. This orientation is typically seen in many of the personal safety programs designed to teach children to protect themselves from abuse (e.g., Poche, Brouwer, & Swearingen, 1981; Wurtele, Marrs, & Miller-Perrin, 1987) as well as programs aimed to reduce injury resulting from pedestrian accidents (e.g., Yeaton & Bailey, 1978; Peterson, 1984). Peterson (1984) has developed a multicomponent program that targets the child's behavior in several areas including safe behavior for daily activities (e.g., fixing snacks), transportation activities (e.g., bicycle safety), emergency activities (e.g., exiting from a fire), and encounters with a stranger (e.g., answering the telephone or door). Multiple studies with this program suggested that children were able to learn the necessary behaviors successfully when extensive behavioral rehearsal was a component of the prevention program. However, they did not learn the necessary behaviors when the program relied on self-help texts (Peterson, 1984), one-day workshops (Peterson, Mori, Selby, & Rosen, 1988), or instruction by unmotivated parents (Peterson et al., 1988). Peterson and Cook (1994) emphasized repeatedly that the key ingredient in successful prevention programs targeting the child's behavior appears to be extensive behavioral rehearsal over several sessions.

Prevention of Illness

A second area of primary prevention related to children's health is the prevention of illness. These prevention efforts target both the child's health as well as the health of the adult that the child will become. Targets of these prevention efforts include increasing immunization levels as well as the promotion of healthful eating habits and reduction of cigarette smoking.

One of the first proactive steps that can be taken to ward off illness is to obtain immunizations as scheduled. However, a sizable number of children do not receive well-child care and routine immunizations. Research suggests that prompting parents to obtain immunizations is unsuccessful unless personal contact is included. Peterson (1986) found that sending reminders to parents and offering free clinic appointments did not increase immunization compliance, but telephone calls were effective. Rewarding compliance has also been shown to increase prompt immunizations (Yokley, Glenwick, Hedrick, & Page, 1980).

A second problem that threatens the health of children is unhealthy eating behaviors. Research suggests that the incidence of eating disorders in children and adolescents is staggering, with estimates that 1% of female adolescents have anorexia nervosa (Li, 1994) and as many as 15% of "healthy" adolescents have bulimia nervosa (Grey & Ford, 1985). Surveys suggest that children begin dieting at an early age, with approximately 32% of third-graders reporting intentional dieting behaviors (Maloney, McGuire, Daniels, & Specker, 1989). Although little empirical data are available on the prevention of eating disorders, data suggest that behavioral programs are helpful in teaching children to eat nutritious meals and snacks. For example, The Traffic Light Diet has repeatedly been shown to be an effective weight-control diet (Epstein, Masek, & Marshall, 1978; Epstein, Wing, Koeske, Ossip, & Beck, 1982) and has even been successful in helping preschoolers choose nutritious snacks (Stark, Collins, Osnes, & Stokes, 1986). Clearly, further research on the prevention of eating disorders is needed.

A third important target for prevention is cigarette smoking cessation. Tobacco use has been labeled as the single most important preventable cause of death in this country (U.S. Department of Health and Human Services, 1991). Prevention efforts have utilized strategies such as social skills training (Evans et al., 1978), anxiety reduction (Botvin & Eng, 1980, 1982), and a public commitment not to smoke (Hurd et al., 1980). For example, Evans (1988) utilized a social learning model to develop recurrent film and poster messages against smoking. In a 3-year follow-up study of seventh- to ninth-graders exposed to

these messages, he found an 8% reduction in smoking acquisition. Although this finding is promising, because of the severity of health problems eventually experienced by cigarette smokers, future work in the prevention of smoking behavior is indeed warranted.

We have previously labeled prevention as the intervention of the future (Peterson & Harbeck, 1988) and believe that it is a promising direction for future pediatric psychologists to pursue. Other directions for the future are explored in this final section.

FUTURE DIRECTIONS

When examining the research base of the field of childhood health, it is clear that studies have become increasingly methodologically sophisticated in the last several decades. The current research is often explicative or descriptive in nature, with an emphasis on examining the relationship between physical and psychological phenomena (Roberts, 1992b). Much of this research is multifactorial and attempts to consider the many factors (e.g., temperament, cognitions, family, peer systems) that affect a child's acquisition of physical symptoms or adaptation to a chronic illness. Recently, these research programs have advanced one stage further and become more theoretically based. It is likely that in the next decade, more of the research programs in this field will emphasize the development and testing of theoretical models that can predict the development and treatment of somatoform disorders, elimination disorders, feeding disorders, adaptation to physical disease, and coping with painful procedures.

Future challenges in this area include the development of multisite research programs to increase statistical power (low n is one of the most common methodological weaknesses in this data) and to better evaluate the complex relationships between variables, as well as longitudinal studies that follow children from diagnosis through young adulthood and beyond. Furthermore, researchers in this area must continue the quest for appropriate measures of psychosocial adjustment. Currently, many studies rely on normed instruments such as the Child Behavior Checklist (CBCL) and the Children's Depression Inventory (CDI). However, as noted elsewhere (Perrin, Stein, & Drotar, 1991; Worchel et al., 1988), measures developed for healthy populations are not always directly transferable to populations with a chronic illness. Both the CDI and CBCL, for example, contain multiple somatic items that may be influenced by physical disease and thus must be interpreted cautiously when used with the pediatric population. Future researchers need to weigh carefully the risks and benefits of reliable instruments normed in a healthy population versus new instruments that do not yet have extensive reliability and validity support that may be more appropriate for pediatric participants.

As Roberts (1992b) noted, a relatively small amount of research in the field of health disorders focuses on intervention or prevention activities. Clearly, it is important to the future of child health psychology that, in addition to doing descriptive work, researchers document the efficacy of their interventions. An emphasis on behavioral techniques and time-limited interventions will be especially important (Peterson & Harbeck, 1988). Although research in this area is sparse, examples of recent outcome studies do exist. For example, Varni, Katz, Colegrove, and Dolgin (1993) evaluated social skills training for children with cancer, and Boardway, Delamater, Tomakowsky, and Gutai (1993) evaluated a stress-management program for children with diabetes mellitus. Hopefully, the pace of documenting the efficacy of such clinical interventions will increase in the next decade.

With the advent of managed health care and other public policy that values empirically validated and time-limited treatment and prevention, pediatric researchers seem in an ideal position for additional growth and contributions. The continued maturation of the field will be best accomplished through emphasis on the strengths that have always underlain this field—a sound knowledge of development, the use of behavioral methods, and emphasis on research-based conclusions.

REFERENCES

Abrahamian, R. P., & Lloyd-Still, J. D. (1984). Chronic constipation in childhood: A longitudinal study of 186 patients. *Journal of Pediatric Gastroenterology and Nutrition, 3,* 460–467.

American Psychiatric Association. (1987). *Diagnostic and statistical manual of mental disorders* (3rd ed., rev.). Washington, DC: Author.

American Psychiatric Association. (1994). *Diagnostic and statistical manual of mental disorders* (4th ed.). Washington, DC: Author.

Amsterdam, B. (1979). Chronic encopresis: A system based psychodynamic approach. *Child Psychiatry and Human Development, 9,* 137–144.

Apley, J. (1975). *The child with abdominal pains.* Oxford: Blackwell Scientific.

Apley, J., & Hale, B. (1973). Children with recurrent abdominal pain: How do they grow up? *British Medical Journal, 3,* 7–9.

Bakwin, H. (1973). The genetics of enuresis. In I. Kolvin, R. C. MacKeith, & R. Meadow (Eds.), *Bladder control and enuresis* (pp. 73–77). Philadelphia: Lippincott.

Bandura, A. (1977). *Social learning theory.* Englewood Cliffs, NJ: Prentice-Hall.

Barakat, L. P., & Linney, J. A. (1992). Children with physical handicaps and their mothers: The interrelations of social support, maternal adjustment, and child adjustment. *Journal of Pediatric Psychology, 17,* 725–739.

Bennett, P. H. (1981). The epidemiology of diabetes mellitus. In H. Rifkin & P. Raskin (Eds.), *Diabetes mellitus* (Vol. 5, pp. 87–94). Bowie, MD: Prentice-Hall.

Berwick, D. M. (1980). Nonorganic failure to thrive. *Pediatrics in Review, 1,* 265–270.

Billie, B. (1981). Migraine in childhood and its prognosis. *Cephalgia, 1,* 71–75.

Blomfield, J. M., & Douglas, J. W. B. (1956). Bedwetting: Prevalence among children aged 4–7 years. *Lancet, 1,* 237–247.

Blount, R. L., Corbin, S. M., Sturges, J. W., Wolfe, V. V., Prater, J. M., & James, L. D. (1989). The relationship between adults' behavior and child coping and distress during BMA/LP procedures: A sequential analysis. *Behavior Therapy, 20,* 585–601.

Blount, R. L., Davis, N., Powers, S. W., & Roberts, M. C. (1991). The influence of environmental factors and coping style on children's coping and distress. *Clinical Psychology Review, 11,* 93–116.

Blount, R. L., Sturges, J. W., & Powers, S. W. (1990). Analysis of child and adult behavioral variations by phase of medical procedure. *Behavior Therapy, 20,* 585–601.

Boardway, R. H., Delamater, A. M., Tomakowsky, J., & Gutai, J. P. (1993). Stress management training for adolescents with diabetes. *Journal of Pediatric Psychology, 18,* 29–46.

Botvin, G. J., & Eng, A. (1980). A comprehensive school-based smoking prevention program. *The Journal of School Health, 50,* 209–213.

Botvin, G. J., & Eng, A. (1982). The efficacy of a multi-component approach to the prevention of cigarette smoking. *Preventive Medicine, 11,* 199–211.

Brown, F., Golding, J. M., & Smith, R. (1990). Psychiatric comorbidity in primary care somatization disorder. *Psychosomatic Medicine, 52,* 445–451.

Brownlee-Duffeck, M., Peterson, L., Simonds, J. F., Goldstein, D., Kilo, C., & Hoett, N. (1987). The role of health beliefs in the regimen adherence and metabolic control of adolescents and adults with diabetes mellitus. *Journal of Consulting and Clinical Psychology, 55,* 139–144.

Bruenlin, D. C., Desai, V. J., Stone, M. E., & Swilley, J. (1983). Failure to thrive with no organic etiology: A critical review. *International Journal of Eating Disorders, 2,* 25–49.

Budd, K. S., McGraw, T. E., Farbisz, R., Murphy, T. B., Hawkins, D., Heilman, N., Werle, M., & Hochstadt, N. J. (1992). Psychosocial concomitants of children's feeding disorders. *Journal of Pediatric Psychology, 17,* 81–94.

Bush, J. P., Melamed, B. G., Sheras, P. L., & Greenbaum, P. E. (1986). Mother–child patterns of coping with anticipatory medical stress. *Health Psychology, 5,* 137–157.

Cecalupo, A. (1994). Childhood cancers: Medical issues. In R. A. Olson, L. L. Mullins, J. B. Gillman, & J. M. Chaney (Eds.), *The sourcebook of pediatric psychology* (pp. 90–97). Boston: Allyn & Bacon.

Chamberlin, R. W. (1974). Management of preschool behavior problems. *Pediatric Clinics of North America, 21,* 33–47.

Chan, D. A., Salcedo, J. R., Atkins, D. M., & Ruley, E. J. (1986). Munchausen syndrome by proxy: A review and case study. *Journal of Pediatric Psychology, 11,* 71–80.

Christopherson, E. R., & Rapoff, M. A. (1983). Toileting problems in children. In C. E. Walker & M. C. Roberts (Eds.), *Handbook of clinical child psychology* (pp. 593–615). New York: Wiley.

Coury, D. L. (1994). Munchausen syndrome by proxy: Medical issues. In R. A. Olson, L. L. Mullins, J. B. Gillman, & J. M. Chaney (Eds.), *The sourcebook of pediatric psychology* (pp. 355–360). Boston: Allyn & Bacon.

Craig, K. (1983). Modeling and social learning factors in chronic pain. In J. J. Bonica, A. Iggo, & U. Lindblom (Eds.), *Proceedings of the Third World Congress on Pain* (pp. 813–827). New York: Raven Press.

Craig, K. D., McMahon, R. J., Morison, J. D., & Zaskow, C. (1984). Developmental changes in infant pain expression during immunization injections. *Social Science and Medicine, 19,* 1331–1337.

Craig, T. K. J., Boardman, A. P., Mills, K., Daly-Jones, O., & Drake, H. (1993). The South London somatization study I: Longitudinal course and the influence of early life experiences. *British Journal of Psychiatry, 163,* 579–588.

Crist, W., McDonnell, P., Beck, M., Gillespie, C. T., Barrett, P., & Mathews, J. (1994). Behavior at mealtimes and the young child with cystic fibrosis. *Journal of Developmental and Behavioral Pediatrics, 15,* 157–161.

Crist, W., McDonnell, P., Beck, M., Gillespie, C. T., & Mathews, J. (1992). Behavior at mealtimes and nutritional intake in the young child with cystic fibrosis. *Pediatric Pulmonary, 14*(Suppl. 8), 321.

Cystic Fibrosis Foundation Patient Registry. (1995). *1994 Annual data report.* Bethesda, MD: Author.

Dodge, J. A. (1988). Nutritional requirements in cystic fibrosis: A review. *Journal of Pediatric Gastroenterology and Nutrition, 7,* S8–S11.

Drotar, D. (1988). Failure to thrive. In D. K. Routh (Ed.), *Handbook of pediatric psychology* (pp. 71–107). New York: Guilford Press.

Drotar, D., & Sturm, L. (1994). Failure to thrive. In R. A. Olson, L. L. Mullins, J. B. Gillman, & J. M. Chaney (Eds.), *The sourcebook of pediatric psychology* (pp. 29–41). Boston: Allyn & Bacon.

Eland, J. M., & Anderson, J. E. (1977). The experience of pain in children. In A. Jacox (Ed.), *Pain: A source book for nurses and other professionals* (pp. 453–473). Boston: Little, Brown.

Elliott, C. H., & Olson, R. A. (1983). The management of children's distress in response to painful medical treatment for burn injuries. *Behaviour Research and Therapy, 21,* 675–683.

Epstein, L. H., Masek, B. J., & Marshall, W. R. (1978). A nutritionally based school program for control of eating in obese children. *Behavior Therapy, 9,* 766–788.

Epstein, L. H., Wing, R. R., Koeske, R., Ossip, D., & Beck, S. (1982). A comparison of lifestyle change and programmed aerobic exercise on weight and fitness changes in obese children. *Behavior Therapy, 13,* 651–665.

Ernst, A. R., Routh, D. K., & Harper, D. C. (1984). Abdominal pain in children and symptoms of somatization disorder. *Journal of Pediatric Psychology, 9,* 77–86.

Escobar, J. L., Golding, J. M., & Hough, R. L. (1987). Somatization in the community: Relationship to disability and use of services. *American Journal of Public Health, 77,* 837–840.

Escobar, J. I., Rubio-Stipec, M., Canino, G., & Karno, M. (1989). Somatic Symptom Index: A new and abridged somatization construct. *Journal of Nervous and Mental Disorders, 177,* 140–146.

Evans, R. I. (1988). How can health life-styles in adolescents be modified? Some implications from a smoking prevention program. In D. K. Routh (Ed.), *Handbook of pediatric psychology* (pp. 321–331). New York: Guilford Press.

Evans, R. I., Rozelle, R. M., Mittelmark, M. B., Hansen, W. B., Bane, A. L., & Havis, J. (1978). Deterring the onset of smoking in children: Knowledge of immediate physiological effects and coping with peer pressure, media pressure, and parent modeling. *Journal of Applied Social Psychology, 8,* 125–135.

Ewigman, B., Kivlahan, C., & Land, G. (1993). The Missouri Child Fatality Study: Underreporting of maltreatment fatalities among children under five years of age. *Pediatrics, 91,* 330–337.

Fernald, C. D., & Corry, J. J. (1981). Empathetic versus directive preparation of children for needles. *Journal of the Association for the Care of Children's Health, 10,* 44–47.

Field, T., Alpert, B., Vega-Lahr, N., Goldstein, S., & Perry, S. (1988). Hospitalization stress in children: Sensitizer and repressor coping styles. *Health Psychology, 7,* 433–445.

Fisher, S. M. (1979). Encopresis. In J. D. Noshpitz (Ed.), *Basic handbook of child psychiatry* (pp. 556–568). New York: Basic Books.

Ford, C. V., & Folks, D. G. (1985). Conversion disorders: An overview. *Psychosomatics, 26,* 371–383.

Forsythe, W. I., & Redmond, A. (1974). Enuresis and spontaneous cure rate: Study of 1129 enuretics. *Archives of Disease in Childhood, 49,* 259–263.

Gallmeier, T. M., & Bonner, B. L. (1992). University-based interdisciplinary training in child abuse and neglect. *Child Abuse and Neglect, 16,* 513–521.

Gardner, T. M., Morrell, J. A., Jr., & Ostrowski, T. A. (1990). Somatization tendencies and ability to detect internal body cues. *Perceptual and Motor Skills, 71,* 364–366.

Geffken, G., & Johnson, S. B. (1994). Diabetes: Psychological issues. In R. A. Olson, L. L. Mullins, J. B. Gillman, & J. M. Chaney (Eds.), *The sourcebook of pediatric psychology* (pp. 118–129). Boston: Allyn & Bacon.

Gil, K. M., Williams, D. A., Thompson, R. J., Jr., & Kinney, T. R. (1991). Sickle cell disease in children and adolescents: The relation of child and parent pain coping strategies to adjustment. *Journal of Pediatric Psychology, 16,* 643–664.

Ginsberg, A. J. (1988). Feeding disorders in the developmentally disabled population. In D. C. Russo & J. H. Kedesdy (Eds.), *Behavioral medicine with the developmentally disabled* (pp. 21–41). New York: Plenum Press.

Gonzalez, J. C., Routh, D. K., Saab, P. G., Armstrong, F. D., Shifman, L., Guerra, E., & Fawcett, N. (1989). Effects of parent presence on children's reactions to injections: Behavioral, physiological, and subjective aspects. *Journal of Pediatric Psychology, 14,* 449–462.

Gorman, R. L., Charney, E., Holtzman, N. A., & Roberts, K. B. (1985). A successful city-wide smoke-detector giveaway program. *Pediatrics, 75,* 14–18.

Grey, J. J., & Ford, K. (1985). The incidence of bulimia in a college sample. *International Journal of Eating Disorders, 4,* 201–210.

Gross, A. M., Stern, R. M., Levin, R. B., Dale, J., & Wojnilower, D. A. (1983). The effect of mother–child separation on the behavior of children experiencing a diagnostic medical procedure. *Journal of Consulting and Clinical Psychology, 51,* 783–785.

Gurwitz, D., Corey, M., Francis, P. S., Crozier, D., & Levison, H. (1979). Perspectives in cystic fibrosis. *Pediatric Clinics of North America, 26,* 603–615.

Guyer, B. (1989). The application of morbidity data in the Massachusetts statewide childhood injury prevention program. *Canadian Journal of Public Health, 80,* 432–434.

Guyer, B., & Ellers, B. (1990). Childhood injuries in the United States. *American Journal of Diseases of Children, 144,* 649–652.

Hallgren, B. (1956). Enuresis: I. A study with reference to morbidity, risk, and symptomatology: II. A study with reference to certain physical, mental and social factors possibly associated with enuresis. *Acta Psychiatrica Scandinavica, 31,* 379–436.

Hammill, P. B. B., Drizd, T. A., Johnson, C. L., Reed, R. B., Roche, A. F., & Moore, W. M. (1979). Physical growth: National Center for Health Statistics percentiles. *American Journal of Clinical Nutrition, 32,* 607–629.

Hanson, C. L. (1992). Developing systemic models of the adaptation of youths with diabetes. In A. M. La Greca, L. J. Siegel, J. L. Wallander, & C. E. Walker (Eds.), *Stress and coping in child health* (pp. 212–241). New York: Guilford Press.

Hanson, C. L., Henggeler, S. W., & Burghen, G. A. (1987). Social competence and parental support as mediators of the link between stress and metabolic control in adolescents with insulin-dependent diabetes mellitus. *Journal of Consulting and Clinical Psychology, 55,* 529–533.

Hanson, C. L., Henggeler, S. W., Harris, M. A., Burghen, G. A., & Moore, M. (1989). Family system variables and the health status of adolescents with IDDM. *Health Psychology, 8,* 239–253.

Hanson, C. L., Henggeler, S. W., Harris, M. A., Cigrang, J. A., Schinkel, A. M., Rodrigue, J. R., & Klesges, R. C. (1992). Contributions of sibling relations to the adaptation of youth with insulin-dependent diabetes mellitus. *Journal of Consulting and Clinical Psychology, 60,* 104–112.

Harbeck-Weber, C., & McKee, D. H. (1995). Prevention of emotional and behavioral distress in children experiencing hospitalization and chronic illness. In M. C. Roberts (Ed.), *Handbook of pediatric psychology* (2nd ed., pp. 167–184). New York: Guilford Press.

Hersov, L. (1977). Fecal soiling. In M. Rutter & L. Hersov (Eds.), *Child psychiatry: Modern approaches* (pp. 613–627). Oxford, UK: Blackwell Scientific Publications.

Hodges, K., & Burbach, D. J. (1991). Recurrent abdominal pain. In J. P. Bush & S. W. Harkins (Ed.), *Children in pain: Clinical and research issues from a developmental perspective* (pp. 251–274). New York: Springer-Verlag.

Hodges, K., Kline, J. J., Barbero, G., & Flanery, R. (1984). Life events occurring in families of children with recurrent abdominal pain. *Journal of Psychosomatic Research, 28,* 185–188.

Homer, C., & Ludwig, S. (1980). Categorization of etiology of failure to thrive. *American Journal of Diseases of Children, 135,* 848–852.

Howe, A. C., & Walker, C. E. (1992). Behavioral management of toilet training, enuresis, and encopresis. *Pediatric Clinics of North America, 39,* 413–432.

Hughes, M. C., & Zimin, R. (1978). Children with psychogenic abdominal pain and their families. *Clinical Pediatrics, 17,* 569–573.

Hurd, P. D., Johnson, C. A., Pechacek, T., Bast, L. P., Jacobs, D. R., & Luepker, R. V. (1980). Prevention of cigarette smoking in seventh grade students. *Journal of Behavioral Medicine, 3,* 15–28.

Johnson, C. C., & Strada, M. E. (1986). Acute pain response in infants: A multidimensional description. *Pain, 24,* 373–382.

Johnson, S. B. (1988). Diabetes mellitus in childhood. In R. K. Routh (Ed.), *Handbook of pediatric psychology* (pp. 9–31). New York: Guilford Press.

Johnson, S. B. (1990). Adherence behaviors and health status in childhood diabetes. In C. S. Holmes (Ed.), *Neuropsychological and behavioral aspects of diabetes* (pp. 30–57). New York: Springer-Verlag.

Katz, E. R. (1980). Illness impact and social reintegration. In J. Kellerman (Ed.), *Psychological aspects of childhood cancer* (pp. 14–46). Springfield, IL: Charles C. Thomas.

Kaufman, K. (1990, August). *Munchausen syndrome by proxy: A Clinical overview.* Parental falsification of pediatric symptoms: Munchausen syndrome by proxy. Symposium conducted at the meeting of the American Psychological Association, Boston.

Kaufman, K. L. (1994). Munchausen syndrome by proxy: Psychological issues. In R. A. Olson, L. L. Mullins, J. B. Gillman, & J. M. Chaney (Eds.), *The sourcebook of pediatric psychology* (pp. 361–375). Boston: Allyn & Bacon.

Kazak, A. E. (1992). The social context of coping with childhood chronic illness: Family systems and social support. In A. M. La Greca, L. J. Siegel, J. L. Wallander, & C. E. Walker (Eds.), *Stress and coping in child health* (pp. 262–278). New York: Guilford Press.

Kellerman, J., Rigler, D., & Siegel, S. E. (1979). Psychological response of children to isolation in a protected environment. *Journal of Behavioral Medicine, 2,* 263–274.

Kempe, C. J., & Helfer, R. E. (1972). *Helping the battered child and his family.* Philadelphia: Lippincott.

Kirmayer, L. J., Robbins, J. M., & Paris, J. (1994). Somatoform disorders: Personality and the social matrix of somatic distress. *Journal of Abnormal Psychology, 103,* 125–136.

Knopf, I. J. (1979). *Childhood psychopathology: A developmental approach.* Englewood Cliffs, NJ: Prentice-Hall.

Kronenberger, W. G., Carter, B. D., Morrow, C., Stewart, J., Martin, K., & Sender, L. (1993, April). *Stress, coping, and psychological adjustment of children undergoing bone marrow transplantation.* Poster presented at the Fourth Florida Conference on Child Health Psychology, Gainesville, FL.

La Greca, A. (1988). Children with diabetes and their family: Coping and disease management. In T. Field, P. McCabe, & N. Schneiderman (Eds.), *Stress and coping across development* (Vol. II, pp. 139–159). Hillsdale, NJ: Erlbaum.

La Greca, A. M., Siegel, L. J., Wallander, J. L., & Walker, C. E. (1992). *Stress and coping in child health.* New York: Guilford Press.

LaMontagne, L. L. (1984). Children's locus of control beliefs as predictors of preoperative coping. *Nursing Research, 33,* 76–79.

LaMontagne, L. L. (1987). Children's preoperative coping: Replication and extension. *Nursing Research, 36,* 163–167.

Larson, D. G., & Chastain, R. L. (1990). Self-concealment: Conceptualization, measurement and health implications. *Journal of Social and Clinical Psychology, 9,* 439–455.

Lavigne, J. V., & Faier-Routman, J. (1992). Psychological adjustment to pediatric physical disorders: A meta-analytic review. *Journal of Pediatric Psychology, 17,* 133–158.

Lehman, E. (1944). Psychogenic incontinence of feces (encopresis) in children: Report of recovery of four patients following psychotherapy. *American Journal of Diseases of Children, 687,* 190–199.

Levine, M. D. (1975). Children with encopresis: A descriptive analysis. *Pediatrics, 56,* 412–416.

Li, B. U. K. (1994). Anorexia nervosa: Medical issues. In R. A. Olson, L. L. Mullins, J. B. Gillman, & J. M. Chaney (Eds.), *The sourcebook of pediatric psychology* (pp. 317–321). Boston: Allyn & Bacon.

Lifshitz, M., & Chovers, A. (1972). Encopresis among Israeli kibbutz children. *Israel Annals of Psychiatry and Related Disciplines, 10,* 326–340.

Linscheid, T. R., Budd, K. S., & Rasnake, L. K. (1995). Pediatric feeding disorders. In M. C. Roberts (Ed.), *Handbook of pediatric psychology* (2nd ed., pp. 501–515). New York: Guilford Press.

Loening-Baucke, V. (1990). Modulation of abnormal defecation dynamics by biofeedback treatment in chronically constipated children with encopresis. *Journal of Pediatrics, 116,* 214–222.

Lumley, M. (1987). *Age, previous experience, and presurgical behavior as predictors of a child's reaction to anesthesia induction.* Unpublished master's thesis, University of Florida, Gainesville.

Luxem, M., & Christophersen, E. (1994). Behavioral toilet training in early childhood: Research, practice, and implications. *Journal of Developmental and Behavioral Pediatrics, 15,* 370–378.

MacDonald, A., Holden, C., & Harris, G. (1991). Nutritional strategies in cystic fibrosis: Current issues. *Journal of the Royal Society of Medicine, 84*(Suppl. 18), 28–35.

MacLean, W. E., Jr., Perrin, J. M., Gortmaker, S., & Pierre, C. B. (1992). Psychological adjustment of children with asthma: Effects of illness severity and recent stressful life events. *Journal of Pediatric Psychology, 17,* 159–172.

Maier, S. F., Watkins, L. R., & Fleshner, M. (1994). Psychoneuroimmunology: The interface between behavior, brain, and immunity. *American Psychologist, 49,* 1004–1017.

Maloney, M. J. (1980). Diagnosing hysterical conversion reactions in children. *Journal of Pediatrics, 97,* 1016–1020.

Maloney, M. J., McGuire, J., Daniels, S. R., & Specker, B. (1989). Dieting behavior and eating attitudes in children. *Pediatrics, 84,* 482–487.

Margo, K. L., & Margo, G. M. (1994). The problem of somatization in family practice. *American Family Physician, 49,* 1873–1879.

Maron, M., & Bush, J. P. (1991). Burn injury and treatment pain. In J. P. Bush & S. W. Harkins (Eds.), *Children in pain: Clinical and research issues from a developmental perspective* (pp. 275–296). New York: Springer-Verlag.

Matarazzo, J. D. (1984). Behavioral immunogens and pathogens in health and illness. In B. L. Hannonds & C. J. Scheirer (Eds.), *Psychology and health* (pp. 5–44). Washington, DC: American Psychological Association.

McGrath, P. A. (1990). *Pain in children: Nature, assessment, and treatment.* New York: Guilford Press.

McGrath, P. J. H., Goodman, J. K., Firestone, P., Shipman, R., & Peters, S. (1983). Recurrent abdominal pain: A

psychogenic disorder? *Archives of Disease in Childhood, 58*, 888–890.

Melamed, B. G. (1992). Family factors predicting children's reaction to anesthesia induction. In A. M. La Greca, L. J. Siegel, J. L. Wallander, & C. E. Walker (Eds.), *Stress and coping in child health* (pp. 140–156). New York: Guilford Press.

Melamed, B. G., Dearborn, M., & Hermecz, D. A. (1983). Necessary considerations for surgery preparation: Age and previous experience. *Psychosomatic Medicine, 45*, 517–525.

Melamed, B. G., & Siegel, L. J. (1975). Reduction of anxiety in children facing hospitalization and surgery by use of filmed modeling. *Journal of Consulting and Clinical Psychology, 43*, 511–521.

Melamed, B. G., & Siegel, L. J. (1980). *Behavioral medicine: Practical application in health care.* New York: Springer.

Mesibov, G. B., Schroeder, C. S., & Wesson, L. (1977). Parental concerns about their children. *Journal of Pediatric Psychology, 2*, 13–17.

Muir, I. F. K., & Barclay, T. L. (1974). *Burns and their treatment* (2nd ed.). Chicago: Yearbook.

Mulhern, R. K., Carpentieri, S., Shema, S., Stone, P., & Fairclough, D. (1993). Factors associated with social and behavioral problems among children recently diagnosed with brain tumor. *Journal of Pediatric Psychology, 18*, 339–350.

Mullins, L. L., Gillman, J., & Harbeck, C. (1992). Multiple-level interventions in pediatric psychology settings: A behavioral–systems perspective. In A. M. La Greca, L. J. Siegel, J. L. Wallander, & C. E. Walker (Eds.), *Stress and coping in child health* (pp. 377–400). New York: Guilford Press.

Mullins, L. L., & Olson, R. A. (1990). Familial factors in the etiology, maintenance, and treatment of somatoform disorders in children. *Family Systems Medicine, 8*, 159–175.

Mullins, L. L., Olson, R. A., & Chaney, J. M. (1992). A social learning–family systems approach to the treatment of somatoform disorders in children and adolescents. *Family Systems Medicine, 10*, 1–5.

National Committee for the Prevention of Child Abuse. (1991, April). NCPCA releases new child abuse statistics and prevention trends. *NCPCA Memorandum*, p. 1.

Newacheck, P. W., & Taylor, W. R. (1992). Childhood chronic illness: Prevalence, severity, and impact. *American Journal of Public Health, 82*, 364–371.

Noll, R. B., Bukowski, W. M., Rogosch, F. A., LeRoy, S., & Kulkarni, R. (1990). Social interactions between children with cancer and their peers: Teacher ratings. *Journal of Pediatric Psychology, 15*, 43–56.

Noll, R. B., LeRoy, S., Bukowski, W. M., Rogosch, F. A., & Kulkarni, R. (1991). Peer relationships and adjustment in children with cancer. *Journal of Pediatric Psychology, 16*, 307–326.

Olatawura, M. O. (1973). Encopresis: A review of thirty-two cases. *Acta Paediatrica Scandinavica, 62*, 358–364.

Olson, R. A., Mullins, L. L., Gillman, J. B., & Chaney, J. M. (1994). *The sourcebook of pediatric psychology*. Boston: Allyn & Bacon.

Oppel, W. C., Harper, P. A., & Rider, R. V. (1968). Social, psychological and neurological factors associated with nocturnal enuresis. *Pediatrics, 42*, 627–641.

Osborne, R. B., Hatcher, J. W., & Richtsmeier, A. J. (1989). The role of social modeling in unexplained pediatric pain. *Journal of Pediatric Psychology, 14*, 43–61.

Oster, J. (1972). Recurrent abdominal pain, headache and limb pains in children and adolescents. *Pediatrics, 50*, 429–436.

Outwater, K. M., Lipnick, R. N., Luban, N. C., Ravenscroft, K., & Ruley, E. J. (1981). Factitious hematuria: Diagnosis by minor blood group typing. *Journal of Pediatrics, 98*, 95–97.

Palmer, S., Thompson, R. J., & Linscheid, T. R. (1975). Applied behavior analysis in the treatment of childhood feeding problems. *Developmental Medicine and Child Neurology, 17*, 333–339.

Pennebaker, J. W. (1982). *The psychology of physical symptoms.* New York: Springer.

Perlmutter, D. (1985). Enuresis. In P. D. Kelalis, L. R. King, & A. B. Belman (Eds.), *Clinical pediatric urology* (2nd ed., pp. 311–325). Philadelphia: Saunders.

Perrin, E. C., Stein, R. E. K., & Drotar, D. (1991). Cautions in using the Child Behavior Checklist: Observations based on research about children with a chronic illness. *Journal of Pediatric Psychology, 16*, 411–422.

Peterson, L. (1984). The "Safe at Home" game: Training comprehensive prevention skills in latchkey children. *Behavior Modification, 8*, 474–494.

Peterson, L. (1986). Prevention and community compliance to immunization schedules. *Prevention in Human Services, 5*, 79–95.

Peterson, L., & Brown, D. (1994). Integrating child injury and abuse-neglect research: Common histories, etiologies, and solutions. *Psychology Bulletin, 116*, 293–315.

Peterson, L., & Cook, S. C. (1994). Preventing injuries: Psychological issues. In R. A. Olson, L. L. Mullins, J. B. Gillman, & J. M. Chaney (Eds.), *The sourcebook of pediatric psychology* (pp. 304–313). Boston: Allyn & Bacon.

Peterson, L., & Harbeck, C. (1988). *The pediatric psychologist: Issues in professional development and practice.* Champaign, IL: Research Press.

Peterson, L., Harbeck, D., Farmer, J., & Zink, M. (1991). Developmental contributions to the assessment of children's pain: Conceptual and methodological implications. In J. P. Bush & S. W. Harkins (Eds.), *Children in pain: Clinical and research issues from a developmental perspective* (pp. 33–58). New York: Springer-Verlag.

Peterson, L., & Mori, L. (1985). Prevention of child injury: An overview of targets, methods, and tactics for psychologists. *Journal of Consulting and Clinical Psychology, 53*, 586–595.

Peterson, L., Mori, L., Selby, V., & Rosen, B. (1988). Community intervention in children's injury prevention: Differing costs and differing benefits. *Journal of Community Psychology, 16*, 62–73.

Peterson, L., Schultheis, K., Ridley-Johnson, R., Miller, D. J., & Tracy, K. (1984). Comparison of three modeling procedures on the presurgical and postsurgical reactions of children. *Behavior Therapy, 15*, 197–203.

Peterson, L., & Shigetomi, C. (1981). The use of coping techniques to minimize anxiety in hospitalized children. *Behavior Therapy, 12*, 1–14.

Peterson, L., & Toler, S. M. (1986). An information seeking disposition in child surgery patients. *Health Psychology, 5*, 343–358.

Peterson, L., Zink, M., & Downing, J. (1993). Childhood injury prevention. In D. S. Glenwick & L. A. Jason (Eds.), *Promoting health and mental health: Behavioral approaches to prevention* (pp. 51–74). New York: Springer.

Phipps, S., & DeCuir-Whalley, S. (1990). Adherence issues

in pediatric bone marrow transplantation. *Journal of Pediatric Psychology, 15,* 459–475.

Poche, C., Brouwer, R., & Swearingen, M. (1981). Teaching self-protection to young children. *Journal of Applied Behavior Analysis, 14,* 169–176.

Poster, E. C. (1983). Stress immunization: Techniques to help children cope with hospitalization. *Maternal–Child Nursing Journal, 12,* 119–134.

Powazek, M., Goff, J. R., Schyving, J., & Paulson, M. A. (1978). Emotional reactions of children to isolation in a cancer hospital. *Pediatrics, 92,* 834–837.

Quittner, A. L., DiGirolamo, A. M., & Winslow, E. B. (1991, April). *Problems in parenting a child with cystic fibrosis: A contextual analysis.* Paper presented at the meeting of the Florida Conference on Child Health Psychology, Gainesville, FL.

Ramsey, B., Farrell, P., & Pencharz, P. (1992). Nutritional assessment and management in cystic fibrosis: Consensus conference. *American Journal of Clinical Nutrition, 55,* 108–116.

Rasnake, L. K., & Linscheid, T. R. (1989). Anxiety reduction in children receiving medical care: Developmental considerations. *Developmental and Behavioral Pediatrics, 10,* 169–175.

Rief, W., Schaefer, S., Hiller, W., & Fichter, M. M. (1992). Lifetime diagnoses in patients with somatoform disorders: Which came first? *European Archives of Psychiatry and Clinical Neuroscience, 241,* 236–240.

Ringdahl, I. C. (1980). Hospital treatment of the encopretic child. *Psychosomatics, 21,* 65–71.

Riordan, M. M., Iwata, B. A., Finney, J. W., Wohl, M. K., & Stanley, A. E. (1984). Behavioral assessment and treatment of chronic food refusal in handicapped children. *Journal of Applied Behavior Analysis, 17,* 327–341.

Rivara, F. P. (1982). Minibikes: A case study in underregulation. In S. B. Bergman (Ed.), *Preventing childhood injuries* (pp. 61–63). Columbus, OH: Ross Laboratories.

Robbins, J. M., & Kirmayer, L. J. (1991). Cognitive and social factors in somatization. In L. J. Kirmayer & J. M. Robbins (Eds.), *Current concepts of somatization: Research and clinical perspectives* (pp. 107–141). Washington, DC: American Psychiatric Press.

Roberts, M. C. (1986). *Pediatric psychology: Psychological interventions for pediatric problems.* New York: Pergamon.

Roberts, M. C. (1992a). Theory-driven research in pediatric psychology [Special issue]. *Journal of Pediatric Psychology, 17,* (5 & 6).

Roberts, M. C. (1992b). Vale Dictum: An editor's view of the field of pediatric psychology and its journal. *Journal of Pediatric Psychology, 17,* 785–806.

Roberts, M. C. (Ed.). (1995). *Handbook of pediatric psychology* (2nd ed.). New York: Guilford Press.

Robertson, L. S. (1983). *Injuries: Causes, control strategies, and public policy.* Lexington, MA: Lexington Books.

Rodriguez, J. G. (1990). Childhood injuries in the United States: A priority issue. *American Journal of Diseases of Children, 144,* 625–626.

Rosen, C. L., Frost, J. D., Bricker, T., Tarnow, J. D., Gillette, P. C., & Dunlavy, S. (1983). Two siblings with recurrent cardiorespiratory arrest: Munchausen syndrome by proxy or child abuse? *Pediatrics, 71,* 715–720.

Rosenberg, D. A. (1987). Web of deceit: A literature review of Munchausen syndrome by proxy. *Child Abuse and Neglect, 11,* 547–563.

Ross, D. M. (1988, June). Aversive treatment procedures: The school-aged child's view. *Newsletter of the Society of Pediatric Psychology,* pp. 3–6.

Ross, D. M., & Ross, S. A. (1984). Childhood pain: The school-aged child's viewpoint. *Pain, 20,* 179–191.

Rost, K. M., Akins, R. N., Brown, F. W., & Smith, G. R. (1992). The comorbidity of DSM-III personality disorders in somatization disorder. *General Hospital Psychiatry, 14,* 322–326.

Routh, D. K. (Ed.). (1988). *Handbook of pediatric psychology.* New York: Guilford Press.

Routh, D. K., & Ernst, A. R. (1984). Somatization disorder in relatives of children and adolescents with functional abdominal pain. *Journal of Pediatric Psychology, 9,* 427–437.

Routh, D. K., Ernst, A. R., & Harper, D. C. (1988). Recurrent abdominal pain in children and somatization disorder. In D. K. Routh (Ed.), *Handbook of pediatric psychology* (pp. 492–504). New York: Guilford Press.

Saile, H., Burgmeier, R., & Schmidt, L. R. (1988). A meta-analysis of studies on psychological preparation of children facing medical procedures. *Psychology and Health, 2,* 107–132.

Schaefer, C. E. (1979). *Childhood encopresis and enuresis.* New York: Van Nostrand Reinhold.

Schroeder, C. S., & Gordon, B. N. (1991). *Assessment and treatment of childhood problems: A clinician's guide.* New York: Guilford Press.

Schultheis, K., Peterson, L., & Selby, V. (1987). Preparation for stressful medical procedures and person × treatment interactions. *Clinical Psychology Review, 7,* 329–352.

Shaffer, D. (1973). The association between enuresis and emotional disorder: A review of the literature. In I. Kolvin, R. C. MacKeith, & S. R. Meadow (Eds.), *Bladder control and enuresis.* Philadelphia: Lippincott.

Shaw, E. G., & Routh, D. K. (1982). Effect of mother presence on children's reaction to adverse procedures. *Journal of Pediatric Psychology, 7,* 33–42.

Siegel, L. J. (1981, April). *Naturalistic study of coping strategies in children facing medical procedures.* Paper presented at the meeting of the Southeastern Psychological Association, Atlanta.

Siegel, M., & Barthel, R. P. (1986). Conversion disorders on a child psychiatry consultation service. *Psychosomatics, 27,* 201–204.

Silber, D. L. (1969). Encopresis: Discussion of etiology and management. *Clinical Pediatrics, 8,* 225–231.

Sils, R. H. (1978). Failure to thrive: The role of clinical and laboratory evaluation. *American Journal of Diseases of Children, 132,* 967–969.

Silverstein, P., & Lack, B. (1987). Fire prevention in the United States. In J. A. Boswick, Jr. (Ed.), *The surgical clinics of North America* (pp. 1–14). Philadelphia: Saunders.

Smith, G. R., Jr., Monson, R. A., & Ray, D. C. (1986). Patients with multiple unexplained symptoms: Their characteristics, functional health, and health care utilization. *Archives of Internal Medicine, 146,* 69–72.

Spierings, C., Pels, P. J. E., Sijben, N., Gabreels, F. J., & Renier, W. O. (1990). Conversion disorders in childhood: A retrospective follow-up study of 84 inpatients. *Developmental Medicine and Child Neurology, 32,* 865–871.

Stark, L. J., Collins, F. L., Osnes, P. G., & Stokes, T. F. (1986). Using reinforcement and cuing to increase healthy snack food choices in preschoolers. *Journal of Applied Behavior Analysis, 19,* 367–379.

Stehbens, J. A. (1988). Childhood cancer. In D. K. Routh

(Ed.), *Handbook of pediatric psychology* (pp. 135–161). New York: Guilford Press.

Swartz, M., Blazer, D., George, L., Woodbury, M. A., & Manton, K. G. (1988). Somatization disorder in a community population. *American Journal of Psychiatry, 143,* 1403–1408.

Thomas, K. A., Hassanein, R. S., & Christophersen, E. R. (1984). Evaluation of group well-child care for improving burn prevention in the home. *Pediatrics, 74,* 879–882.

Thompson, R. J., Jr., Gustafson, K. E., Hamlett, K. W., & Spock, A. (1992). Psychological adjustment of children with cystic fibrosis: The role of child cognitive processes and maternal adjustment. *Journal of Pediatric Psychology, 17,* 741–755.

Twardosz, S., Weddle, K., Border, L., & Stevens, E. (1986). A comparison of three methods of preparing children for surgery. *Behavior Therapy, 17,* 14–25.

U.S. Department of Health & Human Services. (1991). *Healthy people 2000: National health promotion and disease prevention objectives* (DHHS Publication No. PHS 91–50213). Washington, DC: U.S. Government Printing Office.

Varni, J. W., Katz, E. R., Colegrove, R., Jr., & Dolgin, M. (1993). The impact of social skills training on the adjustment of children with newly diagnosed cancer. *Journal of Pediatric Psychology, 18,* 751–768.

Vaughan, B. C., McKay, R. J., & Behrman, R. E. (1979). *Nelson textbook of pediatrics* (11th ed.). Philadelphia: Saunders.

Verhulst, F. C., Van Der Lee, J. J., Akkerhuis, G. W., Sandersj-Woudstna, J. A., Timmer, F. C., & Donkhorst, J. D. (1985). The prevalence of nocturnal enuresis: Do DSM-III criteria need to be changed: A brief research report. *Journal of Child Psychology and Psychiatry, 26,* 989–993.

Vernon, D. T. S., & Thompson, R. H. (1993). Research on the effect of experimental interventions on children's behavior after hospitalization: A review and synthesis. *Developmental and Behavioral Pediatrics, 14,* 36–44.

Walker, C. E., Kenning, M., & Faust-Campanile, J. (1989). Enuresis and encopresis. In E. J. Mash & R. A Barkley (Eds.), *Treatment of childhood disorders* (pp. 423–448). New York: Guilford Press.

Walker, C. E., Milling, L. S., & Bonner, B. L. (1988). Incontinence disorders: Enuresis and encopresis. In D. K. Routh (Ed.), *Handbook of pediatric psychology* (pp. 363–398). New York: Guilford Press.

Walker, L. S., Garber, J., & Greene, J. W. (1994). Somatic complaints in pediatric patients: A prospective study of the role of negative life events, child social and academic competence, and parental somatic symptoms. *Journal of Consulting and Clinical Psychology, 62,* 1213–1221.

Walker, L. S., & Greene, J. W. (1991). Negative life events and symptom resolution in pediatric abdominal pain patients. *Journal of Pediatric Psychology, 16,* 341–360.

Wallander, J. L., & Varni, J. W. (1992). Adjustment in children with chronic physical disorders: Programmatic research on a disability–stress–coping model. In A. M. La Greca, L. J. Siegel, J. L. Wallander, & C. E. Walker (Eds.), *Stress and coping in child health* (pp. 279–300). New York: Guilford Press.

Wallander, J. L., Varni, J. W., Babani, L., Banis, H. T., DeHaan, C. B., & Wilcox, K. T. (1989). Disability parameters, chronic strain, and adaptation of physically handicapped children and their mothers. *Journal of Pediatric Psychology, 14,* 25–42.

Wallander, J. L., Varni, J. W., Babani, L. V., Banis, H. T., & Wilcox, K. T. (1988). Children with chronic physical disorders: Maternal reports of their psychological adjustment. *Journal of Pediatric Psychology, 13,* 197–212.

Walton, W. W. (1982). An evaluation of the Poison Prevention Packaging Act. *Pediatrics, 69,* 363–370.

Warner, J. E., & Hansen, D. J. (1994). The identification and reporting of physical abuse by physicians: A review and implications for research. *Child Abuse and Neglect, 18,* 11–25.

Wasserman, A. L., Whitington, P. F., & Rivara, F. P. (1988). Psychogenic basis for abdominal pain in children and adolescents. *Journal of American Academy of Child and Adolescent Psychiatry, 27,* 179–184.

Wolfe, D. A. (1987). *Child abuse: Implications for child development and psychopathology.* Newbury Park, CA: Sage.

Woolston, J. (1985). Diagnostic classification: The current challenge in failure to thrive syndrome research. In D. Drotar (Ed.), *New directions in failure to thrive: Implications for research and practice* (pp. 225–233). New York: Plenum Press.

Worchel, F. F., Nolan, B. F., Wilson, V. L., Purser, J. S., Copeland, D. R., & Pfefferbaum, B. (1988). Assessment of depression in children with cancer. *Journal of Pediatric Psychology, 13,* 101–112.

World Health Organization. (1993). *The ICD-10 classification of mental and behavioral disorders: Diagnostic criteria for research.* Geneva, Switzerland: Author.

Wurtele, S. K., Marrs, S. R., & Miller-Perrin, C. L. (1987). Practice makes perfect? The role of participant modeling in sexual abuse prevention programs. *Journal of Consulting and Clinical Psychology, 54,* 599–602.

Wysocki, T. (1993). Associations among teen-parent relationships, metabolic control, and adjustment to diabetes in adolescents. *Journal of Pediatric Psychology, 18,* 441–452.

Yeaton, W. H., & Bailey, J. S. (1978). Teaching pedestrian safety skills to young children: An analysis and one year follow-up. *Journal of Applied Behavior Analysis, 11,* 315–329.

Yokley, J. M., Glenwick, D. W., Hedrick, T. E., & Page, N. D. (1980, November). *Increasing the immunization of high risk preschoolers: An evaluation of applied community interventions.* Paper presented at the meeting of the Association for Advancement of Behavior Therapy, New York.

Zastowny, T. R., Kirschenbaum, D. S., & Meng, A. L. (1986). Coping skills training for children: Effects on distress before, during, and after hospitalization for surgery. *Health Psychology, 5,* 231–247.

Author Index

Aaronson, B. A., 447, *452*
Aase, J. M., *388*
Abbott, R. D., 17, *57*, 421, 422, *427*
Abbott, R., *52*
Abe, K., 197, 198, *234*
Abe, T., 326, *338*
Aber, J. L., 498, 500, 512, 521, 530, *531*
Ablon, S., *104*
Abrahamian, R. P., 582, 583, *595*
Abramowicz, H. K., 371, *384*
Abramson, L. Y., 171, *186*, *191*, *194*, 228, *234*, 259, *269*
Achenbach, T. M., 6, 10, 11, 12, 13, 22, 23, 24, 25, 28, 29, 31, 32, 35, 36, 43, *51*, 66, 76, 79, 80, 99, 100, *102*, 113, 116, 117, 118, 121, 128, *144*, 158, 159, 160, 161, *186*, 213, 216, 230, 231, *234*, *241*, 263, *269*, 280, *301*, 446, *450*
Ackerman, B. J., 273, *534*
Ackerman, B. P., *53*
Ackerman, P. T., 425, *427*
Ackman, D., *270*
Adam, B. S., 253, 263, *269*
Adam, T., 172, *191*
Adams, A., 313, *335*
Adams, H. E., 28, *51*, *305*
Adams, M. J., 416, *427*
Adams, P., *334*
Adan, A. M., *54*

Addalli, K. A., *147*
Addison, S., 375, *388*
Addy, C. L., 162, *189*, *241*
Adelman, H. S., 16, 26, 37, 38, *51*
Adelson, E., 464, *490*
Adolphs, R., 331, *333*
Adrian, C., 166, 171, 176, 183, 184, *186*, *189*, *190*
Agras, S., *570*
Agras, W. S., 217, *234*, 545, 548, 550, 552, *566*, *569*, *570*
Ahadi, S. A., 19, *58*, 100, *106*
Ahearn, M. B., *109*
Ahlawat, K. S., 221, *234*
Ahrens, A. H., 182, *189*
Aiken, L. R., 425, *427*
Ainsworth, M. D. S., 313, *333*, *334*, 477, *484*, 493, 503, *531*, *532*
Akins, R. N., 575, *600*
Akiskal, H. S., 154, *191*
Akkerhuis, G. W., 11, *59*, 220, *241*, *446*, *454*, *601*
Akman, D., *531*
Akshoomofff, N. A., *335*
Al-Shabbout, M., *189*
Alain, M., 284, *301*
Alansky, J. A., 291, *303*
Albano, A. M., 4, 16, 202, 204, 206, 209, 211, 212, 213, 219, 231, 232, 233, *234*, *237*
Albert, N., 162, *186*

Alberta Mental Health Research Fund, 50
Albin, R. L., 448, *450*
Albus, K. E., *359*
Alder, R. J., 125, *148*
Alessandri, S. M., 512, *531*
Alessi, N. E., 212, 233, *234*
Alexander, D., 464, *490*
Alexander, G. E., *432*, 449, *450*
Alexander, L., 423, *427*
Alexander, P. C., 493, 505, 516, 522, 523, *531*, *533*
Alger, S. A., 564, *570*
Algozzine, B., 397
Allan, W. D., 212, 237
Allen, D. M., 501, 513, *531*
Allen, J. P., 500, 512, *531*
Allen, J., *335*
Allen, L., 10, *56*, 197, 239, *388*
Allen, R. P., 449, *450*
Allen, R., 229, 235
Allen, T. W., 67, 96, *110*
Allen, V., *334*
Allgood-Merten, B., 157, 164, *186*
Alloy, L. B., 171, *186*, *194*, 198, 225, 228, *234*
Alnæs, R., 230, *234*
Alpern, G., *335*
Alpern, L., 139, *147*, 473, 482, *484*, *488*
Alpert, B., 593, *597*

Alpert, J., 501, *532*
Altaus, M., 11, *59*
Altemeier, W. A. III, 465, *484*
Altepeter, T. S., 68, *102*
Alterman, A. I., 517, *536*
Altham, P. M. E., 176, 180, 182, 184, 189
Althaus, M., 220, *241*, 446, *454*
Altmann, E. O., 174, *187*, 284, *301*
Altschuler, L., 350, *361*
Aman, M. G., 93, *109*, 380, *384*
Amanat, E., 179, *187*
Amato, P. R., 138, *144*
Ambonetti, A., *271*
Ambrosini, P., *187, 188, 189, 193, 194*
Ameli, R., 317, 331, *334*
American Association on Mental Retardation, 362, 365, 366, 367, 368, *384*
American Psychiatric Association, 16, 21, 23, 24, 26, 28, 29, *51*, 64, 65, 66, 67, 76, 77, *102*, 113, 115, 118, 119, 120, 121, 123, 124, 130, *144*, 154, 155, 158, *187*, 196, 197, 199, 201, 203, 204, 205, 207, 208, 209, 210, 212, 215, 218, *234*, 243, 244, 245, 246, 247, 253, 255, 258, 266, *269, 270*, 280, 281, 286, *301*, 320, 321, *334*, 341, 342, 343, 344, 357, 364, 366, 367, 368, 370, 383, *384*, 397, 398, 400, 401, 406, 420, 421, 423, 424, *427*, 438, 439, *450*, 458, 468, 470, 472, *484*, 496, 497, 505, *531*, 541, 542, 543, 544, 546, 547, 548, 549, 550, 552, 561, 565, *566*, 574, 575, 576, 577, 578, 579, 581, 585, 587, *595*
Amir, N., 90, *106*
Ammerman, R. T., 3, *53, 54, 57, 146*, 274, 498, 528, *531*
Amsterdam, B., 583, *595*
An Der Heiden, W., *360*
Anastopoulos, A. D., 86, 91, 92, 94, *102, 103*
Anders, T. F., 459, 467, *484, 490*
Andersen, A., *567*
Anderson, C. A., 9, 64, 67, 69, 92, *102*, 139, *144*, 165, *187*, 481
Anderson, C., 476, *484*
Anderson, D. J., 196, 218, 219, 220, 222, 231, *235*
Anderson, E., *453*
Anderson, G. M., 271, 327, 328, 333, *334, 339*, 451, 452, 453, *567*
Anderson, I. M., 554, *567*
Anderson, J. C., 11, 32, *51*, 130, *144*
Anderson, J. E., 590, *596*
Anderson, J., *147*, 163, 164, 171, 179, *187, 192, 193*
Anderson, K. E., 138, *144*
Anderson, L. T., *334*
Anderson, M., *339*
Anderson, R. F., 85, *108*
Anderson, R. L., *56*
Anderson, S. R., 333, *334*

Anderson, T., 75, *103*
Anderson, W. F., 379, *385*
Andersson, L., *338*
Andreasen, N. C., *191*
Andreski, P., 242, *270*
Andrews, C. E., 326, *338*
Andrews, G., 229, *235*
Andrews, J. A., 83, *108, 162, 163, 171, 190, 192, 193*, 219, *238*
Andrews, L. K., 356, *360*
Angel, B., 264, *272*
Angell, R. H., 249, 252, *273*
Angold, A., 10, *53*, 125, *145*, 160, 161, 162, 164, *187*
Anhalt, J. M., 425, *427*
Anker, M., *359*
Anthony, A., *147*
Anthony, E. J., 268, *270*
Antony, M., 209, *235*
Apel, K., 403, *430*
Apicella, A., *429*
Apley, J., 578, *596*
Appelbaum, A. S., 499, *531*
Appelbaum, M. I., 413, *428*
Apple, R., *568*
Applegate, B., *56, 79, 102, 107*, 134, *147*
Apter, A., *241*, 443, 445, *450*
Aragona, J. A., 515, *531*
Aram, D. M., 413, *427*
Arcus, D., 476, 484, *484*
Arend, R. A., 291, *304*, 478, *488*
Aries, P., 7, *51*
Arkowitz, H., 6, *51*
Armelagos, J., *192*
Armsden, G. C., 174, 176, 179, 180, 186, *187*
Armstrong, F. D., *597*
Armstrong, K. J., 94, *111*
Armsworth, M. W., 247, 269, *270*
Arnold, D., *570*
Arnold, M. M., 424, 425, *432*
Arnow, B., *566*
Arny, L., 19, *55*
Arrindell, W. A., 230, *237*, 283, *301*
Arroyo, W., 256, 268, *274*
Arsenault, L., 93, *109*
Arthur, J., *190*
Artiles, A. J., 365, *385*
Arunkumar, R., 19, *60*
Asamen, J., *358*
Asarnow, J. R., 166, 171, 172, 173, 175, 176, 179, 180, 181, *187*, 324, 341, 344, 345, 348, 350, 353, 354, 355, 356, 357, 358, *360*
Asarnow, R. F., 324, 326, 334, *338*, 341, 344, 348, 349, 351, 352, *358, 359, 360*
Aseltine, R. H., 165, 183, *189*
Asendorpf, J. B., *52*, 277, 279, 280, 284, 292, 293, 300, *301, 302, 303, 305, 306, 307*
Asher, J., 48, 49, *52*
Asher, S. J., 498, 504, 508, *531*
Asher, S. R., 132, *148*, 280, 284, 293, *301, 305, 306*

Asnes, R. S., 463, *484*
Asperger, H., 311, 312, 322, *334*
Atkins, D. M., 584, *596*
Atkins, M. S., *108*, 249, 262, 271, 273, 505, *535*
Attie, I., 558, 561, *566*
Attili, G., *301, 306*
Audette, D. P., 175, *187*
August, G. J., 97, *102*, 326, *334*, 381, *385*
Ayalon, O., 255, 256, 267, *270*
Ayers, R. R., 418, *428*
Aylward, E. H., *451, 454*
Ayoub, C., 265, *271*
Ayoub, E. M., *454*
Azar, S. T., 511, *531*
Azrin, N. H., 377, *386*, 450, *450*
Azuma, S. D., 384, *386*

Baak, K., 291, 303, *305*
Babani, L. V., 587, *601*
Babigian, H. M., 551, *568*
Bachevalier, J., 316, 317, 329, 331, *334*
Bachorowski, J., 140, *145*
Backman, J. E., 442, *454*
Badian, N. A., 425, *427*
Baer, D. M., 38, *52*
Baer, L., *452*
Bagnoto, S., *272*
Bailet, L., *429*
Bailey, A., *148, 338*
Bailey, D., 375, *385*
Bailey, J. S., 594, *601*
Bailey, P., *110*
Bain, A., *429*
Baird, T. D., 326, *334*
Baker, A. G., 21, *55*
Baker, B., 377, *385*
Baker, G. B., *435*
Baker, L. A., 218, *238*
Baker, L., 90, *102, 104*, 217, 218, 220, *236*, 315, *334*, 405, *428*, 560, 569
Baker, R. W., 510, 513, *536*
Baker, W., *429*
Bakermans-Kranenburg, M. J., 475, *484, 490*
Bakker, D. J., *104*, 410, 411, *427*
Bakwin, H., 580, *596*
Baldwin, A., 58, 262, *275*
Baldwin, C. P., 4, 58, 262, *275*
Bale, S. J., *107*
Ball, E. W., 403, 416, *427*
Balla, D. A., 363, 388, *389*
Ballenger, J. C., 212, *235*, 554, *568*
Bally, H., 416, *435*
Baloh, R., 98, *102*
Balthasar. K., 448, *450*
Bamford, K. A., *451*
Bandura, A., 38, *52*, 228, *235*, 262, 579, *596*
Bane, A. L., *597*
Banis, H. T., 587, *601*
Bank, L., 481, *489*
Banks, S. R., 327, *335*
Barabas, G., 442, 449, *450*

Barahal, R., 499, 501, 515, *531*
Barakat, L. P., 588, *596*
Barbero, G. J., 464, *490*, 580, *597*
Barchas, J. D., 262, *270*
Barclay, T. L., 591, *599*
Barglow, P., 478, *491*
Barkley, R. A., 4, 11, 21, 33, 37, 51,
    51, 52, 53, 56, 59, 65, 66, 67, 68,
    69, 70, 71, 72, 73, 74, 75, 76, 77,
    78, 79, 80, 83, 86, 87, 88, 89, 91,
    92, 93, 94, 95, 96, 97, 99, 100, *102*,
    103, *105*, *106*, *107*, *108*, *109*, *110*,
    111, 132, 133, *143*, *144*, 235, *301*,
    302, 418, 425, *427*, *432*, *433*, *601*
Barlow, D. H., 4, 16, 197, 198, 202,
    206, 209, 211, 212, 213, 216, 218,
    221, 222, 224, 225, 226, 227, 228,
    229, 231, 233, 233, 234, *234*, 235,
    236, *237*, *239*, 260, 261, 262, 272,
    564, *570*
Barnes, K. T., 511, *531*
Barnett, D., 20, 56, 479, 481, *485*,
    486, 511, 514, 515, *532*, *535*, *536*
Barnett, P. A., 174, *187*
Barnum, R., 265, *271*
Baron, J., 416, *435*
Baron-Cohen, S., 316, 317, 318, *334*,
    337, *339*, 443, *450*
Barr, C. E., 352, *358*
Barr, H. M., *111*
Barr, L., *452*
Barr, R. G., 462, 463, *484*
Barrera, M., 174, 179, 180, *187*
Barrett, C. L., 197, *239*
Barrett, C., 448, *454*
Barrett, J. E., *568*
Barrett, J., 298, *303*
Barrett, M. J., *533*
Barrett, O. L., 217, *237*
Barrett, P. M., 230, *235*
Barrett, P., *109*, *596*
Barrett, R. P., 328, *339*
Barrios, B. A., 196, 197, 213, *235*,
    284, *301*
Barron, J., *338*
Barron, R. W., 415, *430*
Barros-Beck, J., *270*
Bartak, L., 319, 323, 324, 325, 326,
    334, *338*
Barth, C., 330, 331, *334*
Barthel, R. P., 577, *600*
Barthelemy, C., *335*
Bartko, J. J., *109*, *146*, *238*
Bartlett, D. P., 216, *240*
Bartolucci, G., 322, 325, *338*
Barton, L. M., 464, *485*
Barton, M. L., 503, *531*
Barton, S., 20, *52*, *335*
Bartusen, D., *149*
Basham, R. B., 287, *302*
Bashir, M. R., *148*
Baskiewicz, A., 375, *385*
Bassiri, M., 345, *359*
Basso, A., 421, *427*
Bast, L. P., *598*
Bastian, H. C., 392, *427*

Bates, J. E., 18, *53*, 138, 141, *145*,
    478, *484*, 511, *532*
Bates, S., 172, 173, *187*
Bauer, D. H., *235*
Baum, A., 47, 48, *52*, 520, 521, *531*
Bauman, M., *329*
Baumberger, T., *339*
Baumeister, A. A., 384, 377, *385*
Baumgaertel, A., 85, *103*
Baumgarten, R., *104*
Baumrind, D., 267, *270*, 298, *301*
Bawden, H. N., 442, *454*
Bax, M., 466, *487*
Beardslee, W. R., 41, *58*, 178, *187*,
    191, *238*
Beasley, M. C., 248, *270*
Beck, A. T., 23, 35, 38, 42, 43, *52*, 55,
    162, 170, 182, 186, *187*
Beck, M., 586, *596*
Beck, N. C., *191*
Beck, S., 594, *596*
Becker, J. V., 527, *531*
Beckman, P., 375, *385*
Beckwith, L., 481, *484*
Bedi, G., 68, *106*
Beeghly, M., 372, 373, *385*, *386*, 387,
    451, 510, 511, 513, *531*, *532*
Befera, M., 91, 92, *103*
Begab, M. J., 364, *388*
Beglin, S. J., 542, 551, 552, *566*, 567
Behar, D., 212, *241*
Behar, J., *452*
Behrman, R. E., 581, *601*
Beidel, D. C., 49, *57*, 69, 89, *110*,
    198, 202, 204, 220, 232, 231, *235*,
    239, *241*, 283, 284, *304*
Beilke, R. L., 506, *533*
Beitchman, J. H., 80, 86, 90, *103*,
    211, *235*, 253, *270*, 341, 345, *358*,
    504, 505, 515, 516, *531*
Bekken, K., *110*
Beliard, D., 550, *566*
Bell, M. A., 289, *303*
Bell, R. Q., 4, *54*, *58*, 443, *450*
Bell, R., 501, *534*
Bell-Berti, F., 406, *430*
Bell-Dolan, D., 196, 198, 199, 200,
    211, *235*, 284, 285, *301*
Bellack, A. S., 53, 56, 59, 355, *358*
Bellugi, U., 374, *385*, *388*
Belman, A. B., *599*
Belsky, J., *146*, 291, *301*, *303*, 306,
    473, 474, 476, 478, *484*, *485*, *490*,
    530, *531*, *532*
Bem, D. J., 299, *302*
Bemporad, J. R., 178, *187*, 449, *451*
Ben, R., 252, *273*
Ben-Meir, S., 344, 354, *358*
Benaroya, S., 315, *338*
Benbow, C. P., 426, *434*
Bender, L., 343, *358*
Bender, M. E., 87, 93, *109*, 176, *193*,
    260, *272*
Benedek, E. P., 247, *270*
Benjamin, L. S., 561, *566*
Benness, B. B., 92, *105*

Bennett, L. A., 99, *103*
Bennett, P. H., 588, *596*
Bennett, S., 342, *358*
Benoit, D., 464, 465, 466, 468, 475,
    485, 502, 503, 508, 515, *531*
Benson, D. F., 69, 95, *111*, *452*
Benton, A. L., 69, 95, *103*, *433*
Bentzen, F. A., 394, *428*
Bereiter, C., 421, *427*
Berg, C., 206, 218, *235*
Berg, I., 223, *235*
Berger, M., *149*
Bergman, A., 514, *536*
Bergman, L. R., 142, *147*
Bergman, S. B., *600*
Berk, L. E., 69, 73, *103*
Berkell, D. E., *337*
Berkowitz, C. D., 464, *485*
Berkowitz, R., 355, *359*
Berkson, G., 438, *450*
Berkson, J. B., 231, *235*, 442, *450*
Berlin, L. J., 477, *485*
Berliner, L., 505, *531*
Berman, A., 158, *187*
Berman, S. R., 262, *273*
Bernal, J., 468, *485*
Bernheimer, C., 369, *385*
Bernheimer, L., 376, *386*
Berninger, V. W., 419, 420, 421, 422,
    423, *427*, *432*
Bernstein, G. A., *52*, 198, 199, 228,
    232, *235*
Berry, M. F., 400, *427*
Bertenthal, B. I., 445, *450*
Berthier, M. L., *337*
Berwick, D. M., 465, *485*, 585, *596*
Bessler, A., 86, *108*
Best, K. M., 228, *239*
Bettelheim, B., 9, *52*, 312, 326, *334*
Beuchler, S., 228, *237*
Beumont, P., 549, *566*
Bevin, T., 470, *485*
Beyer, H., 93, *110*
Beyreiss, J., 93, *110*
Bhatia, M. S., 85, *103*
Bialer, I., *109*, *112*, *193*
Bice, H. V., 394, *428*
Biederman, J., 48, *52*, 54, *58*, 80, 81,
    89, 93, 97, 98, 101, *102*, *103*, *104*,
    105, *107*, *110*, 115, 120, 132, 135,
    137, *144*, *145*, 217, 222, 223, 224,
    235, *237*, 240, 284, *301*, *303*, 305,
    481, *485*, *487*
Bierman, J. M., 10, *60*
Bifulco, A., 472, *485*
Biglan, A., *190*
Bihrle, A., 374, *385*
Bijou, S. W., 38, *52*
Bijur, P., 94, *104*
Billie, B., 579, *596*
Billings, A. G., 179, 180, 181, *187*
Bingham, R. D., 458, *486*
Binkoff, J. A., 4, *54*
Birch, H., 19, *59*
Bird, H. R., 10, 11, 32, *52*, 163, 164,
    187, 219, 220, *235*

Birmaher, B., 169, 170, *187*
Bishop, D. V., 323, *334, 385*
Bissette, G., *451*
Bithoney, W. G., 465, *485*
Bixler, E. O., 272
Bjorck, J. P., 180, 183, *188*
Bjorkqvist, K., 116, 130, *144*
Blacher, J., 376, *385*
Blachman, B. A., 402, 403, 416, *427*
Black, B., 217, *235, 236*
Black, D., 470, *487*
Blackman, J. A., 466, *485*
Blackwell, C., *359*
Blaine, D., 20, *54*
Blake, D. D., *269, 274*
Blalock, J., 418, *430*
Blanchard, E. B., 229, *236*
Bland, R. C., 166, *187*
Blank, A. S., Jr., 245, *270*
Blanz, B., 481, *485*
Blasco, P., 375, *385*
Blashfield, R. K., 32, *52*, 398, 410, 413, *427, 432*
Blaszczynski, A., 230, *240*
Blatt, B., 362, *385*
Blatt, S. J., 177, 178, 179, 181, 182, 184, 186, *187*
Blazer, D., 575, *601*
Blechman, E. A., 175, *187*, 284, *301*
Blehar, M. C., 313, *334*, 477, *484*
Bleich, A., *241, 450*
Bleuler, E., 311, *334*, 341, 345, *358*
Bloch, D. A., 242, 267, 268, *270, 275*
Block, D., 480, *488*
Block, J. H., 136, 141, *143, 144, 148, 492, 536*
Bloedau, L., 183, *190*
Blom, G. E., 248, 252, 253, 263, 264, *270*
Blomfield, J. M., 580, *596*
Blondis, T. A., 15, *59*, 87, *110*
Bloomingdale, L. M., *104, 109, 110, 148*
Blount, R. L., 590, 591, *596*
Blue, J., 525, *531*
Blum, H. M., *57, 192*
Blum, N., 32, *52*
Blumensohn, R., *360*
Boardman, A. P., 575, *596*
Boardway, R. H., 595, *596*
Boder, E., 410, 411, *427, 428*
Bogues, J., 464, *487*
Bohman, M., *338*
Bohr, Y., 552, *567*
Bohra, N., 85, *103*
Boisjoly, C., 462, *484*
Boivin, M., 284, 293, *301*
Bol, A., 329, *335*
Bolduc, E. A., *54*, 222, 223, 224, *235, 237, 240, 303, 487*
Bolduc-Murphy, E. A., *52, 235, 301*
Bolten, P., 81, *110*, 117, *148*
Bolton, P., 326, *334, 338*
Bolyard, K., 350, *361*
Bonagura, N., 86, *106, 147*

Bond, M. H., 300, *303, 304*
Bond, S., 325, *338*
Bonett, D., 353, *359*
Bonica, J. J., *596*
Bonner, B. L., 580, 584, *597, 601*
Bonvillian, J. D., 515, *532*
Boomsma, D. I., 97, *111*
Boon, C., 509, *536*
Booth, C. L., 288, 291, 297, *301, 304, 306*, 480, *490*
Boothe, T., *429*
Borchardt, C. M., *52*, 198, 199, 228, *235*
Border, L., 592, *601*
Borduin, C. M., 178, *188*
Borgstedt, A. D., 96, *107*
Borison, R. L., *104*
Borner, H., 96, *108*
Bornstein, M., 306, *387*
Bornstein, R. A., 443, *451*
Borstelmann, L. J., 7, *52*
Bortner, M., *427*
Borus, J. F., 248, 264, *270*
Bos, C., *431, 433*
Boswick, J. A., Jr., *600*
Botein, S., 479, *488*
Both, L., 178, *194*, 293, *306*
Bott, L., 344, *360*
Botvin, G. J., 594, *596*
Boucher, C., 468, *485*
Boucher, J., 317, *334*
Boukydis, C. F. Z., 462, 463, *488*
Boulton, A. A., *435*
Bowen, R. C., 200, 220, *236*
Bower, E. M., 285, *301*
Bower, G., 186, *187*
Bowers, M. B., 439, *454*
Bowers, N. D., 68, *112, 112*
Bowers, P., 416, *428*
Bowes, J. M., 169, *195*
Bowker, A., 284, 288, 294, *303, 306*
Bowlby, J., 17, 38, 40, 41, *52*, 177, *187*, 225, 228, 230, *236*, 290, *302*, 477, *485*, 524, *531*
Boyd, H., 260, *275*
Boyd, J. L., *358*
Boyko, K. A., 288, 292, *307*
Boyle, M. H., 9, 10, 12, 47, *52, 57, 59*, 81, *111, 125, 148*, 164, *189, 192*, 200, *236*
Braafladt, N., 175, *189*
Bradburn, I. S., 249, 253, *270*, 550, *569*
Bradley, L., 403, 416, *428*
Bradley, S. J., 212, *236*
Bradshaw, J., *148*
Brady, E. U., 4, 33, *52*, 160, *187*, 224, *236*
Brady, S. A., 416, *433*
Braff, D. L., 449, *454*
Bragg, R., 421, *427*
Braiman, S., *195, 235, 241*
Brams, J. S., 466, *488*
Brand, S., *54*
Brandenburg, N. A., 9, *52*
Brander, T., 243, 247, *270*

Brandl, B., 547, *567*
Brandt, H. A., 554, *568*
Brasher, C., *194*
Brassard, M. R., 493, 496, *531, 533*
Braun, A. R., 448, *451*
Braunwald, K. G., 479, *485*, 514, *532, 535*
Bray, J. H., 21, *52*
Brazeal, T. J., 196, 199, 200, 211, *235*
Brazelton, T. B., 462, 463, *485*
Bream, L., 293, *306*
Breaux, A. M., 67, *104*
Breedveld, G. J., *453*
Breen, M. J., 68, 69, *102, 104*
Bregman, J. D., 381, *385*
Breier, A., 218, *236*
Breiling, J., *146*
Brelsford, K. A., *336*
Bremner, R., 325, *338*
Brennan-Quattrock, J., *193*
Brent, D., 164, *188*
Breslau, N., 242, *270*
Bretherton, I., 4, 39, 40, *52, 145*, 305, *484, 488, 489*
Brett, E. A., 243, *270*
Brewerton, T. D., 554, *568*
Brewin, C. R., 260, *272*
Breznitz, Z., 178, *187*
Brhar, D., *109*
Bricker, T., *600*
Bridges, L. J., 291, *307*
Briere, J., 516, 517, *531*
Brilman, E., 283, *301*
Britton, H., 480, *487*
Broberg, A., 291, 300, *302*
Broca, P. P., 391, 392, *428*
Brody, G. H., 165, *189*
Brody, L. E., 426, *434*
Brody, L., 445, *452*
Broman, H., *335*
Broman, S. H., 371, *385*
Bromet, E., 265, *270*
Bromfield, R., 374, *389*
Bronfenbrenner, U., 4, *52*
Bronfman, E. T., 480, *485, 488*
Bronowski, J., 71, 72, 73, 74, *104*
Bronson, W. C., 293, *302*
Broocks, A., 554, *566*
Brook, J., *188*
Brooks-Gunn, J., 9, *53*, 164, *187*, 445, *453*, 558, 561, *566*
Brophy, C. J., *104*
Brothers, L., 331, *334*
Brouwer, R., 594, *600*
Brown, A., *484*
Brown, D. R., 221, *236*
Brown, D., 57, 515, *535*, 584, *599*
Brown, E., 273, *534*
Brown, F. W., 575, *600*
Brown, F., 575, *596*
Brown, G. L., *147*
Brown, G. W., 181, *187*, 472, *485*
Brown, G., 166, *190*
Brown, I. S., 403, *428*
Brown, J. D., 181, 182, *194*
Brown, J. E., 449, *450*

Brown, J., *454*
Brown, L. M., 41, *59*
Brown, M. M., 482, *486, 489*
Brown, P. J., 294, *305*
Brown, P., 258, *275*
Brown, R. T., 364, *388*
Brown, S., *145*
Brown, T. A., 231, *236*
Brown, T. E., *111*
Brown, W. S., 351, *360*
Brown, W. T., 382, *385*
Browne, A., 496, 504, 506, 508, 512, 513, 516, 517, *531, 533*
Brownell, K., *570, 571*
Brownlee-Duffeck, M., 589, *596*
Bruce, B., 548, *570*
Bruch, H., 558, 560, *566*
Bruck, M., 404, 410, 416, 418, *428*
Bruenlin, D. C., 465, *485*, 585, *596*
Bruhn, P., 96, *108*
Bruininks, R., 368, *387*
Brumley, H. E., 178, *189*
Bruner, J., 313, *334*
Brunk, M. A., 295, *302*
Bruun, R. D., *104*, 439, 441, 442, 448, *451, 452, 454*
Bryan, R. N., *451, 454*
Bryan, T. H., 418, *428*
Bryans, B. N., 414, *428*
Bryant, P., 403, 416, *428*
Bryson, C. Q., *335*
Bryson, S. E., 313, 316, 325, 326, *334, 338*
Buchsbaum, M. S., *240*, 329, *334*
Budd, K. S., 584, 585, *596, 598*
Budin, L. E., 528, *531*
Budman, C. L., 441, 442, *451*
Buela-Casal, G., *57*
Bugental, D. B., 37, *52*, 296, *302*, 523, 524, 525, *531*
Buhrmeister, D., 69, 91, 92, *104, 107*, 174, 178, 179, 180, *188*
Bujas-Petkovic, Z., 326, *334*
Bukowski, W. M., 589, *599*
Bullard, D. M., 465, *487*
Bunney, W. E., Jr., *109*
Burack, J. A., 318, *334*, 372, 377, 379, 380, *385, 386, 387, 388, 389*
Burbach, D. J., 178, *188, 191*, 578, *597*
Burd, L., 345, 355, *358*, 442, 442, 445, *451*
Burge, D., 166, 172, 174, 178, 181, 184, *188, 189, 190, 194*
Burgess, A. W., 242, 248, 268, *270, 271*, 504, 505, 506, 508, 509, 510, 512, 513, 514, 516, 517, 527, *534*
Burgess, K., 292, *307*
Burgess, R., 515, *532*
Burghen, G. A., 587, 589, *597*
Burgmeier, R., 592, *600*
Burk, G. S., 468, 470, *491*
Burke, A. E., 230, 232, *236, 240*
Burke, J. C., 312, *336*
Burke, J. D., 166, *188*, 248, 264, 267, *270*

Burke, K. C., 166, 167, *188*,
Burke, P. M., 154, 156, 174, *187, 192*
Burke, P., 171, *192*
Burks, H., 65, *104*
Burlingame, W. V., *195*
Burlingham, D. T., 242, 247, 255, 267, *271*
Burnam, M. A., 218, *237*
Burney, E., 166, *190*
Burns, B. J., 164, *188*, 248, 264, *270*
Burroughs, J., 555, *570*
Burt, C. E., 180, 181, 183, 184, *188*, 242, 243, 247, *270*
Burton, N., 153, *191*
Busch, J., 325, *336*
Bush, J. P., 591, 592, *596, 597, 598, 599*
Bush, L., *486*
Bush, M., 500, *532*
Butler, C., 179, *187*
Butler, G., 230, *236*
Butler, M. G., *387*
Butow, P., 549, *566*
Butterworth, G., 445, *451*
Byles, J. A., *52, 57, 192*
Byrne, C., *57, 192*
Byrne, T., 96, *110*

Caballo, V. E., *57*
Caddell, J. M., 260, *272*
Cadman, D. T., *52, 57*, 28, *192*
Cadoret, R. J., 97, *104*
Cadorette, T., *334*
Cahill, C., 253, *270*
Caine, E. D., 439, 445, 447, 449, *451, 453*
Caine, S. B., 449, *454*
Cairns, B. D., 125, *145*
Cairns, R. B., 125, *145*
Calam, R., 561, *566, 570*
Calderon, R., *192*
Calkins, S. D., 31, *58*, 277, 287, 289, 291, 292, *302, 303, 306*, 339, 478, 484, 485
Call, J. D., 247, 253, 267, *272*, 489
Callaway, E., *335*
Cameron, J., 369, *386*
Cameron, O. G., 204, 228, 233, *241*
Camfield, P. R., 442, *454*
Camino, G., *52*
Camparo, L., 91, *104*
Campbell, J. P., 35, *54*
Campbell, M., 328, *334, 336*, 355, *358, 359, 360*
Campbell, S. B., 36, *52*, 67, 75, 79, 80, 86, 86, 87, *104*, 129, *145*, 481, 485
Campbell, S., 333, *334*
Campos, J., 290, *305*, 478, *489*
Camras, L. A., 510, *532*
Canino, G., *52, 187*, 219, *235*, 575, *597*
Cann, W., 291, 299, *306*
Cannon, B. O., 333, *334*
Cannon, T. D., 352, 353, *358*
Cantor, D. S., 330, *334*
Cantor, N., 15, 28, *52*

Cantor, S., 341, 345, 352, 355, *358*
Cantwell, D. P., 90, 97, *102, 104*, 153, 154, *188, 193*, 217, 218, 220, *236*, 315, 323, *334*
Capaldi, D. M., 129, 135, 139, 141, *145*
Caplan, P. J., 499, *532*
Caplan, R., 327, *338*, 345, 355, *358*
Cappella, B., 75, *104*
Capps, L., 313, *334*
Caputo, G. C., 560, *569*
Carbonari, C. M., *452*
Cardarelli, A. P., 253, *272*
Cardon, L. R., 417, *428*
Carek, D. J., 212, *235*
Carella, E. T., 175, *187*, 284, *301*
Carey, G., 32, 46, *52*
Carey, M., *194*
Carey, W. B., 462, 463, 467, *485*
Carlsmith, J. M., *567*
Carlson, C. L., 66, 67, 89, 99, 100, 101, *104, 107*
Carlson, E. A., 475, *491*, 514, *535*
Carlson, G. A., 89, *104*, 153, 154, 156, 157, 158, 162, 171, 180, *187, 188, 191, 193, 489*
Carlson, J. G., 258, *270*
Carlson, V., *270*, 479, *485*, 514, *532, 535, 536*
Carlsson, A., 350, *358*
Carmen, E. H., 242, *270*, 516, *532*
Carnine, D., 425, *428*
Carntwell, D. P., 405, *428*
Carole, L. F., *274*
Caron, C., 32, 33, *52*, 131, 132, 135, *145*, 160, *188*, 231, 232, *236*
Carosella, N., 350, *358*
Carpentieri, S., 161, 176, *188*, 284, *302*, 588, *599*
Carr, E. G., 4, *54*
Carr, T. H., 56, 172, *195*
Carriere, R., 531, *534*
Carrigan, S., 134, *149*
Carrobles, J. A., *57*
Carroll, B. J., 448, *452*
Carroll, E. M., 262, *271*
Carroll-Wilson, M., 171, *192*
Carrougher, J., 81, *109*
Carskadon, M. A., 467, *484*
Carson, R. E., *451*
Carte, E. T., 91, *107*
Carter, A., 444, *451*
Carter, B. D., *598*
Carter, B., 403, *430*
Carter, J. D., 41, *52*
Carter, R. A., 69, *111*
Carter, W. G., 233, *241*
Carton, A. S., 372, *388*
Cartwright, A., *427*
Caruso, D. R., 363, *385*
Casanova, M. F., 350, *358*
Casey, J. E., 426, *428*
Casey, P. H., 465, *485*
Cash, R., 172, *194*
Cashmore, J., 296, *303*
Caspi, A., 131, 135, *143, 145, 149*, 287, 299, *302*, 473, 476, *486*

Cass, L. K., 29, *52*
Cassano, G. B., 223, *236*
Cassavia, E., *270*, *531*
Cassidy, J., 44, 45, 46, *52*, 177, *192*, 477, 478, 481, *484*, *485*, 488, 513, *532*
Cassidy, S. B., 370, 382, *385*, *386*, *387*
Castellan, J., 460, 461, *486*
Castellanos, F. X., 449, *451*
Castelloe, P., 330, 332, *334*, *335*
Castiglione, C. M., *453*
Castino, R. J., 480, *487*
Castle, D., 480, *489*
Catalano, R. F., 13, *52*
Cataldo, M. F., 93, *104*
Catlin, G. P., *52*
Cattell, R. B., 7, 22, *52*
Catts, H. W., 402, 403, 416, *428*, *430*
Caul, W. F., 66, 69, *106*
Cawley, J. F., 426, *428*
Cecalupo, A., 586, *596*
Ceci, J., *428*, *429*
Celano, M. P., 510, *532*
Cerny, J. A., 229, 230, *240*
Chadwick-Dias, A., *339*
Chaiyasit, W., *241*, 300, *307*
Chaloff, J., *52*, 222, 223, 235, *240*, *301*
Chamberlin, R. W., 580, *596*
Chambers, W. J., 157, 159, 188, 193
Champeaux, M., 476, *490*
Champoux, M., 225, *239*
Chan, B., *454*
Chan, D. A., 584, *596*
Chan, J., 300, *302*
Chandler, M., 279, *302*, 443, *454*
Chaney, J. M., 572, 574, *596*, *597*, *598*, *599*
Chansky, T. E., *238*
Chapel, J. L., *148*
Chapin, H. N., 217, *234*
Chapman, M., 178, *193*
Chappell, P., 449, *451*
Chard, L., 345, *361*
Charney, D. S., 218, *236*, 554, *567*
Charney, E., 594, *597*
Charnock, D. J. K., 559, *566*
Chase, T. N., 442, *451*, *452*, *453*, *454*
Chasnoff, I. J., 384, *386*
Chastain, R. L., 575, *598*
Chatillon, M., 416, *430*
Chatoor, I., 464, 465, 466, 469, *485*, *486*
Chaudhry, D. R., 229, *237*, *239*
Chavoya, G. A., 247, *272*
Chazan, R., 139, *145*
Chee, E., *454*
Chee, P., 68, *104*
Chemtob, C., 258, 259, *270*
Chen, R., *336*
Chen, S., 290, *305*, 478, *489*
Chen, W. J., 80, *104*, *105*, *109*
Chen, X., 14, 49, *53*, 58, 277, 287, 290, 294, 300, *302*, *306*
Chen, Y., *429*

Chernauzan, N., *360*
Cheslow, D. L., 204, 206, *238*, *240*, *454*
Chesney-Lind, M., 130, 138, *145*
Chess, S., 19, 35, 48, *59*, 65, *104*, 444, *454*
Chevron, E. S., 179, *187*
Cheyne, J. A., 93, *104*
Chhabra, V., 405, *431*
Chhun, B., *274*
Chiat, S., 315, *336*
Chibaiwa, D., 221, *241*
Chisholm, Y., 291, *303*
Chisum, H., 17, *53*
Chiverton, P., *451*
Choate, M., 98, *105*
Chorpita, B. F., 4, 16, 211, 219, 225, 228, 231, 232, *234*, 235, *236*
Choudry, I. Y., 552, *569*
Chovers, A., 583, *598*
Christ, M. A. G., 68, *108*, 126, *146*, *147*, *149*, *304*
Christensen, A., 91, *104*
Christensen, L., 319, *337*
Christoffel, K. K., 462, *491*
Christopher, J., 186, *194*
Christophersen, E. R., 580, 582, 594, *596*, *598*, *601*
Chrousos, G. P., 170, *189*
Chu, J. A., 242, *270*
Chun, Z. F., 552, *566*
Chung, S. Y., 326, *334*
Churchill, D. W., *335*
Cialdella, P., 326, *335*
Cibelli, C., 482, 483, *488*
Cicchetti, D. V., 3, 5, 6, 11, 15, 16, 18, 20, 36, 38, 44, 45, 46, *53*, *54*, 56, *57*, 58, 113, 117, 121, 129, 135, 142, *145*, 148, 177, 184, *186*, *188*, 265, 266, *270*, *304*, *306*, *335*, *337*, 358, 363, 372, 373, *385*, *386*, *387*, *388*, *451*, 479, 481, *485*, *486*, *488*, 493, 495, 498, 500, 501, 509, 510, 511, 513, 514, 515, 519, 521, 530, *531*, *532*, *533*, *534*, *535*, *536*
Cigrang, J. A., *597*
Ciminero, A. R., *51*
Clairborne, J. H., 392, *428*
Clark, B. S., 316, *334*
Clark, C., 17, *55*
Clark, L. A., 224, *241*, *286*, *302*
Clark, M. L., 93, *104*
Clarke, C., 290, *304*
Clarke, G., 249, 252, *270*, *273*
Clarkin, J. F., 286, *307*
Clarren, S. K., *388*
Claussen, A. H., 20, *53*
Claussen, A. K., 492, *532*
Cleckley, H., 115, 118, 124, *145*
Clegg, M., 90, *103*
Clements, C. M., 198, *234*
Clementz, B. A., 28, 29, *53*
Cloninger, C. R., *191*, *234*, *236*, 447, *451*, 560, *566*
Clubb, M., *452*
Clum, G. A., 517, *536*

Cobb, J. C., 462, *491*
Cobham-Portorreal, C. S., *147*
Cohen, A., 91, *108*, 437, *451*
Cohen, C., *145*
Cohen, D. J., 3, 36, *53*, 96, 99, *109*, *110*, 240, 241, 312, 316, 319, 324, 328, *334*, *335*, 337, 339, 345, 355, *360*, 380, 388, 436, 437, 438, 439, 445, 446, 436, 437, 441, 442, 443, 444, 447, *450*, *451*, *452*, *453*, *454*, *567*
Cohen, D., 313, *335*, *387*
Cohen, I. L., 382, *385*
Cohen, J. A., 252, 262, *273*
Cohen, J., 24, *53*, *188*, *568*
Cohen, L. H., 175, 180, 183, *188*, *189*
Cohen, M., 413, *434*
Cohen, N. J., 67, 81, 92, *104*, *110*
Cohen, P., 12, *59*, 84, *111*, 162, 164, *188*, 219, *241*, 466, *488*
Cohen, R. M., *105*, *112*
Cohen, R., 172, *193*, *195*
Cohen, S., 252, 275, 287, *302*
Cohn, J. F., 178, *188*
Coie, J. D., 116, 141, *145*, *306*
Colbus, D., 174, *191*, 501, *534*
Cole, C. M., 12, 21, *60*
Cole, D. A., 161, 165, 172, 173, 175, 176, 179, 180, 182, 183, *188*, *194*, 284, *302*
Cole, D., *52*
Cole, J. O., *358*
Cole, P. M., 44, 45, *53*, 69, *104*, 265, 266, *270*, 513, 522, *532*
Colegrove, R., Jr., 595, *601*
Coles, G., 391, 405, *428*
Colheart, M., *429*, *433*
Collins, B. E., 93, *111*
Collins, F. L., 594, *600*
Colon, E., 549, *569*
Colton, M. E., 165, 183, *189*
Comings, B. E., 439, 441, 442, 447, *451*
Comings, B. G., 89, *104*, 446, *451*
Comings, D. E., 89, 98, *104*, 439, 441, 442, 446, 447, *451*
Compas, B. E., 21, 57, 158, 159, 160, 161, 175, 184, *188*, *190*, 267, *270*, 287, *302*
Conger, R. D., 4, *54*
Conger, R., 515, *532*
Congneau, M., 329, *335*
Conley, C., 466, *485*
Connell, D. B., 178, *188*, *192*, 478, 479, *488*
Connell, J. P., 262, *270*, 291, *307*
Conners, C. K., 10, *51*, 66, 68, 69, *104*, *106*
Conners, M. E., 560, *568*
Connolly, J., 171, *192*
Connor, R., *147*
Connors, F., 404, *432*
Conolly, J., 341, *358*
Conrad, M., 159, *188*
Conte, J. R., 263, 267, *270*, 493, 528, *532*

Conte, R. A., 94, *107*
Cook, A., 19, *55*
Cook, E. H., 98, *104*
Cook, S. C., 593, 594, *599*
Cooley, E. J., 418, *428*
Cooper, F. S., 402, *430*
Cooper, P. J., 156, 157, 162, 164, *188, 189*, 542, 546, *567*
Copeland, A. P., 68, 69, *103, 104*
Copeland, D. R., *601*
Copeland, P. M., 553, *567*
Coplan, R. J., 31, *58*, 277, 279, 280, 287, 292, 302, *306*
Corbin, S. M., *596*
Corcoran, C. M., *191*
Cordas, T. A., 556, *569*
Cordisco, L. K., 333, *338*
Corey, M., 586, *597*
Corkum, P. V., 67, 68, *105*
Cornblatt, B. A., *189*
Cornely, P., 265, *270*
Cornish-McTighe, D., 212, *235*
Cornsweet, C., 91, *107*
Coromina, J., 242, 247, *270*
Corry, J. J., 591, *597*
Cortez, V., *531*
Costa, D. C., 329, *335*
Costa, P. T., 286, 302, *307*
Costello, A. J., 80, *105*, 159, 164, *188*, 198, *241*
Costello, E. J., 9, 10, 13, *53*, 81, *105*, 125, *145*, 158, 160, 161, 162, 163, 164, 165, *187, 188*, 220, *236*, 284, 302
Coulter, M. L., 267, *271*
Courchesne, E., 16, *53*, 4, 317, 328, 329, 330, *334, 335, 336*
Coury, D. L., 584, *596*
Cowen, E. L., 262, *276*
Cowen, P. J., 554, *567, 568*
Cox, A., 178, *192*, 323, *334*
Cox, M. J., 474, *486*
Cox, N. J., *104*
Coyne, J. C., 137, *145*, 174, 176, *188*, 287, 302, 483, *486*
Craft, P., 460, 461, *486*
Crago, M., 565, *570*
Craig, A. G., 91, *111*
Craig, K. D., 579, 590, *596*
Craig, T. K. J., 575, *596*
Craighead, W. E., *195*
Crawford, J. W., 4, 5, 37, 41, 42, 43, 52, 57, *192*
Crawford, S. L., 200, *238*
Crawshaw, R., 255, 267, *270*
Creak, M., 342, *358*
Crick, N. R., 116, 140, *145*
Criqui, M. H., *106*
Crisp, A. H., 551, 558, 560, *567*
Crist, W., 586, *596*
Crittenden, P. M., 20, *53*, 464, 465, *486*, 492, 500, 501, 503, 513, 515, 523, 524, *532*
Crnic, K. A., 233, *241*, 287, 302, 375, *385*
Crockenberg, S. B., 228, *236*, 478, *486*

Crocker, A., *388*
Crockett, L., 16, *55*
Crocq, M., 251, *270*
Crosby, R. B., *567*
Crosby, R. D., 559, *569*
Cross, P., *450*
Cross-National Collaborative Group, *188*,
Crouch, J. L., 503, *532*
Crouse-Novak, M. A., 160, 166, 167, 180, 183, 184, *191*
Crowe, J., *239*
Crowe, R. R., 228, 229, *236, 237*
Crowell, J., 491, 511, *536*
Crowson, M., *450*
Crozier, D., 586, *597*
Cruickshank, W. M., 65, *105*, 391, 393, 394, *428, 429*
Cruse, R. P., 449, *452*
Crutcher, D., *388*
Cruttenden, L., 71, *105*
Cuffe, S. P., *241*
Cullinan, D., 380, *385*
Culpepper, L., 448, *452*
Cummings, E. M., 4, 11, 37, 44, *53*, 138, *145*, 177, 184, 178, *188, 193, 194*, 488, 509, *534*
Cummings, J., *452*
Cummings, M., 297, *306*
Cunningham, C. E., 67, 93, 92, 99, 103, 104, *105*
Curcio, F., 313, *335*
Curry, J. F., *195*
Curry, S. L., 267, *270*
Curtis, G. C., 204, 228, 233, *241*
Curtiss, S., 374, *385*
Cutler, N. R., *338*
Cvejic, H., *110*
Cystic Fibrosis Foundation Patient Registry, 586, *596*
Cytryn, L., 229, 237, *307*

DaCosta, G. A., 270, *531*
DaCosta, M., 557, 560, *567*
Dadds, M. R., 172, 180, *189, 194*, 228, 230, *235, 236*
Dagenbach, D., *56*
Dahl, M., 465, *486*
Dahl, R. E., 169, 170, 187, 189, 193, 194
Daily, J. M., 285, *301*
Dale, J., 590, *597*
Daleiden, E. L., 41, *59*
Daley, S. E., *190*
Daltroff, W., 436, *453*
Daly, K., 320, *338*
Daly, T., 333, *337*
Daly-Jones, O., 575, *596*
Damasio, A. R., 331, *333, 335, 337*
Damasio, H., 331, *333, 337*
Damon, W., 279, *302*
Dandes, S. K., 284, *304*
Dandoy, A. c., *237*
Danforth, J. S., 69, 91, 93, *105*
Daniels, S. R., 594, *598*
Daniels, T., 292, *307*

Daniels-Beirness, T., 293, *306*
Dannals, R. F., *454*
Darby, B. L., *111*
Dare, C., 38, *53*
Darling, N., 298, *307*
Data, P. C., *338*
Dauber, S. L., 426, *434*
Daugherty, T. K., 136, *145*
Davenport, C. W., 243, *272*
Davenport, D., *307*
David, O. J., 98, *105*
Davidson, B. J., 409, *432*
Davidson, C. E., 139, *145*
Davidson, D., *487*
Davidson, J. R., 261, *270, 272, 273*, 468, *486*
Davidson, K. C., 10, *54*
Davidson, K. S., 221, *240*
Davidson, L. L., 94, *105, 531*
Davidson, R., *240*, 289, 302, *303*
Davies, M., 59, 80, *110*, 157, 163, 165, 167, *188, 190, 193, 195, 235, 236, 241*, 570
Davies, P. T., 4, 11, 37, 44, *53*
Davies, S. P., 363, *385*
Davila, J., 166, *190*
Davis, D., 350, *360*
Davis, G. C., 242, *270*
Davis, H., 183, *190*
Davis, N. S., 467, *488*
Davis, N., 590, *596*
Davis, T., 462, *491*
Dawson, G., 5, *53*, 312, 313, 314, 316, 317, 330, 331, 332, 333, *334, 335, 336, 337, 339, 342*
Day, N. L., 384, *388*
Dayson, D., 550, *568*
De Bellis, M. D., 260, *270*
de Groen, J. H. M., *271*
de Hirsch, K., 400, *428*
de la Burde, B., 98, *105*
De Sanctis, S., 341, *358*
De Vellis, R., 320, *338*
De Vries, A., *452*
de Zwaan, M., 550, 564, 565, *567, 569*
Dearborn, M., 593, *599*
deAzevedo, M. H., 553, *567*
Deblinger, E., 249, 262, *271, 273*, 505, *535*
Decker, S., 411, *428*
DeCuir-Whalley, S., 590, *599*
Deering, C. G., 177, *191*
DeFries, J. C., 90, *106, 111*, 403, 404, 407, 411, 417, *428, 433*
DeGangi, G. A., 460, 461, *486*
DeGroff, L., 410, *430*
DeHaan, C. B., *601*
DeJong, A. R., 264, *271*
DeKlyen, M., 139, *146*, 149, 483, *487, 490*
Dekry, S. J., 380, *385*
Del Dotto, J., 412, *428*
Delamater, A. M., 595, *596*
Delaney, H. D., 8, 33, 34, *57*
Delaney, M. A., 212, *241*

Delgado, P. L., 554, *567*
DeLisi, L. E., 352, *358*
Dell, L., 350, *359*
DeLong, G. R., 317, *335*
Delong, M. R., 449, *450*
Delprato, D. J., *149*
Deltito, J. A., 223, *236*
DeLucca, J., 412, *428*
Demb, H. B., 82, *105*
Dement, W. C., 467, *484*
DeMulder, E. K., 178, *189*, *194*, 479, *486*
DeMyer, M. K., 312, 313, 316, *335*, *336*
DeMyer, W. E., *335*
den Velde, W. O., 251, *271*
Denckla, M. B., 67, 69, *105*, 411, 443, 449, *451*, *454*
Denhoff, E., 65, *108*
Denson, R., 99, *105*
DePaola, L. M., *271*
Depue, R. A., *193*
Derrick, A., 134, *149*
Desai, V. J., 465, *485*, 585, *596*
Desch, L. W., 414, *434*
Detlor, J., 436, 447, *451*, *453*
Detwilet, A. C., 462, *491*
Deutsch, C. K., 47, *53*
Devinsky, O., 449, *451*
Devlin, M., *570*
DeVolder, A., 329, *335*
Devor, E. J., 447, *451*
Devost, L, Brickell, C., *486*
Deykin, E., 501, *532*
deYoung, M., 492, 509, *532*
Diamond, A., 71, *104*, *105*
Diamond, R., 69, *106*
Diaz-Guerrero, R., 221, *240*
DiBartolo, P. M., 202, 204, 211, 213, *234*
Dibble, E. D., *567*
Dick, T., 506, *535*
Dickson, L., 465, 466, *485*
DiClemente, R. J., 264, *274*
Dienstbier, R. A., 228, *236*
Dieruf, W., 91, *111*
Dietz, G., *104*
DiGirolamo, A. M., 586, *600*
DiLalla, D. L., 32, 46, 52, 333, *338*, 500, 503, *532*
DiLalla, L. F., 137, *145*
Dill, D. L., 242, *270*
Dillon, M., 511, *534*
Dilsaver, S. C., 212, *234*
DiMascio, A., *358*
Dinardo, L., 499, *532*
DiNardo, P. A., 229, *236*
Dinges, N. G., 222, *236*
Dingman, H. F., 378, *385*
DiPietro, J. A., 461, *486*
Dishion, T. J., 4, 17, *56*, *57*, 134, 139, 143, *145*, *148*
Diskin, S. D., 473, *487*
Divoky, D., 82, *110*
Dix, T. H., 296, *302*, 482, *486*
Dixon, J. F., 182, *189*

Dobson, K. S., 39, 41, 42, 43, *53*, *55*
Dobyns, W. B., *386*
Docherty, J. P., 259, *276*
Dodge, J. A., 586, *596*
Dodge, K. A., 4, 5, 18, 37, 41, 42, 43, 44, *53*, *54*, *56*, *59*, *106*, 116, 136, 138, 139, 140, 141, *145*, *147*, *148*, 161, *189*, *193*, 278, 283, *302*, 482, *486*, *489*, *489*, 511, 514, 523, 525, *532*, *536*
Doehring, D. G., 410, 414, *428*
Doerfler, L. A., 175, *189*
Dohrenwend, B. P., 346, *358*
Doidge, N., *570*
Doise, W., 279, *302*
Dolgin, M., 595, *601*
Dolinsky, A., *195*, *241*
Doll, H. A., 545, *567*, *568*
Dollinger, S. J., 253, *271*
Dolnansky, E. S., *452*
Dolphin, J. E., 65, *105*
Domenech, J., *335*
Donahue, M., 418, *428*
Donald, A., *452*
Donaldson, S. K., *56*
Dondis, E. H., 364, *388*
Donkhorst, J. D., *601*
Donnellan, A. M., 319, *334*, *335*
Donnelly, M., 81, *109*
Donoghue, D., *334*
Donohue, B., 3, 6, 7, *53*
Dooley, J. M., 442, *454*
Dorer, D. L., *191*
Doris, J. L., 391, 393, 395, 405, *428*, 511, 512, *533*
Dorland's Illustrated Medical Dictionary, *357*
Dornbusch, S. M., 298, *307*, 557, *567*
Dosen, A. 381, *385*, *387*
Doster, J. A., 28, *51*
Dotemoto, S., 93, *112*
Douglas, E., 80, *108*, 281, *304*
Douglas, J. W. B., 580, *596*
Douglas, P., 170, *190*
Douglas, V. I., 21, *55*, 65, 66, 67, 68, 69, 75, *104*, *105*, *109*
Downey, G., 4, 27, *53*, *54*, 137, *145*, 186, *189*, 287, *302*, 473, 483, *486*, 514, 516, *532*, *536*
Downing, J., 593, *599*
Dozier, M., 23, *53*
Dozois, D. J. A., *50*
Draeger, S., 68, *105*
Draguns, J. G., 216, *240*, 398, *427*
Drake, H., 575, *596*
Drell, M. J., 265, *274*, 468, 469, 470, *486*, *490*
Drenowski, A., 551, *567*
Drew, N., 531, *533*
Drizd, T. A., *597*
Droegenmueller, W., 494, *534*
Drotar, D., 375, *385*, 464, 465, *484*, *485*, *486*, *489*, *491*, *486*, 526, 529, 530, *532*, *533*, 585, 595, *596*, *599*, *601*
du Verglas, G., 327, *335*

Duane, D. D., *428*, *429*, *431*, *435*
Duara, R., *338*, *429*, *431*
Dubbert, B. K., 565, *571*
DuBois, D. L., *54*
Dubowitz, H., 465, *485*
Dugas, F., 83, *111*
Dugdale, R. L., 363, *385*
Dulcan, M. K., 159, 164, *188*
Dumas, J. E., 4, *53*, 139, *144*, *149*
Duncan, G. J., 9, 11, *53*
Duncan, J. S., *453*
Duncan, P. D., *567*
Dunlavy, S., *600*
Dunn, G., *109*
Dunn, J., *307*
Dunner, D. L., 305, *307*
Dunsdon, M. I., 243, 247, *271*
Dunst, C. J., 373, *385*
Duong, T., *338*
Duong-Tran, Q., 222, *236*
DuPaul, G. J., 52, 66, 67, 68, 69, 70, 79, 83, 86, 89, 90, 93, 94, 95, 97, 99, 100, *103*, *105*, *109*
Durand, V. M., 216, 222, *235*
Duval, F., *270*
Dweck, C., 198, *236*, 293, *303*
Dworkin, R. H., *189*
Dwyer, J. T., 557, *567*
Dycian, A., *450*
Dyck, D. G., 172, *192*
Dykens, E. M., 363, 369, 371, 372, 374, 375, 376, 379, 380, 381, 382, 384, *385*, *386*, *387*, 442, 443, 444, *450*, *451*
Dykes, L., 508, *533*
Dykman, R. A., 425, *427*
Dziuba-Leatherman, J., 492, 498, *533*

Eales, M. J., 315, *335*
Eapen, V., 447, *452*
Eardley, D. A., 43, *58*
Earls, F., 10, *53*, 129, *149*, 242, 249, 253, 262, 263, *271*, *568*
Early-Zald, M. B., 13, *56*
Easterbrooks, M. A., 139, *145*, 482, 483, *488*
Eaton, W. W., 221, *236*
Eaves, L. J., 229, *238*, 570
Eaves, L., *569*
Ebata, A. T., 175, *189*
Ebaugh, F. G., 65, *105*
Eberenz, K. P., 517, *533*
Eberhart-Wright, A., *487*
Ebert, M. H., 439, 449, *453*, 553, *567*, *568*
Eckenrode, J., 262, *274*, 511, 512, *533*
Eckerle, D., *486*
Eckert, E. D., *568*, *569*
Eckman, T., *359*
Ecob, K. C., 363, *385*
Edelbrock, C. S., 5, 10, 12, 13, 17, 22, 23, 28, 36, *51*, *53*, 66, 68, 76, 79, 80, 95, 98, 99, *102*, *103*, *105*, *106*, 116, 132, 137, *144*, 158, 159, 164, *186*, *188*, 216, 230, 231, *234*, 263, 269, 280, 284, *301*, *302*, 446, *450*

Edelsohn, G. A., 16, *55*, 267, *271*
Edelstein, W., 481, *487*
Edgell, H. G., 345, *358*
Edison, M., 383, *389*
Edwards, N. B., 273, *534*
Efron, D. H., *358*
Egaas, B., *335*
Egan, J., 464, 465, *485*
Egeland, B., 17, *54*, 125, 139, *145*, *148*, 291, *302*, 305, 473, 476, 481, 482, *486*, 489, 492, 493, 500, 501, 503, 514, *533*, *535*
Egeland, J. A., *107*
Eggers, C., 345, 355, 356, 357, *358*
Ehiobuche, I., 230, *236*
Ehlers, A., 235, *239*
Ehly, S. W., 380, *385*
Ehri, L., *434*
Einbender, A. J., 263, *271*, 511, 514, *533*
Eisen, A. E., 216, 232, *240*, *241*
Eisen, A. R., 211, 213, 216, 220, *234*, *236*, 237, *241*
Eisenberg, L., 298, *302*
Eisenhauer, G., 350, *361*
Eisenson, J., 400, *427*
Eisler, I., *570*
Eisler, R. M., *239*
Eitinger, L., 251, *275*
Ekvall, S., *489*
El-Amin, D., *486*
Eland, J. M., 590, *596*
Elder, G. H., 4, *54*, 287, 299, *302*, 473, 474, *486*
Eldredge, K., 552, *566*, *571*
Eldredge, R., 500, *534*, 439, 447, *452*, *453*
Eliopulos, D., 96, *107*
Elizur, E., 248, 252, *271*
Elkind, D., 445, *452*
Elkind, G. S., 67, *111*
Elkins, R., *240*
Ell, P. J., 329, *335*
Ellers, B., 593, *597*
Ellicott, A., 166, *190*
Elliott, C. H., 592, *596*
Elliott, G. R., 332, *338*
Ellis, A. W., 421, *428*
Ellis, N. R., *385*
Ellis, W. W., *428*
Elman, M., *110*
Elmer, E., 247, 268, *271*
Emde, R. N., 458, 459, 460, 470, 472, *484*, *486*, 490, *491*
Eme, R. F., 11, *54*
Emery, G., 35, 52, 170, *187*
Emery, R. E., 4, *54*, 138, *145*, 242, 268, *271*, 287, *302*
Emmelkamp, P. M. G., 230, *237*, 283, *301*
Emmerich, W., 296, *302*
Emmett, G. A., 264, *271*
Emslie, G., 43, *59*
Endicott, J., *191*
Endriga, M. C., 139, *146*, 483, *487*
Eng, A., 594, *596*

Engfer, A., 299, *302*
Engler, L. B., 211, *236*
Englert, C. S., 421, *428*
Epps, J., 42, *55*
Epstein, L. H., 556, *567*, 594, *596*
Epstein, M. H., 380, *385*
Epstein, S., 258, 259, *259*, *271*
Erenberg, G., 449, *452*
Erickson, M. F., 125, 139, *145*, 291, 295, *302*, 492, 493, 499, 500, 503, *533*, *535*
Erikson, E. H., 445, *452*
Erlenmeyer-Kimling, L., *336*, *359*
Ernberg, G., 346, *359*, *360*
Ernst, A. R., 575, 579, 580, *597*, *600*
Ernst, M., 96, *105*, *334*
Erol, N., 221, *236*
Eron, L. D., 11, *54*, 137, *146*
Eschler, J., 332, *338*
Escobar, J. I., 575, *597*
Escobar, M. D., 403, *433*
Eshleman, S., *238*
Eskinazi, B., 98, *106*
Eslinger, P. J., 95, *106*
Esman, A., 38, *58*
Esser, G., 481, *485*
Esveldt-Dawson, K., 174, 176, *191*
Eth, S., 242, 247, 256, 266, 267, 268, 270, *271*, 272, 274, 470, *489*
Ettinger, L., 245, *271*
Evans, C. D., 549, *569*
Evans, D. D., *104*
Evans, D. W., 89, 369, *386*, 445, *452*
Evans, E. G., *54*
Evans, R. I., 594, *597*
Evans, T., 171, 183, *191*, *192*
Everett, B. L., 253, *269*
Everly, G. S., 286, *305*
Everson, M. D., 267, *271*
Ewigman, B., 583, *597*
Ewing, L. J., 67, 86, *104*, 129, *145*, *569*
Ey, S., 158, *188*
Eyberg, S. M., 515, *531*
Eyman, R. K., 370, *386*
Eysenck, H. J., 116, *145*
Eysenck, S. B. G., 300, *302*

Faed, J. M., 98, *110*
Fagot, B. I., 139, *145*
Fahy, T. A., 562, *567*
Faier-Routman, J., 587, *598*
Fairbairn, W., 177, *189*
Fairbank, J. A., 247, 260, *272*, J. A., 468, *486*
Fairbanks, L., 250, *274*, *567*
Fairburn, C. G., 541, 542, 545, 546, 547, 549, 550, 551, 552, 554, 556, 558, 559, 562, 566, *566*, *567*, 568, 569, 570, *571*
Fairclough, D., 588, *599*
Falger, P. R. J., *271*
Fallahi, C., *191*
Falloon, I. R. H., 355, *358*
Famularo, R., 249, 252, 255, 265, 267, *271*, 498, *533*

Fantuzzo, J. W., 268, *271*, J. W., 498, 500, *533*
Faraone, S. V., 52, *54*, 80, 81, 90, 93, 98, *103*, *104*, *105*, *110*, 137, *145*, 222, 224, 235, 237, *240*, *301*, *303*, *487*
Faraone, V., *454*
Faravelli, C., 255, *271*
Farber, B., 375, *386*
Farbisz, R., *596*
Farmer, J., 580, *599*
Farrell, P., 586, *600*
Farrington, D. P., 115, 125, 132, 133, *146*
Farris, A. M., *304*
Fassbender, L. L., 319, *335*
Fatkenheuer, B., *360*
Fauber, R. L., 8, *54*, 165, *189*
Faust-Campanile, J., 59, 581, *601*
Fava, M., 553, *567*
Faw, G. D., *388*
Fawcett, N., *597*
Feagans, L., 410, 413, 425, 426, *428*, *432*
Feehan, M., 79, *108*, 130, *147*, 164, *192*, *304*
Feeman, D. J., 410, *434*
Fehan, M., *239*
Fein, D., 330, *331*
Fein, G., 290, *306*
Feinberg, M., 448, *452*
Feinberg, T. E., 437, 441, *454*
Feinberg, T. L., 160, 166, 167, 180, 183, 184, *191*
Feindel, E., 436, *453*
Feinstein, C., 328, *339*
Feldman, J. J., 557, *567*
Feldman, P. M., *36*
Feldman, S., 37, *54*
Feldman, M., 255, 262, 267, *275*
Felner, R. D., 4, *54*, R. D., 268, *271*
Felton, R. H., 90, *112*, 399, 403, *428*, *435*
Femina, D. B., 530, *534*
Feng, Y. L., 300, *303*
Fenichel, E., *491*
Fenton, T., 249, 265, *271*, 498, *533*
Ferber, R., *486*
Ferguson, B., 83, 90, *103*, *111*
Ferguson, L. L., 125, *145*
Fergusson, D. M., 98, *105*, 114, 120, 132, *146*
Fergusson, I. E., 98, *105*
Fernald, C. D., 591, *597*
Ferrari, M., 442, *450*
Ferreira, C. P., 553, *567*
Feschbach, S., 115, 116, *146*
Fewell, R., 375, *386*
Fichter, M. M., 547, 549, 551, 554, 562, *566*, *567*, 569, 575, *600*
Fiedorowicz, A. M., 414, *428*
Fiegenbaum, W., 235, *239*
Field, T. M., 313, *335*
Field, T., 177, 178, *188*, *189*, *192*, 593, *597*, *598*
Figley, C. R., 243, 245, *271*, 272, *274*

Filice, G. A., 566
Filipek, P. A., 110, 404, 429
Filloux, F., 318, 337
Finch, A. J., 194, 250, 273, 275
Fincham, F. D., 138, 146
Fine, E. J., 451
Fine, S., 171, 190, 268, 274, 516, 535
Fingerhut, L. A., 113, 146
Finkelhor, D., 242, 256, 271, 273, 492, 495, 496, 498, 503, 504, 506, 508, 509, 512, 513, 516, 517, 520, 522, 527, 528, 531, 533, 534
Finkelstein, R., 160, 166, 167, 180, 183, 184, 191, 197, 238
Finlayson, M. A. J., 322, 338, 425, 411, 433
Finley, C., 330, 335
Finlon, M. A., 464, 486
Finn, T., 179, 193
Finney, J. W., 23, 54, 104, 584, 600
Finucane, B. M., 382, 386
Firestone, P., 580, 598
Fischer, F. W., 403, 430
Fischer, M. L., 316, 337
Fischer, M., 68, 77, 79, 86, 87, 88, 89, 90, 92, 95, 97, 103, 106, 132, 144
Fischer, S., 164, 179, 192, 194
Fischoff, S., 179, 191
Fish, B., 341, 342, 343, 344, 345, 346, 349, 352, 353, 355, 356, 358, 359
Fish-Murray, C. C., 266, 271
Fisher, C., 545, 569
Fisher, G. L., 414, 432
Fisher, K. W., 445, 450
Fisher, P., 159
Fisher, S. M., 583, 597
Fisher, W., 445, 451
Fisk, J. L., 410, 412, 429
Fisman, S., 338
Fitzgerald, G. A., 105, 112
Fitzgerald, H., 531
Fitzgibbon, M. L., 550, 566
Flament, M. F., 197, 204, 218, 220, 231, 236
Flanagan, S. D., 104
Flanery, R., 580, 597
Flavell, J. H., 69, 106, 278, 303
Fleck, K., 531
Fleeson, J., 493, 500, 521, 536
Fleisher, M. H., 380, 387
Fleishner, J. E., 423, 424, 425, 426, 429
Fleming, A., 178, 189
Fleming, J. E., 57, 157, 161, 162, 164, 165, 189, 192
Fleming, J., 429
Flemming, P., 285, 303
Fleshner, M., 573, 598
Fletcher, J. M., 10, 54, 391, 394, 396, 397, 398, 403, 407, 408, 409, 410, 416, 417, 426, 429, 433
Fletcher, K. E., 250, 251, 257, 258, 259, 271, 468, 496
Fletcher, K. F., 86, 92, 103
Fletcher, K., 68, 77, 92, 106
Fletcher, R. J., 385, 387

Flett, G., 178, 189
Flood, M., 571
Florin, I., 235, 239
Flower, L. S., 421, 429
Flowers, L., 399, 435
Flynn, J. M., 398, 410, 415, 416, 431
Foa, D., 247, 271, 272, 273
Foa, E. B., 243, 249, 258, 259, 260, 262, 271, 272, 486, 505, 520, 533, 535
Foch, T., 98, 109
Fodor, J., 374, 386
Fogelson, D. L., 359
Folkman, S., 259, 273
Folks, D. G., 573, 597
Follett, C., 212, 217, 239
Folstein, S., 326, 327, 335, 337
Foltz, G., 409, 432
Fonagy, P., 475, 486
Fondacaro, K. M., 175, 188
Fonesca, A. C., 221, 236
Fonnesu, F., 271
Ford, C. V., 573, 597
Ford, K., 594, 597
Ford-Black, M. M., 32, 33, 60
Forehand, R., 165, 174, 175, 176, 179, 189, 194, 198, 240, 284, 307
Fornari, V., 562, 564, 567
Forness, S., 391, 393, 394, 397, 398, 405, 430
Forrest, D., 465, 489
Forsberg, H., 404, 432
Forsyth, B. W. C., 463, 486
Forsythe, W. I., 580, 597
Fossey, M. D., 568
Foster, G. D., 560, 570
Foster, S. L., 13, 54
Fowler, A., 369, 373, 374, 386, 429
Fowles, D. C., 136, 145, 146, 147, 148, 149
Fox, L. W., 168, 194
Fox, M. M., 551, 568
Fox, N. A., 12, 31, 44, 45, 46, 47, 49, 52, 54, 58, 60, 277, 287, 289, 291, 302, 306, 471, 478, 486
Fox, N., 240, 289, 292, 302, 303, 304, 478, 484, 485
Foxx, R. M., 377, 386
Foy, D. W., 262, 271
Fraiberg, S., 464, 490
Frame, C. L., 132, 140, 145, 149, 176, 194, 198, 240, 284, 307, 380, 387
Frances, A. J., 213, 231, 236, 255, 271, 286, 307
Francis, D. J., 10, 54, 396, 398, 403, 408, 410, 417, 429
Francis, G., 47, 56, 197, 200, 204, 211, 219, 232, 236, 238, 240
Francis, P. S., 586, 597
Francoeur, T. E., 462, 484
Frank, A., 259, 276
Frank, B., 426, 429
Frank, D. A., 465, 486
Frank, L., 287, 303
Frank, Y., 96, 106

Franke, S., 284, 293, 303
Frankel, K. A., 478, 484
Frankel, M., 443, 452
Frankenburg, F. R., 564, 568
Franklin, J., 43, 56
Franks, C. M., 55
Frazier, J. A., 344, 345, 350, 355, 359
Frederick, C. J., 242, 247, 249, 250, 255, 264, 271, 274
Fredrickson, B. L., 175, 192
Freedheim, D. K., 51
Freedman, D., 327, 338, 410, 412, 431
Freeman, B. J., 327, 335, 338
Freeman, R. J., 171, 190
Fremmer-Bombik, E., 476, 481, 487, 491
French, D. C., 141, 146, 284, 288, 293, 303
French, F. E., 10, 60
French, J. H., 410, 411, 432
French, R. deS., 15, 52
French, V., 7, 54
Frenkel, O. J., 476, 491
Frensch, P., 551, 570
Freud, A., 197, 236, 242, 247, 255, 267, 271
Freud, S., 177, 189, 196, 236, 243, 258, 271
Freund, L., 382, 386, 388
Frey, K., 5, 53, 375, 386
Frick, P. J., 56, 68, 95, 102, 106, 107, 108, 126, 127, 133, 135, 137, 144, 146, 147, 304
Friedel, R. O., 360
Friedhoff, A. J., 442, 451, 452, 453, 454
Friedin, M. R., 93, 111
Friedlander, M. L., 171, 194
Friedman, H. S., 94, 106
Friedman, L., 190
Friedman, P., 255, 272
Friedman, R. M., 4, 9, 52, 54, 192
Friedman, S., 221, 236
Friedrich, W. N., 263, 271, 375, 385, 386, 493, 505, 506, 508, 511, 514, 515, 516, 527, 528, 533, 536
Friman, P. C., 23, 54
Fristad, M. A., 169, 195
Frith, U., 316, 334, 411, 416, 429
Frodi, A., 501, 509, 525, 533
Frost, A. K., 164, 193
Frost, J. D., 448, 449, 452, 600
Frost, J., 416, 431
Fry, A. F., 72, 106
Fudge, H., 167, 190
Fujii, K., 85, 107
Fulker, D., 404, 428, 432
Fulkerson, J. A., 13, 56
Fuller, B., 443, 454
Fuller, F., 422, 427
Fuller, P., 330, 335
Fullerton, C. S., 242, 275
Fulop, G., 454
Fulton, M., 111
Fusco, J., 487

Fuster, J. M., 69, 71, 72, 74, 95, 102, *106*
Fyer, M. R., 213, *236*

Gabreels, F. J., 577, *600*
Gaddes, W. H., 425, *429*
Gadot, N., *450*
Gadow, K., 108, 109, 112, *193*
Gaensbauer, T. J., 468, 469, 470, *486*, 515, *533*
Gaffney, G. R., 329, *335*
Gaines, R., 527, *533*
Galaburda, A. M., 417, *429*
Galambos, R., 330, *335*
Galante, R., 247, *272*
Galenson, E., *489*
Gallimore, R., 376, *386*
Gallmeier, T. M., 584, *597*
Galpert, L., 314, 330, *335*
Gamble, W., 179, *191*
Gammon, D., *194*
Ganiban, J., 515, *532*
Garbarino, J., 496, 531, *533*
Garber, H. J., 329, *335*
Garber, J. A., *489*
Garber, J., 5, 16, 22, 28, 40, 44, *54*, *106*, 161, 167, 168, 171, 172, 175, 176, 182, 184, *189, 193, 194, 532*, 580, *601*
Garcia-Coll, C. T., 17, 55, 283, 290, *303, 304*, 462, *488*
Gardner, H., 374, *386*
Gardner, S., 476, *484*
Gardner, T. M., 575, *597*
Garfinkel, B. D., 228, 232, *235*
Garfinkel, B., *102, 489*
Garfinkel, P. E., 551, 552, 556, 558, 562, *567, 569, 570*
Gariepy, J., 125, *145*
Garmezy, N., 15, 18, 19, 26, 33, 35, *53, 54, 58*, 225, 228, *236, 239, 242, 243, 272, 273, 274, 280, 305, 306*
Garner, D. M., 542, 551, 552, 556, 558, 559, 562, *567, 570*
Garralda, M. E., 345, *359*
Garreau, B., 328, *335*
Garrison, C. Z., 162, 165, 167, 179, 181, 182, *189, 241*
Garrison-Jones, C., 174, 179, 180, *187*
Gatepost Foundation, *450*
Gath, A., 375, *386*
Gatsonis, C., 134, *146, 154, 191, 160*
Gattaz, W. F., 358, 359, *360*
Gautier, M., 363, *387*
Gayol, M., *359*
Gdowski, C. L., 69, *111*
Ge, X., 4, 12, *54*
Geertsma, M. A., 466, *486*
Geffken, G., 589, *597*
Gehl, J. J., *360*
Gelder, M. G., 207, *239*
Gelernter, J. O., 98, *106*
Gelfand, D. M., 12, *54*, 177, 178, *189, 194*
Gelinas, D. J., 513, *533*

Geller, B., 168, *194*
Geller, E., 327, *335*
Gelles, R. J., 494, 523, *533, 534*
Gentile, C., 259, 275, 276, 292, *307, 505, 537*
Gentile, J. R., 75, *104*
Gentry, B. F., 403, *430*
George, C., 464, 470, 475, *486, 487, 488*, 500, 501, 514, *533, 535*
George, D. T., 553, 568, *569*
George, L., 575, *601*
George, M. S., 329, *335*
Gerald, P., 381, *387*
Gerber, A., 400, 401, 402, 405, *429*
Gerber, G., *531*
Gerbing, D. W., 100, *106*
Gerhard, D. S., *107*
Gerlsma, C., 230, *237*
Germain, R., 496, *531*
German, M. L., 369, *387*
Gerner, R. H., 553, *567*
Gernert, J., *451*
Gershenson, H. P., 508, *533*
Gershon, E. S., 453, 555, *567*
Gershon, E., 163, *189*
Gersten, M., 58, 223, 235, 237, *240, 305*
Getson, P., 464, *485*
Geyer, M. A., 449, *454*
Ghiselli, E. E., 35, *54*
Ghublikian, M., 425, *427*
Giaconia, R. M., 163, 164, 165, 183, *193*
Giampiccolo, J., 364, *388*
Giampino, T. L., *147*
Gibbons, J. L., 170, *190*, 223, *237*, 283, *291, 304*
Giberson, R. S., 268, *274*
Gibson, D., 369, *386*
Gibson, J. J., 445, 449, *452*
Giedd, J., *359*
Gielen, J. M., 381, *385*
Gil, D. G., 494, 519, *533*
Gil, K. M., 588, *597*
Giles, S., 81, *111*
Gilger, J. W., 90, 98, *106, 111*, 407, *433*
Gilies, J. J., 90, *106, 111*
Gillberg, C., 316, 322, 324, 325, 328, *336, 338*
Gillberg, I. C., 326, *338*
Gillen, J. C., *453*
Giller, E. L., 260, 273, *276*
Gilles de la Tourette, G., 436, 447, *452*
Gillespie, C. T., 586, *596*
Gillespie, J. F., 268, *271*
Gillette, P. C., *600*
Gillin, J. C., *240*
Gillis, C., 551, *570*
Gillis, J. J., 403, *428*
Gillman, J. B., 572, 573, *596, 597, 598, 599*
Gilmore, M., *52*
Ginns, E. I., *107*
Ginsberg, A. J., 584, *597*

Ginsburg, G. S., 211, *240*
Ginsburg, H. P., 425, *433*
Girgus, J. S., 164, 165, 171, *192*
Giroux, B., *147*
Girshick, L. B., *533*
Gislason, I. L., 247, 253, 267, *272*
Gitlin, M., 166, *190*
Gittelman, R., 86, 89, 91, 98, *106*, 217, 237, 239, *240*
Gittelman-Klein, R., 86, *108*
Giunta, C. T., 184, *188*
Gjerde, P., 143, *144*
Gladow, K. D., *454*
Gladstone, T., 247, *275*
Glaser, G. H., 517, *534*
Glaser, H. H., 465, *487*
Glaze, D. G., 448, 449, *452*
Gleaves, D. H., 517, *533*
Gleitman, L. R., 402, *429*
Glenwick, D. S., *599*
Glenwick, D. W., 594, *601*
Gleser, G., 98, *102, 245, 272, 272*
Glick, M., 381, *386*, 445, *454*
Glod, C. A., *194*
Glow, P. H., 66, *106*
Glow, R. A., 66, *106*
Gluck, D. S., 67, *104*
Glyshaw, K., 175, *189*
Gnagy, E. M., 83, *109*
Goddard, H. H., 362, 363, *386*
Goetz, C. C., 449, *452*
Goetz, D., *193*
Goetz, R., *189, 193*
Goetz, T., 293, *303*
Goff, B., 249, *270*
Goff, J. R., 590, *600*
Goffinet, A. M., 329, *335*
Golby, B., *491*
Gold, E. R., 242, *272*
Gold, J. M., 442, *453*
Gold, M. S., 562, *568*
Gold, P. W., 170, 186, *189, 571*
Goldberg, S., 17, *54*, 290, *303*, 376, *386*, 476, 490, *491*
Goldberg, T. E., 442, *453*
Goldberger, E. L., 206, *238*
Goldetsky, G., 476, *487*
Goldgar, D. E., 414, *435*
Golding, J. M., 218, *237*, 575, 596, *597*
Golding, J., 94, *104*
Goldman-Rakic, P. S., 71, *106*
Goldsmith, H. H., 291, *303*
Goldstein, A. M., *107*
Goldstein, D. S., 553, *569*
Goldstein, D., *596*
Goldstein, G., 317, 331, *337*
Goldstein, J., *454*
Goldstein, K., 419, *429*
Goldstein, M. J., 179, 181, *187*, 345, 348, 350, 353, 354, 356, *358, 359, 360*
Goldstein, M., 80, *106, 187*
Goldstein, S., 80, 94, *106, 107*, 177, *189*, 593, *597*
Goldston, D., 175, *191*

Goldwyn, R., 475, 479, *488*
Gomes-Schwartz, B., 248, 253, 272
Gomez, R., 68, 91, *106*
Gong, Y., 300, *303*
Gonzalez, J. C., 590, 597
Gonzalez, J. J., *107*
Gonzalez, L. S., 91, *104*
Gonzalez, N. M., *334*
Goode, S., *336*
Gooding, W., *569*
Goodman, J. F., 369, *386*
Goodman, J. K., 580, *598*
Goodman, J. R., 95, *106*
Goodman, K. S., 409, 410, *429*
Goodman, K., *429*
Goodman, S. H., 116, 130, *145, 146, 147, 148, 149*, 177, 178, 181, *189*
Goodman, W. K., 438, *452*
Goodman, W., 285, *305*, 451, *453*
Goodman-Brown, T., 182, *190*
Goodnow, J. J., 296, *303, 306*
Goodwin, F. K., 170, *189*
Goodwin, G. M., 554, *568*
Goodwin, J., 468, *487*
Goodyear, P., 66, 67, 95, 99, 100, *106*
Goodyer, I. M., 156, 157, 162, 164, 176, 180, 181, 184, *188, 189*, 228, *237*
Gopnik, A., 313, 318, *337*
Gordon, A. H., *487*
Gordon, B. N., 581, 582, 583, *600*
Gordon, C. T., 344, 345, 350, 352, 355, *359*
Gordon, C., 551, *568*
Gordon, D., 178, *189, 190*
Gordon, R. G., *58*
Gore, S., 165, 183, *189*
Gorman, J. M., 48, *55*
Gorman, R. L., 594, *597*
Gorrell, R. W., 465, *489*
Gortmaker, S., 588, *598*
Gotlib, I. H., 160, 164, 171, 172, 173, 174, 181, 182, 184, *187, 189, 190, 192*, 284, *301*
Gottesman, I. I., 137, *145*
Gottlieb, H., 179, *191*
Gottman, J. M., 12, 19, *55*, 138, *146*
Gough, P., *434*
Gough, R., 517, 530, *537*
Gould, J., 319, 325, 326, 332, *339*
Gould, M. S., 10, *52*, 187, 219, *235*
Goyer, P., 449, *453*
Goyette, C. H., 66, 79, *106*
Grace, M. C., 272
Grady, C., *338*
Grafman, J., *335, 385*
Graham, P. J., 10, 17, *54, 58*, 467, *489*
Graham, P., 86, *109*, 249, *274*, 380, *388*
Graham, S., 420, 421, *429*
Granger, D. A., 170, 173, 186, *190, 195*
Granger, D., *112*
Granholm, E., 351, *358*
Grant, K. E., 158, 175, *188*

Grant, N. I. R., 57, *193*
Grattan, L. M., 95, *106*
Graves, D. J., 175, *194*
Gray, D. B., *336*, 390, *428, 429, 430, 431, 432, 434, 435*
Gray, G., 134, *147*
Gray, J. A., 69, *106*, 225, 228, *237*
Greden, J. F., *192*
Green, A. H., 242, 268, 272, 501, 511, 527, *533*
Green, B. L., 242, 245, 247, 249, 252, 253, 255, 259, 263, 265, 268, 272
Green, B., 98, *102*
Green, L., 72, *106*
Green, R., 443, *452*
Green, S. M., *56*, 68, *108*, 121, 126, *147, 149*
Green, S., *107*
Green, W. H., 324, *336*
Green, W., 344, 345, *359*
Greenbaum, P. E., 4, *54*, 591, *596*
Greenberg, F., 382, *386, 387*
Greenberg, J. W., 285, *305*
Greenberg, L. M., 83, *106*
Greenberg, M. T., 139, *146, 149*, 174, 186, *187, 188*, 287, *302*, 483, *487, 488, 490*
Greenberg, M., 260, *275*, 375, 385, *386*
Greenberg, R. A., 465, *489*
Greenberg, R., 313, *335*
Greene, J. W., 268, *275*, 580, *601*
Greene, R. W., 293, *305*
Greenfeld, D., 343, *360*
Greenhill, L., *102, 104, 107*
Greenslade, K. E., 83, *109*
Greenspan, S. I., 30, *54*, 290, *303*, 460, 461, 462, 467, 486, *487*
Greenswag, L. R., *387*
Grega, D. M., *336, 359*
Gregg, N., 420, 422, 427, *429*
Greiz, E., 233, *241*
Grellong, B. A., *54*
Gresham, F. M., 300, *303*, 365, 368, *386, 387*, 405, *429*
Grey, J. J., 594, *597*
Gribble, P. A., *276*
Grice, D., *452*
Grice, H. P., 475, *487*
Griegel, L. E., 212, *237*
Griffin, N. J., 175, *189*
Griffith, D. R., 384, *386*
Grillon, C., 317, *334*
Grimm, S., *147*
Grinker, R. R., 243, 272
Grodzinsky, G., 4, *52*, 66, 67, 69, 70, 95, 99, 100, *103, 106*
Groisser, D., 404, *433*
Gross, A. M., 590, *597*
Gross, J., 557, *569*
Gross, R. T., *567*
Gross-Glenn, K., 404, *429, 431*
Gross-Tsur, V., 90, 93, *106*
Gross., M., *112*
Grossman, H., 365, 367, 368, 372, *386*

Grossmann, K. E., 476, 478, 479, 481, 487, 488, 490, 491
Groteluschen, A., *274*
Grotpeter, J. K., 116, *145*
Group for the Advancement of Psychiatry, 28, *54*
Groves, W. B., 141, *149*
Gruenberg, A. M., *359*
Gruenberg, E., 364, *386*
Grunberg, N. E., 47, *52*
Grunebaum, H. U., 178, *192*
Grusec, J. E., 296, *302, 303*
Gruzelier, J. H., *358*
Gualtieri, C. T., 93, *111*
Guerra, E., *597*
Guerra, N. G., 11, 13, *54*
Guevremont, D. G., 86, 92, 94, *103*
Guida, F. V., 221, *237*
Guilleminault, C., *491*
Guinon, G., 436, *452*
Guite, J., 93, *104*
Gulbinat, W., 346, *359, 360*
Gull, W. N., 541, *568*
Gullone, E., 224, *238*
Gunnar, M., 5, *54*, 225, *239, 489*
Gunnoe, C., *109*
Guralnick, M. J., *303, 335, 429*
Gurland, B., 287, *303*
Guroff, J., 163, *189*
Gurtman, M. B., 176, *190*
Gurwitz, D., 586, *597*
Gustafson, K. E., 588, *601*
Gutai, J. P., 595, *596*
Guthertz, M., 178, *189*
Guthrie, D., 171, 179, 181, *187*, 338, 351, 354, *358, 360*
Guttman, E., 496, *533*
Guyer, B., 593, *597*
Guyer, K. E., 327, *335*
Guze, S. B., *568*
Guzzetts, V., *386*
Gwirtsman, H. E., 553, 554, *568*
Gysin, R., *104*

Haaf, R. G., 425, *434*
Haas, R. H., *335*
Haas-Givler, B., 382, *386*
Hadzi-Pavlovic, D., 230, *240*
Haenlein, M., 66, 69, *106*
Hafner, H., *358, 359, 360*
Hagerman, R. J., 382, *386, 387*
Hahn, I.-H., 449, *454*
Haier, R., *334*
Haigler, E. D., 67, *109*
Hale, B., 578, *596*
Hale, G. A., *104*
Haley, G. M., 171, 172, *190*
Haley, G., 268, *274*, 516, *535*
Hall, G. C. N., 527, *533*
Hallahan, D. P., 391, 393, *429*
Hallgren, B., 580, *597*
Hallowell, E. M., 72, *106*
Halmi, K. A., 557, 560, 562, 567, *568*
Halperin, J. M., 68, 91, *106*
Ham, M., 174, *191*, 356, *360*

Hamada, R. S., 258, *270*
Hamburger, S. D., 238, *359, 451*
Hamburger, S., *112, 146, 147,* 318, 338
Hamer, R. M., *360*
Hamilton, D. I., 197, *238*
Hamilton, E. B., 179, *187,* 354, *358, 359*
Hamilton, V., *272*
Hamilton-Hellberg, C., 328, *336*
Hamlett, K. W., 69, *106,* 588, *601*
Hammeke, T. A., 425, *432*
Hammen, C. L., 3, 159, 160, 161, 164, 165, 166, 168, 171, 172, 173, 174, 176, 177, 178, 180, 181, 182, 183, 184, 186, *186, 187, 188, 189, 190, 194*
Hammer, L. D., *237*
Hammett, E., 261, *270*
Hammill, D. D., 391, 397, 400, 422, *429, 432*
Hammill, P. B. B., 585, *597*
Hamovit, J. R., *163, 189, 567*
Hampe, E., 197, 217, 237, *239*
Hamra, B. J., *239*
Hanchett, J. M., *387*
Handal, P. J., 179, *193*
Handford, H., 259, 265, 267, *272*
Handleman, J., 333, *336, 337, 338*
Hann, D. M., 141, *144, 149,* 480, 483, *487*
Hannan, T., 314, *336*
Hannonds, B. L., *598*
Hansen, D. J., 584, 569, 601
Hansen, W. B., *597*
Hanson, C. L., 573, 587, 588, 589, *597*
Hanson, K., *146, 304*
Happe, F., 316, *336*
Harbeck, C., 573, 580, 595, *599*
Harbeck-Weber, C., 593, *597*
Harden, M. T., *454*
Hardesty, A., 345, *336, 359*
Hardin, M. T., *240,* 444, 451, 452, *453, 454*
Hardwick, N., 415, *431*
Hare, R. D., 115, 119, 124, *146, 148*
Hare, T. A., *567*
Harel, Z., 251, *272*
Harkins, S. W., *597, 598, 599*
Harkness, L., 260, *273*
Harkness, S., 376, *388*
Harlow, H., 49
Harman, G., *487*
Harmon, R. J., 458, *486,* 515, *533*
Harper, D. C., 580, *597, 600*
Harper, D., *194*
Harper, L. V., *54*
Harper, P. A., 580, *599*
Harpur, T. J., 115, *146*
Harrington, R., *110, 148,* 167, *190, 338*
Harris, B., 197, 229, *237*
Harris, E. L., 229, *237, 239, 451, 454*
Harris, G. S., 462, *491*
Harris, G. T., 115, 117, 119, *146*
Harris, G., 586, *598*

Harris, J. R., 542, *570*
Harris, K. S., 406, *430*
Harris, K., 420, 421, *429*
Harris, M. A., 589, *597*
Harris, S., 333, *336, 337, 338*
Harris, T. O., 472, *485*
Harris, T., 181, *187*
Harrison, P., 368, *386*
Harrison, S. I., 243, 267, *272*
Hart, E. L., 4, *54, 56,* 68, 78, 87, *102, 107,* 115, 117, 134, *146, 147, 304*
Hart, H., 466, *487*
Hart, J., 5, *54*
Hart, S. D., 115, *146*
Hart, S. N., 493, 496, *531, 533*
Hart, T., 421, 422, *427*
Hartdagen, S. E., *108,* 138, *147*
Harter, S., 161, 171, 182, 183, 184, *190, 193,* 445, *452,* 516, *533*
Hartman, C. R., 242, 248, *270, 271,* 504, 505, 506, 508, 509, 510, 512, 513, 514, 516, 517, 527, *534*
Hartmann, A. H., 11, *58*
Hartmann, D. P., 197, 213, *235*
Hartmark, C., *188*
Hartsough, C. S., 90, 93, *107*
Hartung, C. M., 67, *109*
Hartup, W. W., 279, *303, 536*
Hasin, D., *570*
Haskell, P. H., 362, *386*
Haslum, M., 94, *104*
Hassanein, K. M., 329, *335*
Hassanein, R. S., 594, *601*
Hastings, J., 96, *107*
Hatch, A., 506, *535*
Hatcher, J. W., 579, *599*
Hatfield, E., 557, *568*
Hatsukami, D., *569*
Havis, J., *597*
Hawkins, D., *596*
Hawkins, J. D., 17, *52, 57*
Hay, D., 98, *108*
Hay, P. J., 541, 545, 546, 547, 551, 552, *567, 568*
Hayes, J. R., 421, *429*
Hayes, S., 66, *107*
Haymaker, W., 449, *453*
Haynes, O. M., 291, *303*
Haynes, S. N., 20, *54*
Hayward, C., 212, *237*
Hayward, M. E., 551, *570*
Hazel, S., 404, 405, *429*
Hazen, N., 476, *487*
Hazlett, E., *334*
Hazzard, A., 511, 517, *534, 536*
Head, H., 391, 419, *429*
Heagarty, M. C., 465, *487*
Healey, J. M., Jr., *271*
Health, A. C., *570*
Healy, H., 177, *189*
Heard, P. M., 228, *236*
Heath, A. C., 229, *238, 569*
Hebb, D. O., 197, 228, *237*
Heber, R., *386*
Hechtman, L., 66, 77, 86, 89, 90, 94, 95, *111*

Hecimovic, A., 319, *337*
Hedrick, T. E., 594, *601*
Heemsbergen, J., *336*
Heffernan, K., 552, 558, *568*
Heffron, W. A., 98, *107*
Heger, A., 505, *534*
Hegg, A. P., 554, *568*
Heilman, K. M., 69, 95, *107, 433*
Heilman, N., *596*
Heimberg, R. G., 202, *234*
Heimbuch, R., 447, *453*
Heinecke, C. M., 473, *487*
Heird, W., 466, *488*
Heister, M., 17, *54*
Helfer, R. E., *534, 535,* 580, *598*
Heller, T., 69, 75, *107*
Hellgren, L., *338*
Helsel, W. J., 174, 200, *190, 239*
Hemming, M., 446, *454*
Henderson, A. S., 229, *235*
Henderson, J., *566*
Hendren, R. L., 350, *359*
Hendrick, I. G., 372, *387*
Hendriks, J. H., 470, *487*
Henggeler, S. W., 284, 295, 302, 305, 587, 589, *597*
Heninger, G. R., 218, *236*
Henker, B., 91, 93, *111, 112*
Hennessy, K. D., 11, 53, 509, *534*
Henninger, G. R., 554, *567*
Henriksen, L., 96, *108*
Henriques, J., 289, *303*
Henry, A., 91, *110*
Henry, D., 249, *273*
Hensley, R., 174, *191,* 284, *304*
Hepburn, W. S., *111*
Herbel, B., 233, *239*
Herbsman, C., 69, *107*
Herdy, S., 179, *193*
Herman, C. P., 559, *569*
Herman, J. B., *58,* 240, *305*
Herman, J. L., 242, *272,* 492, 493, 497, 506, 508, 509, 510, 511, 512, 513, 514, 515, 516, 517, *534, 536*
Herman, S., 69, *109*
Hermecz, D. A., 593, *599*
Hern, K. L., *107*
Herscovitch, P., *112, 451*
Hersen, M., 3, 47, *51, 51,* 52, 53, 54, 56, 57, 59, 60, 89, *108, 146,* 197, 211, 217, 218, 219, 220, 224, 229, *238, 239,* 240, *241, 273,* 302, *303, 306*
Hersov, L., *53, 272, 452, 491,* 583, *597*
Hertzog, C., 474, *484*
Hervada, A. R., 264, *271*
Herzberger, S. D., 511, *534*
Herzog, D. B., 550, 551, 553, 562, 564, *567, 568, 569*
Hesse, E., 480, *488*
Hesselink, J. R., 328, *335*
Hessl, D., 5, *53*
Heston, J., 249, *273,* 498, *534*
Hetherington, E. M., 21, *54, 58,* 148, 168, *193, 273,* 295, 297, *303, 304, 306, 535*

Hetherington, M., *454*
Heutink, P., *453*
Hewitt, D., *452*
Hewitt, L. E., 118, *146*
Hewson, P., 463, *487*
Hibbs, E. D., 10, *54*, *146*, *147*, 233, 237, 354, *359*
Hickok, J., 168, *194*
Hicks, C., 414, *434*
Hide, D. W., 463, *487*
Higuchi, S., 563, *568*
Hill, D., 314, *335*
Hill, J., 167, *190*
Hill, J. L., 562, *570*
Hill, J. O., *570*
Hill, M., *452*
Hiller, W., 575, *600*
Hillson, J. M. C., 526, *534*
Himes, J. A., 446, *451*
Hinde, R. A., 298, 299, 300, *303*, *305*, 306, *307*, 485, *487*
Hingtgen, N. J., *335*
Hinkley, K., 171, 173, *194*
Hinshaw, S. P., 9, 64, 67, 69, 75, 80, 83, 87, 91, *102*, *104*, *107*, *110*, 114, 115, 117, 119, 120, 121, 126, 127, 128, 132, 133, 134, 139, *143*, *144*, *146*, 216, 237, 481
Hinshelwood, J., 392, 406, *429*
Hiroto, D., 171, *189*, *190*
Hirsch, M., *188*
Hirschfeld, R. M. A., 48, *191*
Hirschi, T., 113, *146*
Hirshfeld, D., *305*
Hirshfeld, D. R., 17, *52*, *54*, *58*, 222, 223, 224, *235*, *237*, *240*, 283, *301*, *303*, 484, *487*
Hiscock, M., *435*
Hjern, A., 264, *272*
Ho, D. Y. F., 300, *303*
Hobbes, G., 90, *108*
Hobbs, N., *240*
Hoberman, H. M., 166, *192*, 228, *235*
Hobson, R. P., 314, 315, *336*, *339*, 480, *489*
Hochstadt, N. J., *596*
Hockman, C. C., *453*
Hodapp, R. M., 363, 364, 365, 370, 368, 369, 371, 372, 374, 375, 376, 378, 379, 380, 381, 382, 383, *385*, *386*, *387*, *388*, *389*
Hodde-Vargas, M. S., 350, *359*
Hodges, J., 470, *490*
Hodges, K., 175, *192*, 229, 237, 578, 580, *597*
Hoehler, F. K., *338*
Hoek, H. W., 551, *568*
Hoeper, E. W., *191*
Hoeppner, J. B., 94, *111*
Hoett, N., *596*
Hoffman, H. G., *52*
Hoffman, M. L., 298, *303*
Hoffman, M., 248, *274*
Hoffman, R., 551, *567*
Hoffman, V., 481, *487*
Hoffman-Plotkin, D., 499, 503, 512, *534*

Hoffmann, W., 318, *337*
Hogan, K. L., 321, 332, *338*
Hohman, L. B., 65, *107*
Höjer, B., 264, *272*
Holaday, M., 247, 269, *270*
Holahan, C. J., 267, *272*
Holahan, J. M., 408, *433*
Holcomb, W. R., 156, *191*
Holden, C., 586, *598*
Holden, E. W., *532*
Hole, W. T., 328, *339*, 462, *488*
Holliman, W. B., 413, *434*
Hollingshead, A. B., 11, *54*
Holm, V. A., 382, *387*
Holmes, C. S., *598*
Holmes, W. M., *193*
Holt, C. S., 202, *234*
Holtzman, N. A., 594, *597*
Holtzworth-Munroe, A., 480, *487*
Homann, E., 177, 178, 179, 181, 182, 184, *187*
Homatidis, S., 325, *336*
Homer, C., 585, *597*
Hommer, D., *359*
Hong, W., *359*
Honzik, M. P., *56*
Hood, J., 80, 90, *103*, 211, 212, *235*, 236, 270, *531*
Hook, R. J., *104*
Hooper, S. R., 410, 411, 414, 415, 416, 419, 420, 421, 422, 423, *429*, *430*
Hope, D. A., 233, 234, *234*, *235*, 237, *239*
Hope, R. A., 550, *567*
Hopkins, J., 550, *569*
Hoppe, C. M., 86, *110*, 132, *149*
Hops, H., 12, 13, 44, *54*, *55*, 83, *108*, 157, 162, 163, 164, 165, 166, 171, 173, 175, 178, 179, 181, 182, *186*, *190*, *192*, *193*, 219, *238*
Horn, S., 467, *489*
Horne, R. L., *570*
Hornstein, N., 341, *358*
Horowitz, F. D., *454*
Horowitz, F., *304*
Horowitz, H. A., 34, 35, *57*
Horowitz, J. M., 248, 253, 258, *272*
Horowitz, M. J., *272*, 498, 520, *534*
Horowitz, M., *272*
Horwood, L. J., 98, *105*, 114, *146*
Hoshino, Y., *327*, *334*, 345, *360*
Hoshko, I. M., 410, 414, *428*
Hosier, D. M., *454*
Hotaling, G. T., 242, *271*, 514, *534*
Hough, R. L., 575, *597*
Houle, L., 517, *536*
Houts, A. C., 4, *54*
Hovens, J. E., *271*
Howard, B. L., 42, *55*, 228, *238*
Howard, L. J., 564, *570*
Howard, R., 480, *489*
Howard, S., 443, *454*
Howe, A. C., 582, *598*
Howell, C. T., 10, 22, *51*, *51*, 80, *102*, 113, *144*, 158, *186*

Howell, D. C., 184, *188*
Howes, C., 500, *534*
Hoznik, M., 197, *239*
Hrybyk, M., 330, *334*
Hsiao, H. K., *451*
Hsu, F. L. K., 300, *307*
Hsu, G., *568*
Hsu, L. K. G., 545, 548, 551, 552, 557, 558, 562, 566, *568*, *569*
Hsu, M., 328, *336*
Huan, Z. Z., *566*
Hubbard, J., *274*
Hubbard, M., *454*
Hubbs-Tait, L., 483, *487*
Huber, F., 478, *487*
Hudson, J. I., 556, 564, 565, *568*, *569*
Huertas-Goldman, S., *52*, *187*
Huesmann, L. R., 11, *54*, 137, *146*
Hufton, I., 465, *487*
Hughes, C. W., 43, *59*
Hughes, H. M., 268, *272*
Hughes, J. N., 43, *57*
Hughes, M. C., 580, *598*
Hughes, M., *238*
Hughes, P., 98, *110*
Hughes, S. J., 94, *105*
Hulme, C., 416, *430*
Hulse, S. H., 517, *535*
Humphrey, F. J., *272*
Humphrey, L. L., 186, *194*, 561, *568*, *570*
Humphrey, M., 343, *359*
Humphries, T., 90, 93, *107*
Hunsley, J., 28, *56*
Hunt, J. Mc V., *385*
Hunter, R., *111*
Hunter, W. M., 267, *271*
Huntzinger, R. M., 200, *239*
Hurd, P. D., 594, *598*
Hurley, P., 506, *535*
Hurst, C. R., *109*
Hussey, D. L., 528, *536*
Hutchins, H., 121, *146*
Hutchinson, G., 480, *487*
Hutton, H. E., 551, *568*
Huttunen, M. O., 352, *359*
Hwang, P., 291, *302*
Hyams, J. S., 466, *486*
Hyde, T. M., 442, 447, *452*, *453*
Hyler, S. E., *570*
Hymel, S., 49, *55*, *58*, 277, 283, 284, 287, 288, 292, 293, 294, *303*, *306*
Hynd, G. W., 4, *54*, 66, 67, 95, 96, 97, 99, 100, *102*, *106*, *107*, *108*, 132, *147*, *149*, 392, 414, *428*, *429*, *430*, 432, *434*
Hynd, S. R., *388*

Iaboni, F., 21, *55*
Iacono, W. G., 28, 29, 16, *53*
Ialongo, N., *55*
Iannotti, R., 279, *303*
Iggo, A., *596*
Ika, E. R., 418, (Ika or Okla? see p. 418), *433*
Ikeda, S., 170, *190*

Illingworth, R. S., 463, *487*
Imboden, J. B., 517, *535*
Incagnoli, T., 443, *452*
Ingersoll, B. D., 72, 94, *107*
Inglis, A., 90, *103*
Ingram, R. E., 42, *55*
Inhelder, B., 266, *274*, 372, *387*, *388*
Inoff-Germain, G., 178, *190*
Institute of Medicine, 9, 11
Inui, T. S., 80, *108*, 281, *304*
Irvin, N., 375, *385*
Irwin, C. P., 248, *273*
Isabella, R., 178, *194*
Ismond, D. R., *109*
Israel, A. C., 32, *56*, 231, *238*
Israeli, R., 247, *276*
Itard, J. M. G., 436, *452*
Iwata, B. A., 584, *600*
Iyengar, S., *194*
Izard, C. E., 4, 38, 44, 53, *55*, 153, *188*, *194*, 228, *237*, 291, *303*, 485

Jablensky, A., 346, *359*, *360*
Jackson, E., 392, *430*
Jackson, E. B., 462, *491*
Jackson, K. L., 162, *189*, *241*
Jackson, T., *109*
Jackson, Y. K., 95, *106*, 135, 137, *144*, *146*
Jacob, T., 38, 39, *55*, *149*
Jacobs, C., 555, *570*
Jacobs, D. R., *598*
Jacobs, H. A., 333, *337*
Jacobsen, J. W., 366, 368, 380, 381, 383, *387*
Jacobsen, R. H., 174, *190*, 284, *303*
Jacobsen, T., 481, *487*
Jacobson, R. S., 501, *536*
Jacobvitz, D., 16, 18, *59*, 476, *486*, *487*
Jacoby, C. G., *109*
Jacox, A., *596*
Jaenicke, C., 173, *189*, *190*
Jaffe, P., 263, 268, *272*, 275, 521, 522, *537*
Jagger, J., 439, 440, 449, *452*
Jakobsson, G., *338*
Jallad, B., *431*
James, H. E., *335*
James, H. T., 423, *427*
James, L. D., *596*
James, W., 75, *107*
Jameson, J. C., *487*
Janiszewski, S., 164, *188*
Jankovic, J., 438, 448, 449, *452*
Janoff-Bulman, R., 258, 259, *272*, 509, *534*
Jansky, J., 400, *428*
Janzarik, W., *358*, *360*
Jaremko, M. E., *275*
Jarosinski, J., 480, *487*
Jason, L. A., *599*
Javors, M. A., 136, *148*
Jenkins, E. C., 382, *385*
Jenkins, R. L., 118, *146*
Jenkins, S., 466, 467, *487*

Jensen, A. R., 364, *387*
Jensen, P. S., 10, 50, *55*, 183, 184, *190*, 233, 237
Jernigan, T. L., 328, *335*, 374, *385*
Jessor, R., 530, *534*
Jewell, L., 174, *191*
Jimerson, D. C., 553, 554, *568*, *569*
Jobes, D., 158, *187*
Joels, T., *490*
John, K., *194*, *452*
Johns, M. S., 415, *431*
Johnson, B., 16, 32, 33, *55*
Johnson, C., 560, *568*
Johnson, C. A., *598*
Johnson, C. C., 590, *598*
Johnson, C. F., 528, *531*
Johnson, C. L., *597*
Johnson, D. J., 394, 400, 411, 412, 418, 421, *422*, *430*
Johnson, J., 12, *59*, 84, *111*, *188*, *195*, 219, *240*, *241*
Johnson, J. H., 228, *237*
Johnson, M. O., 283, *291*, *304*
Johnson, S. B., 588, 589, *597*, *598*
Johnson-Sabine, E., 550, 551, *568*
Johnston, B. M., 172, *194*
Johnston, C., 11, 21, *57*, 87, 91, 92, *108*
Jonas, J. M., 562, 563, 564, *568*
Jones, B., 19, *55*, 530, *534*
Jones, D. J., 551, *568*
Jones, D. P. H., 463, *487*
Jones, J. C., 260, 261, 262, *272*
Jones, J. E., 353, *359*
Jones, M. B., *338*
Jones, M. C., 197, *237*
Jones, N., 289, *303*, *304*
Jones, R., 550, *567*
Jones, R. T., 242, 249, 253, 259, *272*
Jordan, H., *336*
Jordan, J. V., 557, *568*
Jorm, A. F., 402, 409, *430*, *433*
Joschko, M., 443, *452*
Joseph, L., 286, *304*
Joseph, S. A., 260, *272*
Joshi, R. M., *427*
Joshko, M., 412, *430*
Jouriles, E. N., 253, 268, *272*, 287, *304*
Juarez, L. J., 85, *108*
Juliano, D. B., 75, *104*
Jun, Z., *566*
Jung, K. G., 242, *271*
Jutkowitz, R., 439, *454*

Kaffman, M., 248, 252, *271*
Kaftantaris, V., 355, *360*
Kagan, J., 4, 5, 10, 13, 17, 20, 28, 31, 32, 33, 34, 35, 37, 40, 44, 45, 47, 48, 49, 52, 54, *55*, 58, 117, *146*, 170, *190*, 222, 223, 225, 235, *237*, *240*, 266, *272*, 277, 283, 288, 289, 290, 291, 292, 293, 298, 300, *301*, *303*, *304*, *305*, 469, *487*
Kahana, B., 251, *272*
Kaiser, A. P., *336*

Kalas, R., 159, *188*
Kales, J. D., *272*
Kalikow, K., *195*, *241*, *236*
Kalkoske, M., 514, *535*
Kallman, F. J., 341, 345, 352, 353, *359*
Kalman, E., 212, *239*
Kalucy, R. S., 551, *567*
Kamhi, A. G., 402, 403, 416, *430*
Kamil, M. L., *434*
Kamphaus, R. W., *146*
Kanbayashi, Y., 85, *107*
Kandel, D. B., 163, 165, 167, *190*
Kane, M. T., 228, *238*
Kane, R., 443, *452*
Kanfer, F. H., 28, *55*, 69, *107*
Kang, T. K., 300, *303*
Kaniasty, K., 258, 259, *274*
Kanner, L., 7, *55*, 311, 312, 315, 324, 326, *336*, 342, 343, *359*
Kantor, G. K., 530, *536*
Kaplan, A. G., 557, *568*
Kaplan, B. J., 94, *107*
Kaplan, F., *362*
Kaplan, H. I., *55*
Kaplan, M., *567*
Kaplan, M. D., *489*
Kaplan, M. S., 527, *531*
Kaplan, N., 177, *192*, 464, 478, *486*, *488*
Kaplan, S., 499, *535*
Kaplan, T., 470, *487*
Kardiner, A., 243, *272*
Karlsson, J., 67, 91, 92, 93, *103*, *111*
Karno, M., 218, *237*, 575, *597*
Karoly, P., 69, *107*
Kasari, C., 314, 315, 318, *336*, *337*, 374, *388*
Kasen, S., *188*
Kashani, J. H., 156, 157, 158, 161, 162, 179, 180, 181, *188*, *190*, *191*, 196, 200, 218, 219, 228, *237*, 284, *304*
Kaslow, N. J., 171, 172, 175, 177, 179, 183, 186, *191*, *194*, 510, *534*
Kasser, T., *570*
Katic, M., *191*
Katsui, T., 327, *336*
Katz, E. R., 589, 595, *598*, *601*
Katz, J. L., 562, 564, 567, *570*
Katz, L., *429*, *453*
Katz, L. F., 12, 19, *55*, 138, *146*
Katz, L. M., *237*
Katz, M., *192*, 380, *388*
Katzman, M. A., 560, *568*
Kaufman, A. S., 317, *334*
Kaufman, D. W., 442, *451*
Kaufman, J., 19, 22, *55*, *193*, 500, 501, 502, 513, 514, 515, 517, 519, 530, *534*
Kaufman, K. L., 584, *598*
Kaufman, S., 376, *386*
Kaukianinen, A., 116, *144*
Kauneckis, D., 170, 186, *190*
Kavale, K. A., 391, 393, 394, 397, 398, 405, 420, *430*, *431*

Kavanagh, J. F., 390, 391, *427*, *428*, *429*, *430*, *431*, *432*, *434*, *435*
Kavanagh, K. A., 13, 55, 139, *145*
Kavanagh, M. E., 328, *339*
Kawi, A., 448, *453*
Kaye, H., 330, *334*
Kaye, W. H., 548, 553, 554, 559, 562, 563, *567*, *568*, *569*
Kaysen, D. L., *451*
Kaysen, D., *359*
Kazak, A. E., 376, *387*, 573, *598*
Kazdin, A. E., 89, *104*, *108*, 197, 218, 219, 224, 229, 238, 240, 5, 8, 10, 13, 16, 20, 22, 28, 31, 32, 33, 34, 35, 37, 40, 47, 51, *51*, *55*, 56, 114, 117, *146*, *147*, 174, 176, *190*, *191*, 487, 501, 532, 534
Keane, T. M., 247, 260, 272
Kearney, C. A., 207, 211, 212, 213, 216, 220, 232, 233, *234*, *236*, 237, *238*, 240, 241
Kearney-Cooke, A., 561, *570*
Kedesdy, J. H., *597*
Keefe, P. H., 550, *569*
Keele, S. W., 317, *337*
Keenan, K., 32, *56*, 81, *103*, *105*, 121, 126, 137, *145*, *147*
Keenan, V., 376, *388*
Keens, S., 92, *104*
Keith, B., 138, *144*
Kelalis, P. D., *599*
Kellam, S., 16, *55*
Keller, C. E., 423, 425, *430*
Keller, J., *187*
Keller, M. B., 161, 166, 167, 178, *187*, *191*, 198, 217, 218, *238*, 550, 562, *568*, *569*
Kellerman, J., 590, *598*
Kellman, H. D., *570*
Kelly, J., *108*, *192*, 239, *304*
Kelly, K. A., 198, *234*
Kelly, M., 499, 510, 511, *536*
Kelsoe, J. R., 98, *107*
Kempe, C. H., 494, *534*, *535*
Kempe, C. J., 580, *598*
Kemper, T., 329, *334*
Kendall, P. C., 4, 33, 39, 41, 42, 43, *52*, *53*, *55*, *59*, 160, 172, 173, 175, *187*, *191*, 196, 198, 224, 228, 233, *236*, 238
Kendall-Tackett, K. A., 256, 267, *273*, 504, 505, 509, 513, 514, 517, *534*
Kendler, K. S., 168, *191*, 229, 230, *238*, 341, 353, 355, *359*, 563, *569*, *570*
Kennedy, D., *110*, 404, *429*
Kennedy, E., 174, 175, 176, *191*, 284, *304*
Kennedy, J. L., *106*
Kennedy, R. E., 157, *193*
Kennedy, S. H., 562, 567, *569*
Kennedy, W., 371, *385*
Kennell, J., 375, *385*
Kenning, M., 59, 581, *601*
Keogh, B. K., 369, *385*, 395, *430*, *431*, *434*

Kephart, N. C., 65, *111*
Kerbeshian, J., 345, 355, *358*, 442, 442, 445, *451*
Kerdyk, L., *102*
Kern, E., *569*
Kerr, D., 464, *487*
Kerr, M., 464, *487*
Kessen, W., 52, *57*
Kessler, D. B., *489*
Kessler, J. W., 29, *55*, 65, *107*
Kessler, R. C., 204, 229, *238*, *569*, 570
Kestenbaum, C. J., *239*
Keyes, S., 141, *144*
Keysor, C. S., *146*, *359*
Khazam, C., 545, *569*
Kidd, J. R., 452, 453
Kidd, K. K., *109*, 178, *193*, 447, 452, 453
Kieffer, J. E., *104*
Kiely, K., *104*
Kiely, M., 365, *387*
Kiessling, L. S., 448, *452*
Kihlstrom, J. F., 262, *274*
Killam, K. F., *358*
Killen, J. D., *237*
Kilman, B. A., 330, *335*
Kilo, C., *596*
Kilpatrick, D. G., 250, 251, 259, *273*, 275
Kim, R., *238*
Kimberlin, C., *335*
Kimberling, W. J., *428*
Kimmerly, N. L., 471, *486*
King, A. C., *105*, *112*
King, A. Y. C., 300, *304*
King, C. A., 171, 173, 183, *191*, *192*
King, L. R., *599*
King, M. B., 551, *569*
King, N. J., 16, *57*, 197, 207, 212, 224, 230, *236*, *238*, *239*
King, R., *240*, 443, 448, *452*, *453*
Kinney, T. R., 588, *597*
Kinsbourne, M., 47, *53*, 93, *107*, 411, *430*
Kinscherff, R., 249, 265, *271*, 498, 533
Kinzett, N. G., 98, *105*
Kinzie, J. D., 249, 252, 253, 256, 259, 264, 265, *273*
Kirchner, G. L., *111*
Kirk, S. A., 121, *146*, 394, 400, *430*
Kirk, W. D., 400, *430*
Kirmayer, L. J., 575, *598*, *600*
Kirschenbaum, D. S., 550, *566*, 592, *601*
Kiser, L. J., 249, 255, 259, 263, 264, 268, *273*, 498, 505, *534*
Kishore, P. R., *360*
Kissileff, H. R., *571*
Kita, M., 85, *107*, 444, *453*
Kittl, S., 562, *569*
Kivlahon, C., 583, *597*
Klaric, S. H., 159, *188*
Klaus, M., 375, *385*
Klawans, H. L., 449, *452*

Klebanov, P. K., 9, *53*
Kleiman, M. D., 329, *336*
Klein, D. F., 48, *55*, 217, *237*
Klein, D. N., *104*
Klein, D., *56*
Klein, H. R., 342, *358*
Klein, L., 315, *338*
Klein, N., *147*
Klein, R., 87, 88, 89, *108*
Klein, S. B., 39, *55*
Klein, T. P., 11, *58*
Kleinerman, R., 465, *485*
Kleinknecht, R. A., 219, *239*
Kleinman, J. C., 113, *146*
Kleinman, J. E., 350, *358*
Klepper, T., *193*
Klerman, G. L., *145*, 163, 177, 178, *187*, 191, *194*
Klesges, R. C., *597*
Kliegel, R., 409, *432*
Klima, E., 374, *388*
Klindworth, L. M., 384, *385*
Kline, J. J., 229, *237*, 580, *597*
Kline, M. A., *452*
Klinger, L. G., 316, 317, 330, *335*, *336*, 342
Klorman, R., 96, 100, *107*
Kluft, R. P., 242, *273*
Knee, D., 120, *144*, 481, *485*
Knell, E., *104*
Knight, R., 296, *303*
Knights, R., *104*
Knobel, M., 65, *107*
Knopf, I. J., 583, *598*
Knox, L. S., 206, *234*
Knutson, J. F., 499, *536*
Kobak, R. R., 179, 186, *191*
Kobayashi, R., 324, 325, *336*
Koby, E. V., 266, *271*
Koch, M., 167, *189*
Kochanska, G., 178, 181, *191*, 287, 291, 297, *304*
Kocsis, P., *104*
Koegel, L. K., 312, 316, *336*
Koegel, R. L., 316, *336*
Koenig, L. J., 171, 172, *191*
Koeske, R., 594, *596*
Kog, E., 561, *569*
Kohlsdorf, B., 116, 130, *146*
Kohn, A., 82, 83, *107*
Koizumi, T., 327, *336*
Kolb, L. C., 260, *273*
Kolko, D. J., 114, *146*, 500, 508, 514, 516, *534*
Koller, H., 380, *388*
Koller, M. M., *360*
Kolvin, I., 83, *108*, 324, *336*, 343, 344, 345, 352, *358*, *359*, 596, *600*
Konar, D., 382, *386*
Kondo, I., *386*
Kono, H., 563, *568*
Konstantareas, M. M., 325, *336*
Koot, H. M., 10, 50, *59*
Kopeiken, H., *531*

Koplowitz, S., 75, 87, *103, 107*
Kopp, C. B., 73, *107*
Koren-Karie, N., *490*
Korenblum, M., 171, *192*
Koretz, D., 55
Korol, M., *272*
Korten, A., *359*
Kortlander, E., *238*
Kosc, L., 424, 425, *430*
Kostelny, K., 531, *533*
Kosten, T. R., 260, *273*
Kotelchuck, M., 465, *487*
Kotler, M., *450*
Kouris, K., 329, *335*
Kovacs, B. W., *104*
Kovacs, M., 23, 55, 134, *146*, 154, 157, 159, 160, *160*, 161, 166, 175, 180, 183, *184*, *191*, 295, *304*
Koverola, C., 505, *534*
Kovitz, K., 11, *57*
Kowalski, J. M., 242, 247, 249, 250, 253, 259, 260, *269*, *274, 275*
Kozak, M. J., 505, 520, *533*
Kozuch, P. L., *451*
Kraemer, G. W., 41, *56*
Kraepelin, E., 341, 345, *359*
Krahenbuhl, V., 178, *193*
Krahn, D. D., 551, *567*
Krahn, G. L., 50, *57*
Kramer, J. R., 499, *536*
Kramer, J., 86, 100, *108, 109*
Kramer, M. S., 462, *484*
Kramer, T. L., *272*
Krantz, P., 333, *336*
Kranzler, H. R., *106*
Krasnegor, N. A. *390, 428, 429, 431, 432, 434, 435, 490*
Krasner, L., 39, *56*
Krasnewich, D., 352, *359*
Krasnor, L. R., 293, 296, *306*
Krasowski, M. D., *104*
Kratochwill, T. R., *433*
Kraus, I., *104, 105*
Krauss, M. W., 375, *375*, 376, *387, 388*
Krenz, C., *52*
Kreusi, M. J. P., *359*
Krieger, R., 499, *535*
Kriegler, J. A., *269, 274*
Krifcher, B., *105*
Krishnan, R. R., 261, *270*
Kriss, M. R., 167, *189*
Krocker-Tuskman, M., 249, *274*
Kron, S., *241, 450*
Krone, H., *236*
Kronenberger, W. G., 590, *598*
Kroonenberg, P. M., 476, 477, *490, 491*
Kruesi, M. J. P., 136, *146, 147*
Kruger, E., *110*
Kruger, S. D., *109*
Krupa, M., 41, *58*
Krusei, M. J. P., 68, *112*
Krystal, J., *106*, 260, *273, 275*
Kuczynski, L., 178, *191, 193*, 287, 296, *303, 304*

Kuehnel, T., *359*
Kuhn, T. S., 33, *56*
Kuiper, N. A., 526, *534*
Kuipers, L., 355, *359*
Kulkarni, R., 589, *599*
Kulm, G., 425, *430*
Kung, M. P., *453*
Kuperman, S., 329, *335*
Kupstas, F. D., 384, *385*
Kurita, H., 316, *336*
Kurlan, R., 447, *451, 452, 453*
Kurtz, L. F., *58*
Kurtz, M., 382, *386*
Kurtzberg, D., 330, *337*
Kurzon, M., 94, *104*
Kusama, H., 248, *275*
Kushch, M., *431*
Kussmaul, A., 392, *430*
Kutcher, S., 169, *169*, 171, *191, 192*

L'Heureux, F., 562, *570*
La Greca, A. M., 211, *240*, 284, *304*, 573, 587, 597, 598, 599, *601*
Labhart, A., 382, *388*
Lacey, G. N., 243, 247, *273*
Lacey, J. H., 549, *569*
Lachar, D., 69, *111*, 359
Lachiewicz, A., *387*
Lack, B., 591, *600*
LaDue, R. A., *388*
Laessle, R. G., 562, 564, *569*
LaFreniere, P. J., 4, *53*
Lagunas-Solar, M., *334*
Lahey, B. B., 4, 13, 17, *54, 56*, 66, 67, 68 76, 77, 89, 92, 97, 99, 100, 101, *102*, *104, 107, 108*, 115, 117, 118, 121, 126, 127, 132, 134, 135, 136, 137, 138, *146, 147, 149*, 175, *190*, *238, 240*, 284, *303, 304*, 481, *487*, 532
Lahr, M., *388*
Laird, M., 511, *533*
Lake, C. R., 447, *452, 568*
Lake, R., *240*, 553, *568*
Lamb, M. E., 291, *302, 306*, 478, *484, 489*, 525, *533*
Lambert, L., *271*
Lambert, M, C., 14, *56*
Lambert, N. M., 81, 83, 84, 85, 90, 93, *107, 108*, 372, *387*
Lamborn, S. D., 298, *307*
Lamon, R., 442, *453*
Lamont, J., 179, 180, *191*
LaMontagne, L. L., 593, *598*
Lamparelli, M., 91, *110*
Lamparski, D. M., 247, *272*
Lampert, C., 157, *194*, 555, *570*
Lan, Y. D., *566*
Land, G., 583, *597*
Landau, S., 141, *148*, 285, *304*
Landis, H. D., 339, 554, *567*
Lang, A. E., *454*
Lang, A. R., 92, *109*
Lang, A., 437, *452*
Langer, D. H., *240*
Langsdorf, R., 85, *108*

Langsford, W., 400, *428*
Lann, I. S., *240*
Lanning, K., 528, *534*
Lapa, L. M., 288, *304*
LaPadula, M., 86, *108*
Lapey, K., 81, *103*
Lapouse, R., 10, *56*, 83, *108*, 197, *238*
Laraia, M. T., *568*
Larkin, K., *273*
Larrieu, J. A., 265, 468, *274, 490*
Larry P. v. Wilson Riles, 372, *387*
Larsen, A., *273*
Larsen, S., 397, 422, *429*
Larson, D. G., 575, *598*
Larson, D. W., 43, *56*
Larson, R. W., 174, 179, *191*
Larzelere, R., 23, *54*
Lasschuit, L. J., *271*
Last, C. G., 47, 49, *56*, 89, *108*, 197, 198, 200, 202, 204, 206, 207, 209, 211, 213, 217, 218, 219, 220, 224, 229, 231, 232, 233, *235, 236, 238*, *239, 240, 241*
Laufer, M., 65, *108*
Laughon, P., 402, *435*
Laurent, J., 171, 172, 186, *191, 194*
Laux, L., *236*
Lavigne, J. V., 587, *598*
Lavori, P. W., *191, 238*, 550, 562, *568, 569*
Laxen, D. P. H., *111*
Lay, K., 511, *536*
Lazar, J. W., 96, *106*
Lazarus, R. S., 259, *273*
Le Couteur, A., *110, 148*, 321, *336, 338*
Lease, C. A., 5, 36, *56*, 211, 224, 233, *240*
Lebedinskaya, K. S., 326, *336*
LeBlanc, M., *59*
Leckman, J. F., 46, *56*, *104, 109*, 240, 354, *360*, 363, 369, 371, 372, 374, 379, 381, 382, *385, 386, 387*, 436, 437, 438, 439, 441, 442, 443, 444, 445, 446, 447, 448, 449, *450, 451*, *452, 453, 454*
Ledingham, J. E., *59*, 280, 285, *303*, *304, 305, 306*, 483, *487*
LeDoux, J., 289, *304*
Leduc, D., 462, *484*
Lee, A., 314, 315, *336*
Lee, F., *143, 149*
Lee, P. W. H., 326, *334*
Lee, S., 23, *53, 453*
Lees, A. J., 449, *454*
Leet, M., 549, *571*
Lefebvre, L., 501, *537*
Lefever, G. B., 478, *491*
Leff, J. P., 346, 354, 355, *359, 360*
Lefkowitz, E. S., 164, *193*
Lefkowitz, M. M., 137, *146*, 153, 179, *191, 192*
Lefter, L., 260, *270*
Lehman, B., 93, *105, 110*
Lehman, E., 583, *598*
Lehtinen, L. E., 65, *111*, 393, *434*
Leigh, J., 397, *429*

Leitenberg, H., 171, 172, *192*, 545, 569
Lejeune, J., 363, *387*
Lelord, G., *335*
LeMare, L., 49, *55*, 277, 293, *303, 304, 306*
Lenane, M. C., *147*, 204, 235, *240*, 359, 443, *453*
Lennox, C., 411, *430*
Lenox, K. F., 141, *145*
Leon, A., *489*
Leon, G. R., 13, *56*
Leonard, A. C., 272
Leonard, H. L., 204, 206, 207, 218, 235, 238, 239, 240, 443, 448, *453, 454*
Leonard, M. A., 297, *307*
Leonard, M. F., 465, *487*
Leong, C. K., 427
Lerner, J. A., 80, *108*, 281, *304*
Lerner, M. J., 509, *534*
LeRoy, S., 589, *599*
Lesem, M. D., 553, 554, *568, 569*
Leslie, A. M., 316, *334*
Lesser, S. T., 39, *56*
Lessers, S., 568
Lester, B. M., 462, 463, 464, *487, 488, 531*
Letizia, K. A., 560, *570*
Leu, D. J., 410, *430*
Leung, F. Y. K., 517, *536*
Levendosky, A. A., 11, *57*
Leventhal, B. L., *104*
Leventhal, J. M., 463, *486*
Levin, B., *431*
Levin, P. M., 69, *108*
Levin, R. B., 590, *597*
Levine, J., *358*
Levine, M. D., 80, *109*, 582, *598*
Levine, M., *429*
Levison, H., 586, *597*
Leviton, A., *109*
Levy, D. L., *104*
Levy, D. M., 297, *304*
Levy, F., 90, 98, *108*
Levy, J. C., 465, *485*
Levy, J. S., 466, *488*
Lewine, R. R. J., 346, *359*
Lewinsohn, P. M., 43, *56*, 83, 84, *108*, 157, 158, 160, 162, 163, 164, 165, 166, 167, 171, 173, 174, 175, 176, *186*, 190, *192*, 193, *194*, 219, 238
Lewis M., 532
Lewis, B. A., 404, *430*
Lewis, D. O., 131, *147*, 517, 530, *534*
Lewis, J. C., *531*
Lewis, J. M., *486*
Lewis, J., 525, 531, *531, 534*
Lewis, K., 242, *273*
Lewis, M., 3, 16, 18, 34, 35, 36, 37, 46, *51, 51, 53, 55, 56, 58, 104*, 280, *304*, 445, 452, *453*
Lewy, A., 317, 330, *335*
Li, B. U. K., 594, *598*
Li, B., 300, *302*
Li, K., *566*

Li, Z. Y., 14, *53*
Liberman, A. M., 402, 405, *430*
Liberman, I. Y., 402, 403, 405, 406, 416, *429, 430, 433*
Liberman, R. P., 355, *359*
Libow, J. A., 502, *535*
Lichter, D., *452*
Liddell, A., 209, *238*
Liddle, C., 476, *489*
Liebenauer, L. L., *105, 112*
Lieberman, A. F., 290, *303*, 471, *488, 491*
Lieberman, P., 416, *430*
Liebert, D. E., 285, *305*
Liebowitz, M. R., *234*
Lifshitz, M., 583, *598*
Lifton, R. J., 245, *273*
Light, R., 494, *534*
Lightfall, F. F., 221, *240*
Lilienfeld, S. O., 15, 32, 33, *56*, 119, 132, *147*, 231, *238*
Lilly, R. S., 220, *239*
Lincoln, A. J., 317, 330, *334, 335*, 514, *534*
Lindamood, P. C., 421, *430*
Lindblom, U., *596*
Lindholm, K. J., 264, *273*
Lindholm, L., 167, *189*
Lindsay, K. A., *192*
Lindsay, P., 68, *104*
Lindy, J., 253, *272*
Link, B. G., 346, *358*
Links, P. S., 52, *57, 192*
Linn, L., 255, *272*
Linney, J. A., 588, *596*
Linnoila, M., 567
Linscheid, T. R., 466, *488*, 584, 585, 593, 599, *598, 600*
Lion, J. R., *306*
Lipman, E. L., *57, 193*
Lipnick, R. N., 584, *599*
Lipovsky, J. A., 497, *535*
Lipscombe, P., 283, *305*
Lipsedge, M., 223, *235*
Lipsett. L. P., *104*
Lipton, M. A., *358*
Lipton, R. C., 470, *489*
Litt, I. F., *237*
Livingston, R., 42, *59*, 186, *194*, 200, *238*, 268, *273*
Lizardi, H., 18, *56*
Llewelyn, S. P., 253, *270*
Lloyd, M., 114, *146*
Lloyd-Still, J. D., 582, 583, *595*
Lo, E. E. S., *187*
Lo, W. H., 206, *239*
Lobato, D., 375, *387*
Lobell, C. M., 517, *535*
Lochman, J. E., 43, *56*, 140, *147*, 482, *486*
Locke, B. Z., 55
Lockhart, L. H., 381, *385*
Lockyer, L., 316, *336*, 343, *360*
Loeber, R., 4, 5, 16, 17, 18, 32, *54, 56*, 68, 81, 86, 87, 88, 89, *105, 107, 108*, 116, 118, 121, 125, 126, 127,

129, 130, 132, 133, 138, *146, 147, 149*, 304, 517, *535*
Loening-Baucke, V., 583, *598*
Loffler, W., *360*
Logan, G. D., 31, *56*, 66, 67, 68, 69, 70, *104, 110*
Lojkasek, M., 376, *386*
Lollis, S., 277, 292, *306*
Lombroso, P. J., 46, 47, 48, *56*, 448, 449, *453*
Loney, J., 86, *108, 109*, 114, 121, *147*
Long, N., 54, 165, *189*
Lonigan, C. J., 250, 253, 263, 268, 269, 273, 275
Lopez, R., 98, *108*
Lorch, E. P., 67, *109*
Lord, C., 320, 321, 325, 327, 333, 336, 337, 339
Lorenz, F. O., 4, *54*
Lorys, A. R., 96, *107*
Lorys-Vernon, A., *108*
Lott, I., *334*
Lotter, V., 325, *336*
Lou, H. C., 96, *108*
Lourie, R. I., 460, *487*
Lovaas, I., 95, *112*, 333, *336*
Lovegrove, W., 416, *430, 432*
Lovejoy, M. C., 178, *186, 192*
Loveland, K. A., 313, *336*
Lovely, R., 530, *534*
Lovett, M. W., 406, 410, 411, 415, *430, 431*
Lovett, M., 352, *358*
Low, J. F., 470, *489*
Lowe, C. B., 11, *58*
Lowe, M. R., 559, 560, *569*
Lowry, J. A., 492, 509, *532*
Lozoff, B., 467, *488*
Luban, N. C., 584, *599*
Lubensky, A. W., 285, *307*
Lubin, R. A., 365, *387*
Lubs, H., 417, *429, 431*
Lubs, M. L., *431*
Ludlow, C., *240*
Ludlow, L. H., 221, *237*
Ludolph, P., 492, *536*
Ludwig, S., 585, *597*
Luecke, W. J., 511, 516, *533*
Luepker, R. V., *598*
Lufi, D., 91, *108*
Luk, S. L., 326, *334*
Luk, S., 67, 68, *108*
Luke, J. A., 436, *453*
Lukens, E., *193*
Lumley, M., 593, *598*
Lundberg, I., 405, 416, *431*
Lupisiki, J. R., *386*
Lupowski, A. E., 426, *434*
Luria, A. R., 415, 425, *431*
Luthar, S. S., 18, 19, *56*, 262, *273*
Lutz, J., 345, *359*
Luxem, M., 580, *598*
Lydiard, R. B., 568
Lynam, D., 91, *108*, 131, 136, 137, 144, 145, *147, 148*
Lynch, G., 83, *111*

Lynch, M., 514, 530, *532, 535*
Lyon, G. R., 101, *104, 108,* 390, 394, 395, 396, 397, 398, 399, 402, 404, 405, 407, 408, 409, 410, 412, 415, 416, 417, 418, 419, 422, 424, 425, 426, *427, 427, 428,* 429, *430, 431, 432, 433, 434, 435*
Lyon, J., *531*
Lyons, M., 209, *238*
Lyons-Ruth, K., 4, 16, 30, *56,* 139, *147,* 178, *188, 192,* 473, 474, 476, 477, 478, 479, 480, 481, 482, 483, *484,* 488, 502
Lytle, C., 505, *534*
Lytton, H., 138, *144, 147*
Lyytinen, H., *107*

Ma, X., 260, *276*
Maas, J. W., 136, *148, 339*
MacArthur, C., 420, *429*
Macaulay, J. L., 219, *239*
Maccoby, E. E., 266, 267, 268, *273,* 296, 298, *304*
MacDonald, A., 586, *598*
Macdonald, H., 81, *110,* 137, *148, 338*
MacDonald, J. P., 42, 43, *55*
MacDonald, K., 298, *304*
Macedo, C. A., 136, *148*
MacFarlane, J. W., 10, 12, 16, 23, *56,* 197, *239, 388*
MacGregor, D., 376, *386*
Macher, J., *270*
Machon, R. A., 352, *359*
Mack, G., 448, *453*
MacKeith, R. C., *596, 600*
MacKinnon, G. E., *432*
MacLean, C., *569*
MacLean, G., 468, *488*
MacLean, R., 409, *433*
MacLean, W. E., Jr., 377, *385,* 588, *598*
MacMillan, D. L., 365, 366, 368, 371, 372, 383, *386, 387*
MacMillan, H. L., *57, 193*
MacMurray, J., *104*
Madrigal, J. F., 85, *108*
Magee, V., *533*
Magen, J., 212, 233, *234*
Magenis, R. E., *386, 388*
Magnus, E., *194*
Magnusson, D., 118, 120, 132, 142, *147, 149, 334*
Maguire, L., 287, *304*
Maguire, R., 223, *235*
Maharaj, S., 180, *192*
Maher, C., *109*
Maher, M. C., 91, *102*
Mahler, S. M., 436, *453*
Mahoney, E. M., 550, *569*
Mahoney, W., *338*
Maier, S. F., 573, *598*
Main, M., 177, *192,* 464, 470, 475, 477, 478, 479, 480, 481, *486, 487, 488, 480, 490,* 500, 501, 514, *533, 535*

Maisto, A. A., 369, *387*
Majoni, C., 221, *241*
Makari, G. J., 8, *56*
Makuch, R., 403, *433*
Malatesha, R. N., *431*
Malcarne, V. L., 175, *188*
Malik, S. C., 85, *103*
Malison, R. T., 449, *453*
Malkin, A., *191*
Malkin, D., *191*
Malla, S., 506, *535*
Malloy, P., 86, *108, 147*
Malmquist, C. P., 249, 253, *273*
Malone, C. A., *486*
Malone, M. A., 67, 90, *107, 108*
Maloney, M. J., 577, 594, *598*
Mamelle, N., *326*
Mammen, O., 471, *491*
Manassis, K., 212, *239*
Mandeli, J., *454*
Mangelsdorf, S., 139, *148,* 291, *305,* 481, *489*
Mangweth, B., 556, *569*
Manicavasagar, V., 230, *240*
Manku, M., 93, *109*
Manly, J. T., 20, *56,* 501, 514, *535, 536*
Mann, A., 551, *568*
Mann, L., 391, 416, *431, 435*
Mann, V. A., 405, *431*
Mannarino, A. P., 252, 262, 263, *273,* 530, *534*
Mannuzza, S., 86, 87, 88, 89, *106, 108,* 133, *147*
Mans-Wagener, L., 373, *385*
Manson, S., 249, *273*
Manton, K. G., 575, *601*
Mantz-Clumpner, L., *486*
March, C. L., 86, *104*
March, J. S., 207, 218, 219, 233, 233, 234, *235, 239, 240,* 448, *453*
Marchi, M., 466, *488*
Marchi, P., *568*
Marcotte, A. C., 448, *452*
Marcovitch, S., 376, *386*
Marcus, M. D., 546, 549, 550, 559, 560, 565, *569, 570*
Marek, K. L., 437, *454*
Maremmani, I., 223, *236*
Marenco, S., *454*
Marfo, K., *387*
Margo, G. M., 575, *598*
Margo, K. L., 575, *598*
Margolin, R. A., *338*
Margraf, J., 235, *239*
Mariani, M., 69, 76, 90, 91, *108*
Marino, L., 15, 32, *56*
Marks, I. M., 207, 220, 223, *235, 239,* 562, *567*
Marks, S., 374, *385*
Marnell, M., *566*
Marold, D. B., 182, *190*
Maron, M., 592, *598*
Marriage, K., 171, *190,* 268, *274,* 516, *535*
Marrs, S. R., 594, *601*

Marsh, J. T., 351, *360*
Marshall, J. C., 411, *431*
Marshall, J., *429, 433*
Marshall, R., *107*
Marshall, T., 289, *302*
Marshall, W. R., 594, *596*
Marsteller, F., 162, *189*
Marten, P. A., 202, 233, *234*
Martin, B., 295, 297, 298, *303, 304*
Martin, C. A., 98, *107*
Martin, C., *452*
Martin, D. C., *111*
Martin, E. W., 395, *432*
Martin, F., 416, *430*
Martin, H. P., 499, *531*
Martin, J. A., 268, *273,* 296, 298, *304,* 567
Martin, K., *598*
Martin, L. R., *106*
Martin, M., 345, *360*
Martin, N., 374, *388*
Martinez, C. R., Jr., 13, *54*
Martinez, P. E., 23, *59,* 113, 141, *148,* 178, *194,* 268, *273*
Martino, T., *271*
Marton, P., 169, 171, 172, 173, 174, 175, 176, 180, *191, 192*
Marvin, R. S., *484*
Marvin, R., 376, *387*
Marvinney, D., 139, *148,* 291, *305,* 481, *489*
Masek, B. J., 594, *596*
Maser, J. D., *146, 191, 234, 236, 237*
Mash, E. J., 4, 5, 8, 9, 10, 11, 21, 22, 23, 29, 30, 31, 49, 50, 51, *51, 53, 56, 57, 59,* 87, 91, 92, *108,* 235, *301, 302,* 495, 518, 530, *535, 537, 601*
Maslin, C. A., 478, *484*
Maslin-Cole, C., 313, *338*
Mason, E., 65, *107*
Mason, J. W., 260, *273, 276*
Masse, B., *59*
Masten, A. S., 19, *53, 54,* 228, *239,* 262, 268, *273,* 293, 294, 299, 300, *304, 305*
Masui, T., 197, 198, *234*
Masukume, C., 221, *241*
Matarazzo, J. D., 573, *598*
Matas, L., 291, *304,* 478, *488*
Mathews, A., 230, *236*
Mathews, J., 586, *596*
Mathews, W., *454*
Matias, R., 178, *188*
Matier, K., 68, *106*
Matrin, A., 67, *109*
Matson, J. L., 174, 176, *190, 191, 200, 239,* 377, 380, *385, 387, 388*
Mattes, J. A., 69, 95, *108*
Matthews, M., *567*
Matthews, R., 409, *433*
Matthews, W. S., 442, *450*
Mattis, S. G., 4, *57,* 212, *239*
Mattis, S., 410, 411, *432*
Mattison, R. E., 90, *102,* 272, *388,* 405, *428*

Mauer, D., 403, *430*
Maughan, B., 134, *147, 147,* 476, 480, 489
Maurer, K., *360*
Maurice, C., 311, *336*
Mawhood, L., 315, *334, 336*
Maxwell, S. E., 8, 21, 33, 34, *52, 57*
Mayer, J. A., 232, *239*
Mayer, J. D., 44, *57*
Mayer, J., 557, *567*
Mayes, S. D., *272*
Mayfield, A., *307*
Mayseless, O., *490*
McAdoo, W. G., 312, *336*
McAllister, J. A., *191*
McArdle, P., 83, *108*
McAuliffe, S., 93, *111*
McBride, M. C., *451*
McBride-Chang, C., 512, *536*
McBurnett, K., 4, *54, 102, 107,* 134, 136, *147, 149,* 283, *304*
McCabe, M., 174, 176, *195,* 284, *307*
McCabe, P., *598*
McCalley-Whitters, M., *109*
McCann, I. L., 258, 259, *273*
McCarthy, J. J., 400, *430*
McCarthy, P. L., 463, *486*
McCaughey, B. G., 242, *275*
McCauley, E., 154, 156, 157, 165, 166, 171, 172, 173, 174, 177, *187, 192*
McCausland, M. P., 248, *270*
McChesney, C. M., *239*
McClannahan, L., 333, *336*
McClaskey, C. L., 482, *486*
McClearn, G. E., 542, *570*
McClellan, J. M., 341, 345, 355, 356, 357, *359, 360, 361*
McClelland, D. C., 285, *307*
McCluskey, K., 478, *486*
McColgan, E., *534*
McConaha, C., *569*
McConaughy, S. H., 22, *51,* 80, *102,* 158, *186*
McCord, J., *145, 146,* 518, *535*
McCormack, A., 242, *270*
McCracken, J. T., 170, *190*
McCrae, R. R., 286, *302*
McCrary, M. D., 297, *307*
McCrone, E. R., 514, *535*
McCurley, J., 556, *567*
McCutchen, D., 422, *432*
McCutcheon, S. M., 228, *237*
McDermott, J. F., 243, *272*
McDermott, M., 447, *452, 569*
McDermott, P. A., 9, 24, 31, *57*
McDonnell, P., 586, *596,* 294, *306*
McDougle, C., *451, 452*
McElgin, W., *453*
McElroy, R. A., Jr., 32, *52*
McEnroe, M. J., 175, *187,* 284, *301*
McEvoy, L., 117, 121, *148*
McEvoy, R. E., 314, 318, *337*
McEwan, J. L., 286, *302*
McFall, R. M., 39, 40, *59*
McFarlane, A. C., 242, 248, 249, 252, 263, 265, 267, *273*

McGavran, L., *388*
McGee, G., 333, *337*
McGee, R., *51,* 79, 83, 84, 91, 93, *108, 109,* 130, 134, *144, 147,* 148, 163, 164, 165, 171, 175, *187, 192,* 196, 218, 220, 235, 239, 284, *304,* 409, *434,* 492, 530, 495, *535, 537*
McGill, C. W., *358*
McGillicuddy-deLisi, A., *306*
McGonagle, K., *238*
McGrath, P. A., *598*
McGrath, P. J. H., 578, 580, *598*
McGraw, T. E., *596*
McGrew, K., 368, *387*
McGuire, J., 594, *598*
McGuire, M., *359*
McHale, J. P., 75, *107*
McKay, M. C., 449, *451*
McKay, R. J., 581, *601*
McKee, D. H., 593, *597*
McKee, M., *569*
McKeown, R. E., 162, *189, 241*
McKinney, J. D., 413, 425, 426, *428, 432*
McKinnon, J., 291, 294, *301, 306*
McKnew, D. H., 229, 237, *307*
McLaren, J., 380, *388*
McLeer, S. V., 212, *24,* *241,* 249, 262, 271, *273,* 505, *535*
McLennan, J. D., 325, *337*
McLeod, S., 479, *488*
McMahon, R. J., 590, *596*
McMahon, W. M., 318, *337*
McMurray, M. B., 66, 67, 68, 69, 75, 86, 89, 90, 93, 97, 100, *103*
McNamara, J., 501, *532*
McNay, A., 343, *359*
McNeil, T. F., 352, *359*
McNichol, J., 94, *107*
McNutt, G., 397, *429*
McPherson, A. E., 179, *188*
McWatters, M. A., 99, *105*
Meacham, M. L., 414, *432*
Mead, G. H., 279, *304*
Meadow, S. R., *596, 600*
Medical Research Council of Canada, 51
Medin, D. L., 317, *338*
Mednick, S. A., 352, *358, 359, 360*
Medved, L., *452*
Mefford, I. N., 262, *270*
Meichenbaum, D., 41, *57, 275*
Meige, H., 436, *453*
Melamed, B. G., 591, 592, 593, *596, 599*
Melnick, S., 69, *107*
Meltzer, L., 410, *428*
Meltzoff, A. N., 313, 314, 318, *335, 337*
Meminger, S. R., *58,* 235, *240, 305*
Menahem, S., 463, *487, 488*
Mendelson, W. B., *240,* 449, *453*
Meng, A. L., 592, *601*
Menolascino, F. J., 380, *387*
Menvielle, E., 464, *485*
Mercer, J., 370, 376, *387*
Mercurio, A., 328, *339*

Merikangas, K. R., 106, *194*
Merlo, M., 68, *109*
Meryash, D. L., 381, *387*
Mesaros, R. A., 319, *335*
Mesibov, G. B., *335, 336, 337, 338,* 339, 580, *599*
Meskill, R. H., 416, *430*
Messer, S. C., 49, *57,* 231, *239,* 283, 284, *304*
Messick, S., 20, 22, *57,* 560, *570*
Messinger, D., 178, *194*
Mester, R., *360*
Metalsky, G. I., 171, *186*
Meyer, J. E., 463, *488*
Meyer, N. E., 172, 173, 175, *192*
Meyer, V. A., *189*
Meyers, A. W., 172, *193*
Meyers, C. E., 364, 376, *386, 387,* 388
Meyerson, J., 72, *106*
Mezzich, J., 15, *52*
Michael, C. M., 285, *304*
Michel, C., 329, *335*
Michel, G., 416, *435*
Michel, M. K., 44, *53*
Michelli, J. A., 93, *111*
Michelman, J. D., 324, *337,* 355, *360*
Michienzi, T., 259, *275*
Michon, J., 71, *109*
Mick, R., *104*
Mignani, V., 223, *236*
Mikkelsen, E., 328, *337*
Miklowitz, D. J., *360*
Milberger, S., 93, *104, 110*
Milgram, N. A., 247, 254, 263, *273*
Milgram, R. M., 247, 263, *273*
Milich, R., 67, 69, 83, 86, 100, *108, 109,* 140, 141, *148*
Miller, C. A., 370, *386*
Miller, D. J., 592, *599*
Miller, J. B., 557, *568, 569*
Miller, J. H., 426, *428*
Miller, L. C., 197, 217, 237, *239*
Miller, P. M., *239*
Miller, S. M., 3, 46, *51, 51, 53, 55, 56,* 58, 262, 273, 280, *304, 532*
Miller-Perrin, C. L., 594, *601*
Millich, R., 285, *304*
Millichap, J. B., *112*
Milling, L. S., 580, *601*
Millon, T., *145,* 286, *304, 305*
Mills, K., 575, *596*
Mills, M., 178, *192*
Mills, R. S. L., 49, *58,* 277, 284, 285, 287, 288, 291, 292, 293, 294, 295, 296, 297, 298, *305, 306*
Mills, T., 242, *270,* 516, *532*
Millsap, P. A., 249, *273,* 498, *534*
Millstein, K. H., 248, *270*
Milne, G., 247, *273*
Milner, J. S., 503, 523, 525, 526, *532,* 535
Minchin, S., 329, *335*
Minde, K. K., 67, 81, 92, *104,* 457, 468, *485, 488*
Minde, R., 457, *488*

Mindera, R., *452*
Mineka, S. M., 198, 222, 225, *234*, *239*, 260, 262, *274*
Minichiello, W. E., 228, *240*
Minichiello, W. O., *452*
Mink, I., 376, *387*
Minkunas, D. V., *112*
Minnes, P., 375, 376, *387*
Minshew, N. J., 317, 331, *337*
Minuchin, S., 560, 561, *569*
Mirenda, P. L., 319, *335*
Mischel, W., 20, *57*
Misle, B., 492, *536*
Missel, K. A., 136, *146*
Mitchell, E. A., 93, *109*
Mitchell, J. E., 549, 550, 559, 564, 566, 567, *569*
Mitchell, J. R., 171, 174, *187*, *192*
Mitchell, J., 154, 156, 157, 158, 160, 161, *192*, *192*, *570*
Mitchell, W. B., 209, *234*
Mitchell, W. G., 465, 465, *489*
Mittelmark, M. B., *597*
Mitterer, J. O., 411, *432*
Miyake, K., 290, 291, *305*, 478, *489*
Mizokowa, D. T., 421, *427*
Moats, L. C., 390, 394, 395, 396, 397, 398, 401, 407, 408, 420, 421, *429*, *431*, *432*
Moccia, P., 264, *270*
Modolfsky, H., 442, *453*
Moeykens, B. A., *193*
Moffitt, T. E., 91, *108*, *109*, 114, 115, 117, 122, 123, 125, 126, 129, 130, 131, 133, 134, 135, 136, 137, 141, 143, *143*, *145*, *147*, 148, 149, 482, *489*
Mogford, K., *385*
Moghadam, H. K., 94, *107*
Moldofsky, H., 556, *567*
Molnar, J., 11, *58*
Mones, R. L., 463, *484*
Monk, M. A., 10, *56*, 83, *108*, 197, *238*
Monsma, A., 283, *301*
Monson, R. A., 575, *600*
Montgomery, J. W., 404, *429*, *432*
Moore, C., *105*
Moore, L. A., 43, *57*
Moore, M. K., 313, *337*
Moore, M., 589, *597*
Moore, W. M., *597*
Moore-Motily, S., 252, *273*
Moos, R. H., 175, 179, 180, 181, *187*, 267, *272*
Moran, P. B., 262, *274*
Moran, T. M., 449, *454*
Moras, K., 225, *239*
Moreau, D., 212, 217, *239*
Moretti, M. M., 171, *190*
Morgan, W. P., 392, 405, *432*
Morganstern, G., 67, *104*
Mori, L., 593, 594, *599*
Moriarty, A. E., 267, *274*
Morison, J. D., 590, *596*
Morison, P., 293, 294, 299, 300, *305*

Morrell, J. A., Jr., 575, *597*
Morrell, W., 157, *194*, 555, *570*
Morris, D. P., 285, *304*
Morris, N., *147*
Morris, R. J., 42, *55*
Morris, R., 391, 394, 396, 397, 398, 407, 409, 410, 412, 413, 416, *429*, *432*, *433*, *435*
Morris, T. L., 202, 220, *235*
Morrison, D. C., 91, *107*
Morrison, D., *52*
Morrison, J., 89, 97, *109*
Morrison, M., 180, *189*
Morrison, S. R., 391, *432*
Morrow, C., *598*
Morrow, J., 175, *192*
Moscoso, M., 52, *187*
Mosenthal, P., *434*
Moser, H., 378, *387*
Moser, J., 501, 508, *534*
Mosk, M. D., 11, *60*, 511, 512, 516, 537
Moskowitz, D. S., 280, 293, *305*
Moss, H. A., 293, 298, *304*
Moss, S. J., 154, 156, 171, *189*, *192*
Mower, R. R., 39, *55*
Mowrer, O. H., 260, *274*
Moyal, B. R., 171, *192*
Mozes, T., 355, *360*
Mrazek, D. A., 504, 515, *533*, *535*
Mrazek, P. J., 502, 504, *535*
Mueller, E., 470, *489*
Mueser, K. T., 355, *358*
Mugny, G., 279, *302*
Muhleman, D., *104*
Muir, I. F. K., 591, *599*
Mulhall, P. F., *54*
Mulhern, R. K., 588, *599*
Mulick, J., 366, 368, 383, *387*, *388*
Mulle, K., 233, *239*
Mullins, L. L., 175, 181, *189*, *192*, 285, *305*, 572, 573, 574, 577, *596*, 597, 598, *599*
Mulloy, C., 327, *336*
Mumford, D, B., 552, *569*
Mundy, E., *104*
Mundy, P., 37, *57*, 312, 313, 314, 315, 318, *334*, *336*, *337*, *338*, 374, 388
Munir, K., 120, *144*, 481, *485*
Munk-Jorgensen, P., *360*
Murakami, J. W., *335*, *336*
Murata, T., 324, *336*
Murphy, C. M., 253, *272*, *304*
Murphy, D. L., *240*, 562, *570*
Murphy, H. A., *108*
Murphy, J. M., 253, *275*
Murphy, J. V., 93, *103*
Murphy, K., 78, *109*
Murphy, L. B., 267, *274*
Murphy, T. B., *596*
Musachio, J., *454*
Musick, J. S., *533*
Mussell, M. P., 559, *569*
Mussen, P. H., 52, *57*, *58*, *148*, 273, *303*, *304*, *306*, *452*

Myers, C. S., 243, *274*
Myers, K., 177, *192*
Myers, P., 391, *432*
Myklebust, H., 394, 400, 411, 421, 422, *430*, *431*, *432*

Nadeau, S. E., 69, *107*
Nadel, J., *301*, *306*
Nadel, L., *386*
Nader, K., 249, 250, 252, 253, 255, 263, *269*, *274*, *275*
Nahm, F. K., 331, *337*
Nair, R., 90, *103*
Nakamura, C. Y., 197, *240*
Nakata, Y., 85, *107*
Nanson, J. L., 99, *105*
Narcombe, B., 247, *275*
Nasby, W., 260, *276*
Nash, L. J., 382, *386*
Nasrallah, H. A., 96, *109*
Nasser, M., 552, *569*
Nation, J. E., 413, *427*
National Advisory Committee on Handicapped Children, 396, 400, 423, *432*
National Commission on Children, 9, 57
National Committee for the Prevention of Child Abuse, 583, 599
National Institute for Child Health and Human Development, 102
National Institute of Mental Health, 16, 50, *57*, 102, 143, 204, 234, 357, 360, 450
National Joint Committee on Learning Disabilities, 397, 400, 423, *432*
National Research Council, 492, 494, 495, 502, 503, 508, 515, 516, 517, 523, 527, 529, *535*
Nau, P. A., *104*
Nausieda, P. A., 449, *452*
Nauta, W. J. H., 449, *453*
Naylor, C., 399, *435*
Naylor, M. W., 169, 171, 173, 183, *191*, *192*
Neal, A. M., 220, 221, 222, *239*
Neal, M. E., 565, *570*
Neale, J., 285, *305*
Neale, M. C., 229, *238*, 569, *570*
Neckerman, H. J., 125, *145*
Nee, L. E., 439, 447, *453*
Needleman, H. L., 98, *109*
Needles, D., *149*
Neese, R. M., 204, 228, 232, 233, *241*
Neff, S., 329, *336*
Negrao, A. B., 556, *569*
Negray, J., *486*
Nehme, E., *337*
Neiderman, D., 71, *105*
Neimeyer, R. A., 516, *533*
Neiuwenhuys, R., 449, *453*
Nelles, W. B., 212, 229, 230, *239*, *240*
Nelson, B., *187*, *189*, *193*, *194*
Nelson, C. B., *238*

Nelson, C. L. A., 466, *485*
Nelson, H. E., 411, *432*
Nelson, J. E., 565, *571*
Nelson, J. Y., 465, *485*
Nelson, W. M., *194*
Neuman, R., 168, *194*
Neville, J. K., 4, *57*
Newacheck, P. W., 586, *599*
Newberger, E. H., 465, *487*
Newby, R. F., 410, 415, 416, *432*
Newcomb, M., 511, *537*
Newcombe, F., 411, *431*
Newcomer, P., 400, *432*
Newcorn, J. H., 68, *102*, *106*, 115, *144*
Newman, C. J., 247, 267, *274*
Newman, J. M., 140, *145*
Newman, J. P., 41, *53*
Newman, S. C., 166, *187*
Newton, T., 561, *566*
Neziroglu, F., 443, *454*
Nezworski, T., *146*, *303*, *306*, 490, 532
Nguyen, N. A., *189*
Nichols, P. L., *109*, 371, *385*
Nicholson, T., 410, *432*
Nielsen, J. B., 96, *108*
Niemala, P., *144*
Nigam, V. R., 85, *103*
Nigg, J., 69, *107*
Nihira, C., 376, *387*
Nikolskaya, O. S., 326, *336*
Nir, Y., 242, 255, 268, *274*
Nisi, A., 85, *109*
Nkoma, E., 221, *241*
Noam, G., 445, *452*
Noble, H., *197*, *217*, *237*, *239*
Nolan, B. F., *601*
Nolan, D. R., 425, *432*
Nolen, P., 422, *432*
Nolen-Hoeksema, S., 164, 165, 171, 173, 175, 176, 182, *192*, 221, 228, *239*
Nolin, T., *339*
Noll, R. B., 589, *599*
Nomura, Y., 444, *453*
Nonas, C. A., 549, *570*, *571*
Nordahl, T. E., *112*
Nordlie, J., *454*
Norman, C. A., 425, *432*
Norman, D. K., 253, 275, 551, *568*
Norman, D., *105*
Norman, P. A., *567*
Norris, F. H., 242, 258, 259, *274*
North, C. S., 250, 251, *275*
Noshpitz, J. D., *359*, 443, *452*
Nottelmann, E. D., 178, *190*
Novacenko, H., *187*, *189*, *193*
Novak, C., 92, *104*
Novey, E. S., 96, *107*
Novick, B. Z., 330, *337*, 424, 425, *432*
Nowak, M., *486*
Noyes, R., 228, 229, *236*, *237*, *239*
Nucci, L. P., 69, *109*
Nuechterlein, K. H., *304*, 341, 346, 348, *360*
Num, J. P., *335*

Nunez, F., *274*
Nunn, R. G., 450, *450*
Nurnberger, J. I., 163, *189*, *567*
Nutzinger, D. O., 550, *567*
Nye, C., 397, *430*

O'Brien, G. T., 229, *236*
O'Brien, G., 83, *108*
O'Brien, M. A., 473, *486*
O'Brien, M. M., 286, *305*
O'Connor, E., *491*
O'Connor, M., 98, *109*, 550, *567*
O'Connor, P. A., 94, *105*
O'Connor, S., 465, *484*
O'Dell, S. L., *196*, *197*, *235*, 284, *301*
O'Donnell, J., 17, *57*
O'Donnell, R., 464, *485*
O'Hare, A., *359*
O'Keefe, M., *531*
O'Leary, D., 253, *272*
O'Leary, K. D., 85, *109*
O'Malley, S., *106*
O'Neal, E., 253, *269*
O'Neil, P., *568*
O'Neill, R. E., 312, *336*
Oates, D. S., 473, *487*
Oates, K., 465, *487*
Oates, R. K., 465, *487*
Oberklaid, F., 291, 299, *306*, 463, *487*
Obrzut, J. E., *428*, *430*, *432*
Oca-Luna, R. M., *386*
Offord, D. R., 9, 10, 11, 12, 13, 17, 22, 32, 47, *52*, *57*, *59*, 81, 93, *105*, *111*, 125, 132, 134, *148*, 157, 161, 162, 163, 164, 165, *189*, *192*, 200, *236*
Ogan, T., 314, *339*
Ogbu, J., 364, *388*
Ogle, J. W., 419, *432*
Ohman, A., *147*
Okuda, M., 327, *336*
Okun, A., *57*
Olatawura, M. O., 582, *599*
Oldham, J. M., *570*
Oliveau, D. C., 217, *234*
Oliver, J. M., 179, *193*
Olkon, D. M., *104*
Ollendick, D. G., 248, *273*, *274*
Ollendick, T. H., 3, 4, 5, 16, 36, *51*, *51*, *52*, *53*, *55*, 56, *57*, *60*, *102*, *109*, 197, 200, 212, 217, 219, 220, 221, 224, 229, 232, 233, *236*, *238*, *239*, *241*, 293, 294, *302*, *305*
Olmstead, M. A., 552, 558, *567*
Olmstead, M. P., *567*
Olofsson, A., 405, *431*
Olsen, K., 493, *532*
Olson, R. A., 572, 573, 574, 577, 592, *596*, *597*, *598*, *599*
Olson, R. K., 404, 407, 409, 410, 417, *428*, *432*, *433*
Olson, S. C., *109*
Olson, S. L., 100, *109*
Olweus, D., 11, 17, *57*, 125, 138, *144*, *148*, 284, 293, 298, 300, *305*, 481, *489*

Oostra, B. A., *453*
Oppel, W. C., 580, *599*
Oppenheim, D., 478, *489*
Orlando, C., 406, *430*
Orn, H., 166, *187*
Ornitz, E. M., 320, 324, 337, 355, *360*
Orrison, W. W., 350, *359*
Ort, S. I., 240, 369, 381, *385*, 386, 387, 444, *453*, *454*
Ortegon, J., *336*
Orton, S., 392, 393, 406, *432*
Orvaschel, H., 89, *108*, 156, 178, 179, *191*, *193*, *194*, 196, 198, 200, 218, 219, 222, 229, *237*, *238*, *239*, 249, 273, 284, *304*
Osacar, A., 562, *567*
Osborne, L. N., 138, *146*
Osborne, R. B., 579, *599*
Osmon, B. B., *104*
Osnes, P. G., 594, *600*
Osofsky, J. D., 469, 470, 487, *489*, *491*
Ossip, D., 594, *596*
Öst, L-G., 209, 217, 228, *239*
Osteen, V., *190*
Oster, J., 578, *599*
Osterling, J., 314, 332, 333, 335, *337*
Osterman, K., 116, *144*
Ostroff, R. B., 260, *273*
Ostrowski, T. A., 575, *597*
Oswald, D. P., 293, *305*
Otto, M. W., 218, *240*
Ouimette, P. C., *56*
Ounsted, C., 343, *359*
Ouston, J., 314, *336*
Outwater, K. M., 584, *599*
Overall, J. E., 328, *334*
Overton, W. F., 34, 35, *57*
Overtoom, C. C. E., 31, *59*
Ovrut, M., 416, *435*
Owen, M. T., *486*
Ozer, D., *271*
Ozols, E. J., 425, *433*
Ozonoff, S., 5, 16, 17, 38, 44, 48, *57*, 313, 314, 316, 318, 319, 322, *337*, *338*

Padron-Gayol, M., *336*, 345, 355, *359*, *360*
Paek, J., *334*
Paez, P., *188*
Pagan, A., *52*, *187*
Page, H., *274*
Page, N. D., 594, *601*
Pahlavan, K., *194*
Pakiz, B., 163, 164, 165, 183, *193*
Pakstis, A., *453*
Palazzoli, M. S., 560, *569*
Paley, B., *190*
Palfrey, J. S., 80, 86, *109*
Palkes, H., 91, *111*
Pallotta, J., *486*
Palmer, R. L., 551, *567*
Palmer, S., 466, 467, *489*, 584, *599*
Panagiotides, H., 330, *335*
Panak, W. F., 161, 182, *193*, *193*

Panella, D., 284, *305*
Panksepp, J., 328, *337*
Paolicelli, L. M., *454*
Papousek, H., *488*
Pappini, D., 179, 186, *193*
Paradis, C. M., 221, *236*
Paradise, J. L., 463, *489*
Pardo, C., 531, *533*
Parent, W. S., 377, *388*
Paret, I., 467, 468, *489*
Paris, J., 575, *598*
Paris, S., 418, *433*
Parish-Plass, J., 91, *108*
Park, L. C., 517, *535*
Park, T. J., 517, *535*
Parke, R. D., 115, 116, 130, *148*, 298, 304, 499, *535*
Parker K., 475, *485*
Parker, G. R., 262, *276*
Parker, G., 179, 186, *193*, 222, 228, 230, 231, 239, *240*, 283, *305*
Parker, J. B., 284, *307*
Parker, J. G., 11, *57*, 132, *148*, 280, 297, *305*
Parkhurst, J. T., 293, *305*
Parkinson, D., 268, *272*
Parmelee, D. X., *195*
Parnas, J., 352, *360*
Parrish, K., 563, *568*
Parrish, R. T., 204, 217, *241*
Parrone, P. L., 154, *191*
Parry, P. A., 66, 68, *105*, *109*
Parsons, E., 480, *488*
Partridge, F., *108*, *192*, 239, *304*
Pasamanick, B., 448, *453*
Pastor, D. L., 291, *305*
Patel, P. G., 90, *103*, 414, *428*
Patel, P. I., *386*
Patrick, M., 480, *489*
Patterson, G. R., 4, 5, *57*, 116, 125, 129, 134, 135, 138, 139, 141, *144*, *145*, *148*, 175, *193*, 287, *305*, 481, *489*, 529, *535*
Patterson, K., 429, *433*
Patton, G. C., 551, 558, 559, *568*, *569*
Patton, J. H., 100, *106*
Paul, R., 312, 316, 319, *335*, *337*, *339*
Paulauskas, S. L., 134, *146*, 160, 166, 167, 180, 183, 184, *191*
Pauls, D. L., 46, *56*, 90, 97, *107*, *109*, 228, *236*, *241*, 438, 442, 443, 444, 447, 450, 451, 452, 453, *454*
Paulson, M. A., 590, *600*
Paykel, E. S., 177, 181, *193*, *194*
Payton, J. B., 249, *274*
Peacok, A., 465, *489*
Pearl, T., 418, *428*, *433*
Pearlman, L. A., 258, 259, *273*
Pearlson, G., *337*
Pearson, C., 253, *270*
Pearson, D. A., *336*
Pearson, P. D., *434*
Pechacek, T., *598*
Pedersen, N. L., 542, *570*
Pedlow, R., 291, 299, *306*
Pekarik, E. G., 285, *305*

Pelcovitz, D., 499, *535*
Pelham, W. E., 83, 87, 93, 92, *108*, *109*, 176, *193*
Pellegrin, A., 506, *537*
Pellegrini, D. S., 69, *106*, *273*
Pelletier, J. M., 466, *486*
Pels, P. J. E., 577, *600*
Pencharz, P., 586, *600*
Pendergrast, M., 85, *109*
Pennebaker, J. W., 575, *599*
Pennington, B. F., 5, 16, 38, 44, 48, *57*, 69, 90, *106*, *111*, 313, 314, 318, 319, 322, 337, *338*, 404, 407, 416, 428, *433*
Penny, J. B., 448, *450*
Pensky, E., 473, 476, *484*, 530, *531*
Pepler, D. J., *145*
Pepose, M., 551, *568*
Perel, J., *189*
Peresie, H., *109*
Perez, C. M., 512, *535*
Perfetti, C. A., 409, 410, 416, *430*, *433*
Perkins, S. C., 172, *193*
Perlmutter, D., 580, *599*
Perlmutter, M., *303*, *306*
Perret-Clermont, A., 279, 302, *306*
Perrin, E. C., 595, *599*
Perrin, J. M., 588, *598*
Perrin, J., *105*
Perrin, S., 89, *108*, 213, 218, 219, 220, 229, *238*, *240*
Perron, D., *59*
Perry, B. D., *273*
Perry, C. L., 13, *56*
Perry, E. C., 516, *536*
Perry, J. C., 242, *272*
Perry, S. E., 242, 267, *270*, *275*
Perry, S., 593, *597*
Perugi, G., 223, *236*
Peters, K. G., 65, *105*
Peters, S. D., 515, *535*
Peters, S., 580, *598*
Petersen, A. C., 157, 164, *193*
Peterson, A. L., 450, *450*
Peterson, B., 443, 447, 448, 449, 450, *453*, *454*
Peterson, C., *191*, *194*, 259, 262, *274*, 522, *535*
Peterson, E., 242, *270*
Peterson, L., 9, *57*, 93, *110*, 284, 285, *301*, *305*, 515, *535*, 573, 580, 583, 591, 592, 593, 594, 595, *599*, *600*, *596*
Peterson, M., 90, *103*
Peterson, O., 416, *431*
Petrauskas, R., 410, 412, *433*
Petrinack, R. J., 172, *192*
Petti, T. A., 255, *271*
Pettit, G. S., 18, *53*, 138, 141, *145*, 482, *486*, *489*, 511, *532*
Petty, L. K., 324, *337*
Petty, L. P., 355, *360*
Peveler, R. C., 550, *567*
Pfeffer, C. R., 169, *193*
Pfefferbaum, B., *601*

Pfohl, B., 32, *52*
Phares, V., 21, *57*, 184, *188*
Phillips, J. E., 47, 49, *56*
Phillips, L., 216, *240*
Phillips, R. A., *454*
Phillips, S., 330, *335*
Phipps, S., 590, *599*
Piacentini, J. C., 137, 159, *147*, *194*, 481, *487*
Piaget, J., 266, *274*, 278, *305*, 372, *388*
Pianta, R., 473, *486*, 492, 493, *533*, *535*
Picard, E. M., 426, *428*
Pickar, J., *338*
Pickles, A., 120, *149*, 167, *190*, 476, *489*
Pierce, E. W., 86, *104*
Pierce, L. H., 264, *274*
Pierce, P., 463, *489*
Pierce, R. L., 264, *274*
Pierre, C. B., 588, *598*
Pigott, T. A., 562, *570*
Pilkonis, P. A., 286, *305*
Pilner, C., 332, *338*
Pincus, J. H., 517, *534*
Pines, A. M., 517, *536*
Pinyerd, B. J., 463, *489*
Pirke, K. M., 554, 561, 562, *566*, *568*, *569*
Pirozzolo, F. J., *433*
Pitman, R., 443, *452*
Pittinsky, T., 19, *55*
Pittman, R. K., 260, *274*
Pitts, F. N., 91, *111*
Pivchik, E. C., 465, *487*
Piven, J., 329, *337*
Plapp, J. M., *148*
Platts, M., 552, *569*
Pless, I. B., 93, *109*, 462, *484*
Pliszka, S. R., 89, *109*, 134, *147*
Plomin, R., 4, 21, 46, *54*, *57*, 95, 98, *105*, *109*, 116, *145*, 168, *193*, *307*
Ploog, D., *568*
Plum, F., *429*
Poche, C., 594, *600*
Poderefsky, D., 41, *58*
Polan, H. J., 464, *489*
Policansky, S., 248, *273*
Polinsky, R. J., 439, *453*
Politano, M., *194*
Polivy, J., 552, 558, 559, 567, *569*
Pollack, M. H., 218, *240*
Pollack, M., 285, *305*
Pollack, S. L., 510, *534*
Pollard, S., 91, 92, 93, *103*
Pollin, R., 285, *307*
Pollock, M., 166, 167, 184, *191*
Pomeroy, C., 549, 566, *569*
Poncher, J., 462, *491*
Pontius, W., *335*
Ponton, L. E., 264, *274*
Pope, H. G., 556, 564, *568*, *569*
Pope-Cordle, J., *570*
Porch, B., 410, *431*
Porges, S. W., 461, *486*, *489*

Porrino, L. J., 67, 68, *109*
Posada, G., 511, *536, 491*
Posner, M. I., 317, *337*
Poster, E. C., 590, *600*
Pottash, A. L. C., 562, *568*
Potter, H. W., 342, 343, *360*
Potter, W. Z., *147*
Potts, D. A., 511, *534*
Potts, M. K., 69, 73, *103*
Pound, A., 178, *192*
Pound, J., 505, *534*
Powazek, M., 590, *600*
Powell, G. F., 470, *489*
Powell, G. J., 533, *535*
Powell, T. H., 319, *337*
Power, E., 527, *533*
Power, T. G., 268, *275*
Powers, P., 248
Powers, S. W., 590, 591, *596*
Poznanski, E. O., 178, *193*
Prader, A., 382, *388*
Prange, M. E., 4, *54*
Prasse, D. P., 372, *388*
Prater, J. M., *596*
Pratt, A. C., 416, *433*
Press, G. A., 328, 329, *335, 336*
Price, J. M., 140, *145*
Price, L. H., 554, *567*
Price, R. A., 447, *452, 453, 454*
Price-Bonham, S., 375, *388*
Prinz, R. J., 55, *103, 109, 238, 241,* 285, *305*
Prior, M., 68, *105,* 291, 299, *306,* 318, *337,* 341, *360*
Prizant, B. M., 315, *337, 338*
Proffitt, V. D., 172, 173, 175, *193, 195*
Provence, S., 470, *489*
Pruett, K. D., 468, 470, *489*
Pruitt, D. B., 249, *273,* 498, *534*
Prusoff, B. A., *194,* 447, *452*
Prutting, C., 314, *339*
Puckering, C., 178, *192*
Pueschel, S., 370, *388*
Pugh, R., *273, 534*
Puig-Antich, J., 134, *148,* 157, 159, 161, 165, 168, 169, 170, 174, 175, 176, 179, 180, 181, *187, 188, 189, 193, 194*
Purdue, S., *187*
Purser, J. S., *601*
Putnam, F. W., Jr., 260, 265, 266, 270, 512, 513, 522, 532, *536*
Pyle, R. L., 558, *566, 567, 569*
Pynoos, R. S., 242, 247, 249, 250, 252, 253, 255, 260, 263, 266, 267, *269, 270, 271, 272, 274, 275,* 468, 470, *489*

Quadflieg, N., 547, *567*
Quay, H. C., 10, 26, *51, 51, 58,* 69, 83, *109, 111,* 114, 115, 118, 126, 132, 135, 136, *145, 147, 148,* 198, *241, 280, 303, 305, 360,* 459, *489*
Quiggle, N. L., 161, 171, 172, 175, *193*

Quinlan, D. M., 179, *187*
Quinsey, V. L., 115, *146*
Quinton, D., 120, *149,* 476, *489*
Quittner, A. L., 586, *600*

Rabb, G. M., *111*
Rabian, B., 207, *240*
Rabideau, G. J., 11, *53,* 509, *534*
Rabin, M., *431*
Rabinovich, H., *187, 189, 193, 194*
Racine, Y. A., 10, *57, 192*
Rack, J., 404, *432*
Racusin, G. R., 177, *191*
Radbill, S. X., 493, *535*
Radford, J., 531, *534*
Radke-Yarrow, M., 23, 55, 59, *144, 148,* 178, 181, 186, *189, 190, 191, 193, 194,* 291, 299, *304, 305, 307,* 479, *486*
Radloff, L., 159, *193*
Rado, S., 243, *274*
Radojevic, M., *489*
Rae, D. S., 166, *188*
Rae-Grant, N. I., 52, *57, 192*
Raeburn, S. D., *566*
Raffaelli, M., 174, *191*
Ragozen, A. S., 287, *302*
Ragusa, D. M., 95, *110*
Raleigh, M., 553, *568*
Ralphe, D. L., 249, 262, *271, 273,* 505, *535*
Ramey, C., 370, *388*
Ramey, S. L., 370, 375, *387, 388*
Ramsey, B., 586, *600*
Ramsey-Klee, D. M., 473, *487*
Randels, S. P., *388*
Randolph, C., 442, 443, 447, *451, 452, 453*
Ransby, M. J., 415, *430, 431*
Rao, K., 264, *274*
Raoof, A., *276*
Rapee, R. M., 228, 230, *235, 236*
Raphael, B., 270, 271, 272, *275*
Rapin, I., 316, 332, *337,* 410, 411, *432*
Rapoff, M. A., 582, *596*
Rapoport, J. L., 68, 81, *109, 112, 146, 147, 195,* 204, 206, 207, *235, 236, 238, 240,* 338, 359, *451, 453, 454*
Rapoport, S. I., *338*
Rappaport, M., *241*
Rapport, M. D., 68, *109*
Rashotte, C. A., 402, *435*
Raskin, A., 55
Raskin, P., *596*
Rasmussen, S. A., *452*
Rasnake, L. K., 466, *488,* 585, 593, *598, 600*
Ratey, J. J., 72, *106*
Rath, B., 249, *273*
Rathbun, J. M., 465, *489*
Ratzburg, F. H., 394, *428*
Ratzoni, G., *241, 450*
Ravenscroft, K., 584, *599*
Ray, D. C., 575, *600*
Raymond, C., 443, *453*

Raymond, N. C., 559, *567, 569*
Rayner, P., 197, *241*
Read, P. B., 153, *188, 194, 236, 485*
Reader, M. J., 451, *454*
Realmuto, G. M., 249, 260, 265, *274*
Reaven, N. M., 284, 285, *301, 305*
Rebgetz, M., 180, *189*
Rediess, S., *451*
Redlich, F. C., 11, *54*
Redmond, A., 580, *597*
Redner, J. E., 171, *190*
Reed, E. W., 371, *388*
Reed, M., *429*
Reed, R. B., *597*
Reed, R., *109*
Reed, S. C., 371, *388*
Rees, J. R., 7, 8, *58*
Rees, J., 470, *490*
Reese, H. W., *104*
Reeves, J. S., 67, *111*
Regier, D. A., 117, *148,* 166, *188*
Rehm, L. P., 171, 172, 173, 178, 180, *188, 191, 193,* 510, *534*
Reiber, R. W., 372, *388*
Reich, T., *191, 194*
Reich, W., 242, *271*
Reichler, R., 312, 320, *338*
Reid, D. H., *388*
Reid, J. B., 4, *57*
Reid, J. C., 134, *148,* 156, *191,* 218, *237*
Reid, J., *191,* 517, *535*
Reilly, J. S., 374, *388*
Reinherz, H. Z., 162, 163, 164, 165, 183, *193*
Reiss, A. L., 382, *386, 388,* 451, *454*
Reiss, D., 21, *54,* 99, *103,* 168, *193,* 550, *568*
Reiss, S., 381, 383, *388*
Reiter, S., 466, *486*
Reitzel-Jaffe, D., 501, 517, 530, *537*
Remschmidt, H. E., 345, 345, 346, 355, *360*
Remy, E., *427*
Rende, R. D., 19, *58,* 98, *105,* 116, *145,* 168, *193,* 345, *360*
Renier, W. O., 577, *600*
Renken, B., 139, *148,* 291, 299, *305,* 320, *338,* 481, *489*
Renouf, A. G., 161, 171, *193*
Renshaw, P. D., *110,* 294, *305*
Repacholi, B., 139, *147,* 473, 479, *488*
Reschly, D. J., 368, 372, *388*
Resnick, H. S., 250, 251, 262, *271, 273*
Resnick, J. S., 4, 17, *55*
Resnick, L. B., *430*
Resnick, S., *58*
Rettew, D. C., *238, 453*
Rey, J. M., 118, *148*
Reynolds, C. R., 364, *388*
Reynolds, W. M., 24, *58*
Reznick, J. S., *54,* 170, *190,* 222, 223, *235, 237. 240,* 283, 288, 289, 290, 291, *303, 304, 305, 307, 487*
Rhea, P., 345, *360*

Rhode, P., 171, *190, 192*
Rhodes, J., 410, *431*
Rhymes, J. P., 465, *487*
Ribbe, D. P., 242, 249, 253, 259, 272
Ribera, J., 52, *187*
Ribordy, S., 510, *532*
Rice, J., *191*
Rice, M. E., 115, *146*
Rich, S., 325, *338*
Richard, K., 284, *307*
Richards, C. S., 134, *146*, 160, 175, *189, 191*
Richards, I. N., *148*
Richards, M. H., 174, *191*
Richardson, D. T., 23, *59*
Richardson, E. P., 448, *454*
Richardson, G. A., 384, *388*
Richardson, S. A., 380, *388*
Richardson, S., 371, *384*
Richman, G. S., *104*
Richman, N., 10, *58*, 86, *109*, 467, 467, *489*
Richter, S. F., *386*
Richters, J. E., 6, 15, 16, 23, 36, 46, 53, 55, *58*, 113, 117, 121, 129, 135, 141, 142, *144, 145, 148*, 159, 183, 190, 193, 268, 273, 299, 304, 305, 504, *535*
Richtsmeier, A. J., 579, *599*
Rickler, K. C., 447, *452, 453*
Ricks, D. F., 285, *303, 307*
Riddle, M. A., 204, 231, *240*, 442, *451, 452, 453, 454*
Rider, R. V., 580, *599*
Ridley-Johnson, R., 285, *305*, 592, *599*
Rie, E., *104*
Rie, H. E., 7, 8, 55, *58, 104*
Rieben, L., *430*
Riecher, A., 345, *360*
Riedel, C., *486*
Rief, W., 575, *600*
Rieker, P. P., 242, *270*, 516, *532*
Rietta, S., 410, *431*
Rifkin, H., *596*
Rigamer, E. F., 243, 247, *274*
Rigler, D., 523, *536*, 590, *598*
Riguet, C., 315, 324, *338*
Riley, A. W., *104*
Rimland, B., 312, *338*
Ring, B., 331, *334*
Ring, H. A., 329, *335*
Ringdahl, I. C., 583, *600*
Rintoul, B., 172, *195*
Riordan, M. M., 584, *600*
Risch, C., *304*
Risch, N., *106*
Riso, L. P., *56*
Risucci, D., 398, 410, 411, *431, 435*
Ritchett, D., 531, *535*
Ritter, P. L., *567*
Ritvo, E. R., 327, 329, *335, 338*, 341, 342, 343, 346, 353, 356, *359*
Rivara, F. P., 580, 594, *600, 601*
Rizley, R., 519, 530, *532*
Robbins, D. R., 212, 217, *234, 236*

Robbins, J. M., 575, *598, 600*
Roberts, A. R., 8, *58*
Roberts, K. B., 594, *597*
Roberts, M. A., 68, 69, *109*
Roberts, M. C., *58*, 573, 585, 595, 590, *596, 597, 598, 600*
Roberts, M. D., *239*
Roberts, R. E., 83, *108*, 162, 163, 171, 173, 174, 175, 176, *190, 192*, *193*, 219, *238*
Roberts, R., 162, *193*
Roberts, W., 90, *107*
Robertson, G. M., *359*
Robertson, J., 472, *489*
Robertson, L. S., 593, *600*
Robertson, M. M., 439, 442, 447, 452, *454*
Robins, C. J., 171, 173, *194*
Robins, L. N., 4, 32, *58*, 117, 118, 120, 121, 128, 130, 131, *146, 147, 148*
Robins, L., 129, *149*
Robinson, D., *194*
Robinson, H., *338*
Robinson, J., *388*
Robinson, M. M., 287, *302*
Roche, A. F., *597*
Rochlin, G., 153, *194*
Rochon, J., 90, *103*
Rodin, J., 551, 557, 561, *569, 570*, *571*
Rodning, C., 481, *484*
Rodrigue, J. R., *597*
Rodriguez, J. G., 593, *600*
Roeltgen, D. P., 421, 422, *433*
Roff, M., *303, 307*
Rogeness, G. A., 136, *148*
Rogers, S. J., 313, 314, 318, 322, 333, 337, *338*
Roggman, L., 179, *193*
Rogoff, B., *484*
Rogosch, F. A., 589, *599*
Rohde, P., 158, 160, 161, 164, 171, *194*
Roitblat, H. C., 258, *270*
Roizen, N. J., 15, *59*, 87, *110*
Rojas, M., *188*
Rolf, J., 53, *304*
Romaniello, G., *453*
Romney, D. M., 138, *144*
Ronan, K., *238*
Rong, Z. Y., *566*
Rose, R. M., 260, *274*
Rose-Krasnor, L., 277, 278, 288, 290, 291, 295, 296, *301, 304, 306*
Rosemier, R. A., 380, *385*
Rosen, B. N., 93, *110*
Rosen, B., 594, *599*
Rosen, C. L., 584, *600*
Rosen, J. C., 545, 557, *569*
Rosen, P., 402, *429*
Rosenbaum, D., 439, *454*
Rosenbaum, J. F., 48, 49, 52, 54, *58*, 218, 222, 223, 224, 235, 237, *240*, 283, 284, *301, 303, 305, 487*
Rosenbaum, M., 166, *192*

Rosenberg, A., *305*
Rosenberg, C., 355, *360*
Rosenberg, D. A., 584, *600*
Rosenberg, D., *533*
Rosenberg, L. A., 442, *454*
Rosenberg, M. S., 268, *270, 274*
Rosenberg, M., *532*
Rosenberg, R. S., 94, *111*
Rosenberg, T. K., 156, 179, 180, *188*, *191*, 218, *237*
Rosenblum, G., 549, *571*
Rosenthal, D., 352, *360*
Rosenthal, R. H., 67, 96, *110*
Rosenthal, S. L., 22, 34, *58*
Rosman, B. L., 560, *569*
Rosman, N. P., 329, *336*
Ross, C. J., *531*
Ross, D. M., 84, 94, 96, *110*, 590, 591, *600*
Ross, H. S., *305*
Ross, R. T., 364, 369, *388*
Ross, S. A., 84, 94, 96, *110*, 590, *600*
Rossiter, E. M., 545, 548, 549, 559, 560, *569, 570*
Rossman, B. B. R., 265, 266, 267, *274*
Rossman, P., 528, *535*
Rost, K. M., 575, *600*
Roth, B., 341, 345, 352, 353, *359*
Roth, J., *238*
Roth, N., 93, *110*
Rothbart, M. K., 19, *58*
Rothbaum, B. O., 243, 262, 271, 520, *533*
Rothman, S., 96, *110*
Rothner, A. D., 449, *452*
Rothstein, J. A., 94, *111*
Rotman, A., 327, *338*, 462, *484*
Rotter, J. B., 262, *274*
Rourke, B. P., 398, 408, 410, 411, 412, 424, 425, 426, *428, 429, 430*, *431, 432, 433, 434, 435*, 443, *452*
Rouse, L. W., 42, *59*
Routh, D. K., 26, 29, *58, 103, 109*, *110, 144*, 573, 575, 579, 580, 590, 596, 597, 598, 600, *601*
Rovine, M., 291, *301*, 474, 478, *484*, *485*
Rowden, L., 49, 55, 277, 293, *303*, *306*
Rowitz, L., *387*
Rowlands, O., *149*
Rozelle, R. M., *597*
Ruben, D. H., *149*
Rubenstein, C. S., 562, 564, *570*
Rubin, K. H., 14, 16, 31, 44, 45, 48, 49, *53, 55, 58, 145*, 178, *194*, 222, 277, 278, 279, 280, 283, 284, 285, 287, 288, 290, 291, 292, 293, 294, 295, 296, 297, 298, 299, 300, *301*, 302, *303, 304, 305, 306, 307*
Rubin, Z., *536*
Rubino, K. K., *533*
Rubins, A., *148*
Rubinstein, B., 380, *388*
Rubinstein, E., 7, *58*
Rubio-Stipec, M., 52, *187*, 575, *597*

Ruble, D. N., 178, *189*, 296, *302*
Ruch-Ross, H. S., *533*
Rudel, R. G., 67, 69, *105*
Rudolph, J., 476, *487*
Rudolph, K. D., 3, 172, 173, 174, 175, 176, 177, 186, *190*, *194*, *195*
Ruebush, B. K., 221, *240*
Ruffins, S., 492, *536*
Ruley, E. J., 584, *596*, *599*
Rumsey, J., *112*, 318, 329, *338*, *431*
Rumsey, J. M., *55*, 404, *433*
Runtz, M., 516, 517, *531*
Runyan, D. K., 267, *271*
Rush, A. J., 35, *52*, 170, *187*
Russ, S. W., 267, *270*
Russell, A. T., 341, 344, 345, 355, 358, *360*
Russell, D. E. H., 517, *535*
Russell, G., 541, *570*
Russell, R., 425, *433*
Russo, D. C., *597*
Russo, M. F., *56*, 69, 89, *108*, *110*, *149*, 481, *487*
Ruthberg, J., *427*
Rutter, M., 5, 9, 10, 15, 16, 17, 18, 19, 20, 22, 26, 32, 33, 35, 36, 39, 41, *52*, 53, 54, *58*, 59, 81, 93, 97, *104*, *110*, 117, 120, 125, 130, 132, 134, 135, 137, 140, *145*, *146*, *147*, *148*, *149*, 153, 159, 160, 162, 164, 167, *187*, *188*, *190*, *194*, 213, 218, 219, 225, 231, 232, 236, *240*, 242, 243, 249, 263, 265, 266, 267, 272, *273*, *274*, 280, 287, *305*, *306*, *307*, 315, 316, 319, 321, 323, 324, 325, 326, 327, *334*, *335*, *336*, *338*, *339*, 341, 343, *359*, *360*, 380, *388*, 407, 409, *433*, 446, 452, *454*, 459, 470, 476, *485*, *489*, *491*, 520, *536*, *597*
Ryan, E., 411, *434*
Ryan, N. D., 156, 157, 158, 161, 164, 167, *187*, *189*, *193*, *194*
Ryan, S., 230, *235*
Rydell, P. J., 315, *337*
Rynders, A., *388*
Ryshon, K. L., 414, *435*

Saab, P. G., *597*
Sabalesky, D., *334*
Sabatino, D. A., *435*
Sabo, H., 374, *385*
Sacco, W. P., 175, *194*
Sachs, G. S., 218, *240*
Sack, W. H., 249, 252, *270*, *273*
Sacks, N. R., 562, *568*
Sadeh, A., 467, *490*
Sadock, B. J., *55*
Sagi, A., 475, 478, *489*, *490*
Sahley, T. L., 328, *337*
Saigh, P. A., 242, 248, 249, 253, *274*
Saile, H., 592, *600*
Saitoh, O., *335*
Salam, M. M., 449, *450*
Salcedo, J. R., 584, *596*
Sale, P., 377, *388*

Sallee, F. R., 250, *273*
Salovey, P., 44, *57*
Salter, A. C., 527, *535*
Salzinger, S., 499, 512, *535*
Salzman, L. F., 96, *107*
Sameroff, A. J., 4, 34, 35, *58*, 262, 275, 348, *360*
Sameroff, A., 443, *454*, 457, 459, 460, 484, *490*
Samit, C., 499, *535*
Sammons, C., 344, *360*
Sampson, R. J., 141, *149*
Sampugnaro, V., *568*
Samuelson, H., *191*
Sanchez-Lacay, A., *52*, *187*
Sandberg, D. E., *567*
Sandberg, S. T., 81, 94, *105*, *111*
Sanders, M. R., 172, 180, *189*, *194*
Sandersj-Woudstna, J. A., *601*
Sanderson, C., 286, *307*
Sandgrund, A., 527, *533*
Sandkuyl, L. A., *453*
Sandler, A., *429*
Sandman, B. M., *111*
Sandman, C. A., 328, *338*
Sandoval, J., 81, 90, *108*
Sands, M., 470, *486*
Sanford, M. N., 57, *193*
Sanson, A. V., 68, 91, *105*, *106*, 291, 299, *306*
Sansonnet-Hayden, H., 268, *274*, 516, *535*
Santangelo, S., 448, *454*
Santelli, R., 559, *569*
Saperstein, G., 221, 237, *240*
Sarason, S. B., 221, 237, *240*
Sarigiani, P. A., 157, *193*
Sarsgard, E., 463, *491*
Sartorius, N., 346, *359*, *360*
Sas, L., 259, *275*, 505, 506, 515, *535*, *537*
Saslow, G., 28, *55*
Sassone, D., 81, *108*
Satola, J., *486*
Satterfield, J. H., 86, 90, *104*, *110*, 132, *143*, *149*
Satz, P., 410, 412, 413, *432*, *433*, *435*
Sauvage, D., *335*
Sauzier, M., 248, 253, *272*
Savilahti, E., 462, *490*
Savoie, T., 350, *360*
Sbrocco, T., *570*
Scahill, L., *240*, 437, 441, 442, 444, 448, 449, 450, 451, 453, *454*
Scalf-McIver, L., *486*
Scanlon, D. M., 405, 410, 416, *435*
Scarr-Salapatek, S., *454*
Sceery, W., 109, 236, *240*
Schachar, R. J., 66, 67, 68, 69, 70, 81, 93, *104*, *110*
Schaefer, C. A., 216, *234*, 236, 237, *240*, *241*
Schaefer, C. E., 582, *600*
Schaefer, S., 465, *485*, 575, *600*
Schafer, W. D., 471, *486*
Schaffer, D., *241*

Schain, R. J., 327, *338*
Schalling, D., *148*
Scharf, M., *490*
Schaughency, E. A., *108*
Scheerenberger, R. C., 362, *388*
Scheeringa, M. S., 265, *274*, 468, 469, 470, *490*
Scheibel, A. B., *338*
Scheinin, M., *567*
Schell, A. M., 86, *110*, 132, *143*, *149*
Scherer, M. W., 197, *240*
Schetky, D. H., 470, *490*
Schiefelbusch, R., *338*
Schinkel, A. M., *597*
Schleifer, M., 87, *104*, *110*
Schlenzka, K., 93, *110*, *192*
Schlundt, D. G., 550, *570*
Schmaling, K. B., 116, *147*
Schmidt, L. R., 592, *600*
Schmidt, M. H., 481, *485*
Schmidt, S., 157, *194*
Schneider, B. H., *301*, *303*, *305*, 306
Schneider, J. A., 552, *570*
Schneider, S., *55*
Schneider-Rosen, K., 184, *188*, 513, 514, *535*
Schneiderman, N., *598*
Schneier, F. R., *234*
Schnell, C., 409, *433*
Schoenbeck, G., 550, *567*
Scholten, C. A., 66, *110*
Schopler, E., 312, 320, 325, 326, 327, 333, *335*, 336, *337*, *338*, *339*
Schouten, E. G. W., *271*
Schowalter, J. E., *360*
Schrag, P., 82, *110*
Schreiber, J. L., *567*
Schreiber, M., *386*
Schreibman, L., 312, *335*, *336*
Schreier, H. A., 502, *535*
Schreiner, R., *387*
Schroeder, C. S., 69, *110*, 580, 581, 582, 583, *599*, *600*
Schroeder, S. R., 93, *111*
Schteingart, J. S., 11, *58*
Schuerman, J. R., 263, 267, *270*
Schuler, A., 315, *338*
Schulsinger, F., *360*
Schulsinger, H., *360*
Schulterbrandt, J. G., *55*
Schultheis, K., 592, 593, *599*, *600*
Schultz, L. G., *535*
Schultz, L. H., 41, *58*
Schulz, E., 345, *360*
Schulz, S. C., *334*, 350, *360*
Schupack, H., 416, *430*
Schwab-Stone, M., 159, *194*
Schwalberg, M. D., 564, 565, *570*
Schwartz, C. E., *238*
Schwartz, D., 377, *388*
Schwartz, J. E., *106*
Schwartz, S., 420, *429*, *451*
Schwartzman, A. E., 59, 280, 285, *305*, *306*

Schwarz, E. D., 242, 247, 249, 250, 253, 259, 260, *269*, *274*, *275*
Schwarz, M., *148*
Schweiger, U., 553, 567
Schyving, J., 590, *600*
Scott, C. I., 382, *386*
Scott, K. D., 516, *535*
Scott, P. M., 298, *307*
Scott, W. O., 247, *272*
Scruggs, T. E., *428*
Scurfield, R. M., 245, *275*
Sears, M. R., 93, *108*
Sebring, N. G., 550, 559, *571*
Seeley, J. R., 83, *108*, 158, 160, 162, 163, 164, 171, *190*, *194*, *192*, *193*, 219, 238, 496, *533*
Segal, H. G., 171, 183, *191*
Segawa, M., 444, *453*
Seiden, J. A., 96, *106*
Seidman, L. J., *105*
Seifer, R., 4, *58*, 262, 263, 267, 268, *275*, 478, *491*
Seim, H. C., *567*
Seitz, V., 370, *388*, 593, 594, *599*, *600*
Seligman, M. E. P., 165, 171, 173, 182, *186*, *191*, *192*, *194*, 228, *234*, 259, 262, *269*, *274*, 522, *535*
Selman, R. L., 41, *58*, 278, *306*
Seltzer, C. C., 557, *567*
Seltzer, M., 376, *388*
Semel, E. M., 402, *435*
Semple, W. E., *112*
Semrud-Clikeman, M., 96, *107*, *110*
Sender, L., *598*
Senf, G. M., 397, *433*
Senior, N., 247, *275*
Senter, S. A., 464, *485*
Serbin, L., 285, *306*
Sergeant, J., 66, 69, *110*
Serketich, W. J., 4, *53*
Sesman, M., *52*, *187*
Sessa, F., *238*
Sessarego, A., *271*
Sgroi, S. M., 527, *536*
Shaffer, D., *102*, 159, *194*, *195*, *236*, 581, *600*
Shaffi, N., 134, *149*
Shafii, M., 448, *454*
Shah, A. B., *452*
Shah, N. S., *452*
Shahbahrami, B., *104*
Shaheen, E., 464, *490*
Shain, B. N., 171, *191*, *192*
Shalev, R. S., 90, *106*
Shallice, T., 419, *433*
Shanahan, M., 4, *54*
Shankweiler, D. P., , 402, 403, 405, 406, 416, *428*, *429*, *430*, *433*
Shanley, N., 171, *189*
Shannon, M. P., 250, 255, 258, 262, 264, 268, *269*, *273*, *275*
Shapiro, A. K., 437, 439, 441, 447, 448, *452*, *454*
Shapiro, E. S., 437, 439, 441, 447, 448, *454*

Shapiro, L., *386*
Shapiro, S. K., 26, *58*
Shapiro, T., 38, *58*
Shapiro, W., 464, *490*
Share, D. J., 409, *433*
Share, D. L., 402, *430*
Sharma, V., 68, *106*
Shaughnessy, P., 371, *385*
Shaul, D., 178, *189*
Shaver, B. A., 463, *490*
Shaw, B. F., 35, 43, *52*, *53*, 170, *187*
Shaw, C. A., 463, *490*
Shaw, D. S., 4, *58*
Shaw, E. G., 590, *600*
Shaw, K., 284, *304*
Shaw-Lamphear, V. S., 500, *536*
Shaywitz, B. A., 96, 99, 104, 107, 110, 328, *339*, 396, 398, 403, 408, 409, 410, 426, *429*, *433*, 436, *451*, 567
Shaywitz, S. E., 96, 99, *104*, *107*, *110*, 396, 398, 403, 408, 409, 410, 416, 417, 426, *429*, *433*
Sheehan, D. V., 228, *240*
Sheehan, K. E., 228, *240*
Shelden, R. G., 130, 138, *145*
Shell, J., *359*
Shellhammer, T. A., 285, *301*
Shelton, M. R., 176, 184, *194*
Shelton, T. L., 94, *103*, 418, *433*
Shema, S., 588, *599*
Shenker, R., 86, *106*
Shennum, W. A., 524, *531*, 296, *302*
Sheras, P. L., 591, *596*
Shereslefsky, P., *490*
Sherick, R. B., 174, *191*
Sherman, L., *190*
Sherman, T., 178, *187*, 314, 337, 351, *358*
Sherrod, K. B., 465, *484*
Sherrod, L., *486*
Sherry, T., 98, *109*
Shiao, S., *451*
Shifman, L., *597*
Shigetomi, C., 591, 592, *599*
Shih, B., *454*
Shindledecker, R., 169, *193*
Shinn-Strieker, T., 413, *434*
Shipman, R., 580, *598*
Shirk, S. R., 500, *536*
Shisslak, C., 565, *570*
Short, E., 410, 413, *428*, *432*
Shoulson, I., *452*
Showalter, B. A., *147*
Shrout, P. E., 346, *358*
Shulman, S., *306*
Shumaker, J. B., 404, 405, *429*
Shumway, J., *430*
Sickel, R. Z., 461, *486*
Siegel, A. W., 171, *191*, 510, *534*
Siegel, B. V., *334*
Siegel, B., 332, *338*
Siegel, C. H., 468, *486*
Siegel, D., 469, *486*
Siegel, G., *454*
Siegel, J. M., 181, 182, *194*

Siegel, L. J., 175, *189*, *192*, 573, 592, 593, *597*, *598*, *599*, *601*
Siegel, L. S., 67, 68, 92, 93, *105*, 391, 398, 407, 408, 411, 416, *430*, *432*, *434*
Siegel, M., 577, *600*
Siegel, S. E., 590, *598*
Siegel-Gorelick, B., *567*
Siever, L. J., 286, *305*, *306*
Sigel, I., 302, *306*, *428*
Sigman, M., 14, 59, 312, 313, 314, 315, 317, 318, *334*, *336*, *337*, *338*, *339*
Sijben, N., 577, *600*
Silber, D. L., 583, *600*
Silber, E., 242, 267, 268, 270, *275*
Silberfeld, M., 230, *240*
Silberstein, L. R., 551, 557, *570*
Silbert, M. H., 517, *536*
Silove, D., 230, *240*
Sils, R. H., *600*
Silva, E., 479, *488*
Silva, P. A., 11, *51*, 91, 98, *108*, *109*, 110, 131, 136, *144*, *145*, 148, 171, *192*, 196, 235, 239, *304*, 409, *434*
Silva, P., 129, 130, *149*, *187*, *192*
Silver, H. K., 494, *534*
Silver, R., 509, *536*
Silver, S. E., 4, *52*, *54*
Silverberg, J., *191*
Silverman, F. N., 494, *534*
Silverman, I. W., 95, *110*
Silverman, J. A., 43, *58*
Silverman, J. S., 43, *58*
Silverman, N., 470, *489*
Silverman, W. K., 171, *194*, 207, 211, 212, 216, 219, 229, 230, 232, 233, *236*, *237*, *238*, *240*
Silverstein, A. B., 369, *388*
Silverstein, P., 591, *600*
Simeonsson, R. J., 22, 34, *58*, 375, *385*, *387*
Simmel, C., 67, 69, *102*, *107*, *110*, 139, *144*
Simmonds, B., *237*
Simmons, H. D., 410, *430*
Simmons, K., 402, *435*
Simonds, J. F., *596*
Simonoff, E., *110*, *148*
Simpson, J. C., *359*
Simpson, K. S., 138, *145*
Simson, R., 330, *337*
Singer, H. S., 442, 448, 449, *450*, *451*, *454*
Singer, J. E., 47, *52*
Singer, L., *490*
Singer, M. I., 528, *536*
Singer, M. T., 353, *360*
Siperstein, G. N., 365, 368, *386*, *387*
Sipprelle, R. C., 262, *271*
Siqueland, L., 228, *238*
Sirbasku, S., 333
Sirles, E. A., 248, *275*
Sisson, L. A., *146*
Sivage, C., 68, *103*
Siverman, A. B., *193*

Skeels, H. M., 470, *490*
Skiner, H., 398, *434*
Skinner, B. F., 38, 59, 66, 69, *110*, 377, *388*
Skinner, J. R., 43, *59*
Skodol, A. E., 346, *358*, 563, 565, *570*
Skolnick, N., *567*
Slaby, R. G., 115, 116, 130, *148*, 499, 535
Slade, P., 561, *566*, *570*
Slaghuis, W., 416, *430*
Slater, M. A., 268, *275*
Slymen, D., 228, *236*
Small, A. M., 328, *334*
Smalley, S. L., 326, 327, *338*
Smallish, L., 68, 77, 79, 92, 95, *103*, 106, 132, *144*
Smetana, J. G., 499, 501, 509, 510, 511, *533*, *536*
Smith, A. C. M., 382, *388*
Smith, A. E., *386*
Smith, A., 81, *110*, *195*
Smith, D. A., *304*
Smith, D. E., 559, *569*
Smith, D. F., *388*
Smith, D., 69, *104*
Smith, E. E., 15, 52, 317, *338*
Smith, E. M., 250, 251, *275*
Smith, E., 242, *271*
Smith, F., 409, 410, *434*
Smith, G. R., Jr., 575, *600*
Smith, I. M., 313, 316, *334*, *338*
Smith, J. A., 248, 252, 273, *275*
Smith, J. C., *453*
Smith, M., *104*
Smith, R. S., 19, 20, *60*, 262, 267, *275*
Smith, R., 268, *271*, 575, *596*
Smith, S. D., 404, *428*, *433*
Smith, S. J. M., 449, *454*
Smith, Y. S., 69, *112*
Smitson-Cohen, S., *272*
Snidman, N., 4, 17, 48, *54*, *55*, *58*, 222, 223, *235*, *237*, *240*, 283, 288, 289, 290, 291, 292, *303*, *304*, *305*, *487*
Snow, J. H., 413, 414, *434*
Snowling, M. J., 416, *434*
Sokol, M. S., 328, *334*
Solnit, A. J., 375, 376, *360*, *388*, 465, *487*
Solomon, J., 477, 479, *488*
Solomons, G., 65, *108*
Soltys, S. M., *237*
Solyom, C., 230, *240*
Solyom, L., 230, *240*
Somberg, D. R., 41, *53*
Sonuga-Barke, E. J., 91, *110*
Sorensen, A., *486*
Sorenson, S. B., 218, *237*
Soroker, E., 285, *304*
Southwick, S., 260, 273, *276*
Sovner, R., 380, 381, *388*
Spaccarelli, S., 510, 522, *532*, *536*
Spangler, G., 478, 479, *487*, *490*
Sparkes, R. S., *453*
Sparrow, S. S., 325, *339*, 363, 366, *387*, *388*

Specker, B., 594, *598*
Specker, S. M., 564, 567, *569*
Speece, D. L., 410, 414, *431*, *434*
Speers, M. A., 470, *489*
Spellman, M., *359*
Speltz, M. L., 139, *146*, *149*, 483, *487*, *490*
Spence, A., 326, *338*
Spence, S. H., 174, *191*, 284, *304*
Spencer, A., 314, *335*
Spencer, E. K., 355, *360*
Spiegel, J. P., 243, *272*
Spieker, S. J., 480, *490*
Spielberger, C. D., 221, 229, *237*, *240*
Spierings, C., 577, *600*
Spinetta, J. J., 523, *536*
Spisto, M. A., 91, *102*
Spitzer, R. L., 11, 31, 32, *59*, 80, *110*, 286, *307*, 542, 546, 547, 549, 551, 565, *570*, *571*
Spock, A., 588, *601*
Sprague, D. J., 69, *111*
Sprecher, S., 557, *568*
Spreen, O., 425, *434*
Sprenger, J., 436, *454*
Sprich, S. E., 115, *105*, *144*
Spring, B., 346, *361*
Springer, T., 262, *275*
Springs, F. E., 508, *536*
Sroufe, A., 501, 503, *533*
Sroufe, L. A., 5, 16, 17, 18, 22, 36, 40, *59*, 125, 139, *145*, *148*, 225, 228, *240*, 287, 290, 291, *302*, *304*, *305*, *306*, *307*, 476, 477, 478, 481, *486*, *488*, *489*, *490*, 493, 500, 520, 521, *533*, *536*
Stabenau, J., 285, *307*
Staghezza, B., 10, *52*, 219, *235*
Stahl, J., 478, *488*
Stahlberg, M. R., 462, 463, *490*
Stanley, A. E., 584, *600*
Stanley, J. C., 426, *434*
Stanovich, K. E., 397, 398, 407, 408, 409, 410, 416, *434*, *435*
Stansbury, K., 181, *190*
Stanton, W. R., 93, *108*
Stark, K. D., 42, 43, *59*, 171, 172, 186, *191*, *194*
Stark, L. J., 594, *600*
Stark, M., 375, 376, *388*
Stark, R. E., 404, *432*
Starkstein, S. E., *337*
Statfeld, A., 47, 49, *56*
Stattin, H., 118, 120, *149*
Steele, B. F., 494, *534*
Steele, H., 475, *486*, *490*
Steele, J. J., 212, *235*
Steele, M., 475, *486*, *490*
Steele, R., *335*
Stefani, R., 510, *532*
Steffenburg, S., 316, 324, 325, 326, *336*, *338*
Stehbens, J. A., 589, *600*
Steiger, H., 517, *536*
Stein, M. A., 15, *59*, 87, 91, *104*, *110*

Stein, R. E. K., 595, *599*
Steinberg, E. R., *427*, *429*
Steinberg, L., 298, *307*
Steingard, R., *110*
Steinhauer, S. R., *358*
Steinkamp, M. W., 67, *110*
Steinmetz, J. L., 43, *56*
Steketee, G., 243, *271*, 520, *533*
Stephenson, S., 392, *434*
Stern, D. N., 313, *338*, 469, *489*, *490*
Stern, J., 447, *452*
Stern, L., 229, *237*
Stern, R. M., 590, *597*
Sternberg, R. J., 386, *388*
Steubing, K. K., 396, *429*
Stevens, E., 592, *601*
Stevens, H. A., *386*
Stevens, J. S., *195*
Stevens, V., *568*
Stevenson, J. E., 10, *54*, *58*
Stevenson, J., 86, 90, 91, 95, 98, *106*, 109, *110*, *111*, 443, *452*, *453*, 467, *489*
Stevenson-Hinde, J., 299, *305*, *306*, 307, 485, *487*
Stewart, A. J., *271*
Stewart, G. W., *148*
Stewart, G., 229, *235*
Stewart, J., *598*
Stewart, M. A., 64, 93, 91, 93, 94, 97, *102*, *104*, *111*, 89, 91, 97, *109*, *111*
Stewart, N., 410, 412, *431*
Stewart, S. L., 16, 45, 48, 222, 277, 287, 288, 290, 293, 295, 296, *302*, *306*, *307*
Stewart, S. M., 43, *59*
Stewart, S., 292, *302*
Stewart-Berghauer, G., *193*
Stieglitz, E., 530, *534*
Stierlin, H., 560, *570*
Stiffman, A. R., 248, 255, *275*
Still, G. F., 64, 69, 75, 95, *111*
Stipek, D. J., 171, *195*
Stiver, I. P., 557, *568*
Stoddard, F. J., 253, *275*
Stoetter, B., *451*
Stoff, D. M., *146*
Stokes, A., 442, 444, 450, *454*
Stokes, P., 169, *193*
Stokes, T. F., 69, *105*, 594, *600*
Stoller, R., 510, *536*
Stolorow, R. D., 285, *307*
Stolz, L. M., 296, *307*
Stone, A., 287, *303*
Stone, M. E., 465, *485*, 585, *596*
Stone, M. H., 286, *307*
Stone, N., 501, *536*
Stone, P., 147, 588, *599*
Stone, W. L., 284, *304*, 321, 332, *338*
Stoner, G., 68, *109*
Stones, M., 509, *536*
Stoolmiller, M., 175, *193*
Storck, M., 261, *270*
Stouthamer-Loeber, M., 81, 91, *105*, *108*, 116, 136, 138, *146*, *147*, *148*, *149*

Strada, M. E., 590, *598*
Strage, A., 480, *490*
Strain, P. S., 303, 333, *338*
Strain, P., *429*
Straker, G., 501, *536*
Strandburg, R. J., 351, *358, 360*
Strang, J. D., 424, 425, *433, 434*
Strassberg, Z., 5, *59*, 523, 525, *536*
Straus, M. A., 514, 530, *534, 536*
Strauss, A. A., 65, *111*, 393, *434*
Strauss, C. C., 47, *56*, 175, 176, *190, 194*, 197, 198, 200, 202, 204, 206, 207, 209, 211, 219, 220, 224, 233, 231, 232, *235, 236, 238, 240*, 284, *303, 307*
Strayer, D. L., 318, *337*
Streissguth, A. P., 99, *111*, 384, *388*
Strelau, J., 221, *240*
Streuning, E. L., *188*
Strick, P. L., 449, *450*
Striegel-Moore, R. H., 551, 557, 558, 561, *570*
Strober, M., 89, 157, 166, *194*, 554, 555, 556, 557, 560, 561, 562, 564, *570*
Strom, K. J., 528, *536*
Stromgren, E., *360*
Strupp, K., 326, *338*
Stryker, S., 65, *111*
Stuart, G. L., 480, *487*
Stuart, G. W., *568*
Stubbe, D. E., 354, *360*
Stuber, M. L., 252, 253, *275*
Studdert-Kennedy, M., 402, *430*
Stuebing, K. K., 10, *54*
Stunkard, A. J., 542, 560, *570*
Stunkard, A., 547, *570*
Sturgeon, D., 355, *359*
Sturges, J. W., 591, *596*
Sturm, C., 418, *428*
Sturm, L., 585, *596*
Sturm, R., 98, *102*
Stuss, D. T., 69, 95, *111*
Subotnick, K., *359*
Sudhalter, V., 382, *385*
Sudler, N., 179, *191*
Suelzle, M., 376, *388*
Suess, G. J., 478, 481, 487, *490, 491*
Sugar, M., 267, 268, *275*, 468, 469, *490*
Sugarman, D. B., 20, *53*
Sugarman, S., 313, *338*
Sugiyama, T., 326, *338*
Sullivan, H. S., 279, *307*
Sullivan, J., 92, *104*
Sullivan, M., 80, *109*
Sullivan, R. C., 319, *338*
Sun, Y., 277, *302*
Sundelin, C., 465, *486*
Suomi, S. J., 49, 223, *240*, 476, *490*
Super, C., 376, *388*
Surrey, J. L., 557, *568*
Surwillo, W., 448, *454*
Susman, E. L., 135, *149*
Sussman, L., 221, *236*
Suster, A., *486*

Sutker, P. B., 115, 124, *145, 146, 147, 148, 149*, 305
Sutton, J. P., 423, 425, *430*
Sutton, S., *271*
Suwanlert, S., 11, 13, 14, *59, 60, 241*, 300, *307*
Suzuki, K., 563, *568*
Svennerholm, L., 328, *336*
Sverd, J., *104*, 449, *454*
Swain, B., 565, *570*
Swanson, H. L., 41, *52*, 431, 432, *434*
Swanson, J. M., 67, *108, 112, 148*, 338
Swanson, J., 93, *107, 143, 149*
Swartz, C., *429*
Swartz, M., 261, *270, 601*
Swearingen, M., 594, *600*
Swedo, S. E., 204, 206, 207, 217, 220, *235, 238, 239, 240*, 443, 448, *453, 454*
Sweeney, J. E., 411, *434*
Sweeney, L., 172, 173, *195*
Sweeney, M. D., 562, *568*
Sweet, R. D., 448, *454*
Sweet, R., 439, 447, *452, 454*
Swerdlow, N. R., 449, *454*
Swilley, J., 465, *485*, 585, *596*
Szalai, J., 169, *191*
Szasz, T. S., 7, 8, *59*
Szatmari, P., 47, *52, 57, 59*, 81, 83, 84, 85, 90, 93, 101, *111, 192, 193*, 322, 325, 326, *338, 339*
Szekely, G. A., 327, *338*
Szmuckler, G. I., 551, *570*
Szumowski, E. K., 15, *59, 67*, 86, 87, *104, 110*
Szymanski, L. S., 381, *387*

Taborelli, A., 421, *427*
Tabrizi, M., 157, 159, *188, 193*
Tager-Flusberg, H., 315, 316, 317, *337, 339*
Tallal, P., 402, 418, *434*
Tallmadge, J., 91, *111*
Talovic, S. A., *359*
Tamminga, C. A., *334*
Tamplin, A., 298, *303*
Tanenbaum, R. L., *191, 194*
Tanguay, P. E., 341, 349, *334, 360*
Tannenbaum, T. E., *146*
Tannenhauser, M. T., 394, *428*
Tanner, C. M., 449, *452*
Tannock, R., 67, 69, 70, 89, *110, 111*
Tantum, D., 322, *339*
Tanzman, M. S., 410, *435*
Tarjan, G., 378, *385*
Tarnow, J. D., *600*
Tarnowski, K. J., 466, *488*, 501, 513, *531*
Tartaglini, A., 527, *531*
Tarter, R. E., 517, *536*
Tarullo, L. B., 23, *59*, 178, 181, *194*
Tarver-Behring, S., 91, 92, *111*
Tast, D., *104*
Taylor, C. B., 237, 262, *270*
Taylor, C. M., 250, *273, 275*

Taylor, D., 478, *485, 570*
Taylor, E. A., 94, *105*
Taylor, E., 65, 81, 86, 87, 88, 89, 90, 91, 92, 93, *109, 110, 111*, 452, *491*
Taylor, H. G., 93, *109*
Taylor, J. L., 200, *238*
Taylor, L., 37, 38, *51*
Taylor, N., 315, *338*
Taylor, R. L., 372, *388*
Taylor, W. R., 586, *599*
Teasdale, J. D., 171, 186, *186, 194*, 228, 234, 259, *269*
Teasdale, T. W., *360*
Teicher, M. H., 169, *194*
Telch, C. F., 548, 550, *566, 570*
Tellegen, A., 19, *54, 273*
Tems, C. L., 43, *59*
Tenke, C. E., 527, *531*
Terdal, L. G., 4, 29, 30, 31, 49, 51, *51, 57, 235, 537*
Terr, L. C., 45, *59*, 243, 247, 248, 252, 253, 255, 256, 259, 275, 468, 469, 470, *490*, 492, 497, 498, 505, *536*
Tesiny, E. P., 179, *192*
Teti, D. M., 12, *54*, 177, 178, 186, 189, *194*
Teti, L. O., 44, *53*
Thach, B. T., 93, *111*
Thaler, M., 463, *488*
Thatcher, R. W., 330, *334*
The New York Times, 113, *148*
Thelen, E., *489*
Thomas, A., 19, 35, 48, *59*, 444, *454*
Thomas, C. B., 29, *52*
Thomas, C., 118, 121, *147*
Thomas, H., *57, 192, 193*
Thomas, K. A., 594, *601*
Thomas, P., 17, *59*
Thomassin, L., 284, *301*
Thompson, L. A., 116, *145*
Thompson, L., 98, *105*
Thompson, M. E., 411, 414, *434*
Thompson, M., 91, *110*
Thompson, N. M., 10, *54*
Thompson, R. A., 44, 45, *59*, 291, *307*
Thompson, R. H., 592, *601*
Thompson, R. J., 466, *489*, 584, 588, 597, 599, *601*
Thompson, R., *532*
Thomson, G. O. B., *111*
Thorley, G., 81, 93, 94, *105, 110, 111*
Thorn, B., *333*
Thyer, B. A., 204, 217, 228, 232, 233, *241*
Timmer, F. C., *601*
Tingey, C., *388*
Tinsley, B., 284, *301*
Tizard, B., 470, *490*
Tizard, J., 10, *58*, 130, *148*, 218, *240*, 249, 274, 380, *388, 454*
Tobin, D. L., 560, *570*
Todak, G., *193*
Todd, R. D., 168, *194*
Tolan, P. H., 11, 17, *54, 59*
Tolan, W., 478, *488*

Tomakowsky, J., 595, *596*
Tomasini, L., 478, *488*
Tomlinson-Keasey, C., *106*
Tompson, M. C., 345, 350, 353, 354, 356, *358, 360*
Tompson, M., 179, 181, *187*
Toner, B. B., 562, 563, *570*
Tonry, M., *147*
Toomey, F., 422, *431*
Topol, D., *453*
Toren, P., *360*
Torgersen, S., 5, 38, 46, 47, 48, 49, 59, 229, 230, *234, 241*
Torgesen, J. K., 69, *111*, 391, 392, 393, 395, 396, 397, 400, 402, 405, 406, 416, *431, 433, 435*
Tosk, J. M., *104*
Toth, S. L., 52, 56, 57, *186, 306*, *335, 485, 488, 500, 501, 502, 532, 536*
Tourette Syndrome Association, *450*
Touyz, S., 549, *566*
Towbes, L. C., 175, *189*
Towbin, K. E., *240*
Towle, V. R., 409, *433*
Towns, K., 531, *535*
Townsend, J., 17, *53*
Townsend, J. P., *335*
Tracy, K., 592, *599*
Tranel, D., 331, *337*
Treboux, D., *491*
Treder, R., *192*
Treiman, R., 416, *428, 434, 435*
Tremblay, R. E., 12, *59, 145*
Trent, S. C., 365, *385*
Trepper, T. S., *533*
Trestman, R. L., 286, *305*
Trickett, P. K., 260, *270*, 512, *536*
Trimble, M., 452, *454*
Trites, R. L., 83, 84, 85, *111*, 414, *428*
Trocme, N., 519, *536*
Trommer, B. L., 94, *111*
Tronick, E., 178, *188, 192*
Trott, G., 345, *360*
Trull, T. J., 286, *307*
Trupin, E. W., 80, *108*, 281, *304*
Truskowsky, M., 464, *490*
Truss, T. J., 391, *429, 430, 434*
Trzepacz, P. T., 510, 513, *536*
Tsai, L. Y., 316, 327, 329, *335, 339*
Tseng, W. S., *304*
Tsuang, M. T., 80, 81, *103, 104, 105*, 137, *145, 359, 454*
Tsunematsu, N., 376, *388*
Tucker, D., 5, 36, *53*
Tucker, D. M., *450*
Tucker, J. S., *106*
Tucker, S. B., 68, *109*
Tuff, L., 322, *338*
Tullis, C., 442, *453*
Tuma, A. H., 213, 237, *240*
Tuma, J., 198, *241*
Tunali-Kotoski, B., *336*
Turbott, S. H., 93, *109*
Turkal, I. D., 286, *307*
Turner, J. E., 182, 183, *188, 194*

Turner, S. M., 198, 220, 221, 222, 229, 230, 232, *235, 239, 241*
Turovsky, J., 225, *235*
Turpin, R., 363, *387*
Twardosz, S., 592, *601*
Twentyman, C. T., 258, *270*, 499, 503, 511, 512, *531, 534, 536*
Twomey, J., *189, 193, 194*

U.S. Advisory Board on Child Abuse and Neglect, 9, *59*, 494, *536*
U.S. Bureau of the Census, 11, *59*
U.S. Department of Education, 390, *435*
U.S. Department of Health and Human Services, 492, 508, 518, 519, *536*, 594, *601*
U.S. General Accounting Office, 9, *59*
U.S. Office of Education, 397, 406, 423, *435*
Udwin, O., 374, *388*
Ullman, D. G., 67, 68, *103*
Ulrich, R. F., 66, *106*
Unger, H. T., 517, *535*
Ungerer, J. A., 312, 313, 314, 315, 317, *337, 338, 339*
Unzner, L., 478, *487*
Urquiza, A. J., 506, *533*
Ursano, R. J., 242, 243, 253, *275*
Ussery, T., 183, *190*
Usuda, S., 327, *336*
Uzgiris, I., *385*

Vaasen, M., 422, *431*
Vaidya, A. F., *237*
Valenstein, E., *433*
Valenzuela, M., 464, *490*, 503, *536*
Valez, C. N., 219, *241*
Valleni-Basile, Garrison, C. Z., 206, 218, 219, 220, 231, *241*
Valoski, A., 556, *567*
Van Acker, R., 11, *54*, 322, 323, *339*
van Aken, M. A. G., 293, *301*
van de Wetering, B. J. M., *453*
van den Hout, M. A., 233, *241*
van den Oord, E. J. C. G., 97, *111*
van der Ende, J., 32, 33, *59*, 167, *194*
van der Hart, O., 258, *275*
van der Kolk, B. A., 242, 255, 258, 260, 266, *271, 272, 275*, 516, 517, *534, 536*
Van Der Lee, J. J., *601*
van der Meere, J. P., 69, *110*
van der Molen, G. M., 233, *241*
Van Der Vlugt, H., 412, 413, *435*
van Dieren, A. C., 233, *241*
Van Duijn, H., *271*
Van Hasselt, V. B., *303, 306*
Van Horn, Y., *146*
van Huijzen, C., 449, *453*
van IJzendoorn, M. H., 464, 475, 476, 477, 479, *484, 490, 491*
Van Kammen, W. B., 132, *146, 147*
Van Nguyen, T., 287, *302*, 476, *486*
van Praag, H. M., *145*
Van Wort, M. H., 439, *454*

Vandenberg, B., 290, *306*
Vandereycken, W., 561, *568, 569*
Vargas, L. A., 350, *359*
Vargo, M., 268, *272*
Varni, J. W., 587, 588, 595, *601*
Vary, M. G., *272*
Vasey, M. W., 41, *59*, 202, 232, 233, *241*
Vaughan, B. C., 581, 583, *601*
Vaughn, B. E., 478, *491*
Vaughn, C., 354, *359*
Vaughn, H. G., 330, *337*
Vaughn, S., *431, 433*
Vaux, A., 93, *111*
Vega-Lahr, N., 593, *597*
Velez, C. N., 12, 13, *59*, 84, *111, 188*
Vellutino, F. R., 405, 410, 416, *435*
Venter, A., 325, *339*
Verbaten, M. N., 31, *59*
Verduyn, D. M., 463, *487*
Verhulst, F. C., 10, 11, 32, 33, 50, *59*, 97, *111*, 167, *194*, 220, *241*, 446, *454*, 580, *601*
Vernon, D. T. S., 592, *601*
Vernon, M. D., 411, *435*
Vernon, P., *369, 388*
Veronen, L. J., 259, *275*
Vertommen, H., 561, *569*
Vessotskie, J. M., *453*
Vietze, P. M., 382, 385, 465, *484*
Vignolo, L. A., 421, *427*
Viken, R. J., 39, 40, *59*
Vincent, J. P., *275*
Vinogradov, S., 382, *386*
Vitale, A., *450*
Vitiello, A. B., 212, *241*
Vitulano, L., 530, *534*
Vivian, D., 85, *109*
Vladar, K., *451*
Voelker, S. L., 69, *111*
Voeller, K. K. S., 69, *107*
Volkmar, F. R., 312, 319, 323, 324, 325, 327, 328, *335, 339*, 345, 355, *360, 380, 388*, 470, *491*
Vondra, J. A., 511, *536*
Voogd, J., 449, *453*
Vorhies, L., 286, *302*
Vosk, B., 284, *307*
Vygotsky, L. S., 73, *111*

Wachsmuth, R., 68, *104*
Wada, K., 85, *107*
Waddell, M. T., 229, *236*
Wadden, R., *570*
Wadden, T. A., 560, *570*
Wagner, R. K., 402, 405, 416, *435*
Wagner, W., 506, *537*
Wahler, R. G., 138, 139, 141, *144, 149*
Wahlsten, D., 476, *491*
Waite, R. R., 221, *240*
Wakefield, J. C., 15, *59*, 83, *111*, 122, 128, *143, 149*
Wakeling, A., 551, *568*
Walchter, D., 85, *108*
Wald, E. R., *454*

Walden, T., 314, *339*
Walder, L. O., 137, *146*
Waldman, I. D., 32, *56*, 68, *102*, *106*, 132, *147*, 231, *238*
Waldman, W. H., 463, *491*
Waldstein, G., *388*
Walk, A., 341, *360*
Walker, C. E., 8, 16, 46, *58*, *59*, *60*, 239, 573, 580, 581, 582, 583, *596*, *597*, *598*, *599*, *601*
Walker, D., *453*
Walker, D. E., 437, 438, *451*, *453*
Walker, D. K., 80, *109*
Walker, E. F., *189*, 350, *358*, *360*
Walker, E., 186, *189*, 514, 516, *532*, *536*
Walker, H., *429*
Walker, H. M., *303*
Walker, J. L., 132, 134, *149*, 481, *487*
Walker, L. S., 268, *275*, 580, *601*
Walker, L., *531*, *533*
Walkup, J. T., 442, *452*, *453*, *454*
Wall, S., 313, *334*, 405, *431*, 477, *484*
Wallace, C., *359*
Wallace, M., *486*
Wallander, J. L., 93, *111*, 573, 587, *587*, 588, *597*, *598*, *599*, *601*
Wallen, N. E., 394, *428*
Waller, G., 561, *566*, *570*
Waller, J. L., *241*
Waller, T. G., *432*
Walsh, B. T., *195*, *241*, 548, *570*, *571*
Walsh, D., *359*
Walsh, K., 382, *386*
Walter, B. R., *241*
Walters, A. S., 328, *339*
Walters, E. E., 545, 546, 555, 564, *570*
Walton, W. W., 593, *601*
Wang, P., 374, *385*
Wannon, M. 276
Warburton, D. M., *272*
Warburton, R., 93, *104*
Ward, L. G., 171, 175, *194*
Ward, M. J., 475, *489*, *491*
Ware, L., *487*
Warne, V., *194*
Warner, J. E., 584, *601*
Warner, V., 212, *239*
Warnke, A., 345, *360*
Warren, R., 219, *241*
Warrenburg, S., 330, *335*
Warrington, E. K., 317, *334*, 411, *430*, *432*
Wartner, U. G., 478, 481, *487*, *491*
Wasileski, T., *429*
Wasserman, A. A., 171, *195*
Wasserman, A. L., 580, *601*
Wasserstein, S., 211, *240*
Waterman, J., 499, *531*
Waters, E., 22, *59*, *145*, 291, *304*, *305*, *307*, 313, *334*, 475, 477, *484*, *488*, *489*, *491*, 511, 512, *536*
Watkins, A., 372, *387*
Watkins, J. M., 349, 350, *358*, *360*
Watkins, L. R., 573, *598*

Watrous, B. G., 300, *307*
Watson, B. U., 410, 412, 414, 415, 429, 431, 435
Watson, D., 224, *241*
Watson, J. B., 197, *241*
Watson, L., 314, *335*
Watt, N. F., 285, *307*
Waxler, C. Z., 298, *307*
Waychik, J., *486*
Wayland, K. K., 43, *56*
Weaver, P. A., *430*
Weaver, T. L., 517, *536*
Webb, N. B., *485*
Webb, T., *271*
Weber, G., 560, *570*
Weber, J., *453*
Wechsler, V., 259, *276*
Weddle, K., 592, *601*
Weeks, S. J., *314, 339*
Wehman, P., 377, *388*
Weigel, C., 255, 262, 263, 267, *275*
Wein, S. J., 179, *187*
Weinberger, D. R., 345, 349, 350, *360*, 442, 447, *452*, *453*
Weinberger, E., 550, *569*
Weiner, J. M., *238*
Weiner, W. J., 449, *452*, *454*
Weinert, F., *486*
Weintraub, S., 53, 285, *304*, *305*
Weisath, L., 251, *275*
Weiselberg, M., 93, *109*, *110*
Weisner, T., 376, *386*
Weiss, B., 125, *149*, 157, 171, *189*, *194*, *195*, *241*, 300, *307*, 374, *389*
Weiss, G., 66, 67, 77, 86, 87, 89, 90, 94, 95, *103*, *104*, *108*, *110*, *111*
Weiss, R. V., 9, 24, *57*
Weiss, S. R., 553, *568*
Weiss-Perry, M., 373, *385*
Weissberg, R. P., *301*, *306*
Weissbluth, M., 462, *491*
Weissman, M. M., 159, 166, 177, 178, *193*, *194*, 196, 198, 212, *239*
Weissman, W., 517, *535*
Weist, M. D., 293, *305*
Weisz, J. R., 11, 13, 14, *56*, *59*, *60*, 125, *149*, 170, 171, 172, 173, 175, *186*, *190*, *193*, *194*, *195*, 222, *241*, 300, *307*, 373, 374, *389*
Weizman, A., *241*, *360*, *450*
Wekerle, C., 9, 18, 80, *103*, 211, *235*, 494, 501, 505, 517, 530, 531, *536*, *537*, 583, 584, *601*
Welch, S. L., 541, 546, *567*
Weldy, S., 508, *534*
Weller, E., *489*
Weller, E. B., 169, *195*
Weller, R. A., 169, *195*
Wellman, H. M., 317, *339*
Wells, E., 52
Welner, A., 91, *111*, 297, *307*
Welner, Z., 91, 97, *111*, 297, *307*
Welsh, J. D., 12, *60*, 178, *191*
Welsh, M. C., 69, *111*
Welsh, M., 319, *337*, 404, *433*
Welsh, R. J., 98, *107*

Weltzin, T. E., 553, 554, 562, *569*
Wendelboe, M., 327, *336*
Werle, M., *596*
Werner, E. E., 10, 12, 19, 20, *60*, 262, 267, *275*
Werner, H., 372, *389*, *393*, *434*
Wernicke, C., 392, *435*
Werry, J. S., 67, 68, 83, 91, *111*, *148*, 198, *241*, 341, 344, 345, 346, 355, 356, 357, 359, 360, 361
Werry, J., 280, *303*, *305*
Werthamer-Larsson, L., 16
Wertlieb, D., 255, 262, 267, *275*
Wessel, M. A., 462, 463, *491*
Wesson, L., 580, *599*
West, R. F., 410, 416, *434*, *435*
Westen, D., 492, *536*
Weston, D. R., 478, *488*
Wetherby, A., 314, *339*
Wetzles, R., *453*
Wexler, B. E., 443, *454*
Whalen, C. K., 91, 93, *111*, *112*
Wheeler, V. A., 284, *301*
Whissell, C., 531, *534*
Whitaker, A., 163, 164, 165, *195*, 206, 219, 235, 236, *241*
Whitaker, H. A., *431*
White, B., *359*
White, J. L., 129, 133, *149*
White, K. J., 43, *56*
White, P. J., 463, *491*
Whitehouse, A. M., 552, *569*
Whitehurst, G. J., *303*
Whitesell, N. R., 182, *190*
Whitington, P. F., 580, *601*
Whitman, L., *387*
Whitmore, E. A. W., 499, *536*
Whitmore, K., 10, *58*, 130, *148*, 218, *240*, 249, *274*, 380, *388*, *454*
Whittinghill, J. R., 134, *149*
Wick, P., 284, *304*
Wickman, E. K., 285, *307*
Wickramarante, P., *194*
Wicks, J., 159, *194*
Widiger, T. A., 32, 33, *60*, 213, *236*, 286, *302*, *307*
Widom, C. S., *512*, *514*, 517, 518, *530*, *535*, *536*, *537*
Widom, K. S., 138, *149*
Wieder, S., 30, *54*, 460, 461, 462, 467, *487*
Wiederholt, J. L., 391, 405, *435*
Wierzbicki, M., 168, 174, 176, *195*, 284, *307*
Wiig, E. H., 402, *435*
Wikler, L., 376, *389*
Wilcox, K. T., 587, *601*
Wilfley, D. E., *566*
Wilk, J. E., 560, *570*
Wilkenheiser, M., 445, *451*
Wilkinson, M., 178, *194*, 297, *306*
Willerman, L., 47, *60*, 98, *112*
Willey, R., 264, *273*
Willi, H., 382, *388*
Williams, D. A., 588, *597*
Williams, D. T., *239*

Williams, J. B. W., 286, *307*
Williams, L. L., 41, *59*
Williams, L. M., 256, *273*, 504, *534*
Williams, M., *358*
Williams, R. A., 184, *188*
Williams, R. M., 255, *276*
Williams, R., 260, *272*
Williams, S. L., 262, *270*
Williams, S., 11, *51*, 79, 91, 98, *108*, *109*, *110*, 130, *144*, *147*, *148*, 164, 171, *187*, *192*, 196, 235, 239, *304*, 409, *434*
Williamson, D. E., *187*, *189*, *193*, *194*
Williamson, P., 169, *191*
Willis, D. J., 46, *60*, *532*
Willis, T. J., 95, *112*
Willis, W. G., 392, 410, 411, 414, 415, 416, *430*
Wills, T. A., 287, *302*
Wilmore, J. H., *571*
Wilsher, C., 414, *434*
Wilson, A., 138, *145*
Wilson, B. C., 411, *435*
Wilson, D. J., 221, *241*
Wilson, D. M., *237*
Wilson, G. T., 542, 543, 546, 549, 550, 552, 556, 559, 562, 563, 565, 566, *566*, *567*, 569, *570*, *571*
Wilson, J. P., 243, 245, 251, 253, 270, 271, *272*, *275*
Wilson, P. G., *388*
Wilson, S. A. K., *453*
Wilson, S. K., 242, 263, 272, *275*
Wilson, S., *275*
Wilson, V. L., *601*
Wilson, W. E., 299, *305*
Windsor, J., 404, *432*
Wing, L., 315, 319, 323, 325, 326, 332, *339*
Wing, R. R., 550, 556, 567, 569, 594, *570*, *596*
Wingard, D. L., *106*
Winget, C., 245, *272*
Winslow, E. B., 586, *600*
Winsten, N. E., 517, *536*
Winters, R. W., 466, *488*
Wise, B., 404, *432*
Wish, E., 91, *111*
Wittchen, H. -U., *238*, 562, *569*
Wittenborn, J. R., *358*
Wittrock, M. C., *433*
Woerner, M. G., 285, *305*
Wohl, M. K., 584, *600*
Wojnilower, D. A., 590, *597*
Wolchik, S. S., 560, *568*
Wolf, A. W., 467, *488*
Wolf, M., 416, *428*, *435*
Wolfe, D. A., 9, 11, 18, 57, *60*, 242, 259, 263, 268, *272*, *275*, *276*, 492, 494, 495, 498, 500, 501, 503, 504, 505, 506, 510, 511, 512, 516, 517, 518, 520, 521, 522, 523, 526, 527, 529, 530, 531, *535*, *536*, *537*, 583, 584, *601*

Wolfe, V. V., 259, 260, 275, *276*, 503, 504, 505, 506, 510, 514, 537, *596*
Wolff, R., 207, *241*
Wolfson, S., 212, *241*
Wolin, S. J., 99, *103*
Wolman, B. B., *56*
Wolman, M. B., 65, *107*
Wonderlich, S. A., 285, *305*
Wong, B. Y. L., 419, *428*, *431*, *433*, *435*, *435*
Wong, D. F., 449, *454*
Wood, F. B., 90, *112*, 399, 404, 410, 418, *435*
Wood, K., 551, *568*
Woodbury, M. A., 575, *601*
Woodbury, M., *52*, *187*
Woodson, R., 313, *335*
Woodward, C. A., 57, *192*, *193*
Woody, E., 284, 288, *303*
Woody, R. C., 350, *361*
Wooley, S. C., 542, *567*
Woolston, J. L., 465, *491*
Woolston, J., 584, *601*
Worchel, F. F., 595, *601*
Work, W. C., 262, *276*
World Health Organization, 21, 23, 28, *60*, 81, 82, *112*, 123, *149*, 154, 155, 158, *195*, 197, 201, 203, 205, 208, 210, 215, *241*, 243, 245, 246, *276*, 280, 283, *307*, 320, 321, *339*, 341, *361*, 365, 367, *389*, 397, 398, 406, 407, 420, 423, 424, *435*, 438, 440, *454*, 465, *491*, 543, 544, 546, *571*, 574, 576, 577, 578, 579, 581, 582, 585, 587, *601*
Worthman, B., 465, *485*
Wortman, C., 198, *236*
Wozencraft, T., 506, *537*
Wozniak, J., *104*
Wren, F., *194*
Wright, C., 176, 180, *189*
Wu, D. Y. H., *304*
Wu, J. C., *334*
Wunder, J., *191*, *238*
Wung, P., 116, 129, *147*
Wurtele, S. K., 594, *601*
Wyatt, B., *486*
Wyatt, G. E., 511, *533*, *535*, *537*
Wyman, P. A., 262, 267, 268, *276*
Wynne, L. C., 353, *360*
Wyshogrod, D., 550, *569*
Wysocki, T., 588, *601*

Yager, T., 10, *52*, 219, *235*
Yahr, M. D., *454*
Yamada, E. M., *112*
Yamada, J. E., 374, *389*
Yamada, K., 563, *568*
Yang, E., *335*
Yang, V., 443, *451*
Yanovski, J. A., *571*
Yanovski, S. Z., 549, 550, 559, 565, *571*
Yanovski, S., 546, *570*
Yaremko, J., 462, *484*

Yarrow, L. J., *490*
Yarrow, M. R., 298, *307*
Yaryura-Tobias, J., 443, *454*
Yasuda, P., 252, *275*
Yates, C., *427*
Yates, J. L., 260, *276*
Yazgan, Y., 443, 448, *454*
Yeager, C. A., *147*
Yeager, C., 530, *534*
Yeager, T. D., 465, *484*
Yeates, K., 374, *389*
Yeaton, W. H., 594, *601*
Yee, D. K., 551, *567*
Yeh, C. J., 562, *568*
Yehuda, R., 260, *276*
Yeung-Courchesne, R., 328, 329, *335*, *336*
Yirmiya, N., 314, *336*
Yockey, W., *487*
Yogman, M., *531*
Yokley, J. M., 594, *601*
Yokoi, F., *454*
Yoran-Hegesh, R., *360*
Yorkston, N., 287, *303*
Yoshii, F., *429*
Yoshinaga, K., 324, *336*
Yost, L. W., 171, *192*
Young, A. B., 448, *450*
Young, J. G., 328, 339, 437, 441, *454*, *567*
Youngblade, L., 476, *485*, 530, *531*
Younger, A. J., 288, 292, *307*
Ysseldyke, J. E., 397, *435*
Yu, W. M., *566*
Yule, B., *149*
Yule, W., *149*, 221, 236, 255, 260, 272, *276*, 374, 380, 388, 409, *433*
Yung, B., *454*
Yurgelun-Todd, D., 564, *568*
Yuwiler, A., 327, *335*

Zagar, R., 68, *112*
Zahen, T., *359*
Zahn, T. P., 68, *112*, 146, *240*
Zahn-Waxler, C., 12, *60*, 69, *104*, 131, *149*, 178, *194*, 287, *307*
Zahn-Waxler, E. C., 297, *306*
Zahner, G., 354, *360*
Zak, L., 242, 263, 272, *275*
Zakis, S., 220, *239*
Zambarano, R. J., 296, *302*
Zametkin, A. J., 81, 96, *109*, *105*, *112*, *359*
Zamvil, L. S., 259, *276*
Zarate, R., 209, *234*
Zaskow, C., 590, *596*
Zastowny, T. R., 592, *601*
Zeanah, C. H., 58, 265, 274, 457, 464, 458, 468, 469, 470, 471, 472, *485*, *486*, *487*, *488*, 490, *491*, 502, 503, 531, *535*
Zedeck, S., 35, *54*
Zeitlin, H., 341, 345, 355, 356, *361*
Zelinsky, D., *387*
Zeman, J., 175, *189*

Zentall, S. S., 67, 68, 69, *112*
Zeremba-Berg, C., *236*
Zero to Three/National Center for Clinical Infant Programs, 28, 30, *60*, 457, 458, 459, 469, 471, *491*
Zgourides, G., 219, *241*
Zhang, Q., *56*
Ziegler, M., 447, *452*
Ziesel, S. H., 465, *486*
Zigler, E., 365, 369, 370, 372, 373, 374, 377, 378, 379, 383, *385, 386*, *387, 388, 389*, 445, *454*, 500, 517, 519, *531, 534*
Zigmond, N., 394, 395, 425, *432, 435*
Zimering, R. T., 260, *272*
Zimin, R., 580, *598*
Zimmerman, E. G., 324, 337, 355, *360*
Zimmerman, M. A., 19, *60*
Zimmerman, R., *569*
Zinbarg, R., 225, *239, 262, 271*
Zink, M., 580, *593, 599*
Zipf, W. B., 463, *489*
Ziv, A., 247, *276*
Zoccolillo, M., 11, *60*, 120, 125, 128, 130, 131, 134, *149*
Zohar, A. H., 218, *241, 450*
Zoll, D., 178, *192*, 478, *488*
Zonona, J., *388*
Zrull, J. P., 178, *193*
Zubin, J., 346, *358, 361*
Zucker, K. J., *270, 531*
Zupan, B. A., 114, *146*, 171, *190*

Subject Index

Abecedarian Project, 370
Academic functioning (*see* School performance)
Accident prevention, 593, 594
Accident proneness, 93, 94
Acute lymphoblastic leukemia, 589
Adaptational failure
  concept and definition, 22
  healthy functioning comparison, 15, 16
  psychopathology theme, 5, 22
Adoption studies, 47, 48
  attention-deficit/hyperactivity disorder, 97
  genetic paradigm, 47, 48
Adult Attachment Interview, 475, 479, 480
Affect regulation
  abused children, 515
  and depression, 175
Affect sensitivity, abused children, 501, 510
"Affectionless control," 230
Affective communication, 480
Affective models, 43–46
Affective numbing (*see* Numbing reactions)
Affective sharing, autism, 314
African-American children
  abuse and neglect, 518
  anxiety disorders, 220

attention-deficit/hyperactivity disorder, 85
depression, 165
eating disorders, 552
mental retardation, 365, 371, 372
phonological deficits, 404
posttraumatic stress disorder, 264, 265
problem behaviors, overview, 13
reading disabilities, 399, 404
Age differences, overview, 10, 11
Age of onset
  antisocial behavior, 122, 123
  attention-deficit/hyperactivity disorder, 79, 86, 87
  conduct disorder, 17, 122, 123, 136
  depression, 166
  obsessive–compulsive disorder, 206
  oppositional defiant disorder, 126
  tic disorders, 439–441
Aggression
  abused children, 500, 514
  and attachment quality, 139, 482, 483
  attention-deficit/hyperactivity disorder, 132, 133
  and cognitive distortion, 139, 140
  depression comorbidity, 161
  and disorganized attachment, 482, 483
  gender differences, 129–131

intergenerational transmission, 473, 474
internalizing disorders relationship, 134, 135
peer group influences, 141
psychobiology, 135–137
psychopathology dimension, 24, 25
risk factors, infancy, 481, 483
and social withdrawal, 285
subtypes, 115, 116
Agoraphobia, and panic disorder, 212, 213, 215
Alcohol use/abuse
  abused children, 516, 517
  eating disorders comorbidity, 562–564
  parents of ADHD children, 92
Ambivalent attachment profile, 477–479
American Association on Mental Retardation
  founding of, 362
  mental retardation definition, 365–368, 383
Amnesic syndrome, autism, 317
Amygdala
  autism, 329–332
  hippocampal interaction, 331, 332
  social cognition role, 331, 332
Anger, abused children, 509
Animal models, autism, 329

Animal phobia, 207, 209
Anorexia nervosa
   adolescent developmental factors,
      558
   affective disorders comorbidity,
      562, 563
   binge eating/purging subtype, 543
   biology, 553
   clinical characteristics, 548
   comorbidity, 562, 563
   cultural variations, 552, 553
   developmental course/prognosis,
      549, 550
   diagnostic criteria, 543, 544
   epidemiology, 551–553
   etiology, 553–562
   family role, 560–562
   gender differences, 551, 552, 557,
      558
   genetics, 554, 555
   medical complications, 548
   and obsessive–compulsive disorder,
      562
   personality characteristics, 560
   prevention, 565, 566, 594
   psychopathology, 548
   restricting subtype, 543
   sexual abuse outcome, 517
   sociocultural pressures, 557, 558
   and substance abuse, 562
   treatment, 566
Antisocial behavior
   academic underachievement, 133,
      134
   age of onset, 122, 123
   coercion theory, 138, 139
   comorbidity, 131–135
   contextual factors, 140, 141
   definitional criteria, 118–124
   definitional terminology, 114, 115
   dimensional versus categorical
      issue, 116–118
   gender differences, 129–131
      long-term outcome, 131
   heterotypic continuity, 125, 126, 128
   intergenerational transmission, 517,
      518
   and internalizing disorders, 134, 135
   peer group influences, 141
   physically abused children, 514,
      517, 518
   prevalence, 124, 125
   social information processing, 139,
      140
   subtypes, 115, 116
Antisocial personality disorder
   definitional criteria, 119
   DSM-IV criteria, 124
   progression from conduct disorder,
      128, 129
Anxiety, and behavioral inhibition, 48,
   49
Anxiety disorders
   attention-deficit/hyperactivity
      disorder comorbidity, 89
   attachment quality, 230

behavioral inhibition model, 222–
   224, 283, 284
biological factors, 222–224
categorical versus dimensional
   classification, 213, 216
cognitive factors, 224–228
comorbidity, 231–233
conduct disorder comorbidity, 134
control-related factors, 225–228
cultural factors, 221, 222
depression comorbidity, 160, 233
developmental course, 217, 218
DSM-IV problems, 216
eating disorders comorbidity, 562–
   564
epidemiology, 218–222
etiological models, 222–231
family factors, 228–231
gender differences, 220
genetics, 228–231
historical context, 196–198
prognosis, 217, 218
psychosocial factors, 224–228
and social withdrawal, 284
sociodemographic variables, 219,
   220
and stress, 225–228
Anxiety proneness, 223
Anxious depression
   chronicity, 167
   psychopathology dimension, 24, 25,
      158, 160
Appraisals, traumatic stressors, 258,
   259
Arithmetic skills disorder, 423–425
Arousal (see also Overarousal)
   and behavioral inhibition, 223
   conduct disorder mechanism, 136
   posttraumatic stress disorder, 497,
      498
Articulation disorders, 323
Asian children, PTSD, 264, 265
Asperger disorder, 322
   autism relationship, 322
   core symptoms, 322
Assertiveness skills
   depression, 174
   socially withdrawn children, 293, 294
Assortative mating, Tourette
   syndrome, 447
Athletes, eating disorders, 552
Atopic rhinitis, 4
Attachment relationship, 40, 41, 470–
   472, 475–481
   and aggression risk, 482, 483
   antisocial behavior link, 139
   anxiety disorders, 230
   autism, 312, 314
   caregiver role, 40
   clinical disorders of, 470–472
   depression, 177, 185, 186
   developmental aspects, 472
   disinhibited subtype, 470, 471
   disorganized/disoriented subtype,
      476–481
   DSM approach, 471, 472

failure to thrive, 464, 465
   inhibited subtype, 470, 471
   intergenerational transmission, 475,
      476
   key issues, 41
   and loss, 472
   neglected children, 503
   "pattern of organization" influence,
      17, 18
   patterns of, 477, 478
   physically abused children, 500, 501
   psychodynamic theory relationship,
      39
   and social cognition, abused
      children, 510, 511
   social withdrawal relationship, 290–
      292
   and temperament, 290, 291, 478
   theoretical aspects, 40, 41, 477–479
Attention-deficit/hyperactivity
   disorder, 63–112
   academic functioning, 90
   adult outcome, 86–88
   age of onset, 79, 80
   associated conditions, 88–94
   biological factors in, 94–99
   categorical versus dimensional
      approach, 80
   comorbidity, 89, 90, 132, 133, 442
   conduct disorder relationship, 132,
      133
   contextual effects, 21
   core symptoms, 322
   depression comorbidity, 161
   developmental aspects, 78, 79, 86–88
   DSM-IV criteria, 76–81
   environmental toxins, 98, 99
   epidemiology, 83–85
   ethnic/cultural issues, 85
   gender differences, 79, 84
   genetics, 97, 98
   historical context, 64–67
   ICD-10 criteria, 81, 82
   inattentive type, 99–101
   and intelligence, 90, 91
   medical risks, 93
   as mental disorder, 82, 83
   neurological factors, 95–97
   parent–child relations, 91–93
      and medication, 93
   physical abuse link, 499, 500
   prevalence, 83, 84
   and reading disability, 418
   socioeconomic differences, 84, 85
   theoretical framework, 69–76
Attention-deficit/hyperactive
   disorder—combined type, 76,
      78, 87, 99–101
Attention-deficit/hyperactive
   disorder—inattentive type, 76–
      78, 87, 99–101
Attentional problems
   in attention-deficit/hyperactivity
      disorder, 67
   childhood schizophrenia, 351
   psychopathology dimension, 24, 25

Attributional distortions
    abused children, 510, 511
    and aggressive behavior, 140
    depression, 171–173, 182
    stress interaction, depression, 182
    traumatic stress effects, 259, 260
Atypical autism, 323
Auditory hallucinations, depression, 157
Australian bushfire impact, 248, 249
Authoritarian parenting, 296–298
Authoritative parenting, 298
Autism Diagnostic Interview—Revised, 321, 322
Autism Diagnostic Observation Schedule, 320, 321
Autistic disorder, 311–339
    attachment quality, 312, 313
    autopsy studies, 329
    biochemical findings, 327, 328
    and childhood schizophrenia, 355
    cognitive ability, 316–319
    core symptoms, 312–319
    cultural factors, 326
    definitional/diagnostic issues, 320–324
    developmental course, 324, 325
    differential diagnosis, 323, 324
    DSM-IV, 320, 321
    early diagnosis, 332
    early intervention, 332, 333
    electroencephalography, 329, 330
    epidemiology, 325, 326
    etiology, 326–332
    event-related potentials, 330
    genetics, 326, 327
    high-functioning subtype, prognosis, 325
    historical context, 311, 312
    ICD-10 criteria, 320
    language impairments, 315, 316
    neuroanatomical findings, 328, 329
    neuropsychology, 330–332
    positron emission tomography, 329
    social class factors, 326
    socioemotional impairments, 3123–315
    subgroups, 332
    theory of mind, 317, 318
"Automatic processing," 525, 526
Autonomic reactivity
    and behavioral inhibition, 223
    conduct disorder mechanism, 136
Autopsy studies, autism, 329
Avoidant attachment profile, 477–479
Avoidant behavior (see also Social withdrawal)
    family studies, 230
    and separation anxiety disorder, 199, 200
    and specific phobias, 207
Avoidant personality disorder
    eating disorders comorbidity, 563, 565
    and social withdrawal, 286

"Battered child syndrome," 494
Behavior genetics, paradigm, 46, 47
Behavior therapy, bulimia nervosa, 550
Behavioral activation system, 136
Behavioral inhibition, 48, 49, 222–224
    anxiety risk factor, 48, 49, 22–224, 283, 284
    and attachment quality, 290, 291
    attention-deficit/hyperactivity disorder model, 70–76
    conduct disorder mechanism, 136
    heritability, 283
    paradigm of, 48, 49, 222–224
    phenotypes, 224
    physiology, 48, 223, 289
    predictive value, 224
    predictors of, 289
    and social withdrawal, 283, 284, 288–292
Behavioral problems (see also Conduct disorder)
    abused children, 500
    continuity, 17
    sex differences, overview, 12
Behavioral–systems approach, 573, 586, 587
Behavioral techniques
    mental retardation, 377
    surgery preparation programs, 592
Behavioral theories
    depression, 174–177
    health-related disorders, 573
Belief in a just world
    abused children, 509
    and traumatic stress, 259
Binge eating disorder, 541–571
    comorbidity, 565
    definitional issues, 542, 543
    diagnostic issues, 542, 543, 546–548
    dieting behavior, 559, 560
    epidemiology, 551
    episodes versus days issue, 548
    food consumption, 549
Binge-eating/purging anorexia subtype
    definition, 543
    overweight risk, 556, 557
    parental substance abuse, 557
    personality characteristics, 560
    psychopathology, 548
    substance abuse, 562
Bipolar disorder
    attention-deficit/hyperactivity disorder comorbidity, 89
    diagnostic features, 157
Birth complications
    schizophrenia, 352
    Tourette syndrome, 447, 448
Birth weight, 447, 448
Blood phobia, 209, 220
Body rocking, 438
Bone marrow aspirations, 591
Bone marrow transplant, 589, 590

Borderline personality disorder, 517
Brain damage
    attention-deficit/hyperactivity disorder, 97
    learning disabilities theory, 393
Brainstem abnormalities, schizophrenia, 350
Buffalo Creek dam collapse, 252, 263
Bulimia nervosa, 541–571
    and affective disorder, 564, 565
    binge definition, 545
    biology, 553, 554
    clinical characteristics, 548, 549
    comorbidity, 549, 563–565
    cultural variations, 552, 553
    developmental course/outcome, 550
    diagnostic issues, 543–546
    epidemiology, 551–553
    etiology, 553–562
    family role, 560–562
    gender differences, 551, 552, 557, 558
    genetics, 554, 555
    medical complications, 549
    nonpurging type, 543–546
    overweight history, 556, 557
    personality characteristics, 560
    prevention, 565, 566, 594
    psychopathology, 548, 549
    purging type, 543–546
    sexual abuse link, 517, 556
    and substance abuse, 563, 564
    treatment, 550, 566
Burn hydrotherapy, 591, 592

Cambodian refugees, 264, 265
Cancer, 589, 590, 595
Carbohydrate consumption, bulimia, 548, 549
Catecholamine levels, PTSD, 260
Categorical diagnostic approach, 28–32, 213, 216
    antisocial behavior, 116–118
    attention-deficit/hyperactivity disorder, 80
    anxiety disorders, 213, 216
    child maltreatment, 5219, 530
    conduct disorder, 116–118
    depression, 158
    disorders of infancy, 459
    DSM-IV system, 24, 26–30
    general issues, 28–32, 213, 216
    reading disabilities, 408, 409
Categorization ability, autism, 316, 317
Caudate nucleus, ADHD, 97
Center for Epidemiological Studies—Depression scores, 159
Cerebellar hypoplasia, autism, 328, 329
Cerebral blood flow, ADHD, 96
Cerebral cortex malformations, autism, 329
Chemotherapy, 589

Child abuse (*see* Child maltreatment)
Child–Adult Medical Procedure
    Interaction Scale, 591
Child Behavior Checklist, 31
Child Depression Inventory, 295
Child maltreatment, 492–537 (*see
    also* Child neglect; Physical
    abuse; Sexual abuse)
    adult outcome, 516–518
    antisocial behavior link, 138, 514
    attachment quality interaction, 510,
        511, 514
    betrayal dynamic, 513, 514
    categorical classification
        weaknesses, 529, 530
    child characteristics, 528, 529
    classification, 495
    cognitive development, 508–512
        outcome, 511, 512
    contextual factors, 20
    costs, 494
    definitions, 495, 496
    developmental consequences, 18,
        506–515
    developmental psychopathology
        model, 521, 522
    epidemiology, 9, 518, 519
    etiology, 522–529
    family context, 515, 516
    historical context, 493, 494
    intergenerational transmission, 517,
        518
    internal attributions, 510, 511
    medical problems, 583, 584
    parental characteristics, 523–528
    physical development, 508
    posttraumatic stress disorder
        model, 256, 257, 496–506
        theory, 520, 521
    prevention, 530, 531
    self-concept, 512, 513
    social cognition, 510, 511
    socioemotional development/
        outcome, 512–515
    survivor symptoms, 516–518
Child neglect, 502, 503, 507
    betrayal dynamics, 514
    child characteristics, 528, 529
    cognitive-behavioral development,
        503, 512
    depression, 502
    epidemiology, 518, 519
    failure to thrive, 502, 503
    medical problems, 583, 584
    moral reasoning, 499
    outcome, 20
    parental characteristics, 526, 527
    prevention, 530, 531
Child rearing (*see* Parenting)
Childhood Autism Rating Scale, 320
Childhood disintegrative disorder,
    323
Childhood schizophrenia, 340–361
    and autism, 324, 355
    biological factors, 349–352
    comorbidity, 354, 355

core symptoms, 343
cultural variation, 346
developmental issues, 344, 345
diagnostic issues, 344, 345
dopamine hypothesis, 350
DSM-IV criteria, 344
environmental stressors, 352, 353
epidemiology, 345, 346
etiologies, 348–354
genetics, 352
historical context, 341–343
imaging studies, 350
neurodevelopmental model, 349,
    350
outcome and prognostic factors,
    356, 357
pharmacological treatment, 355
psychosocial stress, 353, 354
psychosocial treatment, 355, 356
related symptoms, 344
sex differences, 345, 346
social class factors, 346
spectrum of, 345
theoretical framework, 346–348
vulnerability–stress model, 346–
    348
Chinese children
    cultural influences, 14
    shyness, 300
Chowchilla kidnapping, 247, 248
Chromosome 6, 418
Chronic illness, 586–595
Chronic motor/vocal tic disorder,
    438–440
Chronic stress, and trauma, 256, 257
Cigarette smoking, prevention, 594,
    595
Circadian rhythms, depression, 168,
    169
Classification, 26–33
    categorical approaches, 28–32
    comorbidity issue, 32, 33
    dimensional approaches, 31, 32
    overview, 26–33
Clinging behavior, abused children,
    514
Clozapine, 355
Coarticulation, 402, 403
"Code-emphasis" interventions, 416,
    418
Coercive behaviors
    and antisocial behavior, 138, 139,
        144*n*13
    risk factor, infancy, 482, 483
Cognitions Checklist, 172
Cognitive-behavioral theories, 42, 43
Cognitive-behavioral therapy
    bulimia nervosa, 550
    surgery preparation programs, 592
Cognitive deficits, 43
Cognitive development
    abused children, 499, 500, 508–
        512
    and disorganized attachment, 481
    neglected children, 503
    and trauma reactions, 266, 267

Cognitive distortions
    and aggressive behavior, 139, 140
    cognitive deficits distinction, 43
    depression, 165, 171, 173, 182, 183
    stress interaction, depression, 182,
        183
Cognitive impairments
    abused children, 511, 512
    attention-deficit/hyperactivity
        disorder, 69
    autism, 316–319
Cognitive mediation model, 182, 183
Cognitive schemata
    depression theory, 170, 171
    theory of, 42
Cognitive theories, 41–43
    anxiety disorders, 224–228
    depression, 170–173
        shortcomings, 173
    overview, 41–43
Cohort effects
    attention-deficit/hyperactivity
        disorder, 86
    depression, 163, 164
Colic, 461–464
    cry characteristics, 463, 464
    description of, 462
    developmental course, 462
    diagnostic considerations, 462
    epidemiology, 463
    etiology, 462, 464
Communication deviance, 353, 354
Communication disorders, 400
Comorbidity, 32, 33 (*see also under
    specific disorders*)
    anxiety disorders, 231, 233
    attention-deficit/hyperactivity
        disorder, 89, 90, 132, 133
    childhood schizophrenia, 354, 355
    and classification, 32, 33
    conduct disorder, 131–135
    depression, 160–162
    eating disorders, 548, 549, 562–565
    gender paradox, 12
    mental retardation, 380–384
Compliant behavior, abused children,
    500
Compulsions, and tic disorders, 438
"Compulsive compliance," 500
Concentration camps, 264, 265
Concentration difficulties, and
    trauma, 252
Concept formation, autism, 316, 317
Conditioning
    abused children, 520, 521
    in families, anxiety, 230
    and posttraumatic stress disorder,
        260, 261, 520, 521
Conduct disorder, 113–149 (*see also
    Externalizing problems*)
    academic underachievement, 133,
        134
    age of onset, 17, 122, 123, 126
    antisocial personality disorder link,
        128, 129
    attachment quality, 139, 482, 483

attention-deficit/hyperactivity
   disorder
   comorbidity, 89, 132, 133
   comorbidity, 131–135
   contextual factors, 140, 141
   continuity, 17
   definitional criteria, 118–124
   definitional terminology, 114, 115
   depression comorbidity, 161
   developmental progression, 125–
      129
      and gender, 130, 131
   dimensional versus categorical
      issue, 116–118
   DSM-IV criteria, 119–123
   etiologies, 135–142
   familial influences, 137–139
   gender differences, 129–131
      long-term outcome, 131
   heterotypic continuity, 125, 126
   ICD-10 criteria, 123, 124
   as mental disorder, 122
   oppositional disorder link, 126–128
   overt and covert symptomatology,
      121
   peer group influences, 141
   positive predictive power, 127, 128
   prevalence, 124, 125
   psychobiology, 135–137
   risk factors, infancy, 481–483
   social and environmental
      considerations, 121, 122
Conduction aphasia, 392
Conflict negotiation, 480
Confrontational communications, 69
Connecticut Longitudinal Study, 409
Constitutional models, overview, 46–
   49
Contextual factors, 20, 21
   antisocial behavior, 140, 141
   attention-deficit/hyperactivity
      disorder, 68
   conduct disorders, 121, 122, 140,
      141
   research findings, overview, 20, 21
"Contingency-shaped attention," 75
Continuous performance tests, 68
Control-related factors
   animal studies, 225
   anxiety disorders, 225–228
   depression, 171, 172
   and stress responsivity, 262
Conversational impairments, autism,
   315
Conversion disorder, 577, 578
Coping style
   depression, 175
   and surgery preparation, 593
Coprolalia
   age of onset, 440, 441
   definition, 437
Copropraxia, 437, 439
Corpus callosum, ADHD, 96
Cortisol levels
   avoidant infants, 478
   childhood depression, 169, 170

conduct disorder, 136
disorganized attachment, 479
Covert antisocial behavior
   and anxiety symptomatology, 134
   and attention-deficit/hyperactivity
      disorder, 132
   developmental trajectory, 116
   gender differences, 130
   heritability, 137
   versus overt antisocial behavior,
      116
Crack babies, 384
Cultural factors, 14, 15
   anxiety disorders, 221, 222
   attention-deficit/hyperactivity
      disorder, 85
   autism, 326
   child maltreatment, 518
   childhood schizophrenia, 346
   depression, 165
   eating disorders, 552, 535
   learning disabilities, 399
   posttraumatic stress disorder, 264,
      265
   research findings, overview, 14, 15
   social withdrawal, 299, 300
Cystic fibrosis, 585, 586

Daily hassles, 184
DC:0–3 approach, 30, 31
Delinquent behavior (see also
   Conduct disorder)
   age of onset, 122, 123
   attention-deficit/hyperactivity
      disorder
      as predictor, 132
   child abuse outcome, 517, 518
   contextual factors, 140, 141
   covert aggression relationship, 116
   heritability, 137
   peer group influences, 141
Denial
   abused children, 511
   and surgery preparation, 593
Dependency needs, depression, 182
Depressed mothers
   antisocial behavior link, 137
   avoidant attachment, 482
   and childhood depression, 177–
      181, 482
   as informants, 23, 159
Depression, 153–195
   abused children, 501, 502, 505, 506
   adult outcome, 516
   age of onset, 166
   age-related effects, 162, 163
   anxiety disorders comorbidity, 160,
      233
   attachment theory, 177
   behavioral theory, 174–177
   biological models, 169, 170
   cognitive theories, 170–173
   cohort effects, 163, 164
   comorbidity, 160–162
   conduct disorder comorbidity, 134,
      135, 161

continuity over time, 167
definitional issues, 158–162
developmental course, 18, 165–167
diagnostic criteria, 154–158
eating disorders comorbidity, 562–
   565
epidemiology, 162–165
family theories, 177–181
gender differences, 164
genetic models, 168
informant sources, 158
interpersonal theories, 174–177
multifactorial models, 184–186
prognosis, 165–167
and social withdrawal, 157, 284,
   285, 294, 295
Developmental continuity/
   discontinuity, 16–18
Developmental language disorders,
   323, 324
Developmental psychopathology
   abused children, 521, 522
   assumptions, 36, 37
   as model, 36, 37
Developmental sequences, 372, 373
Developmental Trends Study, 126–
   128, 134
Dexamethasone suppression test, 169
Diabetes mellitus, 588, 589, 595
Diagnostic Interview Schedule for
   Children, 159
Diagnostic systems, 26–33
   categorical approaches, 28–31
   and child psychopathology
      definition, 21
   dimensional approach, 31
   overview, 26–33
   performance-based measures, 31,
      32
Diathesis–stress models
   anxiety disorders, 225–228
   depression, 182, 184–186
Dieting
   adolescent girls, 557
   eating disorders role, 558–560
   in families, 561, 562
   preventive interventions, 594
Dimensional diagnostic approach, 24,
   25, 31, 32
   antisocial behavior, 116–18
   anxiety disorders, 213, 216, 230
      family studies, 230
   attention-deficit/hyperactivity
      disorder, 80
   conduct disorder, 116–118
   disorders of infancy, 459
   general issues, 31, 32, 213, 216
   reading disabilities, 408, 409
   research overview, 24, 25
Direct aggression
   gender differences, 130
   indirect aggression comparison,
      116
"Discrepancy" concept
   learning disorders, 398, 399
   reading disorders, 407, 408

Disinhibition
  age-related declines, 68
  attachment disorder subtype, 470,
    471
  in attention-deficit/hyperactivity
    disorder, 67, 68, 70–76
Disorder-specific models, 37
Disorganized/disoriented attachment
  aggression predictor, 482, 483
  and fear, 480
  heart rate/cortisol levels, 479
  indices, 479
  and risk, 476–481
Dissociation, 509, 510
  abused children, 509–511
  age-related differences, 266
  traumatic stress reaction, 258, 266,
    497
Diurnal enuresis, 580, 581
Divorce
  antisocial behavior link, 138
  and attention-deficit/hyperactivity
    disorder, 92
Domestic violence (see Family
  violence)
Dopamine transporter gene, 98
Dopaminergic system
  autism, 327, 328
  schizophrenia, 350
  Tourette syndrome, 448, 449
"Double ABCX" model, 375, 376
Double depression, 167
Down syndrome
  adaptive behavior levels, 369
  behavioral phenotype, 379
  developmental sequences, 373
  IQ stability, 369
  maternal adaptation, 376
  "modular" deficits, 374
Drug use/abuse
  abused children, outcome, 516, 517
  eating disorders comorbidity, 562–
    564
DSM system, history, 28–30
DSM-IV, 24, 26–30
  anorexia nervosa, 543
  antisocial personality disorder, 124
  anxiety disorders, 216, 217
  attachment disorders approach, 471
  attention-deficit/hyperactivity
    disorder, 76–81
  binge eating disorder, 546–548
  bulimia nervosa, 543–545
  categorical approach in, 24, 26–30,
    216
  comorbidity issue, 33
  conduct disorder, 119–123
  conversion disorder, 578
  critical evaluation, 29, 30, 216
  depressive disorders, 154, 155
  encopresis, 582
  enuresis, 580, 581
  feeding disorder, 585
  generalized anxiety disorder, 210
  infancy disorders, 458
  language disorders, 400, 401

  learning disabilities, 397, 398
  mathematics disorder, 423
  mental retardation, 366, 367
  obsessive–compulsive disorder, 205
  oppositional defiant disorder, 119–
    121
  pain disorder, 579
  panic disorder, 214, 215
  posttraumatic stress disorder, 244,
    246, 247
  and infants, 468, 469
  reading disorder, 406
  schizophrenia, 343, 344
  separation anxiety disorder, 201
  social phobia, 203
  social withdrawal, 280, 281
  somatization disorder, 576
  specific phobias, 208
  spelling disorder, 420
  tic disorder, 438, 439
  undifferentiated somatization
    disorder, 577
  written expression disorder, 420
"Dual self," 513
Dunedin, New Zealand, study, 163
Dyscalculia, 424
Dyslexia (see Reading disabilities)
Dysphoria, child abuse outcome, 516
Dysthymia
  abused children, 501
  age of onset, 166
  chronicity, 167
  developmental pathways, 18
  diagnostic criteria, 155

Early intervention, autism, 332, 333
Eating Attitudes Test, 552
Eating Disorder Examination, 542
Eating disorder not otherwise
  specified, 541, 542, 565
Eating disorders, 541–571
  adolescent developmental factors,
    558
  athletes, 552
  biology, 553, 554
  clinical characteristics, 548, 549
  comorbidities, 562–565
  cultural variations, 552, 553
  developmental course/prognosis,
    549–551
  diagnostic issues, 542–548
  epidemiology, 551–553
  etiology, 553–562
  family role, 560–562
  genetics, 554, 555
  personality characteristics, 560
  prevention, 565, 566, 594
  sexual abuse outcome, 517
  treatment, 566
Eating Disorders Inventory, 552
Echolalia, 440, 441
  age of onset, 440, 441
  autism, 315
Education of the Handicapped Act
  (1971), 395, 396
EEG asymmetry, 289

Egocentrism, and peer interactions,
  278, 279
Electroencephalography
  autism, 329, 330
  behavioral inhibition, 289
Elimination disorders, 580–583
Emotion
  in autism, 314, 315
  psychopathology models, 43–46
  reactivity, 44, 45
Emotion regulation
  development of, 45
  emotion reactivity distinction, 44,
    45
  physiology, 289
  and social withdrawal, 287
Emotional abuse (see Psychological
  abuse)
Emotional expression, autism, 314,
  315
Emotional problems
  abused children, 500–502, 512–515
  sex differences, overview, 12
Empathy, abused children, 514
Encopresis, 582, 585
  diagnostic criteria, 582
  etiology, 582, 583
  prevalence, 582
  treatment, 583
Endogenous depression, 157
Endogenous opioids, autism, 328
Endorphins, autism, 328
Enmeshed families, 560, 561
Enuresis, 580, 581
  diagnostic criteria, 580, 581
  etiologies, 580, 581
  prevalence, 580
Environmental factors
  conduct disorder, 121, 122
  depression, 181–184
Environmental toxins, 98, 99
Epidemiology, 10–15 (see also under
  specific disorders)
Epistemology, 34
Ethan Has an Operation film, 592
Ethnic factors
  anxiety disorders, 219, 220
  attention-deficit/hyperactivity
    disorder, 85
  child maltreatment, 518
  depression, 165
  learning disabilities, 399
  mental retardation, 371, 372
  posttraumatic stress disorder, 264,
    265
  research findings, overview, 13, 14
Etiological models, 5, 6
Event-related potentials
  attention-deficit/hyperactivity
    disorder, 96, 100
  autism, 330
  childhood schizophrenia, 351
Executive functions
  and antisocial behavior, 136
  attention-deficit/hyperactivity
    disorder model, 70–76

autism, 318, 319
  behavioral inhibition link, 70–76
  childhood schizophrenia, 351
Exit events, and depression, 182
Expectancies, and child abuse, 529
Expressed emotion
  childhood schizophrenia, 354
  and depression, 179, 180
Expressive language disorders, 392, 400, 401
  abused children, 511
  and autism, 323
  early medical studies, 392
  phonological processing, 403
Externalizing problems
  academic failure association, 133, 134
  and attachment, 482, 483
  cognitive deficits, 43
  continuities, 16, 17
  and oppositional behavior, 114
  risk factors, infancy, 481–483
  sex differences, overview, 11, 12

Facial expression, 314
Failure to thrive, 464–466, 585
  description of, 464, 465
  diagnosis, 465
  epidemiology, 465
  etiology, 465
  family relationships, 464, 465
  medical aspects, 585
  neglected children, 502, 503
False affect, abused children, 513
Familial aggregation
  anxiety disorders, 228–230
  attention-deficit/hyperactivity disorder, 97
  childhood schizophrenia, 352
  depression, 168
  eating disorders, 555
  genetic paradigm, 47
  Tourette syndrome, 447
Familial mental retardation, 377, 378
Family cohesion
  depression link, 179
  and posttraumatic stress disorder, 268
Family coping
  Down syndrome, 376
  mental retardation, 375–377
Family dieting, 561, 562
Family-of-origin variables, 474
Family relationships
  abused children, 515, 516
  antisocial behavior, 137–139
  anxiety disorders, 230, 231
  attention-deficit/hyperactivity disorder, 91–93
  depression, 177–181
  eating disorders, 560–562
  failure to thrive, 464, 465
  infant risk factor, 472–483
  intergenerational continuity, 473–476
  intergenerational discontinuity, 476

microsocial analysis, anxiety, 230, 231
  posttraumatic stress disorder, 268
  research trends, 21
  resilient children, 19, 20
  tic disorders, 443, 444
Family studies (see Familial aggregation)
Family violence
  aggressive behavior link, 138
  and child maltreatment, 519
  and posttraumatic stress disorder, 268
Father–child relationship
  attention-deficit/hyperactivity disorder, 91, 92
  intergenerational transmission, 475
Fatigue, and task performance, ADHD, 68
Fear of novelty, 289
Fear structures, 259
Fear Survey Schedule for Children—Revised, 221
Fears
  in autism, 319, 320
  and disorganized attachment, 480
  prevalence, 198
Feeding disorders, 464–467, 584–586
  and cystic fibrosis, 585, 586
  diagnostic criteria, 584, 585
  and failure to thrive, 464–466
  subtypes, 584, 585
Felt security, 290, 294
Fenfluramine, in autism, 327
Fetal alcohol syndrome, 384
Focal psychotherapy, 550
Food preferences, autism, 319
Fragile X syndrome
  adaptive behavior levels, 369
  and autism, 327
  behavioral abnormalities, 381, 382
  behavioral phenotype, 379
  dual diagnosis, 381, 382
  IQ stability, 369
  "modular" deficits, 374
  sex differences, 371
Friendship, depressed children, 174

Gall's influence, 391
Gang membership, 118
Gaze impairments, autism, 314
Gender differences, 11–13
  antisocial behavior, 129–131
  anxiety disorders, 220
  attention-deficit/hyperactivity disorder, 79, 84
  autism, 325, 326
  child maltreatment factor, 518
  childhood schizophrenia, 345, 346
  conduct disorder, 129–131
  depression, 164
  eating disorders, 551, 552, 557, 558
  obsessive–compulsive disorder, 206
  overview, 11–13
  posttraumatic stress disorder, 263, 264
  reading disabilities, 417

social withdrawal, 299
  somatization disorder, 575
"Gender paradox," 12
Generalized anxiety disorder
  comorbidity, 232
  core symptoms, 209, 211
  developmental course, 218
  DSM-IV criteria, 210
  epidemiology, 218, 219
  gender differences, 220
  genetics, 229
  ICD-10 criteria, 210
  related symptoms, 211, 212
  social class factors, 220
Genetics, 46–48 (see also under specific disorders)
Germany, ADHD prevalence, 85
Gestural impairment, autism, 313, 314
Goal-directed behavior, 74
Grief response, young children, 472
Growth hormone, depression, 169
Guilt
  abused children, 510, 511
  age-related differences, PTSD, 266
  and trauma, 259, 266

Haloperidol
  childhood schizophrenia, 355
  Tourette syndrome neurobiology, 448, 449
Handwashing rituals, 204
Hay fever, 4
Headaches, 578, 579
Health-related disorders, 572–601
Healthy functioning, overview, 15, 16
Heart period, 461
Heart rate
  avoidant infants, 478
  and behavioral inhibition, 223
  and disorganized attachment, 479
Heller syndrome, 323
"Heterotypic continuity"
  conduct disorder, 125, 126
  oppositional defiant disorder, 128
5-HIAA levels, anorexia nervosa, 553
Hippocampus
  amygdala interactions, 331, 332
  autism, 329–332
  social cognition role, 331, 332
Hispanic children
  attention-deficit/hyperactivity disorder, 85
  maltreatment, 518
  posttraumatic stress disorder, 264
  problem behaviors, 11
Home environment (see also Family relationships)
  childhood schizophrenia, 353
  and depression, 179, 180
Homotypic correspondence, 17
Homovanillic acid, autism, 328
"Hopelessness" depression, 171
Hormonal influences, antisocial behavior, 136
Hostile aggression, 116

Hurricane Hugo disaster, 250, 258,
263, 264
Hyperactive behavior
antisocial behavior predictor, 132,
133
attention-deficit/hyperactivity
disorder
symptom, 67, 68
Hyperarousal (see Overarousal)
Hyperserotonemia, autism, 327
Hypersomnia, childhood depression,
156
Hypervigilance
abused children, 509
posttraumatic stress disorder, 251
Hypoglycemia episodes, 588
Hypothalamic–pituitary–adrenal axis,
169, 170

ICD-10 criteria
anorexia nervosa, 543, 544
arithmetic skills disorder, 423, 424
attention-deficit/hyperactivity
disorder, 81, 82
bulimia nervosa, 546
conduct disorder, 123, 124
depressive disorders, 154, 155
encopresis, 582
enuresis, 580, 581
feeding disorder, 585
generalized anxiety disorder, 210
learning disabilities, 397, 398
mental retardation, 366, 367
obsessive–compulsive disorder, 205
pain disorder, 579
panic disorder, 214
phobic anxiety disorder of
childhood, 208
posttraumatic stress disorder, 245–
247
reading disorder, 406, 407
separation anxiety disorder, 201
social anxiety disorder of childhood,
203
and social withdrawal, 280, 282,
283
somatization disorder, 576
somatoform autonomic
dysfunction, 578
spelling disorder, 420
tic disorders, 438–441
Identity formation
eating disorders, 558
and trauma, 266
Illinois Test of Psycholinguistic
Abilities, 400
Illness prevention programs, 594, 595
Imitation skills, autism, 313
Immune system, 573
Immunization programs, 594
Impulsive behavior
antisocial behavior predictor, 132,
133
attention-deficit/hyperactivity
disorder, 67, 68
and bulimia nervosa, 565

Inattention
antisocial behavior predictor, 132,
133
and attention-deficit/hyperactivity
disorder, 67, 68
Incest (see Sexual abuse)
India, ADHD prevalence, 85
Indirect aggression, 116, 130
Individual differences, learning
disabilities, 391–394
Infancy, 457–491
attachment relationships, 475–
481
colic, 461–464
diagnostic classification, 458–460
disorganized attachment, 476–481
failure to thrive, 464–466
family context risk factor, 472–483
feeding disorders, 464–467
posttraumatic stress disorder, 468–
470
reactive attachment disorder, 470–
472
regulatory disorders, 460, 461
risk factors, family, 472–483
sleep disorders, 467, 468
Informant agreement, 22, 23
Information processing model, 41, 42
(see also Social information
processing)
and child abuse, 523–525
childhood schizophrenia, 351
depression, 170, 171
overview, 41, 42
Inhibited attachment subtype, 470,
471
Injections
distress reactions, 590, 591
and parental presence, 590
phobia, 209
Injury prevention programs, 593, 594
Institutionalized children, 470, 471
Instrumental aggression, 116
Insulin-dependent diabetes mellitus,
588, 589
Intelligence (see also IQ)
and attention-deficit/hyperactivity
disorder, 90, 91
autism, 316
stress mitigation, 262
Intergenerational transmission, 472–
476
antisocial behavior, 138
attachment quality, 475, 476
child maltreatment, 138, 500, 501
discontinuity factors, 476
longitudinal studies, 473–475
relational behavior, 473–476
Internal attributions, abused children,
510, 511
Internal working models
and attachment theory, 40, 41
and depression, 185, 186
intergenerational transmission, 475
stability of, 17, 18
Internalization of speech, 69, 73

Internalizing problems
antisocial behavior comorbidity,
134, 135
cognitive distortions, 43
continuities, 16, 17
dimensional approach, 216
gender differences, 11, 12, 131
life stress link, 184
and social dysfunction, 176
Interpersonal orientation, 557, 558
Interpersonal psychotherapy, 566
Interpersonal relationships,
depression, 174–177
Intrauterine growth retardation, 93
Introversion, 286
Intrusive memories
age-related differences, 266, 267
learning theory, 261
posttraumatic stress disorder, 261,
266, 267
IQ
abused children, 499, 512
and attachment quality, 481
attention-deficit/hyperactivity
disorder, 91
autism, 316
conduct disorder, 136
mental retardation, 369
and minority groups, 371, 372
Irritability, 156
Isle of Wight Study, 10

Japan, ADHD prevalence, 85
Joint attention, autism, 313, 314
"Just world" beliefs
abused children, 509
and posttraumatic stress disorder,
259

Kenyan children, 14
Kiddie-SADS, 159

Language comprehension, autism,
316
Language disorders, 400–405
abused children, 511
attention-deficit/hyperactivity
disorder, 90
and autism, 315, 316, 323, 324, 330
comorbidities, 405
diagnostic criteria, 400, 401
historical aspects, 400
Larry P. case, 372
Lead levels, 98, 99
Learned alarms, 260, 261
Learned helplessness
abused children, 522
depression, 171, 172
victimization effects, 259, 522
Learning disabilities, 390–435
antisocial behavior link, 133, 134
attention-deficit/hyperactivity
disorder
association, 90
classification, 396–398
comorbidity, 404, 405, 442

definitional problems, 396–398
discrepancy concept, 398, 399, 407, 408
historical context, 391–395
mathematics, 423–426
oral language, 400–405
reading, 405–419
research impediments, 395–400
social and political aspects, 394, 395
social skill deficits, 405
and tic disorders, 442
written expression, 419–423
Learning theory (*see also* Conditioning)
encopresis, 583
enuresis, 581
posttraumatic stress disorder, 260, 261
Lesbians, eating disorders, 558
Life expectancy, ADHD, 94
Life stress, and depression, 181–186
Linear models, 35
Linguistic deficits, 401, 402
Listening comprehension, 408
"Little Hans," 196, 197
Locomotor activity, depression, 169
Locus of control
depression, 171, 172
stress responsivity role, 262
Logical positivism, 34, 35
London Epidemiological study, 10
Loneliness, 292–295
Lumbar punctures, 591

Magnetic resonance imaging
attention-deficit/hyperactivity disorder, 96
autism, 328, 329
childhood schizophrenia, 350
Main effects model, 35
Major depression (*see* Depression)
Mania, diagnostic criteria, 157
Manipulative soiling, 582, 583
Marital conflict
antisocial behavior link, 137, 138
and attention-deficit/hyperactivity disorder, 92
and childhood depression, 179, 180
failure to thrive, 464
Marital support, protective effect, 476
"Masked" depression, 161
Mastery orientation
anxiety disorders, 228
depression, 175
Masturbatory insanity, 7, 8
Maternal characteristics (*see also* Mothers)
intergenerational transmission, 473–475
sexual abuse mitigating factor, 514, 515
and social withdrawal, 296–298
Maternal depression (*see* Depressed mothers)
Mathematics disorder, 423–426
characteristics, 424, 425

comorbidities, 426
definitions/diagnostic criteria, 423, 424
epidemiology, 425, 426
etiologies, 425
history, 423
neuropsychology, 425
Mechanistic models, 34
Medial temporal lobe, autism, 331, 332
Medical problems
physiological etiology, 586–595
psychosocial etiology, 583–586
Medical procedures, 590–593
Melancholic depression, 157
Memory
and autism, 317, 330–332
trauma sequelae, 497, 498
Menarche onset
and delinquent behavior, 131
and eating disorders, 558
Mental computation, ADHD, 69
Mental retardation, 362–389
AAMR definition, 366–368
and attention-deficit/hyperactivity disorder, 81, 82
autism differential diagnosis, 323
behavioral research "cultures," 379, 380, 383, 384
behavioral techniques, 377
classification, 363, 364
contextual issues, 364, 365
core features, 363
definitional and diagnostic issues, 365–368, 383
developmental course, 368–370
developmental theory, 372–376
DSM-IV and ICD-10 definitions, 366, 367
dual diagnosis, 380–384
ecocultural perspective, 376
epidemiology, 370–372
etiologies, 377–380
family stress-and-coping model, 375, 376
IQ stability, 369
levels of functioning, 363, 364, 368
mild subtype, 363, 364, 369–372
levels of functioning, 363, 364
prevalence, 370, 371
minority group overrepresentation, 376, 371, 372
moderate subtype, 363, 369, 371
prognosis, 368–370
and psychopathology, 380, 381, 384
service delivery, 383
severe subtype, 364, 369, 371
sex differences, 371
social role theory, 376, 377
two-group approach, 377, 378
Metatheoretic principles, 34
MHPG (3-methoxy-4-hydroxyphenylglycol) levels
autism, 328
eating disorders, 553, 554
Migraine, 579
Minimal brain dysfunction, 65, 393

Minority groups (*see* Ethnic factors)
Modeling, in families, 230
Modeling techniques, surgery preparation, 592
"Modular" theory, 374, 375
Moral reasoning
abused children, 499
attention-deficit/hyperactivity disorder, 69
Mother–child relationship
antisocial behavior link, 137–139, 144
attention-deficit/hyperactivity disorder, 91–93
and depression, 178–181
disorganized attachment, 476–481
failure to thrive, 464
intergenerational transmission, 473–476
attachment model, 475, 476
sexual abuse mitigating factor, 514, 515
and social withdrawal, 296–298
Mothers (*see also* Depressed mothers)
beliefs of, 296–298
characteristics of, intergenerational effects, 473–476
coercive behaviors, 138, 139
as informants, 22, 23
intrusive control, 482
mental retardation coping, 375, 376
and social withdrawal, 296–298
Motor coordination, ADHD, 69, 74
Motor sequencing, ADHD, 69, 74
Motor stereotypies, autism, 319
Motor tics
age of onset, 439–441
classification, 438–440
definition, 436, 437
"Multidimensionally impaired," 345
Munchausen by proxy syndrome, 502, 584
Mutism, 315

Naloxone, autism, 328
Naltrexone, autism, 328
Negative affect
abused children, 513
anxious behavior predictor, 289
Negative cognitions
depression, 170, 171, 173
generalization of, 173
stress interaction, depression, 182, 183
Neglected children (*see* Child neglect)
Neurobiological models, overview, 46–49
Neurodevelopmental model, schizophrenia, 349, 350
Neuroendocrine models, depression, 169
Neuroleptics
childhood schizophrenia, 355
Tourette syndrome neurobiology, 448, 449

Neurological factors, ADHD, 95–97
Neuropsychology, conduct disorder, 136, 137
New Jersey Study, *163*
New York Child Longitudinal Study, *163*
New Zealand, ADHD prevalence, 85
Nocturnal enuresis, 580, 581
Nonorganic failure to thrive, 585
Nonverbal communication, autism, 313, 314
Nonverbal learning disabilities, 426
Norepinephrine
    autism, 328
    eating disorders, 553, 554
    and posttraumatic stress disorder, 260
Normality, definitional issues, 15
Northeastern U.S. Longitudinal Study, *163*
Novel stimulation, fear response, 289
"Numbing" reactions, 46
    adaptive functioning problem, 46
    age-related differences, 266
    and child maltreatment, 497, 522
    posttraumatic stress disorder, 251, 252, 266, 497
Nutrition, 594

Obesity, 542, 556, 557
Object-oriented children, 286
Object relations, depression, 177
Obsessive–compulsive disorder
    age of onset, 206
    comorbidity, 231, 443
    core symptoms, 204, 206
    developmental course, 217, 218
    DSM-IV criteria, 205
    eating disorders comorbidity, 562–564
    epidemiology, 218, 219
    gender differences, 206, 220
    ICD-10 criteria, 205
    prognosis, 217, 218
    related symptoms, 206, 207
    and tic disorders, 443
"Off task" behaviors, 67
Ontario Child Health Study, 10, *163*
Operant conditioning models
    health-related disorders, 573
    manipulative soiling, 583
Oppositional defiant disorder, 113–149
    academic underachievement association, 133, 134
    age of onset, 126
    antisocial personality disorder link, 128, 129
    attachment quality, 483
    attention-deficit/hyperactivity disorder
        comorbidity, 81, 89, 132, 133
    comorbidity, 131–135
    definitional criteria, 118–124
    developmental progression, 125–129
    and gender, 130, 131

dimensional versus categorical issue, 116–118
    DSM-IV criteria, 118–124
    etiology, 135–142
    and family relationships, 92, 93
    heterotypic continuity, 125, 126
    internalizing disorders comorbidity, 134, 135
    positive predictive power, 127, 128
    prevalence, 124, 125
    progression to conduct disorder, 126–128
    psychobiology, 135–137
    validity of category, 120, 121
Oral language disorders, 400–405
Oregon Adolescent Depression Project, *163*
Organic mental retardation, 377–380
Orienting behavior, autism, 313, 314
Overanxious disorder, 232 (*see also* Generalized anxiety disorder)
Overarousal
    genetic component, 262
    learning theory, 260, 261
    posttraumatic stress disorder, 252, 260–262, 497, 498
Overprotective parents, 295–298
Overt antisocial behavior
    attention-deficit/hyperactivity disorder
        relationship, 132
    versus covert antisocial behavior, 116
    gender differences, 130
    heritability, 137

P300
    attention-deficit/hyperactivity disorder, 100
    autism, 330
Pain disorder, 577–580
    diagnostic criteria, 577, 579
    epidemiology, 578
    family factors, 579, 580
    social learning framework, 579
Pain sensitivity, autism, 320
Palilalia, 441
Panic disorder
    and agoraphobia, 212, 213, 215, 229, 230, 232, 233
    and bulimia nervosa, 564
    core symptoms, 212
    developmental course, 218
    DSM-IV criteria, 214, 215
    epidemiology, 219
    genetics, 229
    ICD-10 criteria, 214
    puberty relationship, 212
    related symptoms, 212, 213
    separation anxiety relationship, 232, 233
Panic disorder with agoraphobia
    behavioral inhibition association, 223
    DSM-IV criteria, 215

epidemiology, 219
    genetics, 229, 230
    separation anxiety relationship, 232, 233
Parent–child relationship (*see also* Mother–child relationship)
    abused children, 515, 516
    antisocial behavior link, 137–139
    anxiety disorders, 230, 231
    attention-deficit/hyperactivity disorder, 91–93
    childhood schizophrenia, 354
    depression, 177–181
    and social withdrawal, 296, 298
    tic disorders, 443, 444
Parent–Infant Relationship Global Assessment Scale, 459, 460
Parent Interview for Autism, 321
Parental characteristics, and child abuse, 523–528
Parental death, 180
Parental education, 219
Parental informants, 22, 23
    attention-deficit/hyperactivity disorder, 80, 81
    research findings, overview, 22, 23
Parental overcontrol
    aggression risk factor, 482
    and social withdrawal, 295–297
Parental psychopathology (*see also* Depressed mothers)
    antisocial behavior link, 137
    and depression, 178–180
Parenting
    aggression influence, 481–483
    antisocial behavior bidirectional influences, 138, 139
    anxiety disorders, 230, 231
    and depression, 177–181
    intergenerational transmission, 473–476
    maltreated children, 522–528
    and posttraumatic stress disorder, 267, 268
Passive behavior
    maladaptation predictor, 294, 299
    neglected children, 503
    sex differences, 299
Paternal psychopathology, 137
Pedophiles, 527
Peer relationships
    depression, 174–177
    normal development significance, 278, 279
    protective effects, 476
    and social withdrawal, 288, 292–294
    Tourette syndrome, 444
Perception of control (*see* Control-related factors)
Perfectionism
    bulimia nervosa, 556
    eating disorders, 556, 560
Performance-based measures, 31, 32
Performance IQ, autism, 316

Perinatal complications
  attention-deficit/hyperactivity
    disorder, 93
  autism, 327
  childhood schizophrenia, 352
  tic disorders, 447, 448
Perseverative behavior, autism, 319
Personal control (see Control-related
    factors)
Personality, and eating disorders,
    560
Personality disorders
  abused children, outcome, 517
  eating disorders comorbidity, 563–
    565
  social withdrawal relationship, 286,
    287
Perspective-taking ability, 278, 279
Pervasive developmental disorder,
    320
Pervasive developmental disorder,
    NOS, 323
Phenylketonuria, and autism, 327
Phobic disorders
  and behavioral inhibition, 223, 224
  developmental course/prognosis,
    217
  epidemiology, 218, 219
  gender differences, 220
  historical context, 196–198
Phonemes, 402
Phonic tics
  age of onset, 439–441
  classification, 438–440
  definition, 436, 437
Phonological deficits, 400–405
  developmental aspects, 403
  diagnostic criteria, 400, 401
  epidemiology, 403, 404
  genetics, 404
  neurobiology, 404
  and reading disability, 402, 403,
    405, 416, 417
Physical abuse, 492–537
  antisocial behavior, 514
  attention-deficit/hyperactivity
    disorder
    link, 499, 500
  behavioral development, 500
  betrayal dynamic, 514
  and borderline personality disorder,
    517
  child risk characteristics, 528, 529
  cognitive development, 499, 500,
    511, 512
  definition, 496
  depression link, 501, 502
  developmental pathways, 18
  epidemiology, 518, 519
  intergenerational transmission, 517,
    518
  and internal attributions, 511
  parent characteristics, 522–528
  physical signs, 498, 499, 508
  self-blame, 511
  and social class, 11

Physical aggression
  and anxiety symptoms, 134
  and attention-deficit/hyperactivity
    disorder, 132
  versus verbal aggression, 115, 116
Physical attractiveness
  and eating disorders, 557
  and parenting, 476
Piagetian stages
  mental retardation, 373, 374
  "modular" view comparison, 374,
    375
Pica, 466
Pittsburgh HMO Study, 163
Planning ability, ADHD, 69, 74
Planum temporale, ADHD, 96
Play behavior, autism, 315
Positron emission tomography
  attention-deficit/hyperactivity
    disorder, 96
  autism, 329
  childhood schizophrenia, 350
Postnatal stress, and tics, 448
Posttraumatic play, 256, 266
Posttraumatic stress disorder, 242–
    276
  age-specific symptomatology, 247,
    265–267
  associated disorders, 252
  biological changes, 260
  biological vulnerability, 261, 262
  and child maltreatment, 256, 257,
    496–506
    theory, 520, 521
  cognitive effects, 258–260
  conditioning theory, 260, 261
  context of, model, 253, 254
  delayed onset, 247
  developmental course, 252, 253
    infants, 469, 470
  developmental differences, 265–
    267
  DSM-IV, 244, 246, 247, 250–252,
    468, 469
  emotional reactions, 258
  evolution of concept, 243–247
  experiential vulnerability, 263
  gender differences, 263, 264
  historical overview, 247–249
  ICD-10, 245–247
  infants and toddlers, 468–470
  prevalence, 250–252
  prognosis, 252, 253
    infants, 469, 470
  psychoanalytic theory, 243
  psychological vulnerability, 262,
    263
  social environment role, 268
  social support role, 267
  and stressor type, 254–258
  subtypes, 497, 498
Poverty
  child maltreatment factor, 518, 519
  research findings, overview, 11
Powerlessness, abused children, 512,
    513

Prader–Willi syndrome, 382
  behavioral phenotype, 379
  developmental phases, 382
  maladaptive behaviors, 382
Pragmatic conversation, autism, 315
Prefrontal cortex, ADHD, 95, 96
Premonitory sensory urges, 437, 438,
    441
Prenatal problems
  attention-deficit/hyperactivity
    disorder, 93
  autism, 327
  childhood schizophrenia, 352, 353
  tic disorders, 447, 448
Prepotent responses, behavioral
    inhibition, 70, 71
Preschool-age children (see also
    Infancy)
  attention-deficit/hyperactivity
    disorder, 79, 80, 86, 87
  posttraumatic stress disorder, 265,
    266
  social withdrawal, 281
Pretend play, autism, 315
Prevention
  child abuse, 530, 531
  eating disorders, 565, 566
  illness, 594, 595
  injury, 593, 594
  surgery preparation, 592, 593
Proactive aggression 116
Problem-specific models, 37
Profound mental retardation, 364,
    369, 371
Pronoun usage, autism, 315
Prosody impairment, autism, 315
Protective factors, overview, 18–20
Psychoanalytic theory (see
    Psychodynamic theory)
Psychodynamic theory, 38, 39
  attachment theory relationship,
    39
  depression, 177
  and DSM system, 29
  posttraumatic stress disorder, 243
Psychological abuse
  definition, 496
  depression link, 501, 502
  personality disorders, 517
  versus sexual abuse, outcome, 20
Psychological factors affecting
    physical condition, 586, 587
Psychomotor agitation, 156
Psychoneuroimmunology, 573
Psychopathy, 118, 119 (see also
    Antisocial personality disorder)
Psychostimulants, 93
Psychotic symptoms
  and schizophrenia, 341
  sexually abused children, 506
PTSD Reaction Index, 249
Puberty
  and depression onset, 164
  panic disorder progression, 212
Puerto Rico Child Epidemiologic
    Study, 163

Pupil Evaluation Inventory, 285
"Pure" depression 160, 162

Quantitative EEG, autism, 329, 330
Questionnaires, and depression, 159, 160

Racial factors (see Ethnic factors)
Rate-disabled readers, 415
Rationalism, 34
Reactive attachment disorder, 470–472
Reactivity profile
  behaviorally inhibited children, 223
  depression, 170
Reading achievement, abused children, 511, 512
Reading comprehension, 409, 410, 415
Reading disabilities, 405–419
  and attention-deficit/hyperactivity disorder, 90, 418
  categorical versus dimensional models, 408, 409
  clinical subtyping, 415
  comorbidities, 418
  core deficits, 409, 410
  definitions, 406–409
  developmental course, 417
  diagnostic criteria, 406–409
  empirical subtyping, 415, 416
  epidemiology, 417
  ethnic factors, 399
  etiology, 417, 418
  history, 405, 406
  longitudinal studies, 417
  models, 409–417
  neurobiology, 417, 418
  Orton's influence, 392, 393, 406
  phonological processing, 402, 403, 405, 416, 417
  subtypes, 410–416
Realism, and epistemology, 34
Receptive language disorders, 392, 400, 401
Reexperiencing the trauma
  learning theory, 260, 261
  maltreated children, 497
  and posttraumatic stress disorder, 250, 251
Regressive behaviors, PTSD, 266
Regulatory disorders, 460, 461
  developmental course and prognosis, 461
  diagnosis, 460, 461
  epidemiology, 461
Religion, 7, 8
REM latency, depression, 169
Repetitive behavior
  autism, 319, 327, 328
  and depression, 327, 328
"Repressor" coping style, 593
Resilience
  genetic component, 262
  models, 19

research findings, overview, 18–20
  and self-efficacy, 228
  sex differences, 12
Restricting anorexia subtype
  definition, 543
  dieting, 559
  personality characteristics, 560
  psychopathology, 548
Retaliatory aggression, 116, 138, 140
Retentive encopresis, 582, 583
Rett disorder, 322, 323
Right frontal EEG, 289
Risk, 457–491
  attachment relationship role, 475–483
  family context, infants, 472–483
  protective factors, overview, 18–20
Ritualistic behaviors, autism, 319
Rule-governed behavior, ADHD, 73
"Rule of 3," 462
Rumination disorder, 466
Rural–urban differences, 13

Safety programs, 594
Schemata (see Cognitive schemata)
Schizoid personality disorder, 286
Schizophrenia (see Childhood schizophrenia)
Schizotypal personality disorder, 353, 354
School behavior, ADHD, 68
School performance
  abused children, 499, 511, 512
  antisocial behavior link, 133, 134
  attention-deficit/hyperactivity disorder, 90
  depression, 165, 175
School refusal behavior
  anxiety disorders relationship, 232
  categorical and dimensional approach, 216
  comorbidity, 232
  functional approach, 216
  and separation anxiety disorder, 200
  and social phobia, 204
Secure attachment profile, 477–479
Self-blame, abused children, 510, 511
Self-concept
  abused children, 512, 513
  eating disorders, 558
  tic disorders, 445
Self-control theory, depression, 172
Self-destructive behavior, 501, 515, 516
Self-directed aggression, 134
Self-efficacy
  abused children, 513
  stress responsivity role, 262
Self-esteem
  abused children, 502, 513
  depression, 171, 173
  and social withdrawal, 191–195
  tic disorders, 445
Self-injurious behaviors
  abused children, 515
  autism, 319

Self-mutilation, 515, 516
Self-regulation
  abused children, 515
  attention-deficit/hyperactivity disorder, 69–75
Self-report, and depression, 159, 160
Semantics, and autism, 315, 316
"Sensitizer" coping style, 593
Separation anxiety disorder
  behavioral inhibition model, 223
  core symptoms, 199, 200
  cross-cultural study, 222
  developmental course/prognosis, 217
  DSM-IV criteria, 201
  epidemiology, 218, 219
  ICD-10 criteria, 201
  panic disorder relationship, 232, 233
  racial and social class factors, 219, 220
  related symptoms, 200
Sequential development, 372, 373
Serotonin
  autism, 327
  eating disorders, 553, 554
Severe mental retardation, 364, 369, 371
Sex differences (see Gender differences)
Sex-role stereotypes, 557, 558
Sexual abuse, 503–506
  acute symptoms, 504, 505
  adult outcome, 516–518
  antisocial behavior risk, 138
  betrayal dynamic, 513, 514
  bulimia nervosa link, 517, 556
  versus child neglect, outcome, 20
  child risk characteristics, 528, 529
  definition, 496
  depression link, 505, 506
  developmental psychopathology model, 521, 522
  etiology, 522–529
  ethnic differences in PTSD, 264
  maternal relationship as mitigating factor, 514, 515
  medical problems, 583, 584
  offender characteristics, 527, 528
  parental characteristics, 527, 528
  physical development/outcome, 508
  posttraumatic stress symptoms, 256, 257, 505, 520, 521
    gender differences, 263, 264
  preconditions, 527, 528
  prevention, 530, 531
  secondary symptoms, 505–507
  self-concept, 512, 513
  and sexual behavior, 256, 257, 508, 517
  survivor symptoms, 516–518
Sexual offender characteristics, 527, 528
Sexualized behaviors, 505, 508

Shyness (*see also* Social withdrawal)
and behavioral inhibition, 48, 49
bulimia nervosa, 556
cultural attitudes, 300
definition, 279
sex differences, 299
Siblings
attention-deficit/hyperactivity
disorder, 92
autism genetics, 326
inhibited children, 224
"Similar sequence hypothesis," 373
"Similar structure hypothesis," 373,
374
Simple phobia (*see* Specific phobias)
Single parents, 519
Single word reading, 409, 410
Situation-specific attributions, 171
Situational factors, ADHD, 68
Sleep architecture, depression, 169
Sleep disturbances
attention-deficit/hyperactivity
disorder, 94
autism, 319
infants, 467, 468
posttraumatic stress disorder, 251
Sleep latency, depression, 169
Smith–Magenis syndrome, 382
Smoking prevention, 594, 595
Social class factors
anxiety disorders, 219, 220
attention-deficit/hyperactivity
disorder, 84
autism, 326
childhood schizophrenia, 346
depression, 164, 165
Social cognition
autism neuropsychology, 331, 332
and peer interaction, 279
Social development
abused children, 500–502, 512–
515
and peer interaction, 279
and traumatic reactions, 266
Social dysfunction
abused children, 512–515
autism, 312–315
depression, 174–177
psychopathology dimension, 24, 25
Tourette syndrome, 444
Social exploration, 291, 292
Social imitation, autism, 313
Social information processing
aggressive behavior link, 140
autism, 312–315, 331, 332
neuropsychology, 331, 332
child abuser characteristics, 523–
525
as model, 41, 42
Social inhibition, and attachment,
291, 470
Social isolation (*see also* Social
withdrawal)
definition, 279
depression, 174
and schizophrenia, 285

Social phobia
comorbidity, 231
core symptoms, 200, 202–204
DSM-IV criteria, 203
epidemiology, 218
gender differences, 220
ICD-10 criteria, 203
related symptoms, 204
simple phobia difference, 202
Social problem solving, 175
Social sensitivity, abused children,
501
Social skills
depression, 174–177
learning disabilities, 405
Social skills training, 595
Social support
and depression, 183
and posttraumatic stress disorder, 267
Social withdrawal, 277–307
and aggression, 285
anxiety disorders relationship, 284
attachment security role, 290, 291
behavioral inhibition role, 283, 284,
288–290
clinical significance, 280–287
correlates and consequences, 292–
295
sex differences, 299
cultural variation, 299, 300
definition, 279, 280
and depression, 157, 284, 285
developmental course, 287–295
in DSM-IV disorders, 280, 281
emotional dysregulation, 287, 288
etiological factors, 288–292
in familiar peer group, 294
fear of novelty, 289, 290
in ICD-10 disorders, 282, 283
motivations, 280
neglected children, 503
and parental beliefs, 296–298
and peer rejection, 288
and personality disorders, 286, 287
and schizophrenia, 285
sex differences, 299
stability data, 292, 293
Sociocultural factors, overview, 14
Socioeconomic factors, 11
anxiety disorders, 219, 220
attention-deficit/hyperactivity
disorder, 84, 85
autism, 326
child maltreatment, 518, 519
childhood schizophrenia, 346
depression, 164, 165
mental retardation, 365, 371, 372
significance of, overview, 11
Socioemotional impairments (*see*
Social dysfunction)
Sociometric status, depression, 174
Sociopathy (*see* Psychopathy)
Sociotropy, 182
Solitary behavior, 280
Somatic complaints
conduct disorder outcome, girls, 131

depression, 156, 157
posttraumatic stress disorder, 251
psychopathology dimension, 24, 25
separation anxiety disorder, 200
Somatization disorder, 574, 575
comorbidity, 575
definition, 574, 575
diagnostic criteria, 576
etiology, 575
gender differences, 575
Somatoform disorders, 574
Span of apprehension task, 351
Spatial reversal, autism, 318
Specific phobias
core symptoms, 207, 209
developmental course, 217
DSM-IV criteria, 208
epidemiology, 218, 219
gender differences, 220
ICD-10 criteria, 208
prognosis, 217
related symptoms, 209
subtypes, 209
Speech disorders, 400–405
attention-deficit/hyperactivity
disorder, 90
autism, 315, 316
comorbidity, 405
Spelling disorders, 419–423
attention-deficit/hyperactivity
disorder
association, 90
definitions, 419
developmental aspects, 421
diagnostic criteria, 420
phonological processing, 402, 403
Spinal taps, 591
Splitting, abused children, 513
Startle response, PTSD, 251, 267
State–Trait Anxiety Inventory for
Children, 221
Stereotyped behavior
autism, 319, 328, 329
and dopamine, 328, 329
and tic disorder, 438
Stigma, and trauma, 255
Stimulant medication, 93
Strange Situation assessment, 477
Streptococcal infection, and tic
disorders, 448
Stress-and-coping model, 375, 376
Stress-generation model, 183, 184
Stress-inoculation, 592
Stress management, diabetes, 595
Stress models
anxiety disorders, 225–228
childhood schizophrenia, 346–348
depression, 181–184
family adaptation, mental
retardation, 375, 376
Stress reactivity, depression, 170
Substance abuse
abused children, outcome, 516, 517
developmental progression, 129
eating disorders comorbidity, 562–
564

Suicidal behavior
    abused children, 501, 516
    conduct disorder and depression,
        134
    cortisol dysregulation, 169
    depression criterion, 158
Surgery preparation programs, 592,
    593
Sustained attention, 75
Symbolic play, autism, 315

Task performance, ADHD, 68
Teacher informants, 22, 80, 81
Temperament (see also Behavioral
    inhibition)
    attachment quality relationship,
        290, 291, 478
    and stress responsivity, 262
Templates, in cognitive theory, 42
Test anxiety
    comorbidity, 232
    cross cultural aspects, 221, 222
Test Anxiety Scale for Children, 221,
    222
Testosterone, and aggression, 136
Thai children
    cultural influences, 13
    shyness, 300
Theory of mind, autism, 317, 318
Three Mile Island disaster, 259
Thyroid-stimulating hormone
    secretion, 169
Tic disorders, 436–454
    age of onset, 439–441
    attention-deficit/hyperactivity
        disorder
        comorbidity, 89, 90, 442
    comorbidity, 442, 443
    epidemiology, 445, 446
    natural history, 439–442
    neurobiology, 448, 449
    neuropsychological correlates,
        443
    nosology, 437–441
    and obsessive–compulsive disorder,
        443
    parental acceptance, 443, 444
    pathogenesis, 446–449
    peer group acceptance, 444
    perinatal factors, 447, 448
    premonitory sensory urges, 437,
        438
    school environment, 444
    self-esteem, 445
Toddlerhood, 457–491
    disorganized attachment effects,
        475–481
    family context risk factor, 472–483
    feeding disorders, 464–467
    posttraumatic stress disorder, 468–
        470
    reactive attachment disorder, 470–
        472
    sleep disorders, 467, 468
Toilet training, 580

Tourette syndrome, 436–454
    age of onset, 439–441
    assortative mating, 447
    attention-deficit/hyperactivity
        disorder
        comorbidity, 89, 90, 442
    comorbidity, 442, 443
    environmental risk factors, 447, 448
    epidemiology, 445, 446
    family environment, 443, 444
    genetics, 447
    natural history, 439–442
    neurobiology, 448, 449
    neuropsychological correlates, 443
    nosology, 437–441
    and obsessive–compulsive disorder,
        443
    parental acceptance, 443, 444
    pathogenesis model, 446
    peer group acceptance, 444
    perinatal factors, 447, 448
    premonitory sensory urges, 437,
        438
    school environment, 444
    self-esteem, 445
Tower of Hanoi task, autism, 318
Traffic accidents, ADHD risk, 94
Traffic Light Diet, 594
Trait anxiety
    cultural variation, 221
    stress vulnerability, 262, 263
Transient tic disorder, 438–440
Traumatic events, 254–258 (see also
        Posttraumatic stress disorder)
Tryptophan, bulimia nervosa, 554
Tuberous sclerosis, and autism, 327
Turn-taking behavior, autism, 314
Twin studies
    anxiety disorders, 229
    attention-deficit/hyperactivity
        disorder, 97, 98
    autism, 326
    childhood schizophrenia, 352
    eating disorders, 555
    as genetic paradigm, 47
    phonological deficits, 404
    Tourette syndrome, 447, 448
"Two-group approach," 377, 378

Uncontrollability (see Control-related
        factors)
Undersocialized antisocial behavior,
        118
Undifferentiated somatoform
        disorder, 575, 577
Urban–rural differences, 13

Vagal tone, 461
Vasovagal fainting response, 209
Venipunctures
    distress reactions, 590, 591
    and parental presence, 590
Ventricular enlargement
    autism, 329
    childhood schizophrenia, 350

Verbal aggression, 115, 116
Verbal fluency deficits
    antisocial behavior, 136
    attention-deficit/hyperactivity
        disorder, 69, 74, 136
Verbal intelligence
    attention-deficit/hyperactivity
        disorder, 91
    autism, 316
    mothers of deviant children, 482
Victimization, betrayal dynamic, 514
Vigilance
    abused children, 509
    attention-deficit/hyperactivity
        disorder, 96
Violence, intergenerational
        transmission, 517, 518
Viral infection, and schizophrenia,
        352, 353
Visual naming deficits, 416
Vocal tics, 436–441
Vocational training, mental
        retardation, 377
Vulnerability, 18–20
    anxiety disorders, 225–228
    childhood schizophrenia model,
        346–348
    diathesis-stress model, depression,
        182
    posttraumatic stress disorder, 261–
        263
    protective factors, overview, 18–20

War trauma, 264, 265
Washing rituals, 204
Waterloo Longitudinal Project, 292–
        294
"Wessel colic," 462
Williams syndrome, 374
Wisconsin Card Sorting Test, autism,
        318
Withdrawal (see Social withdrawal)
Witnessing of violence, 469, 470
Word recognition deficits, 409, 410,
        415
Working memory
    attention-deficit/hyperactivity
        disorder
        model, 69, 71, 72
    and behavioral inhibition, 71, 72
Written expression disorder, 419–423
    characteristics, 420, 421
    comorbidities, 422, 423
    definitions/diagnostic criteria, 419,
        420
    developmental aspects, 421
    discrepancy model, 420
    epidemiology, 421, 422
    etiology, 422
    historical context, 419
    reading deficits dissociation, 422
    theoretical models, 421

Zero to Three classification, 30, 31.
        458, 459, 471